P9-DIH-212

Biological Psychology 12e

JAMES W. KALAT
North Carolina State University

CENGAGE Learning®

Australia • Brazil • Mexico • Singapore • United Kingdom • United States

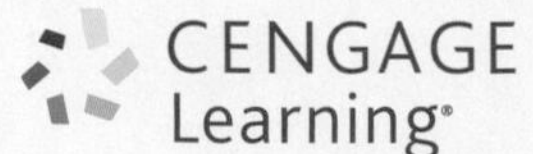

Biological Psychology, **Twelfth Edition**
James W. Kalat

Product Director: Jon-David Hague
Product Manager: Timothy Matray
Content Developer: Carolyn Lewis
Product Assistant: Nicole Richards
Media Developer: Jasmin Tokatlian
Marketing Manager: Melissa Larmon
Content Project Manager: Samen Iqbal
Art Director: Vernon Boes
Manufacturing Planner: Karen Hunt
Production Service: Jill Traut, MPS Limited
Photo Researcher: Carly Bergey, Lumina Datamatics Ltd.
Text Researcher: Nandhini Srinivasagopalan, Lumina Datamatics Ltd.
Copy Editor: Heather McElwain
Illustrator: Argosy Publishing Inc./MPS Limited
Text Designer: Lisa Buckley
Cover Designer: Irene Morris
Cover Images: Hippocampal neuron: Dr. Kieran Boyle; Ghosted Man: Darius Turek © 123RF.com
Compositor: MPS Limited

For product information and technology assistance, contact us at
Cengage Learning Customer & Sales Support, 1-800-354-9706
For permission to use material from this text or product,
submit all requests online at **www.cengage.com/permissions**
Further permissions questions can be e-mailed to
permissionrequest@cengage.com

Library of Congress Control Number: 2014941994

Student Edition:
ISBN-13: 978-1-305-10540-9

Loose-leaf Edition:
ISBN-13: 978-1-305-63365-0

Cengage Learning
20 Channel Center Street
Boston, MA 02210
USA

Cengage Learning is a leading provider of customized learning solutions with office locations around the globe, including Singapore, the United Kingdom, Australia, Mexico, Brazil, and Japan. Locate your local office at **www.cengage.com/global**

Cengage Learning products are represented in Canada by Nelson Education, Ltd.

To learn more about Cengage Learning Solutions, visit **www.cengage.com**

Purchase any of our products at your local college store or at our preferred online store **www.cengagebrain.com**

Printed in the United States of America
Print Number: 02 Print Year: 2014

About the Author

James W. Kalat (rhymes with ballot) is professor emeritus of psychology at North Carolina State University, where he taught courses in introduction to psychology and biological psychology from 1977 through 2012. Born in 1946, he received a BA summa cum laude from Duke University in 1968, and a PhD in psychology from the University of Pennsylvania in 1971. He is also the author of *Introduction to Psychology* (10th edition) and co-author with Michelle Shiota of *Emotion* (2nd edition). In addition to textbooks, he has written journal articles on taste-aversion learning, the teaching of psychology, and other topics. He was twice the program chair for the annual convention of the American Psychological Society, now named the Association for Psychological Science. A remarried widower, he has three children, two stepsons, and four grandchildren.

To my grandchildren.

Brief Contents

Introduction 3

1 Nerve Cells and Nerve Impulses 15

2 Synapses 39

3 Anatomy and Research Methods 65

4 Genetics, Evolution, Development, and Plasticity 103

5 Vision 147

6 Other Sensory Systems 187

7 Movement 227

8 Wakefulness and Sleep 261

9 Internal Regulation 293

10 Reproductive Behaviors 325

11 Emotional Behaviors 355

12 The Biology of Learning and Memory 391

13 Cognitive Functions 423

14 Psychological Disorders 465

A Appendix A: Brief, Basic Chemistry 503

B Appendix B: Society for Neuroscience Policies on the Use of Animals and Human Subjects in Research 509

Contents

Overview and Major Issues 3

The Biological Approach to Behavior 4
The Field of Biological Psychology 5
Three Main Points to Remember from This Book 6
Biological Explanations of Behavior 6
Career Opportunities 8
The Use of Animals in Research 9
Degrees of Opposition 10
IN CLOSING: Your Brain and Your Experience 12

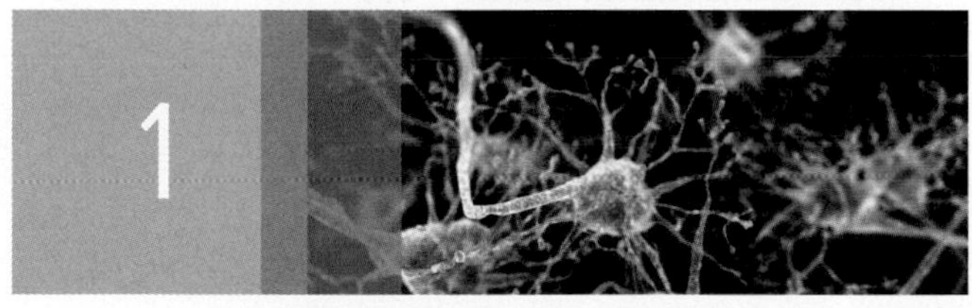

Nerve Cells and Nerve Impulses 15

MODULE 1.1 **The Cells of the Nervous System** 16
Neurons and Glia 16
Santiago Ramón y Cajal, a Pioneer of Neuroscience 16
The Structures of an Animal Cell 17
The Structure of a Neuron 17
Variations among Neurons 19
Glia 19
The Blood–Brain Barrier 21
Why We Need a Blood–Brain Barrier 21
How the Blood–Brain Barrier Works 22
Nourishment of Vertebrate Neurons 23
IN CLOSING: Neurons 23

MODULE 1.2 **The Nerve Impulse** 26
The Resting Potential of the Neuron 26
Forces Acting on Sodium and Potassium Ions 27
Why a Resting Potential? 29
The Action Potential 29
The Molecular Basis of the Action Potential 29
The All-or-None Law 31
The Refractory Period 31
Propagation of the Action Potential 32
The Myelin Sheath and Saltatory Conduction 32
Local Neurons 34
IN CLOSING: Neurons and Messages 35

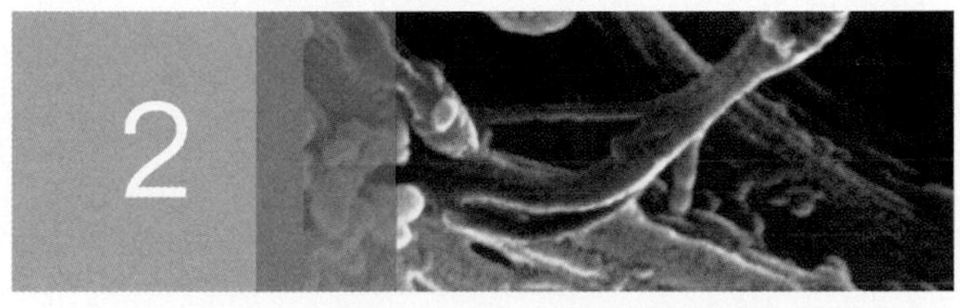

Synapses 39

MODULE 2.1 **The Concept of the Synapse** 40
Properties of Synapses 40
Speed of a Reflex and Delayed Transmission at the Synapse 41
Temporal Summation 41
Spatial Summation 41
Inhibitory Synapses 43
Relationship among EPSP, IPSP, and Action Potentials 44
IN CLOSING: The Neuron as Decision Maker 46

MODULE 2.2 **Chemical Events at the Synapse** 48
The Discovery of Chemical Transmission at Synapses 48
The Sequence of Chemical Events at a Synapse 49
Types of Neurotransmitters 50
Synthesis of Transmitters 50
Storage of Transmitters 51
Release and Diffusion of Transmitters 51
Activating Receptors of the Postsynaptic Cell 52
Ionotropic Effects 52
Metabotropic Effects and Second Messenger Systems 53
Neuropeptides 53
Variation in Receptors 54
Drugs that Act by Binding to Receptors 54
Inactivation and Reuptake of Neurotransmitters 55
Negative Feedback from the Postsynaptic Cell 56
Electrical Synapses 57

Hormones 57
IN CLOSING: Neurotransmitters and Behavior 60

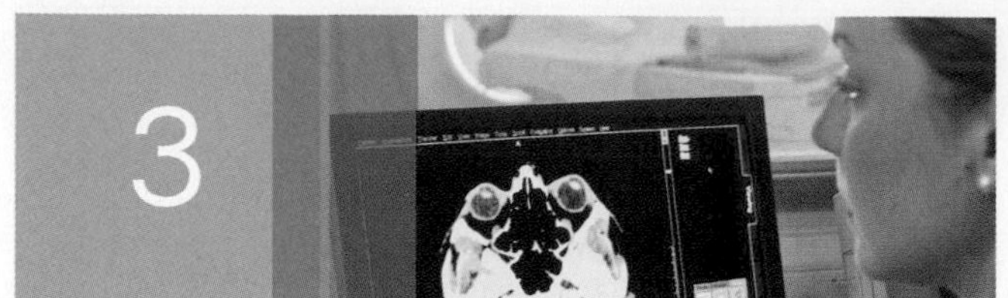

3 Anatomy and Research Methods 65

MODULE 3.1 **Structure of the Vertebrate Nervous System** 66
- Terminology to Describe the Nervous System 66
- The Spinal Cord 68
- The Autonomic Nervous System 69
- The Hindbrain 71
- The Midbrain 71
- The Forebrain 72
  - Thalamus 74
  - Hypothalamus 75
  - Pituitary Gland 75
  - Basal Ganglia 75
  - Basal Forebrain 76
  - Hippocampus 76
- The Ventricles 77
- IN CLOSING: Learning Neuroanatomy 78

MODULE 3.2 **The Cerebral Cortex** 80
- Organization of the Cerebral Cortex 80
- The Occipital Lobe 82
- The Parietal Lobe 83
- The Temporal Lobe 83
- The Frontal Lobe 84
  - The Rise and Fall of Prefrontal Lobotomies 85
  - Functions of the Prefrontal Cortex 85
- How Do the Parts Work Together? 85
- IN CLOSING: Functions of the Cerebral Cortex 87

MODULE 3.3 **Research Methods** 89
- Effects of Brain Damage 89
- Effects of Brain Stimulation 90
- Recording Brain Activity 91
- Correlating Brain Anatomy with Behavior 94
- Brain Size and Intelligence 96
  - Comparisons across Species 96
  - Comparisons among Humans 97

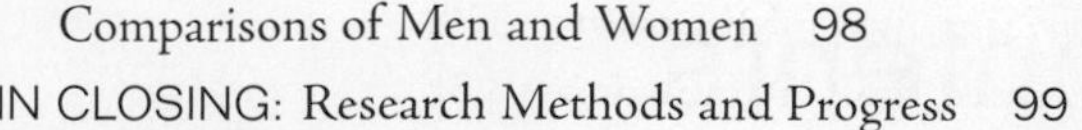

  - Comparisons of Men and Women 98
- IN CLOSING: Research Methods and Progress 99

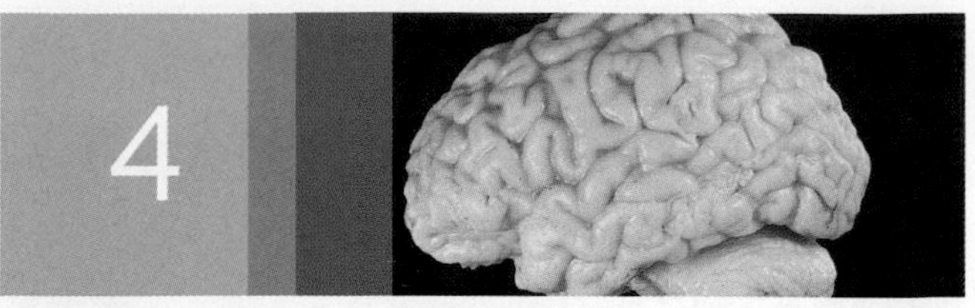

4 Genetics, Evolution, Development and Plasticity 103

MODULE 4.1 **Genetics and Evolution of Behavior** 104
- Mendelian Genetics 104
  - Sex-Linked and Sex-Limited Genes 106
  - Genetic Changes 107
  - Epigenetics 107
- Heredity and Environment 108
  - Environmental Modification 109
  - How Genes Affect Behavior 109
- The Evolution of Behavior 110
  - Common Misunderstandings about Evolution 110
  - Brain Evolution 111
  - Evolutionary Psychology 112
- IN CLOSING: Genes and Behavior 114

MODULE 4.2 **Development of the Brain** 117
- Maturation of the Vertebrate Brain 117
  - Growth and Development of Neurons 117
  - New Neurons Later in Life 118
- Pathfinding by Axons 119
  - Chemical Pathfinding by Axons 119
  - Competition among Axons as a General Principle 121
- Determinants of Neuronal Survival 122
- The Vulnerable Developing Brain 123
- Differentiation of the Cortex 124
- Fine-Tuning by Experience 125
  - Experience and Dendritic Branching 125
  - Effects of Special Experiences 127
- Brain Development and Behavioral Development 131
  - Adolescence 131
  - Old Age 132
- IN CLOSING: Brain Development 132

MODULE 4.3 **Plasticity after Brain Damage** 136
- Brain Damage and Short-Term Recovery 136
  - Reducing the Harm from a Stroke 136

Later Mechanisms of Recovery 138
Increased Brain Stimulation 138
Regrowth of Axons 139
Axon Sprouting 139
Denervation Supersensitivity 139
Reorganized Sensory Representations and the Phantom Limb 140
Learned Adjustments in Behavior 142
IN CLOSING: Brain Damage and Recovery 142

Vision 147

MODULE 5.1 Visual Coding 148
General Principles of Perception 148
The Eye and Its Connections to the Brain 149
Route within the Retina 149
Fovea and Periphery of the Retina 149
Visual Receptors: Rods and Cones 152
Color Vision 153
The Trichromatic (Young-Helmholtz) Theory 154
The Opponent-Process Theory 155
The Retinex Theory 156
Color Vision Deficiency 158
IN CLOSING: Visual Receptors 158

MODULE 5.2 How the Brain Processes Visual Information 162
An Overview of the Mammalian Visual System 162
Processing in the Retina 162
Further Processing 165
The Primary Visual Cortex 166
Simple and Complex Receptive Fields 167
The Columnar Organization of the Visual Cortex 169
Are Visual Cortex Cells Feature Detectors? 169
Development of the Visual Cortex 170
Deprived Experience in One Eye 171
Deprived Experience in Both Eyes 171
Uncorrelated Stimulation in the Two Eyes 171
Early Exposure to a Limited Array of Patterns 172
Impaired Infant Vision and Long-Term Consequences 173
IN CLOSING: Understanding Vision by Understanding the Wiring Diagram 173

MODULE 5.3 Parallel Processing in the Visual Cortex 177
The Ventral and Dorsal Paths 177
Detailed Analysis of Shape 178
The Inferior Temporal Cortex 178
Recognizing Faces 179
Color Perception 181
Motion Perception 181
The Middle Temporal Cortex 181
Motion Blindness 182
IN CLOSING: Aspects of Vision 183

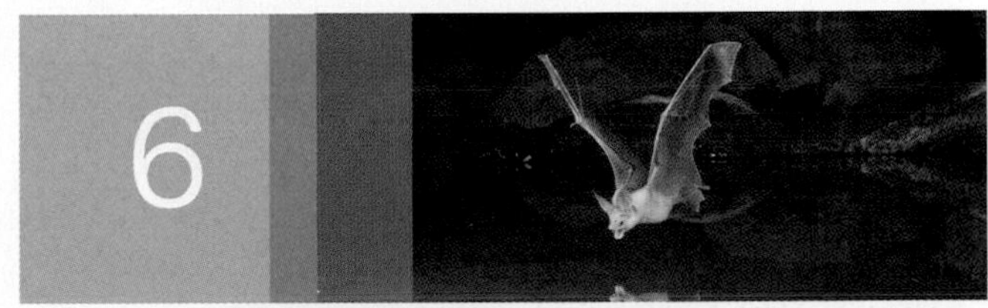

Other Sensory Systems 187

MODULE 6.1 Audition 188
Sound and the Ear 188
Physics and Psychology of Sound 188
Structures of the Ear 189
Pitch Perception 190
The Auditory Cortex 192
Hearing Loss 193
Deafness 193
Hearing, Attention, and Old Age 194
Sound Localization 194
IN CLOSING: Functions of Hearing 196

MODULE 6.2 The Mechanical Senses 198
Vestibular Sensation 198
Somatosensation 198
Somatosensory Receptors 199
Tickle 201
Somatosensation in the Central Nervous System 201
Pain 202
Stimuli and Spinal Cord Paths 202
Emotional Pain 203
Ways of Relieving Pain 204
Sensitization of Pain 207
Itch 207
IN CLOSING: The Mechanical Senses 208

MODULE 6.3 The Chemical Senses 211
Chemical Coding 211
Taste 212
Taste Receptors 212

How Many Kinds of Taste Receptors? 213
Mechanisms of Taste Receptors 214
Taste Coding in the Brain 214
Variations in Taste Sensitivity 215
Olfaction 216
Olfactory Receptors 218
Implications for Coding 219
Messages to the Brain 219
Individual Differences 220
Pheromones 220
Synesthesia 221
IN CLOSING: Senses as Ways of Knowing the World 222

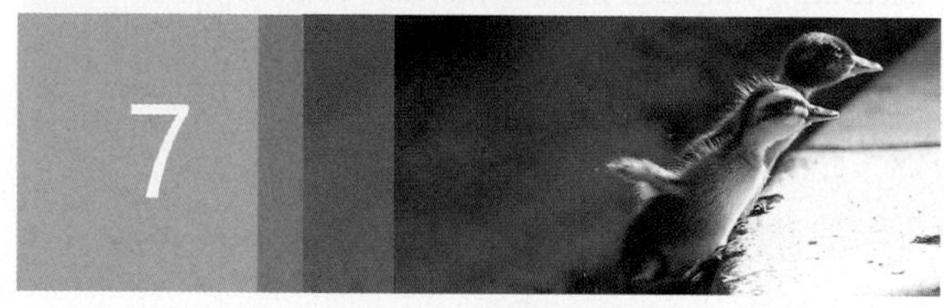

Movement 227

MODULE 7.1 The Control of Movement 228
Muscles and Their Movements 228
Fast and Slow Muscles 230
Muscle Control by Proprioceptors 231
Units of Movement 232
Voluntary and Involuntary Movements 232
Movements Varying in Sensitivity to Feedback 232
Sequences of Behaviors 232
IN CLOSING: Categories of Movement 233

MODULE 7.2 Brain Mechanisms of Movement 235
The Cerebral Cortex 235
Planning a Movement 237
Inhibiting a Movement 238
Mirror Neurons 238
Connections from the Brain to the Spinal Cord 239
The Cerebellum241
Functions Other than Movement 242
Cellular Organization 243
The Basal Ganglia 243
Brain Areas and Motor Learning 246
Conscious Decisions and Movement 246
IN CLOSING: Movement Control and Cognition 248

MODULE 7.3 Movement Disorders 252
Parkinson's Disease 252
Causes 253
L-Dopa Treatment 253
Other Therapies 254
Huntington's Disease 254
Heredity and Presymptomatic Testing 255
IN CLOSING: Heredity and Environment in Movement Disorders 257

Wakefulness and Sleep 261

MODULE 8.1 Rhythms of Waking and Sleeping 262
Endogenous Rhythms 262
Setting and Resetting the Biological Clock 264
Jet Lag 265
Shift Work 265
Morning People and Evening People 265
Mechanisms of the Biological Clock 266
The Suprachiasmatic Nucleus (SCN) 267
How Light Resets the SCN 268
The Biochemistry of the Circadian Rhythm 268
Melatonin 269
IN CLOSING: Sleep–Wake Cycles 270

MODULE 8.2 Stages of Sleep and Brain Mechanisms 272
Sleep and Other Interruptions of Consciousness 272
The Stages of Sleep 272
Paradoxical or REM Sleep 273
Brain Mechanisms of Wakefulness, Arousal, and Sleep 275
Brain Structures of Arousal and Attention 275
Sleep and the Inhibition of Brain Activity 276
Brain Function in REM Sleep 278
Sleep Disorders 279
Sleep Apnea 279
Narcolepsy 280
Periodic Limb Movement Disorder 280
REM Behavior Disorder 280
Night Terrors and Sleepwalking 281
IN CLOSING: Stages of Sleep 281

MODULE 8.3 Why Sleep? Why REM? Why Dreams? 284
Functions of Sleep 284
Sleep and Energy Conservation 284
Analogous to Sleep: Hibernation 284
Species Differences in Sleep 285
Sleep and Memory 286

Functions of REM Sleep 287
Biological Perspectives on Dreaming 288
The Activation-Synthesis Hypothesis 288
The Clinico-Anatomical Hypothesis 288
IN CLOSING: Our Limited Self-Understanding 289

Internal Regulation 293

MODULE 9.1 **Temperature Regulation** 294
Homeostasis and Allostasis 295
Controlling Body Temperature 296
Surviving in Extreme Cold 297
The Advantages of Constant High Body Temperature 297
Brain Mechanisms 298
Fever 299
IN CLOSING: Combining Physiological and Behavioral Mechanisms 300

MODULE 9.2 **Thirst** 302
Mechanisms of Water Regulation 302
Osmotic Thirst 302
Hypovolemic Thirst and Sodium-Specific Hunger 304
IN CLOSING: The Psychology and Biology of Thirst 305

MODULE 9.3 **Hunger** 307
Digestion and Food Selection 307
Consumption of Dairy Products 308
Food Selection and Behavior 308
Short- and Long-Term Regulation of Feeding 309
Oral Factors 309
The Stomach and Intestines 310
Glucose, Insulin, and Glucagon 310
Leptin 312
Brain Mechanisms 313
The Arcuate Nucleus and Paraventricular Hypothalamus 313
The Lateral Hypothalamus 315
Medial Areas of the Hypothalamus 316
Eating Disorders 317
Genetics and Body Weight 318
Weight Loss 318
Bulimia Nervosa 319
IN CLOSING: The Multiple Controls of Hunger 320

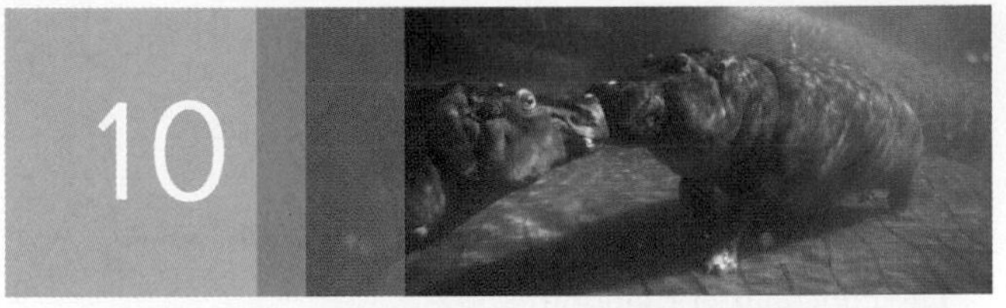

Reproductive Behaviors 325

MODULE 10.1 **Sex and Hormones** 326
Organizing Effects of Sex Hormones 328
Sex Differences in the Hypothalamus 329
Sex Differences in Childhood Behavior 330
Activating Effects of Sex Hormones 331
Males 331
Females 332
Effects of Sex Hormones on Nonsexual Characteristics 334
Parental Behavior 336
IN CLOSING: Reproductive Behaviors and Motivations 338

MODULE 10.2 **Variations in Sexual Behavior** 341
Evolutionary Interpretations of Mating Behavior 341
Interest in Multiple Mates 341
What Men and Women Seek in a Mate 342
Differences in Jealousy 342
Evolved or Learned? 342
Gender Identity and Gender-Differentiated Behaviors 343
Intersexes 343
Interests and Preferences of CAH Girls 344
Testicular Feminization 344
Issues of Gender Assignment and Rearing 344
Discrepancies of Sexual Appearance 345
Sexual Orientation 346
Behavioral and Anatomical Differences 346
Genetics 346
An Evolutionary Question 347
Prenatal Influences 348
Brain Anatomy 348
IN CLOSING: We Are Not All the Same 350

Emotional Behaviors 355

MODULE 11.1 **What Is Emotion?** 356
Emotions and Autonomic Arousal 356

Is Physiological Arousal *Necessary* for Emotional Feelings? 357
Is Physiological Arousal *Sufficient* for Emotions? 358
Is Emotion a Useful Concept? 359
Do People Have a Limited Number of Basic Emotions? 361
The Functions of Emotion 362
Emotions and Moral Decisions 362
Decision Making after Brain Damage that Impairs Emotions 363
IN CLOSING: Emotions and the Nervous System 365

MODULE 11.2 Attack and Escape Behaviors 367
Attack Behaviors 367
Effects of Hormones 368
Serotonin Synapses and Aggressive Behavior 368
Heredity and Environment in Violence 370
Fear and Anxiety 371
Role of the Amygdala 371
Studies of Rodents 371
Studies of Monkeys 373
Response of the Human Amygdala to Visual Stimuli 373
Individual Differences in Amygdala Response and Anxiety 373
Damage to the Human Amygdala 374
Anxiety Disorders 376
Relief from Anxiety 377
Pharmacological Relief 377
Alcohol as an Anxiety Reducer 378
Learning to Erase Anxiety 378
IN CLOSING: Doing Something about Emotions 379

MODULE 11.3 Stress and Health 383
Stress and the General Adaptation Syndrome 383
Stress and the Hypothalamus-Pituitary-Adrenal Cortex Axis 383
The Immune System 384
Effects of Stress on the Immune System 385
Stress Control 386
IN CLOSING: Emotions and Body Reactions 387

12

The Biology of Learning and Memory 391

MODULE 12.1 Learning, Memory, and Amnesia 392
Localized Representations of Memory 392
Lashley's Search for the Engram 392
The Modern Search for the Engram 394
Types of Memory 395
Short-Term and Long-Term Memory 395
Our Changing Views of Consolidation 396
Working Memory 397
The Hippocampus 397
People with Hippocampal Damage 398
Theories of the Function of the Hippocampus 401
Other Types of Amnesia 403
Korsakoff's Syndrome 403
Alzheimer's Disease 404
What Patients with Amnesia Teach Us 406
The Basal Ganglia 406
Other Brain Areas and Memory 407
IN CLOSING: Types of Memory 408

MODULE 12.2 Storing Information in the Nervous System 412
Blind Alleys and Abandoned Mines 412
Learning and the Hebbian Synapse 413
Single-Cell Mechanisms of Invertebrate Behavior Change 414
Aplysia as an Experimental Animal 414
Habituation in *Aplysia* 414
Sensitization in *Aplysia* 414
Long-Term Potentiation in Vertebrates 415
Biochemical Mechanisms 415
Improving Memory 419
IN CLOSING: The Physiology of Memory 420

13

Cognitive Functions 423

MODULE 13.1 Lateralization of Function 424
The Left and Right Hemispheres 424
Visual and Auditory Connections to the Hemispheres 425
The Corpus Callosum and the Split-Brain Operation 426
Split Hemispheres: Competition and Cooperation 428

The Right Hemisphere 429
Hemispheric Specializations in Intact Brains 430
Development of Lateralization and Handedness 431
Anatomical Differences between the Hemispheres 431
Maturation of the Corpus Callosum 431
Avoiding Overstatements 432
IN CLOSING: One Brain, Two Hemispheres 432

MODULE 13.2 **Evolution and Physiology of Language** 435
Nonhuman Precursors of Language 435
Common Chimpanzees 435
Bonobos 436
Nonprimates 437
How Did Humans Evolve Language? 437
Language: By-product of Intelligence, or Specialized Adaptation? 438
A Sensitive Period for Language Learning 440
Brain Damage and Language 440
Broca's Aphasia (Nonfluent Aphasia) 440
Wernicke's Aphasia (Fluent Aphasia) 442
Music and Language 443
Dyslexia 444
IN CLOSING: Language and the Brain 445

MODULE 13.3 **Conscious and Unconscious Processes and Attention** 448
The Mind–Brain Relationship 448
Consciousness of a Stimulus 449
Experiments Using Masking 450
Experiments Using Binocular Rivalry 450
The Fate of an Unattended Stimulus 451
Consciousness as a Threshold Phenomenon 452
The Timing of Consciousness 452
Conscious and Unconscious People 453
Attention 453
Brain Areas Controlling Attention 454
Spatial Neglect 454
IN CLOSING: Attending to Attention and Being Conscious of Consciousness 456

MODULE 13.4 **Social Neuroscience** 459
The Biology of Love 459
Empathy and Altruism 460
IN CLOSING: The Social Brain 461

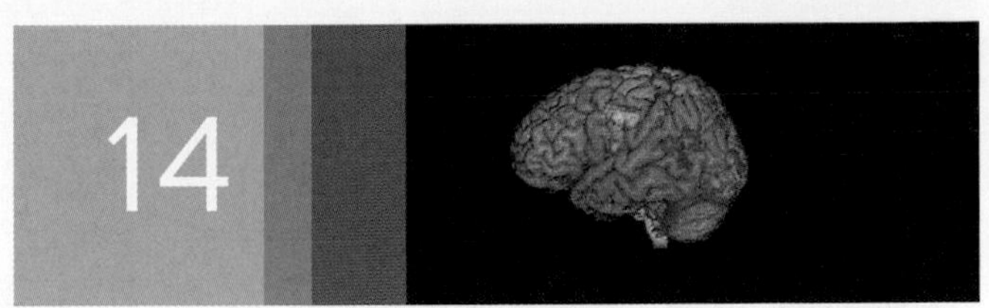

Psychological Disorders 465

MODULE 14.1 **Substance Abuse and Addiction** 466
Drug Mechanisms 466
Similarities and Differences among Addictive Substances 466
Cravings 468
Tolerance and Withdrawal 468
Predispositions 469
Genetic Influences 469
Environmental Influences 469
Behavioral Predictors of Abuse 470
Treatments 471
Medications to Combat Alcohol Abuse 471
Medications to Combat Opiate Abuse 472
In the Experimental Stage 472
IN CLOSING: The Psychology and Biology of Addiction 472

MODULE 14.2 **Mood Disorders** 475
Major Depressive Disorder 475
Genetics 475
Abnormalities of Hemispheric Dominance 476
Antidepressant Drugs 477
How Effective Are Antidepressants? 479
Alternatives to Antidepressant Drugs 480
Bipolar Disorder 482
Treatments 482
Seasonal Affective Disorder 483
IN CLOSING: The Biology of Mood Swings 484

MODULE 14.3 **Schizophrenia** 487
Diagnosis 487
Differential Diagnosis of Schizophrenia 488
Demographic Data 488
Genetics 489
Family Studies 489
Adopted Children Who Develop Schizophrenia 490
Efforts to Locate a Gene 490

The Neurodevelopmental Hypothesis 491
- Prenatal and Neonatal Environment 491
- Mild Brain Abnormalities 492
- Long-term Course 493
- Early Development and Later Psychopathology 493

Treatments 493
- Antipsychotic Drugs and Dopamine 493
- Role of Glutamate 495
- Other Medications 495

IN CLOSING: Many Remaining Mysteries 496

MODULE 14.4 Autism Spectrum Disorders 499

Symptoms and Characteristics 499

Genetics and Other Causes 500

Treatments 500

IN CLOSING: Developmental Disorders 501

APPENDIX A

Brief, Basic Chemistry 503

APPENDIX B

Society for Neuroscience Policies on the Use of Animals and Human Subjects in Research 509

References 512

Name Index 567

Subject Index/Glossary 593

Preface

In the first edition of this text, published in 1981, I remarked, "I almost wish I could get parts of this text . . . printed in disappearing ink, programmed to fade within ten years of publication, so that I will not be embarrassed by statements that will look primitive from some future perspective." I would say the same thing today, except that I would like for the ink to fade faster. Biological psychology progresses rapidly, and much that we thought we knew becomes obsolete.

Biological psychology is the most interesting topic in the world. No doubt many people in other fields think their topic is the most interesting, but they are wrong. This really is the most interesting. Unfortunately, it is easy to get so bogged down in memorizing facts that one loses the big picture. The big picture here is fascinating and profound: Your brain activity *is* your mind. I hope that readers of this book will remember that message even after they forget some of the details.

Each chapter is divided into modules; each module begins with an introduction and finishes with a summary. This organization makes it easy for instructors to assign part of a chapter per day instead of a whole chapter per week. Modules can also be covered in a different order. Indeed, of course, whole chapters can be taken in different orders.

I assume that readers have a basic background in psychology and biology and understand such terms as classical conditioning, reinforcement, vertebrate, mammal, gene, chromosome, cell, and mitochondrion. I also assume a high school chemistry course. Those with a weak background in chemistry or a fading memory of it may consult Appendix A.

MindTap for *Biological Psychology*, 12th Edition

MindTap for *Biological Psychology*, 12th Edition, engages and empowers students to produce their best work—consistently. By seamlessly integrating course material with videos, activities, apps, and much more, MindTap creates a unique learning path that fosters increased comprehension and efficiency.

For students:

- MindTap delivers real-world relevance with activities and assignments that help students build critical thinking and analytic skills that will transfer to other courses and their professional lives.
- MindTap helps students stay organized and efficient with a single destination that reflects what's important to the instructor, along with the tools students need to master the content.
- MindTap empowers and motivates students with information that shows where they stand at all times—both individually and compared to the highest performers in class.

Additionally, for instructors, MindTap allows you to:

- Control what content students see and when they see it with a learning path that can be used as-is or matched to your syllabus exactly.
- Create a unique learning path of relevant readings and multimedia and activities that move students up the learning taxonomy from basic knowledge and comprehension to analysis, application, and critical thinking.
- Integrate your own content into the MindTap Reader using your own documents or pulling from sources like RSS feeds, YouTube videos, websites, Googledocs, and more.
- Use powerful analytics and reports that provide a snapshot of class progress, time in course, engagement, and completion.

Changes in this Edition

One new feature in this edition is a set of multiple-choice review questions at the end of each module. This edition also includes several changes in organization and many changes in content, to reflect the rapid progress in biological psychology. It includes well over 600 new references, more than 85 percent of them from 2011 or later, and many new or revised illustrations. Here are a few noteworthy items:

The module on genetics and evolution of behavior has been moved from the first chapter to the chapter on development (Chapter 4). The remainder of the first chapter (introduction to the field, concept of mind–body monism, job opportunities, ethics of animal research, etc.) is now labeled "Introduction." The introduction is brief, but I believe important. Note especially the section "Three Main Points to Remember from this Book."

The discussion of addictions, previously in the Synapses chapter, is now a module in the chapter on Psychological Disorders (Chapter 14). Material about how drugs exert their effects is integrated into the second module of the Synapses chapter (Chapter 2).

Chapter 3 (Anatomy and Research Methods) has an expanded treatment of optogenetics, rapidly becoming a more important method in neuroscience. The discussion of fMRI has new examples and a clearer emphasis that we need to be cautious about the conclusions we draw from fMRI studies.

Chapter 4 (Genetics, Evolution, Development and Plasticity) now includes a short section on brain evolution. The discussion of behavioral evolution now acknowledges that group selection is sometimes plausible. Important updates are added to the discussions of new neurons in the adult brain, fetal alcohol syndrome, and brain changes in adulthood.

Chapter 5 (Vision) is rearranged at the start to emphasize a fundamental point that a third of college students miss, sometimes even after taking courses in physics, perception, and biological psychology: We see because light enters the eyes, not because we send out sight rays! This chapter also has a revised description of the distinction between the ventral and dorsal pathways.

Chapter 6 (Other Sensory Systems) has a new section on the role of attention in hearing loss, and a new study showing that some people developed synesthesia by playing with colored refrigerator magnets during childhood.

Chapter 7 (Movement) has a substantial revision of the section about the basal ganglia, stressing their role in motivating movements.

Chapter 10 (Reproductive Behaviors) has a new section on how sex hormones affect nonsexual behaviors. The section on activating effects of hormones is reorganized in terms of males versus females instead of rodents versus humans.

Chapter 11 (Emotional Behavior) begins with a reorganized and reconsidered discussion of the relationship between emotion and autonomic arousal. A new section is titled, "Do People Have a Limited Number of Basic Emotions?" An expanded treatment of reconsolidation relates it to the possibility of alleviating learned fears.

Chapter 12 (The Biology of Learning and Memory) has some reorganization, and a more thorough explanation of the role of the basal ganglia in probabilistic learning.

Chapter 13 (Cognitive Functions) has a new short module on social neuroscience. It also has a new discussion of what Michael Gazzaniga calls "the interpreter," the tendency of the left hemisphere to invent explanations, correct or not, for unconsciously influenced behaviors. The discussion of consciousness is reorganized.

Chapter 14 (Psychological Disorders) has a new module on addictions and a new short module on autism spectrum disorders. The modules on depression and schizophrenia have been updated in many ways.

A Comprehensive Teaching and Learning Package

Biological Psychology, 12th edition, is accompanied by an array of supplements developed to facilitate both instructors' and students' best experience inside as well as outside the classroom. All of the supplements continuing from the 11th edition have been thoroughly revised and updated; other supplements are new to this edition. Cengage Learning invites you to take full advantage of the teaching and learning tools available to you and has prepared the following descriptions of each.

Online Instructor's Resource Manual

This manual, updated and expanded for the 12th edition, is designed to help streamline and maximize the effectiveness of your course preparation. It provides chapter outlines and learning objectives; class demonstrations and projects, including lecture tips and activities, with handouts; a list of video resources, additional suggested readings and related websites, discussion questions designed to work both in class and on message boards for online classes; key terms from the text; and James Kalat's answers to the "Thought Questions" that conclude each module.

Cengage Learning Testing, powered by Cognero for *Biological Psychology*, 12th Edition

Cognero is a flexible, online system that allows you to author, edit, and manage test bank content as well as create multiple test versions in an instant. You can deliver tests from your school's learning management system, your classroom, or wherever you want.

Acknowledgments

Let me tell you something about researchers in this field: As a rule, they are amazingly cooperative with textbook authors. Many colleagues sent me comments and helpful suggestions. I thank especially Glenn Weisfeld, Wayne State University.

I appreciate the helpful comments provided by the following reviewers in preparation of the 12th edition: John Alden, Lipscomb University; Jeremy Cohen, Xavier University of Louisiana; Robert Fisher, Lee University; and Lorenz Neuwirth, The College of Staten Island (CUNY).

I appreciate the helpful comments provided by instructors who reviewed previous editions of the text, as well as those who participated in a survey that gave us valuable insights on the issues in this course.

Text Reviewers and Contributors:

- John Agnew, *University of Colorado at Boulder*
- John Dale Alden III, *Lipscomb University*
- Joanne Altman, *Washburn University*
- Kevin Antshel, *SUNY–Upstate Medical University*
- Ryan Auday, *Gordon College*
- Susan Baillet, *University of Portland*
- Teresa Barber, *Dickinson College*
- Christie Bartholomew, *Kent State University*
- Howard Bashinski, *University of Colorado*
- Bakhtawar Bhadha, *Pasadena City College*
- Chris Brill, *Old Dominion University*
- J. Timothy Cannon, *The University of Scranton*
- Lore Carvajal, *Triton College*
- Sarah Cavanagh, *Assumption College*
- Linda Bryant Caviness, *La Sierra University*
- Cathy Cleveland, *East Los Angeles College*
- Elie Cohen, *The Lander College for Men (Touro College)*
- Howard Cromwell, *Bowling Green State University*
- David Crowley, *Washington University*
- Carol DeVolder, *St. Ambrose University*
- Jaime L. Diaz-Granados, *Baylor University*
- Carl DiPerna, *Onondaga Community College*
- Francine Dolins, *University of Michigan–Dearborn*
- Timothy Donahue, *Virginia Commonwealth University*
- Michael Dowdle, *Mt. San Antonio College*
- Jeff Dyche, *James Madison University*
- Gary Felsten, *Indiana University–Purdue University Columbus*
- Erin Marie Fleming, *Kent State University*
- Laurie Fowler, *Weber State University*
- Deborah Gagnon, *Wells College*
- Jonathan Gewirtz, *University of Minnesota*
- Jackie Goldstein, *Samford University*
- Peter Green, *Maryville University*
- Jeff Grimm, *Western Washington University*
- Amy Clegg Haerich, *Riverside Community College*
- Christopher Hayashi, *Southwestern College*
- Suzane Helfer, *Adrian College*
- Alicia Helion, *Lakeland College*
- Jackie Hembrook, *University of New Hampshire*
- Phu Hoang, *Texas A&M International University*
- Richard Howe, *College of the Canyon*
- Barry Hurwitz, *University of Miami*
- Karen Jennings, *Keene State College*
- Craig Johnson, *Towson University*
- Robert Tex Johnson, *Delaware County Community College*
- Kathryn Kelly, *Northwestern State University*
- Shannon Kendey, *Hood College*
- Craig Kinsley, *University of Richmond*
- Philip Langlais, *Old Dominion University*
- Jerry Lee, *Albright College*
- Robert Lennartz, *Sierra College*
- Hui-Yun Li, *Oregon Institute of Technology*
- Cyrille Magne, *Middle Tennessee State University*
- Michael Matthews, *U.S. Military Academy (West Point)*
- Estelle Mayhew, *Rutgers University–New Brunswick*
- Daniel McConnell, *University of Central Florida*
- Maria McLean, *Thomas More College*
- Elaine McLeskey, *Belmont Technical College*
- Corinne McNamara, *Kennesaw State University*
- Brian Metcalf, *Hawaii Pacific University*
- Richard Mills, *College of DuPage*
- Daniel Montoya, *Fayetteville State University*
- Paulina Multhaupt, *Macomb Community College*
- Walter Murphy, *Texas A&M University–Central Texas*
- Joseph Nedelec, *Florida State University*
- Ian Norris, *Murray State University*
- Marcia Pasqualini, *Avila University*
- Susana Pecina, *University of Michigan–Dearborn*

- Linda Perrotti, *The University of Texas–Arlington*
- Terry Pettijohn, *The Ohio State University*
- Jennifer Phillips, *Mount St. Mary's University*
- Edward Pollak, *West Chester University*
- Brian Pope, *Tusculum College*
- Mark Prendergast, *University of Kentucky*
- Jean Pretz, *Elizabethtown College*
- Mark Prokosch, *Elon University*
- Adam Prus, *Northern Michigan University*
- Khaleel Razak, *University of California–Riverside*
- John Rowe, *Florida Gateway College*
- David Rudek, *Aurora University*
- Jeffrey Rudski, *Muhlenberg College*
- Karen Sabbah, *California State University–Northridge*
- Sharleen Sakai, *Michigan State University*
- Ron Salazar, *San Juan College*
- Shanon Saszik, *Northeastern University*
- Steven Schandler, *Chapman University*
- Sue Schumacher, *North Carolina A&T State University*
- Vicki Sheafer, *LeTourneau University*
- Timothy Shearon, *The College of Idaho*
- Stephanie Simon-Dack, *Ball State University*
- Steve Smith, *University of California–Santa Barbara*
- Suzanne Sollars, *University of Nebraska–Omaha*
- Gretchen Sprow, *University of North Carolina–Chapel Hill*
- Jeff Stowell, *Eastern Illinois University*
- Gary Thorne, *Gonzaga University*
- Chris Tromborg, *Sacramento City College and University of California–Davis*
- Lucy Troup, *Colorado State University*
- Joseph Trunzo, *Bryant University*
- Sandy Venneman, *University of Houston–Victoria*
- Beth Venzke, *Concordia University*
- Ruvanee Vilhauer, *Felician College*
- Jacquie Wall, *University of Indianapolis*
- Zoe Warwick, *University of Maryland–Baltimore County*
- Jon Weimer, *Columbia College*
- Rosalyn Weller, *The University of Alabama–Birmingham*
- Adam Wenzel, *Saint Anselm College*
- David Widman, *Juniata College*
- Steffen Wilson, *Eastern Kentucky University*
- Joseph Wister, *Chatham University*
- Jessica Yokley, *University of Pittsburgh*

My product manager, Timothy Matray, has been as helpful and supportive as he could possibly be. Bob Jucha, my content developer for this edition, carefully oversaw this complex project, and has my highest respect and appreciation. Jill Traut supervised the production, a major task for a book like this one. As art editor, Vernon Boes's considerable artistic abilities helped to compensate for my complete lack. The production phases of the 12th edition were skillfully overseen by Samen Iqbal, content product manager. Brittani Hall had charge of permissions, a major task for a book like this. Carly Berger was the photo manager; I hope you enjoy the new photos in this text as much as I do. I thank the rest of the entire team at Cengage Learning for their contributions, including Melissa Larmon, executive marketing manager; Jasmin Tokatian, media developer; and Nicole Richards, product assistant. I have been fortunate to have Heather McElwain as my copy editor. All of these people have been splendid colleagues, and I thank them immensely.

I thank my wife, Jo Ellen, for keeping my spirits high, and my department head, Douglas Gillan, and my son Sam for many original and insightful ideas about brain functioning.

I welcome correspondence from both students and faculty. Write James W. Kalat, Department of Psychology, Box 7650, North Carolina State University, Raleigh, NC 27695–7801, USA. E-mail: james_kalat@ncsu.edu

James W. Kalat

Renee Lynn/Corbis

Overview and Major Issues

Introduction

OUTLINE

The Biological Approach to Behavior
Biological Explanations of Behavior
Career Opportunities
The Use of Animals in Research
In Closing: Your Brain and Your Experience

LEARNING OBJECTIVES

After studying this introduction, you should be able to:

1. Briefly state the mind–brain problem and contrast monism with dualism.
2. List three general points that are important to remember from this text.
3. Give examples of physiological, ontogenetic, evolutionary, and functional explanations of behavior.
4. Discuss the ethical issues of research with laboratory animals.

It is often said that Man is unique among animals. It is worth looking at this term *unique* before we discuss our subject proper. The word may in this context have two slightly different meanings. It may mean: Man is strikingly different—he is not identical with any animal. This is of course true. It is true also of all other animals: Each species, even each individual, is unique in this sense. But the term is also often used in a more absolute sense: Man is so different, so "essentially different" (whatever that means) that the gap between him and animals cannot possibly be bridged—he is something altogether new. Used in this absolute sense, the term is scientifically meaningless. Its use also reveals and may reinforce conceit, and it leads to complacency and defeatism because it assumes that it will be futile even to search for animal roots. It is prejudging the issue.

Niko Tinbergen (1973, p. 161)

Biological psychologists study the animal roots of behavior, relating actions and experiences to genetics and physiology. In this chapter, we consider three major issues: the relationship between mind and brain, the roles of nature and nurture, and the ethics of research. We also briefly consider career opportunities in this and related fields.

OPPOSITE: It is tempting to try to "get inside the mind" of people and other animals, to imagine what they are thinking or feeling. In contrast, biological psychologists try to explain behavior in terms of its physiology, development, evolution, and function. *Source: C. D. L. Wynne, 2004*

The Biological Approach to Behavior

Of all the questions that people ask, two stand out as the most profound and the most difficult. One of those questions deals with physics. The other pertains to the relationship between physics and psychology.

Gottfried Leibniz (1714) posed the first of these questions: "Why is there something rather than nothing?" It would seem that nothingness would be the default state. Evidently, the universe—or whoever or whatever created the universe—had to be self-created.

So . . . how did that happen?

That question is supremely baffling, but a subordinate question is more amenable to discussion: Given the existence of a universe, why this particular kind of universe? Could the universe have been fundamentally different? Our universe has protons, neutrons, and electrons with particular dimensions of mass and charge. It has four fundamental forces—gravity, electromagnetism, the strong nuclear force, and the weak nuclear force. What if any of these properties had been different?

Beginning in the 1980s, specialists in a branch of physics known as *string theory* set out to prove mathematically that this is the only possible way the universe could be. Succeeding in that effort would have been theoretically satisfying, but alas, as string theorists worked through their equations, they concluded that this is not the only possible universe. The universe could have taken a vast number of forms with different laws of physics. How vast a number? Imagine the number 1 followed by about 500 zeros. And that's the *low* estimate.

Of all those possible universes, how many could have supported life? Very few. Consider the following (Davies, 2006):

- If gravity were weaker, matter would not condense into stars and planets. If it were stronger, stars would burn brighter and use up their fuel too quickly for life to evolve.
- If the electromagnetic force were stronger, the protons within an atom would repel one another so strongly that atoms would burst apart.
- In the beginning was hydrogen. The other elements formed by fusion within stars. The only way to get those elements out of stars and into planets is for a star to explode as a supernova and send its contents out into the galaxy. If the weak nuclear force were *either* a bit stronger *or* a bit weaker, a star could not explode.
- Because of the exact ratio of the electromagnetic force to the strong nuclear force, helium (element 2 on the periodic table) and beryllium (element 4) go into resonance within a star, enabling them to fuse easily into carbon (element 6), which is essential to life as we know it. (It's hard to talk about life as we don't know it.) If either the electromagnetic force or the strong nuclear force changed slightly (less than 1 percent), the universe would have almost no carbon.
- The electromagnetic force is 10^{40} times stronger than gravity. If gravity were a bit stronger relative to the electromagnetic force, planets would not form. If it were a bit weaker, planets would consist of only gases.

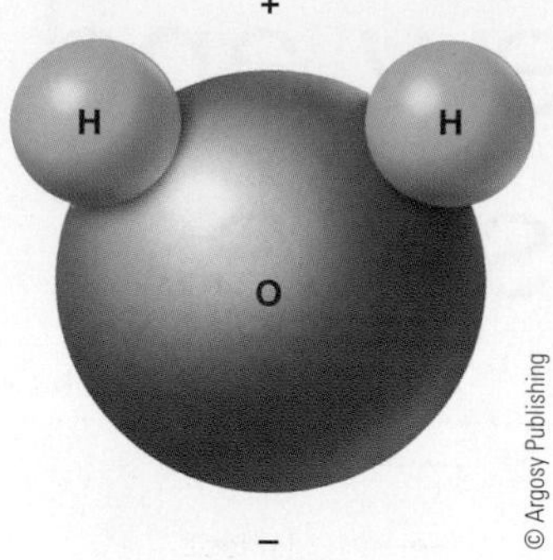

FIGURE INTRO.1 A water molecule
Because of the hydrogen-oxygen-hydrogen angle, one end of a water molecule is more positive and the other negative. The exact difference in charge causes water molecules to attract one another just enough to be a liquid.

- Why is water (H_2O) a liquid? Other light molecules, such as carbon dioxide, nitric oxide, ozone, and methane are gases except at extremely low temperatures. In a water molecule, the two hydrogen ions form a 104.5° angle (Figure Intro.1). As a result, one end of the water molecule has a slight positive charge and the other a slight negative charge. The difference is enough for water molecules to attract one another electrically. If they attracted one another a bit less, all water would be a gas (steam). But if water molecules attracted one another a bit more strongly, water would always be a solid (ice).

In short, the universe could have been different in many ways, nearly all of which would have made life impossible. Why is the universe the way it is? Maybe it's just a coincidence. (Lucky for us, huh?) Or maybe intelligence of some sort guided the formation of the universe. That hypothesis clearly goes beyond the reach of empirical science. A third possibility that many physicists favor is that a huge number of other universes (perhaps an infinite number) really *do* exist, and we of course know about only the kind of universe in which we could evolve. That hypothesis, too, goes beyond the reach of empirical science, as we cannot know about other universes. Will we ever know why the universe is the way it is? Maybe or maybe not, but the question is fascinating.

At the start I mentioned two profound and difficult questions. The second one is called the **mind–brain problem** or the **mind–body problem**, the question of how mind relates to brain activity. Put another way: Given a universe composed of matter and energy, why is there such a thing as consciousness? We can imagine how matter came together to form molecules, and how certain kinds of carbon compounds came together to form a primitive type of life, which then evolved into animals with brains and complex behaviors. But why are certain types of brain activity conscious?

So far, no one has offered a convincing explanation of consciousness. A few scholars have suggested that we abandon the concept of consciousness altogether (Churchland, 1986; Dennett, 1991). That proposal seems to avoid the question, not answer it. Chalmers (2007) and Rensch (1977) proposed, instead, that we regard consciousness as a fundamental property of matter. A fundamental property is one that cannot be reduced to something else. For example, mass and electrical charge are fundamental properties. Maybe consciousness is like that.

But it's an unsatisfying answer. First, consciousness isn't like other fundamental properties. Matter has mass all the

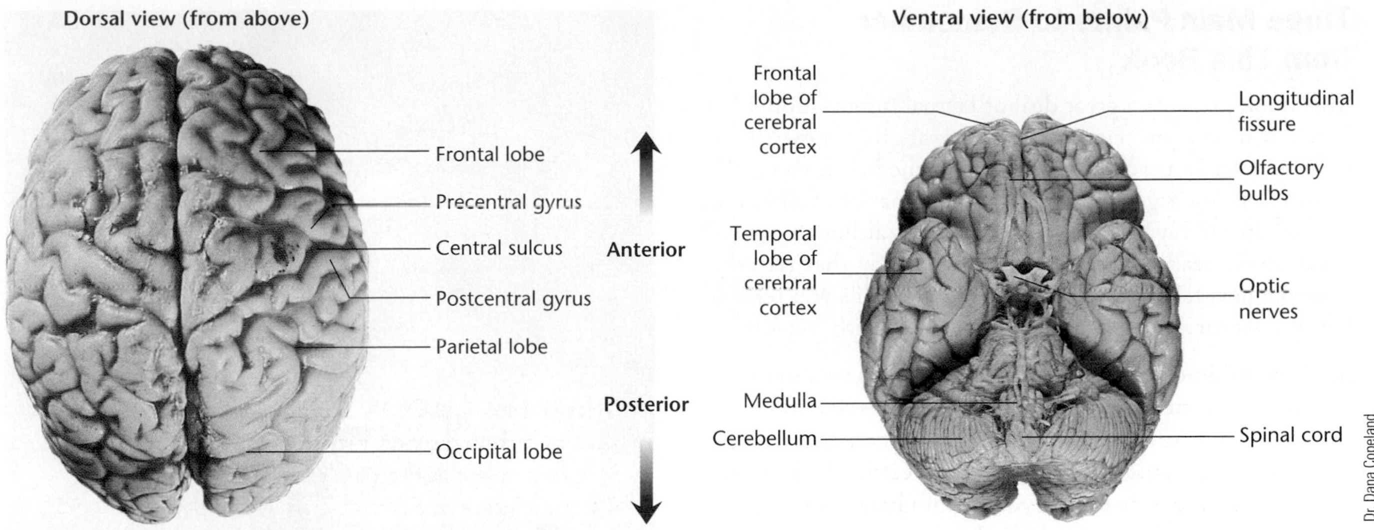

FIGURE INTRO.2 Two views of the human brain
The brain has an enormous number of divisions and subareas; the labels point to a few of the main ones on the surface of the brain.

time, and protons and electrons have charge all the time. So far as we can tell, consciousness occurs only in certain parts of certain kinds of nervous systems, just some of the time—not when you are in a dreamless sleep, and not when you are in a coma. Besides, it's unsatisfying to call *anything* a fundamental property, even mass or charge. To say that mass is a fundamental property doesn't mean that there is no reason. It means that we have given up on finding a reason. And, in fact, contemporary physicists have not given up. They are trying to explain mass and charge in terms of the Higgs boson and other elements of the universe. To say that consciousness is a fundamental property would mean that we have given up on explaining it. Certainly it is too soon to give up. After we learn as much as possible about the nervous system, maybe someone will have a brilliant insight and understand what consciousness is all about. Even if not, the research will teach us much that is useful and interesting.

The Field of Biological Psychology

Biological psychology is the study of the physiological, evolutionary, and developmental mechanisms of behavior and experience. It is approximately synonymous with the terms *biopsychology, psychobiology, physiological psychology,* and *behavioral neuroscience.* The term *biological psychology* emphasizes that the goal is to relate biology to issues of psychology. *Neuroscience* includes much that is relevant to behavior but also includes more detail about anatomy and chemistry.

Biological psychology is not only a field of study, but also a point of view. It holds that we think and act as we do because of brain mechanisms that we evolved because ancient animals with these mechanisms survived and reproduced better than animals with other mechanisms.

Biological psychology deals mostly with brain activity. Figure Intro.2 offers a view of the human brain from the top (what anatomists call a *dorsal* view) and from the bottom (a *ventral* view). The labels point to a few important areas that will become more familiar as you proceed through this text. An inspection of a brain reveals distinct subareas. At the microscopic level, we find two kinds of cells: the *neurons* (Figure Intro.3) and the *glia.* Neurons, which convey messages to one another and to muscles and glands, vary enormously in size, shape, and functions. The glia, generally smaller than neurons, have many functions but do not convey information over great distances. The activities of neurons and glia somehow produce an enormous wealth of behavior and experience. This book is about researchers' attempts to elaborate on that word *somehow.*

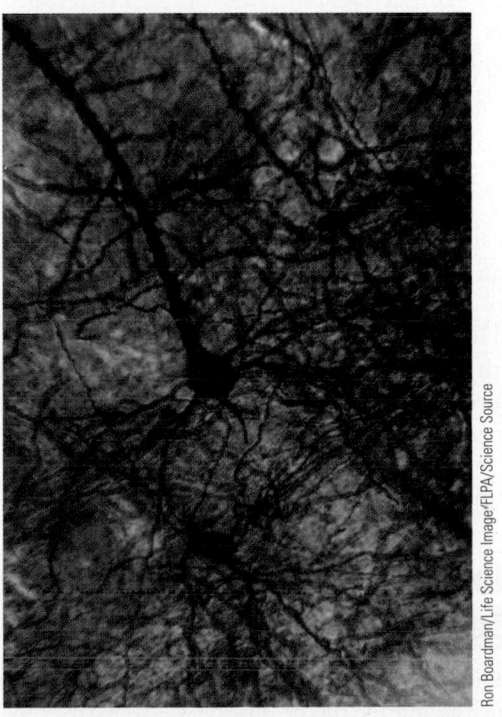

FIGURE INTRO.3 Neurons, magnified
The brain is composed of individual cells called neurons and glia.

Three Main Points to Remember from This Book

This book presents a great deal of factual information. How much of it will you remember a few years from now? If you have a career in psychology, biology, or medicine, you might continue using a great deal of the information. Otherwise, you will inevitably forget many of the facts (although you will occasionally read about a new research study that refreshes your memory). Regardless of how many details you remember, at least three general points should stick with you forever:

1. Perception occurs in your brain. When something contacts your hand, the hand sends a message to your brain. You feel it in your brain, not your hand. (Electrical stimulation of your brain could produce a hand experience even if you had no hand. A hand disconnected from your brain has no experience.) Similarly, when you see something, the experience is in your head, not "out there." You do NOT send "sight rays" out of your eyes, and even if you did, they wouldn't do you any good. The chapter on vision elaborates on this point.
2. Mental activity and certain types of brain activity are, so far as we can tell, inseparable. This position is known as **monism**, the idea that the universe consists of only one type of being. (The opposite is **dualism**, the idea that minds are one type of substance and matter is another.) Nearly all neuroscientists and philosophers support the position of monism. Whether you agree is up to you, but you should at least understand monism and the evidence behind it. The chapter on consciousness considers this issue directly, but nearly everything in the book pertains to the mind–brain relationship in one way or another.
3. We should be cautious about what is an explanation and what is not. For example, consider a study that shows us that certain brain areas are less active than usual in people with depression. Does that evidence tell us *why* people became depressed? No, it does not, unless and until we know a great deal more. For illustration, on average, the legs are also less active than average in people with depression, but inactive legs do not cause depression. Another study might tell us that certain genes are more common in people with depression than in others. Would that explain depression? Not at all, until we understand what those genes do, how they interact with the environment, and so forth. We should avoid overstating the conclusions from any research study.

Biological Explanations of Behavior

Commonsense explanations of behavior often refer to intentional goals such as, "He did this because he was trying to . . ." or "She did that because she wanted to. . . ." But often, we have no reason to assume intentions. A 4-month-old bird migrating south for the first time presumably does not know why. The next spring, when she lays an egg, sits on it, and defends it from predators, again she doesn't know why. Even humans don't always know the reasons for their own behaviors. Yawning and laughter are two examples. You do them, but can you explain what they accomplish?

Researchers continue to debate the function of yawning. Brain mechanisms produce many behaviors that we engage in without necessarily knowing why.

In contrast to commonsense explanations, biological explanations of behavior fall into four categories: physiological, ontogenetic, evolutionary, and functional (Tinbergen, 1951). A **physiological explanation** relates a behavior to the activity of the brain and other organs. It deals with the machinery of the body—for example, the chemical reactions that enable hormones to influence brain activity and the routes by which brain activity controls muscle contractions.

The term *ontogenetic* comes from Greek roots meaning the origin (or genesis) of being. An **ontogenetic explanation** describes how a structure or behavior develops, including the influences of genes, nutrition, experiences, and their interactions. For example, the ability to inhibit impulses develops gradually from infancy through the teenage years, reflecting gradual maturation of the frontal parts of the brain.

An **evolutionary explanation** reconstructs the evolutionary history of a structure or behavior. The characteristic features of an animal are almost always modifications of something found in ancestral species (Shubin, Tabin, & Carroll, 2009). For example, bat wings are modified arms, and porcupine quills are modified hairs. In behavior, monkeys use tools occasionally, and humans evolved elaborations on those abilities that enable us to use tools even better (Peeters et al., 2009). Evolutionary explanations call attention to behavioral similarities among related species.

A **functional explanation** describes *why* a structure or behavior evolved as it did. Within a small, isolated population, a gene can spread by accident through a process called *genetic drift*. For example, a dominant male with many offspring spreads all his genes, including some that helped him become dominant and other genes that were irrelevant or even disadvantageous. However, a gene that is prevalent in a large population probably provided some advantage—at least in the past, though not necessarily today. A functional explanation identifies that advantage. For example, many species have an appearance that matches their background (see Figure Intro.4). A functional explanation is that camouflaged appearance makes the animal inconspicuous to predators. Some species use their behavior as part of the camouflage. For example, zone-tailed hawks, native to Mexico and the southwestern United States, fly among vultures and hold their wings in the same posture as vultures. Small mammals and birds run for cover when they see a hawk, but they learn to ignore vultures, which pose no threat to healthy animals. Because the zone-tailed hawks resemble vultures in both appearance and flight behavior, their prey disregard them, enabling the hawks to pick up easy meals (W. S. Clark, 2004).

To contrast the four types of biological explanation, consider how they all apply to one example, birdsong (Catchpole & Slater, 1995):

Steve Maslowski/Science Source

Unlike all other birds, doves and pigeons can drink with their heads down. (Others fill their mouths and then raise their heads.) A physiological explanation would describe these birds' unusual pattern of nerves and throat muscles. An evolutionary explanation states that all doves and pigeons share this behavioral capacity because they inherited their genes from a common ancestor.

Krzysztof Wiktor/Shutterstock.com

FIGURE INTRO.4 A seadragon, an Australian fish related to the seahorse, lives among kelp plants, looks like kelp, and usually drifts slowly, *acting* like kelp.
A functional explanation is that potential predators overlook a fish that resembles inedible plants. An evolutionary explanation is that genetic modifications expanded smaller appendages that were present in these fish's ancestors.

Type of Explanation	Example from Birdsong
Physiological	A particular area of a songbird brain grows under the influence of testosterone; hence, it is larger in breeding males than in females or immature birds. That brain area enables a mature male to sing.
Ontogenetic	In many species, a young male bird learns its song by listening to adult males. Development of the song requires certain genes and the opportunity to hear the appropriate song during a sensitive period early in life.
Evolutionary	Certain pairs of species have similar songs. For example, dunlins and Baird's sandpipers, two shorebird species, give their calls in distinct pulses, unlike other shorebirds. The similarity suggests that the two evolved from a single ancestor.
Functional	In most bird species, only the male sings. He sings only during the reproductive season and only in his territory. The functions of the song are to attract females and warn away other males.

STOP & CHECK

1. How does an evolutionary explanation differ from a functional explanation?

ANSWER

1. An evolutionary explanation states what evolved from what. For example, humans evolved from earlier primates and therefore have certain features that we inherited from those ancestors, even if the features are not useful to us today. A functional explanation states why something was advantageous and therefore evolutionarily selected.

TABLE INTRO.1 Fields of Specialization

Specialization	Description
Research fields	**Research positions ordinarily require a PhD. Researchers are employed by universities, hospitals, pharmaceutical firms, and research institutes.**
Neuroscientist	Studies the anatomy, biochemistry, or physiology of the nervous system. (This broad term includes any of the next five, as well as other specialties not listed.)
Behavioral neuroscientist (almost synonyms: psychobiologist, biopsychologist, or physiological psychologist)	Investigates how functioning of the brain and other organs influences behavior.
Cognitive neuroscientist	Uses brain research, such as scans of brain anatomy or activity, to analyze and explore people's knowledge, thinking, and problem solving.
Neuropsychologist	Conducts behavioral tests to determine the abilities and disabilities of people with various kinds of brain damage and changes in their condition over time. Most neuropsychologists have a mixture of psychological and medical training; they work in hospitals and clinics.
Psychophysiologist	Measures heart rate, breathing rate, brain waves, and other body processes and how they vary from one person to another or one situation to another.
Neurochemist	Investigates the chemical reactions in the brain.
Comparative psychologist (almost synonyms: ethologist, animal behaviorist)	Compares the behaviors of different species and tries to relate them to their habitats and ways of life.
Evolutionary psychologist (almost synonym: sociobiologist)	Relates behaviors, especially social behaviors, including those of humans, to the functions they have served and, therefore, the presumed selective pressures that caused them to evolve.
Practitioner fields of psychology	**In most cases, their work is not directly related to neuroscience. However, practitioners often need to understand it enough to communicate with a client's physician.**
Clinical psychologist	Requires PhD or PsyD; employed by hospital, clinic, private practice, or college; helps people with emotional problems.
Counseling psychologist	Requires PhD or PsyD. Employed by hospital, clinic, private practice, or college. Helps people make educational, vocational, and other decisions.
School psychologist	Requires master's degree or PhD. Most are employed by a school system. Identifies educational needs of schoolchildren, devises a plan to meet the needs, and then helps teachers implement it.
Medical fields	**Practicing medicine requires an MD plus about four years of additional study and practice in a specialization. Physicians are employed by hospitals, clinics, medical schools, and in private practice. Some conduct research in addition to seeing patients.**
Neurologist	Treats people with brain damage or diseases of the brain.
Neurosurgeon	Performs brain surgery.
Psychiatrist	Helps people with emotional distress or troublesome behaviors, sometimes using drugs or other medical procedures.
Allied medical field	**These fields ordinarily require a master's degree or more. Practitioners are employed by hospitals, clinics, private practice, and medical schools.**
Physical therapist	Provides exercise and other treatments to help people with muscle or nerve problems, pain, or anything else that impairs movement.
Occupational therapist	Helps people improve their ability to perform functions of daily life, for example, after a stroke.
Social worker	Helps people deal with personal and family problems. The activities of a social worker overlap those of a clinical psychologist.

Career Opportunities

If you want to consider a career related to biological psychology, you have a range of options relating to research and therapy. Table Intro.1 describes some of the major fields.

A research position ordinarily requires a PhD in psychology, biology, neuroscience, or other related field. People with a master's or bachelor's degree might work in a research laboratory but would not direct it. Many people with a PhD hold college or university positions, where they perform some combination of teaching and research. Others have pure research positions in laboratories sponsored by the government, drug companies, or other industries.

Fields of therapy include clinical psychology, counseling psychology, school psychology, medicine, and allied medical practice such as physical therapy. These fields range from neurologists (who deal exclusively with brain disorders) to social workers and clinical psychologists, who need to recognize possible signs of brain disorder so they can refer a client to a proper specialist.

Anyone who pursues a career in research needs to stay up to date on new developments by attending conventions, consulting with colleagues, and reading research journals, such as *The Journal of Neuroscience, Neurology, Behavioral Neuroscience, Brain Research, Nature Neuroscience,* and *Archives of General Psychiatry*. But what if you are entering a field on the outskirts of neuroscience, such as clinical psychology, school psychology, social work, or physical therapy? In that case, you probably don't want to wade through technical journal articles, but you do want to stay current on major developments, at least enough to converse intelligently with medical colleagues. You can find much information in the magazine *Scientific American Mind* or at websites such as the Dana Foundation at www.dana.org.

The Use of Animals in Research

Certain ethical disputes resist agreement. One is abortion. Another is the use of animals in research. In both cases, well-meaning people on each side of the issue insist that their position is proper and ethical. The dispute is not a matter of the good guys against the bad guys. It is between two views of what is good.

Animals are used in many kinds of research studies, some dealing with behavior and others with the functions of the nervous system.

Given that most biological psychologists and neuroscientists are primarily interested in the human brain and human behavior, why do they study nonhumans? Here are four reasons:

1. *The underlying mechanisms of behavior are similar across species and sometimes easier to study in a nonhuman species.* If you want to understand a complex machine, you might begin by examining a simpler machine. We also learn about brain–behavior relationships by starting with simpler cases. The brains and behavior of nonhuman vertebrates resemble those of humans in their chemistry and anatomy (see Figure Intro.5). Even invertebrate

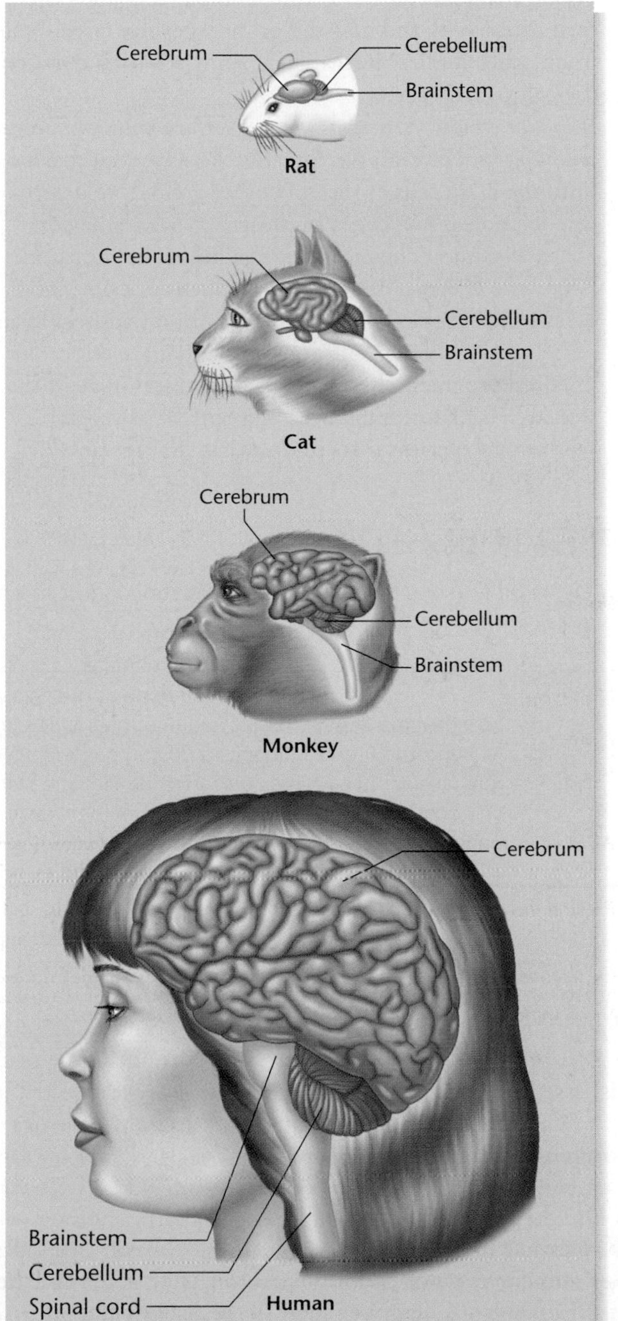

FIGURE INTRO.5 Brains of several species
The general plan and organization of the brain are similar for all mammals, even though the size varies from species to species.

neurons and their connections resemble our own. Much research has been conducted on squid nerves, which are thicker than human nerves and therefore easier to study.

2. *We are interested in animals for their own sake.* Humans are naturally curious. We would love to know about life, if any, elsewhere in the universe, regardless of whether that knowledge would have any practical use. Similarly, we would like to understand how bats chase insects in the dark, how migratory birds find their way over unfamiliar territory, and how schools of fish manage to swim in unison.
3. *What we learn about animals sheds light on human evolution.* How did we come to be the way we are? What makes us different from chimpanzees and other primates? Why and how did primates evolve larger brains than other species? Researchers approach such questions by comparing species.
4. *Legal or ethical restrictions prevent certain kinds of research on humans.* For example, investigators insert electrodes into the brain cells of rats and other animals to determine the relationship between brain activity and behavior. They also inject chemicals, extract brain chemicals, and study the effects of brain damage. Such experiments answer questions that investigators cannot address in any other way, including some questions that are critical for medical progress. They also raise an ethical issue: If the research is unacceptable with humans, is it acceptable with other species? If so, under what circumstances?

STOP&CHECK

2. Describe reasons biological psychologists conduct much of their research on nonhuman animals.

ANSWER

2. Sometimes the mechanisms of behavior are easier to study in a nonhuman species. We are curious about animals for their own sake. We study animals to understand human evolution. Certain procedures that might lead to important knowledge are illegal or unethical with humans.

In some cases, researchers simply observe animals in nature as a function of times of day, seasons of the year, changes in diet, and so forth. These procedures raise no ethical problems. In other studies, however, including many discussed in this book, animals have been subjected to brain damage, electrode implantation, injections of drugs or hormones, and other procedures that are clearly not for their own benefit. Anyone with a conscience (including scientists) is bothered by this fact. Nevertheless, experimentation with animals has been critical to the medical research that led to methods for the prevention or treatment of polio, diabetes, measles, smallpox, massive burns, heart disease, and other serious conditions. Most Nobel Prizes in physiology or medicine have been awarded for research conducted on nonhuman animals. The hope of finding methods to treat or prevent AIDS, Alzheimer's disease, stroke, and many other disorders depends largely on animal research. In much of medicine and biological psychology, research would progress slowly or not at all without animals.

Degrees of Opposition

Opposition to animal research ranges considerably in degree. "Minimalists" tolerate certain types of animal research but wish to prohibit others depending on the probable value of the research, the amount of distress to the animal, and the type of animal. (Few people have serious qualms about hurting an insect, for example.) They favor firm regulations on research. Researchers agree in principle, although they might differ in where they draw the line between acceptable and unacceptable research.

The legal standard emphasizes "the three Rs": *reduction* of animal numbers (using fewer animals), *replacement* (using computer models or other substitutes for animals, when possible), and *refinement* (modifying the procedures to reduce pain and discomfort). In the United States, every college or other institution that receives government research funds is required to have an Institutional Animal Care and Use Committee, composed of veterinarians, community representatives, and scientists that evaluate proposed experiments, decide whether they are acceptable, and specify procedures to minimize pain and discomfort. Similar regulations and committees govern research on human subjects. In addition, research laboratories must abide by national laws requiring standards of cleanliness and animal care. Similar laws apply in other countries, and scientific journals accept publications only after researchers state that they followed all the laws and regulations. Professional organizations such as the Society for Neuroscience publish guidelines for the use of animals in research (see Appendix B).

In contrast to "minimalists," the "abolitionists" see no room for compromise. Abolitionists maintain that all animals have the same rights as humans. They regard killing an animal as murder, regardless of whether the intention is to eat it, use its fur, or gain scientific knowledge. Keeping an animal in a cage (presumably even a pet) is, in their view, slavery. Because animals cannot give informed consent to research, abolitionists insist it is wrong to use them in any way, regardless of the circumstances. According to one opponent of animal research, "We have no moral option but to bring this research to a halt. Completely. . . . We will not be satisfied until every cage is empty" (Regan, 1986, pp. 39–40). Advocates of this position sometimes claim that most animal research is painful and that it never leads to important results. However, for a true abolitionist, neither of those points really matters. Their moral imperative is that people have no right to use animals at all, even if the research is highly useful and totally painless.

The disagreement between abolitionists and animal researchers is a dispute between two ethical positions: "Never knowingly harm an innocent" and "Sometimes a little harm leads to a greater good." On the one hand, permitting research has the undeniable consequence of inflicting pain or distress. On the other hand, banning the use of animals means a great setback in medical research as well as the end of animal-to-human transplants (e.g., transplanting pig heart valves to prolong lives of people with heart diseases).

It would be nice to say that this ethical debate has always proceeded in an intelligent and mutually respectful way. Unfortunately, it has not. Over the years, the abolitionists have sometimes advanced their cause through intimidation. Examples include vandalizing laboratories (causing millions of dollars of damage), placing a bomb under a professor's car, placing a bomb on a porch (intended for a researcher but accidentally placed on the neighbor's porch), banging on a researcher's children's windows at night, and inserting a garden hose through a researcher's window to flood the house (G. Miller, 2007a). Michael Conn and James Parker (2008, p. 186) quote a spokesperson for the Animal Defense League as follows: "I don't think you'd have to kill—assassinate—too many [doctors involved with animal testing]. . . . I think for 5 lives, 10 lives, 15 human lives, we could save a million, 2 million, 10 million nonhuman lives." One researcher, Dario Ringach, finally agreed to stop his research on monkeys, if animal-rights extremists would stop harassing and threatening his children. He emailed them, "You win." In addition to researchers who quit in the face of attacks, many colleges and other institutions have declined to open animal research laboratories because of their fear of violence. Researchers have replied to attacks with campaigns such as the one illustrated in Figure Intro.6.

The often fervent and extreme nature of the argument makes it difficult for researchers to express intermediate or nuanced views. Many remark that they really do care about animals, despite using them for research. Some neuroscientists are even vegetarians (Marris, 2006). But admitting to doubts seems almost like giving in to intimidation. The result is extreme polarization that interferes with open-minded contemplation of the difficult issues.

We began this chapter with a quote from the Nobel Prize–winning biologist Niko Tinbergen, who argued that no fundamental gulf separates humans from other animal species. Because we are similar in many ways to other species, we learn much about ourselves from animal studies. Also because of that similarity, we wish not to hurt them. Neuroscience researchers who decide to conduct animal research do not, as a rule, take this decision lightly. They believe it is better to inflict distress under controlled conditions than to permit ignorance and disease to inflict greater distress. In some cases, however, it is a difficult decision.

FIGURE INTRO.6 In defense of animal research
For many years, opponents of animal research have been protesting against experimentation with animals. This ad defends such research. *Source:* Courtesy of the Foundation for Biomedical Research

STOP&CHECK

3. What are the "three Rs" in the legal standards for animal research?

4. How does the "minimalist" position differ from the "abolitionist" position?

ANSWERS

3. Reduction, replacement, and refinement. **4.** A "minimalist" wishes to limit animal research to studies with little discomfort and much potential value. An "abolitionist" wishes to eliminate all animal research regardless of how the animals are treated or how much value the research might produce.

Your Brain and Your Experience

The goal in this introduction has been to preview the kinds of questions biological psychologists hope to answer. In the next several chapters, we shall go through a great deal of technical information of the type you need to know before we can start applying it to interesting questions about why people do what they do and experience what they experience.

Biological psychologists are ambitious, hoping to explain as much as possible of psychology in terms of brain processes, genes, and the like. The guiding assumption is that the pattern of activity that occurs in your brain when you see a rabbit *is* your perception of a rabbit. The pattern that occurs when you feel fear *is* your fear. This is not to say "your brain physiology controls you" any more than "you control your brain." Rather, your brain *is* you! The rest of this book explores how far we can go with this guiding assumption.

Summary

1. Two profound, difficult questions are why the universe exists, and why consciousness exists. Regardless of whether these questions are answerable, they motivate research on related topics. **4**
2. Three key points are important to remember: Perception occurs in the brain, not in the skin or in the world. As far as we can tell, brain activity is inseparable from mental activity. It is important to be cautious about what is or is not an explanation of behavior. **6**
3. Biological psychologists address four types of questions about any behavior. Physiological: How does it relate to the physiology of the brain and other organs? Ontogenetic: How does it develop within the individual? Evolutionary: How did the capacity for the behavior evolve? Functional: Why did the capacity for this behavior evolve? (That is, what function does it serve or did it serve?) **6**
4. Many careers relate to biological psychology, including various research fields, certain medical specialties, and counseling and psychotherapy. **8**
5. Researchers study animals because the mechanisms are sometimes easier to study in nonhumans, because they are interested in animal behavior for its own sake, because they want to understand the evolution of behavior, and because certain kinds of experiments are difficult or impossible with humans. **9**
6. Using animals in research is ethically controversial. Some research does inflict stress or pain on animals; however, many research questions can be investigated only through animal research. **10**
7. Animal research today is conducted under legal and ethical controls that attempt to minimize animal distress. **10**

Key Terms

Terms are defined in the module on the page number indicated. They're also presented in alphabetical order with definitions in the book's Subject Index/Glossary. Interactive flash cards, audio reviews, and crossword puzzles are among the online resources available to help you learn these terms and the concepts they represent.

biological psychology **5**
dualism **6**
evolutionary explanation **7**
functional explanation **7**
mind–body or mind–brain problem **4**
monism **6**
ontogenetic explanation **6**
physiological explanation **6**

Thought Questions

Thought questions are intended to spark thought and discussion. In most cases, there is no clearly right answer, but several fruitful ways to think about the question.

1. Is consciousness useful? That is, what (if anything) can we do because of consciousness that we couldn't do otherwise?
2. What are the special difficulties of studying the evolution of behavior, given that behavior doesn't leave fossils (with a few exceptions such as footprints showing an animal's gait)?

INTRODUCTION End of Introduction Quiz

1. What is meant by "monism"?
   - a. The idea that all forms of life evolved from a single ancestor
   - b. The idea that conscious and unconscious motivations combine to produce behavior
   - c. The idea that the mind is made of the same substance as the rest of the universe
   - d. The idea that the mind is one type of substance as matter is another

2. Of the following, which one is an example of an evolutionary explanation (as opposed to a functional explanation)?
   - a. People evolved a fear of snakes because many snakes are dangerous.
   - b. Humans have a (tiny) tailbone because our ancient monkey-like ancestors had a tail.
   - c. People evolved an ability to recognize faces because that ability is essential for cooperative social behaviors.
   - d. People evolved a tendency to form long-term male–female bonds because human infants benefit from the help of two parents during their long period of dependence.

3. Of the following, which is a reason favoring the use of animals in biological psychology research aimed at solving human problems?
   - a. Nonhuman animals engage in all the same behaviors as humans.
   - b. One human differs from another, but nonhumans are nearly the same as one another.
   - c. The nervous system of nonhuman animals resembles that of humans in many ways.

4. What does a "minimalist" favor with regard to animal research?
   - a. All research should have a minimum of at least 10 animals per group.
   - b. A minimum of three people should review each research proposal.
   - c. Interference with animal research should be held to a minimum.
   - d. Animal research is permissible but should be held to a minimum.

ANSWERS: 1c, 2b, 3c, 4d.

Suggestions for Further Reading

de Waal, F. (2005). *Our inner ape.* New York: Riverhead. An exploration of evolutionary psychology, especially with regard to how human behavior compares to that of related species.

Morrison, A. R. (2009). *An odyssey with animals: A veterinarian's reflections on the animal rights & welfare debate.* New York: Oxford University Press. A defense of animal research that acknowledges the difficulties of the issue and the competing values at stake.

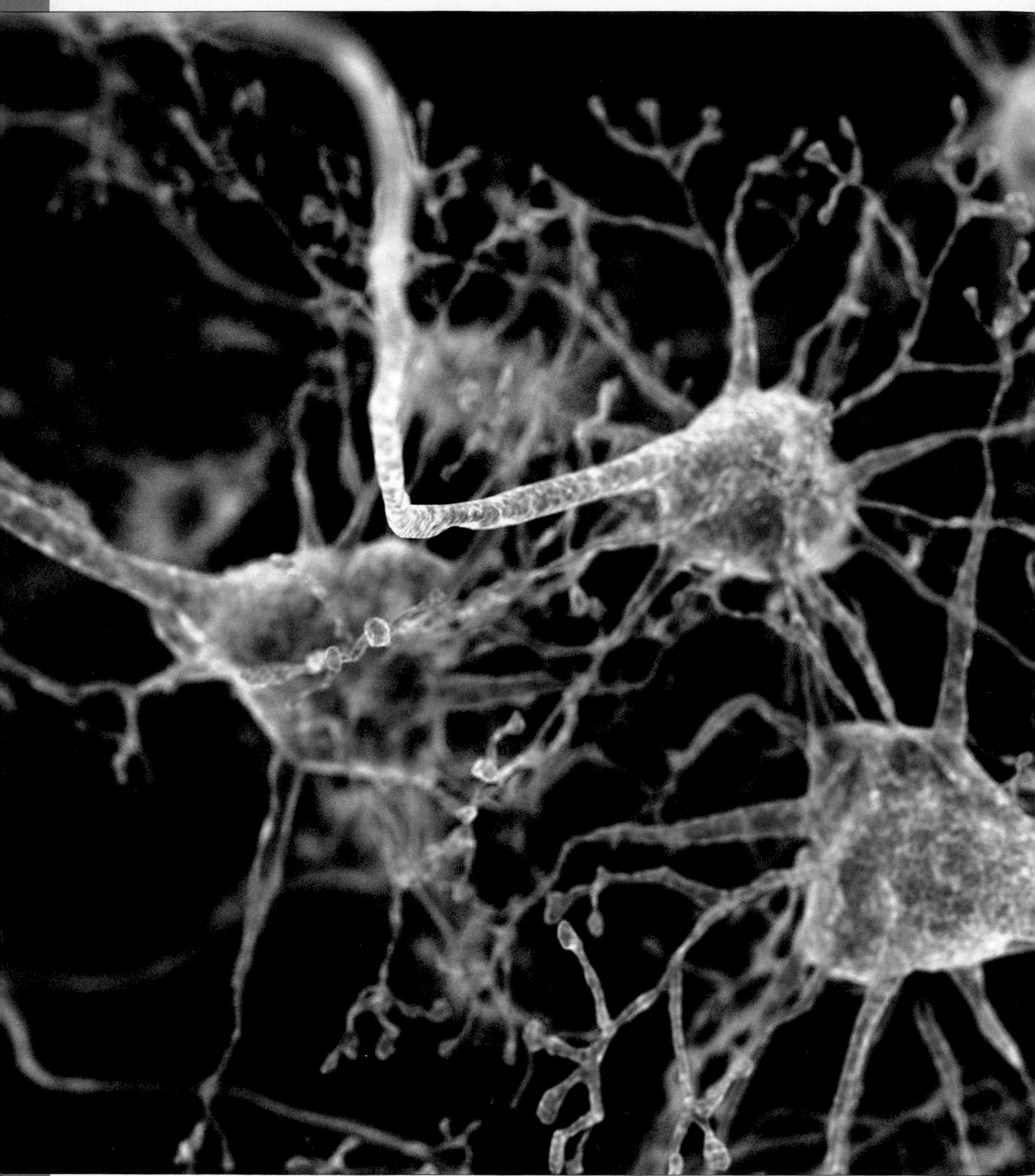

Juan Gaertner/Shutterstock.com

Nerve Cells and Nerve Impulses

1

People talk about growing into adulthood and becoming independent, but in fact almost no human life is truly independent. How often do you hunt your own meat and cook it on a fire you made from scratch? Do you grow your own vegetables? Could you build your own house (with tools you made yourself)? Have you ever made your own clothing (with materials you gathered in the wild)? Of all the activities necessary for your survival, which ones—if any—could you do completely on your own, other than breathe? People can do an enormous amount together, but very little by themselves.

The cells of your nervous system are like that, too. Together they accomplish amazing things, but one cell by itself is helpless. We begin our study of the nervous system by examining single cells. Later, we examine how they act together.

Advice: Parts of this chapter and the next assume that you underst and the basic principles of chemistry. If have never studied chemistry or if you have forgotten what you did study, read Appendix A.

OPPOSITE: An electron micrograph of neurons, magnified tens of thousands of times. The color is added artificially. For objects this small, it is impossible to focus light to obtain an image. It is possible to focus an electron beam, but electrons do not show color.

CHAPTER OUTLINE

MODULE 1.1 **The Cells of the Nervous System**
Neurons and Glia
The Blood–Brain Barrier
Nourishment of Vertebrate Neurons
In Closing: Neurons

MODULE 1.2 **The Nerve Impulse**
The Resting Potential of the Neuron
The Action Potential
Propagation of the Action Potential
The Myelin Sheath and Saltatory Conduction
Local Neurons
In Closing: Neurons and Messages

LEARNING OBJECTIVES

After studying this chapter, you should be able to:

1. Describe neurons and glia, the cells that constitute the nervous system.
2. Summarize how the blood–brain barrier relates to protection and nutrition of neurons.
3. Explain how the sodium–potassium pump and the properties of the membrane lead to the resting potential of a neuron.
4. Discuss how the movement of sodium and potassium ions produces the action potential and recovery after it.
5. State the all-or-none law of the action potential.

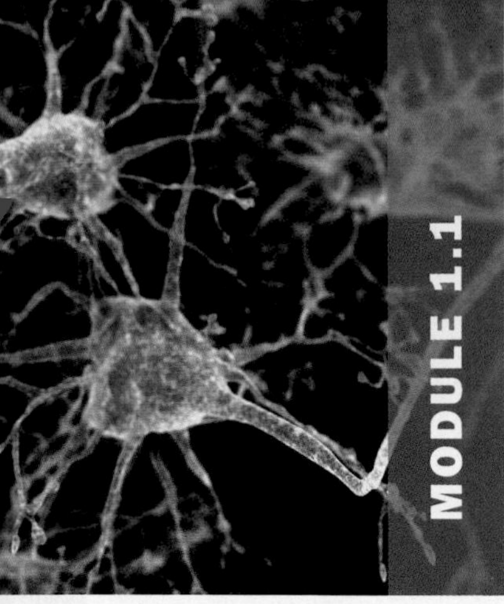

MODULE 1.1

The Cells of the Nervous System

No doubt you think of yourself as an individual. You don't think of your mental experience as being composed of pieces . . . but it is. Your experiences depend on the activity of a huge number of separate but interconnected cells. Researchers are far from fully understanding how they achieve all that they do, but the place to begin is by trying to understand the cells of the nervous system.

Neurons and Glia

The nervous system consists of two kinds of cells, neurons and glia. **Neurons** receive information and transmit it to other cells. Glia serve many functions that are difficult to summarize, and we shall defer that discussion until later in this module. For a round number, the adult human brain contains approximately 100 billion neurons (R. W. Williams & Herrup, 1988; see Figure 1.1). The exact number varies from person to person.

We now take it for granted that the brain is composed of individual cells, but the idea was in doubt as recently as the early 1900s. Until then, the best microscopic views revealed little detail about the brain. Observers noted long, thin fibers between one cell body and another, but they could not see whether a fiber merged into the next cell or stopped before it (Albright, Jessell, Kandel, & Posner, 2001). In the late 1800s, Santiago Ramón y Cajal used newly developed staining techniques to show that a small gap separates the tips of one neuron's fibers from the surface of the next neuron. The brain, like the rest of the body, consists of individual cells.

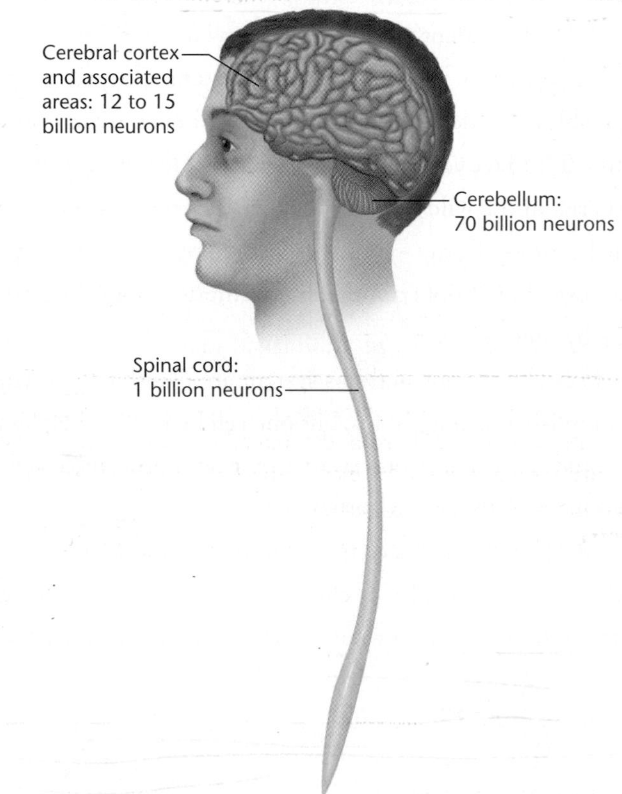

FIGURE 1.1 Estimated numbers of neurons in humans
Because of the small size of many neurons and the variation in cell density from one spot to another, obtaining an accurate count is difficult. *Source:* R. W. Williams & Herrup, 1988

Santiago Ramón y Cajal, a Pioneer of Neuroscience

Two scientists are widely recognized as the main founders of neuroscience—Charles Sherrington, whom we shall discuss in Chapter 2, and the Spanish investigator Santiago Ramón y Cajal (1852–1934). Cajal's early education did not progress smoothly. At one point, he was imprisoned in a solitary cell, limited to one meal a day, and taken out daily for public floggings—at the age of 10—for the crime of not paying attention during his Latin class (Cajal, 1901–1917/1937). (And *you* complained about *your* teachers!)

Santiago Ramón y Cajal

(1852–1934)

How many interesting facts fail to be converted into fertile discoveries because their first observers regard them as natural and ordinary things! . . . It is strange to see how the populace, which nourishes its imagination with tales of witches or saints, mysterious events and extraordinary occurrences, disdains the world around it as commonplace, monotonous and prosaic, without suspecting that at bottom it is all secret, mystery, and marvel. (Cajal, 1937, pp. 46-47).

Cajal wanted to become an artist, but his father insisted that he study medicine as a safer way to make a living. He managed to combine the two fields, becoming an outstanding anatomical researcher and illustrator. His detailed drawings of the nervous system are still considered definitive today.

Before the late 1800s, microscopy revealed few details about the nervous system. Then the Italian investigator Camillo Golgi found a way to stain nerve cells with silver salts. This method, which completely stains some cells without affecting others at all, enabled researchers to examine the structure of a single cell. Cajal used Golgi's methods but applied them to infant brains, in which the cells are smaller and therefore easier to examine on a single slide. Cajal's research demonstrated that nerve cells remain separate instead of merging into one another.

Philosophically, we see the appeal of the old idea that neurons merge. We describe our experience as undivided, not the sum of separate parts, so it seems right that all the cells in the brain might be joined together as one unit. How the separate cells combine their influences is a complex and still mysterious process.

The Structures of an Animal Cell

Figure 1.2 illustrates a neuron from the cerebellum of a mouse (magnified enormously, of course). Neurons have much in common with the rest of the body's cells. The surface of a cell is its **membrane** (or *plasma membrane*), a structure that separates the inside of the cell from the outside environment. Most chemicals cannot cross the membrane, but protein channels in the membrane permit a controlled flow of water, oxygen, sodium, potassium, calcium, chloride, and other important chemicals.

Except for mammalian red blood cells, all animal cells have a **nucleus,** the structure that contains the chromosomes. A **mitochondrion** (plural: mitochondria) is the structure that performs metabolic activities, providing the energy that the cell uses for all activities. Mitochondria require fuel and oxygen. **Ribosomes** are the sites at which the cell synthesizes new protein molecules. Proteins provide building materials for the cell and facilitate chemical reactions. Some ribosomes float freely within the cell, but others are attached to the **endoplasmic reticulum**, a network of thin tubes that transport newly synthesized proteins to other locations.

The Structure of a Neuron

The most distinctive feature of neurons is their shape, which varies enormously from one neuron to another (see Figure 1.3). Unlike most other body cells, neurons have long branching extensions. The larger neurons have dendrites, a soma (cell body), an axon, and presynaptic terminals. The tiniest neurons lack axons, and some lack well-defined dendrites. Contrast the motor neuron in Figure 1.4 and the sensory neuron in Figure 1.5. A **motor neuron**, with its soma in the spinal cord, receives excitation through its dendrites and conducts impulses along its axon to a muscle. A **sensory neuron** is specialized at one end to be highly sensitive to a particular type of stimulation, such as light, sound, or touch. The sensory neuron shown in Figure 1.5 conducts touch information from the skin to the spinal cord. Tiny branches lead directly from the receptors into the axon, and the cell's soma is located on a little stalk off the main trunk.

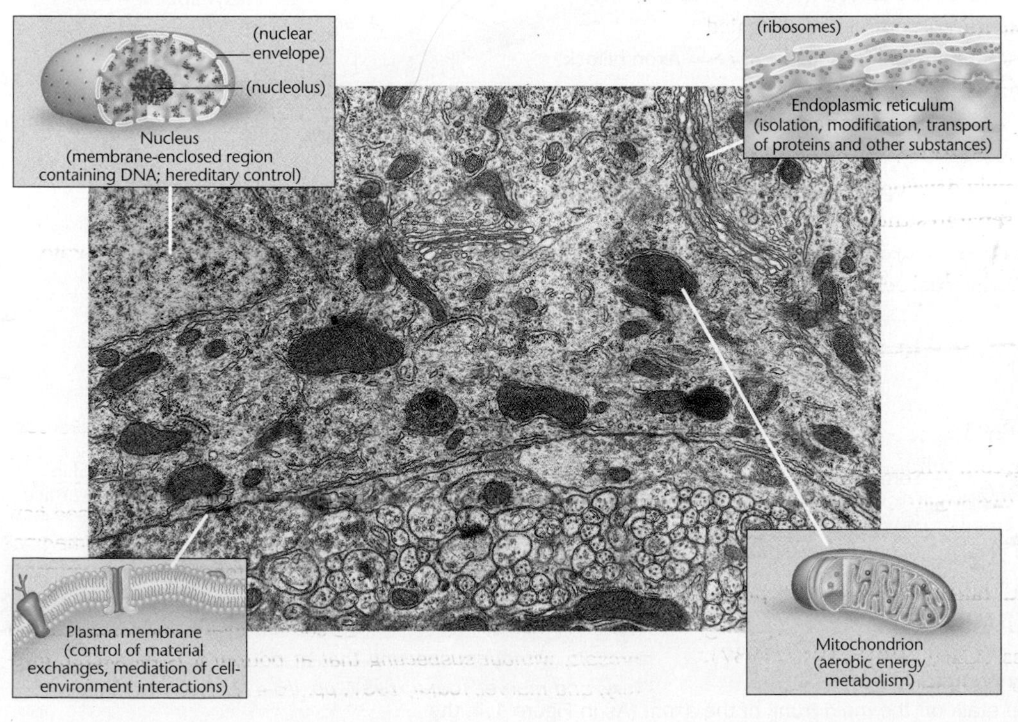

FIGURE 1.2 An electron micrograph of parts of a neuron from the cerebellum of a mouse
The nucleus, membrane, and other structures are characteristic of most animal cells. The plasma membrane is the border of the neuron. Magnification approximately x 20,000. *Source:* Micrograph from Dr. Dennis M.D. Landis.

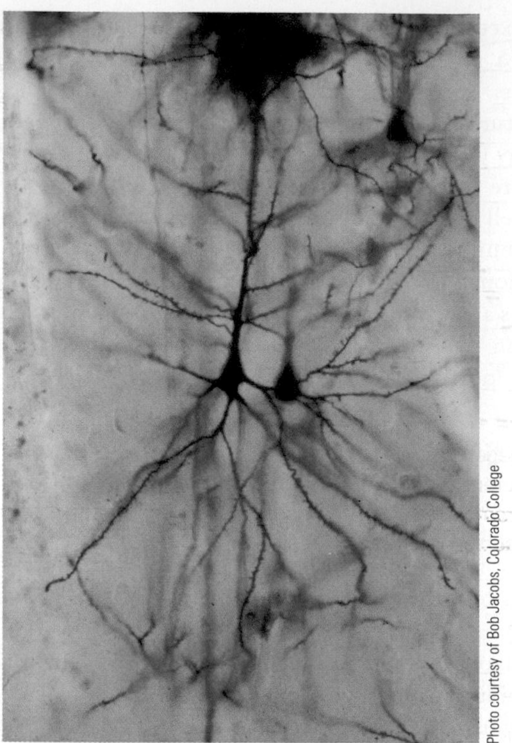
Photo courtesy of Bob Jacobs, Colorado College

FIGURE 1.3 Neurons, stained to appear dark
Note the small fuzzy-looking spines on the dendrites.

Dendrites are branching fibers that get narrower near their ends. (The term *dendrite* comes from a Greek root word meaning "tree." A dendrite branches like a tree.) The dendrite's surface is lined with specialized *synaptic receptors,* at which the dendrite receives information from other neurons. (Chapter 2 concerns synapses.) The greater the surface area of a dendrite, the more information it can receive. Many dendrites contain **dendritic spines,** short outgrowths that increase the surface area available for synapses (see Figure 1.6).

The **cell body,** or **soma** (Greek for "body"; plural: somata), contains the nucleus, ribosomes, and mitochondria. Most of a neuron's metabolic work occurs here. Cell bodies of neurons range in diameter from 0.005 millimeter (mm) to 0.1 mm in mammals and up to a millimeter in certain invertebrates. Like the dendrites, the cell body is covered with synapses on its surface in many neurons.

The **axon** is a thin fiber of constant diameter. (The term *axon* comes from a Greek word meaning "axis.") The axon conveys an impulse toward other neurons, an organ, or a muscle. Axons range up to more than a meter in length, as in the case of axons from your spinal cord to your feet. That is, the length of an axon is enormous in comparison to its width—like that of a narrow highway across a continent. Many vertebrate axons are covered with an insulating material called a **myelin sheath** with interruptions known as

FIGURE 1.4 The components of a vertebrate motor neuron
The cell body of a motor neuron is located in the spinal cord. The parts are not drawn to scale; a real axon is much longer in proportion to the soma.

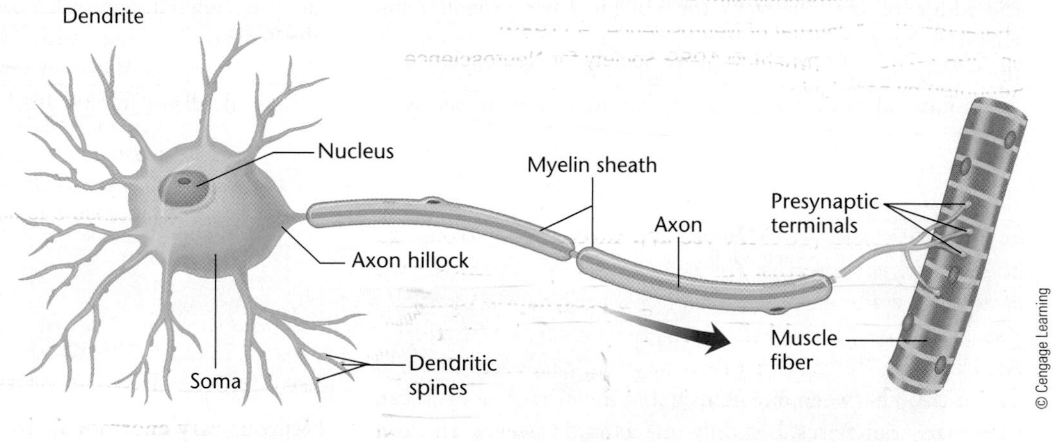

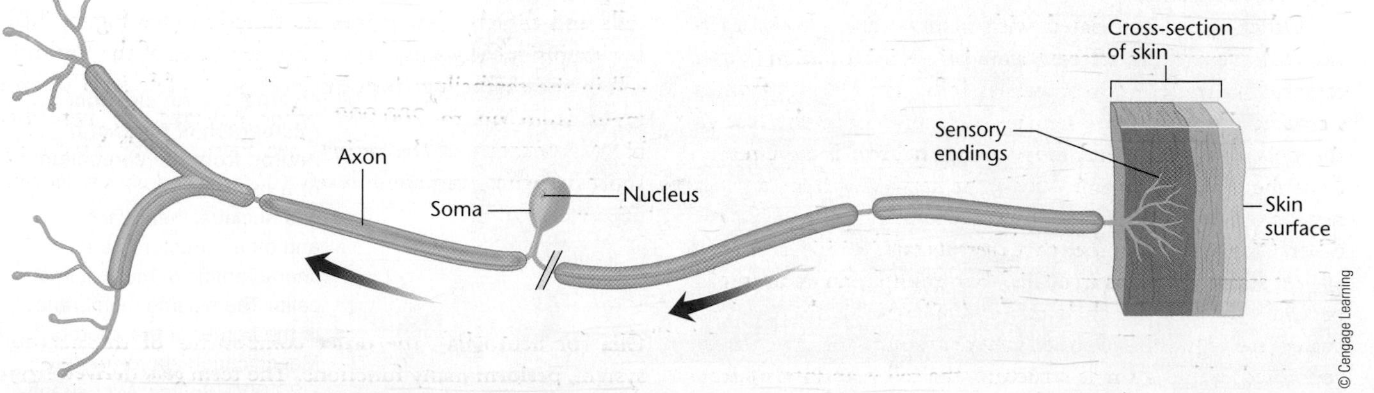

FIGURE 1.5 A vertebrate sensory neuron
Note that the soma is located on a stalk off the main trunk of the axon. (As in Figure 1.4, the structures are not drawn to scale.)

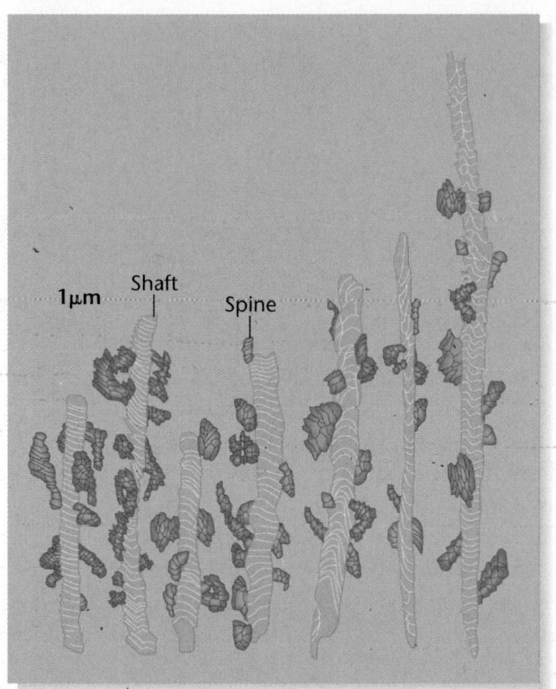

FIGURE 1.6 Dendritic spines
Many dendrites are lined with spines, short outgrowths that receive incoming information. *Source:* From K. M. Harris and J. K. Stevens, Society for Neuroscience, "Dendritic Spines of CA1 Pyramidal Cells in the Rat Hippocampus: Serial Electron Microscopy with Reference to Their Biophysical Characteristics." *Journal of Neuroscience*, 9 (1989), pp. 2982–2997. Copyright © 1989 Society for Neuroscience. Reprinted by permission.

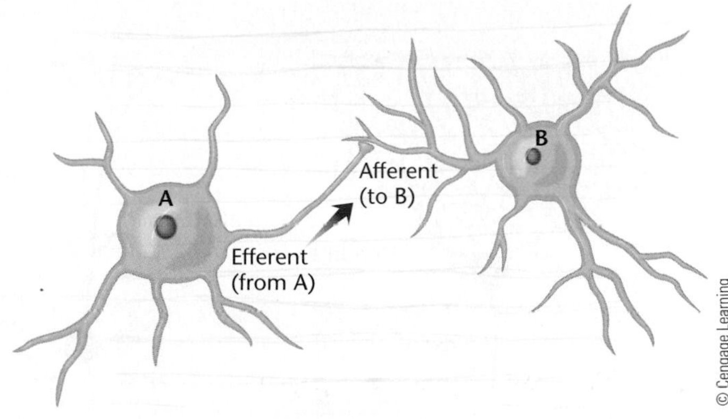

FIGURE 1.7 Cell structures and axons
It all depends on the point of view. An axon from A to B is an efferent axon from A and an afferent axon to B, just as a train from Washington to New York is exiting Washington and approaching New York.

nodes of Ranvier (RAHN-vee-ay). Invertebrate axons do not have myelin sheaths. An axon has many branches, each of which swells at its tip, forming a **presynaptic terminal**, also known as an *end bulb* or *bouton* (French for "button"). At that point the axon releases chemicals that cross through the junction between one neuron and the next. A neuron can have many dendrites, but only one axon. However, an axon may have branches.

Other terms associated with neurons are *afferent, efferent,* and *intrinsic.* An **afferent axon** brings information into a structure; an **efferent axon** carries information away from a structure. Every sensory neuron is an afferent to the rest of the nervous system, and every motor neuron is an efferent from the nervous system. Within the nervous system, a given neuron is an efferent from one structure and an afferent to another. (You can remember that *efferent* starts with *e* as in *exit; afferent* starts with *a* as in *admit.*) For example, an axon might be efferent from the thalamus and afferent to the cerebral cortex (see Figure 1.7). If a cell's dendrites and axon are entirely contained within a single structure, the cell is an **interneuron** or **intrinsic neuron** of that structure. For example, an intrinsic neuron of the thalamus has its axon and all its dendrites within the thalamus.

STOP&CHECK

1. What are the widely branching structures of a neuron called? And what is the long, thin structure that carries information to another cell called?

2. Which animal species would have the longest axons?

ANSWERS

1. The widely branching structures of a neuron are called *dendrites*, and the long thin structure that carries information to another cell is called an *axon*. 2. The longest axons occur in the largest animals. For example, giraffes and elephants have axons that extend from the spinal cord to the feet, nearly 2 meters away.

Variations among Neurons

Neurons vary enormously in size, shape, and function. The shape of a neuron determines its connections with other cells and thereby determines its function (see Figure 1.8). For example, the widely branching dendrites of the Purkinje cell in the cerebellum (see Figure 1.8a) enable it to receive input from up to 200,000 other neurons. By contrast, bipolar neurons in the retina (see Figure 1.8d) have only short branches, and some receive input from as few as two other cells.

Glia

Glia (or neuroglia), the other components of the nervous system, perform many functions. The term *glia*, derived from a Greek word meaning "glue," reflects early investigators' idea that glia were like glue that held the neurons together (Somjen, 1988). Although that concept is obsolete, the term

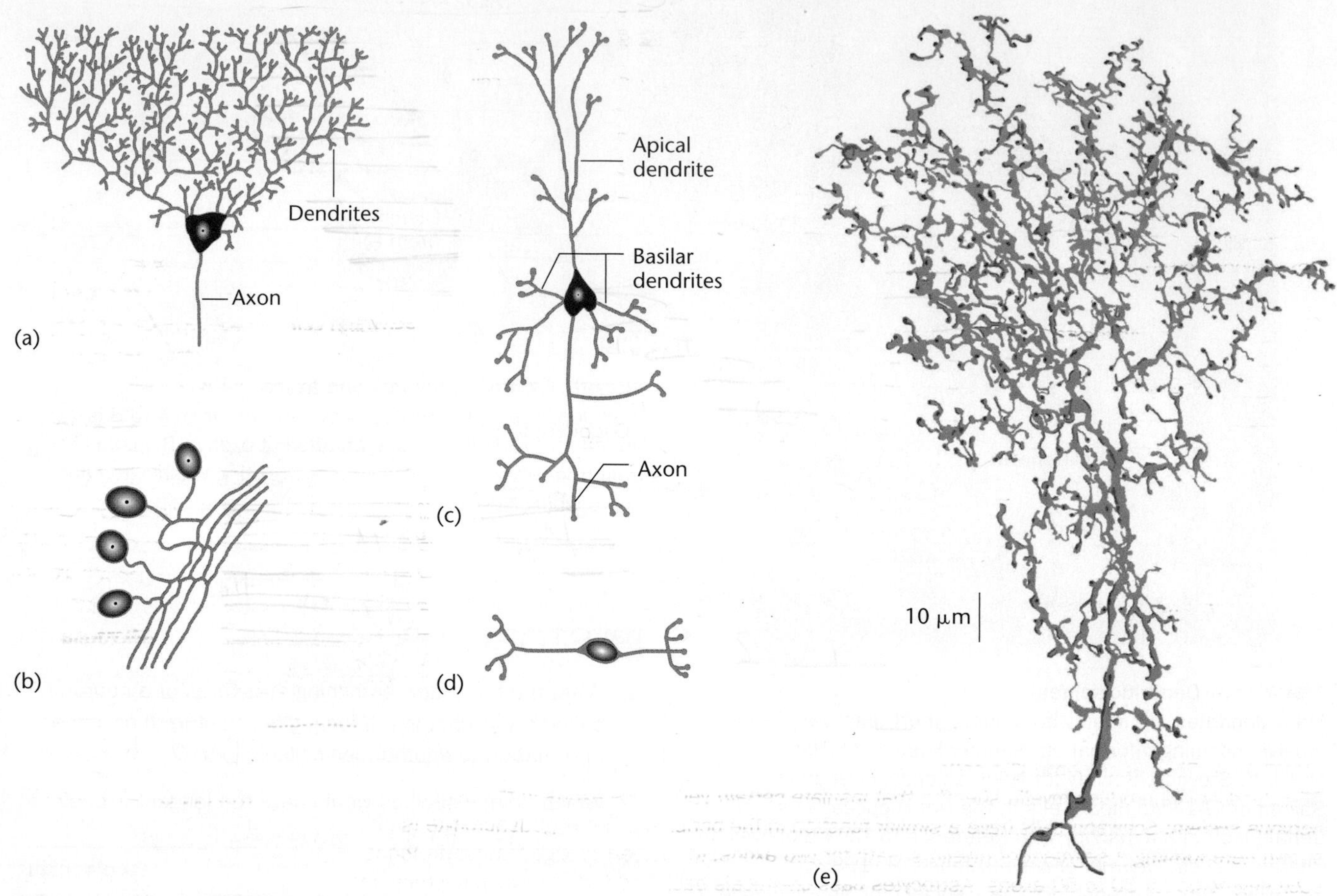

FIGURE 1.8 The diverse shapes of neurons
(a) Purkinje cell, a cell type found only in the cerebellum; (b) sensory neurons from skin to spinal cord; (c) pyramidal cell of the motor area of the cerebral cortex; (d) bipolar cell of retina of the eye; (e) Kenyon cell, from a honeybee. *Source:* Part **e** courtesy of R. G. Goss

remains. Glia are smaller but more numerous than neurons (see Figure 1.9).

The brain has several types of glia (Haydon, 2001). The star-shaped **astrocytes** wrap around the presynaptic terminals of a group of functionally related axons, as shown in Figure 1.10. By surrounding a synapse between neurons, an astrocyte shields it from chemicals circulating in the surround (Nedergaard & Verkhatsky, 2012). Also, by taking up ions released by axons and then releasing them back, an astrocyte helps synchronize the activity of the axons, enabling them to send messages in waves (Angulo, Kozlov, Charpak, & Audinat, 2004; Antanitus, 1998). Astrocytes also guide the formation and elimination of synapses (Clarke & Barres, 2013). They remove waste material created when neurons die and control the amount of blood flow to each brain area (Mulligan & MacVicar, 2004). An additional function is that during periods of heightened activity in some brain area, astrocytes dilate the blood vessels to bring more nutrients into that area (Filosa et al., 2006; Takano et al., 2006). A possible role in information processing is less certain. According to a popular hypothesis known as the *tripartite synapse,* the tip of an axon releases chemicals that cause the neighboring astrocyte to release chemicals of its own, thus magnifying or modifying the message to the next neuron (Ben Achour & Pascual, 2012). However, the evidence for this idea is based on some uncertain assumptions, and it remains controversial (Nedergaard & Verkhatsky, 2012).

Tiny cells called **microglia** act as part of the immune system, removing waste material, viruses, and fungi from the brain. They proliferate after brain damage and in most brain diseases (Aguzzi, Barres, & Bennett, 2013). Microglia are necessary for the survival of certain neurons early in life (Ueno et al., 2013). They also contribute to learning by removing the weakest synapses. **Oligodendrocytes** (OL-i-go-DEN-druh-sites) in the brain and spinal cord and **Schwann cells** in the periphery of the body build the myelin sheaths that surround and insulate certain vertebrate axons. They also supply an axon with nutrients necessary for its functioning (Y. Lee et al., 2012). **Radial glia** guide the migration of neurons and their axons and dendrites during embryonic development. When embryological development finishes, most radial glia differentiate into neurons, and a smaller number differentiate into astrocytes and oligodendrocytes (Pinto & Götz, 2007).

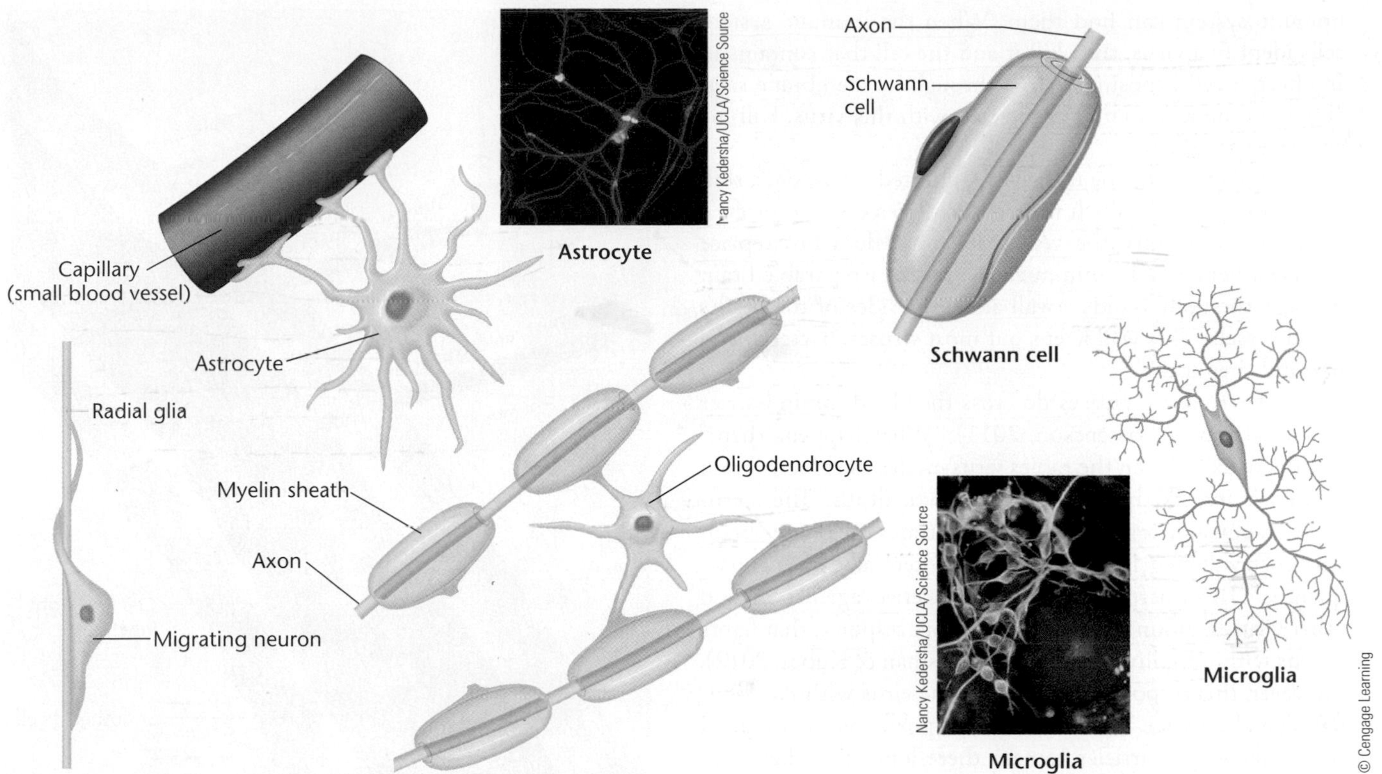

FIGURE 1.9 Shapes of some glia cells
Oligodendrocytes produce myelin sheaths that insulate certain vertebrate axons in the central nervous system; Schwann cells have a similar function in the periphery. The oligodendrocyte is shown here forming a segment of myelin sheath for two axons; in fact, each oligodendrocyte forms such segments for 30 to 50 axons. Astrocytes pass chemicals back and forth between neurons and blood and among neighboring neurons. Microglia proliferate in areas of brain damage and remove toxic materials. Radial glia (not shown here) guide the migration of neurons during embryological development. Glia have other functions as well.

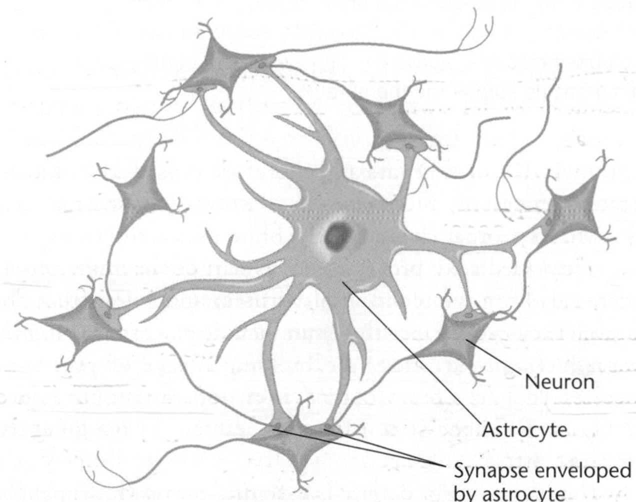

FIGURE 1.10 How an astrocyte synchronizes associated axons
Branches of the astrocyte (in the center) surround the presynaptic terminals of related axons. If a few of them are active at once, the astrocyte absorbs some of the chemicals they release. It then temporarily inhibits all the axons to which it is connected. When the inhibition ceases, all of the axons are primed to respond again in synchrony. *Source:* Based on Antanitus, 1998

STOP & CHECK

3. Identify the four major structures that compose a neuron.

4. Which kind of glia cell wraps around the synaptic terminals of axons?

ANSWERS

3. Dendrites, soma (cell body), axon, and presynaptic terminal. **4.** Astrocytes.

The Blood–Brain Barrier

Although the brain, like any other organ, needs to receive nutrients from the blood, many chemicals cannot cross from the blood to the brain (Hagenbuch, Gao, & Meier, 2002). The mechanism that excludes most chemicals from the vertebrate brain is known as the **blood–brain barrier.** Before we examine how it works, let's consider why we need it.

Why We Need a Blood–Brain Barrier

When a virus invades a cell, mechanisms within the cell extrude virus particles through the membrane so that the immune system can find them. When the immune system cells identify a virus, they kill it and the cell that contains it. In effect, a cell exposing a virus through its membrane says, "Look, immune system, I'm infected with this virus. Kill me and save the others."

This plan works fine if the virus-infected cell is, say, a skin cell or a blood cell, which the body replaces easily. However, with few exceptions, the vertebrate brain does not replace damaged neurons. To minimize the risk of irreparable brain damage, the body builds a wall along the sides of the brain's blood vessels. This wall keeps out most viruses, bacteria, and harmful chemicals.

However, some viruses do cross the blood–brain barrier in several ways (Kristensson, 2011). "What happens then?" you might ask. When the rabies virus evades the blood–brain barrier, it infects the brain and leads to death. The spirochete responsible for syphilis also penetrates the blood–brain barrier, producing long-lasting and potentially fatal consequences. The microglia are more effective against certain other viruses, mounting an inflammatory response that fights a virus without killing the neuron (Ousman & Kubes, 2012). However, this response may control the virus without eliminating it altogether. When the chicken pox virus enters spinal cord cells, virus particles remain there long after they have been exterminated from the rest of the body. The virus may emerge from the spinal cord decades later, causing a painful condition called shingles. Similarly, the virus responsible for genital herpes hides in the nervous system, producing little harm there but periodically emerging to cause new genital infections.

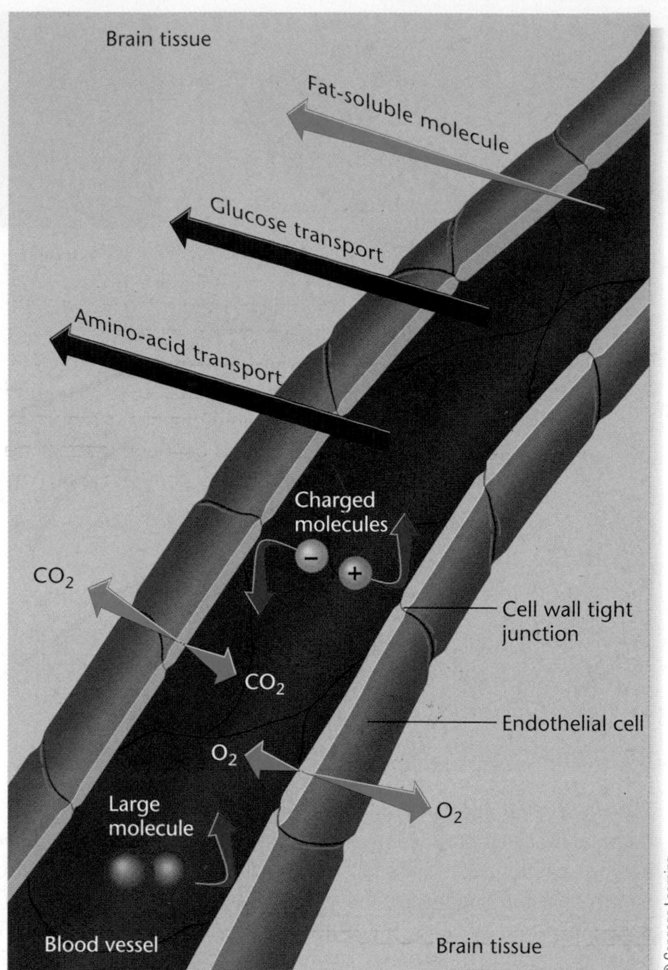

FIGURE 1.11 The blood–brain barrier
Most large molecules and electrically charged molecules cannot cross from the blood to the brain. A few small, uncharged molecules such as O_2 and CO_2 cross easily, as can certain fat-soluble molecules. Active transport systems pump glucose and amino acids across the membrane.

How the Blood–Brain Barrier Works

The blood–brain barrier (see Figure 1.11) depends on the endothelial cells that form the walls of the capillaries (Bundgaard, 1986; Rapoport & Robinson, 1986). Outside the brain, such cells are separated by small gaps, but in the brain, they are joined so tightly that they block viruses, bacteria, and other harmful chemicals from passage.

"If the blood–brain barrier is such a good defense," you might ask, "why don't we have similar walls around all our other organs?" The answer is that the barrier keeps out useful chemicals as well as harmful ones. Those useful chemicals include all fuels and amino acids, the building blocks for proteins. For the brain to function, it needs special mechanisms to get these chemicals across the blood–brain barrier.

The brain has several such mechanisms. *Small, uncharged molecules,* including oxygen and carbon dioxide, cross freely. Water crosses through special protein channels in the wall of the endothelial cells (Amiry-Moghaddam & Ottersen, 2003). Also, *molecules that dissolve in the fats of the membrane* cross easily. Examples include vitamins A and D and all the drugs that affect the brain—from antidepressants and other psychiatric drugs to illegal drugs such as heroin. How fast a drug takes effect depends partly on how readily it dissolves in fats and therefore crosses the blood–brain barrier.

For a few other chemicals, the brain uses **active transport,** a protein-mediated process that expends energy to pump chemicals from the blood into the brain. Chemicals that are actively transported into the brain include glucose (the brain's main fuel), amino acids (the building blocks of proteins), purines, choline, a few vitamins, iron, and certain hormones (Abbott, Rönnback, & Hansson, 2006; A. R. Jones & Shusta, 2007).

The blood–brain barrier is essential to health. In people with Alzheimer's disease or similar conditions, the endothelial cells lining the brain's blood vessels shrink, and harmful chemicals enter the brain (Zipser et al., 2007). However, the barrier also poses a difficulty in medicine because it keeps out many medications. Brain cancers are difficult to treat because nearly all the drugs used for chemotherapy fail to cross the blood–brain barrier.

STOP & CHECK

5. Identify one major advantage and one disadvantage of having a blood–brain barrier.

6. Which chemicals cross the blood–brain barrier passively?

7. Which chemicals cross the blood–brain barrier by active transport?

ANSWERS

5. The blood–brain barrier keeps out viruses (an advantage) and also most nutrients (a disadvantage). **6.** Small, uncharged molecules such as oxygen, carbon dioxide, and water cross the blood–brain barrier passively. So do chemicals that dissolve in the fats of the membrane. **7.** Glucose, amino acids, purines, choline, certain vitamins, iron, and a few hormones.

Nourishment of Vertebrate Neurons

Most cells use a variety of carbohydrates and fats for nutrition, but vertebrate neurons depend almost entirely on **glucose,** a sugar. (Cancer cells and the testis cells that make sperm also rely overwhelmingly on glucose.) Because the metabolic pathway that uses glucose requires oxygen, neurons need a steady supply of oxygen. Although the human brain constitutes only about 2 percent of the body's weight, it uses about 20 percent of its oxygen.

Why do neurons depend so heavily on glucose? They can and sometimes do use ketones (a kind of fat) and lactate for fuel (Wyss, Jolivet, Buck, Magistretti & Weber, 2011). However, glucose is the only nutrient that crosses the blood–brain barrier in large quantities.

Although neurons require glucose, glucose shortage is rarely a problem. The liver makes glucose from many kinds of carbohydrates and amino acids, as well as from glycerol, a breakdown product from fats. The only likely problem is an inability to *use* glucose. To use glucose, the body needs vitamin B_1, **thiamine.** Prolonged thiamine deficiency, common in chronic alcoholism, leads to death of neurons and a condition called *Korsakoff's syndrome,* marked by severe memory impairments.

MODULE 1.1 ■ IN CLOSING

Neurons

What does the study of individual neurons tell us about behavior? One important principle is that our experience and behavior do not follow from the properties of any one neuron. Just as a chemist must know about atoms to make sense of compounds, a biological psychologist or neuroscientist must know about cells to understand the nervous system. However, the nervous system is more than the sum of the individual cells, just as water is more than the sum of oxygen and hydrogen. Our behavior emerges from the communication among neurons.

Summary

1. Neurons receive information and convey it to other cells. The nervous system also contains *glia,* cells with a variety of functions. **16**
2. In the late 1800s, Santiago Ramón y Cajal used newly discovered staining techniques to establish that the nervous system is composed of separate cells, now known as neurons. **16**
3. Neurons contain the same internal structures as other animal cells. **17**
4. Neurons have four major parts: a cell body, dendrites, an axon, and presynaptic terminals. Their shapes vary greatly depending on their functions and their connections with other cells. **17**
5. Because of the blood–brain barrier, many molecules cannot enter the brain. The barrier protects the nervous system from viruses and many dangerous chemicals. **21**
6. The blood–brain barrier consists of an unbroken wall of cells that surround the blood vessels of the brain and spinal cord. A few small, uncharged molecules such as water, oxygen, and carbon dioxide cross the barrier freely. So do molecules that dissolve in fats. Active transport proteins pump glucose, amino acids, and a few other chemicals into the brain and spinal cord. **22**
7. Adult neurons rely heavily on glucose, the only nutrient that crosses the blood–brain barrier in large quantities. They need thiamine (vitamin B1) to use glucose. **23**

Key Terms

Terms are defined in the module on the page number indicated. They're also presented in alphabetical order with definitions in the book's Subject Index/Glossary. Interactive flash cards, audio reviews, and crossword puzzles are among the online resources available to help you learn these terms and the concepts they represent.

active transport **22**
afferent axon **19**
astrocytes **20**
axon **18**
blood–brain barrier **21**
cell body **18**
dendrites **18**
dendritic spines **18**
efferent axon **19**
endoplasmic reticulum **17**
glia **19**
glucose **23**
interneuron **19**
intrinsic neuron **19**
membrane **17**
microglia **20**
mitochondrion **17**
motor neuron **17**
myelin sheath **18**
neurons **16**
nodes of Ranvier **19**
nucleus **17**
oligodendrocytes **20**
presynaptic terminal **19**
radial glia **20**
ribosomes **17**
Schwann cells **20**
sensory neuron **17**
thiamine **23**

Thought Question

Although heroin and morphine are similar in many ways, heroin exerts faster effects on the brain. What can we infer about those drugs with regard to the blood–brain barrier?

MODULE 1.1: End of Module Quiz

1. Santiago Ramón y Cajal was responsible for which of these discoveries?
   a. The human cerebral cortex has many specializations to produce language.
   b. The brain's left and right hemispheres control different functions.
   c. The nervous system is composed of separate cells.
   d. Neurons communicate at specialized junctions called synapses.

2. What does an afferent axon do?
   a. It controls involuntary behavior.
   b. It controls voluntary behavior.
   c. It carries output from a structure.
   d. It brings information into a structure.

3. Of these species, which probably has the longest axons?
   a. Humans
   b. Chimpanzees
   c. Cheetahs
   d. Giraffes

4. Which of the following is NOT one of the four major structures that compose a neuron?
   a. Dendrites
   b. Glia
   c. Soma
   d. Axon
   e. Presynaptic terminal

5. Which of the following is something that glia do NOT do?
   a. Synchronize activity of a group of axons
   b. Remove waste material
   c. Dilate blood vessels to increase blood flow to the most active brain areas
   d. Conduct action potentials

6. An advantage of the blood–brain barrier is that it keeps out most _______. A disadvantage is that it also keeps out ______.
   a. viruses . . . most nutrients
   b. small molecules . . . fat-soluble molecules
   c. harmful gases . . . oxygen
   d. waste products . . . water

7. Which of these chemicals cross the blood–brain barrier by active transport?
   a. Oxygen, water, and fat-soluble molecules
   b. Glucose and amino acids
   c. Proteins
   d. Viruses

8. What makes brain cancers so difficult to treat?
   a. Nearly all chemotherapy drugs fail to cross the blood–brain barrier.
   b. Brain cancers spread more rapidly than other cancers.
   c. The brain includes more pain receptors than other organs.
   d. The brain has a very low metabolic rate.

9. What is the brain's main source of fuel?
   a. Glucose
   b. Glutamate
   c. Thiamine
   d. Proteins

ANSWERS: 1c, 2d, 3d, 4b, 5d, 6a, 7b, 8a, 9a.

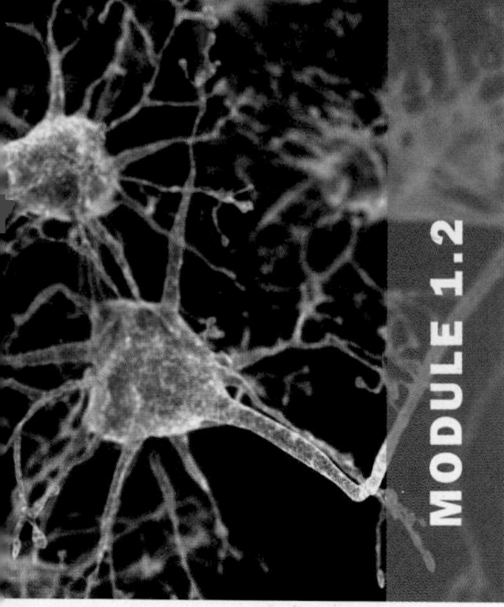

MODULE 1.2

The Nerve Impulse

Think about the axons that convey information from your feet's touch receptors toward your spinal cord and brain. If the axons used electrical conduction, they could transfer information at a velocity approaching the speed of light. However, given that your body is made of water and carbon compounds instead of copper wire, the strength of the impulse would decay rapidly as it traveled. A touch on your shoulder would feel stronger than a touch on your abdomen. Short people would feel their toes more strongly than tall people could—if either could feel their toes at all.

The way your axons actually function avoids these problems. Instead of conducting an electrical impulse, the axon regenerates an impulse at each point. Imagine a long line of people holding hands. The first person squeezes the second person's hand, who then squeezes the third person's hand, and so forth. The impulse travels along the line without weakening because each person generates it anew.

Although the axon's method of transmitting an impulse prevents a touch on your shoulder from feeling stronger than one on your toes, it introduces a different problem: Because axons transmit information at only moderate speeds (varying from less than 1 meter per second (m/s) to about 100 m/s), a touch on your shoulder reaches your brain *sooner* than will a touch on your toes, although you will not ordinarily notice the difference. Your brain is not set up to register small differences in the time of arrival of touch messages. After all, why should it be? You almost never need to know whether a touch on one part of your body occurred slightly before or after a touch somewhere else.

In vision, however, your brain *does* need to know whether one stimulus began slightly before or after another one. If two adjacent spots on your retina—let's call them A and B—send impulses at almost the same time, an extremely small difference between them in timing tells your brain whether light moved from A to B or from B to A. To detect movement as accurately as possible, your visual system compensates for the fact that some parts of the retina are slightly closer to your brain than other parts are. Without some sort of compensation, simultaneous flashes arriving at two spots on your retina would reach your brain at different times, and you might perceive movement inaccurately. What prevents this illusion is the fact that axons from more distant parts of your retina transmit impulses slightly faster than those closer to the brain (Stanford, 1987)!

In short, the properties of impulse conduction in an axon are amazingly well adapted to your needs for information transfer. Let's examine the mechanics of impulse transmission.

The Resting Potential of the Neuron

Messages in a neuron develop from disturbances of the resting potential. Let's begin by understanding the resting potential.

All parts of a neuron are covered by a membrane about 8 nanometers (nm) thick (just less than 0.00001 mm), composed of two layers (free to float relative to each other) of phospholipid molecules (containing chains of fatty acids and a phosphate group). Embedded among the phospholipids are cylindrical protein molecules through which various chemicals can pass (see Figure 1.12). The structure of the membrane and its proteins controls the flow of chemicals between the inside and outside of the cell.

When at rest, the membrane maintains an **electrical gradient**, also known as **polarization**—a difference in electrical charge between the inside and outside of the cell. The

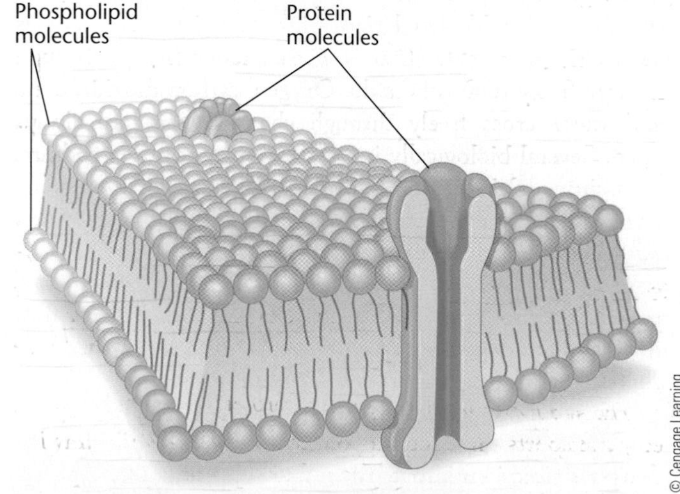

FIGURE 1.12 The membrane of a neuron
Embedded in the membrane are protein channels that permit certain ions to cross through the membrane at a controlled rate.

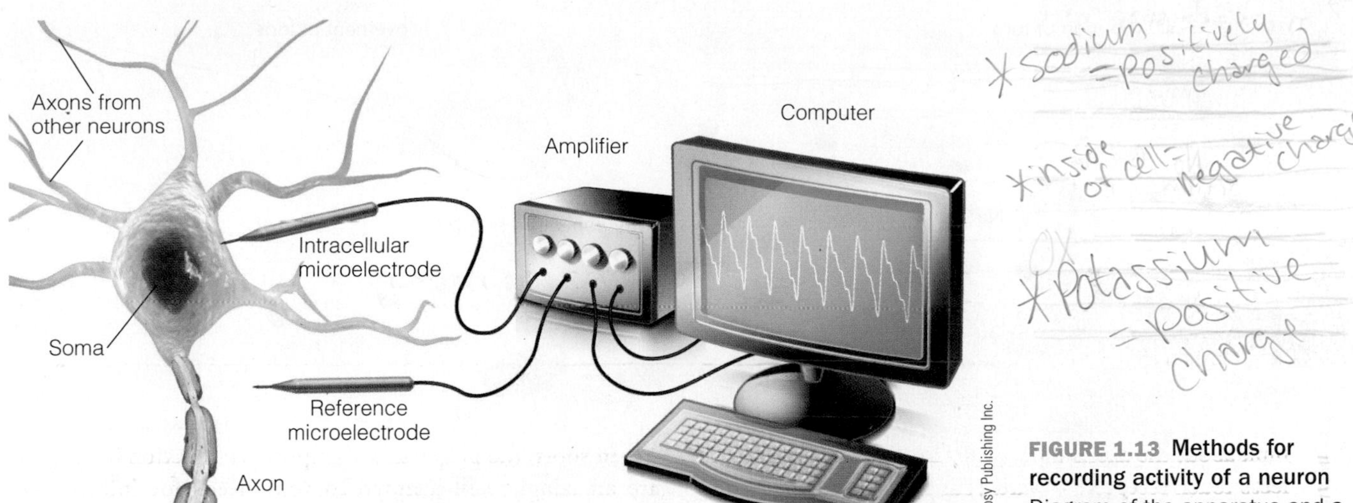

FIGURE 1.13 Methods for recording activity of a neuron Diagram of the apparatus and a sample recording.

neuron inside the membrane has a slightly negative electrical potential with respect to the outside, mainly because of negatively charged proteins inside the cell. This difference in voltage is called the **resting potential**.

Researchers measure the resting potential by inserting a very thin *microelectrode* into the cell body, as Figure 1.13 shows. The diameter of the electrode must be as small as possible so that it enters the cell without causing damage. The most common electrode is a fine glass tube filled with a salt solution, tapering to a tip diameter of 0.0005 mm or less. A reference electrode outside the cell completes the circuit. Connecting the electrodes to a voltmeter, we find that the neuron's interior has a negative potential relative to its exterior. A typical level is −70 millivolts (mV), but it varies from one neuron to another.

Forces Acting on Sodium and Potassium Ions

If charged ions could flow freely across the membrane, the membrane would depolarize. However, the membrane is **selectively permeable**. That is, some chemicals pass through it more freely than others do. Oxygen, carbon dioxide, urea, and water cross freely through channels that are always open. Several biologically important ions, including sodium, potassium, calcium, and chloride, cross through membrane channels (or gates) that are sometimes open and sometimes closed, as shown in Figure 1.14. When the membrane is at rest, the sodium and potassium channels are closed, permitting almost no flow of sodium and only a small flow of potassium. Certain types of stimulation can open these channels, permitting freer flow of both ions.

The **sodium–potassium pump**, a protein complex, repeatedly transports three sodium ions out of the cell while drawing two potassium ions into it. The sodium–potassium pump is an active transport that requires energy. As a result of the sodium–potassium pump, sodium ions are more than 10 times more concentrated outside the membrane than inside, and potassium ions are similarly more concentrated inside than outside.

The sodium–potassium pump is effective only because of the selective permeability of the membrane, which prevents the sodium ions that were pumped out of the neuron from leaking right back in again. When sodium ions are pumped out, they stay out. However, some of the potassium ions in the neuron slowly leak out, carrying a positive charge with them. That leakage increases the electrical gradient across the membrane, as shown in Figure 1.15.

When the neuron is at rest, two forces act on sodium, both tending to push it *into* the cell. First, consider the electrical gradient. Sodium is positively charged and the inside of the cell is negatively charged. Opposite electrical charges attract, so the electrical gradient tends to pull sodium into the cell. Second, consider the **concentration gradient**, the difference in distribution of ions across the membrane. Sodium is more concentrated outside than inside, so just by the laws of probability, sodium is more likely to enter the cell than to leave it. Given that both the

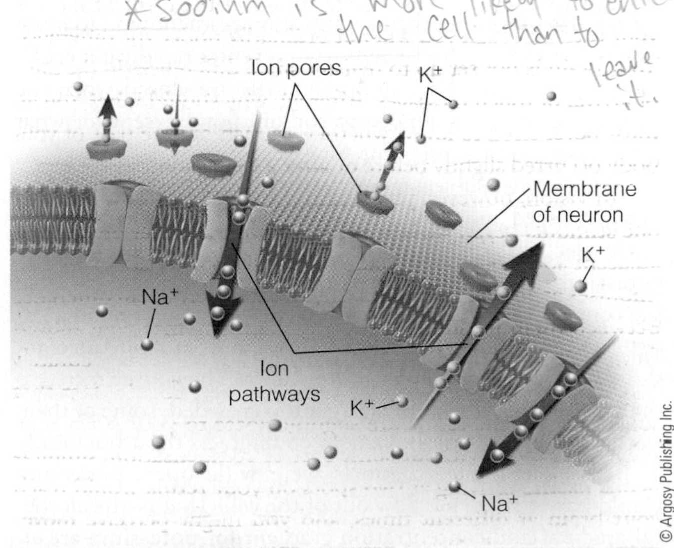

FIGURE 1.14 Ion channels in the membrane of a neuron When a channel opens, it permits some type of ion to cross the membrane. When it closes, it prevents passage of that ion.

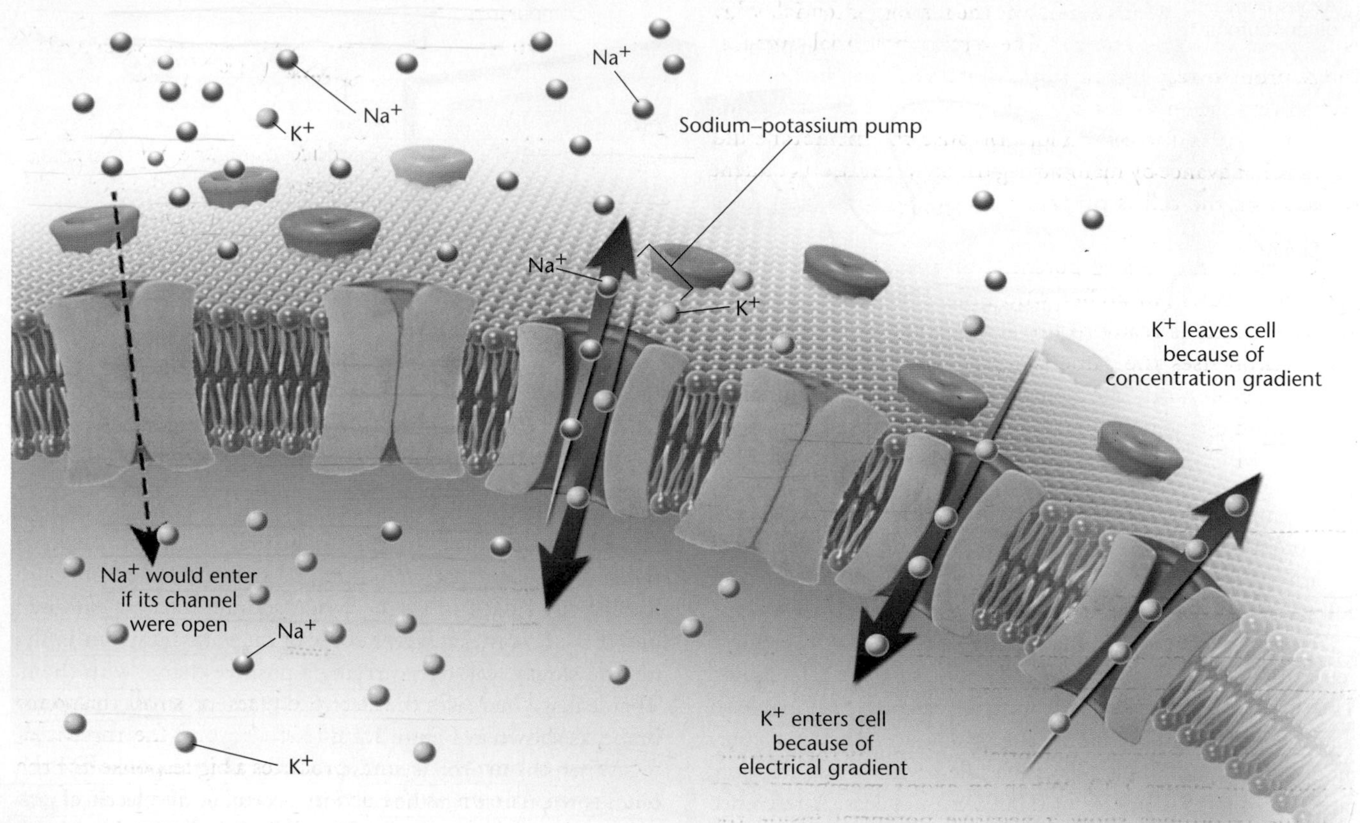

FIGURE 1.15 The sodium and potassium gradients for a resting membrane
Sodium ions are more concentrated outside the neuron, and potassium ions more concentrated inside. Protein and chloride ions (not shown) bear negative charges inside the cell. At rest, almost no sodium ions cross the membrane except by the sodium–potassium pump. Potassium tends to flow into the cell because of an electrical gradient but tends to flow out because of the concentration gradient. However, potassium gates retard the flow of potassium when the membrane is at rest.

electrical gradient and the concentration gradient tend to move sodium ions into the cell, sodium would enter rapidly if it could. However, because the sodium channels are closed when the membrane is at rest, almost no sodium flows except for what the sodium–potassium pump forces *out of* the cell.

Potassium is subject to competing forces. Potassium is positively charged and the inside of the cell is negatively charged, so the electrical gradient tends to pull potassium in. However, potassium is more concentrated inside the cell than outside, so the concentration gradient tends to drive it out. (For an analogy, imagine a number of women inside a room. Men can enter the room or leave through a narrow door. They are attracted to the women, but when the men get too crowded, some of them leave. The concentration gradient counteracts the attraction.)

If the potassium channels were wide open, potassium would have a small net flow out of the cell. That is, the electrical gradient and concentration gradient for potassium are almost in balance, but not quite. The sodium–potassium pump continues pulling potassium into the cell, so it always remains a little extra concentrated inside.

The cell has negative ions, too. Negatively charged proteins inside the cell are responsible for the membrane's polarization. Chloride ions, being negatively charged, are mainly outside the cell. When the membrane is at rest, the concentration gradient and electrical gradient balance, so opening the chloride channels would produce little effect. However, chloride does have a net flow when the membrane's polarization changes.

STOP&CHECK

8. When the membrane is at rest, are the sodium ions more concentrated inside the cell or outside? Where are the potassium ions more concentrated?

9. When the membrane is at rest, what tends to drive the potassium ions out of the cell? What tends to draw them into the cell?

ANSWERS

8. Sodium ions are more concentrated outside the cell, and potassium is more concentrated inside. **9.** When the membrane is at rest, the concentration gradient tends to drive potassium ions out of the cell, and the electrical gradient draws them into the cell. The sodium–potassium pump also draws them into the cell.

Why a Resting Potential?

The body invests much energy to operate the sodium–potassium pump, which maintains the resting potential. Why is it worth so much energy? The resting potential prepares the neuron to respond rapidly. As we shall see in the next section, excitation of the neuron opens channels that allow sodium to enter the cell rapidly. Because the membrane did its work in advance by maintaining the concentration gradient for sodium, the cell is prepared to respond vigorously to a stimulus.

Compare the resting potential of a neuron to a poised bow and arrow: An archer who pulls the bow in advance and then waits is ready to fire at the appropriate moment. The neuron uses the same strategy. The resting potential remains stable until the neuron is stimulated. Ordinarily, stimulation of the neuron takes place at synapses, which we consider in Chapter 2. In the laboratory, it is also possible to stimulate a neuron by inserting an electrode into it and applying current.

The Action Potential

Messages sent by axons are called **action potentials.** To understand action potentials, let's begin by considering what happens when the resting potential is disturbed. We can measure a neuron's potential with a microelectrode, as shown in Figure 1.13. When an axon's membrane is at rest, the recordings show a negative potential inside the axon. If we now use another electrode to apply a negative charge, we can further increase the negative charge inside the neuron. The change is called **hyperpolarization,** which means increased polarization. When the stimulation ends, the charge returns to its original resting level. The recording looks like this:

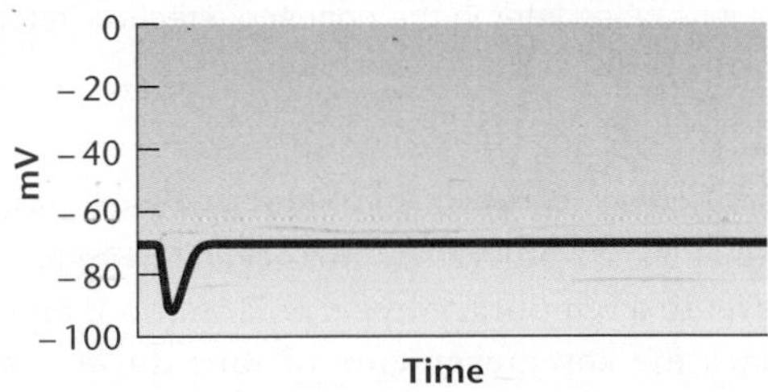

Now let's apply a current to **depolarize** the neuron—that is, reduce its polarization toward zero. If we apply a small depolarizing current, we get a result like this:

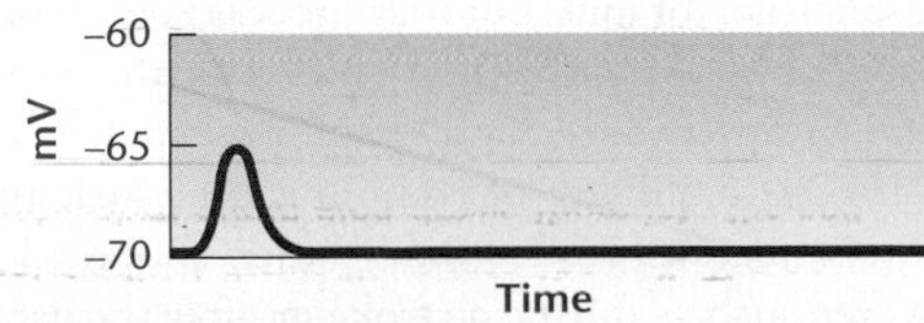

With a slightly stronger depolarizing current, the potential rises slightly higher but again returns to the resting level as soon as the stimulation ceases:

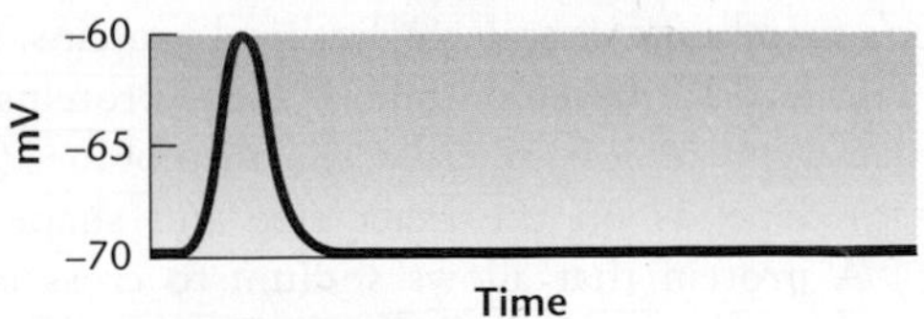

Now let's apply a still stronger current: Stimulation beyond the **threshold** of excitation produces a massive depolarization of the membrane. When the potential reaches the threshold, the membrane opens its sodium channels and permits sodium ions to flow into the cell. The potential shoots up far beyond the strength of the stimulus:

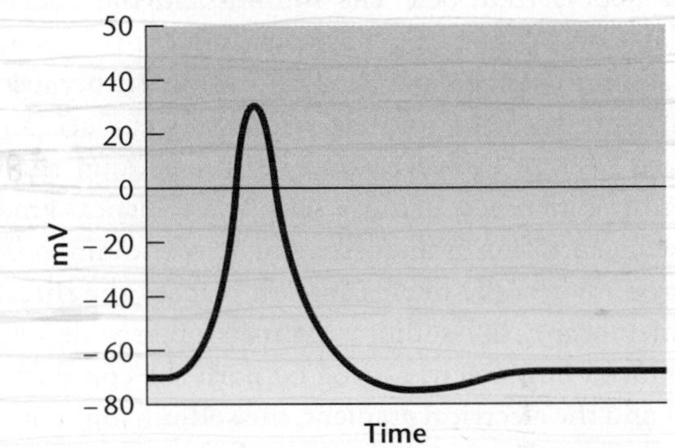

Any *subthreshold* stimulation produces a small response that quickly decays. Any stimulation beyond the threshold, regardless of how far beyond, produces a big response like the one shown, known as the action potential. The peak of the action potential, shown as +30 mV in this illustration, varies from one axon to another, but it is consistent for a given axon.

STOP&CHECK

10. What is the difference between a hyperpolarization and a depolarization?

11. What is the relationship between the threshold and an action potential?

ANSWERS

10. A hyperpolarization is an exaggeration of the usual negative charge within a cell (to a more negative level than usual). A depolarization is a decrease in the amount of negative charge within the cell. **11.** A depolarization that passes the threshold produces an action potential. One that falls short of the threshold does not produce an action potential.

The Molecular Basis of the Action Potential

The chemical events behind the action potential may seem complex, but they make sense if you remember three principles:

1. At the start, sodium ions are mostly outside the neuron, and potassium ions are mostly inside.
2. When the membrane is depolarized, sodium and potassium channels in the membrane open.
3. At the peak of the action potential, the sodium channels close.

A neuron's membrane contains cylindrical proteins, like the ones in Figure 1.12. Opening one of these proteins allows a particular type of ion to cross the membrane. (Which ion crosses depends on the exact size and shape of the opening.) A protein that allows sodium to cross is called a sodium channel, one that allows potassium to cross is a potassium channel, and so forth. The ones regulating sodium and potassium are **voltage-gated channels.** That is, their permeability depends on the voltage difference across the membrane. At the resting potential, the sodium channels are closed and the potassium channels are almost closed (allowing only a little flow of potassium). As the membrane becomes depolarized, both the sodium and the potassium channels begin to open, allowing freer flow. At first, opening the potassium channels makes little difference, because the concentration gradient and electrical gradient are almost in balance anyway. However, opening the sodium channels makes a big difference, because both the electrical gradient and the concentration gradient tend to drive sodium ions into the neuron. When the depolarization reaches the threshold of the membrane, the sodium channels open wide enough for sodium to flow freely. Driven by both the concentration gradient and the electrical gradient, the sodium ions enter the cell rapidly, until the electrical potential across the membrane passes beyond zero to a reversed polarity, as shown in the following diagram:

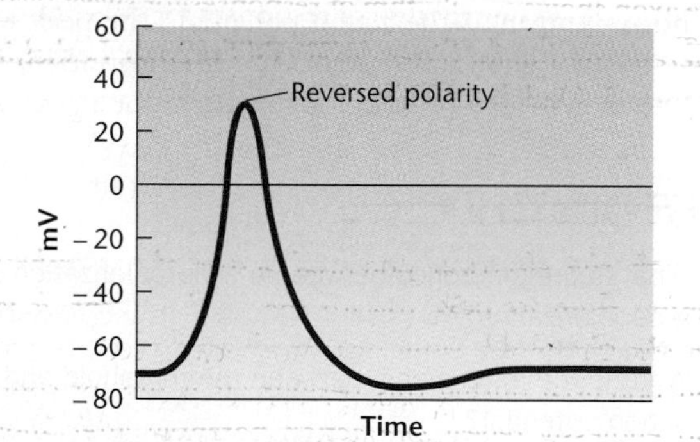

Of the total number of sodium ions near the axon, less than one percent cross the membrane during an action potential. Even at the peak of the action potential, sodium ions continue to be far more concentrated outside the neuron than inside. Because of the persisting concentration gradient, sodium ions should still tend to diffuse into the cell. However, at the peak of the action potential, the sodium gates snap shut and resist reopening for the next millisecond.

Then what happens? Remember that depolarizing the membrane also opens potassium channels. At first, opening those channels made little difference. However, after so many sodium ions have crossed the membrane, the inside of the cell has a slight positive charge instead of its usual negative charge. At this point both the concentration gradient and the electrical gradient drive potassium ions out of the cell. As they flow out of the axon, they carry with them a positive charge. Because the potassium channels remain open after the sodium channels close, enough potassium ions leave to drive the membrane beyond its usual resting level to a temporary hyperpolarization. Figure 1.16 summarizes the key movements of ions during an action potential.

At the end of this process, the membrane has returned to its resting potential, but the inside of the neuron has slightly more sodium ions and slightly fewer potassium ions than before. Eventually, the sodium–potassium pump restores the original distribution of ions, but that process takes time. After an unusually rapid series of action potentials, the pump cannot keep up with the action, and sodium accumulates within the axon. Excessive buildup of sodium can be toxic to a cell. (Excessive stimulation occurs only under abnormal conditions, however, such as during a stroke or after the use of certain drugs. Don't worry that thinking too hard will explode your brain cells!)

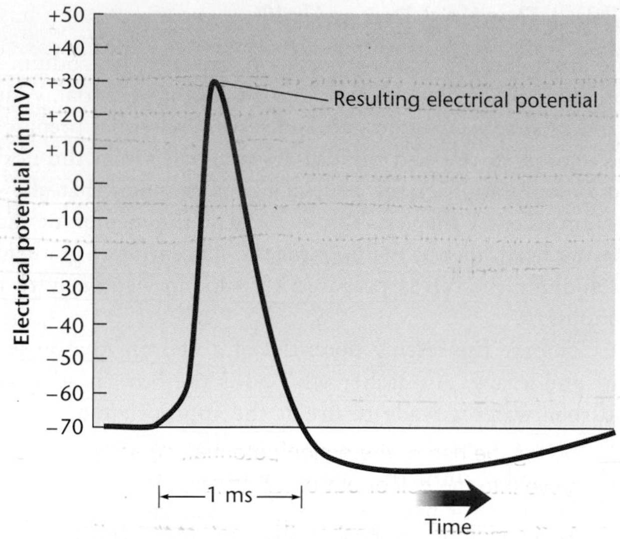

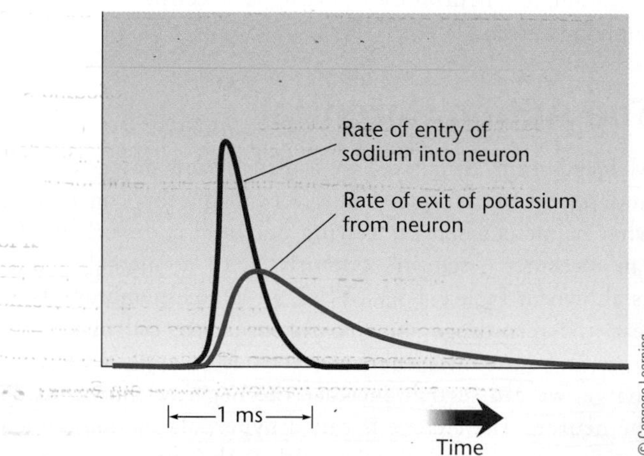

FIGURE 1.16 The movement of sodium and potassium ions during an action potential
Sodium ions cross during the peak of the action potential, and potassium ions cross later in the opposite direction, returning the membrane to its original polarization.

Action potentials require the flow of sodium and potassium. **Local anesthetic** drugs, such as Novocain and Xylocaine, attach to the sodium channels of the membrane, preventing sodium ions from entering, and thereby stopping action potentials (Ragsdale, McPhee, Scheuer, & Catterall, 1994). When a dentist administers Novocain before drilling into one of your teeth, your receptors are screaming, "pain, pain, pain!" but the axons cannot transmit the message to your brain, and so you don't feel it.

STOP & CHECK

12. During the rise of the action potential, do sodium ions move into the cell or out of it? Why?

13. As the membrane reaches the peak of the action potential, what brings the membrane down to the original resting potential?

ANSWERS

12. During the action potential, sodium ions move into the cell. The voltage-dependent sodium gates have opened, so sodium can move freely. Sodium is attracted to the inside of the cell by both an electrical and a concentration gradient. **13.** After the peak of the action potential, potassium ions exit the cell, driving the membrane back to the resting potential. Important note: The sodium–potassium pump is NOT responsible for returning the membrane to its resting potential. The sodium–potassium pump is too slow for this purpose.

The All-or-None Law

An action potential always starts in an axon and propagates without loss along the axon. However, once it starts, it "back-propagates" into the cell body and dendrites (Lorincz & Nusser, 2010). The cell body and dendrites do not conduct action potentials in the same way that axons do, but they passively register the electrical event happening in the nearby axon. This back-propagation is important: When an action potential back-propagates into a dendrite, the dendrite becomes more susceptible to the structural changes responsible for learning.

Here, we concentrate on the axon. When the voltage across an axon membrane reaches the threshold, voltage-gated sodium channels open wide enough to let sodium ions enter, and the incoming sodium depolarizes the membrane to produce an action potential. For a given neuron, all action potentials are approximately equal in amplitude (intensity) and velocity. More properly stated, the **all-or-none law** is that the amplitude and velocity of an action potential are independent of the intensity of the stimulus that initiated it, provided that the stimulus reaches the threshold. By analogy, imagine flushing a toilet: You have to make a press of at least a certain strength (the threshold), but pressing harder does not make the toilet flush faster or more vigorously.

Although the amplitude, velocity, and shape of action potentials are consistent over time for a given axon, they vary from one neuron to another. Thicker axons convey action potentials at greater velocities. Thicker axons can also convey more action potentials per second. The ability to do so is important for certain kinds of sensory information (Perge, Niven, Mugnaini, Balasubramanian, & Sterling, 2012).

The all-or-none law puts constraints on how an axon can send a message. To signal the difference between a weak stimulus and a strong stimulus, the axon cannot send bigger or faster action potentials. All it can change is the timing. By analogy, you might send signals to someone by flashing the lights in your room on and off, varying the speed of flashing to indicate something. You could also convey information by a rhythm.

Flash-flash . . . [long pause] . . . flash-flash

might mean something different from

Flash . . . [pause] . . . flash . . . [pause] . . . flash . . . [pause] . . . flash.

The nervous system uses both kinds of coding. For example, a taste axon shows one rhythm of responses for sweet tastes and a different rhythm for bitter tastes (Di Lorenzo, Leshchinskiy, Moroney, & Ozdoba, 2009).

The Refractory Period

Although the electrical potential across the membrane is returning from its peak toward the resting point, it is still above the threshold. Why doesn't the cell produce another action potential during this period? (If it did, of course, it would endlessly repeat one action potential after another.) Immediately after an action potential, the cell is in a **refractory period** during which it resists the production of further action potentials. In the first part of this period, the **absolute refractory period**, the membrane cannot produce an action potential, regardless of the stimulation. During the second part, the **relative refractory period**, a stronger-than-usual stimulus is necessary to initiate an action potential. The refractory period depends on two facts: The sodium channels are closed, and potassium is flowing out of the cell at a faster-than-usual rate.

In most of the neurons that researchers have tested, the absolute refractory period is about 1 millisecond (ms), and the relative refractory period is another 2 to 4 ms. (To return to the toilet analogy, during a short time right after you flush a toilet, you cannot make it flush again—an absolute refractory period. Then follows a period when it is possible but difficult to flush it again—a relative refractory period—before it returns to normal.)

STOP&CHECK

14. State the all-or-none law.

15. Does the all-or-none law apply to dendrites? Why or why not?

16. Suppose researchers find that axon A can produce up to 1,000 action potentials per second (at least briefly, with maximum stimulation), but axon B can never produce more than 100 per second (regardless of the strength of the stimulus). What could we conclude about the refractory periods of the two axons?

ANSWERS

14. According to the all-or-none law, the size and shape of the action potential are independent of the intensity of the stimulus that initiated it. That is, every depolarization beyond the threshold of excitation produces an action potential of about the same amplitude and velocity for a given axon. **15.** The all-or-none law does not apply to dendrites because they do not have action potentials. **16.** Axon A must have a shorter absolute refractory period, about 1 ms, whereas B has a longer absolute refractory period, about 10 ms.

Propagation of the Action Potential

Up to this point, we have considered how the action potential occurs at one point on the axon. Now let us consider how it moves down the axon. Remember, it is important for axons to convey impulses without any loss of strength over distance.

During an action potential, sodium ions enter a point on the axon. Temporarily, that spot is positively charged in comparison with neighboring areas along the axon. The positive ions flow within the axon to neighboring regions. The positive charges slightly depolarize the next area of the membrane, causing it to reach its threshold and open its voltage-gated sodium channels. Then the membrane regenerates the action potential at that point. In this manner, the action potential travels along the axon, as in Figure 1.17.

The term **propagation of the action potential** describes the transmission of an action potential down an axon. The propagation of an animal species is the production of offspring. In a sense, the action potential gives birth to a new action potential at each point along the axon.

Let's reexamine Figure 1.17 for a moment. What is to prevent the electrical charge from flowing in the direction opposite that in which the action potential is traveling? Nothing. In fact, the electrical charge does flow in both directions. Then what prevents an action potential near the center of an axon from reinvading the areas that it has just passed? The answer is that the areas it just passed are still in their refractory period.

Let's review the action potential:

- When an area of the axon membrane reaches its threshold of excitation, sodium channels and potassium channels open.
- At first, the opening of potassium channels produces little effect.
- Opening sodium channels lets sodium ions rush into the axon.
- Positive charge flows down the axon and opens voltage-gated sodium channels at the next point.
- At the peak of the action potential, the sodium gates snap shut. They remain closed for the next millisecond or so, despite the depolarization of the membrane.
- Because voltage-gated potassium channels remain open, potassium ions flow out of the axon, returning the membrane toward its original depolarization.
- A few milliseconds later, the voltage-dependent potassium channels close.

All of this may seem like a lot to memorize, but it is not. Everything follows logically from the facts that voltage-gated sodium and potassium channels open when the membrane is depolarized and that sodium channels snap shut at the peak of the action potential.

The Myelin Sheath and Saltatory Conduction

In the thinnest axons, action potentials travel at a velocity of less than 1 m/s. Increasing the diameter brings conduction velocity up to about 10 m/s. At that speed, an impulse along an axon to or from a giraffe's foot takes about half a second. To increase the speed still more, vertebrate axons evolved a special mechanism: sheaths of **myelin**, an insulating material composed of fats and proteins.

Consider the following analogy. Suppose your job is to take written messages over a long distance without using any mechanical device. Taking each message and running with it would be reliable but slow, like the propagation of an action potential along an unmyelinated axon. If you tied each message to a ball and threw it, you could increase the speed, but your throws would not travel far enough. The best solution is to station people at moderate distances along the route and throw the message-bearing ball from person to person until it reaches its destination.

The same principle applies to **myelinated axons**, those covered with a myelin sheath. Myelinated axons, found only in vertebrates, are covered with layers of fats and proteins. The myelin sheath is interrupted periodically by short sections of axon called nodes of Ranvier, each one about 1 micrometer wide, as shown in Figure 1.18. In myelinated axons, the action potential starts at the first node of Ranvier (Kuba, Ishii, & Ohmari, 2006).

Suppose an action potential occurs at the first myelin segment. The action potential cannot regenerate along the membrane between nodes because sodium channels are virtually absent between nodes (Catterall, 1984). After an action potential occurs at a node, sodium ions enter the axon and diffuse, pushing a chain of positive charge along the axon to the next node, where they regenerate the action potential (see Figure 1.19). This flow of charge moves considerably faster

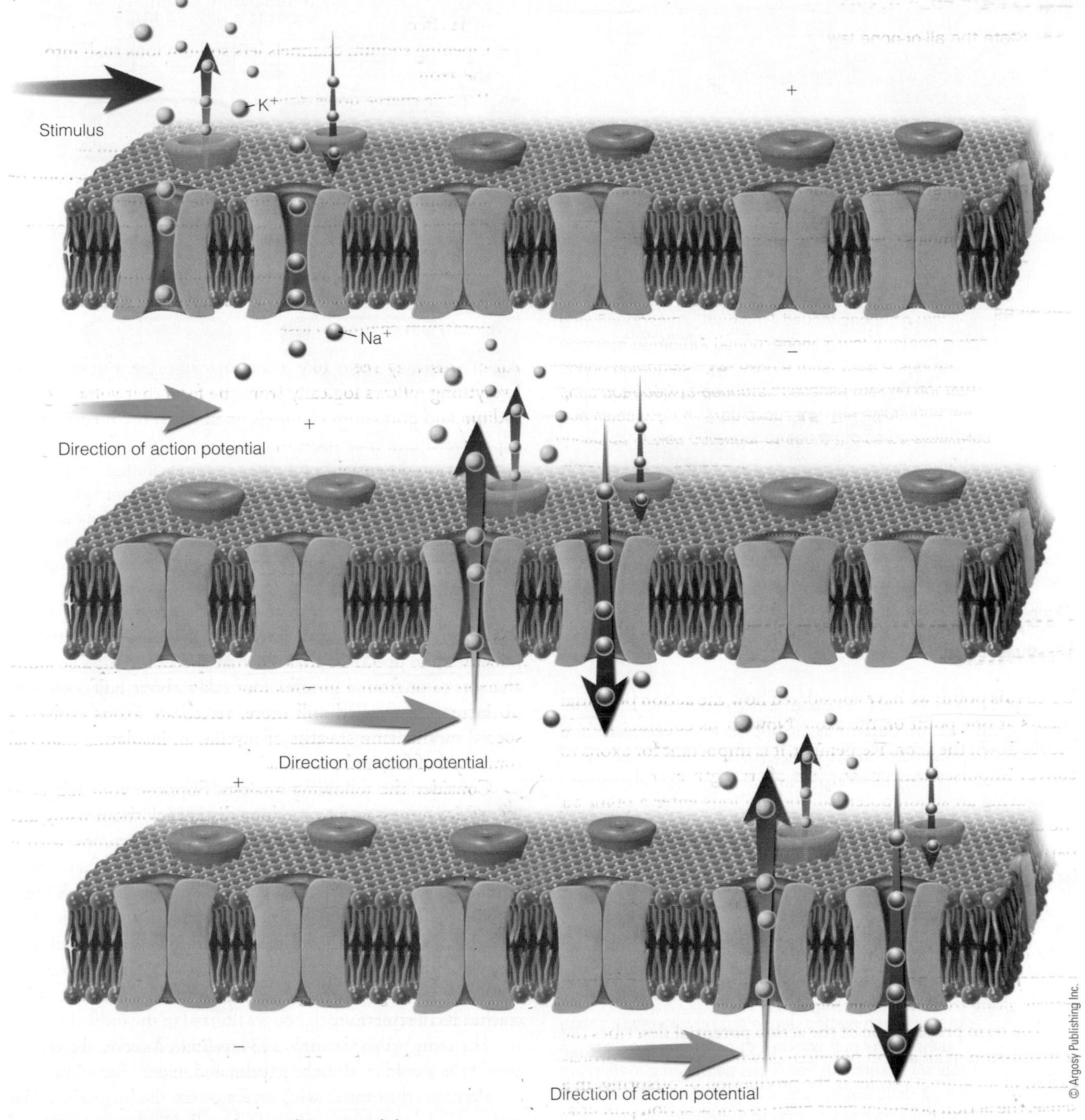

FIGURE 1.17 Propagation of an action potential
As an action potential occurs at one point on the axon, enough sodium enters to depolarize the next point to its threshold, producing an action potential at that point. In this manner the action potential flows along the axon, remaining at equal strength throughout. Behind each area of sodium entry, potassium ions exit, restoring the resting potential.

than the regeneration of an action potential at each point along the axon. The jumping of action potentials from node to node is referred to as **saltatory conduction**, from the Latin word *saltare,* meaning "to jump." (The same root shows up in the word *somersault.*) In addition to providing rapid conduction of impulses, saltatory conduction conserves energy: Instead of admitting sodium ions at every point along the axon and then having to pump them out via the sodium–potassium pump, a myelinated axon admits sodium only at its nodes.

In multiple sclerosis, the immune system attacks myelin sheaths. An axon that never had a myelin sheath conducts impulses slowly but steadily, but an axon that has lost its myelin is not the same, because it lacks sodium channels where

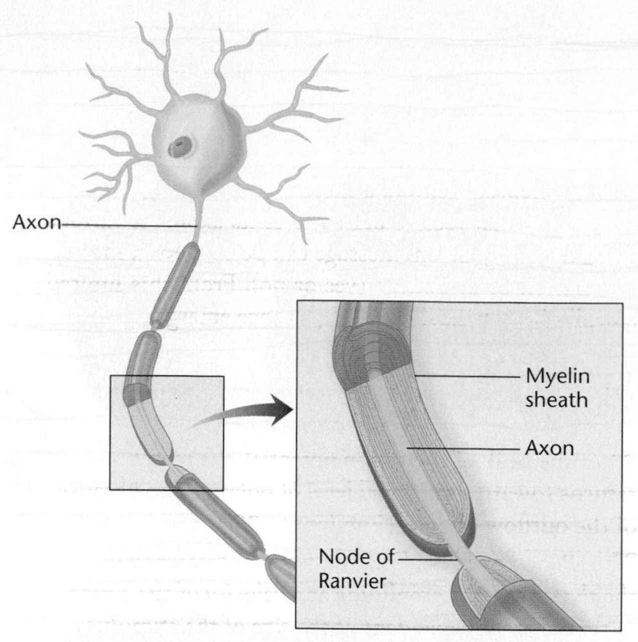

FIGURE 1.18 An axon surrounded by a myelin sheath and interrupted by nodes of Ranvier
The inset shows a cross-section through both the axon and the myelin sheath. The anatomy is distorted here to show several nodes; in fact, the distance between nodes is generally at least 100 times as long as a node.

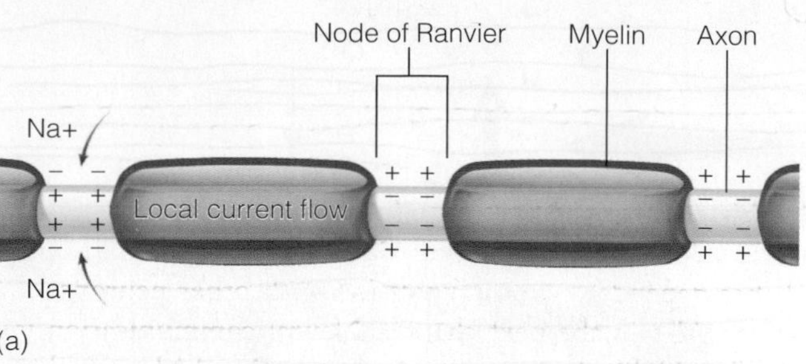

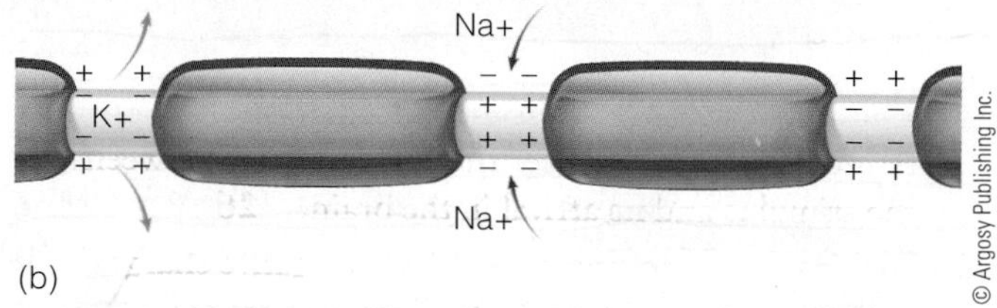

FIGURE 1.19 Saltatory conduction in a myelinated axon
An action potential at the node triggers flow of current to the next node, where the membrane regenerates the action potential. In reality, a myelin sheath is much longer than shown here, relative to the size of the nodes of Ranvier and to the diameter of the axon.

the myelin used to be (Waxman & Ritchie, 1985). Consequently, most action potentials die out between one node and the next. People with multiple sclerosis suffer a variety of impairments, ranging from visual impairments to poor muscle coordination.

STOP&CHECK

17. In a myelinated axon, how would the action potential be affected if the nodes were much closer together? How might it be affected if the nodes were much farther apart?

ANSWER

17. If the nodes were closer, the action potential would travel more slowly. If they were much farther apart, the action potential would be faster if it could successfully jump from one node to the next. When the distance becomes too great, the current cannot diffuse from one node to the next and still remain above threshold, so the action potentials would stop.

Local Neurons

Axons produce action potentials. However, many small neurons have no axon (Le Magueresse, et al., 2011). Neurons without an axon exchange information with only their closest neighbors. We therefore call them **local neurons.** Because they do not have an axon, they do not follow the all-or-none law. When a local neuron receives information from other neurons, it has a **graded potential,** a membrane potential that varies in magnitude in proportion to the intensity of the stimulus. The change in membrane potential is conducted to adjacent areas of the cell, in all directions, gradually decaying as it travels. Those various areas of the cell contact other neurons, which they excite or inhibit.

Local neurons are difficult to study because it is almost impossible to insert an electrode into a tiny cell without damaging it. Most of our knowledge, therefore, has come from large neurons, and that bias in our research methods may have led to a misconception. Many years ago, all that neuroscientists knew about local neurons was that they were small. Given their focus on larger neurons, many scientists assumed that the small neurons were immature. As one textbook author put it, "Many of these [neurons] are small and apparently undeveloped, as if they constituted a reserve stock not yet utilized in the individual's cerebral activity" (Woodworth, 1934, p. 194). In other words, the small cells would contribute to behavior only if they grew.

Perhaps this misunderstanding was the origin of that widespread, nonsensical belief that "they say we use only 10 percent of our brain." (Who are "they," incidentally?) Other origins have also been suggested for this belief. Regardless of how it started, it has been remarkably persistent, given its total lack of justification. Surely, it cannot be true that someone could lose 90 percent of the brain and still behave normally. Nor is it true that only 10 percent of neurons are active at any given moment. You use all of your brain, even at times when you might not be using it very well. The belief that we use only a small part of the brain became popular, presumably because people wanted to believe it. Eventually, people were simply quoting one another long after everyone forgot where the idea originated.

MODULE 1.2 ■ IN CLOSING

Neurons and Messages

In this chapter, we have examined what happens within a single neuron. However, everything that a neuron accomplishes depends on communication with other neurons, as we consider in the next chapter. Neural communication is amazing. Unlike human communication, in which a speaker sometimes presents a complicated message to an enormous audience, a neuron delivers a mere on/off message to only those neurons that receive branches of its axon. At various receiving neurons, an "on" message can be converted into either excitation or inhibition (yes or no). From this limited system, all of our behavior and experience emerge.

Summary

1. The action potential transmits information without loss of intensity over distance. The cost is a delay between the stimulus and its arrival in the brain. 26
2. The inside of a resting neuron has a negative charge with respect to the outside. Sodium ions are actively pumped out of the neuron, and potassium ions are pumped in. 26
3. When the membrane is at rest, the electrical gradient and concentration gradient act in competing directions for potassium, almost balancing out. Potassium ions have a slow net flow out of the cell. Both gradients tend to push sodium into the cell, but sodium ions do not cross while the membrane is at rest. 27
4. When the charge across the membrane is reduced, sodium and potassium channels begin to open. When the membrane potential reaches the threshold of the neuron, sodium ions enter explosively, suddenly reducing and reversing the charge across the membrane. This event is known as the action potential. 29
5. After the peak of the action potential, the membrane returns toward its original level of polarization because of the outflow of potassium ions. 30
6. The all-or-none law: For any stimulus greater than the threshold, the amplitude and velocity of the action potential are independent of the size of the stimulus that initiated it. 31
7. Immediately after an action potential, the membrane enters a refractory period during which it is resistant to starting another action potential. 31
8. The action potential is regenerated at successive points along the axon as sodium ions flow through the core of the axon and stimulate the next point along the axon to its threshold. The action potential maintains a constant magnitude as it passes along the axon. 32
9. In axons that are covered with myelin, action potentials form only in the nodes that separate myelinated segments. Transmission in myelinated axons is faster than in unmyelinated axons. 32

Key Terms

Terms are defined in the module on the page number indicated. They're also presented in alphabetical order with definitions in the book's Subject Index/Glossary. Interactive flash cards, audio reviews, and crossword puzzles are among the online resources available to help you learn these terms and the concepts they represent.

absolute refractory period 31
action potentials 29
all-or-none law 31
concentration gradient 27
depolarize 29
electrical gradient 26
graded potential 34
hyperpolarization 29
local anesthetic 31
local neurons 34
myelin 32
myelinated axons 32
polarization 26
propagation of the action potential 32
refractory period 31
relative refractory period 31
resting potential 27
saltatory conduction 33
selectively permeable 27
sodium–potassium pump 27
threshold 29
voltage-gated channels 30

Thought Questions

1. Suppose the threshold of a neuron were the same as the neuron's resting potential. What would happen? At what frequency would the cell produce action potentials?

2. In the laboratory, researchers can apply an electrical stimulus at any point along the axon, making action potentials travel in both directions from the point of stimulation. An action potential moving in the usual direction, away from the axon hillock, is said to be traveling in the *orthodromic* direction. An action potential traveling toward the axon hillock is traveling in the antidromic direction. If we started an orthodromic action potential at the start of the axon and an antidromic action potential at the opposite end of the axon, what would happen when they met at the center? Why?
3. If a drug partly blocks a membrane's potassium channels, how does it affect the action potential?

MODULE 1.2 End of Module Quiz

1. When the neuron's membrane is at rest, sodium ions are more concentrated _____ the cell, and potassium ions are more concentrated _____.
   a. inside . . . outside
   b. inside . . . inside
   c. outside . . . inside
   d. outside . . . outside
2. When the membrane is at rest, the concentration gradient tends to draw potassium ions ____ the cell, and the electrical gradient draws them ____ the cell.
   a. into . . . out of
   b. into . . . into
   c. out of . . . into
   d. out of . . . out of
3. When the membrane is at rest, the concentration gradient tends to draw sodium ions ____ the cell, and the electrical gradient draws them ____ the cell.
   a. into . . . out of
   b. into . . . into
   c. out of . . . into
   d. out of . . . out of
4. The sodium–potassium pump moves sodium ions _____ and moves potassium ions _____.
   a. into the cell . . . out of the cell
   b. into the cell . . . into the cell
   c. out of the cell . . . into the cell
   d. out of the cell. . . out of the cell
5. Suppose a neuron has a resting potential of −70 mV. If the potential goes to −80 mV, the change would be a _____.
   a. depolarization
   b. hyperpolarization
6. Under what conditions does an axon produce an action potential?
   a. Whenever the membrane is hyperpolarized
   b. Whenever the membrane's potential reaches the threshold
   c. Whenever the membrane is depolarized
   d. Whenever the membrane's potential reaches zero
7. During the rising portion of the action potential, which ions are moving across the membrane and in which direction?
   a. Sodium ions move out.
   b. Sodium ions move in.
   c. Both sodium and potassium ions move in.
   d. Potassium ions move in.
8. After the action potential reaches its peak, the potential across the membrane falls toward its resting level. What accounts for this recovery?
   a. The sodium–potassium pump removes the extra sodium.
   b. Potassium ions move out because their channels are open and the electrical gradient pushes them out.
   c. Potassium ions move out because their channels are open and the concentration gradient pushes them out.
   d. Potassium ions move in.

9. Which of the following is one way of stating the all-or-none law?

a. The amplitude of the action potential in one axon is the same as that in another axon.

b. At a given time, either all axons produce action potentials, or none do.

c. All stimuli that exceed the threshold produce equivalent responses in the axon.

d. During an action potential, all sodium channels open at the same time.

10. To which part or parts of a neuron does the all-or-none law apply?

a. Axons

b. Dendrites

c. Both axons and dendrites

11. What does the myelin sheath of an axon accomplish?

a. It enables an axon to communicate with other axons.

b. It enables action potentials to travel both directions along an axon.

c. It enables nutrients to enter the axon.

d. It enables action potentials to travel more rapidly.

12. Is it true that we use only 10 percent of our brain? If so, what does that mean?

a. At any moment, only 10 percent of brain cells are active.

b. You could lose 90 percent of your brain and still do what you are doing now.

c. About 90 percent of the brain's neurons are immature and not yet functional.

d. No, the statement is false and nonsensical.

ANSWERS: 1c, 2c, 3b, 4c, 5b, 6b, 7b, 8c, 9c, 10a, 11d, 12d.

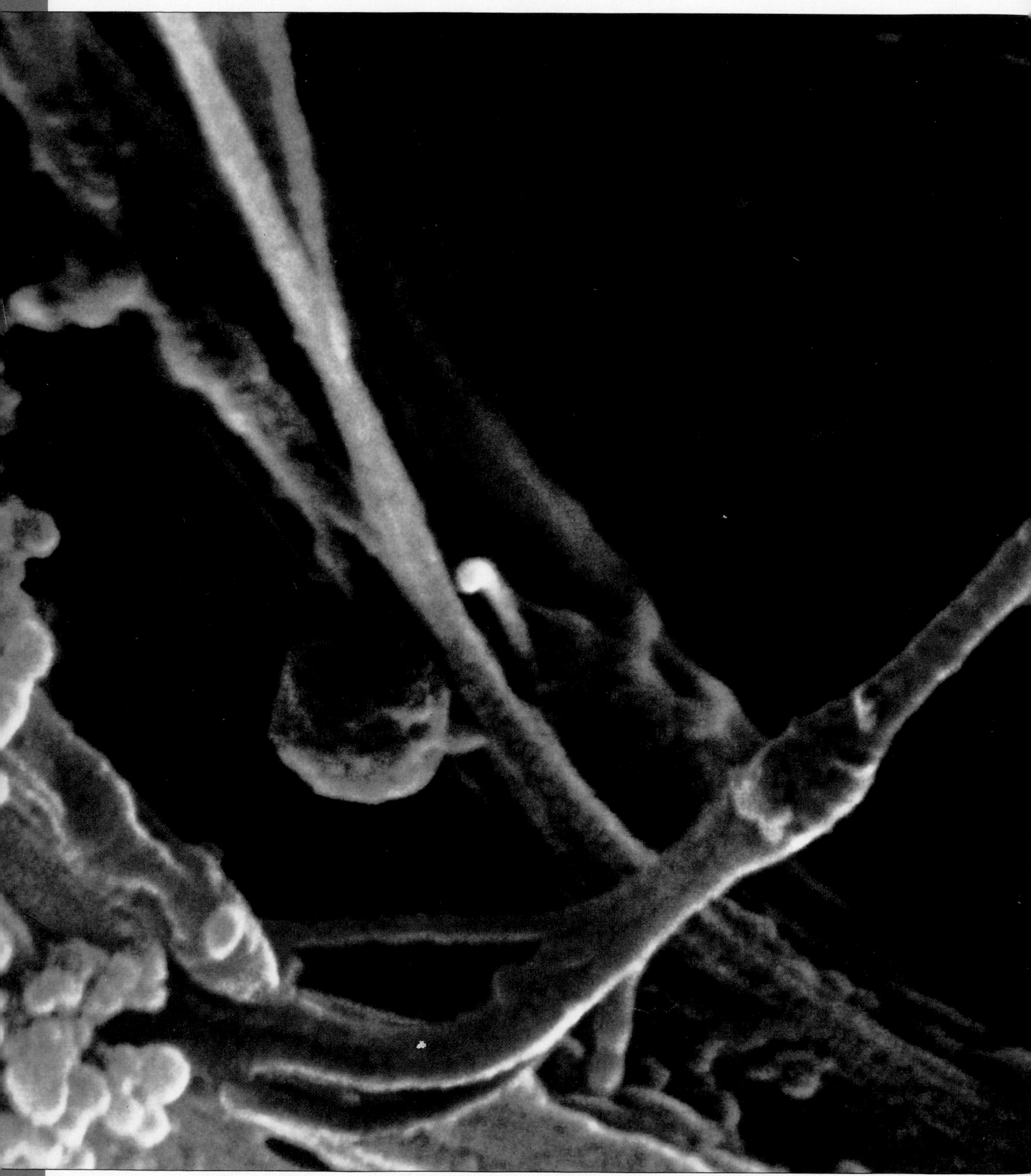
Eye of Science/Science Source

Synapses

2

I f you had to communicate with someone without sight or sound, what would you do? Chances are, your first choice would be a touch code or a system of electrical impulses. You might not even think of passing chemicals back and forth. Chemicals are, however, the main way your neurons communicate. They communicate by transmitting chemicals at specialized junctions called *synapses*.

OPPOSITE: This electron micrograph, with color added artificially, shows branches of an axon making contacts with other cells.

CHAPTER OUTLINE

MODULE 2.1 **The Concept of the Synapse**
Properties of Synapses
Relationship among EPSP, IPSP, and Action Potentials
In Closing: The Neuron as Decision Maker
MODULE 2.2 **Chemical Events at the Synapse**
The Discovery of Chemical Transmission at Synapses
The Sequence of Chemical Events at a Synapse
Hormones
In Closing: Neurotransmitters and Behavior

LEARNING OBJECTIVES

After studying this chapter, you should be able to:

1. Describe how Charles Sherrington used behavioral observations to infer the major properties of synapses.
2. Relate the activities at a synapse to the probability that a neuron will produce an action potential.
3. List and explain the sequence of events at a synapse, from synthesis of neurotransmitters, through stimulation of receptors, to the later disposition of the transmitter molecules.
4. Discuss how certain drugs affect behavior by altering events at synapses.
5. Contrast neurotransmitters, neuropeptides, and hormones.

The Concept of the Synapse

In the late 1800s, Ramón y Cajal anatomically demonstrated a narrow gap separating one neuron from another. In 1906, Charles Scott Sherrington physiologically demonstrated that communication between one neuron and the next differs from communication along a single axon. He inferred a specialized gap between neurons and introduced the term **synapse** to describe it. Cajal and Sherrington are regarded as the great pioneers of modern neuroscience, and their nearly simultaneous discoveries supported each other: If communication between neurons is special in some way, then there can be no doubt that neurons are anatomically separate from one another. Sherrington's discovery was an amazing feat of scientific reasoning, as he used behavioral observations to infer the major properties of synapses half a century before researchers had the technology to measure those properties directly.

Properties of Synapses

Sherrington studied **reflexes**, automatic muscular responses to stimuli. In a leg flexion reflex, a sensory neuron excites a second neuron, which in turn excites a motor neuron, which excites a muscle, as in Figure 2.1. The circuit from sensory neuron to muscle response is called a **reflex arc.** If one neuron is separate from another, as Cajal had demonstrated, a reflex must require communication between neurons, and therefore, measurements of reflexes might reveal some of the special properties of that communication.

Sherrington strapped a dog into a harness above the ground and pinched one of the dog's feet. After a fraction of a second, the dog *flexed* (raised) the pinched leg and *extended* the other legs. Sherrington

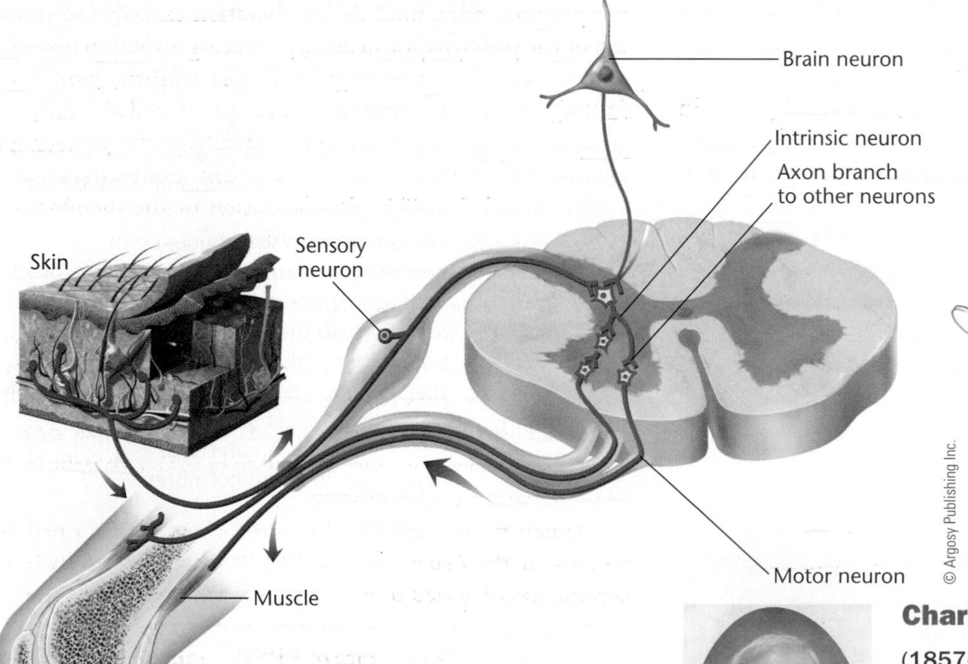

FIGURE 2.1 A reflex arc for leg flexion
The anatomy has been simplified to show the relationship among sensory neuron, intrinsic neuron, and motor neuron.

Hulton Archive/Getty Images

Charles Scott Sherrington

(1857–1952)

A rainbow every morning who would pause to look at? The wonderful which comes often or is plentifully about us is soon taken for granted. That is practical enough. It allows us to get on with life. But it may stultify if it cannot on occasion be thrown off. To recapture now and then childhood's wonder is to secure a driving force for occasional grown-up thoughts. (Sherrington, 1941, p. 104) found the same reflexive movements after he made a cut that disconnected the spinal cord from the brain. Evidently, the spinal cord controlled the flexion and extension reflexes. In fact, the movements were more consistent after he separated the spinal cord from the brain. (In an intact animal, messages descending from the brain modify the reflexes, making them stronger at some times and weaker at others.)

Sherrington observed several properties of reflexes suggesting special processes at the junctions between neurons: (1) Reflexes are slower than conduction along an axon. (2) Several weak stimuli presented at nearby places or times produce a stronger reflex than one stimulus alone does. (3) When one set of muscles becomes excited, a different set becomes relaxed. Let's consider each of these points and their implications.

Speed of a Reflex and Delayed Transmission at the Synapse

When Sherrington pinched a dog's foot, the dog flexed that leg after a short delay. During that delay, an impulse had to travel up an axon from the skin receptor to the spinal cord, and then an impulse had to travel from the spinal cord back down the leg to a muscle. Sherrington measured the total distance that the impulse traveled from skin receptor to spinal cord to muscle and calculated the speed at which the impulse traveled to produce the response. He found that the speed of conduction through the reflex arc varied but was never more than about 15 meters per second (m/s). In contrast, previous research had measured action potential velocities along sensory or motor nerves at about 40 m/s. Sherrington concluded that some process must be slowing conduction through the reflex, and he inferred that the delay occurs where one neuron communicates with another (see Figure 2.2). This idea is critical, as it established the existence of synapses. Sherrington, in fact, introduced the term *synapse*.

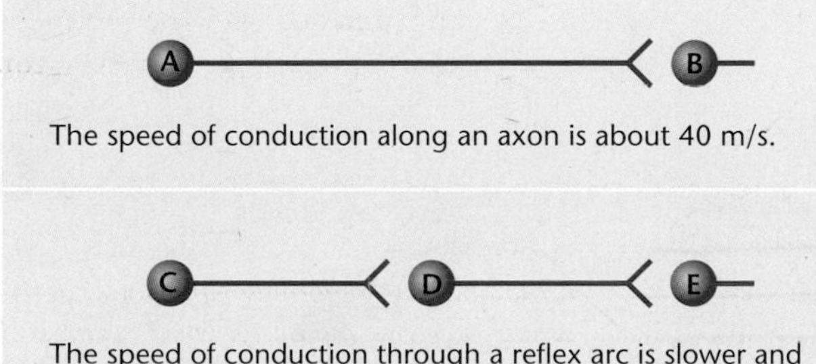

FIGURE 2.2 Sherrington's evidence for synaptic delay
An impulse traveling through a synapse in the spinal cord is slower than one traveling a similar distance along an uninterrupted axon.

STOP&CHECK

1. What evidence led Sherrington to conclude that transmission at a synapse is different from transmission along an axon?

ANSWER

1. Sherrington found that the velocity of conduction through a reflex arc was slower than the velocity of an action potential along an axon. Therefore, some delay must occur at the junction between one neuron and the next.

Temporal Summation

Sherrington found that repeated stimuli within a brief time have a cumulative effect. He referred to this phenomenon as **temporal summation** (summation over time). A light pinch of the dog's foot did not evoke a reflex, but a few rapidly repeated pinches did. Sherrington surmised that a single pinch did not reach the threshold of excitation for the next neuron. The neuron that delivers transmission is the **presynaptic neuron**, and the one that receives it is the **postsynaptic neuron**. Sherrington proposed that although the subthreshold excitation in the postsynaptic neuron decays over time, it can combine with a second excitation that follows it quickly. With a rapid succession of pinches, each adds its effect to what remained from the previous ones, until the combination exceeds the threshold of the postsynaptic neuron, producing an action potential.

Decades later, Sherrington's former student, John Eccles (1964), attached microelectrodes to stimulate axons of presynaptic neurons while he recorded from the postsynaptic neuron. For example, after he had briefly stimulated an axon, Eccles recorded a slight depolarization of the membrane of the postsynaptic cell (point 1 in Figure 2.3).

Note that this partial depolarization is a graded potential. Unlike action potentials, which are always depolarizations, graded potentials may be either depolarizations (excitatory) or hyperpolarizations (inhibitory). A graded depolarization is known as an **excitatory postsynaptic potential (EPSP)**. It results from a flow of sodium ions into the neuron. If an EPSP does not cause the cell to reach its threshold, the depolarization decays quickly.

When Eccles stimulated an axon twice, he recorded two EPSPs. If the delay between EPSPs was short enough, the second EPSP added to what was left of the first one (point 2 in Figure 2.3), producing temporal summation. At point 3 in Figure 3.3, a quick sequence of EPSPs combines to exceed the threshold and produce an action potential.

Spatial Summation

Sherrington also found that synapses have the property of **spatial summation**—that is, summation over space. Synaptic inputs from separate locations combine their effects on a neuron. Sherrington again began with a pinch too weak to elicit a reflex. This time, instead of pinching one point twice, he pinched two points at once. Although neither pinch alone

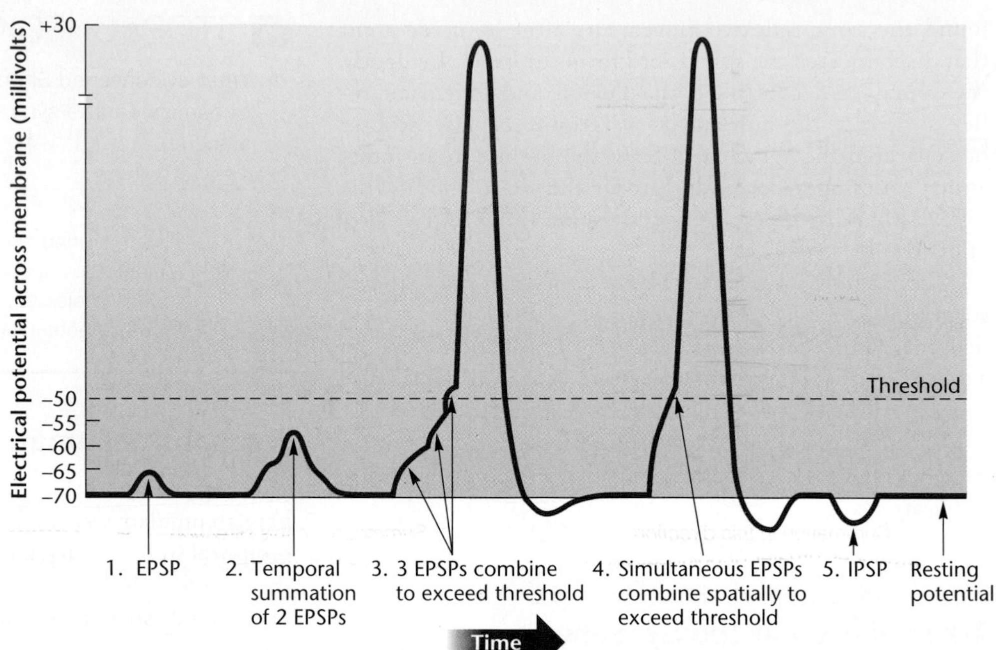

FIGURE 2.3 Recordings from a postsynaptic neuron during synaptic activation

produced a reflex, together they did. Sherrington concluded that pinching two points activated separate sensory neurons, whose axons converged onto one neuron in the spinal cord. Excitation from either sensory axon excited that spinal neuron, but not enough to reach the threshold. A combination of excitations exceeded the threshold and produced an action potential (point 4 in Figure 2.3). Again, Eccles confirmed Sherrington's inference, demonstrating that EPSPs from several axons summate their effects on a postsynaptic cell (see Figure 2.4).

Spatial summation is critical to brain functioning. Sensory input to the brain arrives at synapses that individually produce weak effects. However, each neuron receives many incoming axons that might produce synchronized responses (Bruno & Sakmann, 2006). Spatial summation assures that those synchronized inputs excite a neuron enough to activate it.

Temporal summation and spatial summation ordinarily occur together. That is, a neuron might receive input from several axons in succession. Integrating these inputs provides complexity. As Figure 2.5 shows, a series of axons active in

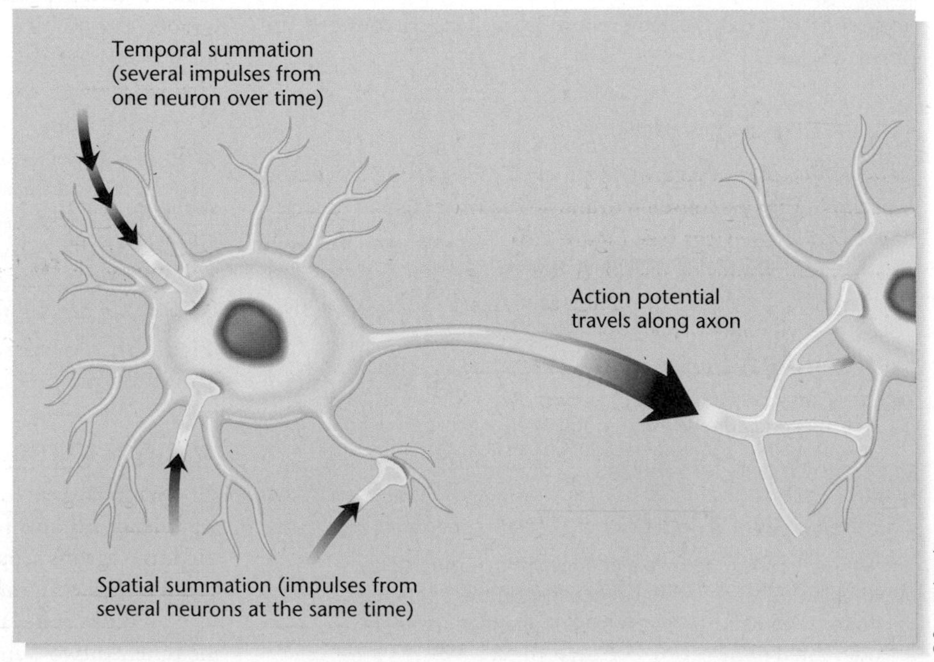

FIGURE 2.4 Temporal and spatial summation

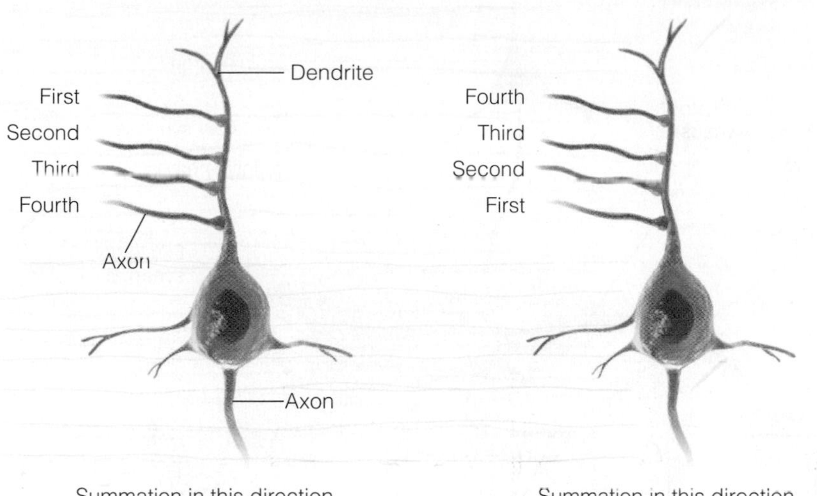

FIGURE 2.5 Summation effects can depend on the order of stimuli

one order can have a different result from the same axons in a different order. For example, a neuron in the visual system could respond to light moving in one direction and not another (Branco, Clark, & Häusser, 2010).

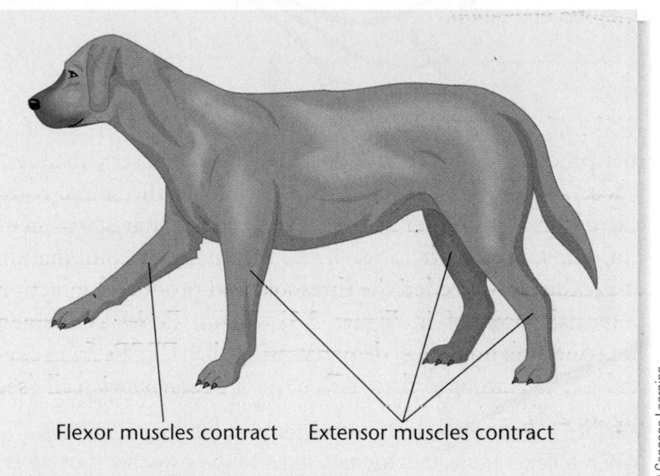

FIGURE 2.6 Antagonistic muscles
Flexor muscles draw an extremity toward the trunk of the body, whereas extensor muscles move an extremity away from the body.

STOP&CHECK

2. What is the difference between temporal summation and spatial summation?

ANSWER

2. Temporal summation is the combined effect of quickly repeated stimulation at a single synapse. Spatial summation is the combined effect of several nearly simultaneous stimulations at several synapses onto one neuron.

Inhibitory Synapses

When Sherrington vigorously pinched a dog's foot, the flexor muscles of that leg contracted, and so did the extensor muscles of the other three legs (see Figure 2.6). (You can see how this arrangement would be useful. A dog raising one leg needs to apply pressure with the other legs to maintain balance.) At the same time, the dog relaxed the extensor muscles of the stimulated leg and the flexor muscles of the other legs. Sherrington's explanation assumed certain connections in the spinal cord: A pinch on the foot sends a message along a sensory neuron to an *interneuron* (an intermediate neuron) that excites the motor neurons connected to the flexor muscles of that leg and the extensor muscles of the other legs (see Figure 2.7). Also, the interneuron sends messages to inhibit the extensor muscles in that leg and the flexor muscles of the three other legs.

Later researchers physiologically demonstrated the inhibitory synapses that Sherrington had inferred. At these synapses, input from an axon hyperpolarizes the postsynaptic cell. That is, it increases the negative charge within the cell, moving it further from the threshold and decreasing the probability of an action potential (point 5 in Figure 2.3). This temporary hyperpolarization of a membrane—called an **inhibitory postsynaptic potential**, or **IPSP**—resembles an EPSP. An IPSP occurs when synaptic input selectively opens the gates for potassium ions to leave the cell (carrying a positive charge with them) or for chloride ions to enter the cell (carrying a negative charge).

Today, we take for granted the concept of inhibition, but at Sherrington's time, the idea was controversial, as no one could imagine a mechanism to accomplish it. Establishing the idea of inhibition was critical not just for neuroscience but for psychology as well.

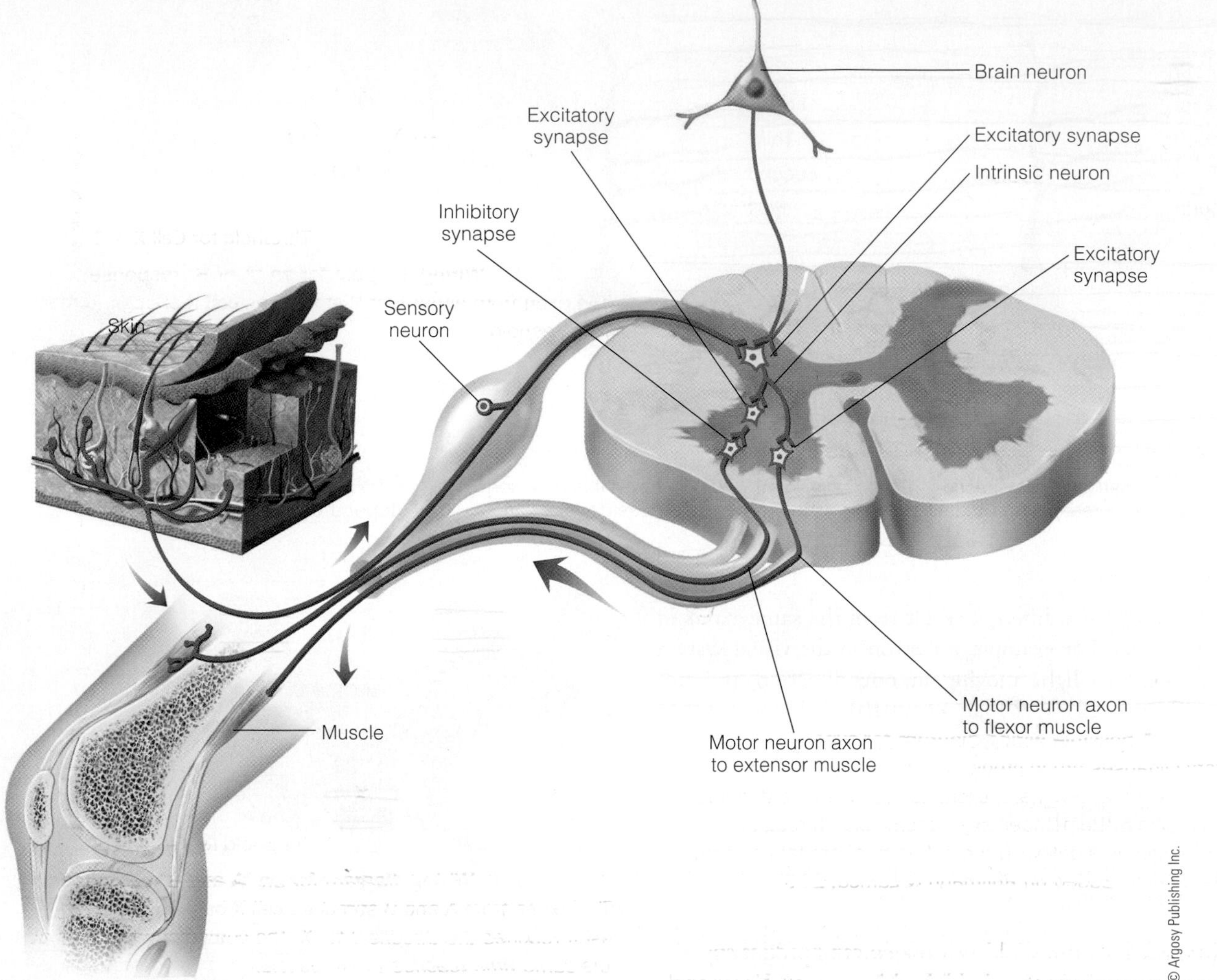

FIGURE 2.7 Sherrington's inference of inhibitory synapses
When a flexor muscle is excited, input to the extensor muscle is inhibited. Sherrington inferred that the interneuron that excited a motor neuron to the flexor muscle also inhibited a motor neuron connected to the extensor muscle. Not shown here are the connections to motor neurons controlling the other three legs.

STOP & CHECK

3. What was Sherrington's evidence for inhibition in the nervous system?
4. What ion gates in the membrane open during an EPSP? What gates open during an IPSP?
5. Can an inhibitory message flow along an axon?

ANSWERS

3. Sherrington found that a reflex that stimulates a flexor muscle prevents contraction of the extensor muscles of the same limb. He therefore inferred that an interneuron that excited motor neurons connected to the flexor muscle also inhibited the input to the extensor muscle. **4.** During an EPSP, sodium gates open. During an IPSP, potassium or chloride gates open. **5.** No. Only action potentials propagate along an axon. Inhibitory messages—IPSPs—decay over time and distance.

Relationship among EPSP, IPSP, and Action Potentials

Sherrington's work opened the way to exploring the wiring diagram of the nervous system. Consider the neurons shown in Figure 2.8. When neuron 1 excites neuron 3, it also excites neuron 2, which inhibits neuron 3. The excitatory message reaches neuron 3 faster because it goes through just one synapse instead of two. The result is a burst of excitation (EPSP) in neuron 3, which quickly slows or stops. You see how inhibitory messages can regulate the timing of activity.

The nervous system has complex patterns of connections that produce varied responses. To see how the wiring diagram controls responses, consider Figures 2.9 through 2.11. In Figure 2.9, the axon from either cell A or cell B stimulates cell X enough to reach its threshold. Therefore, cell X responds to "A or B." In Figure 2.10, neither A nor B stimulates cell X

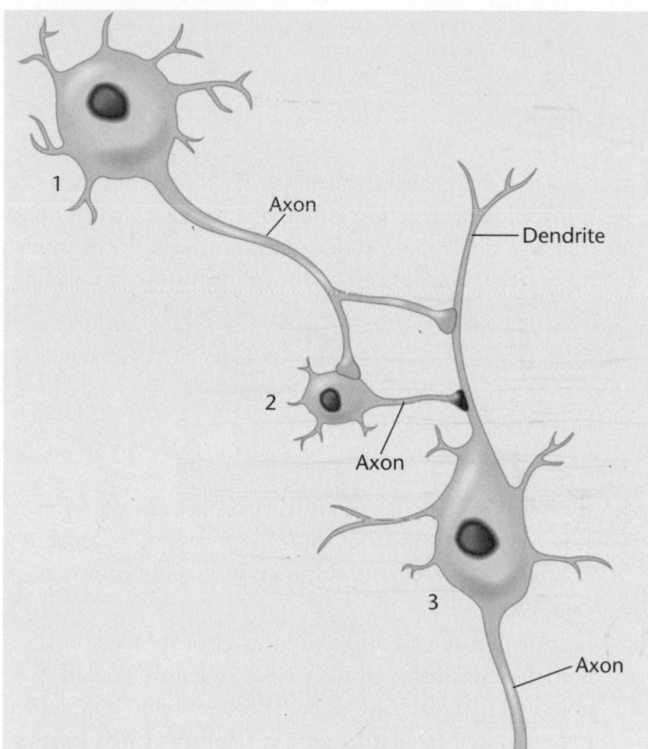

FIGURE 2.8 A possible wiring diagram for synapses
Excitatory synapses are in green, and inhibitory synapses in red. In the circuit shown here, excitation reaches the dendrite before inhibition. (Remember, any transmission through a synapse produces a delay.) The result is brief excitation of the dendrite. *Source:* Based on Kullmann & Lamsa, 2007

enough to reach its threshold, but the two can produce spatial summation to reach the threshold. In this case, cell X responds to "A and B." In Figure 2.11, cell X responds to "A and B if not C." With a little imagination, you can construct other possibilities.

Mathematical models of the nervous system are based on connections like these. However, many of these models ignore complexities that researchers discovered long after the time of Sherrington. Some synapses produce fast, brief effects, and others produce slow, long-lasting effects. In many cases, the effect of two synapses at the same time can be more than double the effect of one, or less than double (Silver, 2010). Certain combinations of synapses summate with one another more strongly than others do (Lavzin, Rapoport, Polsky, Garion, & Schiller, 2012). Also, the strength of a synapse can vary from one time to another. The nervous system is indeed complex.

Most neurons have a **spontaneous firing rate,** a periodic production of action potentials even without synaptic input. In such cases, the EPSPs increase the frequency of action potentials above the spontaneous rate, whereas IPSPs decrease it. For example, if the neuron's spontaneous firing rate is 10 action potentials per second, a stream of EPSPs might increase the rate to 15 or more, whereas a preponderance of IPSPs might decrease it to 5 or fewer.

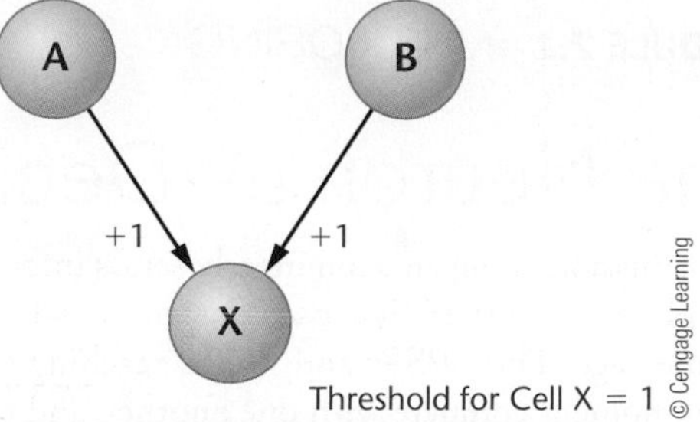

FIGURE 2.9 Wiring diagram for an "A or B" response
The axon from either A or B stimulates cell X enough to reach its threshold.

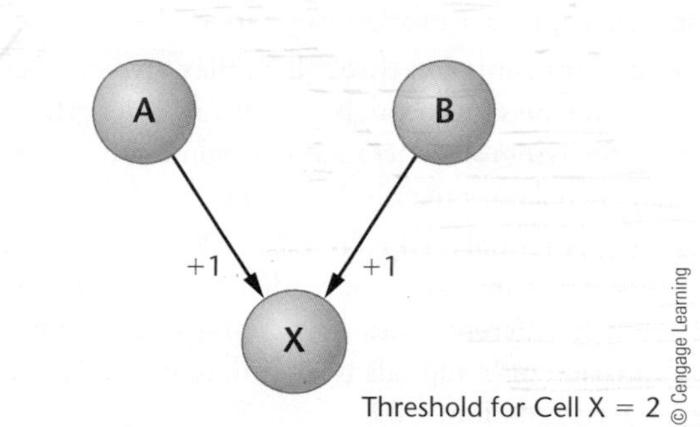

FIGURE 2.10 Wiring diagram for an "A and B" response
The axons from A and B stimulate cell X but neither one by itself reaches the threshold for X. The combination of both at the same time reaches the threshold.

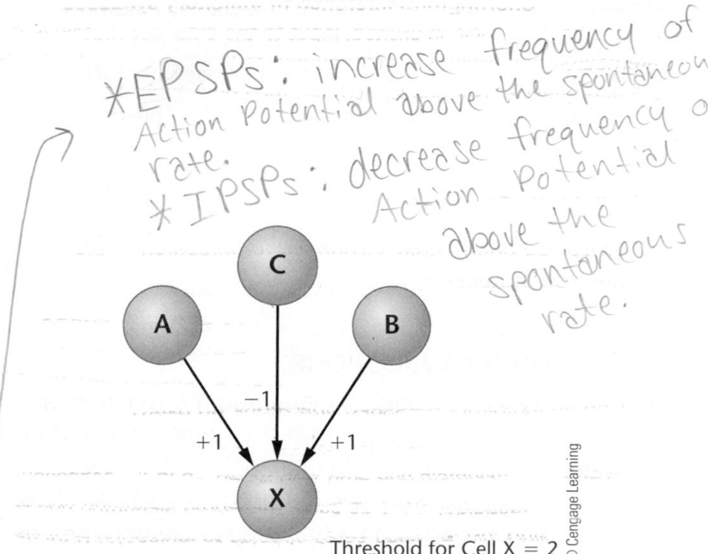

FIGURE 2.11 Wiring diagram for an "A and B if not C" response
The axons from A and B can combine to reach the threshold for X, but the axon from C can inhibit X enough to prevent a response.

MODULE 2.1 ■ IN CLOSING

The Neuron as Decision Maker

Transmission along an axon merely sends information from one place to another. Synapses determine whether to send the message. The EPSPs and IPSPs reaching a neuron at a given moment compete with one another, and the net result is a complicated, not exactly algebraic summation of their effects. We could regard the summation of EPSPs and IPSPs as a "decision" because it determines whether or not the postsynaptic cell fires an action potential. However, do not imagine that any single neuron decides what to eat for breakfast. Complex behaviors depend on the contributions from a huge network of neurons.

Summary

1. The synapse is the point of communication between two neurons. Charles S. Sherrington's observations of reflexes enabled him to infer the existence of synapses and many of their properties. **40**
2. Because transmission through a reflex arc is slower than transmission through an equivalent length of axon, Sherrington concluded that some process at the synapses delays transmission. **41**
3. Graded potentials (EPSPs and IPSPs) summate their effects. The summation of graded potentials from stimuli at different times is temporal summation. The summation of potentials from different locations is spatial summation. **41**
4. Inhibition is more than just the absence of excitation. It is an active brake that suppresses excitation. Within the nervous system, inhibition is just as important as excitation. **43**
5. Stimulation at a synapse produces a brief graded potential in the postsynaptic cell. An excitatory graded potential (depolarizing) is an EPSP. An inhibitory graded potential (hyperpolarizing) is an IPSP. An EPSP occurs when gates open to allow sodium to enter the neuron's membrane. An IPSP occurs when gates open to allow potassium to leave or chloride to enter. **41, 43**
6. The EPSPs on a neuron compete with the IPSPs; the balance between the two increases or decreases the neuron's frequency of action potentials. **44**

Key Terms

Terms are defined in the module on the page number indicated. They're also presented in alphabetical order with definitions in the book's Subject Index/Glossary. Interactive flash cards, audio reviews, and crossword puzzles are among the online resources available to help you learn these terms and the concepts they represent.

excitatory postsynaptic potential (EPSP) **41**
inhibitory postsynaptic potential (IPSP) **43**
postsynaptic neuron **41**
presynaptic neuron **41**
reflex arc **40**
reflexes **40**
spatial summation **41**
spontaneous firing rate **45**
synapse **40**
temporal summation **41**

Thought Questions

1. When Sherrington measured the reaction time of a reflex (i.e., the delay between stimulus and response), he found that the response occurred faster after a strong stimulus than after a weak one. Can you explain this finding? Remember that all action potentials—whether produced by strong or weak stimuli—travel at the same speed along a given axon.
2. Suppose neuron X has a synapse onto neuron Y, which has a synapse onto Z. Presume that no other neurons or synapses are present. An experimenter finds that stimulating neuron X causes an action potential in neuron Z after a short delay. However, she determines that the synapse of X onto Y is inhibitory. Explain how the stimulation of X might produce excitation of Z.

3. Figure 2.11 shows synaptic connections to produce a cell that responds to "A and B if not C." Construct a wiring diagram so that a cell responds to "A *or* B if not C." This is trickier than it sounds. If you simply shift the threshold of cell X to 1, it will respond to "A if not C, or B if not C, or A and B even if C." Can you get X to respond to either A or B, but only if C is inactive? (Hint: You might need to introduce one or two additional cells on the way to X.)

→ MODULE 2.1 End of Module Quiz

1. What evidence led Sherrington to conclude that transmission at a synapse is different from transmission along an axon?
   a. Chemicals that alter a synapse are different from those that affect action potentials.
   b. The velocity of a reflex is slower than the velocity of an action potential.
   c. Stains and microscopic observations demonstrate a gap at the synapse.
   d. Reflexes can go in either direction, whereas axons transmit in only one direction.
2. Although one pinch did not cause a dog to flex its leg, a rapid sequence of pinches did. Sherrington cited this observation as evidence for what?
   a. Temporal summation
   b. Spatial summation
   c. Inhibitory synapses
3. Although one pinch did not cause a dog to flex its leg, several simultaneous pinches at nearby locations did. Sherrington cited this observation as evidence for what?
   a. Temporal summation
   b. Spatial summation
   c. Inhibitory synapses
4. When a vigorous pinch excited a dog's flexor muscle, it decreased excitation of the extensor muscles of the same leg. Sherrington cited this observation as evidence for what?
   a. Temporal summation
   b. Spatial summation
   c. Inhibitory synapses
5. During an EPSP, the _____ gates in the membrane open. During an IPSP, the _____ gates open.
   a. sodium . . . potassium or chloride
   b. potassium . . . sodium or chloride
   c. chloride . . . sodium or potassium
6. In what way were Sherrington's conclusions important for psychology as well as neuroscience?
   a. He demonstrated the importance of unconscious motivations.
   b. He demonstrated the importance of inhibition.
   c. He demonstrated the phenomenon of classical conditioning.
   d. He demonstrated the evolution of intelligence.

ANSWERS: 1b, 2a, 3b, 4c, 5a, 6b.

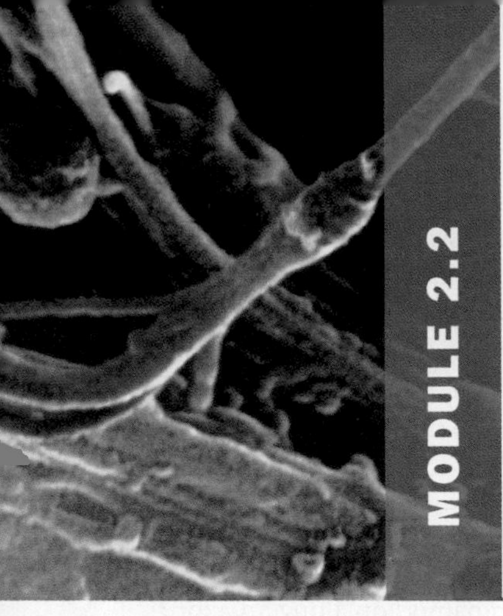

Chemical Events at the Synapse

Although Charles Sherrington accurately inferred many properties of the synapse, he was wrong about one important point: Although he knew that synaptic transmission was slower than transmission along an axon, he thought it was still too fast to depend on a chemical process and therefore concluded that it must be electrical. We now know that the great majority of synapses rely on chemical processes, which are much faster and more versatile than Sherrington or anyone else of his era would have guessed. Over the years, our concept of activity at synapses has grown in many ways.

The Discovery of Chemical Transmission at Synapses

A set of nerves called the sympathetic nervous system accelerates the heartbeat, relaxes the stomach muscles, dilates the pupils of the eyes, and regulates other organs. T. R. Elliott, a young British scientist, reported in 1905 that applying the hormone *adrenaline* directly to the surface of the heart, the stomach, or the pupils produces the same effects as those of the sympathetic nervous system. Elliott therefore suggested that the sympathetic nerves stimulate muscles by releasing adrenaline or a similar chemical.

However, this evidence was not convincing. Perhaps adrenaline merely mimicked effects that are ordinarily electrical in nature. At the time, Sherrington's prestige was so great that most scientists ignored Elliott's results and continued to assume that synapses transmitted electrical impulses. Otto Loewi, a German physiologist, liked the idea of chemical synapses but did not see how to demonstrate it more decisively. Then in 1920, he awakened one night with an idea. He wrote himself a note and went back to sleep. Unfortunately, the next morning he could not read his note! The following night he awoke at 3 A.M. with the same idea, rushed to the laboratory, and performed the experiment.

Loewi repeatedly stimulated the vagus nerve, thereby decreasing a frog's heart rate. He then collected fluid from that heart, transferred it to a second frog's heart, and found that the second heart also decreased its rate of beating, as shown in Figure 2.12. Then Loewi stimulated the accelerator nerve to the first frog's heart, increasing the heart rate. When he collected fluid from that heart and transferred it to the second frog's heart, its heart rate increased. That is, stimulating one nerve released something that inhibited heart rate, and stimulating a different nerve released something that increased heart rate. He knew he was collecting and transferring chemicals, not loose electricity. Therefore, Loewi concluded, nerves send messages by releasing chemicals.

Loewi later remarked that if he had thought of this experiment in the light of day, he probably would have dismissed it as unrealistic (Loewi, 1960). Even if synapses did release chemicals, his daytime reasoning went, they probably did not release much. Fortunately, by the time he realized that the experiment should not work, he had already completed it, and it did work. It earned him a Nobel Prize.

Despite Loewi's work, most researchers over the next three decades continued to believe that most synapses were electrical and that chemical synapses were the exception. Finally, in the 1950s, researchers established that chemical transmission predominates throughout the nervous system. That discovery revolutionized our understanding and encouraged research developing drugs for psychiatric uses (Carlsson, 2001). (A small number of electrical synapses do exist, however, as discussed later in this module.)

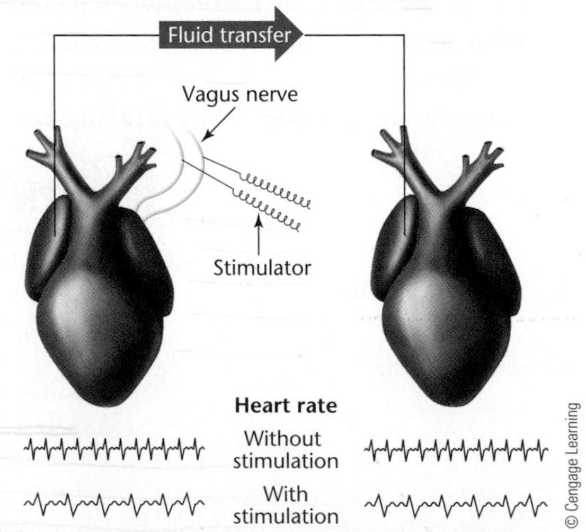

FIGURE 2.12 Loewi's experiment demonstrating that nerves send messages by releasing chemicals
Loewi stimulated the vagus nerve to one frog's heart, decreasing the heartbeat. When he transferred fluid from that heart to another frog's heart, he observed a decrease in its heartbeat.

STOP&CHECK

6. What was Loewi's evidence that neurotransmission depends on the release of chemicals?

ANSWER

6. When Loewi stimulated a nerve that increased or decreased a frog's heart rate, he could withdraw fluid from the area around the heart, transfer it to another frog's heart, and thereby increase or decrease its rate also.

The Sequence of Chemical Events at a Synapse

Understanding the chemical events at a synapse is fundamental to understanding the nervous system. Every year, researchers discover more and more details about synapses, their structure, and how those structures relate to function. Here are the major events:

1. The neuron synthesizes chemicals that serve as neurotransmitters. It synthesizes the smaller neurotransmitters in the axon terminals and synthesizes neuropeptides in the cell body.
2. Action potentials travel down the axon. At the presynaptic terminal, an action potential enables calcium to enter the cell. Calcium releases neurotransmitters from the terminals and into the *synaptic cleft*, the space between the presynaptic and postsynaptic neurons.
3. The released molecules diffuse across the cleft, attach to receptors, and alter the activity of the postsynaptic neuron.
4. The neurotransmitter molecules separate from their receptors.
5. The neurotransmitter molecules may be taken back into the presynaptic neuron for recycling or they may diffuse away.
6. Some postsynaptic cells send reverse messages to control the further release of neurotransmitter by presynaptic cells.

Figure 2.13 summarizes these steps. Let's now consider each step in more detail. As we do, we shall also consider drugs that affect one step or another in this process. Nearly all drugs that affect behavior or experience do so by altering synaptic transmission.

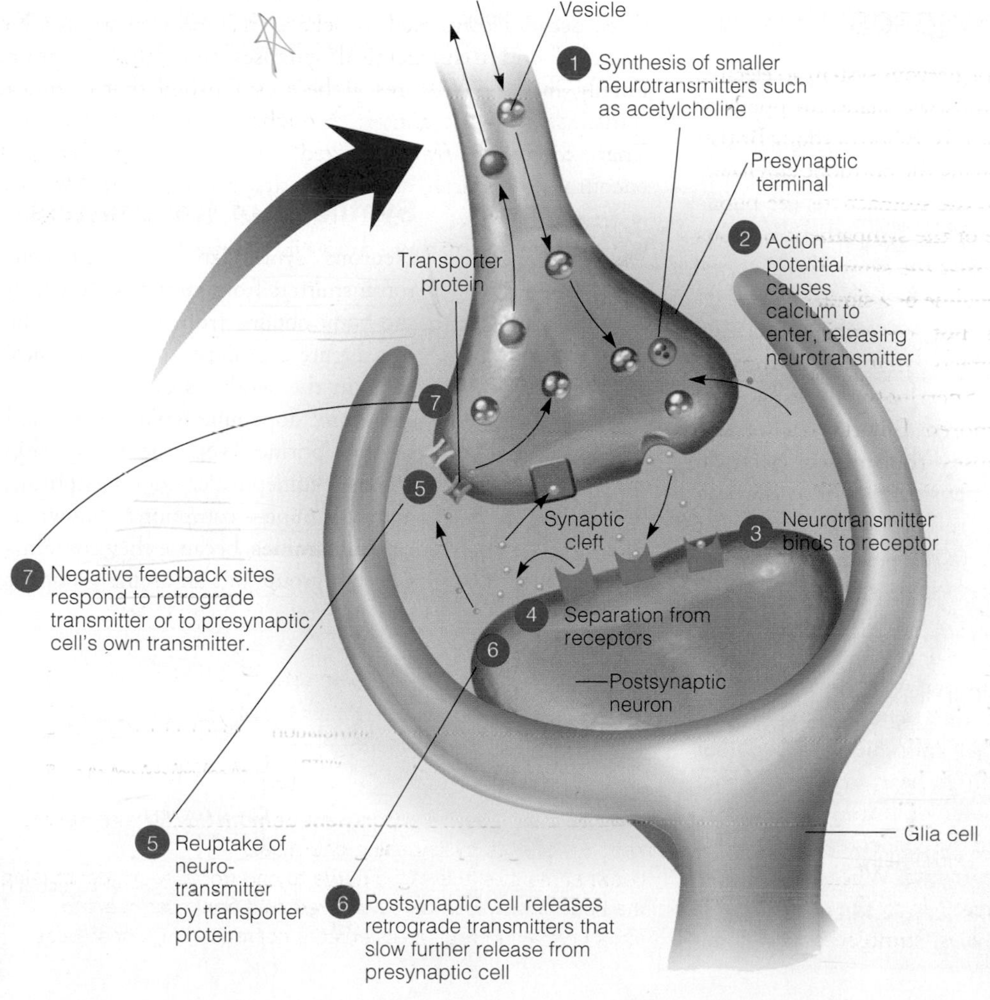

FIGURE 2.13 Some major events in transmission at a synapse
The structure shown in green is an astrocyte that shields the synapse from outside chemicals.

TABLE 2.1 Neurotransmitters

Amino acids	glutamate, GABA, glycine, aspartate, maybe others
A modified amino acid	acetylcholine
Monoamines (also modified from amino acids)	indoleamines: serotonin
	catecholamines: dopamine, norepinephrine, epinephrine
Neuropeptides (chains of amino acids)	endorphins, substance P, neuropeptide Y, many others
Purines	ATP, adenosine, maybe others
Gases	NO (nitric oxide), maybe others

Types of Neurotransmitters

At a synapse, a neuron releases chemicals that affect another neuron. Those chemicals are known as **neurotransmitters**. A hundred or so chemicals are known or suspected to be neurotransmitters, as shown in Table 2.1 (Borodinsky et al., 2004). Here are the major categories:

amino acids Acids containing an amine group (NH_2)
monoamines Chemicals formed by a change in certain amino acids
acetylcholine (a one-member "family") A chemical similar to an amino acid, except that it includes an $N(CH_3)_3$ group instead of an NH_2
neuropeptides Chains of amino acids
purines A category of chemicals including adenosine and its derivatives
gases Nitric oxide and possibly others

The oddest transmitter is **nitric oxide** (chemical formula NO), a gas released by many small local neurons. (Do not confuse nitric oxide, NO, with nitrous oxide, N_2O, sometimes known as "laughing gas.") Nitric oxide is poisonous in large quantities and difficult to make in a laboratory. Yet, many neurons contain an enzyme that enables them to make it efficiently. One special function of nitric oxide relates to blood flow: When a brain area becomes highly active, blood flow to that area increases. How does the blood know which brain area has become more active? The message comes from nitric oxide. Many neurons release nitric oxide when they are stimulated. In addition to influencing other neurons, nitric oxide dilates the nearby blood vessels, thereby increasing blood flow to that brain area (Dawson, Gonzalez-Zulueta, Kusel, & Dawson, 1998).

STOP&CHECK

7. What does a highly active brain area do to increase its blood supply?

ANSWER

7. In a highly active brain area, many stimulated neurons release nitric oxide, which dilates the blood vessels in the area and thereby increases blood flow to the area.

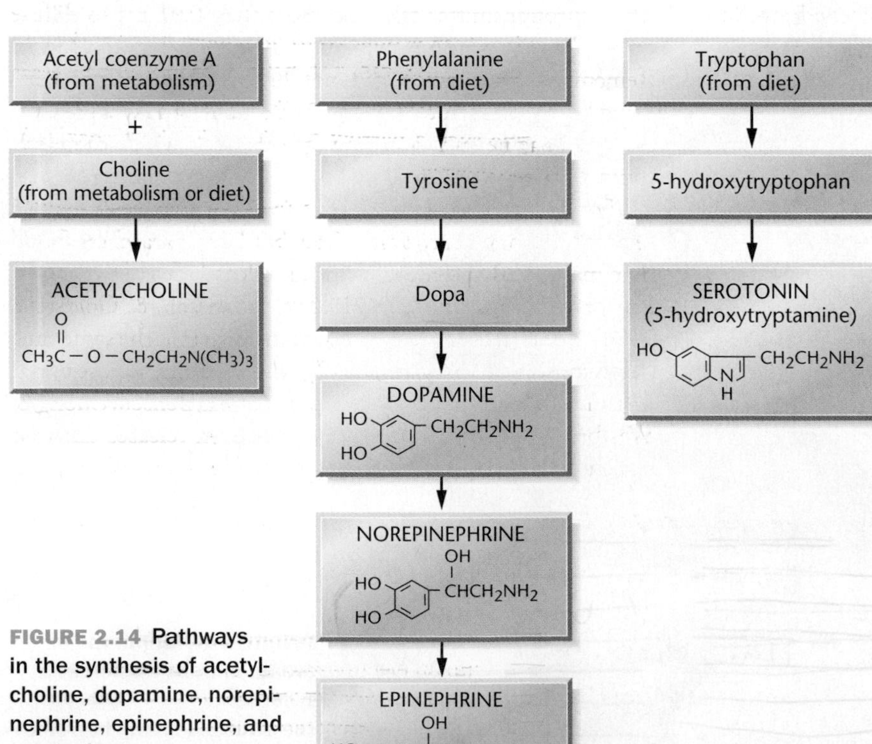

FIGURE 2.14 Pathways in the synthesis of acetylcholine, dopamine, norepinephrine, epinephrine, and serotonin
Arrows represent chemical reactions.

Synthesis of Transmitters

Neurons synthesize nearly all neurotransmitters from amino acids, which the body obtains from proteins in the diet. Figure 2.14 illustrates the chemical steps in the synthesis of acetylcholine, serotonin, dopamine, epinephrine, and norepinephrine. Note the relationship among epinephrine, norepinephrine, and dopamine—compounds known as **catecholamines**, because they contain a catechol group and an amine group, as shown here:

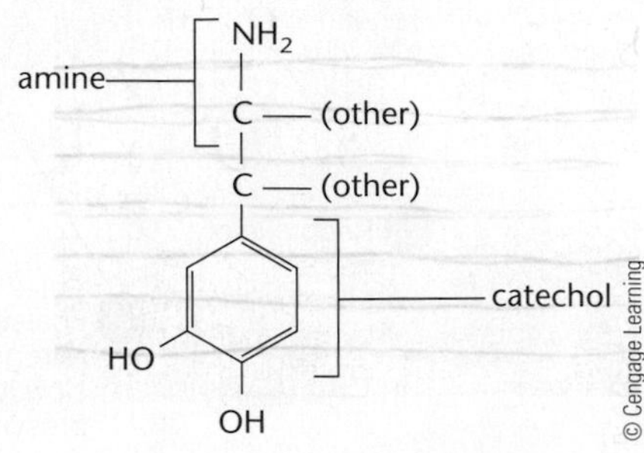

Each pathway in Figure 2.14 begins with substances found in the diet. Acetylcholine, for example, is synthesized from choline, which is abundant in milk, eggs, and peanuts. The amino acids phenylalanine and tyrosine, present in proteins, are precursors of dopamine, norepinephrine, and epinephrine. People with phenylketonuria lack the enzyme that converts phenylalanine to tyrosine. They can get tyrosine from their diet, but they need to minimize intake of phenylalanine.

The amino acid *tryptophan*, the precursor to serotonin, crosses the blood–brain barrier by a special transport system that it shares with other large amino acids. The amount of tryptophan in the diet controls the amount of serotonin in the brain (Fadda, 2000), so your serotonin levels rise after you eat foods richer in tryptophan, such as soy, and fall after something low in tryptophan, such as maize (American corn). However, tryptophan has to compete with other, more abundant large amino acids, such as phenylalanine, that share the same transport system, so increasing intake of tryptophan is not always an effective way to increase serotonin. One way to increase tryptophan entry to the brain is to decrease consumption of phenylalanine. Another is to eat carbohydrates. Carbohydrates increase the release of the hormone *insulin*, which takes several competing amino acids out of the bloodstream and into body cells, thus decreasing the competition against tryptophan (Wurtman, 1985).

Several drugs act by altering the synthesis of transmitters. L-dopa, a precursor to dopamine, helps increase the supply of dopamine. It is a helpful treatment for people with Parkinson's disease. AMPT (alpha-methyl-para-tyrosine) temporarily blocks the production of dopamine. It has no therapeutic use, but it helps researchers study the functions of dopamine.

STOP&CHECK

8. Name the three catecholamine neurotransmitters.

ANSWER

8. Epinephrine, norepinephrine, and dopamine

Storage of Transmitters

Most neurotransmitters are synthesized in the presynaptic terminal, near the point of release. The presynaptic terminal stores high concentrations of neurotransmitter molecules in **vesicles**, tiny nearly spherical packets (see Figure 2.15). (Nitric oxide is an exception to this rule. Neurons release nitric oxide as soon as they form it instead of storing it.) The presynaptic terminal also maintains much neurotransmitter outside the vesicles.

It is possible for a neuron to accumulate excess levels of a neurotransmitter. Neurons that release serotonin, dopamine, or norepinephrine contain an enzyme, **MAO** (monoamine oxidase), that breaks down these transmitters into inactive chemicals. The first antidepressant drugs that psychiatrists discovered were MAO inhibitors. By blocking MAO, they increase the brain's supply of serotonin, dopamine, and norepinephrine. However, MAO inhibitors also have other effects, and exactly how they help relieve depression is still not certain.

Release and Diffusion of Transmitters

At the end of an axon, an action potential itself does not release the neurotransmitter. Rather, depolarization opens voltage-dependent calcium gates in the presynaptic terminal. Within 1 or 2 milliseconds (ms) after calcium enters the terminal, it causes **exocytosis**—bursts of release of neurotransmitter from the presynaptic neuron. An action potential often fails to release any transmitter, and even when it does, the amount varies (Craig & Boudin, 2001).

After its release from the presynaptic cell, the neurotransmitter diffuses across the synaptic cleft to the postsynaptic membrane, where it attaches to a receptor. The neurotransmitter takes no more than 0.01 ms to diffuse across the cleft, which is only 20 to 30 nanometers (nm) wide. Remember, Sherrington did not believe chemical processes could be fast enough to account for the activity at synapses. He did not imagine such a narrow gap through which chemicals could diffuse so quickly.

For many years, investigators believed that each neuron released just one neurotransmitter, but later researchers found that many, perhaps most, neurons release a combination of two or more transmitters (Hökfelt, Johansson, & Goldstein, 1984). Some neurons release two transmitters at the same time (Tritsch, Ding, & Sabatini, 2012), whereas some release one at first and another one slowly later (Borisovska, Bensen, Chong, & Westbrook, 2013). In some cases a neuron releases different transmitters from different branches of its axon (Nishimaru,

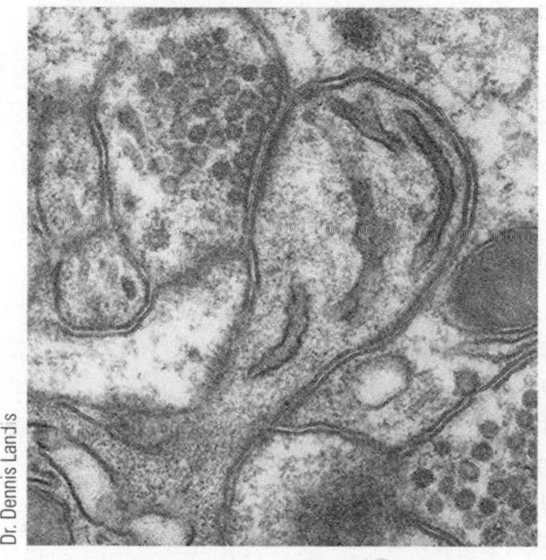

Dr. Dennis Landis

(a)

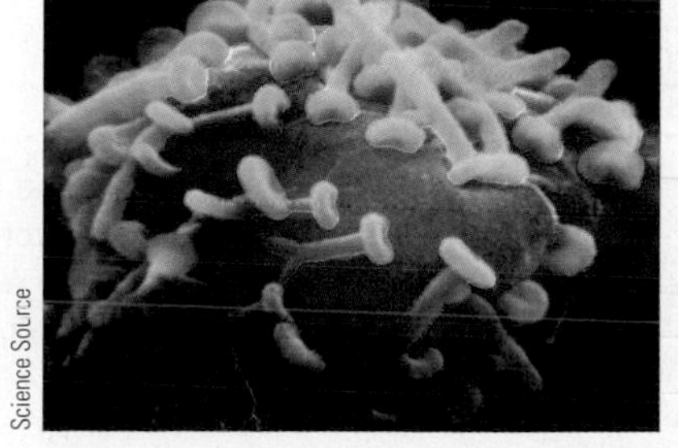

Science Source

(b)

FIGURE 2.15 Anatomy of a synapse
(a) An electron micrograph showing a synapse from the cerebellum of a mouse. The small round structures are vesicles. (b) Electron micrograph showing axon terminals onto the soma of a neuron.

Restrepo, Ryge, Yanagawa, & Kiehn, 2005). A pattern of experience can cause a neuron to stop releasing one transmitter and release another one instead (Dulcis, Jamshidi, Leutgeb, & Spitzer, 2013; Spitzer, 2012). Presumably, the postsynaptic neuron changes its receptors as well. All these processes make it possible for the nervous system to be amazingly flexible.

STOP&CHECK

9. When the action potential reaches the presynaptic terminal, which ion must enter the presynaptic terminal to evoke release of the neurotransmitter?

*Calcium

ANSWER

9. Calcium

Activating Receptors of the Postsynaptic Cell

Sherrington's concept of the synapse was simple: Input produced excitation or inhibition—in other words, on/off. When Eccles recorded from individual cells, he happened to choose cells that produced only brief EPSPs and IPSPs—again, just on/off. The discovery of chemical transmission at synapses didn't change that, at first. Researchers discovered more and more neurotransmitters and wondered, "Why does the nervous system use so many chemicals, if they all produce the same type of message?" Eventually they found that the messages are more complicated and more varied.

The effect of a neurotransmitter depends on its receptor on the postsynaptic cell. When the neurotransmitter attaches to its receptor, the receptor may open a channel—exerting an *ionotropic* effect—or it may produce a slower but longer effect—a *metabotropic* effect.

Ionotropic Effects

At one type of receptor, neurotransmitters exert **ionotropic effects**, corresponding to the brief on/off effects that Sherrington and Eccles studied. Imagine a paper bag that is twisted shut at the top. If you untwist it, the opening grows larger so that something can go into or come out of the bag. An ionotropic receptor is like that. When the neurotransmitter binds to an ionotropic receptor, it twists the receptor enough to open its central channel, which is shaped to let a particular type of ion pass through. In contrast to the sodium and potassium channels along an axon, which are voltage-gated, the channels controlled by a neurotransmitter are **transmitter-gated** or **ligand-gated** channels. (A *ligand* is a chemical that binds to another chemical.) That is, when the neurotransmitter attaches, it opens a channel.

Ionotropic effects begin quickly, sometimes within less than a millisecond after the transmitter attaches (Lisman, Raghavachari, & Tsien, 2007). The effects decay with a half-life of about 5 ms. They are well suited to conveying visual information, auditory information, and anything else that needs to be updated as quickly as possible.

Most of the brain's excitatory ionotropic synapses use the neurotransmitter *glutamate*. In fact, glutamate is the most abundant neurotransmitter in the nervous system. Most of the inhibitory ionotropic synapses use the neurotransmitter GABA (gamma-aminobutyric acid), which opens chloride gates, enabling chloride ions, with their negative charge, to cross the membrane into the cell more rapidly than usual. Glycine is another common inhibitory transmitter, found mostly in the spinal cord (Moss & Smart, 2001). Acetylcholine, another transmitter at many ionotropic synapses, is excitatory in most cases. Figure 2.16a shows an acetylcholine receptor (hugely magnified, of course), as it would appear if you were looking down at it from within the synaptic cleft. Its outer portion (in red) is embedded in the neuron's membrane; its inner portion (in purple) surrounds the sodium channel. When the receptor is at rest, the inner portion coils together tightly enough to block sodium passage. When acetylcholine attaches as in Figure 2.16b, the receptor folds outward, widening the sodium channel (Miyazawa, Fujiyoshi, & Unwin, 2003).

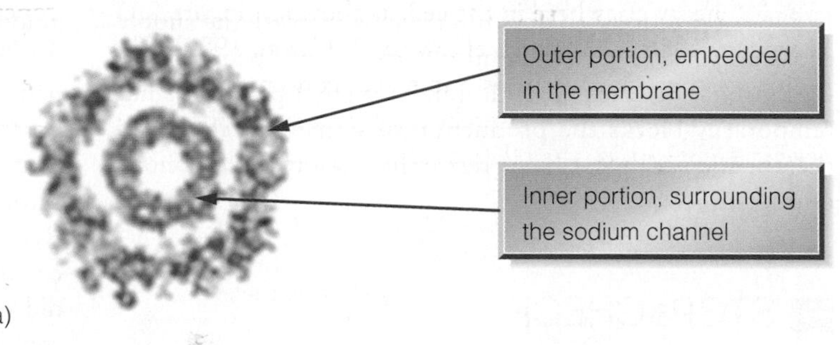

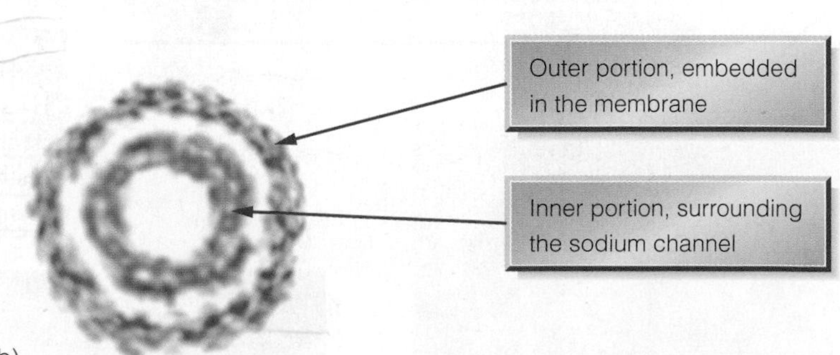

FIGURE 2.16 The acetylcholine receptor
(a) A cross-section of the receptor at rest, as viewed from the synaptic cleft. The membrane surrounds it. (b) A similar view after acetylcholine has attached to the side of the receptor, opening the central channel wide enough for sodium to pass through. *Source*: Adapted from A. Miyazawa, Y. Fujiyoshi, and N. Unwin (2003). "Structure and gating mechanism of the acetylcholine receptor pore," *Nature*, 423, pp. 949–955

Metabotropic Effects and Second Messenger Systems

At other receptors, neurotransmitters exert **metabotropic effects** by initiating a sequence of metabolic reactions that are slower and longer lasting than ionotropic effects (Greengard, 2001). Metabotropic effects emerge 30 ms or more after the release of the transmitter (North, 1989). Typically, they last up to a few seconds, but sometimes longer. Whereas most ionotropic effects depend on either glutamate or GABA, metabotropic synapses use many neurotransmitters, including dopamine, norepinephrine, and serotonin . . . and sometimes glutamate and GABA too.

Apologies if you find this analogy silly, but it might help clarify metabotropic synapses: Imagine a large room. You are outside the room holding a stick that goes through a hole in the wall and attaches to the hinge of a cage. If you shake the stick, you open that cage and release an angry dog. The dog runs around waking up all the rabbits in the room, which then scurry around causing all kinds of further action. A metabotropic receptor acts a little like that. When a neurotransmitter attaches to a metabotropic receptor, it bends the receptor protein that goes through the membrane of the cell. The other side of that receptor is attached to a **G protein**—that is, a protein coupled to guanosine triphosphate (GTP), an energy-storing molecule. Bending the receptor protein detaches that G protein, which is then free to take its energy elsewhere in the cell, as shown in Figure 2.17 (Levitzki, 1988; O'Dowd, Lefkowitz, & Caron, 1989). The result of that G protein is increased concentration of a **second messenger**, such as cyclic adenosine monophosphate (cyclic AMP), inside the cell. Just as the "first messenger" (the neurotransmitter) carries information to the postsynaptic cell, the second messenger communicates to many areas within the cell. It may open or close ion channels in the membrane or activate a portion of a chromosome. Note the contrast: An ionotropic synapse has effects localized to one point on the membrane, whereas a metabotropic synapse, by way of its second messenger, influences activity in much or all of the cell and over a longer time.

Ionotropic and metabotropic synapses contribute to different aspects of behavior. For vision and hearing, the brain needs rapid, quickly changing information, the kind that ionotropic synapses bring. In contrast, metabotropic synapses are better suited for more enduring effects such as taste (Huang et al., 2005), smell, and pain (Levine, Fields, & Basbaum, 1993), where the exact timing isn't important anyway. Metabotropic synapses are also important for many aspects of arousal, attention, pleasure, and emotion—again, functions that arise more slowly and last longer than a visual or auditory stimulus.

Neuropeptides

Researchers often refer to the neuropeptides as **neuromodulators**, because they have several properties that set them apart from other transmitters (Ludwig & Leng, 2006). Whereas the neuron synthesizes most other neurotransmitters in the presynaptic terminal, it synthesizes neuropeptides in the cell body and then slowly transports them to other parts of the cell. Whereas other neurotransmitters are released at the axon terminal, the neuropeptides are released mainly by dendrites, and also by the cell body and the sides of the axon. A single action potential can release other

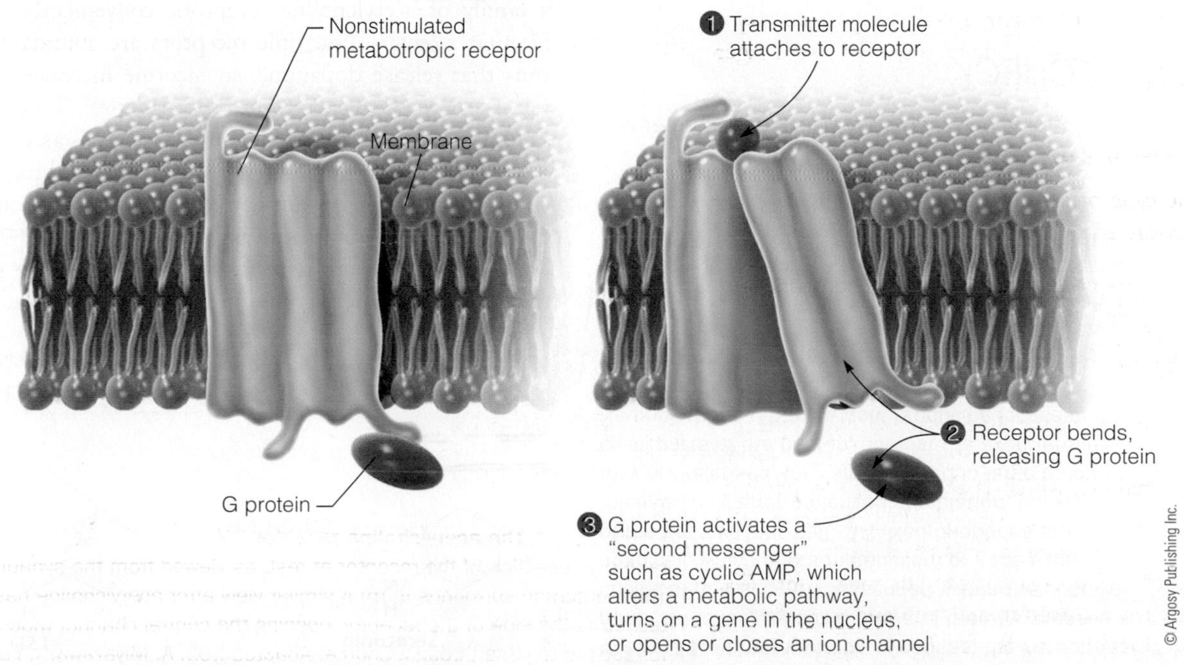

FIGURE 2.17 Sequence of events at a metabotropic synapse, using a second messenger within the postsynaptic neuron

TABLE 2.2 Distinctive features of neuropeptides

	Neuropeptides	Other Neurotransmitters
Place synthesized	Cell body	Presynaptic terminal
Place released	Mostly from dendrites, also cell body and sides of axon	Axon terminal
Released by	Repeated depolarization	Single action potential
Effect on neighboring cells	They release the neuropeptide too	No effect on neighbors
Spread of effects	Diffuse to wide area	Effect mostly on receptors of the adjacent postsynaptic cell
Duration of effects	Many minutes	Less than a second to a few seconds

neurotransmitters, but neuropeptide release requires repeated stimulation. However, after a few dendrites release a neuropeptide, the released chemical primes other nearby dendrites to release the same neuropeptide also, including dendrites of other cells. Thus, neurons containing neuropeptides do not release them often, but when they do, they release substantial amounts. Furthermore, unlike other transmitters that are released immediately adjacent to their receptors, neuropeptides diffuse widely, slowly affecting many neurons in their region of the brain. In that way they resemble hormones. Because many of them exert their effects by altering gene activity, their effects are long-lasting, in the range of 20 minutes or more. Neuropeptides are important for hunger, thirst, and other long-term changes in behavior and experience. Table 2.2 summarizes differences between other neurotransmitters and neuropeptides.

STOP&CHECK

10. How do ionotropic and metabotropic synapses differ in speed and duration of effects?

11. What are second messengers, and which type of synapse relies on them?

12. How are neuropeptides special compared to other transmitters?

ANSWERS

10. Ionotropic synapses act more quickly and more briefly. **11.** At metabotropic synapses, the neurotransmitter attaches to its receptor and thereby releases a chemical (the second messenger) within the postsynaptic cell, which alters metabolism or gene expression of the postsynaptic cell. **12.** Neuropeptides are released only after prolonged stimulation, but when they are released, they are released in large amounts by all parts of the neuron, not just the axon terminal. Neuropeptides diffuse widely, producing long-lasting effects on many neurons.

Variation in Receptors

The brain has a great variety of receptors, including at least 26 types of GABA receptors and at least 7 families of serotonin receptors, differing in their structure (C. Wang et al., 2013). Receptors differ in their chemical properties, responses to drugs, and roles in behavior. Because of this variation in properties, it is possible to devise drugs with specialized effects on behavior. For example, the serotonin receptor type 3 mediates nausea, and the drug *ondansetron* that blocks this receptor helps cancer patients undergo treatment without nausea.

A given receptor can have different effects for different people, or even in different parts of one person's brain, because of differences in the hundreds of proteins associated with the synapse (O'Rourke, Weiler, Micheva, & Smith, 2012). The synapse is a complicated place, where proteins tether the presynaptic neuron to the postsynaptic neuron and guide neurotransmitter molecules to their receptors. Abnormalities of these scaffolding proteins have been linked to increased anxiety, sleep disorders, and other behavioral problems. Because of the importance of all these proteins, people can vary genetically in a huge number of ways that influence behavior.

Drugs that Act by Binding to Receptors

A drug that chemically resembles a neurotransmitter can bind to its receptor. Many **hallucinogenic drugs**—that is, drugs that distort perception, such as lysergic acid diethylamide (LSD)—chemically resemble serotonin (see Figure 2.18). They attach to serotonin type 2A (5-HT_{2A}) receptors and provide stimulation at inappropriate times or for longer-than-usual durations. (Why and how the inappropriate stimulation of those receptors leads to distorted perceptions is an unanswered question.)

Nicotine, a compound present in tobacco, stimulates a family of acetylcholine receptors, conveniently known as *nicotinic receptors*. Nicotinic receptors are abundant on neurons that release dopamine, so nicotine increases dopamine release there (Levin & Rose, 1995; Pontieri, Tanda, Orzi, & DiChiara, 1996). Because dopamine release is associated with reward, nicotine stimulation is rewarding also. Typical antipsychotic drugs block dopamine receptors, often producing side effects of decreased pleasure and motivation.

Opiate drugs are derived from, or chemically similar to those derived from, the opium poppy. Familiar opiates include

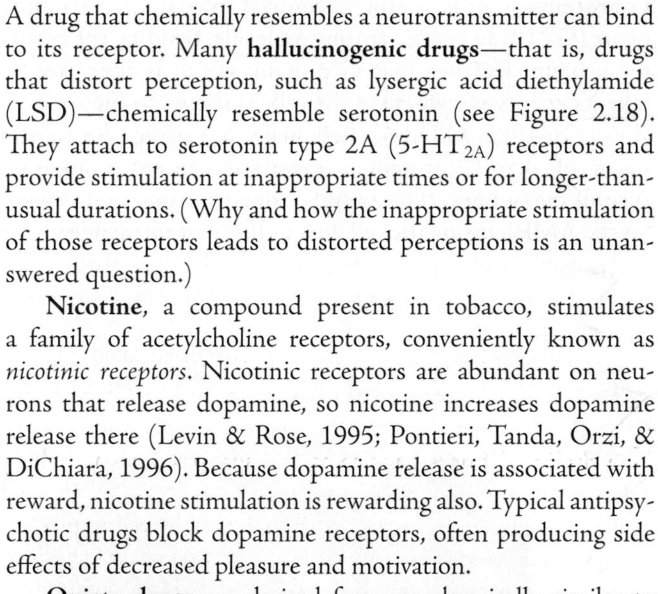

HO — $CH_2CH_2NH_2$ N H **Serotonin**

$O{=}C$ — $N(C_2H_5)_2$ NCH_3 N H **LSD**

FIGURE 2.18 Resemblance of the neurotransmitter serotonin to LSD, a hallucinogenic drug

morphine, heroin, and methadone. People used morphine and other opiates for centuries without knowing how the drugs affected the brain. Then researchers found that opiates attach to specific receptors in the brain (Pert & Snyder, 1973). It was a safe guess that vertebrates had not evolved such receptors just to enable us to become drug addicts; the brain must produce its own chemical that attaches to these receptors. Soon investigators found that the brain produces certain neuropeptides now known as *endorphins*—a contraction of *endogenous morphines*. Opiate drugs exert their effects by binding to the same receptors as endorphins. This discovery was important because it indicated that opiates relieve pain by acting on receptors in the brain, not in the skin. This finding also paved the way for the discovery of other neuropeptides that regulate emotions and motivations.

STOP&CHECK

13. How do LSD, nicotine, and opiate drugs influence behavior?

ANSWER

13. LSD binds to one type of serotonin receptor. Nicotine binds to one type of acetylcholine receptor. Opiates bind to endorphin receptors.

Inactivation and Reuptake of Neurotransmitters

A neurotransmitter does not linger at the postsynaptic membrane. If it did, it might continue exciting or inhibiting the receptor. Various neurotransmitters are inactivated in different ways. (The neuropeptides, however, are not inactivated. They simply diffuse away. Because these large molecules are resynthesized slowly, a neuron can temporarily exhaust its supply.)

After acetylcholine activates a receptor, it is broken down by the enzyme **acetylcholinesterase** (a-SEE-til-ko-lih-NES-teh-raze) into two fragments: acetate and choline. The choline diffuses back to the presynaptic neuron, which takes it up and reconnects it with acetate already in the cell to form acetylcholine again. Although this recycling process is highly efficient, it takes time, and the presynaptic neuron does not reabsorb every molecule it releases. A sufficiently rapid series of action potentials at any synapse depletes the neurotransmitter faster than the presynaptic cell replenishes it, thus slowing or interrupting transmission (G. Liu & Tsien, 1995).

Serotonin and the catecholamines (dopamine, norepinephrine, and epinephrine) do not break down into inactive fragments at the postsynaptic membrane. They simply detach from the receptor. At that point, the next step varies. The presynaptic neuron takes up much or most of the released neurotransmitter molecules intact and reuses them. This process, called **reuptake**, occurs through special membrane proteins called **transporters**. The activity of transporters varies among individuals and from one brain area to another. Any transmitter molecules not taken up by transporters are broken down by an enzyme called **COMT** (catechol-o-methyltransferase). The breakdown products wash away and eventually show up in the blood and urine.

Stimulant drugs, including **amphetamine** and **cocaine**, inhibit the transporters for dopamine, thus decreasing reuptake and prolonging dopamine's effects (Beuming et al., 2008; Schmitt & Reith, 2010; Zhao et al., 2010). Amphetamine also blocks the serotonin and norepinephrine transporters. Methamphetamine's effects are like those of amphetamine, but stronger. Most antidepressant drugs also block the dopamine transporter, but much more weakly than amphetamine and cocaine do.

When stimulant drugs increase the accumulation of dopamine in the synaptic cleft, COMT breaks down the excess dopamine faster than the presynaptic cell can replace it. A few hours after taking a stimulant drug, a user has a deficit of dopamine and enters a withdrawal state, marked by reduced energy, reduced motivation, and mild depression.

Methylphenidate (Ritalin), another stimulant drug, is often prescribed for people with attention deficit/hyperactivity disorder. Methylphenidate and cocaine block the reuptake of dopamine in the same way at the same brain receptors. The differences between the drugs relate to dose and time course. Cocaine users typically sniff it or inject it to produce a rapid rush of effect on the brain. People taking methylphenidate pills experience a gradual increase in the drug's concentration over an hour or more, followed by a slow decline. Therefore, methylphenidate does not produce the sudden rush of excitement that cocaine does. However, anyone who injects methylphenidate experiences effects similar to cocaine's, including the risk of addiction.

STOP&CHECK

14. What happens to acetylcholine molecules after they stimulate a postsynaptic receptor?

15. What happens to serotonin and catecholamine molecules after they stimulate a postsynaptic receptor?

16. How do amphetamine and cocaine influence dopamine synapses?

17. Why is methylphenidate generally less disruptive to behavior than cocaine is despite the drugs' similar mechanisms?

ANSWERS

14. The enzyme acetylcholinesterase breaks acetylcholine molecules into two smaller molecules, acetate and choline, which are then reabsorbed by the presynaptic terminal. **15.** Most serotonin and catecholamine molecules are reabsorbed by the presynaptic terminal. Some of their molecules are broken down into inactive chemicals, which then diffuse away. **16.** They interfere with reuptake of released dopamine. **17.** The effects of a methylphenidate pill develop and decline in the brain much more slowly than do those of cocaine.

Negative Feedback from the Postsynaptic Cell

Suppose someone sends you an email message and then, worried that you might not have received it, sends it again and again. To prevent cluttering your inbox, you might add a system that provides an automatic answer, "Yes, I got your message. Don't send it again."

A couple of mechanisms in the nervous system serve that function. First, many presynaptic terminals have receptors sensitive to the same transmitter they release. These receptors are known as **autoreceptors**—receptors that respond to the released transmitter by inhibiting further synthesis and release. That is, they provide negative feedback (Kubista & Boehm, 2006).

Second, some postsynaptic neurons respond to stimulation by releasing chemicals that travel back to the presynaptic terminal to inhibit further release of transmitter. Nitric oxide is one such transmitter. Two others are **anandamide** (from the Sanskrit word *anana*, meaning "bliss") and **2-AG** (*sn*-2 arachidonylglycerol).

Cannabinoids, the active chemicals in marijuana, bind to anandamide or 2-AG receptors on presynaptic neurons (Kreitzer & Regehr, 2001; R. I. Wilson & Nicoll, 2002) or GABA (Földy, Neu, Jones, & Soltesz, 2006; Oliet, Baimouknametova, Piet, & Bains, 2007). When cannabinoids attach to these receptors, they indicate, "The cell got your message. Stop sending it." The presynaptic cell, unaware that it hadn't sent any message at all, stops sending. In this way, the chemicals in marijuana decrease both excitatory and inhibitory messages from many neurons. (Exactly how this effect produces all marijuana's experiential effects remains largely uncertain.)

Figure 2.19 summarizes some of the ways in which drugs affect dopamine synapses, including effects on synthesis,

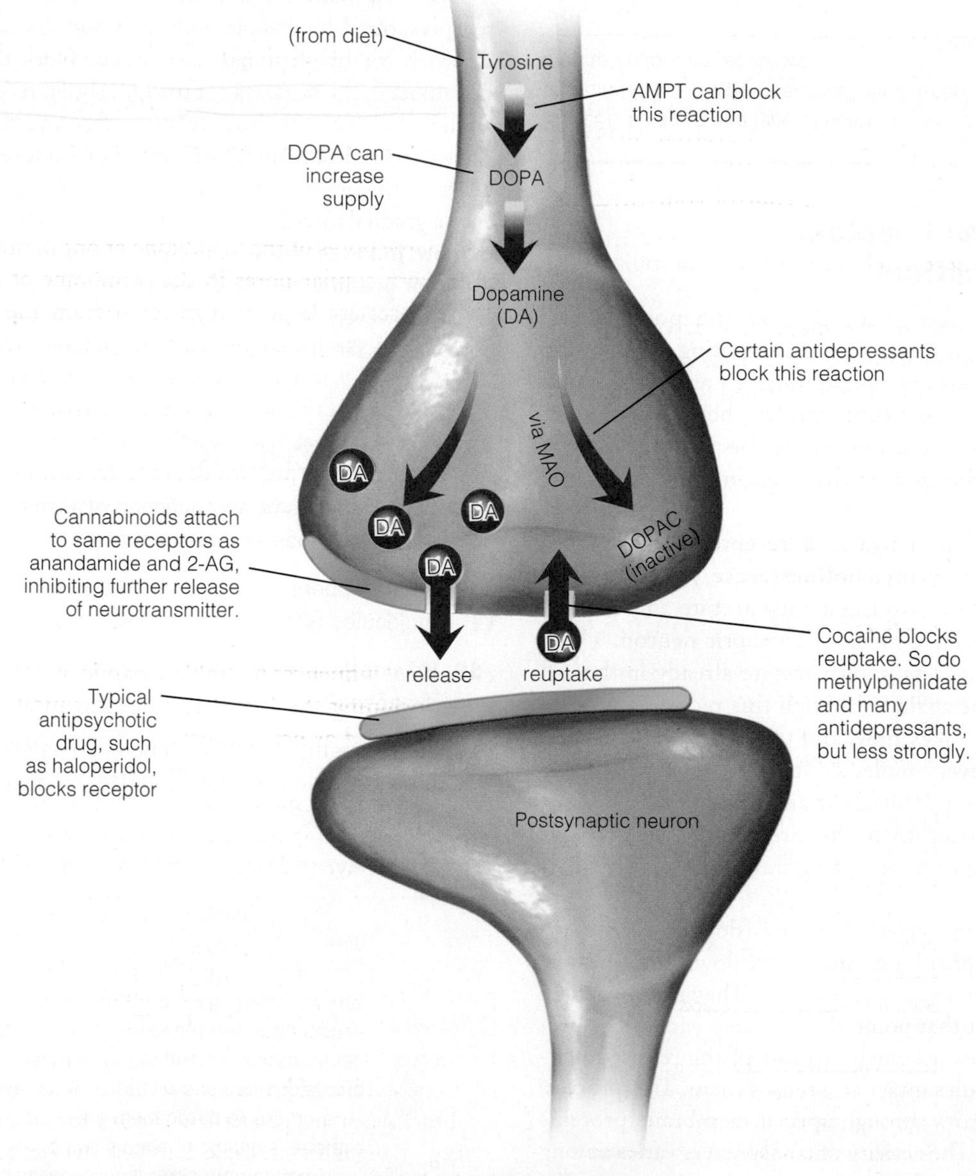

FIGURE 2.19 Effects of some drugs at dopamine synapses
Drugs can alter transmission at a synapse in many ways.

STOP&CHECK

16. How do cannabinoids affect neurons?

ANSWER

16. Cannabinoids released by the postsynaptic neuron attach to receptors on presynaptic neurons, where they inhibit further release of both glutamate and GABA.

release, action on postsynaptic receptors, reuptake, and breakdown. Table 2.3 also summarizes effects of some common drugs.

Electrical Synapses

At the start of this module, you learned that Sherrington was wrong to assume that synapses convey messages electrically. Well, he wasn't completely wrong. A few special-purpose synapses do operate electrically. Because electrical transmission is faster than even the fastest chemical transmission, electrical synapses have evolved in cases where exact synchrony between two cells is important. For example, some of the cells that control your rhythmic breathing are synchronized by electrical synapses. (It's important to inhale on the left side at the same time as on the right side.)

At an electrical synapse, the membrane of one neuron comes into direct contact with the membrane of another, as shown in Figure 2.20. This contact is called a **gap junction**.

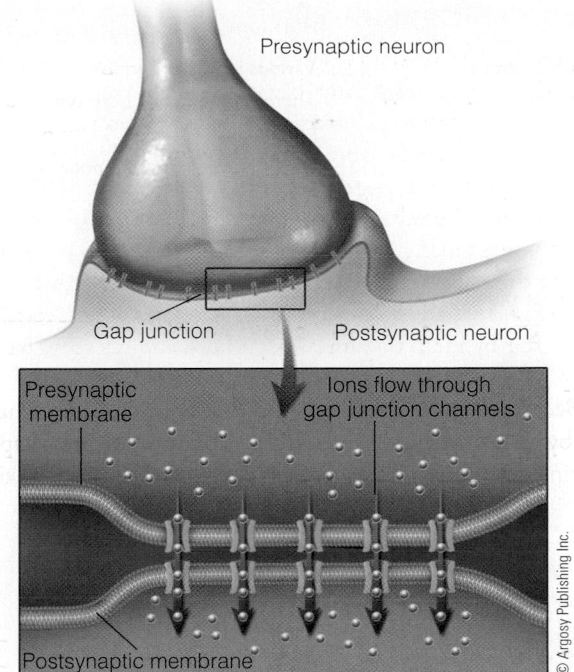

FIGURE 2.20 A gap junction for an electrical synapse

Fairly large pores of the membrane of one neuron line up precisely with similar pores in the membrane of the other cell. These pores are large enough for sodium and other ions to pass readily, and unlike the other membrane channels we have considered, these pores remain open constantly. Therefore, whenever one of the neurons is depolarized, sodium ions from that cell can pass quickly into the other neuron and depolarize it, too. As a result, the two neurons act almost as if they were a single neuron. Again we see the great variety of synapses in the nervous system.

TABLE 2.3 Summary of some drugs and their effects

Drugs	Main Synaptic Effects
Amphetamine	Blocks reuptake of dopamine and several other transmitters
Cocaine	Blocks reuptake of dopamine and several other transmitters
Methylphenidate (Ritalin)	Blocks reuptake of dopamine and others, but gradually
MDMA ("Ecstasy")	Releases dopamine and serotonin
Nicotine	Stimulates nicotinic-type acetylcholine receptor, which (among other effects) increases dopamine release in nucleus accumbens
Opiates (e.g., heroin, morphine)	Stimulates endorphin receptors
Cannabinoids (marijuana)	Excites negative-feedback receptors on presynaptic cells; those receptors ordinarily respond to anandamide and 2AG
Hallucinogens (e.g., LSD)	Stimulates serotonin type 2A receptors (5-HT_{2A})

Hormones

Hormonal influences resemble synaptic transmission in many ways, including the fact that many chemicals serve both as hormones and as neurotransmitters. A **hormone** is a chemical secreted by cells in one part of the body and conveyed by the blood to influence other cells. A neurotransmitter is like a telephone signal: It conveys a message from the sender to the intended receiver. Hormones function more like a radio station: They convey a message to any receiver tuned to the right station. Neuropeptides are intermediate. They diffuse only within the brain, and the blood doesn't carry them to other parts of the body. Figure 2.21 presents the major **endocrine** (hormone-producing) **glands**. Table 2.4 lists only those hormones that become relevant in other chapters of this book. (A complete list of hormones would be lengthy.)

Hormones are particularly useful for coordinating long-lasting changes in multiple parts of the body. For example, birds that are preparing for migration secrete hormones that change their eating and digestion to store extra energy for a

TABLE 2.4 Selective list of hormones

Organ	Hormone	Hormone Functions (Partial)
Hypothalamus	Various releasing hormones	Promote/inhibit release of hormones from pituitary
Anterior pituitary	Thyroid-stimulating hormone	Stimulates thyroid gland
	Luteinizing hormone	Stimulates ovulation
	Follicle-stimulating hormone	Promotes ovum maturation (female), sperm production (male)
	ACTH	Increases steroid hormone production by adrenal gland
	Prolactin	Increases milk production
	Growth hormone	Increases body growth
Posterior pituitary	Oxytocin	Uterine contractions, milk release, sexual pleasure
	Vasopressin	Raises blood pressure, decreases urine volume
Pineal	Melatonin	Sleepiness; also role in puberty
Adrenal cortex	Aldosterone	Reduces release of salt in the urine
	Cortisol	Elevated blood sugar and metabolism
Adrenal medulla	Epinephrine, norepinephrine	Similar to actions of sympathetic nervous system
Pancreas	Insulin	Helps glucose enter cells
	Glucagon	Helps convert stored fats into blood glucose
Ovary	Estrogens and progesterone	Female sexual characteristics and pregnancy
Testis	Testosterone	Male sexual characteristics and pubic hair
Kidney	Renin	Regulates blood pressure, contributes to hypovolemic thirst
Fat cells	Leptin	Decreases appetite

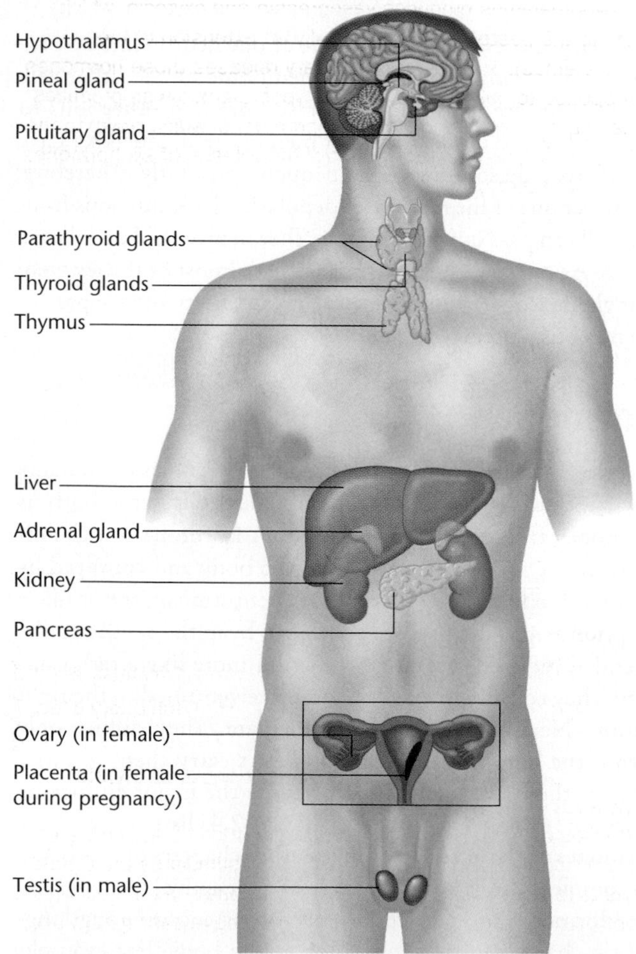

FIGURE 2.21 Location of some major endocrine glands
Source: Starr & Taggart, 1989

long journey. Two types of hormones are **protein hormones** and **peptide hormones**, composed of chains of amino acids. (Proteins are longer chains and peptides are shorter.) Protein and peptide hormones attach to membrane receptors, where they activate a second messenger within the cell—exactly like a metabotropic synapse.

Just as circulating hormones modify brain activity, hormones secreted by the brain control the secretion of many other hormones. The **pituitary gland**, attached to the hypothalamus (see Figure 2.22), has two parts, the **anterior pituitary** and the **posterior pituitary**, which release different sets of hormones. The posterior pituitary, composed of neural tissue, can be considered an extension of the hypothalamus. Neurons in the hypothalamus synthesize the hormones **oxytocin** and **vasopressin** (also known as antidiuretic hormones), which migrate down axons to the posterior pituitary, as shown in Figure 2.23. Later, the posterior pituitary releases these hormones into the blood.

The anterior pituitary, composed of glandular tissue, synthesizes six hormones, although the hypothalamus controls their release (see Figure 2.23). The hypothalamus secretes **releasing hormones**, which flow through the blood to the anterior pituitary. There they stimulate or inhibit the release of other hormones.

The hypothalamus maintains fairly constant circulating levels of certain hormones through a negative feedback system. For example, when the level of thyroid hormone is low, the hypothalamus releases *TSH-releasing hormone*, which stimulates the anterior pituitary to release TSH, which in turn causes the thyroid gland to secrete more thyroid hormones (see Figure 2.24).

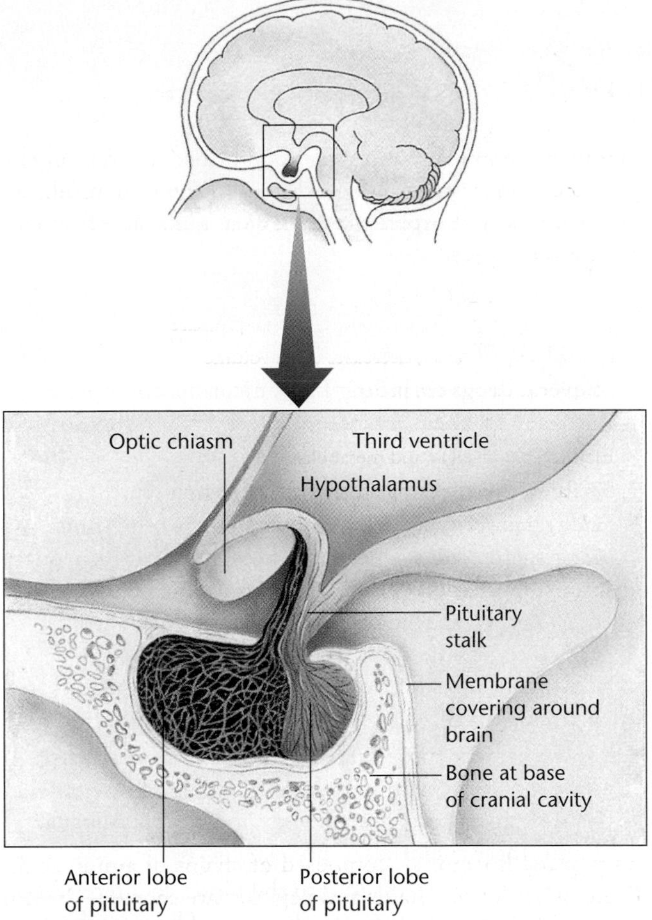

FIGURE 2.22 Location of the hypothalamus and pituitary gland in the human brain
Source: Starr & Taggart, 1989

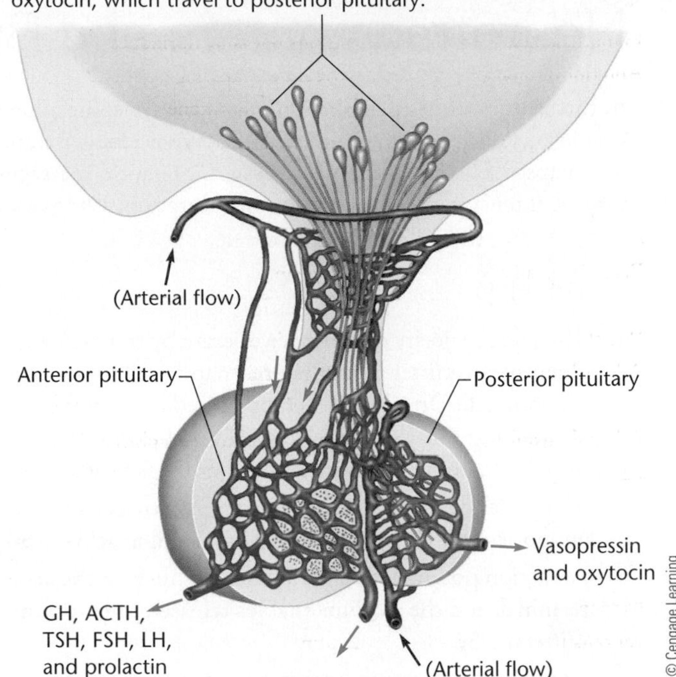

FIGURE 2.23 Pituitary hormones
The hypothalamus produces vasopressin and oxytocin, which travel to the posterior pituitary (really an extension of the hypothalamus). The posterior pituitary releases those hormones in response to neural signals. The hypothalamus also produces releasing hormones and inhibiting hormones, which travel to the anterior pituitary, where they control the release of six hormones synthesized there.

STOP&CHECK

17. Which part of the pituitary—anterior or posterior—is neural tissue, similar to the hypothalamus? Which part is glandular tissue and produces hormones that control the secretions by other endocrine organs?

18. In what way is a neuropeptide intermediate between neurotransmitters and hormones?

ANSWERS

17. The posterior pituitary is neural tissue, like the hypothalamus. The anterior pituitary is glandular tissue and produces hormones that control several other endocrine organs. **18.** Most neurotransmitters are released in small amounts close to their receptors. Neuropeptides are released into a brain area in larger amounts or not at all. When released, they diffuse more widely. Hormones are released into the blood for diffuse delivery throughout the body.

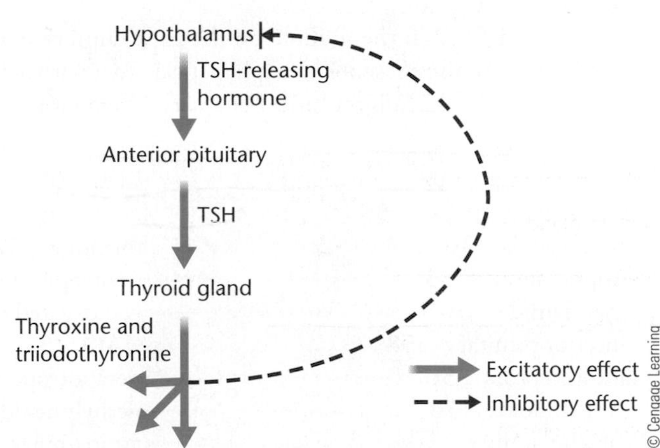

FIGURE 2.24 Negative feedback in the control of thyroid hormones
The hypothalamus secretes a releasing hormone that stimulates the anterior pituitary to release TSH, which stimulates the thyroid gland to release its hormones. Those hormones, in turn, act on the hypothalamus to decrease its secretion of the releasing hormone.

MODULE 2.2 ■ IN CLOSING

Neurotransmitters and Behavior

In the century plus since Sherrington, we have come a long way in our understanding of synapses. We no longer think of synapses as simple on/off messages. Synaptic messages vary in intensity, speed of onset, and duration. Drugs can modify them in many ways, for good or bad, but so can experiences. Understanding how the nervous system produces our behavior and experiences is largely a matter of understanding synapses.

Summary

1. The great majority of synapses operate by transmitting a neurotransmitter from the presynaptic cell to the postsynaptic cell. Otto Loewi demonstrated this point by stimulating a frog's heart electrically and then transferring fluids from that heart to another frog's heart. **48**
2. Many chemicals are used as neurotransmitters. Most are amino acids or chemicals derived from amino acids. **50**
3. An action potential opens calcium channels in the axon terminal, and the calcium enables release of neurotransmitters. **51**
4. At ionotropic synapses, a neurotransmitter attaches to a receptor that opens the gates to allow a particular ion, such as sodium, to cross the membrane. Ionotropic effects are fast and brief. At metabotropic synapses, a neurotransmitter activates a second messenger inside the postsynaptic cell, leading to slower but longer-lasting changes. **52**
5. Neuropeptides diffuse widely, affecting many neurons for a period of minutes. Neuropeptides are important for hunger, thirst, and other slow, long-term processes. **53**
6. Several drugs including LSD, nicotine, and opiate drugs exert their behavioral effects by binding to receptors on the postsynaptic neuron. **54**
7. After a neurotransmitter (other than a neuropeptide) has activated its receptor, many of the transmitter molecules reenter the presynaptic cell through transporter molecules in the membrane. This process, known as reuptake, enables the presynaptic cell to recycle its neurotransmitter. Stimulant drugs and many antidepressant drugs inhibit this process. **55**
8. Postsynaptic neurons send chemicals to receptors on the presynaptic neuron to inhibit further release of neurotransmitter. Cannabinoids, found in marijuana, mimic these chemicals. **56**
9. Hormones are released into the blood to affect receptors scattered throughout the body. Their mechanism of effect resembles that of a metabotropic synapse. **57**

Key Terms

Terms are defined in the module on the page number indicated. They are also presented in alphabetical order with definitions in the book's Subject Index/Glossary. Interactive flash cards, audio reviews, and crossword puzzles are among the online resources available to help you learn these terms and the concepts they represent.

2-AG **56**
acetylcholine **50**
acetylcholinesterase **55**
amino acids **50**
amphetamine **55**
anandamide **56**
anterior pituitary **58**
autoreceptors **56**
cannabinoids **56**
catecholamines **50**
cocaine **55**
COMT **55**
endocrine glands **57**
exocytosis **51**
gap junction **57**
G protein **53**
gases **50**
hallucinogenic drugs **54**
hormone **57**
ionotropic effects **52**
ligand-gated channels **52**
MAO **51**
metabotropic effects **53**
methylphenidate **55**
monoamines **50**
neuromodulators **53**
neuropeptides **50**
neurotransmitters **50**
nicotine **54**
nitric oxide **50**
opiate drugs **54**
oxytocin **58**
peptide hormones **58**
pituitary gland **58**
posterior pituitary **58**
protein hormones **58**
purines **50**
releasing hormones **58**
reuptake **55**
second messenger **53**
transmitter-gated channels **52**
transporters **55**
vasopressin **58**
vesicles **51**

Thought Questions

1. Suppose axon A enters a ganglion (cluster of neurons) and axon B leaves on the other side. An experimenter who stimulates A shortly thereafter records an impulse traveling down B. We want to know whether B is just an extension of axon A or whether A formed an excitatory synapse on some neuron in the ganglion, whose axon is axon B. How could an experimenter determine the answer? Try to think of more than one good method. Presume that the anatomy within the ganglion is so complex that you cannot simply trace the course of an axon through it.
2. If incoming serotonin axons were destroyed, LSD would still have its full effects. However, if incoming dopamine axons were destroyed, amphetamine and cocaine would lose their effects. Explain the difference.

MODULE 2.2: End of Module Quiz

1. What was Loewi's evidence that neurotransmission depends on the release of chemicals?
   a. He applied adrenaline to muscles and saw them contract.
   b. He applied drugs at various synapses and observed excitatory and inhibitory postsynaptic potentials.
   c. He stimulated one frog's heart, collected fluid around it, transferred it to another frog's heart, and saw change in its heart rate.
   d. He stimulated certain nerves, collected the fluid around their terminals, and analyzed the contents chemically.
2. Which of the following is NOT one of the brain's neurotransmitters?
   a. Glutamate
   b. GABA
   c. Glucose
   d. Serotonin
3. The amino acid tryptophan is a precursor to which neurotransmitter?
   a. Serotonin
   b. Dopamine
   c. Glutamate
   d. Acetylcholine
4. Suppose you want to cause the presynaptic terminal of an axon to release its transmitter. How could you do so *without* an action potential?
   a. Decrease the temperature at the synapse.
   b. Use an electrode to produce IPSPs in the postsynaptic neuron.
   c. Inject water into the presynaptic terminal.
   d. Inject calcium into the presynaptic terminal.
5. The brain's most abundant excitatory neurotransmitter is ______, and its most abundant inhibitory neurotransmitter is ______.
   a. GABA . . . serotonin
   b. serotonin . . . dopamine
   c. dopamine . . . glutamate
   d. glutamate . . . GABA
6. In which of these ways does a metabotropic synapse differ from an ionotropic synapse?
   a. Its effects are slower to start and last longer.
   b. Its effects are faster to start and last longer.
   c. Its effects are slower to start and briefer in duration.
   d. Its effects are faster to start and briefer in duration.
7. What is a second messenger?
   a. A chemical released by the presynaptic neuron a few milliseconds after release of the first neurotransmitter
   b. A chemical released inside a cell after stimulation at a metabotropic synapse
   c. A chemical that travels from the postsynaptic neuron back to the presynaptic neuron

8. Which of the following is true of neuropeptides?

a. They are released close to their receptors.

b. A neuron releases them at a steady rate almost constantly.

c. They produce rapid, brief effects.

d. They are released either in large quantities or not at all.

9. Which of these drugs exerts its behavioral effects by binding to the same receptor as a neurotransmitter?

a. Amphetamine

b. Cocaine

c. Nicotine

d. Marijuana

10. Which neurotransmitter is broken into two pieces to inactivate it, after it excites the postsynaptic neuron?

a. Dopamine

b. Acetylcholine

c. Glutamate

d. Serotonin

11. What does a transporter protein do at a synapse?

a. It carries neurotransmitter molecules from the presynaptic neuron to the postsynaptic neuron.

b. It carries neurotransmitter molecules from the cell body to the presynaptic terminal.

c. It carries neurotransmitter molecules from neurons that have too much into neurons that need more.

d. It pumps used neurotransmitter molecules back into the presynaptic neuron.

12. Except for the magnitude and speed of effects, methylphenidate (Ritalin) affects synapses the same way as which other drug?

a. Heroin

b. Cocaine

c. Nicotine

d. Marijuana

13. Which of these drugs acts by inhibiting release of neurotransmitters from the presynaptic neuron?

a. Opiates such as morphine

b. Cannabinoids (found in marijuana)

c. Nicotine

d. Amphetamine and cocaine

14. In contrast to the posterior pituitary, the anterior pituitary . . .

a. is neural tissue that releases oxytocin and vasopressin.

b. is glandular tissue that releases oxytocin and vasopressin.

c. is neural tissue that produces hormones that control other endocrine organs.

d. is glandular tissue that produces hormones that control other endocrine organs.

15. In what way is a neuropeptide intermediate between neurotransmitters and hormones?

a. A neuropeptide diffuses more widely than other neurotransmitters but less than a hormone.

b. A neuropeptide is larger than other neurotransmitters but smaller than a hormone.

c. A neurotransmitter produces excitatory effects, a neuropeptide produces neutral effects, and a hormone produces negative effects.

d. A neurotransmitter produces slow effects, a neuropeptide produces faster effects, and a hormone produces still faster effects.

ANSWERS:

1c, 2c, 3a, 4d, 5d, 6a, 7b, 8d, 9c, 10b, 11d, 12b, 13b, 14d, 15a.

Suggestion for Further Reading

Snyder, S. (1989). *Brainstorming: The science and politics of opiate research*. Cambridge, MA: Harvard University Press.

Fascinating history of the discovery of opiate receptors.

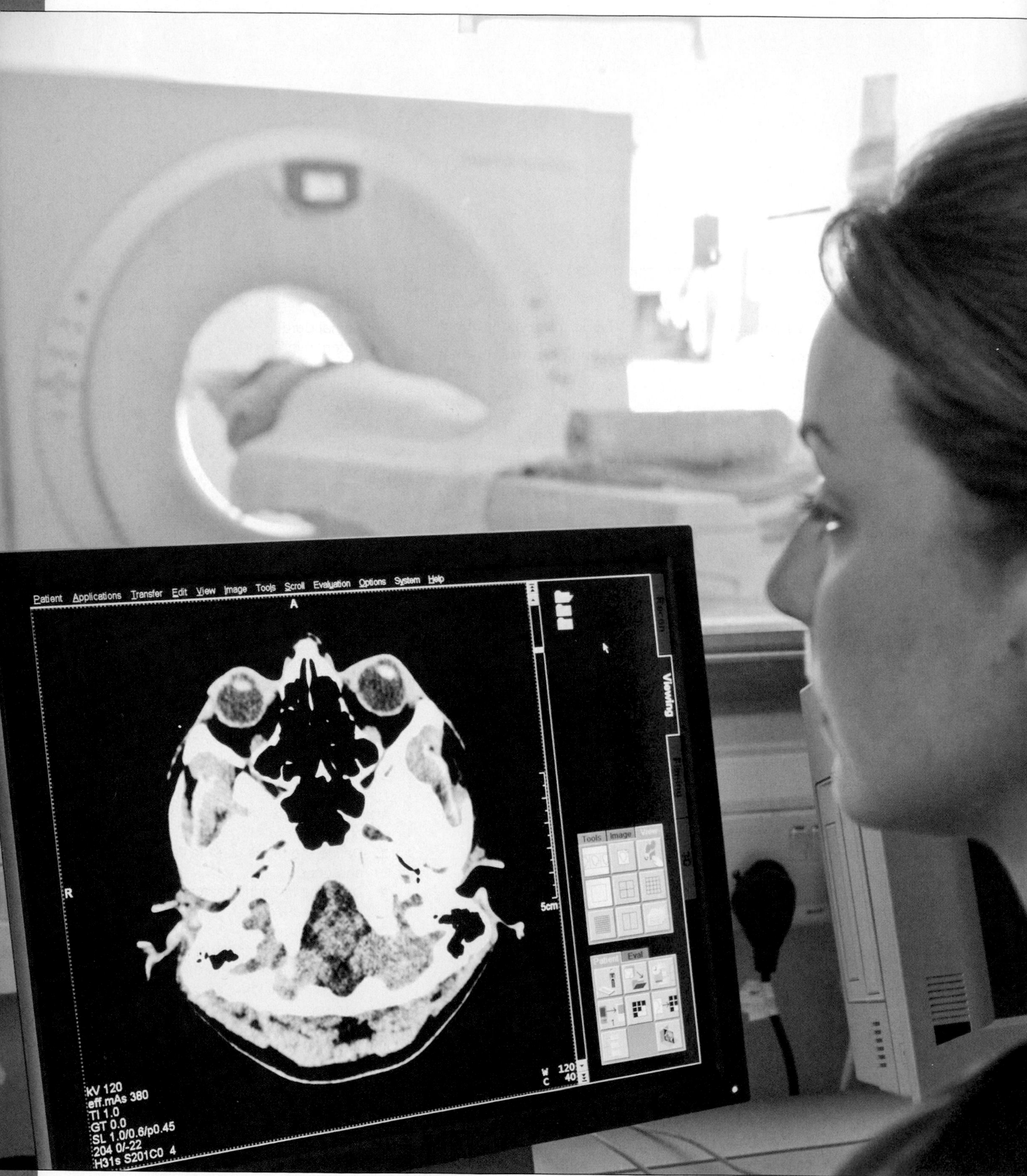

Jupiterimages/Getty Images

Anatomy and Research Methods

3

CHAPTER OUTLINE

MODULE 3.1 Structure of the Vertebrate Nervous System
Terminology to Describe the Nervous System
The Spinal Cord
The Autonomic Nervous System
The Hindbrain
The Midbrain
The Forebrain
The Ventricles
In Closing: Learning Neuroanatomy
MODULE 3.2 The Cerebral Cortex
Organization of the Cerebral Cortex
The Occipital Lobe
The Parietal Lobe
The Temporal Lobe
The Frontal Lobe
How Do the Parts Work Together?
In Closing: Functions of the Cerebral Cortex
MODULE 3.3 Research Methods
Effects of Brain Damage
Effects of Brain Stimulation
Recording Brain Activity
Correlating Brain Anatomy with Behavior
Brain Size and Intelligence
In Closing: Research Methods and Progress

LEARNING OBJECTIVES

After studying this chapter, you should be able to:

1. Define the terms used to describe brain anatomy.
2. Describe the principal functions of certain brain areas.
3. List the four lobes of the cerebral cortex and name their principal functions.
4. Describe the binding problem and explain its theoretical importance.
5. Cite examples of several methods for studying the relationship between brain activity and behavior.
6. Discuss why it is so difficult to draw any firm conclusion about the relationship between brain size and intelligence.

Trying to learn **neuroanatomy** (the anatomy of the nervous system) from a book is like trying to learn geography from a road map. A map can tell you that Mystic, Georgia, is about 40 km north of Enigma, Georgia. Similarly, a book can tell you that the habenula is about 4.6 mm from the interpeduncular nucleus in a rat's brain (proportionately farther in a human brain). But these little gems of information will seem both mysterious and enigmatic unless you are concerned with that part of Georgia or that area of the brain.

This chapter does not provide a detailed road map of the nervous system. It is more like a world globe, describing the large, basic structures (analogous to the continents) and some distinctive features of each.

The first module introduces key neuroanatomical terms and outlines overall structures of the nervous system. In the second module, we concentrate on the cerebral cortex, the largest part of the mammalian central nervous system. The third module deals with the main methods that researchers use to discover the functions of brain areas.

Be prepared: This chapter contains a huge number of new terms. You should not expect to memorize all of them at once, and you should review this chapter repeatedly.

OPPOSITE: New methods allow researchers to examine living brains.

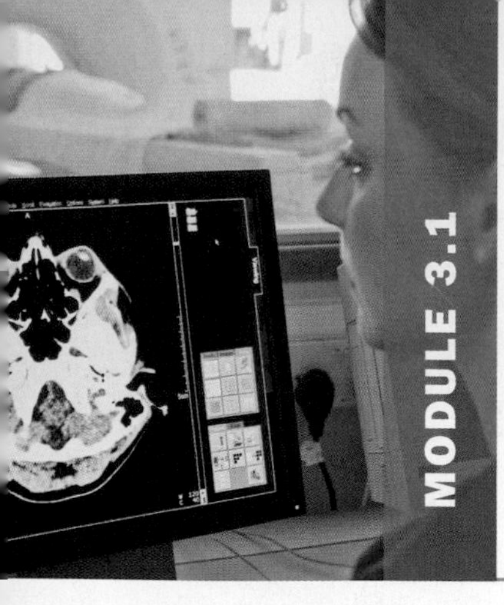

MODULE 3.1

Structure of the Vertebrate Nervous System

Your nervous system consists of many substructures, a huge number of neurons, and an even huger number of synapses. How do all the parts work together to make one behaving unit? Does each neuron have an independent function? Or does the brain operate as an undifferentiated whole?

The answer is something between those extremes. Consider an analogy to human society: Each individual has a special role, such as teacher, farmer, or nurse, but no one performs any function without the cooperation of many other people. Similarly, brain areas and neurons have specialized roles, but they also depend on connections with other areas.

Terminology to Describe the Nervous System

For vertebrates, we distinguish the central nervous system from the peripheral nervous system (see Figure 3.1). The **central nervous system (CNS)** is the brain and the

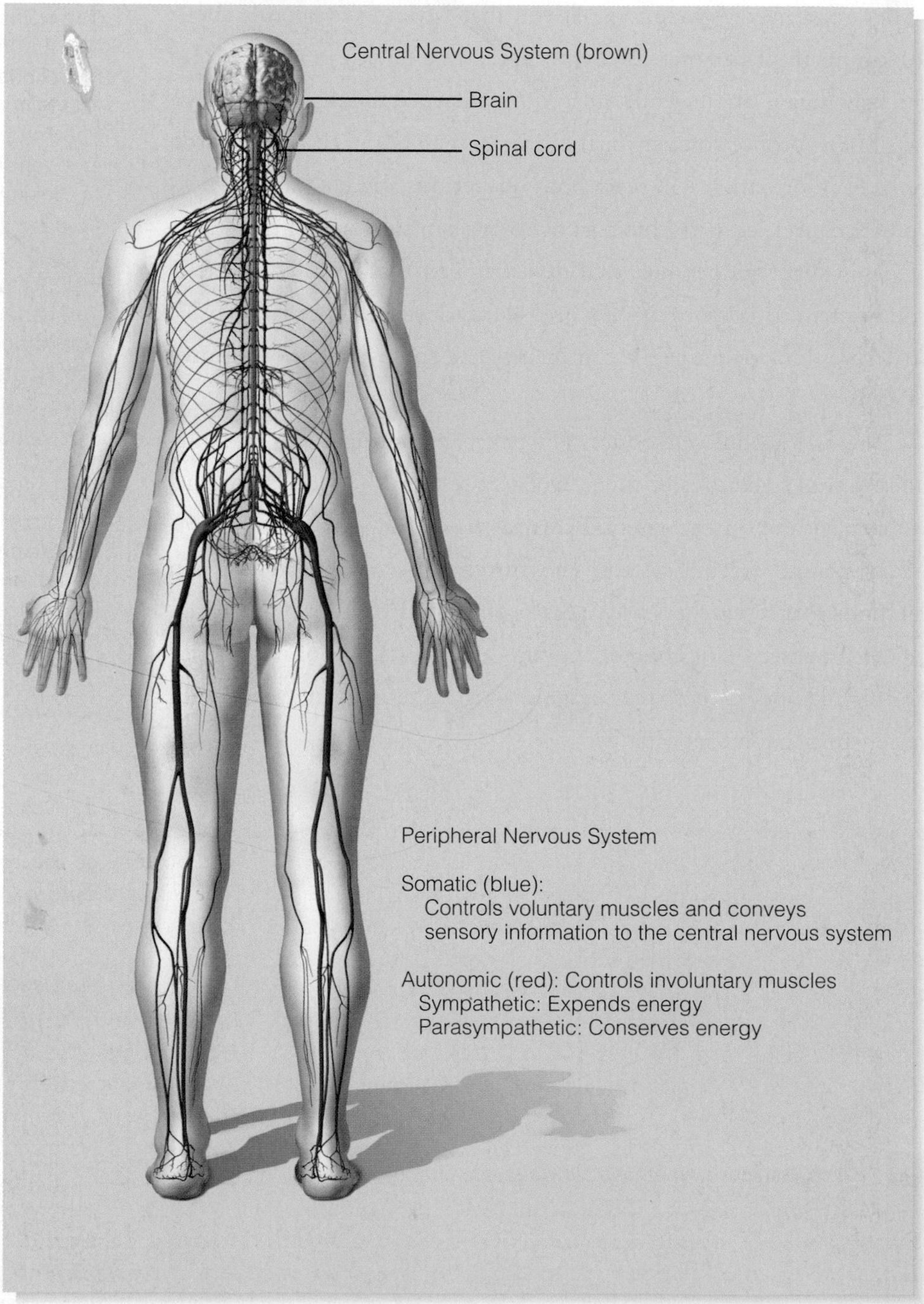

Central Nervous System (brown)
Brain
Spinal cord

Peripheral Nervous System

Somatic (blue):
Controls voluntary muscles and conveys sensory information to the central nervous system

Autonomic (red): Controls involuntary muscles
Sympathetic: Expends energy
Parasympathetic: Conserves energy

FIGURE 3.1 The human nervous system
The central nervous system consists of the brain and spinal cord. The peripheral nervous system is the nerves outside the brain and spinal cord.

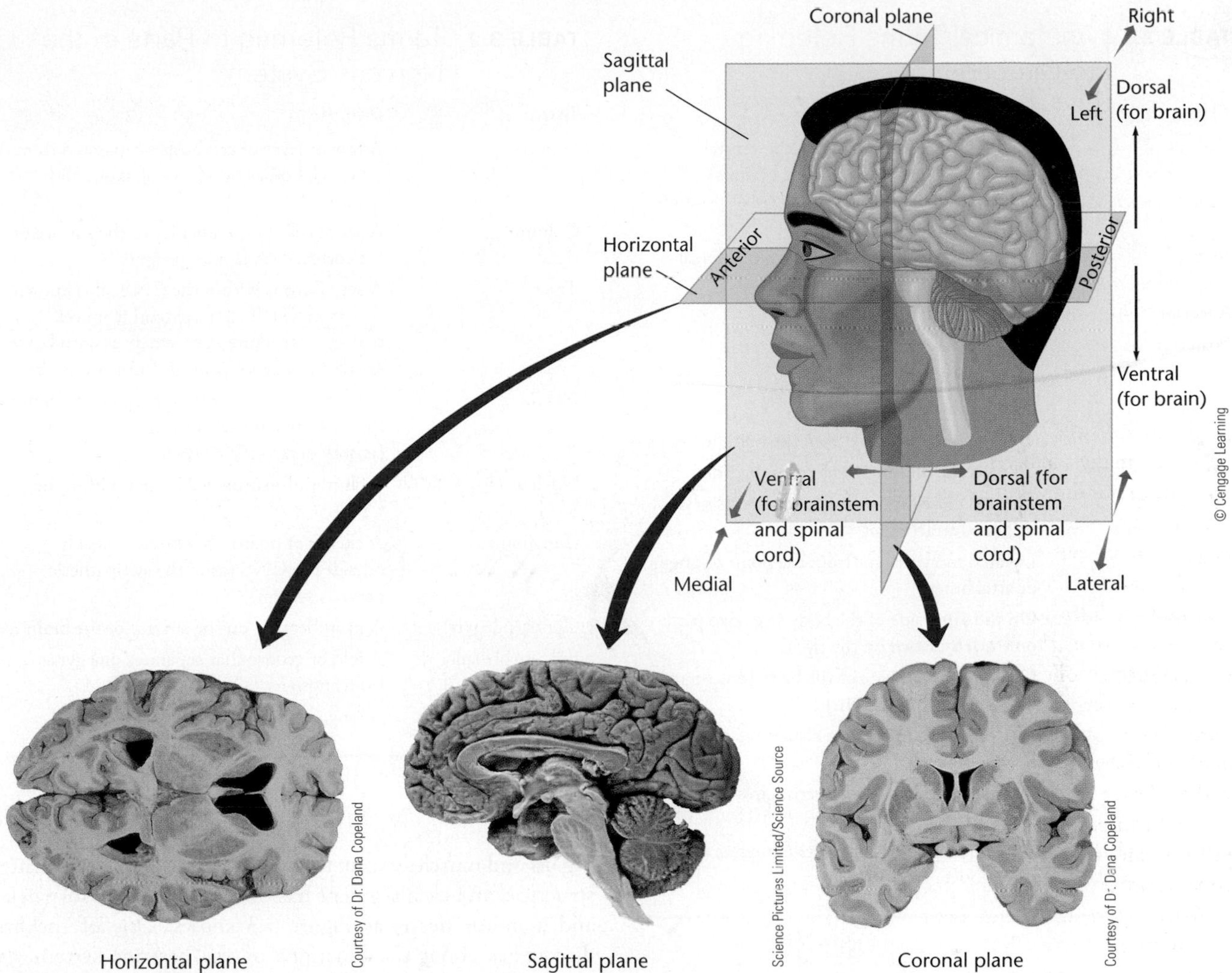

FIGURE 3.2 Terms for anatomical directions in the nervous system
In four-legged animals, the dorsal and ventral axes for the head are parallel to those for the rest of the body. However, humans' upright posture has tilted the head, so the dorsal and ventral directions of the head are at right angles to those of the spinal cord.

spinal cord. The **peripheral nervous system (PNS)** connects the brain and spinal cord to the rest of the body. Part of the PNS is the **somatic nervous system,** which consists of the axons conveying messages from the sense organs to the CNS and from the CNS to the muscles. Another part of the PNS, the **autonomic nervous system,** controls the heart, intestines, and other organs. The autonomic nervous system has some of its cell bodies within the brain or spinal cord and some in clusters along the sides of the spinal cord.

To follow a map, you must understand *north, south, east,* and *west.* Because the nervous system is three-dimensional, we need more terms to describe it. As Figure 3.2 and Table 3.1 indicate, **dorsal** means toward the back and **ventral** means toward the stomach. (A *ventri*loquist is literally a "stomach talker.") In a four-legged animal, the top of the brain is dorsal (on the same side as the animal's back), and the bottom of the brain is ventral (on the stomach side). The same would be true for you if you crawled on your knees. However, when humans evolved upright posture, the position of the head changed relative to the spinal cord. For convenience, we still apply the terms *dorsal* and *ventral* to the same parts of the human brain as other vertebrate brains. Consequently, the dorsal–ventral axis of the human brain is at a right angle to the dorsal–ventral axis of the spinal cord. Figure 3.2 also illustrates the three ways of taking a plane through the brain, known as horizontal, sagittal, and coronal (or frontal).

Table 3.2 introduces additional terms that are worth learning. Tables 3.1 and 3.2 require careful study and review. After you think you have mastered the terms, check yourself with the following "Stop & Check" questions.

TABLE 3.1 Anatomical Terms Referring to Directions

Term	Definition
Dorsal	Toward the back, away from the ventral (stomach) side. The top of the brain is considered dorsal because it has that position in four-legged animals.
Ventral	Toward the stomach, away from the dorsal (back) side
Anterior	Toward the front end
Posterior	Toward the rear end
Superior	Above another part
Inferior	Below another part
Lateral	Toward the side, away from the midline
Medial	Toward the midline, away from the side
Proximal	Located close (approximate) to the point of origin or attachment
Distal	Located more distant from the point of origin or attachment
Ipsilateral	On the same side of the body (e.g., two parts on the left or two on the right)
Contralateral	On the opposite side of the body (one on the left and one on the right)
Coronal plane (or frontal plane)	A plane that shows brain structures as seen from the front
Sagittal plane	A plane that shows brain structures as seen from the side
Horizontal plane (or transverse plane)	A plane that shows brain structures as seen from above

TABLE 3.2 Terms Referring to Parts of the Nervous System

Term	Definition
Lamina	A row or layer of cell bodies separated from other cell bodies by a layer of axons and dendrites
Column	A set of cells perpendicular to the surface of the cortex, with similar properties
Tract	A set of axons within the CNS, also known as a *projection*. If axons extend from cell bodies in structure A to synapses onto B, we say that the fibers "project" from A onto B.
Nerve	A set of axons in the periphery, either from the CNS to a muscle or gland or from a sensory organ to the CNS
Nucleus	A cluster of neuron cell bodies within the CNS
Ganglion	A cluster of neuron cell bodies, usually outside the CNS (as in the sympathetic nervous system)
Gyrus (pl.: gyri)	A protuberance on the surface of the brain
Sulcus (pl.: sulci)	A fold or groove that separates one gyrus from another
Fissure	A long, deep sulcus

STOP&CHECK

1. What does *dorsal* mean, and what is its opposite?

2. What term means *toward the side, away from the midline*, and what is its opposite?

3. If two structures are both on the left side of the body, they are _____ to each other. If one is on the left and the other is on the right, they are _____ to each other.

4. The bulges in the cerebral cortex are called _____. The grooves between them are called _____.

ANSWERS

1. Dorsal means toward the back, away from the stomach side. Its opposite is ventral. **2.** lateral; medial **3.** ipsilateral; contralateral **4.** gyri; sulci. To remember sulcus, think of the word *sulk*, meaning "to pout" (and therefore lie low).

The Spinal Cord

The **spinal cord** is the part of the CNS within the spinal column. The spinal cord communicates with all the sense organs and muscles except those of the head. It is a segmented structure, and each segment has on each side a sensory nerve and a motor nerve, as Figure 3.3 shows. One of the first discoveries about the functions of the nervous system was that the entering dorsal roots (axon bundles) carry sensory information, and the exiting ventral roots carry motor

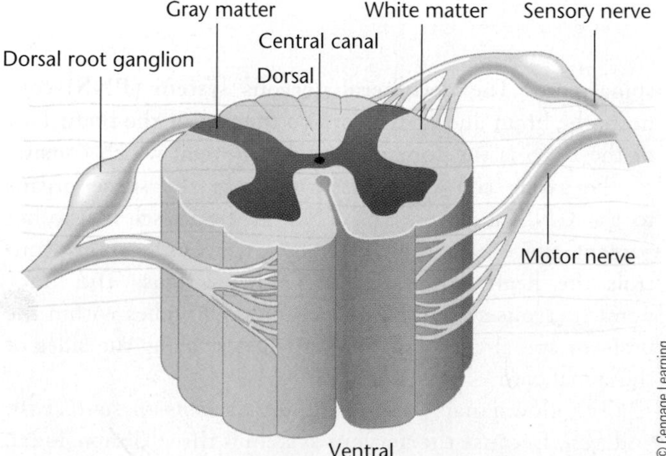

FIGURE 3.3 Diagram of a cross-section through the spinal cord

The dorsal root on each side conveys sensory information to the spinal cord; the ventral root conveys motor commands to the muscles.

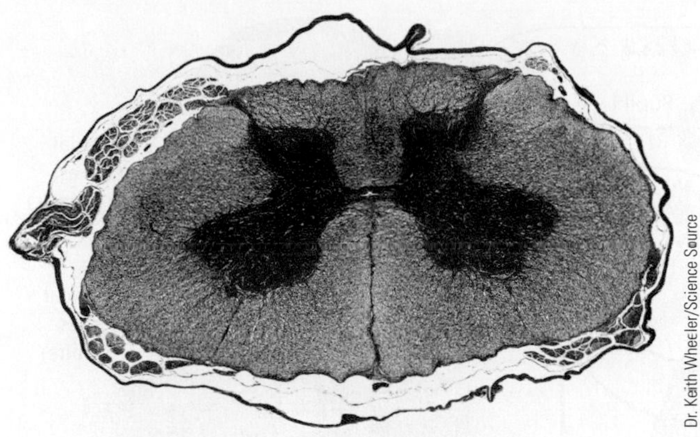

FIGURE 3.4 Photo of a cross-section through the spinal cord
The H-shaped structure in the center is gray matter, composed largely of cell bodies. The surrounding white matter consists of axons.

information. The cell bodies of the sensory neurons are in clusters of neurons outside the spinal cord, called the **dorsal root ganglia.** (*Ganglia* is the plural of *ganglion*, a cluster of neurons. In most cases, a neuron cluster outside the CNS is called a ganglion, and a cluster inside the CNS is called a nucleus.) Cell bodies of the motor neurons are inside the spinal cord.

In the cross-section through the spinal cord shown in Figures 3.4 and 3.5, the H-shaped **gray matter** in the center of the cord is densely packed with cell bodies and dendrites. Many neurons from the gray matter of the spinal cord send axons to the brain or to other parts of the spinal cord through the **white matter,** containing myelinated axons.

Each segment of the spinal cord sends sensory information to the brain and receives motor commands from the brain. All that information passes through tracts of axons in the spinal

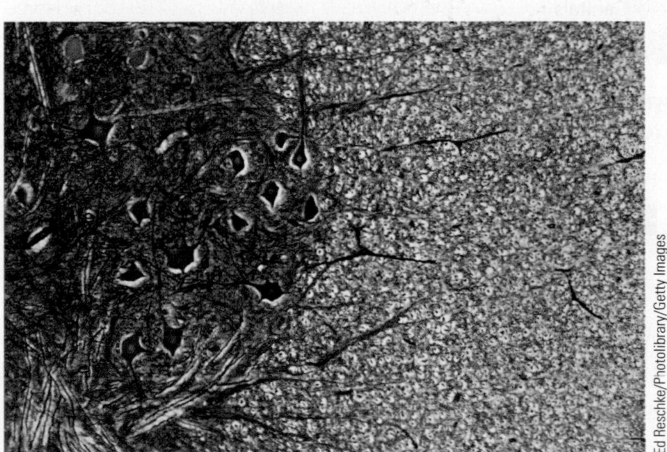

FIGURE 3.5 A section of gray matter of the spinal cord (left) and white matter surrounding it
Cell bodies and dendrites reside entirely in the gray matter. Axons travel from one area of gray matter to another in the white matter.

cord. If the spinal cord is cut at a given segment, the brain loses sensation from that segment and below. The brain also loses motor control over all parts of the body served by that segment and the lower ones.

The Autonomic Nervous System

The autonomic nervous system consists of neurons that receive information from and send commands to the heart, intestines, and other organs. Its two parts are the sympathetic and parasympathetic nervous systems (see Figure 3.6). The **sympathetic nervous system,** a network of nerves that prepare the organs for vigorous activity, consists of chains of ganglia just to the left and right of the spinal cord's central regions (the thoracic and lumbar areas). These ganglia are connected by axons to the spinal cord. Sympathetic axons prepare the organs for "fight or flight"—increasing breathing and heart rate and decreasing digestive activity. Because the sympathetic ganglia are closely linked, they often act as a single system "in sympathy" with one another, although an event may activate some parts more than others. The sweat glands, the adrenal glands, the muscles that constrict blood vessels, and the muscles that erect the hairs of the skin have sympathetic input but no parasympathetic input.

The **parasympathetic nervous system** facilitates vegetative, nonemergency responses. The term *para* means "beside" or "related to," and parasympathetic activities are related to, and generally the opposite of, sympathetic activities. For example, the sympathetic nervous system increases heart rate, but the parasympathetic nervous system decreases it. The parasympathetic nervous system increases digestive activity, whereas the sympathetic nervous system decreases it. The parasympathetic system also promotes sexual arousal, including erection in males. Although the sympathetic and parasympathetic systems produce contrary effects, both are constantly active to varying degrees, and many stimuli arouse parts of both systems.

The parasympathetic nervous system is also known as the craniosacral system because it consists of the cranial nerves and nerves from the sacral spinal cord (see Figure 3.6). Unlike the ganglia in the sympathetic system, the parasympathetic ganglia are not arranged in a chain near the spinal cord. Rather, long *preganglionic* axons extend from the spinal cord to parasympathetic ganglia close to each internal organ. Shorter *postganglionic* fibers then extend from the parasympathetic ganglia into the organs themselves. Because the parasympathetic ganglia are not linked to one another, they act more independently than the sympathetic ganglia do. Parasympathetic activity decreases heart rate, increases digestive rate, and in general, conserves energy.

The parasympathetic nervous system's axons release the neurotransmitter acetylcholine onto the organs. Most sympathetic nervous system axons release norepinephrin although a few, such as those onto the sweat glands,

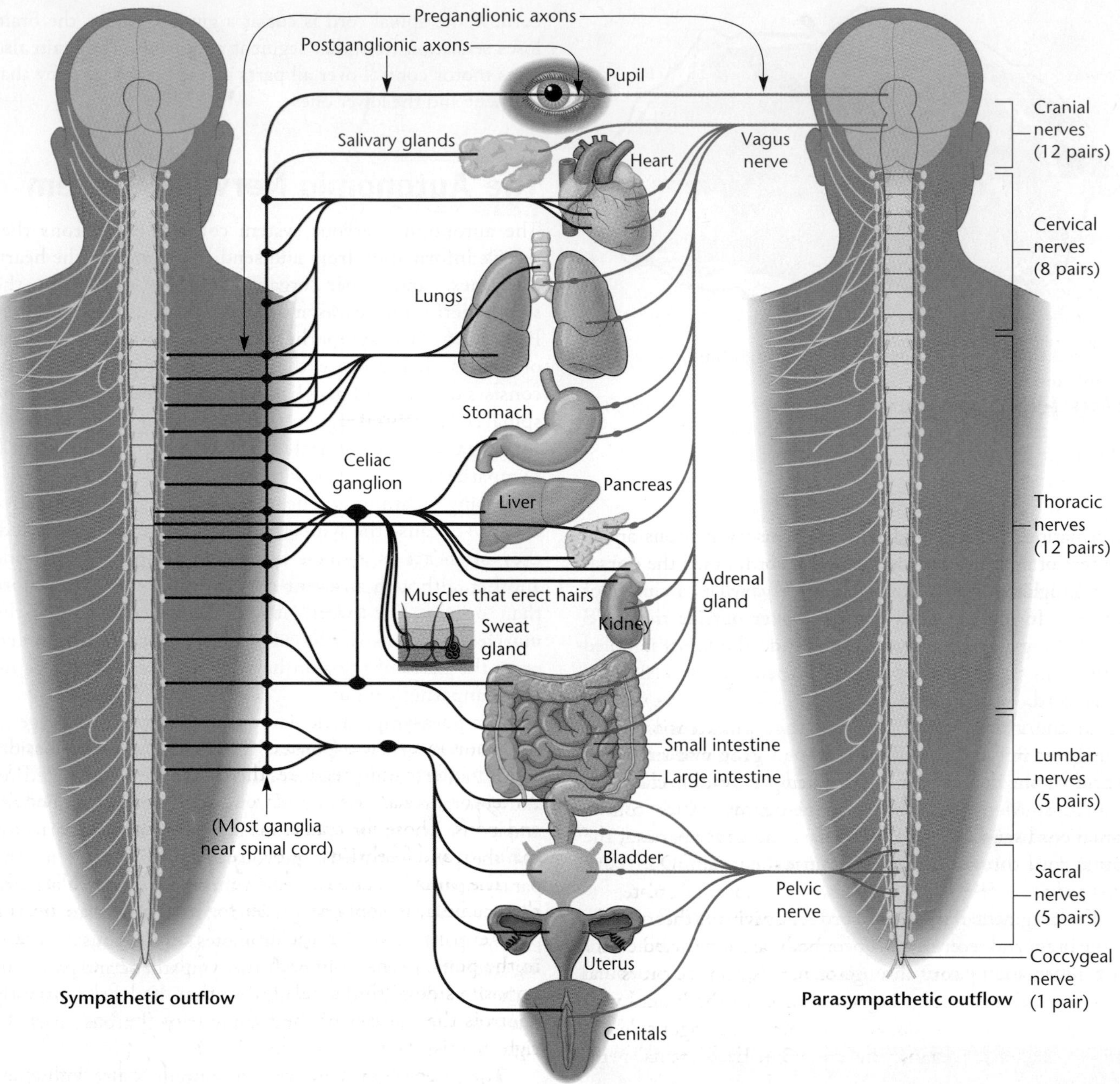

FIGURE 3.6 The sympathetic nervous system (red lines) and parasympathetic nervous system (blue lines)
Note that the adrenal glands, sweat glands, and hair erector muscles receive sympathetic input only. *Source:* Starr & Taggart, 1989

acetylcholine. Because the two systems use different transmitters, certain drugs excite or inhibit one system or the other. For example, over-the-counter cold remedies exert most of their effects by blocking parasympathetic activity or increasing sympathetic activity. Because the flow of sinus fluids is a parasympathetic response, drugs that block the parasympathetic system inhibit sinus flow. The side effects of cold remedies stem from their pro-sympathetic, anti-parasympathetic activities: They increase heart rate, blood pressure, sweating, and arousal. They inhibit salivation and digestion. Certain decongestant pills containing pseudoephedrine have been withdrawn or restricted because of their potential for abuse.

STOP & CHECK

5. Sensory nerves enter which side of the spinal cord, dorsal or ventral?

6. Which functions are controlled by the sympathetic nervous system? Which are controlled by the parasympathetic nervous system?

ANSWERS

5. Dorsal **6.** The sympathetic nervous system prepares the organs for vigorous fight-or-flight activity. The parasympathetic system increases vegetative responses such as digestion.

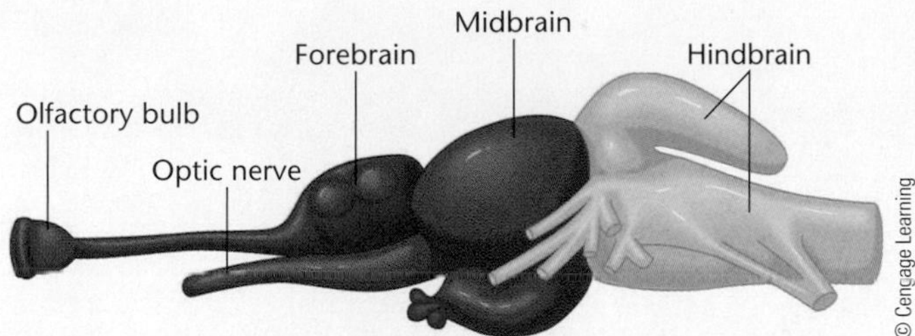

FIGURE 3.7 Major divisions of the vertebrate brain
In a fish brain, as shown here, the forebrain, midbrain, and hindbrain are clearly visible as separate bulges. In adult mammals, the forebrain grows and surrounds the entire midbrain and part of the hindbrain.

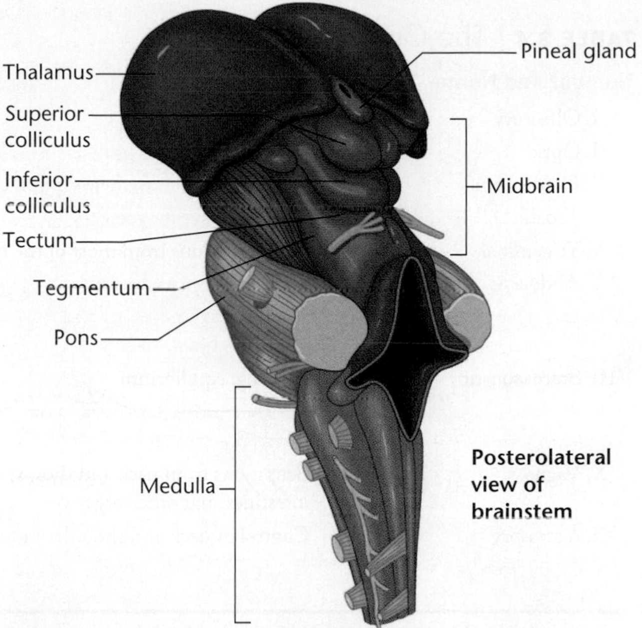

FIGURE 3.8 The human brainstem
This composite structure extends from the top of the spinal cord into the center of the forebrain. The pons, pineal gland, and colliculi are ordinarily surrounded by the cerebral cortex.

The Hindbrain

The brain has three major divisions—the hindbrain, the midbrain, and the forebrain (see Figure 3.7 and Table 3.3). Some neuroscientists prefer terms with Greek roots: rhombencephalon (hindbrain), mesencephalon (midbrain), and prosencephalon (forebrain). You may encounter these terms in other reading.

The **hindbrain**, the posterior part of the brain, consists of the medulla, the pons, and the cerebellum. The medulla and pons, the midbrain, and certain central structures of the forebrain constitute the **brainstem** (see Figure 3.8).

The **medulla**, or medulla oblongata, is just above the spinal cord and can be regarded as an enlarged extension of the spinal cord into the skull. The medulla controls vital reflexes—including breathing, heart rate, vomiting, salivation, coughing, and sneezing—through the **cranial nerves**, which control sensations from the head, muscle movements in the head, and much of the parasympathetic output to the organs. Damage to the medulla is frequently fatal, and large doses of opiates are life-threatening because they suppress activity of the medulla.

Just as the lower parts of the body are connected to the spinal cord via sensory and motor nerves, the receptors and muscles of the head and organs connect to the brain by 12 pairs of cranial nerves (one of each pair on the right side and one on the left), as shown in Table 3.4. Each cranial nerve originates in a *nucleus* (cluster of neurons) that integrates the sensory information, regulates the motor output, or both. The nuclei for cranial nerves V through XII are in the medulla and pons. Those for cranial nerves I through IV are in the midbrain and forebrain (see Figure 3.9).

TABLE 3.3 Major Divisions of the Vertebrate Brain

Area	Also Known as	Major Structures
Forebrain	Prosencephalon ("forward-brain")	
	Diencephalon ("between-brain")	Thalamus, hypothalamus
	Telencephalon ("end-brain")	Cerebral cortex, hippocampus, basal ganglia
Midbrain	Mesencephalon ("middle-brain")	Tectum, tegmentum, superior colliculus, inferior colliculus, substantia nigra
Hindbrain	Rhombencephalon (literally, "parallelogram-brain")	Medulla, pons, cerebellum

© Cengage Learning

The **pons** lies anterior and ventral to the medulla. Like the medulla, it contains nuclei for several cranial nerves. The term *pons* is Latin for "bridge," reflecting the fact that in the pons, axons from each half of the brain cross to the opposite side of the spinal cord so that the left hemisphere controls the muscles of the right side of the body and the right hemisphere controls the left side.

The **cerebellum** is a large hindbrain structure with many deep folds. It has long been known for its contributions to the control of movement, and many older textbooks describe the cerebellum as important for "balance and coordination." True, people with cerebellar damage are clumsy and lose their balance, but the functions of the cerebellum extend far beyond balance and coordination. People with damage to the cerebellum have trouble shifting their attention back and forth between auditory and visual stimuli (Courchesne et al., 1994). They have difficulty with timing, such as judging whether one rhythm is faster than another.

The Midbrain

As the name implies, the **midbrain** starts in the middle of the brain, although in adult mammals it is dwarfed and surrounded by the forebrain. The midbrain is more prominent in birds, reptiles, amphibians, and fish. The roof of the

TABLE 3.4 The Cranial Nerves

Number and Name	Major Functions
I. Olfactory	Smell
II. Optic	Vision
III. Oculomotor	Control of eye movements; pupil constriction
IV. Trochlear	Control of eye movements
V. Trigeminal	Skin sensations from most of the face; control of jaw muscles for chewing and swallowing
VI. Abducens	Control of eye movements
VII. Facial	Taste from the anterior two thirds of the tongue; control of facial expressions, crying, salivation, and dilation of the head's blood vessels
VIII. Statoacoustic	Hearing; equilibrium
IX. Glossopharyngeal	Taste and other sensations from throat and posterior third of the tongue; control of swallowing, salivation, throat movements during speech
X. Vagus	Sensations from neck and thorax; control of throat, esophagus, and larynx; parasympathetic nerves to stomach, intestines, and other organs
XI. Accessory	Control of neck and shoulder movements
XII. Hypoglossal	Control of muscles of the tongue

Cranial nerves III, IV, and VI are coded in red to highlight their similarity: control of eye movements. Cranial nerves VII, IX, and XII are coded in green to highlight their similarity: taste and control of tongue and throat movements. Cranial nerve VII has other important functions as well. Nerve X (not highlighted) also contributes to throat movements, although it is primarily known for other functions.

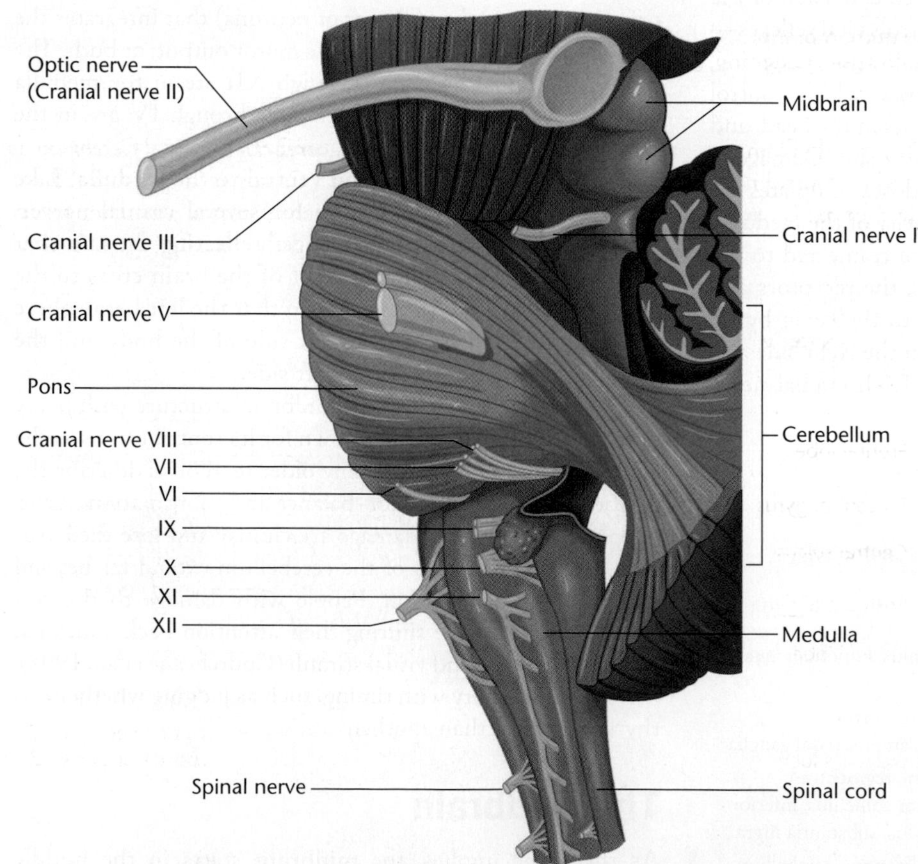

FIGURE 3.9 Cranial nerves II through XII
Cranial nerve I, the olfactory nerve, connects directly to the olfactory bulbs of the forebrain.
Source: Based on Braus, 1960

midbrain is called the **tectum.** (*Tectum* is the Latin word for "roof." The same root occurs in the geological term *plate tectonics.*) The swellings on each side of the tectum are the **superior colliculus** and the **inferior colliculus** (see Figures 3.8 and 3.10). Both are important for sensory processing—the inferior colliculus for hearing and the superior colliculus for vision.

Under the tectum lies the **tegmentum,** the intermediate level of the midbrain. (In Latin, *tegmentum* means a "covering," such as a rug on the floor. The tectum covers the tegmentum, but the tegmentum covers several other midbrain structures.) Another midbrain structure, the **substantia nigra,** gives rise to a dopamine-containing pathway that facilitates readiness for movement.

The Forebrain

The **forebrain,** the most prominent part of the mammalian brain, consists of two cerebral hemispheres, one on the left and one on the right (see Figure 3.11). Each hemisphere

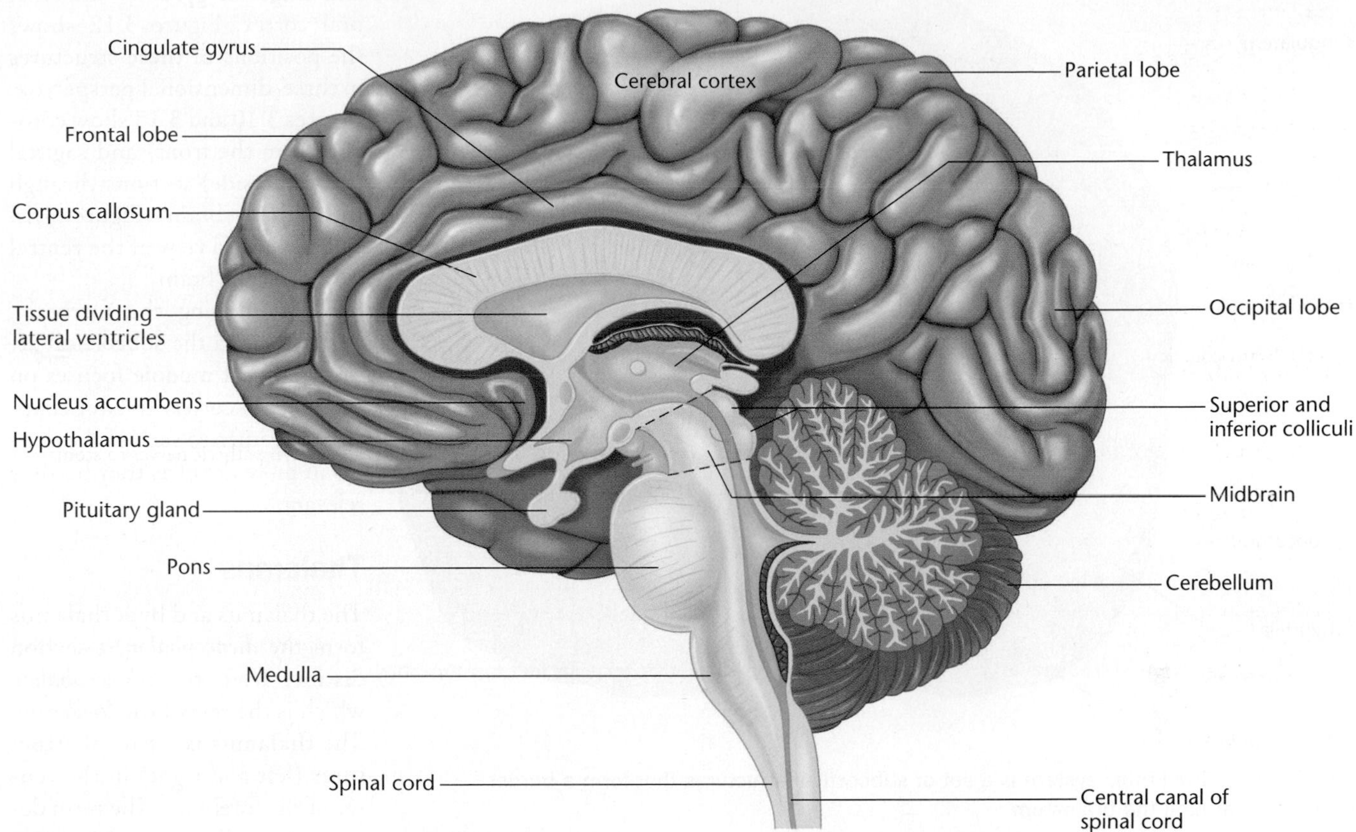

FIGURE 3.10 A sagittal section through the human brain
Source: Based on Nieuwenhuys, Voogd, & vanHuijzen, 1988

is organized to receive sensory information, mostly from the contralateral (opposite) side of the body, and to control muscles, mostly on the contralateral side, by way of axons to the spinal cord and the cranial nerve nuclei.

The outer portion is the cerebral cortex. (*Cerebrum* is a Latin word meaning "brain." *Cortex* is a Latin word for "bark" or "shell.") Under the cerebral cortex are other structures, including the thalamus and the basal ganglia. Several

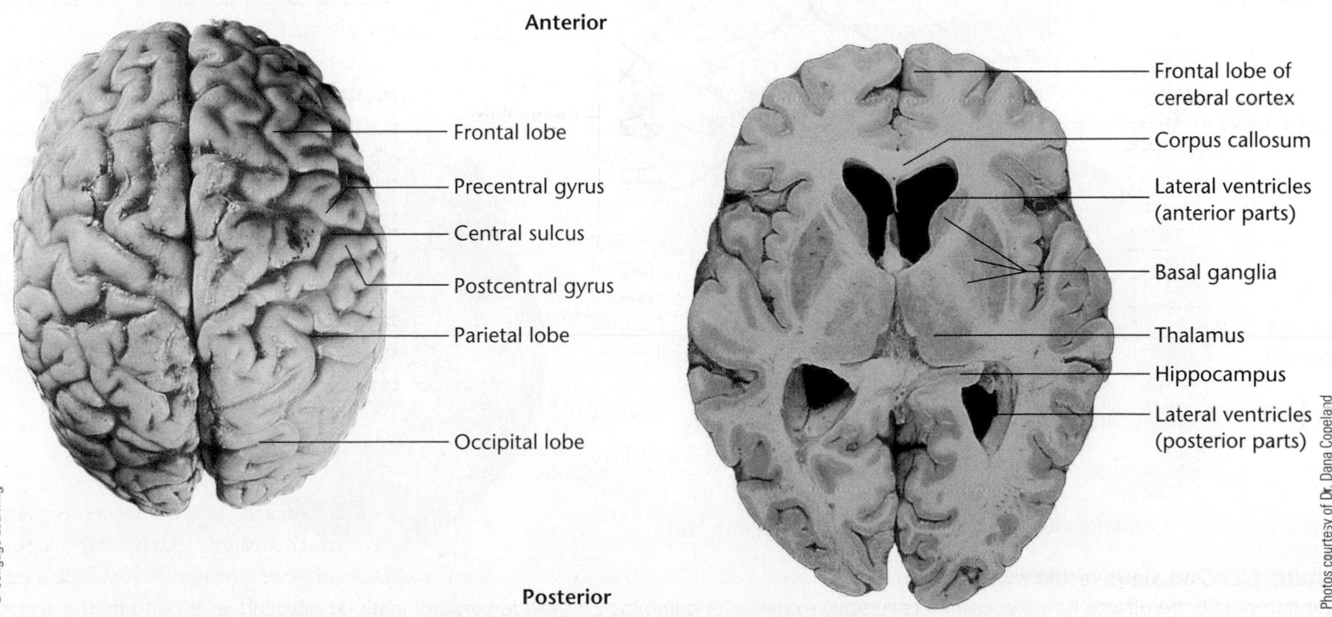

FIGURE 3.11 Dorsal view of the brain surface and a horizontal section through the brain

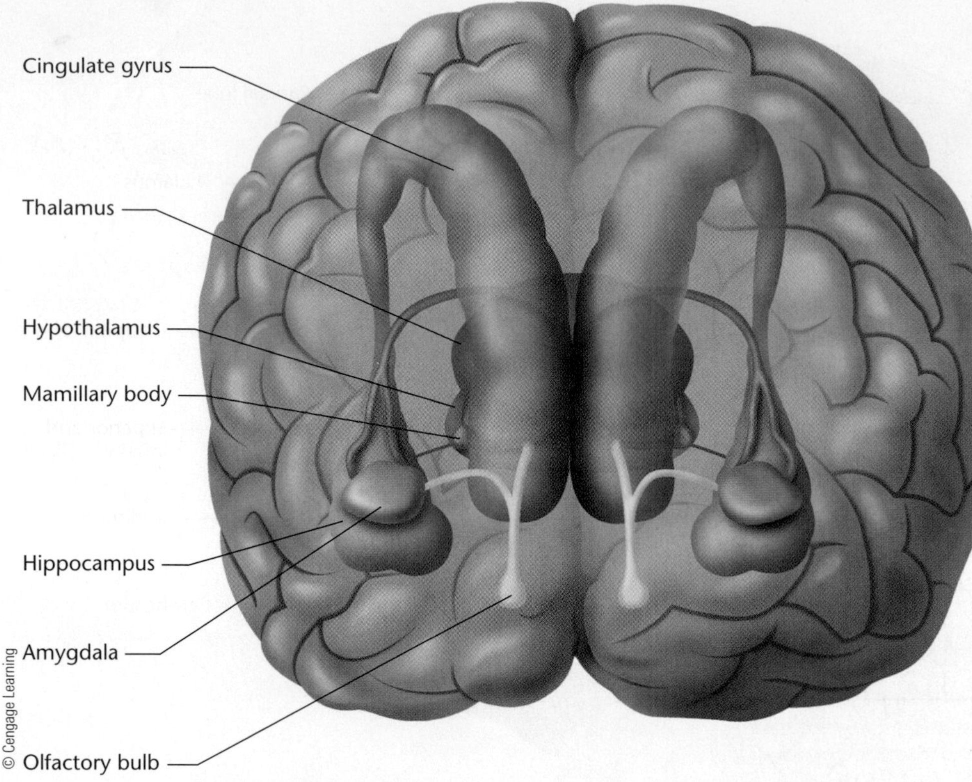

FIGURE 3.12 **The limbic system is a set of subcortical structures that form a border (or limbus) around the brainstem**

interlinked structures, known as the **limbic system**, form a border (or *limbus*, the Latin word for "border") around the brainstem. These structures are particularly important for motivations and emotions, such as eating, drinking, sexual activity, anxiety, and aggression. The limbic system includes the olfactory bulb, hypothalamus, hippocampus, amygdala, and cingulate gyrus of the cerebral cortex. Figure 3.12 shows the positions of these structures in three-dimensional perspective. Figures 3.10 and 3.13 show coronal (from the front) and sagittal (from the side) sections through the human brain. Figure 3.13 also includes a view of the ventral surface of the brain.

In describing the forebrain, we begin with the subcortical areas. The next module focuses on the cerebral cortex. In later chapters, we return to each of these areas in more detail as they become relevant.

Thalamus

The thalamus and hypothalamus form the *diencephalon*, a section distinct from the *telencephalon*, which is the rest of the forebrain. The **thalamus** is a pair of structures (left and right) in the center of the forebrain. The term derives from a Greek word meaning "anteroom," "inner chamber," or "bridal bed." It resembles two small avocados joined side by side, one in the left hemisphere and one in the right. Most sensory information goes first to the thalamus, which processes it and sends output to the cerebral cortex. An exception to this rule is olfactory information, which progresses from the olfactory receptors to the olfactory bulbs and then directly to the cerebral cortex.

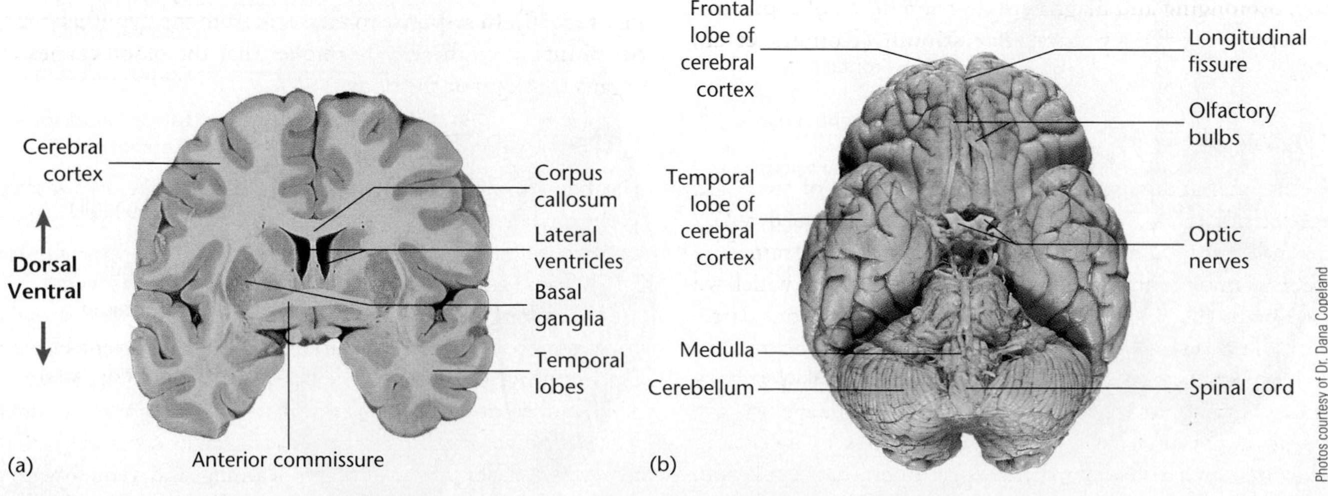

FIGURE 3.13 **Two views of the human brain**
(a) A coronal section. Note how the corpus callosum and anterior commissure provide communication between the left and right hemispheres. (b) The ventral surface. The optic nerves (cut here) extend to the eyes.

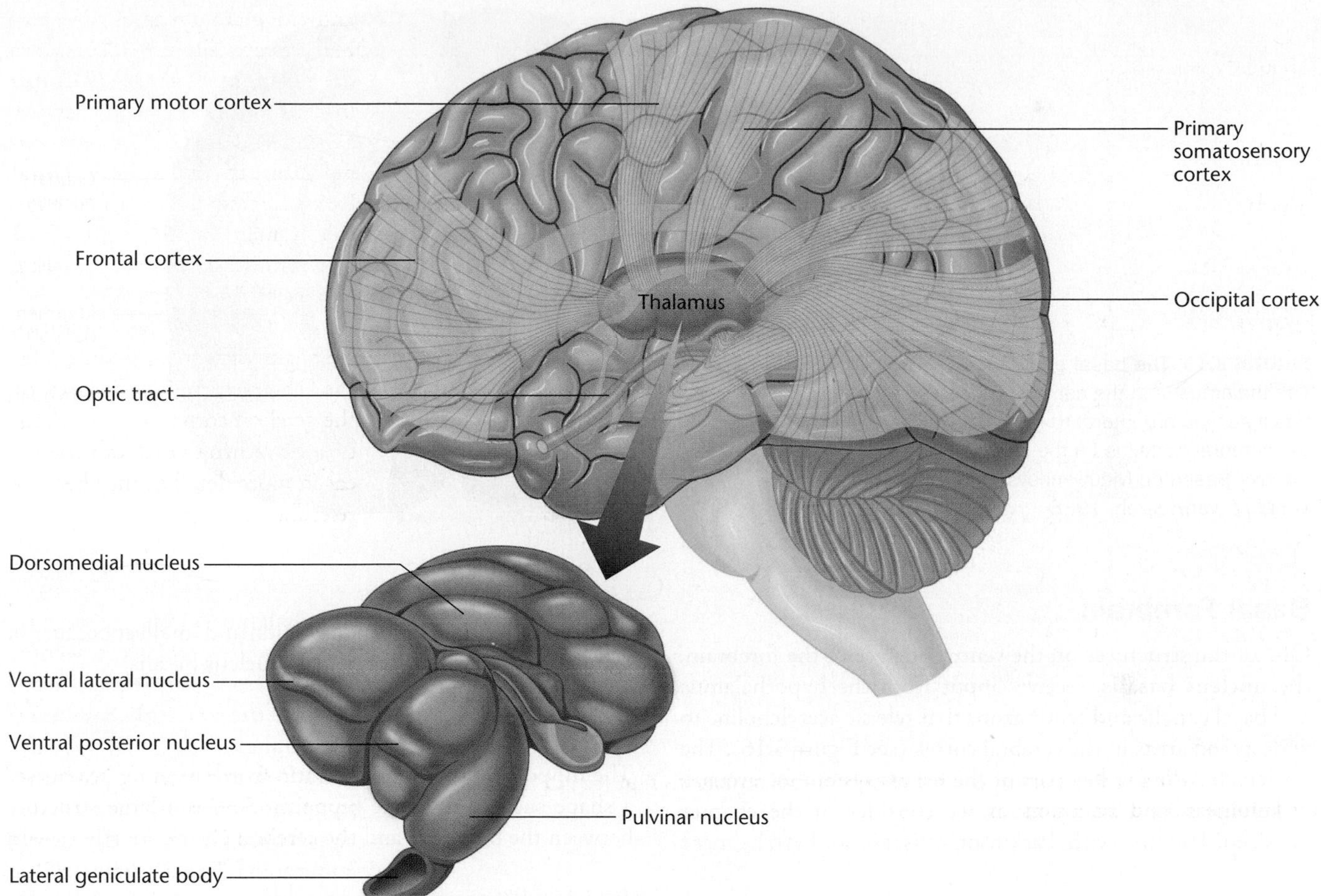

FIGURE 3.14 Routes of information from the thalamus to the cerebral cortex
Each thalamic nucleus projects its axons to a different part of the cortex. *Source:* After Nieuwenhuys, Voogd, & vanHuijzen, 1988

Many nuclei of the thalamus receive their input from a sensory system, such as vision, and transmit information to a single area of the cerebral cortex, as in Figure 3.14. The cerebral cortex sends information back to the thalamus, prolonging and magnifying certain kinds of input and focusing attention on particular stimuli (Komura et al., 2001).

Hypothalamus

The **hypothalamus**, a small area near the base of the brain just ventral to the thalamus (see Figures 3.10 and 3.12), has widespread connections with the rest of the brain. The hypothalamus contains a number of distinct nuclei, which we examine in the chapters on motivation and emotion. Partly through nerves and partly through hypothalamic hormones, the hypothalamus conveys messages to the pituitary gland, altering its release of hormones. Damage to any hypothalamic nucleus leads to abnormalities in motivated behaviors, such as feeding, drinking, temperature regulation, sexual behavior, fighting, or activity level. Because of these important behavioral effects, the small hypothalamus attracts much research attention.

Pituitary Gland

The **pituitary gland** is an endocrine (hormone-producing) gland attached to the base of the hypothalamus by a stalk that contains neurons, blood vessels, and connective tissue (see Figure 3.10). In response to messages from the hypothalamus, the pituitary synthesizes hormones that the blood carries to organs throughout the body.

Basal Ganglia

The **basal ganglia**, a group of subcortical structures lateral to the thalamus, include three major structures: the caudate nucleus, the putamen, and the globus pallidus (see Figure 3.15). Some authorities include other structures as well.

It has long been known that damage to the basal ganglia impairs movement, as in conditions such as Parkinson's disease and Huntington's disease. The basal ganglia integrate motivational and emotional behavior to increase the vigor of selected actions. However, the role of the basal ganglia extends beyond movement. They are critical for learning and remembering skills and habits, as well as other types of learning that develop gradually with extended experience. We return to the basal ganglia in more detail in the chapters on movement and memory.

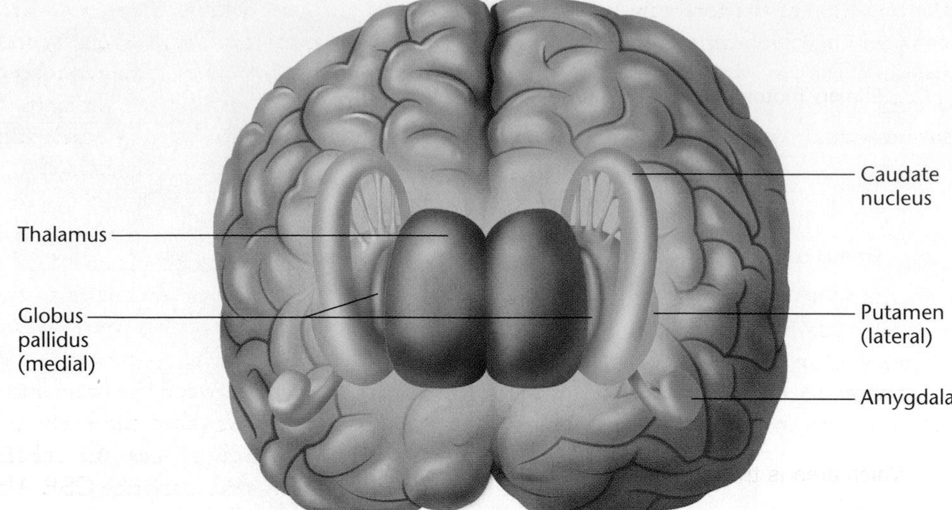

FIGURE 3.15 The basal ganglia
The thalamus is in the center, the basal ganglia are lateral to it, and the cerebral cortex is on the outside. *Source*: Based on Nieuwenhuys, Voogd, & vanHuijzen, 1988

Basal Forebrain

One of the structures on the ventral surface of the forebrain, the **nucleus basalis**, receives input from the hypothalamus and basal ganglia and sends axons that release acetylcholine to widespread areas in the cerebral cortex (see Figure 3.16). The nucleus basalis is a key part of the brain's system for arousal, wakefulness, and attention, as we consider in the chapter on sleep. Patients with Parkinson's disease and Alzheimer's disease have impairments of attention and intellect because of inactivity or deterioration of their nucleus basalis.

Hippocampus

The **hippocampus** (from the Latin word meaning "sea horse," a shape suggested by the hippocampus) is a large structure between the thalamus and the cerebral cortex, mostly toward

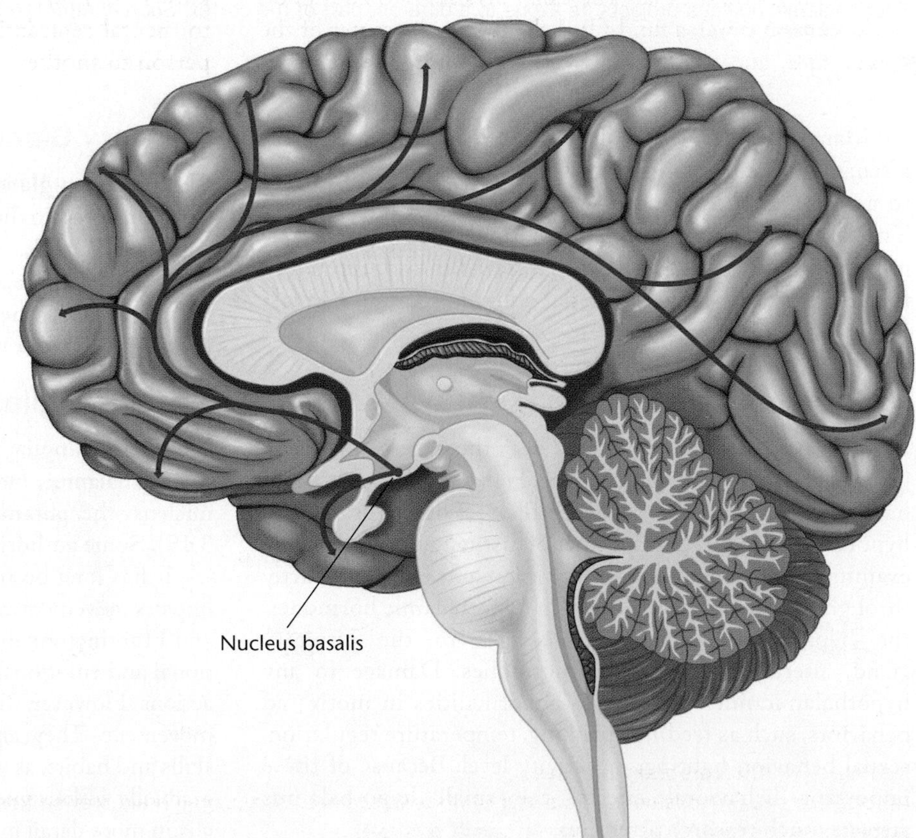

FIGURE 3.16 The basal forebrain
The nucleus basalis and other structures in this area send axons throughout the cortex, increasing its arousal and wakefulness through release of the neurotransmitter acetylcholine. *Source*: Based on Woolf, 1991

the posterior of the forebrain, as shown in Figure 3.12. We consider the hippocampus in more detail in the chapter on memory. The gist of that discussion is that the hippocampus is critical for certain types of memories, especially memories for individual events.

STOP&CHECK

7. Of the following, which are in the hindbrain, which in the midbrain, and which in the forebrain: basal ganglia, cerebellum, hippocampus, hypothalamus, medulla, pituitary gland, pons, substantia nigra, superior and inferior colliculi, tectum, tegmentum, thalamus?
8. Which area is the main source of input to the cerebral cortex?

ANSWERS

7. Hindbrain: cerebellum, medulla, and pons. Midbrain: substantia nigra, superior and inferior colliculi, tectum, and tegmentum. Forebrain: basal ganglia, hippocampus, hypothalamus, pituitary, and thalamus. **8.** Thalamus

The Ventricles

The nervous system begins its development as a tube surrounding a fluid canal. The canal persists into adulthood as the **central canal**, a fluid-filled channel in the center of the spinal cord, and as the **ventricles**, four fluid-filled cavities within the brain. Each hemisphere contains one of the two large lateral ventricles (see Figure 3.17). Toward their posterior, they connect to the third ventricle, positioned at the midline, separating the left thalamus from the right thalamus. The third ventricle connects to the fourth ventricle in the center of the medulla.

Cells called the *choroid plexus* inside the four ventricles produce **cerebrospinal fluid (CSF)**, a clear fluid similar to blood plasma. CSF fills the ventricles, flowing from the lateral ventricles to the third and fourth ventricles. From the fourth ventricle, some of it flows into the central canal of the spinal cord, but more goes into the narrow spaces between the brain and the thin **meninges**, membranes that surround the brain and spinal cord. In one of those narrow spaces, the subarachnoid space, the blood gradually reabsorbs the CSF. Although the brain has no pain receptors, the meninges do, and meningitis—inflammation of the meninges—is painful. Swollen blood vessels in the meninges are responsible for the pain of a migraine headache (Hargreaves, 2007).

Cerebrospinal fluid cushions the brain against mechanical shock when the head moves. It also provides buoyancy. Just as a person weighs less in water than on land, cerebrospinal fluid helps support the weight of the brain. It also provides a reservoir of hormones and nutrition for the brain and spinal cord.

If the flow of CSF is obstructed, it accumulates within the ventricles or in the subarachnoid space, increasing pressure on the brain. When this occurs in infants, the skull bones spread, causing an overgrown head. This condition, known as *hydrocephalus* (HI-dro-SEFF-ah-luss), can lead to mental retardation, although the results vary from one person to another.

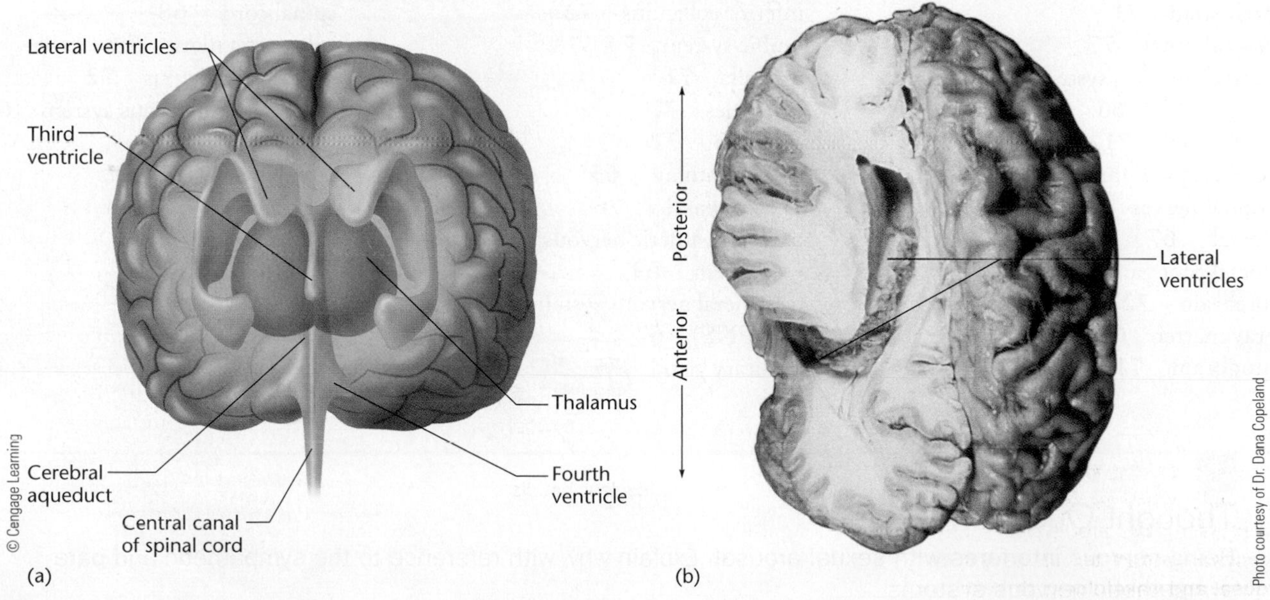

FIGURE 3.17 The cerebral ventricles
(a) Diagram showing positions of the four ventricles. (b) Photo of a human brain, viewed from above, with a horizontal cut through one hemisphere to show the position of the lateral ventricles.

MODULE 3.1 ■ IN CLOSING

Learning Neuroanatomy

The brain is a complex structure. This module has introduced a great many terms and facts; do not be discouraged if you have trouble remembering them. It will help to return to this module to review anatomy as you encounter structures again in later chapters. Gradually, the material will become more familiar.

Summary

1. The vertebrate nervous system has two main divisions, the central nervous system and the peripheral nervous system. **66**
2. Each segment of the spinal cord has a sensory nerve and a motor nerve on both the left and right sides. Spinal pathways convey information to the brain. **68**
3. The sympathetic nervous system (one of the two divisions of the autonomic nervous system) activates the body's internal organs for vigorous activities. The parasympathetic system (the other division) promotes digestion and other nonemergency processes. **69**
4. The central nervous system consists of the spinal cord, the hindbrain, the midbrain, and the forebrain. **71**
5. The hindbrain consists of the medulla, pons, and cerebellum. The medulla and pons control breathing, heart rate, and other vital functions through the cranial nerves. The cerebellum contributes to movement and timing short intervals. **71**
6. The cerebral cortex receives its sensory information (except for olfaction) from the thalamus. **72**
7. The subcortical areas of the forebrain include the thalamus, hypothalamus, pituitary gland, basal ganglia, and hippocampus **74**
8. The cerebral ventricles contain fluid that provides buoyancy and cushioning for the brain. **77**

Key Terms

Terms are defined in the module on the page number indicated. They're also presented in alphabetical order with definitions in the book's Subject Index/Glossary. Interactive flash cards, audio reviews, and crossword puzzles are among the online resources available to help you learn these terms and the concepts they represent.

autonomic nervous system **67**
basal ganglia **75**
brainstem **71**
central canal **77**
central nervous system (CNS) **66**
cerebellum **71**
cerebrospinal fluid (CSF) **77**
cranial nerves **71**
dorsal **67**
dorsal root ganglia **68**
forebrain **72**
gray matter **68**
hindbrain **71**
hippocampus **77**
hypothalamus **75**
inferior colliculus **72**
limbic system **74**
medulla **71**
meninges **77**
midbrain **71**
neuroanatomy **65**
nucleus basalis **76**
parasympathetic nervous system **69**
peripheral nervous system (PNS) **67**
pituitary gland **75**
pons **71**
somatic nervous system, **67**
spinal cord **68**
substantia nigra **72**
superior colliculus **72**
sympathetic nervous system **69**
tectum **72**
tegmentum **72**
thalamus **74**
ventral **67**
ventricles **77**
white matter **68**

Thought Question

Being nervous interferes with sexual arousal. Explain why, with reference to the sympathetic and parasympathetic nervous systems.

MODULE 3.1 End of Module Quiz

1. The term meaning *toward the stomach side* is ______, and its opposite is ______.
   - a. medial . . . lateral
   - b. lateral . . . medial
   - c. ventral . . . dorsal
   - d. dorsal . . . ventral

2. The term meaning *toward the midline* is ______, and its opposite is ______.
   - a. medial . . . lateral
   - b. lateral . . . medial
   - c. ventral . . . dorsal
   - d. dorsal . . . ventral

3. If two structures are on the same side of the body, they are ______ to each other. If they are on opposite sides, they are ______.
   - a. medial . . . lateral
   - b. lateral . . . medial
   - c. ipsilateral . . . contralateral
   - d. contralateral . . . ipsilateral

4. A plane that shows structures as viewed from the left or right side is called what?
   - a. Sagittal
   - b. Frontal
   - c. Coronal
   - d. Horizontal

5. What is the difference between the dorsal and ventral roots of the spinal cord?
   - a. The dorsal roots control "fight-or-flight" activity, and the ventral roots control vegetative, nonemergency responses.
   - b. The dorsal roots control vegetative, nonemergency responses, and the ventral roots control "fight-or-flight" activity.
   - c. The dorsal roots contain sensory input, and the ventral roots contain motor output.
   - d. The dorsal roots contain motor output, and the ventral roots contain sensory input.

6. Why do most cold remedies increase heart rate and blood pressure?
   - a. These drugs block the sympathetic nervous system.
   - b. These drugs block the parasympathetic nervous system.
   - c. These drugs block the ventral roots of the spinal cord.
   - d. These drugs block the dorsal roots of the spinal cord.

7. Of the following, which one is part of the forebrain?
   - a. Cerebellum
   - b. Pons
   - c. Superior colliculus
   - d. Hippocampus

8. The pituitary gland is attached to which brain structure?
   - a. Cerebellum
   - b. Medulla
   - c. Thalamus
   - d. Hypothalamus

ANSWERS: 1c, 2a, 3c, 4a, 5c, 6b, 7d, 8d.

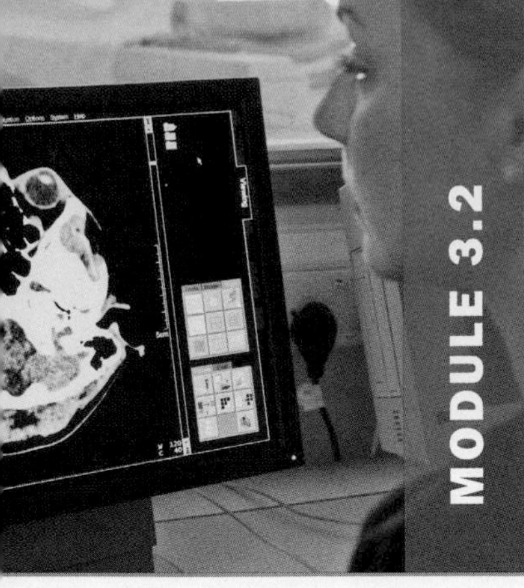

The Cerebral Cortex

The most prominent part of the mammalian brain is the **cerebral cortex.** The cells on the outer surface of the cerebral cortex are gray matter, and their axons extending inward are white matter (see Figure 3.13a). Neurons in each hemisphere communicate with neurons in the corresponding part of the other hemisphere through two bundles of axons, the **corpus callosum** (see Figures 3.10, 3.11, and 3.13) and the smaller **anterior commissure** (see Figure 3.13). Several other commissures (pathways across the midline) link subcortical structures.

The basic organization of the brain is remarkably similar across vertebrate species. The visual cortex is in the same place, the auditory cortex is in the same place, and so forth. Even the brains of insects show detailed similarities to vertebrate brains, implying evolutionary derivation from a common ancestor (Strausfeld & Hirth, 2013). However, brains vary enormously in size. The largest mammalian brains are 100,000 times larger than the smallest ones (Herculano-Houzel, 2011).

If we compare mammalian species, we see differences in the size of the cerebral cortex and the degree of folding (see Figure 3.18). Compared to other mammals of comparable size, **primates**—monkeys, apes, and humans—have a larger cerebral cortex, more folding, and more neurons per unit of volume (Herculano-Houzel, 2011). Figure 3.19 shows the size of the cerebral cortex in comparison to the rest of the brain for insectivores and two suborders of primates (Barton & Harvey, 2000). Figure 3.20 compares species in another way (D. A. Clark, Mitra, & Wang, 2001). The investigators arranged the insectivores and primates from left to right in terms of what percentage of their brain was devoted to the forebrain, including the cerebral cortex. They also inserted tree shrews, a species often considered intermediate. Note that as the proportion devoted to the forebrain increases, the relative sizes of the midbrain and medulla decrease. Curiously, the cerebellum occupies a remarkably constant percentage—approximately 13 percent of any mammalian brain (D. A. Clark et al., 2001). A comparison of 28 mammalian species found 4.2 neurons in the cerebellum for every one in the cerebral cortex, for each species (Herculano-Houzel, 2011). Why? Good question.

Organization of the Cerebral Cortex

The microscopic structure of the cells of the cerebral cortex varies from one cortical area to another, as does the density of neurons per volume (Collins, 2011). Much research has been directed toward understanding the relationship between structure and function.

In humans and most other mammals, the cerebral cortex contains up to six distinct **laminae,** layers of cell bodies that

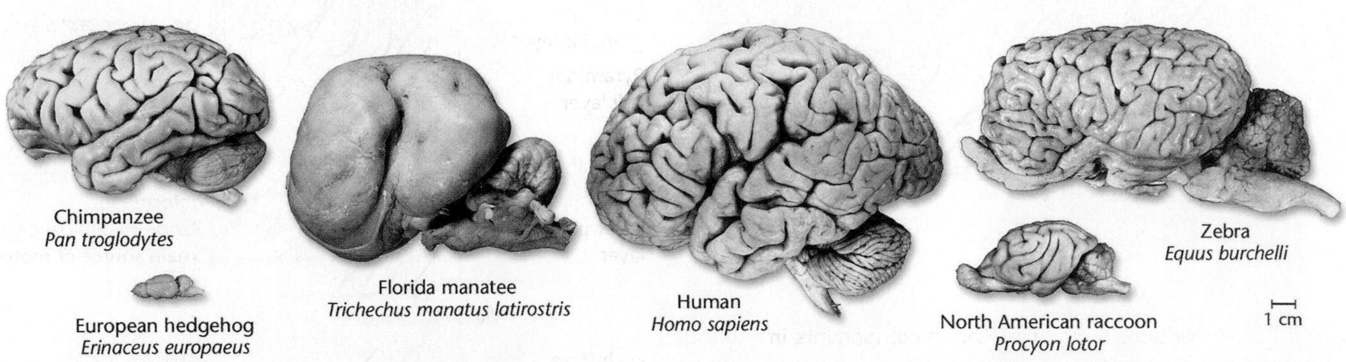

FIGURE 3.18 Comparison of mammalian brains
The human brain is the largest of those shown, although whales, dolphins, and elephants have still larger brains. All mammals have the same brain subareas in the same locations. From the University of Wisconsin—Madison Comparative Mammalian Brain Collection, Wally Welker, Curator. Project supported by the Natural Science Foundation

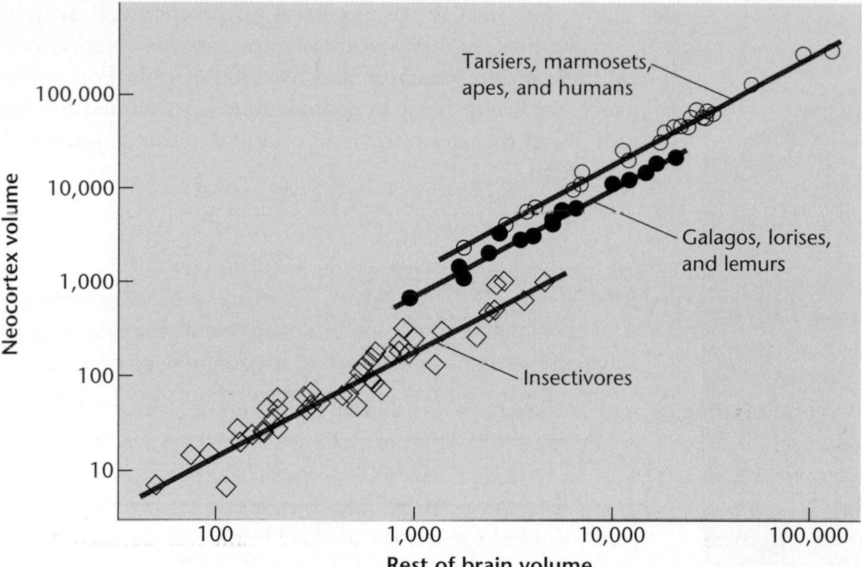

FIGURE 3.19 Relationship between volume of the cortex and volume of the rest of the brain
For each of the three groups, cortical volume increases quite predictably as a function of the volume of the rest of the brain. However, the lines for the two primate groups are displaced upward. *Source:* Fig. 1, p. 1055 in R. A. Barton & R. H. Harvey, "Mosaic evolution of brain structure in mammals." *Nature, 405*, pp. 1055–1058.

are parallel to the surface of the cortex and separated from each other by layers of fibers (see Figure 3.21). The laminae vary in thickness and prominence from one part of the cortex to another, and a given lamina may be absent from certain areas. Lamina V, which sends long axons to the spinal cord and other distant areas, is thickest in the motor cortex, which has the greatest control of the muscles. Lamina IV, which receives axons from the sensory nuclei of the thalamus, is prominent in the sensory areas of the cortex (visual, auditory, and somatosensory) but absent from the motor cortex.

The cells of the cortex are also organized into **columns** of cells perpendicular to the laminae. Figure 3.22 illustrates the idea of columns, although in nature they are not so straight. The cells within a given column have similar properties to one another. For example, if one cell in a column responds to touch on the palm of the left hand, then the other cells in that column do, too. If one cell responds to a horizontal pattern of light at a particular location, then other cells in the column respond to the same pattern in nearby locations.

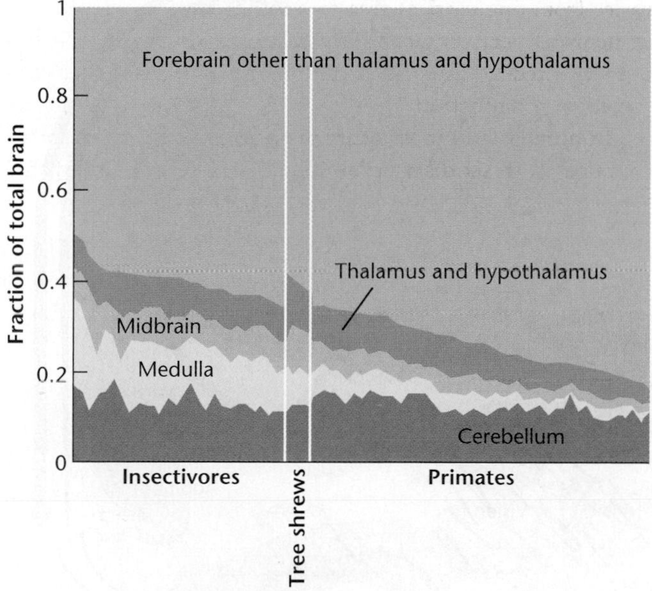

FIGURE 3.20 Relative sizes of five brain components in insectivores and primates
The forebrain composes a larger percentage of primate than insectivore brains. Note also the near constant fraction devoted to the cerebellum. *Source:* Fig. 1, p. 189 in D. A. Clark, P. P. Mitra, & S. S.-H. Wong, "Scalable architecture in mammalian brains." *Nature, 411*, pp. 189–193.

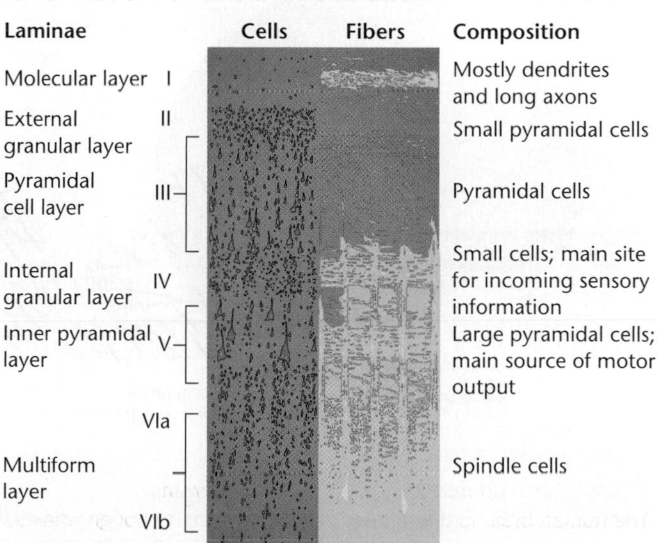

FIGURE 3.21 The six laminae of the human cerebral cortex
Source: Adapted from Ranson & Clark, 1959

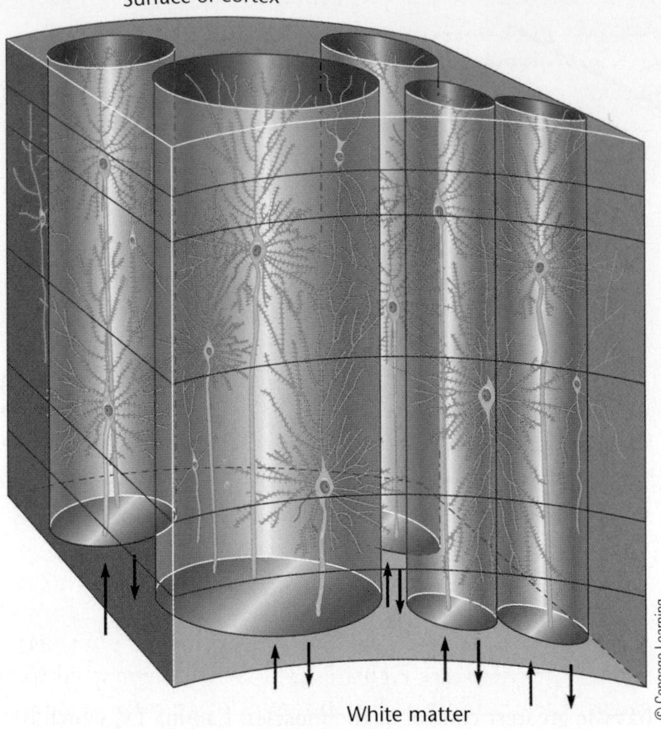

FIGURE 3.22 Columns in the cerebral cortex
Each column extends through several laminae. Neurons within a given column have similar properties. For example, in the somatosensory cortex, all the neurons within a given column respond to stimulation of the same area of skin.

We now turn to specific parts of the cortex. Researchers make fine distinctions among areas of the cerebral cortex based on the structure and function of cells. For convenience, we group these areas into four *lobes* named for the skull bones that lie over them: occipital, parietal, temporal, and frontal.

STOP&CHECK

9. If several neurons of the visual cortex all respond best when the retina is exposed to horizontal lines of light, then those neurons are probably in the same _____.

ANSWER

9: Column

The Occipital Lobe

The **occipital lobe**, at the posterior (caudal) end of the cortex (see Figure 3.23), is the main target for visual information. The posterior pole of the occipital lobe is known as the *primary visual* cortex, or *striate cortex,* because of its striped appearance in cross-section. Destruction of any part of the striate cortex causes *cortical blindness* in the related part of the visual field. For example, extensive damage to the striate cortex of the right hemisphere causes

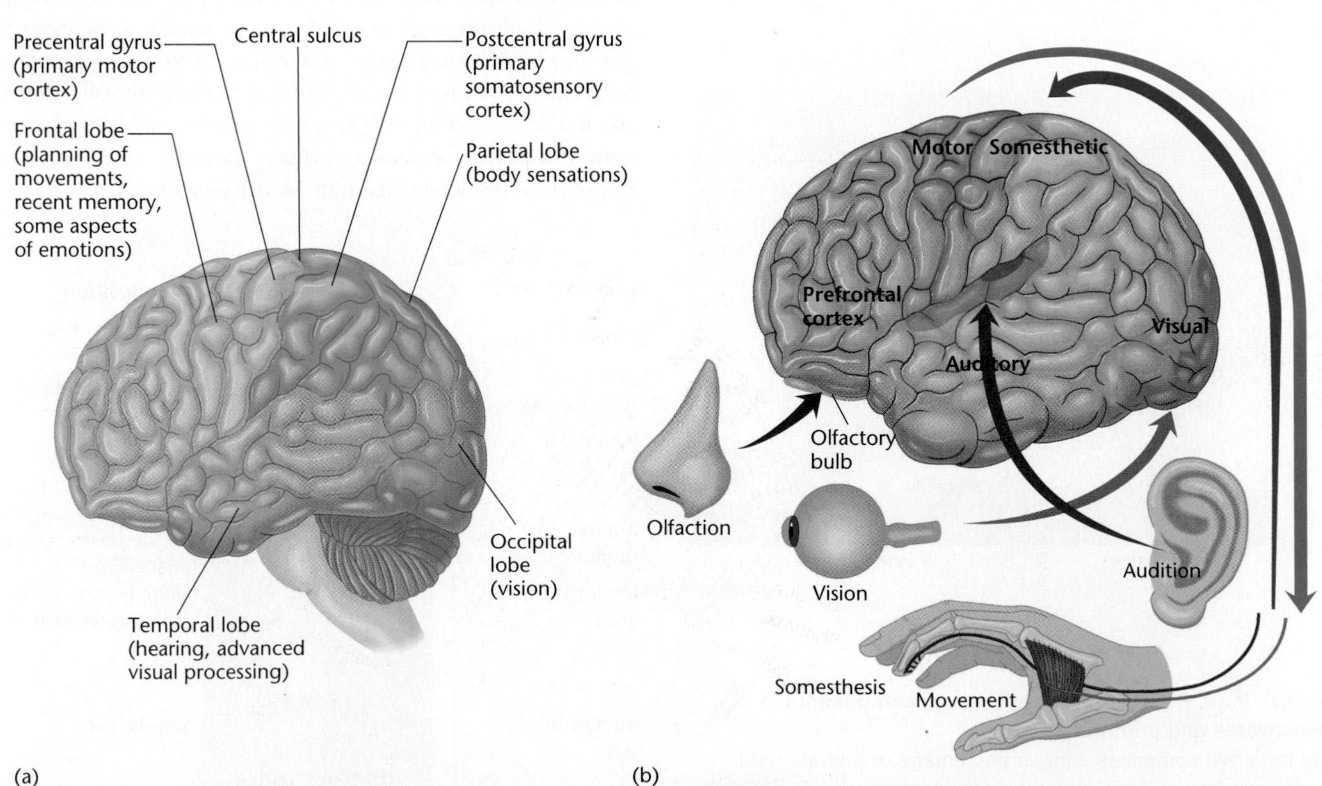

FIGURE 3.23 Areas of the human cerebral cortex
(a) The four lobes: occipital, parietal, temporal, and frontal. (b) The primary sensory cortex for vision, hearing, and body sensations; the primary motor cortex; and the olfactory bulb, responsible for the sense of smell. *Source* for part b: T. W. Deacon, 1990

blindness in the left visual field (that is, the left side of the world from the viewer's perspective). A person with cortical blindness has normal eyes and pupillary reflexes, but no conscious visual perception and no visual imagery (not even in dreams). People who suffer eye damage become blind, but if they have an intact occipital cortex and previous visual experience, they can still imagine visual scenes and can still have visual dreams (Sabo & Kirtley, 1982). In short, the eyes provide the stimulus, and the visual cortex provides the experience.

The Parietal Lobe

The **parietal lobe** lies between the occipital lobe and the **central sulcus**, a deep groove in the surface of the cortex (see Figure 3.23). The area just posterior to the central sulcus, the **postcentral gyrus**, or *primary somatosensory cortex*, receives sensations from touch receptors, muscle-stretch receptors, and joint receptors. Brain surgeons sometimes use only local anesthesia (anesthetizing the scalp but leaving the brain awake). If during this process they lightly stimulate the postcentral gyrus, people report tingling sensations on the opposite side of the body.

The postcentral gyrus includes four bands of cells parallel to the central sulcus. Separate areas along each band receive simultaneous information from different parts of the body, as shown in Figure 3.24a (Nicolelis et al., 1998). Two of the bands receive mostly light-touch information, one receives deep-pressure information, and one receives a combination of both (Kaas, Nelson, Sur, Lin, & Merzenich, 1979). In effect, the postcentral gyrus represents the body four times.

Information about touch and body location is important not only for its own sake but also for interpreting visual and auditory information. For example, if you see something in the upper-left portion of the visual field, your brain needs to know which direction your eyes are turned, the position of your head, and the tilt of your body before it can determine the location of whatever you see. The parietal lobe monitors all the information about eye, head, and body positions and passes it on to brain areas that control movement (Gross & Graziano, 1995). The parietal lobe is essential not only for spatial information but also numerical information (Hubbard, Piazza, Pinel, & Dehaene, 2005). That overlap makes sense when you consider all the ways in which numbers relate to space—including the fact that we initially use our fingers to count.

The Temporal Lobe

The **temporal lobe** is the lateral portion of each hemisphere, near the temples (see Figure 3.23). It is the primary cortical target for auditory information. The human temporal lobe—in most cases, the left temporal lobe—is essential for understanding spoken language. The temporal lobe also contributes to complex aspects of vision, including perception of movement and recognition of faces. A tumor in the temporal lobe may give rise to elaborate auditory or visual hallucinations, whereas a tumor in the occipital lobe

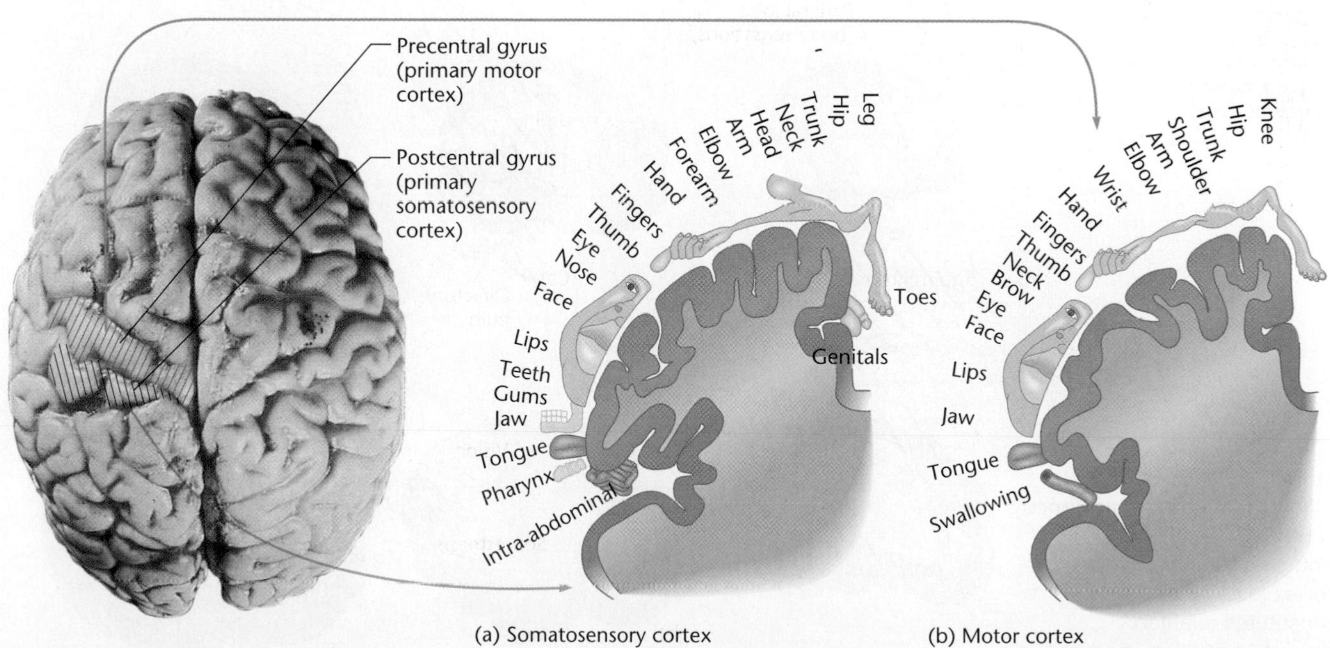

FIGURE 3.24 Approximate representation of sensory and motor information in the cortex
(a) Each location in the somatosensory cortex represents sensation from a different body part. (b) Each location in the motor cortex regulates movement of a different body part. *Source:* Based on Penfield & Rasmussen, 1950

ordinarily evokes only simple sensations, such as flashes of light. When psychiatric patients report hallucinations, brain scans detect extensive activity in the temporal lobes (Dierks et al., 1999).

The temporal lobes are also important for emotional and motivational behaviors. Temporal lobe damage can lead to a set of behaviors known as the **Klüver-Bucy syndrome** (named for the investigators who first described it). Previously wild and aggressive monkeys fail to display normal fears and anxieties after temporal lobe damage (Klüver & Bucy, 1939). They put almost anything they find into their mouths and attempt to pick up snakes and lighted matches (which intact monkeys consistently avoid). Interpreting this behavior is difficult. For example, a monkey might handle a snake because it is no longer afraid (an emotional change) or because it no longer recognizes what a snake is (a cognitive change). We explore these issues in the chapter on emotion.

The Frontal Lobe

The **frontal lobe**, containing the primary motor cortex and the prefrontal cortex, extends from the central sulcus to the anterior limit of the brain (see Figure 3.23). The posterior portion of the frontal lobe just anterior to the central sulcus, the **precentral gyrus**, is specialized for the control of fine movements, such as moving one finger at a time. Separate areas are responsible for different parts of the body, mostly on the contralateral (opposite) side but also with slight control of the ipsilateral (same) side. Figure 3.24b shows the traditional map of the precentral gyrus, also known as the *primary motor cortex*. However, the map is only an approximation. For example, within the arm area, there is no one-to-one relationship between brain location and specific muscles (Graziano, Taylor, & Moore, 2002).

The most anterior portion of the frontal lobe is the **prefrontal cortex**. In general, the larger a species' cerebral cortex, the larger percentage that the prefrontal cortex occupies (see Figure 3.25). For example, it forms a larger portion of the cortex in humans and the great apes than in other species (Semendeferi, Lu, Schenker, & Damasio, 2002). The dendrites in the prefrontal cortex have up to 16 times as many dendritic spines (see Figure 1.7) as neurons in other cortical areas (Elston, 2000). As a result, the prefrontal cortex integrates an enormous amount of information.

STOP&CHECK

10. Which lobe of the cerebral cortex includes the primary auditory cortex?

11. Which lobe of the cerebral cortex includes the primary somatosensory cortex?

12. Which lobe of the cerebral cortex includes the primary visual cortex?

13. Which lobe of the cerebral cortex includes the primary motor cortex?

ANSWERS

10. Temporal lobe **11.** Parietal lobe **12.** Occipital lobe **13.** Frontal lobe

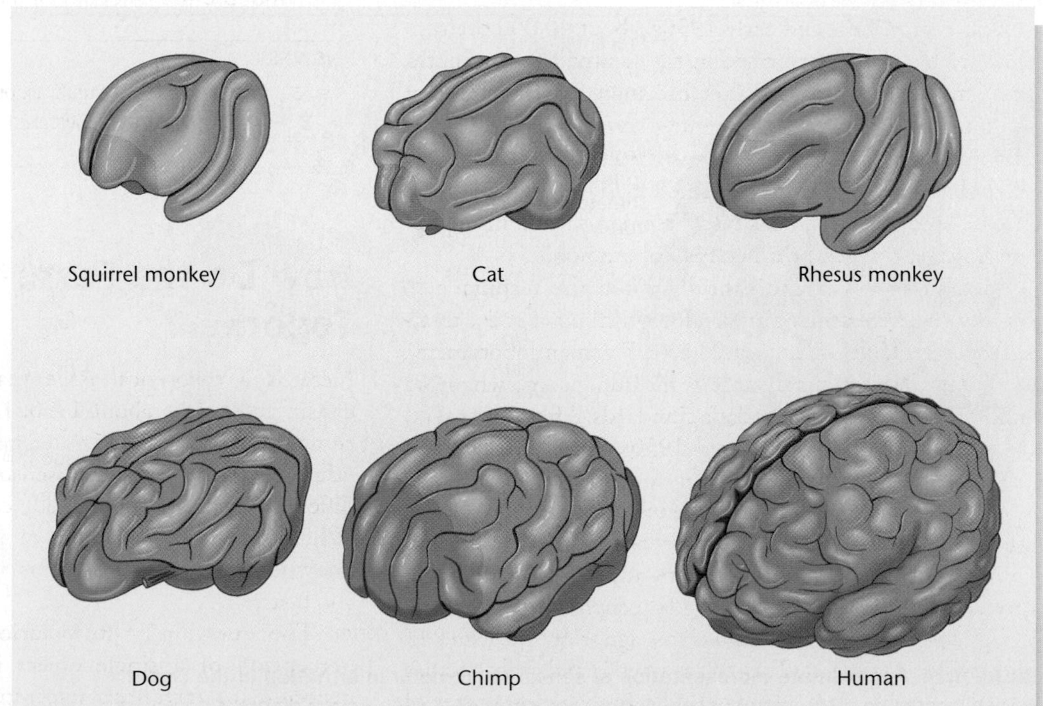

FIGURE 3.25 Species differences in prefrontal cortex
Note that the prefrontal cortex (blue area) constitutes a larger proportion of the human brain than of these other species. *Source:* Based on Fuster, 1989

The Rise and Fall of Prefrontal Lobotomies

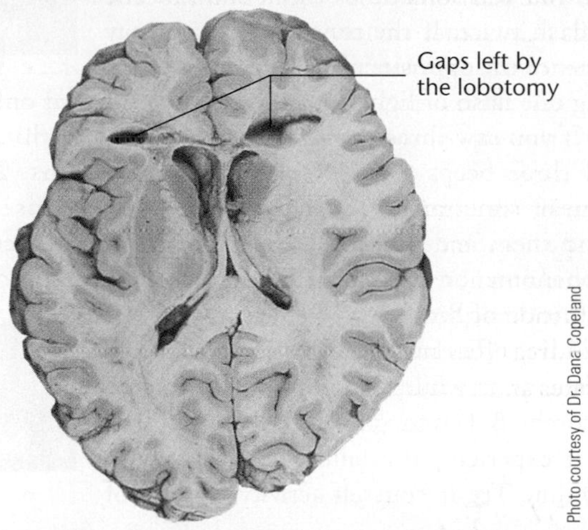

A horizontal section of the brain of a person who had a prefrontal lobotomy many years earlier. The two holes in the frontal cortex are the visible results of the operation.

You may have heard of the infamous procedure known as **prefrontal lobotomy**—surgical disconnection of the prefrontal cortex from the rest of the brain. The surgery consisted of damaging the prefrontal cortex or cutting its connections to the rest of the cortex. Lobotomy began with a report that damaging the prefrontal cortex of laboratory primates made them tamer without noticeably impairing their sensations or coordination. A few physicians reasoned loosely that the same operation might help people who suffered from severe, untreatable psychiatric disorders.

In the late 1940s and early 1950s, about 40,000 prefrontal lobotomies were performed in the United States (Shutts, 1982), many of them by Walter Freeman, a medical doctor untrained in surgery. His techniques were crude, even by the standards of the time, using such instruments as an electric drill and a metal pick. He performed many operations in his office or other nonhospital sites. (Freeman carried his equipment in his car, which he called his "lobotomobile.")

At first, Freeman and others limited the technique to people with severe schizophrenia, for which no effective treatment was available at the time. Later, Freeman lobotomized people with less serious disorders, including some whom we would consider normal by today's standards. After drug therapies became available in the mid-1950s, lobotomies quickly dropped out of favor.

Among the common consequences of prefrontal lobotomy were apathy, a loss of the ability to plan and take initiative, memory disorders, distractibility, and a loss of emotional expressions (Stuss & Benson, 1984). People with prefrontal damage lost their social inhibitions, ignoring the rules of polite, civilized conduct. They often acted impulsively because they failed to calculate adequately the probable outcomes of their behaviors.

Functions of the Prefrontal Cortex

The prefrontal cortex contributes to many functions. One of them is attention—that is, enhancing the response of other brain areas to the most relevant information and decreasing the response to distractors (Zanto, Rubens, Thangavel, & Gazzaley, 2011). Another is *working memory*, the ability to remember recent events, such as where you parked your car or what you were talking about before an interruption. People with damage to the prefrontal cortex have trouble on the **delayed-response task**, in which they see or hear something, and then have to respond to it after a delay.

The prefrontal cortex is also important for making decisions and planning movements. When you decide whether to do something, you consider the difficulty of the action, the probabilities of success and failure, and how valuable the possible reward would be to you right now. (For example, the chance to win a pizza becomes less valuable if you have just finished a meal. An opportunity to win a few extra-credit points is valuable if you think you are on the borderline between two grades, but less valuable otherwise.) Cells in the prefrontal cortex respond to all these complex factors (Hunt et al., 2012; Wallis, 2012). An unexpected outcome highly arouses many of these cells, as they update their response-outcome predictions (Alexander & Brown, 2011). People with prefrontal cortical damage often make decisions that seem impulsive, because they failed to weigh all the likely pros and cons.

STOP&CHECK

14. What are the functions of the prefrontal cortex?

ANSWER

14. The prefrontal cortex is especially important for attention, working memory, and weighing the pros and cons of a possible action.

How Do the Parts Work Together?

Here is a theoretical issue that researchers hardly even considered before about 1990: How do various brain areas combine to produce integrated behavior and experience? The visual, auditory, and somatosensory areas of the cortex are in different locations, only weakly connected with one another. When you hold your radio or iPod, how does your brain know that the object you see is also what you feel and what you hear?

The question of how various brain areas produce a perception of a single object is known as the **binding problem**, or *large-scale integration* problem. In an earlier era, researchers thought that various kinds of sensory information converged onto what they called the association areas of the cortex. Their guess was that those areas "associate" one sensation with another, or current sensations with memories of previous experiences. Later research found that the association areas perform advanced processing on a particular sensory system, such as vision or hearing, but relatively few cells combine one sense with another (Blanke, 2012). If different sensory paths don't converge, then how do you know that something you see is also what you hear or feel?

Although researchers cannot fully explain binding, they know what is necessary for it to occur: It occurs if you perceive two sensations as happening at the same time and in approximately the same place. For example, when a skilled ventriloquist makes the dummy's mouth move at the same time as his or her own speech, in nearly the same place, you perceive the sound as coming from the dummy. As part of this illusion, the visual stimulus alters the response of the auditory cortex, so that the sound really does seem to come from the same location as the dummy's mouth (Bonath et al., 2007; Bruns, Liebnau, & Röder, 2011). In contrast, if you watch a poorly dubbed foreign-language film, the lips do not move at the same time as the speech, and you perceive that the words did *not* come from those lips.

Applying these principles, researchers arranged a camera to video someone's back and sent the pictures to a three-dimensional display mounted to the person's head. The person viewed his or her own back, apparently 2 meters in front. Then someone stroked the participant's back, so that the person simultaneously felt the touch and saw the action, apparently 2 meters in front. After awhile, the person had what you might call an "out of body" experience, perceiving the body as being 2 meters in front of its real position. When asked, "please return to your seat," the person walked to a spot displaced from the actual seat, as if he or she had actually been forward (Lenggenhager, Tadi, Metzinger, & Blanke, 2007; see Figure 3.26).

Here is a demonstration you can try: If you see a light flash once while you hear two beeps, you will sometimes think you saw the light flash twice. If the tone is soft, you may experience the opposite: The tone beeps twice during one flash of light, and you think you heard only one beep. If you saw three flashes of light, you might think you heard three beeps (Andersen, Tiippana, & Sams, 2004). The near simultaneity of lights and sounds causes you to bind them and perceive an illusion. You can experience this phenomenon with the Online Try It Yourself activity, "Illustration of Binding."

Binding often fails if the displays are flashed very briefly or while the viewer is distracted (Holcombe & Cavanagh, 2001; Lehky, 2000). You can experience this failure of binding with the Online Try It Yourself activity "Failure of Binding."

Here is another great demonstration (I. H. Robertson, 2005). Position yourself parallel to a large mirror, as in Figure 3.27, so that you see your right hand and its reflection in the mirror. Keep your left hand out of sight. Now repeatedly clench and unclench both hands in unison. Wiggle your fingers, touch your thumb to each finger, and so forth, in each case doing the same thing with both hands at the same time. You will continually feel your left hand doing the same thing you see the hand in the mirror doing, which (being the mirror image of your right hand) looks like your left hand. After 2 or 3 minutes, you may start to feel that the hand in the mirror is your own left hand.

In a variant of this procedure, researchers arranged to touch someone's real right hand at the same time and in the same way as touching a rubber hand next to it, allowing the person to see both hands. Within minutes, people reported feeling that they had two right hands, in addition to the

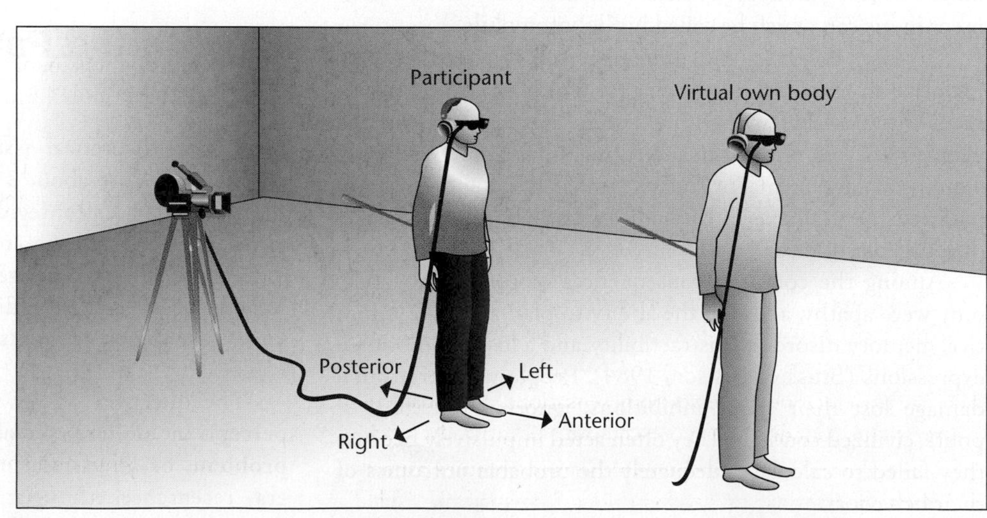

FIGURE 3.26 Where Am I? As someone stroked the person's back, a video camera relayed the information so the person could view it, appearing to be a few feet ahead. After a few minutes, the person felt as if the body were in fact a few feet ahead of where it was. Based on B. Lenggenhager, T. Tadi, T. Metzinger, & O. Blanke (2007). Video ergo sum: Manipulating bodily self-consciousness. *Science, 317,* pp. 1096–1099.

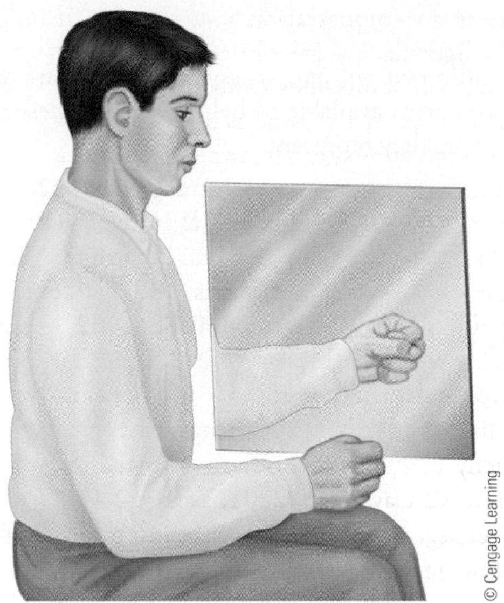

FIGURE 3.27 An illusion to demonstrate binding
Clench and unclench both hands while looking at your right hand and its reflection in the mirror. Keep your left hand out of sight. After a couple of minutes, you may start to experience the hand in the mirror as being your own left hand.

unseen left hand (Guterstam, Petkova, & Ehrsson, 2011). So, the evidence indicates that we bind two experiences that occur at the same time. Still, the theoretical question remains of exactly how we do so.

STOP & CHECK

15. What is meant by the binding problem, and what is necessary for binding to occur?

ANSWER

15. The binding problem is the question of how the brain combines activity in different brain areas to produce unified perception and coordinated behavior. Binding requires identifying the location of an object and perceiving sight, sound, and other aspects of a stimulus as being simultaneous. When the sight and sound appear to come from the same location at the same time, we bind them as a single experience.

MODULE 3.2 ■ IN CLOSING

Functions of the Cerebral Cortex

The human cerebral cortex is so large that we easily slip into thinking of it as "the" brain. In fact, only mammals have a true cerebral cortex, and many animals produce impressive, complex behaviors without a cerebral cortex.

What, then, is the function of the cerebral cortex? The primary function seems to be one of elaborating sensory material. Even fish, which have no cerebral cortex, can see, hear, and so forth, but they do not recognize and remember all the complex aspects of sensory stimuli that mammals do. The cerebral cortex takes information and analyzes it in great detail.

Summary

1. Although brain size varies among mammalian species, the overall organization is similar. **80**
2. The cerebral cortex has six laminae (layers) of neurons. A given lamina may be absent from certain parts of the cortex. For example, the lamina responsible for sensory input is absent from the motor cortex. The cortex is organized into columns of cells arranged perpendicular to the laminae. **80**
3. The occipital lobe of the cortex is primarily responsible for vision. Damage to part of the occipital lobe leads to blindness in part of the visual field. **82**
4. The parietal lobe processes body sensations. The postcentral gyrus contains four representations of the body. **83**
5. The temporal lobe contributes to hearing, complex aspects of vision, and processing of emotional information. **83**
6. The frontal lobe includes the precentral gyrus, which controls fine movements. It also includes the prefrontal cortex, which contributes to memories of recent stimuli and planning of movements. **84**
7. The prefrontal cortex is important for working memory and for planning actions that depend on the context. **85**
8. The binding problem is the question of how we connect activities in different brain areas, such as sights and sounds. The various brain areas do not all send their information to a single central processor. **85**
9. Binding requires perceiving that two aspects of a stimulus (such as sight and sound) occurred at the same place at the same time. **86**

Key Terms

Terms are defined in the module on the page number indicated. They're also presented in alphabetical order with definitions in the book's Subject Index/Glossary. Interactive flash cards, audio reviews, and crossword puzzles are among the online resources available to help you learn these terms and the concepts they represent.

anterior commissure **80**
binding problem **85**
central sulcus **82**
cerebral cortex **80**
columns **81**
corpus callosum **80**
delayed-response task **85**
frontal lobe **84**
Klüver-Bucy syndrome **84**
laminae **80**
occipital lobe **82**
parietal lobe **82**
postcentral gyrus **82**
prefrontal cortex **84**
prefrontal lobotomy **85**
primates **80**
temporal lobe **82**

Thought Question

When monkeys with Klüver-Bucy syndrome pick up lighted matches and snakes, we do not know whether they are displaying an emotional deficit or an inability to identify the object. What kind of research method might help answer this question?

MODULE 3.2 End of Module Quiz

1. If we compare the brains of humans to those of smaller mammals, which of these patterns do we find?
   a. The location of the visual cortex varies relative to other brain areas.
   b. The proportion of the brain devoted to the cerebral cortex is smaller in humans.
   c. The proportion of the brain devoted to the cerebellum is about the same.
   d. The relative size of the midbrain is larger in humans.
2. Which of these is in the temporal lobe of the cerebral cortex?
   a. Primary visual cortex
   b. Primary auditory cortex
   c. Primary somatosensory cortex
   d. Primary motor cortex
3. Which of these is in the parietal lobe of the cerebral cortex?
   a. Primary visual cortex
   b. Primary auditory cortex
   c. Primary somatosensory cortex
   d. Primary motor cortex
4. Which of these is in the occipital lobe of the cerebral cortex?
   a. Primary visual cortex
   b. Primary auditory cortex
   c. Primary somatosensory cortex
   d. Primary motor cortex
5. Which of these is in the frontal lobe of the cerebral cortex?
   a. Primary visual cortex
   b. Primary auditory cortex
   c. Primary somatosensory cortex
   d. Primary motor cortex
6. The main functions of the prefrontal cortex include which of the following?
   a. Perceiving the location of body parts in space
   b. Providing a pool of immature neurons to replace those damaged in other brain areas
   c. Coordination of slow, repetitive movements
   d. Working memory and weighing the pros and cons of a possible action
7. Which of the following is necessary for binding to occur?
   a. Perceiving different aspects of a sensation as coming from the same location
   b. Correctly perceiving the size and shape of a stimulus
   c. Perceiving the direction of movement of an object
   d. Correctly perceiving the color of an object

ANSWERS:
1c, 2b, 3c, 4a, 5d, 6d, 7a.

MODULE 3.3

Research Methods

Describing the structure of the brain is difficult enough, but the real challenge is to discover how it works. Throughout the text, we shall consider many research methods as they become relevant. However, most methods fall into a few categories. This module provides an overview of those categories and the logic behind them:

1. *Examine the effects of brain damage.* After damage or temporary inactivation, what aspects of behavior are impaired?
2. *Examine the effects of stimulating a brain area.* Ideally, if damaging some area impairs a behavior, stimulating that area should enhance the behavior.
3. *Record brain activity during behavior.* We might record changes in brain activity during fighting, sleeping, finding food, solving a problem, or any other behavior.
4. *Correlate brain anatomy with behavior.* Do people with some unusual behavior also have unusual brains? If so, in what way?

Effects of Brain Damage

In 1861, the French neurologist Paul Broca found that a patient who had lost the ability to speak had damage in part of his left frontal cortex. Additional patients with loss of speech also showed damage in and around that area, now known as *Broca's area*. This discovery revolutionized neurology, as many other physicians at the time doubted that different brain areas had different functions at all.

Since then, researchers have made countless reports of behavioral impairments after brain damage. Brain damage can produce an inability to recognize faces, an inability to perceive motion, a shift of attention to the right side of the body and world, changes in motivation and emotion, memory impairments, and a host of other highly specialized effects.

Many of the most interesting results come from humans with brain damage, but human studies have their limitations. Few people have damage confined to just one brain area, and no two people have exactly the same damage. Therefore researchers often turn to producing carefully localized damage in laboratory animals. An **ablation** is a removal of a brain area, generally with a surgical knife. Because surgical removal is difficult for tiny structures below the surface of the brain, researchers sometimes make a **lesion**, meaning damage, by means of a **stereotaxic instrument,** a device for the precise placement of electrodes in the brain (see Figure 3.28). By consulting a stereotaxic atlas (map) of a species' brain, a researcher aims an electrode at the desired position relative to landmarks on the skull. The researcher anesthetizes an animal, drills a small hole in the skull, inserts the electrode (insulated except at the tip), lowers it to the target, and passes an electrical current just sufficient to damage that area. For example, researchers have made lesions in parts of the hypothalamus to explore their contributions to eating and drinking. After the death of the animal, someone takes slices of its brain, applies stains, and verifies the actual location of the damage.

Suppose a researcher makes a lesion and reports some behavioral deficit. You might ask, "How do we know the deficit wasn't caused by anesthetizing the animal, drilling a hole in its skull, and lowering an electrode to this target?" To test this possibility, an experimenter produces a *sham lesion* in a control

James W. Kalat

FIGURE 3.28 A stereotaxic instrument for locating brain areas in small animals
Using this device, researchers can insert an electrode to stimulate, record from, or damage any point in the brain.

group, performing all the same procedures except for passing the electrical current. Any behavioral difference between the two groups must result from the lesion and not the other procedures.

An electric lesion is a crude technique that damages axons passing by that area as well as the neurons in the area itself. Researchers use this method less often today than in the past. Instead, they might inject chemicals that kill neurons, or disable them temporarily, without harming the passing axons (Rudebeck, Saunders, Prescott, Chau, & Murray, 2013). Another option is the *gene-knockout approach* that directs a mutation to a gene that is important for one type of cell, transmitter, or receptor (Joyner & Guillemot, 1994).

Transcranial magnetic stimulation (**TMS**), the application of magnetic stimulation to a portion of the scalp, inactivates neurons in a narrow area below the magnet, producing a "virtual lesion" that outlasts the magnetic stimulation itself (Dayan, Censor, Buch, Sandrini, & Cohen, 2013). This procedure enables researchers to study behavior with some brain area active, then inactive, and then active again. Figure 3.29 shows the apparatus. For example, one study found that after TMS silenced the hand area of the motor cortex, people had trouble with a task of mentally rotating the hand in a picture to imagine how it would look from a different angle (Ganis, Keenan, Kosslyn, & Pascual-Leone, 2000). That is, when you imagine seeing your hand from a different angle, you imagine moving it, not just seeing it move.

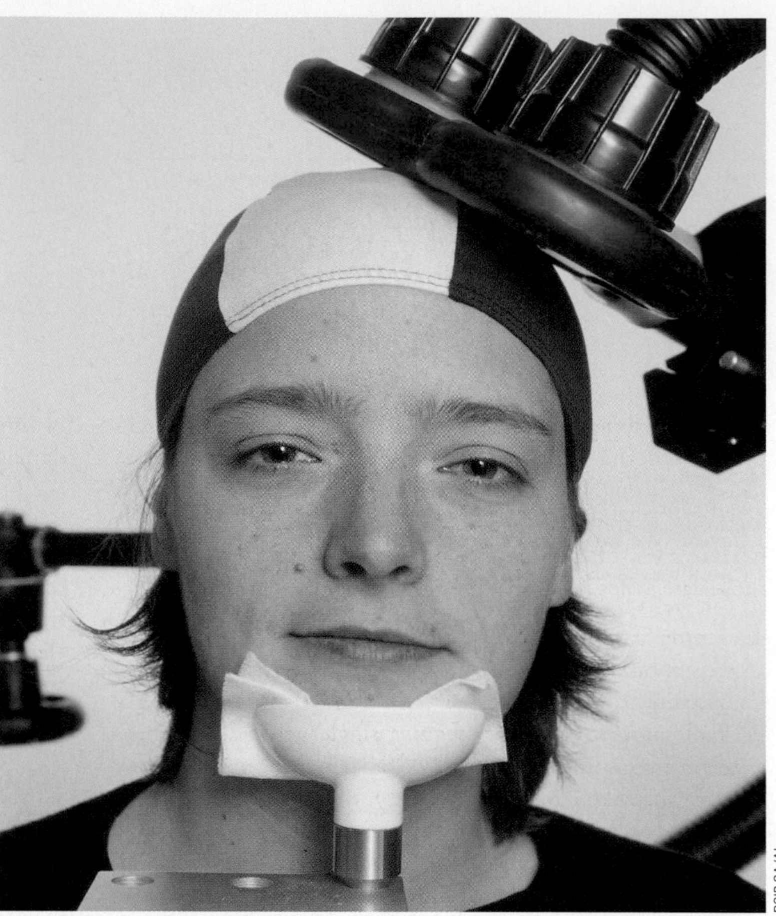

BSIP SA/Alamy

FIGURE 3.29 Apparatus for magnetic stimulation of a human brain
The procedure is known as transcranial magnetic stimulation, or TMS.

After any kind of brain damage or inactivation, the problem for psychologists is to specify the exact behavioral deficit. By analogy, suppose you cut a wire in a television and the picture disappears. Evidently that wire is necessary for the picture, but why? Similarly, if you damage a brain area and the animal stops eating, you don't know why. Did it lose its hunger? Its ability to taste food? Its ability to find the food? Its ability to move at all? You would need further behavioral tests to narrow down the possibilities.

STOP&CHECK

16. What is the difference between a lesion and an ablation?

ANSWER

16. A lesion is damage to a structure. An ablation is removal of the structure. For example, a blood clot might produce a lesion, whereas surgery could produce an ablation.

Effects of Brain Stimulation

If brain damage impairs some behavior, stimulation should increase it. The old-fashioned way is to insert an electrode into an animal's brain and deliver brief, mild currents to stimulate one area or another. That method has some value, but its limitation is that a given area may have many types of neurons with varying functions. The electrical current stimulates all of them, as well as passing axons.

In the early 2000s, Karl Deisseroth pioneered a method called **optogenetics**, using light to control a limited population of neurons. First the researcher uses a specially manipulated virus to insert light-sensitive proteins into the membrane of a given type of neuron. One protein reacts to light by opening a sodium channel, exciting the neuron. Another reacts by opening a chloride channel, producing inhibition. The virus can be altered chemically so that it delivers one of these proteins only to a certain type of neuron, or even to just one part of the neuron, such as the axon or the dendrites (Packer, Roska, & Häusser, 2013). The investigator implants a very thin optical fiber into the brain, making it possible to shine light that affects only the type of neuron containing the light-sensitive protein. The investigator can then control the excitation or inhibition of those cells in a small brain area with millisecond accuracy. This method lets researchers study the function of given cells in greater detail than ever before. A few physicians have begun applying optogenetics to human patients to try to control narcolepsy (a sleep disorder) and other conditions.

STOP&CHECK

17. What determines whether optogenetic stimulation excites a neuron or inhibits it?

ANSWER

17. Optogenetic stimulation activates a light-sensitive protein. If that protein opens a sodium channel in the membrane, the result is excitation of the neuron. If it opens a chloride channel, the result is inhibition.

Recording Brain Activity

Suppose damage to some brain area impairs a behavior (eating, for example) and stimulation of that area increases the behavior. We can strengthen the conclusion by showing that the area increases its activity during spontaneous occurrences of the behavior. We might also use brain recordings for exploratory purposes: During a given behavior or cognitive activity, which brain areas increase their activity?

With laboratory animals, one method is to insert an electrode to record activity from a single neuron. We shall consider examples of this method in the chapter on vision. Another technique takes advantage of the fact that zebra fish during their larval stage have transparent bodies. By modifying one gene, researchers can cause neurons to fluoresce when they produce action potentials. They can then watch as one neuron after another responds to some event, such as a visual stimulus (Muto, Ohkura, Abe, Nakai, & Kawakami, 2013).

Studies of human brains almost always use noninvasive methods—that is, recordings from outside the skull. An **electroencephalograph (EEG)** records electrical activity of the brain through electrodes—ranging from just a few to more than a hundred—attached to the scalp (see Figure 3.30). Electrodes glued to the scalp measure the average activity at any moment for the population of cells under the electrode. The output is then amplified and recorded. This device can record spontaneous brain activity or activity in response to a stimulus, in which case we call the results **evoked potentials** or **evoked responses**. Evoked responses are useful for many purposes, including studies of infants too young to give verbal answers (Parise & Csibra, 2012).

A **magnetoencephalograph (MEG)** is similar, but instead of measuring electrical activity, it measures the faint magnetic fields generated by brain activity (Hari, 1994). Like EEG, an MEG recording identifies the approximate location of activity to within about a centimeter. An MEG has excellent temporal resolution, showing changes from one millisecond to the next.

Figure 3.31 shows an MEG record of brain responses to a brief tone heard in the right ear. The diagram represents a human head as viewed from above, with the nose at the top (Hari, 1994). Researchers using an MEG can identify the times at which various brain areas respond and thereby trace a wave of brain activity from its point of origin to the other areas that process it (Salmelin, Hari, Lounasmaa, & Sams, 1994).

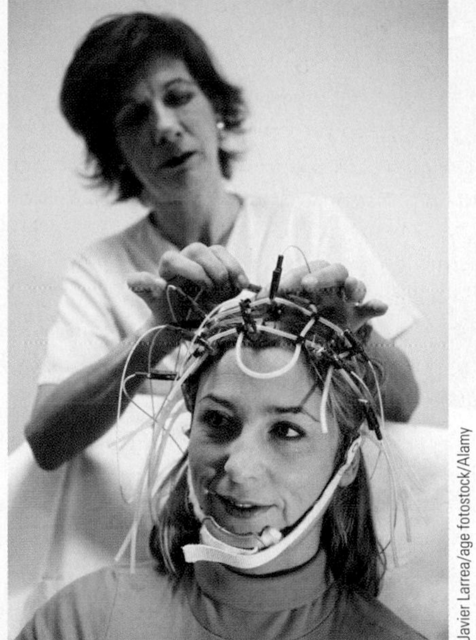

Javier Larrea/age fotostock/Alamy

FIGURE 3.30 Electroencephalography
An electroencephalograph records the overall activity of neurons under various electrodes attached to the scalp.

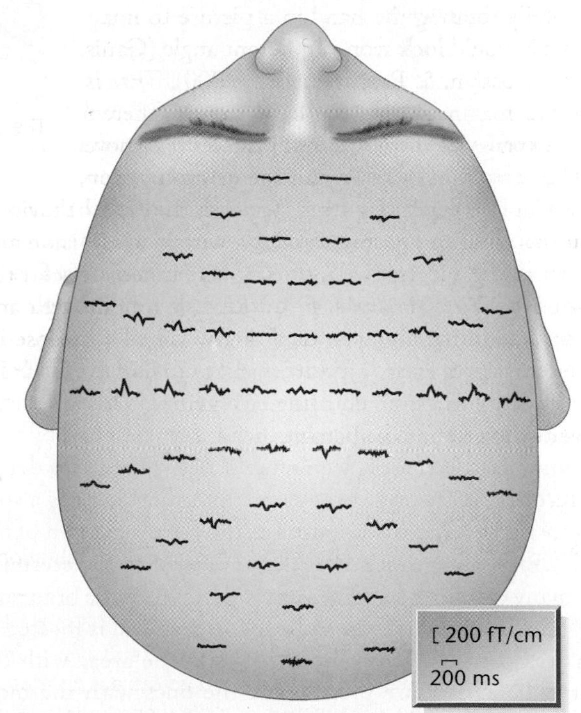

FIGURE 3.31 A result of magnetoencephalography, showing responses to a tone in the right ear
The nose is shown at the top. For each spot on the diagram, the display shows the changing response over a few hundred milliseconds following the tone. (Note calibration at lower right.) The tone evoked responses in many areas, with the largest responses in the temporal cortex, especially on the left side. *Source:* Based on *Neuroscience: From the Molecular to the Cognitive*, by R. Hari, 1994, p. 165.

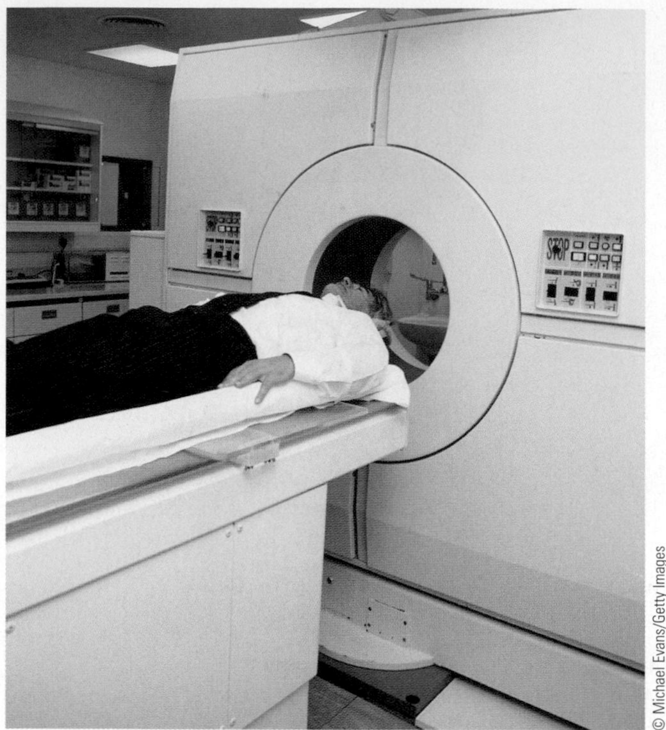

FIGURE 3.32 A PET scanner
A person engages in a cognitive task while attached to this apparatus that records which areas of the brain become more active and by how much.

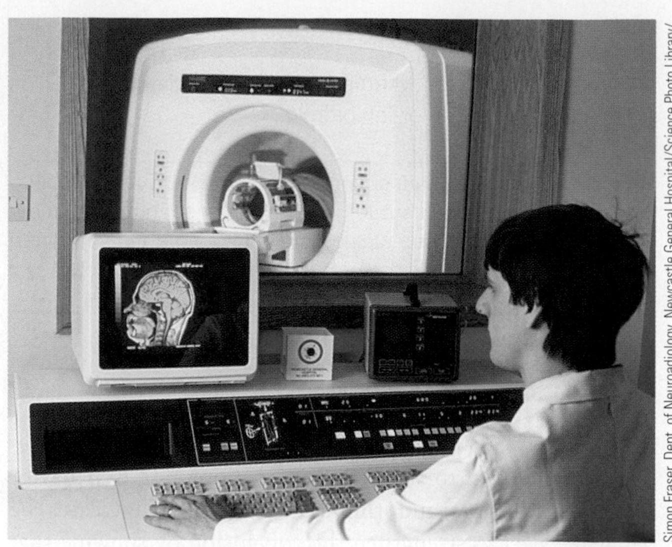

FIGURE 3.33 An fMRI scan of a human brain
An fMRI produces an image with a spatial resolution of 1 to 2 mm and temporal resolution of about a second.

Positron-emission tomography (PET) provides a high-resolution image of activity in a living brain by recording the emission of radioactivity from injected chemicals. First, the person receives an injection of glucose or some other chemical containing radioactive atoms. Glucose use increases in the most active brain areas, so tracking the levels of glucose tells us something about brain activity. When a radioactive atom decays, it releases a positron that immediately collides with a nearby electron, emitting two gamma rays in exactly opposite directions. The person's head is surrounded by a set of gamma ray detectors (see Figure 3.32). When two detectors record gamma rays at the same time, they identify a spot halfway between those detectors as the point of origin of the gamma rays. A computer uses this information to determine how many gamma rays came from each spot in the brain and therefore how much of the radioactive chemical is located in each area (Phelps & Mazziotta, 1985). The areas with the most radioactivity are presumably the ones with the most active neurons.

PET scans use radioactive chemicals with a short half-life, made in a device called a cyclotron. Because cyclotrons are expensive, PET is available only at research hospitals. Furthermore, PET requires exposing the brain to radioactivity. For most purposes, researchers have replaced PET scans with **functional magnetic resonance imaging (fMRI)**, which is less expensive and less risky. Standard MRI scans record the energy released by water molecules after removal of a magnetic field. (We consider more details about this method later.) An fMRI is a modified version of MRI based on hemoglobin (the blood protein that binds oxygen) instead of water (Detre & Floyd, 2001). Hemoglobin with oxygen reacts to a magnetic field differently from hemoglobin without oxygen. Researchers set the fMRI scanner to detect the amount of hemoglobin with oxygen (Viswanathan & Freeman, 2007). When a brain area becomes more active, two relevant changes occur: First, blood vessels dilate to allow more blood flow to the area. Second, as the brain area uses oxygen, the percentage of hemoglobin with oxygen decreases. An fMRI scan responds to both of these processes (Sirotin, Hillman, Bordier, & Das, 2009). Figure 3.33 shows an example.

An fMRI while you were, for example, reading would mean nothing without a comparison to something else. Researchers would record your brain activity while you were reading and during a comparison task and then subtract the brain activity during the comparison task to determine which areas are more active during reading. As a comparison task, for example, researchers might ask you to look at a page written in a language you do not understand. That task would activate visual areas just as the reading task did, but it presumably would not activate the language areas of your brain. Figure 3.34 illustrates the idea.

The fMRI method produces spectacular pictures, but the importance of the provided information is in many cases debatable (Rugg & Thompson-Schill, 2013). For example, researchers found that people who crave chocolate show a greater than average brain response to the sight of chocolate (Rolls & McCabe, 2007). Does this result tell us *why* some people like chocolate so much? Hardly. Nevertheless, fMRI does sometimes provide valuable

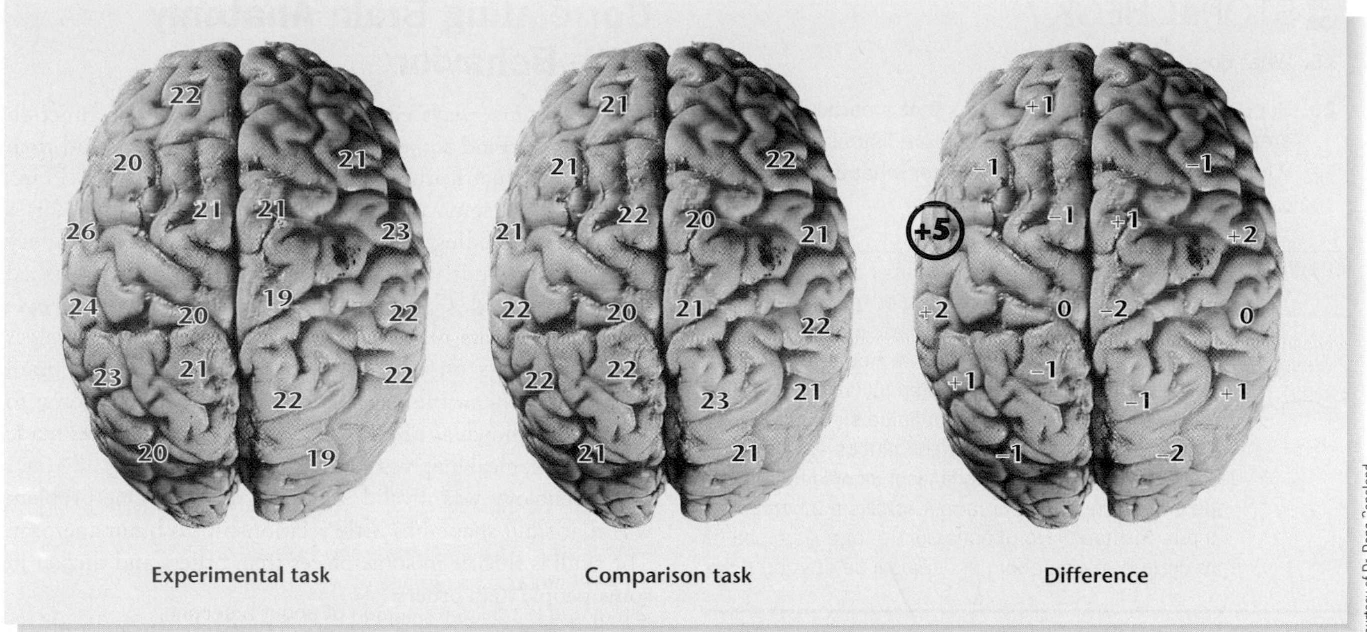

Courtesy of Dr. Dana Copeland

FIGURE 3.34 Subtraction for a brain scan procedure
Numbers on the brain at the left show hypothetical levels of arousal during some task, measured in arbitrary units. The brain at the center shows activity during the same brain areas during a comparison task. The brain at the right shows the differences. The highlighted area shows the largest difference. In actual data, the largest increases in activity would be one-tenth or two-tenths of a percent.

psychological information. Let's quickly consider some examples:

1. Many people in pain report decreased pain after they receive a placebo (a drug with no pharmacological activity). Do they really feel less pain, or are they just saying so? Studies with fMRI show that brain areas responsible for pain really do decrease their response (Wager & Atlas, 2013).
2. As we shall consider in more detail in the memory chapter, psychologists find it useful to distinguish several types of memory, such as implicit versus explicit and declarative versus procedural. One view is that any given task falls into one category or the other. In that case, we might expect that one type of memory activates one set of brain areas and another type activates other areas. An alternative view is that we process memory with several components, some of which pertain mostly to one type of memory and others that pertain to a different type of memory. The fMRI data fit that view better: Most memory tasks activate a wide array of brain areas to varying degrees (Cabeza & Moscovitch, 2013).
3. When you are just sitting there with nothing expected of you, is your brain really doing nothing? Definitely not. You do "mind wandering," which activates diffuse areas called the brain's "default system" (Corballis, 2012; M. F. Mason et al., 2007). These same areas are also active when people recall past experiences or imagine future experiences (Immordino-Yang, Christodoulou, & Singh, 2012). However, a task requiring focused attention decreases the activity of this default system, unless your mind is wandering (Weissman, Roberts, Visscher, & Woldorff, 2006)!

Interpreting fMRI results is a complex task. Suppose researchers find that some area becomes more active while people process emotional information. If we see that area active again at a later time, can we assume that the person is feeling an emotion? We cannot, unless we are sure the area is active *only* during emotional processing.

The best way to test our understanding is this: If we think we know what a given fMRI pattern means, we should be able to use that pattern to identify what someone is doing or thinking. That is, we should be able to use it to read someone's mind, to a limited degree. In one study, researchers used fMRI to record brain activity from people as they were falling asleep. People typically have some visual imagery at that time, but not quite a dream. The researchers repeatedly awakened these people, asked them to report their visual imagery, and compared the reports to the fMRI data. After enough repetitions, they were able to use the fMRI data to predict approximately what imagery the people were about to report (Horikawa, Tamaki, Miyawaki, & Kamitani, 2013).

How far can this procedure go? At this point we can read people's minds in only this very limited way, and only after prolonged testing on a given individual. It would be hazardous to guess how far the procedure might or might not develop in the future. The main point is that trying to read people's minds (in this limited way) tests how well we understand what the brain recordings mean.

STOP&CHECK

19. What does fMRI measure?

20. Suppose someone demonstrates that a particular brain area becomes active when people are listening to music. When that area becomes active later, what if anything can we conclude?

ANSWER

19. It detects an increase in blood flow to a brain area immediately after an increase in brain activity, and it also detects a slightly slower increase in the percentage of hemoglobin lacking oxygen. **20.** Without further evidence, we should not draw any conclusion. Perhaps the person is listening to music again, but this area may perform functions other than listening to music. A good test of how well we understand the area would be to find out whether we can use fMRI recordings to guess which type of music someone is hearing (or whether they are listening at all).

Correlating Brain Anatomy with Behavior

One of the first ways ever used for studying brain function sounds easy: Find someone with unusual behavior and then look for unusual features of the brain. In the 1800s, Franz Gall observed some people with excellent verbal memories who had protruding eyes. He inferred that verbal memory depended on brain areas behind the eyes that had pushed the eyes forward. Gall then examined the skulls of people with other talents or personalities. He assumed that bulges and depressions on their skull corresponded to the brain areas below them. His process of relating skull anatomy to behavior is known as **phrenology**. One of his followers made the phrenological map in Figure 3.35.

Phrenology was invalid for many reasons. One problem was that skull shape has little relationship to brain anatomy. The skull is thicker in some places than others and thicker in some people than others.

Today, researchers examine detailed brain anatomy in detail in living people. One method is **computerized axial tomography**, better known as a **CT** or **CAT scan** (Andreasen, 1988). A physician injects a dye into the blood (to increase contrast in the image) and then places the person's head into a CT scanner like the one shown in Figure 3.36a. X-rays are passed through the head and recorded by detectors on the opposite side. The CT scanner is rotated slowly until a measurement has been taken at each angle over 180 degrees. From the measurements, a computer constructs images of the brain. Figure 3.36b is an example. CT scans help detect tumors and other structural abnormalities.

Another method is **magnetic resonance imaging (MRI)** (Warach, 1995), based on the fact that any atom with an odd-numbered atomic weight, such as hydrogen, has an axis of rotation. An MRI device applies a powerful magnetic field (about 25,000 times the magnetic field of the Earth) to align all the axes of rotation, and then tilts them with a brief radio frequency field. When the radio frequency field is turned off, the atomic nuclei release electromagnetic energy as they relax and return to their original axis. By measuring that energy, MRI devices form an image of the brain, such as the one in Figure 3.37. MRI shows anatomical details smaller than a millimeter in diameter. One drawback is that the person must

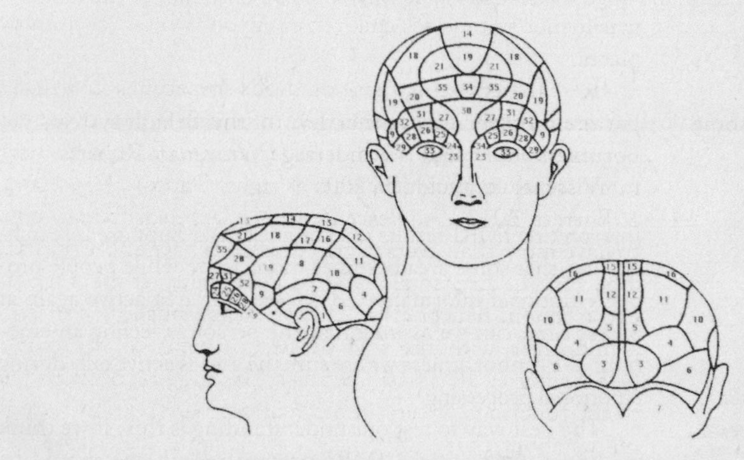

Affective Faculties		Intellectual Faculties	
Propensities	**Sentiments**	**Perceptive**	**Reflective**
? Desire to live	10 Cautiousness	22 Individuality	34 Comparison
• Alimentiveness	11 Approbativeness	23 Configuration	35 Causality
1 Destructiveness	12 Self-esteem	24 Size	
2 Amativeness	13 Benevolence	25 Weight and resistance	
3 Philoprogenitiveness	14 Reverence	26 Coloring	
4 Adhesiveness	15 Firmness	27 Locality	
5 Inhabitiveness	16 Conscientiousness	28 Order	
6 Combativeness	17 Hope	29 Calculation	
7 Secretiveness	18 Marvelousness	30 Eventuality	
8 Acquisitiveness	19 Ideality	31 Time	
9 Constructiveness	20 Mirthfulness	32 Tune	
	21 Imitation	33 Language	

FIGURE 3.35 A phrenologist's map of the brain
Neuroscientists today also try to localize functions in the brain, but they use more careful methods and they study such functions as vision and hearing, not "secretiveness" and "marvelousness." *Source:* From Spurzheim, 1908

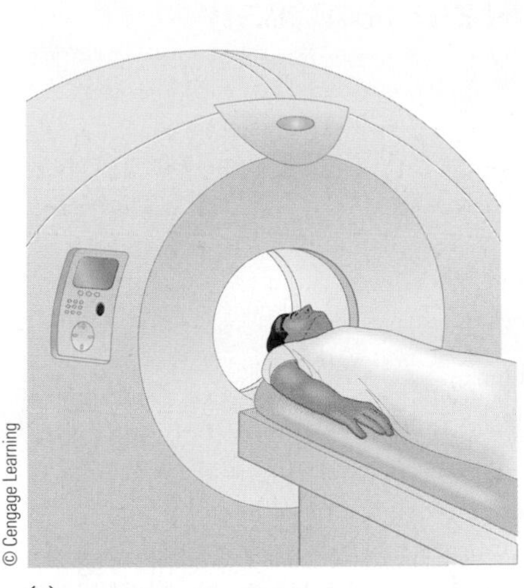

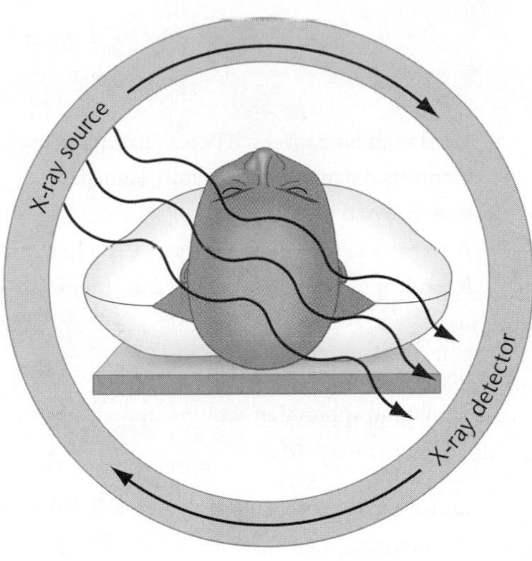

(a)

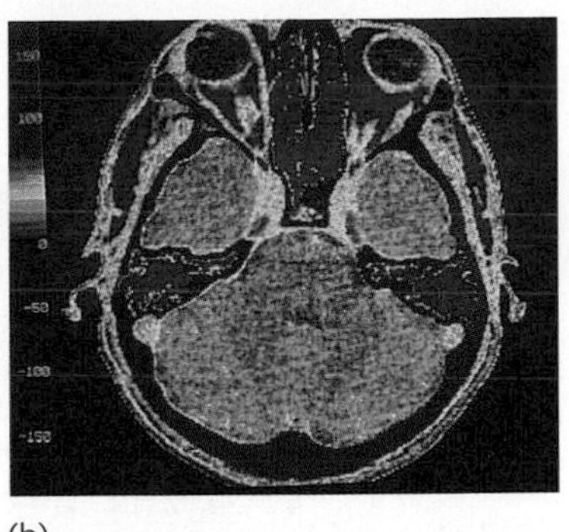

(b)

FIGURE 3.36 CT scanner
(a) A person's head is placed into the device and then a rapidly rotating source sends X-rays through the head while detectors on the opposite side make photographs. A computer then constructs an image of the brain. (b) A view of a normal human brain generated by computerized axial tomography CT scanning. *Source:* Dan McCoy/Rainbow

FIGURE 3.37 A view of a living brain generated by magnetic resonance imaging
Any atom with an odd-numbered atomic weight, such as hydrogen, has an inherent rotation. An outside magnetic field can align the axes of rotation. A radio frequency field can then make all these atoms move like tiny gyros. When the radio frequency field is turned off, the atomic nuclei release electromagnetic energy as they relax. By measuring that energy, we can obtain an image of a structure such as the brain without damaging it.

lie motionless in a confining, noisy apparatus. The procedure is usually not suitable for children or anyone who fears enclosed places.

Researchers using these methods sometimes find that a particular brain area is enlarged in certain types of people. For example, people with a larger amygdala tend to have more social contacts (Bickart, Wright, Dautoff, Dickerson, & Barrett, 2011). Adolescents with a large vocabulary tend to have more than average gray matter in part of the parietal lobe (H. L. Lee et al., 2007). Personality traits such as extraversion, neuroticism, and conscientiousness correlate significantly with the size of certain areas of the cortex (De Young et al., 2010). Studies like these give us a hint to the functions of certain brain areas. However, they don't tell us about cause and effect. For example, we don't know whether having much gray matter in the parietal lobe helps people develop a large vocabulary, or whether developing a large vocabulary leads to growth of relevant gray matter. Table 3.5 summarizes various methods of studying brain-behavior relationships.

STOP&CHECK

21. What are the similarities and differences between MRI and fMRI?

ANSWER

21. Both methods measure the responses of brain chemicals to a magnetic field. MRI shows the anatomy of the brain. The fMRI method shows which brain areas are most active at the moment.

TABLE 3.5

Examine Effects of Brain Damage	
Study victims of stroke, etc.	Used with humans; each person has different damage
Lesion	Controlled damage in laboratory animals
Ablation	Removal of a brain area
Gene knockout	Affects wherever that gene is active (e.g., a receptor)
Transcranial magnetic stimulation	Intense application temporarily inactivates a brain area
Examine Effects of Stimulating a Brain Area	
Stimulating electrodes	Invasive; used with laboratory animals, seldom with humans
Transcranial magnetic stimulation	Brief, mild application activates underlying brain area
Record Brain Activity during Behavior	
Record from electrodes in brain	Invasive; used with laboratory animals, seldom humans
Electroencephalograph (EEG)	Records from scalp; measures changes by milliseconds, but with low resolution of location of the signal
Evoked potentials	Similar to EEG but in response to stimuli
Magnetoencephalograph (MEG)	Similar to EEG but measures magnetic fields
Positron emission tomography (PET)	Measures changes over both time and location but requires exposing brain to radiation
Functional magnetic resonance imaging (fMRI)	Measures changes over about 1 second, identifies location within 1 to 2 mm, no use of radiation
Correlate Brain Anatomy with Behavior	
Computerized axial tomography (CAT)	Maps brain areas, but requires exposure to X-rays
Magnetic resonance imaging (MRI)	Maps brain areas in detail, using magnetic fields

Brain Size and Intelligence

Let's consider in more detail a specific example of correlating brain structure with behavior: What is the relationship between brain size and intelligence? It seems natural to assume that bigger brains are better, but it's not that simple.

In the 1800s and early 1900s, several societies arose whose members agreed to donate their brains after death for research into the brains of eminent people. No conclusion resulted. The brains of the eminent varied considerably, as did those of less eminent people. If brain anatomy was related to intellect in any way, the relation wasn't obvious (Burrell, 2004). (Of course, achieving eminence depends largely on opportunity and luck, not just intellectual ability.) Still, the idea lingers: Even if brain size isn't strongly related to intelligence, shouldn't it have *some* relationship?

Comparisons across Species

All mammalian brains have the same organization, but they differ greatly in size. Do variations in brain size relate to animal intelligence? We humans like to think of ourselves as the most intelligent animals—after all, we get to define what intelligence means! However, humans do not have the largest brains. Sperm whales' brains are eight times larger than ours, and elephants' are four times larger. Perhaps, many people suggest, intelligence depends on brain-to-body ratio. Figure 3.38 illustrates the relationship between logarithm of body mass and logarithm of brain mass for various vertebrates (Jerison, 1985). Note that the species we regard as most intelligent—such as, ahem, ourselves—have larger brains in proportion to body size than do the species we consider less impressive, such as frogs.

However, brain-to-body ratio has problems also: Chihuahuas have the highest brain-to-body ratio of all dog breeds, not because they were bred for intelligence but because

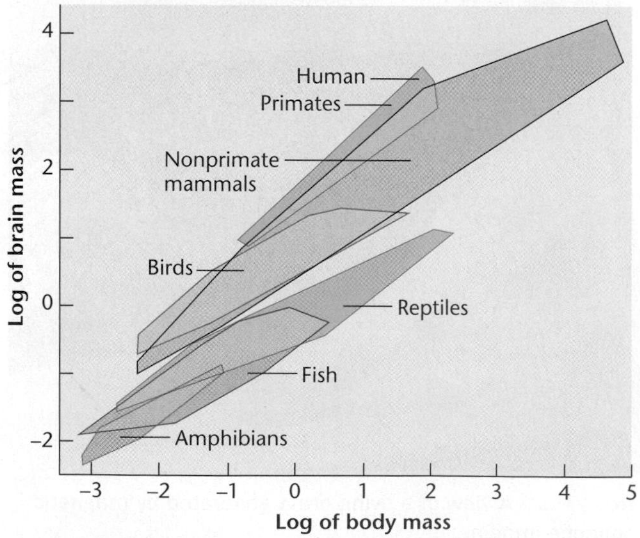

FIGURE 3.38 Relationship of brain mass to body mass across species
Each species is one point within one of the polygons. In general, log of body mass is a good predictor of log of brain mass. Primates in general and humans in particular have a large brain mass in proportion to body mass. *Source:* Adapted from Jerison, 1985

they were bred for small bodies (Deacon, 1997). Squirrel monkeys, which are also very thin, have a higher brain-to-body ratio than humans. (And with the increasing prevalence of human obesity, our brain-to-body ratio is declining!) The elephant-nose fish, which you might keep in an aquarium, has a 3 percent brain-to-body ratio compared to 2 percent for humans (Nilsson, 1999). The tiniest ants have a 15 percent brain-to-body ratio (Seid, Castillo, & Wcislo, 2011). So neither total brain mass nor brain-to-body ratio puts humans in first place.

Further problems: Some species have larger neurons than others, so brain size is a poor indicator of the number of neurons (Herculano-Houzel, 2011). Also, we lack a useful definition of animal intelligence (Macphail, 1985). No test could fairly compare elephants, chimpanzees, and dolphins; each species is intelligent in its own way. Given that studies of brain and behavior in nonhumans are not helping, let's abandon that effort and turn to humans.

STOP & CHECK

22. Why are both brain size and brain-to-body ratio unsatisfactory ways of estimating animal intelligence?

ANSWER

22. If we consider ourselves to be the most intelligent species, we are confronted with the fact that we have neither the largest brains nor the highest brain-to-body ratios. Brain-to-body ratio depends on selection for thinness as well as selection for brain size. Furthermore, animal intelligence is undefined, so we cannot determine what correlates with it.

Comparisons among Humans

For many years, studies of human brain size and intelligence found correlations barely above zero. However, a low correlation between two variables can mean either that they are unrelated, or that at least one of the variables was measured poorly. Most early studies measured skull size instead of brain size. Today, using more accurate measurements based on MRI, most studies find a moderate positive correlation between brain size and IQ, typically around 0.3 (McDaniel, 2005).

Presumably certain brain areas are more important than others for intelligence. Several researchers have looked for particular brain areas that might be larger in people who score higher on intelligence tests. Many areas emerged as important, but the areas identified were not exactly the same from one study to the next (Colom et al., 2009, 2013; Frangou, Chitins, & Williams, 2004; Haier et al., 2009; Karama et al., 2009). In one case, investigators used MRI to measure the size of gray matter and white matter areas throughout the brains of 23 young adults from one university campus and 24 middle-aged or older adults from another campus. In Figure 3.39, the areas highlighted in red showed a statistically significant correlation with IQ, and those highlighted in yellow showed an even stronger correlation. Note the differences between the two samples, even though the procedures were the same for both (Haier, Jung, Yeo, Head, & Alkire, 2004). The discrepancies point out a problem with this type of research: If we record from all brain areas during a task, it is like testing hundreds of hypotheses at the same time. The evidence will confirm some of them, just by chance. (The protection against this kind of error is to try to replicate the results.)

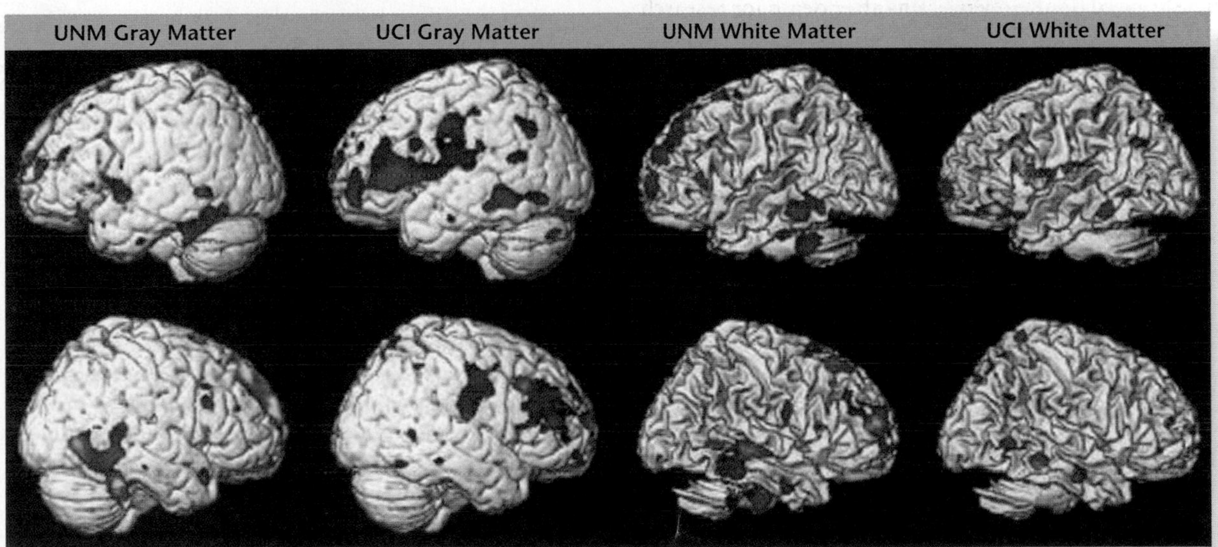

FIGURE 3.39 Cortical areas whose size correlated with IQ
The top row shows the left hemisphere; the bottom row shows the right. UNM and UCI columns show the results for two universities (University of New Mexico and University of California at Irvine). Areas whose size was significantly associated with IQ are shown in red; areas with the strongest relationship are shown in yellow. Adapted from NeuroImage, 23, Haier, R.J., Jung, R.E., Yeo, R.A., Head, K., & Alkire, M.T., Structural brain variation and general intelligence, pp. 425–433, Copyright 2004

STOP&CHECK

23. Why do recent studies show a stronger relationship between brain size and IQ than older studies did?

ANSWER

23. The use of MRI greatly improves the measurement of brain size, in comparison to measurements based on the skull.

Comparisons of Men and Women

Now for the most confusing part: If we examine intelligence test scores and brain size for just men, or for just women, we find a moderate positive correlation. If we combine results for men and women, the correlation declines. Men on average have larger brains than women but equal IQs (Burgaleta et al., 2012; Gilmore et al., 2007; Willerman, Schultz, Rutledge, & Bigler, 1991; Witelson, Beresh, & Kigar, 2006). Even if we take into account differences in height, men's brains remain larger (Ankney, 1992).

Although male and female brains differ on average, behavioral differences are smaller than most people expect (Hyde, 2005). For example, vastly more men than women become grand masters in chess. Does that fact indicate a difference in abilities? No. Boys and girls start at an equal level in playing chess and progress at equal rates. Apparently the only reason more men reach the highest level is that vastly more boys than girls *start* playing chess (Chabris & Glickman, 2006). The difference in chess performance pertains to interests, not abilities.

Many people believe that men tend to be better than women at mathematics. In countries where men and women have roughly equal opportunities, their performance on math tests is about equal (Guiso, Monte, Sapienza, & Zingales, 2008). In the United States, girls on average do at least as well as boys in all math courses from elementary school through college, except for certain aspects of geometry, such as the items in Figure 3.40 (Hyde, Lindberg, Linn, Ellis, & Williams, 2008; Spelke, 2005). Even that difference may reflect differences in interests rather than ability. From an early age, most boys spend more time on activities related to angles and distances. In one study, young women who spent 10 hours playing action video games significantly improved on the kind of item shown in Figure 3.40 (Feng, Spence, & Pratt, 2007).

How can we explain why men and women are equal in intellect, but men have larger brains? One potentially relevant factor pertains to relative amounts of gray matter (cell bodies) and white matter (axons). Women average more and deeper sulci on the surface of the cortex, especially in the frontal and parietal areas (Luders et al., 2004). Consequently, the surface area of the cortex is almost equal for men and women. Because the surface is lined with neurons (gray matter), the sexes have nearly the same number of neurons, despite differences in brain volume (Allen, Damasio, Grabowski, Bruss, & Zhang, 2003). This idea would provide a convincing explanation *if* intelligence depended only on gray matter. However, the research points to important contributions from both gray matter and white matter (Chiang et al., 2009; Narr et al., 2007; van Leeuwen et al., 2009). We are left, then, with the apparent conclusion that women's brains and men's brains differ structurally but accomplish the same thing, presumably because they are organized differently. Male and female brains differ in much more than overall size. Certain brain areas are relatively larger in men, and others in women. Also, the pattern of connections differs between the sexes, on average (Gong, He, & Evans, 2011).

In short, the data do not support any simple summary of the relationship between overall brain size and overall intelligence. We have better success in relating specific brain areas to more detailed aspects of behavior. In the rest of this text, we concentrate on those questions.

Can the set of blocks on the left be rotated to match the set at the right?

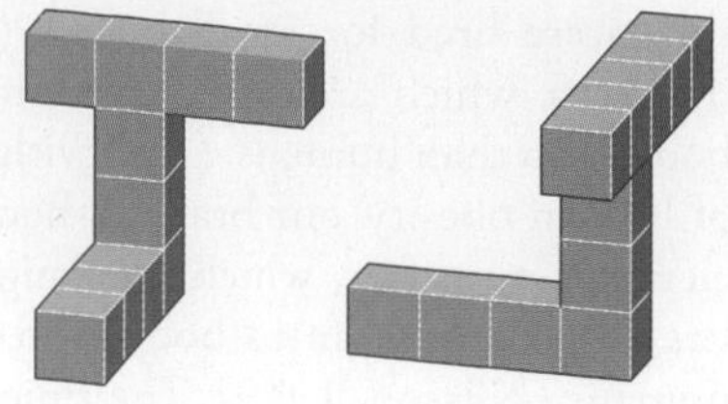

Which of the lines at the left has the same angle as the one at the right?

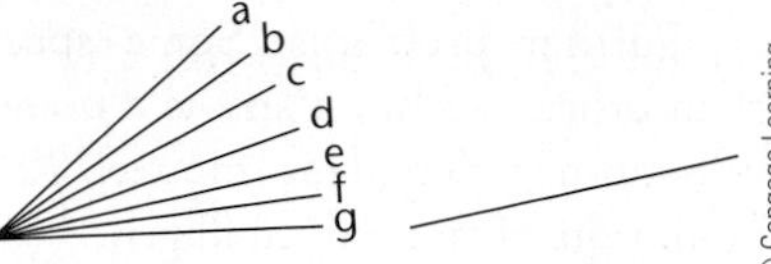

FIGURE 3.40 A spatial rotation task
People are presented with a series of pairs such as this one and asked whether the first figure could be rotated to match the second one. Here the answer is *no*. For the line-angle question, the correct answer is *e*.

STOP&CHECK

24. In which way do men and women differ most—intellectual performance, total gray matter, or total white matter?

ANSWER

24. Men have more white matter, and therefore larger brains. However, men and women are equal in intellectual performance and nearly equal in gray matter.

Research Methods and Progress

In any scientific field—indeed, any field of knowledge—progress almost always depends on improvements in measurement. In astronomy, for example, improvements in both ground-based and satellite-based astronomy have established conclusions that even science-fiction writers couldn't have imagined a few decades ago. Weather prediction is vastly more accurate than it used to be. Similarly, our understanding of the brain has advanced greatly because of the introduction of PET scans, fMRI, optogenetics, and other modern technologies. Future progress will continue to depend on improvements in our methods of measurement.

Summary

1. One way to study brain-behavior relationships is to examine the effects of brain damage. If someone suffers a loss after some kind of brain damage, then that area contributes in some way to that behavior. **89**
2. If stimulation of a brain area increases some behavior, presumably that area contributes to the behavior. Optogenetics is a relatively new method that enables researchers to stimulate a particular type of cell at a particular moment. **90**
3. Researchers try to understand brain-behavior relationships by recording activity in various brain areas during a given behavior. Many methods are available, including EEG, MEG, and fMRI. **91**
4. People who differ with regard to some behavior sometimes also differ with regard to their brain anatomy. MRI is one modern method of imaging a living brain. However, correlations between behavior and anatomy should be evaluated cautiously. **94**
5. Research using modern methods to measure brain size suggests a low to moderate relationship between brain size and intelligence, although many puzzles and uncertainties remain. **96**
6. Men and women are equal on average in their IQ scores, despite men's having larger brains. **98**

Key Terms

Terms are defined in the module on the page number indicated. They're also presented in alphabetical order with definitions in the book's Subject Index/Glossary. Interactive flash cards, audio reviews, and crossword puzzles are among the online resources available to help you learn these terms and the concepts they represent.

ablation **89**
computerized axial tomography (CT or CAT scan) **94**
electroencephalograph (EEG) **91**
evoked potentials or evoked responses **91**
functional magnetic resonance imaging (fMRI) **92**
lesion **89**
magnetic resonance imaging (MRI) **94**
magnetoencephalograph (MEG) **91**
phrenology **94**
Positron-emission tomography (PET) **92**
stereotaxic instrument **89**
Transcranial magnetic stimulation (TMS) **90**

Thought Question

Certain unusual aspects of brain structure were observed in the brain of Albert Einstein (Falk, Lepore, & Noe, 2013). One interpretation is that he was born with certain specialized brain features that encouraged his scientific and intellectual abilities. What is an alternative interpretation?

MODULE 3.3 End of Module Quiz

1. Which of the following is a method to inactivate a brain area temporarily?
   a. Stereotaxic instrument
   b. Transcranial magnetic stimulation
   c. Lesion
   d. Ablation

2. Which of these is the first step in using the optogenetic technique?
   a. Inject a radioactive chemical into the blood.
   b. Insert an electrode into the brain.
   c. Subject the brain to a strong magnetic field.
   d. Attach light-sensitive proteins to a virus.

3. Which of these is the first step for positron-emission tomography (PET)?
   a. Inject a radioactive chemical into the blood.
   b. Insert an electrode into the brain.
   c. Subject the brain to a strong magnetic field.
   d. Attach light-sensitive proteins to a virus.

4. What is one advantage of fMRI over PET scans?
   a. The fMRI technique measures activity on a millisecond-by-millisecond basis.
   b. The fMRI technique does not require inserting an electrode into the head.
   c. The fMRI technique does not expose the brain to radioactivity.
   d. The fMRI technique identifies which brain areas are most active at a given moment.

5. Suppose someone demonstrates that a particular brain area becomes active when people listen to music. What would be a good way to test whether this brain area is really specialized for music perception?
   a. Test whether the fMRI recordings are stronger in people who enjoy music more than others do.
   b. Test whether this brain area becomes silent when someone is not listening to music.
   c. Examine the size of this brain area in nonhuman animals.
   d. Test whether we can use fMRI recordings to guess what kind of music someone is hearing.

6. Which of these methods measures brain anatomy but NOT brain activity?
   a. EEG
   b. PET
   c. MRI
   d. fMRI

7. Comparing MRI and fMRI, which one(s) measure the responses of brain chemicals to a magnetic field? Which one(s) show which brain areas are most active at the moment?
   a. Only MRI measures responses of brain chemicals to a magnetic field. Both show which brain areas are most active at the moment.
   b. Only fMRI measures responses of brain chemicals to a magnetic field. Only MRI shows which brain areas are most active at the moment.
   c. Both measure responses of brain chemicals to a magnetic field. Only fMRI shows which brain areas are most active at the moment.
   d. Both measure responses of brain chemicals to a magnetic field. Both show which brain areas are most active at the moment.

8. In which regard, if either, do human brains exceed those of all other species?
   a. Humans have the largest brains in total mass.
   b. Humans have the largest brain-to-body ratio.
   c. Humans do not exceed all other species in either regard.

9. Most studies using modern methods show a moderate positive correlation between brain size and IQ scores. Nevertheless, interpreting these results is problematic. Why?
   a. As children grow older, their brain size increases but their IQ decreases.
   b. When people are sleepy or sick, their brain size remains the same but their IQ performance drops.
   c. On average, men have larger brains than women, but equal IQ scores.
   d. Some parts of the brain are more important for IQ than other parts are.

10. In which way do men and women differ most, on the average?
    a. Intellectual performance
    b. Gray matter (neuron cell bodies)
    c. White matter (axons)

ANSWERS:

1b, 2d, 3a, 4c, 5d, 6c, 7c, 8c, 9c, 10c

Suggestions for Further Reading

Burrell, B. (2004). *Postcards from the brain museum.* New York: Broadway Books.

Fascinating history of the attempts to collect brains of successful people and try to relate their brain anatomy to their success.

DeSalle, R., & Tattersall, I. (2012). *The brain.* New Haven, CT: Yale University Press.

Discussion of the human brain with emphasis on how it may have evolved.

Klawans, H. L. (1988). *Toscanini's fumble and other tales of clinical neurology.* Chicago: Contemporary Books.

Description of illustrative cases of brain damage and their behavioral consequences.

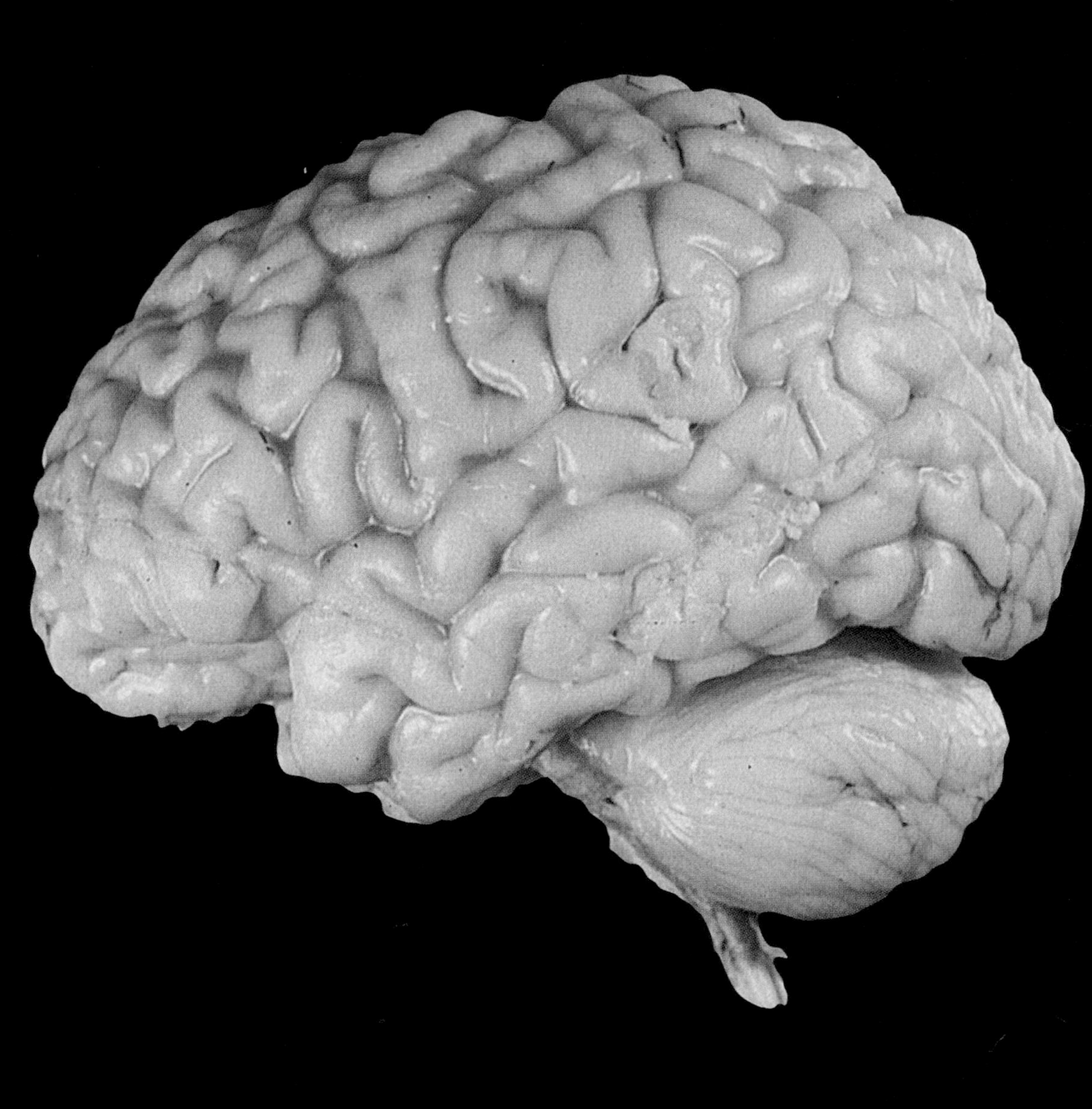

Dr. Dana Copeland

Genetics, Evolution, Development and Plasticity

4

CHAPTER OUTLINE

MODULE 4.1 Genetics and Evolution of Behavior
Mendelian Genetics
Heredity and Environment
The Evolution of Behavior
In Closing: Genes and Behavior
MODULE 4.2 Development of the Brain
Maturation of the Vertebrate Brain
Pathfinding by Axons
Determinants of Neuronal Survival
The Vulnerable Developing Brain
Differentiation of the Cortex
Fine-Tuning by Experience
Brain Development and Behavioral Development
In Closing: Brain Development
MODULE 4.3 Plasticity after Brain Damage
Brain Damage and Short-Term Recovery
Later Mechanisms of Recovery
In Closing: Brain Damage and Recovery

LEARNING OBJECTIVES

After studying this chapter, you should be able to:

1. Distinguish between genetic and epigenetic influences on development.
2. Describe the types of evidence researchers use to infer heritability.
3. Give examples of evolutionary explanations in psychology.
4. Discuss the formation of new neurons in a mature brain.
5. Describe the evidence showing that axons seek specific targets.
6. Define apoptosis and explain how neurotrophins prevent it.
7. Cite examples of how experiences alter brain anatomy and function.
8. Discuss brain changes during adolescence and old age, and how they might relate to behavior.
9. List several possible mechanisms of recovery after brain damage.
10. Explain how remodeling in the cerebral cortex produces the phantom limb experience.

"Some assembly required." Have you ever bought a package with those ominous words? Sometimes, all you have to do is attach a few parts, but other times, you face page after page of barely comprehensible instructions.

The human nervous system requires an enormous amount of assembly, and the instructions are different from those for the objects we assemble from a kit. Instead of, "Put this piece here and that piece there," the instructions are, "Put these axons here and those dendrites there, and then wait to see what happens. Keep the connections that work the best and discard the others. Continue making new connections and keeping only the successful ones."

Therefore, we say that the brain's anatomy is *plastic*. It changes rapidly in early development and continues changing throughout life.

OPPOSITE: An enormous amount of brain development has already occurred by the time a person is 1 year. This is a brain of a one-year old.

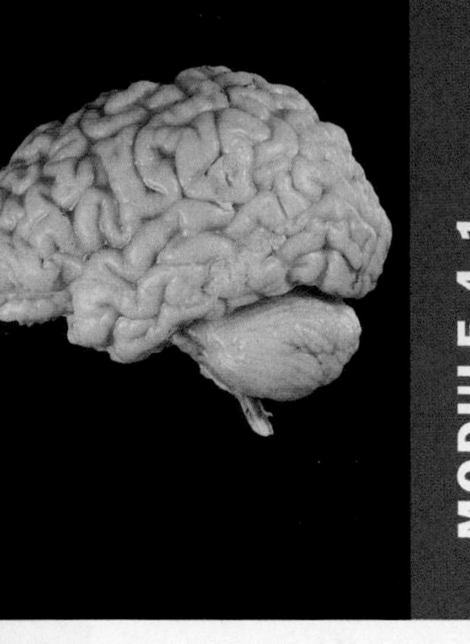

MODULE 4.1

Genetics and Evolution of Behavior

Everything you do depends on both your genes and your environment. Consider facial expressions. A contribution of the environment is obvious: You smile more when the world is treating you well and frown when things are going badly. Does heredity influence your facial expressions? Researchers examined facial expressions of people who were born blind and therefore could not have learned to imitate facial expressions. The facial expressions of the people born blind were remarkably similar to those of their sighted relatives, as shown in Figure 4.1 (Peleg et al., 2006). These results suggest a major role for genetics in controlling facial expressions.

Controversies arise when we move beyond the generalization that both heredity and environment are important. For example, do differences in human intelligence depend mostly on genetic differences, environmental influences, or both about equally? Similar questions arise for sexual orientation, alcoholism, weight gain, and much else that interests psychologists. This module should help you understand these issues as they arise later in this text or elsewhere. We begin with a review of genetics, a field that has become more and more complicated as research has progressed.

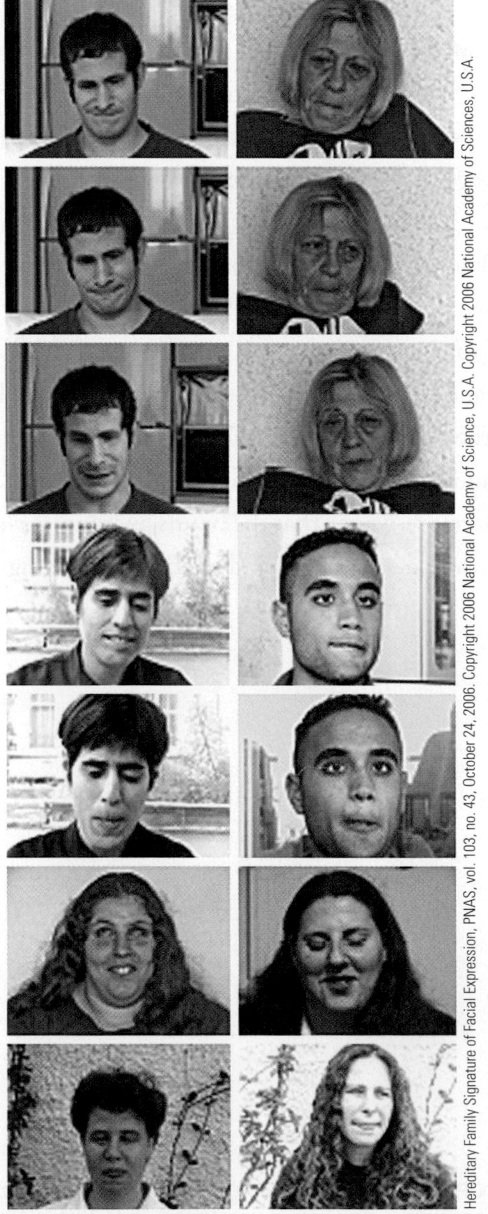

FIGURE 4.1 Facial expressions by people born blind (left) and their sighted relatives (right)
The similarities imply a genetic contribution to facial expressions.

Mendelian Genetics

Prior to the work of Gregor Mendel, a late 19th-century monk, scientists thought that inheritance was a blending process in which the properties of the sperm and the egg simply mixed, like two colors of paint.

Mendel demonstrated that inheritance occurs through **genes**, units of heredity that maintain their structural identity from one generation to another. As a rule, genes come in pairs because they are aligned along **chromosomes** (strands of genes) that also come in pairs. (As an exception to this rule, a male mammal has unpaired X and Y chromosomes with different genes.) Classically, a gene has been defined as part of a chromosome composed of the double-stranded molecule **deoxyribonucleic acid (DNA)**. However, many genes do not have the discrete locations we once imagined (Bird, 2007). Sometimes several genes overlap on a stretch of chromosome. Sometimes a genetic outcome depends on parts of two or more chromosomes. In many cases, part of a chromosome alters the expression of a gene without coding for any protein of its own.

A strand of DNA serves as a template (model) for the synthesis of **ribonucleic acid (RNA)** molecules, a single-strand chemical. One type of RNA molecule—messenger RNA—serves as a template for the synthesis of protein molecules. DNA contains four "bases"—adenine, guanine, cytosine, and thymine. The order of those bases determines the order of corresponding bases along an RNA molecule—adenine, guanine, cytosine, and uracil. The order of bases along an RNA molecule in turn determines the order of amino acids that compose a protein. For example, if three RNA bases are in order cytosine, adenine, and guanine, then the protein adds the amino acid *glutamine*. If the next three RNA bases are uracil, guanine, and guanine, the next amino acid on the protein is *tryptophan*. In total, proteins consist of 20 amino acids, and the order of those amino acids depends on the order of DNA and RNA bases. It's an amazingly simple code, considering the complexity of body structures and functions that result from it.

Figure 4.2 summarizes the main steps in translating information from DNA through RNA into proteins. Some proteins form part of the structure of the body. Others serve as *enzymes*, biological catalysts that regulate chemical reactions in the body. Not all RNA codes for proteins. Many RNA molecules perform regulatory functions.

Anyone with an identical pair of genes on the two chromosomes is **homozygous** for that gene. An individual with an unmatched pair of genes is **heterozygous** for that gene. For example, you might have a gene for blue eyes on one chromosome and a gene for brown eyes on the other.

Genes are dominant, recessive, or intermediate. A **dominant** gene shows a strong effect in either the homozygous or heterozygous condition. A **recessive** gene shows its effects only in the homozygous condition. For example, a gene for brown eyes is dominant and a gene for blue eyes is recessive. If you have one gene for brown eyes and one for blue, the result is brown eyes. The gene for high sensitivity to the taste of phenylthiocarbamide (PTC) is dominant, and the gene for low sensitivity is recessive. Only someone with two recessive genes has trouble tasting it (Wooding et al., 2004). Figure 4.3 illustrates the possible results of a mating between people who are both heterozygous for the PTC-tasting gene. Because each has one high taste sensitivity gene—let's abbreviate it "T"—the parents can taste PTC. However, each parent transmits either a high taste sensitivity gene (T) or a low taste sensitivity gene (t) to any child. Therefore, a child in this family has a 25 percent chance of two T genes, a 50 percent chance of the heterozygous condition, and a 25 percent chance of being homozygous for the t gene.

However, an example like this can be misleading, because it implies that a single gene produces a single outcome, regardless of the environment. Even in the case of eye color, that is not true. Researchers have identified at least 10 genes that contribute to variations in eye color (Liu et al., 2010). At least 180 genes contribute to differences in people's height (Allen et al., 2010). Each gene that contributes to eye color or height affects other characteristics as well. Furthermore, it is also possible to express a gene in some cells and not others, or under some circumstances and not others, depending on the environment. Genetic influences are more complex than we once imagined.

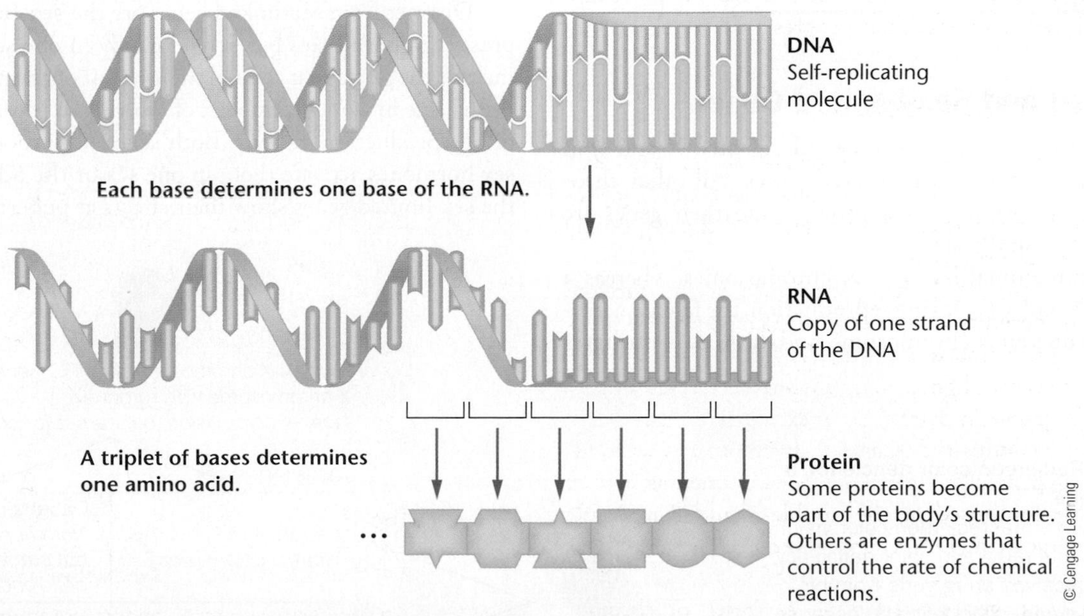

FIGURE 4.2 How DNA controls development of the organism
The sequence of bases along a strand of DNA determines the order of bases along a strand of RNA; RNA in turn controls the sequence of amino acids in a protein molecule.

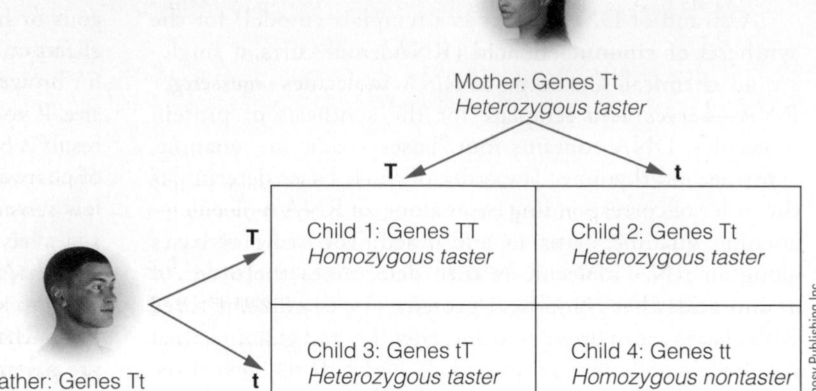

FIGURE 4.3 Four equally likely outcomes of a mating between parents who are heterozygous for a given gene (Tt)
A child in this family has a 25 percent chance of being homozygous for the dominant gene (TT), a 25 percent chance of being homozygous for the recessive gene (tt), and a 50 percent chance of being heterozygous (Tt).

STOP&CHECK

1. Suppose you have high sensitivity to tasting PTC. If your mother can also taste it easily, what (if anything) can you predict about your father's ability to taste it?

2. Suppose you have high sensitivity to the taste of PTC. If your mother has low sensitivity, what (if anything) can you predict about your father's taste sensitivity?

ANSWERS

1. If your mother has high sensitivity to the taste of PTC, we can make no predictions about your father. You may have inherited a high-sensitivity gene from your mother, and because the gene is dominant, you need only one copy of the gene to taste PTC. **2.** If your mother has low sensitivity, you must have inherited your high-sensitivity gene from your father, so he must have high sensitivity.

Sex-Linked and Sex-Limited Genes

The genes on the sex chromosomes (designated X and Y in mammals) are known as **sex-linked genes**. All other chromosomes are autosomal chromosomes, and their genes are known as **autosomal genes**.

A female mammal has two X chromosomes, whereas a male has an X and a Y. During reproduction, the female necessarily contributes an X chromosome, and the male contributes either an X or a Y. If he contributes an X, the offspring is female; if he contributes a Y, the offspring is male. (Exceptions to this rule are possible, but uncommon.)

When biologists speak of sex-linked genes, they usually mean X-linked genes. The Y chromosome is small, with genes for far fewer proteins than other chromosomes. However, the Y chromosome also has many sites that influence the functioning of genes on other chromosomes.

One human sex-linked gene controls red-green color vision deficiency (see Figure 4.4). Any man with the recessive form of this gene on his X chromosome is red-green color deficient because he has no other X chromosome. A woman is color deficient only if she has that recessive gene on both of her X chromosomes. So, for example, if 8 percent of human X chromosomes contain the gene for color vision deficiency, then 8 percent of men will be color deficient, but less than one percent of women will be (0.08×0.08).

Distinct from sex-linked genes are the **sex-limited genes**, present in both sexes but active mainly in one sex. Examples include the genes that control the amount of chest hair in men, breast size in women, amount of crowing in roosters, and rate of egg production in hens. Both sexes have those genes, but sex hormones activate them in one sex or the other. Many of the sex-limited genes show their effects at puberty.

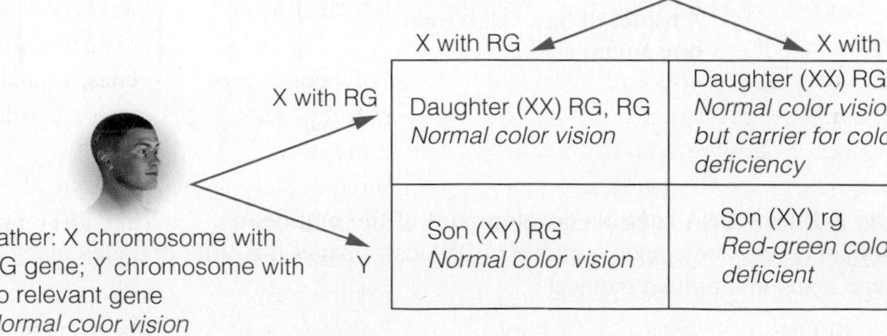

FIGURE 4.4 Red-green color deficiency, a sex-linked gene
RG represents normal red-green color vision, and rg represents red-green color deficiency. Any son who receives an rg gene from his mother is red-green color deficient, because the Y gene has no gene for color vision. A daughter could be color deficient only if her father has color deficiency and her mother is a carrier for the condition.

STOP & CHECK

3. How does a sex-linked gene differ from a sex-limited gene?
4. Suppose someone identifies a "gene for" certain aspects of sexual development. In what ways might that statement be misleading?

ANSWERS

3. A sex-linked gene is on the X or Y chromosome. A sex-limited gene is on an autosomal chromosome, but activated in one sex more than in the other. **4.** Almost any characteristic depends on more than one gene, as well as influences from the environment.

Genetic Changes

Genes change in several ways. One way is by **mutation**, a heritable change in a DNA molecule. Changing just one base in DNA to any of the other three types means that the mutant gene will code for a protein with a different amino acid at one location in the molecule. Given that evolution has already had eons to select the best makeup of each gene, a mutation is rarely advantageous. Still, those rare exceptions are important. The human *FOXP2* gene differs from the chimpanzee version of that gene in just two bases, but those two mutations modified the human brain and vocal apparatus in several ways that facilitate language development (Konopka et al., 2009).

Another kind of mutation is a duplication or deletion. During the process of reproduction, part of a chromosome that ordinarily appears once might instead appear twice or not at all. When this process happens to just a tiny portion of a chromosome, we call it a microduplication or microdeletion. Although it is possible for a duplication to be helpful, microduplications and microdeletions of certain brain-relevant genes are a possible explanation for schizophrenia (International Schizophrenia Consortium, 2008; Stefansson et al., 2008).

Epigenetics

In addition to these permanent changes in genes, the field of **epigenetics** deals with changes in gene expression. Every cell in your body has the same DNA as every other cell (except red blood cells, with no DNA). However, the activity of a gene can vary. The genes active in your brain are not the same as those active in your lungs or kidneys. At puberty, certain genes that had been almost silent become much more active (Lomniczi et al., 2013). Bees working as nurses have the same genes as those working as foragers, but they differ in which genes are active or inactive (Herb et al., 2012).

Various experiences can turn a gene on or off. For example, if a mother rat is malnourished during pregnancy, her offspring alter the expression of certain genes to conserve energy and adjust to a world in which food will presumably be hard to find. If in fact rich food becomes abundant later in life, those offspring are predisposed, because of their gene expression, to a high probability of obesity and heart disease (Godfrey, Lillycrop, Burdge, Gluckman, & Hanson, 2007). Rat pups with a low degree of maternal care early in life alter the expression of certain genes in a brain area called the hippocampus, resulting in high vulnerability to emotional stress reactions later in life (Harper, 2005; Weaver et al., 2004; Zhang et al., 2010).

Epigenetics is a new, growing field that will almost certainly play an increasingly important role in our understanding of behavior. For example, one study examined 40 female mice from an inbred strain, living in the same large enclosure. They were virtually identical genetically and they were exposed to the same environment. Nevertheless, as time went on, their behavior became more and more different. For whatever reason, some of them were slightly more active at the start. That activity led to epigenetic changes in certain brain areas, leading to still more activity, changes in muscle growth and body weight, and so on (Freund et al., 2013). In short, even when individuals have virtually the same genes and apparently the same environment, they can turn out differently, and the mechanism is epigenetics.

Epigenetic changes in humans are also critical. When you learn something, your brain stores the information by increasing activity in certain genes in certain cells while decreasing it in others (Feng, Fouse, & Fan, 2007). Drug addiction also produces epigenetic changes in the brain (Sadri-Vakili et al., 2010; Tsankova, Renthal, Kumar, & Nestler, 2007). The experience of feeling socially isolated or rejected alters the activity of hundreds of genes (Slavich & Cole, 2013).

How could an experience modify gene expression? First, let's look at how gene expression is regulated, and then see how environmental factors can influence that regulation. Standard illustrations of the DNA molecule, as in Figure 4.2, show it as a straight line, which is an oversimplification. In fact, proteins called **histones** bind DNA into a shape that is more like string wound around a ball (see Figure 4.5). The histone molecules in the ball have loose ends to which certain chemical groups can attach. To activate a gene, the DNA must partially unwind from the histones.

The result of an experience—maternal deprivation, cocaine exposure, new learning, or whatever—in some way alters the chemical environment within a cell. In some cases the outcome adds acetyl groups ($COCH_3$) to the histone tails near a gene, causing the histones to loosen their grip on the DNA, and facilitating the expression of that gene. Removal of the acetyl group causes the histones to tighten their grip on the DNA, and turns the gene off. Another possibility is to add or remove methyl groups from DNA, usually at the promoter regions at the beginning of a gene. Adding methyl groups (CH_3) to promoters turns genes off, and removing them turns on a gene (Tsankova et al., 2007). For example, severe traumatic experiences in early childhood decrease methylation of many brain genes, increasing the later risk of depression, post-traumatic stress disorder, and so forth (Klengel et al., 2013).

The general point is that what you do at any moment not only affects you now, but also produces epigenetic effects that alter gene expression for longer periods of time. Furthermore, the line between "genetic" effects and "experiential" effects has become blurrier than ever. Experiences act by altering the activity of genes.

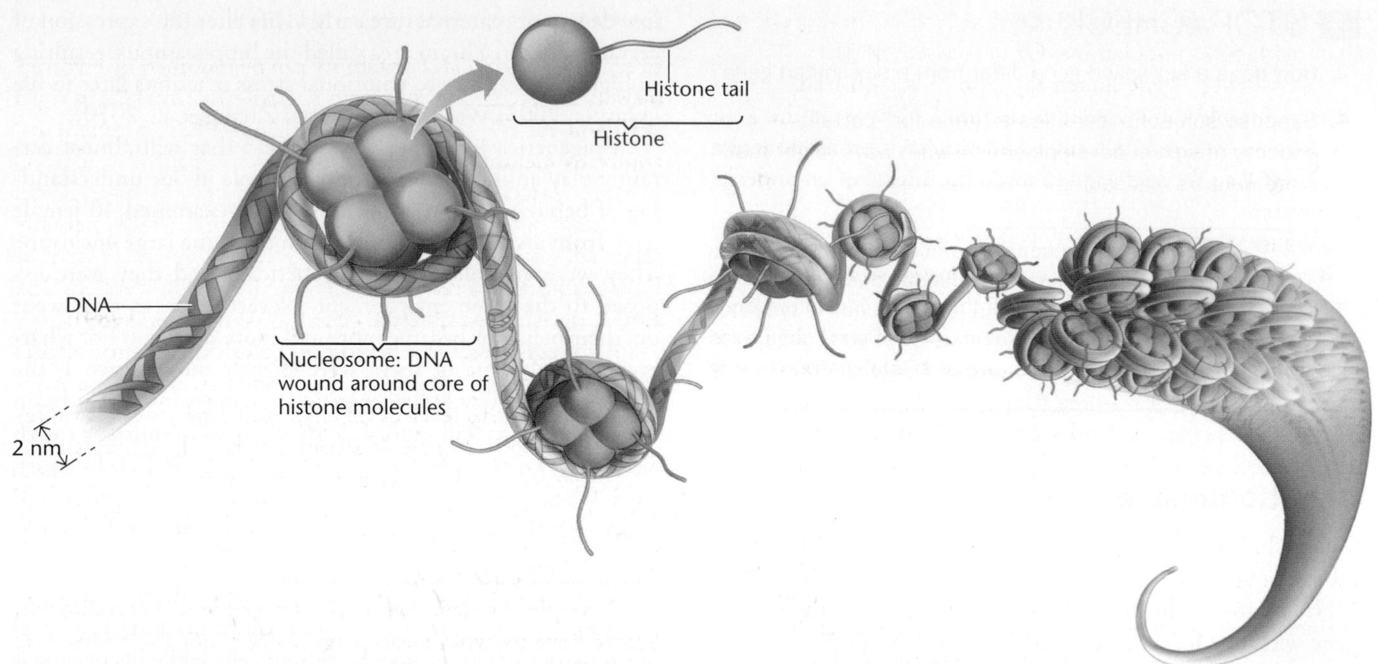

FIGURE 4.5 DNA bound into a ball shape by histone proteins
Acetyl groups that attach to a loose end of a histone molecule loosen the histone's grip on DNA, exposing more genes to the possibility of being active.

STOP&CHECK

5. How does an epigenetic change differ from a mutation?

6. How does adding a methyl or acetyl group to a histone protein alter gene activity?

ANSWERS

5. A mutation is a permanent change in part of a chromosome. An epigenetic change is an increase or decrease in the activity of a gene or group of genes. **6.** Adding a methyl group turns genes off. An acetyl group loosens histone's grip and increases gene activation.

Heredity and Environment

Suppose someone asks whether singing ability depends on heredity or environment. That question as stated is meaningless. Unless you had both heredity and environment, you couldn't sing at all. However, we can rephrase the question meaningfully: Do the observed *differences* among individuals depend more on *differences* in heredity or *differences* in environment? For example, if you sing better than someone else, the reason could be different genes, better training, or both. If the variations in some characteristic depend largely on genetic differences, the characteristic has high **heritability**.

To determine the heritability of any characteristic, researchers rely mainly on three kinds of evidence. First, they compare **monozygotic** ("from one egg") twins and **dizygotic** ("from two eggs") twins. People usually call monozygotic twins "identical" twins, but that term is misleading, because identical twins often differ in important ways. Some are mirror images of each other. Also, for epigenetic reasons, certain genes may be activated more in one twin than the other (Raj, Rifkin, Andersen, & van Oudenaarden, 2010). Still, they have the same genes, whereas dizygotic twins do not. A stronger resemblance between monozygotic than dizygotic twins suggests a genetic contribution. However, it is not totally decisive, because people who look alike tend to be treated alike. Researchers sometimes also examine "virtual twins"—children of the same age, adopted at the same time into a single family. They grow up in the same environment from infancy, but without any genetic similarity. Any similarities in behavior imply environmental influences. However, the behavioral differences—which are in many cases substantial—suggest genetic influences (Segal, 2000).

A second kind of evidence is studies of adopted children. Any tendency for adopted children to resemble their biological parents suggests a hereditary influence. However, again the evidence is not always decisive. The biological mother contributes not only her genes, but also the prenatal environment. A mother's health, diet, and smoking and drinking habits during pregnancy can greatly influence her child's development, especially the brain development. A similarity between an adopted child and the genetic mother could reflect both genetic influences and prenatal environment.

A third type of evidence is to identify specific genes linked to some behavior. In some cases, researchers test a hypothesis, such as "a gene that decreases the activity of the serotonin transporter may be linked to an increased risk of depression." In other cases, they examine all the genes of people with some condition (such as depression or schizophrenia), looking for any gene that is more common than in the rest of the population. However, this procedure tests thousands of hypotheses at once (one for each gene), and risks reporting a false association. We should be skeptical of the conclusions until researchers have replicated them with other populations (Chablis et al., 2012).

Identifying a gene linked to some condition leads to further questions: How strong is the link? How does the gene produce its effect? Which environmental conditions moderate its effect? Can we find ways to undo the effects of an undesirable gene?

We can draw a firmer conclusion if more than one type of evidence supports it, such as both adoption studies and twin studies. Using these methods, researchers have found evidence for significant heritability of almost every behavior they have tested, including loneliness (McGuire & Clifford, 2000), neuroticism (Lake, Eaves, Maes, Heath, & Martin, 2000), television watching (Plomin, Corley, DeFries, & Fulker, 1990), childhood misbehavior (Burt, 2009), social attitudes (Posner, Baker, Heath, & Martin, 1996), cognitive performance (Plomin et al., 2013), educational attainment (Rietveld et al., 2013), and speed of learning a second language (Dale, Harlaar, Haworth, & Plomin, 2010). About the only behavior anyone has tested that has *not* shown a significant heritability is religious affiliation—such as Protestant or Catholic (Eaves, Martin, & Heath, 1990).

Any estimate of the heritability of a trait is specific to a given population. Consider alcohol abuse, which has moderate heritability in the United States. Imagine a population somewhere in which some families teach very strict prohibitions on alcohol use, perhaps for religious reasons, and other families are more permissive. With such strong environmental differences, the genetic influences exert less effect, and heritability will be relatively low. Then consider another population where all families have the same rules, but people happen to differ substantially in genes that affect their reactions to alcohol. In that population, heritability will be higher. In short, estimates of heritability are never absolute. They apply to a particular population at a particular time.

STOP & CHECK

7. What are the main types of evidence to estimate the heritability of some behavior?

8. Suppose someone determines the heritability of IQ scores for a given population. Then society changes in a way that provides the best possible opportunity for everyone within that population. Will heritability of IQ increase, decrease, or stay the same?

ANSWERS

7. One type of evidence is greater similarity between monozygotic twins than dizygotic twins. Another is resemblance between adopted children and their biological parents. A third is a demonstration that a particular gene is more common than average among people who show a particular behavior. **8.** Heritability will *increase*. Heritability estimates how much of the variation is due to differences in genes. If everyone has the same environment, then differences in environment cannot account for much of the remaining differences in IQ scores. Therefore, the relative role of genetic differences will be greater.

Environmental Modification

Even a trait with high heritability can be modified by environmental interventions. A prime example is **phenylketonuria** (FEE-nil-KEET-uhn-YOOR-ee-uh), or **PKU**, a genetic inability to metabolize the amino acid phenylalanine. If PKU is not treated, phenylalanine accumulates to toxic levels, impairing brain development and leaving a child mentally retarded, restless, and irritable. Approximately one percent of Europeans carry a recessive gene for PKU. Fewer Asians and almost no Africans have the gene (T. Wang et al., 1989).

Although PKU is a hereditary condition, environmental interventions can modify it. Physicians in many countries routinely test the level of phenylalanine or its metabolites in babies' blood or urine. If a baby has high levels, indicating PKU, physicians advise the parents to put the baby on a strict low-phenylalanine diet to protect the brain (Waisbren, Brown, de Sonneville, & Levy, 1994). The success of this diet shows that *heritable* does not mean *unmodifiable*.

A couple of notes about PKU: The required diet is difficult. People have to avoid meats, eggs, dairy products, grains, and especially aspartame (NutraSweet), which is 50 percent phenylalanine. Instead, they eat an expensive formula containing the other amino acids. Physicians long believed that children with PKU could quit the diet after a few years. Later experience has shown that high phenylalanine levels damage mature brains, too. A woman with PKU should be especially careful during pregnancy and when nursing. Even a genetically normal baby cannot handle the enormous amounts of phenylalanine that an affected mother might pass through the placenta.

STOP & CHECK

9. What example illustrates the point that even if some characteristic is highly heritable, a change in the environment can alter it?

ANSWER

9. Keeping a child with the PKU gene on a strict low-phenylalanine diet prevents the mental retardation that the gene ordinarily causes. The general point is that sometimes a highly heritable condition can be modified environmentally.

How Genes Affect Behavior

A biologist who speaks of a "gene for brown eyes" does not mean that the gene directly produces brown eyes. The gene produces a protein that makes the eyes brown, assuming normal health and nutrition. If we speak of a "gene for alcoholism," we should not imagine that the gene itself causes alcoholism. Rather, it produces a protein that under certain circumstances increases the probability of alcoholism. It is important to specify these circumstances as well as we can.

Exactly how a gene increases the probability of a given behavior is a complex issue. Some genes control brain chemicals, but others affect behavior indirectly. Suppose your genes make you unusually attractive. As a result, strangers smile at you and many people want to get to know you. Their reactions to your appearance may change your personality, and if so, the genes altered your behavior by altering your environment!

For another example, imagine a child born with genes promoting greater than average height, running speed, and coordination. The child shows early success at basketball, and soon spends more and more time playing basketball. Soon the child spends less time on other pursuits—including television, playing chess, or anything else you might imagine. Thus, the measured heritability of several behaviors might depend partly on genes that affect leg muscles. This is a hypothetical example, but it illustrates the point: Genes influence behavior in roundabout ways. We should not be amazed by reports that nearly every human behavior has some heritability.

The Evolution of Behavior

Charles Darwin, known as the founder of evolutionary theory, didn't like the term *evolution*. He preferred *descent with modification*, emphasizing the idea of changes without necessarily implying improvement. **Evolution** is a change over generations in the frequencies of various genes in a population.

We distinguish two questions about evolution: How *did* some species evolve, and how *do* species evolve? To ask how a species did evolve is to ask what evolved from what, basing our answers on inferences from fossils and comparisons of living species. For example, biologists find that humans are more similar to chimpanzees than to other species, and they infer a common ancestor. As new evidence becomes available, biologists change their opinions about the evolutionary relationship between one species and another (Xu, You, & Han, 2011).

The question of how species *do* evolve is a question of how the process works, and that process is a necessary outcome from what we know about reproduction. The reasoning goes as follows:

- Offspring generally resemble their parents for genetic reasons. That is, "like begets like."
- Mutations, recombinations, and microduplications of genes introduce new heritable variations that help or harm an individual's chance of surviving and reproducing.
- Certain individuals reproduce more than others do, thus passing on their genes to the next generation. Any gene that is associated with greater reproductive success will become more prevalent in later generations. That is, the current generation of any species resembles the individuals who reproduced in the past. If the environment changes such that a different gene increases the probability of survival and reproduction, that gene will spread in the population. You can witness and explore these principles with the interactive Try It Yourself activity "Genetic Generations."

TRY IT YOURSELF ONLINE

Because plant and animal breeders have long understood this idea, they choose individuals with a desired trait and make them the parents of the next generation through a process called **artificial selection**. Over many generations, breeders have produced exceptional racehorses, hundreds of kinds of dogs, chickens that lay huge numbers of eggs, and so forth. Darwin's (1859) insight was that nature also selects. If certain individuals are more successful than others in finding food, escaping enemies, attracting mates, or protecting their offspring, then their genes will become more prevalent in later generations. Given a huge amount of time, this process can produce the wide variety of life that we in fact encounter.

Common Misunderstandings about Evolution

Let's clarify the principles of evolution by addressing a few misconceptions:

- *Does the use or disuse of some structure or behavior cause an evolutionary increase or decrease in that feature?* You may have heard people say something like, "Because we hardly ever use our little toes, they get smaller and smaller in each succeeding generation." This idea is a carryover of biologist Jean-Baptiste Lamarck's theory of evolution through the inheritance of acquired characteristics, known as **Lamarckian evolution**. According to this idea, if you exercise your arm muscles, your children will be born with bigger arm muscles, and if you fail to use your little toes, your children's little toes will be smaller than yours. However, biologists have found no mechanism for Lamarckian evolution to occur and no evidence that it does. Using or failing to use some body structure does not change the genes. People's little toes will shrink in future generations only if people with genes for smaller little toes manage to reproduce more than other people do.
- *Have humans stopped evolving?* Because modern medicine can keep almost anyone alive, and because welfare programs in prosperous countries provide the necessities

Barry Lewis/Alamy Limited

China's policy to limit each family to one child decreases the possibility of genetic changes between generations.

of life for almost everyone, some people assert that humans are no longer subject to the principle of "survival of the fittest." Therefore, the argument goes, human evolution has slowed or stopped.

The flaw in this argument is that evolution depends on reproduction, not just survival. If people with certain genes have more than the average number of children, their genes will spread in the population.

- *Does "evolution" mean "improvement"?* It depends on what you mean by "improvement." By definition, evolution improves **fitness**, which is operationally defined as *the number of copies of one's genes that endure in later generations.* If you have more children than average (and they survive long enough to reproduce), you are evolutionarily fit, regardless of whether you are successful in any other way. You also increase your fitness by supporting your relatives, who share many of your genes and spread them by their own reproduction. Any gene that spreads is, by definition, fit. However, genes that increase fitness at one time and place might be disadvantageous after a change in the environment. For example, the colorful tail feathers of the male peacock enable it to attract females but might become disadvantageous in the presence of a new predator that responds to bright colors. In other words, the genes of the current generation evolved because they were fit for *previous* generations. They may or may not be adaptive in the future.
- *Does evolution benefit the individual or the species?* Neither: It benefits the genes! In a sense, you don't use your genes to reproduce yourself. Rather, your genes use *you* to reproduce *themselves* (Dawkins, 1989). Imagine a gene that causes you to risk your life to protect your children. If that gene enables you to leave behind more surviving children than you would have otherwise, then that gene will increase in prevalence within your population.

F.J. Hierscha/Science Source

Sometimes, a sexual display, such as a peacock's spread of its tail feathers, improves reproductive success and spreads the associated genes. In a changed environment, this gene could become maladaptive. For example, if an aggressive predator with good color vision enters the range of the peacock, the bird's colorful feathers could seal its doom.

STOP & CHECK

10. Many people believe the human appendix is useless. Will it become smaller and smaller with each generation?

ANSWER

10. No. Failure to need a structure does not make it smaller in the next generation. The appendix will shrink only if people with a gene for a smaller appendix reproduce more successfully than other people do.

Brain Evolution

Humans have bigger and better brains (at least we think so) than other species. We, and to a large extent our primate relatives also, create new solutions to problems we have never faced before (Rumbaugh, Savage-Rumbaugh, King, & Tagliatela, 2010). How did we manage to evolve this advantage? One explanation is that our ancestors managed to get enough nutrition to provide a big brain with all the fuel it needs. Researchers selectively bred guppies (small fish) for larger brains. Within a few generations, they did indeed have guppies with bigger brains and better performance on some (not all) learning tasks. However, these guppies had less energy available for other organs and functions. In particular, they produced fewer offspring than average (Kotrschal et al., 2013). In a world where most baby fish get eaten, sacrificing babies for big brains is a bad bet, evolutionarily.

Humans may have been able to evolve such big brains without sacrificing other functions, because of our diet. At some point in our early evolutionary history, our ancestors learned to cook their food, making it easier to digest. They hunted in groups, bringing back more food than one person alone could find, and many of them probably ate seafood, rich in nutrition. Also, humans differ from chimpanzees in two genes responsible for glucose transport: We have more of the protein that transports glucose into the brain, and less of the protein that transports it into the muscles (Fedrigo et al., 2011). Thus, we devote more energy to our brains and less to physical strength.

In addition to having large brains, our brains are different in ways that are not yet well understood. Primates in general have many genes active in brain development that do not occur in other mammals, and humans have a few that don't occur even in other primates (Zhang, Landback, Vibranovski, & Long, 2011). These genes exert their effects especially in the prefrontal cortex, an area important for memory, attention, speech, and decision making.

Evolutionary Psychology

Evolutionary psychology concerns how behaviors evolved. The emphasis is on *evolutionary* and *functional* explanations—that is, the presumed genes of our ancestors and why natural selection might have favored genes that promote certain behaviors. The assumption is that any behavior characteristic of a species arose through natural selection and presumably provided some advantage, at least in ancestral times. Consider these examples:

- Some animal species have better color vision than others, and some have better peripheral vision. Species evolve the kind of vision they need for their way of life (Chapter 5).
- Animals that are in danger of being attacked while they sleep get little sleep per night (and apparently need little sleep), as compared to lions, bats, and armadillos, which are unlikely to be attacked in their sleep, and sleep many hours (Chapter 8).
- Bears eat all the food they can find, and small birds eat only enough to satisfy their immediate needs. Eating habits relate to the needs of each species (Chapter 9).

Certain human behaviors make no sense except in terms of evolution. For example, people get "goose bumps"—erections of the hairs, especially on their arms and shoulders—when they are cold or frightened. Goose bumps produce little if any benefit to humans because our shoulder and arm hairs are short and usually covered by clothing. In most other mammals, however, erected hairs make a frightened animal look larger and more intimidating (see Figure 4.6). They also provide extra insulation when the air is cold. We explain human goose bumps by saying that the behavior evolved in our remote ancestors and we inherited the mechanism.

Also consider the infant grasp reflex (see Figure 4.7). An infant will grasp tightly onto a finger, pencil, or similar object placed in the palm of the hand. What good does that accomplish? Little or none for humans, but for our monkey-like ancestors, it was critical. A mother monkey often needs all four limbs to climb a tree for food or to run away from a predator. An infant monkey that couldn't hold on would jeopardize its life.

Jane Burton/Nature Picture Library

FIGURE 4.6 A frightened cat with erect hairs
For animals with long hairs, erecting those hairs increases insulation from cold and makes the animal look larger and more dangerous. We humans continue to erect our hairs in those same situations as a remnant from our evolutionary past.

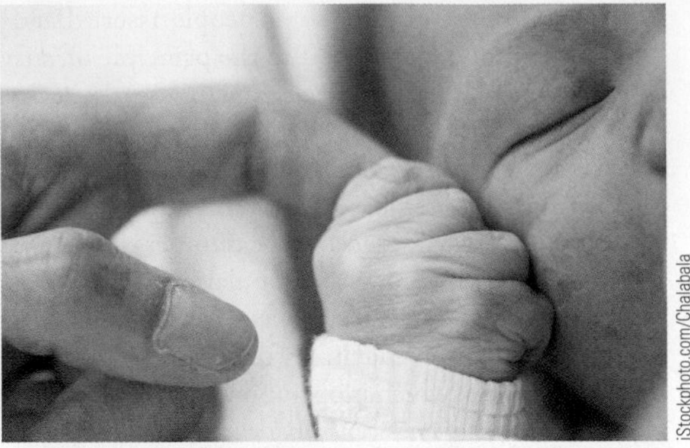
iStockphoto.com/Chalabala

Jo Ellen Kalat

FIGURE 4.7 Grasp reflex in human and monkey infants
The grasp reflex, which accomplishes little or nothing for human infants, makes sense as an evolutionary remnant of a behavior necessary for the survival of our monkey-like ancestors.

On the other hand, some proposed evolutionary explanations are speculative and controversial. Consider two examples:

- More men than women enjoy the prospect of casual sex with multiple partners. Theorists have related this tendency to the fact that a man can spread his genes by impregnating many women, whereas a woman cannot multiply her children by having more sexual partners (Buss, 1994). Are men and women prewired to have different sexual behaviors? We shall explore this controversial and uncertain topic in a later chapter.
- People grow old and die, with an average survival time of 70 to 80 years under favorable circumstances. However, people vary in how rapidly they deteriorate in old age, and part of that variation is under genetic control. Researchers have identified several genes that are significantly more common among people who remain healthy and alert at ages 85 and beyond (Halaschek-Wiener et al., 2009; Poduslo, Huang, & Spiro, 2009; Puca et al., 2001). Why don't we all have those genes? Perhaps living many years after the end of your reproductive years is evolutionarily disadvantageous. Did we evolve a tendency to grow old and die in order to

get out of the way and stop competing with our children and grandchildren? Curiously, a few species of turtles and deep-ocean fish continue reproducing throughout their lives, and they do not seem to grow old. That is, so far as we can tell from limited samples, they are no more likely to die when they are 100 years old than when they are 50 or 20. One rockfish is known to have lived more than 200 years (Finch, 2009). Again, the idea is that old-age deterioration might be an evolved mechanism, and its presence or absence could be under genetic control.

To further illustrate evolutionary psychology, consider the theoretically interesting example of **altruistic behavior,** an action that benefits someone other than the actor. A gene that encourages altruistic behavior would help *other* individuals survive and spread *their* genes. Could a gene for altruism spread, and if so, how?

How common is altruism? It certainly occurs in humans: We contribute to charities. We try to help people in distress. A student may explain something to a classmate who is competing for a good grade in a course. Some people donate a kidney to save the life of someone they didn't even know (MacFarquhar, 2009).

Among nonhumans, altruism is harder to find. Cooperation occurs, certainly. A pack of animals may hunt together or forage together. A flock of small birds may "mob" an owl or hawk to drive it away. Chimpanzees sometimes share food (Hamann, Warneken, Greenberg, & Tomasello, 2011). Bur real altruism, in the sense of helping a nonrelative without immediately getting something in return, is rare in nonhumans (Cheney, 2011). In one study, a chimpanzee could pull one rope to bring food into its own cage or a second rope that would bring food to itself and additional food to a familiar but unrelated chimpanzee in a neighboring cage. Most often, chimps pulled whichever rope happened to be on the right at the time—suggesting right-handedness—apparently indifferent to the welfare of the other chimpanzee, even when the other made begging gestures (Silk et al., 2005).

Even when animals do appear altruistic, they often have a selfish motive. When a crow finds food on the ground, it caws loudly, attracting other crows that will share the food. Altruism? Not really. A bird on the ground is vulnerable to attack by cats and other enemies. Having other crows around means more eyes to watch for dangers.

Also consider meerkats (a kind of mongoose). Periodically, one or another member of a meerkat colony stands and, if it sees danger, emits an alarm call that warns the others (see Figure 4.8). Its alarm call helps the others (including its relatives), but the one who sees the danger first and emits the alarm call is the one most likely to escape (Clutton-Brock et al., 1999).

For the sake of illustration, let's suppose—without evidence—that some gene increases altruistic behavior. Could it spread within a population? One common reply is that most altruistic behaviors cost very little. True, but costing little is not good enough. A gene spreads only if the individuals with it reproduce more than those without it. Another common reply is that the altruistic behavior benefits the species. True

FIGURE 4.8 Sentinel behavior: altruistic or not?
As in many other prey species, meerkats sometimes show sentinel behavior in watching for danger and warning the others. However, the meerkat that emits the alarm is the one most likely to escape the danger.

again, but the rebuttal is the same. A gene that benefits the species but fails to help the individual dies out with that individual.

A better explanation is **kin selection**—selection for a gene that benefits the individual's relatives. A gene spreads if it causes you to risk your life to protect your children, who share many of your genes, including perhaps a gene for altruism. Natural selection can also favor altruism toward other relatives—such as brothers and sisters, cousins, nephews, and nieces (Dawkins, 1989; Hamilton, 1964; Trivers, 1985). In both humans and nonhumans, helpful behavior is more common toward relatives than toward unrelated individuals (Bowles & Posel, 2005; Krakauer, 2005).

Another explanation is **reciprocal altruism**, the idea that individuals help those who will return the favor. Researchers find that people are prone to help not only those who helped them but also people whom they observed helping someone else (Nowak & Sigmund, 2005). The idea is not just "you scratched my back, so I'll scratch yours," but also "you scratched someone else's back, so I'll scratch yours." By helping others, you build a reputation for helpfulness, and others are willing to cooperate with you. This system works only if individuals recognize one another. Otherwise, an uncooperative individual can accept favors, prosper, and never repay the favors. In other words, reciprocal altruism requires an ability to identify individuals and remember them later. Humans, of course, are excellent at recognizing one another even over long delays.

A more controversial hypothesis is *group selection*. According to this idea, altruistic groups thrive better than less cooperative ones (Bowles, 2006; Kohn, 2008). Although this idea is certainly true, it faces a problem: Even if cooperative groups do well, wouldn't an uncooperative individual within the cooperative group gain an advantage? Nevertheless, theorists have concluded that group selection does work under certain circumstances, such as when cooperative individuals do most of their interactions with one another (Simon, Fletcher, & Doebeli, 2013). Group selection works especially well for humans, because of our ability to punish or expel uncooperative people.

At its best, evolutionary psychology leads to research that helps us understand a behavior. The search for a functional explanation directs researchers to explore species' different habitats and ways of life until we understand why they behave differently. The approach is criticized when its practitioners propose explanations without testing them (Schlinger, 1996).

STOP&CHECK

11. What are plausible ways for possible altruistic genes to spread in a population?

ANSWER

11. Altruistic genes could spread because they facilitate care for one's kin or because they facilitate exchanges of favors with others (reciprocal altruism). Group selection may also work under some circumstances, especially if the cooperative group has some way to punish or expel an uncooperative individual.

MODULE 4.1 ■ IN CLOSING

Genes and Behavior

In the control of behavior, genes are neither all important nor irrelevant. Certain behaviors have a high heritability, such as the ability to taste PTC. Many other behaviors are influenced by genes but also subject to strong influence by experience. Our genes and our evolution make it possible for humans to be what we are today, but they also give us the flexibility to change our behavior as circumstances warrant.

Understanding the genetics of human behavior is important but also especially difficult, because researchers have such limited control over environmental influences and *no* control over who mates with whom. Inferring human evolution is also difficult, partly because we do not know enough about the lives of our ancient ancestors. Inferring behavioral evolution has the additional difficulty that behavior does not fossilize.

Finally, we should remember that the way things *are* is not necessarily the same as the way they *should be*. For example, even if our genes predispose us to behave in a particular way, we can still decide to try to overcome those predispositions if they do not suit the needs of modern life.

Summary

1. Genes are chemicals that maintain their integrity from one generation to the next and influence the development of the individual. A dominant gene affects development regardless of whether a person has pairs of that gene or only a single copy per cell. A recessive gene affects development only in the absence of the dominant gene. **104**
2. Genes can change by mutations, microduplications, and microdeletions. **107**
3. Gene expression can also change in a process called epigenetics, as chemicals activate or deactivate parts of chromosomes. **107**
4. Most behavioral variations reflect the combined influences of genes and environmental factors. Heritability is an estimate of the amount of variation that is due to genetic variation as opposed to environmental variation. **108**
5. Researchers estimate heritability of a human condition by comparing monozygotic and dizygotic twins and by comparing adopted children to their biological and adoptive parents. They also identify genes that are more common in people with one type of behavior than another. **108**
6. Even if some behavior shows high heritability for a given population, a change in the environment might significantly alter the behavioral outcome. **109**

7. Genes influence behavior directly by altering brain chemicals and indirectly by affecting other aspects of the body and therefore the way other people react to us. **109**
8. The process of evolution through natural selection is a necessary outcome, given what we know about reproduction: Mutations sometimes occur in genes, and individuals with certain sets of genes reproduce more successfully than others do. **110**
9. The human brain has evolved to be as large as it is partly because we can provide a large amount of fuel to the brain. Human brains also have certain genes not active in other species. **111**
10. Evolution spreads the genes of the individuals who have reproduced the most. Therefore, if some characteristic is widespread within a population, it is reasonable to look for ways in which that characteristic is or has been adaptive. However, we cannot take it for granted that all common behaviors are the product of our genes. We need to distinguish genetic influences from learning. **112**

Key Terms

Terms are defined in the module on the page number indicated. They're also presented in alphabetical order with definitions in the book's Subject Index/Glossary. Interactive flash cards, audio reviews, and crossword puzzles are among the online resources available to help you learn these terms and the concepts they represent.

altruistic behavior **113**
artificial selection **110**
autosomal genes **106**
chromosomes **104**
deoxyribonucleic acid (DNA) **104**
dizygotic **108**
dominant **105**
epigenetics **107**
evolution **110**
evolutionary psychology **112**
fitness **111**
genes **104**
heritability **108**
heterozygous **105**
homozygous **105**
kin selection **113**
Lamarckian evolution **110**
monozygotic **108**
mutation **107**
phenylketonuria (PKU) **109**
recessive **105**
reciprocal altruism **113**
ribonucleic acid (RNA) **105**
sex-limited genes **106**
sex-linked genes **106**

Thought Questions

1. For what human behaviors, if any, are you sure that heritability would be extremely low?
2. Genetic differences probably account for part of the difference between people who age slowly and gracefully and others who grow old more rapidly and die younger. Given that the genes controlling old age have their onset long after people have stopped having children, how could evolution have any effect on such genes?

MODULE 4.1 End of Module Quiz

1. Suppose you have high sensitivity to the taste of PTC. If your mother also has high sensitivity, what (if anything) can you predict about your father's taste sensitivity?
   a. He has high taste sensitivity.
   b. He has low taste sensitivity.
   c. We do not have enough information to make a prediction.
2. Suppose you have high sensitivity to the taste of PTC. If your mother has low sensitivity, what (if anything) can you predict about your father's taste sensitivity?
   a. He has high taste sensitivity.
   b. He has low taste sensitivity.
   c. We do not have enough information to make a prediction.
3. What is a sex-limited gene?
   a. A gene on the X chromosome
   b. A gene on the Y chromosome
   c. A gene that sex hormones activate
   d. A gene that becomes active during sexual activity

4. Suppose someone identifies a "gene for" certain aspects of sexual development. In what ways might that statement be misleading?
   a. The statement didn't specify whether the gene was dominant or recessive.
   b. Many aspects of sexual development are not apparent until puberty.
   c. Almost any characteristic depends on many genes, as well as influences from the environment.

5. How does an epigenetic change differ from a mutation?
   a. An epigenetic change is a duplication or deletion of part of a gene.
   b. An epigenetic change is an alteration of gene activity without structurally replacing any part of the gene itself.
   c. An epigenetic change alters more than one gene at a time.
   d. An epigenetic change is beneficial, whereas a mutation is harmful.

6. How does adding a methyl or acetyl group to a histone protein alter gene activity?
   a. A methyl group turns genes off. An acetyl group loosens histone's grip and increases gene activation.
   b. A methyl group turns genes on. An acetyl group tightens histone's grip and decreases gene activation.
   c. A methyl group increases the probability of a mutation, whereas an acetyl group decreases the probability.
   d. A methyl group decreases the probability of a mutation, whereas an acetyl group increases the probability.

7. Which of the following is NOT one of the main types of evidence to estimate the heritability of some behavior?
   a. Comparisons between monozygotic and dizygotic twins
   b. Similarities between adopted children and their biological parents
   c. Examination of identified genes that might vary between people showing one behavior and another
   d. Comparisons of people living in different cultures

8. Suppose someone determines the heritability of IQ scores for a given population. Then society changes in a way that provides the best possible opportunity for everyone within that population. How will the heritability of IQ change, if at all?
   a. Heritability will increase.
   b. Heritability will decrease.
   c. Heritability will stay the same.

9. The information about phenylketonuria (PKU) supports which of these conclusions?
   a. Several genes active in the human brain are not found in other species.
   b. Each brain area controls a different behavioral function.
   c. A change in the environment can alter the effects of a gene.
   d. Epigenetic changes depend on methyl and acetate groups.

10. What, if anything, can we predict about the future of human evolution?
   a. People will get smarter, wiser, and more cooperative.
   b. People will not change, because evolution no longer affects humans.
   c. People will become more like whichever people tend to have the most children.

11. Which of these is the *least* acceptable explanation for how an altruistic gene might spread in a population?
   a. Selection for a gene that benefits the individuals' relatives
   b. Selection for helping individuals who might return the favor
   c. Selection for genes that benefit the species
   d. Selection for groups that are more cooperative than other groups

ANSWERS: 1c, 2a, 3c, 4c, 5b, 6a, 7d, 8a, 9c, 10c, 11c.

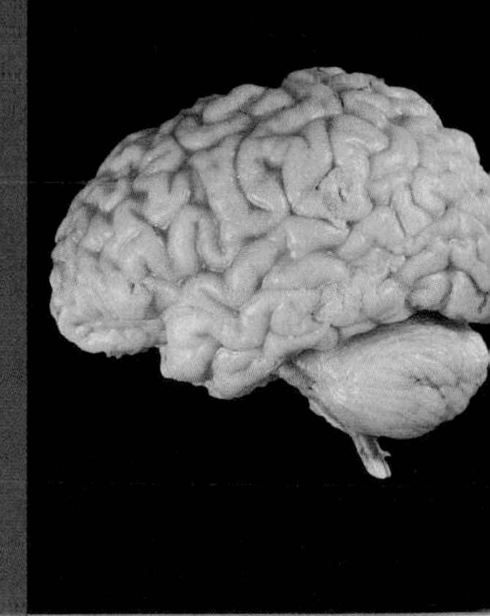

MODULE 4.2

Development of the Brain

Think of all the things you can do that you couldn't have done a few years ago—analyze statistics, read a foreign language, write brilliant critiques of complex issues, and so on. Have you developed these new skills because of brain growth? Many of your dendrites have grown new branches, but your brain as a whole hasn't grown.

Now think of all the things that 1-year-old children can do that they could not do at birth. Have *they* developed their new skills because of brain growth? To a large extent, yes, although the results depend on experiences as well. Brain development depends on experience in complex ways that blur the distinction between learning and maturation. In this module, we consider how neurons develop, how their axons connect, and how experience modifies development.

Maturation of the Vertebrate Brain

The human central nervous system begins to form when the embryo is about 2 weeks old. The dorsal surface thickens and then long thin lips rise, curl, and merge, forming a neural tube that surrounds a fluid-filled cavity (see Figure 4.9). As the tube sinks under the surface of the skin, the forward end enlarges and differentiates into the hindbrain, midbrain, and forebrain (see Figure 4.10). The rest becomes the spinal cord. The fluid-filled cavity within the neural tube becomes the central canal of the spinal cord and the four ventricles of the brain, containing the cerebrospinal fluid (CSF). The first muscle movements start at age 7½ weeks, and their only accomplishment is to stretch the muscles. At that age, spontaneous activity in the spinal cord drives all the muscle movements, as the sensory organs are not yet functional (Provine, 1972). That is, contrary to what we might guess, we start making movements before we start receiving sensations.

At birth, the average human brain weighs about 350 grams. By the end of the first year, it weighs 1000 g, close to the adult weight of 1200 to 1400 g.

Growth and Development of Neurons

Neuroscientists distinguish these processes in the development of neurons: proliferation, migration, differentiation, myelination, and synaptogenesis. **Proliferation** is the production of new cells. Early in development, the cells lining the ventricles of the brain divide. Some cells remain where they are as **stem cells**, continuing to divide. Others become primitive neurons and glia that migrate to other locations.

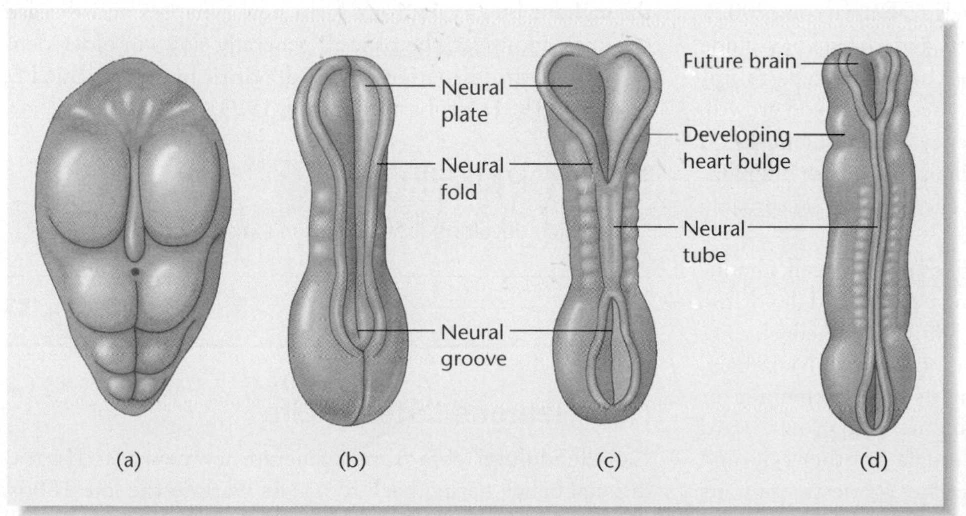

FIGURE 4.9 Early development of the human central nervous system
The brain and spinal cord begin as folding lips surrounding a fluid-filled canal. The stages shown occur at approximately 2 to 3 weeks after conception.

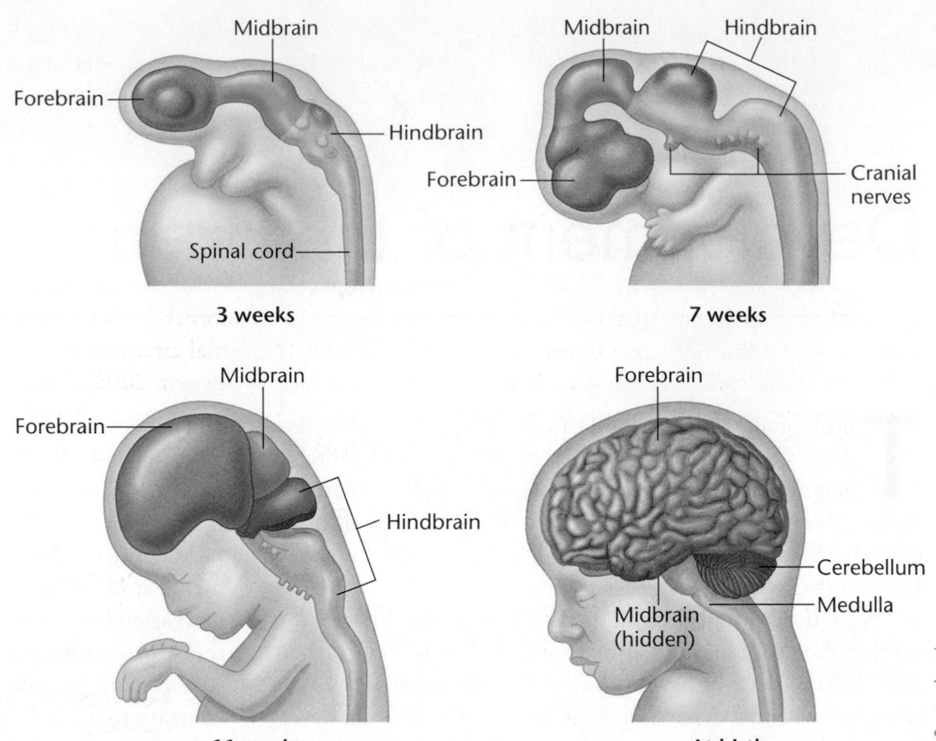

FIGURE 4.10 Human brain at four stages of development
The growing forebrain quickly surrounds the midbrain and part of the hindbrain.

Neuron proliferation is similar among vertebrates, differing mainly in the number of cell divisions. One of the major differences between human brains and chimpanzee brains is that human neurons continue proliferating longer (Rakic, 1998; Vrba, 1998). Nearly all neurons form within the first 28 weeks of gestation, and premature birth before that time inhibits neuron formation (Malik et al., 2013).

Early in development, the primitive neurons begin to **migrate** (move). Some migrate faster than others, and a few of the slowest don't reach their destinations until adulthood (Ghashghaei, Lai, & Anton, 2007). Some neurons move radially from the inside of the brain to the outside, some move tangentially along the surface of the brain, and some move tangentially and then radially (Nadarajah & Parnavelas, 2002). Chemicals known as *immunoglobulins* and *chemokines* guide neuron migration. A deficit in these chemicals leads to impaired migration, decreased brain size, decreased axon growth, and mental retardation (Berger-Sweeney & Hohmann, 1997; Crossin & Krushel, 2000; Tran & Miller, 2003). The brain has many kinds of immunoglobulins and chemokines, presumably reflecting the complexity of brain development.

At first, a primitive neuron looks like any other cell. Gradually, the neuron **differentiates**, forming its axon and dendrites. The axon grows first. In many cases, a migrating neuron tows its growing axon along like a tail (Gilmour, Knaut, Maischein, & Nüsslein-Volhard, 2004), allowing its tip to remain at or near its target. In other cases, the axon needs to grow toward its target, finding its way through a jungle of other cells and fibers. After the migrating neuron reaches its destination, its dendrites begin to form.

A later and slower stage of neuronal development is **myelination**, the process by which glia produce the insulating fatty sheaths that accelerate transmission in many vertebrate axons. Myelin forms first in the spinal cord and then in the hindbrain, midbrain, and forebrain. Unlike the rapid proliferation and migration of neurons, myelination continues gradually through adolescence and early adulthood, and perhaps beyond (Benes, Turtle, Khan, & Farol, 1994; Lebel & Beaulieu, 2011). Myelination is a vulnerable process. The experience of social isolation produces part of its effect by impairing myelination (Liu et al., 2012).

The final stage is **synaptogenesis**, or the formation of synapses. Although this process begins before birth, it continues throughout life, as neurons form new synapses and discard old ones. However, the process generally slows in older people, as does the formation of new dendritic branches (Buell & Coleman, 1981; Jacobs & Scheibel, 1993).

STOP & CHECK

12. Which develops first, a neuron's axon or its dendrites?

ANSWER

12. The axon forms first.

New Neurons Later in Life

Can the adult vertebrate brain generate new neurons? The traditional belief, dating back to Cajal's work in the late 1800s, discussed in Chapter 1, was that vertebrate brains formed all their neurons in embryological development or early infancy at the latest. Beyond that point, neurons could modify their shape, but the brain could not develop new neurons. Later researchers found exceptions.

The first were the olfactory receptors, which, because they are exposed to the outside world and its toxic chemicals, have a half-life of only 90 days. Stem cells in the nose remain immature throughout life. Periodically, they divide, with one cell remaining immature while the other differentiates to replace a dying olfactory receptor. It grows its axon back to the appropriate site in the brain (Gogos, Osborne, Nemes, Mendelsohn, & Axel, 2000; Graziadei & deHan, 1973). Later researchers also demonstrated the formation of new neurons in the olfactory bulb of many species (Gage, 2000) and in an area of the songbird brain necessary for singing. This area loses neurons in fall and winter and regains them the next spring (mating season) (Nottebohm, 2002; Wissman & Brenowitz, 2009). Also, new neurons form in the adult hippocampus of birds (Smulders, Shiflett, Sperling, & DeVoogd, 2000) and mammals (Song, Stevens, & Gage, 2002; van Praag et al., 2002). The hippocampus is an important area for memory formation. A supply of new neurons keeps the hippocampus "young" for learning new tasks (Ge, Yang, Hsu, Ming, & Song, 2007; Schmidt-Hieber, Jonas, & Bischofberger, 2004). Blocking the formation of new neurons (such as by exposing the hippocampus to X-rays) impairs new memories (Clelland et al., 2009; Meshi et al., 2006).

Researchers have also found that certain types of brain damage lead to the production of new neurons in the cerebral cortex of rodents (Ohira et al., 2010; Pan et al., 2013; Vessal & Darian-Smith, 2010). At least some of these neurons persist for at least a year—a long time in the life of a rodent—but they failed to differentiate into mature neurons (Osman, Porritt, Nilsson, & Kuhn, 2011). Although newly formed neurons in the hippocampus and olfactory bulb are behaviorally important (Alonso et al., 2012), researchers are less sure about the new neurons in the damaged cortex.

The early research on formation of new neurons used laboratory rodents, and later research has found somewhat different results with humans. One way to test for newly formed neurons uses measurements of a radioactive isotope of carbon, ^{14}C. The concentration of ^{14}C in the atmosphere, compared to other isotopes of carbon, was nearly constant over time until the era of nuclear bomb testing released much radioactivity. That era ended with the Test Ban Treaty of 1963. The concentration of ^{14}C peaked in 1963 and has been declining since then. If you examine tree rings, you find that a ring that formed in 1963 has the ^{14}C content typical of 1963, a ring that formed in 1990 has the ^{14}C content typical of 1990, and so forth. Researchers examined carbon in the DNA of various human cells. Every cell acquires DNA molecules when it forms and keeps them until it dies. When researchers examined people's skin cells, they found a concentration of ^{14}C corresponding to the year in which they did the test. That is, skin cells turn over rapidly, and all of your skin cells are less than a year old. When they examined skeletal muscle cells, they found a ^{14}C concentration corresponding to 15 years ago, indicating that skeletal muscles are replaced slowly, making the average cell 15 years old. Cells of the heart are, on average, almost as old as the person, indicating that the body replaces no more than one percent of heart cells per year (Bergmann et al., 2009). When researchers examined neurons in the cerebral cortex (of dead people at autopsy), they found a ^{14}C concentration corresponding to the year of the person's birth. These results indicate that the mammalian cerebral cortex forms few or no new neurons after birth, at least under normal circumstances (Spalding, Bhardwaj, Buchholz, Druid, & Frisén, 2005). They also found that the ^{14}C concentration in the human olfactory bulbs corresponded to the year of birth (Bergmann et al., 2012). Evidently, unlike rodents, humans do not make new neurons in the olfactory bulbs. The ^{14}C concentration the human hippocampus indicated that we replace a little less than 2 percent of neurons in that area per year (Spalding et al., 2013).

STOP & CHECK

13. New receptor neurons form in adult rodents for which sensory system?

14. What evidence indicated that new neurons seldom or never form in the human cerebral cortex and olfactory bulb?

ANSWERS

13. Olfaction **14.** The ^{14}C concentration in the DNA of human neurons in the cerebral cortex and olfactory bulbs corresponds to the level during the year the person was born, indicating that all or nearly all of those neurons are as old as the person is.

Pathfinding by Axons

If you asked someone to run a cable from your desk to another desk across the room, your directions could be simple. But imagine asking someone to run a cable to somewhere on the other side of the country. You would have to give detailed instructions about how to find the right city, building, and desk. The developing nervous system faces a similar challenge because it sends axons over great distances. How do they find their way?

Chemical Pathfinding by Axons

A famous biologist, Paul Weiss (1924), conducted an experiment in which he grafted an extra leg to a salamander and then waited for axons to grow into it. (Unlike mammals, salamanders and other amphibians accept transplants of extra limbs and generate new axon branches to the extra limbs. Much research requires finding the right species to study.) After the axons reached the muscles, the extra leg moved in synchrony with the normal leg next to it.

Weiss dismissed the idea that each axon found its way to the correct muscle in the extra limb. He suggested instead that the nerves attached to muscles at random and then sent a variety of messages, each one tuned to a different muscle. The muscles were like radios tuned to different stations: Each muscle received many signals but responded to only one. (The 1920s were the early days of radio, and it was an appealing analogy to think the nervous system might work like a radio. In the 1600s, Descartes thought the nervous system worked like a hydraulic pump, the most advanced technology of the time. Today, many people think the nervous system works like a computer, our own most advanced technology.)

Specificity of Axon Connections

Later evidence supported the interpretation that Weiss had rejected: The salamander's extra leg moved in synchrony with its neighbor because each axon found the correct muscle.

Roger Sperry, a former student of Weiss, performed a classic experiment that showed how sensory axons find their way to their correct targets. The principle is the same as for axons finding their way to muscles. First, Sperry cut the optic nerves of some newts. (Note the importance of choosing the right species: A cut optic nerve grows back in newts and other amphibians, but not in mammals or birds.) The damaged optic nerve grew back and connected with the *tectum*, which is amphibians' main visual area (see Figure 4.11), thereby reestablishing normal vision. So then Sperry's question was: Did they grow at random, or did they grow to a specific target?

Courtesy of the Archives, California Institute of Technology

Roger W. Sperry

(1913–1994)

When subjective values have objective consequences . . . they become part of the content of science. . . . Science would become the final determinant of what is right and true, the best source and authority available to the human brain for finding ultimate axioms and guideline beliefs to live by, and for reaching an intimate understanding and rapport with the forces that control the universe and created man. (Sperry, 1975)

For the next set of newts, Sperry (1943) cut the optic nerve and rotated the eye by 180 degrees. When the axons grew back to the tectum, the axons from what had originally been the dorsal portion of the retina (which was now ventral) grew back to the area responsible for vision in the dorsal retina. Axons from other parts of the retina also grew back to their original targets. The newt now saw the world upside down and backward, responding to stimuli in the sky as if they were on the ground and to stimuli on the left as if they were on the right (see Figure 4.12). Each axon regenerated to the same place where it had originally been, presumably by following a chemical trail.

Chemical Gradients

The next question was: How does an axon find its target? The current estimate is that humans have only about 30,000 genes total—far too few to provide a specific target for each of the brain's billions of neurons.

A growing axon follows a path of cell surface molecules, attracted by some chemicals and repelled by others, in a process that steers the axon in the correct direction (Yu & Bargmann, 2001). Eventually, axons sort themselves over the surface of their target area by following a gradient of chemicals. One protein in the amphibian tectum is 30 times more concentrated in the axons of the dorsal retina than of the ventral retina and 10 times more concentrated in the ventral tectum than in the dorsal tectum. As axons from the retina grow toward the tectum, the retinal axons with the greatest concentration of this chemical connect to the tectal cells with the highest concentration. The axons with the lowest concentration connect to the tectal cells with the lowest concentration. A similar gradient of another protein aligns the axons along the anterior–posterior axis (J. R. Sanes, 1993) (see Figure 4.13). By analogy, you could think of men lining up from tallest to shortest, pairing up with women who lined up from tallest to shortest.

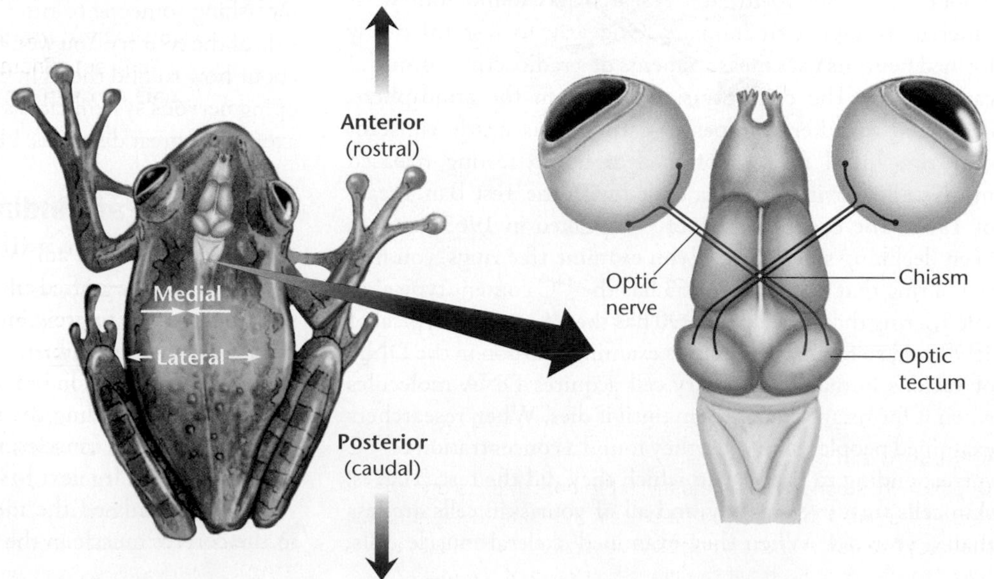

FIGURE 4.11 Connections from eye to brain in a frog
The optic tectum is a large structure in fish, amphibians, reptiles, and birds. Its location corresponds to the midbrain of mammals, but its function is analogous to what the cerebral cortex does in mammals. Note: Connections from eye to brain are different in humans, as described in the module on lateralization. *Source:* From Romer, 1962

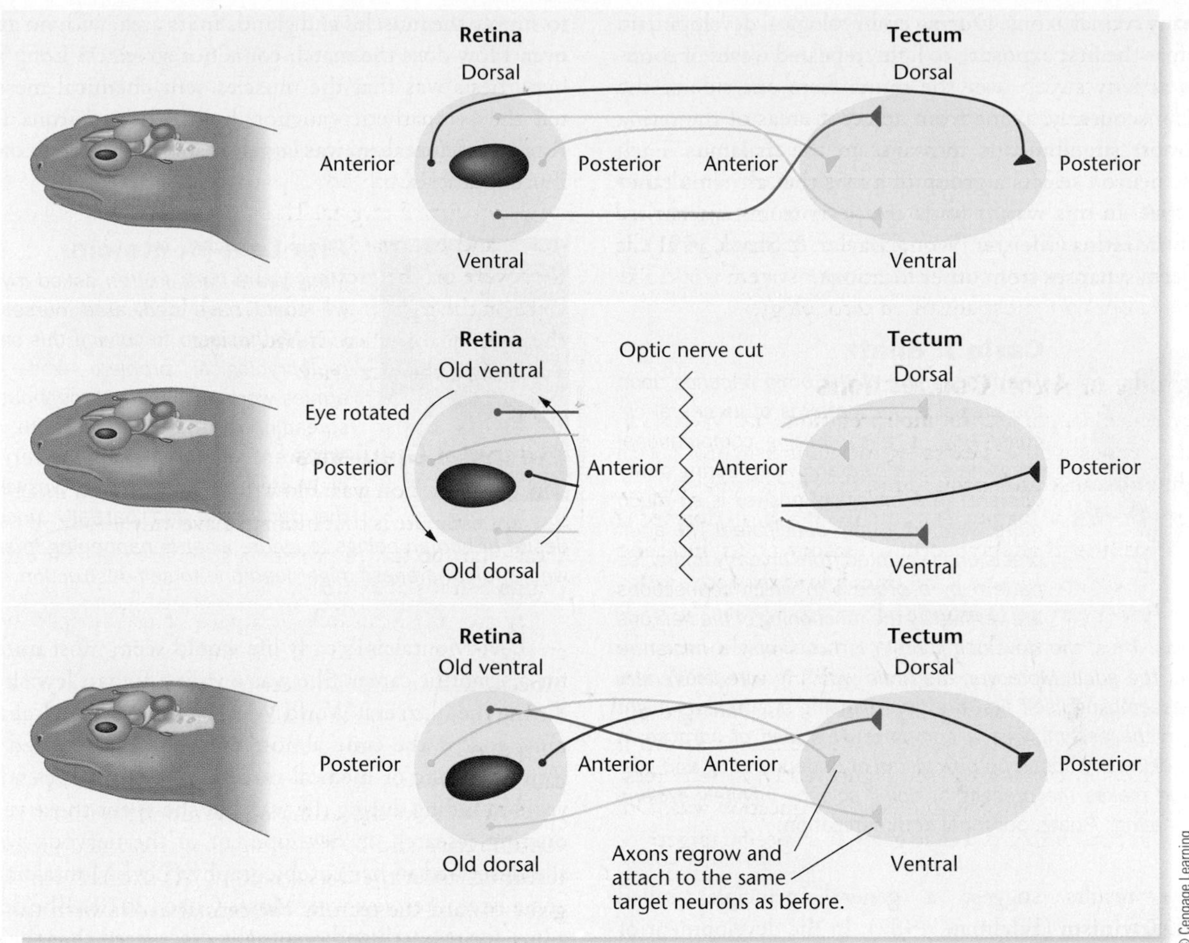

FIGURE 4.12 Sperry's experiment on nerve connections in newts
After he cut the optic nerve and inverted the eye, the axons grew back to their original targets, not to the targets corresponding to the eye's current position.

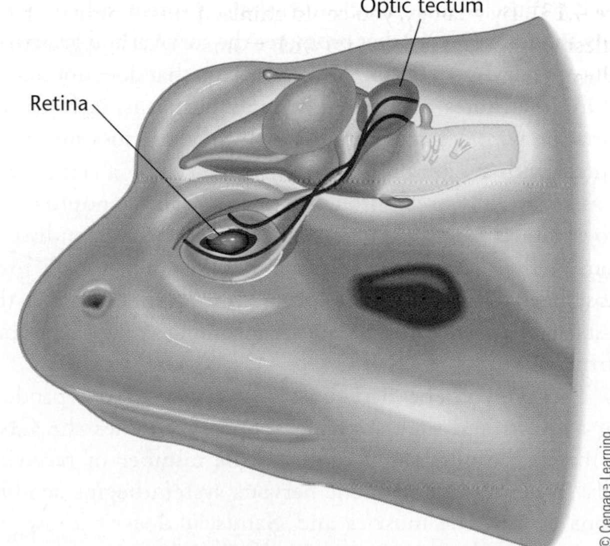

FIGURE 4.13 Retinal axons find targets in the tectum by following chemical gradients
One protein is concentrated mostly in the dorsal retina and the ventral tectum. Axons rich in that protein attach to tectal neurons that are also rich in that chemical. A second protein directs axons from the posterior retina to the anterior portion of the tectum.

STOP&CHECK

15. What was Sperry's evidence that axons grow to a specific target instead of attaching at random?

ANSWER

15. If he cut a newt's eye and inverted it, axons grew back to their original targets, even though the connections were inappropriate to their new positions on the eye.

Competition among Axons as a General Principle

When axons initially reach their targets, chemical gradients steer them to approximately their correct location, but it would be hard to imagine that they achieve perfect accuracy. Instead, each axon forms synapses onto many cells in approximately the correct location, and each target cell receives synapses from many axons. Over time, each postsynaptic cell strengthens the most appropriate synapses and eliminates others (Hua & Smith, 2004). This adjustment depends on the pattern of input from incoming axons (Catalano & Shatz, 1998). For example, one part of the thalamus receives input from many retinal axons. During embryological development, long before the first exposure to light, repeated waves of spontaneous activity sweep over the retina from one side to the other. Consequently, axons from adjacent areas of the retina send almost simultaneous messages to the thalamus. Each thalamic neuron selects a group of axons that are simultaneously active. In this way, it finds receptors from adjacent regions of the retina (Meister, Wong, Baylor, & Shatz, 1991). It then rejects synapses from other locations.

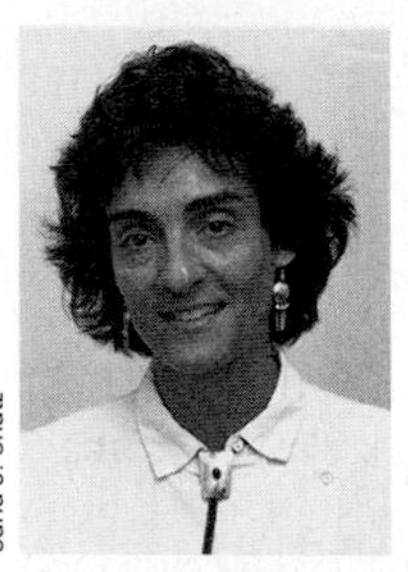
Carla J. Shatz

Carla J. Shatz

The functioning of the brain depends upon the precision and patterns of its neural circuits. How is this amazing computational machine assembled and wired during development? The biological answer is so much more wonderful than anticipated! The adult precision is sculpted from an early imprecise pattern by a process in which connections are verified by the functioning of the neurons themselves. Thus, the developing brain is not simply a miniature version of the adult. Moreover, the brain works to wire itself, rather than assembling itself first and then flipping a switch, as might happen in the assembly of a computer. This kind of surprise in scientific discovery opens up new vistas of understanding and possibility and makes the process of doing science infinitely exciting and fascinating. (Shatz, personal communication)

These results suggest a general principle, called **neural Darwinism** (Edelman, 1987). In the development of the nervous system, we start with more neurons and synapses than we can keep. Synapses form with approximate accuracy, and then a selection process keeps some and rejects others. The most successful axons and combinations survive, and the others fail. The principle of competition among axons is an important one, although we should use the analogy with Darwinian evolution cautiously. Mutations in the genes are random events, but neurotrophins steer new axonal branches and synapses in the right direction.

STOP & CHECK

16. If axons from the retina were prevented from showing spontaneous activity during early development, what would be the probable effect on development of the thalamus?

ANSWER

16. The axons would attach based on a chemical gradient but could not fine-tune their adjustment based on experience. Therefore, the connections would be less precise.

Determinants of Neuronal Survival

Getting the right number of neurons for each area of the nervous system is more complicated than it might seem. Consider an example. The sympathetic nervous system sends axons to muscles and glands. Each ganglion has enough axons to supply the muscles and glands in its area, with no axons left over. How does the match come out so exact? Long ago, one hypothesis was that the muscles sent chemical messages to tell the sympathetic ganglion how many neurons to form. Rita Levi-Montalcini was largely responsible for disconfirming this hypothesis.

Erich Hartmann/Magnum Photos

Rita Levi-Montalcini

Many years later, I often asked myself how we could have dedicated ourselves with such enthusiasm to solving this small neuroembryological problem while German armies were advancing throughout Europe, spreading destruction and death wherever they went and threatening the very survival of Western civilization. The answer lies in the desperate and partially unconscious desire of human beings to ignore what is happening in situations where full awareness might lead one to self-destruction.

Levi-Montalcini's early life would seem most unfavorable for a scientific career. She was a young Italian Jewish woman during the Nazi era. World War II destroyed the Italian economy, and at the time almost everyone discouraged women from scientific or medical careers. She had to spend several years in hiding during the war, but she spent those years conducting research on development of the nervous system, as she described in her autobiography (Levi-Montalcini, 1988) and a later interview with Moses Chao (2010). She developed a love for research and eventually discovered that the muscles do not determine how many axons *form;* they determine how many *survive.*

Initially, the sympathetic nervous system forms far more neurons than it needs. When one of its neurons forms a synapse onto a muscle, that muscle delivers a protein called **nerve growth factor (NGF)** that promotes the survival and growth of the axon (Levi-Montalcini, 1987). An axon that does not receive NGF degenerates, and its cell body dies. That is, each neuron starts life with a "suicide program": If its axon does not make contact with an appropriate postsynaptic cell by a certain age, the neuron kills itself through a process called **apoptosis,**[1] a programmed mechanism of cell death. (Apoptosis is distinct from *necrosis,* which is death caused by an injury or a toxic substance.) NGF cancels the program for apoptosis; it is the postsynaptic cell's way of telling the incoming axon, "I'll be your partner. Don't kill yourself."

The sympathetic nervous system's way of overproducing neurons and then applying apoptosis enables the CNS to match the number of axons to the number of receiving cells. When the sympathetic nervous system begins sending axons toward the muscles and glands, it doesn't know the exact size of the muscles or glands. It makes more neurons than necessary and discards the excess. In fact, all areas of the

[1]Apoptosis is based on the Greek root *ptosis* (meaning "dropping"), which is pronounced TOE-sis. Therefore, most scholars insist that the second *p* in *apoptosis* should be silent, a-po-TOE-sis. Others argue that *helicopter* is also derived from a root with a silent *p* (*pteron*), but we pronounce the *p* in *helicopter,* so we should also pronounce the second *p* in *apoptosis.* Be prepared for either pronunciation.

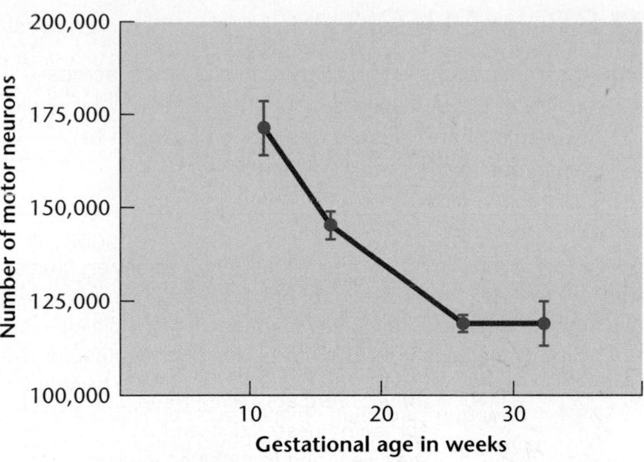

FIGURE 4.14 Cell loss during development of the nervous system

The number of motor neurons in the spinal cord of human fetuses is highest at 11 weeks and drops steadily until about 25 weeks. Axons that fail to make synapses die. *Source:* From N. G. Forger and S. M. Breedlove, Motoneuronal death in the human fetus. *Journal of Comparative Neurology, 264,* 1987, pp. 118–122.

developing nervous system make far more neurons than will survive into adulthood. Each brain area has a period of massive cell death, becoming littered with dead and dying cells (see Figure 4.14). This loss of cells is a natural part of development. In fact, loss of cells in a particular brain area often indicates maturation. For example, teenagers lose cells in parts of the prefrontal cortex while neuronal activity increases in those areas (Sowell, Thompson, Holmes, Jernigan, & Toga, 1999). Maturation of successful cells is linked to simultaneous loss of less successful ones.

Nerve growth factor is a **neurotrophin**, meaning a chemical that promotes the survival and activity of neurons. (The word *trophin* derives from a Greek word for "nourishment.") In addition to NGF, the nervous system responds to *brain-derived neurotrophic factor* (BDNF) and several other neurotrophins (Airaksinen & Saarma, 2002). Neurotrophins are essential for growth of axons and dendrites, formation of new synapses, and learning (Alleva & Francia, 2009; Pascual et al., 2008; Rauskolb et al., 2010). Remember the term BDNF, because it becomes important again in the discussion of depression.

Although neurotrophins are essential to the survival of motor neurons in the periphery, they do not control survival of neurons within the brain. When cortical neurons reach a certain age in early development, a certain percentage of them die. How many neurons are present doesn't seem to matter. Experimenters transplanted extra neurons into mouse cortex with no apparent effect on the survival of the neurons already present (Southwell et al., 2012). What controls neuron death in the brain is not yet understood, but one factor may be that neurons need input from incoming neurons. In one study, researchers examined mice with a genetic defect that prevented release of neurotransmitters. The brains initially assembled normal anatomies, but then the neurons started dying rapidly (Verhage et al., 2000).

STOP&CHECK

17. What process assures that the spinal cord has the right number of axons to innervate all the muscle cells?

18. What class of chemicals prevents apoptosis in the sympathetic nervous system?

19. At what age does a person have the greatest number of neurons—early in life, during adolescence, or during adulthood?

ANSWERS

17. The nervous system builds far more neurons than it needs and discards through apoptosis those that do not make lasting synapses. **18.** Neurotrophins, such as nerve growth factor **19.** The neuron number is greatest early in life.

The Vulnerable Developing Brain

According to Lewis Wolpert (1991), "It is not birth, marriage, or death, but gastrulation, which is truly the most important time of your life." (Gastrulation is one of the early stages of embryological development.) Wolpert's point was that if you mess up in early development, you have problems from then on. Actually, if you mess up during gastrulation, your life is over.

The earliest stages of development are remarkably similar across species. A series of genes known as *homeobox genes*—found in vertebrates, insects, plants, even fungi and yeast—regulate the expression of other genes and control the start of anatomical development, including such matters as which end is the front and which is the rear. All these genes share a large sequence of DNA bases. A mutation in one homeobox gene causes insects to form legs where their antennas should be, or to form an extra set of wings. In humans, mutations in homeobox genes have been linked to many brain disorders including mental retardation, as well as physical deformities (Conti et al., 2011).

During early development, the brain is highly vulnerable to malnutrition, toxic chemicals, and infections that would produce only mild problems at later ages. For example, impaired thyroid function produces lethargy in adults but mental retardation in infants. (Thyroid deficiency was common in the past because of iodine deficiency. It is rare today because table salt is fortified with iodine.) A fever is a mere annoyance to an adult, but it impairs neuron proliferation in a fetus (Laburn, 1996). Low blood glucose decreases an adult's pep, but before birth, it impairs brain development (C. A. Nelson et al., 2000).

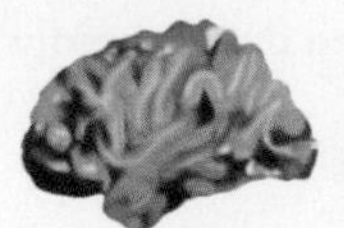 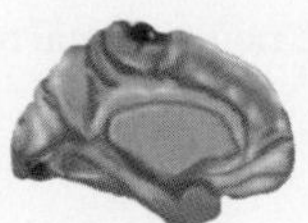  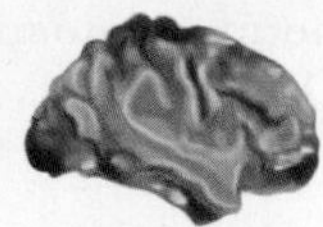

FIGURE 4.15 Cortical thinning as a result of prenatal alcohol exposure
The cortical areas marked in red are thinner, on average, in adults whose mothers drank alcohol during pregnancy.
Adapted from *NeuroImage*, 58, pp. 16–25, Zhou, D., Lebel, C., Lepage, C., Rasmussen, C., Evans, A., Wyper, K., . . . Beaulieu, C., Developmental cortical thinning in fetal alcohol spectrum disorders, 2011, with permission from Elsevier.

The infant brain is highly vulnerable to damage by alcohol. Children of mothers who drink heavily during pregnancy are born with **fetal alcohol syndrome**, a condition marked by hyperactivity, impulsiveness, difficulty maintaining attention, varying degrees of mental retardation, motor problems, heart defects, and facial abnormalities. Drinking during pregnancy leads to thinning of the cerebral cortex that persists to adulthood (Zhou et al., 2011) (see Figure 4.15). More drinking causes greater deficits, but even moderate drinking produces a measurable effect (Eckstrand et al., 2012).

Exposure to alcohol damages the brain in several ways. At the earliest stage of pregnancy, it interferes with neuron proliferation. A little later, it impairs neuron migration and differentiation. Still later, it impairs synaptic transmission (Kleiber, Mantha, Stringer, & Singh, 2013). Alcohol kills neurons partly by apoptosis. To prevent apoptosis, a brain neuron must receive input from incoming axons. Alcohol inhibits receptors for glutamate, the brain's main excitatory transmitter, and enhances receptors for GABA, the main inhibitory transmitter. Because of the decrease in net excitation, many neurons undergo apoptosis (Ikonomidou et al., 2000). Further harm occurs *after* a bout of drinking, while the alcohol is washing out of the system. While alcohol was inhibiting the glutamate receptors, many neurons compensated by quickly building more glutamate receptors. Then, when alcohol leaves, glutamate overexcites its receptors, bringing excess sodium and calcium into the cell and poisoning the mitochondria. The result is increased cell death in several brain areas (Clements et al., 2012).

The immature brain is also highly responsive to influences from the mother. If a mother rat is exposed to stressful experiences, she becomes more fearful, she spends less than the usual amount of time licking and grooming her offspring, and her offspring become permanently more fearful in a variety of situations (Cameron et al., 2005). Analogously, the children of impoverished and abused women have, on the average, increased problems in both their academic and social lives. The mechanisms in humans are not exactly the same as those in rats, but the overall principles are similar: Stress to the mother changes her behavior in ways that change her offspring's behavior.

STOP&CHECK

20. Anesthetic drugs and anxiety-reducing drugs increase activity of GABA, decreasing brain excitation. Why would we predict that exposure to these drugs might be dangerous to the brain of a fetus?

ANSWER

20. Prolonged exposure to anesthetics or anxiety-reducing drugs might increase apoptosis of developing neurons. Increased GABA activity decreases excitation, and developing neurons undergo apoptosis if they do not receive enough excitation. Many studies confirm that anesthetics and anxiety-reducing drugs impair brain development in laboratory animals, although the research is less complete for humans (Sanders, Hassel, Davidson, Robertson, & Ma, 2013; C. Young et al., 2005).

Differentiation of the Cortex

Neurons differ in shape and chemistry. When and how does a neuron "decide" which kind of neuron it is going to be? It is not a sudden decision. Immature neurons experimentally transplanted from one part of the developing cortex to another develop the properties characteristic of their new location (S. K. McConnell, 1992). However, neurons transplanted at a slightly later stage develop some new properties while retaining some old ones (Cohen-Tannoudji, Babinet, & Wassef, 1994). It is like the speech of immigrant children: Those who enter a country when very young master the correct pronunciation, whereas older children retain an accent.

In one fascinating experiment, researchers explored what would happen to the immature auditory portions of the brain if they received input from the eyes instead of the ears. Ferrets—mammals in the weasel family—are born so immature that their optic nerves (from the eyes) have not yet reached the thalamus. On one side of the brain, researchers damaged the superior colliculus and the occipital cortex, the two main targets for the optic nerves. On that side, they also damaged the auditory input. Therefore, the optic nerve could not attach to its usual target, and the auditory area of the thalamus lacked its usual input. As a result, the optic nerve attached to what is usually the auditory area of the thalamus. What would you guess happened? Did the visual input cause auditory sensations, or did the auditory areas of the brain turn into visual areas?

The result, surprising to many, was this: What would have been the auditory thalamus and cortex reorganized, developing some (but not all) of the characteristic appearance of visual areas (Sharma, Angelucci, & Sur, 2000). But how do we know whether the animals treated that activity as vision? Remember that the researchers performed these procedures on one side of the brain. They left the other side intact. The researchers presented stimuli to the normal side of the brain and trained the ferrets to turn one direction when they heard something and the other direction when they saw a light, as shown in Figure 4.16. After the ferrets learned this task well, the researchers presented a light that the rewired side could see.

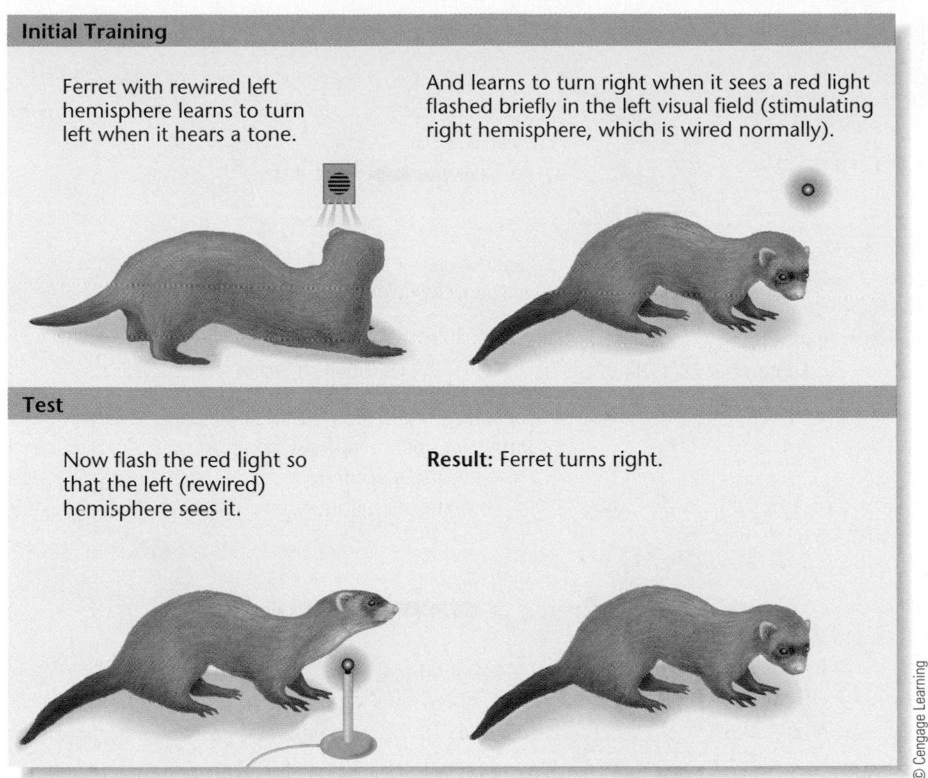

FIGURE 4.16 A ferret with rewired temporal cortex
First, the normal (right) hemisphere is trained to respond to a red light by turning to the right. Then, the rewired (left) hemisphere is tested with a red light. The fact that the ferret turns to the right indicates that it regards the stimulus as light, not sound.

The result: The ferrets turned the way they had been taught to turn when they saw something. In short, the rewired temporal cortex, receiving input from the optic nerve, produced visual responses (von Melchner, Pallas, & Sur, 2000).

STOP&CHECK

21. In the ferret study, how did the experimenters determine that visual input to the auditory portions of the brain actually produced a visual sensation?

ANSWER

21. They trained the ferrets to respond to stimuli on the normal side, turning one direction in response to sounds and the other direction to lights. Then they presented light to the rewired side and saw that the ferret again turned in the direction it had associated with lights.

Fine-Tuning by Experience

The blueprints for a house determine its overall plan, but because architects cannot anticipate every detail, construction workers often have to improvise. The same is true for your nervous system. Because of the unpredictability of life, our brains have evolved the ability to remodel themselves in response to experience (Shatz, 1992).

Experience and Dendritic Branching

Decades ago, researchers doubted that adult neurons substantially changed their shape. Although the central structure of a dendrite becomes stable by adolescence, the peripheral branches of a dendrite remain flexible throughout life (Koleske, 2013). Dale Purves and R. D. Hadley (1985) injected a dye that let them watch the structure of a living mouse neuron over days or weeks. They found that some dendritic branches extended between one viewing and another, whereas others retracted or disappeared (see Figure 4.17). About 6 percent of dendritic spines appear or disappear within a month (Xu, Pan, Yang, & Gan, 2007). The gain or loss of spines means a turnover of synapses, which relates to learning (Yang, Pan, & Gan, 2009).

Experiences guide the neuronal changes. Let's start with a simple example. Decades ago, it was typical for a laboratory rat to live alone in a small gray cage. Imagine by contrast several rats in a larger cage with a few objects to explore. Researchers called this an enriched environment, but it was enriched only in comparison to the deprived experience of a typical rat cage. A rat in the more stimulating environment developed a thicker cortex, more dendritic branching, and improved learning (Greenough, 1975; Rosenzweig & Bennett, 1996). A stimulating environment enhances sprouting of axons and dendrites in many other species also (Coss, Brandon, & Globus, 1980) (see Figure 4.18). As a result of this research, most rats today are kept in a more enriched environment than was typical in the past.

We might suppose that the neuronal changes in an enriched environment depend on interesting experiences and social interactions. No doubt some of them do, but much of the enhancement produced by the enriched environment is due to physical activity. Using a running wheel enhances growth of axons and dendrites, even for rodents in isolation

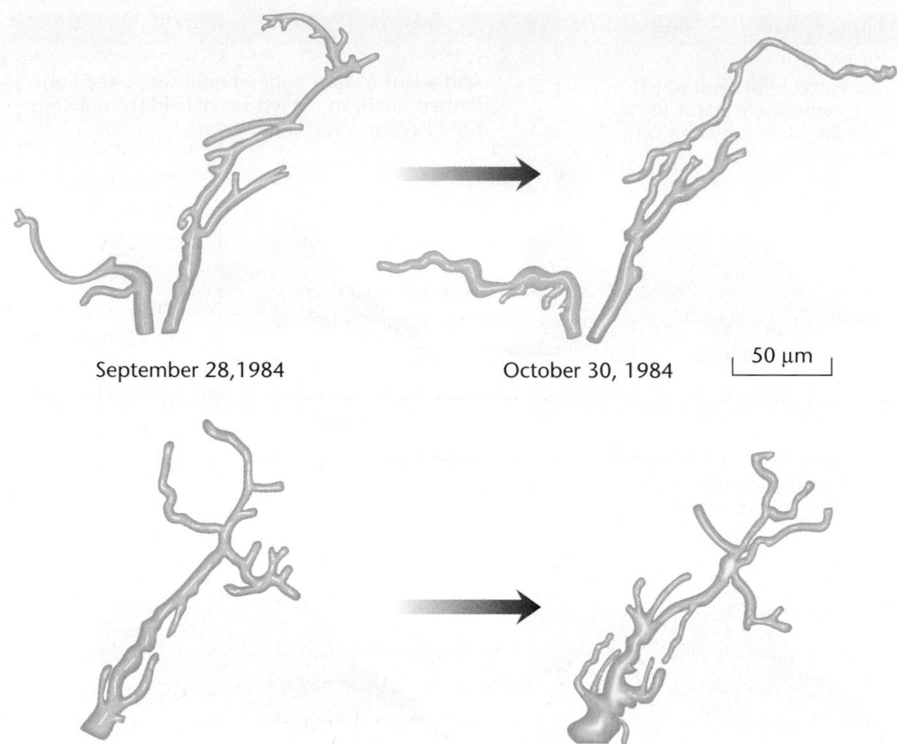

FIGURE 4.17 Changes in dendritic trees of two mouse neurons
During a month, some branches elongated and others retracted. *Source:* Reprinted by permission from Macmillan Publishers Ltd; from "Changes in Dendritic Branching of Adult Mammalian Neurons Revealed by Repeated Imaging in Situ," by D. Purves and R. D. Hadley, *Nature, 315*, pp. 404–406. Reprinted by permission.

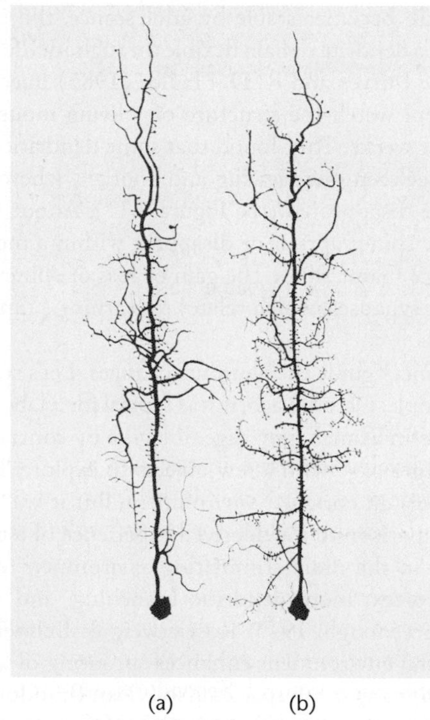

FIGURE 4.18 Effect of a stimulating environment
(a) A jewelfish reared in isolation develops neurons with fewer branches. **(b)** A fish reared with others has more dendritic branches. *Source:* Adapted from image by Richard Coss

(Pietropaolo, Feldon, Alleva, Cirulli, & Yee, 2006; Rhodes et al., 2003; van Praag, Kempermann, & Gage, 1999). In the hippocampus, many old neurons die by apoptosis and new ones form to take their place, accompanied by proliferating blood vessels (Kerr & Swain, 2011). All these changes correlate with improved learning and memory (Marlatt, Potter, Lucassen, & van Praag, 2012; Van der Borght, Havekes, Bos, Eggen, & Van der Zee, 2007).

Can we extend these results to humans? Could we, for example, improve people's intelligence by giving them a more enriched environment? It's not that easy. Educators have long operated on the assumption that training children to do something difficult will enhance their intellect in general. Long ago, British schools taught children Greek and Latin. Today it might be calculus, but in either case, the idea is to teach one thing and hope students get smarter in other ways, too. The psychological term is "far transfer." (*Near transfer* is training on one task and finding improvement on a similar task.) In general, far transfer is a weak effect. Most attempted interventions to improve people's memory and reasoning produce only small benefits (Hertzog, Kramer, Wilson, & Lindenberger, 2009). Your brain isn't like a muscle, where you could exercise it to be bigger and stronger.

Similarly, many people advise old people to do crossword puzzles or sudoku puzzles to "exercise their brains." Correlational studies show that people who engage in such activities do remain mentally alert longer than average, but we cannot conclude cause and effect. Perhaps working puzzles helps keep the brain active, but the other interpretation is that people who already have active brains are more likely than average to work puzzles. Experimental studies suggest that practicing crossword puzzles doesn't improve people's skills at anything other than crossword puzzles (Salthouse, 2006).

One of the best-documented ways to maintain intellectual vigor in old age is the same thing that works so well for laboratory animals—physical activity. Experimental studies, in which older people were randomly assigned to daily aerobic exercise or sedentary activities, confirm that the physical activity enhances both cognitive processes and brain anatomy (Rosano et al., 2010; P. J. Smith et al., 2010).

STOP&CHECK

22. An enriched environment promotes growth of axons and dendrites in laboratory rodents. What is known to be one mportant reason for this effect?

ANSWER

22. Animals in an enriched environment are more active, and their exercise enhances growth of axons and dendrites.

Effects of Special Experiences

Attempts to enhance overall brain development produce at best modest effects. However, prolonged experience of a particular type profoundly enhances the brain's ability to perform the same function again, especially if training begins early in life.

Brain Adaptations in People Blind Since Infancy

What happens to the brain if one sensory system is impaired? Recall the experiment on ferrets, in which axons of the visual system, unable to contact their normal targets, attached instead to the brain areas usually devoted to hearing, and managed to convert them into more or less satisfactory visual areas. Might anything similar happen in the brains of people born deaf or blind?

People often say that blind people become better than usual at touch and hearing. That statement is true in a way, but we need to be more specific. Blind people improve their attention to touch and sound, based on practice. Researchers found that blind people have greater than average touch sensitivity in their fingers, especially blind people who read Braille and therefore practice their finger sensitivity extensively. Touch sensitivity does not increase at all for the lips, where blind people pay no more attention to touch than anyone else does (Wong, Gnanakumaran, & Goldreich, 2011).

In several studies, investigators asked sighted people and people blind since infancy to feel Braille letters or other objects and say whether two items were the same or different. On average, blind people performed more accurately than sighted people, as you would guess. More surprisingly, PET and fMRI scans indicated substantial activity in the occipital cortex of blind people while they performed these tasks (Burton et al., 2002; Sadato et al., 1996, 1998). Evidently, touch information activated this cortical area, which is ordinarily devoted to vision alone.

To double-check this conclusion, researchers asked people to perform the same kind of task during temporary inactivation of the occipital cortex. Intense magnetic stimulation on the scalp temporarily inactivates neurons beneath the magnet. Applying this procedure to the occipital cortex of people who are blind interferes with their ability to identify Braille symbols, whereas it does not impair touch perception in sighted people. In short, blind people, unlike sighted people, use the occipital cortex to help identify what they feel (L. G. Cohen et al., 1997).

In people blind since birth or early childhood, the occipital cortex also responds to auditory information, because of strong connections from the temporal cortex to the occipital cortex (Gougoux et al., 2009; Klinge, Eippert, Roder, & Büchel, 2010; Wan, Wood, Reutens, & Wilson, 2010). As a result, the occipital cortex contributes to language comprehension in blind people, unlike sighted people (Bedny, Pascual-Leone, Dodell-Feder, Fedorenko, & Saxe, 2011).

Just as people who are blind from an early age become more sensitive to touch and sound, people who are deaf from an early age become more responsive to touch and vision. Just as touch and sound come to activate what would be the visual cortex in blind people, touch and vision come to activate what would be the auditory cortex in deaf people (Karns, Dow, & Neville, 2012).

STOP&CHECK

23. Name two kinds of evidence indicating that touch information from the fingers activates the occipital cortex of people blind since birth.

ANSWER

23. First, brain scans indicate increased activity in the occipital cortex while blind people perform tasks such as feeling two objects and saying whether they are the same or different. Second, temporary inactivation of the occipital cortex blocks blind people's ability to perform that task, without affecting the ability of sighted people.

Music Training

People who develop expertise in any area spend enormous amounts of time practicing, generally beginning in childhood, and it seems reasonable to look for corresponding changes in their brains. Of the various kinds of expertise, which would you want to examine? Researchers' favorite choice has been musicians, for two reasons. First, we have a good idea of where in the brain to look for changes—the brain areas responsible for hearing and finger control. Second, serious musicians are numerous and easy to find. Almost any big city has an orchestra, and so do most universities. (And unlike professional athletes, musicians are accustomed to working for low pay!)

One study used magnetoencephalography to record responses of the auditory cortex to pure tones. The responses in musicians were about twice as strong as those in nonmusicians. An examination of their brains, using MRI, found that one area of the temporal cortex in the right hemisphere was about 30 percent larger in the musicians (Schneider et al., 2002).

Other studies found enhanced responses of subcortical brain structures to musical sounds and speech sounds, compared to nonmusicians (Herdener et al., 2010; Lee, Skoe, Kraus, & Ashley, 2009; Musacchia, Sams, Skoe, & Kraus, 2007). Even as little as three years of musical training in childhood produces a measurable increase in brain-stem responses to sounds (Skoe & Kraus, 2012).

These brain changes help musicians attend to key sounds in tonal languages. For example, in Chinese, *nián* (with a rising tone) means year, and *niàn* (with a falling tone) means study. On average, musicians learn to recognize these differences faster than other people do (Wong, Skoe, Russo, Dees, & Kraus, 2007).

According to a study using MRI, gray matter of several cortical areas was thicker in professional musicians than in amateurs and thicker in amateurs than in nonmusicians, as shown in Figure 4.19 (Gaser & Schlaug, 2003). The most strongly affected areas related to hand control and vision (which is important for reading music). A related study on stringed instrument players found that a larger than normal section of the somatosensory cortex in the right hemisphere was devoted to representing the fingers of the left hand, which they use to control the strings (Elbert, Pantev, Wienbruch, Rockstroh, & Taub, 1995). The area devoted to the left fingers was largest in those who began their music practice early and therefore also continued for more years.

These results suggest that practicing a skill reorganizes the brain to maximize performance of that skill. However, an alternative hypothesis is that brain characteristics that were present from birth attract people to one occupation or another. The structure of the auditory cortex predicts who can learn most quickly to distinguish very similar or unfamiliar speech sounds (Golestani, Molko, Dehaene, LeBihan, & Palier, 2007; Golestani, Price, & Scott, 2011). Might it also be the case that inborn brain features attract certain people to music? One way to address that question is with a longitudinal study. Researchers examined 15 6-year-olds who were beginning piano lessons and 16 other children not taking music lessons. At the start of training, neither brain scans nor cognitive tests showed any significant difference between the two groups. After 15 months, the trained group performed better on measures of rhythm and melody discrimination, and they showed enlargements of brain areas responsible for hearing and hand movements, similar to those seen in adult musicians (Hyde et al., 2009a, 2009b). These results imply that the brain differences are the result of musical training, not the cause.

Another issue is whether music training produces bigger effects if it begins early in life, while the brain is more easily modified. Several studies have found major differences between young adults who started music training in childhood and those who began as teenagers. However, those studies do not separate the effects of age at starting from those of total years of practice. Two later studies compared people who started music training before age 7 with people who started later but continued for just as many years. In both studies, those who started younger showed greater changes in sensory discriminations and brain anatomy (Steele, Bailey, Zatorre, & Penhune, 2013; Watanabe, Savion-Lemieux, & Penhune, 2007).

STOP&CHECK

24. Which brain area shows expanded representation of the left hand in people who began practicing stringed instruments in childhood and continued for many years?

ANSWER

24. Somatosensory cortex (postcentral gyrus) of the right hemisphere.

Special Training in Adulthood

Being blind or deaf from birth leads to altered brain anatomy, and so does extensive musical training beginning in childhood. Might adult experiences modify brain anatomy also? In a sense, the answer is, "Yes, of course." Anything you learn must have some effect on the brain. Reading this sentence just now rearranged a few molecules in your brain. The issue is

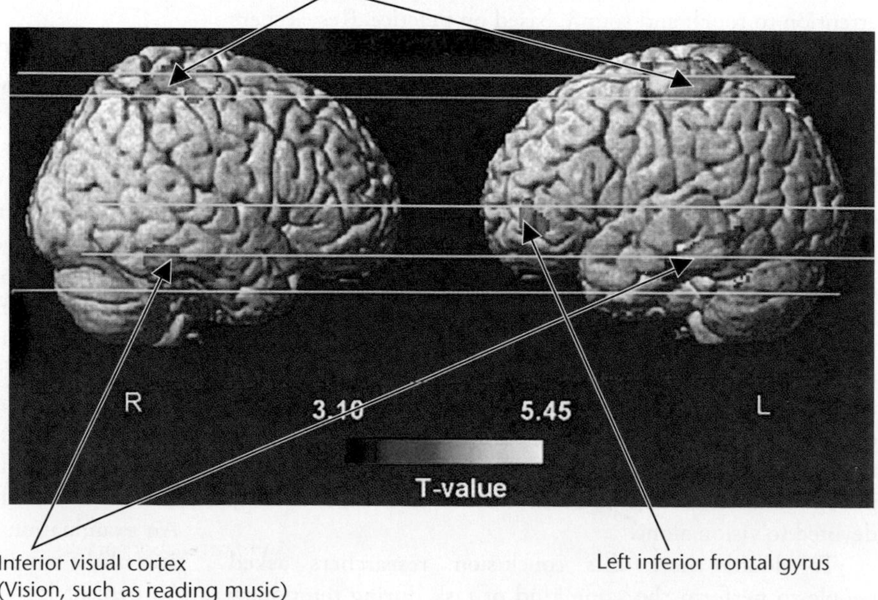

FIGURE 4.19 Brain correlates of music practice
Areas marked in red showed thicker gray matter among professional keyboard players than in amateurs and thicker among amateurs than in nonmusicians. Areas marked in yellow showed even stronger differences in that same direction.
Source: Gaser & Schlaug, 2003

whether an adult experience produces a big enough effect that we might observe it with MRI or similar technology.

Many studies have in fact reported changes in adult brain anatomy from tasks such as learning to juggle three balls (Draganski et al., 2004; Zatorre, Fields, & Johansen-Berg, 2012), 16 hours of playing a complex video game (Colom et al., 2012), or 40 hours of playing golf for the first time (Bezzola, Mérillat, Gaser, & Jäncke, 2011). However, skeptics raise serious objections (Thomas & Baker, 2013): Many of the studies compared mean MRIs of the entire brains of the trained group to the entire brains of a control group. In effect, they tested a huge number of hypotheses at once—one hypothesis for each brain area. That procedure has a high risk of finding an apparent result by accident, especially when we consider that some of the reported brain differences were less than one-tenth of a millimeter. Also, in most cases, no one has reported an attempt to replicate the results, or if they did, the second study did not find the same results as the first study. The only replicated finding is that physical exercise expands part of the hippocampus in older people. In short, we should reserve judgment about most of the reported effects of brief experiences on the adult brain.

When Brain Reorganization Goes Too Far

If playing music, or practicing anything else, expands a relevant brain area, the change is good, right? Usually it is, but not always. As mentioned, when people play piano or string instruments many hours a day for years, the representation of the hand increases in the somatosensory cortex. Imagine the normal representation of the fingers in the cortex:

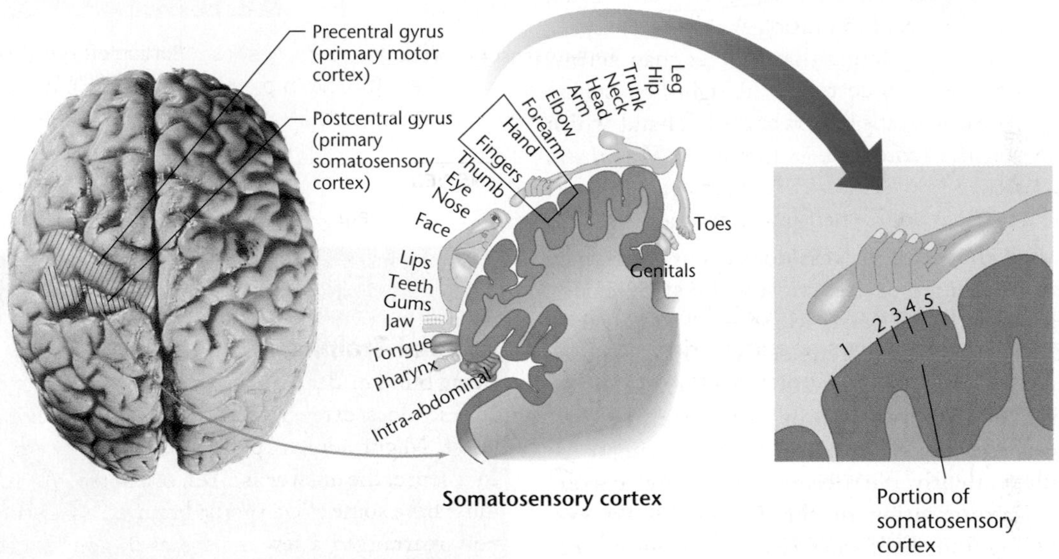

With extensive musical practice, the expanding representations of the fingers might spread out like this:

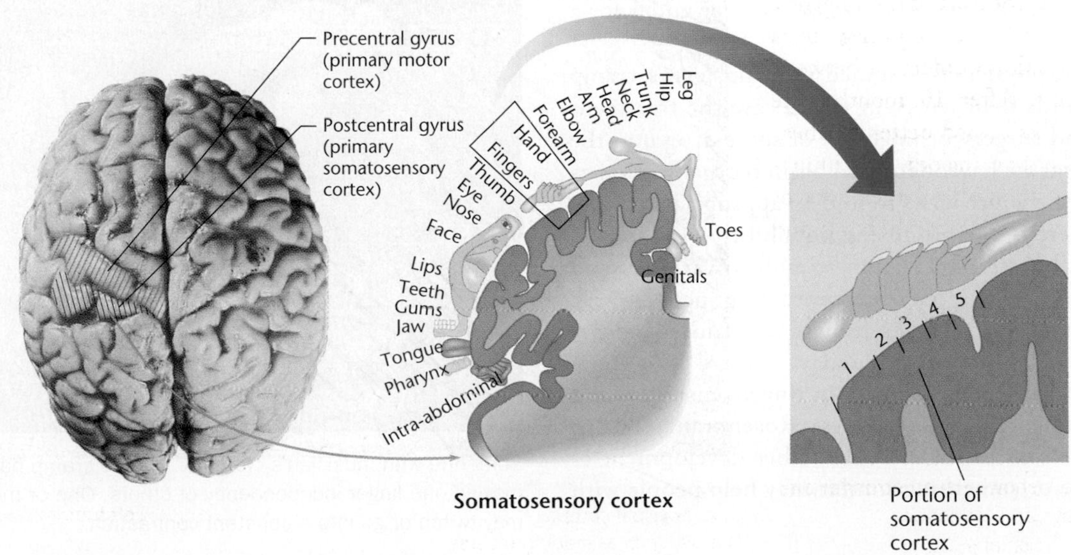

Or the representations of all fingers could grow from side to side without spreading out so that representation of each finger overlaps that of its neighbor:

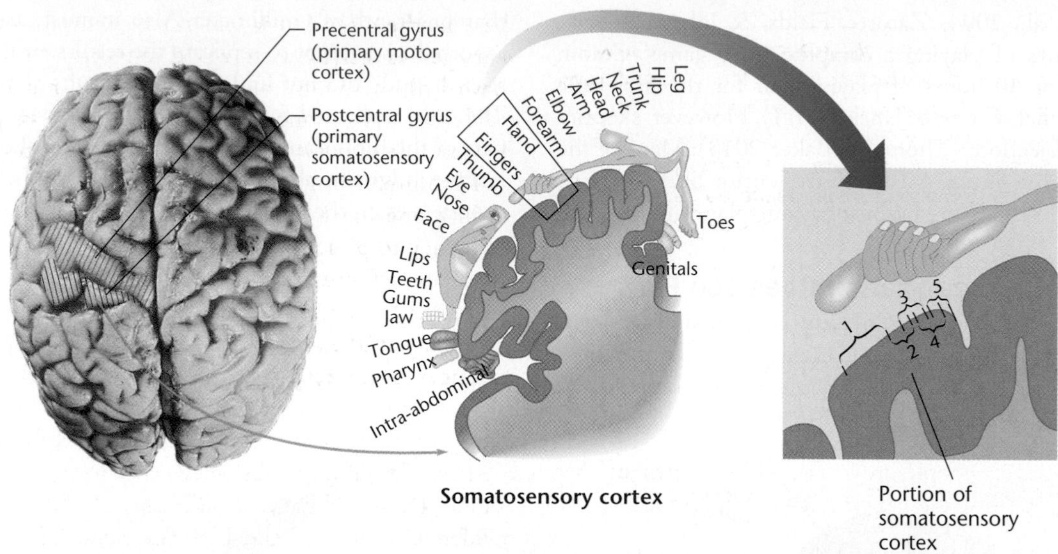

In some cases, the latter process does occur, such that stimulation on one finger excites mostly the same cortical areas as another finger (Byl, McKenzie, & Nagarajan, 2000; Elbert et al., 1998; Lenz & Byl, 1999; Sanger, Pascual-Leone, Tarsy, & Schlaug, 2001; Sanger, Tarsy, & Pascual-Leone, 2001). If you cannot clearly feel the difference between one finger and another, it is difficult to move them independently. Furthermore, the motor cortex changes also. Representation of the middle fingers expands, overlapping and displacing representation of the index finger and little finger. One or more fingers may go into constant contraction (Beck et al., 2008; Burman, Lie-Nemeth, Brandfonbrener, Parisi, & Meyer, 2009). This condition, known as "musician's cramp" or more formally as **focal hand dystonia,** can be a career ender for a musician.

Previously, physicians assumed that musician's cramp was in the hands themselves, in which case the treatment would be hand surgery or injection of some drug into the hand. Now that we have identified brain reorganization as the problem, the approach is to find an appropriate type of retraining. Here is one promising possibility: Researchers gave periodic bursts of vibration stimuli to various hand muscles, in random sequence, instructing people with musician's cramp to attend carefully to the stimuli and any changes in their vibration frequency. A mere 15-minute treatment produced improvement in finger sensations and use, which lasted up to 24 hours (Rosenkranz, Butler, Williamson, & Rothwell, 2009). Further development of this technique or something similar may help people with this disorder.

Someone with musician's cramp or writer's cramp has difficulty moving one finger independently of others. One or more fingers may twitch or go into a constant contraction.

STOP&CHECK

25. What change in the brain is responsible for musician's cramp?

ANSWER

25. Extensive practice of violin, piano, or other instruments causes expanded representation of the fingers in the somatosensory cortex, as well as displacement of representation of one or more fingers in the motor cortex. If the sensory representation of two fingers overlaps too much, the person cannot feel them separately or move them separately.

Brain Development and Behavioral Development

Behavior changes as people grow older. How much of that change has to do with the brain? Let's consider adolescence and old age.

Adolescence

Adolescents are widely regarded as impulsive and prone to seek immediate pleasure, as compared to adults. Impulsiveness is a problem if it leads to risky driving, drinking, sex, spending sprees, and so forth.

In addition to being more impulsive than older adults, adolescents (and children) tend to "discount the future," preferring a smaller pleasure now over a larger one later. Which would you prefer, $100 now or $125 a year from now? What about $100 now versus $150 a year from now? How much bigger would the payoff have to be next year to make you willing to wait? Adolescents are more likely to choose an immediate reward than are older adults, in a variety of situations (Steinberg et al., 2009). However, to be fair, the situation is not the same for people of different ages, especially with regard to money. Most adolescents have little cash on hand and need the money right now. Older adults are more likely to be financially secure and better able to wait for a higher reward. Still, adolescents tend to prefer immediate rewards even with rewards other than money, and adolescent rats and mice show a similar tendency to prefer immediate food instead of a larger portion later (Doremus-Fitzwater, Barretto, & Spear, 2012; Pinkston & Lamb, 2011).

Many studies have found that adolescent humans show stronger brain responses than older adults do when anticipating rewards, and weaker responses in the areas of the prefrontal cortex responsible for inhibiting behaviors (Geier, Terwilliger, Teslovich, Velanova, & Luna, 2010; Luna, Padmanabhan, & O'Hearn, 2010). That type of evidence influenced the U.S. Supreme Court to rule that adolescents are less responsible for their actions than adults are, because they are less able to restrain their impulses (Steinberg, 2013). However, although the prefrontal cortex is indeed less mature in adolescents, its immaturity is at best only part of the explanation for impulsivity. Adolescents are not incapable of restraining their impulses, and in many laboratory tests they inhibit impulses just as well as adults. The heightened impulsivity occurs almost entirely in social situations when adolescents are trying to impress their peers (Casey & Caudle, 2013; Crone & Dahl, 2012; Luna et al., 2010; Reyna & Farley, 2006). Adolescents are highly responsive to social support and social influence.

ZITS BY JERRY SCOTT AND JIM BORGMAN

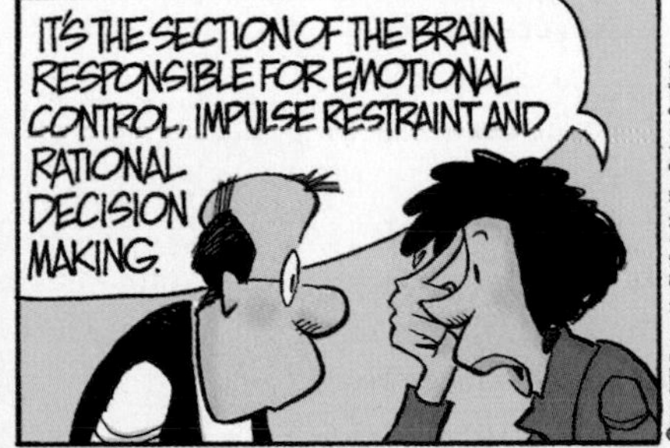

STOP&CHECK

26. Under what circumstances are adolescents most likely to make an impulsive decision?

27. When people claim that adolescents make risky decisions because of a lack of inhibition, which brain area do they point to as being responsible for inhibition?

ANSWERS

26. Adolescents are most likely to make an impulsive decision in the presence of peer pressure. **27.** The prefrontal cortex

Old Age

Many studies confirm that, on average, old people's memory and reasoning begin to fade. Many neurons lose some of their synapses, and the remaining synapses change more slowly than before in response to experiences (Gan, Kwon, Feng, Sanes, & Lichtman, 2003; Grutzendler, Kasthuri, & Gan, 2002; Morrison & Baxter, 2012). Neurons in the prefrontal cortex become less able to maintain a high level of firing while storing a working memory (M. Wang et al., 2011). The thickness of the temporal cortex shrinks by about half a percent per year, on average (Fjell et al., 2009). The frontal cortex begins thinning at age 30 (Brans et al., 2010)!

The volume of the hippocampus also gradually declines in old age, and certain aspects of memory decline in proportion to the loss of hippocampus (Erickson et al., 2010). Old people are apt to decline rapidly after an injury or illness because of brain inflammation, although physical exercise can help to reverse the decline (Barrientos et al., 2011).

In old age, even the blood contains chemicals that impair cognitive function. After researchers transfused blood from old mice into young mice, the young mice showed a temporary impairment of synaptic plasticity and learning (Villeda et al., 2011). So, if you need a blood transfusion, hope that the donor was a healthy young person!

In spite of all these problems, most chief executives of major corporations, world political leaders, and college presidents are over 60 years old. Is this a problem? Should we fire them and replace them with 25-year-olds?

Much of the research underestimates older people, for several reasons. First, some people deteriorate markedly, but others show little sign of loss, partly for genetic reasons (Barzilai, Alzmon, Derby, Bauman, & Lipton, 2006; Pudas et al., 2013). On average, it appears that everyone is decaying a little each year, but averages can be misleading. Second, even someone who may be slower in certain intellectual activities has developed a great base of knowledge and experience. On certain kinds of questions, older people do significantly better than younger people (Queen & Hess, 2010). Third, many older people find ways to compensate for losses, such as by activating more widespread brain areas to compensate for decreased arousal in one or two areas (Park & McDonough, 2013).

STOP&CHECK

28. What is one way in which older adults compensate for less efficient brain functioning?

ANSWER

28. Many of them compensate by activating additional brain areas.

MODULE 4.2 ■ IN CLOSING

Brain Development

Most of the machines you might buy get built, and then they are done. They might need repair, but the construction is finished. Your brain isn't like that. Although the changes are most rapid at first, structural changes continue throughout life. You are forever a work in progress.

Summary

1. In vertebrate embryos, the central nervous system begins as a tube surrounding a fluid-filled cavity. Developing neurons proliferate, migrate, differentiate, myelinate, and generate synapses. Neuron proliferation varies among species mainly by the number of cell divisions. Migration depends on a large number of chemicals that guide immature neurons to their destinations. **117**
2. In adult vertebrates, new neurons can form in the olfactory system, the hippocampus, and the song-producing brain areas of some bird species. Adult humans form new neurons in the hippocampus but few or none in the olfactory bulbs or cerebral cortex. **118**
3. Growing axons find their way close to the right locations by following chemicals. Then they array

themselves over a target area by following chemical gradients. **119**

4. After axons reach their targets based on chemical gradients, the postsynaptic cell adjusts the connections based on experience, accepting certain combinations of axons and rejecting others. This kind of competition among axons continues throughout life. **121**
5. Initially, the nervous system develops far more neurons than will actually survive. Axons of the sympathetic nervous system survive only if they reach a target cell that releases to them nerve growth factor. Otherwise, they die in a process called apoptosis. Apoptosis also occurs in the brain, but the factors controlling it are poorly understood. **122**
6. The developing brain is vulnerable to chemical insult. Many chemicals that produce only mild, temporary problems for adults can permanently impair early brain development. **123**
7. At an early stage of development, the cortex is sufficiently plastic that visual input can cause what would have been the auditory cortex to develop different properties and now respond visually. **124**
8. Enriched experience leads to greater branching of axons and dendrites, partly because animals in enriched environments are more active than those in deprived environments. **125**
9. Specialized experiences can alter brain development, especially early in life. For example, in people who are born blind, representation of touch and hearing expands in areas usually reserved for vision. **127**
10. Extensive practice of a skill expands the brain's representation of sensory and motor information relevant to that skill. For example, the representation of fingers expands in people who regularly practice musical instruments. **127**
11. Controversy remains about whether new adult experiences modify brain structures enough to be visible in MRI scans. **128**
12. Although expanded representation in the brain is ordinarily a good thing, it can be harmful if carried too far. Some musicians and others who use their hands many hours each day develop brain changes that interfere with their ability to feel or use one finger independently of the others. **129**
13. Compared to adults, adolescents tend to be impulsive and centered more on present pleasures than future prospects. Although immaturity of the prefrontal cortex contributes to impulsiveness, impulsiveness occurs mostly under the influence of peer pressure. **131**
14. On average, people in old age show declining memory and reasoning, and shrinkage of certain brain areas. However, these averages do not apply to all individuals or all situations. Many older people compensate for inefficiency of certain brain functions by recruiting activity in additional brain areas. **132**

Key Terms

Terms are defined in the module on the page number indicated. They're also presented in alphabetical order with definitions in the book's Subject Index/Glossary. Interactive flash cards, audio reviews, and crossword puzzles are among the online resources available to help you learn these terms and the concepts they represent.

apoptosis **122**
differentiates **118**
fetal alcohol syndrome **123**
focal hand dystonia **130**
migrate **118**
myelination **118**
nerve growth factor (NGF) **122**
neurotrophin **123**
proliferation **117**
stem cells **117**
synaptogenesis **118**

Thought Question

Biologists can develop antibodies against nerve growth factor (i.e., molecules that inactivate nerve growth factor). What would happen if someone injected such antibodies into a developing nervous system?

MODULE 4.2 End of Module Quiz

1. Which part of a neuron forms first, if either?
   a. The axon forms first.
   b. The dendrites form first.
   c. They form at the same time.

2. What is unusual about the olfactory receptors?

a. Olfactory neurons have more than one axon.

b. Humans do not begin forming olfactory neurons until nearly 2 years old.

c. We continue forming new olfactory neurons throughout life.

d. An unusually strong blood–brain barrier protects olfactory neurons from damage.

3. The ^{14}C concentration in the atmosphere has been declining since 1963. The ^{14}C concentration in neurons of a person's cerebral cortex and olfactory bulbs corresponds to that of _____.

a. the year of the person's birth

b. about halfway between the person's birth and the present year

c. the year the person's education ended

d. the current year

4. When Sperry cut a newt's optic nerve and turned the eye upside down, what happened?

a. Axons of the optic nerve grew randomly and attached diffusely to target cells in the tectum.

b. Axons of the optic nerve grew back to their original targets.

c. Axons of the optic nerve grew back to targets appropriate to their new location in the eye.

d. At first the axons grew back randomly, but then they established appropriate connections by learning.

5. If axons from the retina were prevented from showing spontaneous activity during early development, what would be the probable effect on development of the thalamus?

a. Axon attachment would be more precise than usual.

b. Axons would branch more widely, establishing more connections than usual.

c. Axons would not fine-tune their adjustment based on experience, so their connections would be less precise.

d. Axons would attach in the same way as usual, unaffected by the change.

6. Why does the spinal cord have the right number of axons to innervate all the muscle cells?

a. Each muscle cell sends a chemical message telling the spinal cord to make a neuron.

b. The genes cause a certain number of neurons to form and the same number of muscles to form.

c. Immature cells divide, with one daughter cell becoming a neuron and the other becoming a muscle.

d. The spinal cord makes an excess of neurons, but those that fail to innervate a muscle die.

7. What is apoptosis?

a. A chemical that damages neurons

b. A chemical that keeps neurons alive

c. A programmed mechanism of cell death

d. A machine that records neuron activity

8. Which neurons depend on nerve growth factor to prevent apoptosis in early development?

a. Neurons in the brain

b. Neurons in the sympathetic nervous system

c. Both

d. Neither

9. At what age does a person have the largest number of neurons?

a. Before or shortly after birth

b. Equally at all times of life

c. Adolescence

d. Adulthood

10. If a pregnant woman drinks alcohol, alcohol harms the brain of the fetus not only while it is in the system, but also while it is washing away after drinking. What is the danger while alcohol is washing away?

a. Temperature in the brain may decrease.

b. Blood pressure in the brain may decrease.

c. Excess inhibition at GABA synapses can lead to apoptosis.

d. Overstimulation at glutamate synapses can poison the mitochondria.

11. In the ferret study, what evidence indicated that visual input to the auditory portions of the brain actually produced a visual sensation?

a. Bright flashes of light to the rewired eye caused the ferrets to blink both eyes.

b. Recordings from individual cells of the rewired temporal cortex showed the same patterns usually seen in cells of the occipital cortex.

c. Ferrets could find their way around an unfamiliar room even with the normal eye closed.

d. Ferrets that learned to turn one way in response to light in the normal eye turned the same way to light in the rewired eye.

12. An enriched environment promotes growth of axons and dendrites in laboratory rodents. What is known to be one important reason for this effect?

a. Increased physical activity

b. Increased happiness

c. Increased relaxation

d. Increased empathy with other animals

13. If a person is born blind, in what way do the senses of hearing and touch improve?

a. The person gradually develops more receptors in the ears and skin.

b. The number of receptors does not change, but each of them becomes more responsive to weak stimuli.

c. The receptors in the ears and skin send faster action potentials to the brain.

d. Through practice the person learns to increase attention to hearing and touch, and those sensations come to activate the occipital cortex.

14. Of the following, which is the strongest evidence to indicate that musical training modifies brain anatomy?

a. The gray matter of several cortical areas is thicker in professional musicians than in nonmusicians.

b. A larger than average portion of the right somatosensory cortex responds to the left hand in stringed instrument players than in other people.

c. At age 6, children starting musical training did not differ from average, but 15 months later they showed enlargements of several brain areas.

15. Many studies report brain changes after special experiences in adulthood, such as learning to juggle or learning to play golf. Why are some researchers skeptical of these findings?

a. The adult brain cannot change anatomically.

b. Most of the reported results were small and have not been replicated.

c. Most of the reported studies had no control group.

d. Most of the reported studies required many years of training.

16. What causes musician's cramp?

a. Changes in the muscles and tendons of the hand

b. Rewiring of the cerebral cortex

c. Loss of myelin on the motor nerves to the hand

d. Changes in the touch receptors of the hand

17. Is it reasonable to argue that adolescents are mature enough to make some decisions and not others?

a. No. This argument is based entirely on political leanings.

b. Perhaps. Adolescents reason in a mature way for unimportant decisions, but not for important ones.

c. Perhaps. Adolescents reason in an immature way when they decide quickly under peer pressure.

d. Perhaps. Adolescents reason in a mature way when they are happy but not when they are sad.

18. Immaturity of the prefrontal cortex is a possible explanation for which aspect of adolescent behavior?

a. Impulsivity

b. Increased interest in social contact

c. Increased appetite

d. Sleepiness during the day

19. Why do many older people continue to hold important jobs in spite of the declines in memory and brain function that are known to occur in old age?

a. Laws prevent them from being fired.

b. Although their jobs are important, they don't require much brain activity.

c. Old people take the credit for work that younger people actually do.

d. The declines on average do not apply to all people.

ANSWERS: 1a, 2c, 3a, 4b, 5c, 6d, 7c, 8b, 9a, 10d, 11d, 12a, 13d, 14c, 15b, 16b, 17c, 18a, 19d.

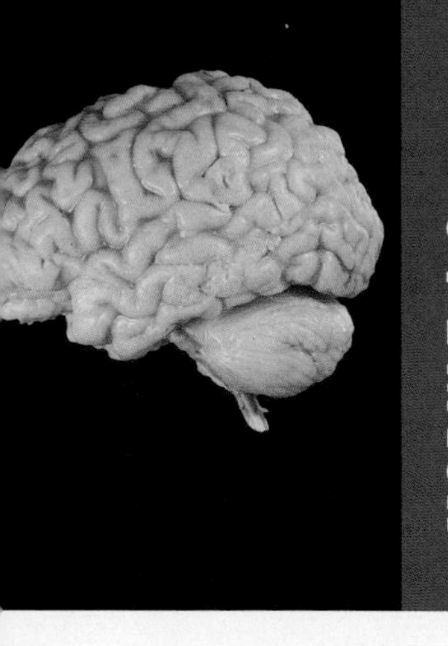

MODULE 4.3

Plasticity after Brain Damage

An American soldier who suffered a wound to the left hemisphere of his brain during the Korean War was at first unable to speak at all. Three months later, he could speak in short fragments. When he was asked to read the letterhead, "New York University College of Medicine," he replied, "Doctors—little doctors." Eight years later, when someone asked him again to read the letterhead, he replied, "Is there a catch? It says, 'New York University College of Medicine'" (Eidelberg & Stein, 1974).

Almost all survivors of brain damage show behavioral recovery to some degree. Some of the mechanisms rely on the growth of new branches of axons and dendrites, similar to the mechanisms of brain development. Understanding the process leads to better therapies for people with brain damage and contributes to our understanding of brain functioning.

Brain Damage and Short-Term Recovery

Possible causes of brain damage include tumors, infections, exposure to radiation or toxic substances, and degenerative conditions such as Parkinson's disease and Alzheimer's disease. In young people, the most common cause is **closed head injury**, a sharp blow to the head that does not puncture the brain. The effects of closed head injury depend on severity and frequency. Many, probably most, children and young adults sustain at least a mild blow to the head from falling off a bicycle or similar accident, from which they recover within a few days. Repeated head injuries, common in certain sports, are more worrisome (Shaughnessy, 2009). After a severe head injury, recovery is slow and often incomplete (Forsyth, Salorio, & Christensen, 2010).

One cause of damage after closed head injury is the rotational forces that drive brain tissue against the inside of the skull. Another cause is blood clots that interrupt blood flow to the brain (Kirkpatrick, Smielewski, Czosnyka, Menon, & Pickard, 1995). Given the dangers from a blow to the head, how do woodpeckers manage to avoid giving themselves concussions? If you banged your head into a tree 20 times per second at a speed strong enough to tear a hole in the bark, you would not be in good shape.

Using slow-motion photography, researchers found that woodpeckers usually start with a couple of quick preliminary taps against the wood, much like a carpenter lining up a nail with a hammer. Then the birds make a hard strike in a straight line, keeping a rigid neck. They almost completely avoid rotational forces and whiplash (May, Fuster, Haber, & Hirschman, 1979). Furthermore, the spongy bone of the woodpecker's head makes an excellent shock absorber (Yoon & Park, 2011).

The implication is that football helmets, racecar helmets, and so forth would give more protection if they extended down to the shoulders to prevent rotation and whiplash. Also, if you see a crash about to happen, you should tuck your chin to your chest and tighten your neck muscles.

Reducing the Harm from a Stroke

A common cause of brain damage, especially in older people, is temporary interruption of normal blood flow to a brain area during a **stroke**, also known as a **cerebrovascular accident**. The more common type of stroke is **ischemia** (iss-KEE-me-uh), the result of a blood clot or other obstruction in an artery. The less common type is **hemorrhage** (HEM-oh-rage), the result of a ruptured artery. Effects of strokes vary from barely noticeable to immediately fatal. Figure 4.20 shows the brains of three people: one who died immediately after a stroke, one who survived long after a stroke, and a bullet wound victim.

In ischemia, the neurons deprived of blood lose much of their oxygen and glucose supplies. In hemorrhage, they are flooded with blood and excess oxygen, calcium, and other chemicals. Both ischemia and hemorrhage lead to many of the same problems, including **edema** (the accumulation of fluid), which increases pressure on the brain and the probability of additional strokes (Unterberg, Stover, Kress, & Kiening, 2004). Both ischemia and hemorrhage also impair the sodium–potassium pump, leading to an accumulation of sodium inside neurons. The combination of edema and excess sodium provokes excess release of the transmitter glutamate (Rossi, Oshima, & Attwell, 2000), which overstimulates neurons, damaging both neurons and synapses (Castro-Alvarez, Gutierrez-Vargas, Darnaudéry, & Cardona-Gómez, 2011). As neurons die, microglia cells proliferate, removing the products

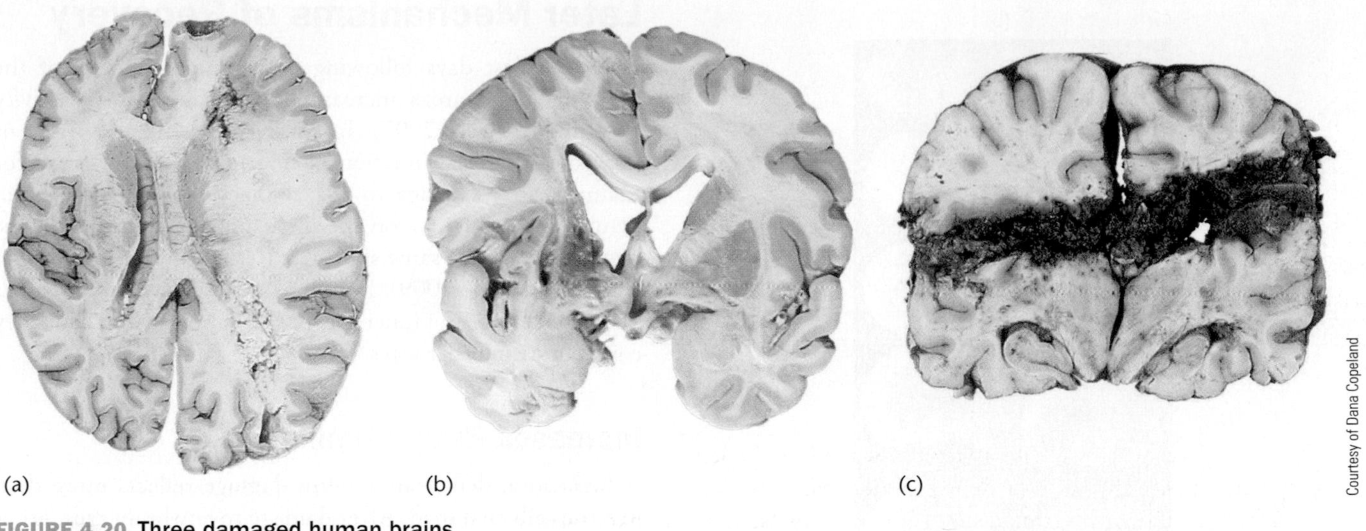

FIGURE 4.20 Three damaged human brains
(a) Brain of a person who died immediately after a stroke. Note the swelling on the right side. (b) Brain of someone who survived for a long time after a stroke. Note the cavities on the left side, where many cells were lost. (c) Brain of a person who suffered a gunshot wound and died immediately.

of dead neurons and supplying neurotrophins that promote survival of the remaining neurons (Lalancette-Hébert, Gowing, Simard, Weng, & Kriz, 2007).

Immediate Treatments

As recently as the 1980s, hospitals had little to offer to stroke patients. Today, prospects are good for ischemia if physicians act quickly. A drug called **tissue plasminogen activator (tPA)** breaks up blood clots (Barinaga, 1996). To get a benefit, a patient should receive tPA quickly, at least within 4.5 hours after a stroke. Emergency wards have improved their response times, but the limiting factor is that most stroke victims don't get to the hospital quickly enough (Evenson, Foraker, Morris, & Rosamond, 2009).

It is difficult to determine whether a stroke was ischemic or hemorrhagic. Given that tPA is useful for ischemia but could only make matters worse in a hemorrhage (and sometimes causes a hemorrhage), what is a physician to do? An MRI scan distinguishes between the two kinds of stroke, but MRIs take time, and time is limited. The usual decision is to give the tPA. Hemorrhage is less common and usually fatal anyway, so the risk of making a hemorrhage worse is small compared to the hope of alleviating ischemia.

What other treatments might be effective shortly after a stroke? Given that stokes kill neurons by overstimulation, one approach has been to decrease stimulation by blocking glutamate synapses or blocking calcium entry. Many such techniques have shown benefits in laboratory animals, but so far none has shown benefits for humans (Minnerup, Sutherland, Buchan, & Kleinschnitz, 2012). Likely reasons include the fact that the lab animals received the drugs immediately after a stroke, whereas human patients receive the drugs hours later. Also, the animals were young and healthy (except for the stroke), whereas most patients are older and have additional health problems. Finally, physicians are reluctant to give humans large doses of experimental drugs, for fear of dangerous side effects.

The most effective known method of preventing brain damage after strokes in laboratory animals is to cool the brain. Cooling protects the brain after ischemia by reducing overstimulation, apoptosis, and inflammation (Yenari & Han, 2012). People can be cooled safely as far as 33°C (91°F). Possible methods of cooling include ice packs on the head, injections of cool liquid into the blood, or drugs that lower body temperature. Each of these methods has its own advantages and risks (M. Zhang et al., 2013). What matters is temperature in the brain, so it is possible to keep the skin warm enough to prevent shivering. This procedure has shown promise in very limited testing, and a larger-scale clinical trial is underway (Neugebauer et al., 2013).

Another procedure might surprise you: Exposure to cannabinoids (the chemicals found in marijuana) minimizes the damage caused by strokes in laboratory animals. You might wonder how anyone thought of trying such a thing. The theoretical rationale was that cannabinoids decrease the release of glutamate. If excessive glutamate is one of the reasons for cell loss, then cannabinoids might be helpful. They do, in fact, minimize the damage after a stroke, as shown in Figure 4.21, although the explanation for the benefit is not yet clear (Schomacher, Müller, Sommer, Schwab, & Schäbitz, 2008). In addition to putting the brakes on glutamate, cannabinoids exert anti-inflammatory effects and alter brain chemistry in several ways that might protect against damage (Capettini et al., 2012; Chung et al., 2011). So far, physicians have made few attempts to apply cannabinoids to human stroke patients, and again the limiting factor is that

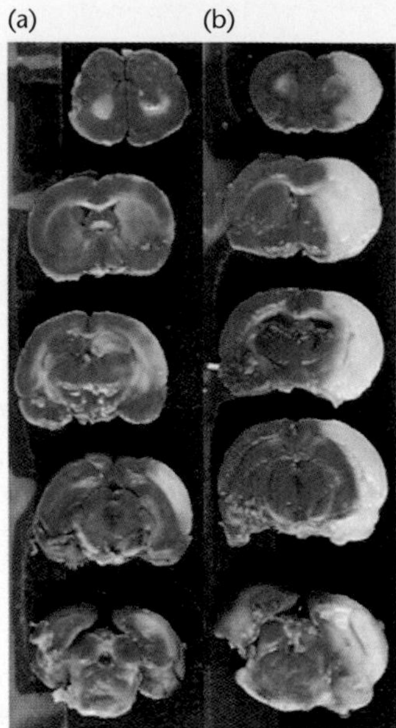

FIGURE 4.21 Effects of a cannabinoid on stroke damage Row (a) shows slices through the brains of five rats treated with a high dose of a cannabinoid shortly after a stroke. Row (b) shows slices for rats not treated with cannabinoids. The white areas on the right of each brain show the extent of the damage. *Source:* From Schomacher, M., Müller, H. D., Sommer, C., Schwab, S., & Schäbitz, W. R. (2008). Endocannabinoids mediate neuroprotection after transient focal cerebral ischemia. *Brain Research, 1240,* pp. 213–220.

the chemicals are effective only within the first hours after a stroke. In fact, the research on laboratory animals indicates that cannabinoids are most effective if taken shortly *before* the stroke. People, of course, cannot predict when a stroke might occur, and remaining permanently stoned as a precaution against stroke would be a bad idea not only for other reasons, but also because prolonged use of marijuana can cause a stroke!

STOP&CHECK

29. What are the two kinds of stroke, and what causes each kind?

30. Why is tPA not helpful in cases of hemorrhage?

31. If one of your relatives has a stroke and a well-meaning person offers a blanket, what should you do?

ANSWERS

29. The more common form, ischemia, is the result of an occlusion of an artery. The other form, hemorrhage, is the result of a ruptured artery. **30.** The drug tPA breaks up blood clots, and hemorrhage results from a ruptured blood vessel, not a blood clot. **31.** Refuse the blanket. Recovery will be best if the stroke victim remains cold.

Later Mechanisms of Recovery

After the first days following brain damage, many of the surviving brain areas increase or reorganize their activity (Nishimura et al., 2007). In some cases, one area more or less takes over the function of another, damaged area. For example, after damage to the connections from one brain hemisphere to the leg on the opposite side of the body, the hemisphere on the same side increases its connections to that leg (Ghosh et al., 2009). In other cases, surviving brain areas do not take over the functions of the damaged area, but they compensate in other ways.

Increased Brain Stimulation

A behavioral deficit after brain damage reflects more than just the cells that died. After damage to any brain area, other areas that have lost part of their normal input become less active. For example, shortly after damage in one brain hemisphere, its input to the other hemisphere declines, and therefore the other hemisphere shows deficits also (van Meer et al., 2010). Recovery from a stroke depends largely on increasing activity for the opposite side of the brain (Takatsuru et al., 2009).

Diaschisis (di-AS-ki-sis, from a Greek term meaning "to shock throughout") refers to the decreased activity of surviving neurons after damage to other neurons. If diaschisis contributes to behavioral deficits following brain damage, then increased stimulation should help. (This stimulation should not occur during the first day or two after the stroke, while neurons may be dying from excess stimulation, but instead during a later period of recovery.) In a series of experiments, D. M. Feeney and colleagues measured the behavioral effects of cortical damage in rats and cats. Depending on the location of the damage, the animals showed impairments in movement or depth perception. Injecting amphetamine significantly enhanced both behaviors, and animals that practiced the behaviors under the influence of amphetamine showed long-lasting benefits. Injecting a drug to block dopamine synapses impaired behavioral recovery (Feeney & Sutton, 1988; Feeney, Sutton, Boyeson, Hovda, & Dail, 1985; Hovda & Feeney, 1989; Sutton, Hovda, & Feeney, 1989). Although amphetamine is too risky for use with human patients, other stimulant drugs are more promising (Whyte et al., 2005).

STOP&CHECK

32. After someone has had a stroke, would it be best (if possible) to direct stimulant drugs to the cells that were damaged or somewhere else?

ANSWER

32. It is best to direct the amphetamine to the cells that had been receiving input from the damaged cells. Presumably, the loss of input has produced diaschisis.

Regrowth of Axons

Damaged axons grow back under certain circumstances. A neuron of the peripheral nervous system has its cell body in the spinal cord (for motor neurons) or in a ganglion near the spinal cord (for sensory neurons). In either case, the axon extends into one of the limbs. A crushed axon grows back toward the periphery at a rate of about 1 mm per day, following its myelin sheath to the original target.

Within a mature mammalian brain or spinal cord, damaged axons do not regenerate, or do so only slightly (Schwab, 1998). However, in many kinds of fish, axons do regenerate across a cut in the spinal cord and restore nearly normal functioning (Bernstein & Gelderd, 1970; Rovainen, 1976; Scherer, 1986; Selzer, 1978). Why do damaged CNS axons regenerate so much better in fish than in mammals? Can we find ways to improve axon regeneration in mammals?

Several problems limit axon regeneration in mammals. First, a cut in the nervous system causes a scar to form (thicker in mammals than in fish), creating a mechanical barrier. Scar tissue is beneficial immediately after the damage, but it blocks regrowth of axons later (Hellal et al., 2011; Rolls, Shechter, & Schwartz, 2009). Second, neurons on the two sides of the cut pull apart. Third, the glia cells that react to CNS damage release chemicals that inhibit axon growth (Yiu & He, 2006).

These problems are formidable, but hope remains if we can find a way to get axons to regrow through or around the scar and then reattach to their appropriate targets. Researchers developed a way to build a protein bridge, providing a path for axons to regenerate across a scar-filled gap. When they applied this technique to hamsters with a cut in the optic nerve, many axons from the eye grew back and established synapses, enabling most hamsters to regain partial vision (Ellis-Behnke et al., 2006). In another study, veterinary researchers took cells from the olfactory mucosa—not the olfactory receptors themselves, but the cells that surround them—and transplanted them into spinal cords of people's pet dogs that had suffered spinal cord injuries months earlier. These dogs regained a substantial degree of walking (Granger, Blamires, Franklin, & Jeffery, 2012). However, the improvement was entirely due to short connections developing across the cut, enabling movements of the front limbs to lead simultaneous movements of the hind limbs. No long axons grew to connect the brain with the lower spinal cord. So, although it is encouraging to see a once-paralyzed dog now walking with all four limbs, the method holds only slight promise for humans. It would not enable victims of spinal injury to move their legs voluntarily, control their bladder, or do the other things they would like to do.

Axon Sprouting

Ordinarily, the surface of dendrites and cell bodies is covered with synapses, and a vacant spot doesn't stay vacant for long. After a cell loses input from an axon, it secretes neurotrophins that induce other axons to form new branches, or **collateral sprouts**, that take over the vacant synapses (Ramirez, 2001) (see Figure 4.22). In the area near the damage, new synapses form at a high rate, especially for the first two weeks (C. E. Brown, Li, Boyd, Delaney, & Murphy, 2007).

Is collateral sprouting helpful or harmful? It depends on whether the sprouting axons convey information similar to those that they replace. For example, the hippocampus receives much input from an area called the entorhinal cortex. If the entorhinal cortex is damaged in one hemisphere, then axons from the entorhinal cortex of the other hemisphere sprout, take over the vacant synapses, and largely restore behavior (Ramirez, Bulsara, Moore, Ruch, & Abrams, 1999; Ramirez, McQuilkin, Carrigan, MacDonald, & Kelley, 1996). However, if the entorhinal cortex is damaged in both hemispheres, then axons from other locations sprout into the vacant synapses, conveying different information. Under those conditions, the sprouting interferes with behavior and prevents recovery (Ramirez, 2001; Ramirez et al., 2007).

Denervation Supersensitivity

Neurons make adjustments to maintain a nearly constant level of arousal. After learning strengthens one set of synapses, other synapses weaken. (If this didn't happen, every time you learned something, your brain would get more and more aroused.) Conversely, if a certain set of synapses

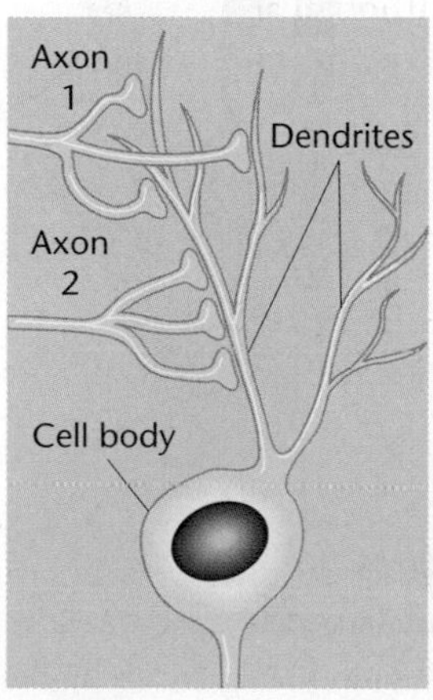

Axon injured, degenerates

Loss of an axon

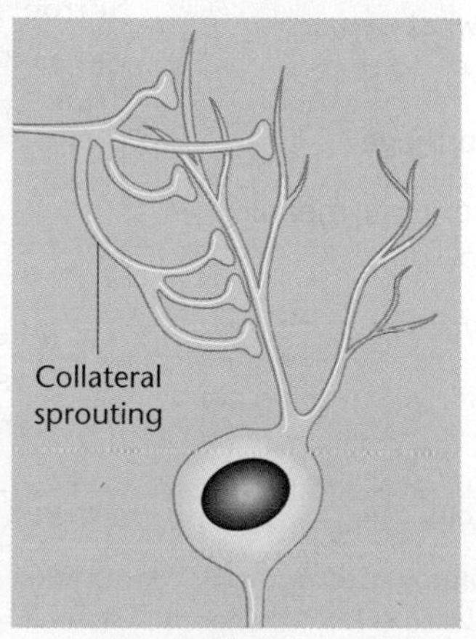

FIGURE 4.22 Collateral sprouting
A surviving axon grows a new branch to replace the synapses left vacant by a damaged axon.

becomes inactive—perhaps because of damage elsewhere in the brain—the remaining synapses become more responsive, more easily stimulated. This process of enhanced response, known as **denervation supersensitivity** or *receptor supersensitivity*, has been demonstrated mostly with dopamine synapses (Kostrzewa, Kostrzewa, Brown, Nowak, & Brus, 2008).

Denervation supersensitivity helps compensate for decreased input. In some cases, it enables people to maintain nearly normal behavior even after losing most of the axons in some pathway (Sabel, 1997). However, it can also have unpleasant consequences, such as chronic pain. Because spinal injury damages many axons, postsynaptic neurons develop increased sensitivity to the remaining ones. Therefore, even mild input produces enhanced responses (Hains, Everhart, Fullwood, & Hulsebosch, 2002).

STOP&CHECK

33. Is collateral sprouting a change in axons or dendritic receptors?

34. Is denervation supersensitivity a change in axons or dendritic receptors?

ANSWERS

33. Axons **34.** Dendritic receptors

Reorganized Sensory Representations and the Phantom Limb

If a brain area loses a set of incoming axons, we can expect some combination of increased response (denervation supersensitivity) by the surviving axons and collateral sprouting by axons that ordinarily attach to some other target. Let's imagine how these processes might apply in the case of an amputation.

Reexamine Figure 3.24: Each section along the somatosensory cortex receives input from part of the body. Within the area marked "fingers" in that figure, a closer examination reveals that each subarea responds more to one finger than to another. Figure 4.23 shows the arrangement for a monkey brain. In one study, experimenters amputated finger 3 of an owl monkey. The cortical cells that previously responded to information from finger 3 lost their input. Soon various cells became more responsive to finger 2, finger 4, or part of the palm, until the cortex developed the pattern of responsiveness shown in Figure 4.23b (Kaas, Merzenich, & Killackey, 1983; Merzenich et al., 1984).

What happens if an entire arm is amputated? For many years, neuroscientists assumed that the cortical area corresponding to that arm would remain permanently silent, because axons from other cortical areas could not sprout far enough to reach the area representing the arm. Then came a surprise. Investigators recorded from the cerebral cortices of monkeys whose sensory nerves from one forelimb had been cut 12 years previously. They found that the stretch of cortex previously responsive to the limb was now responsive to the face (Pons et al., 1991). After loss of sensory input from the forelimb, the axons representing the forelimb degenerated, leaving vacant synaptic sites at several levels of the CNS. Evidently, axons representing the face sprouted into those sites in the spinal cord, brain stem, and thalamus (Florence & Kaas, 1995; E. G. Jones & Pons, 1998). Or perhaps axons from the face were already present but became stronger through denervation supersensitivity. Brain scan studies confirm that the same processes occur with humans. Later studies showed that this process can be much quicker than 12 years.

Now consider what happens when something activates the neurons in a reorganized cortex. Previously, those cells responded to arm stimulation, but now they receive information from the face. Does it feel like stimulation on the face or on the arm? The answer: It feels like the arm (K. D. Davis et al., 1998).

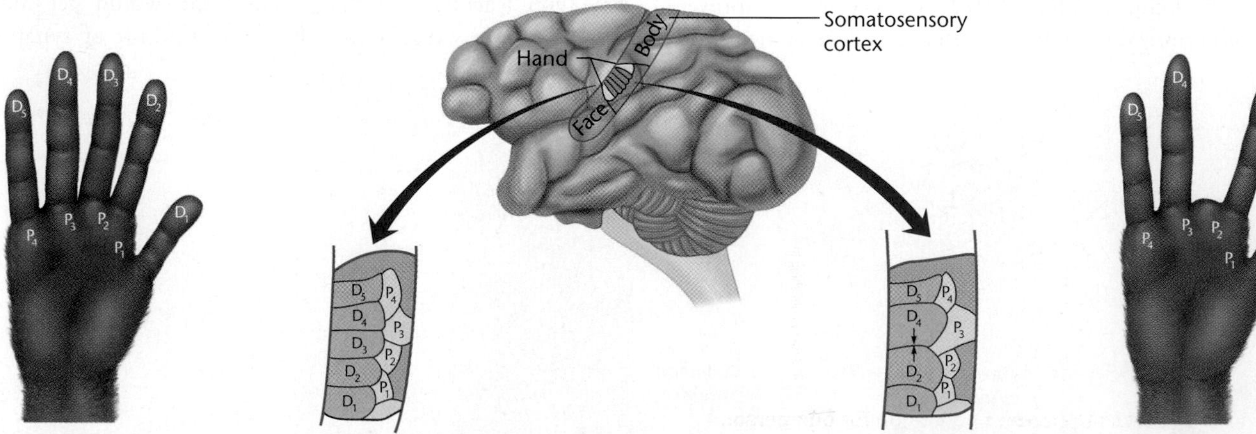

(a) Normal (before amputation)

(b) After amputation of 3rd digit

FIGURE 4.23 Somatosensory cortex of a monkey after a finger amputation
Note that the cortical area previously responsive to the third finger (D_3) becomes responsive to the second and fourth fingers (D_2 and D_4) and part of the palm (P_3). Based on the *Annual Review of Neuroscience*, Vol. 6, 1983.

One patient had a hand amputated at age 19; 35 years later, a new hand was grafted in its place. Within months, he started to feel normal sensations in that hand (Frey, Bogdanov, Smith, Watrous, & Breidenbach, 2008). Evidently the brain areas that start off as arm areas, hand areas, or whatever retain those properties even after decades without normal input.

Physicians have long noted that most people with amputations experience a **phantom limb**, a continuing sensation of an amputated body part. That experience can range from occasional tingling to intense pain, and from occasional to constant experience (Giummarra et al., 2010). It is possible to have a phantom hand, foot, or any other body part. The phantom sensation might last days, weeks, or a lifetime (Ramachandran & Hirstein, 1998).

Until the 1990s, no one knew what caused phantom pains, and most believed that the sensations came from the stump of the amputated limb. Some physicians performed additional amputations, removing more of the limb in a futile attempt to eliminate the phantom sensations. Modern methods show that phantom limbs develop when the relevant portion of the somatosensory cortex reorganizes and becomes responsive to alternative inputs (Flor et al., 1995). For example, suppose axons representing the face come to activate the cortical area previously devoted to an amputated hand. A touch on the face now produces a facial sensation but it also produces a sensation in the phantom hand. Figure 4.24 shows a map of which face area stimulates sensation in which part of the phantom hand, for one person (Aglioti, Smania, Atzei, & Berlucchi, 1997). For some people, seeing someone else being touched can also elicit a sensation in the phantom limb (Goller, Richards, Novak, & Ward, 2013).

Note in Figure 3.24 that the part of the cortex responsive to the feet is adjacent to the part responsive to the genitals. Two patients with foot amputations felt a phantom foot during sexual arousal! One reported feeling orgasm in the phantom foot as well as the genitals—and enjoyed it intensely (Ramachandran & Blakeslee, 1998). Evidently, the representation of the genitals had spread into the cortical area responsible for foot sensation.

Is there any way to relieve a painful phantom sensation? In some cases, yes. Many amputees who learn to use an artificial arm report that their phantom sensations gradually disappear (Lotze et al., 1999). As they start attributing sensations to the artificial arm, they displace the abnormal connections that caused phantom sensations.

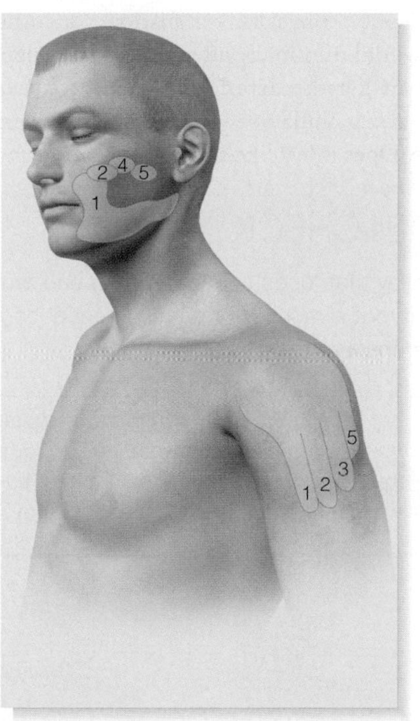

FIGURE 4.24 Sources of phantom sensation for one person
Stimulation in the areas marked on the cheek produced phantom sensations of digits 1 (thumb), 2, 4, and 5. Stimulation on the shoulder also evoked phantom sensations of digits 1, 2, 3, and 5.
Source: Based on Figure 5.29 from *Phantoms in the Brain* by V. S. Ramachandran, MD, PhD and Sandra Blakeslee.

Amputees who feel a phantom limb are likely to lose those phantom sensations if they learn to use an artificial arm.

STOP&CHECK

35. What is responsible for the phantom limb experience?

ANSWER

35. Synapses that used to receive input from the now amputated part become vacant. Axons representing another part of the body take over those synapses. Now stimulation of this other part activates the synapses associated with the amputated area, but that stimulation feels like the amputated area.

Learned Adjustments in Behavior

So far, the discussion has focused on anatomical changes. In fact, much recovery from brain damage is based on learning.

If you cannot find your keys, perhaps you accidentally dropped them into the trash (so they are gone forever), or perhaps you absentmindedly put them in an unusual place (where you will find them if you keep looking). Similarly, someone with brain damage may have lost some ability totally or may be able to find it with enough effort. Much recovery from brain damage depends on learning to make better use of the abilities that were spared. For example, if you lose your peripheral vision, you learn to move your head from side to side to compensate (Marshall, 1985).

Sometimes, a person or animal with brain damage appears unable to do something but is in fact not trying. Consider an animal that incurred damage to the sensory nerves linking a forelimb to the spinal cord, as in Figure 4.25. The animal no longer feels the limb, although the motor nerves still connect to the muscles. We say the limb is **deafferented** because it has lost its afferent (sensory) input. A monkey with a deafferented limb does not spontaneously use it for walking, picking up objects, or any other voluntary behaviors (Taub & Berman, 1968). At first investigators assumed that a monkey *cannot* use a deafferented limb. In a later experiment, however, they cut the afferent nerves of both forelimbs. Despite this more extensive damage, the monkey used both deafferented limbs to walk, climb, and pick up food. Apparently, a monkey fails to use a deafferented forelimb only because walking on three limbs is easier than using an impaired limb. When it has no choice but to use its deafferented limbs, it does.

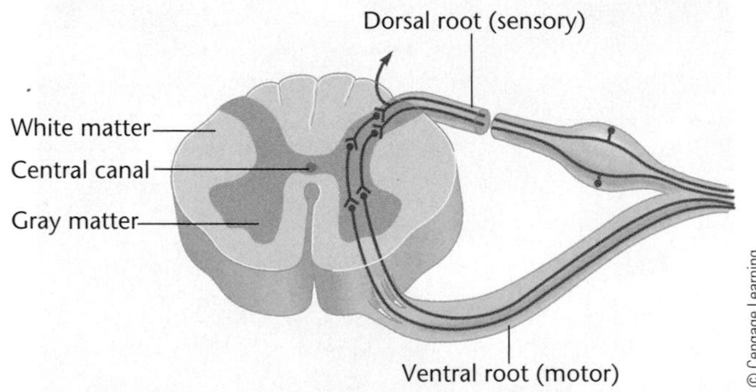

FIGURE 4.25 Cross-section through the spinal cord
A cut through the dorsal root (as shown) deprives the animal of touch sensations from part of the body but leaves the motor nerves intact.

Similarly, one treatment for people recovering from a stroke is to force them to use the weaker limb by preventing them from using the normal limb (Sens et al., 2012). A related therapy begins with careful evaluation of a patient's abilities and disabilities. For example, someone who has trouble carrying out spoken instructions might be impaired in hearing, memory, language, muscle control, or alertness. After identifying the problem, a physical therapist or occupational therapist helps the patient practice the impaired skills. Therapists get their best results if they start soon after a patient's stroke, although later practice can be somewhat helpful also.

Behavior recovered after brain damage is effortful, and its recovery is precarious. A person with brain damage who appears to be functioning normally is working harder than usual. The recovered behavior deteriorates markedly after drinking alcohol, physical exhaustion, or other kinds of stress that would minimally affect most other people (Fleet & Heilman, 1986). It also deteriorates in old age (Corkin, Rosen, Sullivan, & Clegg, 1989).

STOP&CHECK

36. A monkey that loses sensation from one arm stops using it, but a monkey that loses sensation from both arms does use them. Why?

ANSWER

36. A monkey that lost sensation in one arm is capable of moving it, but finds it easier to walk with the three intact limbs. When both arms lose their sensations, the monkey is forced to rely on them.

MODULE 4.3 ■ IN CLOSING

Brain Damage and Recovery

The mammalian body is well equipped to replace lost blood cells or skin cells but poorly prepared to deal with lost brain cells. Even the processes that do occur after brain damage, such as collateral sprouting of axons or reorganization of sensory representations, are not always helpful. It is tempting to speculate that we failed to evolve mechanisms to recover from brain damage because, through most of our evolutionary history, an individual with brain damage was not likely to survive long enough to recover. Today, many people with brain and spinal cord damage survive for years, and we need continuing research on how to improve their lives.

Summary

1. Brain damage has many causes, including blows to the head, obstruction of blood flow to the brain, or a ruptured blood vessel in the brain. Strokes kill neurons largely by overexcitation. **136**
2. During the first hours after an ischemic stroke, tissue plasminogen activator (tPA) can reduce cell loss by breaking up the blood clot. Theoretically, it should also be possible to minimize cell loss by preventing overexcitation of neurons, but so far, procedures based on this idea have been ineffective. Researchers continue seeking ways to facilitate recovery from stroke in human patients. **137**
3. When one brain area is damaged, other areas become less active than usual because of their loss of input. Stimulant drugs can help restore normal function of these undamaged areas. **138**
4. After an area of the CNS loses its usual input, other axons begin to excite it as a result of either sprouting or denervation supersensitivity. In some cases, this abnormal input produces odd sensations such as the phantom limb. **139**
5. The phantom limb experience occurs because axons from another body part invade the cortical area ordinarily devoted to sensation from the now lost body part. Stimulation of the other body part now produces sensation as if it had come from the amputated part. **140**
6. Many individuals with brain damage are capable of more than they show because they avoid using skills that have become impaired or difficult. **142**

Key Terms

Terms are defined in the module on the page number indicated. They're also presented in alphabetical order with definitions in the book's Subject Index/Glossary. Interactive flash cards, audio reviews, and crossword puzzles are among the online resources available to help you learn these terms and the concepts they represent.

cerebrovascular accident **136**
closed head injury **136**
collateral sprouts **139**
deafferented **142**
denervation supersensitivity **140**
diaschisis **138**
denervation supersensitivity **140**
edema **136**
hemorrhage **136**
ischemia **136**
phantom limb **141**
stroke **136**
tissue plasminogen activator (tPA) **137**

Thought Questions

1. Ordinarily, patients with advanced Parkinson's disease (who have damage to dopamine-releasing axons) move very slowly if at all. However, during an emergency (e.g., a fire in the building), they may move rapidly and vigorously. Suggest a possible explanation.
2. Drugs that block dopamine synapses tend to impair or slow limb movements. However, after people have taken such drugs for a long time, some experience involuntary twitches or tremors in their muscles. Based on material in this chapter, propose a possible explanation.

MODULE 4.3 End of Module Quiz

1. What are the two kinds of stroke, and what causes each kind?
   a. Ischemia (blocked blood vessel) and hemorrhage (burst blood vessel)
   b. Hemorrhage (blocked blood vessel) and ischemia (burst blood vessel)
   c. Active (increased brain activity) and passive (decreased brain activity)
   d. Hyperthermic (increased brain temperature) and hypothermic (decreased brain temperature)

2. The drug _____ is helpful for strokes related to _____.
   a. Xanax . . . ischemia
   b. Xanax . . . hemorrhage
   c. tPA . . . ischemia
   d. tPA . . . hemorrhage

3. Name two procedures that decrease the damage caused by strokes in laboratory animals, although physicians so far have seldom tried them with people.
   a. Dehydration and lithium
   b. Increased blood flow and antidepressants
   c. Decreased body temperature and cannabinoids
   d. Increased body temperature and tranquilizers

4. What is diaschisis?
   a. Impaired performance of neurons because neurons that used to provide them with input have been damaged
   b. Improved performance of neurons after they have received extra stimulation
   c. Alternation between activation of the left hemisphere and activation of the right hemisphere
   d. Sprouting of axons to provide input to cells that have lost their normal input

5. After someone has had a stroke, what kind of drug might be helpful, and which brain areas should receive it?
   a. It would be best to deliver tranquilizers to the damaged area of the brain.
   b. It would be best to deliver stimulant drugs to the damaged area of the brain.
   c. It would be best to deliver tranquilizers to cells previously connected to the neurons that have been damaged.
   d. It would be best to deliver stimulant drugs to cells previously connected to the neurons that have been damaged.

6. Where does collateral sprouting take place?
   a. In the cell body
   b. In the axon
   c. In the dendrites
   d. In both the axons and the dendrites

7. Where does denervation supersensitivity take place?
   a. In the cell body
   b. In the axon
   c. In the dendrites
   d. In both the axons and the dendrites

8. What causes the phantom limb experience?
   a. Irritation of receptors at the stump where the amputation occurred
   b. Spontaneous activity of receptors at the stump where the amputation occurred
   c. Reorganization of the sensory cortex
   d. A psychiatric reaction based on denial of the amputation

9. Suppose a patient uses only the right arm following injury that blocked all sensation from the left arm. Of the following, which is the most promising therapy?
   a. Electrically stimulate the skin of the left arm
   b. Tie the right arm behind the person's back
   c. Blindfold the person

ANSWERS: 1a, 2c, 3c, 4a, 5d, 6b, 7c, 8c, 9b.

Suggestions for Further Reading

Levi-Montalcini, R. (1988). *In praise of imperfection.* New York: Basic Books. Autobiography by the discoverer of nerve growth factor.

Ramachandran, V. S., & Blakeslee, S. (1998). *Phantoms in the brain.* New York: Morrow. One of the most thought-provoking books ever written about human brain damage, including the phantom limb phenomenon.

Tom McHugh/Science Source

Vision

5

I magine that you are a piece of iron. So there you are, sitting around doing nothing, as usual, when along comes a drop of water. What will be your perception of the water? Yes, of course, a bar of iron doesn't have a brain, and it wouldn't have any perception at all. But let's ignore that inconvenient fact and imagine what it would be like if a bar of iron could perceive the water. From the standpoint of a piece of iron, water is above all *rustish*.

Now return to your perspective as a human. You know that rustishness is not really a property of water itself but of how it reacts with iron. The same is true of human perception. When you see grass as *green*, the green is no more a property of grass than rustish is a property of water. Green is the experience that results when the light bouncing off grass reacts with the neurons in your brain. Greenness is in us—just as rust is in the piece of iron.

CHAPTER OUTLINE

MODULE 5.1 Visual Coding
General Principles of Perception
The Eye and Its Connections to the Brain
Visual Receptors: Rods and Cones
Color Vision
In Closing: Visual Receptors
MODULE 5.2 How the Brain Processes Visual Information
An Overview of the Mammalian Visual System
Processing in the Retina
Further Processing
The Primary Visual Cortex
Development of the Visual Cortex
In Closing: Understanding Vision by Understanding the Wiring Diagram
MODULE 5.3 Parallel Processing in the Visual Cortex
The Ventral and Dorsal Paths
Detailed Analysis of Shape
Color Perception
Motion Perception
In Closing: Aspects of Vision

LEARNING OBJECTIVES

After studying this chapter, you should be able to:

1. Remember that we see because light strikes the retina, sending a message to the brain.
2. List the properties of cones and rods.
3. Explain the main features of color vision.
4. Trace the route of visual information from the retina to the cerebral cortex.
5. Explain lateral inhibition in terms of the connections among neurons in the retina.
6. Define and give examples of receptive fields.
7. Describe research on how experiences alter development of the visual cortex.
8. Discuss specific deficits, such as impaired facial recognition or impaired motion perception, that can occur after damage to parts of the visual cortex.

OPPOSITE: Later in this chapter, you will understand why this prairie falcon has tilted its head.

Visual Coding

Several decades ago, a graduate student taking his final oral exam for a PhD in psychology was asked, "How far can an ant see?" He turned pale. He did not know the answer, and evidently he was supposed to. He tried to remember everything he knew about insect vision. Finally, he gave up and admitted he did not know.

With an impish grin, the professor told him, "Presumably, an ant can see 93 million miles—the distance to the sun." Yes, this was a trick question. However, it illustrates an important point: How far an ant sees, or how far you see, depends on how far the light travels before it strikes the eyes. You do not send out "sight rays." That principle was probably the first scientific discovery in psychology (Steffens, 2007). About a thousand years ago, the Arab philosopher Ibn al-Haytham (965–1040) observed that when you open your eyes at night, you immediately see the distant stars. He reasoned that if you saw by sending out sight rays, they couldn't get to the stars that fast. Then he demonstrated that light rays bounce off an object in all directions, but you see only those rays that reflect off the object and strike your retina (Gross, 1999).

The point is worth emphasizing, because a distressingly large number of college students believe they send out sight rays from their eyes when they see (Winer, Cottrell, Gregg, Fournier, & Bica, 2002). Even some students who have taken courses in physics or visual perception hold that profound misunderstanding. Here is one of the most important principles to remember from this text: When you see a tree, for example, your perception is not in the tree. It is in your brain. You see something only when light from it alters your brain activity. Even if you did send out rays from your eyes—and you don't—when they struck some object, you wouldn't know about it, unless they bounced back and returned to your eyes. (Similarly, you feel something only when touch information reaches your brain. When you feel something *with* your fingers, you don't feel it *in* your fingers. You feel it in your brain.)

STOP&CHECK

1. What was Ibn al-Haytham's evidence that we see only because light enters the eyes, not by sending out sight rays?

ANSWER

1. First, you can see distant objects such as stars far faster than we could imagine any sight rays reaching them. Second, when light strikes an object, we see only the light rays that reflect off the object and into the eyes.

General Principles of Perception

You see an object when it emits or reflects light that stimulates receptors that transmit information to your brain. How does your brain make sense of that information? The 17th-century philosopher René Descartes believed that the nerves from the eye would send the brain a pattern of impulses arranged like a picture of the perceived object, right side up. In fact, your brain encodes the information in a way that doesn't resemble what you see. A computer's representation of a triangle is a series of 0s and 1s that are in no way arranged like a triangle. Similarly, your brain stores a representation of a triangle in terms of altered activity in many neurons, and if you examine those neurons, you see nothing that looks like a triangle.

One aspect of coding is *which* neurons are active. Impulses in certain neurons indicate light, whereas impulses in others indicate sound, touch, or other sensations. In 1838, Johannes Müller described this insight as the **law of specific nerve energies.** Müller held that whatever excites a particular nerve establishes a special kind of energy unique to that nerve. In modern terms, the brain somehow interprets the action potentials from the auditory nerve as sounds, those from the olfactory nerve as odors, and so forth. Admittedly, that word *somehow* glosses over a deep mystery.

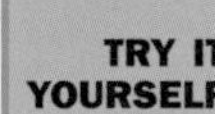

Here is a demonstration: If you rub your eyes, you may see spots or flashes of light even in a totally dark room. You applied mechanical pressure, which excited visual receptors in your eyes. Anything that excites those receptors is perceived as light. (If you try this demonstration, first remove any contact lenses. Shut your eyelids and rub gently.)

Another aspect of coding is the amount of response—that is, how many action potentials a neuron sends per unit of time. Much of sensory coding depends on the frequency of firing. For example, when pain axons fire many action potentials per second, you feel intense pain. Fewer per second would produce less pain.

STOP&CHECK

2. If someone electrically stimulated the auditory receptors in your ear, what would you perceive?
3. If it were possible to flip your entire brain upside down, without breaking any of the connections to sense organs or muscles, what would happen to your perceptions of what you see, hear, and so forth?

ANSWERS

2. Because of the law of specific nerve energies, you would perceive it as sound, not as shock. (Of course, a strong enough shock might spread far enough to excite pain receptors also.) 3. Your perceptions would not change. The way visual or auditory information is coded in the brain does not depend on the physical location within the brain. Seeing something as "on top" or "to the left" depends on which neurons are active but does not depend on the physical location of those neurons.

The Eye and Its Connections to the Brain

Light enters the eye through an opening in the center of the iris called the **pupil** (see Figure 5.1). It is focused by the lens (adjustable) and cornea (not adjustable) and projected onto the **retina**, the rear surface of the eye, which is lined with visual receptors. Light from the left side of the world strikes the right half of the retina, and vice versa. Light from above strikes the bottom half of the retina, and light from below strikes the top half. The inversion of the image poses no problem for the nervous system. Remember, the visual system does not duplicate the image. It codes it by various kinds of neuronal activity.

Route within the Retina

If you were designing an eye, you would probably send the receptors' messages directly back to the brain. In the vertebrate retina, however, messages go from receptors at the back of the eye to **bipolar cells**, located closer to the center of the eye (see Figure 5.2). The bipolar cells send their messages to **ganglion cells**, located still closer to the center of the eye. The ganglion cells' axons join together and travel back to the brain (see Figure 5.3). Additional cells called *amacrine cells* get information from bipolar cells and send it to other bipolar, amacrine, and ganglion cells. Many types of amacrine cells refine the input to ganglion cells, enabling certain ones to respond mainly to particular shapes, directions of movement, changes in lighting, color, and other visual features (Masland, 2012). The retina has more ganglion cells than bipolar cells (Asari & Meister, 2012).

One consequence of this anatomy is that light passes through the ganglion, amacrine, and bipolar cells en route to the receptors. However, these cells are transparent, and light passes through them without distortion. A more important consequence is the *blind spot*. The ganglion cell axons join to form the **optic nerve** that exits through the back of the eye. The point at which it leaves (also where the blood vessels enter and leave) is the **blind spot** because it has no receptors. You can demonstrate your own blind spot with Figure 5.4. Close your left eye and focus your right eye on the top o. Then move the page forward and back. When the page is about 10 inches (25 cm) away, the x disappears because its image strikes the blind spot.

TRY IT YOURSELF

Now repeat with the lower part of the figure. When the page is again about 10 inches away from your eyes, what do you see? The *gap* disappears! When the blind spot interrupts a straight line or other regular pattern, your brain fills in the gap.

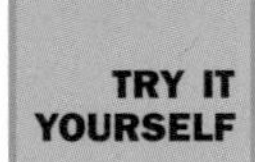

In everyday life, you never notice your blind spot, for two reasons. First, your brain fills in the gap, as you just experienced. Second, anything in the blind spot of one eye is visible to the other eye. Use Figure 5.4 again to locate the blind spot in your right eye. Then close your right eye and open the left one. You will see the spot that the right eye couldn't see.

STOP&CHECK

4. What makes the blind spot of the retina blind?

ANSWER

4. The blind spot has no receptors because it is occupied by exiting axons and blood vessels.

Fovea and Periphery of the Retina

When you look at details such as letters on this page, you fixate them on the central portion of your retina, especially the **fovea** (meaning "pit"), a tiny area specialized for acute, detailed vision (see Figure 5.1). Because blood vessels and ganglion cell axons are almost absent near the fovea, it has nearly unimpeded vision. The tight packing of receptors also aids perception of detail.

More importantly for perceiving detail, each receptor in the fovea connects to a single *bipolar cell*, which in turn connects to a single *ganglion cell*, with an axon to the brain. The ganglion

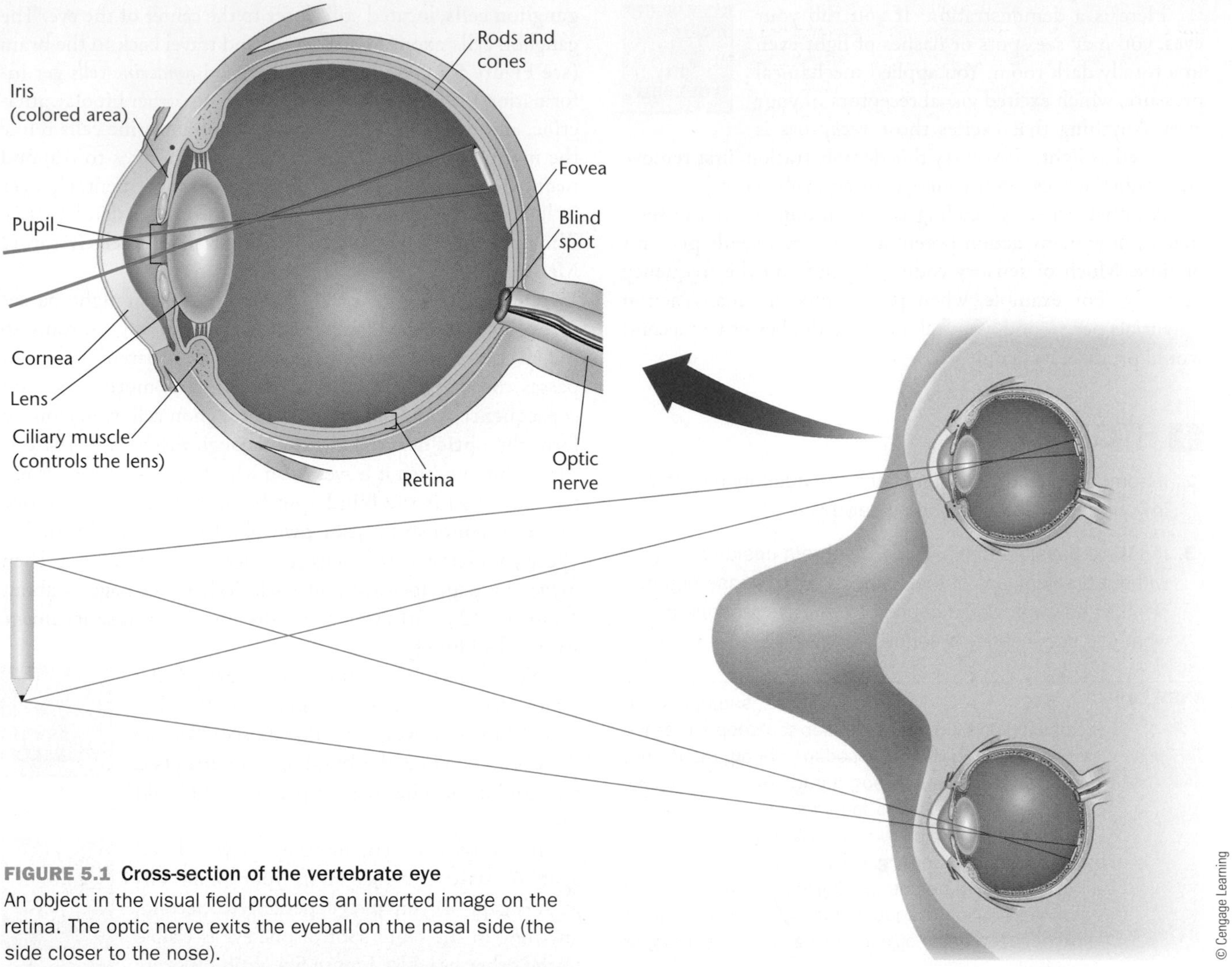

FIGURE 5.1 Cross-section of the vertebrate eye
An object in the visual field produces an inverted image on the retina. The optic nerve exits the eyeball on the nasal side (the side closer to the nose).

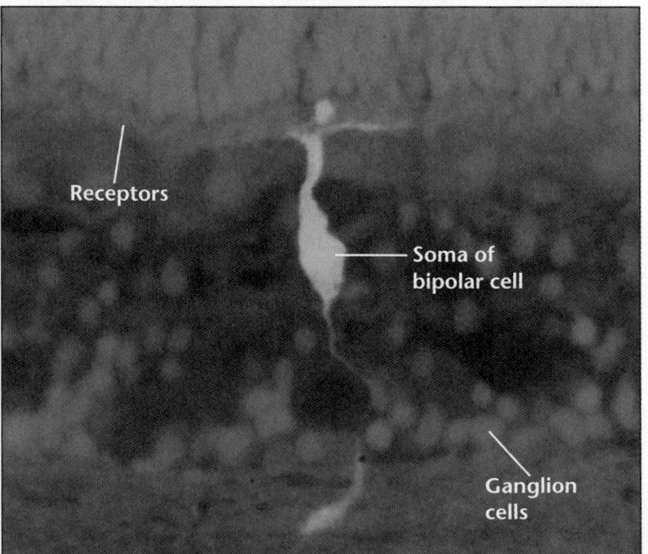

FIGURE 5.2 A bipolar cell from the retina of a carp, stained yellow
Bipolar cells get their name from the fact that a fibrous process is attached to each end (or pole) of the neuron.

cells in the fovea of humans and other primates are called **midget ganglion cells** because each is small and responds to just a single cone. As a result, each cone in the fovea has a direct route to the brain. Because the midget ganglion cells provide 70 percent of the input to the brain, our vision is dominated by what we see in the fovea (Nassi & Callaway, 2009).

You have heard the expression "eyes like a hawk." Many birds' eyes occupy most of the head, compared to only 5 percent of the head in humans. Furthermore, many bird species have two foveas per eye, one pointing ahead and one pointing to the side (Wallman & Pettigrew, 1985). The extra foveas enable perception of detail in the periphery.

Hawks and other predatory birds have a greater density of visual receptors on the top half of their retinas (looking down) than on the bottom half (looking up). That arrangement is adaptive because predatory birds spend most of their day soaring high in the air looking down. However, to look up, the bird must turn its head, as in Figure 5.5 (Waldvogel, 1990). Conversely, many prey species such as rats have most of their receptors on the bottom half of the retina, enabling them to see above better than below (Lund, Lund, & Wise, 1974). You can see the evolutionary advantages for these species.

FIGURE 5.3 Visual path within the eye
Receptors send their messages to bipolar and horizontal cells, which in turn send messages to amacrine and ganglion cells. The axons of the ganglion cells form the optic nerve, which exits the eye at the blind spot and continues to the brain.

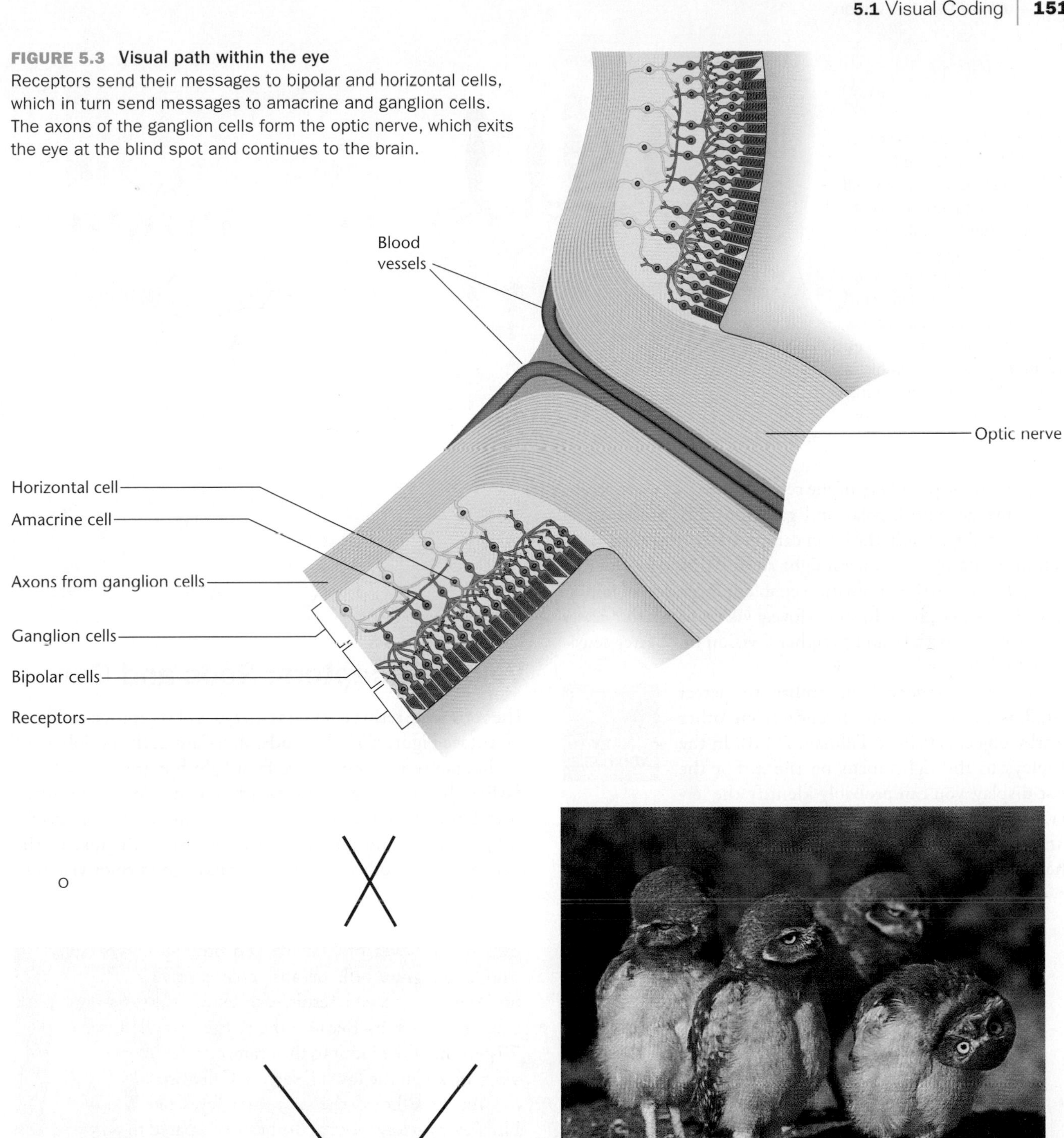

FIGURE 5.4 Demonstrations of the blind spot of the retina
Close your left eye and focus your right eye on the o in the top part. Move the page toward you and away, noticing what happens to the x. At a distance of about 10 inches (25 cm), the x disappears. Now repeat this procedure with the bottom part. At that same distance, what do you see?

FIGURE 5.5 A consequence of how receptors are arranged on the retina
One owlet has turned its head almost upside down to look up. Birds of prey have many receptors on the upper half of the retina, enabling them to see down in great detail during flight. But they see objects above themselves poorly, unless they turn their heads. Take another look at the prairie falcon at the start of this chapter. It is not a one-eyed bird; it is a bird that has tilted its head. Do you now understand why?

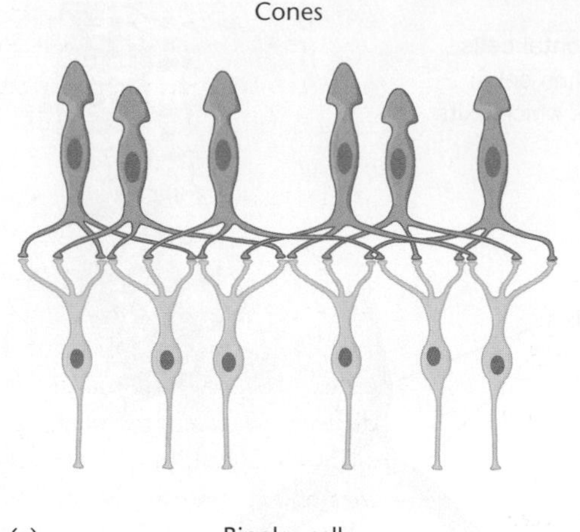

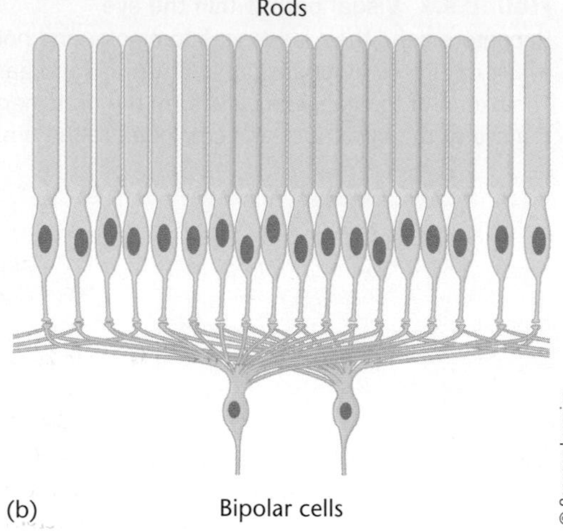

FIGURE 5.6 Convergence of input onto bipolar cells
In the fovea, each bipolar cell receives excitation from just one cone (and inhibition from a few surrounding cones), and relays its information to a single midget ganglion cell. In the periphery, input from many rods converges onto each bipolar cell, resulting in higher sensitivity to faint light and low sensitivity to spatial location.

Toward the periphery of the retina, more and more receptors converge onto bipolar and ganglion cells, as shown in Figure 5.6. As a result, the brain cannot detect the exact location or shape of a peripheral light source (Rossi & Roorda, 2010). However, the summation enables perception of fainter lights in the periphery. In short, foveal vision has better *acuity* (sensitivity to detail), and peripheral vision has better sensitivity to dim light.

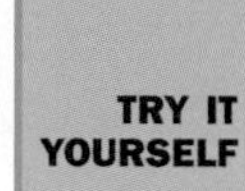

In the periphery, your ability to detect detail is limited by interference from other nearby objects (Pelli & Tillman, 2008). In the displays to the right, focus on the x. For the first display, you can probably identify the letter to its right. For the second display, it is harder to read that same letter in the same location, because of interference from the neighboring letters.

X T

X ATE

Visual Receptors: Rods and Cones

The vertebrate retina contains two types of receptors: rods and cones (see Figure 5.7). The **rods**, abundant in the periphery of the human retina, respond to faint light but are not useful in daylight because bright light bleaches them. **Cones**, abundant in and near the fovea, are less active in dim light, more useful in bright light, and essential for color vision. Because of the distribution of rods and cones, you have good color vision in

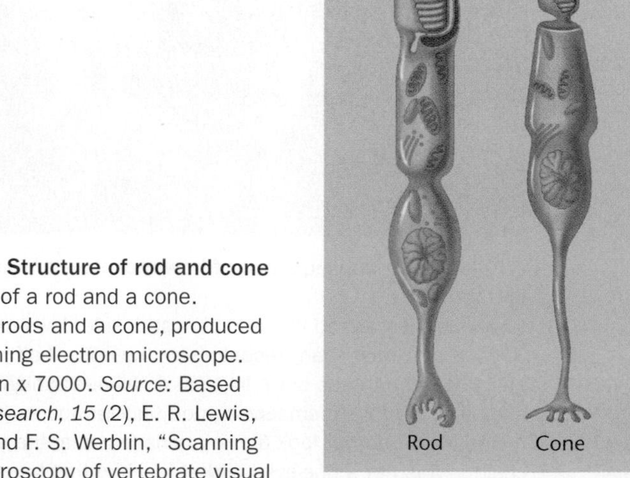

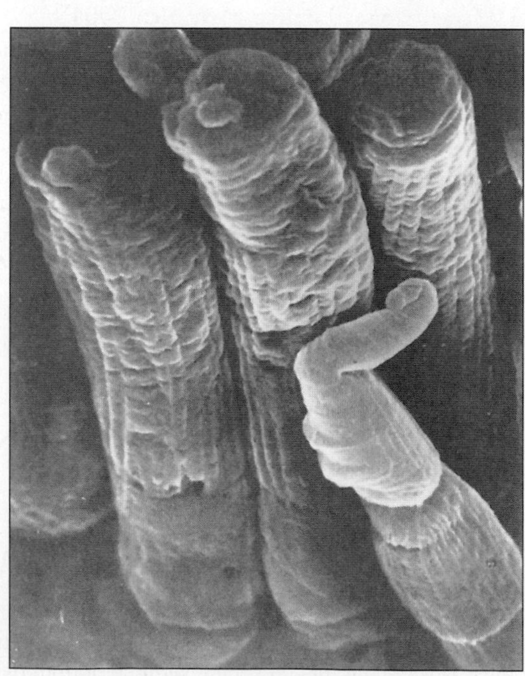

FIGURE 5.7 Structure of rod and cone
(a) Diagram of a rod and a cone.
(b) Photo of rods and a cone, produced with a scanning electron microscope. Magnification x 7000. *Source:* Based on *Brain Research, 15* (2), E. R. Lewis, Y. Y. Zeevi and F. S. Werblin, "Scanning electron microscopy of vertebrate visual receptors," 1969.

TABLE 5.1 Human Foveal and Peripheral Vision

Characteristic	Foveal Vision	Peripheral Vision
Receptors	Cones	Proportion of rods increases toward periphery
Convergence of input	Each ganglion cell excited by a single cone	Each ganglion cell excited by many receptors
Brightness sensitivity	Distinguishes among bright lights; responds poorly to dim light	Responds well to dim light; poor for distinguishing among bright lights
Sensitivity to detail	Good detail vision because each cone's own ganglion cell sends a message to the brain	Poor detail vision because many receptors converge their input onto a given ganglion cell
Color vision	Good (many cones)	Poor (few cones)

the fovea but not in the periphery. Table 5.1 summarizes the differences between foveal and peripheral vision.

Although rods outnumber cones by about 20 to 1 in the human retina, cones provide about 90 percent of the brain's input (Masland, 2001). Remember the midget ganglion cells: In the fovea, each cone has its own line to the brain. In the periphery (mostly rods), each receptor shares a line with tens or hundreds of others. Overall, 120 million rods and 6 million cones converge onto 1 million axons in the optic nerve, on average. A 20:1 ratio of rods to cones may sound high, but the ratio is much higher in species that are active at night. South American oilbirds, which live in caves and emerge only at night, have about 15,000 rods per cone. As a further adaptation to detect faint lights, their rods are packed three deep throughout the retina (G. Martin, Rojas, Ramírez, & McNeil, 2004).

People vary substantially in the number of axons in their optic nerve and the size of the visual cortex, largely for genetic reasons (Bakken et al., 2012). Some people have two or three times as many axons from the eyes to the brain as others do. They also have more cells in their visual cortex (Andrews, Halpern, & Purves, 1997; Stevens, 2001; Sur & Leamey, 2001) and greater ability to detect brief, faint, or rapidly changing visual stimuli (Halpern, Andrews, & Purves, 1999). Heightened visual responses are valuable in many activities, especially in sports that require aim. Researchers find that top performers in tennis, squash, and fencing show faster than average brain responses to visual stimuli. Speed of response to visual stimuli is only about average for top athletes in rowing or cycling, where strength is important but quick reactions are not (Nakata, Yoshie, Miura, & Kudo, 2010).

Both rods and cones contain **photopigments**, chemicals that release energy when struck by light. Photopigments consist of 11-*cis*-retinal (a derivative of vitamin A) bound to proteins called *opsins*, which modify the photopigments' sensitivity to different wavelengths of light. Light converts 11-*cis*-retinal to all-*trans*-retinal, thus releasing energy that activates second messengers within the cell (Q. Wang, Schoenlein, Peteanu, Mathies, & Shank, 1994). (The light is absorbed in this process. It does not continue to bounce around the eye.)

STOP&CHECK

5. You sometimes find that you can see a faint star on a dark night better if you look slightly to the side of the star instead of straight at it. Why?

6. If you found a species with a high ratio of cones to rods in its retina, what would you predict about its way of life?

ANSWERS

5. If you look slightly to the side, the light falls on an area of the retina with more rods and more convergence of input. **6.** We should expect this species to be highly active during the day and seldom active at night.

Color Vision

Visible light consists of electromagnetic radiation within the range from less than 400 nm (nanometer, or 10^{-9} m) to more than 700 nm. We perceive the shortest visible wavelengths as violet. Progressively longer wavelengths are perceived as blue, green, yellow, orange, and red (see Figure 5.8). We call these wavelengths "light" only because the receptors in our eyes are tuned to detecting them. If we had different receptors, we would define light differently. Indeed, many species of birds, fish, and

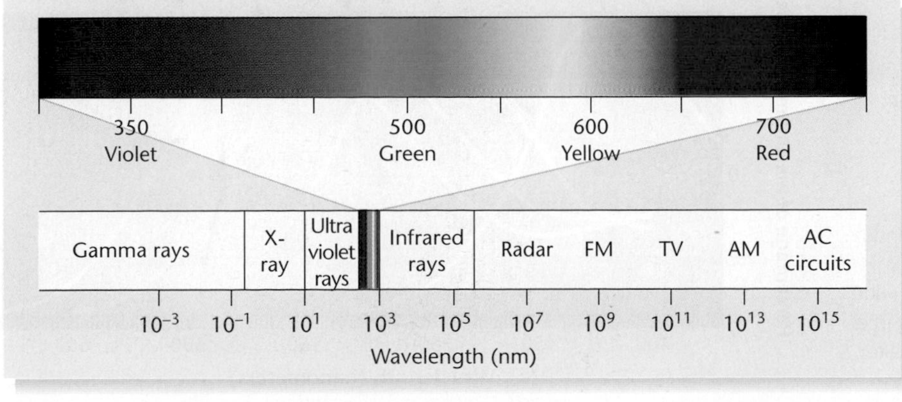

FIGURE 5.8 A beam of light separated into its wavelengths Although the wavelengths vary as a continuum, we perceive distinct colors.

insects have visual receptors sensitive to what we call ultraviolet radiation (Stevens & Cuthill, 2007). Of course, we cannot know what it looks like to them, but it certainly affects their behavior. In some species of birds, the male and female look alike to us, but different to birds, because the male reflects more ultraviolet light.

The Trichromatic (Young-Helmholtz) Theory

People distinguish red, green, yellow, blue, orange, pink, purple, greenish blue, and so forth. Presuming that we don't have a separate receptor for every possible color, how many types do we have?

The first person to advance our understanding on this question was an amazingly productive man named Thomas Young (1773–1829). Young was the first to start deciphering the Rosetta stone. He also founded the modern wave theory of light, defined energy in its modern form, founded the calculation of annuities, introduced the coefficient of elasticity, discovered much about the anatomy of the eye, and made major contributions to other fields (Martindale, 2001). Previous scientists thought they could explain color by understanding the physics of light. Young recognized that color required a biological explanation. He proposed that we perceive color by comparing the responses across a few types of receptors, each of which was sensitive to a different range of wavelengths.

This theory, later modified by Hermann von Helmholtz, is now known as the **trichromatic theory** of color vision, or the **Young-Helmholtz theory**. According to this theory, we perceive color through the relative rates of response by three kinds of cones, each one maximally sensitive to a different set of wavelengths. (*Trichromatic* means "three colors.") How did Helmholtz decide on the number three? He found that people could match any color by mixing appropriate amounts of just three wavelengths. Therefore, he concluded that three kinds of receptors—we now call them cones—are sufficient to account for human color vision.

Figure 5.9 shows wavelength-sensitivity functions for the *short-wavelength*, *medium-wavelength*, and *long-wavelength* cone types. Each cone responds to a broad range of wavelengths but to some more than others.

According to the trichromatic theory, we discriminate among wavelengths by the ratio of activity across the three types of cones. For example, light at 550 nm excites the medium-wavelength and long-wavelength receptors about equally and the short-wavelength receptor almost not at all. This ratio of responses among the three cones determines a perception of yellow-green. More intense light increases the activity of all three cones without much change in their ratio of responses. As a result, the light appears brighter but still the same color. When all three types of cones are equally active, we see white or gray. Think about this example of coding: The perception depends on the frequency of response in one cell *relative to* the frequency of another cell.

The response of any one cone is ambiguous. For example, a low response rate by a middle-wavelength cone might indicate low-intensity 540 nm light or brighter 500 nm light or still brighter 460 nm light. The nervous system determines the color and brightness of the light by comparing the responses of different types of cones.

TRY IT YOURSELF

Given the desirability of seeing all colors in all locations, we might suppose that the three kinds of cones would be equally abundant and evenly distributed. In fact, they are not. Long- and medium-wavelength cones are far more abundant than short-wavelength (blue) cones. Consequently, it is easier to see tiny red, yellow, or green dots than blue dots (Roorda & Williams, 1999). Try this: Look at the dots in the following display, first from close and then from greater distances. You probably will notice that the blue dots look blue when close but appear black from a greater distance. The other colors are still visible when the blue is not.

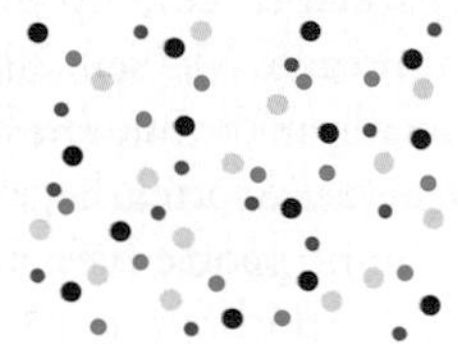

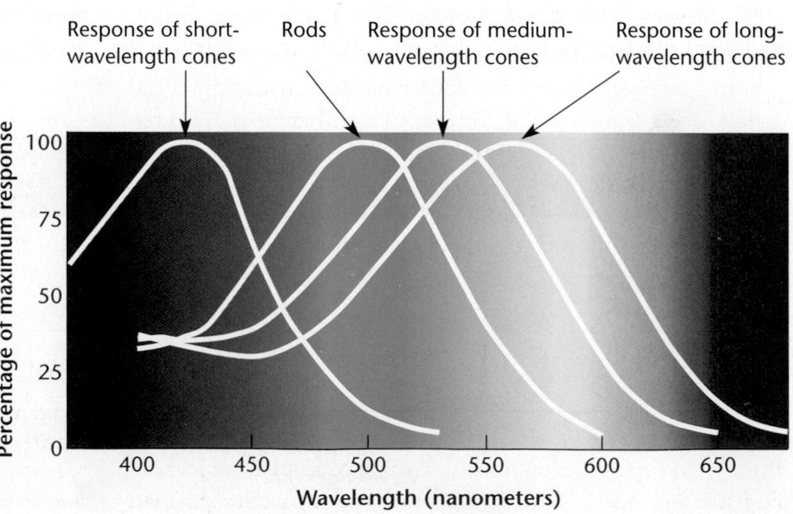

FIGURE 5.9 Responses of rods and three kinds of cones
Note that each kind responds somewhat to a wide range of wavelengths but best to wavelengths in a particular range. *Source:* Adapted from Bowmaker & Dartnall, 1980

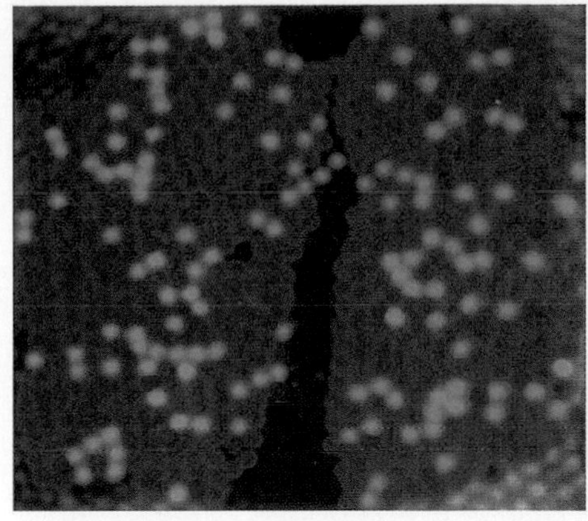
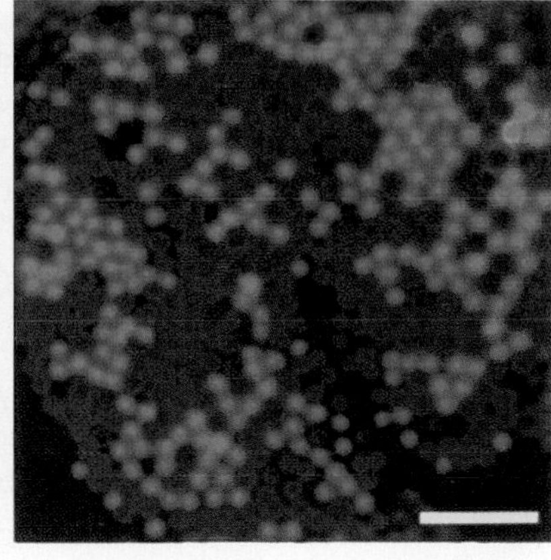

FIGURE 5.10 Distribution of cones in two human retinas
Investigators artificially colored these images of cones from two people's retinas, indicating short-wavelength cones with blue, medium-wavelength cones with green, and long-wavelength cones with red. Note the difference between the two people, the scarcity of short-wavelength cones, and the patchiness of the distributions. *Source:* Reprinted by permission from Macmillan Publishers Ltd.: *Nature*, "The arrangement of the three cone classes in the living human eye," Roorda & Williams, 1999.

Although the short-wavelength (blue) cones are about evenly distributed across the retina, the other two kinds are distributed haphazardly, with big differences among individuals (Solomon & Lennie, 2007). Figure 5.10 shows the distribution of short-, medium-, and long-wavelength cones in two people's retinas, with colors artificially added to distinguish them. Note the patches of all medium- or all long-wavelength cones. Some people have more than 10 times as many of one kind as the other. Surprisingly, these variations produce only small differences in people's color perceptions (Solomon & Lennie, 2007).

In the retina's periphery, cones are so scarce that you have no useful color vision (Diller et al., 2004; P. R. Martin, Lee, White, Solomon, & Rütiger, 2001). Try this: Get someone to put a colored dot on the tip of your finger without telling you the color. A spot of colored ink will do. While keeping your eyes straight ahead, slowly move your finger from behind your head into your field of vision and gradually toward your fovea. At what point do you see the color? Certainly you see your finger before you see the color. The smaller the dot, the farther you have to move it into your **visual field**—that is, the part of the world that you see—before you can identify the color.

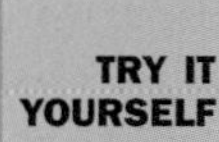

The Opponent-Process Theory

The trichromatic theory is incomplete as a theory of color vision. For example, try the following demonstration: Pick a point near the center of Figure 5.11 and stare at it under a bright light, without moving your eyes, for a minute. (The brighter the light and the longer you stare, the stronger the effect.) Then look at a plain white surface, such as a wall or a blank sheet of paper. Keep your eyes steady. You will see a **negative color afterimage**, a replacement of the red you had been staring at with green, green with red, yellow and blue with each other, and black and white with each other.

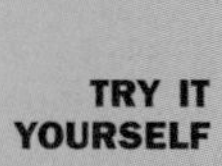

To explain this and related phenomena, Ewald Hering, a 19th-century physiologist, proposed the **opponent-process theory**: We perceive color in terms of opposites (Hurvich & Jameson, 1957). That is, the brain has a mechanism that perceives color on a continuum from red to green, another from yellow to blue, and another from white to black. After you stare at one color in one location long enough, you fatigue that response and tend to swing to the opposite.

Part of the explanation for this process pertains to the connections within the retina. For example, imagine a bipolar cell that receives excitation from a short-wavelength cone and inhibition from long- and medium-wavelength cones. It increases its activity in response to short-wavelength (blue) light and decreases it in response to yellowish light. After prolonged exposure to blue light, the fatigued cell decreases its response. Because a low level of response by that cell usually means yellow, you perceive yellow.

However, that explanation cannot be the whole story. Try this: Stare at the x in the following diagram for a minute or more under a bright light and then look at a white page.

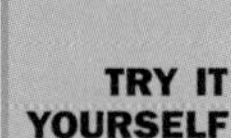

FIGURE 5.11 Stimulus for demonstrating negative color afterimages
Stare at one point under bright light for about a minute, without moving your eyes, and then look at a white field. You should see two oranges, a lime, two bananas, and two apples, all in their normal color.

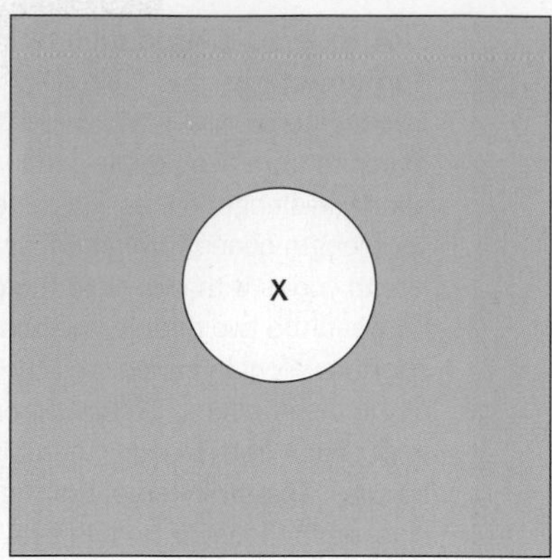

For the afterimage of the surrounding area, you saw red, as the theory predicts. But what about the circle inside? Theoretically, you should see a gray or black afterimage (the opposite of white), but in fact, if you used a bright enough light, you saw a green afterimage. What you saw in the surround influenced what you saw in the center.

Here is another demonstration: First, look at Figure 5.12. Note that although it shows four red quarter circles, you have the illusion of a whole red square. (Look carefully to convince yourself that it is an illusion.) Now stare at the x in Figure 5.12 for at least a minute under bright lights. Then look at a white surface.

People usually report that the afterimage fluctuates. Sometimes, they see four green quarter circles:

And sometimes, they see a whole green square (Shimojo, Kamitani, & Nishida, 2001):

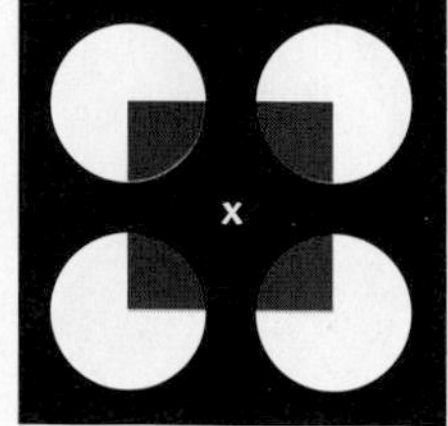

FIGURE 5.12 An afterimage hard to explain in terms of the retina

Stare at the x under bright light for a minute and then look at a white surface. Many people report an alternation between two afterimages, one of them based on the illusion of a red square. *Source:* Based on S. Shimojo, Y. Kamitani, and S. Nishida. Afterimage of perceptually filled-in surface, *Science, 293,* pp. 1677–1680, specifically Figure 1A, p. 1678 (left hand).

If you see a whole green square, it is the afterimage of an illusion! The red square you "saw" wasn't really there. This demonstration suggests that afterimages depend on the whole context, not just the light on individual receptors. The cerebral cortex must be responsible, not the bipolar or ganglion cells.

STOP & CHECK

7. As Figure 5.9 shows, medium-wavelength cones respond most strongly to light that we perceive as green. Long-wavelength cones respond most strongly to light that we perceive as yellow. According to the trichromatic theory, what causes us to perceive yellowish green?

8. According to the opponent-process theory, under what circumstance would you perceive a white object as blue?

ANSWERS

7. We perceive yellowish green when the medium- and long-wavelength cones are about equally active but the short-wavelength cones have very low activity. Each color experience corresponds to a particular ratio of firing by the three types of cones. **8.** If you stared at a bright yellow object for a minute or so and then looked at a similar white object, it would appear blue.

The Retinex Theory

The trichromatic theory and the opponent-process theory cannot easily explain **color constancy**, the ability to recognize colors despite changes in lighting (Kennard, Lawden, Morland, & Ruddock, 1995; Zeki, 1980, 1983). If you wear green-tinted glasses or replace your white light bulb with a green one, you still identify bananas as yellow, paper as white, and so forth. Your brain compares the color of one object with the color of another, in effect subtracting a certain amount of green from each.

To illustrate, examine Figure 5.13 (Purves & Lotto, 2003). Although different colors of light illuminate the two objects at the top, you easily identify the squares as red, yellow, blue, and so forth. Note the result of removing context. The bottom part shows the squares that looked blue in the top left part and yellow in the top right part. Without the context that indicated yellow light or blue light, all these squares look gray. (For this reason, we should avoid talking about the color of a wavelength of light. A certain wavelength of light can appear as different colors depending on the background.)

Similarly, we perceive the brightness of an object by comparing it to other objects. Examine Figure 5.14 (Purves, Shimpi, & Lotto, 1999). The object in the center appears to have a dark gray top and a white bottom. Now cover the border between the top and the bottom with a finger. You see that the top of the object has exactly the same brightness as the bottom! For additional examples like this, visit the website of Dale Purves, Center for Cognitive Neuroscience, Duke University.

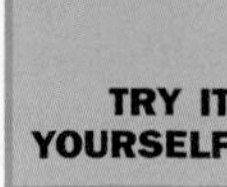

(a)

(b)

(c)

FIGURE 5.13 Effects of context on color perception
After removal of the context, squares that appeared blue on the left or yellow on the right now appear gray. *Source: Why we see what we do,* by D. Purves and R. B. Lotto, Figure 5.10, p. 134. 2003, Sinauer Associates, Inc.

FIGURE 5.14 Brightness constancy
In the center of this figure, do you see a gray object above and a white object below? Place a finger over the border between them and then compare the objects. *Source: From* "An empirical explanation of cornsweet effect," by D. Purves, A. Shimpi, and R. B. Lotto, *Journal of Neuroscience, 19,* pp. 8542–8551.

To account for color and brightness constancy, Edwin Land proposed the **retinex theory** (a combination of the words *retina* and *cortex*): The cortex compares information from various parts of the retina to determine the brightness and color for each area (Land, Hubel, Livingstone, Perry, & Burns, 1983).

Dale Purves and colleagues have expressed a similar idea in more general terms: Whenever we see anything, we make an inference. For example, when you look at the objects in Figures 5.13 and 5.14, you ask yourself, "On occasions when I have seen something that looked like this, what was it really?" You go through the same process for perceiving shapes, motion, or anything else (Lotto & Purves, 2002; Purves & Lotto, 2003). That is, visual perception requires reasoning and inference, not just retinal stimulation.

STOP&CHECK

9. When a television set is off, its screen appears gray. When you watch a program, parts of the screen appear black, even though more light is actually showing on the screen than when the set was off. What accounts for the black perception?

10. Figure 5.9 shows 500 nm light as blue and 550 nm light as yellow. Why should we nevertheless not call them "blue light" and "yellow light"?

ANSWERS

9. The black experience arises by contrast with the other brighter areas. The contrast occurs by comparison within the cerebral cortex, as in the retinex theory of color vision. **10.** Color perception depends not just on the wavelength of light from a given spot but also the light from surrounding areas. As in Figure 5.13, the context can change the color perception.

Color Vision Deficiency

One of the first discoveries in psychology was colorblindness, better described as **color vision deficiency**. (Complete colorblindness, perception of only black and white, is rare.) Today we are familiar with the idea that some people see color better than others do, but before the 1600s, people assumed that everyone sees the same way, and that what we perceive is what the object actually *is* (Fletcher & Voke, 1985). Then investigators demonstrated that some people have otherwise satisfactory vision without seeing all the color that other people do. That is, color is in our brains. It is not in the light or the object itself. In contrast to our three types of cones, most birds have four, and some fish have five (Hárosi & Hashimoto, 1983). So far as they are concerned, all humans are partly color deficient.

Color deficiency results when people with certain genes fail to develop one type of cone, or develop an abnormal type of cone (Nathans et al., 1989). In red-green color deficiency, the most common form of color deficiency, people have trouble distinguishing red from green because their long- and medium-wavelength cones have the same photopigment instead of different ones. The gene causing this deficiency is on the X chromosome. About 8 percent of men are red-green colorblind compared with less than 1 percent of women (Bowmaker, 1998). Women with one normal gene and one color-deficient gene—and that includes all women with a red-green color-deficient father—are slightly less sensitive to red and green than the average for other people (Bimler & Kirkland, 2009).

Suppose an adult with a red-green deficiency suddenly developed all three types of normal cones. Would the brain start seeing in full color? What if mice—which ordinarily have only one kind of cone and therefore no color vision—developed a second kind of cone? Would they start seeing in color?

The answer is yes to both questions. First, the mice: Ordinarily, mice have only one kind of cone, which helps them see differences of brightness but not color. Researchers genetically engineered some mice to have an additional kind of cone. These mice showed behavioral evidence of color vision (Jacobs, Williams, Cahill, & Nathans, 2007).

No one has tested what would happen if people with red-green color deficiency added a third kind of cone, but we do know what would happen for monkeys. Researchers took adult monkeys with red-green color deficiency from birth, and used gene therapy to add a third kind of cone to their retinas. They quickly learned to discriminate red from green (Mancuso et al., 2009). Evidently, the brain adapts to use the information it receives.

STOP&CHECK

11. Why is color vision deficiency a better term than color blindness?

ANSWER

11. Very few people see the world entirely in black and white. The more common condition is difficulty discriminating red from green.

MODULE 5.1 ■ IN CLOSING

Visual Receptors

I remember once explaining to my then teenage son a newly discovered detail about the visual system, only to have him reply, "I didn't realize it would be so complicated. I thought the light strikes your eyes and then you see it." As you should now be starting to realize—and if not, the rest of the chapter should convince you—vision requires complicated processing. If you tried to equip a robot with vision, you would quickly discover that shining light into its eyes accomplishes nothing, unless its visual detectors are connected to devices that identify the useful information and use it to select the proper action. We have such devices in our brains, and they produce the amazing results that we call vision.

Summary

1. You see because light strikes your retina, causing it to send a message to your brain. You send no sight rays out to the object. **148**
2. According to the law of specific nerve energies, the brain interprets any activity of a given sensory neuron as representing a particular type of sensory information. **148**
3. Sensory information is coded so that the brain can process it. The coded information bears no physical similarity to the stimuli it describes. **148**
4. Light passes through the pupil of a vertebrate eye and stimulates the receptors lining the retina at the back of the eye. **149**
5. The axons from the retina loop around to form the optic nerve, which exits from the eye at a point called the blind spot. **149**
6. Visual acuity is greatest in the fovea, the central area of the retina. Because so many receptors in the periphery converge their messages to their bipolar cells, our peripheral vision is highly sensitive to faint light but poorly sensitive to detail. **149**
7. The retina has two kinds of receptors: rods and cones. Rods, more numerous in the periphery of the retina, are more sensitive to faint light. Cones, more numerous in the fovea, are more useful in bright light. **152**
8. People vary in the number of axons from the retina to the brain. Those with more axons show a greater ability to detect brief, faint, or rapidly changing stimuli. **153**
9. According to the trichromatic (or Young-Helmholtz) theory of color vision, color perception begins with a given wavelength of light stimulating a distinctive ratio of responses by the three types of cones. **154**
10. According to the opponent-process theory of color vision, visual system neurons beyond the receptors themselves respond with an increase in activity to indicate one color of light and a decrease to indicate the opposite color. The three pairs of opposites are red-green, yellow-blue, and white-black. **155**
11. According to the retinex theory, the cortex compares the responses across the retina to determine brightness and color of each object. **156**
12. For genetic reasons, certain people are unable to distinguish one color from another. Red-green color deficiency is the most common type. **158**

Key Terms

Terms are defined in the module on the page number indicated. They're also presented in alphabetical order with definitions in the book's Subject Index/Glossary. Interactive flash cards, audio reviews, and crossword puzzles are among the online resources available to help you learn these terms and the concepts they represent.

bipolar cells **149**
blind spot **149**
color constancy **156**
color vision deficiency **158**
cones **152**
fovea **149**
ganglion cells **149**
law of specific nerve energies **148**
midget ganglion cells **150**
negative color afterimage **155**
opponent-process theory **155**
optic nerve **149**
photopigments **153**
pupil **149**
retina **149**
retinex theory **158**
rods **152**
trichromatic theory (or Young-Helmholtz theory) **154**
visual field **155**

Thought Question

How could you test for the presence of color vision in a bee? Examining the retina does not help because invertebrate receptors resemble neither rods nor cones. It is possible to train bees to approach one visual stimulus and not another. However, if you train bees to approach, say, a yellow card and not a green card, you do not know whether they solved the problem by color or by brightness. Because brightness is different from physical intensity, you cannot assume that two colors equally bright to humans are also equally bright to bees. How might you get around the problem of brightness to test color vision in bees?

MODULE 5.1 End of Module Quiz

1. What happens when you see something?
   a. You send out sight rays that strike the object.
   b. Light rays reflect off the object and strike your retina.
   c. You send out sight rays *and* light reflecting off the object strikes your retina.
   d. You neither send out sight rays nor receive light rays onto your retina.

2. If you look at a picture, how do the neurons in your brain represent it?
   a. In a right-side-up pattern
   b. In an upside-down pattern
   c. Neither

3. What is the law of specific nerve energies?
   a. A stronger physical stimulus activates a larger number of sensory neurons.
   b. Prolonged activation of a particular neuron weakens its response and leads to a different type of sensory experience.
   c. The amplitude and velocity of an action potential determines which sensation it conveys, such as light or sound.
   d. Each sensory neuron conveys a particular type of sensation, such as light or sound.

4. What makes the blind spot of the retina blind?
   a. It is at a location where the lens cannot focus the light.
   b. It is usually damaged during the process of birth.
   c. The optic nerve and blood vessels occupy this space, leaving no room for receptors.
   d. It is in the shadow of the pupil.

5. Vision in the periphery of the retina has poor sensitivity to detail but great sensitivity to faint light. Why?
   a. Toward the periphery, the retina has more midget ganglion cells.
   b. Toward the periphery, the retina has more cones and fewer rods.
   c. Toward the periphery, the retina has more convergence of input.
   d. Toward the periphery, the light falls farther from the blind spot.

6. Input to the human visual cortex comes from cones and rods (by way of ganglion cells) in what proportion?
   a. About 95 percent of input to the cortex comes from rods.
   b. About 50 percent comes from rods and 50 percent from cones.
   c. About 90 percent of input to the cortex comes from cones.

7. Suppose you perceive something as red. According to the trichromatic theory, what is the explanation?
   a. Light from the object has excited your long-wavelength cones more strongly than your other cones.
   b. Light from the object has excited your short-wavelength cones more strongly than your other cones.
   c. Ganglion cells that increase response to red and decrease their response to green are firing strongly.
   d. Ganglion cells that increase their response to green and decrease their response to red are responding weakly.

8. If you stare at a white circle surrounded by a green background, and then look at a white surface, you perceive a green circle surrounded by a red background. What does this observation imply about the opponent-process theory?
   a. We perceive colors based on the pattern of input to the bipolar and ganglion cells of the retina.
   b. The mechanisms of color vision vary from one species to another.
   c. Opponent-process color perception depends on the visual cortex, not just the cells in the retina.
   d. The opponent-process theory is wrong.

9. An object that reflects all wavelengths equally ordinarily appears gray, but it may appear yellow, blue, or any other color, depending on what?
   a. Brightness of the light
   b. Contrast with surrounding objects
   c. The culture in which someone grew up

10. Which theory most readily accounts for the observation described in question 9?

a. Trichromatic theory

b. Opponent-process theory

c. Retinex theory

11. What evidence shows that color, such as greenness, is in the brain and not in the light itself?

a. Each wavelength excites a different set of cells in the retina.

b. Each wavelength excites a different set of cells in the visual cortex.

c. Increasing the intensity of the light changes the apparent color.

d. Some people are unable to see certain colors despite otherwise normal vision.

ANSWERS: 1b, 2c, 3d, 4c, 5c, 6c, 7a, 8c, 9b, 10c, 11d.

How the Brain Processes Visual Information

Vision is complicated. We shall go through it in some detail, for two reasons. First, without vision and other senses, you would have no more mental experience than a tree does. Everything in psychology starts with sensations. Second, neuroscientists have developed a relatively detailed understanding of vision. Examining the mechanisms of vision gives us some idea what it means to explain something in biological terms. It provides a model of what we would like to accomplish eventually for other psychological processes.

An Overview of the Mammalian Visual System

Let's begin with a general outline of the anatomy of the mammalian visual system. The rods and cones of the retina make synapses with **horizontal cells** and bipolar cells (see Figures 5.3 and 5.15). The horizontal cells make inhibitory contact onto bipolar cells, which in turn make synapses onto *amacrine cells* and ganglion cells. All these cells are within the eyeball.

The axons of the ganglion cells form the optic nerve, which leaves the retina and travels along the lower surface of the brain. The optic nerves from the two eyes meet at the optic chiasm (see Figure 5.16a), where, in humans, half of the axons from each eye cross to the opposite side of the brain. As shown in Figure 5.16b, information from the nasal half of each eye (the side closer to the nose) crosses to the contralateral hemisphere. Information from the temporal half (the side toward the temporal cortex) goes to the ipsilateral hemisphere. The percentage of crossover varies from one species to another depending on the location of the eyes. In species with eyes far to the sides of the head, such as rabbits and guinea pigs, nearly all axons cross to the opposite side.

Most ganglion cell axons go to the **lateral geniculate nucleus**, part of the thalamus. (The term *geniculate* comes from the Latin root *genu*, meaning "knee." To *genuflect* is to bend the knee. The lateral geniculate looks a little like a knee, if you use some imagination.) A smaller number of axons go to the superior colliculus and other areas, including part of the hypothalamus that controls the waking–sleeping schedule. The lateral geniculate, in turn, sends axons to other parts of the thalamus and the visual cortex. The cortex returns many axons to the thalamus, so the thalamus and cortex constantly feed information back and forth (Guillery, Feig, & van Lieshout, 2001).

STOP&CHECK

12. Where does the optic nerve start and where does it end?

ANSWER

12. It starts with the ganglion cells in the retina. Most of its axons go to the lateral geniculate nucleus of the thalamus; some go to the hypothalamus and superior colliculus.

Processing in the Retina

At any instant, the rods and cones of your two retinas combined send a quarter of a billion messages. You couldn't possibly attend to all of that at once, and you don't need to. You need to extract the meaningful patterns. To understand how the wiring diagram of your retina highlights those patterns, let's start by exploring one example in detail: lateral inhibition.

Lateral inhibition is the retina's way of sharpening contrasts to emphasize the borders of objects. For analogy, suppose 15 people stand in a line. At first, each holds one cookie. Now someone hands 5 extra cookies to the 5 people in the middle of the line, but then each of those 5 people has to throw away one of his or her own cookies, and throw away one cookie that the person on each side is holding. Presuming that you want as many cookies as possible, where is the best place to be? You don't want to be in the middle of the group who receive cookies, because after gaining 5 you would have to throw away one of your own and lose one to each of your neighbors (a total loss of 3). But if you're either the first or last person to receive a cookie, you'll throw one away and lose one to just one neighbor (a total loss of 2). The worst place to be is right before or after the group receiving cookies. You would receive none, and lose the one you already had. The result is a sharp contrast at the border between those receiving cookies and those not.

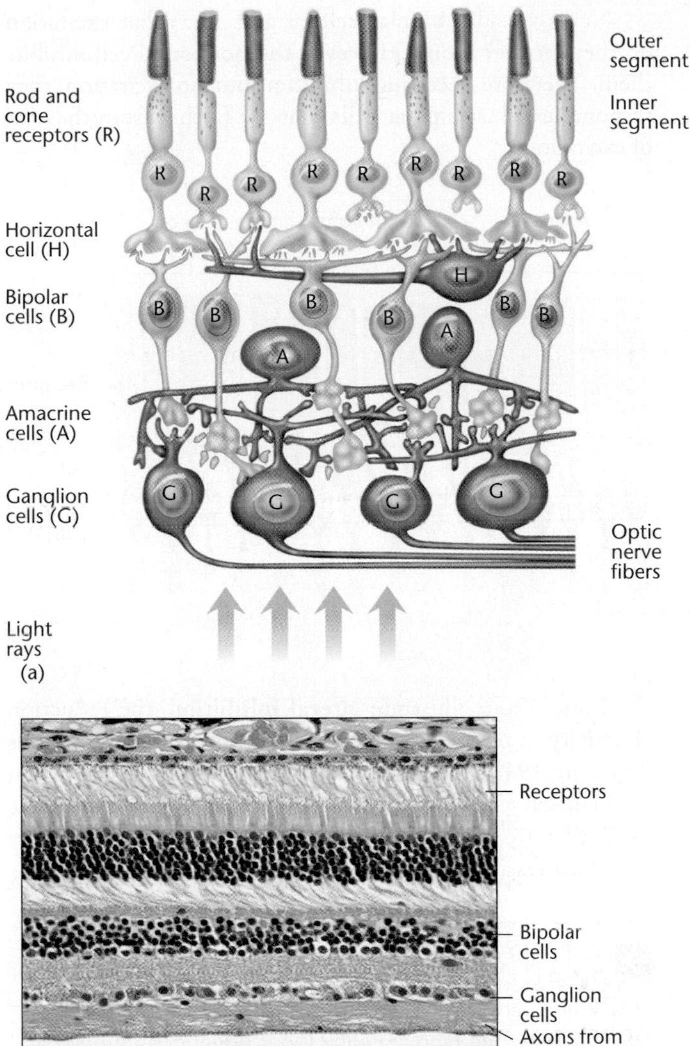

FIGURE 5.15 The vertebrate retina
The top of the figure is the back of the retina. The optic nerve fibers group together and exit through the back of the retina, in the "blind spot" of the eye. Based on "Organization of the Primate Retina," by J. E. Dowling and B. B. Boycott, *Proceedings of the Royal Society of London,* B, 1966, 166, pp. 80–111.

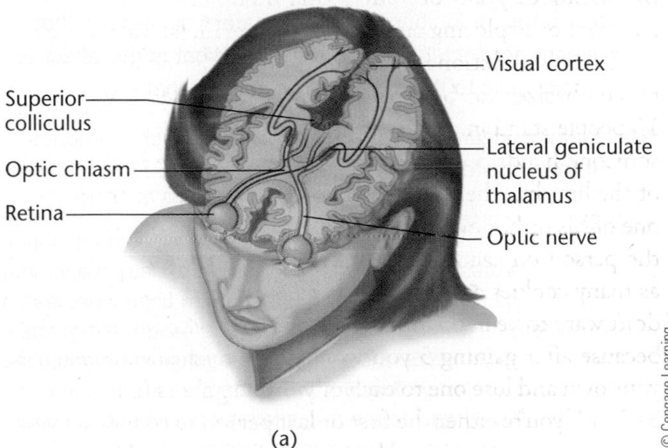

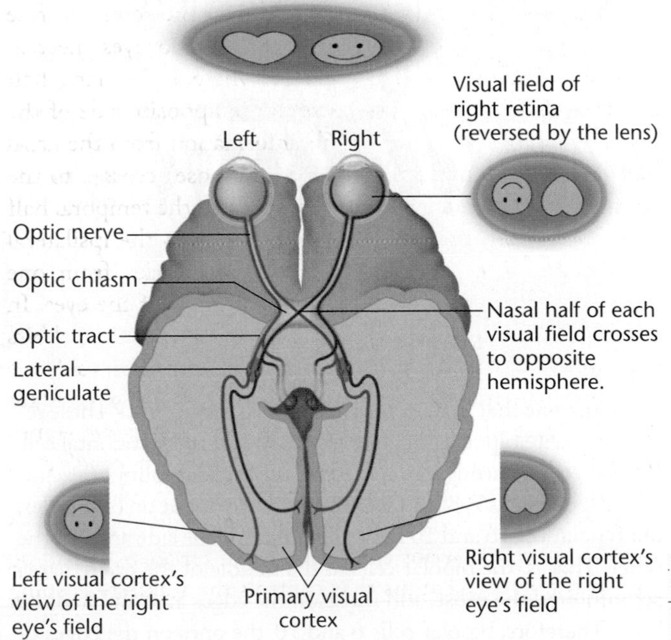

FIGURE 5.16 Major connections in the visual system
(a) Part of the visual input goes to the thalamus and from there to the visual cortex. Another part goes to the superior colliculus. (b) Axons from the retina maintain their relationship to one another—what we call their *retinotopic organization*—throughout their journey from the retina to the lateral geniculate and then from the lateral geniculate to the cortex.

The analogy may sound silly, but it illustrates something that happens in the retina. The receptors send messages to excite the closest bipolar cells (like giving them cookies) and also send messages to slightly inhibit them and the neighbors to their sides (like subtracting cookies). The net result will be to heighten the contrast between an illuminated area and its darker surround.

Actually, light striking the rods and cones *decreases* their spontaneous output. However, they have *inhibitory* synapses onto the bipolar cells, and therefore, light on the rods or cones decreases their inhibitory output. A decrease in inhibition means net excitation, so to avoid double negatives, we'll think of the output as excitation of the bipolar cells. In the fovea, each cone attaches to just one bipolar cell. We'll consider that simple case.

In the following diagram, green arrows represent excitation, and the width of an arrow indicates the amount of excitation. Receptor 8, which is highlighted, excites bipolar cell 8. It also excites a horizontal cell, which *inhibits* the bipolar cells, as shown by red arrows. Because the horizontal cell spreads widely, excitation of any receptor inhibits the surrounding bipolar cells. Because the horizontal cell is a *local cell,* with no axon and no action potentials, its depolarization decays with distance. The horizontal cell inhibits bipolar cells 7 through 9 strongly, bipolars 6 and 10 a bit less, and so on. Bipolar cell 8 shows net excitation, because the excitatory synapse outweighs the effect of the horizontal cell's inhibition. (It's like gaining some cookies and then losing a smaller number.) However, the bipolar cells to the sides (laterally) get no excitation but some inhibition by the horizontal cell. (They gained none and then they lost some.) Bipolar cells 7 and 9 are strongly inhibited, and bipolars 6 and 10 are inhibited less. In this diagram, the thickness of the arrow indicates the amount of excitation or inhibition. The lightness of blue indicates the net amount of excitation in each bipolar cell.

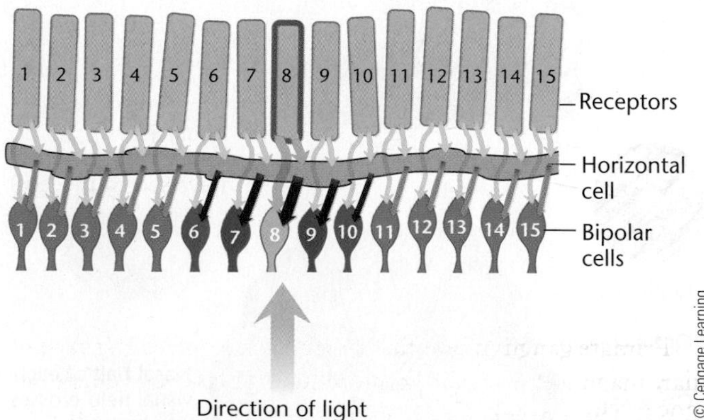

Now imagine that light excites receptors 6 through 10. These receptors excite bipolar cells 6 through 10 and the horizontal cell. Bipolar cells 6 through 10 all receive the same amount of excitation. Bipolar cells 7, 8, and 9 are inhibited by input on both sides, but bipolar cells 6 and 10 are inhibited from one side and not the other. That is, the bipolar cells in the middle of the excited area are inhibited the most, and those on the edges are inhibited the least. Therefore, bipolar cells 6 and 10, the ones on the edges of the field of excitation, respond *more* than bipolars 7 through 9.

Next, consider bipolar cells 5 and 11. What excitation do they receive? None. However, the horizontal cell inhibits them. Therefore, receiving inhibition but no excitation, they respond less than bipolar cells that are farther from the area of excitation.

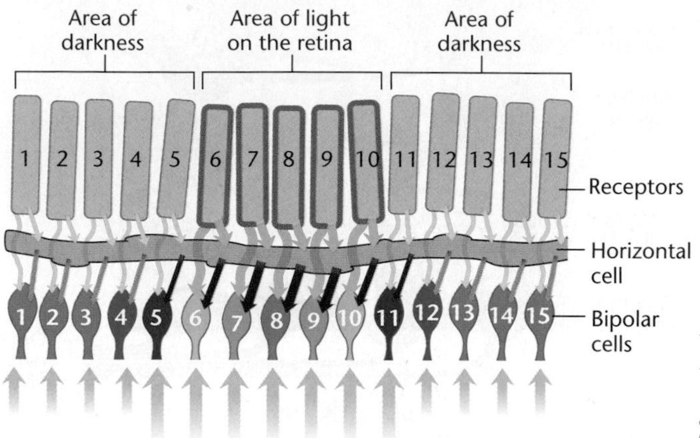

These results illustrate **lateral inhibition**, the reduction of activity in one neuron by activity in neighboring neurons (Hartline, 1949). Lateral inhibition heightens contrast. When light falls on a surface, as shown here, the bipolars just inside the border are most excited, and those outside the border respond the least.

STOP&CHECK

13. When light strikes a receptor, does the receptor excite or inhibit the bipolar cells? What effect does it have on horizontal cells? What effect does the horizontal cell have on bipolar cells?

14. If light strikes only one receptor, what is the net effect (excitatory or inhibitory) on the nearest bipolar cell that is directly connected to that receptor? What is the effect on bipolar cells to the sides? What causes that effect?

15. Examine Figure 5.17. You should see grayish diamonds at the crossroads among the black squares. Explain why.

ANSWERS

13. The receptor excites both the bipolar cells and the horizontal cell. The horizontal cell inhibits the same bipolar cell that was excited plus additional bipolar cells in the surround. **14.** It produces more excitation than inhibition for the nearest bipolar cell. For surrounding bipolar cells, it produces only inhibition. The reason is that the receptor excites a horizontal cell, which inhibits all bipolar cells in the area. **15.** In the parts of your retina that look at the long white arms, each neuron is inhibited by white input on two of its sides (either above and below or left and right). In the crossroads, each neuron is inhibited by input on all four sides. Therefore, the response in the crossroads is decreased compared to that in the arms.

FIGURE 5.17 An illustration of lateral inhibition
Do you see dark diamonds at the "crossroads"?

Further Processing

Each cell in the visual system of the brain has a **receptive field**, an area in visual space that excites or inhibits it. The receptive field of a rod or cone is simply the point in space from which light strikes the cell. Other visual cells derive their receptive fields from the connections they receive. This concept is important, so let's spend some time with it. Suppose you keep track of the events on one city block. We'll call that your receptive field. Someone else keeps track of events on the next block, and another person on the block after that. Now suppose that everyone responsible for a block on your street reports to a supervisor. That supervisor's receptive field is the whole street, because it includes reports from each block on the street. The supervisors for several streets report to the neighborhood manager, whose receptive field is the whole neighborhood. The neighborhood manager reports to a district chief, and so on.

The same idea applies to vision and other sensations. A rod or cone has a tiny receptive field in space to which it is sensitive. Some rods or cones connect to a bipolar cell, with a receptive field that is the sum of those of the cells connected to it (including both excitatory and inhibitory connections). Several bipolar cells report to a ganglion cell, which therefore has a still larger receptive field, as shown in Figure 5.18. The receptive fields of several ganglion cells converge to form the receptive field at the next level, and so on.

To find a cell's receptive field, an investigator records from the cell while shining light in various locations. If light from a particular spot excites the neuron, then that location is part of the neuron's excitatory receptive field. If it inhibits activity, the location is in the inhibitory receptive field.

The receptive field of a typical ganglion cell has a circular center with an antagonistic doughnut-shaped surround. That is, the receptive field might be excited by light in the center and inhibited by light in the surround, or the opposite.

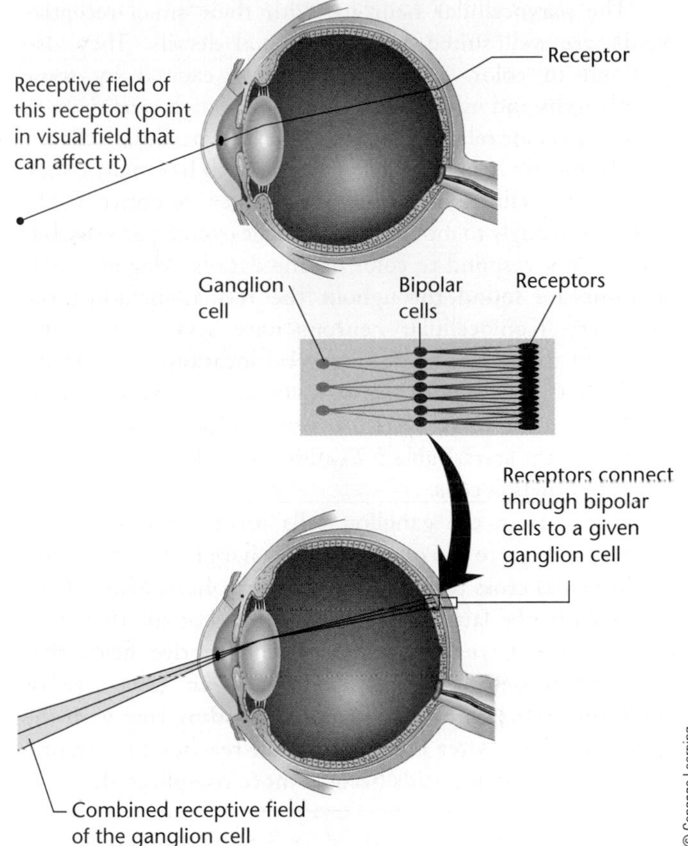

FIGURE 5.18 Receptive fields
The receptive field of any neuron in the visual system is the area of the visual field that excites or inhibits it. Receptors have tiny receptive fields and later cells have progressively larger receptive fields.

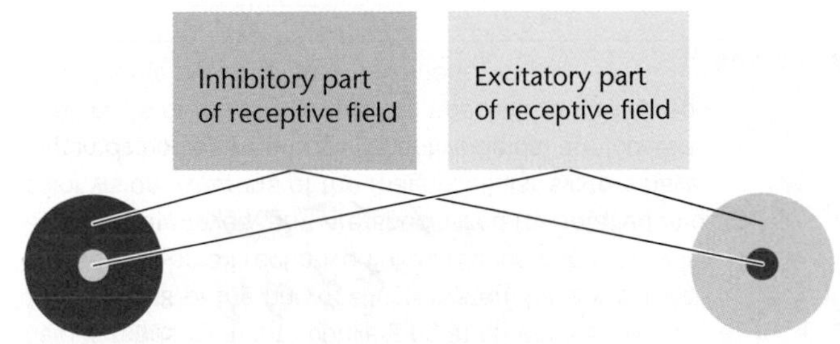

Primate ganglion cells fall into three categories: parvocellular, magnocellular, and koniocellular (Nassi & Callaway, 2009). The **parvocellular neurons**, with small cell bodies and small receptive fields, are mostly in or near the fovea. (Parvocellular means "small celled," from the Latin root *parv*, meaning "small.") The **magnocellular neurons**, with larger cell bodies and receptive fields, are distributed evenly throughout the retina. (Magnocellular means "large celled," from the Latin root *magn*, meaning "large." The same root appears in *magnify*.) The **koniocellular neurons** have small cell bodies, similar to the parvocellular neurons, but they occur throughout the retina. (Koniocellular means "dust celled," from the Greek root meaning "dust." They got this name because of their granular appearance.)

The parvocellular neurons, with their small receptive fields, are well suited to detect visual details. They also respond to color, each neuron being excited by some wavelengths and inhibited by others. The high sensitivity to detail and color relates to the fact that parvocellular cells are located mostly in and near the fovea, which has many cones. The magnocellular neurons, with larger receptive fields, respond strongly to movement and large overall patterns, but they do not respond to color or fine details. Magnocellular neurons are found throughout the retina, including the periphery. Koniocellular neurons have several functions, and their axons terminate in several locations (Hendry & Reid, 2000). The existence of so many kinds of ganglion cells implies that the visual system analyzes information in many ways from the start. Table 5.2 summarizes the three kinds of primate ganglion cells.

Axons from the ganglion cells form the optic nerve, which proceeds to the optic chiasm, where half of the axons (in humans) cross to the opposite hemisphere. Most of the axons go to the lateral geniculate nucleus of the thalamus. Cells of the lateral geniculate have receptive fields that resemble those of the ganglion cells—an excitatory or inhibitory central portion and a surrounding ring with the opposite effect. After the information reaches the cerebral cortex, the receptive fields become more complicated.

TABLE 5.2 Three Kinds of Primate Ganglion Cells

	Parvocellular Neurons	**Magno-cellular Neurons**	**Koniocellular Neurons**
Cell bodies	Smaller	Larger	Small
Receptive fields	Smaller	Larger	Mostly small; variable
Retinal location	In and near fovea	Throughout the retina	Throughout the retina
Color sensitive	Yes	No	Some are
Respond to	Detailed analysis of stationary objects	Movement and broad outlines of shape	Varied

STOP&CHECK

16. As we progress from bipolar cells to ganglion cells to later cells in the visual system, are receptive fields ordinarily larger, smaller, or the same size? Why?

17. What are the differences between the magnocellular and parvocellular systems?

ANSWERS

16. They become larger because each cell's receptive field is made by inputs converging at an earlier level. **17.** Neurons of the parvocellular system have small cell bodies with small receptive fields, are located mostly in and near the fovea, and are specialized for detailed and color vision. Neurons of the magnocellular system have large cell bodies with large receptive fields, are located in all parts of the retina, and are specialized for perception of large patterns and movement.

The Primary Visual Cortex

Information from the lateral geniculate nucleus of the thalamus goes to the **primary visual cortex** in the occipital cortex, also known as **area V1** or the *striate cortex* because of its striped appearance. If you close your eyes and imagine seeing something, activity increases in area V1 in a pattern similar to what happens when you actually see that object (Kosslyn & Thompson, 2003; Stokes, Thompson, Cusack, & Duncan, 2009). If you see an illusion, the activity in area V1 corresponds to what you think you see, not what the object really is (Sperandie, Chouinard, & Goodale, 2012). Although we do not know whether conscious visual perception occurs *in* area V1, area V1 is apparently necessary for it. People with damage to area V1 report no conscious vision, no visual imagery, and no visual images in their dreams (Hurovitz, Dunn, Domhoff, & Fiss, 1999). In contrast, adults who lose vision because of eye damage continue to have visual imagery and visual dreams.

Some people with damage to area V1 show a surprising phenomenon called **blindsight**, the ability to respond in limited ways to visual information without perceiving it consciously. Within the damaged part of their visual field, they have no awareness of visual input, not even to distinguish between bright sunshine and utter darkness. Nevertheless, they might be able to point accurately to something in the area where they cannot see, or move their eyes toward it, while insisting that they are "just guessing" (Bridgeman & Staggs, 1982; Weiskrantz, Warrington, Sanders, & Marshall, 1974). Some blindsight patients can reach for an object they cannot see, avoiding obstacles in the way (Striemer, Chapman, & Goodale, 2009). Some can identify an object's color, direction of movement, and approximate shape, also while insisting that they are just guessing (Radoeva, Prasad, Brainard, & Aguirre, 2008). Some can identify or copy the emotional expression of a face that they insist they do not see (Gonzalez Andino, de Peralta Menendez, Khateb, Landis, & Pegna, 2009; Tamietto et al., 2009).

The research supports two explanations for blindsight: First, in many cases, small islands of healthy tissue remain within an otherwise damaged visual cortex, not large enough to provide conscious perception but enough to support limited visual functions (Fendrich, Wessinger, & Gazzaniga, 1992; Radoeva et al., 2008). Second, the thalamus sends visual input to several other brain areas outside V1, including parts of the temporal cortex. After V1 damage, the connections to these other areas strengthen enough to produce certain kinds of experience (such as "I guess something is moving to the left") despite a lack of conscious visual perception (Bridge, Thomas, Jbabdi, & Cowey, 2008; Cowey & Stoerig, 1995; Gonzalez Andino et al., 2009; Moore, Rodman, Repp, & Gross, 1995; Schmid et al., 2010). In any case, the conclusion remains that conscious visual perception requires activity in area V1.

It is possible for someone with an intact brain to experience blindsight. Researchers arranged an apparatus so that people saw a face or a tool for three-tenths of a second in just one eye, while the other eye was viewing a rapidly changing display, seeing something new ten times a second. In this procedure, known as *continuous flash suppression*, a viewer is conscious of the flashing stimuli and not the steady picture. However, even though people insisted they did not see a face or tool, when they were asked to guess where it was (upper left, upper right, lower left, or lower right), they were correct almost half the time, as opposed to the one-fourth we could expect by chance (Hesselmann, Hebart, & Malach, 2011).

David Hubel

(1926–2013)

Brain science is difficult and tricky, for some reason; consequently one should not believe a result (one's own or anyone else's) until it is proven backwards and forwards or fits into a framework so highly evolved and systematic that it couldn't be wrong. (Hubel, personal communication)

JOSE HUESCA/EPA/Newscom.

Torsten Wiesel

(b. 1924)

Neural connections can be modulated by environmental influences during a critical period of postnatal development. . . . Such sensitivity of the nervous system to the effects of experience may represent the fundamental mechanism by which the organism adapts to its environment during the period of growth and development. (Wiesel, 1982, p. 591)

STOP & CHECK

18. If you were in a darkened room and researchers wanted to "read your mind" just enough to know whether you were having visual fantasies, what could they do?

19. What is an example of an unconscious response to visual information?

ANSWERS

18. Researchers could use fMRI, EEG, or other recording methods to see whether activity increased in your primary visual cortex. **19.** In blindsight, someone can point toward an object or move the eyes toward the object, despite insisting that he or she sees nothing.

Simple and Complex Receptive Fields

In the 1950s, David Hubel and Torsten Wiesel (1959) inserted thin electrodes to record activity from cells in cats' and monkeys' occipital cortex while they shined light patterns on the retina. At first, they presented dots of light, using a slide projector and a screen, but they found little response by cortical cells. They wondered why cells were so unresponsive, when they knew the occipital cortex was essential for vision. Then they noticed a big response while they were moving a slide into place. They quickly realized that the cell was responding to the edge of the slide. It had a bar-shaped receptive field, rather than a circular receptive field like cells in the retina and lateral geniculate (Hubel & Wiesel, 1998). Their research, for which they received a Nobel Prize, has often been called "the research that launched a thousand microelectrodes" because it inspired so much further research. By now, it has probably launched a million microelectrodes.

Hubel and Wiesel distinguished several types of cells in the visual cortex. Figure 5.19 illustrates the receptive field of a **simple cell**. A simple cell has a receptive field with fixed excitatory and inhibitory zones. The more light shines in the excitatory zone, the more the cell responds. The more light shines in the inhibitory zone, the less the cell responds. In Figure 5.19, the receptive field is a vertical bar. Tilting the bar slightly decreases the cell's response because light then strikes inhibitory regions as well. Moving the bar left, right, up, or down also reduces the response. Most simple cells have bar-shaped or edge-shaped receptive fields. More of them respond to horizontal or vertical orientations than to diagonals. That disparity makes sense, considering the importance of horizontal and vertical objects in our world (Coppola, Purves, McCoy, & Purves, 1998).

Unlike simple cells, **complex cells**, located in areas V1 and V2, do not respond to the exact location of a stimulus. A complex cell responds to a pattern of light in a particular orientation (e.g., a vertical bar) anywhere within its large receptive field (see Figure 5.20). It responds most strongly to a moving stimulus—for example, a vertical bar moving horizontally. The best way to classify a cell as simple or complex is to present the stimulus in several locations. A cell that responds to a stimulus in only one location is a simple cell. One that responds equally throughout a large area is a complex cell.

End-stopped, or **hypercomplex**, cells resemble complex cells with one exception: An end-stopped cell has a strong inhibitory area at one end of its bar-shaped receptive field. The cell responds to a bar-shaped pattern of light anywhere in its broad receptive field, provided the bar does not extend beyond a certain point (see Figure 5.21). Table 5.3 summarizes the properties of simple, complex, and end-stopped cells.

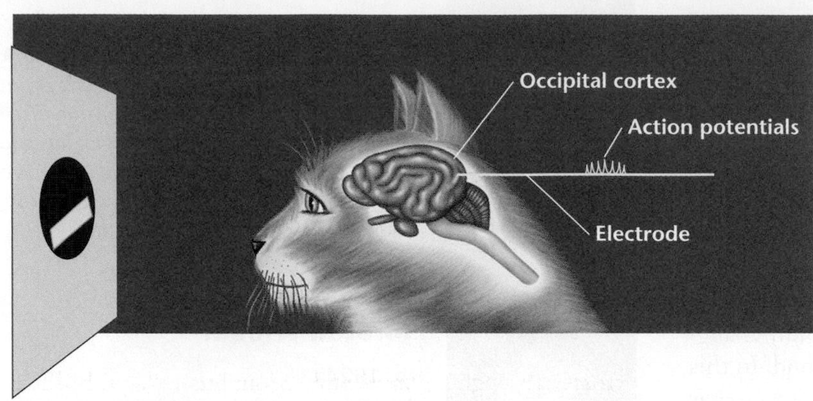

FIGURE 5.19 Responses of a cat's simple cell to a bar of light
This cell responds best to a vertical line in a particular location. Other simple cells respond to lines at other orientations. *Source:* Based on D. H. Hubel and T. N. Wiesel, "Receptive fields of single neurons in the cat's striate cortex," *Journal of Physiology,* 148, 1959, pp. 574-591. 1959, Cambridge University Press

STOP&CHECK

20. How could a researcher determine whether a given neuron in the visual cortex is simple or complex?

ANSWER

20. First identify a stimulus, such as a horizontal line, that stimulates the cell. Then present the stimulus in several locations. If the cell responds strongly in only one location, it is a simple cell. If it responds in several locations, it is a complex cell.

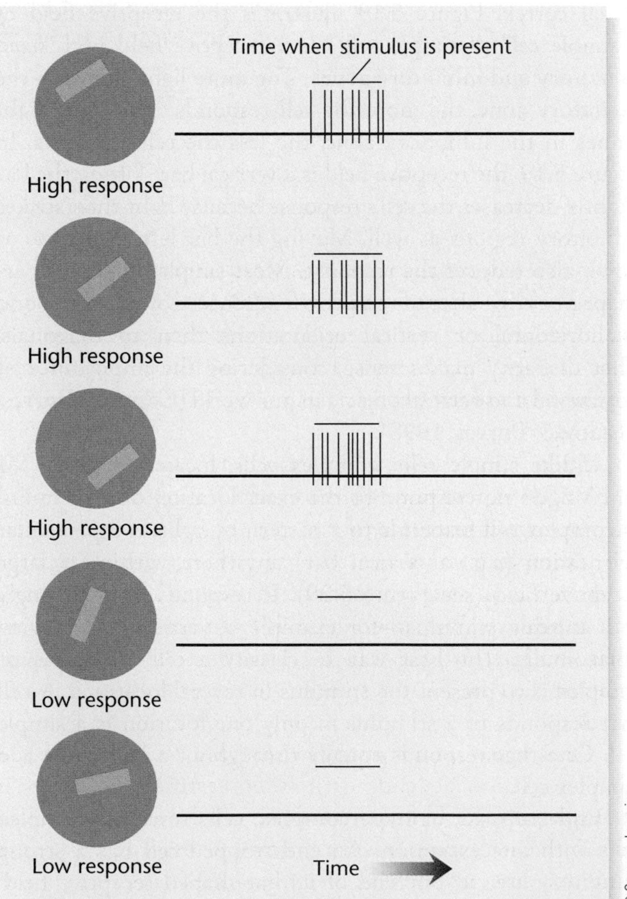

FIGURE 5.20 The receptive field of a complex cell
Like a simple cell, its response depends on a bar of light's angle of orientation. However, a complex cell responds the same for a bar in any location within a large receptive field.

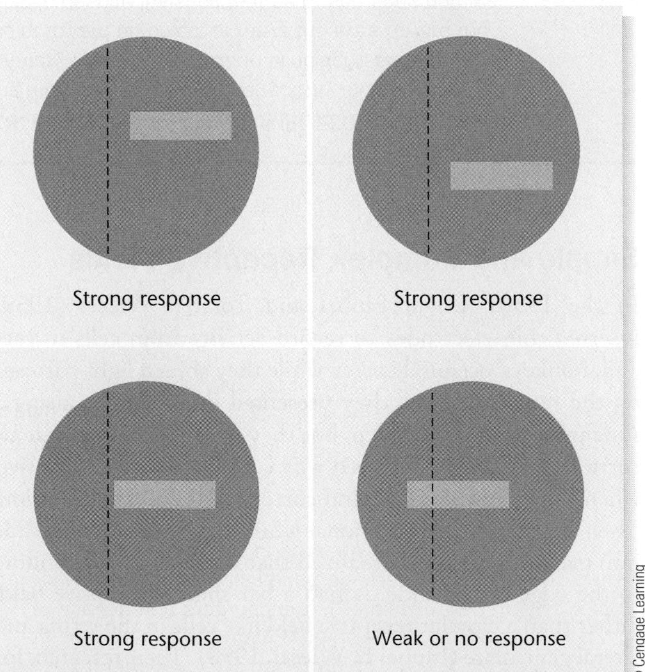

FIGURE 5.21 The receptive field of an end-stopped cell
The cell responds to a bar in a particular orientation (in this case horizontal) anywhere in its receptive field, provided the bar does not extend into a strongly inhibitory area.

TABLE 5.3 Cells in the Primary Visual Cortex

Characteristic	Simple Cells	Complex Cells	End-Stopped Cells
Location	V1	V1 and V2	V1 and V2
Binocular input	Yes	Yes	Yes
Size of receptive field	Smallest	Medium	Largest
Receptive field	Bar- or edge-shaped, with fixed excitatory and inhibitory zones	Bar- or edge-shaped, without fixed excitatory or inhibitory zones	Same as complex cell but with strong inhibitory zone at one end

The Columnar Organization of the Visual Cortex

Cells with similar properties group together in the visual cortex in columns perpendicular to the surface (Hubel & Wiesel, 1977) (see Figure 5.22). For example, cells within a given column might respond to only the left eye, only the right eye, or both eyes about equally. Also, cells within a given column respond best to lines of a single orientation.

Figure 5.22 shows what happens when an investigator lowers an electrode through the visual cortex and records from each cell along the way. Each red line represents a neuron and shows the angle of orientation of its receptive field. In electrode path A, the first series of cells are all in one column and show the same orientation preferences. However, after passing through the white matter, the end of path A invades columns with different preferred orientations. Electrode path B, which is not perpendicular to the surface of the cortex, crosses through columns and encounters cells with different properties. In short, the cells within a given column process similar information.

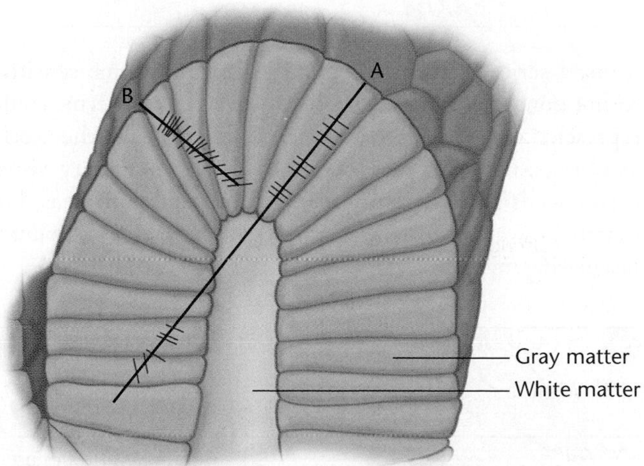

FIGURE 5.22 Columns of neurons in the visual cortex
When an electrode passes perpendicular to the surface of the cortex (first part of line A), it encounters a sequence of neurons responsive to the same orientation of a stimulus. (The colored lines show the preferred stimulus orientation for each cell.) When an electrode passes across columns (B, or second part of A), it encounters neurons responsive to different orientations. Column borders are drawn here to illustrate the point; no such borders are visible in the real cortex. *Source:* Hubel, 1963

STOP & CHECK

21. What do cells within a column of the visual cortex have in common?

ANSWER

21. They respond best to lines in the same orientation. Also, they are similar in their preference for one eye or the other, or both equally.

Are Visual Cortex Cells Feature Detectors?

Given that neurons in area V1 respond strongly to bar- or edge-shaped patterns, we might suppose that the activity of such a cell *is* (or at least is necessary for) the perception of a bar, line, or edge. That is, such cells might be **feature detectors**—neurons whose responses indicate the presence of a particular feature.

Supporting the idea of feature detectors is the fact that prolonged exposure to a given visual feature decreases sensitivity to that feature, as if it fatigued the relevant detectors. For example, if you stare at a waterfall for a minute or more and then look away, the rocks and trees next to the waterfall appear to flow upward. This *waterfall illusion* suggests that you have fatigued the neurons that detect downward motion, leaving unopposed the detectors for the opposite motion.

Long ago, Gestalt psychologists cast doubt on the idea that our vision depends entirely on feature detectors. For example, if you examine Figure 5.23, you might at first see nothing. Then suddenly you exclaim, "Oh, that's a face! [pause] And another face!" Simply looking at these displays (known as Mooney face) should excite whatever feature detectors your brain has, but seeing them as faces requires some interpretation and reorganization of the material. When you start seeing them as faces, the pattern of responses in your visual cortex suddenly changes (Hsieh, Vul, & Kanwisher, 2010).

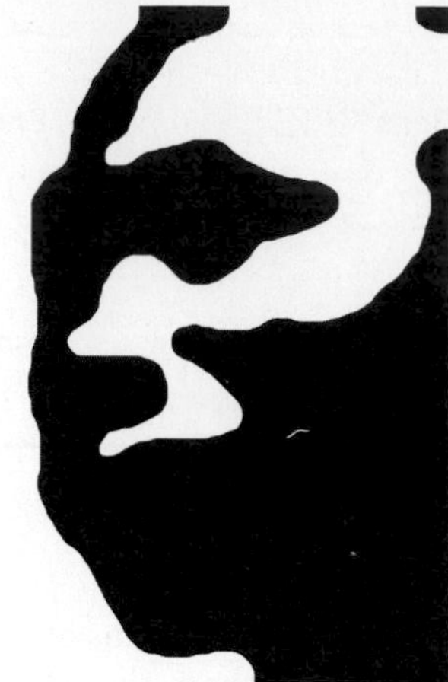
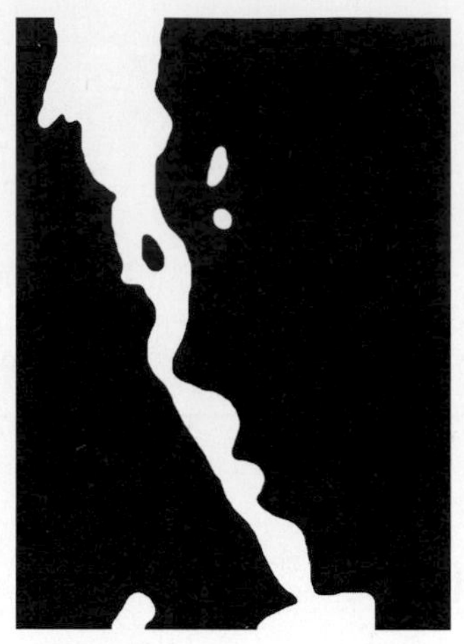
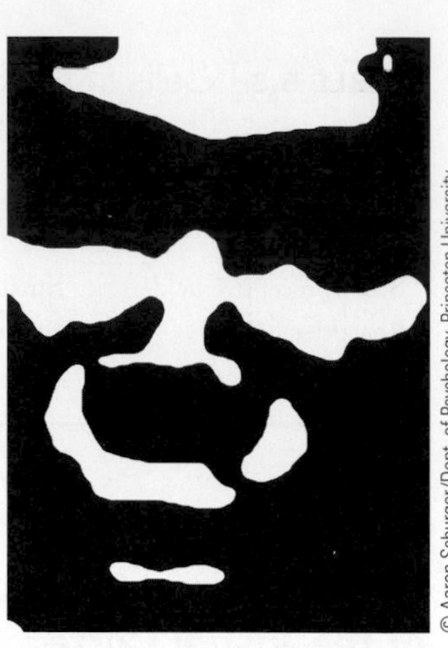

FIGURE 5.23 Mooney faces At first glance, you may see only meaningless blobs. With some time and effort you may get an "Aha" experience when you suddenly see them as faces.

That result implies "top-down" processes in which other brain areas interpret the visual stimulus and send messages back to reorganize the activity in the primary visual cortex. Similarly, when you see an optical illusion, it is due to feedback from other cortical areas to change responses in the primary visual cortex (Wokke, Vandenbroucke, Scholte, & Lamme, 2013). In other words, excitation of feature detectors is not sufficient to explain all of vision.

Furthermore, later researchers found that a cortical cell that responds well to a single bar or line

responds even more strongly to a sine wave grating of bars or lines:

Many cortical neurons respond best to a particular spatial frequency and hardly at all to other frequencies (DeValois, Albrecht, & Thorell, 1982). Most visual researchers therefore believe that neurons in area V1 detect spatial frequencies rather than bars or edges. If so, it is a feature detector for a feature that we don't perceive consciously. How do we translate a series of spatial frequencies into perception? From a mathematical standpoint, sine wave frequencies are easy to work with. A branch of mathematics called Fourier analysis demonstrates that a combination of sine waves can produce an unlimited variety of other patterns. For example, the graph at the top of the following display is the sum of the five sine waves below it:

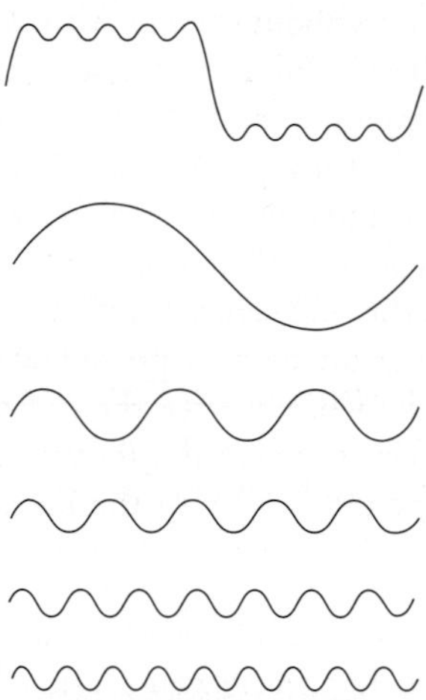

Thus, a series of spatial frequency detectors, some sensitive to horizontal patterns and others to vertical patterns, could represent any possible display. Still, we perceive the world as objects, not sine waves. Output from the primary visual cortex leads to further processing in other brain areas, but exactly how a conscious visual perception emerges remains a fascinating mystery.

STOP & CHECK

22. What is a feature detector?

ANSWER

22. It is a neuron that detects the presence of a particular aspect of an object, such as a shape or a direction of movement.

Development of the Visual Cortex

How do cells in the visual cortex develop their properties? Suppose you had lived all your life in the dark. Then today, for the first time, you came out into the light and looked around. Would you understand anything?

Unless you were born blind, you did have this experience—on the day you were born! At first, presumably you had no idea what you were seeing. Within months, however, you began to recognize faces and crawl toward your favorite toys. How did you learn to make sense of what you saw?

In a newborn mammal, many of the normal properties of the visual system develop normally at first, before birth (Lein & Shatz, 2001; Rakic & Lidow, 1995; Shatz, 1996; White, Coppola, & Fitzpatrick, 2001). Waves of spontaneous activity sweep over the developing retina, synchronizing activity among neighboring receptors and enabling appropriate combinations of receptors to establish connections with cells in the brain (Ackman, Burbridge, & Crair, 2012; Zhang, Ackman, Xu, & Crair, 2012). However, the brain needs visual experience after birth to maintain and fine-tune its connections.

Deprived Experience in One Eye

What would happen if a young animal could see with one eye but not the other? For cats and primates—which have both eyes pointed in the same direction—most neurons in the visual cortex receive **binocular** input (stimulation from both eyes). When a kitten opens its eyes, at about age 9 days, each neuron responds to areas in the two retinas that focus on approximately the same point in space. Most cells in the visual cortex respond to both eyes, although generally better to one eye than the other. However, innate mechanisms cannot make the connections exactly right because the exact distance between the eyes varies from one kitten to another, and the distance changes over age. Therefore, experience is necessary for fine-tuning.

If an experimenter sutures one eyelid shut for a kitten's first 4 to 6 weeks of life, synapses in the visual cortex gradually become unresponsive to input from the deprived eye (Rittenhouse, Shouval, Paradiso, & Bear, 1999). After the deprived eye is opened, the kitten does not respond to it. A similar period of deprivation in older animals weakens the response to the deprived eye, but not as strongly as it does in young ones (Wiesel, 1982; Wiesel & Hubel, 1963).

Deprived Experience in Both Eyes

If *both* eyes stayed shut for the first few weeks, what would you expect? You might guess that the kitten would become insensitive to both eyes, but it does not. When just one eye is open, the synapses from the open eye inhibit the synapses from the closed eye (Maffei, Nataraj, Nelson, & Turrigiano, 2006). If neither eye is active, no axon outcompetes any other. For at least 3 weeks, the kitten's cortex remains responsive to visual input, although most cells become responsive to just one eye or the other and not both (Wiesel, 1982). If the eyes remain shut still longer, the cortical responses start to become sluggish and lose their well-defined receptive fields (Crair, Gillespie, & Stryker, 1998). Eventually, the visual cortex starts responding to auditory and touch stimuli instead.

For each aspect of visual experience, researchers identify a **sensitive period,** when experiences have a particularly strong and enduring influence (Crair & Malenka, 1995; T. L. Lewis & Maurer, 2005; Tagawa, Kanold, Majdan, & Shatz, 2005). The sensitive period ends with the onset of certain chemicals that stabilize synapses and inhibit axonal sprouting (Pizzorusso et al., 2002; Syken, GrandPre, Kanold, & Shatz, 2006). However, even long after the sensitive period, a prolonged experience—such as a full week without visual stimulation to one eye—produces a measurable effect on the visual cortex (Sato & Stryker, 2008). Cortical plasticity is greatest in early life, but it never ends.

STOP&CHECK

23. What is the effect of closing one eye early in life? What is the effect of closing both eyes?

ANSWER

23. If one eye is closed during early development, the cortex becomes unresponsive to it. If both eyes are closed, cortical cells remain somewhat responsive for several weeks and then gradually become sluggish and unselective in their responses.

Uncorrelated Stimulation in the Two Eyes

Most neurons in the human visual cortex respond to both eyes—specifically, to approximately corresponding areas of both eyes. By comparing the inputs from the two eyes, you achieve stereoscopic depth perception.

Stereoscopic depth perception requires the brain to detect **retinal disparity**, the discrepancy between what the left and right eyes see. Experience fine-tunes binocular vision, and abnormal experience disrupts it. Imagine a kitten with weak or damaged eye muscles so that its eyes do not point in the same direction. Both eyes are active, but no cortical neuron consistently receives messages from one eye that match messages from the other eye. Each neuron in the visual cortex becomes responsive to one eye or the other, and few neurons respond to both (Blake & Hirsch, 1975; Hubel & Wiesel, 1965). The behavioral result is poor depth perception.

A similar phenomenon occurs in humans. Certain children are born with **strabismus** (or strabismic amblyopia), also known as "lazy eye," a condition in which the eyes do not point in the same direction. Generally, these children attend to one eye and not the other. The usual treatment is to put a patch over the active eye, forcing attention to the other one. That procedure works to some extent, especially if it is begun early (T. L. Lewis & Maurer, 2005), but many children refuse to wear an eye patch for as long as they need to. In any case, the child is not learning to use both eyes at the same time.

A promising therapy for lazy eye is to ask a child to play action video games that require attention to both eyes. Good performance requires increasing attention to exactly

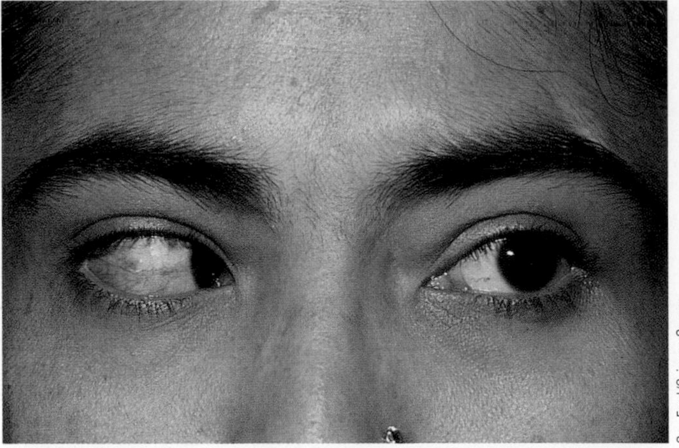

Sue Ford/Science Source

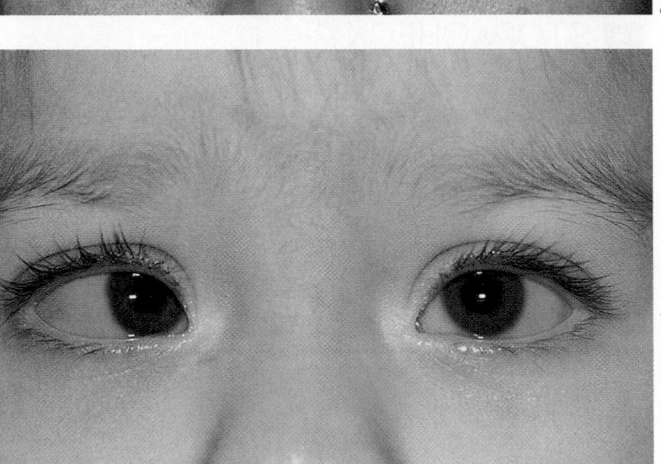

Biophoto Associates/Science Source

Two examples of lazy eye.

the kind of input we want to enhance. Because early results were encouraging (Cleary, Moody, Buchanan, Stewart, & Dutton, 2009), a larger study is measuring the effects with participants randomly assigned to treatment and control groups (Foss et al., 2013).

STOP&CHECK

24. What early experience would cause a kitten or human child to lose stereoscopic depth perception?

ANSWER

24. If the eye muscles cannot keep both eyes focused in the same direction, the developing brain loses the ability for any neuron in the visual cortex to respond to input from both eyes. Instead, each neuron responds to one eye or the other. Stereoscopic depth perception requires cells that compare the input from the two eyes.

Early Exposure to a Limited Array of Patterns

If a kitten spends its entire early sensitive period wearing goggles with horizontal lines painted on them (see Figure 5.24), nearly all its visual cortex cells become responsive only to horizontal lines (Stryker & Sherk, 1975; Stryker, Sherk, Leventhal, & Hirsch, 1978). Even after months of later normal experience, the cat does not respond to vertical lines (D. E. Mitchell, 1980).

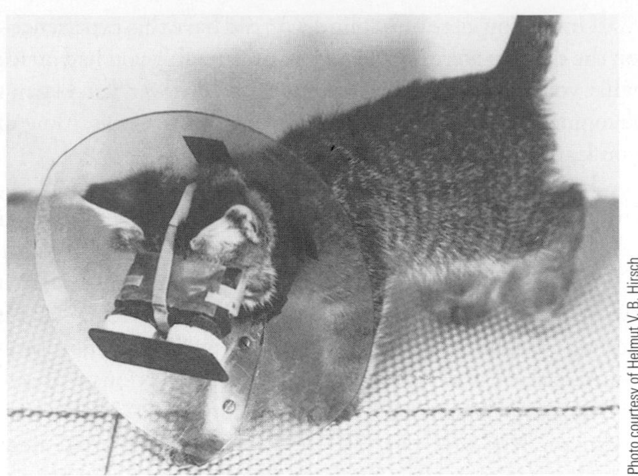

Photo courtesy of Helmut V. B. Hirsch

FIGURE 5.24 Procedure for restricting a kitten's visual experience
For a few hours a day, the kitten wears goggles that show just one stimulus, such as horizontal stripes or diagonal stripes. For the rest of the day, the kitten stays with its mother in a dark room without the mask.

What happens if human infants are exposed mainly to vertical or horizontal lines instead of both equally? They become more sensitive to the kind of line they have seen. You might wonder how such a bizarre thing could happen. No parents would let an experimenter subject their child to such a procedure, and it never happens in nature. Right?

Wrong. In fact, it probably happened to you! About 70 percent of all infants have **astigmatism,** a blurring of vision for lines in one direction (e.g., horizontal, vertical, or one of the diagonals), caused by an asymmetric curvature of the eyes. Normal growth reduces the prevalence of astigmatism to about 10 percent in 4-year-old children.

You can informally test yourself for astigmatism with Figure 5.25. Do the lines in some direction look faint? If so, rotate the page. You will notice that the appearance of the

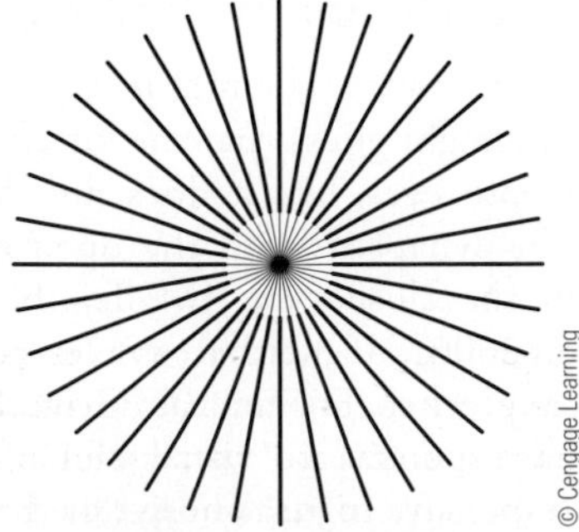

FIGURE 5.25 An informal test for astigmatism
Do the lines in one direction look darker or sharper than the other lines do? If so, notice what happens when you rotate the page. If you wear corrective lenses, try this demonstration both with and without your lenses.

lines depends on their position. If you wear corrective lenses, try this demonstration with and without them. If you see a difference in the lines only without your lenses, then the lenses have corrected your astigmatism.

Impaired Infant Vision and Long-Term Consequences

At the start of this section, we considered the question of what you would see if you lived all your life in the dark and then suddenly could see. Newborn infants have that experience, and we assume they have no idea what they are seeing. We have to assume, because we cannot ask newborns what they see. However, in some countries, a newborn with dense cataracts (cloudy spots on the lenses that prevent perception of anything other than bright versus dark) may have to wait years for surgery to enable vision. When the cataracts are finally removed at age 7 or later, researchers can test what the children see.

For the first couple of days, these children have almost no idea what those visual stimuli mean. In one study, children looked at a picture of a toy building block, and another picture with two blocks. The task was to point to the block in the second picture that matched the first. Children did well on this task, indicating that they could see. However, when the task was to feel a building block and point to the picture of it (of two choices), performance was only a little better than chance. They could see the pictures, but they didn't understand them. A week later, without any special training, they did much better on this task (Held et al., 2011).

Many other aspects of vision also gradually improve over time (Ostrovsky, Meyers, Ganesh, Mathur, & Sinha, 2009), except for motion perception and depth perception, which remain permanently impaired (Dormal, Lepore, & Collignon, 2012; Ellemberg, Lewis, Maurer, Brar, & Brent, 2002). Two people who lived with cataracts until middle adulthood also made some recovery, but continued to find it difficult to recognize objects. Whereas most adults identify the objects they see almost immediately, people who lived most of their lives with cloudy vision say they have to think about it and guess what the objects are (Fine, Smallman, Doyle, & MacLeod, 2002; Fine et al., 2003). For example, when viewing the following display, they say they see three objects, whereas most people say two (a blue ball and a yellow stick running through it). The visual expertise that most of us take for granted depends on practice.

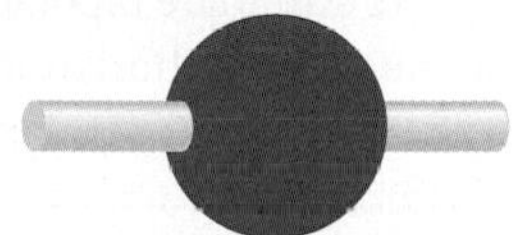

STOP&CHECK

25. What causes astigmatism?

26. If an infant is born with dense cataracts on both eyes and they are surgically removed years later, how well does the child see at first?

ANSWERS

25. Astigmatism results when the eyeball is not quite spherical. As a result, the person sees one direction of lines more clearly than the other. **26.** The child sees well enough to identify whether two objects are the same or different, but the child doesn't understand what the visual information means. In particular, the child cannot answer which visual display matches something the child touches. However, understanding of vision improves with practice.

MODULE 5.2 ■ IN CLOSING

Understanding Vision by Understanding the Wiring Diagram

Your eyes are bombarded with a complex pattern of light emanating from every source in front of you. Out of all this, your brain needs to extract the most useful information. The nervous system from the start identifies the borders between one object and another through lateral inhibition. It identifies lines and their locations by simple and complex cells in the primary visual cortex. Researchers have gone a long way toward mapping out the excitatory and inhibitory connections that make these cells possible. The visual experiences you have at any moment are the result of an awe-inspiring complexity of connections and interactions among a huge number of neurons, but they are also the product of years of experience.

Summary

1. The optic nerves of the two eyes join at the optic chiasm, where half of the axons from each eye cross to the opposite side of the brain. Most of the axons then travel to the lateral geniculate nucleus of the thalamus, which communicates with the visual cortex. **162**
2. Lateral inhibition is a mechanism by which stimulation in any area of the retina suppresses the responses in neighboring areas, thereby enhancing the contrast at light–dark borders. **162**
3. Lateral inhibition in the vertebrate retina occurs because receptors stimulate bipolar cells and also stimulate the much wider horizontal cells, which inhibit both the stimulated bipolar cells and those to the sides. **163**
4. Each neuron in the visual system has a receptive field, an area of the visual field to which it is connected. Light in the receptive field excites or inhibits the neuron depending on the light's location, wavelength, and movement. **165**
5. The mammalian vertebrate visual system has a partial division of labor. In general, the parvocellular system is specialized for perception of color and fine details; the magnocellular system is specialized for perception of depth, movement, and overall patterns. **165**
6. After damage to area V1, people report no vision, even in dreams. However, some kinds of response to light (blindsight) can occur after damage to V1 despite the lack of conscious perception. **166**
7. Within the primary visual cortex, neuroscientists distinguish simple cells with fixed excitatory and inhibitory fields, and complex cells that respond to a light pattern of a particular shape regardless of its exact location. **167**
8. Neurons within a column of the primary visual cortex have similar properties, such as responding to lines in the same orientation. **169**
9. Neurons sensitive to shapes or other visual aspects may or may not act as feature detectors. In particular, cells of area V1 are highly responsive to spatial frequencies, even though we are not subjectively aware of spatial frequencies in our visual perception. **169**
10. The cells in the visual cortex of infant kittens have nearly normal properties. However, experience is necessary to maintain and fine-tune vision. For example, if a kitten has sight in one eye and not in the other during the early sensitive period, its cortical neurons become responsive only to the open eye. **171**
11. Cortical neurons become unresponsive to axons from the inactive eye mainly because of competition with the active eye. If both eyes are closed, each cortical cell remains somewhat responsive to axons from one eye or the other, although that response becomes sluggish and unselective as the weeks of deprivation continue. **171**
12. Abnormal visual experience has a stronger effect during an early sensitive period than later in life. **171**
13. To develop good stereoscopic depth perception, a kitten or human child must have experience seeing the same object with corresponding portions of the two eyes early in life. Otherwise, each neuron in the visual cortex becomes responsive to input from just one eye. **171**
14. If a kitten sees only horizontal or vertical lines during its sensitive period, most of the neurons in its visual cortex become responsive to such lines only. For the same reason, a young child with astigmatism may have decreased responsiveness to one kind of line or another. **172**
15. Some people have cataracts removed after years of cloudy vision. Vision, useless at first, improves with practice but remains imperfect in several ways. **173**

Key Terms

Terms are defined in the module on the page number indicated. They're also presented in alphabetical order with definitions in the book's Subject Index/Glossary. Interactive flash cards, audio reviews, and crossword puzzles are among the online resources available to help you learn these terms and the concepts they represent.

astigmatism **172**
binocular **171**
blindsight **166**
complex cells **167**
end-stopped (or hypercomplex) cells **168**
feature detectors **169**
horizontal cells **162**
koniocellular neurons **166**
lateral geniculate nucleus **162**
lateral inhibition **164**
magnocellular neurons **166**
parvocellular neurons **166**
primary visual cortex (or area V1) **166**
receptive field **165**
retinal disparity **171**
sensitive period **171**
simple cell **167**
strabismus **171**

Thought Questions

1. After a receptor cell is stimulated, the bipolar cell receiving input from it shows an immediate strong response. A fraction of a second later, the bipolar's response decreases, even though the stimulation from the receptor cell remains constant. How can you account for that decrease? (Hint: What does the horizontal cell do?)
2. A rabbit's eyes are on the sides of its head instead of in front. Would you expect rabbits to have many cells with binocular receptive fields—that is, cells that respond to both eyes? Why or why not?

MODULE 5.2 End of Module Quiz

1. What is the order of connections from receptors to visual cortex?
   a. Receptors—bipolar cells—lateral geniculate—ganglion cells—visual cortex
   b. Receptors—lateral geniculate—bipolar cells—ganglion cells—visual cortex
   c. Receptors—ganglion cells—bipolar cells—lateral geniculate—visual cortex
   d. Receptors—bipolar cells—ganglion cells—lateral geniculate—visual cortex

2. Axons from the nasal half of the retina go to the _____ hemisphere of the brain. Axons from the temporal half of the retina go to the _____ hemisphere of the brain.
   a. contralateral . . . ipsilateral
   b. contralateral . . . contralateral
   c. ipsilateral . . . ipsilateral
   d. ipsilateral . . . contralateral

3. When light strikes a receptor, the effect is to _____ the bipolar cells and _____ the horizontal cells. The horizontal cells_____ the bipolar cells.
   a. excite . . . excite . . . excite
   b. inhibit . . . inhibit . . . inhibit
   c. excite . . . inhibit . . . excite
   d. excite . . . inhibit . . . inhibit
   e. excite . . . excite . . . inhibit

4. If light strikes one receptor, the net effect is to _____ the nearest bipolar cell and _____ other bipolar cells to the side because of the contributions from _____ cells.
   a. excite . . . inhibit . . . other receptor
   b. excite . . . inhibit . . . horizontal
   c. excite . . . excite . . . other receptor
   d. excite . . . excite . . . horizontal
   e. inhibit . . . inhibit . . . horizontal

5. Suppose light strikes the retina in a circle, surrounded by dark. Which bipolar cells will show the greatest response, and which will show the least?
   a. Bipolars connected to receptors in the center of the circle respond the most. Those connected to receptors farthest from the circle respond the least.
   b. Bipolars connected to the receptors just outside the circumference of the circle respond most. Those connected to receptors just inside the circumference respond least.
   c. Bipolars connected to the receptors just inside the circumference of the circle respond most. Those connected to receptors just outside the circumference respond least.

6. As we progress from bipolar cells to ganglion cells to later cells in the visual system, what happens to the size of receptive fields?
   a. They become larger.
   b. They become smaller.
   c. They stay the same size.
   d. They vary in size unpredictably.

7. In contrast to parvocellular neurons, magnocellular neurons are more sensitive to _____.
   a. color
   b. small details
   c. movement
   d. the fovea

8. If you were in a darkened room and researchers wanted to know whether you were having visual fantasies (without asking you), they could measure activity in which brain area?
   a. The retina
   b. The lateral geniculate nucleus of the thalamus
   c. The primary visual cortex
   d. The parietal cortex

9. What is meant by blindsight?
   a. Some people with damage to the primary visual cortex accurately guess the location or other properties of objects they say they don't see.
   b. Blind people learn to find their way around by making sounds and listening for echoes.
   c. Blind people on average develop enhancements of hearing, touch, and other senses.
   d. After damage to the eyes, other body parts become sensitive to light.
   e. Incorrect hindsight.

10. How could a researcher determine whether a given neuron in the visual cortex is simple or complex?
   a. If it responds to a line or edge, it is a simple cell. If it responds only to more complex shapes, it is a complex cell.
   b. If it responds to moving stimuli, it is a simple cell. If it responds to stationary objects, it is a complex cell.
   c. If it responds to the same stimulus repeatedly, it is a simple cell. If it responds to a different stimulus each time it is tested, it is a complex cell.
   d. If it responds to a stimulus in just one location, it is a simple cell. If it responds in several locations, it is a complex cell.

11. What do cells within a column of the visual cortex have in common?
   a. They all have action potentials of the same amplitude and velocity.
   b. They are all the same shape.
   c. They are all simple cells, as opposed to complex cells.
   d. They respond best to lines in the same orientation.

12. What is the evidence that certain types of feature detectors operate in the human visual cortex?
   a. When you examine Mooney faces, at first you see only meaningless blobs, but with time and effort you start to perceive faces.
   b. After you stare at a waterfall or other steadily moving display, you see stationary objects as moving in the opposite direction.
   c. An electrode traveling through a section of the cortex may encounter one neuron after another with receptive fields in the same orientation.
   d. Children who are deprived of input in one eye become attentive only to the other eye.

13. If a kitten has one eye shut for its first few weeks of life, its visual cortex becomes insensitive to that eye. Why?
   a. The receptors die.
   b. Any axon that is not used for that long becomes unable to respond.
   c. Activity from the active eye displaces synapses from the inactive eye.

14. What early experience is necessary to maintain binocular input to the neurons of the visual cortex?
   a. Cortical cells will always maintain binocular responsiveness, regardless of their experience.
   b. Cortical cells must receive some input to each eye every day.
   c. Cortical cells must receive an equal amount of input from the two eyes.
   d. Cortical cells must usually receive simultaneous input from the two eyes.

15. Why is it important to correct astigmatism early?
   a. If uncorrected, the eyeball becomes even more asymmetrical over time.
   b. Treatment is less expensive for children than for adults.
   c. The visual cortex becomes more sensitive to the lines it sees best.
   d. Uncorrected astigmatism can develop into cataracts.

16. If someone is born with dense cataracts on both eyes, and the cataracts are removed years later, which of these aspects of vision remains permanently impaired?
   a. Perception of the size of an object
   b. Motion perception and depth perception
   c. Ability to recognize whether two objects are the same or different
   d. Perception of brightness and darkness

ANSWERS: 1d, 2a, 3e, 4b, 5c, 6a, 7c, 8c, 9a, 10d, 11d, 12b, 13c, 14d, 15c, 16b.

Parallel Processing in the Visual Cortex

If you were working on an important project for some business or government, you might receive information on a "need-to-know" basis. For example, if you were told to carry a particular package, you would need to know how heavy it is and whether it is fragile, but you might not need to know much about the object in the package. Someone else who is keeping track of the finances would need to know how much the object costs, but wouldn't need to know anything else. A third person might open the package and check to make sure the color matched the specifications, before handing it on to someone else with a different concern.

Similarly, different parts of the brain's visual system get information on a need-to-know basis. Cells that help your hand muscles reach out to an object need to know the size and location of the object, but they don't need to know about color. They need to know a little about shape, but not in great detail. Cells that help you recognize people's faces need to be extremely sensitive to details of shape, but they can pay less attention to location.

It is natural to assume that anyone who sees something sees everything about it—the shape, color, location, and movement. However, one part of your brain sees its shape, another sees color, another detects location, and another perceives movement (Livingstone, 1988; Livingstone & Hubel, 1988; Zeki & Shipp, 1988). Consequently, after localized brain damage, it is possible to see certain aspects of an object and not others. Neuroscientists have identified at least 80 brain areas that contribute to vision in different ways (Nassi & Callaway, 2009).

The Ventral and Dorsal Paths

The primary visual cortex (V1) sends information to the **secondary visual cortex** (area **V2**), which processes the information further and transmits it to additional areas, as shown in Figure 5.26. The connections in the visual cortex are reciprocal. For example, V1 sends information to V2, and V2 returns information to V1. From V2, the information branches out in several directions for specialized processing.

Researchers distinguish between the ventral stream and the dorsal stream. They call the **ventral stream** through the

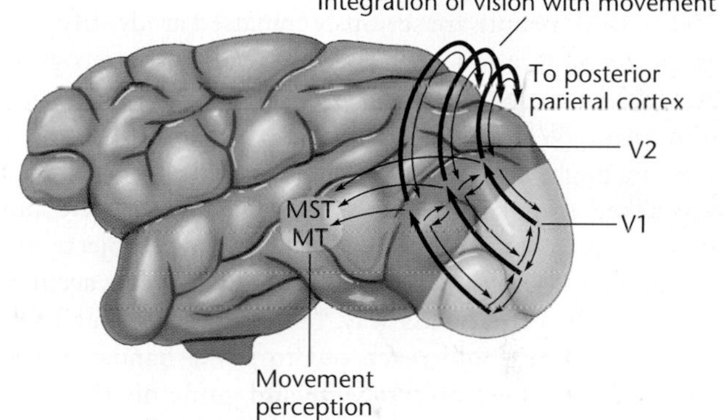

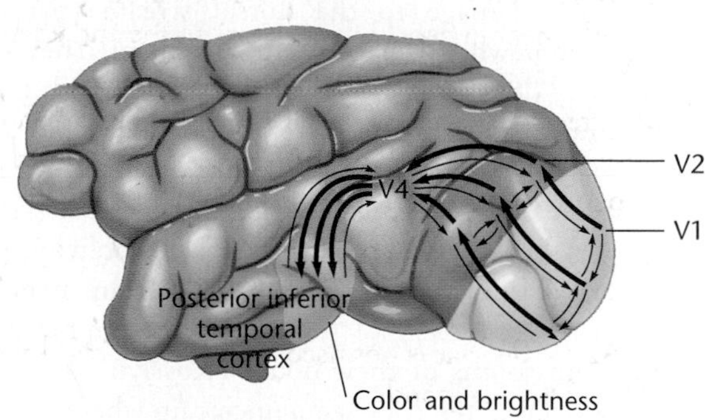

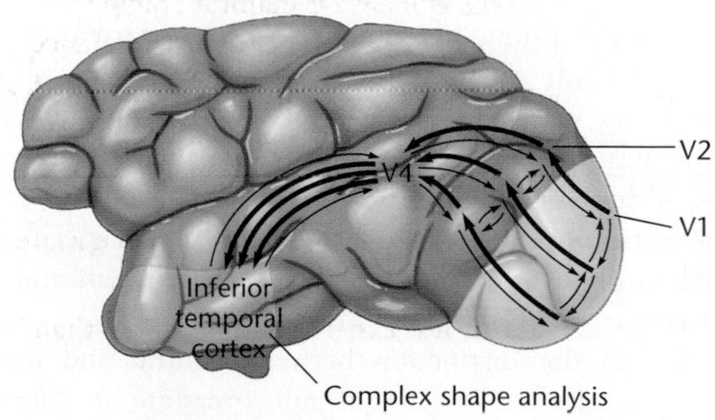

FIGURE 5.26 Visual pathways in the monkey cerebral cortex
After processing in areas V1 and V2 of the occipital cortex, information branches in several directions into the parietal cortex and temporal cortex. *Source:* Based on DeYoe, Felleman, Van Essen, & McClendon, 1994; Ts'o & Roe, 1995; Van Essen & DeYoe, 1995

temporal cortex the "what" pathway, because it is specialized for identifying and recognizing objects. The **dorsal stream** through the parietal cortex, once called the "where" pathway, is now called the "how" pathway, because of its importance for visually guided movements.

The distinction is based partly on animal studies, and partly on MRI and fMRI studies (Milner, 2012), but mostly on observations of a few patients with brain damage. A woman known as patient DF was exposed to carbon monoxide, causing damage to connections between her primary visual cortex and her temporal cortex (Bridge et al., 2013). Another patient, JS, had damage within the temporal lobe (Karnath, Rüter, Mandler, & Himmelbach, 2009). Both people are seriously impaired at identifying the shape or orientation of an object, reading, or recognizing faces. Nevertheless, both can accurately use vision to control movement. When shown a slot in the wall, DF could not state its angle, such as horizontal or vertical, but when she was asked to put an envelope through the slot, she aimed it correctly at once. JS cannot visually locate objects in his room, such as his clothes, but he could take a walk, accurately avoiding obstacles in his way. He could reach out to grab objects, and he could reach out to shake hands. In short, he could see where objects were and guide his movements toward them, even though he had trouble identifying what they were (Karnath et al., 2009).

People with damage to the dorsal stream (parietal cortex) have somewhat the opposite problem: They see objects but they don't integrate their vision well with their arm and leg movements. They can read, recognize faces, and describe objects in detail but they cannot accurately reach out to grasp an object. While walking, they can describe what they see, but they bump into objects, oblivious to their location. Although they can describe from memory what their furniture looks like, they cannot remember how it is arranged in rooms of their house (Kosslyn, Ganis, & Thompson, 2001). Often they seem uncertain where certain parts of their body are (Schenk, 2006). One patient had dorsal stream damage only in his left hemisphere. He showed low accuracy at aiming his right arm or leg toward an object on the right side of his body. However, his accuracy was normal when aiming his left arm or leg toward either side, or when aiming his right arm toward the left side (Cavina-Pratesi, Connolly, & Milner, 2013). So his problem is not with attention, and not exactly vision either. It is specifically a problem of using vision to control certain arm and leg movements.

Although the distinction between ventral and dorsal pathways is useful, we should not overstate it. Normal behavior makes use of both pathways in collaboration (Farivar, 2009), and although damage to either pathway impairs some tasks more than others, it affects all tasks to some degree. For example, although patient DF is much more impaired at identifying objects than at controlling movement, careful testing shows mild impairments in the accuracy of her arm and hand movements also (Himmelbach, Boehme, & Karnath, 2012).

STOP&CHECK

26. Suppose someone can describe an object in detail but stumbles and fumbles when trying to walk toward it and pick it up. Which is probably damaged, the dorsal path or the ventral path?

ANSWER

26. The inability to guide movement based on vision implies damage to the dorsal path.

Detailed Analysis of Shape

In Module 5.2, we encountered simple and complex cells of the primary visual cortex (V1). As visual information goes from the simple cells to the complex cells and then to other brain areas, the receptive fields become more specialized. In the secondary visual cortex (V2), many cells still respond best to lines, edges, and sine wave gratings, but some cells respond selectively to circles, lines that meet at a right angle, or other complex patterns (Hegdé & Van Essen, 2000). Cells in area V2 also respond to complex features such as textures (Freeman, Ziemba, Heeger, Simoncelli, & Movshon, 2013). In later parts of the visual system, receptive properties become still more complex.

The Inferior Temporal Cortex

Cells in the **inferior temporal cortex** (see Figure 5.26) respond to meaningful objects. Examine Figure 5.27. Researchers measured responses in monkeys' inferior temporal cortex

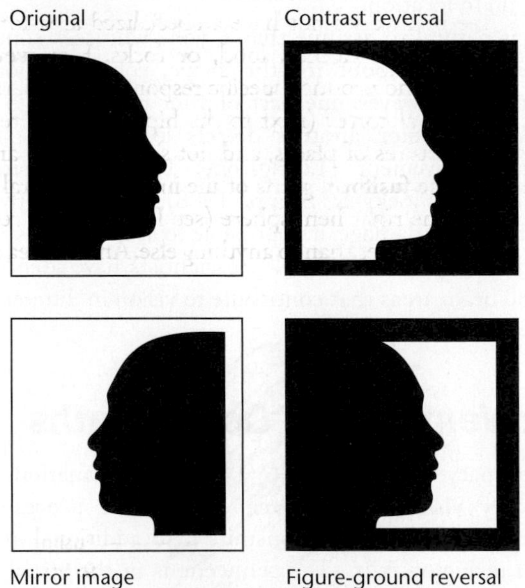

FIGURE 5.27 Transformations of a drawing
In the inferior temporal cortex, cells that respond strongly to the original respond about the same to the contrast reversal and mirror image but not to the figure–ground reversal. Note that the figure–ground reversal resembles the original in terms of the pattern of light and darkness, but it is not perceived as the same object. *Source:* Based on Baylis & Driver, 2001

to several kinds of transformations. A cell that responded to a particular stimulus would respond almost equally to its negative image or mirror image but not to a physically similar stimulus in which the "figure" now appeared to be part of the "background" (Baylis & Driver, 2001). That is, cells in the temporal cortex respond according to what the viewer perceives, not what the stimulus is physically. Cells that respond to the sight of a particular object continue responding about the same way despite changes in its position, size, and angle. Evidently these cells somehow learn to recognize all the different views as being the same object (Li & DiCarlo, 2008).

As we might expect, damage to the shape pathway of the cortex leads to specialized deficits. An inability to recognize objects despite otherwise satisfactory vision is called **visual agnosia** (meaning "visual lack of knowledge"). It usually results from damage in the temporal cortex. Someone might be able to point to visual objects and slowly describe them but fail to recognize what they are. For example, one patient, when shown a key, said, "I don't know what that is. Perhaps a file or a tool of some sort." When shown a stethoscope, he said that it was "a long cord with a round thing at the end." When he could not identify a smoker's pipe, the examiner told him what it was. He then replied, "Yes, I can see it now," and pointed out the stem and bowl of the pipe. Then the examiner asked, "Suppose I told you that the last object was not really a pipe?" The patient replied, "I would take your word for it. Perhaps it's not really a pipe" (Rubens & Benson, 1971).

Within the brain areas specialized for perceiving shape, are there further specializations for particular types of shapes? Researchers used fMRI to record brain activity as people viewed pictures of many objects. Of the various types of objects, most did not activate one brain area more than another. That is, the brain does not have a specialized area for seeing flowers, fish, birds, clothes, food, or rocks. However, three types of objects do produce specific responses. One part of the parahippocampal cortex (next to the hippocampus) responds strongly to pictures of places, and not so strongly to anything else. Part of the **fusiform gyrus** of the inferior temporal cortex, especially in the right hemisphere (see Figure 5.28), responds more strongly to faces than to anything else. And an area close to this face area responds more strongly to bodies than to anything else (Downing, Chan, Peelen, Dodds, & Kanwisher, 2005; Kanwisher, 2010). The brain is amazingly adept at detecting biological motion—the kinds of motion produced by people and animals. If you attach glow-in-the-dark dots to someone's elbows, knees, hips, shoulders, and a few other places, then when that person moves in an otherwise dark room, you perceive a moving person, even though you are actually watching only a few spots of light. You can view a wonderful demonstration by doing an Internet search for Bio Motion Lab and then clicking on Demos.

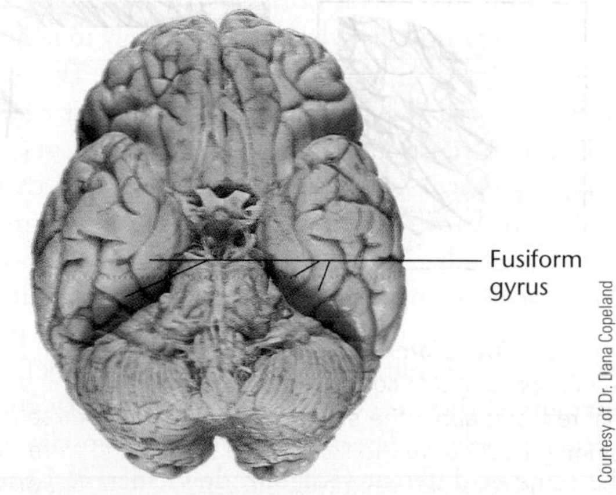

FIGURE 5.28 The fusiform gyrus
Many cells here are especially active during recognition of faces.

Recognizing Faces

Much research on brain mechanisms of vision has focused on how we recognize faces, certainly an important skill for humans. For civilization to succeed, we have to know whom to trust and whom to distrust, and that distinction requires us to recognize people that we haven't seen in months or years. Someday you may attend a high school or college reunion and reunite with people you haven't seen in decades. You will recognize many of them, even if you forget their names, even though they have gained weight, become bald, or dyed their hair (Bruck, Cavanagh, & Ceci, 1991). Computer programmers who have tried to build machines to recognize faces have discovered the difficulty of this task that seems so easy for people.

Human newborns come into the world predisposed to pay more attention to faces than other stationary displays (see Figure 5.29). That tendency supports the idea of a built-in face recognition module. However, the infant's concept of "face" is not like an adult's. Experimenters recorded infants' times of gazing at one face or the other, as shown in Figure 5.30. Newborns showed a strong preference for a right-side-up face over an upside-down face, regardless of whether the face was realistic (left pair) or distorted (central pair). When confronted with two right-side-up faces (right pair), they showed no significant preference between a realistic one and

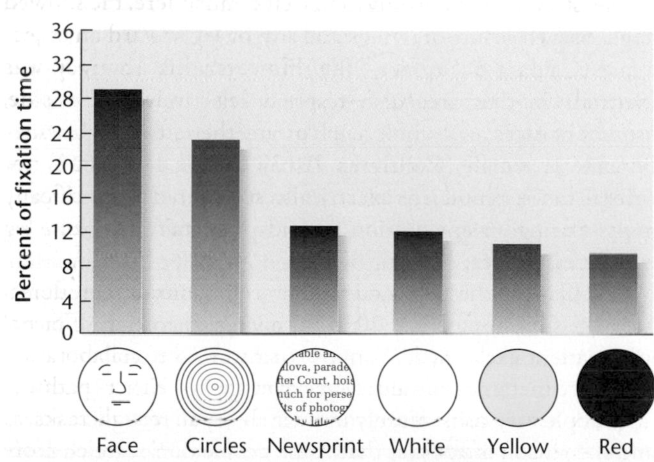

FIGURE 5.29 Amount of time infants spend looking at patterns
Even in the first 2 days after birth, infants look more at faces than at most other stimuli. *Source:* Based on Fantz, 1963

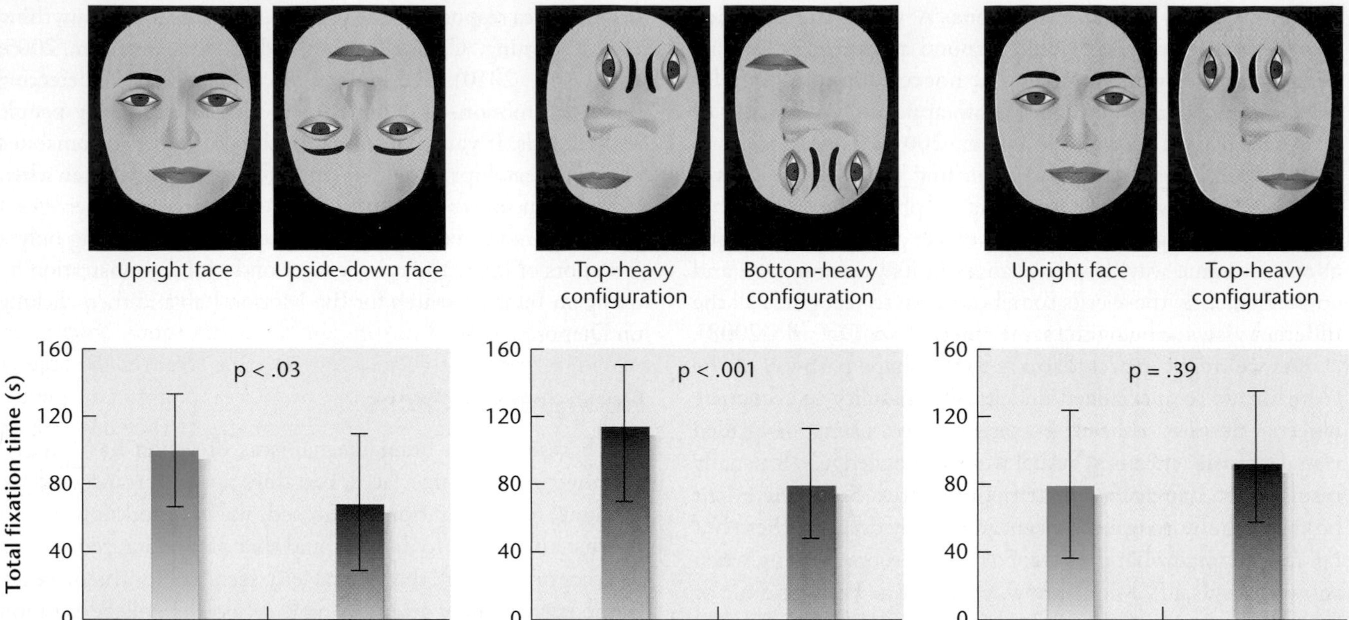

FIGURE 5.30 How infants divided their attention between faces
A right-side-up face drew more attention than an upside-down one, regardless of whether the faces were realistic (left pair) or distorted (central pair). They divided their attention about equally between two right-side-up faces (right pair), even though one was realistic and the other was distorted. *Source:* From "Can a nonspecific bias toward top-heavy patterns explain newborns' face preference?" by V. M. Cassia, C. Turati, & F. Simion, 2004. *Psychological Science, 15,* pp. 379–383

a distorted one (Cassia, Turati, & Simion, 2004). Evidently, a newborn's concept of "face" requires the eyes to be on top, but the face does not have to be realistic.

Face recognition depends on several brain areas, including part of the inferior occipital cortex known as the occipital face area, the amygdala, and parts of the temporal cortex, including the fusiform gyrus, especially in the right hemisphere (Rossion, Hanseeuw, & Dricot, 2012) (see Figure 5.28). The occipital face area responds strongly to parts of a face, such as the eyes and mouth (Arcurio, Gold, & James, 2012). The fusiform gyrus responds strongly to a face viewed from any angle, as well as line drawings and anything else that looks like a face (Caldara & Seghier, 2009; Kanwisher & Yovel, 2006). Neurons in that area also respond selectively to complex aspects of faces as a whole, such as whether a face appears to be male or female (Contreras, Banaji, & Mitchell, 2013). In several cases, physicians electrically stimulated the fusiform gyrus during an exploration to find problems giving rise to epileptic seizures. Varying with the intensity and duration of stimulation, the result was either a difficulty in perceiving faces (S. C. Chong et al., 2013) or a vivid distortion of faces. One patient exclaimed, "You just turned into somebody else. Your face metamorphosed" (Parvizi et al., 2012, p. 14,918).

People vary considerably in their ability to recognize faces, and the reason is not just that some people don't care or don't pay attention. Ability to recognize faces correlates strongly with the strength of connections between the occipital face area and the fusiform gyrus (Zhu et al., 2011). People with stronger connections learn to recognize faces easily, and those with fewer connections have more trouble (Grueter et al., 2007; C. Thomas et al., 2009). People with severe problems, either because of brain damage or because they developed fewer connections, are said to have **prosopagnosia** (PROSS-oh-pag-NOH-see-ah), meaning impaired ability to recognize faces.

Oliver Sacks, famous for writing about other people's neurological problems, is one such case himself. In his words, "I have had difficulty recognizing faces for as long as I can remember. I did not think too much about this as a child, but by the time I was a teenager, in a new school, it was often a cause of embarrassment. . . . My problem with recognizing faces extends not only to my nearest and dearest but also to myself. Thus, on several occasions I have apologized for almost bumping into a large bearded man, only to realize that the large bearded man was myself in a mirror. The opposite situation once occurred at a restaurant. Sitting at a sidewalk table, I turned toward the restaurant window and began grooming my beard, as I often do. I then realized that what I had taken to be my reflection was not grooming himself but looking at me oddly" (Sacks, 2000, p. 37).

People with prosopagnosia can read, so visual acuity is not the problem. They recognize people's voices, so their problem is not memory (Farah, Wilson, Drain, & Tanaka, 1998). Furthermore, if they feel clay models of faces, they are worse than other people at determining whether two clay models are the same or different (Kilgour, de Gelder, & Lederman, 2004). Their problem is not vision in general, but something that relates specifically to faces.

When people with prosopagnosia look at a face, they can describe a few features of the face, but they cannot identify the person. (You would have a similar difficulty if you viewed faces quickly, upside-down.) One patient was shown 34 photographs of famous people and had a choice of two identifications for each. By chance alone, he should have identified 17 correctly; in fact, he got 18. He remarked that he seldom enjoyed watching movies or television programs because he had trouble keeping track of the characters. Curiously, his favorite movie was *Batman*, in which the main characters wore masks much of the time (Laeng & Caviness, 2001).

Much research has focused on the fusiform gyrus, because it responds so much more strongly to faces than to anything else. But did we really evolve a special module devoted to recognizing faces? Or does the fusiform gyrus serve for all types of detailed visual recognition, for which faces are just the best or most typical example? Children with an intense interest in Pokemon cards show strong response in the fusiform gyrus when they look at Pokemon characters (James & James, 2013). Chess experts show a response there when they look at a chessboard (Bilalic, Langner, Ulrich, & Grodd, 2011). People who develop expertise at recognizing cars, identifying bird species, or almost any other type of visual stimulus show fusiform gyrus responses when they look at items within their field of interest (Tarr & Gauthier, 2000), and damage to the fusiform gyrus impairs those types of expertise (Farah, 1990). However, even in people with extreme levels of expertise, many cells in the fusiform gyrus respond more vigorously to faces than anything else (Kanwisher & Yovel, 2006). So face recognition may indeed be special.

STOP&CHECK

27. The brain has no specialized areas for perceiving flowers, clothes, or food. For what items does it have specialized areas?

28. The ability to recognize faces correlates with the strength of connections between which brain areas?

ANSWERS

27. The temporal cortex has specialized areas for perceiving places, faces, and bodies, including bodies in motion. **28.** Ability to recognize faces correlates with the strength of connections between the occipital face area and the fusiform gyrus.

Color Perception

Although neurons in many parts of the visual system show some response to changes in color, one brain area is particularly important, known as area V4 (Hadjikhani, Liu, Dale, Cavanagh, & Tootell, 1998; Zeki, McKeefry, Bartels, & Frackowiak, 1998), although parts of V4 have other functions as well (Tanigawa, Lu, & Roe, 2010). Recall the demonstration in Figure 5.13: The apparent color of an object depends not only on the light reflected from that object, but also on how it compares with objects around it. The responses of cells in V4 correspond to the *apparent* or *perceived* color of an object, which depends on the total context (Brouwer & Heeger, 2009; Kusunoki, Moutoussis, & Zeki, 2006). After damage to area V4, people do not become colorblind, but they lose color constancy. Color constancy is the ability to recognize something as being the same color despite changes in lighting. If you entered a room with green lighting, or if you wore red-tinted sunglasses, you would nevertheless accurately identify the color of all the objects in the room. Your brain would in effect subtract a little green or red from all the objects to construct their natural colors. Both monkeys and people with damage to area V4 lose this ability. If they are trained to reach for a yellow object, they may not be able to find it if the overhead lighting is changed (Rüttiger et al., 1999; Wild, Butler, Carden, & Kulikowski, 1985).

STOP&CHECK

29. Area V4 is important for color constancy. What is color constancy?

ANSWER

29. It is the ability to recognize the color of an object despite changes in the lighting.

Motion Perception

Moving objects often merit immediate attention. A moving object might be a possible mate, something you could hunt and eat, or something that wants to eat you. If you are going to respond, you need to identify what the object is, where it is going, and how fast. The brain is set up to make those calculations quickly and efficiently.

The Middle Temporal Cortex

Viewing a complex moving pattern activates brain areas among all four lobes of the cerebral cortex (Sunaert, Van Hecke, Marchal, & Orban, 1999; Vanduffel et al., 2001). Two areas especially important for motion perception are area **MT** (for middle temporal cortex), also known as area **V5**, and an adjacent region, area **MST** (medial superior temporal cortex) (see Figure 5.26). Areas MT and MST receive input mostly from the magnocellular path (Nassi & Callaway, 2006), which detects overall patterns, including movement over large areas of the visual field. Given that the magnocellular path is color insensitive, MT is also color insensitive.

Most cells in area MT respond selectively when something moves at a particular speed in a particular direction (Perrone & Thiele, 2001). MT cells detect acceleration or deceleration as well as the absolute speed (Schlack, Krekelberg, & Albright, 2007), and they respond to motion in all three dimensions (Rokers, Cormack, & Huk, 2009). Area MT also responds to photographs that imply movement, such as a photo of people running (Kourtzi & Kanwisher, 2000). People who had

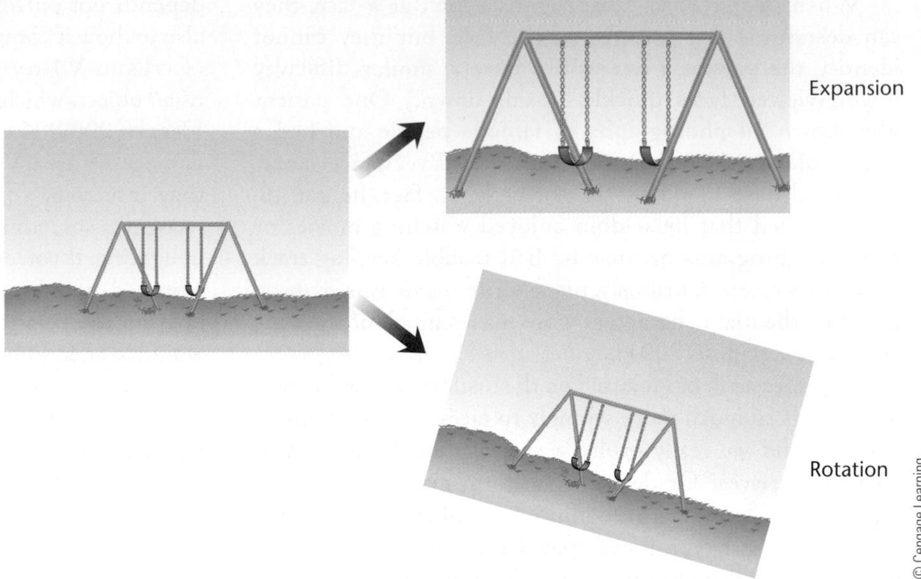

FIGURE 5.31 Stimuli that excite the dorsal part of area MST
Cells here respond if a whole scene expands, contracts, or rotates. That is, they respond if the observer moves forward or backward or tilts his or her head.

electrical stimulation of area MT (while they were undergoing exploratory studies to find the cause of their severe epilepsy) reported seeing vibrations or other movements during the stimulation (Rauschecker et al., 2011). In short, MT activity is apparently central to the experience of seeing motion. Cells in the dorsal part of area MST respond best to more complex stimuli, such as the expansion, contraction, or rotation of a large visual scene, as illustrated in Figure 5.31. That kind of experience occurs when you move forward or backward or tilt your head.

When you move your head or eyes from left to right, everything in your visual field moves across your retina as if the world itself had moved right to left. (Go ahead and try it.) Yet the world seems stationary, because nothing moved relative to anything else. Neurons in areas MT and the ventral part of MST respond briskly if something moves relative to the background, but they show little response if the object and the background both move in the same direction and speed (Takemura, Ashida, Amano, Kitaoka, & Murakami, 2012). In short, MT and MST neurons enable you to distinguish between the result of eye movements and the result of object movements.

Motion Blindness

Given that areas MT and MST respond strongly to moving objects, and only to moving objects, what would happen after damage to these areas? The result is **motion blindness,** ability to see objects but impairment at seeing whether they are moving or, if so, which direction and how fast (Marcar, Zihl, & Cowey, 1997). People with motion blindness are better at reaching for a moving object than at describing its motion (Schenk, Mai, Ditterich, & Zihl, 2000), but in all aspects of dealing with visual motion, they are far behind other people.

People with full color vision can imagine what it would be like to be color deficient, but it is difficult to imagine being motion blind. If something is moving, and you see it, how could you fail to see that it is moving? Because this experience seems so odd, neurologists for many years resisted the idea of motion blindness. Several patients were reported who apparently lost their motion vision as a result of brain damage, but most scientists ignored or disbelieved those reports. After the discovery of area MT, first from monkey research, researchers saw a mechanism whereby motion blindness could (and should) occur. They then became more amenable to the reports of motion blindness in people with brain damage.

Motion perception is a severe impairment. One patient with motion blindness reported that she felt uncomfortable when people walked around because they "were suddenly here or there but I have not seen them moving." She could not cross a street without help: "When I'm looking at the car first, it seems far away. But then, when I want to cross the road, suddenly the car is very near." Pouring coffee became difficult. The flowing liquid appeared to be frozen and unmoving, so she did not stop pouring until the cup overfilled (Zihl, von Cramon, & Mai, 1983).

You wonder what it would be like to be motion blind. Try this demonstration: Look at yourself in a mirror and focus on your left eye. Then shift your focus to your right eye. *(Please do this now.)* Did you see your eyes move? No, you did not. *(Oh, please try the demonstration!)*

Why didn't you see your eyes move? Your first impulse is to say that the movement was too small or too fast. Wrong. Try looking at someone else's eyes while he or she focuses first on your one eye and then the other. You *do* see the other person's eyes move, even though they moved the same distance and the same speed as your own. So an eye movement is neither too small nor too fast for you to see.

You do not see your own eyes move because area MT and parts of the parietal cortex decrease activity during voluntary eye movements, known as **saccades** (Bremmer, Kubischik,

Hoffmann, & Krekelberg, 2009). (Activity doesn't decrease while your eyes are following a moving object.) The brain areas that monitor saccades tell area MT and the parietal cortex, "We're about to move the eye muscles, so take a rest for the next split second." Neural activity and blood flow in MT and part of the parietal cortex begin to decrease 75 milliseconds (ms) before the eye movement and remain suppressed during the movement (Burr, Morrone, & Ross, 1994; Paus, Marrett, Worsley, & Evans, 1995; Vallines & Greenlee, 2006). In short, during a voluntary eye movement, you become temporarily motion blind. Perhaps now you understand a little better what people with motion blindness experience all the time.

The opposite of motion blindness also occurs: Some people are blind *except* for the ability to detect which direction something is moving. How could someone see movement without seeing the object that is moving? Area MT gets some input directly from the lateral geniculate nucleus of the thalamus. Therefore, even after extensive damage to area V1 (enough to produce blindness), area MT still has enough input to permit motion detection (Sincich, Park, Wohlgemuth, & Horton, 2004). Again, we try to imagine this person's experience. What would it be like to see motion without seeing the objects that are moving? (Their answers don't help. When they say which direction something is moving, they insist they are just guessing.) The general point is that different areas of your brain process different kinds of visual information, and it is possible to develop many kinds of disability.

STOP&CHECK

30. When you move your eyes, why does it not seem as if the world is moving?

31. Under what circumstance does someone with an intact brain become motion blind, and what accounts for the motion blindness?

ANSWERS

30. Neurons in areas MT and MST respond strongly when an object moves relative to the background, and not when the object and background move in the same direction and speed. **31.** People become motion blind shortly before and during a saccade (voluntary eye movement), because of suppressed activity in area MT.

MODULE 5.3 ■ IN CLOSING

Aspects of Vision

Anatomists have identified at least nearly a hundred brain areas that contribute to vision in various ways. We have discussed areas responsible for detecting location, shape, faces, color, and movement. Why do we have so many visual areas? We can only infer that the brain, like a human society, benefits from specialization. Life works better if some people become experts at repairing cars, some at baking cakes, some at delivering babies, some at moving pianos, and so forth, than if each of us had to do everything for ourselves. Similarly, your visual system works better because visual areas specialize in a particular task without trying to do everything.

A related question: How do we put it all together? When you watch a bird fly by, you perceive its shape, color, location, and movement all at once. So it seems, anyway. How do you do that? This is the binding problem, as discussed in Chapter 3. Answering that question remains a major challenge.

Summary

1. Many researchers find it useful to distinguish between the ventral visual stream, responsible for identifying objects ("what") and the dorsal stream, responsible for visual guidance of arm and leg movements ("how"). **177**
2. The inferior temporal cortex detects objects and recognizes them despite changes in position, size, and so forth. After damage to this area, people experience visual agnosia, a difficulty in recognizing the objects they see. **178**
3. A circuit including the fusiform gyrus of the temporal cortex is specialized for recognizing faces. People with impairments in this circuit experience prosopagnosia, a difficulty in recognizing faces despite nearly normal vision in other regards. **180**
4. Although the fusiform gyrus is important for recognizing faces, it also contributes to other types of visual expertise. **181**
5. Area V4 is important for color constancy, the ability to perceive the color of an object despite changes in the lighting. **181**

6. The middle temporal cortex (including areas MT and MST) is specialized for detecting the direction and speed of a moving object. People with damage in this area experience motion blindness, an impairment in their ability to perceive movement. **181**

7. People with an intact brain experience a brief period of motion blindness beginning about 75 ms before a voluntary eye movement and continuing during the eye movement. **182**

Key Terms

Terms are defined in the module on the page number indicated. They're also presented in alphabetical order with definitions in the book's Subject Index/Glossary. Interactive flash cards, audio reviews, and crossword puzzles are among the online resources available to help you learn these terms and the concepts they represent.

dorsal stream **178**
fusiform gyrus **179**
inferior temporal cortex **178**
motion blindness **182**
MST **181**
MT (or area V5) **181**
prosopagnosia **180**
saccade **182**
secondary visual cortex **177**
ventral stream **177**
visual agnosia **179**

Thought Questions

1. The visual system has specialized areas for perceiving faces, bodies, and places, but not other kinds of objects. Why might we have evolved specialized areas for these functions but not others?
2. Why is it advantageous to become motion blind during voluntary eye movements? That is, why might we have evolved this mechanism?

MODULE 5.3 End of Module Quiz

1. Within the visual system of the brain, the ventral stream is more important for ________ and the dorsal stream is more important for ________.
   a. perceiving brightness . . . perceiving color
   b. perceiving color . . . perceiving brightness
   c. identifying objects . . . controlling movements
   d. controlling movements . . . identifying objects
2. Visual agnosia usually results from damage to which part of the cortex?
   a. Occipital cortex
   b. Temporal cortex
   c. Parietal cortex
   d. Frontal cortex
3. What impairment is typical after damage to the fusiform gyrus?
   a. Loss of color perception
   b. Impaired perception of movement
   c. Impaired ability to use vision in aiming arm and leg movements
   d. Difficulty recognizing faces
4. Which part of the visual cortex is most important for color vision, especially color constancy?
   a. The fusiform gyrus
   b. The dorsal stream
   c. Area V4
   d. Area MT
5. Why is it difficult to watch your own eyes move when looking in the mirror?
   a. The eye movements are too fast to see.
   b. The eye movements are too small to see.
   c. During a saccadic eye movement, the eyes do not move relative to the background of the rest of the face.
   d. During saccadic eye movements, activity decreases in area MT.

6. What happens after damage limited to area MT? What may occur if MT is intact but area V1 is damaged?
   a. Damage to MT causes prosopagnosia. If MT is intact but V1 is damaged, the person can perceive faces but nothing else.
   b. Damage to MT causes blindness. If MT is intact but V1 is damaged, the person suffers prosopagnosia.
   c. Damage to MT causes motion blindness. If MT is intact but V1 is damaged, the person perceives movement but cannot identify the object.
   d. Damage to MT causes blindness. If MT is intact but V1 is damaged, the person cannot perceive movement.

ANSWERS:

1c, 2b, 3d, 4c, 5d, 6c.

Suggestions for Further Reading

Purves, D., & Lotto, R. B. (2003). *Why we see what we do: An empirical theory of vision.* Sunderland, MA: Sinauer Associates.

This presents a discussion of how our perception of color, size, and other visual qualities depends on our previous experience with objects and not just on the light striking the retina.

Sacks, O. (2010). *Mind's Eye.* New York: Alfred Knopf.

This book includes case histories of people with brain damage who lost the ability to recognize faces, the ability to read, the ability to find their way around, and other specific visual abilities.

Danita Delimont/Gallo Images/Getty Images

Other Sensory Systems

6

CHAPTER OUTLINE

MODULE 6.1 Audition
Sound and the Ear
Pitch Perception
The Auditory Cortex
Hearing Loss
Sound Localization
In Closing: Functions of Hearing

MODULE 6.2 The Mechanical Senses
Vestibular Sensation
Somatosensation
Pain
Itch
In Closing: The Mechanical Senses

MODULE 6.3 The Chemical Senses
Chemical Coding
Taste
Olfaction
Pheromones
Synesthesia
In Closing: Senses as Ways of Knowing the World

LEARNING OBJECTIVES

After studying this chapter, you should be able to:

1. Describe the receptors for hearing, vestibular sensation, the somatic senses, and the chemical senses.
2. Explain the mechanisms of pitch perception and sound localization.
3. Compare physical and emotional pain.
4. Describe methods of relieving pain.
5. Discuss individual differences in taste and olfaction.
6. Define and describe synesthesia.

According to a Native American saying, "A pine needle fell. The eagle saw it. The deer heard it. The bear smelled it" (Herrero, 1985). Each species responds to the most useful kinds of information. Some birds have receptors to detect magnetic fields, useful information when orienting north and south during migration (Wu & Dickman, 2012). The ears of the green tree frog, *Hyla cinerea*, are most sensitive to sounds at the frequencies prominent in the adult male's mating call (Moss & Simmons, 1986). Mosquitoes have a receptor that detects the odor of human sweat—and therefore helps them find us and bite us (Hallem, Fox, Zwiebel, & Carlson, 2004). Bats locate insects by emitting sonar waves at 20,000 to 100,000 hertz (Hz, cycles per second), well above the range of adult human hearing (Griffin, Webster, & Michael, 1960), and then locating the insects from the echoes. Curiously, some moths jam the signals by emitting similar high-frequency calls of their own (Corcoran, Barber, & Conner, 2009).

Humans, too, have important sensory specializations. Our sense of taste alerts us to the bitterness of poisons (Richter, 1950; Schiffman & Erickson, 1971) but does not respond to substances such as cellulose that neither help nor harm us. Our olfactory systems are unresponsive to gases that we don't need to detect (e.g., carbon dioxide) but highly responsive to the smell of rotting meat. This chapter concerns how our sensory systems process biologically useful information.

OPPOSITE: The sensory world of bats—which find insects by echolocation—must be very different from that of humans.

MODULE 6.1

Audition

Evolution has been described as "thrifty." After it has solved one problem, it modifies that solution for other problems instead of starting from scratch. For example, imagine a gene for visual receptors in an early vertebrate. Make a duplicate of that gene, modify it slightly, and presto: The new gene makes receptors that respond to different wavelengths of light, and color vision becomes possible. In this chapter, you will see more examples of that principle. Various sensory systems have their specializations, but they also have much in common.

Sound and the Ear

Hearing alerts us to many sorts of useful information. If you hear a board creak in your home or a twig snap in the forest, you know you are not alone. You hear breathing, and you know some person or animal is close. Then you hear the sound of a familiar friendly voice, and you know that all is well.

Physics and Psychology of Sound

Sound waves are periodic compressions of air, water, or other media. When a tree falls, the tree and the ground vibrate, setting up sound waves in the air that strike the ears. Sound waves vary in amplitude and frequency. The **amplitude** of a sound wave is its intensity. In general, sounds of greater amplitude sound louder, but exceptions occur. For example, a rapidly talking person sounds louder than slow music of the same physical amplitude.

The **frequency** of a sound is the number of compressions per second, measured in hertz (Hz, cycles per second). **Pitch** is the related aspect of perception. Sounds higher in frequency are higher in pitch. Figure 6.1 illustrates the amplitude and frequency of sounds. The height of each wave corresponds to amplitude, and the number of waves per second corresponds to frequency.

Most adult humans hear sounds ranging from about 15 to 20 Hz to somewhat less than 20,000 Hz. Children hear higher frequencies than adults, because the ability to perceive high frequencies decreases with age and exposure to loud noises (B. A. Schneider, Trehub, Morrongiello, & Thorpe, 1986). As a rule, larger animals like elephants hear best at lower pitches, and small animals like mice hear higher pitches, including some well above what we can hear.

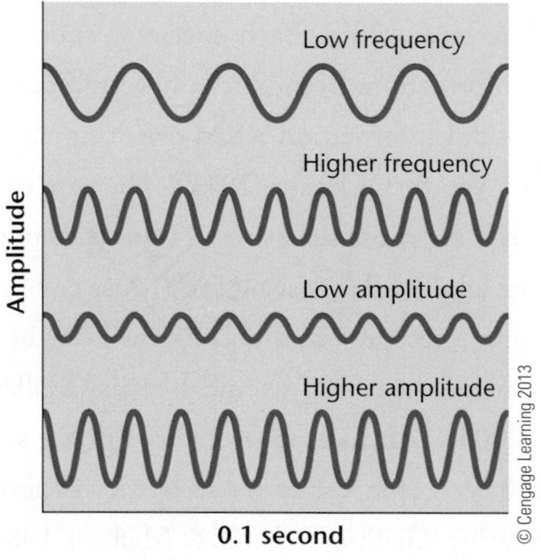

FIGURE 6.1 Four sound waves
The top line represents five sound waves in 0.1 second, or 50 Hz—a low-frequency sound that we experience as a low pitch. The other three lines represent 100 Hz. The vertical extent of each line represents its amplitude, which we experience as loudness.

In addition to amplitude and pitch, the third aspect of sound is **timbre** (TAM-ber), meaning tone quality or tone complexity. Two musical instruments playing the same note at the same loudness sound different, as do two people singing the same note at the same loudness. For example, any instrument playing a note at 256 Hz will simultaneously produce some sound at 128 Hz, 512 Hz, and so forth, known as harmonics of the principal note. The amount of harmonics differs among instruments, providing timbre.

People communicate emotion by alterations in pitch, loudness, and timbre. For example, the way you say "that was interesting" could indicate approval (it really was interesting), sarcasm (it really was boring), or suspicion (you think someone has hinted at something without saying it). Conveying emotional information by tone of voice is known as *prosody*.

Structures of the Ear

Rube Goldberg (1883–1970) drew cartoons of complicated, far-fetched inventions. For example, a person's tread on the front doorstep might pull a string that raised a cat's tail, awakening the cat, which then chases a bird that had been resting on a balance, which swings up to strike a doorbell. The functioning of the ear is complex enough to resemble a Rube Goldberg device, but unlike Goldberg's inventions, the ear actually works.

Anatomists distinguish the outer ear, the middle ear, and the inner ear (see Figure 6.2). The outer ear includes the **pinna**, the familiar structure of flesh and cartilage attached to each side of the head. By altering the reflections of sound waves, the pinna helps us locate the source of a sound. We have to learn to use that information because each person's pinna is shaped differently from anyone else's (Van Wanrooij & Van Opstal, 2005). Rabbits' large movable pinnas enable them to localize sound sources even more precisely.

After sound waves pass through the auditory canal (see Figure 6.2), they strike the **tympanic membrane,** or eardrum, in the middle ear. The tympanic membrane vibrates at the same frequency as the sound waves that strike it. The tympanic membrane connects to three tiny bones that transmit

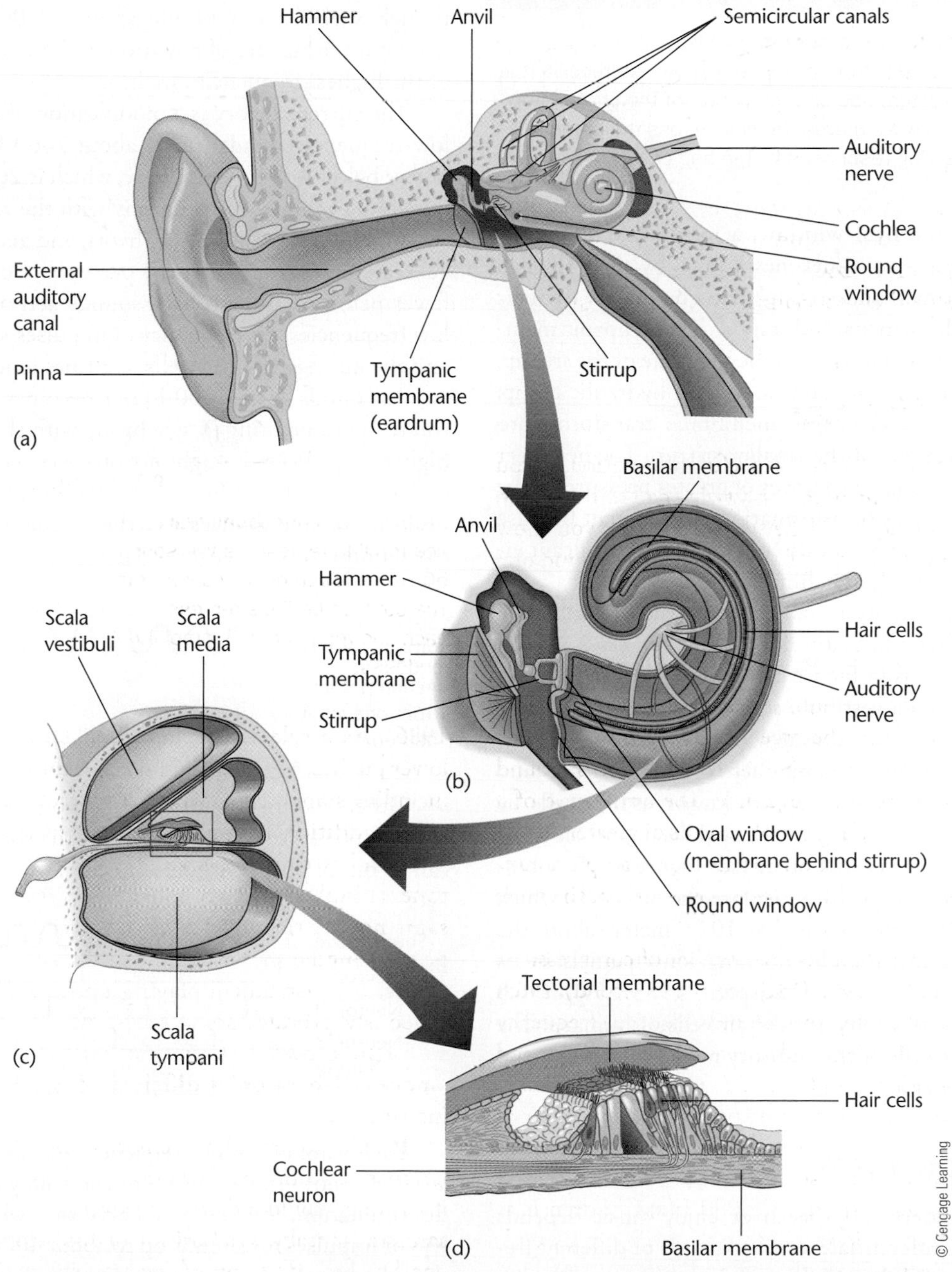

FIGURE 6.2 Structures of the ear
When sound waves strike the tympanic membrane in (a), they vibrate three tiny bones—the hammer, anvil, and stirrup—that convert the sound waves into stronger vibrations in the fluid-filled cochlea (b). Those vibrations displace the hair cells along the basilar membrane in the cochlea. (c) A cross-section through the cochlea. (d) A close-up of the hair cells.

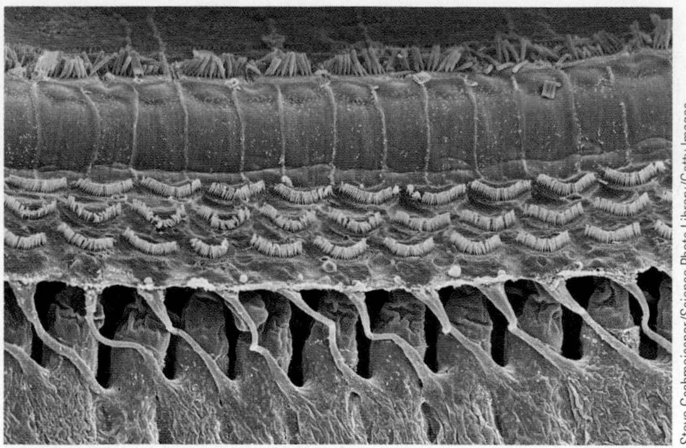

FIGURE 6.3 Hair cells from a human cochlea
This artificially colored electron micrograph shows stereocilia (the crescent-shaped structures across the center of the photo) atop hair cells. As a sound wave moves the fluid across the stereocilia, it bends them, triggering responses by the hair cells.

the vibrations to the **oval window**, a membrane of the inner ear. These bones are sometimes known by their English names (hammer, anvil, and stirrup) and sometimes by their Latin names (malleus, incus, and stapes). The tympanic membrane is about 20 times larger than the footplate of the stirrup, which connects to the oval window. As in a hydraulic pump, the vibrations of the tympanic membrane transform into more forceful vibrations of the smaller stirrup. The net effect converts the sound waves into waves of greater pressure on the small oval window. This transformation is important because vibrations in the air could not directly produce significant vibrations in the viscous fluid behind the oval window.

The inner ear contains a snail-shaped structure called the **cochlea** (KOCK-lee-uh, Latin for "snail"). A cross-section through the cochlea, as in Figure 6.2c, shows three long fluid-filled tunnels: the scala vestibuli, scala media, and scala tympani. The stirrup makes the oval window vibrate at the entrance to the scala vestibuli, thereby setting in motion the fluid in the cochlea. The auditory receptors, known as **hair cells**, lie between the basilar membrane of the cochlea on one side and the tectorial membrane on the other (see Figure 6.2d). Vibrations in the fluid of the cochlea displace the hair cells, which respond to displacements as small as 10^{-10} meter (about the diameter of an atom), thereby opening ion channels in its membrane (Fettiplace, 1990; Hudspeth, 1985). Figure 6.3 shows electron micrographs of the hair cells of humans. The hair cells excite the cells of the auditory nerve, which is part of the eighth cranial nerve.

Pitch Perception

Your ability to understand speech or enjoy music depends on your ability to differentiate among sounds of different frequencies. How do you do it?

According to the **place theory**, the basilar membrane resembles the strings of a piano, with each area along the membrane tuned to a specific frequency. (If you sound a note with a tuning fork near a piano, you vibrate the piano string tuned to that note.) According to this theory, each frequency activates the hair cells at only one place along the basilar membrane, and the nervous system distinguishes among frequencies based on which neurons respond. The downfall of this theory is that the various parts of the basilar membrane are bound together too tightly for any part to resonate like a piano string.

According to the **frequency theory**, the basilar membrane vibrates in synchrony with a sound, causing auditory nerve axons to produce action potentials at the same frequency. For example, a sound at 50 Hz would cause 50 action potentials per second in the auditory nerve. The downfall of this theory in its simplest form is that the refractory period of a neuron, though variable, is typically about 1/1000 second, so the maximum firing rate of a neuron is about 1000 Hz, far short of the highest frequencies we hear.

The current theory is a modification of both theories. For low-frequency sounds (up to about 100 Hz—more than an octave below middle C in music, which is 264 Hz), the basilar membrane vibrates in synchrony with the sound waves, in accordance with the frequency theory, and auditory nerve axons generate one action potential per wave. Soft sounds activate fewer neurons, and stronger sounds activate more. Thus, at low frequencies, the frequency of impulses identifies the pitch, and the number of firing cells identifies loudness.

As sounds exceed 100 Hz, it becomes harder for a neuron to continue firing in synchrony with the sound waves. At higher frequencies, it might fire on every second, third, fourth, or later wave. Its action potentials are phase-locked to the peaks of the sound waves (i.e., they occur at the same phase in the sound wave), as illustrated here:

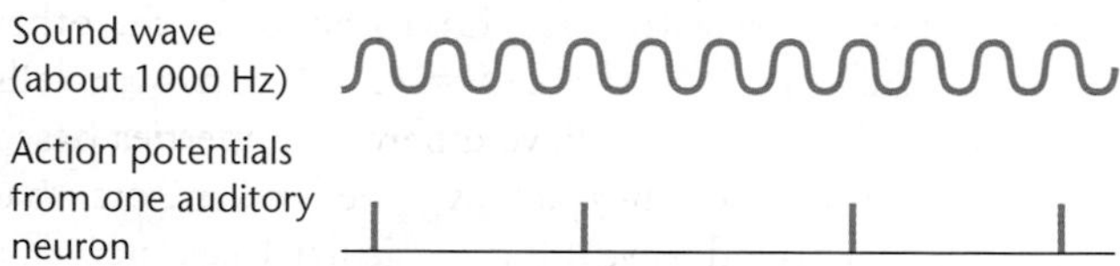

Other auditory neurons also produce action potentials that are phase-locked with peaks of the sound wave, but they can be out of phase with one another:

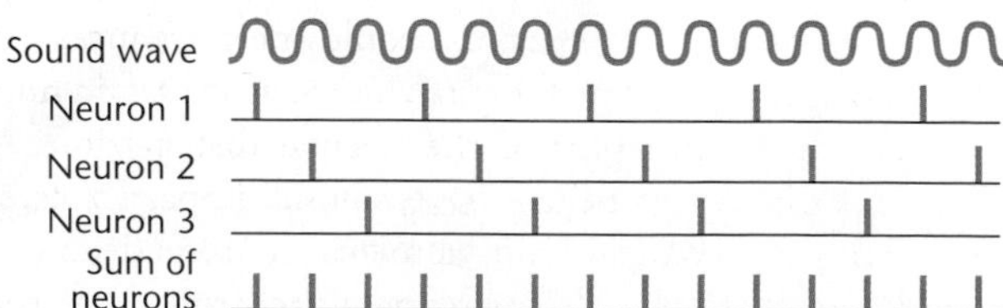

Each wave of a high-frequency tone excites at least a few auditory neurons. According to the **volley principle** of pitch discrimination, the auditory nerve as a whole produces volleys of impulses for sounds up to about 4000 per second, even though no individual axon approaches that frequency (Rose, Brugge, Anderson, & Hind, 1967). However, beyond about 4000 Hz, even staggered volleys of impulses cannot keep pace with the sound waves.

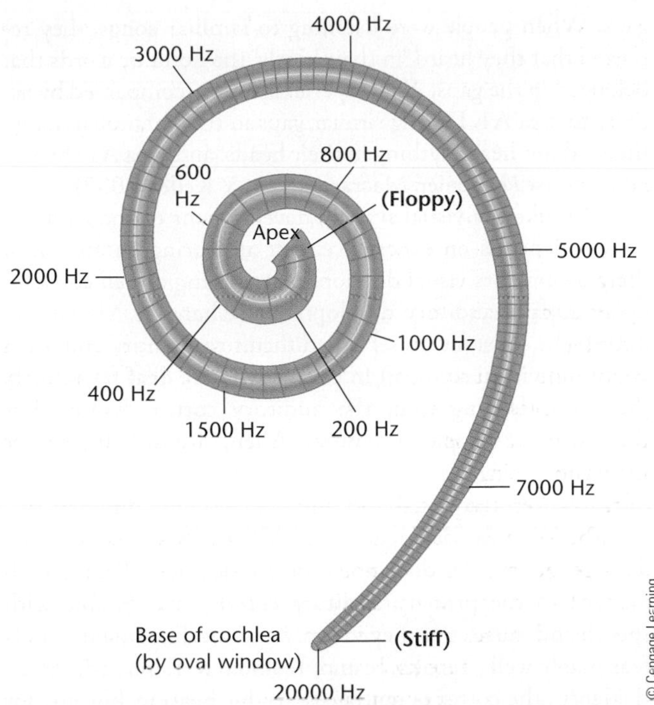

FIGURE 6.4 Basilar membrane of the human cochlea
High-frequency sounds excite hair cells near the base. Low-frequency sounds excite cells near the apex.

Most human hearing takes place below 4000 Hz, the approximate limit of the volley principle. For comparison, the highest key on a piano is 4224 Hz. When we hear still higher frequencies, we use a mechanism similar to the place theory. The basilar membrane varies from stiff at its base, where the stirrup meets the cochlea, to floppy at the other end of the cochlea, the apex (see Figure 6.4). The hair cells along the basilar membrane have different properties based on their location, and they act as tuned resonators that vibrate only for sound waves of a particular frequency. The highest frequency sounds vibrate hair cells near the base, and lower frequency sounds vibrate hair cells farther along the membrane (Warren, 1999). Actually, the mechanisms of hearing high-frequency sounds are more complex, but this is the general idea (Tomo, de Monvel, & Fridberger, 2007).

For most aspects of behavior, people's performances vary along a normal curve, but for pitch perception, a fair number of people are not part of the normal distribution. An estimated 4 percent of people have *amusia*, impaired detection of frequency changes (commonly called "tone deafness") (Hyde & Peretz, 2004). Although not entirely tone-deaf, they generally do not detect a change in sound less than about the difference between C and C-sharp (Loui, Alsop, & Schlaug, 2009). Furthermore, they have trouble recognizing tunes, cannot tell whether someone is singing off-key, and do not detect a "wrong" note in a melody. They also have trouble gauging people's mood, such as happy or sad, from their tone of voice (Thompson, Marin, & Stewart, 2012). However, although they are impaired at consciously recognizing pitch changes—such as saying that this tone is higher than that one, or even different from that one—they have no trouble imitating someone else's intonation (Hutchins & Peretz, 2012). Evidently pitch information reaches some parts of the brain and not others.

Many relatives of a person with amusia have the same condition, so it probably has a genetic basis (Peretz, Cummings, & Dube, 2007). People with amusia have a thicker than average auditory cortex in the right hemisphere but fewer than average connections from it to the frontal cortex (Hyde et al., 2007; Loui et al., 2009). When they hear two tones that slightly differ, the brain's initial response is about the same as in other people, indicating that the ears are properly registering the information, but they fail to process the information further (Moreau, Jolicoeur, & Peretz, 2013). Ordinarily a changed or surprising stimulus produces a strong wave of brain activity about 3/10 second later, called the P300 wave, but a small change in sound fails to produce that wave in people with amusia.

Absolute pitch (or "perfect pitch") is the ability to hear a note and identify it—for example, "That's a B flat." Genetic predisposition contributes (Theusch, Basu, & Gitschier, 2009), but early musical training is also important. Not everyone with musical training develops absolute pitch, but almost everyone with absolute pitch had early musical training (Athos et al., 2007). Absolute pitch is also more common among people who speak tonal languages, such as Vietnamese and Mandarin Chinese (Deutsch, Henthorn, Marvin, & Xu, 2006). In those languages, the meaning of a sound depends on its pitch, and therefore, people learn from infancy to pay close attention to slight changes of pitch.

STOP&CHECK

1. Through which mechanism do we perceive low-frequency sounds (up to about 100 Hz)?
2. How do we perceive middle-frequency sounds (100 to 4000 Hz)?
3. How do we perceive high-frequency sounds (above 4000 Hz)?
4. What evidence suggests that amusia depends on special experiences?

ANSWERS

1. At low frequencies, the basilar membrane vibrates in synchrony with the sound waves, and each responding axon in the auditory nerve sends one action potential per sound wave. **2.** At intermediate frequencies, no single axon fires an action potential for each sound wave, but different axons fire for different waves, and so a volley (group) of axons fires for each wave. **3.** At high frequencies, the sound causes maximum vibration for the hair cells at one location along the basilar membrane. **4.** Absolute pitch occurs almost entirely among people who had early musical training and is also more common among people who speak tonal languages, which require greater attention to pitch.

The Auditory Cortex

As information from the auditory system passes through subcortical areas, axons cross over in the midbrain to enable each hemisphere of the forebrain to get most of its input from the opposite ear (Glendenning, Baker, Hutson, & Masterton, 1992). The information ultimately reaches the **primary auditory cortex (area A1)** in the superior temporal cortex, as shown in Figure 6.5.

The organization of the auditory cortex strongly parallels that of the visual cortex (Poremba et al., 2003). For example, just as the visual system has a "what" pathway and a "where" pathway, the auditory system has a "what" pathway sensitive to patterns of sound in the anterior temporal cortex, and a "where" pathway sensitive to sound location in the posterior temporal cortex and the parietal cortex (Lomber & Malhotra, 2008). Just as patients with damage in area MT become motion blind, patients with damage in parts of the superior temporal cortex become motion deaf. They hear sounds, but they do not detect that a source of a sound is moving (Ducommun et al., 2004).

Just as the visual cortex is active during visual imagery, area A1 responds to imagined sounds as well as real ones. It becomes active when people view short silent videos that suggest sound—such as someone playing a piano, or a glass vase shattering on the ground (K. Meyer et al., 2010). In one study, people listened to several familiar and unfamiliar songs. At various points, parts of each song were replaced by 3- to 5-second gaps. When people were listening to familiar songs, they reported that they heard "in their heads" the notes or words that belonged in the gaps. That experience was accompanied by activity in area A1. During similar gaps in the unfamiliar songs, they did not hear anything in their heads, and area A1 showed no response (Kraemer, Macrae, Green, & Kelley, 2005).

Also like the visual system, development of the auditory system depends on experience. Just as rearing an animal in the dark impairs visual development, rearing one in constant noise impairs auditory development (Chang & Merzenich, 2003). (In constant noise, it is difficult to identify and learn about individual sounds.) In people who are deaf from birth, the axons leading from the auditory cortex develop less than in other people (Emmorey, Allen, Bruss, Schenker, & Damasio, 2003).

However, the visual and auditory systems differ in this respect: Whereas damage to area V1 leaves someone blind, damage to area A1 does not produce deafness. People with damage to the primary auditory cortex have trouble with speech and music, but they identify and localize single sounds reasonably well (Tanaka, Kamo, Yoshida, & Yamadori, 1991). Evidently, the cortex is not necessary for hearing, but just for processing the information.

When researchers record from cells in the primary auditory cortex while playing pure tones, they find that most cells have a preferred tone, as shown in Figure 6.6. Note the gradient from an area responsive to lower tones up to areas responsive to higher and higher tones. The auditory cortex provides what researchers call a *tonotopic* map of sounds.

Properties vary from cell to cell in the auditory cortex. Some cells are tuned sharply to a single tone, and others respond also to some neighboring tones. Some neurons respond to one tone at one synapse and a different tone at an adjacent synapse (Chen, Leischner, Rochefort, Nelken, & Konnerth, 2011). Most cells respond best to a complex sound, such as a dominant tone and several harmonics (Barbour & Wang, 2003; Griffiths, Uppenkamp, Johnsrude, Josephs, & Patterson, 2001; Penagos, Melcher, & Oxenham, 2004; Wessinger et al., 2001). For example, for a tone of 400 Hz, the harmonics are 800 Hz, 1200 Hz, and so forth. We experience a tone with harmonics as "richer" than one without them. Surrounding the primary auditory cortex are additional auditory areas that respond best to what we might call auditory "objects"—sounds such as animal cries, machinery noises, music, and other identifiable, meaningful sounds (Gutschalk, Patterson, Scherg, Uppenkamp, & Rupp, 2004; Zatorre, Bouffard, & Belin, 2004).

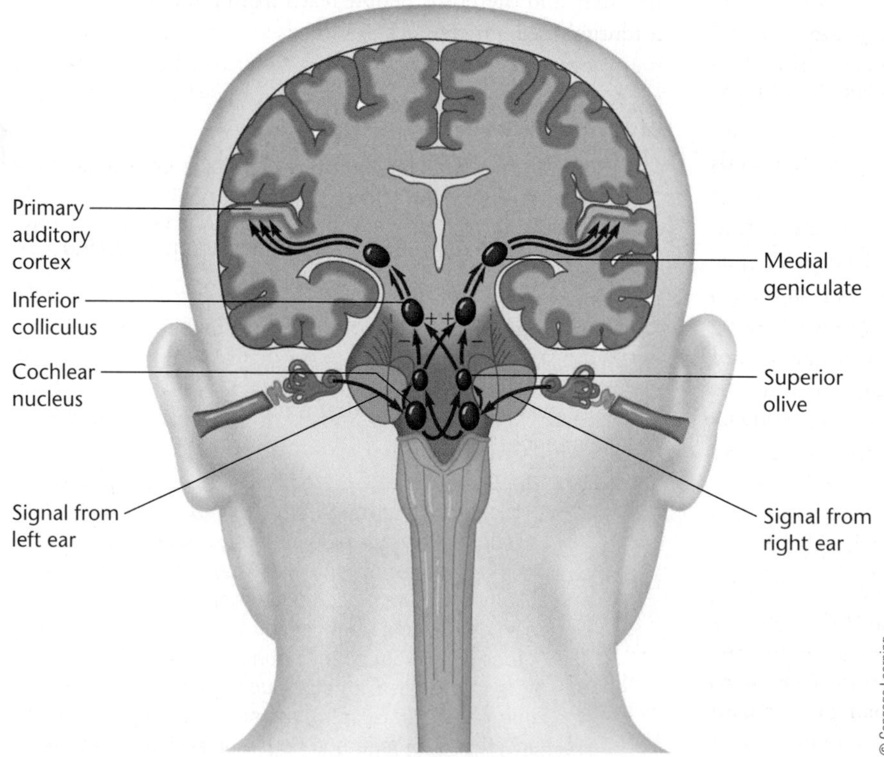

FIGURE 6.5 Route of auditory impulses from the receptors in the ear to the auditory cortex
The cochlear nucleus receives input from the ipsilateral ear only (the one on the same side of the head). All later stages have input from both ears, but more strongly from the contralateral ear.

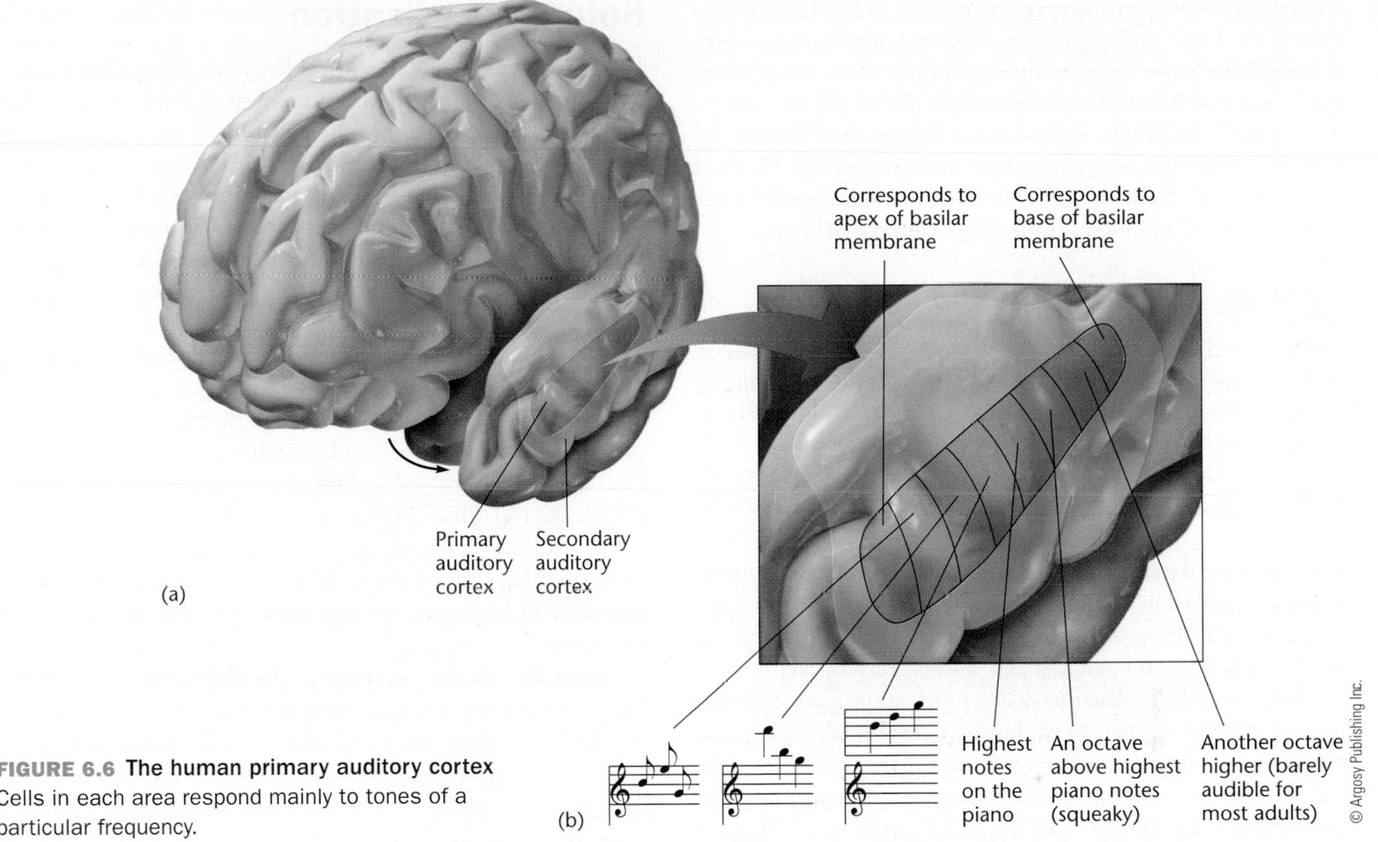

FIGURE 6.6 The human primary auditory cortex Cells in each area respond mainly to tones of a particular frequency.

STOP & CHECK

5. How is the auditory cortex like the visual cortex?
6. What is one way in which the auditory and visual cortices differ?
7. What kinds of sounds most strongly activate the auditory cortex?

ANSWERS

5. Any of the following: (a) Both vision and hearing have "what" and "where" pathways. (b) Areas in the superior temporal cortex analyze movement of both visual and auditory stimuli. Damage there can cause motion blindness or motion deafness. (c) The visual cortex is essential for visual imagery, and the primary auditory cortex is essential for auditory imagery. (d) Both the visual and auditory cortices need normal experience early in life to develop normal sensitivities. **6.** Damage to the primary visual cortex leaves someone blind, but damage to the primary auditory cortex merely impairs perception of complex sounds without making the person deaf. **7.** Most cells respond best to complex sounds that include harmonics. Outside the primary auditory cortex, most cells respond to "auditory objects" that mean something.

Hearing Loss

Many factors can impair hearing. Identifying the cause of hearing loss can help find a remedy.

Deafness

Although few people are totally insensitive to all sounds, many people have enough impairment to reduce or prevent speech comprehension. The two categories of hearing loss are conductive deafness and nerve deafness.

Diseases, infections, or tumorous bone growth can prevent the middle ear from transmitting sound waves properly to the cochlea. The result, **conductive deafness** or **middle-ear deafness,** is sometimes temporary. If it persists, it can be corrected by surgery or by hearing aids that amplify the stimulus. Because people with conductive deafness have a normal cochlea and auditory nerve, they readily hear their own voices, conducted through the bones of the skull directly to the cochlea, bypassing the middle ear. Because they hear themselves clearly, they may accuse others of mumbling or talking too softly.

Nerve deafness, or **inner-ear deafness,** results from damage to the cochlea, the hair cells, or the auditory nerve. It can occur in any degree and may be confined to one part of the cochlea, which impairs hearing of certain frequencies and not others. Nerve deafness can be inherited, it can result from disease, or it can result from exposure to loud noises. For example, many soldiers, construction workers, and fans of loud rock music expose themselves to noise levels that damage the synapses and neurons of the auditory system. Gradually people begin to notice ringing in the ears, extreme sensitivity to noise, or impaired hearing (Kujawa & Liberman, 2009).

Nerve deafness often produces **tinnitus** (tin-EYE-tus)—frequent or constant ringing in the ears. In some cases, tinnitus is due to a phenomenon similar to phantom limb, discussed in

Chapter 4. Damage to part of the cochlea is like an amputation: If the brain no longer gets its normal input, axons representing other parts of the body may invade a brain area previously responsive to sounds, especially high-frequency sounds. Some people find they can increase or change their tinnitus by clenching their jaw or tensing their neck muscles (Lockwood et al., 1998; Roberts et al., 2010). Presumably, axons representing the jaw and neck invaded their auditory cortex.

Hearing, Attention, and Old Age

Many older people continue to have hearing problems despite wearing hearing aids. The hearing aids make the sounds loud enough, but people still have trouble understanding speech, especially in a noisy room or if someone speaks rapidly.

Part of the explanation is that the brain areas responsible for language comprehension have become less active (Peelle, Troiani, Grossman, & Wingfield, 2011). This trend might be just a natural deterioration, or it might be a reaction to prolonged degradation of auditory input. That is, if someone delays getting hearing aids, the language cortex doesn't get its normal input and it begins to become less responsive.

The rest of the explanation relates to attention. Frequently you want to listen to one person while others are also talking or making noises. The background may include music or other sounds as well. To hear what you care about, you need to filter out all the rest (Mesgarani & Chang, 2013). Many older people have a decrease in their inhibitory neurotransmitters in the auditory portions of the brain. As a result, they have trouble suppressing the irrelevant sounds and attending to the important one. Also, instead of making a quick, crisp response to each sound, the auditory cortex has delayed, spread-out responses to each sound, such that the response to one sound partly overlaps the response to another (Anderson, Parbery-Clark, White-Schwoch, & Kraus, 2012). Attention improves if the listener watches the speaker's face (Golumbic, Cogan, Schroeder, & Poeppel, 2013). We all do more lip-reading than we realize, and focusing on the speaker helps to lock attention onto the corresponding sounds. Also, a computer program is available to help people practice attending to a speaker in a noisy environment (Song, Skoe, Banai, & Kraus, 2012).

STOP & CHECK

8. Which type of hearing loss—conductive deafness or nerve deafness—would be more common among members of rock bands and why?

9. Why do many older people have trouble hearing speech in spite of wearing hearing aids?

ANSWERS

8. Nerve deafness is common among rock band members because their frequent exposure to loud noises causes damage to the cells of the ear. **9.** In some cases the language areas of the cortex have become less responsive. Also, auditory areas of the brain have decreased levels of inhibitory neurotransmitters, and the result is decreased ability to focus attention on one speaker in a noisy environment.

Sound Localization

You are walking alone when suddenly you hear a loud noise. You want to know what produced it (friend or foe), but equally, you want to know where it came from, so you can do something about it. Sound localization is less accurate than visual localization, but nevertheless impressive. You can identify a sound's direction even if it occurs just briefly and while you are turning your head (Vliegen, Van Grootel, & Van Opstal, 2004). Owls localize sound well enough to capture mice in the dark.

Determining the direction and distance of a sound requires comparing the responses of the two ears. One method is the difference in *time of arrival* at the two ears. A sound coming directly from the side reaches the closer ear about 600 microseconds (μs) before the other. A smaller difference in arrival times indicates a sound coming from closer to the midline. Time of arrival is most useful for localizing sounds with a sudden onset. Most birds' alarm calls increase gradually in loudness, making them difficult for a predator to localize.

Another cue for location is the difference in intensity between the ears. For high-frequency sounds, with a wavelength shorter than the width of the head, the head creates a *sound shadow* (see Figure 6.7), making the sound louder for the closer ear. In adult humans, this mechanism produces accurate sound localization for frequencies above 2000 to 3000 Hz and less accurate localizations for progressively lower frequencies.

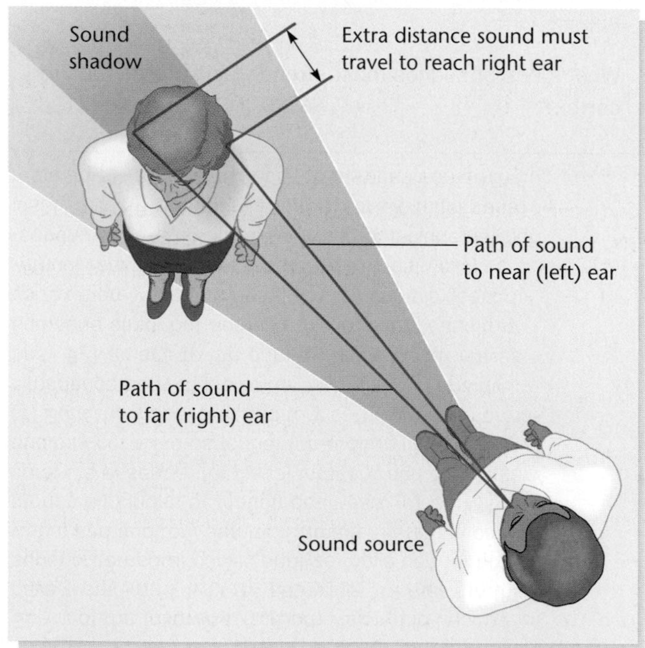

FIGURE 6.7 Loudness and arrival times as cues for sound localization
Sounds reaching the closer ear arrive sooner as well as louder because the head produces a "sound shadow." *Source*: Based on Lindsay & Norman, 1972

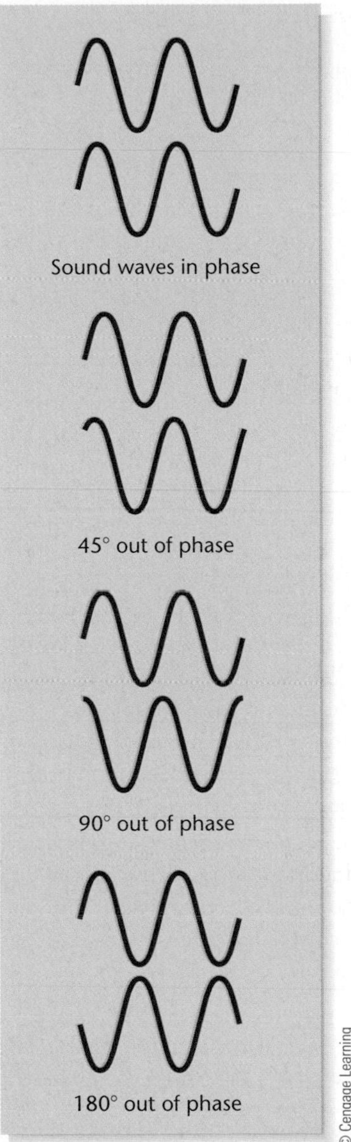

FIGURE 6.8 Sound waves in phase or out of phase
Sound waves that reach the two ears in phase are perceived as coming from directly in front of (or behind) the hearer. The more out of phase the waves, the farther the sound source is from the body's midline.

FIGURE 6.9 Phase differences as a cue for sound localization
A sound coming from anywhere other than straight ahead or straight behind reaches the two ears at different phases of the sound wave. The difference in phase is a signal to the sound's direction. With high-frequency sounds, the phases become ambiguous.

A third cue is the *phase difference* between the ears. Every sound wave has phases with consecutive peaks 360 degrees apart. Figure 6.8 shows sound waves that are in phase and out of phase by different amounts. If a sound originates to the side of the head, the sound wave strikes the two ears out of phase, as shown in Figure 6.9. How much out of phase depends on the frequency of the sound, the size of the head, and the direction of the sound. Phase differences provide information that is useful for localizing sounds with frequencies up to about 1500 Hz in humans.

If your head is under water, you will have trouble localizing low- and medium-frequency sounds. The reason is that sounds travel faster in water than in air, so a sound arrives at the two ears almost simultaneously and the phase differences are small, also.

In short, humans localize low frequencies by phase differences, and high frequencies by loudness differences. We can localize a sound of any frequency by the times of onset if the sound occurs suddenly. All of these methods require learning, because as your head grows, the distance between your ears increases, and you need to recalibrate how you localize sounds (Kumpik, Kacelnik, & King, 2010).

What would happen if you became deaf in one ear? At first, as you would expect, all sounds would seem to come directly from the side of the intact ear. (That ear hears a sound louder and sooner than the other ear because the other ear doesn't hear it at all.) Eventually, however, people learn to interpret loudness cues when they hear familiar sounds in a familiar location. They infer that louder sounds come from the side of the intact ear and softer sounds come from the opposite side. Their accuracy does not match that of people with two ears, but it becomes helpful under some conditions (Van Wanrooij & Van Opstal, 2004).

STOP & CHECK

10. Which method of sound localization is more effective for an animal with a small head? Which is more effective for an animal with a large head? Why?

ANSWER

10. An animal with a small head localizes sounds mainly by differences in loudness because the ears are not far enough apart for differences in onset time to be very large. An animal with a large head localizes sounds mainly by differences in onset time because its ears are far apart and well suited to noting differences in phase or onset time.

MODULE 6.1 ■ IN CLOSING

Functions of Hearing

We spend much of our day listening to language, and we sometimes forget that the original, primary function of hearing has to do with simpler but extremely important issues: What do I hear? Where is it? Is it coming closer? Is it a potential mate, a potential enemy, potential food, or something irrelevant? The organization of the auditory system is well suited to resolving these questions.

Summary

1. Sound waves vibrate the tympanic membrane. Three tiny bones convert these vibrations into more forceful vibrations of the smaller oval window, setting in motion the fluid inside the cochlea. Waves of fluid inside the cochlea stimulate the hair cells that send messages to the brain. **189**
2. We detect the pitch of low-frequency sounds by the frequency of action potentials in the auditory system. At intermediate frequencies, we detect volleys of responses across many receptors. We detect the pitch of the highest-frequency sounds by the area of greatest response along the basilar membrane. **190**
3. The auditory cortex resembles the visual cortex in many ways. Both have a "what" system and a "where" system. Both have specialized areas for detecting motion, and therefore, it is possible for a person with brain damage to be motion blind or motion deaf. The visual cortex is essential for visual imagery, and the auditory cortex is essential for auditory imagery. **192**
4. Each cell in the primary auditory cortex responds best to a particular frequency of tones, although many respond better to complex tones than to a single frequency. **192**
5. Areas bordering the primary auditory cortex analyze the meaning of sounds. **192**
6. Deafness may result from damage to the nerve cells or to the bones that conduct sounds to the nerve cells. **193**
7. Many older people have trouble attending to relevant information and filtering out the distractions, largely because of the loss of inhibitory neurotransmitters in auditory areas of the brain. **194**
8. We localize high-frequency sounds according to differences in loudness between the ears. We localize low-frequency sounds on the basis of differences in phase. If a sound occurs suddenly, we localize it by time of onset in the two ears. **194**

Key Terms

Terms are defined in the module on the page number indicated. They're also presented in alphabetical order with definitions in the book's Subject Index/Glossary. Interactive flash cards, audio reviews, and crossword puzzles are among the online resources available to help you learn these terms and the concepts they represent.

amplitude **188**
cochlea **190**
conductive deafness (middle-ear deafness) **193**
frequency **188**
frequency theory **190**
hair cells **190**
nerve deafness (inner-ear deafness) **193**
oval window **190**
pinna **189**
pitch **188**
place theory **190**
primary auditory cortex (area A1) **192**
timbre **188**
tinnitus **193**
tympanic membrane **189**
volley principle **190**

Thought Questions

1. Why do you suppose that the human auditory system evolved sensitivity to sounds in the range of 20 to 20,000 Hz instead of some other range of frequencies?
2. The text explains how we might distinguish loudness for low-frequency sounds. How might we distinguish loudness for a high-frequency tone?

MODULE 6.1 End of Module Quiz

1. Where are the auditory receptors, known as hair cells?
   a. In the auditory nerve
   b. Along a membrane of the cochlea
   c. On the tympanic membrane
   d. In the pinna

2. The frequency theory of pitch perception applies to what type of sound?
   a. Low-frequency sounds, up to about 100 Hz
   b. Medium-frequency sounds, from about 100 to 4000 Hz
   c. High-frequency sounds, above 4000 Hz
   d. All sounds

3. Which brain abnormality has been demonstrated in people with amusia?
   a. All the axons in the auditory nerve respond equally to every sound.
   b. Information from the auditory nerve does not reach the auditory cortex.
   c. The auditory cortex is smaller than average.
   d. Fewer than average axons connect the auditory cortex to the frontal cortex.

4. Absolute pitch is more common among what type of people?
   a. People who had a period of auditory deprivation during early childhood
   b. People with extensive musical training beginning in early childhood
   c. People who learned two languages beginning in early childhood
   d. People with many older brothers and sisters

5. What happens to people after damage to the primary auditory cortex?
   a. They become totally deaf.
   b. They can identify and localize simple sounds, but they cannot understand speech or enjoy music.
   c. Another part of the brain takes over, restoring normal hearing.

6. What is meant by a "tonotopic map"?
   a. Each location in the auditory cortex responds to a preferred tone, and these areas are arranged in order from low pitches to high pitches.
   b. The auditory cortex has axons back and forth to every other part of the cortex and several nuclei of the thalamus.
   c. Each neuron in the auditory cortex has a distinctive pattern of responding depending on the location of the source of sound in space.
   d. Each cell in the auditory cortex has a "partner" cell in the visual cortex.

7. Infections or bone growth that prevent the middle ear from transmitting sounds properly to the cochlea produce which type of deafness?
   a. Nerve deafness
   b. Conductive deafness

8. Many older people have trouble understanding speech in spite of wearing hearing aids, especially under which circumstance?
   a. Early in the morning
   b. A brightly lit room
   c. A noisy room
   d. A male voice

9. Localizing sounds by intensity differences works best for which pitches?
   a. High-frequency sounds
   b. Intermediate-frequency sounds
   c. Low-frequency sounds

ANSWERS: 1b, 2a, 3d, 4b, 5b, 6a, 7b, 8c, 9a.

The Mechanical Senses

If you place your hand on the surface of your radio, you feel the same vibrations that you hear. If you practiced enough, could you learn to "hear" the vibrations with your fingers? No, they would remain just vibrations. If an earless species had enough time, might its vibration detectors evolve into sound detectors? Yes! In fact, our ears evolved in just that way. Much of evolution consists of taking something that evolved for one purpose and modifying it for another purpose.

The *mechanical senses* respond to pressure, bending, or other distortions of a receptor. They include touch, pain, and other body sensations, as well as vestibular sensation, which detects the position and movement of the head. Audition is also a mechanical sense because the hair cells are modified touch receptors. We considered it separately because of its complexity and importance.

Vestibular Sensation

Try to read a page while you jiggle your head up and down or back and forth. You will find that you can read it fairly easily. Now hold your head steady and jiggle the page up and down, back and forth. Suddenly, you can hardly read it at all. Why?

When you move your head, the vestibular organ adjacent to the cochlea monitors movements and directs compensatory movements of your eyes. When your head moves left, your eyes move right; when your head moves right, your eyes move left. Effortlessly, you keep your eyes focused on what you want to see (Brandt, 1991). When you move the page, however, the vestibular organ cannot keep your eyes on target.

Sensations from the vestibular organ detect the direction of tilt and the amount of acceleration of the head. You use that information automatically for guiding eye movements and maintaining balance. Mice with an impairment of vestibular sensation frequently lose their balance and fall down. They cannot swim or float because they are often upside-down (Mariño et al., 2010).

The vestibular organ, shown in Figure 6.10, consists of the *saccule, utricle,* and three semicircular canals. Like the hearing receptors, the vestibular receptors are modified touch receptors. Calcium carbonate particles called *otoliths* lie next to the hair cells. When the head tilts in different directions, the otoliths push against different sets of hair cells and excite them (Hess, 2001).

The three **semicircular canals**, oriented in perpendicular planes, are filled with a jellylike substance and lined with hair cells. Acceleration of the head at any angle causes the jellylike substance in one of these canals to push against the hair cells. Action potentials initiated by cells of the vestibular system travel through part of the eighth cranial nerve to the brainstem and cerebellum. (The eighth cranial nerve contains both an auditory component and a vestibular component.)

The vestibular organ is nearly the same size for all mammalian species. Whales are 10 million times as massive as mice, but their vestibular organ is only 5 times as large (Squires, 2004). Evidently a small vestibular organ provides all the information we need. For analogy, small thermometers can be nearly as accurate as larger ones.

STOP&CHECK

11. People with damage to the vestibular system have trouble reading street signs while walking. Why?

ANSWER

11. The vestibular system enables the brain to shift eye movements to compensate for changes in head position. Without feedback about head position, a person would not be able to correct the eye movements, and the experience would be like watching a jiggling book page.

Somatosensation

The **somatosensory system**, the sensation of the body and its movements, is not one sense but many, including discriminative touch (which identifies the shape of an object), deep pressure, cold, warmth, pain, itch, tickle, and the position and movement of joints.

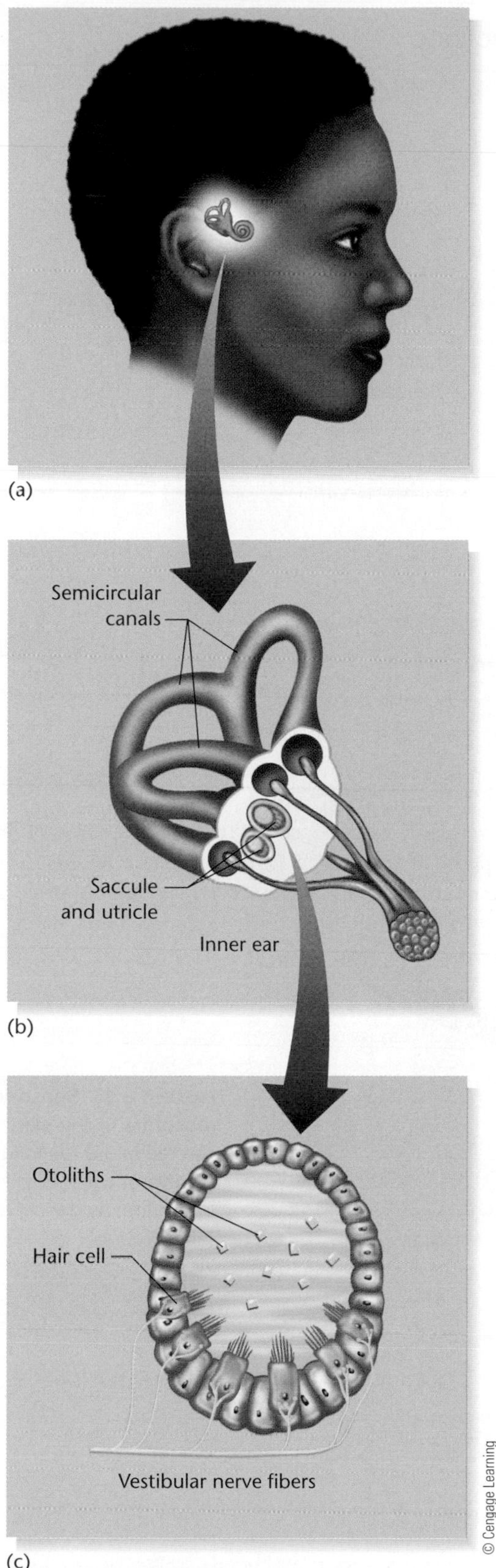

FIGURE 6.10 Structures for vestibular sensation
(a) Location of the vestibular organs. (b) Structures of the vestibular organs. (c) Cross-section through a utricle. Calcium carbonate particles, called otoliths, press against different hair cells depending on the tilt and acceleration of the head.

Somatosensory Receptors

Table 6.1 lists the probable functions of several somatosensory receptors, including those shown in Figure 6.11 (Iggo & Andres, 1982; Paré, Smith, & Rice, 2002). Others not in the table respond to deep stimulation, joint movement, or muscle movements.

A touch receptor may be a simple bare neuron ending (e.g., many pain receptors), a modified dendrite (Merkel disks), an elaborated neuron ending (Ruffini endings and Meissner's corpuscles), or a bare ending surrounded by other cells that modify its function (Pacinian corpuscles). Stimulation of a touch receptor opens sodium channels in the axon, thereby starting an action potential (Price et al., 2000).

Consider the **Pacinian corpuscle,** which detects sudden displacements or high-frequency vibrations on the skin (see Figure 6.12). Inside its outer structure is the neuron membrane. The onion-like outer structure provides mechanical support that resists gradual or constant pressure. It thereby insulates the neuron against most touch stimuli. However, a sudden or vibrating stimulus bends the membrane, enabling sodium ions to enter, depolarizing the membrane (Loewenstein, 1960).

Merkel disks respond to light touch, such as if someone gently strokes your skin or if you feel an object (Maricich et al., 2009). Suppose you feel objects with thin grooves like these, without looking at them, and try to feel whether the grooves go left to right or up and down:

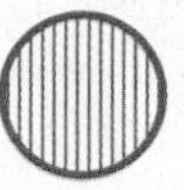 

The experimenter varies the width of the grooves to find what are the narrowest grooves you can discern. On the average, women can detect grooves about 1.4 mm apart, whereas men need the grooves to be about 1.6 mm apart. As sex differences go, this one is not particularly interesting, so your first question might be, "Who cares?" If you get past that question, your second question might be *why* men and women differ. Unlike many sex differences, this one is easy to explain. It reflects the fact that on the average, women have smaller fingers. Apparently they have the same number of Merkel disks compacted into a smaller area. If you compare men and women who have the same finger size, their touch sensitivity is the same (Peters, Hackeman, & Goldreich, 2009).

The body has specialized receptors to detect various degrees of hot or cold. Animals lacking these receptors fail to avoid hot or cold environments (Pogorzala, Mishra, & Hoon, 2013). **Capsaicin**, a chemical found in hot peppers such as jalapeños, stimulates the receptors for painful heat. Capsaicin can produce burning or stinging sensations on many parts of your body, as you may have experienced if you ever touched the insides of hot peppers and then rubbed your eyes. Szechuan peppers also stimulate the heat receptors, and in addition stimulate certain touch receptors that give a tingling sensation (Bautista et al., 2008). Menthol and mint stimulate the coolness receptor (McKemy, Neuhausser, & Julius, 2002). So advertisements mentioning "the cool taste of menthol" are literally correct.

TABLE 6.1 Somatosensory Receptors and Probable Functions

Receptor	Location	Responds to
Free nerve ending (unmyelinated or thinly myelinated axons)	Near base of hairs and elsewhere in skin	Pain, warmth, cold
Hair-follicle receptors	Hair-covered skin	Movement of hairs
Meissner's corpuscles	Hairless areas	Sudden displacement of skin; low-frequency vibration (flutter)
Pacinian corpuscles	Both hairy and hairless skin	Sudden displacement of skin; high-frequency vibration
Merkel's disks	Both hairy and hairless skin	Light touch
Ruffini endings	Both hairy and hairless skin	Stretch of skin
Krause end bulbs	Mostly or entirely in hairless areas, perhaps including genitals	Uncertain

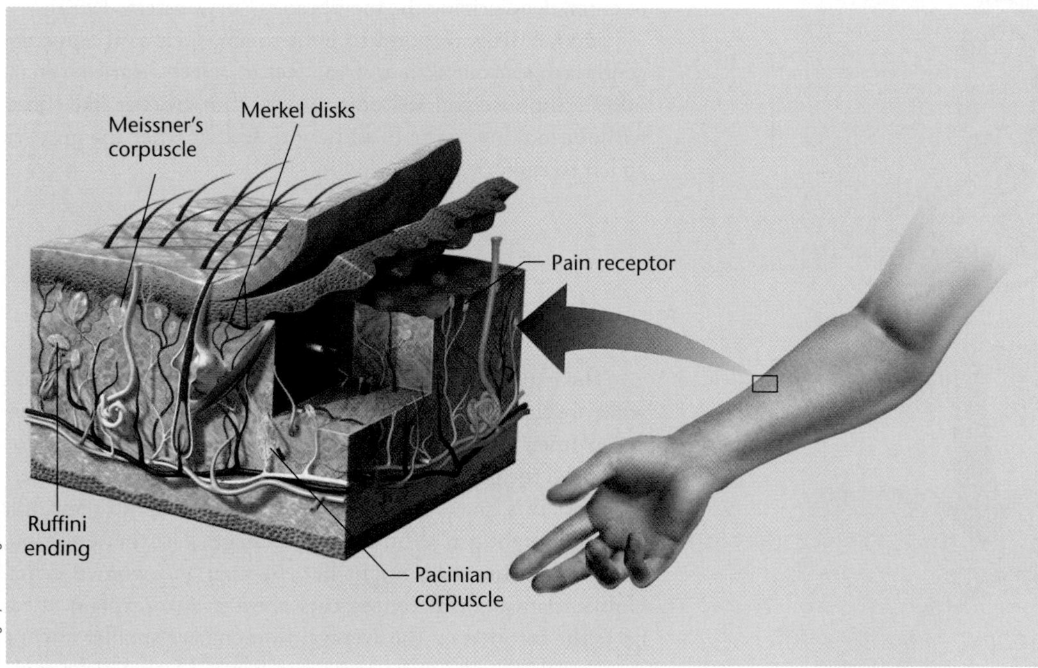

FIGURE 6.11 Sensory receptors in the skin
The receptors respond to several types of skin sensation, as described in Table 6.1.

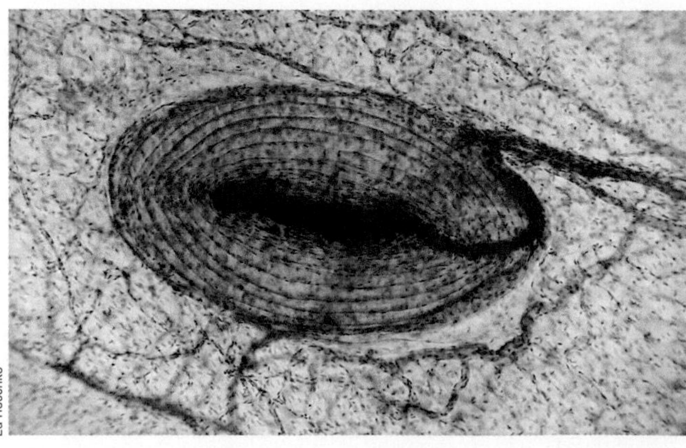

FIGURE 6.12 A Pacinian corpuscle
Pacinian corpuscles are receptors that respond best to sudden displacement of the skin or to high-frequency vibrations. The onion-like outer structure provides a mechanical support to the neuron inside it so that a sudden stimulus can bend it but a sustained stimulus cannot.

STOP & CHECK

12. How do jalapeños produce a hot sensation?

ANSWER

12. Jalapeños and other hot peppers contain capsaicin, which stimulates receptors that are sensitive to heat.

Tickle

The sensation of tickle is interesting but poorly understood. Why does it exist at all? Why do you laugh if someone rapidly fingers your armpit, neck, or the soles of your feet? Chimpanzees respond to similar sensations with bursts of panting that resemble laughter. And yet tickling is unlike humor. We love humor, but most people don't like being tickled, at least not for long. Laughing at a joke makes you more likely to laugh at the next joke. But being tickled doesn't change your likelihood of laughing at a joke (C. R. Harris, 1999).

Why can't you tickle yourself? It is for the same reason that you cannot surprise yourself. When you touch yourself, your brain compares the resulting stimulation to the "expected" stimulation and generates a weaker somatosensory response than you would experience from an unexpected touch (Blakemore, Wolpert, & Frith, 1998). Actually, some people can tickle themselves—a little—if they tickle the right side of the body with the left hand or the left side with the right hand. Also, you might be able to tickle yourself as soon as you wake up, before your brain is fully aroused. See whether you can remember to try that the next time you awaken.

Somatosensation in the Central Nervous System

Information from touch receptors in the head enters the central nervous system (CNS) through the cranial nerves. Information from receptors below the head enters the spinal cord and passes toward the brain through the 31 spinal nerves (see Figure 6.13), including 8 cervical nerves, 12 thoracic nerves, 5 lumbar nerves, 5 sacral nerves, and 1 coccygeal nerve. Each spinal nerve has a sensory component and a motor component.

Each spinal nerve *innervates* (connects to) a limited area of the body called a **dermatome** (see Figure 6.14). For example, the third thoracic nerve (T3) innervates a strip of skin just above the nipples as well as the underarm area. But the borders between dermatomes are less distinct than Figure 6.14 implies. Each dermatome overlaps one-third to one-half of the next dermatome.

The sensory information traveling through the spinal cord follows well-defined pathways toward the brain. The touch path has separate types of axons conveying deep touch and light touch (Löken, Wessberg, Morrison, McGlone, & Olausson, 2009). The pain path has sets of axons conveying sharp pain, slow burning pain, and painfully cold sensations (Abrahamsen et al., 2008; Craig, Krout, & Andrew, 2001).

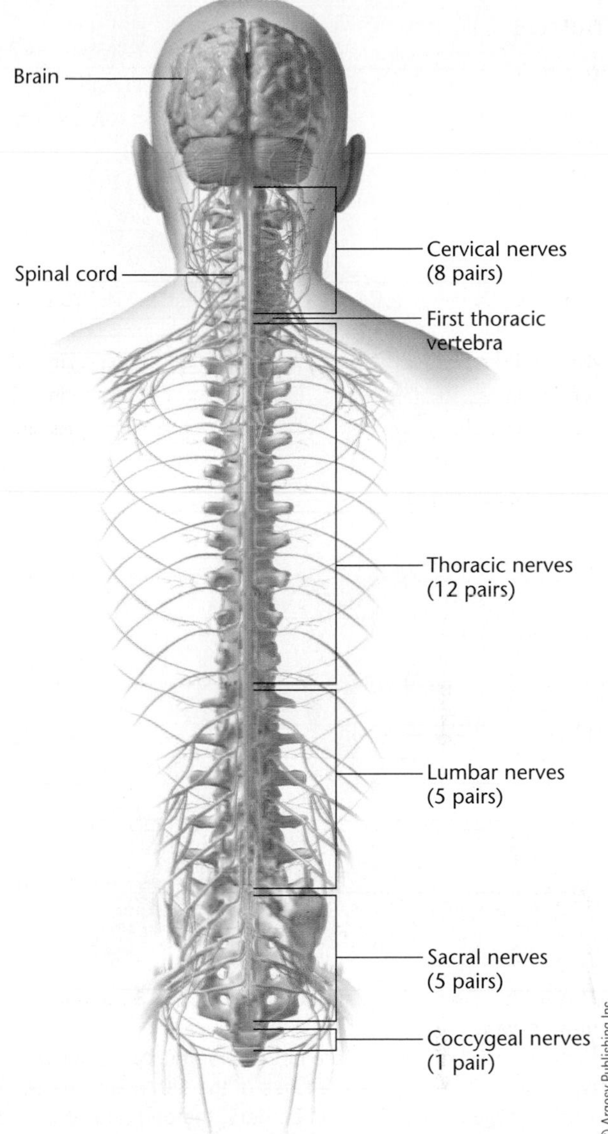

FIGURE 6.13 The human central nervous system (CNS)
Spinal nerves from each segment of the spinal cord exit through the correspondingly numbered opening between vertebrae.

That is, the nervous system codes the differences among these sensations in terms of which cells are active. One patient had an illness that destroyed all the myelinated somatosensory axons from below his nose but spared his unmyelinated axons. He still felt temperature, pain, and itch, because they depend on the unmyelinated axons. However, he had no sense of touch, which depends on myelinated axons. Curiously, if someone lightly stroked his skin, he experienced a vague sense of pleasure. Recordings from his brain indicated no arousal of his primary somatosensory cortex but increased activity in the insular cortex, which responds to light touch and other pleasant emotional experiences (Björnsdotter, Löken, Olausson, Vallbo, & Wessberg, 2009). That is, he experienced the emotional aspect of touch even though he had no conscious sensation of the touch itself.

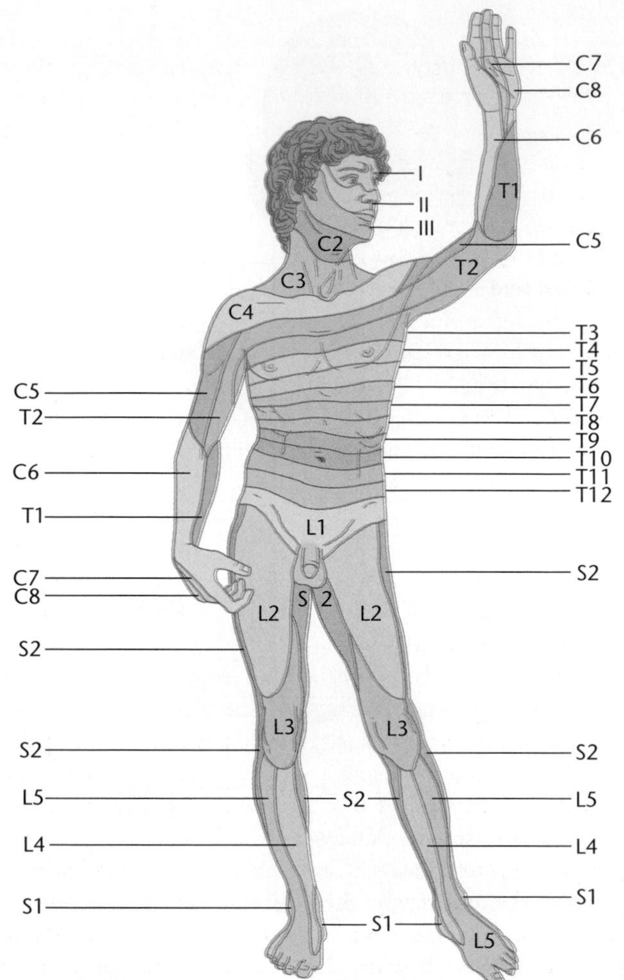

FIGURE 6.14 Dermatomes innervated by the 31 sensory spinal nerves

Areas I, II, and III of the face are not innervated by the spinal nerves but instead by three branches of the fifth cranial nerve. Although this figure shows distinct borders, the dermatomes actually overlap one another by about one-third to one-half of their width.

The various areas of the somatosensory thalamus send their impulses to different areas of the primary somatosensory cortex, located in the parietal lobe. Two parallel strips in the somatosensory cortex respond mostly to touch on the skin. Two other parallel strips respond mostly to deep pressure and movement of the joints and muscles (Kaas, 1983). In short, various aspects of body sensation remain mostly separate all the way to the cortex. Along each strip of somatosensory cortex, different subareas respond to different areas of the body. In that way, the somatosensory cortex acts as a map of body location, as shown in Figure 3.24.

The primary somatosensory cortex is essential for touch experiences. When weak, brief stimuli are applied to the fingers, people are conscious of only those that produce a certain level of arousal in the primary somatosensory cortex (Palva, Linkenkaer-Hansen, Näätäen, & Palva, 2005). If someone touches you quickly on two nearby points on the hand, you will probably have an illusory experience of a single touch midway between those two points. When that happens, the activity in the primary somatosensory cortex corresponds to that midway point (Chen, Friedman, & Roe, 2003). In other words, the activity corresponds to what you experience, not what has actually stimulated your receptors.

Damage to the somatosensory cortex impairs body perceptions. A patient with Alzheimer's disease who had damage in the somatosensory cortex had trouble putting her clothes on correctly. Also she could not point correctly in response to such directions as "show me your elbow," although she pointed correctly to objects in the room. When told to touch her elbow, her most frequent response was to feel her wrist and arm and suggest that the elbow was probably around there, somewhere (Sirigu, Grafman, Bressler, & Sunderland, 1991).

STOP & CHECK

13. In what way is somatosensation several senses instead of one?

14. What evidence suggests that the somatosensory cortex is essential for the conscious perception of touch?

ANSWERS

13. We have several types of receptors, sensitive to touch, heat, and so forth, and different parts of the somatosensory cortex respond to different kinds of skin stimulation. **14.** People are conscious of only those touch stimuli that produce sufficient arousal in the primary somatosensory cortex. Also, cells in the somatosensory cortex respond to what someone experiences, even if it is an illusion.

Pain

Pain, the experience evoked by a harmful stimulus, directs your attention toward a danger. The prefrontal cortex, which is important for attention, typically responds only briefly to any new light, sound, or touch. With pain, it continues responding as long as the pain lasts (Downar, Mikulis, & Davis, 2003).

Have you ever wondered why morphine decreases pain after surgery but not during the surgery itself? Or why some people seem to tolerate pain so much better than others? Or why even the slightest touch on sunburned skin is so painful? Research on pain addresses these and other questions.

Stimuli and Spinal Cord Paths

Pain sensation begins with the least specialized of all receptors, a bare nerve ending (see Figure 6.11). The axons carrying pain information have little or no myelin and therefore conduct impulses relatively slowly, in the range of 2 to 20 meters per second (m/s). The thicker and faster axons convey sharp pain. The thinner ones convey duller pain, such as postsurgical pain. Although pain messages reach the brain more slowly than other sensations, the brain processes pain information rapidly. Motor responses to pain are faster than motor responses to touch stimuli (Ploner, Gross, Timmerman, & Schnitzler, 2006). Mild pain releases the neurotransmitter glutamate, whereas stronger pain also releases several neuropeptides including substance P and CGRP (calcitonin gene-related peptide).

The pain-sensitive cells in the spinal cord relay information to several sites in the brain. One path extends to the ventral posterior nucleus of the thalamus and then to the somatosensory cortex, which responds to painful stimuli, memories of pain (Albanese, Duerden, Rainville, & Duncan, 2007), and signals that warn of impending pain (Babiloni et al., 2005). The spinal paths for pain and touch are parallel, but with one important difference, as illustrated in Figure 6.15: The pain pathway crosses immediately from receptors on one side of the body to a tract ascending the contralateral side of the spinal cord. Touch information travels up the ipsilateral side of the spinal cord to the medulla, where it crosses to the contralateral side. So pain and touch reach neighboring sites in the cerebral cortex. However, consider what happens to pain and touch if someone receives a cut that goes halfway through the spinal cord. You can reason out the answer in the next Stop & Check question.

STOP & CHECK

15. Suppose you suffer a cut through the spinal cord on the right side only. For the part of the body below that cut, will you lose pain sensation on the left side or the right side? Will you lose touch sensation on the left side or the right side?

ANSWER

15. You will lose pain sensation on the left side of the body because pain information crosses the spinal cord at once. You will lose touch sensation on the right side because touch pathways remain on the ipsilateral side until they reach the medulla.

Emotional Pain

Painful stimuli also activate a path that goes through the reticular formation of the medulla and then to several of the central nuclei of the thalamus, the amygdala, hippocampus, prefrontal cortex, and cingulate cortex (see Figure 6.16). These areas react not to the sensation but to its emotional associations (Hunt & Mantyh, 2001). If you watch someone—especially someone you care about—experiencing pain, you experience sympathetic pain that shows up as activity in your cingulate cortex and other cortical areas (Corradi-Dell'Acqua, Hofstetter, & Vuilleumier, 2011; Singer et al., 2004). A hypnotic suggestion to feel no pain decreases the responses in the cingulate cortex without much effect on the somatosensory cortex (Rainville, Duncan, Price, Carrier, & Bushnell, 1997). That is, someone responding to a hypnotic sensation still feels the painful sensation but reacts with emotional indifference. People with damage to the cingulate gyrus still feel pain, but it no longer distresses them (Foltz & White, 1962).

Sometimes you might say that someone hurt your feelings. After a romantic breakup, you might say you feel emotional pain. Many languages use the word for "hurt" or "pain" when referring to social disappointments and frustrations. Is it just an expression, or is emotional distress really like pain?

Hurt feelings do resemble physical pain in important regards. Imagine yourself in this experiment: You sit in front of a computer screen, playing a virtual ball-tossing game with two people your own age. You "catch" a ball and then "throw" it to one of the others, who then tosses it back to someone. Unbeknownst to you, the other two have been paid to play certain roles. At first they throw it to you a fair share of times, but before long they start passing it back and forth between the two of them, leaving you out. Not much is at stake here, but

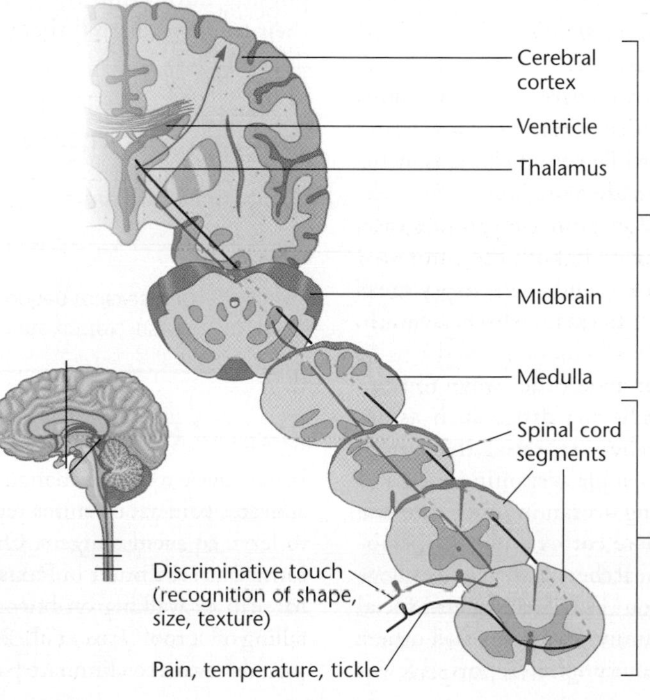

FIGURE 6.15 Spinal pathways for touch and pain
Pain information crosses to the contralateral side of the spinal cord at once, whereas touch information does not cross until the medulla. Touch and pain sensations from the right side of the body (not shown in the figure) are the mirror image of what you see here.

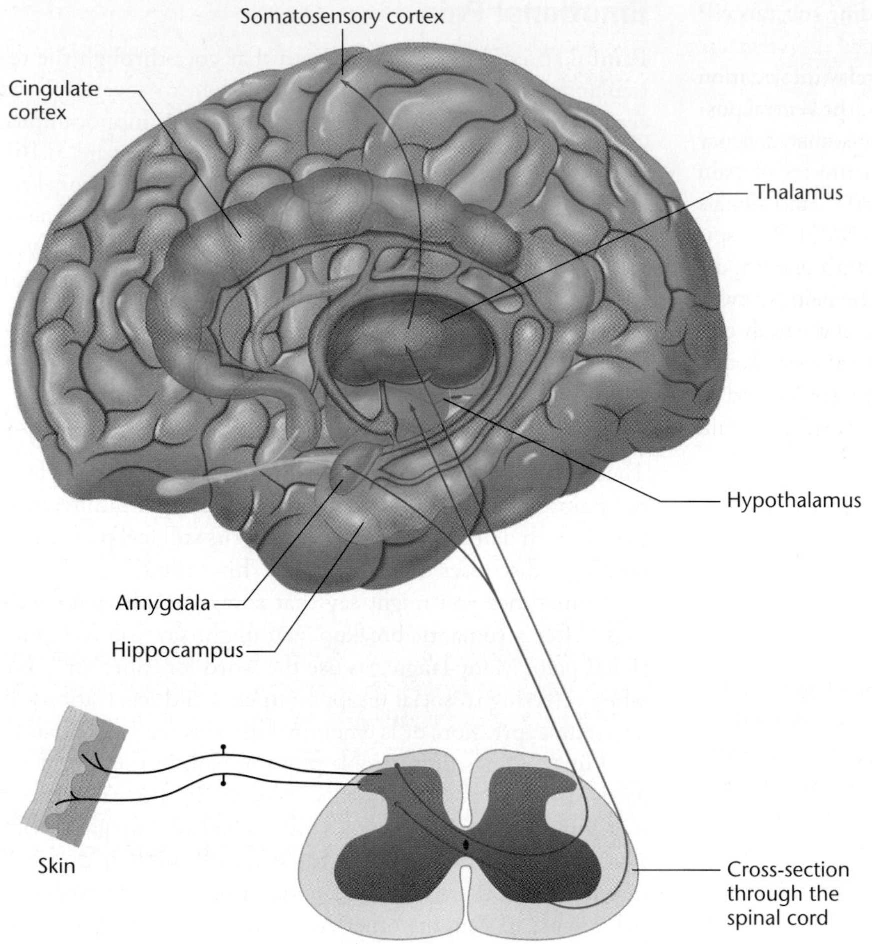

FIGURE 6.16 Pain messages in the human brain
A pathway to the thalamus, and from there to the somatosensory cortex, conveys the sensory aspects of pain. A separate pathway to the hypothalamus, amygdala, and cingulate cortex produces the emotional aspects. *Source*: Hunt & Mantyh, 2001

the experience reminds you of all those times when people left you out of a conversation, times when people didn't invite you to their parties, and so forth since early childhood. It hurts. Experimenters monitored people's brain activity during this virtual ball-throwing task and found significantly increased activity in the cingulate cortex, an area responsive to the emotional aspects of pain (Eisenberger, Lieberman, & Williams, 2003). What happens with more intense hurt feelings? Experimenters measured brain activity while young adults remembered a recent romantic breakup, made more intense by looking at a photo of the ex-boyfriend or girlfriend. In this case, the hurt feelings showed up as activity in both the emotional areas (especially the cingulate cortex) and the sensory areas responsive to physical pain (Kross, Berman, Mischel, Smith, & Wager, 2011).

Hurt feelings are like real pain in another way: You can relieve hurt feelings with pain-relieving drugs such as acetaminophen (Tylenol®)! Researchers repeated the virtual ball-tossing study, but gave some people acetaminophen and the others a placebo. Those taking acetaminophen showed much less response in the cingulate cortex and other emotionally responsive areas. The researchers also asked college students to keep daily records about hurt feelings and social pain, while some took daily acetaminophen pills and others took a placebo. Those taking acetaminophen reported fewer cases of hurt feelings, and the frequency of hurt feelings declined over days as they continued taking the pills (De Wall et al., 2010). In short, hurt feelings are a great deal like physical hurt. (And the next time someone says you hurt their feelings, just tell them to quit complaining and take a Tylenol!)

STOP&CHECK

16. In what ways are hurt feelings similar to physical pain?

ANSWER

16. Hurt feelings activate the cingulate cortex, just as physical pain does. Also, acetaminophen relieves hurt feelings.

Ways of Relieving Pain

Insensitivity to pain is dangerous. People with a gene that inactivates pain axons suffer repeated injuries and generally fail to learn to avoid dangers. One boy with this condition performed street theater in Pakistan by thrusting a knife through his arm or walking on burning coals. He died at age 14 by falling off a roof (Cox et al., 2006). Nevertheless, although we wouldn't want to eliminate pain, we want to control it.

Opioids and Endorphins

After pain alerts you to a danger, continuing pain messages are unnecessary. The brain puts the brakes on prolonged pain by **opioid mechanisms**—systems that respond to opiate drugs and similar chemicals. Candace Pert and Solomon Snyder (1973) discovered that opiates bind to receptors found mostly in the spinal cord and the **periaqueductal gray area** of the midbrain (see Figures 6.17 and 6.18).

The discovery of opiate receptors was important because it showed that opiates act on the nervous system rather than the injured tissue. Furthermore, it implied that the nervous system has its own opiate-type chemicals. The transmitters that attach to the same receptors as morphine are known as **endorphins**—a contraction of *endo*genous mor*phines*. The brain produces several types of endorphins, which relieve different types of pain, such as the pain from a cut versus the pain from a burn (Scherrer et al., 2009).

Inescapable pain is especially potent at stimulating endorphins and inhibiting further pain (Sutton et al., 1997). Presumably, the evolutionary function is that continued intense pain accomplishes nothing when escape is impossible. Endorphins are also released during sex and when you listen to thrilling music that sends a chill down your spine (A. Goldstein, 1980). Those experiences tend to decrease pain. An enjoyable meal also decreases pain sensitivity (Foo & Mason, 2009), probably by releasing dopamine rather than endorphins (Schweinhardt, Seminowicz, Jaeger, Duncan, & Bushnell, 2009).

The discovery of endorphins provided physiological details for the gate theory, proposed decades earlier by Ronald Melzack and P. D. Wall (1965). The gate theory was an attempt to explain why some people withstand pain better than others and why the same injury hurts worse at some times than others. According to the **gate theory**, spinal cord neurons that receive messages from pain receptors also receive input from touch receptors and from axons descending from the brain. These other inputs can close the "gates" for the pain messages—and they do so at least partly by releasing endorphins. You have no doubt noticed that when you have an injury, you can decrease the pain by gently rubbing the skin around it or by concentrating on something else.

Morphine does not affect large-diameter axons that convey sharp pain. For that reason, morphine is ineffective against the sharp pain of a surgeon's knife. However, morphine does block messages from thinner axons that convey slower, duller pain such as postsurgical pain (Taddese, Nah, & McCleskey, 1995).

Placebos

A **placebo** is a drug or other procedure with no pharmacological effects. In medical research, an experimental group receives a potentially active treatment and the control group receives a placebo. Placebos have little effect on most medical conditions, but they often relieve pain or depression (Hróbjartsson & Gøtzsche, 2001). People who receive placebos do not just *say* the pain decreased; scans of the brain and spinal cord also

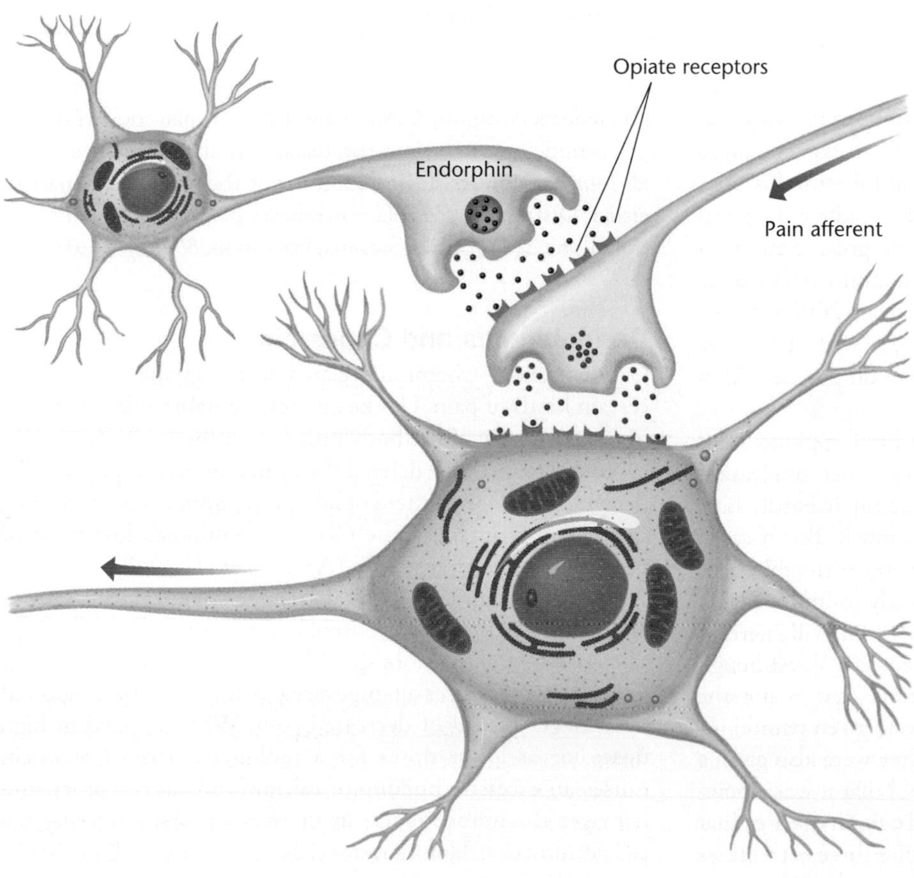

FIGURE 6.17 Synapses for pain and its inhibition
A neuron releases endorphins at presynaptic synapses, thereby inhibiting a cell conveying pain sensations.

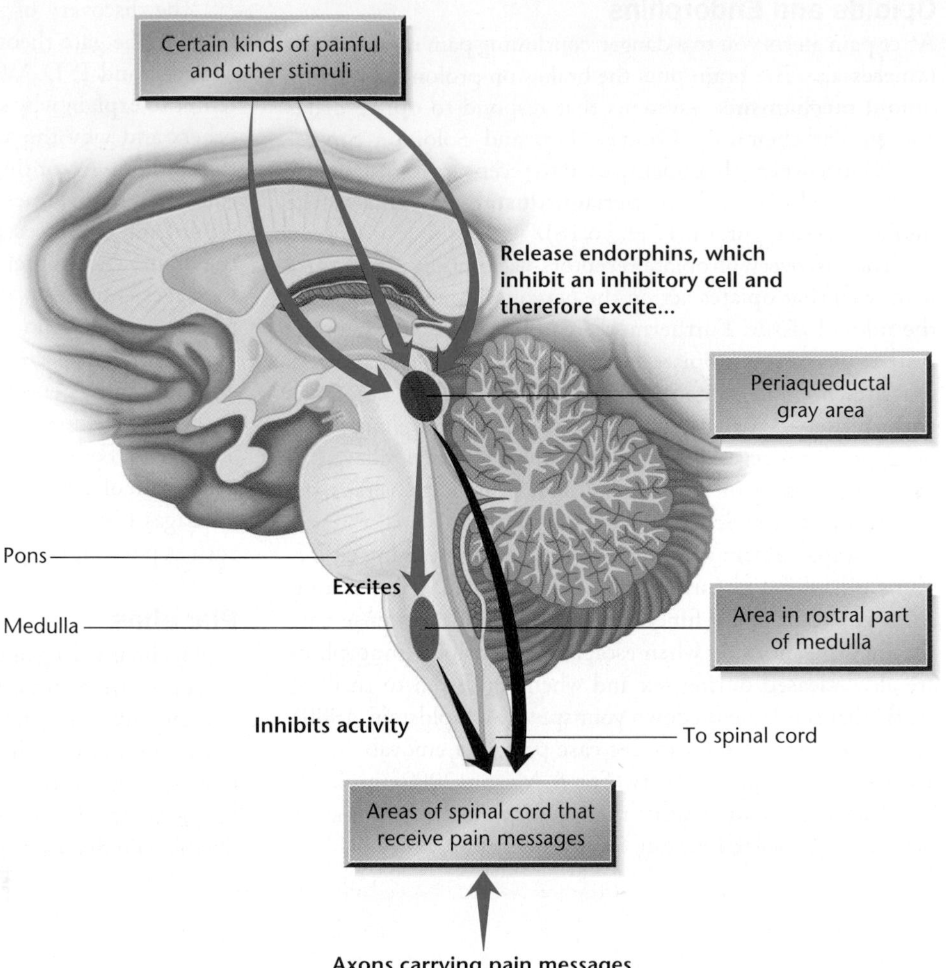

FIGURE 6.18 The periaqueductal gray area, where electrical stimulation relieves pain
Periaqueductal means "around the aqueduct," a passageway of cerebrospinal fluid between the third and fourth ventricles.

show a decreased response (Eippert, Finsterbusch, Binget, & Büchel, 2009). Conversely, if someone is told to expect pain to increase, the spinal cord response to a painful stimulus does increase (Geuter & Büchel, 2013). Placebos reduce the painful sensation but they also produce an even greater effect on the emotional response to pain, as recorded in the cingulate cortex (Petrovic, Kalso, Petersson, & Ingvar, 2002; Wager, Scott, & Zubieta, 2007). Generally, people with a positive outlook on life get more of this effect than do people with a hostile attitude (Peciña et al., 2013).

Suppose you were about to receive a brief application of heat, an injection, a colonoscopy, or some other unpleasant procedure. If you hear several other people say it hardly hurt at all, you relax and it really doesn't hurt much. But if some people say it didn't hurt and others say it was miserable, now you don't know what to expect, you are likely to find it highly painful, and your brain's response to the pain will increase (Yoshida, Seymour, Koltzenburg, & Dolan, 2013). Although placebos decrease pain partly by relaxation, that is not the whole explanation. In one study, people were given painful injections into both hands and both feet. They were also given a placebo cream on one hand or foot and told that it was a powerful painkiller. People reported decreased pain in the area that got the placebo but normal pain on the other three extremities (Benedetti, Arduino, & Amanzio, 1999). If placebos were simply producing relaxation, the relaxation should have affected all four extremities. Distraction is not the whole explanation, either. Distraction plus placebo relieves pain more than distraction alone does (Buhle, Stevens, Friedman, & Wager, 2012).

Cannabinoids and Capsaicin

Cannabinoids—chemicals related to marijuana—also block certain kinds of pain. Unlike opiates, cannabinoids act mainly in the periphery of the body rather than the CNS. Researchers found that if they deleted the cannabinoid receptors in the peripheral nervous system of laboratory animals while leaving the receptors intact in the CNS, cannabinoids lost most of their ability to decrease pain (Agarwal et al., 2007).

Another approach uses capsaicin, a chemical in jalapenos and similar peppers that stimulates receptors for heat. Capsaicin rubbed onto a sore shoulder, an arthritic joint, or other painful area produces a temporary burning sensation followed by a longer period of decreased pain. When applied in high doses, or at lower doses for a prolonged period, capsaicin causes an excessive buildup of calcium in heat receptors, and damages the mitochondria in those receptors, rendering the cell nonfunctional for a substantial time (Anand & Bley, 2011).

Do not try eating hot peppers to reduce pain in, say, your legs. The capsaicin you eat passes through the digestive system without entering the blood. Therefore, eating it will not relieve your pain—unless your tongue hurts (Karrer & Bartoshuk, 1991).

STOP&CHECK

17. Why do opiates relieve dull pain but not sharp pain?

18. How do the pain-relieving effects of cannabinoids differ from those of opiates?

ANSWERS

17. Endorphins block messages from the thinnest pain fibers, conveying dull pain, but not from thicker fibers, carrying sharp pain. **18.** Unlike opiates, cannabinoids exert most of their pain-relieving effects in the peripheral nervous system, not the CNS.

Sensitization of Pain

If you have ever been sunburned, you remember how even a light touch on that sunburned skin became dreadfully painful. Damaged or inflamed tissue, such as sunburned skin, releases histamine, nerve growth factor, and other chemicals that help repair the damage but also magnify the responses of nearby heat and pain receptors (Chuang et al., 2001; Devor, 1996; Tominaga et al., 1998). Stimulation of the facilitated pain receptors releases chemicals that cause swelling and inflammation (Chiu, von Hehn, & Woolf, 2012). Nonsteroidal anti-inflammatory drugs, such as ibuprofen, relieve pain by reducing the release of chemicals from damaged tissues (Hunt & Mantyh, 2001).

Some people suffer chronic pain long after an injury has healed. Chronic pain leads to clinical depression and to decreased activity in the prefrontal cortex and several other brain areas (Henderson et al., 2013; Seminowicz et al., 2011). As we shall see in the chapter on memory, a barrage of stimulation to a neuron can potentiate its synaptic receptors so that they respond more vigorously to the same input in the future. That mechanism is central to learning and memory, but unfortunately, pain activates the same mechanism. A barrage of painful stimuli potentiates the cells responsive to pain so that they respond more vigorously to similar stimulation in the future (Ikeda et al., 2006; Seal et al., 2009; Walters, 2009). In effect, the brain learns how to feel pain, and it gets better at it. In laboratory animals, very high doses of opiate drugs can undo this type of learning, reducing the chronic pain. However, delivering that much opiate to a human would be risky (Drdla-Schutting, Benrath, Wunderbaldinger, & Sandkühler, 2012).

Therefore, to prevent chronic pain, it helps to limit pain from the start. Suppose you are about to undergo major surgery. Which approach is best?

1. Start taking morphine before the surgery.
2. Begin morphine soon after awakening from surgery.
3. Postpone the morphine as long as possible and take as little as possible.

Perhaps surprisingly, the research supports answer 1: Start the morphine before the surgery (Coderre, Katz, Vaccarino, & Melzack, 1993). Allowing pain messages to bombard the brain during and after the surgery increases the sensitivity of the pain nerves and their receptors (Malmberg, Chen, Tonagawa, & Basbaum, 1997). People who begin taking morphine before surgery need less of it afterward.

STOP&CHECK

19. How do ibuprofen and other nonsteroidal anti-inflammatory drugs decrease pain?

20. Why is it preferable to start taking morphine before an operation instead of waiting until later?

ANSWERS

19. Anti-inflammatory drugs block the release of chemicals from damaged tissues, which would otherwise magnify the effects of pain receptors. **20.** The morphine will decrease the barrage of pain stimuli that might sensitize pain neurons.

Itch

Have you ever wondered, "What is itch, anyway? Is it a kind of pain? A kind of touch? Or something else altogether?" The answer is that it is a separate sensation. Researchers have identified special receptors for itch (Y.-G. Sun et al., 2009) and special spinal cord paths conveying itch.

You have two kinds of itch that feel about the same, although their causes are different. First, when you have mild tissue damage, such as when your skin is healing after a cut, your skin releases histamines that dilate blood vessels and produce an itching sensation. Second, contact with certain plants, especially cowhage (a tropical plant with barbed hairs), also produces itch. Antihistamines block the itch that histamines cause but not the itch that cowhage causes. Conversely, rubbing the skin with capsaicin relieves the itch that cowhage causes, but it has little effect on the itch that histamine causes (Johanek et al., 2007).

A particular spinal cord path conveys itch sensation (Andrew & Craig, 2001). Some of its axons respond to histamine itch and some to cowhage itch. Itch axons activate certain neurons in the spinal cord that produce a chemical called *gastrin-releasing peptide*. Blocking that peptide has been shown to decrease scratching in mice without affecting their responses to pain (Sun & Chen, 2007).

The itch pathways are slow to respond, and when they do, the axons transmit impulses at the unusually slow velocity of only half a meter per second. At that rate, an action potential from your foot needs 3 or 4 seconds to reach your head. Imagine the delay for a giraffe or an elephant. You might try lightly rubbing some sandpaper or rough leaves against your ankle. Note how soon you feel the touch sensation and how much more slowly you notice the itch.

Itch is useful because it directs you to scratch the itchy area and remove whatever is irritating your skin. Vigorous scratching produces mild pain, and pain inhibits itch (Davidson, Zhang, Khasabov, Simone, & Giesler, 2009). Opiates, which decrease pain, increase itch (Andrew & Craig, 2001). Morphine and other procedures that decrease pain tend to increase itch (Y. Liu et al., 2010; Moser & Giesler, 2013). This inhibitory relationship between pain and itch is clear evidence that itch is not a type of pain. Further evidence is the demonstration that blocking itch fibers does not reduce pain (Roberson et al., 2013).

This research helps explain an experience that you may have noticed. When a dentist gives you Novocain before drilling a tooth, part of your face becomes numb. An hour or more later, as the drug's effects start to wear off, you may feel an itchy sensation in the numb portion of your face. But when you try to scratch it, you feel nothing because the touch and pain sensations are still numb. Evidently, the effects of Novocain wear off faster for itch than for touch and pain axons. The fact that you can feel itch at this time is evidence that it is not just a form of touch or pain. It is interesting that scratching the partly numb skin does not relieve the itch. Evidently, scratching has to produce some pain to decrease the itch.

STOP&CHECK

21. Do opiates increase or decrease itch sensations?

22. Suppose someone suffers from constant itching. What kinds of drugs might help relieve it?

ANSWERS

21. Opiates increase itch by blocking pain sensations. (Pain decreases itch.) **22.** Two kinds of drugs might help—histamines or capsaicin—depending on the source of the itch. Theoretically, drugs that block gastrin-releasing peptide might help.

MODULE 6.2 ■ IN CLOSING

The Mechanical Senses

The mechanical senses alert you to important information, from heat to cold and from pain to gentle, pleasant touch. The system consists of many receptors, spinal paths, and brain areas. Yet we perceive all this information together—for instance, when you feel the shape and temperature of an object.

You also integrate touch with other senses. For example, suppose someone touches you so lightly that you don't feel it. If at the same time you see a picture of someone touching you in just that way, you do feel it (Serino, Pizzoferrato, & Làdavas, 2008). All the senses combine to give a unified experience.

Summary

1. The vestibular system detects the position and acceleration of the head and adjusts body posture and eye movements accordingly. **198**
2. The somatosensory system has receptors that detect several kinds of stimulation of the skin and internal tissues. **199**
3. The brain maintains several parallel somatosensory representations of the body. **202**
4. Activity in the primary somatosensory cortex corresponds to what someone is experiencing, even if it is illusory. **202**
5. Injurious stimuli excite pain receptors, which are bare nerve endings. Some pain receptors also respond to acids, heat, and capsaicin. **202**
6. Painful information takes two routes to the brain. A route leading to the somatosensory cortex conveys the sensory information, including location in the body. A route to the cingulate cortex conveys the emotional aspect. **203**
7. Hurt feelings are like pain. They activate the cingulate cortex, as physical pain does, and acetaminophen relieves both hurt feelings and physical pain. **203**
8. Opiate drugs attach to the brain's endorphin receptors. Endorphins decrease pain by blocking activity of pain neurons. Both pleasant and unpleasant experiences release endorphins. **205**
9. A harmful stimulus may give rise to a greater or lesser degree of pain depending on other current and recent stimuli. According to the gate theory of pain, other stimuli close gates in the spinal cord and block the transmission of pain. **205**
10. Placebos decrease pain, especially the emotional aspect of pain. **205**

11. Chronic pain bombards pain synapses with repetitive input, and increases their responsiveness to later stimuli through a process like learning. Morphine is most effective as a painkiller if it is used promptly. Allowing the nervous system to be bombarded with prolonged pain messages increases the later sensitivity to pain. **207**

12. Skin irritation releases histamine, which excites a spinal pathway responsible for itch. The axons of that pathway transmit impulses very slowly. They can be inhibited by pain messages. **207**

Key Terms

Terms are defined in the module on the page number indicated. They're also presented in alphabetical order with definitions in the book's Subject Index/Glossary. Interactive flash cards, audio reviews, and crossword puzzles are among the online resources available to help you learn these terms and the concepts they represent.

capsaicin **199**
dermatome **201**
endorphins **205**
gate theory **205**
opioid mechanisms **205**
Pacinian corpuscle **199**
periaqueductal gray area **205**
placebo **205**
semicircular canals **198**
somatosensory system **198**

Thought Question

How could you determine whether hypnosis releases endorphins?

MODULE 6.2 End of Module Quiz

1. Which of the following activities would be most impaired after damage to the vestibular system?
   a. Reading street signs while walking
   b. Detecting changes in the saltiness of foods
   c. Memorizing a poem and saying it aloud
   d. Tying one's shoelaces

2. Why can women on average detect thinner grooves with their fingers than men do?
   a. Most men have calluses on their fingers.
   b. On average, women's fingers are smaller.
   c. Women pay closer attention to the sense of touch than men do.
   d. The somatosensory cortex is larger in women than in men, on average.

3. To what extent does the nervous system maintain separate representations of touch, heat, pain, and other aspects of somatic sensation?
   a. Not at all. A single kind of receptor responds to all kinds of somatic sensation.
   b. The receptors vary, but all kinds of sensation merge in the spinal cord.
   c. The spinal cord maintains separate representations, but the various types merge in the cerebral cortex.
   d. Different types of sensation remain separate even in the cerebral cortex.

4. If a disease damages someone's myelinated somatosensory axons without damaging the unmyelinated axons, what kind of sensation would the person lose?
   a. Temperature
   b. Pain
   c. Itch
   d. Touch

5. Suppose you suffer a cut through the spinal cord on the left side only. For the part of the body below that cut, you will lose pain sensation on the ______ side of the body and touch sensation on the ______ side.
   a. right . . . right
   b. right . . . left
   c. left . . . left
   d. left . . . right

6. Hurt feelings activate the same brain areas as which sensation?
   a. Itch
   b. Hearing
   c. Pain
   d. Olfaction

7. Do placebos relieve pain just by relaxation? And what is the evidence?
   a. Yes. People who are already relaxed gain no benefits from placebos.
   b. Yes. Placebos are effective only for people who are high in neuroticism.
   c. No. A placebo can relieve pain in one body part without affecting another.
   d. No. People who take a placebo become even more nervous than before.

8. Which chemical relieves pain by damaging the mitochondria in heat receptors?
   a. Acetaminophen
   b. Opiates
   c. Cannabinoids
   d. Capsaicin

9. Why do many people suffer chronic pain long after an injury has healed?
   a. The brain has learned to increase its pain perception.
   b. The skin exhausts its supply of histamine.
   c. They took morphine too soon after a surgical operation.

10. Which sense has the slowest axons to the brain?
    a. Itch
    b. Olfaction
    c. Taste
    d. Hearing

11. Which type of sensation inhibits itch sensations?
    a. Olfaction
    b. Taste
    c. Pain
    d. Hearing

ANSWERS: 1a, 2b, 3d, 4d, 5b, 6c, 7c, 8d, 9a, 10a, 11c.

MODULE 6.3

The Chemical Senses

Suppose you had the godlike power to create a new species of animal, but you could equip it with only one sensory system. Which sense would you give it?

Your first impulse might be to choose vision or hearing because of their importance to humans. But an animal with only one sensory system is not going to be much like humans, is it? And if you had only vision, and never tasted anything or felt pain or touch, would you have any idea what those visual stimuli meant? To have any chance of survival, your animal will have to be small, slow, and maybe even one-celled. What sense will be most useful to such an animal?

Most theorists believe that the first sensory system of the earliest animals was a chemical sensitivity (G. H. Parker, 1922). A chemical sense enables a small animal to find food, avoid certain kinds of danger, and even locate mates.

Now imagine that you have to choose one of your senses to lose. Which one will it be? Most of us would not choose to lose vision, hearing, or touch. Losing pain sensitivity can be dangerous. You might choose to sacrifice your smell or taste.

Curious, isn't it? If an animal is going to survive with only one sense, it almost has to be a chemical sense, and yet to humans, with many other well-developed senses, the chemical senses seem dispensable. Perhaps we underestimate their importance.

Chemical Coding

Suppose you run a bakery and need to send messages to your supplier down the street. Suppose further you can communicate only by ringing three large bells on the roof of your bakery. You would have to work out a code.

One possibility would be to label the three bells: The high-pitched bell means, "I need flour." The medium-pitched bell calls for sugar, and the low-pitched bell calls for eggs. The more you need something, the faster you ring the bell. We shall call this system the *labeled-line* code because each bell has a single unchanging label. Of course, you can use it for only flour, sugar, or eggs.

Another possibility would be to set up a code that depends on a relationship among the bells. Ringing the high and medium bells equally means that you need flour. The medium and low bells together call for sugar. The high and low bells call for eggs. Ringing all three together means you need vanilla extract. Ringing mostly the high bell while ringing the other two bells slightly means you need hazelnuts. And so forth. We call this the *across-fiber pattern* code because the meaning depends on the pattern across bells.

A sensory system could theoretically use either type of coding. In a system relying on the **labeled-line principle**, each receptor would respond to a limited range of stimuli, and the meaning would depend entirely on which neurons are active. In a system relying on the **across-fiber pattern principle**, each receptor responds to a wider range of stimuli, and a given response by a given axon means little except in comparison to what other axons are doing (R. P. Erickson, 1982).

In color perception, we encountered a good example of an across-fiber pattern code. For example, the perception of green requires stronger response by the medium-wavelength cones than the long- and short-wavelength cones. In auditory pitch perception, a given receptor responds best to a certain high-frequency tone, but it also responds in phase with a number of low-frequency tones (as do all the other receptors). Each receptor also responds to white noise (static) and to various mixtures of tones. Similarly, a particular taste or smell excites some neurons more than others, but the meaning of a particular neuron's response depends on the context of what other neurons are doing. In short, nearly all perceptions depend on the pattern across an array of axons.

STOP & CHECK

23. Of the following, which one uses an across-fiber pattern code?

a. Flipping a light switch
b. Playing a piano
c. Dialing a telephone number

ANSWER

23. Dialing a telephone number is an example of an across-fiber pattern code, because the result depends on the combination of numbers. No one of its numbers by itself has a clear meaning.

Taste

Vision, hearing, and touch provide information useful for many purposes, but taste is useful for just one function, telling us whether to swallow something or spit it out. We like sweet tastes automatically, even in infancy (Booth, Higgs, Schneider, & Klinkenberg, 2010). We dislike sour and bitter tastes, although we accept them in small amounts. We like salty tastes, although people vary in how salty they like their foods. High concentrations of salt begin to taste sour and bitter as well, triggering an aversion (Oka, Butnaru, von Buchholtz, Ryba, & Zuker, 2013).

Taste results from stimulation of the **taste buds**, the receptors on the tongue. When we talk about the taste of food, we generally mean flavor, which is a combination of taste and smell. Whereas other senses remain separate throughout the cortex, taste and smell axons converge onto many of the same cells in an area called the endopiriform cortex (W. Fu, Sugai, Yoshimura, & Onoda, 2004). That convergence enables taste and smell to combine their influences on food selection.

Taste Receptors

The receptors for taste are not true neurons but modified skin cells. Like neurons, taste receptors have excitable membranes and release neurotransmitters to excite neighboring neurons, which in turn transmit information to the brain. Like skin cells, however, taste receptors are gradually sloughed off and replaced, each one lasting about 10 to 14 days (Kinnamon, 1987).

Mammalian taste receptors are in taste buds located in **papillae** on the surface of the tongue (see Figure 6.19). A given papilla may contain up to 10 or more taste buds (Arvidson & Friberg, 1980), and each taste bud contains about 50 receptor cells.

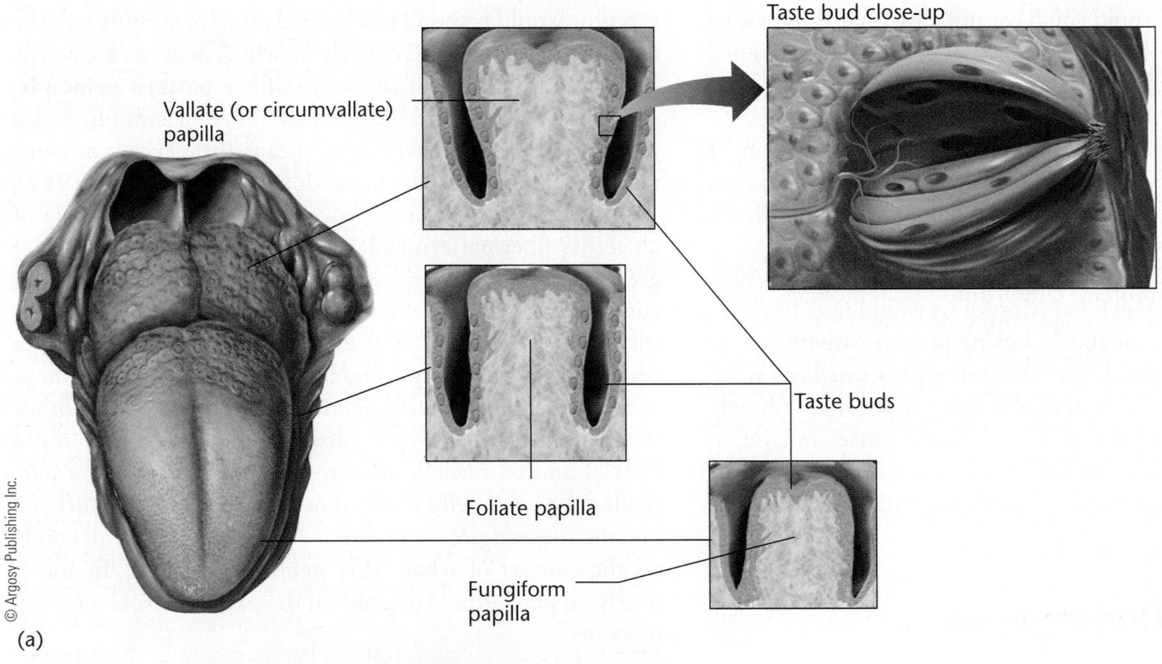

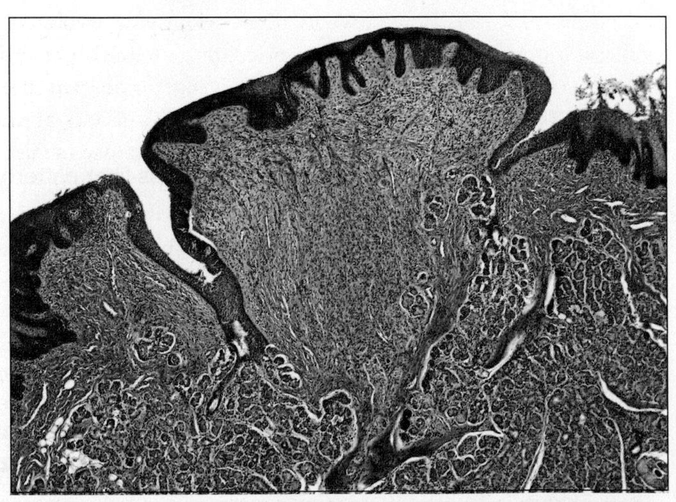

FIGURE 6.19 The organs of taste
(a) The tip, back, and sides of the tongue are covered with taste buds. Taste buds are located in papillae. (b) Photo showing cross-section of a taste bud. Each taste bud contains about 50 receptor cells.

In adult humans, taste buds lie mainly along the edge of the tongue. You can demonstrate this principle as follows: Soak a small cotton swab in sugar water, salt water, or vinegar. Then touch it lightly on the center of your tongue, not too far toward the back. If you get the position right, you will experience little or no taste. Then try it again on the edge of your tongue and notice the taste.

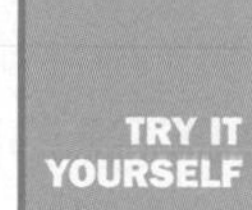

Now change the procedure a bit. Wash your mouth out with water and prepare a cotton swab as before. Touch the soaked portion to one edge of your tongue and then slowly stroke it to the center of your tongue. It will seem as if you are moving the taste to the center of your tongue. In fact, you are getting only a touch sensation from the center of your tongue. You attribute the taste you had on the side of your tongue to every other spot you stroke (Bartoshuk, 1991).

How Many Kinds of Taste Receptors?

Traditionally, people in Western society have described tastes in terms of sweet, sour, salty, and bitter. However, some tastes defy categorization in terms of these four labels (Schiffman & Erickson, 1980; Schiffman, McElroy, & Erickson, 1980). How could we determine how many kinds of taste we have?

One way to identify taste receptor types is to find procedures that alter one receptor but not others. For example, chewing a miracle berry (native to West Africa) gives little taste itself but temporarily changes sweet receptors. Miracle berries contain a protein—miraculin—that modifies sweet receptors, enabling acids to stimulate them (Bartoshuk, Gentile, Moskowitz, & Meiselman, 1974). If you try miracle berry extracts (available via the Internet), anything acidic will taste sweet in addition to its usual sour taste for the next half hour. Some people use these extracts as diet aids, so they can get sweet tastes without the calories.

But don't overdo it. A colleague and I once spent an evening experimenting with miracle berries. We drank straight lemon juice, sauerkraut juice, even vinegar. All tasted extremely sweet, but we awoke the next day with mouths full of ulcers.

Have you ever drunk orange juice just after brushing your teeth? How could something so wonderful suddenly taste so bad? Most toothpastes contain sodium lauryl sulfate, a chemical that intensifies bitter tastes and weakens sweet ones, apparently by coating the sweet receptors and preventing anything from reaching them (DeSimone, Heck, & Bartoshuk, 1980; Schiffman, 1983).

Another taste-modifying substance is an extract from the plant *Gymnema sylvestre* (R. A. Frank, Mize, Kennedy, de los Santos, & Green, 1992). Some health food and herbal remedy stores sell dried leaves of *Gymnema sylvestre*, from which you can brew a tea. (*Gymnema sylvestre* pills won't work for this demonstration.) Soak your tongue in the tea for about 30 seconds and then try tasting various substances. Salty, sour, and bitter substances taste the same as usual, but sugar becomes tasteless. Candies taste sour, bitter, or salty. (Those tastes were already present, but you barely noticed them because of the sweetness.) Curiously, the artificial sweetener aspartame (NutraSweet®) loses only some, not all, of its sweetness, implying that it stimulates an additional receptor besides the sugar receptor (Schroeder & Flannery-Schroeder, 2005). Note: Anyone with diabetes should avoid this demonstration because *Gymnema sylvestre* also alters sugar absorption in the intestines. Also note: One side effect of this demonstration is greenish bowel movements for the next few days. Don't panic if you notice that little souvenir of your experience. The overall point of these demonstrations is that we do have receptors that are sensitive to one taste or another.

Further evidence for separate types of taste receptors comes from studies of the following type: Soak your tongue for 15 seconds in a sour solution, such as unsweetened lemon juice. Then try tasting some other sour solution, such as dilute vinegar. You will find that the second solution tastes less sour than usual. Depending on the concentrations of the lemon juice and vinegar, the second solution may not taste sour at all. This phenomenon, called **adaptation**, reflects the fatigue of receptors sensitive to sour tastes. Now try tasting something salty, sweet, or bitter. These substances taste about the same as usual. In short, you experience little **cross-adaptation**—reduced response to one taste after exposure to another (McBurney & Bartoshuk, 1973). Evidently, the sour receptors are different from the other taste receptors. Similarly, you can show that salt receptors are different from the others and so forth.

Although we have long known that people have at least four kinds of taste receptors, several types of evidence suggest a fifth, glutamate, as in monosodium glutamate (MSG). The tongue has a glutamate receptor that resembles the receptors for glutamate as a neurotransmitter (Chaudhari, Landin, & Roper, 2000). Recall the idea that evolution is "thrifty": After something evolves for one purpose, it can be modified for other purposes. Glutamate tastes somewhat like unsalted chicken broth. The English language had no word for this taste, so English-speaking researchers adopted the Japanese word *umami*.

In addition to the fact that different chemicals excite different receptors, they produce different rhythms of action potentials. For other senses we assume—rightly or wrongly—that what matters is the number of action potentials per unit of time. In taste, the temporal pattern is also important, perhaps more important. Figure 6.20 shows the responses of one brain neuron to five-second presentations of sucrose (sweet), NaCl (salty), HCl (sour), and quinine (bitter). This neuron responded to all four, but with different patterns over time. For example, its response to NaCl faded rapidly, whereas the response to sucrose took longer to start and then remained steady (Di Lorenzo, Chen, & Victor, 2009). Do these patterns actually code taste experiences? Yes. Researchers stimulated rats' brain cells responsive to taste with an electrical pattern matching that for quinine. The rats backed away from whatever they were drinking at the time, reacting as if they were tasting something bitter (Di Lorenzo, Leshchinskiy, Moroney, & Ozdoba, 2009). Electrical stimulation at other temporal patterns did not cause this reaction.

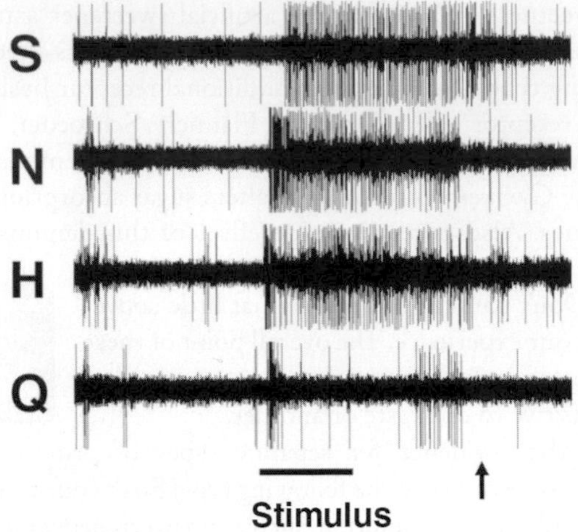

FIGURE 6.20 Responses of a cell in a rat brain to four tastes
Each taste was presented for 5 seconds, marked by the Stimulus line at the bottom. Responses persisted until the tongue was washed with water, at the point marked by the arrow. The four lines represent S = sucrose (sweet), N = NaCl, table salt (salty), H = HCl, hydrochloric acid (sour), and Q = quinine (bitter).
Source: From "Quality time: Representation of a multidimensional sensory domain through temporal coding," by P. M. Di Lorenzo, J.-Y. Chen, & J. D. Victor, 2009, *Journal of Neuroscience, 29*, pp. 9227–9238

Many bitter chemicals also trigger receptors in the nose, provoking coughing and sneezing if you happen to inhale them (Tizzano et al., 2010). That is, bitter chemicals are toxic, and the body does anything it can to expel them.

STOP&CHECK

24. Suppose you find a new, unusual-tasting food. How could you determine whether we have a special receptor for that food or whether we taste it with a combination of the other known taste receptors?

25. If someone injected into your tongue a chemical that blocks the release of second messengers, how would it affect your taste experiences?

ANSWERS

24. You could test for cross-adaptation. If the new taste cross-adapts with others, then it uses the same receptors. If it does not cross-adapt, it may have a receptor of its own. Another possibility would be to find some procedure that blocks this taste without blocking other tastes. **25.** The chemical would block your experiences of sweet, bitter, and umami but should not prevent you from tasting salty and sour.

Mechanisms of Taste Receptors

The saltiness receptor is simple. Recall that a neuron produces an action potential when sodium ions cross its membrane. A saltiness receptor, which detects the presence of sodium, simply permits sodium ions on the tongue to cross its membrane. Chemicals that prevent sodium from crossing the membrane weaken salty tastes (DeSimone, Heck, Mierson, & DeSimone, 1984; Schiffman, Lockhead, & Maes, 1983). Sour receptors detect the presence of acids (Huang et al., 2006).

Sweetness, bitterness, and umami receptors resemble the metabotropic synapses discussed in Chapter 2 (He et al., 2004; Lindemann, 1996). After a molecule binds to one of these receptors, it activates a G protein that releases a second messenger within the cell. Each of these receptors releases adenosine triphosphate (ATP) as a neurotransmitter (Taruno et al., 2013).

Bitter taste used to be a puzzle because bitter substances include a long list of dissimilar chemicals. Their only common factor is that they are to some degree toxic. What receptor could identify such a diverse set of chemicals? The answer is that we have not one bitter receptor but a family of 25 or more (Adler et al., 2000; Behrens, Foerster, Staehler, Raguse, & Meyerhof, 2007; Matsunami, Montmayeur, & Buck, 2000). Each responds to a few related compounds (Born, Levit, Niv, Meyerhof, & Belvens, 2013).

One consequence of having so many bitter receptors is that we detect a great variety of dangerous chemicals. The other is that because each type of bitter receptor is present in small numbers, we don't detect very low concentrations of bitter substances.

Taste Coding in the Brain

Information from the receptors in the anterior two-thirds of the tongue travels to the brain along the chorda tympani, a branch of the seventh cranial nerve (the facial nerve). Taste information from the posterior tongue and the throat travels along branches of the ninth and tenth cranial nerves. What do you suppose would happen if someone anesthetized your chorda tympani? You would no longer taste anything in the anterior part of your tongue, but you probably would not notice, because you would still taste with the posterior part. However, the probability is about 40 percent that you would experience taste "phantoms," analogous to the phantom limb experience discussed in Chapter 4 (Yanagisawa, Bartoshuk, Catalanotto, Karrer, & Kveton, 1998). That is, you might experience taste even when nothing was on your tongue. Evidently, the inputs from the anterior and posterior parts of your tongue interact in complex ways.

The taste nerves project to the **nucleus of the tractus solitarius (NTS)**, a structure in the medulla (Travers, Pfaffmann, & Norgren, 1986). From the NTS, information branches out, reaching the pons, the lateral hypothalamus, the amygdala, the ventral-posterior thalamus, and two areas of the cerebral cortex (Pritchard, Hamilton, Morse, & Norgren, 1986; Yamamoto, 1984). One of these areas, the somatosensory cortex, responds to the touch aspects of tongue stimulation. The other area, known as the insula, is the primary taste cortex. The insula in each hemisphere of the cortex receives input from both sides of the tongue (Stevenson, Miller, & McGrillen, 2013). A few of the major connections are illustrated in Figure 6.21. Although most cells in the NTS respond

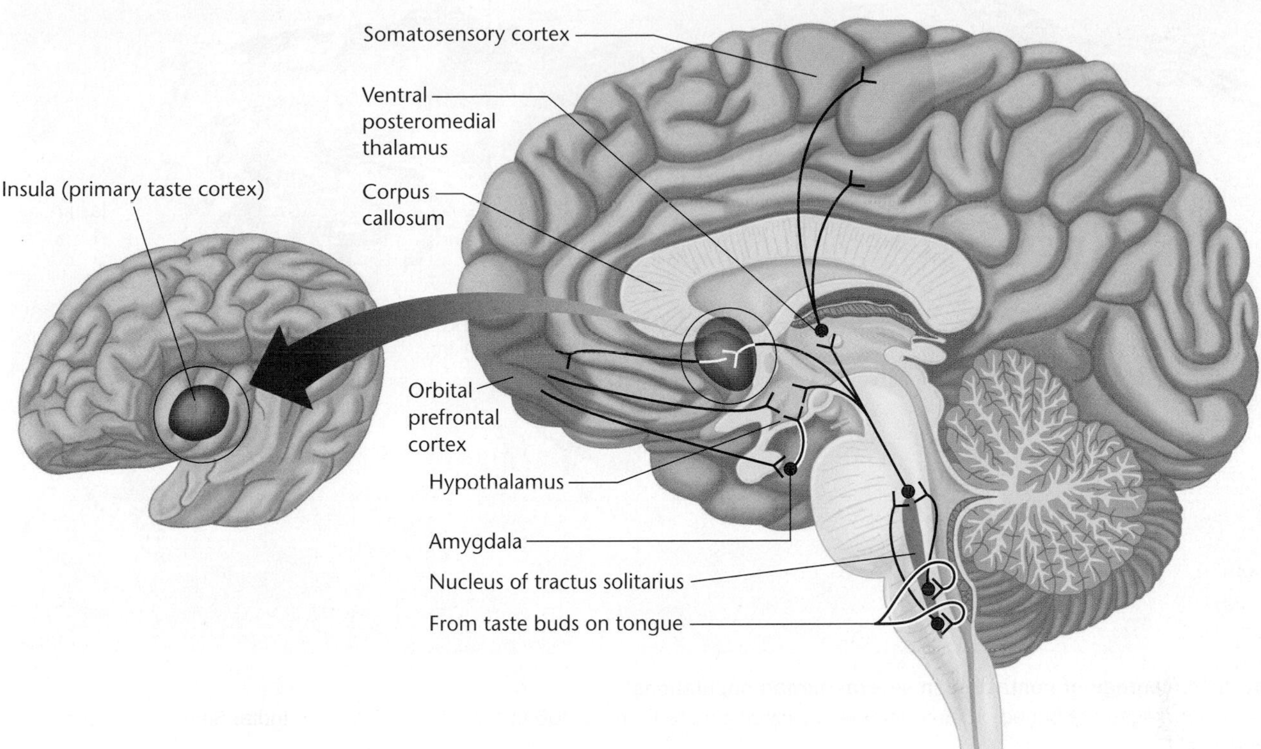

FIGURE 6.21 Major routes of impulses related to taste in the human brain
The thalamus and cerebral cortex receive impulses from both the left and the right sides of the tongue. *Source*: Based on Rolls, 1995

somewhat to a variety of tastes—sweet, sour, salty, bitter, and umami—the insula has areas in which each cell responds mainly to one type of taste, such as sweet or salty (Chen, Gabitto, Peng, Ryba, & Zuker, 2011; Roussin, D'Agostino, Fooden, Victor, & DiLorenzo, 2012).

Variations in Taste Sensitivity

Taste sensitivity varies among animal species (Yarmolinsky, Zuker, & Ryba, 2009). Cats, hyenas, seals, and sea lions have no sweetness receptors (Jiang et al., 2012). Being carnivores (meat eaters), they never choose their food by sweetness. If you see a cat lapping up milk, it is going for the proteins or fats, not the sweetness. Dolphins have few taste receptors of any type (Jiang et al. 2012). They eat only fish, which they swallow whole, and so they have little need for the sense of taste. Over evolutionary time they have decreased their production of functional taste receptors.

Individual people also vary in their taste sensitivity. A demonstration sometimes used in biology laboratory classes is to taste phenylthiocarbamide (PTC) or 6-*n*-propylthiouracil (PROP). Most people—called tasters—taste low concentrations as bitter, but other people—*nontasters*—fail to taste it except at high concentrations. One gene controls most of the variance, although other genes contribute as well (Kim et al., 2003).

Researchers have collected extensive data about the percentage of nontasters in different populations, as shown in Figure 6.22 (Guo & Reed, 2001). The figure shows no obvious relationship between tasting PTC and cuisine. For example, nontasters are common in India, where the food is spicy, and also in Britain, where it is relatively bland.

In the 1990s, researchers discovered that people with low sensitivity to bitter substances are also less sensitive than average to other tastes. People at the opposite extreme, known as **supertasters**, are highly sensitive to all tastes and mouth sensations (Drewnowski, Henderson, Shore, & Barratt-Fornell, 1998). On average, supertasters like their favorite foods more than other people, and avoid their least favorite foods more. Most of them avoid strong-tasting or spicy foods. However, culture and familiarity exert large effects on people's food preferences. Consequently, even after you think about how much you do or do not like strongly flavored foods, you cannot confidently identify yourself as a supertaster, taster, or nontaster.

The difference between tasters and supertasters depends on the number of *fungiform papillae* near the tip of the tongue, with supertasters having the largest number (Hayes, Bartoshuk, Kidd, & Duffy, 2008). (See Figure 6.23.) That anatomical difference depends partly on genetics but also on age, hormones, and other influences. Women's taste sensitivity rises and falls with their monthly hormone cycles and reaches its maximum during early pregnancy, when estradiol levels are high (Prutkin et al., 2000). That tendency is probably adaptive: During pregnancy, a woman needs to be more careful than usual to avoid harmful foods.

If you would like to classify yourself as a taster, nontaster, or supertaster, follow the instructions in Table 6.2.

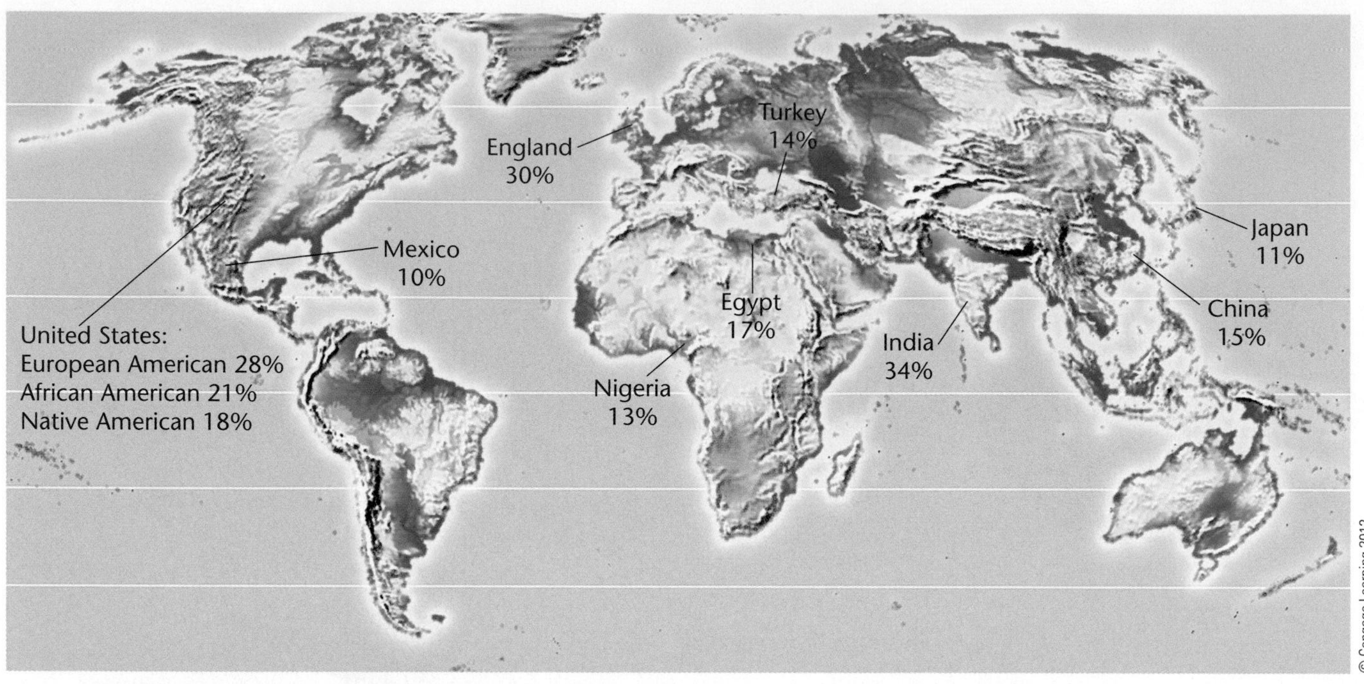

FIGURE 6.22 Percentage of nontasters in several human populations
Most of the percentages are based on large samples, including more than 31,000 in Japan and 35,000 in India. *Source*: Based on Guo & Reed, 2001

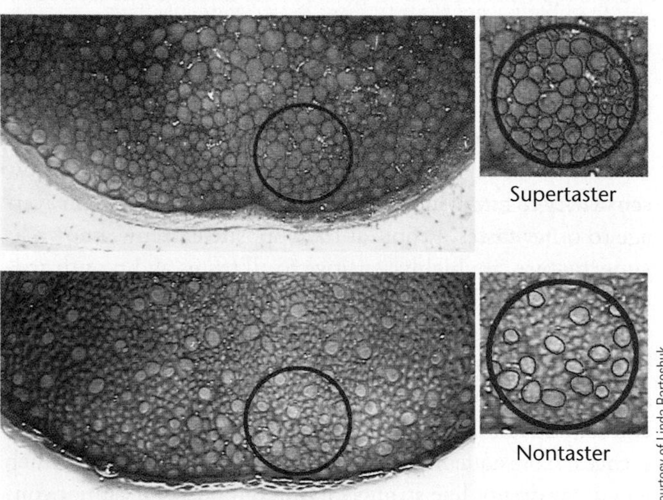

FIGURE 6.23 Fungiform papillae on the human tongue
People with a greater density of papillae (top) are supertasters, with strong reactions to intense tastes. People with fewer papillae are tasters or nontasters (bottom).

STOP&CHECK

26. What causes supertasters to be more sensitive to tastes than other people are?

ANSWER

26. They have more taste buds near the tip of the tongue.

TABLE 6.2 Are You a Supertaster, Taster, or Nontaster?

Equipment: 1/4-inch hole punch, small piece of wax paper, cotton swab, blue food coloring, flashlight, and magnifying glass

Make a 1/4-inch hole with a standard hole punch in a piece of wax paper. Dip the cotton swab in blue food coloring. Place the wax paper on the tip of your tongue, just right of the center. Rub the cotton swab over the hole in the wax paper to dye a small part of your tongue. With the flashlight and magnifying glass, have someone count the number of pink, unstained circles in the blue area. They are your fungiform papillae. Compare your results to the following averages:

Supertasters:	25 papillae
Tasters:	17 papillae
Nontasters:	10 papillae

Olfaction

Olfaction, the sense of smell, is the response to chemicals that contact the membranes inside the nose. For most mammals, olfaction is critical for finding food and mates and for avoiding dangers. For example, rats and mice show an immediate, unlearned avoidance of the smells of cats, foxes, and other predators. Mice that lack certain olfactory receptors fail to avoid, as illustrated in Figure 6.24 (Kobayakawa et al., 2007). Nonrodent species have those same olfactory receptors without the built-in avoidance response (Dewan, Pacifico, Zhan, Rinberg, & Bozza, 2013).

Photo by Ko & Reiko Kobayakawa

FIGURE 6.24 The result of losing one type of olfactory receptor Normal mice innately avoid the smell of cats, foxes, and other predators. This cat had just finished a large meal. *Source:* Kobayakawa et al., 2007

Consider also the star-nosed mole and water shrew, two species that forage along the bottom of ponds and streams for worms, shellfish, and other invertebrates. We might assume that olfaction would be useless under water. However, these animals exhale tiny air bubbles onto the ground and then inhale them again. By doing so, they can follow an underwater trail well enough to track their prey (Catania, 2006).

Terry Whittaker/Alamy

A water shrew

We marvel at feats like this and at the ability of a bloodhound to find someone by following an olfactory trail through a forest. We assume that we could never do anything like that. Of course, we cannot follow an olfactory trail while standing upright, with our noses far above the ground! But what if you got down on your hands and knees and put your nose to the ground? Researchers blindfolded 32 young adults, made them wear gloves, and then asked them to try to follow a scent trail across a field. The scent was chocolate oil. (They decided to use something that people care about.) Most of the participants succeeded and improved their performance with practice. Figure 6.25 shows one example (Porter et al., 2007). So

FIGURE 6.25 A person following a scent trail Most people successfully followed a trail with only their nose to guide them. From: *Nature Neuroscience, 10*, pp. 27-29, "Mechanisms of scent-tracking in humans;" J. Porter et. al, 2007

our olfaction is better than we might guess, if we give it a fair chance (even though bloodhounds are still much better).

Olfaction is especially important for our food selection. Much of what we call "taste" or "flavor" is really the odor of the food. Try holding your nose while you eat, and notice how much flavor you lose.

Olfaction also plays an important role in social behavior. You may have heard the expression "smell of fear," and research supports that idea. Experimenters collected sweat from young men's armpits while the men watched videos that evoked fear, disgust, or no emotion. Later the researchers recorded facial expressions by young women who sniffed the samples. Women smelling the fear samples showed a mild fear expression and those who smelled the disgust samples looked disgusted. Those smelling the neutral samples showed little or no expression (de Groot, Smeets, Kaldewaij, Duijndam, & Semin, 2012). Evidently smells give us a clue to how someone else is feeling.

If you were exposed to the smells of other people (with no other information about them), and you rated their desirability as a potential romantic partner, you would probably prefer people who smell a little different from yourself and your family members (Havlicek & Roberts, 2009). Avoiding a mate who smells like your brother or sister reduces the chance of inbreeding. It also increases the probability that your children will have a good variety of immunities, because chemicals from the immune system contribute to body odors. Curiously, when women start taking contraceptive pills, their preference for a different-smelling mate decreases (Roberts, Gosling, Carter, & Petrie, 2008). One speculation is that women who cannot become pregnant at that moment no longer face the risk of inbreeding.

Olfactory Receptors

The neurons responsible for smell are the **olfactory cells** that line the olfactory epithelium in the rear of the nasal air passages (see Figure 6.26). In mammals, each olfactory cell has cilia (threadlike dendrites) that extend from the cell body into the mucous surface of the nasal passage. Olfactory receptors are located on the cilia.

How many kinds of olfactory receptors do we have? Researchers answered the analogous question for color vision in the 1800s but took much longer for olfaction. Linda Buck and Richard Axel (1991) identified a family of proteins in olfactory receptors, as shown in Figure 6.27. Like metabotropic neurotransmitter receptors, each of these proteins traverses the cell membrane seven times and responds to a chemical outside the cell (here an odorant molecule instead of a neurotransmitter) by triggering changes in a G protein inside the cell. The G protein then provokes chemical activities that lead to an action potential. The best estimate is that humans have several hundred olfactory receptor proteins, whereas rats and mice have about a thousand types (X. Zhang & Firestein, 2002). Correspondingly, rats distinguish among odors that seem the same to humans (Rubin & Katz, 2001).

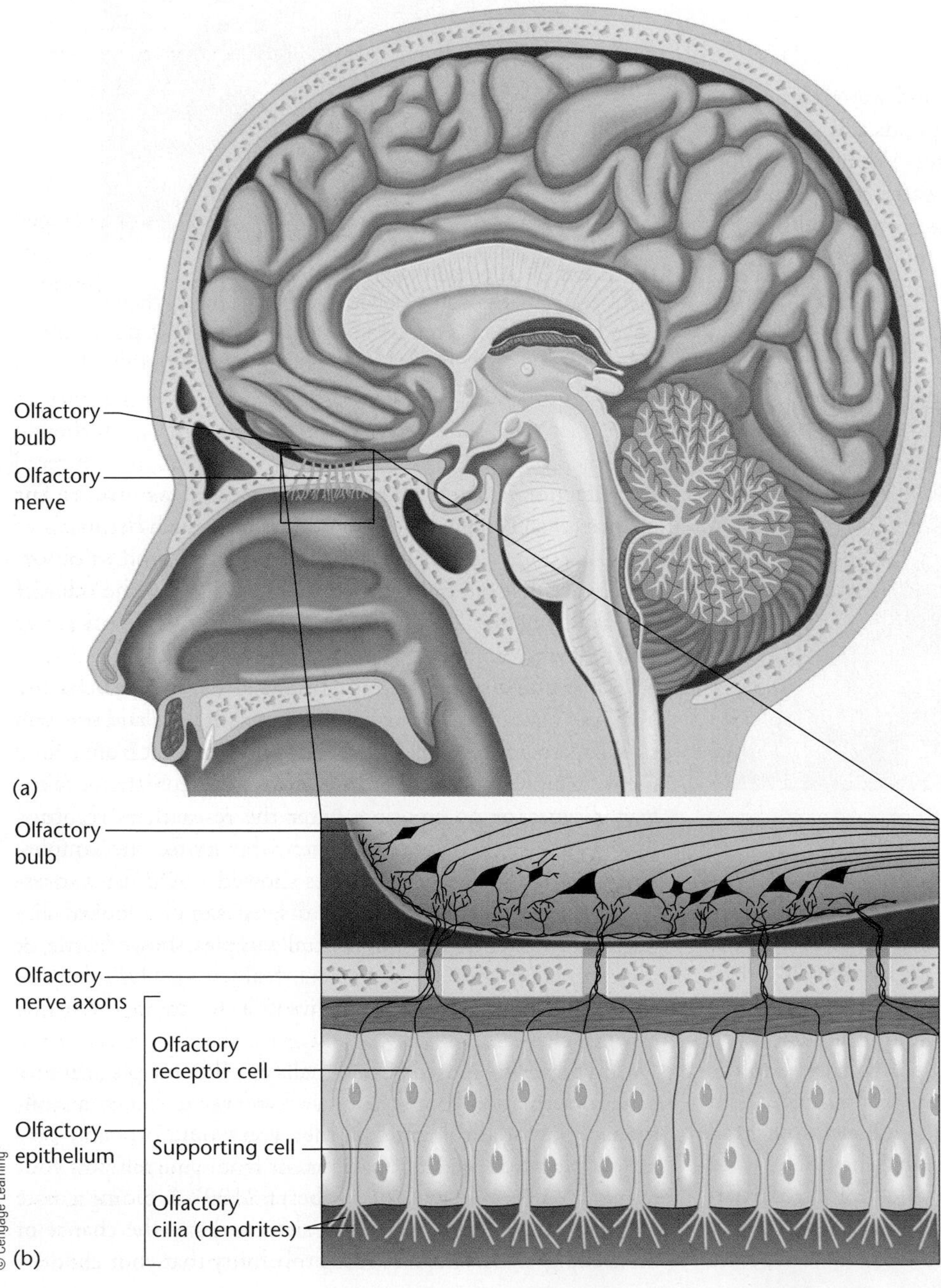

FIGURE 6.26 Olfactory receptors
(a) Location of receptors in nasal cavity. (b) Close-up of olfactory cells.

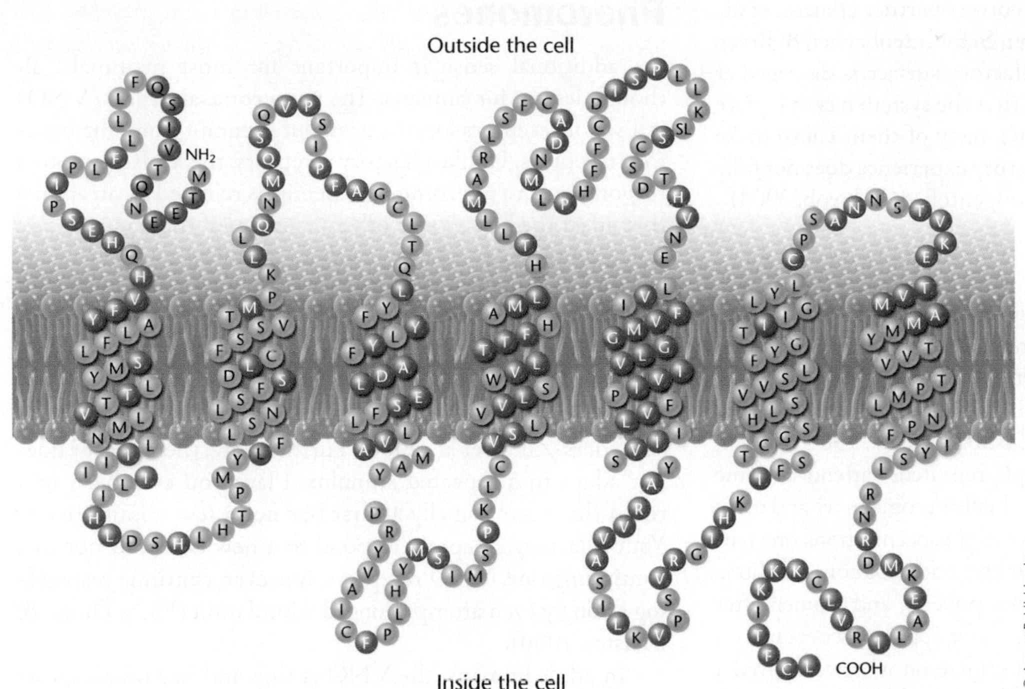

FIGURE 6.27 One of the olfactory receptor proteins
This protein resembles the synaptic receptor protein in Figure 2.17. It responds to a chemical outside the cell and triggers activity of a G protein inside the cell. Different olfactory receptors differ slightly in their structure. Each little circle in this diagram represents one amino acid of the protein. The light green circles represent amino acids that are the same in most of the olfactory receptor proteins. The dark green circles represent amino acids that vary. Reprinted from *Cell, 65*, Buck & Axel, A novel multigene family may encode odorant receptors: A molecular basis for odor recognition, pp. 175–187. (7), 1991 with permission from Elsevier

Although some olfactory receptors respond to a wide range of chemicals, most respond to just a few chemicals with similar structures. Each odor stimulates a small population of receptors (Nara, Saraiva, Ye, & Buck, 2011).

STOP&CHECK

27. In what way do olfactory receptors resemble metabotropic neurotransmitter receptors?

ANSWER

27. Like metabotropic neurotransmitter receptors, an olfactory receptor acts through a G protein that triggers further events within the cell.

Implications for Coding

We have only three kinds of cones and five kinds of taste receptors, so researchers were surprised to find so many kinds of olfactory receptors. That diversity makes possible narrow specialization of functions. To illustrate, because we have only three kinds of cones, each cone contributes to every color perception. Each olfactory receptor responds to only a few stimuli. The response of one receptor might mean, "a fatty acid with a straight chain of three to five carbon atoms." The response of another might mean, "either a fatty acid or an aldehyde with a straight chain of five to seven carbon atoms" (Araneda, Kini, & Firestein, 2000; Imamura, Mataga, & Mori, 1992; Mori, Mataga, & Imamura, 1992). The combined activity of those two receptors identifies a chemical precisely.

The question may have occurred to you, "Why did evolution go to the bother of designing so many olfactory receptor types? After all, color vision gets by with just three types of cones." The main reason is that light energy can be arranged along a single dimension, wavelength. Olfaction processes airborne chemicals that do not range along a single continuum.

Messages to the Brain

When an olfactory receptor is stimulated, its axon carries an impulse to the olfactory bulb (see Figure 3.12). Although the receptors sensitive to a particular chemical are scattered haphazardly in the nose, their axons find their way to the same target cells in the olfactory bulb, such that chemicals of similar smell excite neighboring areas, and chemicals of different smell excite more separated areas (Uchida, Takahashi, Tanifuji, & Mori, 2000). Also, pleasant odors tend to group together, and unpleasant odors together (Lapid et al., 2011). That is, cells of the olfactory bulb code the identity of smells.

The olfactory bulb sends axons to the olfactory area of the cerebral cortex. A complex substance such as a food activates a scattered population of cells (Lin, Shea, & Katz, 2006; Rennaker, Chen, Ruyle, Sloan, & Wilson, 2007). Many cells give their greatest response to a particular kind of food, such as berries or melons (Yoshida & Mori, 2007). As in the olfactory bulb, chemicals that smell similar to us evoke activity in neighboring cells (Howard, Plailly, Grueschow, Haynes, & Gottfried, 2009).

Olfactory receptors are vulnerable to damage because they are exposed to the air. Unlike your receptors for vision and hearing, which remain with you for a lifetime, an olfactory receptor has an average survival time of just over a month. At that point, a stem cell matures into a new olfactory cell in the same location as the first and expresses the same receptor protein (Nef, 1998). Its axon then has to find its way to the correct target in the olfactory bulb. Each olfactory neuron axon contains copies of its olfactory receptor protein, which it uses like an identification card to find its correct partner (Barnea et al., 2004; Strotmann, Levai, Fleischer, Schwarzenbacher, & Breer, 2004). However, if the entire olfactory surface is damaged at once by a blast of toxic fumes so that the system has to replace all the receptors at the same time, many of them fail to make the correct connections, and olfactory experience does not fully recover (Iwema, Fang, Kurtz, Youngentob, & Schwob, 2004).

Individual Differences

In olfaction, as with almost anything else, people differ. On the average, women detect odors more readily than men, and the brain responses to odors are stronger in women than in men. Those differences occur at all ages and in all cultures that researchers have tested (Doty, Applebaum, Zusho, & Settle, 1985; Yousem et al., 1999). In addition, if people repeatedly attend to some faint odor, young adult women gradually become more and more sensitive to it, until they can detect it in concentrations one ten-thousandth of what they could at the start (Dalton, Doolittle, & Breslin, 2002). Men, girls before puberty, and women after menopause do not show that effect, so it apparently depends on female hormones. We can only speculate on why we evolved a connection between female hormones and odor sensitization.

Also, consider this surprising study: Through the wonders of bioengineering, researchers deleted a gene that controls a channel through which most potassium passes in certain neurons of the olfactory bulb. Potassium, as discussed in Chapter 1, leaves a neuron after an action potential, thereby restoring the resting potential. With no particular hypothesis in mind, researchers tested what would happen if they deleted that potassium channel in mice.

Ordinarily, deleting any gene leads to deficits, and deleting an important gene is often fatal. Imagine the researchers' amazement when they found that the mice lacking this potassium channel had a greatly enhanced sense of smell. In fact, you could say they have a superpower: They detect faint smells, less than one-thousandth the minimum that other mice detect. Their olfactory bulb has an unusual anatomy, with more numerous but smaller clusters of neurons (Fadool et al., 2004). Apparently, deleting this potassium gene leads to compensatory enhancement of certain sodium channels that enhance odor sensitivity (Lu, Das, Fadool, & Kaczmarek, 2010). Presumably the mice are deficient in some other way, or evolution would have deleted this gene long ago. Still, it is a remarkable example of how a single gene can make a huge difference.

STOP & CHECK

28. What is the mean life span of an olfactory receptor?

29. What kind of person becomes most sensitive to a smell after sniffing it repeatedly?

ANSWERS

28. Most olfactory receptors survive a little more than a month before dying and being replaced. **29.** Young adult women become highly sensitive to a smell after sniffing it repeatedly.

Pheromones

An additional sense is important for most mammals, although less so for humans. The **vomeronasal organ (VNO)** is a set of receptors located near, but separate from, the olfactory receptors. Unlike olfactory receptors, the VNO receptors respond only to **pheromones**, chemicals released by an animal that affect the behavior of other members of the same species. For example, if you have ever had a female dog that wasn't neutered, whenever she was in her fertile (estrus) period, even though you kept her indoors, your yard attracted every male dog in the neighborhood that was free to roam.

Each VNO receptor responds to just one pheromone, in concentrations as low as one part in a hundred billion (Leinders-Zufall et al., 2000). Furthermore, the receptor does not adapt to a repeated stimulus. Have you ever been in a room that seems smelly at first but not a few minutes later? Your olfactory receptors respond to a new odor but not to a continuing one. VNO receptors, however, continue responding strongly even after prolonged stimulation (Holy, Dulac, & Meister, 2000).

In adult humans, the VNO is tiny and has no receptors (Keverne, 1999; Monti-Bloch, Jennings-White, Dolberg, & Berliner, 1994). It is vestigial—that is, a leftover from our evolutionary past. Nevertheless, part of the human olfactory mucosa contains receptors that resemble other species' pheromone receptors (Liberles & Buck, 2006; Rodriguez, Greer, Mok, & Mombaerts, 2000).

The behavioral effects of pheromones apparently occur unconsciously. That is, people react to certain chemicals in human skin even when they describe them as odorless. The smell of a sweaty woman increases a man's testosterone secretions, especially if the woman was near her time of ovulation (Miller & Maner, 2010). This effect is stronger for heterosexual men than for homosexual men (Savic, Berglund, & Lindström, 2005). The smell of a sweaty man produces several effects on women, although we have no evidence of increased sexual arousal. The smell of a sweaty man activates a woman's hypothalamus, but it does so in men also (Burke, Veltman, Gerber, Hummel, & Bakker, 2012). It also causes women to increase their release of cortisol, a stress hormone (Wyart et al., 2007). Evidently a man reacts to a sweaty woman as a sex signal, and a woman reacts to a sweaty man as a potential danger signal.

The best-documented effect of a human pheromone relates to the timing of women's menstrual cycles. Women who spend much time together find that their menstrual cycles become more synchronized, unless they are taking birth-control pills (McClintock, 1971; Weller, Weller, Koresh-Kamin, & Ben-Shoshan, 1999; Weller, Weller, & Roizman, 1999). To test whether pheromones are responsible for the synchronization, researchers exposed young volunteer women to the underarm secretions of a donor woman. In two studies, most of the women exposed to the secretions became synchronized to the donor's menstrual cycle (Preti, Cutler, Garcia, Huggins, & Lawley, 1986; Russell, Switz, & Thompson, 1980).

Another study dealt with the phenomenon that a woman in an intimate relationship with a man tends to have more regular menstrual periods than women not in an intimate relationship. According to one hypothesis, the man's pheromones promote this regularity. In the study, young women who were not sexually active were exposed daily to a man's underarm secretions. (Getting women to volunteer for this study wasn't easy.) Gradually, over 14 weeks, most of these women's menstrual periods became more regular than before (Cutler et al., 1986). In short, human body secretions probably do act as pheromones, although the effects are more subtle than in most other mammals.

STOP&CHECK

30. What is a major difference between olfactory receptors and those of the vomeronasal organ?

ANSWER

30. Olfactory receptors adapt quickly to a continuous odor, whereas receptors of the vomeronasal organ continue to respond. Also, vomeronasal sensations are apparently capable of influencing behavior even without being consciously perceived.

Synesthesia

Finally, let's consider something that is not one sense but a combination: **Synesthesia** is the experience some people have in which stimulation of one sense evokes a perception of that sense and another one also. For example, someone might perceive the letter J as green or say that each taste feels like a particular shape on the tongue (Barnett et al., 2008). In the words of one person, "To me, the taste of beef is dark blue. The smell of almonds is pale orange. And when tenor saxophones play, the music looks like a floating, suspended coiling snake-ball of lit-up purple neon tubes" (Day, 2005, p. 11).

Various studies attest to the reality of synesthesia. People reporting synesthesia have increased amounts of gray matter in certain brain areas and altered connections to other areas (Jäncke, Beeli, Eulig, & Hänggi, 2009; Rouw & Scholte, 2007; Weiss & Fink, 2009). People who perceive colors in letters and numbers have increased connections between the brain areas responding to colors and those responding to letters and numbers (Tomson, Narayan, Allen, & Eagleman, 2013). They also show behavioral characteristics that would be hard to pretend. Try to find the 2 among the 5s in each of the following displays:

555555555555	555555555555	555555555555
555555555555	555555555555	552555555555
555555525555	555555555555	555555555555
555555555555	555555555525	555555555555

One person with synesthesia was able to find the 2 consistently faster than other people, explaining that he just looked for a patch of orange! However, he was slower than other people to find an 8 among 6s because both 8 and 6 look blue to him (Blake, Palmeri, Marois, & Kim, 2005). Another person had trouble finding an A among 4s because both look red but could easily find an A among 0s because 0 looks black (Laeng, Svartdal, & Oelmann, 2004). Oddly, however, someone who sees the letter P as yellow had no trouble finding it when it was printed in black ink on a yellow page. In some way, he sees the letter both in its real color (black) *and* its synesthetic color (Blake et al., 2005).

In another study, people were asked to identify as quickly as possible the shape formed by the less common character in a display like this:

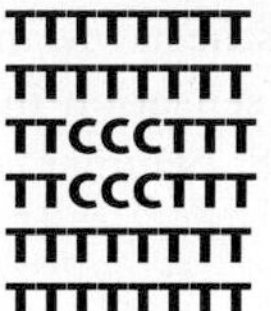

Here, the correct answer is "rectangle," the shape formed by the Cs. People who perceive C and T as different colors find the rectangle faster than the average for other people. However, they do not find it as fast as other people would find the rectangle in this display, where the Cs really are in color:

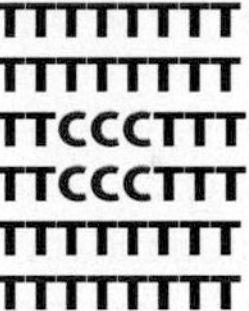

What causes synesthesia? It clusters in families, suggesting a genetic predisposition (Barnett et al., 2008), and it frequently occurs in the same families as people with absolute pitch, suggesting that the two conditions share their genetic predisposition (Gregerson et al., 2013). However, obviously people are not born with a letter-to-color or number-to-color synesthesia. (No one is born knowing the letters of the alphabet.) In some cases, we see where people learned their associations. Researchers found 10 people with synesthesia whose associations matched or nearly matched the colors of Fisher-Price refrigerator magnets they had used as children, such as red A, yellow C, and green D (Witthoft & Winawer, 2013). Only a small percentage of children who play with these magnets develop synesthesia, and most people with synesthesia have different associations, so the toys represent only one part of the explanation.

When people misperceive a stimulus—as in an illusion—the synesthetic experience corresponds to what the person *thought* the stimulus was, not what it actually was (Bargary, Barnett, Mitchell, & Newell, 2009). This result implies that the phenomenon occurs in the cerebral cortex, not in the receptors or their first connections to the nervous system. Furthermore, for some people, the idea of a word triggers a synesthetic experience before they have thought of the word itself. One person who could not think of "castanets" said it was on the tip of the tongue . . . not sure what the word was, but it tasted like tuna (Simner & Ward, 2006). One man with color vision deficiency reports synesthetic colors that he does not see in real life. He calls them "Martian colors" (Ramachandran, 2003). Evidently, his brain can see all the colors, even though his cones cannot send the messages.

One hypothesis is that axons from one cortical area branch into another cortical area. This explanation does apply to at least some cases. One woman suffered damage to the somatosensory area of her right thalamus. Initially she was, as expected, insensitive to touch in her left arm and hand. Over a year and a half, she gradually recovered part of her touch sensation. However, during that period, the somatosensory area of her right cortex was receiving little input. Some axons from her auditory system invaded the somatosensory cortex. As a result, she developed an unusual auditory-to-touch synesthesia. Many sounds cause her to feel an intense tingling sensation in her left arm and hand (Beauchamp & Ro, 2008; Naumer & van den Bosch, 2009).

STOP & CHECK

31. What evidence indicates that people learn their synesthetic associations, at least in some cases?

32. If someone reports seeing a particular letter in color, in what way is it different from a real color?

ANSWERS

31. Some people have letter-color synesthesias that match the colors of refrigerator magnets they played with in childhood. **32.** Someone who perceives a letter as yellow (when it is actually in black ink) can nevertheless see it on a yellow page.

MODULE 6.3 ■ IN CLOSING

Senses as Ways of Knowing the World

Ask the average person to describe the current environment, and you will probably get a description of what he or she sees and hears. If nonhumans could talk, most species would start by describing what they smell. A human, a dog, a bat, and a snail may be in the same place, but the environments they perceive are very different. Our senses are adapted to provide us with information useful to our way of life.

We sometimes underestimate the importance of taste and smell. People who lose their sense of taste say they no longer enjoy eating and find it difficult to swallow (Cowart, 2005). Many people who lose the sense of smell feel permanently depressed. Taste and smell cannot compete with vision and hearing for telling us about what is happening in the distance, but they are essential for telling us about what is right next to us or about to enter our bodies. They are also important for our enjoyment of life.

Summary

1. Sensory information can be coded in terms of either a labeled-line system or an across-fiber pattern system. **211**
2. Taste receptors are modified skin cells inside taste buds in papillae on the tongue. **212**
3. We have receptors sensitive to sweet, sour, salty, bitter, and umami (glutamate) tastes. Taste is coded by the relative activity of different kinds of cells but also by the rhythm of responses within a given cell. **213**
4. Salty receptors respond simply to sodium ions crossing the membrane. Sour receptors respond to a stimulus by blocking potassium channels. Sweet, bitter, and umami receptors act by a second messenger within the cell, similar to the way a metabotropic neurotransmitter receptor operates. **214**
5. Mammals have about 25 kinds of bitter receptors, enabling them to detect many types of harmful substances. **214**
6. Part of the seventh cranial nerve conveys information from the anterior two-thirds of the tongue. Parts of the ninth and tenth cranial nerves convey information from the posterior tongue and the throat. The two nerves interact in complex ways. **214**
7. People known as supertasters, who have more fungiform papillae than average, are more sensitive to tastes. **215**
8. Olfactory receptors are proteins, each of them highly responsive to a few related chemicals and unresponsive to others. Vertebrates have hundreds of olfactory receptors, each contributing to the detection of a few related odors. **218**
9. Olfactory neurons in the cerebral cortex respond to complex patterns, such as those of a food. **219**
10. Olfactory neurons survive only a month or so. The new cells that replace them become sensitive to the same chemicals as the ones they replace, and they send their axons to the same targets. **219**
11. In most mammals, each vomeronasal organ (VNO) receptor is sensitive to only one chemical, a pheromone.

A pheromone is a social signal. Humans also respond somewhat to pheromones, although our receptors are in the olfactory mucosa, not the VNO. **220**

12. Some people experience synesthesia, a sensation in one modality after stimulation in another one. For example, someone might see purple neon tubes while listening to saxophones. In some cases, the explanation is that axons from one sense have invaded brain areas responsible for a different sense. **221**

Key Terms

Terms are defined in the module on the page number indicated. They're also presented in alphabetical order with definitions in the book's Subject Index/Glossary. Interactive flash cards, audio reviews, and crossword puzzles are among the online resources available to help you learn these terms and the concepts they represent.

across-fiber pattern principle **211**
adaptation **213**
cross-adaptation **213**
labeled-line principle **211**
nucleus of the tractus solitarius (NTS) **214**
olfaction **216**
olfactory cells **218**
papillae **212**
pheromones **220**
supertasters **215**
synesthesia **221**
taste bud **212**
vomeronasal organ (VNO) **220**

Thought Questions

1. In the English language, the letter *t* has no meaning out of context. Its meaning depends on its relationship to other letters. Indeed, even a word, such as *to*, has little meaning except in its connection to other words. So is language a labeled-line system or an across-fiber pattern system?
2. Suppose a chemist synthesizes a new chemical that turns out to have an odor. Presumably, we do not have a specialized receptor for that chemical. Explain how our receptors detect it.

MODULE 6.3 End of Module Quiz

1. How long does a taste receptor last?
   a. From one meal to the next
   b. Two weeks or less, the same as skin cells
   c. Approximately a year
   d. A lifetime
2. What do the observations about taste adaptation and cross-adaptation imply about taste receptors?
   a. The receptors sensitive to one taste are different from those for another taste.
   b. The same receptors contribute to all tastes.
3. Umami refers to the taste of which substance?
   a. Sulfates
   b. Chocolate
   c. Fats
   d. Glutamate
4. Why is it possible for us to taste a wide variety of chemicals as bitter?
   a. All bitter substances are chemically similar.
   b. We have 25 or more types of bitter receptors.
   c. We have a bitter receptor that is versatile enough to detect many types of chemicals.
   d. Sweet and sour receptors can detect bitter substances.
5. Which mammalian species is known to have very few taste receptors?
   a. Dolphins
   b. Cats
   c. Rats
   d. Chimpanzees

6. How do we manage to smell a wide variety of chemicals?
   a. An olfactory receptor varies the amplitude and velocity of its action potentials to indicate the type of odor.
   b. The difference in response between the left nostril and the right nostril identifies the odor.
   c. The ratio of firing among three types of olfactory receptors identifies the odor.
   d. We have hundreds of types of olfactory receptors.

7. When a new olfactory receptor forms to replace one that died, does it connect to the same site in the olfactory bulb as the previous receptor? If so, how?
   a. No, it connects at random with a site in the olfactory bulb.
   b. It connects to the correct site because only one neuron in the olfactory bulb has a vacancy.
   c. It finds the correct site by chemical attraction.
   d. Each axon connects to the nearest neuron in the olfactory bulb.

8. On average, who detects odors better than other people?
   a. On average, left-handers detect odors better than right-handers do.
   b. On average, older people detect odors better than young people do.
   c. On average, women detect odors better than men do.
   d. On average, people with Parkinson's disease detect odors better than other people do.

9. To what stimulus does the vomeronasal organ respond?
   a. Pheromones
   b. Pain and temperature
   c. Tilt and acceleration of the head
   d. Taste

10. What is the best-documented example of an effect of pheromones on humans?
   a. The smell of a sweaty man increases a woman's sexual arousal.
   b. People tend to be sexually attracted to someone who smells like members of their own family.
   c. Women who spend much time together tend to synchronize their menstrual cycles.
   d. Men can detect a woman's sexual interest by pheromones she secretes.

11. What behavioral evidence indicates that synesthesia is real, and not just something that people claim to experience?
   a. Some people's associations match the colors of refrigerator magnets they played with in childhood.
   b. Most people change their synesthetic associations from one year to the next.
   c. People with synesthesia can find a 2 among 5s, or a 6 among 8s, faster than usual if they have different synesthetic colors, and slower if they have the same color.
   d. It is easy to teach someone to develop a synesthesia.

12. Is a synesthetic color like seeing a real color? If not, how is it different?
   a. Yes. It is the same as a real color.
   b. No. It is like thinking about the color.
   c. No. Someone who synesthetically sees a certain letter as yellow can still see the letter on yellow paper.
   d. No. It appears only after the person has stared at the letter or word for a few seconds.

ANSWERS: 1b, 2a, 3d, 4b, 5a, 6d, 7c, 8c, 9a, 10c, 11c, 12c.

Suggestions for Further Reading

Henshaw, J. M. (2012). *A tour of the senses.* Baltimore: Johns Hopkins University Press.

Excellent explanation of the physics of hearing and other senses.

Horowitz, S. S. (2012). *The universal sense: How hearing shapes the mind.* New York: Bloomsbury.

Entertaining description of sound, music, and the role of hearing in the lives of humans and other species.

Robertson, L. C., & Sagiv, N. (2005). *Synesthesia: Perspectives from cognitive neuroscience.* Oxford, England: Oxford University Press.

A review of research on this fascinating phenomenon.

Thernstrom, M. (2010). *The pain chronicles.* New York: Farrar, Straus and Giroux.

Why can some people withstand terrible injuries with little apparent pain? Why do others suffer endlessly? This book explores these and other questions about pain.

NELVIN C. CEPEDA/San Diego Union-Tribune/ ZUMA Press, Inc./Alamy

Movement

7

B efore we get started, please try this: Take out a pencil and a sheet of paper, and put the pencil in your nondominant hand. For example, if you are right-handed, put it in your left hand. Now, with that hand, draw a face in profile—that is, facing one direction or the other but not straight ahead. *Please do this now before reading further.*

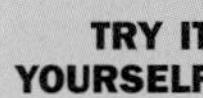

If you tried the demonstration, you probably notice that your drawing is more childlike than usual. It is as if part of your brain stored the way you used to draw as a young child. Now, if you are right-handed and therefore drew the face with your left hand, why did you draw it facing to the right? At least I assume you did, because more than two-thirds of right-handers drawing with their left hand draw the profile facing right. They revert to the pattern shown by young children. Up to about age 5 or 6, children drawing with the right hand almost always draw people and animals facing left, but when using the left hand, they almost always draw them facing right. But *why*? They say, "it's easier that way," but *why* is it easier that way? We have much to learn about the control of movement and how it relates to perception, motivation, and other functions.

OPPOSITE: Ultimately, what brain activity accomplishes is the control of movement—a far more complex process than it might seem.

CHAPTER OUTLINE

MODULE 7.1 **The Control of Movement**
Muscles and Their Movements
Units of Movement
In Closing: Categories of Movement
MODULE 7.2 **Brain Mechanisms of Movement**
The Cerebral Cortex
The Cerebellum
The Basal Ganglia
Brain Areas and Motor Learning
Conscious Decisions and Movement
In Closing: Movement Control and Cognition
MODULE 7.3 **Movement Disorders**
Parkinson's Disease
Huntington's Disease
In Closing: Heredity and Environment in Movement Disorders

LEARNING OBJECTIVES

After studying this chapter, you should be able to:

1. List the types of muscles and the proprioceptors that control them.
2. Describe the cortical mechanisms that control movement and its inhibition.
3. Contrast the anatomy and functions of the lateral and medial corticospinal tracts.
4. Describe the functions of the cerebellum and basal ganglia.
5. Evaluate the evidence regarding the role of consciousness in planning a movement.
6. Discuss the causes of Parkinson's disease and Huntington's disease.

MODULE 7.1

The Control of Movement

Why do we have brains? Plants survive just fine without them. So do sponges, which are animals, even if they don't act like them. But plants don't move, and neither do sponges. A sea squirt (a marine invertebrate) has a brain during its infant stage, when it swims, but when it transforms into an adult, it attaches to a surface, becomes a stationary filter feeder, and digests its own brain, as if to say, "Now that I've stopped traveling, I won't need this brain thing anymore." Ultimately, the purpose of a brain is to control behaviors, and behaviors are movements.

Reinhard Dirscherl/Alamy

Adult sea squirts attach to a surface, never move again, and digest their own brains.

"But wait," you might reply. "We need brains for other things, too, don't we? Like seeing, hearing, understanding speech . . ."

Well, what would be the value of seeing and hearing if you couldn't do anything? Understanding speech wouldn't do you much good unless you could do something about it. A great brain without muscles would be like a computer without a monitor, printer, or other output. No matter how powerful the internal processing, it would be useless.

Muscles and Their Movements

All animal movement depends on muscle contractions. Vertebrate muscles fall into three categories (see Figure 7.1): **smooth muscles** that control the digestive system and other organs, **skeletal** or **striated muscles** that control movement of the body in relation to the environment, and **cardiac muscles** that control the heart.

Each muscle is composed of many fibers, as Figure 7.2 illustrates. Although each muscle fiber receives information from only one axon, a given axon may innervate more than one muscle fiber. For example, the eye muscles have a ratio of about one axon per three muscle fibers, and the biceps muscles of the arm have a ratio of one axon to more than a hundred fibers (Evarts, 1979). This difference allows the eye to move more precisely than the biceps.

A **neuromuscular junction** is a synapse between a motor neuron axon and a muscle fiber. In skeletal muscles, every axon releases acetylcholine at the neuromuscular junction, and acetylcholine always excites the muscle to contract. A deficit of acetylcholine or its receptors impairs movement. Each muscle makes just one movement, contraction. There is no message causing relaxation; the muscle simply relaxes when it receives no message to contract. There is also no message to move a muscle in the opposite direction. Moving a leg or arm back and forth requires opposing sets of muscles, called **antagonistic muscles**. At your elbow, for example, your **flexor** muscle brings your hand toward your shoulder and your **extensor** muscle straightens the arm (see Figure 7.3).

STOP & CHECK

1. Why do we move the eye muscles with greater precision than the biceps muscles?

2. Which transmitter causes a skeletal muscle to contract?

ANSWERS

1. Each axon to the biceps muscles innervates about a hundred fibers; therefore, it is not possible to change the movement by a small amount. In contrast, an axon to the eye muscles innervates only about three fibers. **2.** Acetylcholine. And remember that a muscle's only movement is to contract.

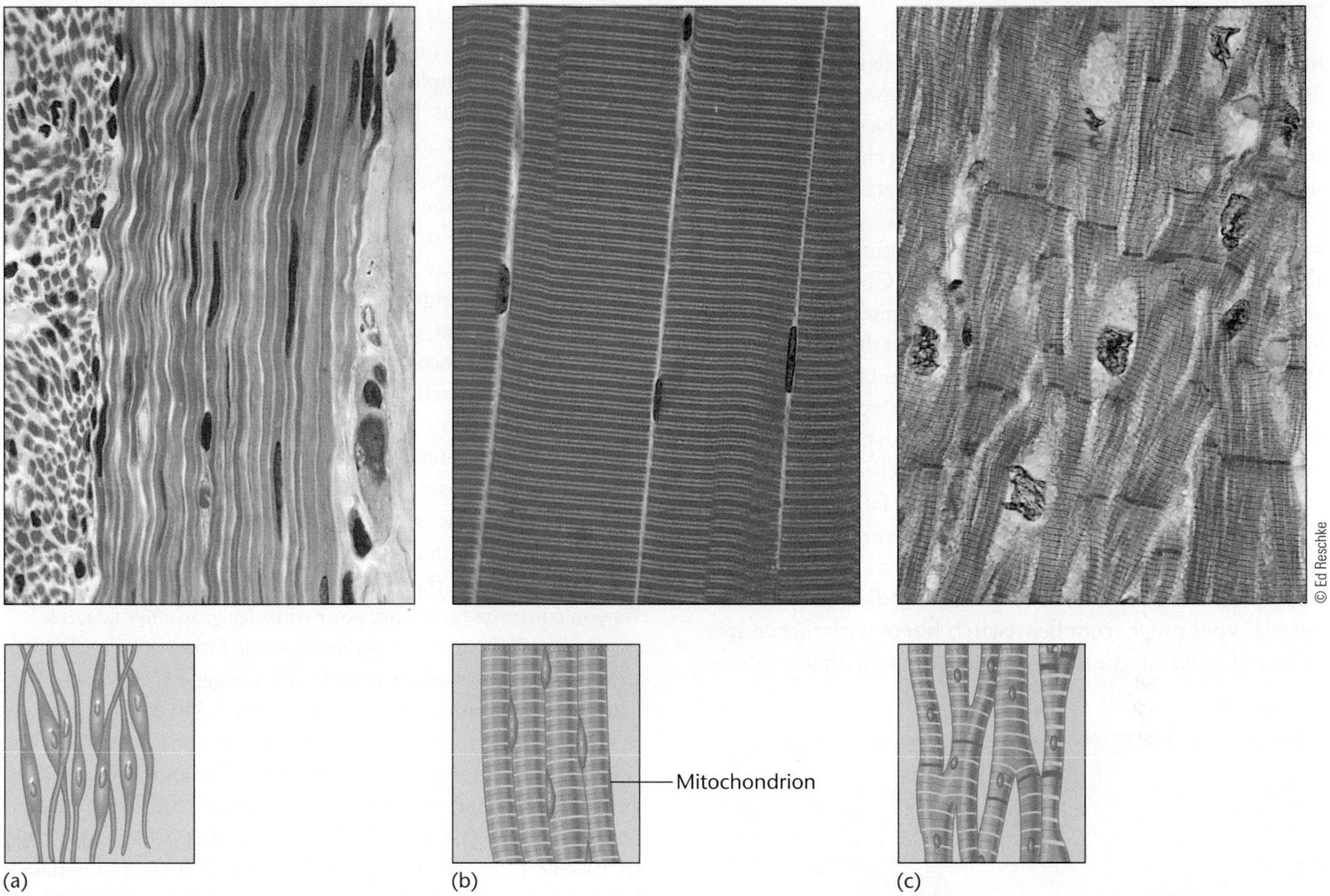

© Ed Reschke

Mitochondrion

(a) (b) (c)

FIGURE 7.1 Vertebrate muscles
(a) Smooth muscle, found in the intestines and other organs, consists of long, thin cells. (b) Skeletal, or striated, muscle consists of long cylindrical fibers with stripes. (c) Cardiac muscle, found in the heart, consists of fibers that fuse together at various points. Because of these fusions, cardiac muscles contract together, not independently. *Source:* Illustrations after Starr & Taggart, 1989

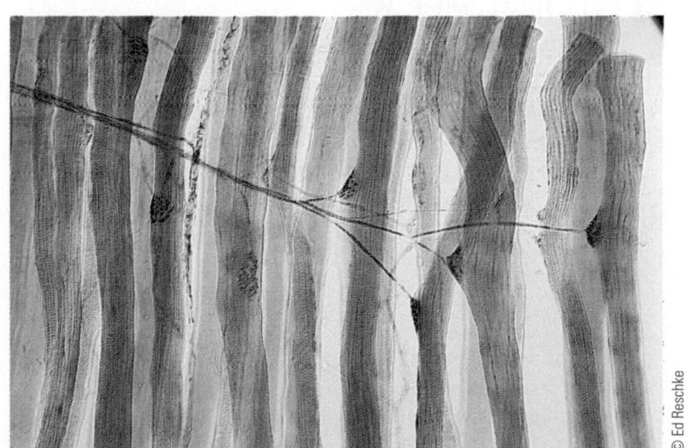

FIGURE 7.2 An axon branching to innervate several muscle fibers
Movements can be more precise where each axon innervates only a few fibers, as with eye muscles, than where it innervates many fibers, as with biceps muscles.

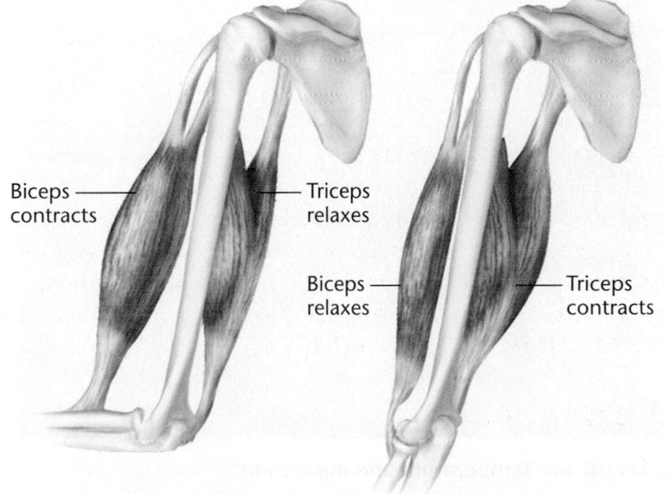

FIGURE 7.3 Antagonistic muscles
The biceps of the arm is a flexor. The triceps is an extensor. Based on Starr & Taggart, 1989

Fast and Slow Muscles

Imagine you are a small fish. Your only defense against bigger fish, diving birds, and other predators is your ability to swim away (see Figure 7.4). Your temperature is the same as the water around you, and muscle contractions, being chemical processes, slowdown in the cold. So when the water gets cold, presumably you will move more slowly, right? Strangely, you will not. You will have to use more muscles than before, but you will swim at about the same speed (Rome, Loughna, & Goldspink, 1984).

A fish has three kinds of muscles: red, pink, and white. Red muscles produce the slowest movements, but they do not fatigue. White muscles produce the fastest movements, but they fatigue rapidly. Pink muscles are intermediate in speed and rate of fatigue. At high temperatures, a fish relies mostly on red and pink muscles. At colder temperatures, the fish relies more and more on white muscles, maintaining its speed but fatiguing faster.

All right, you can stop imagining you are a fish. Human and other mammalian muscles have various kinds of muscle fibers mixed together, not in separate bundles as in fish. Our muscle types range from **fast-twitch fibers** with fast contractions and rapid fatigue to **slow-twitch fibers** with less vigorous contractions and no fatigue (Hennig & Lømo, 1985). We rely on our slow-twitch and intermediate fibers for nonstrenuous activities. For example, you could talk for hours without fatiguing your lip muscles. You might walk for a long time, too. But if you run up a steep hill at full speed, you switch to fast-twitch fibers that fatigue rapidly.

FIGURE 7.4 Temperature and movement
Fish are "cold blooded," but many of their predators (e.g., this pelican) are not. At cold temperatures, each fish muscle contracts more slowly than usual, but a fish compensates by using more muscles.

Slow-twitch fibers do not fatigue because they are **aerobic**—they use oxygen during their movements. You can think of them as "pay as you go." Prolonged use of fast-twitch fibers results in fatigue because the process is **anaerobic**—using reactions that do not require oxygen at the time but need oxygen for recovery. Using them builds up an *oxygen debt*. Imagine yourself bicycling. At first your activity is aerobic, using your slow-twitch fibers. However, your muscles use glucose, and after a while your glucose supplies begin to dwindle. Low glucose activates a gene that inhibits the muscles from using glucose, thereby saving glucose for the brain's use (Booth & Neufer, 2005). You start relying more on the fast-twitch muscles that depend on anaerobic use of fatty acids. As you continue bicycling, your muscles gradually fatigue.

People vary in their percentages of fast-twitch and slow-twitch fibers, for reasons based on both genetics and training. The Swedish ultramarathon runner Bertil Järlaker built up so many slow-twitch fibers in his legs that he once ran 3520 km (2188 mi) in 50 days (an average of 1.7 marathons per day) with only minimal signs of pain or fatigue (Sjöström, Friden, & Ekblom, 1987). Contestants in the Primal Quest race have to walk or run 125 km (77 miles), cycle 250 km (155 miles), kayak 131 km (81 miles), rappel 97 km (60 miles) up canyon walls, swim 13 km (8 miles) in rough water, ride horseback, and climb rocks over 6 days in summer heat. To endure this ordeal, contestants need many adaptations of their muscles and metabolism (Pearson, 2006). In contrast, competitive sprinters have more fast-twitch fibers and other adaptations for speed instead of endurance (Andersen, Klitgaard, & Saltin, 1994; Canepari et al., 2005).

STOP&CHECK

3. In what way are fish movements impaired in cold water?

4. Duck breast muscles are red ("dark meat"), whereas chicken breast muscles are white. Which species probably can fly for a longer time before fatiguing?

5. Why is an ultramarathoner like Bertil Järlaker probably not impressive at short-distance races?

ANSWERS

3. Although a fish can move rapidly in cold water, it fatigues easily. **4.** Ducks can fly great distances, as they often do during migration. The white muscle of a chicken breast has the power necessary to get a heavy body off the ground, but it fatigues rapidly. Chickens seldom fly far. **5.** An ultramarathoner builds up large numbers of slow-twitch fibers at the expense of fast-twitch fibers. Therefore, endurance is great, but maximum speed is not.

Muscle Control by Proprioceptors

As you are walking along on a bumpy road, you occasionally set your foot down a little too hard or not quite hard enough. You adjust your posture and maintain your balance without even thinking about it. How do you do that?

A baby is lying on its back. You playfully tug its foot and then let go. At once, the leg bounces back to its original position. How and why?

In both cases, proprioceptors control the movement (see Figure 7.5). A **proprioceptor** (from the Latin *proprius*, meaning "one's own") is a receptor that detects the position or movement of a part of the body—in these cases, a muscle. Muscle proprioceptors detect the stretch and tension of a muscle and send messages that enable the spinal cord to adjust its signals. When a muscle is stretched, the spinal cord sends a signal to contract it reflexively. This **stretch reflex** is *caused* by a stretch; it does not *produce* one.

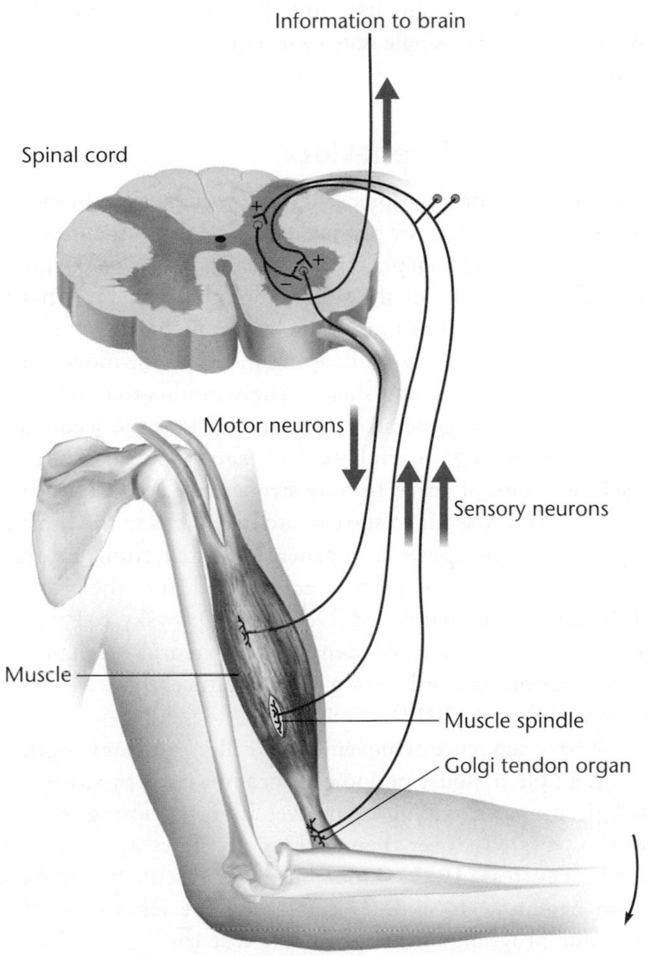

FIGURE 7.5 Two kinds of proprioceptors regulate muscle contractions
When a muscle is stretched, nerves from the muscle spindles transmit impulses that lead to contraction of the muscle. Contraction of the muscle stimulates the Golgi tendon organ, which acts as a brake or shock absorber to prevent a contraction that is too quick or extreme.

One kind of proprioceptor is the **muscle spindle**, a receptor parallel to the muscle that responds to a stretch. Whenever the muscle spindle is stretched, its sensory nerve sends a message to a motor neuron in the spinal cord, which in turn sends a message back to the muscles surrounding the spindle, causing a contraction. Note that this reflex provides for negative feedback: When a muscle and its spindle are stretched, the spindle sends a message that results in a muscle contraction that opposes the stretch.

When you set your foot down on a bump on the road, your knee bends a bit, stretching the extensor muscles of that leg. The sensory nerves of the spindles send action potentials to the motor neuron in the spinal cord, and the motor neuron sends action potentials to the extensor muscle. Contracting the extensor muscle straightens the leg, adjusting for the bump on the road.

A physician who asks you to cross your legs and then taps just below the knee is testing your stretch reflexes (see Figure 7.6). The tap stretches the extensor muscles and their spindles, resulting in a message that jerks the lower leg upward. A leg that jerks excessively or not at all may indicate a neurological problem.

Golgi tendon organs, also proprioceptors, respond to increases in muscle tension. Located in the tendons at opposite ends of a muscle, they act as a brake against an excessively vigorous contraction. Some muscles are so strong that they could damage themselves if too many fibers contracted at once. Golgi tendon organs detect the tension that results during a muscle contraction. Their impulses travel to the spinal cord, where they excite interneurons that inhibit the motor neurons. In short, a vigorous muscle contraction inhibits further contraction by activating the Golgi tendon organs.

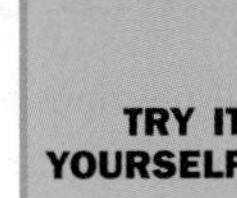

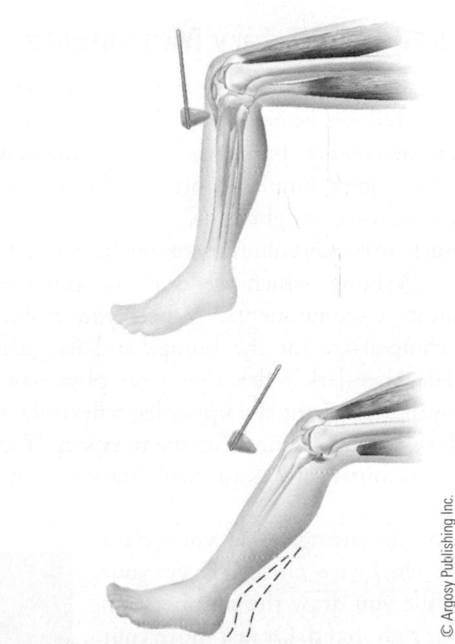

FIGURE 7.6 The knee-jerk reflex
This is one example of a stretch reflex.

The proprioceptors not only control important reflexes but also provide the brain with information. Here is an illusion that you can try: Find a small, dense object and a larger, less dense object that weighs the same as the small one. For example, you might try a lemon and a hollowed-out orange, with the peel pasted back together so it appears to be intact. Drop one of the objects onto someone's hand while he or she is watching. (Watching is essential.) Then remove it and drop the other object onto the same hand. Most people report that the small one felt heavier. The reason is that with the larger object, people set themselves up with an expectation of a heavier weight. The actual weight displaces their proprioceptors less than expected and therefore yields the perception of a lighter object.

STOP&CHECK

6. If you hold your arm straight out and someone pulls it down slightly, it quickly bounces back. Which proprioceptor is responsible?

7. What is the function of Golgi tendon organs?

ANSWERS

6. The muscle spindle **7.** Golgi tendon organs respond to muscle tension and thereby prevent excessively strong muscle contractions.

Units of Movement

Movements include speaking, walking, threading a needle, and throwing a basketball while off balance and evading two defenders. Different kinds of movement represent different kinds of control by the nervous system.

Voluntary and Involuntary Movements

Reflexes are consistent automatic responses to stimuli. We generally think of reflexes as *involuntary* because they are insensitive to reinforcements, punishments, and motivations. The stretch reflex is one example. Another is the constriction of the pupil in response to bright light.

Few behaviors are purely voluntary or involuntary, reflexive or nonreflexive. Walking, which we think of as voluntary, includes involuntary components. When you walk, you automatically compensate for the bumps and irregularities in the road. The knee-jerk reflex that your physician tests contributes to walking; raising the upper leg reflexively moves the lower leg forward in readiness for the next step. You also swing your arms automatically as an involuntary consequence of walking.

Try this: While sitting, raise your right foot and make clockwise circles. Keep your foot moving while you draw the number 6 in the air with your right hand. Or just move your right hand in counterclockwise circles. You will probably reverse the direction of your foot movement. It is difficult to make "voluntary" clockwise and counterclockwise movements on the same side of the body at the same time. However, it is not at all difficult to move your left hand in one direction while moving the right foot in the opposite direction.

Movements Varying in Sensitivity to Feedback

The military distinguishes ballistic missiles from guided missiles. A ballistic missile is launched like a thrown ball: Once it is launched, no one can change its aim. A guided missile detects the target and adjusts its trajectory to correct its aim.

Similarly, some movements are ballistic, and others are corrected by feedback. A **ballistic movement**, such as a reflex, is executed as a whole: Once initiated, it cannot be altered. However, most behaviors are subject to feedback correction. For example, when you thread a needle, you make a slight movement, check your aim, and then readjust. Similarly, a singer who holds a single note hears any wavering of the pitch and corrects it.

Sequences of Behaviors

Many of our behaviors consist of rapid sequences, as in speaking, writing, dancing, or playing a musical instrument. Some of these sequences depend on **central pattern generators**, neural mechanisms in the spinal cord that generate rhythmic patterns of motor output. Examples include the mechanisms that generate wing flapping in birds, fin movements in fish, and the "wet dog shake." The stimulus that activates a central pattern generator does not control the frequency of the alternating movements. For example, a cat scratches itself at a rate of three to four strokes per second, regardless of what caused it to start scratching. Cells in the lumbar segments of the spinal cord generate this rhythm, and they continue doing so even if they are isolated from the brain or if the muscles are paralyzed (Deliagina, Orlovsky, & Pavlova, 1983). Researchers have identified the neural mechanisms of excitation and inhibition that produce these rhythms (Hägglund et al., 2013).

A fixed sequence of movements is called a **motor program**. For example, a mouse periodically grooms itself by sitting up, licking its paws, wiping them over its face, closing its eyes as the paws pass over them, licking the paws again, and so forth (Fentress, 1973). Once begun, the sequence is fixed from beginning to end. By comparing species, we see that a motor program can be gained or lost through evolution. For example, if you hold a chicken above the ground and drop it, its wings extend and flap. Chickens with featherless wings make the same movements, even though they fail to break their fall (Provine, 1979, 1981). Chickens, of course, still have the genetic programming to fly. On the other hand, ostriches, emus, and rheas, which have not used their wings

Nearly all birds reflexively spread their wings when dropped. However, emus—which lost the ability to fly through evolutionary time—do not spread their wings.

for flight for millions of generations, have lost the genes for flight movements and do not flap their wings when dropped (Provine, 1984). (You might pause to think about the researcher who found a way to drop these huge birds to test the hypothesis.)

Do humans have any built-in motor programs? Yawning is one example (Provine, 1986). A yawn includes a prolonged open-mouth inhalation, often accompanied by stretching, and a shorter exhalation. Yawns are consistent in duration, with a mean of just under 6 seconds. Certain facial expressions are also programmed, such as smiles, frowns, and the raised-eyebrow greeting. Hugging is not a built-in motor program, but it is interesting to note that the average nonromantic hug duration is 3 seconds for people throughout the world (Nagy, 2011). That is, even our voluntary behaviors have a surprising degree of regularity and predictability.

MODULE 7.1 ■ IN CLOSING

Categories of Movement

Charles Sherrington described a motor neuron in the spinal cord as "the final common path." He meant that regardless of what sensory and motivational processes occupy the brain, the final result is either a muscle contraction or the delay of a muscle contraction. A motor neuron and its associated muscle participate in a great many kinds of movements, and we need many brain areas to control them.

Summary

1. Vertebrates have smooth, skeletal, and cardiac muscles. **228**
2. All nerve–muscle junctions rely on acetylcholine as their neurotransmitter. **228**
3. Skeletal muscles range from slow muscles that do not fatigue to fast muscles that fatigue quickly. We rely on the slow muscles most of the time, but we recruit the fast muscles for brief periods of strenuous activity. **230**
4. Proprioceptors are receptors sensitive to the position and movement of a part of the body. Two kinds of proprioceptors, muscle spindles and Golgi tendon organs, help regulate muscle movements. **231**
5. Some movements, especially reflexes, proceed as a unit, with little if any guidance from sensory feedback. Other movements, such as threading a needle, are guided and redirected by sensory feedback. **232**

Key Terms

Terms are defined in the module on the page number indicated. They're also presented in alphabetical order with definitions in the book's Subject Index/Glossary. Interactive flash cards, audio reviews, and crossword puzzles are among the online resources available to help you learn these terms and the concepts they represent.

aerobic 230
anaerobic 230
antagonistic muscles 228
ballistic movement 232
cardiac muscles 228
central pattern generators 232
extensor 228
fast-twitch fibers 230
flexor 228
Golgi tendon organ 231
motor program 232
muscle spindle 231
neuromuscular junction 228
proprioceptor 231
reflexes 232
skeletal (striated) muscles 228
slow-twitch fibers 230
smooth muscles 228
stretch reflex 231

Thought Question

Would you expect jaguars, cheetahs, and other great cats to have mostly slow-twitch, nonfatiguing muscles in their legs or mostly fast-twitch, quickly fatiguing muscles? What kinds of animals might have mostly the opposite kind of muscles?

MODULE 7.1 End of Module Quiz

1. After acetylcholine causes a flexor muscle to move your hand toward your shoulder, what would move it the other direction?
   - **a.** A different transmitter causes the muscle to relax.
   - **b.** A different transmitter causes the muscle to move the other direction.
   - **c.** Acetylcholine causes the extensor muscle to contract.
   - **d.** A different transmitter causes the extensor muscle to contract.
2. What happens to a fish's movement speed in colder water?
   - **a.** The fish swims more slowly.
   - **b.** The fish swims at the same speed by making each muscle contract more strongly.
   - **c.** The fish swims at the same speed by recruiting more white muscle fibers.
   - **d.** The fish swims faster.
3. Which of the following is true of mammals' slow-twitch muscle fibers?
   - **a.** Because they are aerobic, they are subject to rapid fatigue.
   - **b.** Because they are anaerobic, they are subject to rapid fatigue.
   - **c.** Because they are aerobic, they do not fatigue rapidly.
   - **d.** Because they are anaerobic, they do not fatigue rapidly.
4. Which of the following describes a stretch reflex?
   - **a.** The receptor detects that a muscle is stretched, and sends a signal to contract it reflexively.
   - **b.** The receptor detects that a muscle is contracted, and sends a signal to stretch it reflexively.
5. A muscle spindle and a Golgi tendon organ are both described as what?
   - **a.** Optic receptors
   - **b.** Metabolic receptors
   - **c.** Proprioceptors
   - **d.** Chemoreceptors

ANSWERS: 1c, 2c, 3c, 4a, 5c.

Brain Mechanisms of Movement

Why do we care how the brain controls movement? One goal is to help people who have spinal cord damage or limb amputations. Suppose we could listen in on their brain messages and decode what movements they would like to make. Then biomedical engineers might route those messages to muscle stimulators or robotic limbs. Sound like science fiction? Not really. Researchers implanted an array of microelectrodes into the motor cortex of a woman who was paralyzed from the neck down. Then they connected electrodes in her primary motor cortex to a robotic arm, enabling her to make simple reaching and grasping movements, as shown in Figure 7.7 (Hochberg et al., 2012). Another woman with a similar device showed gradual improvement over 13 weeks of training, improving her accuracy of arm movements in three dimensions (Collinger et al., 2013). Further progress will depend on both the technology and advances in understanding the brain mechanisms of movement.

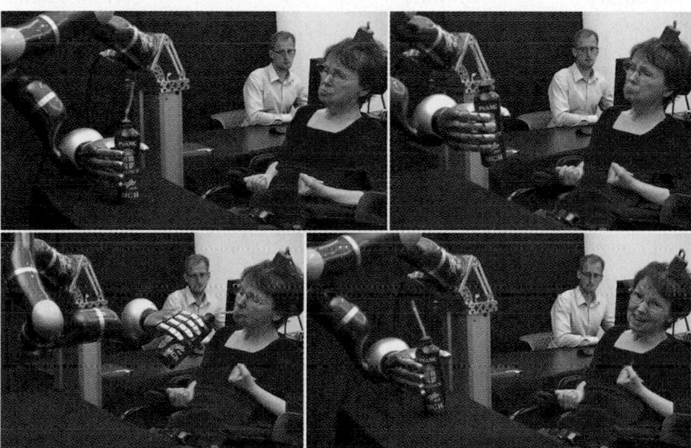

FIGURE 7.7 Recordings from the brain control a robotic arm After a stroke in this woman's midbrain cut off connections from her cortex to the spinal cord, she lost all control of her arm and leg muscles. A neural decoder connected cells in her motor primary motor cortex to a robotic arm, enabling her to pick up a coffee cup, drink from it, and put it back. *Source:* From L. R. Hochberg, D. Bacher, B. Jarosiewicz, N. Y. Masse, J. D. Simeral, J. Vogel, ... J. P. Donoghue (2012). Reach and grasp by people with tetraplegia using aneurally controlled robotic arm. *Nature, 485*, pp. 372-375

Controlling movement depends on many brain areas, as illustrated in Figure 7.8. Don't get too bogged down in details of the figure at this point. We shall attend to each area in due course.

The Cerebral Cortex

Since the pioneering work of Gustav Fritsch and Eduard Hitzig (1870), neuroscientists have known that direct electrical stimulation of the **primary motor cortex**—the precentral gyrus of the frontal cortex, just anterior to the central sulcus (see Figure 7.9)—elicits movements. The motor cortex does not send messages directly to the muscles. Its axons extend to the brainstem and spinal cord, which generate the impulses that control the muscles. In most mammals, these axons connect only to interneurons, which in turn control motor neurons. In humans and other primates, some axons go directly from the cerebral cortex to motor neurons, presumably giving us greater dexterity. Human movements depend on both the axons to motor neurons and axons to interneurons (Kinoshita et al., 2012).

The cerebral cortex is particularly important for complex actions such as talking or writing. It is less important for coughing, sneezing, gagging, laughing, or crying (Rinn, 1984). Perhaps the lack of cerebral control explains why it is hard to perform such actions voluntarily.

Figure 7.10 (which repeats parts of Figure 3.24) shows which areas of the somatosensory cortex feel which parts of the body, and which areas of the motor cortex control muscles in which parts of the body. A key point is the similarity between the two. The motor cortex is just anterior to the somatosensory cortex, and the two match up nicely. That is, the brain area that controls the left hand is near the area that feels the left hand, the area that controls the left foot is near the area that feels the left foot, and so forth. You need to feel a body part to control its movement accurately.

Don't read Figure 7.10 as implying that each spot in the motor cortex controls a single muscle. The region responsible for any finger overlaps the regions responsible for other fingers (Sanes, Donoghue, Thangaraj, Edelman, & Warach, 1995). Furthermore, the output of a given neuron influences movements of the hand, wrist, and arm, and not just a single muscle (Vargas-Irwin et al., 2010).

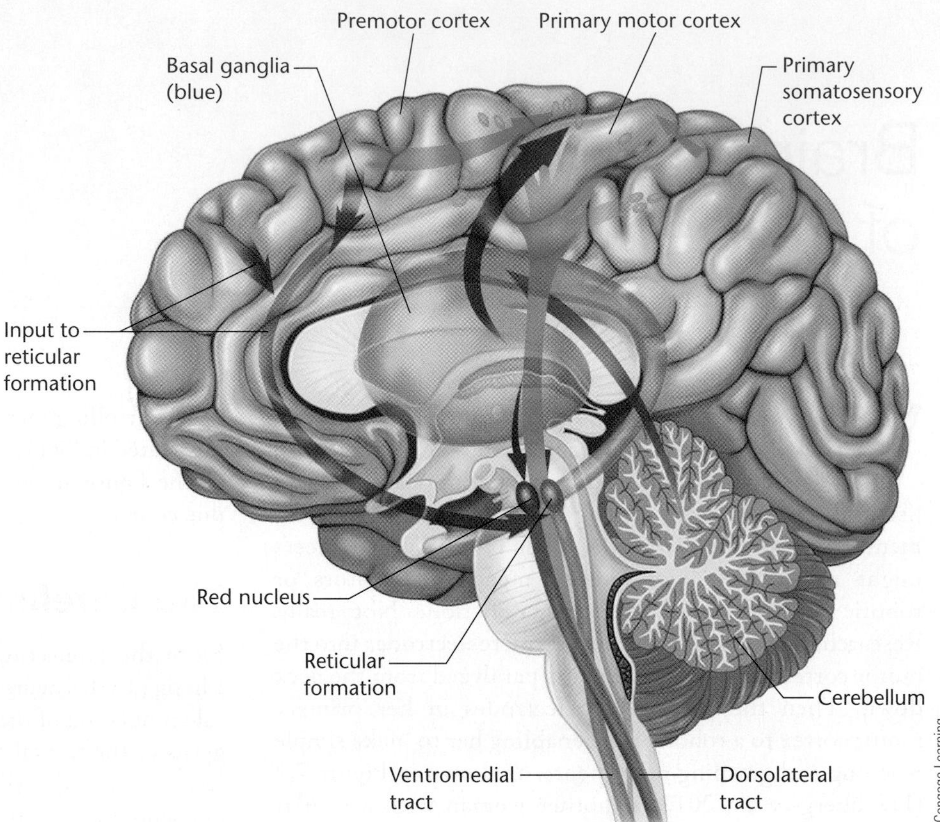

FIGURE 7.8 Motor control in mammals
Motor neurons in the medulla and spinal cord control muscle contractions. Pathways from the primary motor cortex, other cortical areas, midbrain, and medulla control those motor neurons.

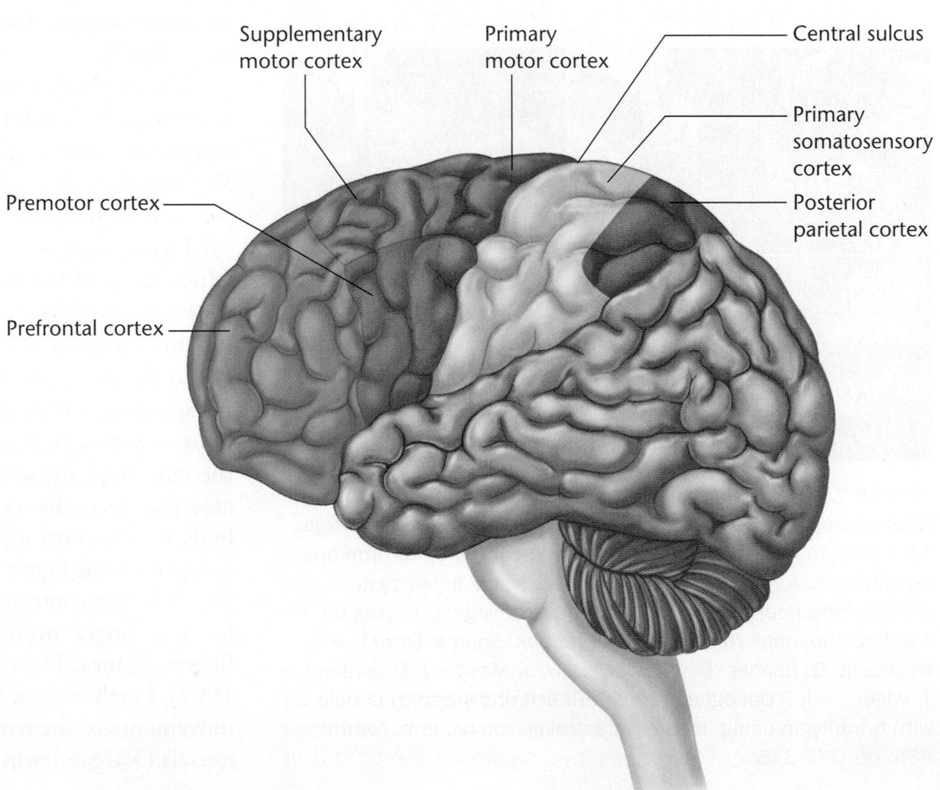

FIGURE 7.9 Principal motor areas of the human cortex
Cells in the premotor cortex and supplementary motor cortex are active during the planning of movements.

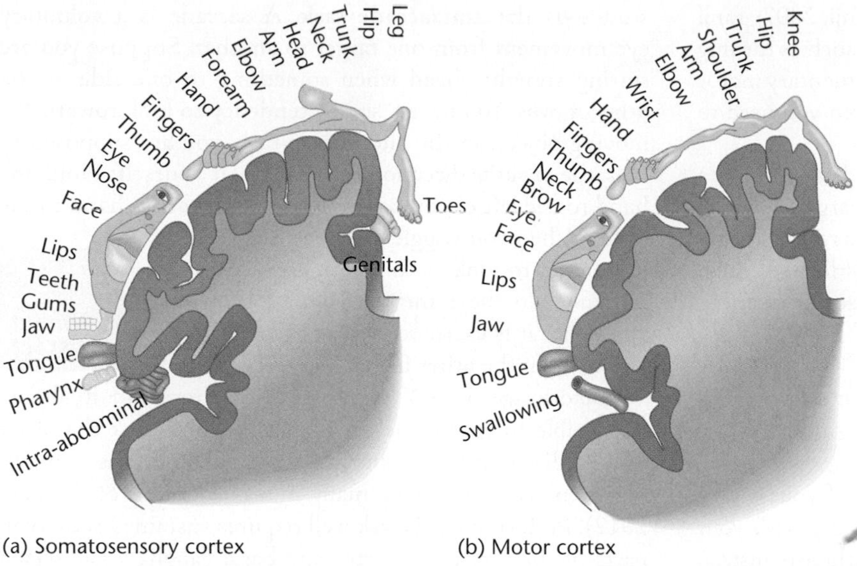

FIGURE 7.10 Coronal section through the primary somatosensory cortex and primary motor cortex
The motor cortex lies just anterior to the somatosensory cortex. The motor area responsible for moving a certain body part is aligned with the somatosensory area responsible for feeling that body part. Communication between sensing and moving is essential. *Source:* Adapted from Penfield & Rasmussen, 1950

For many years, researchers studied the motor cortex in laboratory animals by stimulating neurons with brief electrical pulses, usually less than 50 milliseconds (ms) in duration. The results were brief, isolated muscle twitches. Later researchers found different results when they lengthened the pulses to half a second. Instead of twitches, they elicited complex movement patterns. For example, stimulation of one spot caused a monkey to make a grasping movement with its hand, move its hand to just in front of the mouth, and open its mouth—as if it were picking up something and getting ready to eat it (Graziano, Taylor, & Moore, 2002). Repeated stimulation of this same spot elicited the same result each time, regardless of the initial position of the monkey's hand. That is, the stimulation produced a certain *outcome*, not a particular *muscle movement*. The motor cortex orders an outcome and leaves it to the spinal cord and other areas to find the right combination of muscles (S. H. Scott, 2004).

STOP&CHECK

8. In what way does the brain anatomy facilitate communication between body sensations and body movements?

9. What evidence indicates that cortical activity represents the "idea" of the movement and not just the muscle contractions?

ANSWERS

8. The motor cortex represents muscular control of body areas in close alignment to the way the somatosensory cortex, just posterior to the motor cortex, represents sensations from those areas. **9.** Activity in the motor cortex leads to a particular outcome, such as movement of the hand to the mouth, regardless of what muscle contractions are necessary given the hand's current location.

Planning a Movement

The primary motor cortex is important for making movements, but not for initial planning. One of the first areas to become active in planning a movement is the **posterior parietal cortex** (see Figure 7.9), which monitors the position of the body relative to the world (Snyder, Grieve, Brotchie, & Andersen, 1998). People with posterior parietal damage have trouble finding objects in space, even after describing their appearance accurately. When walking, they frequently bump into obstacles (Goodale, 1996; Goodale, Milner, Jakobson, & Carey, 1991). Beyond helping to control aim, the posterior parietal cortex is also important for planning movements. Brain surgery is sometimes conducted on people who are awake and alert, with only the skin of their scalp anesthetized. (The brain itself has no pain receptors.) During the course of such surgery, physicians can briefly stimulate certain brain areas and record the results. When they stimulate parts of the posterior parietal cortex, people frequently report an *intention* to move—such as an intention to move the left hand. After more intense stimulation at the same locations, people report that they believe they *did* make the movement—although, in fact, they did not (Desmurget et al., 2009).

Several studies used fMRI to measure brain responses while people were preparing to move. The details vary, but the general idea is that people see a first signal that tells them what they are supposed to do, and then they have to wait a few seconds for a second signal that says it is time for the action. Or people see a first signal with partial information about what they will or will not have to do, and then after a short delay a second signal that tells them more precisely what to do. In each of these cases, the posterior parietal cortex is active throughout the delay, evidently preparing for the movement. It is less active during a delay if no movement will be required (Hesse, Thiel, Stephan, & Fink, 2006; Lindner, Iyer, Kagan, & Andersen, 2010).

The prefrontal cortex and the **supplementary motor cortex** are also important for planning and organizing a rapid sequence of movements (Shima, Isoda, Mushiake, & Tanji, 2007; Tanji & Shima, 1994). If you have a habitual action, such as turning left when you get to a certain corner, the supplementary motor cortex is essential for inhibiting that habit when you need to do something else (Isoda & Hikosaka, 2007).

The **premotor cortex** is most active immediately before a movement. It receives information about the target to which the body is directing its movement, as well as information about the body's current position and posture (Hoshi & Tanji, 2000). Both kinds of information are, of course, necessary to direct a movement toward a target.

The **prefrontal cortex**, which is also active during a delay before a movement, stores sensory information relevant to a movement. It is also important for considering the probable outcomes of possible movements (Tucker, Luu, & Pribram, 1995). If you had damage to this area, many of your movements would be disorganized, such as showering with your clothes on or pouring water on the tube of toothpaste instead of the toothbrush (M. F. Schwartz, 1995). Interestingly, this area is inactive during dreams, and the actions we dream about doing are often as illogical as those of people with prefrontal cortex damage (Braun et al., 1998; Maquet et al., 1996). If you do something absent-minded first thing in the morning, it may be that your prefrontal cortex is not fully awake.

STOP&CHECK

10. How does the posterior parietal cortex contribute to movement? The premotor cortex? The supplementary motor cortex? The prefrontal cortex?

ANSWER

10. The posterior parietal cortex is important for perceiving the location of objects and the position of the body relative to the environment. It is also active for planning of a movement. The premotor cortex and supplementary motor cortex are also active in preparing a movement shortly before it occurs. The supplementary motor cortex inhibits a habitual action when it is inappropriate. The prefrontal cortex stores sensory information relevant to a movement and considers possible outcomes of a movement.

Inhibiting a Movement

Finally, consider the situation in which you need to restrain yourself from following some strong impulse. The traffic light changes from red to green, but just as you are about to drive forward, you hear an ambulance siren telling you to get out of the way. Or you start to swing at a tennis ball in a doubles match when your partner shouts, "let it go," because it will land out of bounds. In cases like these, two brain areas are sending competing messages, and the outcome depends on whether the stop message arrives in time to cancel the action message (Schmidt, Leventhal, Mallet, Chen, & Berke, 2013).

Another example—not a particularly important one for its own sake, but a convenient one for psychologists to study—is the **antisaccade task**. A saccade is a voluntary eye movement from one target to another. Suppose you are staring straight ahead when something to one side or the other moves. You have a strong tendency to look toward the moving object. In the antisaccade task, you are supposed to look the *opposite* direction. You can try it yourself: Hold one hand to the left of someone's head and the other hand to the right. When you wiggle a finger, the person is instructed to look at the *other* hand. Or have someone do the same for you. Most people agree that it is easier to look at the finger that moved than the other finger.

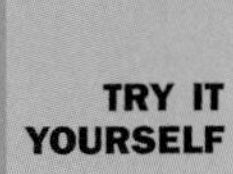

Before age 5 to 7 years, most children find it almost impossible to ignore the wiggling finger and look the other way. Ability to perform this task gradually improves over age, but even teenagers make many mistakes (Bucci & Seessau, 2012). Performing this task well requires sustained activity in parts of the prefrontal cortex and basal ganglia *before* seeing the wiggling finger (Velanova, Wheeler, & Luna, 2009; Watanabe & Munoz, 2010). That is, the brain prepares itself to be ready to inhibit the unwanted action and substitute a different one. Ability to perform the antisaccade task matures slowly because the prefrontal cortex is one of the slowest brain areas to reach maturity. Many adults who have neurological or psychiatric disorders affecting the prefrontal cortex or basal ganglia have trouble on this task (Munoz & Everling, 2004). As you might guess, children with attention deficit/hyperactivity disorder (ADHD), who tend to be impulsive in other ways, also have difficulty with the antisaccade task (Loe, Feldman, Yasui, & Luna, 2009).

Mirror Neurons

Of discoveries in neuroscience, one of the most exciting to psychologists has been **mirror neurons**, which are active both during preparation for a movement and while watching someone else perform the same or a similar movement (Rizzolatti & Sinigaglia, 2010). Mirror neurons were first reported in the premotor cortex of monkeys (Gallese, Fadiga, Fogassi, & Rizzolatti, 1996) and later in other areas and other species, including humans (Dinstein, Hasson, Rubin, & Heeger, 2007; Kilner, Neal, Weiskopf, Friston, & Frith, 2009). These neurons are theoretically exciting because of the idea that they may be important for understanding other people, identifying with them, and imitating them. For example, mirror neurons in part of the frontal cortex become active when people smile or see someone else smile, and they respond especially strongly in people who report identifying strongly with other people (Montgomery, Seeherman, & Haxby, 2009). Many people have speculated that people with autism—who fail to form strong social bonds—might lack mirror neurons. However, one study using fMRI found normal mirror neuron responses in autistic people (Dinstein et al., 2010), so we need to look elsewhere to explain autism.

Mirror neurons are activated not only by seeing an action, but also by any reminder of the action. Certain cells respond to hearing an action as well as seeing or doing it (Kohler et al.,

2002; Ricciardi et al., 2009). Other cells respond to either doing an action or reading about it (Foroni & Semin, 2009; Speer, Reynolds, Swallow, & Zacks, 2009).

The possibilities are exciting, but before we speculate too far, an important question remains: Do mirror neurons *cause* imitation and social behavior, or do they *result from* them? Put another way, are we born with neurons that respond to the sight of a movement and also facilitate the same movement? If so, they could be important for social learning. However, another possibility is that we learn which visible movements correspond to movements of our own. Then seeing others' actions reminds us of our own, and activates brain areas responsible for those actions. In that case, mirror neurons are not responsible for imitation or socialization (Heyes, 2010).

The answer may be different for different movements. Some newborn infants imitate a few facial movements, especially tongue protrusion, as shown in Figure 7.11. That result implies built-in mirror neurons that connect the sight of a movement to the movement itself (Meltzoff & Moore, 1977). However, in both monkey and human infants, many mirror neurons do not respond to observations of others' movements until after the infant has practiced making those movements itself (Shaw & Czekóová, 2013). A mirror neuron cannot be essential for learning to imitate a movement if you have to practice the movement before that neuron develops its mirror properties.

Also, researchers identified mirror neurons that responded both when people moved a certain finger, such as the index finger, and when they watched someone else move the same finger. Then they asked people to watch a display on the screen and move their index finger whenever the hand on the screen moved the little finger. They were to move their little finger whenever the hand on the screen moved the index finger. After some practice, these "mirror" neurons turned into "counter-mirror" neurons that responded to movements of one finger by that person and the sight of a different finger on the screen (Catmur, Walsh, & Heyes, 2007). In other words, at least some mirror neurons modify their properties by learning, and therefore it is possible that they developed their original properties by learning also. How mirror neurons develop their properties will remain a topic for careful research (Shaw & Czekóová, 2013).

STOP&CHECK

11. When expert pianists listen to familiar, well-practiced music, they imagine the finger movements, and the finger area of their motor cortex becomes active, even if they are not moving their fingers (Haueisen & Knösche, 2001). If we regard those neurons as another kind of mirror neuron, what do these results imply about the origin of mirror neurons?

ANSWER

11. These neurons must have acquired these properties through experience. That is, they did not enable pianists to copy what they hear; they developed after pianists learned to copy what they hear.

Connections from the Brain to the Spinal Cord

Messages from the brain must eventually reach the medulla and spinal cord, which control the muscles. Diseases of the spinal cord impair the control of movement in various ways, as listed in Table 7.1. Paths from the cerebral cortex to the spinal cord are called the **corticospinal tracts**. We have two such tracts, the lateral and medial corticospinal tracts. Both tracts contribute in some way to nearly all movements, but a movement may rely on one tract more than the other.

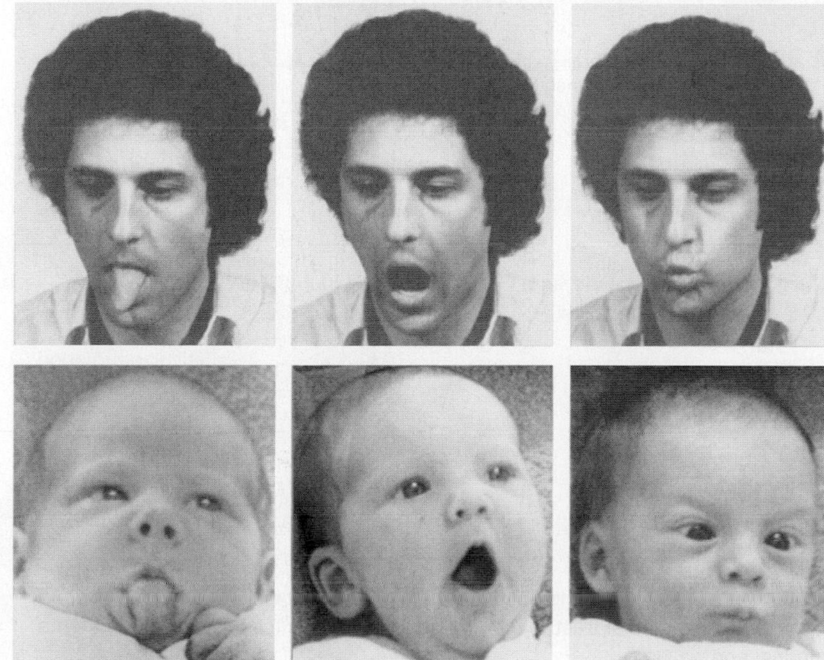

FIGURE 7.11 Infants in their first few days imitate certain facial expressions
These actions imply built-in mirror neurons.
Source: From A.N. Meltzoff & M.K. Moore, "Imitation of facial and manual gestures by human neonates." *Science, 1977, 198,* pp. 75-78

TABLE 7.1 Disorders of the Spinal Cord

Disorder	Description	Cause
Paralysis	Lack of voluntary movement in part of the body.	Damage to spinal cord, motor neurons, or their axons.
Paraplegia	Loss of sensation and voluntary muscle control in both legs. Reflexes remain. Although no messages pass between the brain and the genitals, the genitals still respond reflexively to touch. Paraplegics have no genital sensations, but they can still experience orgasm (Money, 1967).	Cut through the spinal cord above the segments attached to the legs.
Quadriplegia	Loss of sensation and muscle control in all four extremities.	Cut through the spinal cord above the segments controlling the arms.
Hemiplegia	Loss of sensation and muscle control in the arm and leg on one side.	Cut halfway through the spinal cord or (more commonly) damage to one hemisphere of the cerebral cortex.
Tabes dorsalis	Impaired sensation in the legs and pelvic region, impaired leg reflexes and walking, loss of bladder and bowel control.	Late stage of syphilis. Dorsal roots of the spinal cord deteriorate.
Poliomyelitis	Paralysis.	Virus that damages cell bodies of motor neurons.
Amyotrophic lateral sclerosis	Gradual weakness and paralysis, starting with the arms and later spreading to the legs. Both motor neurons and axons from the brain to the motor neurons are destroyed.	Unknown.

The **lateral corticospinal tract** is a pathway of axons from the primary motor cortex, surrounding areas, and the **red nucleus,** a midbrain area that is primarily responsible for controlling the arm muscles (see Figure 7.12). Axons of the lateral tract extend directly from the motor cortex to their target neurons in the spinal cord. In bulges of the medulla called *pyramids,* the lateral tract crosses to the contralateral (opposite) side of the spinal cord. (For that reason, the lateral tract is also called the pyramidal tract.) It controls movements in peripheral areas, such as the hands and feet.

Why does each hemisphere control the contralateral side instead of its own side? We do not know, but all vertebrates

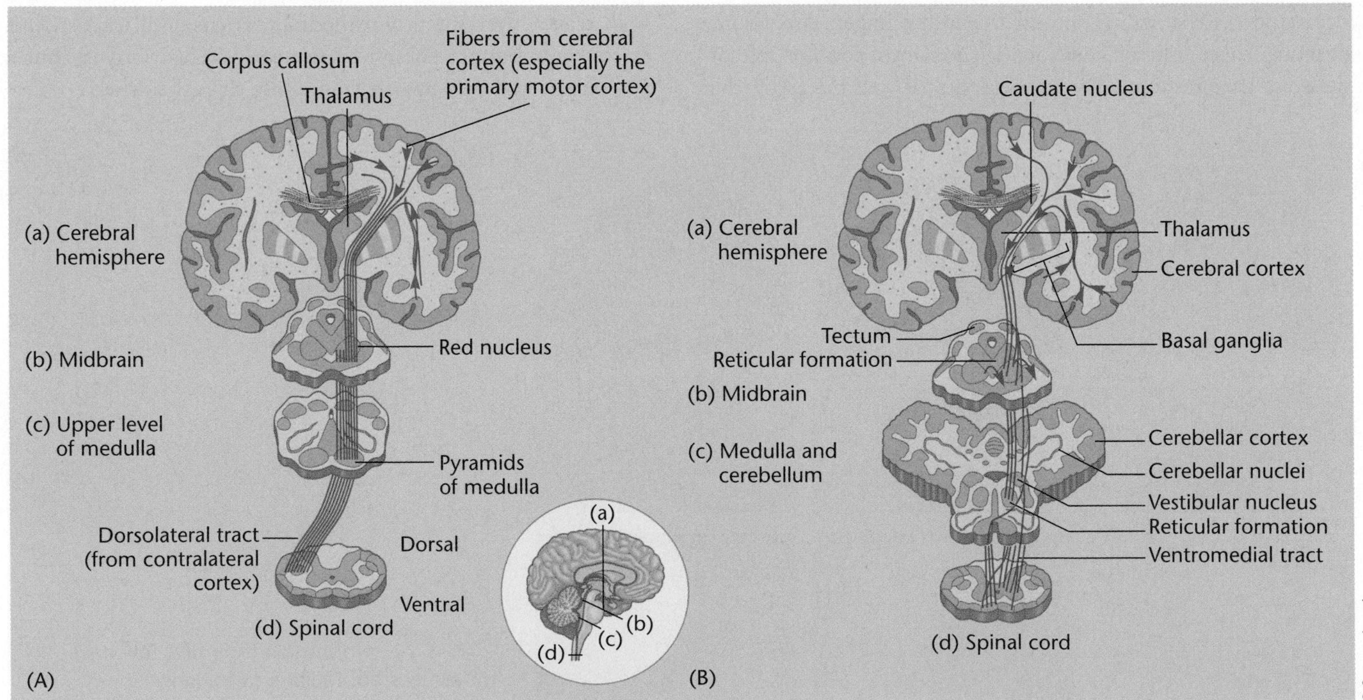

FIGURE 7.12 The lateral and medial corticospinal tracts
The lateral tract (a) crosses from one side of the brain to the opposite side of the spinal cord and controls precise and discrete movements of the extremities, such as hands, fingers, and feet. The medial tract (b) controls trunk muscles for postural adjustments and bilateral movements such as standing, bending, turning, and walking.

and many invertebrates have this pattern. In newborn humans, the immature primary motor cortex has partial control of both ipsilateral and contralateral muscles. As the contralateral control improves over the first year and a half of life, it displaces the ipsilateral control, which gradually becomes weaker. In some children with cerebral palsy, the contralateral path fails to mature, and the ipsilateral path remains relatively strong. The resulting competition causes clumsiness (Eyre, Taylor, Villagra, Smith, & Miller, 2001).

The **medial corticospinal tract** includes axons from many parts of the cerebral cortex, not just the primary motor cortex and its surrounding areas. The medial path also includes axons from the midbrain tectum, the reticular formation, and the **vestibular nucleus**, a brain area that receives input from the vestibular system (see Figure 7.12). Axons of the medial tract go to *both* sides of the spinal cord, not just to the contralateral side. The medial tract controls mainly the muscles of the neck, shoulders, and trunk and therefore bilateral movements as walking, turning, bending, standing up, and sitting down (Kuypers, 1989). You can move your fingers on just one side of the body, but a movement such as standing up or sitting down must include both sides.

The functions of the lateral and medial tracts should be easy to remember: The lateral tract controls muscles in the lateral parts of the body, such as hands and feet. The medial tract controls muscles in the medial parts of the body, including trunk and neck.

Figure 7.12 compares the lateral and medial corticospinal tracts. Figure 7.13 compares the lateral tract to the spinal pathway bringing touch information to the cortex. Note that both paths cross in the medulla and that the touch information arrives at brain areas side by side with those areas responsible for motor control. Touch is obviously essential for movement. You have to know what your hands are doing now in order to control their next action.

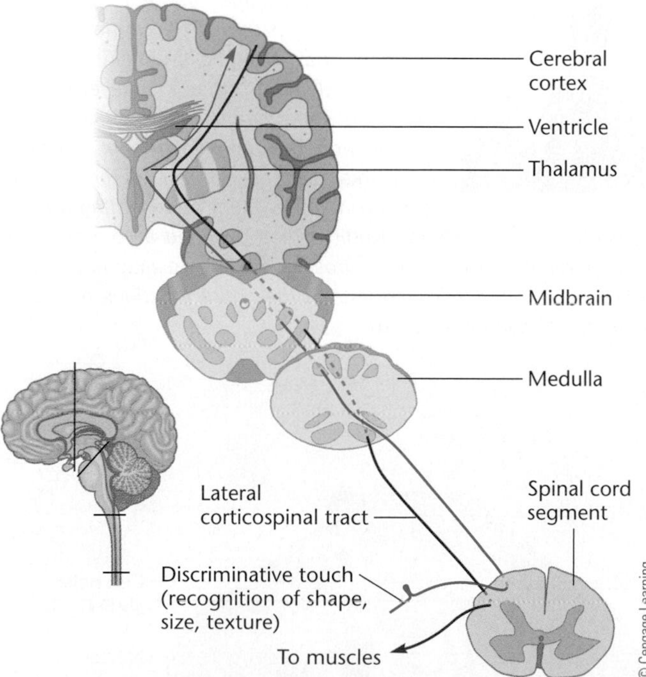

FIGURE 7.13 The touch path and the lateral corticospinal tract Both paths cross in the medulla so that each hemisphere has access to the opposite side of the body. The touch path goes from touch receptors toward the brain; the corticospinal path goes from the brain to the muscles.

Suppose someone suffers a stroke that damages the primary motor cortex of the left hemisphere. The result is a loss of the lateral tract from that hemisphere and a loss of movement control on the right side of the body. Eventually, depending on the location and amount of damage, the person may regain some muscle control from spared axons in the lateral tract. If not, using the medial tract can approximate the intended movement. For example, someone with no direct control of the hand muscles might move the shoulders, trunk, and hips in a way that repositions the hand.

STOP & CHECK

12. What kinds of movements does the lateral tract control? The medial tract?

ANSWER

12. The lateral tract controls detailed movements in the periphery on the contralateral side of the body. (For example, the lateral tract from the left hemisphere controls the right side of the body.) The medial tract controls trunk movements bilaterally.

The Cerebellum

The term *cerebellum* is Latin for "little brain." Decades ago, most texts described the function of the cerebellum as "balance and coordination." Well, yes, people with cerebellar damage do lose balance and coordination, but that description understates the importance of this structure. The cerebellum contains more neurons than the rest of the brain combined (R. W. Williams & Herrup, 1988) and a huge number of synapses. The cerebellum processes far more information than its small size might suggest.

One effect of cerebellar damage is trouble with rapid movements that require aim, timing, and alternations of movements. For example, people with cerebellar damage have trouble tapping a rhythm, clapping hands, pointing at a moving object, speaking, writing, typing, or playing a musical instrument. They are impaired at almost all athletic activities, except ones like weightlifting that do not require aim or timing. Researchers have found enlarged cerebellums in college basketball players (I. Park et al., 2009) and competitive speed skaters (I. Park et al., 2012). The results did not indicate whether that enlargement was a cause or result of their athletic skill.

However, cerebellar damage does not impair *continuous* motor activity (Spencer, Zelaznik, Diedrichsen, & Ivry, 2003). For example, people with such damage can draw continuous circles like the ones shown here, which do not require starting or stopping an action.

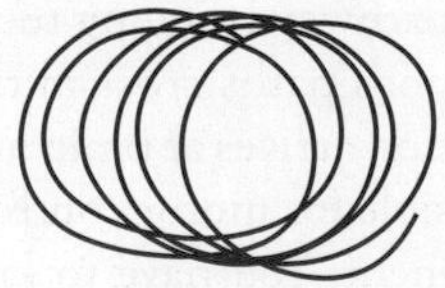

Here is a quick way to test the cerebellum: Ask someone to focus on one spot and then to move the eyes quickly to another spot. Saccades (sa-KAHDS), ballistic eye movements from one fixation point to another, depend on impulses from the cerebellum and the frontal cortex to the cranial nerves. Someone with cerebellar damage has difficulty programming the angle and distance of eye movements (Dichgans, 1984). The eyes make many short movements until, by trial and error, they eventually find the intended spot.

In the *finger-to-nose test,* the person is instructed to hold one arm straight out and then, at command, to touch his or her nose as quickly as possible. A normal person does so in three steps. First, the finger moves ballistically to a point just in front of the nose. This *move* function depends on the cerebellar cortex (the surface of the cerebellum), which sends messages to the deep nuclei (clusters of cell bodies) in the interior of the cerebellum (see Figure 7.14). Second, the finger remains steady at that spot for a fraction of a second. This *hold* function depends on the nuclei alone (Kornhuber, 1974). Finally, the finger moves to the nose by a slower movement that does not depend on the cerebellum.

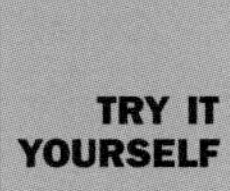

TRY IT YOURSELF

Someone with damage to the cerebellar cortex has trouble with the initial rapid movement. The finger misses the nose, stops too soon, or goes too far. Someone with damage to the cerebellar nuclei has difficulty with the hold segment: The finger reaches a point in front of the nose and then wavers.

The symptoms of cerebellar damage resemble those of alcohol intoxication: clumsiness, slurred speech, and inaccurate eye movements. A police officer testing someone for drunkenness may use the finger-to-nose test or similar tests because the cerebellum is one of the first brain areas that alcohol affects.

Functions Other than Movement

The cerebellum is not only a motor structure. In one study, functional MRI measured cerebellar activity while people performed several tasks (Gao et al., 1996). When they simply lifted objects, the cerebellum showed little activity. When they felt things with both hands to decide whether they were the same or different, the cerebellum was much more active. The cerebellum responded even when the experimenter rubbed an object across an unmoving hand. That is, the cerebellum responds to sensory stimuli even in the absence of movement. The cerebellum also responds to violations of sensory expectations. If you reach out your hand expecting to feel something and then don't feel it, or feel something when you didn't expect to, your cerebellum reacts strongly (Schlerf, Ivry, & Diedrichsen, 2012).

What, then, is the role of the cerebellum? Masao Ito (1984) proposed that a key role is to establish new motor programs that enable one to execute a sequence of actions as a whole. Inspired by this idea, many researchers reported evidence that cerebellar damage impairs motor learning. Richard Ivry and his colleagues have emphasized the importance of the cerebellum for behaviors that depend on precise timing of short intervals (from about a millisecond to 1.5 seconds). Any sequence of rapid movements obviously requires timing. Many perceptual and cognitive tasks also require timing—for example, judging which of two visual stimuli is moving faster or listening to two pairs of tones and comparing the delays between them.

Masao Ito

Brains seem to be built on several principles such that numerous neurons interact with each other through excitation and inhibition, that synaptic plasticity provides memory elements, that multilayered neuronal networks bear a high computational power, and that combination of neuronal networks, sensors, and effectors constitutes a neural system representing a brain function. Thus, Hebbian tradition has provided a very successful paradigm in modern neuroscience, but we may have to go beyond it in order to understand the entire functions of brains. (personal communication)

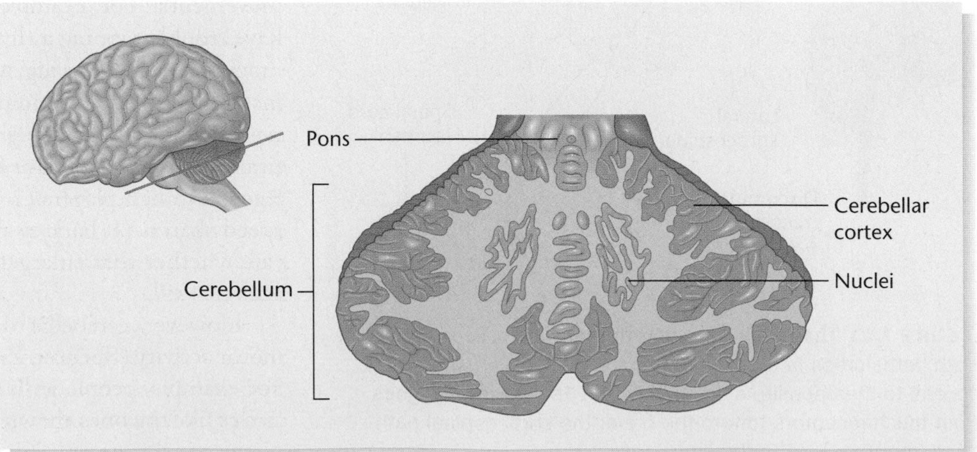

FIGURE 7.14 Location of the cerebellar nuclei relative to the cerebellar cortex
In the inset at the upper left, the line indicates the plane shown in detail at the lower right.

People who are accurate at one kind of timed movement, such as tapping a rhythm with a finger, tend also to be good at other timed movements, such as tapping a rhythm with a foot, and at judging which visual stimulus moved faster and which delay between tones was longer. People with cerebellar damage are impaired at all of these tasks but unimpaired at controlling the force of a movement or at judging which tone is louder (Ivry & Diener, 1991; Keele & Ivry, 1990). In short, the cerebellum is important mainly for tasks that require timing.

The cerebellum also appears critical for certain aspects of attention. In one study, people were told to keep their eyes fixated on a central point. At various times, they would see the letter E on either the left or right half of the screen, and they were to indicate the direction in which it was oriented (E, Ǝ, Ш, or ᗰ) without moving their eyes. Sometimes, they saw a signal telling where the letter would be on the screen. For most people, that signal improved their performance even if it appeared just 100 ms before the letter. For people with cerebellar damage, the signal had to appear nearly a second before the letter to be helpful. Evidently, people with cerebellar damage need longer to shift their attention (Townsend et al., 1999).

STOP&CHECK

13. What kind of perceptual task would be most impaired by damage to the cerebellum?

ANSWER

13. Damage to the cerebellum impairs perceptual tasks that depend on accurate timing.

Cellular Organization

The cerebellum receives input from the spinal cord, from each of the sensory systems by way of the cranial nerve nuclei, and from the cerebral cortex. That information eventually reaches the **cerebellar cortex**, the surface of the cerebellum (see Figure 7.14).

Figure 7.15 shows the types and arrangements of neurons in the cerebellar cortex. The figure is complex, but concentrate on these main points:

- The neurons are arranged in a precise geometrical pattern, with multiple repetitions of the same units.
- The **Purkinje** (pur-KIN-jee) **cells** are flat (two-dimensional) cells in sequential planes, parallel to one another.
- The **parallel fibers** are axons parallel to one another and perpendicular to the planes of the Purkinje cells.
- Action potentials in parallel fibers excite one Purkinje cell after another. Each Purkinje cell then transmits an inhibitory message to cells in the **nuclei of the cerebellum** (clusters of cell bodies in the interior of the cerebellum) and the vestibular nuclei in the brainstem, which in turn send information to the midbrain and the thalamus.
- Depending on which and how many parallel fibers are active, they might stimulate only the first few Purkinje cells or a long series of them. Because the parallel fibers' messages reach different Purkinje cells one after another, the greater the number of excited Purkinje cells, the greater their collective *duration* of response. That is, if the parallel fibers stimulate only the first few Purkinje cells, the result is a brief message to the target cells; if they stimulate more Purkinje cells, the message lasts longer. The output of Purkinje cells controls the timing of a movement, including both its onset and offset (Thier, Dicke, Haas, & Barash, 2000).

STOP&CHECK

14. How are the parallel fibers arranged relative to one another and to the Purkinje cells?

15. If a larger number of parallel fibers are active, what is the effect on the collective output of the Purkinje cells?

ANSWERS

14. The parallel fibers are parallel to one another and perpendicular to the planes of the Purkinje cells. **15.** As a larger number of parallel fibers become active, the Purkinje cells increase their duration of response.

The Basal Ganglia

The term **basal ganglia** applies collectively to a group of large subcortical structures in the forebrain (see Figure 7.16). (*Ganglia* is a plural noun, the plural of *ganglion*.) Various authorities differ in which structures they include as part of the basal ganglia, but everyone includes at least the **caudate nucleus**, the **putamen** (pyuh-TAY-men), and the **globus pallidus**. The caudate nucleus and putamen together are known as the **striatum** or **dorsal striatum**. The striatum receives input from the cerebral cortex and substantia nigra and sends its output to the globus pallidus, which then sends output to the thalamus, which relays it to the frontal cortex. Figure 7.17 shows two pathways, known as the direct and indirect pathways. The direct pathway from the striatum inhibits the globus pallidus, which inhibits part of the thalamus. By inhibiting an inhibitor, the net effect is excitation. Neuroscientists long believed that the direct pathway stimulates movements whereas the indirect pathway inhibits them. However, later evidence found that both pathways are active before a movement and neither is active when the animal is at rest (Cui et al., 2013). Probably the direct pathway enhances the selected movement whereas the indirect pathway inhibits inappropriate competing movements (Kravitz, Tye, & Kreitzer, 2012). The indirect pathway is essential for learned performance. Researchers found that impairing the indirect pathway greatly slowed rats' ability to learn to press one lever or another depending on what tone they heard (Nishizawa et al., 2012).

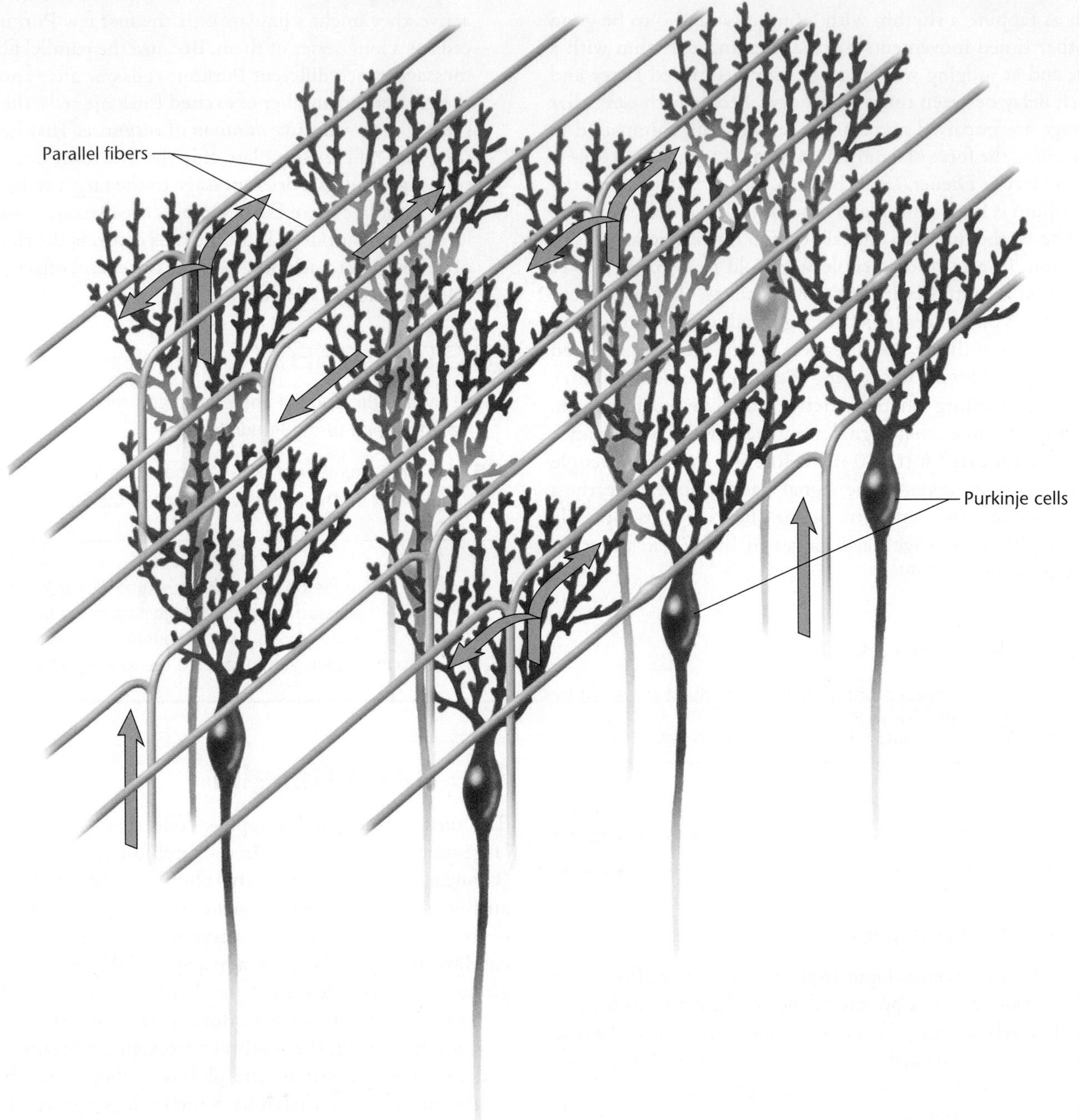

FIGURE 7.15 Cellular organization of the cerebellum
Parallel fibers (yellow) activate one Purkinje cell after another. Purkinje cells (red) inhibit a target cell in one of the nuclei of the cerebellum (not shown, but toward the bottom of the illustration). The more Purkinje cells that respond, the longer the target cell is inhibited. In this way, the cerebellum controls the duration of a movement.

The basal ganglia are particularly important for spontaneous, self-initiated behaviors. For example, a monkey in one study was trained to move one hand to the left or right to receive food. On trials when it heard a signal indicating exactly when to move, the basal ganglia showed little activity. However, on other trials the monkey saw a light indicating that it should start its movement in not less than 1.5 seconds and finish in not more than 3 seconds. Therefore, the monkey had to choose its own starting time. Under those conditions, the basal ganglia were highly active (Turner & Anderson, 2005).

In another study, people used a computer mouse to draw lines on a screen while researchers used PET scans to examine brain activity. Activity in the basal ganglia increased when people drew a new line but not when they

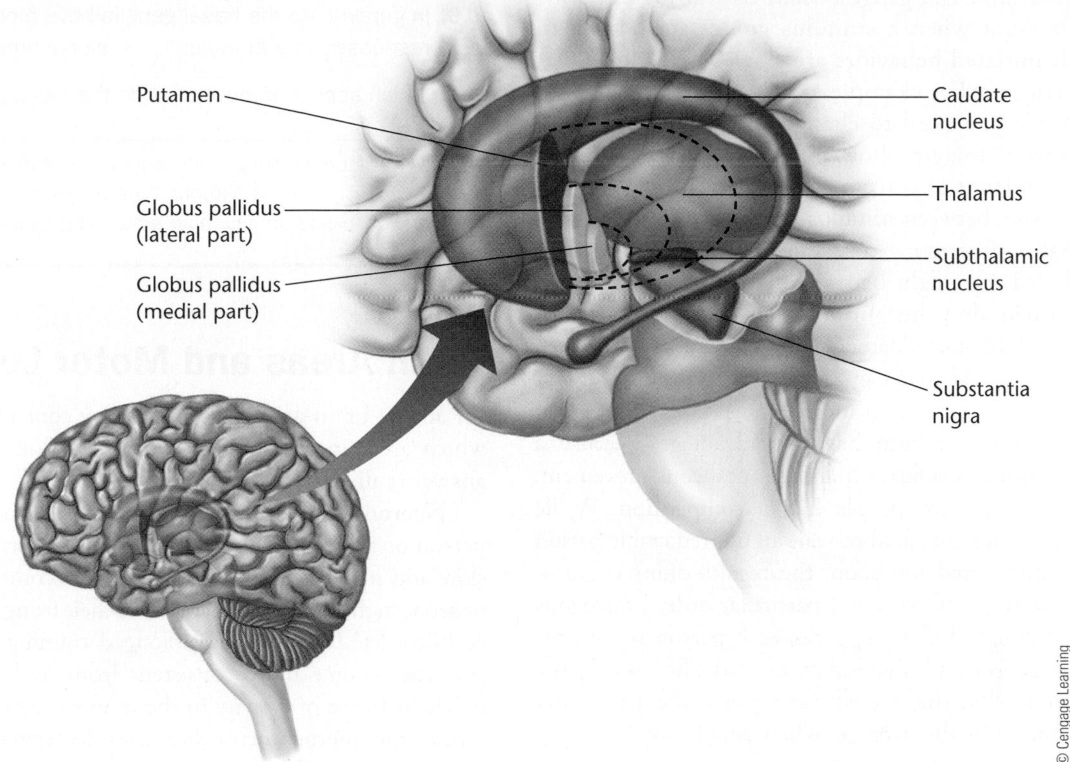

FIGURE 7.16 Location of the basal ganglia
The basal ganglia surround the thalamus and are surrounded by the cerebral cortex.

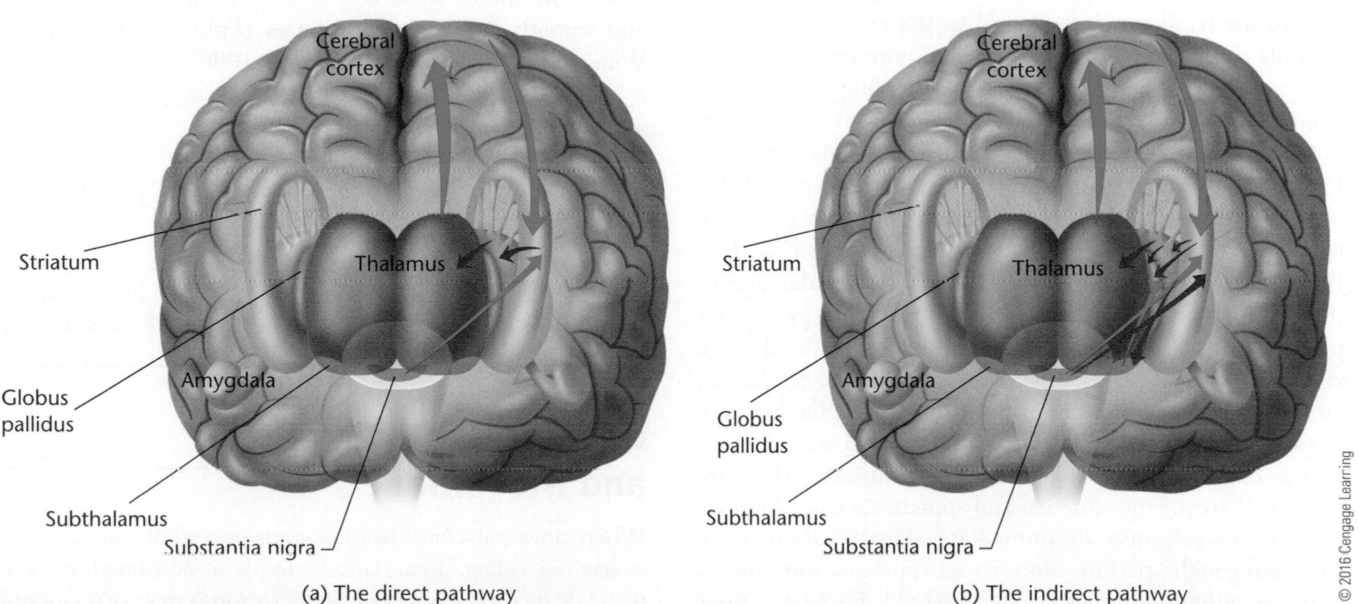

FIGURE 7.17 Two pathways through the basal ganglia
The indirect pathway has extra connections within the globus pallidus and back and forth to the subthalamus.

traced a line already on the screen (Jueptner & Weiller, 1998). Again, the basal ganglia seem critical for initiating an action but not when a stimulus guides the action. In general, self-initiated behaviors are slower than those that a stimulus triggers. For example, if you are driving your car and you decide you need to change lanes to make a turn, you react slowly. Imagine how much faster you react if a deer charges in front of you.

The difference between stimulus-initiated and self-initiated behaviors has an interesting consequence. Many old Western movies included a gunfight between the hero and the villain. Always the villain drew his gun first, but the hero was faster, and even though he started later, he won the draw. Researchers wondered, is that realistic? Could someone draw second and still win? The answer is yes, and in some cases the person drawing second might even have an advantage, because a reaction to a stimulus is faster than a spontaneous movement. In one experiment, two people had a competition. While watching each other, they had to wait an unpredictable period of time—if they acted too soon, the results didn't count—and then press three buttons in a particular order (analogous to drawing a gun and shooting). So, each person sometimes initiated the action and sometimes reacted after seeing the other person act, but the one who completed the action first was the winner. On the average, when people were reacting to the other person's act, they made the movements 9 percent faster (Welchman, Stanley, Schomers, Miall, & Bülthoff, 2010). So, you just learned something useful for the next time you get into a gunfight.

The role of the basal ganglia in movement control has gradually become clearer. Because cells in the primary motor cortex become active before those in the basal ganglia, the basal ganglia must not be responsible for selecting which movement to make. Rather, their role is to regulate the vigor of the movement (Turner & Desmurget, 2010). Many cells in the basal ganglia respond to the reward value of a possible action. That is, cells respond more strongly in the presence of signals indicating that responding will produce a larger or more certain reward (Cromwell & Schultz, 2003; Lau & Glimcher, 2008; Samejima, Ueda, Doya, & Kimura, 2005). Stimulating dopamine type 1 receptors (D1) in the direct pathway of the striatum produces the same behavioral effects that an increase in reward does (Tai, Lee, Benavidez, Bonci, & Wilbrecht, 2012). After damage to the striatum, animals still learn to choose the response that produces the larger reward, but they don't respond more vigorously for the larger reward (Wang, Miura, & Uchida, 2013). Describing the role of the basal ganglia in these terms makes sense of what we see in patients with damage to the basal ganglia, as in Parkinson's disease. They are capable of strong movements, and sometimes they do move strongly, in response to immediate signals. (Remember, the basal ganglia pertain more to self-initiated movements than to stimulus-triggered movements.) However, their spontaneous movements are slow and weak, as if they felt little motivation to move. We consider Parkinson's disease in more detail in the next module.

STOP & CHECK

16. In general, do the basal ganglia have more effect on responses to a stimulus or on self-initiated movements?

17. Which aspect of movement do the basal ganglia control?

ANSWERS

16. The basal ganglia have more influence on self-initiated movements, which are generally slower. **17.** The basal ganglia control the vigor of movements.

Brain Areas and Motor Learning

Of all the brain areas responsible for control of movement, which are important for learning new skills? The apparent answer is all of them.

Neurons in the motor cortex adjust their responses as a person or animal learns a motor skill. At first, movements are slow and inconsistent. As movements become faster, relevant neurons in the motor cortex increase their firing rates (D. Cohen & Nicolelis, 2004). After prolonged training, the movement patterns become more consistent from trial to trial, and so do the patterns of activity in the motor cortex. In engineering terms, the motor cortex increases its signal-to-noise ratio (Kargo & Nitz, 2004).

The basal ganglia are critical for learning new habits (Yin & Knowlton, 2006). For example, when you are first learning to drive a car, you have to think about everything you do. Eventually, you learn to signal for a left turn, change gears, turn the wheel, and change speed all at once. If you try to explain exactly what you do, you will probably find it difficult. People with basal ganglia damage are impaired at learning motor skills and at converting new movements into smooth, "automatic" responses (Poldrack et al., 2005; Willingham, Koroshetz, & Peterson, 1996).

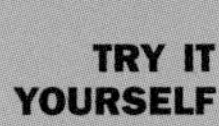

STOP & CHECK

18. What kind of learning depends most heavily on the basal ganglia?

ANSWER

18. The basal ganglia are essential for learning motor habits that are difficult to describe in words.

Conscious Decisions and Movement

Where does conscious decision come into all of this? Each of us has the feeling, "I consciously decide to do something, and then I do it." That sequence seems so obvious that we might not even question it, but research casts doubt on this assumption.

Imagine yourself in the following study (Libet, Gleason, Wright, & Pearl, 1983). You are instructed to flex your wrist

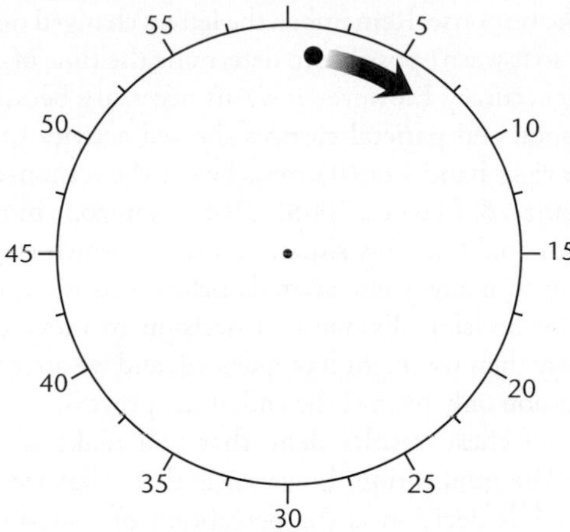

FIGURE 7.18 Procedure for Libet's study of conscious decision and movement

The participant was to make a spontaneous decision to move the wrist and remember where the light was at the time of that decision. Based on "Time of conscious intention to act in relation to onset of cerebral activities (readiness potential): The unconscious initiation of a freely voluntary act," by B. Libet et al., in *Brain, 106*, pp. 623-642

whenever you choose. You don't choose which movement to make, but you choose the time freely. You should not decide in advance when to move but let the urge occur as spontaneously as possible. The researchers take three measurements. First, they attach electrodes to your scalp to record evoked electrical activity over your motor cortex. Second, they attach a sensor to record when your hand starts to move. The third measurement is your self-report: You watch a clocklike device, as shown in Figure 7.18, in which a spot of light moves around the circle every 2.56 seconds. You are to watch that clock. Do not decide in advance that you will flex your wrist when the spot on the clock gets to a certain point. However, when you do decide to move, note where the spot of light is at the moment when you decide, and remember it so you can report it later.

The procedure starts. You think, "Not yet . . . not yet . . . not yet . . . NOW!" You note where the spot was at that critical instant and report, "I made my decision when the light was at the 25 position." The researchers compare your report to their records of your brain activity and your wrist movement. On the average, people report that their decision to move occurred about 200 ms before the actual movement. (The *decision* occurred then. People *report* the decision later.) For example, if you reported that your decision to move occurred at position 25, your decision preceded the movement by 200 ms, and the movement began at position 30. (Remember, the light moves around the circle in 2.56 seconds.) However, your motor cortex produces a kind of activity called a **readiness potential** before any voluntary movement, and on the average, the readiness potential begins at least 500 ms before the movement. In this example, it would start when the light was at position 18, as illustrated in Figure 7.19.

The results varied among individuals, but most were similar. The key point is that the brain activity responsible for the movement apparently began *before* the person's conscious decision! The results seem to indicate that your conscious decision does not cause your action. Rather, you become conscious of the decision after the process leading to action has already been underway for about 300 ms.

As you can imagine, this experiment has sparked much discussion among philosophers as well as psychologists. The result itself has been replicated in several laboratories, so the facts are solid (e.g., Lau, Rogers, Haggard, & Passingham, 2004; Trevena & Miller, 2002). One objection is that people cannot accurately report the time they become conscious of something. However, when people are asked to report the time of a sensory stimulus, or the time that they made a movement

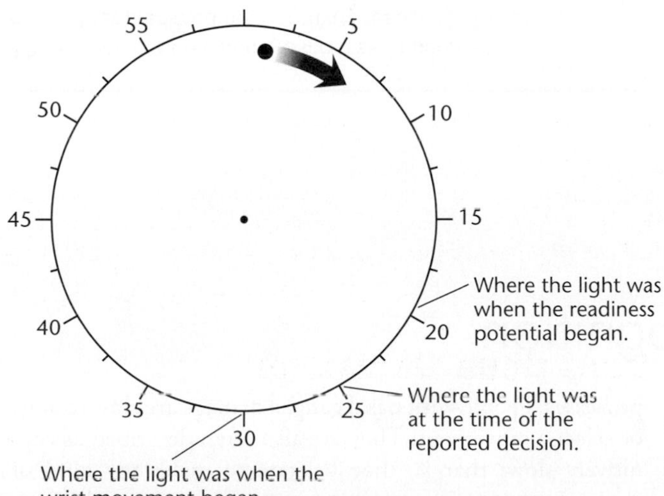

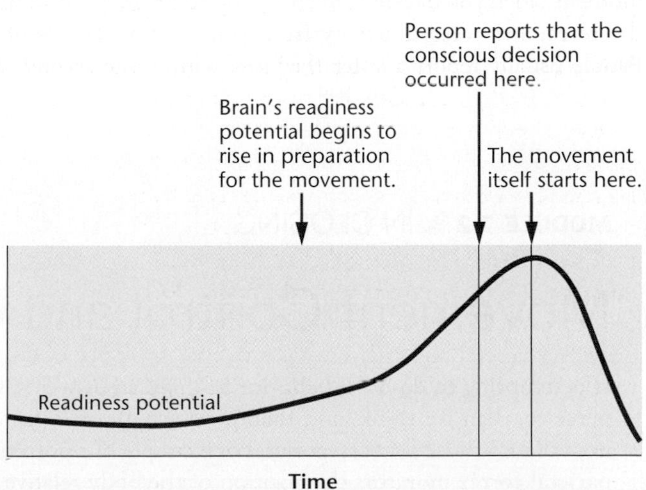

FIGURE 7.19 Results from study of conscious decision and movement

On the average, the brain's readiness potential began at least 300 ms before the reported decision, which occurred 200 ms before the movement. Based on "Time of conscious intention to act in relation to onset of cerebral activities (readiness potential): The unconscious initiation of a freely voluntary act," by B. Libet et al., *in Brain, 106*, pp. 623-642 (instead of the decision to move), their estimates are usually within 30 to 50 ms of the correct time (Lau et al., 2004; Libet et al., 1983). That is, they cannot report the exact time when something happens, but they are close.

Nevertheless, it could easily be that we are less accurate at reporting the time of a conscious decision than the time of a sensory stimulus. After all, we often need to know when something happened, but we seldom need to know exactly when we made a decision. Furthermore, Libet's method asks someone to identify an instant when he or she decided to flex the wrist, as if the decision happened instantaneously. In fact, such a decision builds up gradually (Guggisberg & Mottaz, 2013). The movement is a spontaneous, self-initiated movement, the type that depends on the basal ganglia, the type that generally has a slow onset. Reporting when you decided to make a voluntary movement is like reporting when you fell in love with someone: You can report the time when you were sure of it, but the process developed gradually long before that.

When people report the time of their decision, maybe they are just guessing. Suppose we repeat Libet's experiment with one change: When you make your movement, you will hear a sound, which you naturally assume is simultaneous with your movement. Sometimes it is, but sometimes it is delayed by a fraction of a second after your movement. On occasions when it is delayed, your reported time of making a conscious decision is also delayed! Apparently your report of when you made your decision depends on when you think the movement occurred (Banks & Isham, 2009; Rigoni, Brass, & Sartori, 2010). If your report of when you decided is little more than a guess, then Libet's results don't tell us as much as we thought they did.

Let's consider one more experiment: You watch a screen that displays letters of the alphabet, one at a time, changing every half-second. In this case you choose not just when to act, but which of two acts to do. You should decide at some point whether to press a button on the left or one on the right, press it immediately, and remember what letter was on the screen at the moment when you decided which button to press. Meanwhile, the researchers record activity from your cortex. The result: People usually report a letter they saw within one second of making the response. Remember, the letters changed only twice a second, so it wasn't possible to determine the time of decision with great accuracy. However, it wasn't necessary, because parts of the frontal and parietal cortices showed activity specific to the left or right hand *7 to 10 seconds* before the response (Soon, Brass, Heinze, & Haynes, 2008). That is, someone monitoring your cortex could, in this situation, predict which choice you were going to make a few seconds before you were aware of making the decision. Evidently a decision to move develops more slowly than we might have guessed, and we are conscious of the decision only toward the end of the process.

None of these results deny that you make a *voluntary* decision. The implication, however, is that what we identify as a conscious decision is the perception of a gradual brain process. It probably begins with unconscious processes that build up to a certain level before they become conscious.

Does brain activity always start 7 to 10 seconds before a movement? Of course not. If you see or hear something that calls for an action—such as a pedestrian darting into the road while you are driving—you respond within a split second. Again you see the importance of the distinction between stimulus-triggered movements and self-initiated movements.

STOP&CHECK

19. Explain the evidence that someone's conscious decision to move does not cause the movement.

20. On what basis are some researchers skeptical of this evidence?

ANSWERS

19. Researchers recorded responses in people's cortex that predicted the upcoming response. Those brain responses occurred earlier than the time people reported as "when they made the decision." **20.** The studies assume that people accurately report the times of their intentions. However, people's reports are influenced by events after the movement, and therefore we cannot be confident of their accuracy.

MODULE 7.2 ■ IN CLOSING

Movement Control and Cognition

It is tempting to describe behavior in three steps—first we perceive, then we think, and finally we act. Brain areas do not fall into those neat categories. For example, the posterior parietal cortex monitors the position of the body relative to visual space and thereby helps guide movement. Its functions are sensory, cognitive, and motor. The cerebellum has traditionally been considered a major part of the motor system, but it is now known to be important in timing sensory processes. People with basal ganglia damage are slow to start or select a movement. They are also often described as cognitively slow; that is, they hesitate to make any kind of choice. In short, organizing a movement is not something we tack on at the end of our thinking. It is intimately intertwined with all of our sensory and cognitive processes. The study of movement is not just the study of muscles. It is the study of how we decide what to do.

Summary

1. The primary motor cortex is the main source of brain input to the spinal cord. The spinal cord contains central pattern generators that actually control the muscles. **235**
2. Each area of the motor cortex is closely aligned with a portion of the somatosensory cortex that pertains to the same body part. **235**
3. The primary motor cortex produces patterns representing the intended outcome, not just the muscle contractions. **237**
4. Areas near the primary motor cortex—including the prefrontal, premotor, and supplementary motor cortices—are active in detecting stimuli for movement and preparing for a movement. **237**
5. The ability to inhibit an inappropriate behavior develops gradually in children and adolescents, depending on maturation of the prefrontal cortex and basal ganglia. **238**
6. Mirror neurons in various brain areas respond to both a self-produced movement and an observation of a similar movement by another individual. Although some neurons may have built-in mirror properties, at least some of them acquire these properties by learning. Their role in imitation and social behavior is potentially important but as yet uncertain. **238**
7. The lateral tract, which controls movements in the periphery of the body, has axons that cross from one side of the brain to the opposite side of the spinal cord. The medial tract controls bilateral movements near the midline of the body. **239**
8. The cerebellum is critical for rapid movements that require accurate aim and timing. **241**
9. The cerebellum has multiple roles in behavior, including sensory functions related to perception of the timing or rhythm of stimuli. **242**
10. The cells of the cerebellum are arranged in a regular pattern that enables them to produce outputs of precisely controlled duration. **243**
11. The basal ganglia are a group of large subcortical structures that are important for self-initiated behaviors. The basal ganglia process information about probable rewards and thereby regulate the vigor of responses. **243**
12. The learning of a motor skill depends on changes occurring in both the cerebral cortex and the basal ganglia. **246**
13. When people identify the instant when they formed a conscious intention to move, their time precedes the actual movement by about 200 ms but follows the start of motor cortex activity by about 300 ms. However, it is not clear how accurately people can report the time of a conscious decision. A voluntary decision to move develops gradually, not suddenly. **246**

Key Terms

Terms are defined in the module on the page number indicated. They're also presented in alphabetical order with definitions in the book's Subject Index/Glossary. Interactive flash cards, audio reviews, and crossword puzzles are among the online resources available to help you learn these terms and the concepts they represent.

antisaccade task **238**
basal ganglia **243**
caudate nucleus **243**
cerebellar cortex **243**
corticospinal tracts **239**
globus pallidus **243**
lateral corticospinal tract **240**
medial corticospinal tract **241**
mirror neurons **238**
nuclei of the cerebellum **243**
parallel fibers **243**
posterior parietal cortex **237**
prefrontal cortex **238**
premotor cortex **238**
primary motor cortex **235**
Purkinje cells **243**
putamen **243**
readiness potential **247**
red nucleus **240**
striatum or dorsal striatum **243**
supplementary motor cortex **237**
vestibular nucleus **241**

Thought Question

Human infants are at first limited to gross movements of the trunk, arms, and legs. The ability to move one finger at a time matures gradually over at least the first year. What hypothesis would you suggest about which brain areas controlling movement mature early and which areas mature later?

MODULE 7.2 End of Module Quiz

1. A brief stimulation in the motor cortex, less than 50 ms, produces what kind of result?
   a. Isolated muscle twitches
   b. Contraction of a particular combination of muscles
   c. Contraction of whatever muscles are necessary to produce a particular outcome
   d. Contractions of different muscles that vary unpredictably from one trial to another

2. A half-second stimulation in the motor cortex produces what kind of result?
   a. Isolated muscle twitches
   b. Contraction of a particular combination of muscles
   c. Contraction of whatever muscles are necessary to produce a particular outcome
   d. Contractions of different muscles that vary unpredictably from one trial to another

3. When do the posterior parietal cortex, premotor cortex, and supplementary motor cortex become most active?
   a. During the second or two in preparation for a movement
   b. During the movement itself
   c. During the second or two after a movement

4. What does the antisaccade task measure?
   a. Which brain areas are active during preparation for a movement
   b. The role of mirror neurons in imitation behaviors
   c. Someone's ability to inhibit a movement
   d. The relative contributions of the medial and lateral pathways in the spinal cord

5. The lateral tract of the spinal cord controls ___________. The medial tract controls _________.
   a. peripheral movements on the contralateral side (relative to the side of the brain where the tract originated) . . . trunk movements bilaterally
   b. peripheral movements on the ipsilateral side . . . trunk movements bilaterally
   c. trunk movements bilaterally . . . peripheral movements on the contralateral side
   d. trunk movements bilaterally . . . peripheral movements on the ipsilateral side

6. Where does the medial corticospinal tract originate in the brain?
   a. From the primary motor cortex
   b. From the primary motor cortex plus the red nucleus
   c. From many parts of the cortex, plus the tectum, reticular formation, and vestibular nucleus
   d. From the somatosensory cortex

7. Alcohol intoxication produces clumsiness, poor aim, impaired voluntary eye movements, and slurred speech. Damage to what brain structure yields these same deficits?
   a. Corpus callosum
   b. Ventromedial hypothalamus
   c. Cerebellum
   d. Red nucleus

8. How are the parallel fibers arranged relative to the Purkinje cells?
   a. They are parallel to them.
   b. They are perpendicular to them.
   c. They are arranged at random angles.

9. What is the probable role of the indirect pathway in the basal ganglia?
   a. It is active when the animal is at rest.
   b. It stimulates appropriate movements.
   c. It inhibits inappropriate competing movements.
   d. It produces imitation of other people's movements.

10. Which of the following generally characterizes the movements that depend heavily on the basal ganglia?
    a. Stimulus-triggered, and generally faster than self-initiated movements.
    b. Stimulus-triggered, and generally slower than self-initiated movements.
    c. Self-initiated, and generally faster than responses that a stimulus triggers.
    d. Self-initiated, and generally slower than responses that a stimulus triggers.

11. In what way, if at all, does basal ganglia activity relate to motivation?
   a. The basal ganglia increase vigor of response depending on expected reward value.
   b. The basal ganglia help to maintain constant behavior even when motivation is low.
   c. The basal ganglia become active only when you are competing against someone else.
   d. Basal ganglia activity has nothing to do with motivation.

12. What kind of learning depends most heavily on the basal ganglia?
   a. Learned movements that depend on precise timing
   b. Motor habits that are difficult to describe in words
   c. Learning to recall specific life events
   d. Learning what foods to eat

13. According to Libet's study, what is the order of events in a voluntary movement?
   a. People form an intention, then activity begins in the premotor cortex, and finally the movement starts.
   b. People form an intention at the same time that activity begins in the premotor cortex, and a bit later, the movement starts.
   c. Activity begins in the premotor cortex, and a bit later, people are aware of forming an intention, and finally the movement starts.
   d. Activity begins in the premotor cortex, and a bit later, people are aware of forming an intention, and simultaneously the movement starts.

14. What evidence suggests that people misperceive the time when they made a conscious decision?
   a. People inaccurately report the time of a sensory stimulus.
   b. An event shortly after the movement changes the reported time of the decision.
   c. People who are more highly motivated report earlier decision times.

ANSWERS: 1a, 2c, 3a, 4c, 5a, 6c, 7c, 8b, 9c, 10d, 11a, 12b, 13c, 14b.

Movement Disorders

If you have damage in your spinal cord, peripheral nerves, or muscles, you cannot move, but cognitively you are the same as ever. In contrast, brain disorders that impair movement also impair mood, memory, and cognition. We consider two examples: Parkinson's disease and Huntington's disease.

Parkinson's Disease

The main symptoms of **Parkinson's disease** (also known as *Parkinson disease*) are rigidity, muscle tremors, slow movements, and difficulty initiating physical and mental activity. It becomes more common as people age, striking 1 percent to 2 percent of people over age 65. Early symptoms usually include loss of olfaction (Wattendorf et al., 2009) and psychological depression (Ouchi et al., 1999). Many but not all Parkinson's patients have cognitive deficits, which may include problems with attention, language, or memory (Miller, Neargarder, Risi, & Cronin-Golomb, 2013).

The immediate cause of Parkinson's disease is the gradual loss of neurons in the substantia nigra and therefore a loss of dopamine-releasing axons to the striatum (part of the basal ganglia). With the loss of this input, the striatum decreases its inhibition of the globus pallidus, which therefore increases its inhibitory input to the thalamus, as shown in Figure 7.20. The result is less vigorous voluntary movements. People with Parkinson's disease are still capable of movement, and sometimes they move normally in response to signals or instructions, such as when following a parade (Teitelbaum, Pellis, & Pellis, 1991). However, their spontaneous movements are slow and weak.

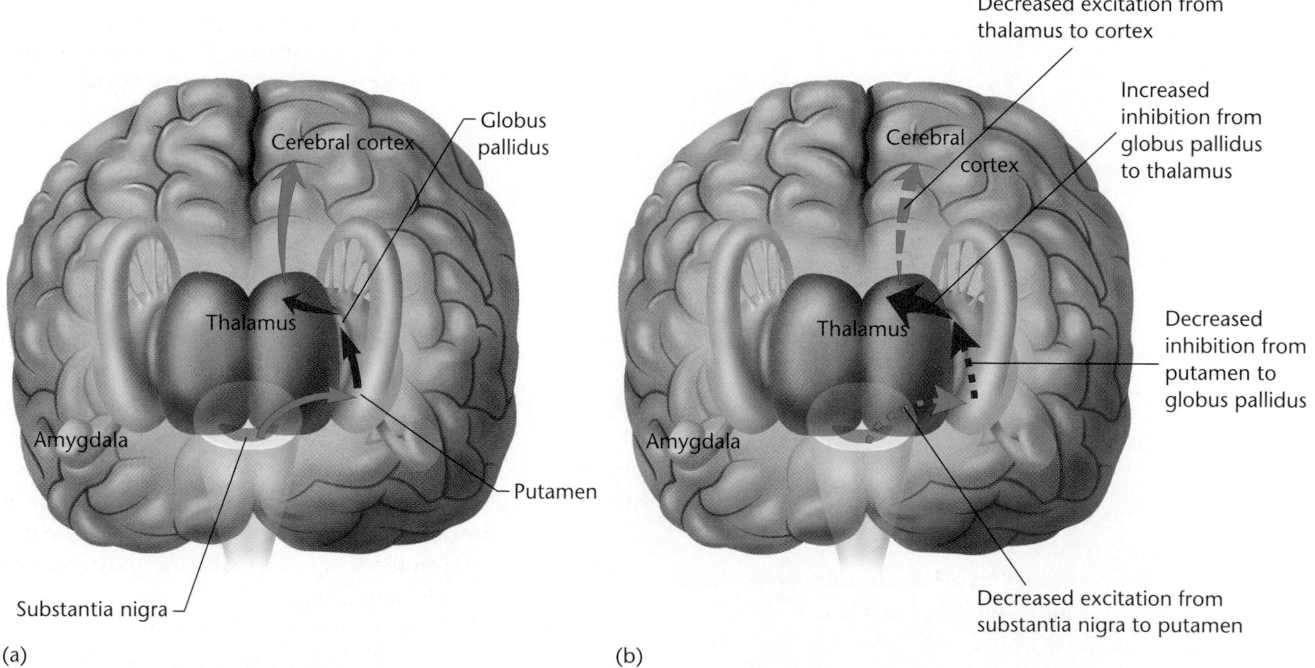

FIGURE 7.20 Connections from the substantia nigra: (a) normal and (b) in Parkinson's disease
Excitatory paths are shown in green; inhibitory are in red. Decreased excitation from the substantia nigra decreases inhibition from the striatum, leading to increased inhibition from the globus pallidus. The net result is decreased excitation from the thalamus to the cortex. *Source:* Based on Yin & Knowlton, 2006

Causes

What causes the damage to the substantia nigra? An early study reported that having a monozygotic twin with early-onset Parkinson's disease greatly increased your probability of getting it, but having a monozygotic twin with late-onset disease had no effect (Tanner et al., 1999). That result implied that genes make little or no contribution to late-onset Parkinson's disease. Later studies have found less extreme results, indicating that genes do influence the late-onset disease, though less strongly than they impact early-onset disease (Thacker & Ascherio, 2008). So far, researchers have identified more than 20 genes that apparently increase the risk of Parkinson's disease, although the results vary from one study to another, and one population to another (Do et al., 2011; Pihlstrom et al., 2013). The results agree, however, that none of these genes by itself produces a high risk.

An accidental discovery implicated exposure to toxins as another factor in Parkinson's disease (Ballard, Tetrud, & Langston, 1985). In northern California in 1982, several young adults developed symptoms of Parkinson's disease after using a drug similar to heroin. Before the investigators could alert the community to the danger, many other users had developed symptoms ranging from mild to fatal (Tetrud, Langston, Garbe, & Ruttenber, 1989). The substance responsible for the symptoms was **MPTP**, a chemical that the body converts to **MPP^+**, which accumulates in, and then destroys, neurons that release dopamine, partly by impairing the transport of mitochondria from the cell body to the synapse[1] (Kim-Han, Antenor-Dorsey, & O'Malley, 2011; Nicklas, Saporito, Basma, Geller, & Heikkila, 1992). Postsynaptic neurons react to the loss of input by increasing their number of dopamine receptors (Chiueh, 1988).

No one supposes that Parkinson's disease often results from using illegal drugs. A more likely hypothesis is that people are sometimes exposed to hazardous environmental chemicals that damage cells of the substantia nigra. Many studies have shown increased risk of Parkinson's disease among people with much exposure to insecticides, herbicides, and fungicides, including paraquat, rotenone, maneb, and ziram (Freire & Koifman, 2012; Pezzoli & Cereda, 2013; Tanner et al., 2011; A. Wang et al., 2011). The disease is more common in farmers and other rural dwellers than in city dwellers, presumably because of increased exposure to these chemicals. Exposure to these chemicals increases the risk especially among people with any of the genes that predispose to Parkinson's (Cannon & Greenamyre, 2013). If someone also had a traumatic head injury, the risk goes up even more (Lee, Bordelon, Bronstein, & Ritz, 2012). In short, most cases result from several influences combined, not just one.

What else might influence the risk of Parkinson's disease? Researchers compared the lifestyles of people who did and didn't develop the disease. One factor that stands out consistently is cigarette smoking and coffee drinking: People who smoke cigarettes or drink coffee have less chance of developing Parkinson's disease (Ritz et al., 2007). (Read that sentence again.) One study took questionnaire results from more than a thousand pairs of young adult twins and compared the results to medical records decades later. Of the twins who had never smoked, 18.4 percent developed Parkinson's disease. In contrast, 13.8 percent of the smokers developed the disease, as did only 11.6 percent of the heaviest smokers (Wirdefeldt, Gatz, Pawitan, & Pedersen, 2005). Needless to say, smoking cigarettes increases the risk of lung cancer and other diseases more than it decreases the risk of Parkinson's disease. One study focusing on coffee found that people who drank 10 or more cups of coffee per day had only one-fourth the risk of Parkinson's disease that other people had (Sääksjärvi, Knekt, Rissanen, Laaksonen, Reunanen, & Männistö, 2008). However, remember that correlation does not mean causation. People who drink that much coffee may differ from other people in other ways as well, including genetics. In short, Parkinson's disease probably results from a mixture of causes that we don't yet fully understand.

[1]The full names of these chemicals are 1-methyl-4 phenyl-1,2,3,6-tetrahydropyridine and 1-methyl-4-phenylpyridinium ion. (Let's hear it for abbreviations.)

STOP & CHECK

21. Is the genetic basis stronger for early-onset or late-onset Parkinson's disease?

22. How does MPTP exposure influence the likelihood of Parkinson's disease? What are the effects of cigarette smoking?

ANSWERS

21. The genetic basis is stronger for early-onset Parkinson's disease. **22.** Exposure to MPTP can induce symptoms of Parkinson's disease. Cigarette smoking is correlated with decreased prevalence of the disease.

L-Dopa Treatment

Because Parkinson's disease results from a dopamine deficiency, a logical goal is to restore the missing dopamine. A dopamine pill would be ineffective because dopamine does not cross the blood–brain barrier. Physicians in the 1950s and 1960s reasoned that **L-dopa**, a precursor to dopamine that does cross the barrier, might be a good treatment. In contrast to all the medicines that were discovered by trial and error, this was the first drug in psychiatry or neurology, and one of the first in all of medicine, to emerge from a plausible theory. Taken as a daily pill, L-dopa reaches the brain, where neurons convert it to dopamine. L-dopa is still the most common treatment for Parkinson's disease.

However, L-dopa treatment is disappointing in several ways (Obeso et al., 2008). It increases dopamine release in all axons, including those that had deteriorated and those that were still functioning normally. It produces spurts of high release alternating with lower release. Even if it adequately replaces lost dopamine, it does not replace other transmitters that are also depleted (Tritsch, Ding, & Sabatinni, 2012). It does not slow the continuing loss of neurons. And it produces unpleasant side effects such as nausea, restlessness, sleep problems, low blood pressure, repetitive movements, and sometimes hallucinations and delusions.

STOP&CHECK

23. How does L-dopa relieve the symptoms of Parkinson's disease?

24. In what ways is L-dopa treatment disappointing?

ANSWERS

23. L-dopa enters the brain, where neurons convert it to dopamine, thus increasing the supply of a depleted neurotransmitter. **24.** L-dopa increases dopamine activity in spurts and in all neurons, not steadily and not just in those that need help. It does not stop the loss of neurons. It has unpleasant side effects.

Other Therapies

Given the limitations of L-dopa, researchers have sought alternatives and supplements. The most common choices are drugs that directly stimulate dopamine receptors and drugs that block the metabolic breakdown of dopamine. To varying degrees, these drugs reduce the symptoms, but none of them halt the underlying disease. Despite many efforts, drugs to prevent the further loss of neurons have been unsuccessful so far (Foltynie & Kahan, 2013). In advanced cases, physicians sometimes implant electrodes to stimulate areas deep in the brain, especially the subthalamic nucleus.

A potentially exciting strategy has been "in the experimental stage" since the 1980s. In a pioneering study, M. J. Perlow and colleagues (1979) injected the chemical 6-OHDA (6-hydroxydopamine, a chemical modification of dopamine) into rats to damage the substantia nigra of one hemisphere, producing Parkinson's-type symptoms on the opposite side of the body. After the movement abnormalities stabilized, the experimenters transplanted substantia nigra tissue from rat fetuses into the damaged brains. Most recipients recovered much of their normal movement within four weeks. Control animals that suffered the same brain damage without receiving grafts showed little or no recovery. This is only a partial brain transplant, but still, the Frankensteinian implications are striking.

If such surgery works for rats, might it also for humans? Ordinarily, scientists test any experimental procedure extensively with laboratory animals before trying it on humans, but with Parkinson's disease, the temptation was too great. People in the late stages have little to lose and are willing to try almost anything. The obvious problem is where to get the donor tissue. Several early studies used tissue from the patient's own adrenal gland. Although that tissue is not composed of neurons, it produces and releases dopamine. Unfortunately, the adrenal gland transplants seldom produced much benefit (Backlund et al., 1985).

Another possibility is to transplant brain tissue from aborted fetuses. Fetal neurons transplanted into the brains of patients with Parkinson's sometimes survive for years and make synapses with the patient's own cells. However, the operation is expensive and difficult, requiring brain tissue from four to eight aborted fetuses, and the benefits to the patient have been small at best (Freed et al., 2001; Olanow et al., 2003). One limitation is that surgeons generally try this procedure only when all else fails, in aged patients with an advanced stage of the disease. Animal studies find that transplants work best if the damaged area is small and the surrounding cells are healthy (Breysse, Carlsson, Winkler, Björklund, & Kirik, 2007). By the time people reach the point when L-dopa and other drugs no longer help, it may be too late for the transplanted tissue to help.

A related approach is to take **stem cells**—immature cells that are capable of differentiating into other cell types—guide their development so that they produce large quantities of L-dopa, and then transplant them into the brain. The idea sounds promising, but researchers will need to overcome several difficulties before this might become an effective treatment (Bjorklund & Kordower, 2013).

The research on brain transplants has suggested yet another possibility for treatment. In several experiments, the transplanted tissue failed to survive, but the recipient showed behavioral recovery anyway (Redmond et al., 2007). Presumably, the transplanted tissue released neurotrophins that stimulated axon and dendrite growth in the recipient's own brain. Work with mice has shown promising results for a neurotrophin to repair Parkinson-like damage (Airavaara et al., 2012). Applying that procedure to humans would still require surgery to deliver the neurotrophin, as neurotrophins do not cross the blood–brain barrier.

STOP&CHECK

25. Why is transfer of fetal tissue more successful in animal models of Parkinson's disease than it is with human patients?

ANSWER

25. In laboratory animals, researchers use young animals at an early stage of the disease. In humans, this is an option when all else has failed, and as a result the patient already has extensive brain damage at the time of surgery.

Huntington's Disease

Huntington's disease (also known as *Huntington disease* or *Huntington's chorea*) is a severe neurological disorder that strikes about 1 person in 10,000 in the United States (A. B. Young, 1995). Motor symptoms usually begin with arm jerks and facial twitches. Then tremors spread to other parts of the body and develop into writhing (M. A. Smith, Brandt, & Shadmehr, 2000). (*Chorea* comes from the same root as *choreography*. The rhythmic writhing of chorea resembles dancing.) Gradually, the tremors interfere more and more with walking, speech, and other voluntary movements. People

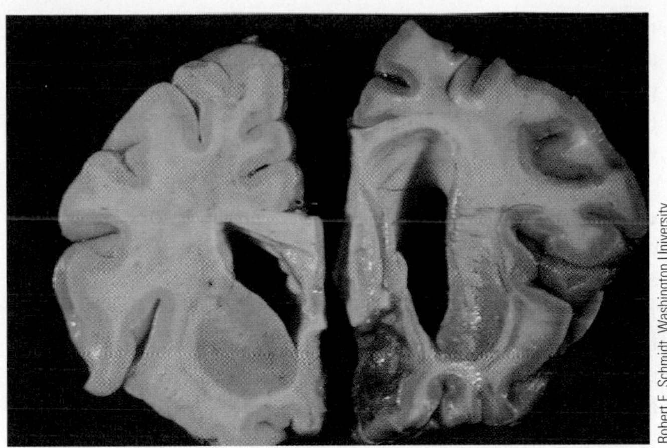

FIGURE 7.21 Brain of a normal person (left) and a person with Huntington's disease (right)
The angle of cut through the normal brain makes the lateral ventricle look larger in this photo than it actually is. Even so, note how much larger it is in the patient with Huntington's disease. The ventricles expand because of the loss of neurons.

lose the ability to learn or improve motor skills (Willingham et al., 1996). The disorder is associated with gradual, extensive brain damage, especially in the basal ganglia but also in the cerebral cortex (Tabrizi et al., 1999) (see Figure 7.21). Because the output from the basal ganglia is inhibitory to the thalamus, damage to the basal ganglia leads to increased activity in motor areas of the thalamus. That increase produces the involuntary jerky movements.

People with Huntington's disease also suffer psychological disorders including depression, sleeplessness, memory impairment, anxiety, hallucinations and delusions, poor judgment, alcoholism, drug abuse, and sexual disorders ranging from complete unresponsiveness to indiscriminate promiscuity (Shoulson, 1990). Occasionally, individuals in the early stages of Huntington's disease are misdiagnosed as having schizophrenia.

Huntington's disease can occur at any age, but most often between the ages of 30 and 50. Once the symptoms emerge, both the psychological and motor symptoms grow progressively worse and culminate in death.

STOP&CHECK

26. Why does damage to the basal ganglia lead to involuntary movements?

ANSWER

26. Output from the basal ganglia to the thalamus is inhibitory. After damage to the basal ganglia, the thalamus, and therefore the cortex, receive less inhibition. Thus, they produce unwanted actions.

Heredity and Presymptomatic Testing

Huntington's disease results from an autosomal dominant gene (i.e., one not on the X or Y chromosome). As a rule, a mutant gene that causes the loss of a function is recessive. The fact that the Huntington's gene is dominant implies that it produces the gain of some undesirable function.

Imagine that as a young adult you learn that your mother or father has Huntington's disease. In addition to your grief about your parent, you know that you have a 50 percent chance of getting the disease yourself. Would you want to know in advance whether or not you were going to get the disease? Knowing the answer might help you decide whether to have children, whether to enter a career that required many years of education, and so forth. However, getting bad news might not be easy to handle.

In 1993, researchers located the gene for Huntington's disease on chromosome number 4, a spectacular accomplishment for the technology available at the time (Huntington's Disease Collaborative Research Group, 1993). Now an examination of your chromosomes can reveal with almost perfect accuracy whether or not you will get Huntington's disease.

The critical area of the gene includes a sequence of bases C-A-G (cytosine, adenine, guanine), which is repeated 11 to 24 times in most people. That repetition produces a string of 11 to 24 glutamines in the resulting protein. People with up to 35 C-A-G repetitions are considered safe from Huntington's disease. Those with 36 to 38 might or might not get it, but probably not before old age (Panegyres & Goh, 2011). People with 39 or more repetitions are likely to get the disease, unless they die of other causes earlier. The more C-A-G repetitions someone has, the earlier the probable onset of the disease, as shown in Figure 7.22 (U.S.–Venezuela Collaborative Research Project, 2004). In short, a chromosomal examination predicts

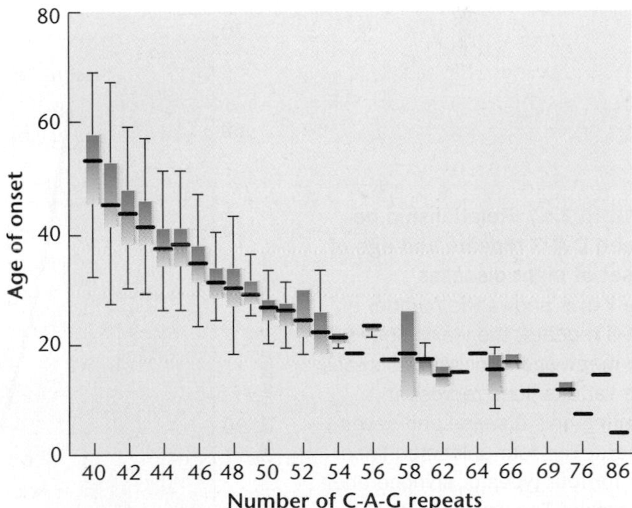

FIGURE 7.22 Relationship between C-A-G repeats and age of onset of Huntington's disease
For each number of C-A-G repeats, the graph shows the age of onset. The green bars show the range that includes the middle 50 percent of observations, from the 75th percentile to the 25th percentile. The vertical lines show the full range of observations. Source: From the U.S. Venezuela Collaborative Research Project (2004). *Proceedings of the National Academy of Sciences, USA, 101*, pp. 3498–3503.

not only whether a person will get Huntington's disease but also approximately when. The graph shows a considerable amount of variation in age of onset, especially for those with fewer C-A-G repeats. A history of drug or alcohol abuse increases the probability of early onset (Byars, Beglinger, Moser, Gonzalez-Alegre, & Nopoulos, 2012). Other genes, stressful experiences, and diet probably contribute also.

Figure 7.23 shows comparable data for Huntington's disease and seven other neurological disorders. Each of them relates to an extended sequence of C-A-G repeats in a gene. An extended sequence of repeats also increases the risk of several other conditions not shown in the figure, including fragile X syndrome and amyotrophic lateral sclerosis (Nelson, Orr, & Warren, 2013). In each case, people with the greatest number of repeats have the earliest onset of disease (Gusella & MacDonald, 2000). Those with a smaller number will be older, if they get the disease at all. Recall that the genetic contribution is greater for early-onset than for late-onset Parkinson's disease. Genetic factors are also important for early-onset Alzheimer's disease, alcoholism, depression, and schizophrenia. For people with later onset, the role of genetics is less pronounced.

Identification of the gene for Huntington's disease led to the discovery of the protein that it codes, which has been designated **huntingtin**. Huntingtin occurs throughout the human body, although its mutant form produces no known harm outside the brain. Within the brain, it occurs inside neurons, not on their membranes. The mutant form impairs neurons in several ways. In the early stages of the disease, it increases neurotransmitter release, sometimes causing overstimulation of the target cells (Romero et al., 2008). Later, the protein forms clusters that impair the neuron's mitochondria (Panov et al., 2002). It also impairs the transport of chemicals down the axon (Morfini et al., 2009).

Identifying the abnormal huntingtin protein and its cellular functions has enabled investigators to search for drugs that reduce the harm. Researchers have developed strains of mice and fruit flies with the same gene that causes Huntington's disease in humans. Research on these animals has found several promising drugs, currently in various stages of investigation (Kordasiewicz et al., 2012; Lu et al., 2013). So far none of them have been approved for human use.

STOP&CHECK

27. What procedure enables physicians to predict who will or will not get Huntington's disease and to estimate the age of onset?

ANSWER

27. Physicians can count the number of consecutive repeats of the combination C-A-G on one gene on chromosome 4. If the number is fewer than 36, the person will not develop Huntington's disease. For repeats of 36 or more, the larger the number, the more certain the person is to develop the disease and the earlier the probable age of onset.

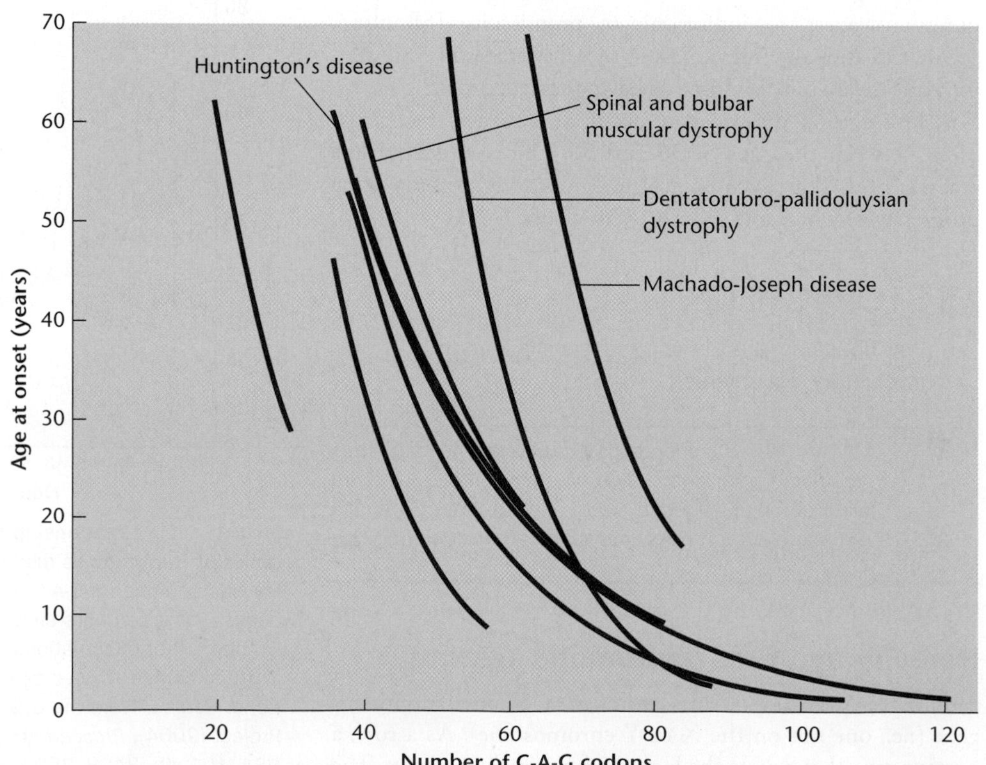

FIGURE 7.23 Relationship between C-A-G repeats and age of onset of eight diseases
The *x* axis shows the number of C-A-G repeats; the *y* axis shows the mean age at onset of disease. The various lines represent Huntington's disease and seven others. The four unlabeled lines are for four types of spinocerebellar ataxia. The key point is that for each disease, the greater the number of repeats, the earlier the probable onset of symptoms. Adapted from "Molecular genetics: Unmasking polyglutamine triggers in neurogenerative disease," by J. F. Gusella and M. E. MacDonald, Fig. 1, p. 111 in *Neuroscience, 1,* pp. 109–115

MODULE 7.3 ■ IN CLOSING

Heredity and Environment in Movement Disorders

Parkinson's disease and Huntington's disease show that genes influence behavior in different ways. Someone who examines the chromosomes can predict almost certainly who will and who will not develop Huntington's disease and with moderate accuracy predict when. A gene has also been identified for early-onset Parkinson's disease, but for the late-onset version, environmental influences appear to be more important. In later chapters, we shall consider other instances in which genes increase the risk of certain disorders, but we will not encounter anything with such a strong heritability as Huntington's disease.

Summary

1. Parkinson's disease is characterized by impaired initiation of activity, slow and inaccurate movements, tremor, rigidity, depression, and cognitive deficits. **252**
2. Parkinson's disease is associated with the degeneration of dopamine-containing axons from the substantia nigra to the caudate nucleus and putamen. **252**
3. A gene has been identified that is responsible for early-onset Parkinson's disease. Heredity plays a smaller role in the more common form of Parkinson's disease, with onset after age 50. **253**
4. The chemical MPTP selectively damages neurons in the substantia nigra and leads to the symptoms of Parkinson's disease. Some cases of Parkinson's disease may result in part from exposure to toxins. **253**
5. The most common treatment for Parkinson's disease is L-dopa, which crosses the blood–brain barrier and enters neurons that convert it into dopamine. However, the effectiveness of L-dopa varies, and it produces unwelcome side effects. **253**
6. Many other treatments are in use or in the experimental stage. The transfer of immature neurons into a damaged brain area seems to offer great potential, but so far, it has provided little practical benefit. **254**
7. Huntington's disease is a hereditary condition marked by deterioration of motor control as well as depression, memory impairment, and other cognitive disorders. **254**
8. By examining a gene on chromosome 4, physicians can determine whether someone is likely to develop Huntington's disease later in life. The more C-A-G repeats in the gene, the earlier is the likely onset of symptoms. **255**
9. The gene responsible for Huntington's disease alters the structure of a protein, known as huntingtin. The altered protein interferes with neurons in several ways. **256**

Key Terms

Terms are defined in the module on the page number indicated. They're also presented in alphabetical order with definitions in the book's Subject Index/Glossary. Interactive flash cards, audio reviews, and crossword puzzles are among the online resources available to help you learn these terms and the concepts they represent.

huntingtin **256**
Huntington's disease **254**
L-dopa **253**
MPP+ **253**
MPTP **253**
Parkinson's disease **252**
stem cells **254**

Thought Question

Haloperidol is a drug that blocks dopamine synapses. What effect would it be likely to have in someone suffering from Parkinson's disease?

MODULE 7.3 End of Module Quiz

1. Parkinson's disease results from damage to _____-releasing axons from the _____ to the striatum.
   a. dopamine . . . substantia nigra
   b. GABA . . . basal forebrain
   c. norepinephrine . . . locus coeruleus
   d. serotonin . . . raphe nucleus

2. People with Parkinson's disease show the greatest impairment with which type of movement?
   a. Reflexes
   b. Spontaneous voluntary movements
   c. Movements in response to a stimulus
   d. Movements when other people are around

3. In what way is L-dopa treatment for Parkinson's disease unusual?
   a. It produces behavioral benefits without entering the brain.
   b. Unlike most drugs, it produces no unpleasant side effects.
   c. The treatment becomes more and more effective over time.
   d. It was based on a theory instead of trial and error.

4. Transplant of brain tissue relieves Parkinson-type symptoms in laboratory animals, but so far this procedure has shown little benefit for humans. What is one reason?
   a. Most patients with Parkinson's disease are unwilling to try this procedure.
   b. Laboratory animals have different neurotransmitters than humans do.
   c. Surgeons use this procedure only in patients with an advanced stage of the disease.
   d. It is difficult to place the transplant into the correct location.

5. What is the most common age of onset for Huntington's disease?
   a. Early childhood (3 to 7 years old)
   b. The teenage years (13 to 19)
   c. Middle age (30 to 50)
   d. Old age (65 to 80)

6. An examination of C-A-G repeats on one gene enables physicians to predict who will develop Huntington's disease. What else does it help them predict?
   a. What other diseases the person will get
   b. The individual's personality
   c. The effectiveness of treatment
   d. The age of onset of symptoms

ANSWERS: 1a, 2b, 3d, 4c, 5c, 6d.

Suggestions for Further Reading

Klawans, H. L. (1996). *Why Michael couldn't hit.* New York: Freeman.

A collection of fascinating sports examples related to the brain and its disorders.

Lashley, K. S. (1951). The problem of serial order in behavior. In L. A. Jeffress (Ed.), *Cerebral mechanisms in behavior* (pp. 112–136). New York: Wiley.

This classic article in psychology is a thought-provoking appraisal of what a theory of movement should explain.

Hoberman Collection/Universal Images Group/Getty Images

Wakefulness and Sleep

8

CHAPTER OUTLINE

MODULE 8.1 **Rhythms of Waking and Sleeping**
Endogenous Rhythms
Setting and Resetting the Biological Clock
Mechanisms of the Biological Clock
In Closing: Sleep–Wake Cycles

MODULE 8.2 **Stages of Sleep and Brain Mechanisms**
Sleep and Other Interruptions of Consciousness
The Stages of Sleep
Paradoxical or REM Sleep
Brain Mechanisms of Wakefulness, Arousal, and Sleep
Brain Function in REM Sleep
Sleep Disorders
In Closing: Stages of Sleep

MODULE 8.3 **Why Sleep? Why REM? Why Dreams?**
Functions of Sleep
Functions of REM Sleep
Biological Perspectives on Dreaming
In Closing: Our Limited Self-Understanding

LEARNING OBJECTIVES

After studying this chapter, you should be able to:

1. Define and describe endogenous rhythms.
2. Explain the mechanisms that set and reset the biological clock.
3. List and characterize the stages of sleep.
4. Describe the brain mechanisms of waking and sleeping.
5. Discuss several consequences of thinking of sleep as a localized phenomenon.
6. List several sleep disorders with their causes.
7. Evaluate possible explanations of the functions of sleep.
8. Describe possible explanations of dreaming.

Anyone deprived of sleep suffers. But if life evolved on another planet with different conditions, could animals evolve life without a need for sleep? Imagine a planet that doesn't rotate on its axis. Some animals evolve adaptations to live in the light area, others in the dark area, and still others in the twilight zone separating light from dark. There would be no need for any animal to alternate active periods with inactive periods on any fixed schedule and perhaps no need for prolonged inactive periods. If you were the astronaut who discovered these sleepless animals, you might be surprised.

Now imagine that astronauts from that planet set out on their first voyage to Earth. Imagine *their* surprise to discover animals like us with long inactive periods resembling death. To someone who hadn't seen sleep before, it would seem mysterious indeed. For the purposes of this chapter, let's adopt their perspective and ask why animals as active as we are spend a third of our lives doing so little.

OPPOSITE: Nearly all animals have daily periods of wakefulness and of sleep.

Rhythms of Waking and Sleeping

You are probably not amazed to learn that your body spontaneously generates its own rhythm of wakefulness and sleep. Psychologists of an earlier era strongly resisted that idea. When radical behaviorism dominated experimental psychology during the mid-1900s, many psychologists believed that every behavior could be traced to external stimuli. For example, alternation between wakefulness and sleep must depend on something in the outside world, such as changes in light or temperature. Research as early as that of Curt Richter (1922) implied that the body generates its own cycles of activity and inactivity, but it took much research to convince the skeptics. The idea of self-generated rhythms was a major step toward viewing animals as active producers of behaviors.

Endogenous Rhythms

An animal that produced its behavior entirely in response to current stimuli would be at a serious disadvantage. Animals often need to anticipate changes in the environment. For example, migratory birds start flying toward their winter homes before their summer territory becomes too cold. A bird that waited for the first frost would be in trouble. Similarly, squirrels begin storing nuts and putting on extra layers of fat in preparation for winter long before food becomes scarce.

Animals' readiness for a change in seasons comes partly from internal mechanisms. Changes in the light–dark pattern of the day tell a migratory bird when to fly south for the winter, but what tells it when to fly back north? In the tropics, the temperature and amount of daylight are nearly the same throughout the year. Nevertheless, migratory birds fly north at the right time. Even if they are kept in a cage with no clues to the season, they become restless in the spring, and if they are released, they fly north (Gwinner, 1986). Evidently, birds generate a rhythm that prepares them for seasonal changes. We refer to that rhythm as an **endogenous circannual rhythm.** (*Endogenous* means "generated from within." *Circannual* comes from the Latin words *circum*, for "about," and *annum*, for "year.")

Animals also produce **endogenous circadian rhythms** that last about a day. (*Circadian* comes from the Latin *circum*, for "about," and *dies*, for "day.") If you go without sleep all night—as most college students do, sooner or later—you feel sleepier and sleepier as the night goes on, but as morning arrives, you feel more alert, not less. The light from the sun helps you feel less sleepy, but also your urge to sleep depends partly on the time of day, not just how long you have been awake (Babkoff, Caspy, Mikulincer, & Sing, 1991).

Figure 8.1 represents the activity of a flying squirrel kept in total darkness for 25 days. Each horizontal line represents one 24-hour day. A thickening in the line represents a period of activity. Even in this unchanging environment, the animal generates a consistent rhythm of activity and sleep. Depending on the individual and the details of the procedure, the self-generated cycle may be slightly shorter than 24 hours, as in Figure 8.1, or slightly longer (Carpenter & Grossberg, 1984).

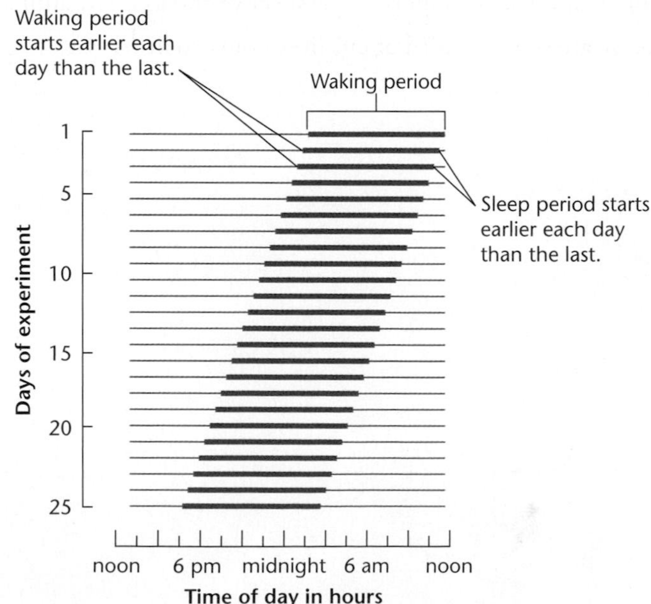

FIGURE 8.1 Activity record of a flying squirrel kept in constant darkness
The thickened segments indicate periods of activity as measured by a running wheel. Note that this free-running activity cycle lasts slightly less than 24 hours. Adapted from "Phase Control of Activity in a Rodent," by P. J. DeCoursey, *Cold Spring Harbor Symposia on Quantitative Biology, 1960, 25*, pp. 49–55

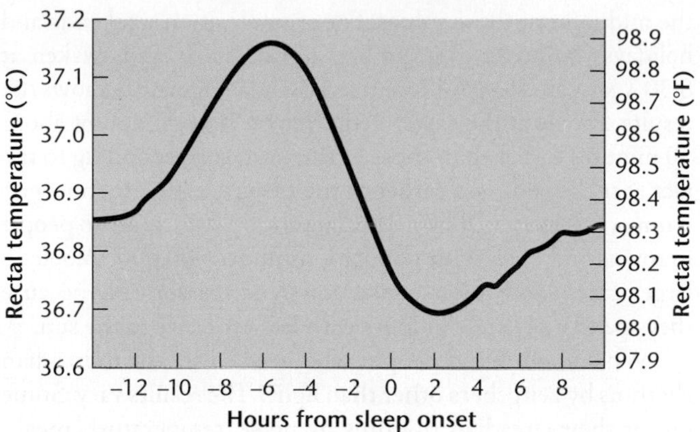

FIGURE 8.2 Mean rectal temperatures for nine adults
Body temperature reaches its low for the day about 2 hours after sleep onset; it reaches its peak about 6 hours before sleep onset. Adapted from "Sleep-Onset Insomniacs Have Delayed Temperature Rhythms," by M. Morris, L. Lack, and D. Dawson, *Sleep, 1990, 13*, pp. 1–14

Humans also generate 24-hour wake–sleep rhythms, and we can modify them only a little. If we ever send astronauts to Mars, they will have to adjust to the Martian day, which lasts about 24 hours and 39 minutes of Earth time. Researchers have found that people can adjust to that schedule fairly easily (Scheer, Wright, Kronauer, & Czeisler, 2007). Circadian rhythms may be the least of our problems if we travel to Mars. However, more severe departures from a 24-hour schedule pose difficulties. Naval personnel on submarines are cut off from sunlight for months at a time, living under faint artificial light. In many cases, they live on a schedule of 6 hours of work, 6 hours of recreation, and 6 hours of sleep. Even though they try to sleep on this 18-hour schedule, their bodies generate rhythms of alertness and body chemistry that average about 24.3 to 24.4 hours (Kelly et al., 1999).

Circadian rhythms affect much more than just waking and sleeping. We have circadian rhythms in our eating and drinking, urination, hormone secretion, metabolism, sensitivity to drugs, and other variables. For example, although we ordinarily think of human body temperature as 37°C, normal temperature fluctuates over the course of a day from a low near 36.7°C during the night to almost 37.2°C in late afternoon (see Figure 8.2). We also have circadian rhythms in mood. In one study, young adults recorded their mood throughout the day. Most showed increases in positive mood (happiness) from waking until late afternoon, and then a slight decline until bedtime. In a follow-up study, the same investigators kept young adults awake for 30 consecutive hours, starting at either 10 A.M. or 5 P.M., in a laboratory setting with constant levels of light and temperature. Regardless of whether people started this procedure at 10 A.M. or 5 P.M., most reported their most pleasant mood around 5 P.M. and their least pleasant mood at around 5 A.M. (Murray et al., 2009). These results suggest a biologically driven circadian rhythm in our emotional well-being (see Figure 8.3).

STOP&CHECK

1. What evidence indicates that humans have an internal biological clock?

ANSWER

1. People who have lived in an environment with a light–dark schedule much different from 24 hours fail to follow that schedule and instead become wakeful and sleepy on about a 24-hour basis.

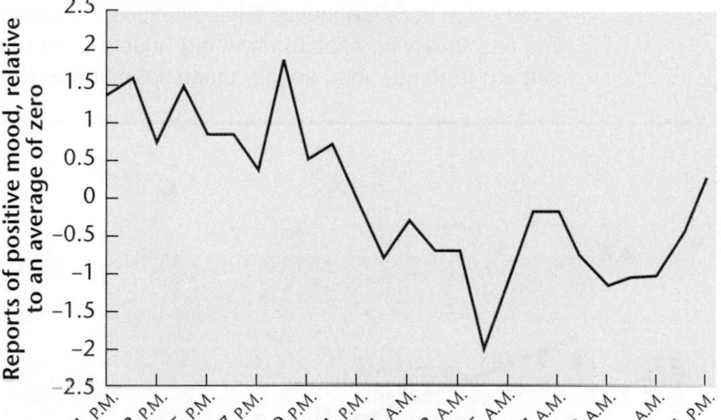

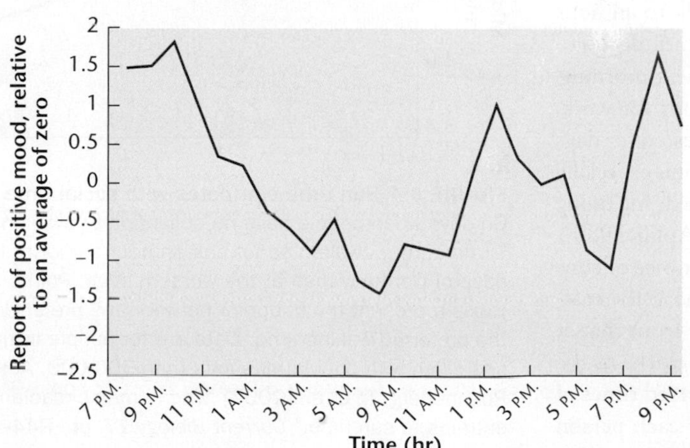

FIGURE 8.3 Reported positive mood over time
During 30 hours in an unchanging laboratory environment, the average young adult reported most pleasant mood in the late afternoon or early evening, and the least pleasant mood around 5 A.M. to 7 A.M. The pattern was similar for those who started the procedure in the morning (above) or in the evening (below). From "Nature's clocks and human mood: The circadian system modulates reward motivation," by G. Murray, C. L. Nicholas, J. Kleiman, R. Dwyer, M. J. Carrington, N. B. Allen, et al., 2009, *Emotion, 9*, pp. 705–716

Setting and Resetting the Biological Clock

Our circadian rhythms generate a period close to 24 hours, but they are not perfect. We readjust our internal workings daily to stay in phase with the world. Sometimes, we misadjust them. On weekends, when most of us are freer to set our own schedules, we expose ourselves to lights, noises, and activity at night and then awaken late the next morning. By Monday morning, when the clock on the table indicates 7 A.M., the biological clock within us may say 5 A.M., and we stagger off to work or school without much pep (Moore-Ede, Czeisler, & Richardson, 1983).

Although circadian rhythms persist without light, light is critical for resetting them. Without something to reset your circadian rhythm, it would gradually drift away from the correct time. The stimulus that resets the circadian rhythm is referred to by the German term **zeitgeber** (TSITE-gay-ber), meaning "time-giver." Light is the dominant zeitgeber for land animals (Rusak & Zucker, 1979), whereas the tides are important for some marine animals. In addition to light, other zeitgebers include exercise (Eastman, Hoese, Youngstedt, & Liu, 1995), arousal of any kind (Gritton, Sutton, Martinez, Sarter, & Lee, 2009), meals, and the temperature of the environment (Refinetti, 2000). Social stimuli—that is, the effects of other people—are ineffective as zeitgebers, unless they induce exercise or other vigorous activity (Mistlberger & Skene, 2004). Although these additional zeitgebers modify the effects of light, they have only weak effects on their own. For example, people who are working in Antarctica during the constant darkness of an Antarctic winter try to maintain a 24-hour rhythm, but they drift away from it. Different people generate different rhythms, until they find it more and more difficult to work together (Kennaway & Van Dorp, 1991). Astronauts in orbit face a special problem: As they orbit the Earth, a 45-minute period of daylight alternates with 45 minutes of darkness. If they retreat from the flight deck to elsewhere in the spacecraft, they have constant dim light. As a result, they are not fully alert during their wakeful periods or deeply asleep during rest periods (Dijk et al., 2001). On long assignments, many experience depression and impaired performance (Mallis & DeRoshia, 2005).

Even when we try to set our wake–sleep cycles by the clock, sunlight has its influence. Consider what happens when we shift to daylight saving time in spring. You set your clock to an hour later, and when it shows your usual bedtime, you dutifully go to bed, even though it seems an hour too early. The next morning, when the clock says it is 7 A.M. and time to get ready for work, your brain registers 6 A.M. Most people remain ill rested for days after the shift to daylight saving time. The adjustment is especially difficult for people who were already sleep deprived, including most college students (Lahti et al., 2006; Monk & Aplin, 1980).

Particularly impressive evidence for the importance of sunlight comes from a study in Germany. The sun time at the eastern end of Germany differs by about half an hour from that at the western edge, even though all people set their clocks to the same time. Researchers asked adults for their preferred times of awakening and going to sleep and determined for each person the midpoint of those values. For example, if on weekends and holidays you prefer to go to bed at 12:30 A.M. and awaken at 8:30 A.M., your sleep midpoint is 4:30 A.M. Figure 8.4 shows the results. People at the eastern edge have a sleep midpoint about 30 minutes earlier than those at the west, corresponding to the fact that the sun rises earlier at the eastern edge (Roenneberg, Kumar, & Merrow, 2007). The data shown here apply to people in towns and cities with populations under 300,000. People in larger cities show a less consistent trend, presumably because they spend more time indoors with less exposure to the sun.

What about blind people, who need to set their circadian rhythms by zeitgebers other than light? The results vary. Some do set their circadian rhythms by noise, temperature, meals, and activity. However, others who are not sufficiently sensitive to these secondary zeitgebers produce circadian rhythms that are a little longer than 24 hours. When their cycles are in phase with the clock, all is well, but when they drift out of phase, they experience insomnia at night and sleepiness during the day (Sack & Lewy, 2001). More than half of all blind people report frequent sleep problems (Warman et al., 2011).

STOP & CHECK

2. Why do people at the eastern edge of Germany awaken earlier than those at the western edge on their weekends and holidays?

ANSWER

2. The sun rises about half an hour earlier at the eastern edge than at the western edge. Evidently, the sun controls waking–sleeping schedules even when people follow the same clock time for their work schedule.

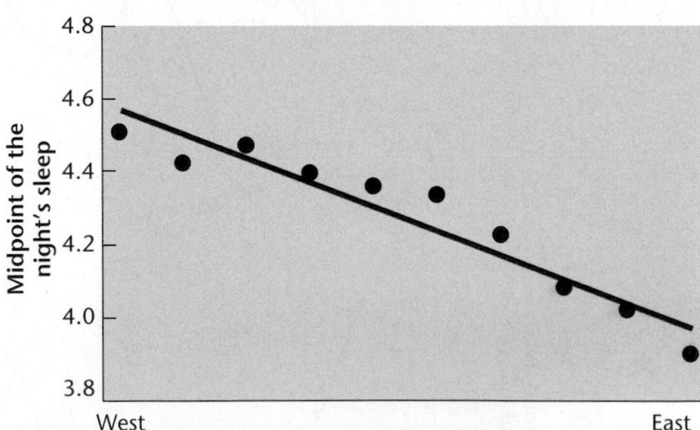

FIGURE 8.4 Sun time competes with social time
On days when people have no obligation to awaken at a particular time, they awaken about half an hour earlier at the eastern edge of Germany than at the western edge. Points along the *y* axis represent the midpoint between the preferred bedtime and the preferred waking time. Data are for people living in towns and cities with populations less than 300,000. Adapted from Roenneberg, T., et al. [2007] "The human circadian clock entrains to sun time." *Current Biology 17*, pp. R44–R45

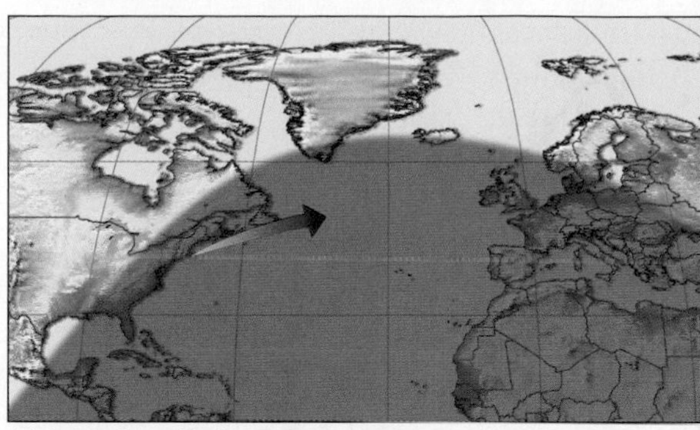

(a) Leave New York at 7 P.M.

(b) Arrive in London at 7 A.M., which is 2 A.M. in New York

FIGURE 8.5 Jet lag
Eastern time is later than western time. People who travel six time zones east fall asleep on the plane and then must awaken when it is morning at their destination but night back home.

Jet Lag

A disruption of circadian rhythms due to crossing time zones is known as **jet lag**. Travelers complain of sleepiness during the day, sleeplessness at night, depression, and impaired concentration. All these problems stem from the mismatch between internal circadian clock and external time (Haimov & Arendt, 1999). Most people find it easier to adjust to crossing time zones going west than east. Going west, we stay awake later at night and then awaken late the next morning, already partly adjusted to the new schedule. We *phase-delay* our circadian rhythms. Going east, we *phase-advance* to sleep earlier and awaken earlier (see Figure 8.5). Most people find it difficult to go to sleep before their body's usual time and difficult to wake up early the next day.

Adjusting to jet lag is often stressful. Stress elevates blood levels of the adrenal hormone *cortisol*, and many studies have shown that prolonged elevations of cortisol damage neurons in the hippocampus, a brain area important for memory. One study examined flight attendants who had spent the previous 5 years making flights across seven or more time zones—such as Chicago to Italy—with mostly short breaks (fewer than 6 days) between trips. On the average, the flight attendants had smaller than average volumes of the hippocampus and surrounding structures, and they showed memory impairments (Cho, 2001). These results suggest a danger from repeated adjustments of the circadian rhythm, although the problem here could be air travel itself. (A good control group would have been flight attendants who flew long north–south routes.)

Shift Work

People who sleep irregularly—such as pilots, medical interns, and shift workers in factories—find that their duration of sleep depends on when they go to sleep. When they have to sleep in the morning or early afternoon, they sleep only briefly, even if they have been awake for many hours (Frese & Harwich, 1984; Winfree, 1983).

People who work on a night shift, such as midnight to 8 A.M., sleep during the day. At least they try to. Even after months or years on such a schedule, many workers adjust incompletely. They continue to feel groggy on the job, they sleep poorly during the day, and their body temperature continues to peak when they are sleeping in the day instead of while they are working at night. In general, night-shift workers have more accidents than day-shift workers.

Working at night does not reliably change the circadian rhythm because most buildings use artificial lighting in the range of 150 to 180 lux, which is only moderately effective in resetting the rhythm (Boivin, Duffy, Kronauer, & Czeisler, 1996). People adjust best to night work if they sleep in a very dark room during the day and work under very bright lights at night, comparable to the noonday sun (Czeisler et al., 1990). Short-wavelength (bluish) light helps to reset the circadian rhythm better than long-wavelength light does (Czeisler, 2013).

Morning People and Evening People

Circadian rhythms differ among individuals. Some people ("morning people," or "larks") awaken early, reach their peak of productivity early, and become less alert later in the day. Others ("evening people," or "owls") warm up more slowly, both literally and figuratively, reaching their peak in the late afternoon or evening. They tolerate staying up all night better than morning people do (Taillard, Philip, Coste, Sagaspe, & Bioulac, 2003). Among shift workers, morning people are most impaired when working the night shift and evening people are most impaired when working the morning shift (Juda, Vetter, & Roenneberg, 2013). Many people are, of course, intermediate between the two extremes.

A convenient way to classify people is to ask, "On holidays and vacations when you have no obligations, what time is the middle of your sleep?" For example, if you sleep from 1 A.M. until 9 A.M. on those days, your middle is 5 A.M. As

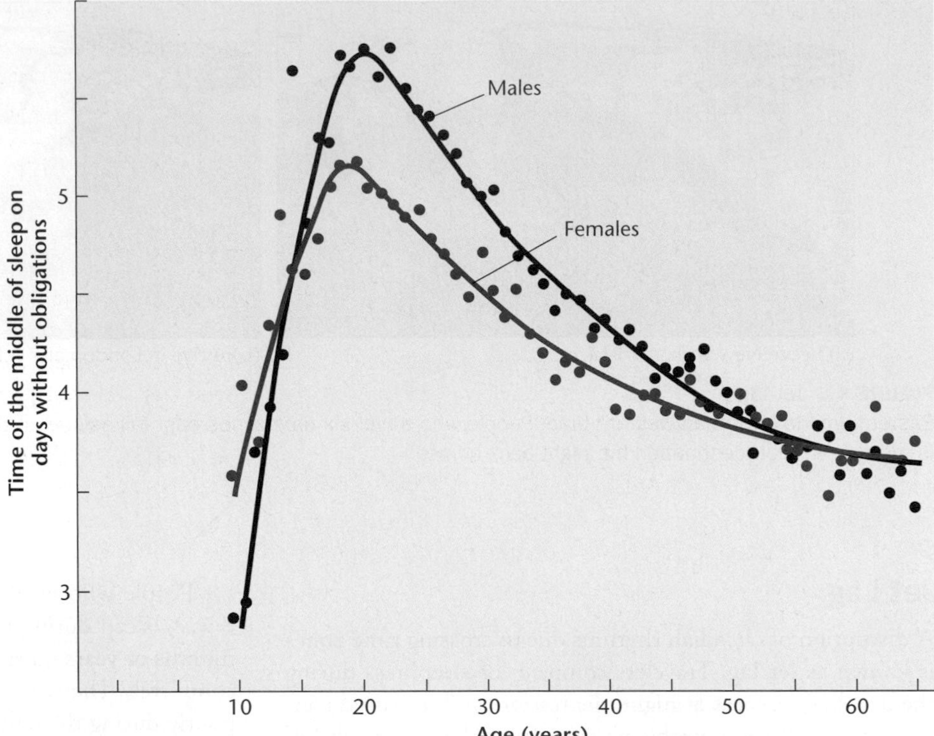

FIGURE 8.6 Age differences in circadian rhythms
People reported the time of the middle of their sleep, such as 3 A.M. or 5 A.M., on days when they had no obligations. Adapted from T. Roenneberg et al., "A Marker for the End of Adolescence," *Current Biology, 14*, pp. R1038–R1039

Figure 8.6 shows, people differ by age. As a child, you almost certainly went to bed early and woke up early. As you entered adolescence, you started staying up later and waking up later, when you had the opportunity. The mean preferred time of going to sleep gets later and later until about age 20 and then gradually reverses (Roenneberg et al., 2004). The tendency to stay up later and awaken later during adolescence occurs in every culture that researchers have studied throughout the world (Gradisar, Gardner, & Dohnt, 2011). The same trend also occurs in rats, monkeys, and other species (Hagenauer & Lee, 2012; Winocur & Hasher, 1999, 2004), apparently resulting from increased levels of sex hormones (Hagenauer & Lee, 2012; Randler et al., 2012). From a functional standpoint, we can only speculate as to why staying up late and waking up late might be more advantageous for adolescents than for children or adults.

So, being a morning person or an evening person depends partly on age. It also depends on genetics and other factors. People who live in a big city, surrounded by bright lights, are more likely to stay up late than are people in rural areas. But the fact that most young people tend to be evening people causes problems. In the United States and many other countries, high school classes start at 8 A.M. or earlier. Most teenagers are at least a bit drowsy at that time, some more than others. Those who are strongly evening types tend to get lower than average grades, in spite of having average or above-average intelligence (Preckel, Lipnevich, Anastasiya, Schneider, & Roberts, 2011; Preckel et al., 2013). They suffer from "social jet lag" every day (Roeser, Scharb, & Kübler, 2013). Possibly as a result of this frustration, or perhaps just as a result of staying up late, they are more likely than others to use alcohol, overeat, and engage in other risky behaviors (Hasler & Clark, 2013; Roenneberg, Allebrandt, Merrow, & Vetter, 2012). When people note that teenagers tend to take impulsive risks, that tendency is especially strong in evening people, and social jet lag is a possible contributing factor. Even beyond the teenage years, morning people report being happier than evening people, on average, possibly because their biological rhythms are more in tune with their 9-to-5 work schedule (Biss & Hasher, 2012). Daylight saving time magnifies the mismatch for evening people (including most young people). Some countries are considering extending daylight saving time to the entire year, making the situation even worse.

Mechanisms of the Biological Clock

How does the body generate a circadian rhythm? Curt Richter (1967) introduced the concept that the brain generates its own rhythms—a biological clock—and he reported that the biological clock is insensitive to most forms of interference. Blind or deaf animals generate circadian rhythms, although they slowly drift out of phase with the external world. The circadian rhythm remains surprisingly steady despite food or water deprivation, X-rays, tranquilizers, alcohol, anesthesia, lack of oxygen, most kinds of brain damage, or the removal of endocrine organs. Even an hour or more of induced hibernation often fails to reset the biological clock (Gibbs, 1983; Richter, 1975). Evidently, the biological clock is a hardy, robust mechanism.

Curt P. Richter

(1894–1988)

I enjoy research more than eating.
(Richter, personal communication)

The Suprachiasmatic Nucleus (SCN)

Although cells throughout the body generate circadian rhythms, the main driver of rhythms for sleep and body temperature is the **suprachiasmatic** (soo-pruh-kie-as-MAT-ik) **nucleus**, or **SCN**, a part of the hypothalamus (Refinetti & Menaker, 1992). It gets its name from its location just above ("supra") the optic chiasm (see Figure 8.7). After damage to the SCN, the body's rhythms become erratic.

The SCN generates circadian rhythms itself in a genetically controlled manner. If SCN neurons are disconnected from the rest of the brain or removed from the body and maintained in tissue culture, they continue to produce a circadian rhythm of action potentials (Earnest, Liang, Ratcliff, & Cassone, 1999; Inouye & Kawamura, 1979). Even a single isolated SCN cell can maintain a circadian rhythm, although interactions among cells sharpen the accuracy of the rhythm (Long, Jutras, Connors, & Burwell, 2005; Yamaguchi et al., 2003).

A mutation in one gene causes hamsters' SCN to produce a 20-hour instead of 24-hour rhythm (Ralph & Menaker, 1988). Researchers surgically removed the SCN from adult hamsters and transplanted SCN tissue from hamster fetuses into the adults. When they transplanted SCN tissue from fetuses with a 20-hour rhythm, the recipients produced a 20-hour rhythm. When they transplanted tissue from fetuses with a 24-hour rhythm, the recipients produced a 24-hour rhythm (Ralph, Foster, Davis, & Menaker, 1990). That is, the rhythm followed the pace of the donors, not the recipients. Again, the results show that the rhythms come from the SCN itself.

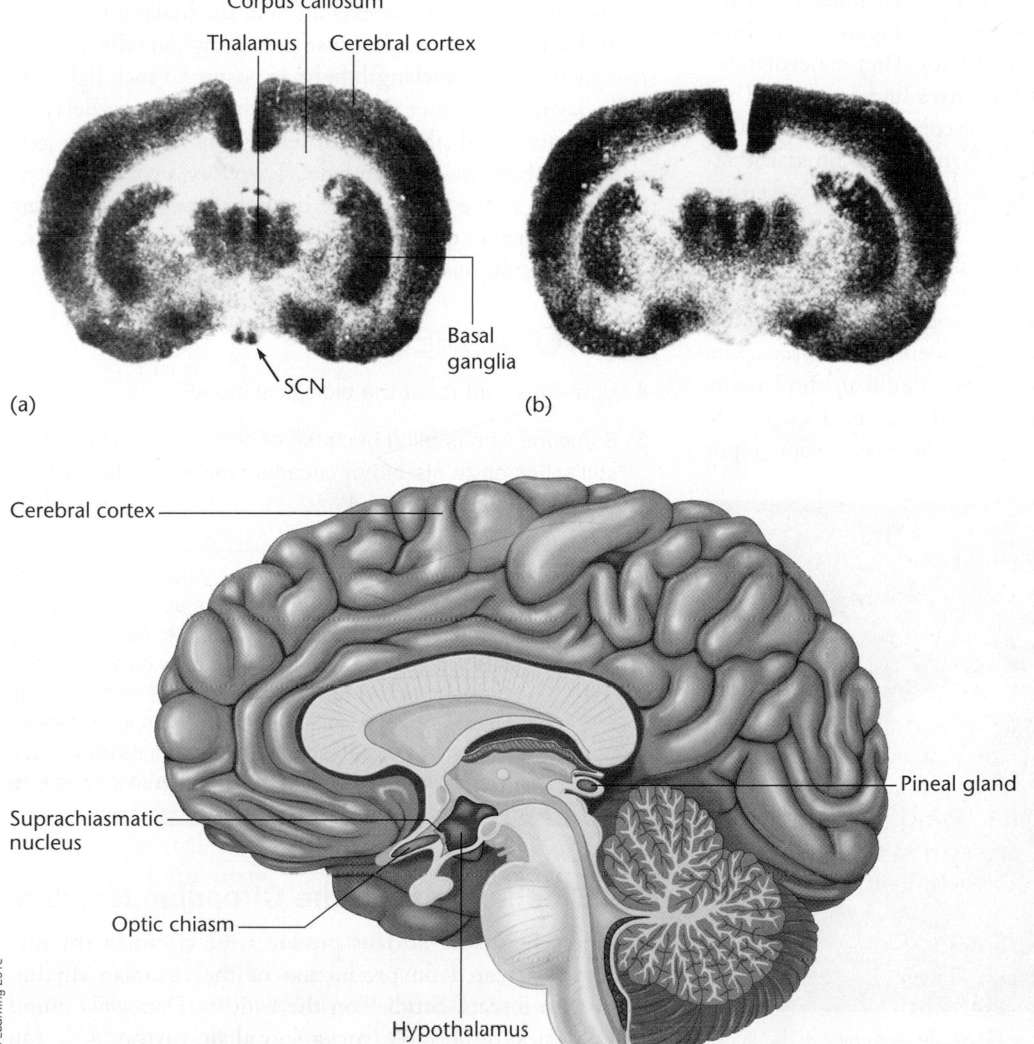

FIGURE 8.7 The suprachiasmatic nucleus (SCN) of rats and humans
The SCN is at the base of the brain, as seen in these coronal sections through the plane of the anterior hypothalamus. Each rat was injected with radioactive 2-deoxyglucose, which is absorbed by the most active neurons. A high level of absorption of this chemical produces a dark appearance on the slide. Note the greater activity in SCN neurons of a rat injected during the day (a), than in one injected at night (b). (c) A sagittal section through a human brain showing the location of the SCN and the pineal gland. Adapted from "Suprachiasmatic nucleus: Use of 14C-labeled deoxyglucose uptake as a functional marker," by W. J. Schwartz & H. Gainer, *Science 1977, 197*: pp. 1089–1091, AAAS/American Association for the Advancement of Science

STOP&CHECK

3. What evidence strongly indicates that the SCN produces the circadian rhythm itself?

ANSWER

3. SCN cells produce a circadian rhythm of activity even if they are kept in cell culture isolated from the rest of the body. Also, when hamsters received transplanted SCN neurons, their circadian rhythm followed the pattern of the donor animals.

How Light Resets the SCN

Figure 8.7 shows the position of the SCN in the human brain, just above the optic chiasm. A small branch of the optic nerve, known as the *retinohypothalamic path,* from the retina to the SCN, alters the SCN's settings.

Most of the input to that path, however, does not come from normal retinal receptors. Mice with genetic defects that destroy nearly all their rods and cones nevertheless reset their biological clocks in synchrony with the light (Freedman et al., 1999; Lucas, Freedman, Muñoz, Garcia-Fernández, & Foster, 1999). Also, consider blind mole rats (see Figure 8.8), whose eyes are covered with folds of skin and fur. They are evolutionarily adapted to spend most of their lives underground. They have fewer than 900 optic nerve axons compared with 100,000 in hamsters. Even a bright flash of light evokes no startle response and no measurable change in brain activity. Nevertheless, light resets their circadian rhythms, enabling them to be awake only at night (de Jong, Hendriks, Sanyal, & Nevo, 1990).

The surprising explanation is that the retinohypothalamic path to the SCN comes from a special population of retinal ganglion cells that have their own photopigment, called *melanopsin,* unlike the ones found in rods and cones (Hannibal, Hindersson, Knudsen, Georg, & Fahrenkrug, 2001; Lucas, Douglas, & Foster, 2001). These special ganglion cells receive some input from rods and cones (Gooley et al., 2010; Güler et al., 2008), but even if they do not receive that input, they respond directly to light (Berson, Dunn, & Takao, 2002). These special ganglion cells are located mainly near the nose, from which they see toward the periphery (Visser, Beersma, & Daan, 1999). They respond to light slowly and turn off slowly when the light ceases (Berson et al., 2002). Therefore, they respond to the overall average amount of light, not to instantaneous changes in light. The average intensity over a period of time is, of course, exactly the information the SCN needs to gauge the time of day. These ganglion cells respond mainly to short-wavelength (blue) light.

Courtesy of Eviatar Nevo

FIGURE 8.8 A blind mole rat
Although blind mole rats are blind in other regards, they reset their circadian rhythms in response to light.

Note several consequences: First, some people who are blind because of damage to the rods and cones, or by damage to the visual cortex, nevertheless have enough input to the melanopsin-containing ganglion cells to entrain their waking and sleeping cycle to the local pattern of sunlight. Second, it was formerly puzzling that bright light aggravates migraine headaches for many blind people. The explanation is that the melanopsin-containing ganglion cells send input to the posterior thalamus, which is part of the pathway producing pain in migraines (Noseda, et al., 2010). Someone with no input to the visual cortex, and therefore no conscious vision, can nevertheless have light-sensitive excitation in the thalamus.

A third consequence: Because these ganglion cells respond strongly to short-wavelength light, exposure to such light late in the day tends to reset the circadian rhythm, phase-delaying it. Computers, cell phones, and televisions emit a high percentage of short-wavelength light. Therefore, people who use those media in the evenings are likely to have trouble falling asleep, and further trouble awakening at the intended time the next morning (Czeisler, 2013).

STOP&CHECK

4. How does light reset the biological clock?

5. Someone who is blind because of cortical damage can still synchronize his or her circadian rhythm to the local pattern of day and night. Why?

ANSWERS

4. A branch of the optic nerve, the retinohypothalamic path, conveys information about light to the SCN. The axons comprising that path originate from special ganglion cells that respond to light by themselves, even if they do not receive input from rods or cones. **5.** If the retina is intact, melanopsin-containing ganglion cells can still send messages to the SCN, resetting its rhythm.

The Biochemistry of the Circadian Rhythm

The suprachiasmatic nucleus produces the circadian rhythm, but how? Research on production of the circadian rhythm began with insects. Studies on the fruit fly *Drosophila* found several genes responsible for a circadian rhythm (X. Liu et al., 1992; Sehgal, Ousley, Yang, Chen, & Schotland, 1999). Two of these genes, known as *period* (abbreviated *PER*) and

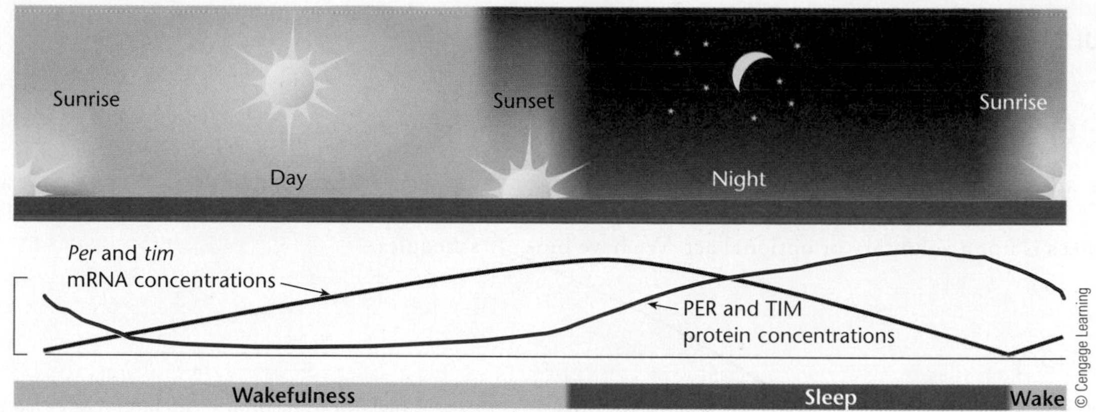

FIGURE 8.9 Feedback between proteins and genes to control sleepiness
In fruit flies (*Drosophila*), the concentrations of the mRNA levels for PER and TIM oscillate over a day, and so do the proteins that they produce.

timeless (*TIM*), produce the proteins PER and TIM. The concentration of these two proteins, which promote sleep and inactivity, oscillates over a day, based on feedback interactions among neurons. Early in the morning, the messenger RNA levels responsible for producing PER and TIM start at low concentrations. As they increase during the day, they increase synthesis of the proteins, but the process takes time, and so the protein concentrations lag hours behind, as shown in Figure 8.9. As the PER and TIM protein concentrations increase, they feed back to inhibit the genes that produce the messenger RNA molecules. Thus, during the night, the PER and TIM concentrations are high, but the messenger RNA concentrations are declining (Nitabach & Taghert, 2008). By the next morning, PER and TIM protein levels are low, the flies awaken, and the cycle is ready to start again. Because the feedback cycle takes about 24 hours, the flies generate a circadian rhythm even in an unchanging environment. However, in addition to the automatic feedback, light activates a chemical that breaks down the TIM protein, thereby increasing wakefulness and synchronizing the internal clock to the external world (Ashmore & Sehgal, 2003).

Why do we care about flies? The reason is that analyzing the mechanism in flies told researchers what to look for in humans and other mammals. Mammals have three versions of the PER protein and several proteins closely related to TIM and the others found in flies (Reick, Garcia, Dudley, & McKnight, 2001; Zheng et al., 1999). Mutations in the genes producing PER proteins lead to alterations of sleep schedules. People with a particular PER mutation have been found to have a circadian rhythm shorter than 24 hours, as if they were moving about a time zone west every day (Chong, Ptácek, & Fu, 2012; C. R. Jones et al., 1999). They consistently get sleepy early in the evening and awaken early in the morning (Toh et al., 2001; Xu et al., 2005). Most people look forward to days when they can stay up late. People with the altered gene look forward to times when they can go to bed early. Most people with this sleep abnormality suffer from depression (Xu et al., 2005). As we see again in Chapter 14 sleep impairments and depression are closely linked. Other known mutations shorten the amount of sleep needed per day or impair people's ability to rebound from temporary sleep deprivation (Dijk & Archer, 2010; Jones, Huang, Ptácek, & Fu, 2013).

STOP & CHECK

6. How do the proteins TIM and PER relate to sleepiness in *Drosophila*?

ANSWER

6. The proteins TIM and PER remain low during most of the day and begin to increase toward evening. They reach high levels at night, promoting sleep. They also feed back to inhibit the genes that produce them, so that their level declines toward morning.

Melatonin

The SCN regulates waking and sleeping by controlling activity levels in other brain areas, including the **pineal gland** (PIN-ee-al; see Figure 8.7), an endocrine gland located just posterior to the thalamus (Aston-Jones, Chen, Zhu, & Oshinsky, 2001; von Gall et al., 2002). The pineal gland releases the hormone **melatonin**, which influences both circadian and circannual rhythms (Butler et al., 2010). The pineal gland secretes melatonin mostly at night, making us sleepy at that time. When people shift to a new time zone and start following a new schedule, they continue to feel sleepy at their old times until the melatonin rhythm shifts (Dijk & Cajochen, 1997). People who have pineal gland tumors sometimes stay awake for days at a time (Haimov & Lavie, 1996).

Melatonin secretion starts to increase about 2 or 3 hours before bedtime. Taking a melatonin pill in the evening has little effect on sleepiness because the pineal gland produces melatonin at that time anyway. However, people who take melatonin earlier start to become sleepy (Crowley & Eastman, 2013). In the process, it shifts the circadian rhythm such that the person starts to become sleepy earlier than usual the next day also. Melatonin pills are sometimes helpful for people who travel across time zones and need to sleep at an unaccustomed time.

MODULE 8.1 ■ IN CLOSING

Sleep–Wake Cycles

Unlike an electric appliance that stays on until someone turns it off, the brain periodically turns itself on and off. Sleepiness is not a voluntary or optional act. We have biological mechanisms that prepare us to wake at certain times and sleep at other times, even if we would prefer other schedules.

Summary

1. Animals, including humans, have circadian rhythms—internally generated rhythms of activity and sleep lasting about 24 hours, even in an unchanging environment. It is difficult to adjust to a sleep schedule much different from 24 hours. **262**
2. Although the biological clock continues to operate in constant light or constant darkness, the onset of light resets the clock. Even when people set their waking and sleeping times by the clock, the timing of sunrise strongly influences their circadian rhythm. **264**
3. It is easier for most people to follow a cycle longer than 24 hours (as when traveling west) than to follow a cycle shorter than 24 hours (as when traveling east). **265**
4. If people wish to work at night and sleep during the day, the best way to shift the circadian rhythm is to have bright lights at night and darkness during the day. **265**
5. Some people are most alert early in the morning, and others become more alert later in the day. On average, people around 20 years old show the greatest preference for staying awake late and sleeping late the next morning. **265**
6. The suprachiasmatic nucleus (SCN), a part of the hypothalamus, generates the body's circadian rhythms for sleep and temperature. **267**
7. Light resets the biological clock partly by a branch of the optic nerve that extends to the SCN. Those axons originate from a special population of ganglion cells that respond directly to light in addition to receiving some input from rods and cones. **268**
8. The genes controlling the circadian rhythm are almost the same in mammals as in insects. Circadian rhythms result from a feedback cycle based on genes that produce the proteins PER and TIM, and the ability of those proteins to inhibit the genes that produce them. **268**
9. The SCN controls the body's rhythm partly by directing the release of melatonin by the pineal gland. The hormone melatonin increases sleepiness; if given at certain times of the day, it can also reset the circadian rhythm. **269**

Key Terms

Terms are defined in the module on the page number indicated. They're also presented in alphabetical order with definitions in the book's Subject Index/Glossary. Interactive flash cards, audio reviews, and crossword puzzles are among the online resources available to help you learn these terms and the concepts they represent.

endogenous circadian rhythms **262**
endogenous circannual rhythm **262**
jet lag **265**
melatonin **269**
pineal gland **269**
suprachiasmatic nucleus (SCN) **267**
zeitgeber **264**

Thought Questions

1. Why would evolution have enabled blind mole rats to synchronize their SCN activity to light, even though they cannot see well enough to make any use of the light?
2. If you travel across several time zones to the east and want to use melatonin to help reset your circadian rhythm, at what time of day should you take it? What if you travel west?

MODULE 8.1 End of Module Quiz

1. What conclusion do researchers draw from the observation that workers on submarines are unable to adjust to a schedule of working 12 hours and resting 6 hours?
   a. Workers on submarines probably need more sleep than most other people do.
   b. People cut off from sunlight need more sleep than most other people.
   c. Body temperature tends to decrease during times when people feel sleepy.
   d. The human body generates a circadian rhythm.
2. Why do people in Antarctica during the winter often find it difficult to work together?
   a. Their work schedules keep them so busy that they cannot sleep enough.
   b. Their circadian rhythms drift out of phase with one another.
   c. After living together in close quarters for so long, they start to irritate one another.
   d. They get homesick.
3. If workers rotate between working shifts at different times of day, what would be a good way to help them adjust to the night shift?
   a. Use dim lighting during the night shift.
   b. Use bright lighting during the night shift.
   c. Rotate from the early morning shift to the night shift, then to the late afternoon shift.
4. What tends to be characteristic of teenagers who are extreme "evening" types?
   a. They have trouble making and keeping friendships.
   b. They adjust more rapidly than average to daylight saving time in the spring.
   c. They get better grades in school than their abilities would predict.
   d. They get worse grades in school than their abilities would predict.
5. What evidence strongly indicates that the SCN produces the circadian rhythm itself?
   a. Damage to the SCN disrupts the circadian rhythm.
   b. SCN cells isolated from the body continue to produce a circadian rhythm.
   c. Animals with a faster circadian rhythm have a larger SCN.
   d. The SCN increases its activity during wakeful periods and decreases it during sleep.
6. Light resets the biological clock by a branch of the optic nerve, beginning with _____ and sending the input to _______.
   a. rods . . . the SCN
   b. cones . . . the SCN
   c. a mixture of rods and cones . . . the visual cortex
   d. ganglion cells that do not require input from rods or cones . . . the SCN
7. If you want to get to sleep on time, what should you avoid?
   a. Long-wavelength light late in the evening
   b. Short-wavelength light late in the evening
   c. Long-wavelength light early in the morning
   d. Short-wavelength light early in the morning
8. The proteins TIM and PER reach their highest levels _______. They _______ the activity of the genes that produce them.
   a. during the day . . . stimulate
   b. during the day . . . inhibit
   c. at night . . . stimulate
   d. at night . . . inhibit

ANSWERS: 1d, 2b, 3b, 4d, 5b, 6d, 7b, 8d.

MODULE 8.2

Stages of Sleep and Brain Mechanisms

Suppose you buy a new radio. After you play it for 4 hours, it suddenly stops. You wonder whether the batteries are dead or whether the radio needs repair. Later, you discover that this radio always stops after playing for 4 hours but operates again a few hours later even without repairs or a battery change. You begin to suspect that the manufacturer designed it this way, perhaps to prevent you from listening to the radio all day. Now you want to find the device that turns it off whenever you play it for 4 hours. You are asking a new question. When you thought that the radio stopped because it needed repairs or new batteries, you did not ask which device turned it off.

Similarly, if we think of sleep as something like wearing out a machine, we do not ask which part of the brain produces it. But if we think of sleep as a specialized state evolved to serve particular functions, we look for the mechanisms that regulate it.

Sleep and Other Interruptions of Consciousness

Let's start with some distinctions. Sleep is a state that the brain actively produces, characterized by decreased response to stimuli. In contrast, **coma** (KOH-muh) is an extended period of unconsciousness caused by head trauma, stroke, or disease. Someone in a coma has a low level of brain activity and little or no response to stimuli. A strong pinch or a loud noise can awaken a sleeping person but not someone in a coma. Typically, someone in a coma either dies or begins to recover within a few weeks.

Someone in a **vegetative state** alternates between periods of sleep and moderate arousal, although even during the more aroused state, the person shows no awareness of surroundings and no purposeful behavior. Breathing is more regular, and a painful stimulus produces at least the autonomic responses of increased heart rate, breathing, and sweating. A **minimally conscious state** is one stage higher, with occasional, brief periods of purposeful actions and a limited amount of speech comprehension. A vegetative or minimally conscious state can last for months or years.

Brain death is a condition with no sign of brain activity and no response to any stimulus. Physicians usually wait until someone has shown no sign of brain activity for 24 hours before pronouncing brain death, at which point most people believe it is ethical to remove life support.

The Stages of Sleep

Nearly every scientific advance comes from new or improved measurements. Researchers did not even suspect that sleep has stages until they accidentally measured them. The electroencephalograph (EEG), as described in Chapter 3, records an average of the electrical potentials of the cells and fibers in the brain areas nearest each electrode on the scalp (see Figure 8.10). If half the cells in some area increase their electrical potentials while the other half decrease, they cancel out. The EEG record rises or falls when most cells do the same thing at the same time. You might compare it to a record of the noise in a sports stadium: It shows only slight fluctuations until some event gets everyone yelling at once. The EEG enables brain researchers to monitor brain activity during sleep.

Figure 8.11 shows data from a **polysomnograph,** a combination of EEG and eye-movement records, for a college student during various stages of sleep. Figure 8.11a presents a period of relaxed wakefulness for comparison. Note the steady series of **alpha waves** at a frequency of 8 to 12 per second. Alpha waves are characteristic of relaxation, not of all wakefulness.

In Figure 8.11b, sleep has just begun. During this period, called stage 1 sleep, the EEG is dominated by irregular, jagged,

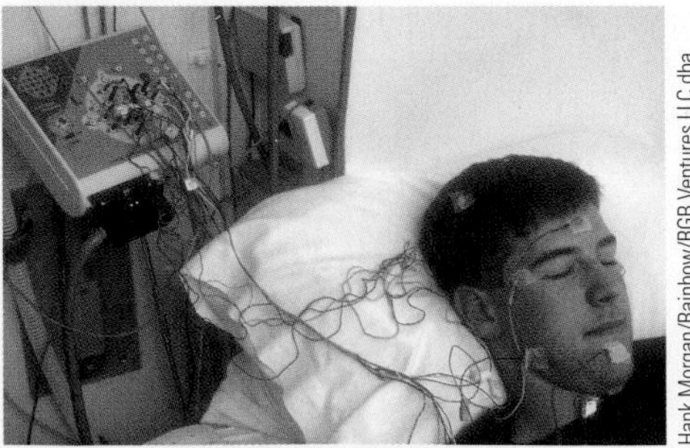

Hank Morgan/Rainbow/RGB Ventures LLC dba SuperStock/Alamy

FIGURE 8.10 Sleeping person with electrodes in place on the scalp for recording brain activity

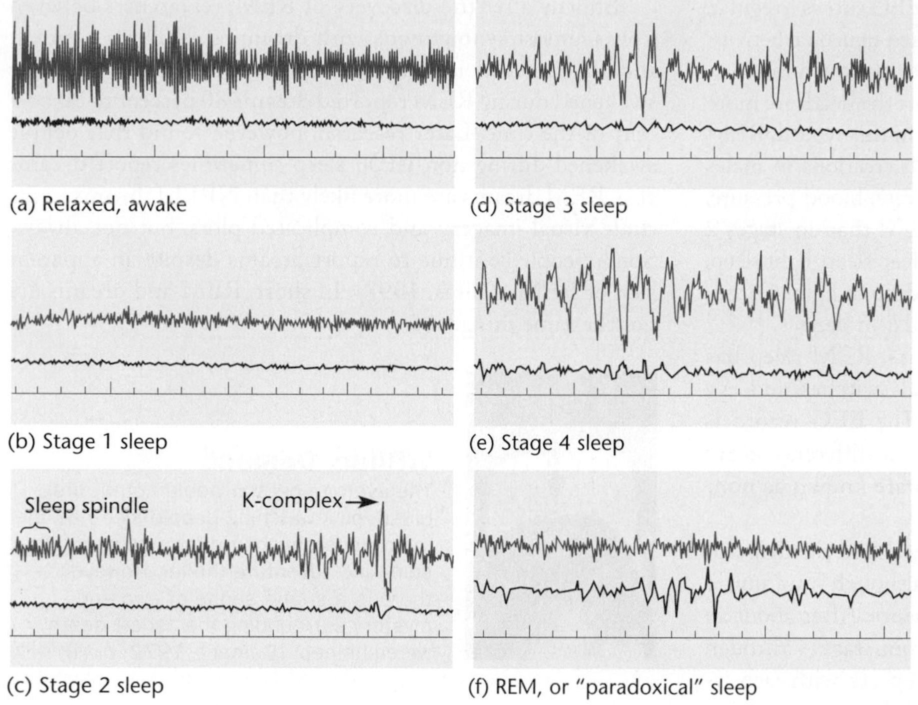

FIGURE 8.11 Polysomnograph records from a college student
For each of these records, the top line is the EEG from one electrode on the scalp. The middle line is a record of eye movements. The bottom line is a time marker, indicating 1-second units. Note the abundance of slow waves in stages 3 and 4.
Source: Records provided by T. E. LeVere

low-voltage waves. Brain activity is less than in relaxed wakefulness but higher than other sleep stages. As Figure 8.11c shows, the most prominent characteristics of stage 2 are sleep spindles and K-complexes. A **sleep spindle** consists of 12- to 14-Hz waves during a burst that lasts at least half a second. Sleep spindles result from oscillating interactions between cells in the thalamus and the cortex. A **K-complex** is a sharp wave associated with temporary inhibition of neuronal firing (Cash et al., 2009).

During stages 3 and 4, heart rate, breathing rate, and brain activity decrease, whereas slow, large-amplitude waves become more common (see Figures 8.11d and e). Stages 3 and 4 differ only in the prevalence of these slow waves, and some authorities combine them as a single stage, **slow-wave sleep (SWS)**.

Slow waves indicate that neuronal activity is highly synchronized. In stage 1 and in wakefulness, the cortex receives much high-frequency input. Because most neurons are out of phase with one another, the EEG is full of short, rapid, choppy waves. During slow-wave sleep, sensory input to the cerebral cortex is greatly reduced, and many cells can synchronize their activity.

STOP&CHECK

7. What do large, slow waves on an EEG indicate?

ANSWER

7. Large, slow waves indicate a low level of activity, with much synchrony of response among neurons.

Paradoxical or REM Sleep

Many discoveries occur when researchers stumble upon something by accident and then see that it might be important. In the 1950s, the French scientist Michel Jouvet was trying to test the learning abilities of cats after removal of the cerebral cortex. Because decorticate mammals don't do much, Jouvet recorded slight movements of the muscles and EEGs from the hindbrain. During certain periods of apparent sleep, the cats' brain activity was relatively high, but their neck muscles were completely relaxed. Jouvet (1960) then recorded the same phenomenon in normal, intact cats and named it **paradoxical sleep** because it is deep sleep in some ways and light in others. (The term *paradoxical* means "apparently self-contradictory.")

Meanwhile, in the United States, Nathaniel Kleitman and Eugene Aserinsky were observing eye movements to determine when someone was asleep, assuming that eye movements stop during sleep. After someone fell asleep, they turned the machine off for most of the night because the recording paper was expensive and they did not expect to see anything interesting in the middle of the night anyway. When they occasionally turned on the machine during the night and saw evidence of eye movements, they at first assumed that something was wrong with their machines. Only after repeated careful measurements did they conclude that periods of rapid eye movements occur during sleep (Dement, 1990). They called these periods **rapid eye movement (REM) sleep** (Aserinsky & Kleitman, 1955; Dement & Kleitman, 1957a), and soon realized that REM sleep was synonymous with what Jouvet called *paradoxical sleep*. Researchers use the term *REM sleep* when referring to humans but often prefer the term *paradoxical sleep* for nonhuman species that lack eye movements.

During paradoxical or REM sleep, the EEG shows irregular, low-voltage fast waves that indicate increased neuronal activity. In this regard, REM sleep is light. However, the postural muscles of the body, including those that support the head, are more relaxed during REM than in other stages. In this regard, REM is deep sleep. REM is also associated with erections in males and vaginal moistening in females. Heart rate, blood pressure, and breathing rate are more variable in REM than in stages 2 through 4. In short, REM sleep combines deep sleep, light sleep, and features that are difficult to classify as deep or light. Consequently, we should avoid the terms *deep* and *light* sleep.

In addition to its steady characteristics, REM sleep has intermittent characteristics such as facial twitches and eye movements, as shown in Figure 9.11f. The EEG record is similar to that for stage 1 sleep, but notice the difference in eye movements. The stages other than REM are known as **non-REM (NREM) sleep**.

When you fall asleep, you start in stage 1 and slowly progress through stages 2, 3, and 4 in order, although loud noises or other intrusions can interrupt the sequence. After about an hour of sleep, you begin to cycle back from stage 4 through stages 3, 2, and then REM. The sequence repeats, with each cycle lasting about 90 minutes. (Some people have inferred that because a cycle lasts 90 minutes, you need to sleep at least 90 minutes to get any benefit. No evidence supports that claim.)

Early in the night, stages 3 and 4 predominate. Toward morning, REM occupies an increasing percentage of the time. Figure 8.12 shows typical sequences. The amount of REM depends on time of day more than how long you have been asleep. That is, if you go to sleep later than usual, you still increase your REM at about the same time that you would have ordinarily (Czeisler, Weitzman, Moore-Ede, Zimmerman, & Knauer, 1980).

Shortly after the discovery of REM, researchers believed it was almost synonymous with dreaming. William Dement and Nathaniel Kleitman (1957b) found that people who were awakened during REM reported dreams 80 percent to 90 percent of the time. Later research, however, found that people awakened during non-REM sleep sometimes report dreams also. REM dreams are more likely than NREM dreams to include visual imagery and complicated plots, but not always. Some people continue to report dreams despite an apparent lack of REM (Solms, 1997). In short, REM and dreams are not the same thing.

William Dement

The average person would not, at first blush, pick watching people sleep as the most apparent theme for a spine-tingling scientific adventure thriller. However, there is a subtle sense of awe and mystery surrounding the "short death" we call sleep. (Dement, 1972, p. xi)

STOP & CHECK

8. How can an investigator determine whether a sleeper is in REM sleep?

9. During which part of a night's sleep is REM most common?

ANSWERS

8. Examine EEG pattern and eye movements. **9.** REM becomes more common toward the end of the night's sleep.

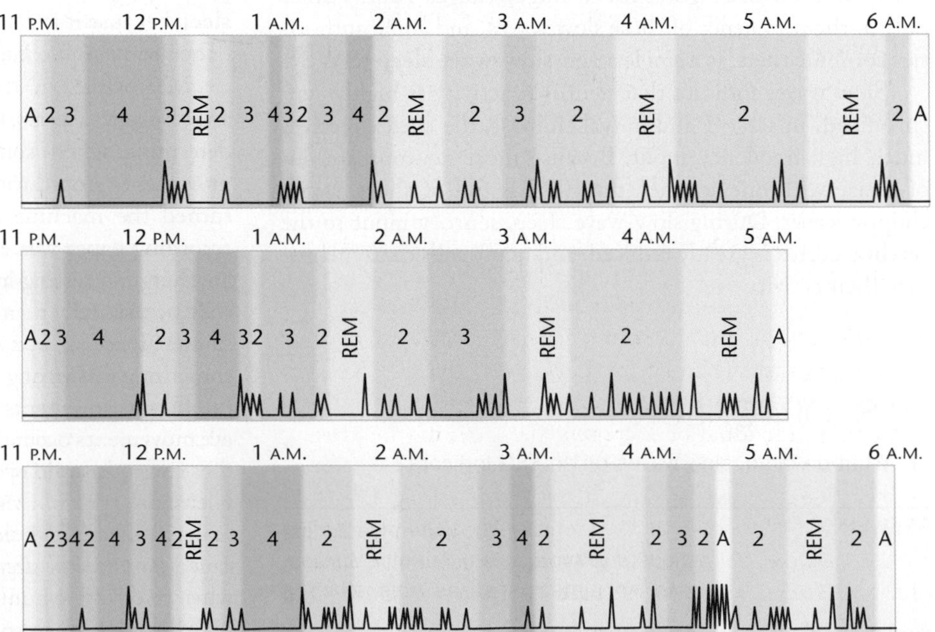

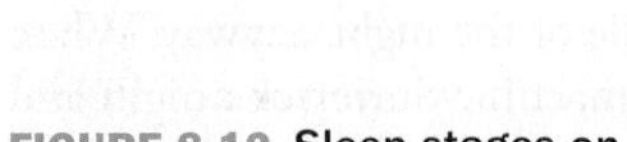

FIGURE 8.12 Sleep stages on three nights

Columns indicate awake (A) and sleep stages 2, 3, 4, and REM. Deflections in the line at the bottom of each chart indicate shifts in body position. Note that slow-wave sleep occurs mostly in the early part of the night's sleep, whereas REM sleep becomes more prevalent toward the end. *Source:* Based on Dement & Kleitman, 1957a

Brain Mechanisms of Wakefulness, Arousal, and Sleep

Philosophers distinguish between the "easy" and "hard" problems of consciousness. The hard problem is why consciousness exists at all. The easy problems include such matters as, "Which brain areas increase overall alertness, and by what transmitters do they do so?" As you are about to see, that question may be philosophically easy, but it is scientifically complex.

Brain Structures of Arousal and Attention

After a cut through the midbrain separates the forebrain and part of the midbrain from all the lower structures, an animal enters a prolonged state of sleep for the next few days. Even after weeks of recovery, the wakeful periods are brief. We might suppose a simple explanation: The cut isolated the brain from the sensory stimuli that come up from the medulla and spinal cord. However, if a researcher cuts each individual tract that enters the medulla and spinal cord, thus depriving the brain of the sensory input, the animal still has normal periods of wakefulness and sleep. Evidently, the midbrain does more than just relay sensory information; it has its own mechanisms to promote wakefulness.

A cut through the midbrain decreases arousal by damaging the **reticular formation,** a structure that extends from the medulla into the forebrain. Some neurons of the reticular formation have axons ascending into the brain, and some have axons descending into the spinal cord. Those with axons descending into the spinal cord form part of the medial tract of motor control, as discussed in Chapter 7. In 1949, Giuseppe Moruzzi and H. W. Magoun proposed that those with ascending axons are well suited to regulate arousal. The term *reticular* (based on the Latin word *rete*, meaning "net") describes the widespread connections among neurons in this system. One part of the reticular formation that contributes to cortical arousal is known as the **pontomesencephalon** (Woolf, 1996). (The term derives from *pons* and *mesencephalon*, or "midbrain.") These neurons receive input from many sensory systems and generate spontaneous activity of their own. Their axons extend into the forebrain, as shown in Figure 8.13, releasing acetylcholine and glutamate, which excite cells in the hypothalamus, thalamus, and basal forebrain. Consequently, the pontomesencephalon maintains arousal during wakefulness and increases it in response to new or challenging tasks (Kinomura, Larsson, Gulyás, & Roland, 1996). Stimulation of the pontomesencephalon awakens a sleeping individual or increases alertness in one already awake, shifting the EEG from long, slow waves to short, high-frequency waves (Munk, Roelfsema, König, Engel, & Singer, 1996). However, subsystems within the pontomesencephalon control different sensory modalities, so a stimulus sometimes arouses one part of the brain more than others (Guillery, Feig, & Lozsádi, 1998).

The **locus coeruleus** (LOW-kus ser-ROO-lee-us; literally, "dark blue place"), a small structure in the pons, is usually inactive, especially during sleep, but it emits bursts of impulses in response to meaningful events, especially those that produce emotional arousal (Sterpenich et al., 2006). Axons from the locus coeruleus release norepinephrine widely throughout the cortex, so this tiny area has a huge influence. Output from the locus coeruleus increases what engineers call "gain." That is, it increases the activity of the most active neurons and decreases the activity of less active neurons. The result is enhanced attention to important information and enhanced memory (Eldar, Cohen, & Niv, 2013).

The hypothalamus has several axon pathways that influence arousal. One pathway releases the excitatory neurotransmitter *histamine* (J.-S. Lin, Hou, Sakai, & Jouvet, 1996), which enhances arousal and alertness throughout the brain (Panula & Nuutinen, 2013). Many antihistamine drugs, often used for allergies, counteract this transmitter and produce drowsiness. Antihistamines that do not cross the blood–brain barrier avoid that side effect.

Another pathway from the hypothalamus, mainly from the lateral and posterior nuclei of the hypothalamus, releases a peptide neurotransmitter called either **orexin** or **hypocretin**. The reason for two names is that two research teams discovered this chemical almost simultaneously in 1998, and each gave it a different name. For simplicity, this text will stick to the term *orexin*, but if you find the term *hypocretin* elsewhere, it means the same thing. The axons releasing orexin extend from the hypothalamus to the basal forebrain and many other areas, enhancing wakefulness (Sakurai, 2007). Orexin is not necessary for waking up, but it is for *staying* awake. That is, most adult humans stay awake for roughly 16 to 17 hours at a time, even when nothing much is happening. Staying awake depends on orexin, especially toward the end of the day (Lee, Hassani, & Jones, 2005). Mice lacking orexin alternate between waking and sleeping, even during an activity that usually sustains arousal, such as running in a running wheel (Anaclet et al., 2009). Optogenetic inhibition of orexin neurons causes mice to go quickly into slow-wave sleep (Tsunematsu et al., 2011).

Drugs that block orexin receptors help people go to sleep, with possibly fewer side effects, compared to other drugs marketed for insomnia (Kukkonen, 2013; Uslaner et al., 2013). In the United States, the Food and Drug Administration is considering approval for one such drug, suvorexant.

Other pathways from the lateral hypothalamus regulate cells in the **basal forebrain** (an area just anterior and dorsal to the hypothalamus). Basal forebrain cells provide axons that extend throughout the thalamus and cerebral cortex (see Figure 8.13). Some of these axons release acetylcholine, which is excitatory and tends to increase arousal (Mesulam, 1995; Szymusiak, 1995). Acetylcholine is released during wakefulness and REM sleep, but not during slow-wave sleep (Hassani, Lee, Henny, & Jones, 2009). During wakefulness, its release sharpens attention—that is, it increases the accurate, reliable detection of sensory stimuli (Goard & Dan, 2009).

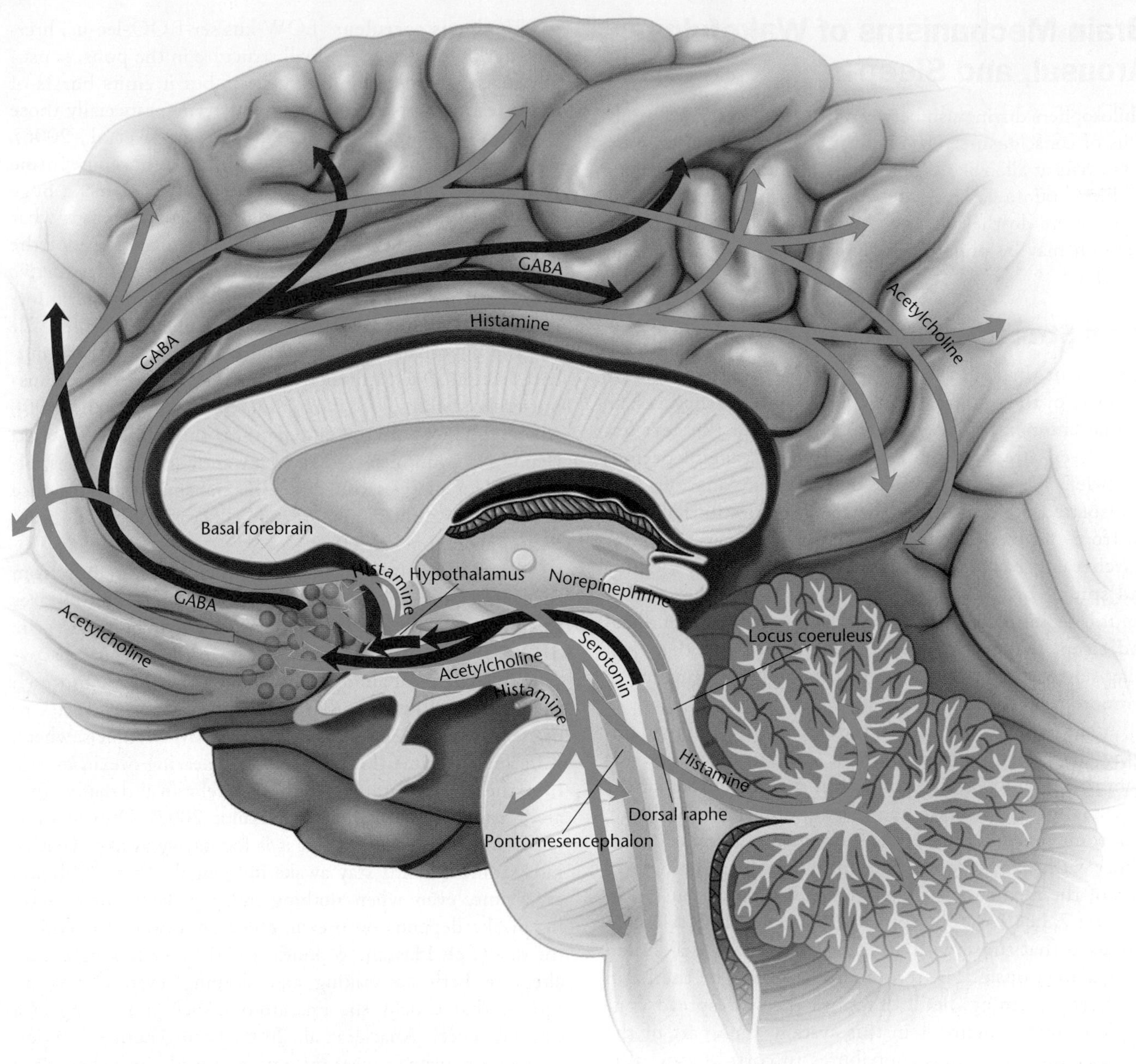

FIGURE 8.13 Brain mechanisms of sleeping and waking
Green arrows indicate excitatory connections. Red arrows indicate inhibitory connections. Neurotransmitters are indicated where they are known. *Source:* Based on J.-S. Lin, Hou, Sakai, & Jouvet, 1996; Robbins & Everitt, 1995; Szymusiak, 1995

STOP&CHECK

10. Why do most antihistamines make people drowsy?

11. What would happen to the sleep–wake schedule of someone who lacked orexin?

ANSWERS

10. Two paths from the hypothalamus—one to the basal forebrain and one to the pontomesencephalon—use histamine as their neurotransmitter to increase arousal. Antihistamines that cross the blood–brain barrier block those synapses. **11.** Someone without orexin would alternate between brief periods of waking and sleeping.

Table 8.1 summarizes the effects of some key brain areas on arousal and sleep.

Sleep and the Inhibition of Brain Activity

Sleep depends partly on decreased sensory input to the cerebral cortex. During sleep, neurons in the thalamus become hyperpolarized, decreasing their readiness to respond to stimuli and decreasing the information they transmit to the cortex (Coenen, 1995). When they do fire, they often fire in synchronous bursts, yielding the high-amplitude waves that characterize slow-wave sleep.

TABLE 8.1 | Brain Structures for Arousal and Sleep

Structure	Neurotransmitter(s) It Releases	Effects on Behavior
Pontomesencephalon	Acetylcholine, glutamate	Increases cortical arousal
Locus coeruleus	Norepinephrine	Increases information storage during wakefulness; suppresses REM sleep
Basal forebrain		
Excitatory cells	Acetylcholine	Excites thalamus and cortex; increases learning, attention; shifts sleep from NREM to REM
Inhibitory cells	GABA	Inhibits thalamus and cortex
Hypothalamus (parts)	Histamine	Increases arousal
(parts)	Orexin	Maintains wakefulness
Dorsal raphe and pons	Serotonin	Interrupts REM sleep

However, although sensory input decreases, a moderate amount remains. In addition, spontaneously active neurons continue firing at only slightly less than their usual rate. How, then, do we remain unconscious in spite of neuronal activity? The answer is inhibition. During sleep, axons that release the inhibitory neurotransmitter GABA, shown in red in Figure 8.13, increase their activity, interfering with the spread of information from one neuron to another (Massimini et al., 2005). Connections from one brain area to another become weaker (Boly et al., 2012; Esser, Hill, & Tononi, 2009). When stimulation doesn't spread, you don't become conscious of it.

Because sleep depends on GABA-mediated inhibition, sleep can be local within the brain (Krueger et al., 2008). That is, you might have substantial inhibition in one brain area and not so much in another. Ordinarily, all brain areas wake up or go to sleep at nearly the same time, but not always. The most extreme case of this principle occurs in dolphins and other aquatic mammals. At night, they need to be alert enough to surface for a breath of air. They have evolved the ability to sleep on one side of the brain at a time. The two hemispheres take turns sleeping, always leaving one awake enough to control swimming and breathing (Rattenborg, Amlaner, & Lima, 2000).

Thinking of sleep as a local phenomenon helps make sense of some otherwise puzzling phenomena. Consider sleepwalking, also known by the fancier term *somnambulism*. Sleepwalkers are asleep in much of the brain, but awake in the motor cortex and a few other areas (Terzaghi et al., 2012). They generally have their eyes open, they orient to the world enough to find their way around, and they often remember at least part of what they thought and did while sleepwalking. Nevertheless, they are confused and sometimes prone to hurt themselves or others, because most of the brain is not alert enough to process information and make reasonable decisions (Zadra, Desautels, Petit, & Montplaisir, 2013).

Another example is lucid dreaming. During lucid dreaming, someone is dreaming but aware of being asleep and dreaming. Evidently some brain area is more awake than usual during dreaming, capable of monitoring dreams that the rest of the brain is generating.

Another example: Have you ever had the experience of waking up but finding that you cannot move your arms or legs? During REM sleep, cells in the pons and medulla send messages that inhibit the spinal neurons that control the body's large muscles (Brooks & Peever, 2012). A cat with damage to those cells moves around awkwardly during REM sleep, as if it were acting out its dreams (Morrison, Sanford, Ball, Mann, & Ross, 1995; see Figure 8.14). Ordinarily, when

FIGURE 8.14 A cat with a lesion in the pons, wobbling about during REM sleep
Cells of an intact pons send inhibitory messages to the spinal cord neurons that control the large muscles. *Source:* From "Stimulus-elicited behavior in rapid eye movement sleep without atonia," by A. R. Morrison, L. D. Sanford, W. A. Ball, G. L. Mann, & R. J. Ross, 1995, *Behavioral Neuroscience, 109*, pp. 972–979. Published by APA and reprinted by permission.

you awaken from a REM period, those cells in the pons shut off and you regain muscle control. But occasionally, most of the brain wakes up while the pons remains in REM. The result is your experience of being temporarily unable to move—a terrifying experience, if you don't understand it (Cheyne & Pennycook, 2013).

STOP&CHECK

12. What would happen to the sleep–wake schedule of someone who took a drug that blocked GABA?

13. Someone who has just awakened sometimes speaks in a loose, unconnected, illogical way. How could you explain this finding?

ANSWERS

12. Someone who took a drug that blocks GABA would remain awake. (Tranquilizers put people to sleep by facilitating GABA.) **13.** People often awaken from a REM period, because REM is abundant toward morning when people usually awaken. Different brain areas don't wake up all at once. Shortly after awakening, parts of the brain may still be in a REM-like state, and thinking may have an illogical, dreamlike quality.

Brain Function in REM Sleep

Researchers interested in the mechanisms of REM decided to use a PET scan to determine which brain areas increased or decreased their activity during REM. Although that research might sound simple, PET requires injecting a radioactive chemical. Imagine trying to give sleepers an injection without awakening them. Further, a PET scan yields a clear image only if the head remains motionless during data collection. If the person tosses or turns even slightly, the image is worthless.

To overcome these difficulties, researchers in two studies persuaded young people to sleep with their heads firmly attached to masks that did not permit any movement. They also inserted a cannula (plastic tube) into each person's arm so that they could inject radioactive chemicals at various times during the night. So imagine yourself in that setup. You have a cannula in your arm and your head is locked into position. Now try to sleep.

Because the researchers foresaw the difficulty of sleeping under these conditions(!), they had their participants stay awake the entire previous night. Someone who is tired enough can sleep even under trying circumstances. (Maybe.)

Now that you appreciate the heroic nature of the procedures, here are the results: During REM sleep, activity increased in the pons (which triggers the onset of REM sleep) and the limbic system (which is important for emotional responses). Activity decreased in the primary visual cortex, the motor cortex, and the dorsolateral prefrontal cortex but increased in parts of the parietal and temporal cortex (Braun et al., 1998; Maquet et al., 1996). REM sleep is associated with a distinctive pattern of high-amplitude electrical potentials known as **PGO waves,** for pons-geniculate-occipital (see Figure 8.15). Waves of neural activity are detected first in the pons, shortly afterward in the lateral geniculate nucleus of the thalamus, and then in the occipital cortex (D. C. Brooks & Bizzi, 1963; Laurent, Cespuglio, & Jouvet, 1974).

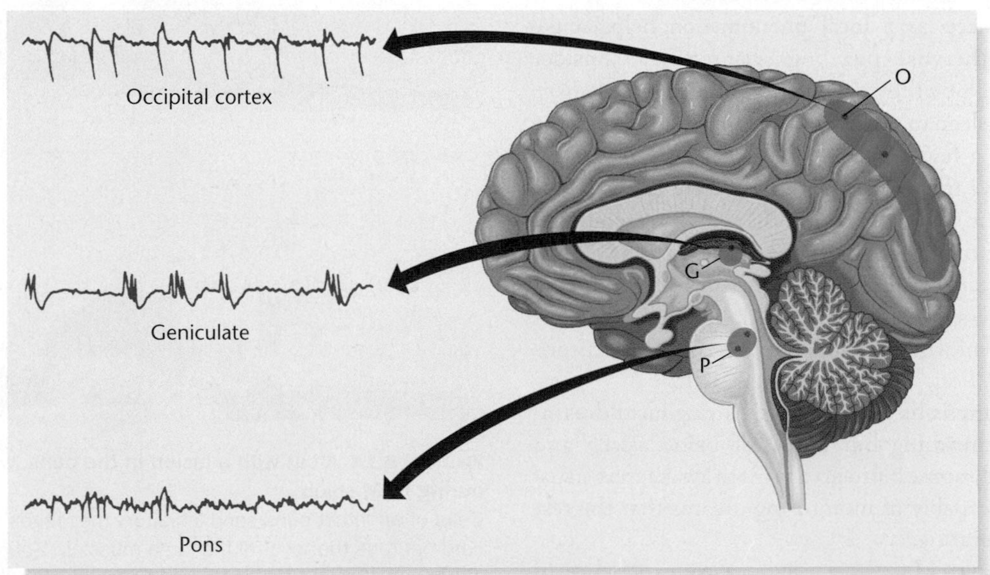

FIGURE 8.15 PGO waves
PGO waves start in the pons (P) and then show up in the lateral geniculate (G) and the occipital cortex (O). Each PGO wave is synchronized with an eye movement in REM sleep.

REM sleep apparently depends on a relationship between the neurotransmitters serotonin and acetylcholine. Injections of the drug *carbachol,* which stimulates acetylcholine synapses, quickly move a sleeper into REM sleep (Baghdoyan, Spotts, & Snyder, 1993). Note that acetylcholine is important for both wakefulness and REM sleep, states of brain arousal. Serotonin and norepinephrine interrupt REM sleep (Boutrel, Franc, Hen, Hamon, & Adrien, 1999; Singh & Mallick, 1996).

Sleep Disorders

How much sleep is enough? The answer isn't the same for everyone. Most adults need about 7½ to 8 hours of sleep per night, but some have been known to do well with less than 3 hours per night (H. S. Jones & Oswald, 1968; Meddis, Pearson, & Langford, 1973). The best gauge of **insomnia**—inadequate sleep—is how someone feels the following day. If you feel tired during the day, you are not sleeping enough at night. Causes of insomnia include noise, uncomfortable temperatures, stress, pain, diet, and medications. Insomnia can also be the result of epilepsy, Parkinson's disease, brain tumors, depression, anxiety, or other neurological or psychiatric conditions. Some children suffer insomnia because they are milk-intolerant, and their parents, not realizing the intolerance, give them milk to drink right before bedtime (Horne, 1992). One man suffered insomnia until he realized that he dreaded going to sleep because he hated waking up to go jogging. After he switched his jogging time to late afternoon, he slept without difficulty. In short, try to identify the reasons for your sleep problems before you try to solve them.

Some cases of insomnia relate to shifts in circadian rhythms (MacFarlane, Cleghorn, & Brown, 1985a, 1985b). Ordinarily, people fall asleep while their temperature is declining and awaken while it is rising, as in Figure 8.16a. Someone whose rhythm is *phase delayed,* as in Figure 8.16b, has trouble falling asleep at the usual time, as if the hypothalamus thinks it isn't late enough (Morris et al., 1990). Someone whose rhythm is *phase advanced,* as in Figure 8.16c, falls asleep easily but awakens early.

Another cause of insomnia is, paradoxically, the use of sleeping pills. Frequent use causes dependence and an inability to sleep without the pills (Kales, Scharf, & Kales, 1978). Similar problems arise when people use alcohol to get to sleep.

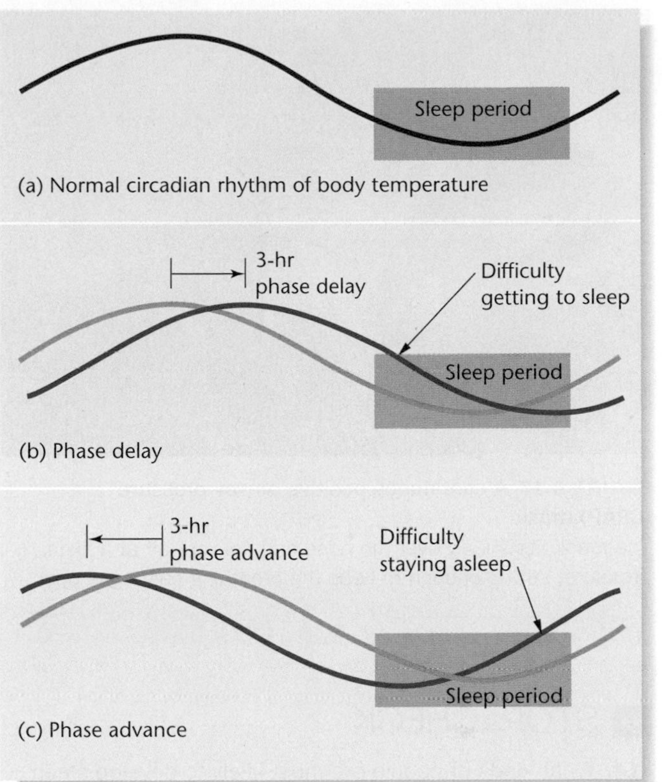

FIGURE 8.16 Insomnia and circadian rhythms
People with a phase delay have trouble getting to sleep. People with a phase advance have trouble staying asleep.

Sleep Apnea

One type of insomnia is **sleep apnea,** impaired ability to breathe while sleeping. People with sleep apnea have breathless periods of a minute or so from which they awaken gasping for breath. They may not remember all their awakenings, although they certainly notice the consequences—sleepiness during the day, impaired attention, depression, and sometimes heart problems. People with sleep apnea have multiple brain areas that appear to have lost neurons, and consequently, they show deficiencies of learning, reasoning, attention, and impulse control (Beebe & Gozal, 2002; Macey et al., 2002). These correlational data do not tell us whether the brain abnormalities led to sleep apnea or sleep apnea led to the brain abnormalities. However, research with rodents suggests the latter: Mice that are subjected to frequent periods of low oxygen (as if they hadn't been breathing) lose some neurons and impair others, especially in areas responsible for alertness (Zhu et al., 2007). Sleep impairments may be responsible for cognitive loss not only in people with sleep apnea but also in some with Alzheimer's disease.

Sleep apnea results from several causes, including genetics, hormones, and old-age deterioration of the brain mechanisms that regulate breathing. Another cause is obesity, especially in middle-aged men. Many obese men have narrower than normal airways and have to compensate by breathing frequently or vigorously. During sleep, they cannot keep up that rate of breathing. Furthermore, their airways become even narrower than usual when they adopt a sleeping posture (Mezzanotte, Tangel, & White, 1992).

People with sleep apnea are advised to lose weight and avoid alcohol and tranquilizers (which impair the breathing muscles). Medical options include surgery to remove tissue that obstructs the trachea (the breathing passage) or a mask that covers the nose and delivers air under enough pressure to keep the breathing passages open (see Figure 8.17).

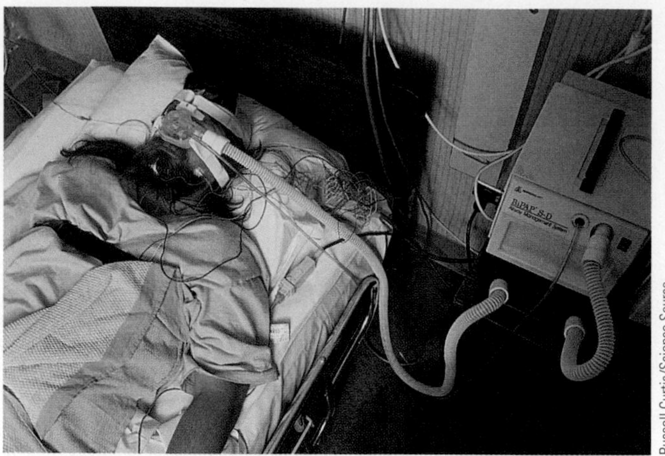

Russell Curtis/Science Source

FIGURE 8.17 A continuous positive airway pressure (CPAP) mask
The mask fits snugly over the nose and delivers air at a fixed pressure, strong enough to keep the breathing passages open.

STOP&CHECK

14. What kinds of people are most likely to develop sleep apnea?

ANSWER

14. Sleep apnea is most common among people with a genetic predisposition, old people, and overweight middle-aged men.

Narcolepsy

Narcolepsy, a condition characterized by frequent periods of sleepiness during the day, strikes about 1 person in 1,000. It sometimes runs in families, but most cases emerge in people with no affected relatives. Narcolepsy has four main symptoms, although not every patient has all four. Each of these symptoms can be interpreted as an intrusion of a REM-like state into wakefulness:

1. Attacks of sleepiness during the day.
2. Occasional cataplexy—an attack of muscle weakness while the person remains awake. Cataplexy is often triggered by strong emotions, such as anger or great excitement. (One man suddenly collapsed during his wedding ceremony.)
3. Sleep paralysis—an inability to move while falling asleep or waking up. Many people have experienced sleep paralysis at least once or twice, but people with narcolepsy experience it frequently.
4. Hypnagogic hallucinations—dreamlike experiences that the person has trouble distinguishing from reality, often occurring at the onset of sleep.

The cause relates to the neurotransmitter orexin. People with narcolepsy lack the hypothalamic cells that produce and release orexin (Thannickal et al., 2000). Why they lack them is unknown, but one possibility is an autoimmune reaction, in which the immune system attacks part of the body—in this case, cells with orexin (Hallmayer et al., 2009). Recall that orexin is important for maintaining wakefulness. Consequently, people lacking orexin alternate between short waking periods and short sleepy periods, instead of staying awake throughout the day. Dogs that lack the gene for orexin receptors have symptoms much like human narcolepsy, with frequent alternations between wakefulness and sleep (L. Lin et al., 1999). The same is true for mice that lack orexin (Hara, 2001; Mochizuki et al., 2004).

As discussed in Chapter 7, people with Huntington's disease have widespread damage in the basal ganglia. In addition, most lose neurons in the hypothalamus, including the neurons that make orexin. As a result, they have problems staying awake during the day and difficulty staying asleep at night (Morton et al., 2005).

So far no one has developed a drug that specifically activates orexin receptors. Administering orexin itself is not a good option, because it does not readily cross the blood–brain barrier. The most common treatment is stimulant drugs such as methylphenidate (Ritalin), which enhance dopamine and norepinephrine activity.

STOP&CHECK

15. What is the relationship between orexin and narcolepsy?

ANSWER

15. Orexin is important for staying awake. Therefore, people or animals lacking either orexin or the receptors for orexin develop narcolepsy, characterized by bouts of sleepiness during the day.

Periodic Limb Movement Disorder

Another sleep disorder is **periodic limb movement disorder**, characterized by repeated involuntary movement of the legs and sometimes the arms during sleep (Edinger et al., 1992). It is distinct from restless leg syndrome, in which people often feel an urge to kick a leg even while awake.

Many people, perhaps most, experience an occasional involuntary kick, especially when starting to fall asleep. Leg movements are not a problem unless they become persistent. In people with periodic limb movement disorder, mostly middle-aged and older, the legs kick once every 20 to 30 seconds for minutes or hours, mostly during NREM sleep.

REM Behavior Disorder

For most people, the major postural muscles are relaxed and inactive during REM sleep. However, people with **REM behavior disorder** move around vigorously during their REM periods, apparently acting out their dreams. They frequently dream about defending themselves against attack, and they may punch, kick, and leap about. They often injure themselves or other people and damage property (Olson, Boeve, & Silber, 2000).

Mice deficient in GABA and other inhibitory neurotransmitters show running, jerking, and chewing movements during REM sleep, and overall disrupted sleep. Because of these similarities to human cases, the results suggest that inadequate inhibitory transmission may be responsible for REM behavior disorder (Brooks & Peever, 2011).

Night Terrors and Sleepwalking

Night terrors are experiences of intense anxiety from which a person awakens screaming in terror. A night terror is more severe than a nightmare, which is simply an unpleasant dream. Night terrors occur during NREM sleep and are more common in children than adults. Dream content, if any, is usually simple, such as a single image.

Sleepwalking runs in families and occurs mostly in children. Most people who sleepwalk, and many of their relatives, have one or more additional sleep difficulties such as chronic snoring, disordered sleep breathing, bed-wetting, and night terrors (Cao & Guilleminault, 2010). The causes of sleepwalking are not well understood, but it is more common when people are sleep deprived or under unusual stress (Zadra & Pilon, 2008). It is most common during slow-wave sleep early in the night and usually not accompanied by dreaming. (It does not occur during REM sleep, when the large muscles are completely relaxed.) Sleepwalking is usually harmless but not always. One teenage girl walked out of her house, climbed a crane, and went back to sleep on a support beam. Fortunately, a pedestrian saw her and called the police. Sleepwalkers have been known to eat, rearrange furniture, fall off balconies, and drive cars—while disregarding lanes and traffic lights. Unlike wakeful actions, the deeds of sleepwalkers are poorly planned and usually not remembered. Evidently, parts of the brain are awake and other parts are asleep (Gunn & Gunn, 2007). Incidentally, contrary to common sayings, it is not dangerous to awaken a sleepwalker. It is not particularly helpful either, but it is not dangerous.

An analogous condition is sleep sex or "sexsomnia," in which sleeping people engage in sexual behavior, either with a partner or by masturbation, and do not remember it afterward. Sexsomnia poses a threat to romances and marriages. As one woman said, "After getting married a few years ago, my husband told me I was masturbating in my sleep. I was mortified, thinking back to all the slumber parties as a girl, and then when I was older and my little sister stayed the night at my house! How many others might have witnessed and not said anything? My new marriage is on the rocks, since I'm having such good sex in my sleep, I have NO desire while I'm awake. This is killing my relationship with my husband" (Mangan, 2004, p. 290).

MODULE 8.2 ■ IN CLOSING

Stages of Sleep

Chemists divide the world into elements, biologists divide life into species, and physicians distinguish one disease from another. Similarly, psychologists try to recognize the most natural or useful distinctions among types of behavior or experience. The discovery of stages of sleep was a major landmark in psychology because researchers found a previously unrecognized distinction that is both biologically and psychologically important. It also demonstrated that external measurements—in this case, EEG recordings—can be used to identify internal experiences. We now take it largely for granted that an electrical or magnetic recording from the brain can tell us something about a person's experience, but it is worth pausing to note what a surprising discovery that was in its time.

Summary

1. During sleep, brain activity decreases, but a stimulus can awaken the person. Someone in a coma cannot be awakened. A vegetative state or minimally conscious state can last months or years, during which the person shows only limited responses. Brain death is a condition without brain activity or responsiveness of any kind. 272
2. Over the course of about 90 minutes, a sleeper goes through stages 1, 2, 3, and 4 and then returns through stages 3 and 2 to a stage called REM. REM is characterized by rapid eye movements, more brain activity than other sleep stages, complete relaxation of the trunk muscles, irregular breathing and heart rate, penile erection or vaginal lubrication, and an increased probability of vivid dreams. 272

3. REM sleep or paradoxical sleep is a condition marked by more cortical activity than other sleep, complete relaxation of the body's postural muscles, and an increased probability of dreaming. **273**
4. The brain has multiple systems for arousal. The pontomesencephalon and parts of the hypothalamus control various cell clusters in the basal forebrain that send axons releasing acetylcholine throughout much of the forebrain. **275**
5. The locus coeruleus is active in response to meaningful events. It facilitates attention and new learning. **275**
6. Orexin is a peptide that maintains wakefulness. Cells in the lateral and posterior nuclei of the hypothalamus release this peptide. **275**
7. During sleep, enhanced release of GABA limits neuronal activity and blocks the spread of activation. Sometimes this suppression is stronger in one brain area than another. That is, sleep can occur in one brain area and not another at a given time. **276**
8. REM sleep is associated with increased activity in a number of brain areas, including the pons, limbic system, and parts of the parietal and temporal cortex. Activity decreases in the prefrontal cortex, the motor cortex, and the primary visual cortex. **278**
9. REM sleep begins with PGO waves, which are waves of brain activity transmitted from the pons to the lateral geniculate to the occipital lobe. **278**
10. People with sleep apnea have long periods without breathing while they sleep. Many have indications of neuronal loss, probably as a result of decreased oxygen while they sleep. **279**
11. People with narcolepsy have attacks of sleepiness during the day. Narcolepsy is associated with a deficiency of the neurotransmitter orexin. **280**

Key Terms

Terms are defined in the module on the page number indicated. They're also presented in alphabetical order with definitions in the book's Subject Index/Glossary. Interactive flash cards, audio reviews, and crossword puzzles are among the online resources available to help you learn these terms and the concepts they represent.

alpha waves **272**
basal forebrain **275**
brain death **272**
coma **272**
insomnia **279**
K-complex **273**
locus coeruleus **275**
minimally conscious state **272**
narcolepsy **280**
night terrors **281**
non-REM (NREM) sleep **274**
orexin (or hypocretin) **275**
paradoxical sleep **273**
periodic limb movement disorder **280**
PGO waves **278**
polysomnograph **272**
pontomesencephalon **275**
rapid eye movement (REM) sleep **273**
REM behavior disorder **281**
reticular formation **275**
sleep apnea **279**
sleep spindle **273**
slow-wave sleep (SWS) **273**
vegetative state **272**

Thought Question

Unlike adults, infants alternate between short waking periods and short naps. What can we infer about their neurotransmitters?

MODULE 8.2 End of Module Quiz

1. Slow, large-amplitude EEG waves characterize which stage or stages of sleep?
   a. Stage 1
   b. REM sleep
   c. Stage 2
   d. Stages 3 and 4
2. Why is REM sleep also known as paradoxical sleep?
   a. Activity in the left hemisphere does not match the activity in the right hemisphere.
   b. We did not know it existed until its discovery in the 1950s.
   c. It is deep sleep in some ways and light in others.
   d. Because a pair of docs discovered it.

3. At which time, if any, is stage 4 sleep most common?
   a. Immediately after falling asleep
   b. Not immediately, but during the early part of the night's sleep
   c. Near the end of the night's sleep
   d. During all parts equally

4. Of the following, which two neurotransmitters increase arousal in the brain?
   a. Acetylcholine and histamine
   b. Acetylcholine and GABA
   c. Histamine and GABA
   d. Orexin and GABA

5. Norepinephrine, released by the locus coeruleus, has which effect on behavior?
   a. It prolongs wakefulness.
   b. It increases attention to important information.
   c. It produces dreams.
   d. It inhibits synapses during sleep.

6. How do dolphins handle breathing while they are asleep?
   a. They store enough oxygen to get through the night without breathing.
   b. They shift to a system of gills, like those of fish.
   c. They sleep with the head out of the water.
   d. Half of the brain sleeps while the other remains awake enough to surface and breathe.

7. What does PGO stand for (with regard to brain function)?
   a. Parasympathetic-Ganglion-Oxytocin
   b. Protein-Glucose-Outcome
   c. Parietal-GABA-Olfaction
   d. Pons-Geniculate-Occipital

8. If you awaken but find you temporarily cannot move your arms or legs, what is happening?
   a. You are probably developing a severe neurological disease.
   b. You are probably just being lazy.
   c. You need more time to get the blood flowing to your muscles.
   d. Most of your brain is awake, but part of your pons and medulla remain in REM sleep.

9. Of the following, which one is *not* associated with an increased probability of sleep apnea?
   a. Having a relative with sleep apnea
   b. Being female
   c. Being overweight
   d. Being middle-aged or older

10. Narcolepsy is linked to a deficit of which neurotransmitter?
   a. Dopamine
   b. GABA
   c. Orexin
   d. Acetylcholine

11. When does sleepwalking usually occur?
   a. During REM sleep
   b. During stage 1 sleep
   c. During slow-wave sleep (stages 3 and 4)
   d. During all sleep stages equally

ANSWERS: 1d, 2c, 3b, 4a, 5b, 6d, 7d, 8d, 9b, 10c, 11c.

Why Sleep? Why REM? Why Dreams?

Why do you sleep? "That's easy," you reply. "I sleep because I get tired." Well, yes, but you are not tired in the sense of muscle fatigue. You need almost as much sleep after a day of sitting around the house as after a day of intense physical or mental activity (Horne & Minard, 1985; Shapiro, Bortz, Mitchell, Bartel, & Jooste, 1981). Furthermore, you could rest your muscles just as well while awake as while asleep. (In fact, if your muscles ache after strenuous exercise, you probably find it difficult to sleep.)

You feel tired at the end of the day because inhibitory processes in your brain force you to become less aroused and less alert. That is, we evolved mechanisms to force us to sleep. Why?

Functions of Sleep

Sleep serves many functions. During sleep, we rest our muscles, decrease metabolism, perform cellular maintenance in neurons (Vyadyslav & Harris, 2013), reorganize synapses, and strengthen memories (Sejnowski & Destexhe, 2000). People who don't get enough sleep react more severely than average to stressful events (Minkel et al., 2012). They may develop symptoms of mental illness or may aggravate symptoms they already had (van der Kloet, Merckelbach, Giesbrecht, & Lynn, 2012). Inadequate sleep is a major cause of accidents by workers and poor performance by college students. Driving while sleep deprived is comparable to driving under the influence of alcohol (Falleti, Maruff, Collie, Darby, & McStephen, 2003). Even one night of sleeplessness activates the immune system (Matsumoto et al., 2001). That is, you react to sleep deprivation as if you were ill. Clearly, we need to sleep. Is there, however, a primary or original reason?

Sleep and Energy Conservation

Even if we identified what seems to be the most important function of sleep for humans today, it might not be the function for which sleep originally evolved. By analogy, consider computers: People use computers today to write papers, send email, search the Internet, play video games, store and display photographs, play music, and find a date. Someone who didn't know the history might not guess that computers were built originally for mathematical calculations.

Similarly, sleep probably started with a simple function to which evolution added others later. Even bacteria have circadian rhythms of activity and inactivity (Mihalcescu, Hsing, & Leibler, 2004). What benefit of sleep applies to species with little or no nervous system?

A likely hypothesis is that sleep's original function—and still an important one—is to save energy (Kleitman, 1963; Siegel, 2009, 2012). Nearly every species is more efficient at some times of day than at others. Those with good vision are more efficient in the day. Those that rely on other senses instead of vision are more efficient at night, when their predators cannot see them. Sleep conserves energy during the inefficient times, when activity would be wasteful and possibly dangerous. NASA's Rover spacecraft, built to explore Mars, had a mechanism to make it "sleep" at night to conserve its batteries. During sleep, a mammal's body temperature decreases by 1°C or 2°C, enough to save a significant amount of energy. Muscle activity decreases, saving more energy. Animals increase their sleep duration during food shortages, when energy conservation is especially important (Berger & Phillips, 1995).

Sleep is therefore in some ways analogous to hibernation. Hibernation is a true need. A ground squirrel that is prevented from hibernating becomes as disturbed as a person who is prevented from sleeping. However, the function of hibernation is simply to conserve energy while food is scarce.

Analogous to Sleep: Hibernation

Hibernating animals decrease their body temperature to only slightly above that of the environment (but not low enough for their blood to freeze). Heart rate drops to almost nothing, brain activity drops to almost nothing, neuron cell bodies shrink, and dendrites lose almost a fourth of their branches, replacing them later when body temperature increases (von der Ohe, Darian-Smith, Garner, & Heller, 2006). A few curious facts about hibernation:

1. Whether or not bears hibernate is a matter of definition. Bears sleep most of the winter, lowering their body temperature a few degrees and decreasing their metabolism and heart rate (Toien et al., 2011), but their state is not as extreme as that of smaller hibernators such as bats and ground squirrels.

2. Hamsters also hibernate. If you keep your pet hamster in a cool, dimly lit place during the winter, and it appears to have died, make sure that it is not just hibernating before you bury it!
3. Hibernating animals come out of hibernation for a few hours every few days, raising their body temperature to about normal. However, they spend most of this time asleep (B. M. Barnes, 1996).
4. Hibernation retards the aging process. Hamsters that spend longer times hibernating have proportionately longer life expectancies than other hamsters do (Lyman, O'Brien, Greene, & Papafrangos, 1981). Hibernation is also a period of relative invulnerability to infection and trauma. Procedures that would ordinarily damage the brain, such as inserting a needle into it, produce little if any harm during hibernation (F. Zhou et al., 2001).

Species Differences in Sleep

If one of the main functions of sleep is to shut down activity at times of relative inefficiency, we might expect to find little or no sleep in species that are equally effective at all times of day. Indeed, evidence supports that expectation. Certain fish have evolved for life in a cave where "day" and "night" have no meaning, because light is always absent and temperature is virtually constant. Observers report that these fish apparently never sleep (Kavanau, 1998).

Several other species turn off their need for sleep under certain circumstances (Siegel, 2009). After a dolphin or whale gives birth, both mother and baby stay awake 24 hours a day for the first couple of weeks while the baby is especially vulnerable. Neither shows any sign of harm from sleep deprivation. During the spring breeding season, while male sandpipers are competing for mates above the Arctic Circle (where it is sunny all day), many of them are active up to 23 hours per day for nearly three weeks, with no apparent harm to their health or alertness (Lesku et al., 2012).

Migratory birds face another kind of problem. During a week or two in fall and spring, they forage for food during the day and do their migratory flying at night. (Flying at night makes sense, because it is cooler then.) That schedule leaves little time for sleep. They apparently decrease their need for sleep during migration. If a bird is kept in a cage during the migration season, it flutters around restlessly at night, sleeping only a third its usual amount. It compensates to some extent with brief drowsy periods (less than 30 seconds each) during the day (Fuchs, Haney, Jechura, Moore, & Bingman, 2006). Still, it gets very little sleep, while remaining alert and performing normally on learning tasks. If the same bird is deprived of sleep during other seasons of the year, its performance suffers (Rattenborg et al., 2004). Exactly how a migratory bird or a mother dolphin decreases its sleep need is unknown, but the fact that it is possible fits with the idea that sleep is primarily a way to conserve energy, rather than a way to fulfill a function that one could not fulfill in other ways.

Animal species vary in their sleep habits in ways that make sense if we ask how many hours the animal needs to be awake, and therefore how long it can afford to spend conserving energy (Allison & Cicchetti, 1976; Campbell & Tobler, 1984). Grazing animals that need to eat for many hours per day get less sleep than carnivores (meat eaters) that can satisfy their nutritional needs with a single meal. Animals that need to be on the alert for predators get little sleep, whereas the predators themselves sleep easily. Insect-eating bats are active in the early evening, when moths and similar insects are most abundant, and then they sleep the rest of the day (see Figure 8.18).

Here's another bit of miscellaneous trivia about animal sleep: Swifts are small, dark birds that chase insects. They get all the nutrition and water they need from the insects. When a baby European swift first takes off from its nest, how long would you guess its first flight lasts, until it comes to land again?

Alan Williams/Alamy

A European swift

The answer: up to 2 years. Except during treacherous storms, it doesn't come down until it is old enough to mate and build a nest. In the meantime, it spends both days and nights in the air. At night it heads into the wind, sticks out its wings, glides, and presumably sleeps—although confirming sleep would require measuring the EEG of a small bird in flight. It picks an altitude where the air is not too cold, accepts the risk of being blown a great distance, and awakens the next morning to resume its chase of flying insects (Bäckman & Alerstam, 2001).

Jo Ellen Kalat

The lion sleeps tonight... and this afternoon... and probably part of the morning, too.

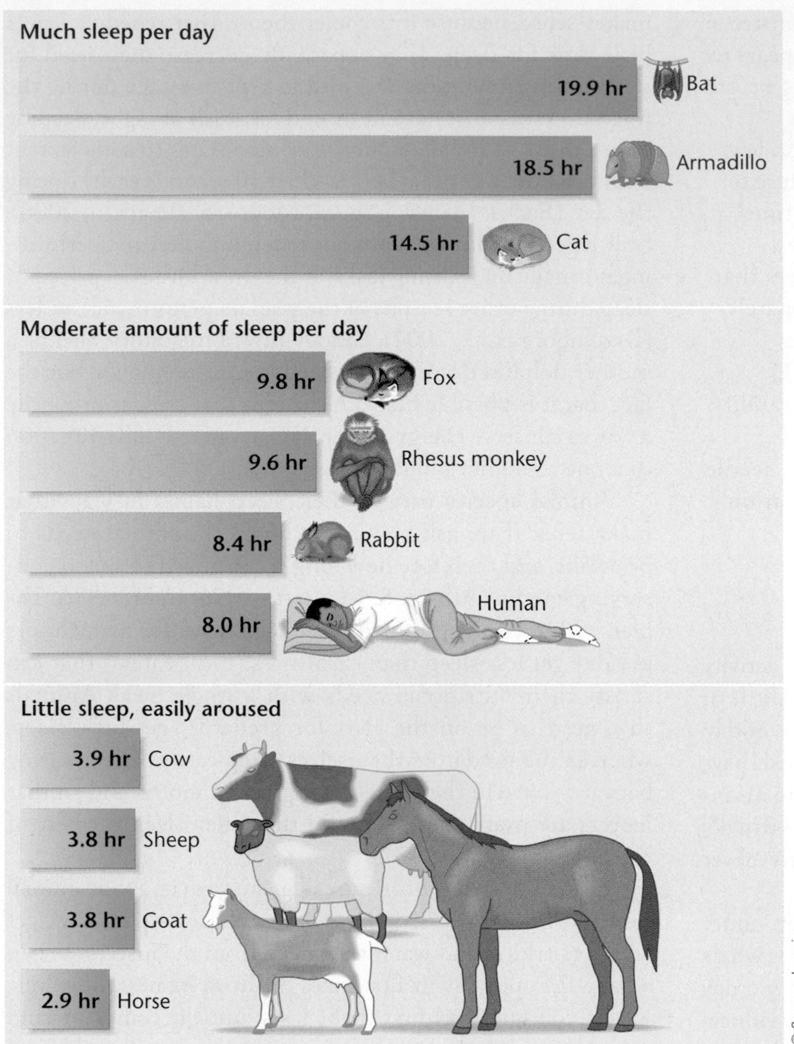

FIGURE 8.18 Hours of sleep per day for various species
Generally, predators and others that are safe when they sleep tend to sleep a great deal. Animals in danger of being attacked while they sleep spend less time asleep.

Sleep and Memory

Another apparent function of sleep is improved memory. Young adults deprived of a night's sleep show deficits on memory tasks (Yoo, Hu, Gujar, Jolesz, & Walker, 2007). In contrast, if people learn something and then go to sleep, or even take a nap, their memory often becomes better than it was before the sleep (Hu, Stylos-Allan, & Walker, 2006; Korman et al., 2007). That is, we see not just an absence of forgetting but also a gain of memory. The amount of improvement varies from one study to another and from one type of learning task to another (Cai & Rickard, 2009; Cai, Shuman, Gorman, Sage, & Anagnostaras, 2009; Doyon et al., 2009). Still, reviewing something right before you go to sleep is a helpful strategy.

In one study, people viewed 50 objects making a sound (such as a cat meowing) in various locations on a computer screen. Then they took a nap, during which they heard some of those sounds again. After the nap, they were tested on their memory for the location of each object on the screen. They showed enhanced memory for the objects whose sounds they heard during the nap (Rudoy, Voss, Westerberg, & Paller, 2009). Evidently the sounds reminded them of the information, and the brain then processed that information again.

Sleep also helps people reanalyze their memories: In one study, people who had just practiced a complex task were more likely to perceive a hidden rule (an "aha" experience) after a period of sleep than after a similar period of wakefulness (Wagner, Gais, Haider, Verleger, & Born, 2004). Another study found that a nap that included REM sleep enhanced performance on certain kinds of creative problem solving (Cai, Mednick, Harrison, Kanady, & Mednick, 2009). However, an afternoon nap also leaves someone less alert than usual for the next half hour (Groeger, Lo, Burns, & Dijk, 2011).

How does sleep enhance memory? Researchers recorded activity in the hippocampus during learning, and then recorded from the same locations during sleep, using microelectrodes within cells for laboratory animals and electrodes on the scalp for humans. The results: Patterns that occurred during sleep resembled those that occurred during learning, except that they were more rapid during sleep. Furthermore, the amount of hippocampal activity during sleep correlated highly with the subsequent improvement in performance (Derégnaucourt, Mitra, Fehér, Pytte, & Tchernichovski, 2005; Euston, Tatsuno, & McNaughton, 2007; Huber, Ghilardi, Massimini, & Tononi, 2004; Ji & Wilson, 2007; Maquet et al., 2000; Peigneux et al., 2004). These results suggest that the brain replays its daily experiences during sleep. However, further research found that the sleeping brain replays its experience backward as often

STOP & CHECK

16. What kind of animal tends to get more than the average amount of sleep?

17. What might one predict about the sleep of fish that live deep in the ocean?

ANSWERS

16. Predators get much sleep, and so do species that are unlikely to be attacked during their sleep (such as armadillos). **17.** The deep ocean, like a cave, has no light and no difference between day and night. These fish might not need to sleep because they are equally efficient at all times of day and have no reason to conserve energy at one time more than another.

as forward, and that it sometimes replays less common experiences more often than more common ones (Gupta, van der Meer, Touretzky, & Redish, 2010). Also, the hippocampus replays recently learned patterns during quiet waking periods, not just during sleep (Karlsson & Frank, 2009). So the role of hippocampal replay during sleep is less clear than it once appeared to be.

One way for sleep to strengthen memory is by weeding out the less successful connections. In the chapter on memory, we shall examine the phenomenon of long-term potentiation, the ability of new experiences to strengthen synaptic connections. Suppose that every time you learn something, your brain strengthened certain synapses without making adjustments elsewhere. As you learned more and more, you would have more and more brain activity. By middle age, your brain might be burning with constant activity. To prevent runaway overactivity, your brain compensates for strengthening some synapses by weakening or removing others, mostly during sleep (Liu, Faraguna, Cirelli, Tononi, & Gao, 2010; Maret, Faraguna, Nelson, Cirelli, & Tononi, 2011; Vyazovskiy, Cirelli, Pfister-Genskow, Faraguna, & Tononi, 2008). Weakening less appropriate synapses emphasizes the ones that were strengthened during wakefulness.

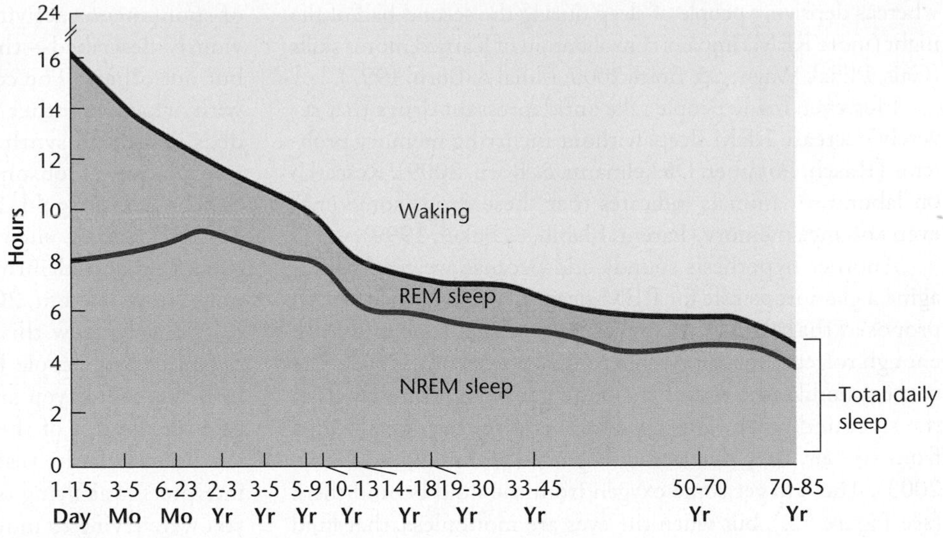

FIGURE 8.19 Sleep patterns for people of various ages
REM sleep occupies about 8 hours a day in newborns but less than 2 hours in most adults. The sleep of infants is not quite like that of adults, however, and the criteria for identifying REM sleep are not the same. *Source:* Based on "Ontogenetic Development of Human Sleep-Dream Cycle," by H. P. Roffwarg, J. N. Muzio, and W. C. Dement, *Science*, 152, 1966, 604–609.

Another aspect of sleep's contribution to memory relates to sleep spindles. Recall that sleep spindles are waves of activity, about 12 to 14 Hz, that are particularly common during stage 2 sleep. They indicate an exchange of information between the thalamus and cerebral cortex. Sleep spindles increase in number after new learning, and the number of sleep spindles correlates positively with improvements in certain types of memory (Eschenko, Mölle, Born, & Sara, 2006; Mednick et al., 2013). Most people are fairly consistent in their amount of spindle activity from one night to another, and the amount of spindle activity correlates more than 0.7 with nonverbal tests of IQ (Fogel, Nader, Cote, & Smith, 2007). Who would have guessed that brain waves during sleep could predict IQ scores?

STOP & CHECK

18. Does sleep improve memory by strengthening or weakening synapses?

ANSWER

18 The evidence so far points to weakening the synapses that were not strengthened during the day. Weakening these less relevant synapses enables the strengthened ones to stand out by contrast.

Functions of REM Sleep

An average person spends about a third of his or her life asleep and about a fifth of sleep in REM, totaling about 600 hours of REM per year. Presumably, REM serves a biological function. But what is it?

One way to approach this question is to compare the people or animals with more REM to those with less. REM sleep is widespread in mammals and birds, indicating that it is part of our ancient evolutionary heritage. Some species, however, have far more than others. As a rule, the species with the most total sleep hours also have the highest percentage of REM sleep (J. M. Siegel, 1995). Cats spend up to 16 hours a day sleeping, much or most of it in REM sleep. Rabbits, guinea pigs, and sheep sleep less and spend little time in REM.

Figure 8.19 illustrates the relationship between age and REM sleep for humans. The trend is the same for other mammalian species. Infants get more REM and more total sleep than adults do, confirming the pattern that more total sleep predicts a higher percentage of REM sleep. Among adult humans, those who sleep 9 or more hours per night have the highest percentage of REM sleep, and those who sleep 5 or fewer hours have the least percentage. This pattern implies that although REM is no doubt important, NREM is more tightly regulated. The amount of NREM varies less among individuals and among species.

One hypothesis is that REM is important for memory storage, especially for weakening the inappropriate connections (Crick & Mitchison, 1983). REM and non-REM sleep may be important for consolidating different types of memories. Depriving people of sleep early in the night (mostly non-REM sleep) impairs verbal learning, such as memorizing a list of words, whereas depriving people of sleep during the second half of the night (more REM) impairs consolidation of learned motor skills (Gais, Plihal, Wagner, & Born, 2000; Plihal & Born, 1997).

However, many people take antidepressant drugs that severely decrease REM sleep, without incurring memory problems (Rasch, Pommer, Diekelmann, & Born, 2009). Research on laboratory animals indicates that these drugs sometimes even enhance memory (Parent, Habib, & Baker, 1999).

Another hypothesis sounds odd because we tend to imagine a glamorous role for REM sleep: David Maurice (1998) proposed that REM just shakes the eyeballs back and forth enough to get sufficient oxygen to the corneas of the eyes. The corneas, unlike the rest of the body, get oxygen directly from the surrounding air. During sleep, because they are shielded from the air, they deteriorate slightly (Hoffmann & Curio, 2003). They do get some oxygen from the fluid behind them (see Figure 5.2), but when the eyes are motionless, that fluid becomes stagnant. Moving the eyes increases the oxygen supply to the corneas. According to this view, REM is a way of arousing a sleeper just enough to shake the eyes back and forth, and the other manifestations of REM are just by-products. This idea makes sense of the fact that REM occurs mostly toward the end of the night's sleep, when the fluid behind the eyes would be the most stagnant. It also makes sense of the fact that individuals who spend more hours asleep devote a greater percentage of sleep to REM. (If you don't sleep long, you have less need to shake up the stagnant fluid.) However, as mentioned, many people take antidepressants that restrict REM sleep. They are not known to suffer damage to the cornea.

STOP&CHECK

19. What kinds of individuals get more REM sleep than others? (Think in terms of age, species, and long versus short sleepers.)

ANSWER

19. Much REM sleep is more typical of the young than the old, and of those who get much sleep than those who get little.

Biological Perspectives on Dreaming

Dream research faces a special problem: All we know about dreams comes from people's self-reports, and researchers have no way to check the accuracy of those reports. In fact, we forget most dreams, and even when we do remember them, the details fade quickly.

The Activation-Synthesis Hypothesis

According to the **activation-synthesis hypothesis,** a dream represents the brain's effort to make sense of sparse and distorted information. Dreams begin with periodic bursts of spontaneous activity in the pons—the PGO waves previously described—that activate some parts of the cortex but not others. The cortex combines this haphazard input with whatever other activity was already occurring and does its best to synthesize a story that makes sense of the information (Hobson & McCarley, 1977; Hobson, Pace-Schott, & Stickgold, 2000; McCarley & Hoffman, 1981). Sensory stimuli, such as sounds in the room, occasionally get incorporated into a dream, although usually they do not (Nir & Tononi, 2010).

Consider how this theory handles a couple of common dreams. Most people have had occasional dreams of falling or flying. While you are asleep, you lie flat, unlike your posture for the rest of the day. Your brain in its partly aroused condition feels the vestibular sensation of your position and interprets it as flying or falling. Have you ever dreamed that you were trying to move but couldn't? Most people have. An interpretation based on the activation-synthesis theory is that during REM sleep (which accompanies most dreams), your motor cortex is inactive and your major postural muscles are virtually paralyzed. That is, when you are dreaming, you really *cannot* move, you feel your lack of movement, and thus, you dream of failing to move.

One criticism is that the theory's predictions are vague. If we dream about falling because of the vestibular sensations from lying down, why don't we *always* dream of falling? If we dream we cannot move because our muscles are paralyzed during REM sleep, why don't we *always* dream of being paralyzed?

The Clinico-Anatomical Hypothesis

An alternative view of dreams has been labeled the **clinico-anatomical hypothesis** because it was derived from clinical studies of patients with various kinds of brain damage (Solms, 1997, 2000). Like the activation-synthesis theory, this theory emphasizes that dreams begin with arousing stimuli that are generated within the brain combined with recent memories and any information the brain is receiving from the senses. However, the clinico-anatomical hypothesis puts less emphasis on the pons, PGO waves, or REM sleep. It regards dreams as thinking that takes place under unusual conditions.

One of those conditions is that the brain is getting little information from the sense organs, and the primary visual and auditory areas of the cortex have lower than usual activity, so other brain areas are free to generate images without constraints or interference. Also, the primary motor cortex is suppressed, as are the motor neurons of the spinal cord, so arousal cannot lead to action. Activity is suppressed in the prefrontal cortex, which is important for working memory (memory of very recent events). Consequently, we not only forget most dreams after we awaken, but we also lose track of what has been happening within a dream, and sudden scene changes are common. We also lose a sense of volition—that is, planning (Hobson, 2009). It seems that events just happen, without any intention on our part.

Meanwhile, activity is relatively high in the inferior (lower) part of the parietal cortex, an area important for visuospatial perception. Patients with damage here have problems binding body sensations with vision. They also report no dreams. Fairly high activity is also found in the areas of visual cortex outside V1. Those areas are presumably important for the visual imagery that accompanies most dreams. Finally, activity is high in the hypothalamus, amygdala, and other areas important for emotions and motivations (Gvilia, Turner, McGinty, & Szymusiak, 2006).

So the idea is that either internal or external stimulation activates parts of the parietal, occipital, and temporal cortex. The arousal develops into a hallucinatory perception, with no sensory input from area V1 to override it. This idea, like the activation-synthesis hypothesis, is hard to test because it does not make specific predictions about who will have what dream and when.

STOP&CHECK

20. What is a key point of disagreement between the activation-synthesis hypothesis and the clinico-anatomical hypothesis?

ANSWER

20. The activation-synthesis hypothesis puts much more emphasis on the importance of the pons.

MODULE 8.3 ■ IN CLOSING

Our Limited Self-Understanding

Without minimizing how much we do understand about sleep, it is noteworthy how many basic questions remain. What is the function of REM sleep? Does dreaming have a function, or is it just an accident? Our lack of knowledge about activities that occupy so much of our time underscores a point about the biology of behavior: We evolved tendencies to behave in certain ways that lead to survival and reproduction. The behavior can serve its function even when we do not fully understand that function.

Summary

1. One important function of sleep is to conserve energy at a time when the individual would be less efficient. Animal species vary in their sleep per day depending on their feeding habits and how much danger they face while asleep. **284**
2. In addition to saving energy, sleep serves other functions, including enhancement of memory. **286**
3. REM sleep occupies the greatest percentage of sleep in individuals and species that sleep the most total hours. **287**
4. According to the activation-synthesis hypothesis, dreams are the brain's attempts to make sense of the information reaching it, based mostly on haphazard input originating in the pons. **288**
5. According to the clinico-anatomical hypothesis, dreams originate mostly from the brain's own motivations, memories, and arousal. The stimulation often produces peculiar results because it does not have to compete with normal visual input and does not get organized by the prefrontal cortex. **288**

Key Terms

Terms are defined in the module on the page number indicated. They're also presented in alphabetical order with definitions in the book's Subject Index/Glossary. Interactive flash cards, audio reviews, and crossword puzzles are among the online resources available to help you learn these terms and the concepts they represent.

activation-synthesis hypothesis **288**

clinico-anatomical hypothesis **288**

Thought Question

Why would it be harder to deprive someone of just NREM sleep than just REM sleep?

MODULE 8.3 End of Module Quiz

1. What do birds do about sleep during the time when they are migrating?
   a. They fly during the day and sleep at night.
   b. They fly at night and sleep during the day.
   c. They eat during the day, fly at night, and suffer from sleep deprivation.
   d. They eat during the day and fly at night, but decrease their need for sleep.
2. If we want to predict how many hours a day some species sleeps, which of these questions would be most helpful in making that prediction?
   a. What color is the animal?
   b. Does the animal live north or south of the equator?
   c. What does the animal eat?
   d. How intelligent is the animal?
3. Which of the following occurs during sleep?
   a. The brain "plays back" certain experiences of the day but more slowly.
   b. Certain synapses become weakened, enabling others to stand out by contrast.
   c. Synapses corresponding to the experiences of the day become strengthened.
   d. Overall brain activity increases.
4. Of the following groups, which one tends to spend the highest percentage of sleep in the REM stage?
   a. Infants
   b. Those who sleep only a few hours per night
   c. Prey animals, such as sheep and horses
   d. Teenagers
5. On which of the following points do the activation-synthesis hypothesis and the clinico-anatomical hypothesis agree?
   a. Dreams are disguised representations of unconscious wishes.
   b. Activity from the pons is essential to the formation of dreams.
   c. Dreams begin with the brain's spontaneous activity combined with recent memories and any information the brain is receiving from the senses.
   d. If we have enough information about a person's recent experiences and current surroundings, we can predict the content of the dreams.

ANSWERS: 1d, 2c, 3b, 4a, 5c.

Suggestions for Further Reading

Dement, W. C. (1992). *The sleepwatchers*. Stanford, CA: Stanford Alumni Association.

Fascinating, entertaining account of sleep research by one of its leading pioneers.

Foster, R. G., & Kreitzman, L. (2004). *Rhythms of life*. New Haven, CT: Yale University Press.

Nontechnical discussion of research on circadian rhythms.

Moorcroft, W. H. (2003). *Understanding sleep and dreaming*. New York: Kluwer.

Excellent review of the psychology and neurology of sleep and dreams.

Refinetti, R. (2005). *Circadian physiology* (2nd ed.). Boca Raton, FL: CRC Press.

Marvelous summary of research on circadian rhythms and the relevance to human behavior.

iStockphoto.com/StockPhotoAstur

Internal Regulation

9

CHAPTER OUTLINE

MODULE 9.1 Temperature Regulation
Homeostasis and Allostasis
Controlling Body Temperature
In Closing: Combining Physiological and Behavioral Mechanisms

MODULE 9.2 Thirst
Mechanisms of Water Regulation
Osmotic Thirst
Hypovolemic Thirst and Sodium-Specific Hunger
In Closing: The Psychology and Biology of Thirst

MODULE 9.3 Hunger
Digestion and Food Selection
Short- and Long-Term Regulation of Feeding
Brain Mechanisms
Eating Disorders
In Closing: The Multiple Controls of Hunger

LEARNING OBJECTIVES

After studying this chapter, you should be able to:

1. List examples of how temperature regulation contributes to behaviors.
2. Explain why a constant high body temperature is worth all the energy it costs.
3. Describe why a moderate fever is advantageous in fighting an infection.
4. Distinguish between osmotic and hypovolemic thirst, including the brain mechanisms for each.
5. Describe the physiological factors that influence hunger and satiety.

What is life? You could define life in many ways depending on whether your purpose is medical, legal, philosophical, or poetic. Biologically, the necessary condition for life is *a coordinated set of chemical reactions*. Not all chemical reactions are alive, but all life has well-regulated chemical reactions.

Every chemical reaction in a living body takes place in a water solution at a rate that depends on the identity and concentration of molecules in the water, and the temperature of the solution. Our behavior is organized to keep the right chemicals in the right proportions and at the right temperature.

OPPOSITE: All life on Earth requires water, and animals drink it wherever they can find it.

MODULE 9.1

Temperature Regulation

Here's an observation that puzzled biologists for years: When a small male garter snake emerges from hibernation in early spring, it emits female pheromones for the first day or two. The pheromones attract larger males that swarm all over him, trying to copulate. Presumably, the tendency to release female pheromones must have evolved to provide the small male some advantage. But what? Biologists speculated about ways in which this pseudo-mating experience might help the small male attract real females. The truth is simpler: A male that has just emerged from hibernation is so cold that it has trouble slithering out of its burrow. The larger males emerged from hibernation earlier and already had a chance to warm themselves in a sunny place. When the larger males swarm all over the smaller male, they warm him and increase his activity level (Shine, Phillips, Waye, LeMaster, & Mason, 2001).

Here are more examples that temperature regulation helps to explain:

- Have you ever noticed gulls, ducks, or other large birds standing on one leg (see Figure 9.1)? Why do they do that, when balancing on two legs would seem easier? One reason is to conserve body heat on cold days. By standing on one leg, they protect the heat in the other leg (Ehrlich, Dobkin, & Wheye, 1988).
- Vultures sometimes defecate onto their own legs. Are they just careless slobs? No. They defecate onto their legs on hot days so that the evaporating excretions will cool their legs (Ehrlich et al., 1988).
- For many years, biologists puzzled about the function of toucans' huge, clumsy bills (see Figure 9.2). The answer is temperature regulation (Tattersall, Andrade, & Abe, 2009). While flying on hot days, a toucan directs more blood flow to the beak, where the passing air cools it. At night the toucan tucks its bill under a wing to prevent undue loss of heat.
- Most lizards live solitary lives, but Australian thick-tailed geckos sometimes form tight huddles. Why? They live in an environment with rapid temperature fluctuations. They huddle only when the environmental temperature is falling rapidly. By huddling, they increase insulation and prevent a rapid drop in body temperature (Shah, Shine, Hudson, & Kearney, 2003).
- The Japanese giant hornet sometimes invades bee colonies, kills one or more bees, and takes them to feed to its larvae. When one of these hornets invades a hive of Japanese honeybees, the bees form a tight swarm of more than 500, surrounding the hornet in a tiny ball. Why? The combined body heat of all those bees raises the temperature to a level that kills the hornet, although bees can survive it (Ono, Igarashi, Ohno, & Sasaki, 1995).
- Migratory birds do most of their migratory flying at night. Why? The nights are cooler. A bird flying in midday would overheat and frequently have to stop for a drink, often in places where fresh water is difficult to find.
- Decades ago, psychologists found that infant rats appeared deficient in certain aspects of learning, eating, and

M+M.Hjelm/F1online digitale Bildagentur GmbH/Alamy

FIGURE 9.1 Why do birds sometimes stand on one foot? One reason is that holding one leg next to the body keeps it warm.

FIGURE 9.2 Why do toucans have such huge bills?
They use their bills to radiate heat when they need to cool the body. They cover the bill at night to decrease heat loss.

FIGURE 9.3 Difficulties of temperature regulation for a newborn rodent
A newborn rat has no hair, thin skin, and little body fat. If left exposed to the cold, it becomes inactive.

drinking. Later results showed that the real problem was temperature control. Researchers generally test animals at room temperature, about 20°C to 23°C (68°F to 73°F), which is comfortable for adult humans but dangerously cold for an isolated baby rat (see Figure 9.3). Infant rats that seem incapable of a task in a cold room do much better in a warmer room (Satinoff, 1991).

- Certain studies found that female rats learned best during their fertile period (estrus). In other studies, they learned best a day or two before their fertile period (proestrus). The difference depends on temperature. Rats in estrus do better in a cooler environment, presumably because they are generating so much heat on their own. Rats in proestrus do better in a warmer environment (Rubinow, Arseneau, Beverly, & Juraska, 2004).

The point is that temperature affects behavior in many ways that we easily overlook. Temperature regulation is more important than you might have guessed.

Homeostasis and Allostasis

Physiologist Walter B. Cannon (1929) introduced the term **homeostasis** (HO-mee-oh-STAY-sis) to refer to temperature regulation and other biological processes that keep body variables within a fixed range. The process resembles the thermostat in a house with heating and cooling systems. Someone sets the minimum and maximum temperatures on the thermostat. When the temperature in the house drops below the minimum, the thermostat triggers the furnace to provide heat. When the temperature rises above the maximum, the thermostat turns on the air conditioner.

Similarly, homeostatic processes in animals trigger physiological and behavioral activities that keep certain variables within a set range. In many cases, the range is so narrow that we refer to it as a **set point**, a single value that the body works to maintain. For example, if calcium is deficient in your diet and its concentration in the blood begins to fall below the set point of 0.16 g/L (grams per liter), storage deposits in your bones release additional calcium into the blood. If the calcium level in the blood rises above 0.16 g/L, you store part of the excess in your bones and excrete the rest. Similar mechanisms maintain constant blood levels of water, oxygen, glucose, sodium chloride, protein, fat, and acidity (Cannon, 1929). Processes that reduce discrepancies from the set point are known as **negative feedback**. Much of motivated behavior can be described as negative feedback: Something causes a disturbance, and behavior proceeds until it relieves the disturbance.

However, the concept of homeostasis is not fully satisfactory, because the body does not maintain complete constancy. True, the concentration of solutes in the blood remains nearly constant most of the time. However, body temperature varies by about half a Celsius degree between its high in mid-afternoon and its low point at night. Most animals maintain a nearly constant body weight from day to day, but add body fat in fall and decrease it in spring. (The increased fat is a good reserve in preparation for probable food shortage during the winter. It also provides insulation against the cold.) We can describe these alterations as changes in the set point, but even changes in the set point don't fully account for many observations. For example, a sign of danger provokes a sudden increase in heart rate, blood pressure, and sweating, preparing the body ready for vigorous activity. Note that the body sweats *before* it starts to overheat, *anticipating* its future need. Similarly, as the air is starting to warm up, a hiker increases thirst and decreases urine production by the kidneys, anticipating probable sweating and dehydration. (Other animals do the same.) To describe these dynamic changes, researchers use the term **allostasis** (from the Greek roots meaning "variable" and "standing"), which means the adaptive way in which the body anticipates needs depending on the situation, avoiding errors rather than just correcting them (McEwen, 2000; Sterling, 2012). As you will see throughout this chapter, much of that control depends on cells in the hypothalamus.

Homeostasis and allostasis don't work perfectly, of course. Obesity, anorexia nervosa, high blood pressure, and diabetes are example of breakdowns of homeostatic processes.

STOP&CHECK

1. How does the idea of allostasis differ from homeostasis?

ANSWER

1. Homeostasis is a set of processes that keep certain body variables within a fixed range. Allostasis is an adjustment of that range, increasing it or decreasing it as circumstances change.

Controlling Body Temperature

If you were to list your strongest motivations in life, you might not think to include temperature regulation, but it has a high priority biologically. An average young adult expends about 2600 kilocalories (kcal) per day. Where do you suppose all that energy goes? It is not to muscle movements or mental activity. Most of it goes to **basal metabolism,** the energy used to maintain a constant body temperature while at rest. Maintaining your body temperature requires about twice as much energy as do all other activities *combined* (Burton, 1994). We produce that much heat largely by metabolism in brown adipose cells, cells that are more like muscle cells than like white fat cells. They burn fuel like muscle cells but release it directly as heat instead of as muscle contractions.

Amphibians, reptiles, and most fish are **poikilothermic** (POY-kih-lo-THER-mik, from Greek roots meaning "varied heat.") That is, their body temperature matches the temperature of their environment. A synonym is *ectothermic,* meaning dependent on external sources for body heat. People often call such animals "cold-blooded," but they are cold only when the environment is cold. A few large fish, including sharks and tuna, are exceptions to the rule, maintaining their core body temperature well above that of the surrounding water most of the time (Bernal, Donley, Shadwick, & Syme, 2005). Poikilothermic animals lack physiological mechanisms of temperature regulation such as shivering and sweating, but they can regulate their body temperature behaviorally. A desert lizard moves between sunny areas, shady areas, and burrows to maintain a fairly steady body temperature. However, behavioral methods do not enable animals to maintain the same degree of constancy that mammals and birds have.

Mammals and birds are **homeothermic** (from Greek roots meaning "same heat"), except that certain species become poikilothermic during hibernation. A synonym is *endothermic,* meaning capable of generating body heat internally. Homeothermic animals use physiological mechanisms to maintain a nearly constant core temperature despite changes in the temperature of the environment. Homeothermy is costly, especially for small animals. An animal *generates* heat in proportion to its total mass, but it *radiates* heat in proportion to its surface area. A small mammal or bird, such as a mouse or a hummingbird, has a high surface-to-volume ratio and therefore radiates heat rapidly. Such animals need much fuel each day to maintain their body temperature.

To cool ourselves when the air is warmer than body temperature, we have only one physiological mechanism, evaporation. Humans sweat to expose water for evaporation. For species that don't sweat, the alternatives are licking themselves and panting. As water evaporates, it cools the body. However, if the air is humid as well as hot, the moisture does not evaporate. Furthermore, you endanger your health if you cannot drink enough to replace the water you lose by sweating. If you sweat without drinking, you start becoming dehydrated (low on water). You then protect your body water by decreasing your sweat, despite the risk of overheating (Tokizawa, Yasuhara, Nakamura, Uchida, Crawshaw, & Nagashima, 2010).

Several physiological mechanisms increase your body heat in a cold environment. One is shivering. Any muscle contractions, such as those of shivering, generate heat. Second, decreased blood flow to the skin prevents the blood from cooling too much. The consequence is warm internal organs but cold skin. A third mechanism works well for most mammals, though not humans: When cold, they fluff out their fur to increase insulation. (We humans also fluff out our "fur" by erecting the tiny hairs on our skin—"goose bumps." That mechanism was more useful back when our remote ancestors had a fuller coat of fur.)

We also use behavioral mechanisms, just as poikilothermic animals do. In fact, we prefer to rely on behavior when we can. The more we regulate our temperature behaviorally, the less energy we need to spend physiologically (Refinetti & Carlisle, 1986). Finding a cool place on a hot day is much better than sweating (see Figure 9.4). Finding a warm place on a cold day is much smarter than shivering. Here are a few other behavioral mechanisms of temperature regulation:

- Put on more clothing or take it off. This human strategy accomplishes what other mammals accomplish by fluffing out or sleeking their fur.
- Become more active to get warmer or less active to avoid overheating.

AP Images/SUN-JOURNAL/KEN LOVE

FIGURE 9.4 One way to cope with the heat
On a hot day, wouldn't you do the same?

FIGURE 9.5 Behavioral regulation of body temperature
An emperor penguin chick is poorly insulated against Antarctic winter temperatures, but when chicks huddle together, they pool their heat. The cold ones on the outside push their way inward, and the warm ones on the inside drift outward. The process is so effective that a cluster of penguin chicks has to move frequently to prevent melting a hole in the ice.

- To get warm, huddle with others. If you are waiting at a bus stop on a cold day, you might feel shy about suggesting to a stranger that you hug each other to keep warm. Other species have no such inhibitions (see Figure 9.5). Spectacled eiders (in the duck family) spend their winters in the Arctic Ocean, which is mostly covered with ice. When more than 150,000 eiders crowd together, they not only keep warm but also melt a big hole in the ice where they can dive for fish (Weidensaul, 1999).

Surviving in Extreme Cold

If the atmospheric temperature drops below 0°C (32°F), you maintain your body temperature by shivering, shifting blood flow away from the skin, and so forth. However, a poikilothermic animal, which by definition takes the temperature of its environment, is vulnerable. If its body temperature drops below the freezing point of water, ice crystals form. Because water expands when it freezes, ice crystals would tear apart blood vessels and cell membranes, killing the animal.

Amphibians and reptiles avoid that risk by burrowing or finding other sheltered locations. However, some frogs, fish, and insects survive through winters in northern Canada where even the underground temperature approaches −40°C (which is also −40°F). How do they do it? Some insects and fish stock their blood with glycerol and other antifreeze chemicals at the start of the winter (Liou, Tocilj, Davies, & Jia, 2000). Wood frogs actually do freeze, but they have several mechanisms to reduce the damage. They start by withdrawing most fluid from their organs and blood vessels and storing it in extracellular spaces. Therefore, ice crystals have room to expand when they form, without tearing blood vessels or cells. Also, the frogs have chemicals that cause ice crystals to form gradually, not in chunks. Finally, they have such extraordinary blood-clotting capacity that they quickly repair any blood vessels that do rupture (Storey & Storey, 1999).

The Advantages of Constant High Body Temperature

As mentioned, we spend about two-thirds of our total energy maintaining body temperature (basal metabolism). A poikilothermic animal, with a much lower level of basal metabolism, needs far less fuel. If we didn't maintain a constant, high body temperature, we could eat less and spend less effort finding food. Given the substantial costs of maintaining our body temperature, it must provide an important advantage, or we would not have evolved these mechanisms. What is that advantage?

For the answer, think back to the chapter on movement: As the water gets colder, a fish recruits more and more fast-twitch muscle fibers to remain active, despite the risk of rapid fatigue. The same is true for amphibians and reptiles. On a very cold day, a lizard has to change its defense strategy: If it ran away from a predator, it would either run more slowly than usual or recruit all of its fast-twitch muscles and fatigue rapidly. So, instead of running, it tries to fight the predator—an act requiring a briefer burst of activity, though often a losing battle (James, 2013).

Birds and mammals keep their bodies warm at all times, regardless of air temperature, and therefore stay constantly ready for vigorous activity. In other words, we eat a great deal to support our high metabolism so that even when the weather is cold, we can still run rapidly without great fatigue. Let's qualify this point, however: On a cold day, you divert blood away from the periphery to protect the internal organs and to avoid losing too much heat to the surrounding air. The result is that your skin is cold, but your muscles are slightly colder than usual, also. A competitive athlete needs to warm up, literally, to increase the muscles' temperature on a cold day.

Why did mammals evolve a body temperature of 37°C (98°F) instead of some other value? From the standpoint of muscle activity, we gain an advantage by being as warm as possible. A warmer animal has warmer muscles and therefore runs faster with less fatigue than a cooler animal. When a reptile has a choice of environments at different temperatures, it usually chooses to warm itself to 37° to 38°C (98° to 100°F) (Wagner & Gleeson, 1997).

If warmer is better, why not heat ourselves to an even higher temperature? First, maintaining a higher temperature requires more fuel and energy. Second, and more importantly, beyond about 41°C (105°F), proteins begin to break their bonds and lose their useful properties. Birds' body temperatures are in fact about 41°C.

It is possible to evolve proteins that are stable at higher temperatures; indeed, odd microscopic animals called thermophiles survive in boiling water. However, to do so, they need many extra chemical bonds to stabilize their proteins. The enzymatic properties of a protein depend on its flexibility, so making proteins rigid enough to withstand high temperatures makes them inactive at more moderate temperatures (Feller, 2010). In short, our body temperature of 37°C (98°F) is a trade-off between the advantages of high temperature for rapid movement and the disadvantages of high temperature for protein stability and energy expenditure.

Reproductive cells require a cooler environment than the rest of the body (Rommel, Pabst, & McLellan, 1998). Birds lay eggs and sit on them, instead of developing them internally, because the birds' internal temperature is too hot for an embryo. Similarly, in most male mammals, the scrotum hangs outside the body, because sperm production requires a cooler temperature than the rest of the body. (It's not just for decoration.) A man who wears his undershorts too tight keeps his testes too close to the body, overheats them, and produces fewer healthy sperm cells. Pregnant women are advised to avoid hot baths and anything else that might overheat a developing fetus.

STOP&CHECK

2. What is the primary advantage of maintaining a constant high body temperature?

3. Why did mammals evolve a temperature of 37°C (98°F) instead of some other temperature?

ANSWERS

2. A constant high body temperature keeps an animal ready for rapid, prolonged muscle activity even in cold weather. **3.** Animals gain an advantage in being as warm as possible and therefore as fast as possible. However, proteins lose stability at temperatures much above 37°C (98°F).

Brain Mechanisms

The physiological changes that regulate body temperature—such as shivering, sweating, and changes in blood flow to the skin—depend on areas in and near the hypothalamus (see Figure 9.6), especially the anterior hypothalamus and the preoptic area, located just anterior to the anterior hypothalamus. (It is called *preoptic* because it is near the optic chiasm, where the optic nerves cross.) Because of the close relationship between the preoptic area and the anterior hypothalamus, researchers often treat them as a single area, the **preoptic area/anterior hypothalamus**, or **POA/AH**. The POA/AH and a couple other hypothalamic areas send output to the hindbrain's raphe nucleus, which controls the physiological mechanisms such as shivering, sweating, changes in heart rate and metabolism, and changes in blood flow to the skin (Yoshida, Li, Cano, Lazarus, & Saper, 2009).

The POA/AH integrates several types of information (Nakamura, 2011). It receives input from temperature receptors in the skin, in the organs, and in the brain especially in the POA/AH itself. If the brain or the skin is hot, an animal sweats or pants vigorously and seeks a cooler location. If either is cold, the animal shivers and seeks a warmer location. The animal reacts most vigorously if the brain and skin are both hot or both cold. The POA/AH also receives input from

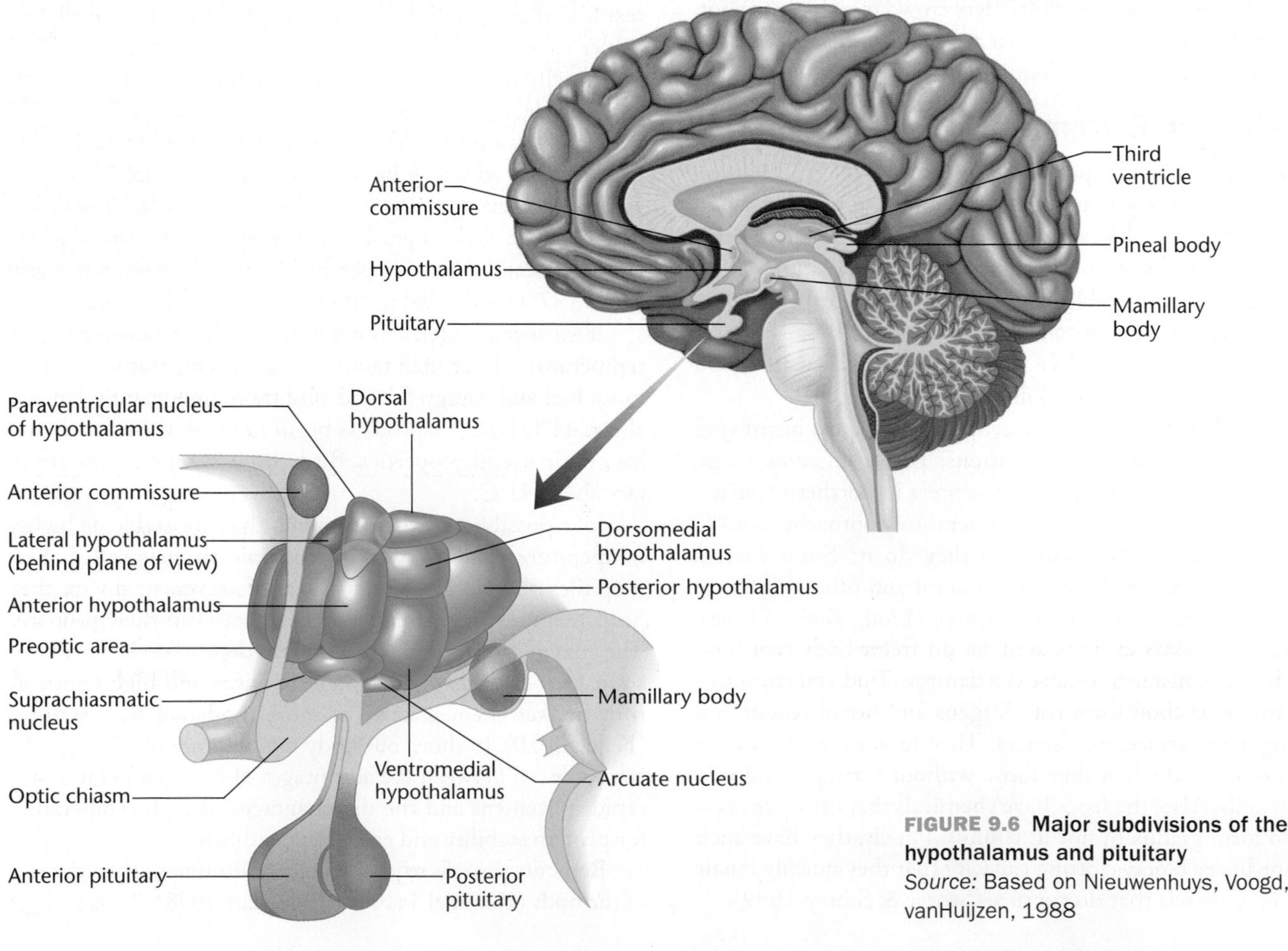

FIGURE 9.6 Major subdivisions of the hypothalamus and pituitary
Source: Based on Nieuwenhuys, Voogd, & vanHuijzen, 1988

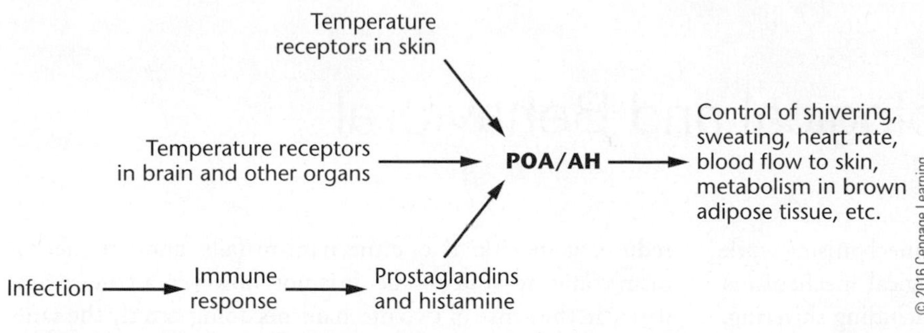

FIGURE 9.7 Integration of temperature information by the POA/AH
If the brain and skin are overheated, the POA/AH sends signals that lead to sweating and other methods of heat loss. If the brain and skin are cooled, or if prostaglandins and histamine indicate an infection, the POA/AH initiates shivering, increased heart rate, decreased blood flow to the skin, and increased metabolism by brown adipose tissue.

the immune system, which reacts to an infection by steps that deliver prostaglandins and histamines to the POA/AH (Ek et al., 2001; Leon, 2002; Tabarean, Sanchez-Alavez, & Sethi, 2012). The delivery of those chemicals is what causes shivering, increased metabolism, and other processes that produce a fever. People lacking the appropriate receptors for those chemicals fail to develop a fever, even when they have pneumonia or similar diseases (Hanada, et al., 2009). Figure 9.7 summarizes the role of the POA/AH.

The POA/AH is not the only brain area that detects temperature, but it is the primary area for controlling physiological mechanisms of temperature regulation such as sweating or shivering. After damage to the POA/AH, mammals can still regulate body temperature, but only by the same behavioral mechanisms that a lizard might use, such as seeking a warmer or colder location (Satinoff & Rutstein, 1970; Van Zoeren & Stricker, 1977).

STOP&CHECK

4. What are the sources of input to the POA/AH?
5. How can an animal regulate body temperature after damage to the POA/AH?

ANSWERS

4. The POA/AH receives input from temperatures in the skin, the organs, and the brain including cells in the POA/AH itself. It also receives prostaglandins and histamines when the immune system detects an infection. **5.** It can regulate temperature through behavior, such as by finding a warmer or cooler place.

Fever

A fever represents an increased set point for body temperature. Just as you shiver or sweat when your body temperature goes below or above its usual 37°C (98°F), when you have a fever of, say, 39°C (102°F), you shiver or sweat whenever your temperature deviates from that level. In other words, fever is not something an infection does to the body; it is something the hypothalamus directs the body to produce. Moving to a cooler room does not lower your fever. Your body just works harder to keep its temperature at the feverish level.

Because newborn rabbits have an immature hypothalamus, they do not shiver in response to infections. If they are given a choice of environments, however, they select a spot warm enough to raise their body temperature and produce a fever by behavioral means (Satinoff, McEwen, & Williams, 1976). Fish and reptiles with an infection also choose a warm enough environment, if they can find one, to produce a feverish body temperature (Kluger, 1991). Again, the point is that fever is something the animal does to fight an infection.

Does fever do any good? Certain types of bacteria grow less vigorously at high temperatures than at normal mammalian body temperatures. Also, the immune system works more vigorously at an increased temperature (Skitzki, Chen, Wang, & Evans, 2007). Other things being equal, developing a moderate fever increases an individual's chance of surviving a bacterial infection (Kluger, 1991). However, a fever above about 39°C (103°F) in humans does more harm than good, and a fever above 41°C (109°F) is life threatening (Rommel et al., 1998).

STOP&CHECK

6. What evidence indicates that fever is an adaptation to fight illness?

ANSWER

6. The body will shiver or sweat to maintain its elevated temperature at a nearly constant level. Also, fish, reptiles, and immature mammals with infections use behavioral means to raise their temperature to a feverish level. Furthermore, a moderate fever inhibits bacterial growth and increases the probability of surviving a bacterial infection.

MODULE 9.1 ■ IN CLOSING

Combining Physiological and Behavioral Mechanisms

Physiological mechanisms and behavioral mechanisms work together. Your body has various physiological mechanisms to maintain constant body temperature, including shivering, sweating, and changes in blood flow. You also rely on behavioral mechanisms, such as finding a cooler or warmer place, adding or removing clothing, and so forth. Redundancy reduces your risk: If one mechanism fails, another mechanism comes to your rescue. It is not, however, a true redundancy in the sense of two mechanisms doing exactly the same thing. Each of your mechanisms of temperature regulation solves an aspect of the problem in a different way. We shall see this theme again in the discussions of thirst and hunger.

Summary

1. It is easy to overlook the importance of temperature regulation. Many seemingly odd animal behaviors make sense as ways to heat or cool the body. **294**
2. Homeostasis is a tendency to maintain a body variable near a set point. Temperature, hunger, and thirst are almost homeostatic, but the set point changes in varying circumstances. **295**
3. A high body temperature enables a mammal or bird to move rapidly without excessive fatigue even in a cold environment. **297**
4. From the standpoint of muscle activity, the higher the body temperature, the better. However, as temperatures increase, protein stability decreases, and more energy is needed to maintain body temperature. Mammalian body temperature of 37°C is a compromise between these competing considerations. **297**
5. The preoptic area and anterior hypothalamus (POA/AH) are critical for temperature control. Cells there monitor both their own temperature and that of the skin and spinal cord. They also receive input regarding infection, and initiate actions that produce a fever. **298**
6. All animals rely partly on behavioral mechanisms for temperature regulation. **299**
7. A moderate fever helps an animal combat an infection. **299**

Key Terms

Terms are defined in the module on the page number indicated. They're also presented in alphabetical order with definitions in the book's Subject Index/Glossary. Interactive flash cards, audio reviews, and crossword puzzles are among the online resources available to help you learn these terms and the concepts they represent.

allostasis **295**
basal metabolism **296**
homeostasis **295**
homeothermic **296**
negative feedback **295**
poikilothermic **296**
preoptic area/anterior hypothalamus (POA/AH) **298**
set point **295**

Thought Question

Speculate on why birds have higher body temperatures than mammals.

→ **MODULE 9.1** End of Module Quiz

1. What does negative feedback do?
   a. It establishes a set point.
   b. It changes the set point.
   c. It eliminates the set point.
   d. It reduces discrepancies from a set point.

2. How do poikilothermic (ectothermic) animals regulate their body temperature, if at all?
   a. They move to a location with a more favorable temperature.
   b. They use physiological mechanisms such as shivering and sweating.
   c. They increase their metabolic rate.
   d. They do not regulate their body temperature at all.

3. What is the primary advantage of maintaining a constant high body temperature?
   a. It saves us the energy from having to look for a comfortable temperature.
   b. It enables us to survive in warmer climates.
   c. It keeps the muscles ready for rapid, prolonged activity even in cold weather.
   d. Other things being equal, animals with a higher body temperature live longer than those with a lower temperature.

4. If we inserted a probe into the POA/AH and directly heated that area, what if anything would happen?
   a. The animal would shiver.
   b. The animal would sweat or pant.
   c. The animal would not react physiologically, but it would seek a cooler location.
   d. The animal would not react in any way that affects body temperature.

5. When you have an infection, what causes the fever?
   a. The infective agent directly stimulates the heart to beat faster.
   b. The infective agent directly stimulates the muscles to shiver.
   c. The immune system increases delivery of prostaglandins and histamine to the POA/AH.
   d. The immune system decreases blood flow to the brain.

6. Which of the following is the most correct description of a fever?
   a. Fever is one way by which the body fights against bacteria.
   b. Fever is one way in which bacteria cause damage to the body.
   c. Fever is an indication that the POA/AH is not functioning properly.
   d. Fever occurs only in homeothermic animals.

ANSWERS: 1d, 2a, 3c, 4b, 5c, 6a.

MODULE 9.2

Thirst

Water constitutes about 70 percent of the mammalian body. Because the concentration of chemicals in water determines the rate of all chemical reactions in the body, the water must be regulated within narrow limits. The body also needs enough fluid in the circulatory system to maintain normal blood pressure. People sometimes survive for weeks without food, but not long without water.

Mechanisms of Water Regulation

Species differ in their strategies for maintaining water. Beavers and other species that live in rivers or lakes drink plenty of water, eat moist foods, and excrete dilute urine. In contrast, most gerbils and other desert animals go through life without drinking at all. They gain water from their food and they have many adaptations to avoid losing water, including the ability to excrete dry feces and concentrated urine. Unable to sweat, they avoid the heat of the day by burrowing under the ground. Their highly convoluted nasal passages minimize water loss when they exhale.

We humans vary our strategy depending on circumstances. If you cannot find enough to drink or if the water tastes bad, you conserve water by excreting more concentrated urine and decreasing your sweat, somewhat like a gerbil, although not to the same extreme. Your posterior pituitary (see Figure 9.6) releases the hormone **vasopressin** that raises blood pressure by constricting blood vessels. (The term *vasopressin* comes from *vas*cular *pressure*.) The increased pressure helps compensate for the decreased blood volume. Vasopressin is also known as **antidiuretic hormone (ADH)** because it enables the kidneys to reabsorb water from urine and therefore make the urine more concentrated. (*Diuresis* means "urination.") You also increase your secretion of vasopressin while sleeping to preserve body water at a time when you cannot drink (Trudel & Bourque, 2010). (Vasopressin helps you get through the night without going to the toilet.)

In most cases, our strategy is closer to that of beavers: We drink more than we need and excrete the excess. (However, if you drink extensively without eating, as many alcoholics do, you may excrete enough body salts to harm yourself.) Most of our drinking is with meals or in social situations, and most people seldom experience intense thirst.

STOP & CHECK

7. If you lacked vasopressin, would you drink like a beaver or like a gerbil? Why?

ANSWER

7. If you lacked vasopressin, you would have to drink more like a beaver. You would excrete much fluid, so you would need to drink an equal amount to replace it.

Osmotic Thirst

We distinguish two types of thirst. Eating salty foods causes *osmotic* thirst, and losing fluid by bleeding or sweating induces *hypovolemic* thirst.

The combined concentration of all *solutes* (molecules in solution) in mammalian body fluids remains at a nearly constant level of 0.15 M (molar). (Molarity is a measure of the number of particles per unit of solution, regardless of the size of each particle. A 1.0 M solution of sugar and a 1.0 M solution of sodium chloride have the same number of molecules per liter.) This fixed concentration of solutes is a set point, similar to the set point for temperature. Any deviation activates mechanisms that restore the concentration of solutes to the set point.

Osmotic pressure is the tendency of water to flow across a semipermeable membrane from the area of low solute concentration to the area of higher concentration. A semipermeable membrane is one through which water can pass but solutes cannot. The membrane surrounding a cell is almost a semipermeable membrane because water flows across it freely and various solutes flow either slowly or not at all between the *intracellular fluid* inside the cell and the *extracellular fluid* outside it. Osmotic pressure occurs when solutes are more concentrated on one side of the membrane than on the other.

If you eat something salty, sodium ions spread through the blood and the extracellular fluid but do not cross the membranes into cells. The result is a higher concentration of solutes (including sodium) outside the cells than inside. The resulting osmotic pressure draws water from the cells into the extracellular fluid. Certain neurons detect their own loss of water and then trigger **osmotic thirst**, a drive for water that helps restore the normal state (see Figure 9.8). The kidneys

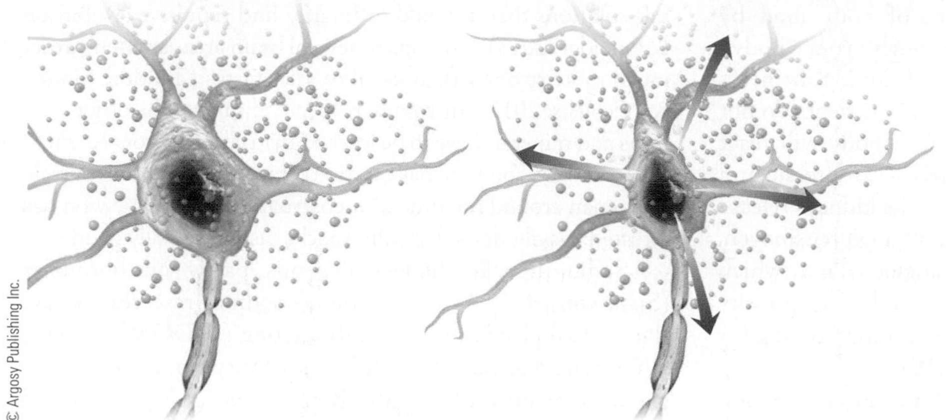

FIGURE 9.8 The consequence of a difference in osmotic pressure
(a) Suppose a solute such as NaCl is more concentrated outside the cell than inside. (b) Water flows by osmosis out of the cell until the concentrations are equal. Neurons in certain brain areas detect their own dehydration and trigger thirst.

also excrete more concentrated urine to rid the body of excess sodium and maintain as much water as possible. An additional, surprising effect occurs at least in rats: Rats with strong osmotic thirst show decreased anxiety, decreased responses to stress, and increased attempts at social interactions with unfamiliar rats (Krause et al., 2011). Humans have not been tested for similar effects. The reasons for a relationship between thirst and anxiety are not obvious, and you are welcome to speculate.

How does the brain detect osmotic pressure? It gets part of the information from receptors around the third ventricle, including the **OVLT** (organum vasculosum laminae terminalis) and the **subfornical organ (SFO)** (Hiyama, Watanabe, Okado, & Noda, 2004) (see Figure 9.9). Those receptors detect osmotic pressure and the sodium content of the blood (Tiruneh, Huang, & Leenen, 2013). The OVLT also receives input from receptors in the digestive tract, enabling it to anticipate an osmotic need before the rest of the body experiences it (Bourque, 2008).

The brain areas surrounding the third ventricle are in a good position to monitor the contents of the blood, because the blood–brain barrier is weak in this area, enabling chemicals to enter that would not reach neurons elsewhere in the brain. The danger, of course, is that a weak blood–brain barrier exposes neurons to potential harm. At least in mice, new neurons form in this area, replacing ones that may have died (Hourai & Miyati, 2013). Other species have not yet been tested.

Receptors in the OVLT, the subfornical organ, the stomach, and elsewhere relay their information to several parts of the hypothalamus, including the **supraoptic nucleus** and the **paraventricular nucleus (PVN)**, which control the rate at which the posterior pituitary releases vasopressin. Receptors also relay information to the **lateral preoptic area** and surrounding parts of the hypothalamus, which control drinking (Saad, Luiz, Camargo, Renzi, & Manani, 1996).

After osmotic pressure triggers thirst, how do you know when to stop drinking? You do *not* wait until water has restored normal osmotic pressure for the receptors in the brain. The water you drink has to be absorbed through the digestive system and then pumped through the blood to the brain. That process takes 15 minutes or so, and if you continued drinking

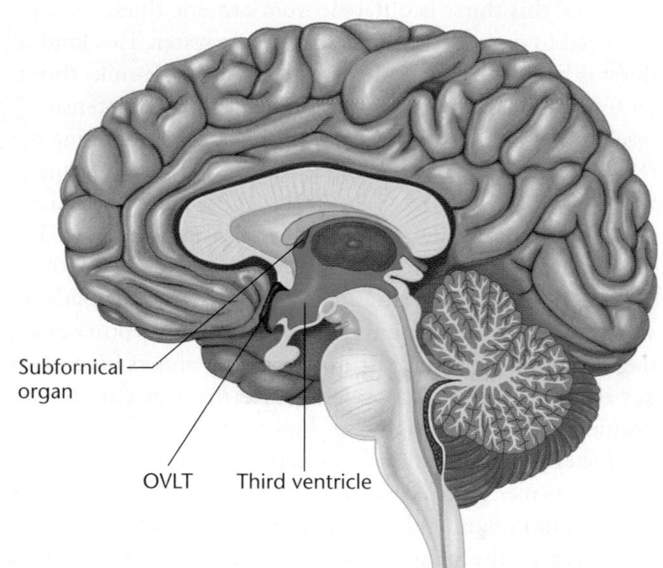

FIGURE 9.9 The brain's receptors for osmotic pressure and blood volume
These neurons are in areas surrounding the third ventricle of the brain, where no blood–brain barrier prevents blood-borne chemicals from entering the brain. *Source:* Based in part on DeArmond, Fusco, & Dewey, 1974; Weindl, 1973

for that long, you would drink far more than you need. The body monitors swallowing and detects the distension of the stomach and upper part of the small intestine. Those messages limit drinking to not much more than you need at a given time (Stricker & Hoffmann, 2007).

STOP & CHECK

8. Would adding salt to the body's extracellular fluids increase or decrease osmotic thirst?

ANSWER

8. Adding salt to the extracellular fluids would increase osmotic thirst because it would draw water from the cells into the extracellular spaces.

Hypovolemic Thirst and Sodium-Specific Hunger

Suppose you lose a significant amount of body fluid by bleeding, diarrhea, or sweating. Although your body's osmotic pressure stays the same, you need fluid. Your heart has trouble pumping blood to the head, and nutrients do not flow as easily as usual into your cells. Your body will react with hormones that constrict blood vessels—vasopressin and *angiotensin II*. When blood volume drops, the kidneys release the enzyme *renin*, which splits a portion off angiotensinogen, a large protein in the blood, to form angiotensin I, which other enzymes convert to **angiotensin II**. Like vasopressin, angiotensin II constricts the blood vessels, compensating for the drop in blood pressure (see Figure 9.10).

Angiotensin II also helps trigger thirst, in conjunction with receptors that detect blood pressure in the large veins. However, this thirst is different from osmotic thirst, because you need to restore lost salts and not just water. This kind of thirst is known as **hypovolemic** (HI-po-vo-LEE-mik) **thirst**, meaning thirst based on low volume. When angiotensin II reaches the brain, it stimulates neurons in areas adjoining the third ventricle (Fitts, Starbuck, & Ruhf, 2000; Mangiapane & Simpson, 1980; Tanaka et al., 2001). Those neurons send axons to the hypothalamus, where they release angiotensin II as their neurotransmitter (Tanaka, Hori, & Nomura, 2001). That is, the neurons surrounding the third ventricle both respond to angiotensin II and release it. As in many other cases, the connection between a neurotransmitter and its function is not arbitrary. The brain uses a chemical that was already performing a related function elsewhere in the body.

Whereas an animal with osmotic thirst needs water, one with hypovolemic thirst cannot drink much pure water. Pure water would dilute its body fluids and lower the solute concentration in the blood. The animal therefore increases its preference for salty water (Stricker, 1969).

An animal that becomes deficient in sodium shows an immediate strong preference for salty tastes, known as **sodium-specific hunger** (Richter, 1936), even for extremely concentrated salt solutions that it would ordinarily find repulsive (Robinson & Berridge, 2013). Neurons in several brain areas suddenly react much more strongly than usual to salty tastes (Tandon, Simon, & Nicolelis, 2012). In contrast, specific hungers for other vitamins and minerals have to be learned by trial and error (Rozin & Kalat, 1971). You may have noticed this phenomenon yourself. A woman around the time of menstruation, or anyone who has sweated heavily, finds that salty snacks taste especially good.

Sodium-specific hunger depends partly on hormones (Schulkin, 1991). When the body's sodium reserves are low, the adrenal glands produce **aldosterone** (al-DOSS-ter-one), a hormone that causes the kidneys, salivary glands, and sweat glands to retain salt (Verrey & Beron, 1996). Aldosterone and angiotensin II together change the properties of taste receptors on the tongue, neurons in the nucleus of the tractus solitarius (part of the taste system), and neurons elsewhere in the brain to increase salt intake (Krause & Sakal, 2007). Note that aldosterone indicates low sodium, and angiotensin II indicates low blood volume. Either one by itself produces only a small increase in salt intake, but their combined effect is substantial, sometimes producing a preference for salt over sugar or anything else (Geerling & Loewy, 2008). Table 9.1 summarizes the differences between osmotic thirst and hypovolemic thirst.

STOP&CHECK

9. Who would drink more pure water—someone with osmotic thirst or someone with hypovolemic thirst?

ANSWER

9. Someone with osmotic thirst would drink more water. Someone with hypovolemic thirst would drink more of a solution containing salts.

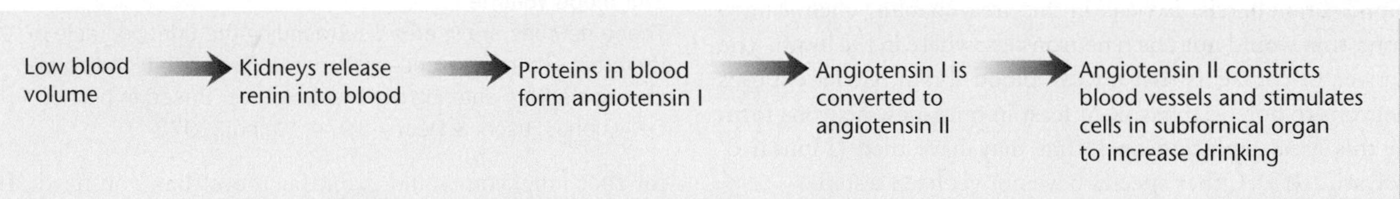

FIGURE 9.10 Hormonal response to hypovolemia

TABLE 9.1 Osmotic and Hypovolemic Thirst

Type of Thirst	Stimulus	Best Relieved by Drinking	Receptor Location	Hormone Influences
Osmotic	High solute concentration outside cells causes loss of water from cells	Water	OVLT, a brain area adjoining the third ventricle	Accompanied by vasopressin secretion to conserve water
Hypovolemic	Low blood volume	Water containing solutes	1. Receptors measuring blood pressure in the veins 2. Subfornical organ, a brain area adjoining the third ventricle	Increased by angiotensin II

MODULE 9.2 ■ IN CLOSING

The Psychology and Biology of Thirst

You may have thought that temperature regulation happens automatically and that water regulation depends on your behavior. You can see now that the distinction is not entirely correct. You control your body temperature partly by automatic means, such as sweating or shivering, but also partly by behavioral means, such as choosing a warm or a cool place. You control your body water partly by the behavior of drinking but also by hormones that alter kidney activity. If your kidneys cannot regulate your water and sodium adequately, your brain gets signals to change your drinking or sodium intake. In short, keeping your body's chemical reactions going depends on both skeletal and autonomic controls.

Summary

1. Mammalian species have evolved ways of maintaining body water, ranging from frequent drinking (beavers) to extreme conservation of fluids (gerbils). Humans alter their strategy depending on the availability of acceptable fluids. **302**
2. An increase in the osmotic pressure of the blood draws water out of cells, causing osmotic thirst. Neurons in areas adjoining the third ventricle detect changes in osmotic pressure and send information to hypothalamic areas responsible for vasopressin secretion and for drinking. **302**
3. Loss of blood volume causes hypovolemic thirst. Animals with hypovolemic thirst drink more water containing solutes than pure water. **304**
4. Hypovolemic thirst is triggered by the hormone angiotensin II, which increases when blood pressure falls. **304**
5. Loss of sodium salts from the body triggers a craving for salty tastes. **304**

Key Terms

Terms are defined in the module on the page number indicated. They're also presented in alphabetical order with definitions in the book's Subject Index/Glossary. Interactive flash cards, audio reviews, and crossword puzzles are among the online resources available to help you learn these terms and the concepts they represent.

aldosterone **304**
angiotensin II **304**
antidiuretic hormone (ADH) **302**
hypovolemic thirst **304**
lateral preoptic area **303**
osmotic pressure **302**
osmotic thirst **302**
OVLT **303**
paraventricular nucleus (PVN) **303**
sodium-specific hunger **304**
subfornical organ (SFO) **303**
supraoptic nucleus **303**
vasopressin **302**

Thought Questions

1. An injection of concentrated sodium chloride triggers osmotic thirst, but an injection of equally concentrated glucose does not. Why not?
2. If all the water you drank leaked out through a tube connected to the stomach, how would your drinking change?
3. Many women crave salt during pregnancy. Why?

MODULE 9.2 End of Module Quiz

1. If you lacked vasopressin, how would your drinking change, if at all?
   a. Your drinking would not change.
   b. You would drink less.
   c. You would drink more.

2. What would happen as a result of adding salt to the body's extracellular fluids?
   a. Increased osmotic thirst
   b. Decreased osmotic thirst
   c. Increased hypovolemic thirst
   d. Decreased hypovolemic thirst

3. How does hypovolemic thirst differ from osmotic thirst?
   a. Hypovolemic thirst is stronger.
   b. Osmotic thirst is stronger.
   c. Someone with hypovolemic thirst prefers slightly salty water.
   d. Someone with hypovolemic thirst prefers pure water.

ANSWERS: 1c, 2a, 3c.

Hunger

Species differ in their eating strategies. A snake or crocodile might devour a huge meal and then eat nothing more for months (see Figure 9.11). Predators in general have large digestive systems capable of handling infrequent but huge meals (Armstrong & Schindler, 2011). Bears eat as much as they can whenever they can. It is a sensible strategy because bears' main foods—fruits and nuts—are available in large quantities for only short times. Bears' occasional feasts tide them over through times of starvation. You might think of it as survival of the fattest. (Sorry about that one.)

A small bird, at the other extreme, eats only what it needs at the moment. The advantage of restraint is that low weight helps it fly away from predators and even a few extra milligrams might make a difference (see Figure 9.12). However, in some climates, a bird needs to store a substantial amount to get through the night. Tiny chickadees manage to survive through Alaska winters. Every night, a chickadee finds a hollowed tree or other nesting site that provides as much insulation as possible, and it lowers its body temperature into a state almost like hibernation. Still, it has to shiver throughout the night to prevent its body from freezing, and all that shivering requires energy. During Alaskan winters, a chickadee eats enough each day to increase its body weight by 10 percent and then loses that amount at night (Harrison, 2008; Sharbaugh, 2001). For comparison, imagine a 50 kg (110-lb) person gaining 5 kg (11 lb) during the day and then shivering it off at night.

As a rule, people neither limit their diet like small birds nor stuff themselves like bears, but we are probably closer to acting like bears than like small birds. One interpretation of the increased prevalence of obesity is that our ancient hunter-gatherer ancestors frequently faced food shortages. Therefore, they would have evolved a tendency to eat all the high-calorie foods they could find, whenever they were available (King, 2013). We still have that tendency today, even if food is readily available throughout the year.

Choosing which food to eat and how much is an important decision. We use a wide array of learned and unlearned mechanisms to help in the process.

Digestion and Food Selection

Examine the digestive system, as diagramed in Figure 9.13. Its function is to break food into smaller molecules that the cells can use. Digestion begins in the mouth, where enzymes

Okapia/Robert Harding

FIGURE 9.11 A python swallowing a gazelle
The gazelle weighed about 50 percent more than the snake. Many reptiles eat huge but infrequent meals. Their total intake over a year is far less than that of a mammal. We mammals need far more fuel because we use so much more energy, mainly for maintaining basal metabolism.

Arco Images/Rolfes, W./Arco Images GmbH / Alamy

FIGURE 9.12 A great tit, a small European bird
Ordinarily, when food is abundant, tits eat just what they need each day and maintain very low fat reserves. When food is harder to find, they eat all they can and live off fat reserves between meals. During an era when their predators were scarce, tits started putting on more fat regardless of the food supplies.

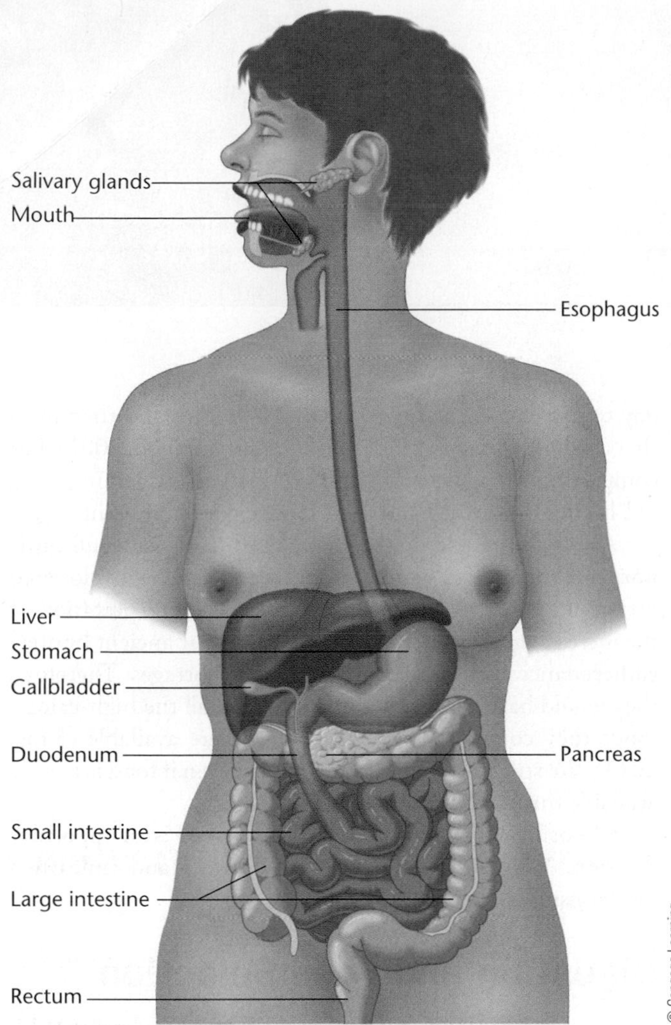

FIGURE 9.13 The human digestive system

in the saliva break down carbohydrates. Swallowed food travels down the esophagus to the stomach, where it mixes with hydrochloric acid and enzymes that digest proteins. The stomach stores food for a time, and then a round sphincter muscle opens at the end of the stomach to release food to the small intestine.

The small intestine has enzymes that digest proteins, fats, and carbohydrates. It is also the site for absorbing digested materials into the bloodstream. The blood carries those chemicals to body cells that either use them or store them for later use. The large intestine absorbs water and minerals and lubricates the remaining materials to pass as feces.

Consumption of Dairy Products

Newborn mammals survive at first on mother's milk. As they grow older, they stop nursing for several reasons: The milk supply declines, the mother pushes them away, and they begin to eat other foods. Most mammals at about the age of weaning lose the intestinal enzyme **lactase**, which is necessary for metabolizing **lactose**, the sugar in milk. Adult mammals can drink a little milk, as you may have noticed with a pet dog or cat. However, consuming too much causes stomach cramps, gas, and diarrhea (Ingram, Mulcare, Itan, Thomas, & Swallow, 2009; Rozin & Pelchat, 1988). The declining level of lactase may be an evolved mechanism to encourage weaning at the appropriate time.

Humans are a partial exception to this rule. Many adults have enough lactase levels to consume milk and other dairy products throughout life. However, prevalence of the necessary genes varies. Nearly all the adults in China and surrounding countries are unable to metabolize lactose, as do varying numbers of people in other parts of the world (Curry, 2013; Flatz, 1987; Rozin & Pelchat, 1988). People who are lactose intolerant can consume a little milk, and larger amounts of cheese and yogurt, which are easier to digest, but they generally learn to limit their intake.

The genetic ability to metabolize lactose in adulthood is common in societies with a long history of domesticated cattle. Within Africa, the distribution of ability to digest lactose varies sharply from place to place. Whereas Europeans who can digest lactose in adulthood all have variants of the same gene, people in various parts of Africa have genes that differ from one another and from Europeans, indicating that genes for adult lactose digestion evolved independently several times as various groups began domesticating cattle (Tishkoff et al., 2007). When cow's milk became available, the selective pressure was strong in favor of genes enabling people to digest it. Figure 9.14 shows the distribution of lactose tolerance across the Eastern hemisphere. About 25 percent of Native Americans can digest lactose in adulthood. For other residents of the Americas, the probability of digesting lactose depends on the origins of their ancestors.

STOP&CHECK

10. What genetic difference is most important for variants in likelihood of drinking milk in adulthood?

ANSWER

10. Likelihood of drinking milk in adulthood depends largely on a gene that controls the ability to digest lactose, the main sugar in milk.

Food Selection and Behavior

Does your food selection change your behavior? Many people have unsubstantiated beliefs in this regard. For example, many people believe that eating sugar makes children hyperactive. The best way to test this claim is to have children eat snacks with sugar on some days, randomly selected, and artificially sweetened snacks on other days, so that neither they nor their parents and teachers know when the child has eaten sugar. Studies of this type have found no significant effect of sugar on children's activity level, play behaviors, or school performance (Ells et al., 2008; Milich & Pelham, 1986). Presumably the belief that sugar causes hyperactivity is an illusion based on

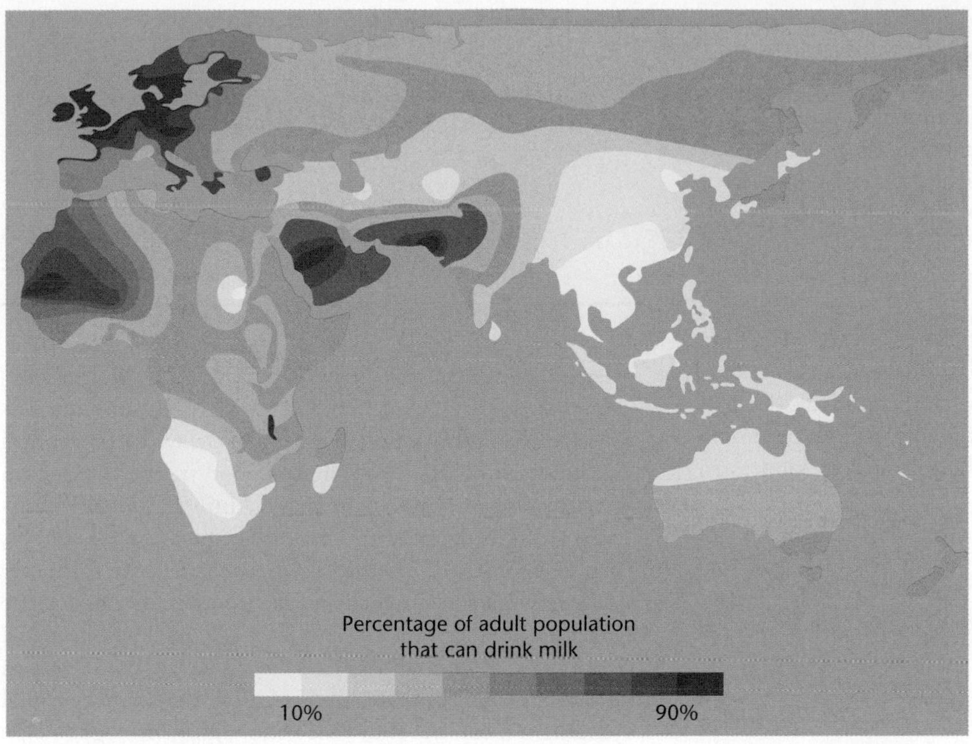

FIGURE 9.14 Percentage of adults who are lactose tolerant People in areas with high lactose tolerance (e.g., Scandinavia) are likely to enjoy milk and other dairy products throughout their lives. Adults in areas with low tolerance (including Southeast Asia) drink less milk, if any. *Source:* Curry, 2013

people's tendency to remember the observations that fit their expectation and disregard the others.

Another common misconception is that eating turkey increases the body's supply of tryptophan, which enables the brain to make chemicals that make you sleepy. That idea probably originated from the observation that many people in the United States feel sleepy after turkey dinner on Thanksgiving. The sleepiness comes from overeating, not from turkey itself, which has only an average amount of tryptophan. However, the rest of that idea is correct: Increasing tryptophan does help the brain produce melatonin, which induces sleepiness. Other than taking tryptophan pills, the most reliable way to increase tryptophan in the brain is to eat a diet high in carbohydrates. Here is the explanation: Tryptophan enters the brain by an active-transport protein that it shares with phenylalanine and other large amino acids. When you eat carbohydrates, your body reacts by increasing secretion of insulin, which moves sugars into storage, and also moves phenylalanine into storage (in liver cells and elsewhere). By reducing the competition from phenylalanine, this process makes it easier for tryptophan to reach the brain, inducing sleepiness (Silber & Schmitt, 2010). In short, it's mainly the dessert at your big meal that induces sleepiness.

On the other hand, one old belief, long dismissed as nonsense, may turn out to be partly true. That belief is that fish is brain food. Many fish, especially salmon, contain oils that are helpful for brain functioning, and several research studies have found that eating more fish helps some people improve their memory and reasoning abilities (Ells et al., 2008).

Short- and Long-Term Regulation of Feeding

Eating is far too important to be entrusted to just one mechanism. Your brain gets messages from your mouth, stomach, intestines, fat cells, and elsewhere to regulate your eating.

Oral Factors

You're a busy person, right? If you could get all the nutrition you need by swallowing a pill, would you do it? Once in a while you might, but not often. People like to eat. In fact, people like to taste and chew even when they are not hungry. Figure 9.15 shows a piece of 6500-year-old chewing gum made from birch-bark tar. The small tooth marks indicate that a child or teenager chewed it. Anthropologists don't know how the ancient people removed the sap to make the gum, and they aren't sure why anyone would chew something that tasted as bad as this gum probably did (Battersby, 1997). Clearly, the urge to chew is strong.

FIGURE 9.15 Chewing gum from about 4500 B.C. The gum, made from birch-bark tar, has small tooth marks indicating that a child or adolescent chewed it. *Source:* Reprinted by permission from Macmillan Publishers Ltd., "Plus c'est le meme chews," by Stephen Battersby, *Nature,* 1997

Could you become satiated without tasting your food? In one experiment, college students consumed lunch five days a week by swallowing one end of a rubber tube and then pushing a button to pump a liquid diet into the stomach (Jordan, 1969; Spiegel, 1973). (They were paid for participating.) After a few days of practice, each person established a consistent pattern of pumping in a constant volume of the liquid each day and maintaining a constant body weight. Most found the untasted meals unsatisfying, however, and reported a desire to taste or chew something (Jordan, 1969).

Could you be satisfied from taste alone? In **sham-feeding** experiments, everything an animal swallows leaks out of a tube connected to the esophagus or stomach. Sham-feeding animals eat and swallow almost continually without becoming satiated (G. P. Smith, 1998). In short, taste contributes to satiety, but it is not sufficient.

STOP&CHECK

11. What evidence indicates that taste is not sufficient for satiety?

ANSWER

11. It is not sufficient, because animals that sham-feed chew and taste their food but do not become satiated.

The Stomach and Intestines

Ordinarily, we end a meal before the food reaches the blood, much less the muscles, brain, or other organs. The main signal to end a meal is distension of the stomach. That was always a likely hypothesis, but it wasn't easy to demonstrate. In a decisive experiment, researchers attached an inflatable cuff at the connection between the stomach and the small intestine (Deutsch, Young, & Kalogeris, 1978). When they inflated the cuff, food could not pass from the stomach to the duodenum. They carefully ensured that the cuff was not traumatic to the animal and did not interfere with feeding. The key result was that, with the cuff inflated, an animal ate a normal-size meal and then stopped. Evidently, stomach distension is sufficient to produce satiety.

The stomach conveys satiety messages to the brain via the vagus nerve and the splanchnic nerves. The **vagus nerve** (cranial nerve X) conveys information about the stretching of the stomach walls, providing a major basis for satiety. The **splanchnic** (SPLANK-nik) **nerves** convey information about the nutrient contents of the stomach (Deutsch & Ahn, 1986).

However, people who have had their stomach surgically removed (because of stomach cancer or other disease) still report satiety, so mechanisms other than stomach distension are capable of producing satiety. Later researchers found that meals end after distension of either the stomach or the duodenum (Seeley, Kaplan, & Grill, 1995). The **duodenum** (DYOU-oh-DEE-num or dyuh-ODD-ehn-uhm) is the part of the small intestine adjoining the stomach. It is the first digestive site that absorbs a significant amount of nutrients.

STOP&CHECK

12. What evidence shows that stomach distension is sufficient for satiety?

ANSWER

12. If a cuff is attached to the junction between the stomach and duodenum so that food cannot leave the stomach, an animal becomes satiated when the stomach is full.

Fat in the duodenum releases a hormone called *oleoylethanolamide* (OEA), which stimulates the vagus nerve, sending a message to the hypothalamus that delays the next meal (Gaetani et al., 2010). Any kind of food in the duodenum also releases the hormone **cholecystokinin** (ko-leh-SIS-teh-KI-nehn) **(CCK),** which limits meal size in two ways (Gibbs, Young, & Smith, 1973). First, CCK constricts the sphincter muscle between the stomach and the duodenum, causing the stomach to hold its contents and fill more quickly than usual (McHugh & Moran, 1985; G. P. Smith & Gibbs, 1998). In that way it facilitates stomach distension, the primary signal for ending a meal. Second, CCK stimulates the vagus nerve to send signals to the hypothalamus, causing cells there to release a neurotransmitter that is a shorter version of the CCK molecule itself (Kobelt et al., 2006; G. J. Schwartz, 2000). The process is something like sending a fax: The CCK in the intestines cannot cross the blood–brain barrier, but it stimulates cells to release something almost like it. As in the case of angiotensin and thirst, the body uses the same chemical in the periphery and in the brain for closely related functions.

Given that CCK helps to end a meal, could we use it to help people who are trying to lose weight? Unfortunately, no. CCK produces short-term effects only. It limits the size of the meal, but an animal that has eaten a smaller than usual meal compensates by overeating at the next meal (Cummings & Overduin, 2007).

STOP&CHECK

13. What are two mechanisms by which CCK increases satiety?

ANSWER

13. When the duodenum is distended, it releases CCK, which closes the sphincter muscle between the stomach and duodenum. CCK therefore increases the rate at which the stomach distends. Also, neural signals from the intestines cause certain cells in the hypothalamus to release CCK as a neurotransmitter, and at its receptors, it triggers decreased feeding.

Glucose, Insulin, and Glucagon

Digestion converts much of a meal into glucose, an important source of energy throughout the body and nearly the only fuel of the brain. Two pancreatic hormones, insulin and glucagon, regulate the flow of glucose into cells. Immediately before, during, and after a meal, the pancreas increases release of **insulin**, which enables glucose to enter the cells, except for brain cells, where glucose does not need insulin to enter. Some of the excess glucose produced by a meal enters the liver, which converts it to glycogen and stores it. Some also enters fat cells, which convert it to fat and store it. The net effect prevents blood glucose levels from rising too sharply.

As time passes after a meal, the blood glucose level falls, insulin levels drop, glucose enters the cells more slowly, and hunger increases (Pardal & López-Barneo, 2002) (see Figure 9.16). The pancreas increases release of **glucagon**, stimulating the liver to convert some of its stored glycogen back to glucose.

If the insulin level stays constantly high, the body continues moving blood glucose into the cells, including the liver cells and fat cells, long after a meal. Before too long, blood glucose drops, because glucose is leaving the blood without any new glucose entering. The result is increased hunger. In autumn, animals that are preparing for hibernation have constantly high insulin levels. They rapidly deposit much of each meal as fat and glycogen, grow hungry again, and continue gaining weight (see Figure 9.17). That weight gain is a valuable preparation for a season when the animal will have to survive off its fat reserves. Most humans also eat more in autumn than in other seasons, as shown in Figure 9.18 (de Castro, 2000). In the United States, we tend to blame our autumn weight gain on the Halloween and Thanksgiving holidays, but the real reason may be an evolved drive to increase our reserves in preparation for winter. (Our ancestors didn't have good food year-round, as we do.)

If the insulin level remains constantly low, as in people with type 1 diabetes, blood glucose levels may be three or more times the normal level, but little of it enters the cells

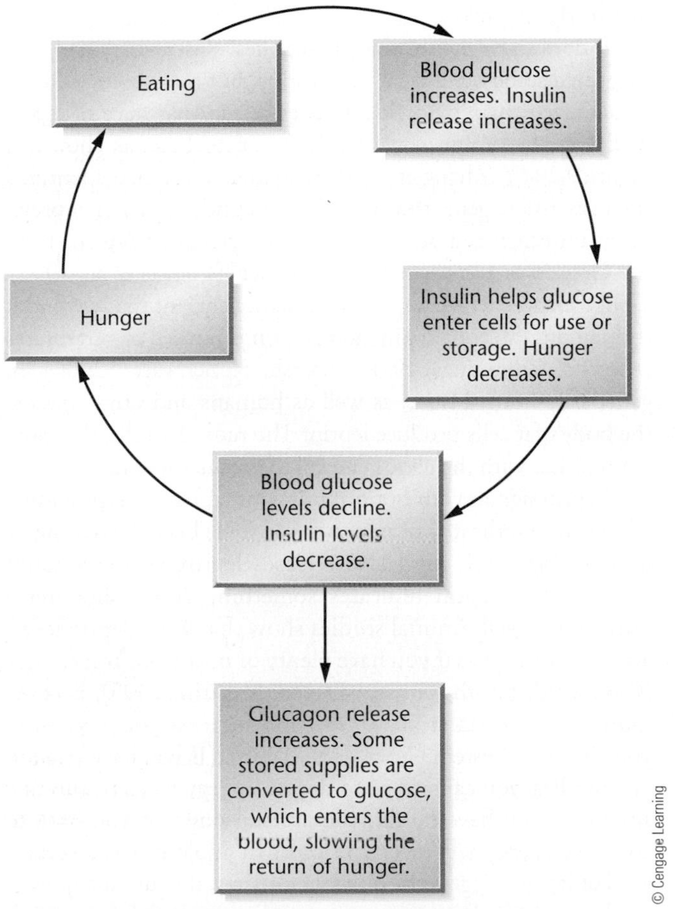

FIGURE 9.16 Insulin and glucagon feedback system
When glucose levels rise, the pancreas releases the hormone insulin, which helps glucose enter cells, including liver cells and fat cells that store fuel for future use. The entry of glucose into cells suppresses hunger and decreases eating, thereby lowering the glucose level.

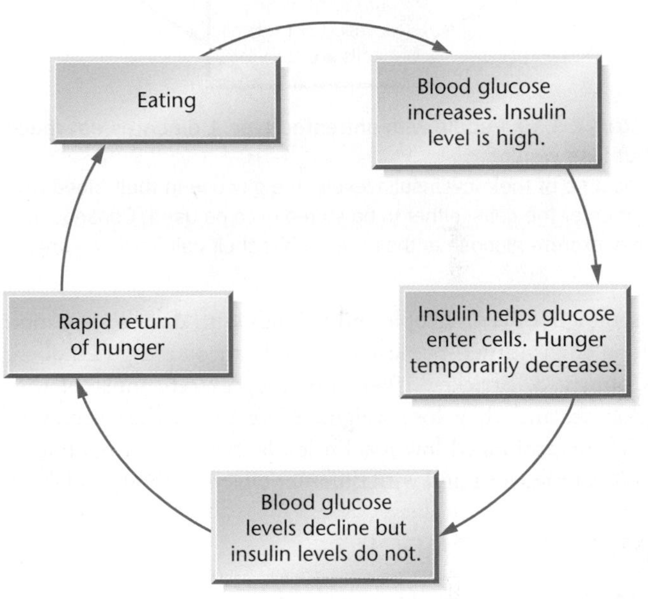

FIGURE 9.17 Effects of steady high insulin levels on feeding
Constantly high insulin causes blood glucose to be stored as fats and glycogen. Because it becomes difficult to mobilize the stored nutrients, hunger returns soon after each meal.

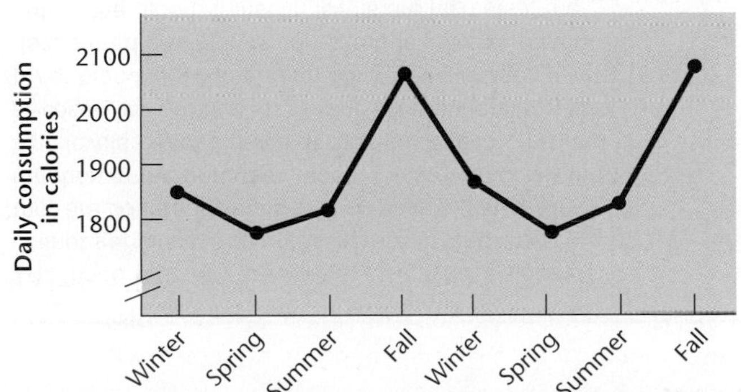

FIGURE 9.18 People eat more in fall than in other seasons
Mean intake increases by more than 10 percent, on the average, according to people's eating diaries. *Source:* Based on de Castro, J. M. (2000). Eating behavior: Lessons from the real world of humans. *Nutrition, 16*, pp. 800–813

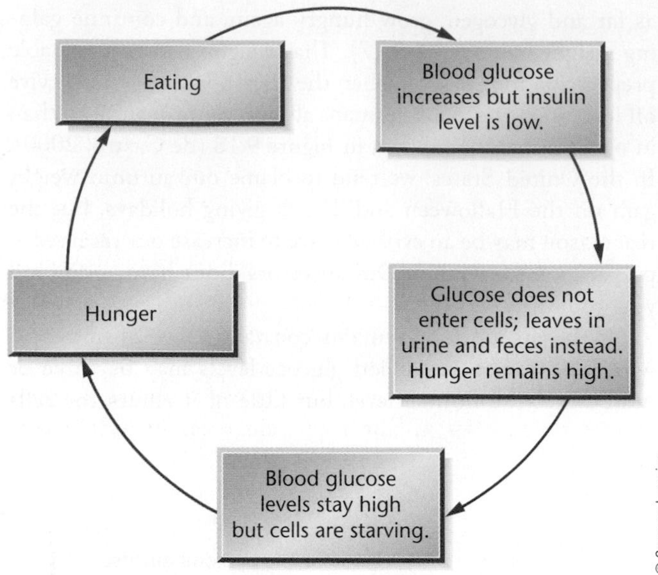

FIGURE 9.19 People with untreated type 1 diabetes eat much but lose weight
Because of their low insulin levels, the glucose in their blood cannot enter the cells, either to be stored or to be used. Consequently, they excrete glucose in their urine while their cells are starving.

(see Figure 9.19). People and animals with diabetes eat more food than normal because their cells are starving (Lindberg, Coburn, & Stricker, 1984), but they excrete most of their glucose, and they lose weight. Note that either prolonged high or prolonged low insulin levels increase eating, but for different reasons and with different effects on body weight.

STOP & CHECK

14. Why do people with very low insulin levels eat so much? Why do people with constantly high levels eat so much?

15. What would happen to someone's appetite if insulin levels and glucagon levels were both high?

ANSWERS

14. Those with very low levels, as in type 1 diabetes, cannot get glucose to enter their cells, and therefore, they are constantly hungry. They pass much of their nutrition in the urine and feces. Those with constantly high levels deposit much of their glucose into fat and glycogen, so within a short time after a meal, the supply of blood glucose drops. **15.** When glucagon levels rise, stored glycogen is converted to glucose, which enters the blood. If insulin levels are high also, the glucose entering the blood is free to enter all the cells. So the result would be decreased appetite.

Leptin

Taste, stomach distension, duodenum distension, and insulin help regulate the onset and offset of a meal. However, we cannot expect those mechanisms to be completely accurate. If you consistently eat either a little more or less than necessary,

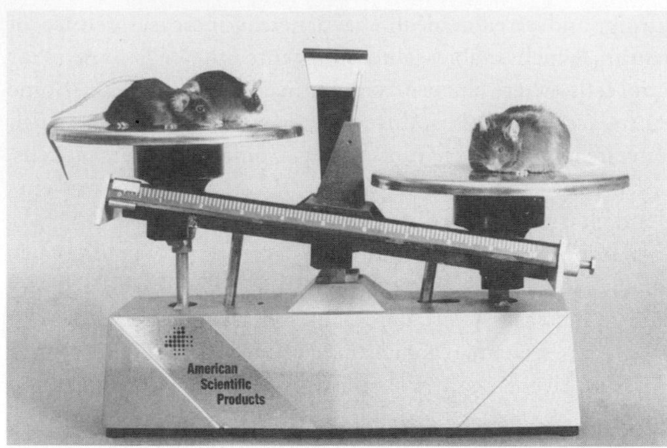

FIGURE 9.20 The effects of the obese gene on body weight
Mice with this gene eat more, move around less, and gain weight. *Source:* Reprinted with permission from Macmillan Publishers Ltd., "Positional cloning of the mouse obese gene and its human homologue," by Zhang et al., 1994, *Nature*

eventually, you would be much too heavy or much too thin. The body needs a long-term mechanism to compensate for day-to-day mistakes.

It does so by monitoring fat supplies. Researchers had long suspected some kind of fat monitoring, but they discovered the actual mechanism by accident. They found that mice of a particular genetic strain consistently become obese, as shown in Figure 9.20 (Y. Zhang et al., 1994). After researchers identified the responsible gene, they found the peptide it makes, a previously unrecognized substance that they named **leptin**, from the Greek word *leptos,* meaning "slender" (Halaas et al., 1995). Unlike insulin, which is so evolutionarily ancient that we find it throughout the animal kingdom, leptin is limited to vertebrates (Morton, Cummings, Baskin, Barsh, & Schwartz, 2006). In genetically normal mice, as well as humans and other species, the body's fat cells produce leptin: The more fat cells, the more leptin. Mice with the *obese* gene fail to produce leptin.

Leptin signals your brain about your fat reserves, providing a long-term indicator of whether you have been overeating or undereating. Each meal also releases leptin, so the amount of circulating leptin indicates something about short-term nutrition as well. Animal studies show that when leptin levels are high, you act as if you have plenty of nutrition. You eat less (Campfield, Smith, Guisez, Devos, & Burn, 1995), become more active (Elias et al., 1998), and increase the activity of your immune system (Lord et al., 1998). (If you have enough fat supplies, you can afford to devote energy to your immune system. If you have no fat, you are starving and you have to conserve energy wherever you can.) In adolescence, a certain level of leptin triggers the onset of puberty. If your fat supply is too low to provide for your own needs, you don't have enough energy to provide for a baby. On the average, thinner people enter puberty later. Leptin also activates the sympathetic nervous system and increases blood pressure (Mark, 2013).

Because a mouse with the *obese* gene does not make leptin, its brain reacts as if its body has no fat stores and must be starving.

The mouse eats as much as possible, conserves its energy by not moving much, and fails to enter puberty. Injections of leptin reverse these symptoms: The mouse then eats less, becomes more active, and enters puberty (Pelleymounter et al., 1995).

As you might imagine, news of this research inspired pharmaceutical companies to hope they could make a fortune by selling leptin. After all, the body makes leptin all the time, so it should not have unpleasant side effects. However, researchers soon discovered that almost all overweight people already produce plenty of leptin (Considine et al., 1996). The problem is that they have become less sensitive to it.

Leptin sensitivity declines during pregnancy and in animals preparing for hibernation. In those cases, increased intake makes sense. Unfortunately, leptin sensitivity also declines as a result of obesity (Ernst et al., 2009; Tups, 2009). In fact, as obesity develops, the effect of leptin actually reverses so that it increases eating (S. J. Lee et al., 2013). The only known way to undo that effect is prolonged physical exercise, which increases production of certain chemicals of the immune system and decreases inflammation of the hypothalamus (Chiarreotto-Ropelle et al., 2013).

STOP&CHECK

16. Why are leptin injections less helpful for most overweight people than for mice with the *obese* gene?

ANSWER

16. Nearly all overweight people produce leptin in proportion to body fat. However, they have low sensitivity to it.

Brain Mechanisms

How does your brain decide when you should eat and how much? Hunger depends on the contents of your stomach and intestines, the availability of glucose to the cells, and your body's fat supplies, as well as your health and body temperature. Your appetite also depends on more than your need for food. If someone offers you a tasty treat, you might eat it even if you are not hungry. Just seeing a picture of highly appealing food increases your appetite (Harmon-Jones & Gable, 2009). People eat more on weekends than on other days, and more when eating with friends or family than when eating alone (de Castro, 2000). Somehow, the brain combines all these types of information. The key brain areas include several nuclei of the hypothalamus (see Figure 9.6).

As shown in Figure 9.21, many kinds of information impinge onto two kinds of cells in the arcuate nucleus of the hypothalamus, which is regarded as the master area for controlling appetite (Mendieta-Zéron, López, & Diéguez, 2008). Axons extend from the arcuate nucleus to other areas of the hypothalamus. Even though this figure leaves out some of the neurotransmitters and other complexities, it may be intimidating. Let's go through the key mechanisms step by step.

The Arcuate Nucleus and Paraventricular Hypothalamus

The **arcuate nucleus** of the hypothalamus has one set of neurons sensitive to hunger signals and a second set sensitive to satiety signals. Damage to one set or the other can lead to starvation or excessive eating (Wu, Clark, & Palmiter, 2012). In Figure 9.21,

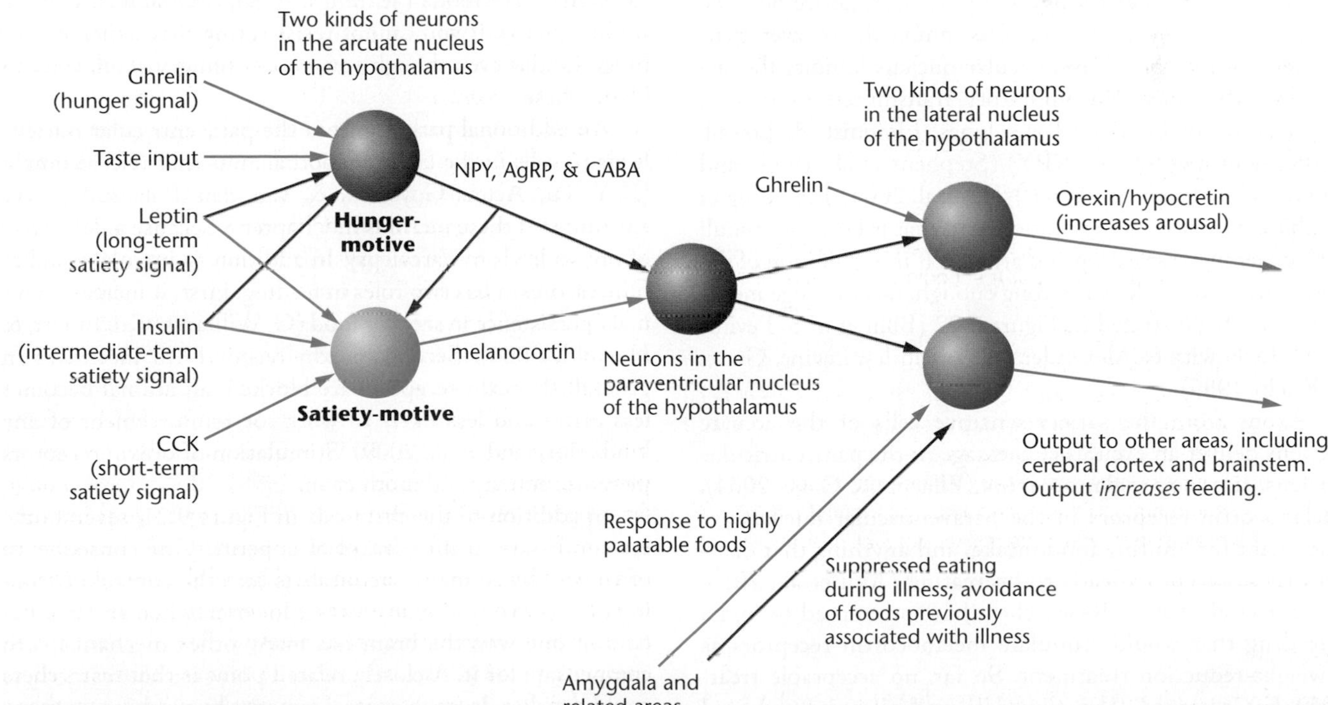

FIGURE 9.21 Hypothalamic transmitters of feeding
Hunger signals increase feeding by inhibiting inhibitory messages to the lateral hypothalamus. *Source:* Based on reviews by Horvath, 2005; Minokoshi et al., 2004

excitatory paths are noted in green, and inhibitory paths are in red. The hunger-sensitive cells receive excitatory input from the taste pathway and from axons releasing the neurotransmitter **ghrelin** (GRELL-in). This odd-looking word takes its name from the fact that it binds to the same receptors as growth-hormone releasing hormone (GHRH). The stomach releases ghrelin during a period of food deprivation, where it triggers stomach contractions. Ghrelin also acts on the hypothalamus to increase appetite. People who produce greater than average amounts of ghrelin respond more strongly than average to the sight of food, and they are almost twice as likely as other people to become obese (Karra et al., 2013).

Nicotine also stimulates the satiety neurons in the arcuate nucleus (Mineur et al., 2011). The result is that cigarette smoking decreases appetite, and quitting smoking increases appetite, leading to weight gain.

Signals of both short-term and long-term satiety provide input to the satiety-sensitive cells of the arcuate nucleus. Distension of the intestines triggers neurons to release the neurotransmitter CCK, a short-term signal (Fan et al., 2004). Blood glucose (a short-term signal) stimulates satiety cells in the arcuate nucleus (Parton et al., 2007) and leads to increased secretion of insulin, which also stimulates the satiety cells. Body fat (a long-term signal) releases leptin, which stimulates the satiety neurons and inhibits the hunger neurons (Diéguez, Vazquez, Romero, López, & Nogueiras, 2011).

Much of the output from the arcuate nucleus goes to the paraventricular nucleus of the hypothalamus. The paraventricular nucleus (PVN) inhibits the lateral hypothalamus, an area important for eating. In Figure 9.21, notice how the hunger cells in the arcuate nucleus inhibit the paraventricular nucleus and the paraventricular nucleus inhibits the lateral hypothalamus. The inhibitory transmitters here are a combination of GABA (Tong, Jones, Elmquist, & Lowell, 2008), **neuropeptide Y (NPY)** (Stephens et al., 1995), and **agouti-related peptide (AgRP)** (Kas et al., 2004). Inhibiting an inhibitor produces net excitation, and that is how the stimuli for hunger increase eating and arousal. If the inhibition of the paraventricular nucleus is strong enough, rats eat huge meals, as tastelessly illustrated in Figure 9.22 (Billington & Levine, 1992; Leibowitz & Alexander, 1991; Morley, Levine, Grace, & Kneip, 1985).

Axons from the satiety-sensitive cells of the arcuate nucleus deliver an excitatory message to the paraventricular nucleus, releasing **melanocortins** (Ellacott & Cone, 2004). Melanocortin receptors in the paraventricular nucleus are important for limiting food intake, and anything that damages these receptors leads to overeating (Asai et al., 2013; Huszar et al., 1997). Researchers have attempted to find a safe drug that would stimulate melanocortin receptors as a weight-reduction treatment. So far, no acceptable treatment has emerged. The amygdala and related areas send two kinds of input to the lateral hypothalamus. One path inhibits eating during illness and mediates aversion to foods previously associated with illness (Carter, Soden, Zweifel, & Palmiter, 2013). The other path stimulates eating in response to highly tasty foods (Jennings, Rizzi, Stamatakis, Ung, & Stuber, 2013). If you cannot resist eating that delicious hot fudge sundae even though you weren't hungry at all, you can blame these axons.

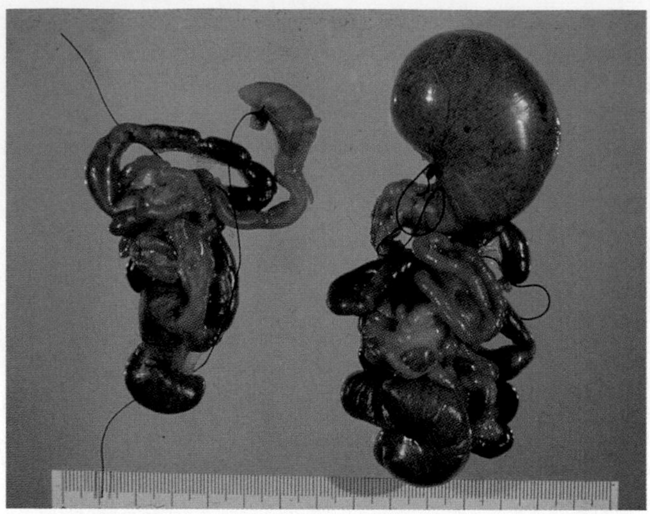

FIGURE 9.22 Effects of inhibiting the paraventricular nucleus of the hypothalamus
On the left is the digestive system of a normal rat. On the right is the digestive system of a rat that had its paraventricular hypothalamus chemically inhibited. The rat continued eating even though its stomach and intestines distended almost to the point of bursting. *(Yeah, this is a little bit disgusting.) Source:* Reprinted from *Brain Research*, 341/1, J. E. Morley, A. S. Levine, M. Grace, and J. Kneip, "Peptide YY PYY, a potently orexigenic agent," pp. 200–203, 1985, with permission of Elsevier

An additional pathway from the paraventricular nucleus leads to cells in the lateral hypothalamus that release orexin (L.-Y. Fu, Acuna-Goycolea, & van den Pol, 2004). We encountered these neurons in Chapter 8 because a deficiency of orexin leads to narcolepsy. In addition to its role in wakefulness, orexin has two roles in feeding. First, it increases animals' persistence in seeking food (G. Williams, Cai, Elliott, & Harrold, 2004). Second, orexin responds to incentives in general. If orexin receptors are blocked, an animal becomes less active and less likely to work for reinforcement of any kind (Borgland et al., 2009). Stimulation of orexin receptors increases activity and motivation.

In addition to the chemicals in Figure 9.21, several others contribute to the control of appetite. One consequence of control by so many chemicals is that the control of feeding can go wrong in many ways. However, when an error occurs in one way, the brain has many other mechanisms to compensate for it. A closely related point is that researchers could develop drugs to control appetite by working on many routes—leptin, insulin, NPY, and so forth—but changing any one circuit might be ineffective because of compensations by the others.

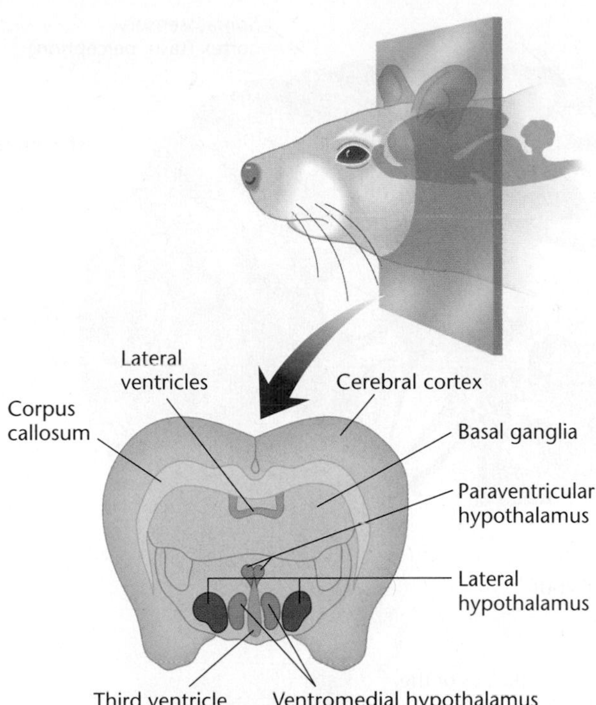

FIGURE 9.23 The lateral hypothalamus, ventromedial hypothalamus, and paraventricular hypothalamus
The side view above indicates the plane of the coronal section of the brain below. *Source:* Based on Hart, 1976

STOP&CHECK

17. Name three hormones that increase satiety and one that increases hunger.

18. Which neuropeptide from the arcuate nucleus to the paraventricular nucleus is most important for satiety?

ANSWERS

17. Insulin, CCK, and leptin increase satiety. Ghrelin increases hunger. **18.** Melanocortin

The Lateral Hypothalamus

Output from the paraventricular nucleus acts on the **lateral hypothalamus** (see Figure 9.23), which includes so many neuron clusters and passing axons that it has been compared to a crowded train station (Leibowitz & Hoebel, 1998). The lateral hypothalamus controls insulin secretion, alters taste responsiveness, and facilitates feeding in other ways. An animal with damage in this area refuses food and water, averting its head as if the food were distasteful. The animal may starve to death unless it is force-fed, but if kept alive, it gradually recovers much of its ability to eat (see Figure 9.24). In contrast, stimulation of the lateral hypothalamus increases the drive to eat.

Many axons containing dopamine pass through the lateral hypothalamus, so damage to the lateral hypothalamus interrupts these fibers. To separate the roles of hypothalamic cells from those of passing fibers, experimenters used chemicals that damage only the cell bodies, or induced lesions in very young rats, before the dopamine axons reached the lateral hypothalamus. In both cases, damaging the cell bodies without damaging the passing dopamine axons produced a loss of feeding without loss of arousal and activity (Almli, Fisher, & Hill, 1979; Grossman, Dacey, Halaris, Collier, & Routtenberg, 1978; Stricker, Swerdloff, & Zigmond, 1978). The lateral hypothalamus contributes to feeding in several ways, as shown in Figure 9.25 (Leibowitz & Hoebel, 1998):

- Axons from the lateral hypothalamus to the NTS (nucleus of the tractus solitarius), part of the taste pathway, alter the taste sensation and the salivation response to the tastes. When the lateral hypothalamus detects hunger, it sends messages that make the food taste better.

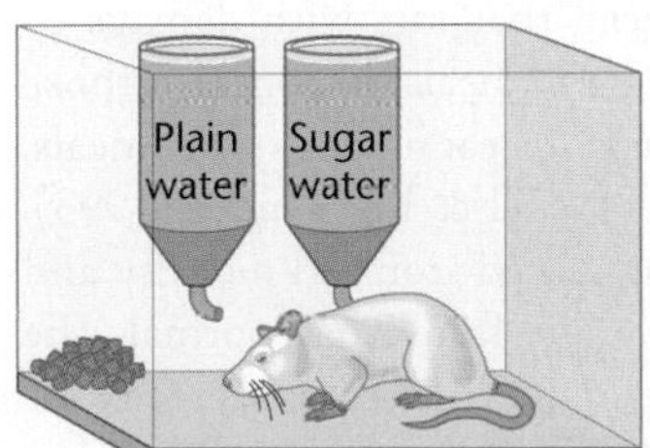

Stage 1. *Aphagia and adipsia.* Rat refuses all food and drink; must be force-fed to keep it alive.

Stage 2. *Anorexia.* Rat eats a small amount of palatable foods and drinks sweetened water. It still does not eat enough to stay alive.

Stage 3. *Adipsia.* The rat eats enough to stay alive, though at a lower-than-normal body weight. It still refuses plain water.

Stage 4. *Near-recovery.* The rat eats enough to stay alive, though at a lower-than-normal body weight. It drinks plain water, but only at mealtimes to wash down its food. Under slightly stressful conditions, such as in a cold room, the rat will return to an earlier stage of refusing food and water.

FIGURE 9.24 Recovery after damage to the lateral hypothalamus
At first, the rat refuses all food and drink. If kept alive for several weeks or months by force-feeding, it gradually recovers its ability to eat and drink enough to stay alive. However, even at the final stage of recovery, its behavior is not the same as that of normal rats. *Source:* Based on Teitelbaum & Epstein, 1962

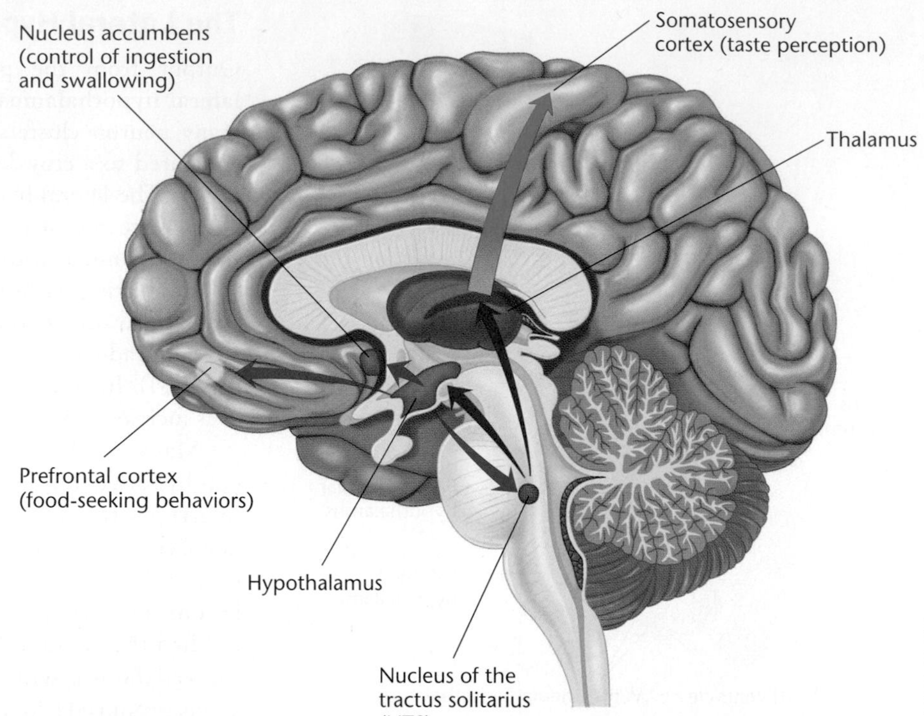

FIGURE 9.25 Pathways from the lateral hypothalamus
Axons from the lateral hypothalamus modify activity in several other brain areas, changing the response to taste, facilitating ingestion and swallowing, and increasing food-seeking behaviors. Also (not shown), the lateral hypothalamus controls stomach secretions.

- Axons from the lateral hypothalamus extend into several parts of the cerebral cortex, facilitating ingestion and swallowing and causing cortical cells to increase their response to the taste, smell, or sight of food (Critchley & Rolls, 1996).
- The lateral hypothalamus increases the pituitary gland's secretion of hormones that increase insulin secretion.
- The lateral hypothalamus sends axons to the spinal cord, controlling autonomic responses such as digestive secretions (van den Pol, 1999). An animal with damage to the lateral hypothalamus has trouble digesting foods.

STOP&CHECK

19. In what ways does the lateral hypothalamus facilitate feeding?

ANSWER

19. Activity of the lateral hypothalamus improves taste, enhances cortical responses to food, and increases secretions of insulin and digestive juices.

Medial Areas of the Hypothalamus

Output from the **ventromedial hypothalamus (VMH)** inhibits feeding (Chee, Myers, Price, & Colmers, 2010), and therefore damage to this nucleus leads to overeating and weight gain (see Figure 9.22). Some people with a tumor in that area have gained more than 10 kg (22 lbs) per month (Al-Rashid, 1971; Killeffer & Stern, 1970; Reeves & Plum, 1969). Rats with similar damage sometimes double or triple their weight (see Figure 9.26). Eventually, body weight levels off at a stable but high set point, and total food intake declines to nearly normal levels. Although these symptoms have been known as the *ventromedial hypothalamic syndrome,* damage limited to just the ventromedial hypothalamus does not consistently increase eating or body weight. To produce a large effect, the lesion must extend outside the ventromedial nucleus to invade nearby axons (Ahlskog & Hoebel, 1973; Ahlskog, Randall, & Hoebel, 1975; Gold, 1973).

Rats with damage in and around the ventromedial hypothalamus show an increased appetite compared to undamaged rats of the same weight (B. M. King, 2006; Peters, Sensenig, & Reich, 1973). Recall that rats with damage to the paraventricular nucleus eat large meals. In contrast, those with damage in the ventromedial area eat normal-sized meals, but they eat more frequently (Hoebel & Hernandez, 1993). One reason is that they have increased stomach motility and secretions, and their stomachs empty faster than normal. The faster the stomach empties, the sooner the animal is ready for its next meal. Another reason for their frequent meals is that the damage increases insulin production (B. M. King, Smith, & Frohman, 1984), and therefore, much of each meal is stored as fat. If animals with this kind of damage are prevented from overeating, they gain weight anyway! According to Mark Friedman and Edward Stricker (1976), the problem is not that the rat gets fat from overeating. Rather, the rat overeats because it is storing so much fat. The high insulin levels keep moving blood glucose into storage, even when the blood glucose level is low. Despite the weight gain, most of the body's cells are starving for nutrition. The result is increased hunger.

Table 9.2 summarizes the effects of lesions in several areas of the hypothalamus.

TABLE 9.2 Effects of Hypothalamic Lesions

Hypothalamic Area	Effect of Lesion
Preoptic area	Deficit in physiological mechanisms of temperature regulation
Lateral preoptic area	Deficit in osmotic thirst due partly to damage to cells and partly to interruption of passing axons
Lateral hypothalamus	Undereating, weight loss, low insulin level (because of damage to cell bodies); underarousal, underresponsiveness (because of damage to passing axons)
Ventromedial hypothalamus	Increased meal frequency, weight gain, high insulin level
Paraventricular nucleus	Increased meal size, especially increased carbohydrate intake during the first meal of the active period of the day

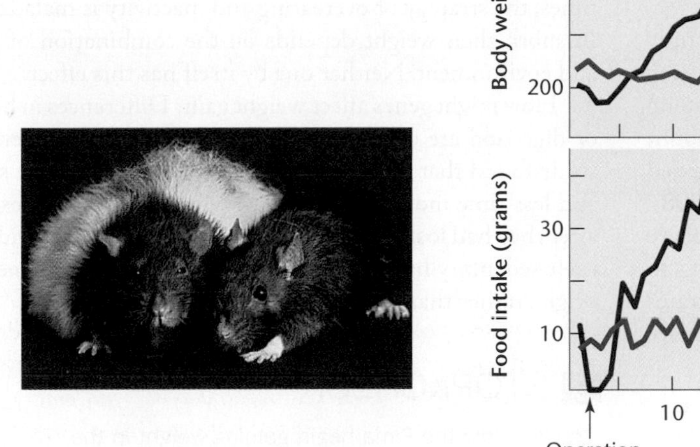

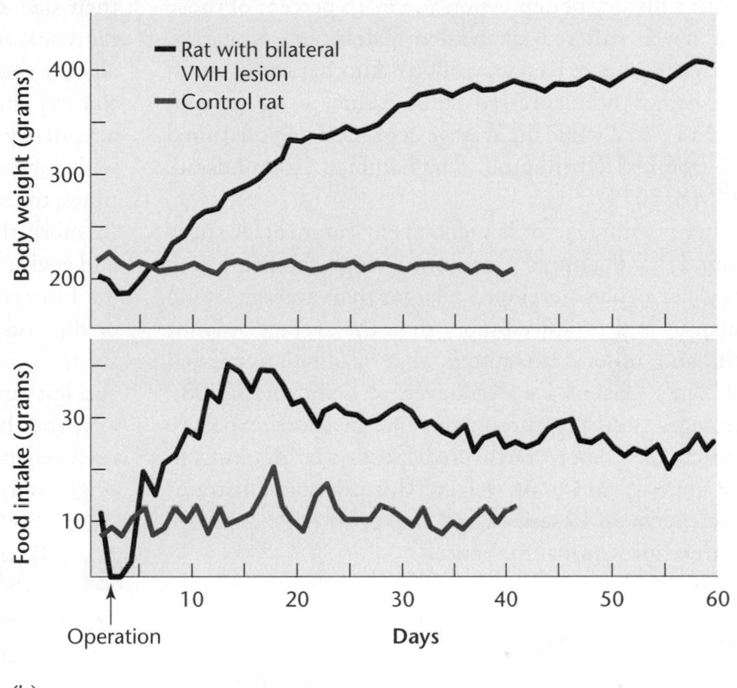

(a)

(b)

FIGURE 9.26 Effects of damage to the ventromedial hypothalamus
(a) On the right is a normal rat. On the left is a rat after damage to the ventromedial hypothalamus. A brain-damaged rat may weigh up to three times as much as a normal rat. *Sources:* Yoav Levy/Phototake (b) Weight and eating after damage to the ventromedial hypothalamus. Within a few days after the operation, the rat begins eating much more than normal. Based on "Disturbances in feeding and drinking behavior after hypothalamic lesions," by P. Teitelbaum, pp. 39–69, in M. R. Jones, Ed., 1961, *Nebraska Symposium on Motivation.* University of Nebraska Press, 1988

STOP&CHECK

20. In what way does eating increase after damage in and around the ventromedial hypothalamus? After damage to the paraventricular nucleus?

ANSWER

20. Animals with damage to the ventromedial hypothalamus eat more frequent meals. Animals with damage to the paraventricular nucleus of the hypothalamus eat larger meals.

Eating Disorders

Obesity has become a serious problem in more and more countries. Simultaneously, other people suffer from anorexia, in which they refuse to eat enough to survive, or bulimia, in which they alternate between eating too much and eating too little. Evidently, our homeostatic or allostatic mechanisms are not fully doing their job.

Through most of human existence, starvation has been a bigger worry than obesity. Most of our ancestors worked all day at manual labor, and they never heard of an all-you-can-eat buffet. The increasing prevalence of obesity obviously relates to the increased availability of our diet and our sedentary lifestyle. It is possible (in fact, easy) to make rats obese by giving them what researchers call a "cafeteria" consisting of chocolate, cheese, salami, peanut butter, marshmallows, and other tasty, high-calorie foods (Geiger et al., 2009). It is hard for rats to pass up these treats, and hard for us, too. When rats become obese on this regimen, they tend to lose interest in rewards other than food (Johnson & Kenny, 2010). Many people show the same tendency.

Still, some people become obese while others do not, even when all have access to the same foods, so it is reasonable to ask what makes some people more vulnerable than others. For a time, it was popular to assume that obesity was a reaction to psychological distress. True, many distressed people cheer themselves up temporarily by eating rich foods. The sight of tasty food activates reward centers in almost anyone's brain, and the effect is bigger in dieters who have just had a bad experience (Wagner, Boswell, Kelley, & Heatherton, 2012). However, in the long run, mood has only a weak relationship to weight gain. One study found obesity in 19 percent of people with a history of depression and in 15 percent of those who had never suffered depression (McIntyre, Konarski, Wilkins, Soczynska, & Kennedy, 2006). Another study found that the average nondepressed adult gained 4 kg (almost 9 lbs) over 11 years, while the average depressed person gained 5 kg (11 pounds) (Brumpton, Langhammer, Romundstad, Chen, & Mai, 2013).

Another possible factor is prenatal environment. A study in rats found that if a mother consumed a high-fat diet during pregnancy, her babies developed a larger than average lateral hypothalamus and produced more than the average amount of orexin and other transmitters that facilitate increased eating (Chang, Gasinskaya, Karatayev, & Leibowitz, 2008). These changes persisted throughout life. In short, exposure to a high-fat diet before birth predisposes the offspring to increased appetite and body weight. This example illustrates epigenetic effects, as described in Chapter 4: An experience can alter the expression of the genes.

Genetics and Body Weight

You have probably noticed that most thin parents have thin children, and most heavy parents have heavy children. A Danish study found that the weights of 540 adopted children correlated more strongly with that of their biological relatives than with that of their adoptive relatives (Stunkard et al., 1986). That result has generally been taken as evidence for a genetic influence, although it could also be evidence for the effects of prenatal environment.

In some cases, obesity can be traced to the effects of a single gene. The most common of these is a mutated gene for the receptor to melanocortin, a neuropeptide important for satiety. People with a mutation in that gene overeat and become obese from childhood onward (Mergen, Mergen, Ozata, Oner, & Oner, 2001). People with a variant form of one gene called *FTO* weigh 3 kg (6 to 7 lb) more than other people, on the average, and have about a two-thirds greater probability of becoming obese (Frayling et al., 2007). However, single-gene mutations account for only about 5 percent of cases of severe obesity (Yeo & Heisler, 2012). Most cases relate to many genes, each with a small effect (Körner, Kiess, Stumvoll, & Kovacs, 2008).

Syndromal obesity is obesity that results from a medical condition. For example, Prader-Willi syndrome is a genetic condition marked by mental retardation, short stature, and obesity. People with this syndrome have blood levels of ghrelin four to five times higher than average (Cummings et al., 2002). Ghrelin, you will recall, is a peptide related to food deprivation. The fact that people with Prader-Willi syndrome overeat and still produce high ghrelin levels suggests that their problem relates to an inability to turn off ghrelin release.

Most cases of obesity relate to the combined influences of genes and environment. Consider the Native American Pima of Arizona and Mexico. Most are seriously overweight, and researchers have identified several genes associated with the increased risk (Bian et al., 2010; Muller et al., 2010). However, obesity was uncommon among them in the early 1900s, when their diet consisted of desert plants that ripen in the brief rainy season. The Pima apparently evolved a strategy of eating all they could when food was available, because it would have to carry them through periods of scarcity. They also evolved a tendency to conserve energy by limiting their activity. Now, with a more typical U.S. diet that is equally available at all times, the strategy of overeating and inactivity is maladaptive. In short, their weight depends on the combination of genes and environment. Neither one by itself has this effect.

How might genes affect weight gain? Differences in hunger or digestion are one possibility, but exercise is another. One study found that mildly obese people spent more time sitting and less time moving about, both while they were obese and after they had lost weight (J. A. Levine et al., 2005). Evidently, their sedentary habits were a lifelong trait, perhaps genetic in origin, rather than a reaction to being overweight.

STOP & CHECK

21. Why did the Pima begin gaining weight in the mid-1900s?

ANSWER

21. They shifted from a diet of local plants that were seasonally available to a calorie-rich diet that is available throughout the year.

Weight Loss

In the United States, obesity is considered a disease, and never mind the fact that we don't have a clear definition of what we mean by *disease*. One positive consequence of calling it a disease is that people are relieved from thinking of themselves as morally guilty for being overweight. A possible negative consequence is that some may decide that they have no control and may as well quit trying to lose weight. Another consequence is that insurance companies will now pay treatment providers to help obese patients.

Dieting by itself is not reliably effective, mainly because most people don't stick to their diet for long (Wyatt, 2013). You will hear advocates of a particular diet plan brag that many people on their plan lost a significant amount of weight. That statement may be true, but it means little unless we know how many other people tried the plan and failed to lose weight. We also need to know how many people who lost weight gained it back. According to one review of the literature, few people on any diet maintain a significant weight loss for years (Mann et al., 2007). Many psychologists now recommend small changes in diet ("eat a little less than usual") on the expectation that more people will stick to this diet, and making a small change is better than failing to make a large change (Stroebele et al., 2008). It is also possible to start with a small change and then add another small change, and so forth.

The most successful treatments require a change of lifestyle, including increased exercise as well as decreased eating. That combination does help people lose weight, although still only 20 percent to 40 percent keep the weight off for at least 2 years (Powell, Calvin, & Calvin, 2007). For exercise to be helpful, it does not need to be strenuous, but it needs to be sustained, such as brisk walking for an hour a day on most days (Wyatt, 2013).

Particularly important advice is to reduce or eliminate the intake of soft drinks. Researchers have found that people who consume at least one soft drink per day are more likely than others to be overweight, and if they are not already overweight, they are more likely than others to become overweight (Dhingra et al., 2007; Liebman et al., 2006). Around 1970, American companies began sweetening their beverages with high-fructose corn syrup instead of sugar. Fructose is somewhat sweeter than common table sugar, and the hope was that people could satisfy their craving for sweets without quite as many calories. Clearly, this idea didn't work, as obesity has become more common, not less common, since then. Some researchers believe that fructose actually increases the problem. Whereas glucose (another common sugar) stimulates release of leptin and insulin that help reduce hunger, fructose has little effect on leptin or insulin (Teff et al., 2004). Therefore, if you drink something with fructose, you gain calories without feeling satiety. Also, if you drink much fructose, the body stores most of it as fat (Bray, Nielsen, & Popkin, 2004). Laboratory studies have shown that rats that are offered drinks containing fructose develop obesity, type 2 diabetes, and high blood pressure (Tappy & Lê, 2010).

Another idea is to sweeten beverages with nonnutritive sweeteners, as in the diet beverages. Again, this idea has been ineffective. Since the advent of diet drinks, obesity has continued to increase in prevalence, and consumption of sugars has *increased*. That is, many people seem to be drinking the diet drinks in addition to their usual sugar intake, and maybe even increasing their sugar intake. Why? In one study, rats mostly ate the usual laboratory diet, but sometimes one group ate naturally sweetened yogurt while the other group ate yogurt sweetened with saccharin (noncaloric). Overall, the rats eating the noncaloric ("diet") yogurt gained *more* weight. The interpretation is complex: Ordinarily, rats, like people, learn to calibrate the calories in their food. They learn that when they eat sweets, they gain a good deal of energy, and so they learn either to limit their intake of sweets or to compensate by eating less of something else. Rats that consumed noncaloric sweeteners lost this tendency. They learned that taste is a poor predictor of energy, and so they overate other foods and stopped compensating afterward. They also became less active (Swithers & Davidson, 2008). A similar study found that rats that sometimes ate "light" potato chips containing a fat substitute reacted by increasing their consumption of real fat, when it was available, and gaining weight (Swithers, Ogden, & Davidson, 2011).

If diet and exercise fail to help someone lose weight, another option is weight-loss drugs. Unfortunately, most of the drugs that help people lose weight produce unpleasant side effects. A new drug, lorcaserin, which stimulates one type of serotonin receptor, has relatively few side effects, but it is only modestly helpful in promoting weight loss. Other drugs are still in the experimental stage (Wyatt, 2013).

If someone with extreme obesity fails to respond to other treatments, an option is gastric bypass surgery, in which part of the stomach is removed or sewed off so that food cannot enter. Remember that stomach distension is a major contributor to satiety. By decreasing stomach size, the surgery makes it possible for a smaller meal to produce satiety. The most common result is that someone goes from being "morbidly obese" to just "obese," and that is a meaningful benefit. However, 10 percent to 20 percent of people experience serious side effects, including infections, bowel obstruction, leakage of food, and nutritional deficiencies (Powell et al., 2007). Surgery is worth considering only in severe cases of obesity.

Here is still another option, definitely experimental and controversial: People's digestive systems have thousands of species of microorganisms that help digest the foods and perform many other functions, some helpful to us and some harmful (Cryan & Dinan, 2012). The types of microorganisms found in obese people differ from those in leaner people. Researchers working with mice found that transferring microorganisms from lean mice to obese mice helped the obese mice lose weight (Ridaura et al., 2013). Umm . . . to be more specific, what they did was to transplant feces from one to another. Might this work with humans?

STOP&CHECK

22. In one study, rats eating the less-caloric yogurt gained more weight than those eating the more-caloric type. What explanation was proposed?

ANSWER

22. The rats unlearned their usual calibration that more sweets mean more energy and therefore stopped compensating after eating other sweets.

Bulimia Nervosa

Bulimia nervosa is a condition in which people alternate between binges of overeating and periods of strict dieting. Many, but not all, induce themselves to vomit. About 95 percent of people with bulimia also suffer from depression, anxiety, or other emotional problems (Hudson, Hiripi, Pope, & Kessler, 2007). In the United States, about 1.5 percent of women and 0.5 percent of men develop bulimia at some time in life. It has become more common over the years. That is, bulimia is more common among young people today than it ever was in their parents' generation and more common in their parents' generation than in their grandparents'. The increase is presumably due to the ready availability of large quantities of tasty high-calorie foods that were less abundant in previous eras.

On average, people with bulimia show a variety of biochemical abnormalities, including increased production of ghrelin, a hormone associated with increased appetite (Monteleone, Serritella, Scognamiglio, & Maj, 2010). The biochemistry is probably a result of the binges and purges, rather than a cause. After therapy that decreases the symptoms of bulimia, the ghrelin and other body chemicals return toward normal levels (Tanaka et al., 2006).

In important ways, bulimia resembles drug addiction (Hoebel, Rada, Mark, & Pothos, 1999). Eating tasty foods activates the same brain areas as addictive drugs, such as the nucleus accumbens. Drug addicts who cannot get drugs sometimes overeat instead, and food-deprived people or animals become more likely than others to use drugs.

Researchers examined rats that were food deprived for 12 hours a day, including the first 4 hours of their wakeful period, and then offered a very sweet, syrupy sugar solution. Over several weeks on this regimen, the rats drank more and more each day, especially during the first hour of availability each day. The intake released dopamine and opioid (opiatelike) compounds in the brain, similar to the effects of highly addicting drugs (Colantuoni et al., 2001, 2002). It also increased the levels of dopamine type 3 receptors in the brain—again, a trend resembling that of rats that receive morphine (Spangler et al., 2004). If they were then deprived of this sweet liquid, they showed withdrawal symptoms, including head shaking, teeth chattering, and tremors. An injection of morphine relieved these symptoms. In short, the rats showed clear indications of an addiction to big doses of sugar (Avena, Rada, & Hoebel, 2008). Similarly, we can regard bulimic cycles of dieting and binge eating as an addiction.

STOP&CHECK

23. What evidence from rats suggests that bulimia resembles an addiction?

ANSWER

23. Rats that alternate between food deprivation and a very sweet diet gradually eat more and more, and they react to deprivation of the sweet diet with head shaking and teeth chattering, like the symptoms of morphine withdrawal.

MODULE 9.3 ■ IN CLOSING

The Multiple Controls of Hunger

The brain areas that control eating monitor blood glucose, stomach distension, duodenal contents, body weight, fat cells, hormones, and more. Because the system is so complex, it can produce errors in many ways. However, the complexity of the system also provides a kind of security: If one part of the system makes a mistake, another part can counteract it. We notice people who choose a poor diet or eat the wrong amount. Perhaps we should be even more impressed by how many people eat appropriately. The regulation of eating succeeds not in spite of its complexity but because of it.

Summary

1. The ability to digest a food is one major determinant of preference for that food. For example, people who cannot digest lactose generally do not like to eat dairy products. **308**
2. Widespread beliefs that sugar causes hyperactivity and that turkey causes sleepiness are unfounded. However, research does support the idea that eating fish enhances some people's memory and reasoning. **308**
3. People and animals eat partly for the sake of taste. However, a sham-feeding animal, which tastes its foods but does not absorb them, eats far more than normal. Taste is not sufficient to satisfy hunger. **309**
4. Factors controlling hunger include distension of the stomach and intestines, secretion of CCK by the duodenum, and the availability of glucose and other nutrients to the cells. **310**
5. Appetite depends partly on the availability of glucose and other nutrients to the cells. The hormone insulin increases the entry of glucose to the cells, including cells that store nutrients for future use. Glucagon mobilizes

stored fuel and converts it to glucose in the blood. Thus, the combined influence of insulin and glucagon determines how much glucose is available at any time. **310**

6. Fat cells produce a peptide called leptin, which provides the brain with a signal about weight loss or gain and therefore corrects day-to-day errors in the amount of feeding. Deficiency of leptin production leads to obesity and inactivity. However, leptin deficiency is rare among humans. **312**
7. The arcuate nucleus of the hypothalamus receives signals of both hunger and satiety. Good-tasting foods and the transmitter ghrelin stimulate neurons that promote hunger. Glucose, insulin, leptin, and CCK stimulate neurons that promote satiety. **313**
8. Axons from the two kinds of neurons in the arcuate nucleus send competing messages to the paraventricular nucleus, releasing neuropeptides that are specific to the feeding system. The paraventricular nucleus inhibits the lateral nucleus of the hypothalamus. Hunger signals increase feeding by decreasing the inhibition from the paraventricular nucleus. **314**
9. The lateral nucleus of the hypothalamus facilitates feeding by axons that enhance taste responses elsewhere in the brain and increase the release of insulin and digestive juices. **315**
10. The ventromedial nucleus of the hypothalamus and the axons passing by it influence eating by regulating stomach emptying time and insulin secretion. Animals with damage in this area eat more frequently than normal because they store much of each meal as fat and then fail to mobilize their stored fats for current use. **316**
11. Obesity is partly under genetic control, although no single gene accounts for many cases of obesity. **317**
12. Dieting is seldom an effective means of long-term weight loss. Dieting combined with exercise is more effective, although at best it helps less than half of people. Reducing consumption of soft drinks is highly recommended. In more severe cases of obesity, people consider weight-loss drugs or surgery. **318**
13. Bulimia nervosa is characterized by alternation between undereating and overeating. It has been compared to addictive behaviors. **319**

Key Terms

Terms are defined in the module on the page number indicated. They're also presented in alphabetical order with definitions in the book's Subject Index/Glossary. Interactive flash cards, audio reviews, and crossword puzzles are among the online resources available to help you learn these terms and the concepts they represent.

agouti-related peptide (AgRP) **314**
arcuate nucleus **313**
bulimia nervosa **319**
cholecystokinin (CCK) **310**
duodenum **310**
ghrelin **314**
glucagon **311**
insulin **311**
lactase **308**
lactose **308**
lateral hypothalamus **315**
leptin **312**
melanocortin **314**
neuropeptide Y (NPY) **314**
sham-feeding **310**
splanchnic nerves **310**
vagus nerve **310**
ventromedial hypothalamus (VMH) **316**

Thought Question

For most people, insulin levels tend to be higher during the day than at night. Use this fact to explain why people grow hungry a few hours after a daytime meal but not so quickly at night.

MODULE 9.3 End of Module Quiz

1. People differ in their likelihood of consuming milk products in adulthood because of what type of genetic difference?
   a. Genetic variants in taste buds
   b. Genetic variants in neurotransmitters of the hypothalamus
   c. Genetic variants in ability to metabolize lactose
   d. Genetic variants in mechanisms of hypovolemic thirst

2. Which of the following describes the relationship between taste and eating?

a. Taste is sufficient to control eating.
b. Taste is necessary for eating.
c. Taste is both necessary and sufficient for eating.
d. Taste is neither necessary nor sufficient for eating, although it contributes.

3. After surgical removal of someone's stomach, what mechanism if any can produce satiety?

a. Distension of the duodenum
b. Entry of nutrients into the muscles and organs
c. None. The person stops eating altogether.
d. None. The person starts eating constantly.

4. When food distends the duodenum, the duodenum releases the hormone CCK. By what *peripheral* (non-CNS) mechanism does it increase satiety?

a. CCK increases stomach contractions.
b. CCK tightens the sphincter muscle between the stomach and the duodenum.
c. CCK increases the ability of nutrients to enter cells.
d. Cells in the hypothalamus release CCK as a neurotransmitter.

5. Increased blood glucose causes increased release of _____, which _____ the ability of glucose to enter the cells.

a. insulin ... increases
b. insulin ... decreases
c. glucagon ... increases
d. glucagon ... decreases

6. People with untreated type 1 diabetes have _____ levels of insulin, _____ levels of blood glucose, and _____ levels of hunger.

a. high ... high ... high
b. low ... high.... high
c. low ... low ... high
d. low ... low ... low
e. low ... high ... low

7. Leptin is produced by the _____ cells. In most cases it tends to _____ appetite.

a. fat ... decrease
b. hypothalamic ... decrease
c. pancreas ... increase
d. intestinal ... increase

8. Which is the only neuropeptide that increases hunger?

a. Ghrelin
b. Melanocortin
c. Leptin
d. Insulin

9. How do taste and ghrelin promote eating and arousal?

a. They increase excitation from the paraventricular nucleus to the arcuate nucleus, an area that excites the lateral hypothalamus.
b. They increase inhibition from the paraventricular nucleus to the arcuate nucleus, an area that inhibits the lateral hypothalamus.
c. They increase excitation from the arcuate nucleus to the paraventricular nucleus, an area that excites the lateral hypothalamus.
d. They increase inhibition from the arcuate nucleus to the paraventricular nucleus, an area that inhibits the lateral hypothalamus.

10. If researchers could find a safe drug that stimulates melanocortin receptors, what would be the probable benefit?

a. Improving memory
b. Helping people go to sleep
c. Combatting anorexia nervosa
d. Helping people lose weight

11. The lateral hypothalamus facilitates feeding in several ways. Which of the following is *not* one of them?

a. It alters taste sensations.
b. It enhances responses to food in the cerebral cortex.
c. It increases insulin secretion.
d. It decreases digestive secretions.

12. Damage to the ventromedial hypothalamus produces a steady increase in the release of insulin. Which of the following is a consequence?

a. The animal decreases its appetite for carbohydrates.
b. More of each meal is stored as fat.
c. The animal eats fewer, but larger meals.
d. Body temperature increases.

13. What evidence suggests that high ghrelin levels lead to weight gain in Prader-Willi syndrome?
   a. People with this syndrome continue to have high ghrelin levels regardless of whether they gain or lose weight.
   b. A mutated gene for melanocortin causes nearly 5 percent of cases of severe obesity.
   c. Ghrelin stimulates hunger-related neurons in the arcuate nucleus.
   d. People with Prader-Willi syndrome have other problems in addition to weight gain.

14. How has the prevalence of obesity changed since the availability of high-fructose corn syrup and artificially sweetened diet beverages?
   a. Each of them helped lower the prevalence of obesity.
   b. High-fructose corn syrup helped lower obesity rates, but diet drinks did not.
   c. Diet drinks helped lower obesity rates, but high-fructose corn syrup did not.
   d. The prevalence of obesity has increased after the availability of both of these.

15. People with bulimia have elevated ghrelin levels. Is this abnormality a likely cause of bulimia? And what is the evidence?
   a. No. It is probably not a cause. The abnormality is common in the ethnic groups who are most likely to develop bulimia.
   b. No. It is probably not a cause. As people recover from bulimia, their ghrelin level returns toward normal.
   c. Yes. It is probably a cause. People who show high ghrelin early in life are likely to develop bulimia later.
   d. Yes. It is probably a cause. Inducing high ghrelin in rats causes the rats to develop bulimia.

ANSWERS: 1c, 2d, 3a, 4b, 5a, 6b, 7a, 8a, 9d, 10d, 11d, 12b, 13a, 14d, 15b.

Suggestions for Further Reading

Allen, J. S. (2012). *The omnivorous mind: Our evolving relationship with food*. Cambridge, MA: Harvard University Press.

A discussion of all the ways eating affects our lives.

Gisolfi, C. V., & Mora, F. (2000). *The hot brain: Survival, temperature, and the human body*. Cambridge, MA: MIT Press.

Discusses research on temperature regulation.

Widmaier, E. P. (1998). *Why geese don't get obese (and we do)*. New York: Freeman.

Lighthearted and often entertaining discussion of the physiology of eating, thirst, and temperature regulation.

Kevin Schafer/Getty Images

Reproductive Behaviors

10

CHAPTER OUTLINE

MODULE 10.1 Sex and Hormones
Organizing Effects of Sex Hormones
Activating Effects of Sex Hormones
Parental Behavior
In Closing: Reproductive Behaviors and Motivations
MODULE 10.2 Variations in Sexual Behavior
Evolutionary Interpretations of Mating Behavior
Gender Identity and Gender-Differentiated Behaviors
Sexual Orientation
In Closing: We Are Not All the Same

LEARNING OBJECTIVES

After studying this chapter, you should be able to:

1. Describe the role of the SRY gene in mammalian sexual development.
2. Distinguish between organizing and activating effects of hormones.
3. Explain the role of testosterone in the development of genital anatomy.
4. List some examples of activating effects on the behavior of males and females.
5. Describe the roles of hormones and experiences in rodent parental behavior.
6. Discuss possible evolutionary explanations of men's and women's sexual behaviors.
7. Explain the relevance of intersexes for understanding the role of hormones in the development of sex-typed behaviors.
8. Discuss possible biological influences on the development of sexual orientation.

What good is sex? Well, yes, of course: We enjoy it. Presumably we evolved to enjoy it because sexual activity sometimes leads to reproduction, which passes on genes. You evolved from a long line of ancestors who engaged in sexual activity at least once.

But why did we evolve to reproduce sexually instead of individually? In some species of reptiles, a female sometimes has offspring by herself, using only her own genes and none from a male (Booth, Johnson, Moore, Schal, & Vargo, 2011). Reproduction without sex would be easier and would produce offspring exactly like yourself, instead of only half like yourself. What advantage does sex provide?

You might suggest the advantage of having a partner while you rear children. In humans, that kind of cooperation is usually helpful. However, many species reproduce sexually even though the male doesn't help at all with the young, and in some fish species, *neither* sex cares for the young—they just release their sperm and eggs in the same place and then depart.

Biologists' explanation is that sexual reproduction increases variation and thereby enables quick evolutionary adaptations to changes in the environment, especially new viruses and parasites (Morran, Schmidt, Gelarden, Parrish, & Lively, 2011). Certain invertebrates reproduce sexually when they live in a complex and changing environment, but reproduce without sex when they live in a constant environment (Becks & Agrawal, 2010). Sex also corrects errors: If you have a disadvantageous mutation in one gene and your mate has a disadvantageous mutation in a different gene, your children could have a normal copy of both genes.

In this chapter, we consider many questions about sexual reproduction that we often ignore or take for granted. We also consider some of the ways in which being biologically male or female influences our behavior.

OPPOSITE: Humans may be the only species that plans parenthood, but all species have a strong biological drive that leads to parenthood.

Sex and Hormones

Being male or female influences many aspects of your life. For humans and other mammals, it all begins with your genes. Females have two X chromosomes, whereas males have an X and a Y chromosome. Biologists used to believe that the chromosomes determine sexual differentiation entirely through hormones. Let's examine that story, and then see how it is incomplete.

Male and female mammals start with the same anatomy during an early stage of prenatal development. Both have a set of **Müllerian ducts** (precursors to female internal structures) and a set of **Wolffian ducts** (precursors to male internal structures), as well as undifferentiated gonads that are on their way to becoming either testes or ovaries. If you look at an embryo at an early stage of development, you cannot tell whether it is male or female. A little later, a gene on the male's Y chromosome, the **SRY** (sex-determining region on the Y chromosome) **gene**, causes those primitive gonads to develop into **testes**, the sperm-producing organs. The testes produce **androgens** (hormones that are more abundant in males) that increase the growth of the testes, causing them to produce more androgens and so forth. That positive feedback cannot go on forever, but it lasts for a period of early development. Androgens also cause the primitive Wolffian ducts, precursors for other male reproductive structures, to develop into *seminal vesicles* (saclike structures that store semen) and the *vas deferens* (a duct from the testis into the penis). The testes also produce *Müllerian-inhibiting hormone (MIH)*, which causes the Müllerian ducts to degenerate. The final result is the development of a penis and scrotum. Because females do not have the SRY gene, their gonads develop into **ovaries** instead of testes, and their Wolffian ducts degenerate. Because their ovaries do not produce MIH, females' Müllerian ducts develop and mature into oviducts, uterus, and the upper vagina. Figure 10.1 shows how the primitive unisex structures develop into male or female external genitals.

From then on, the males' testes produce more androgens than **estrogens** (hormones that are more abundant in females), whereas the females' ovaries produce more estrogens than androgens. The adrenal glands also produce both androgens and estrogens. These two types of hormones have similar effects in some ways and opposing effects in others.

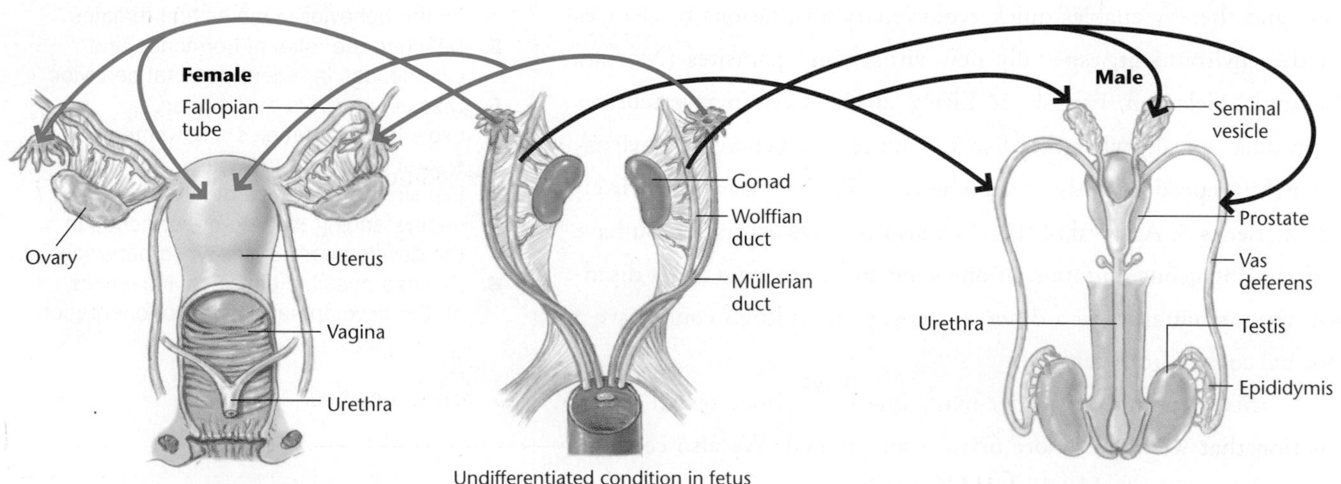

FIGURE 10.1 Differentiation of human genitals
We begin life with undifferentiated structures, as shown in the center. The gonad shown in blue for the fetus develops into either the ovaries, as shown on the left, or the testes, as shown on the right. The Müllerian ducts of the fetus develop into a female's uterus, oviducts, and the upper part of the vagina. The Wolffian ducts of the fetus develop into a male's seminal vesicles (which store semen) and vas deferens, a duct from the testis into the penis. The Müllerian ducts degenerate in males, and the Wolffian ducts degenerate in females. *Source:* Based on Netter, 1983

They are **steroid hormones**, containing four carbon rings, as in Figure 10.2.

Steroids exert their effects in three ways (Nadal, Díaz, & Valverde, 2001). First, they bind to membrane receptors, like neurotransmitters, exerting rapid effects. Second, they enter cells and activate certain kinds of proteins in the cytoplasm. Third, they bind to receptors that bind to chromosomes, where they activate or inactivate certain genes (see Figure 10.3).

Androgens and estrogens are categories of chemicals; neither androgen nor estrogen is a specific chemical itself. The most widely known androgen is **testosterone.** The most prominent type of estrogen is **estradiol. Progesterone**, another predominantly female hormone, prepares the uterus for the implantation of a fertilized ovum and promotes the maintenance of pregnancy.

For many years, biologists assumed that hormones account for all the biological differences between males and females. Later research demonstrated that some differences depend directly on control by the X and Y chromosomes independently of hormones (Arnold, 2009). At least three genes on the Y chromosome (found only in men) are active in specific brain areas, and at least one gene on the X chromosome is active only in the female brain (Arnold, 2004; Carruth, Reisert, & Arnold, 2002; Vawter et al., 2004). In both humans and nonhumans, the Y chromosome has many sites that alter the expression of genes on other chromosomes (Lemos, Araripe, & Hartl, 2008). In short, genes on the X and Y chromosomes produce sex differences in addition to those that we can trace to androgens and estrogens.

Backbone of all steroid molecules

CH_2OH C=O OH HO O

Cortisol

OH O

Testosterone (an androgen)

OH HO

Estradiol (an estrogen)

CH_3 C=O O

Progesterone

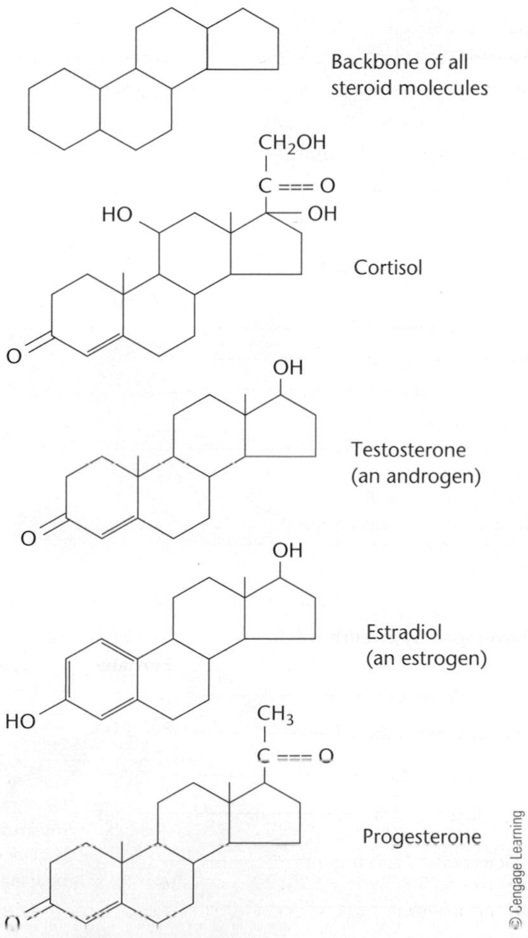

FIGURE 10.2 Steroid hormones
Note the chemical similarity between testosterone and estradiol.

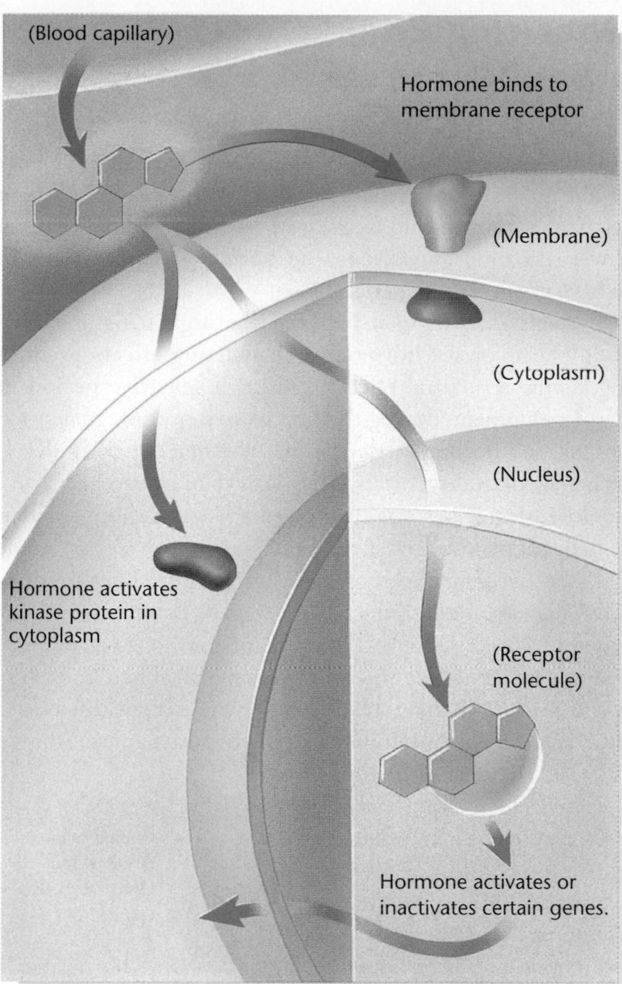

FIGURE 10.3 Routes of action for steroid hormones
Steroid hormones such as estrogens and androgens bind to membrane receptors, activate proteins in the cytoplasm, and activate or inactivate certain genes. *Source:* Revised from Starr & Taggart, 1989

STOP&CHECK

1. What does the SRY gene do?

2. How do sex hormones affect neurons?

ANSWERS

1. The SRY gene (sex-determining region on the Y chromosome) causes the undifferentiated gonad of a mammal to develop into a testis, which then produces testosterone and MIH to direct development toward the male pattern. **2.** Sex hormones, which are steroids, bind to receptors on the membrane, activate certain proteins in the cell's cytoplasm, and activate or inactivate particular genes.

Organizing Effects of Sex Hormones

If we injected estrogens into adult males and androgens into adult females, could we make males act like females or females act like males? Researchers of the 1900s, working with a variety of mammals and birds, were surprised to find that the answer was almost always *no*. But hormones injected early in life have much stronger effects.

Biologists distinguish between the organizing and activating effects of sex hormones. **Organizing effects** produce long-lasting structural effects. During a **sensitive period** in early development, during the first trimester of pregnancy for humans, sex hormones determine whether the body develops female or male genitals. They lead to more receptors, and therefore greater sensitivity, around the female nipples than the male nipples (Liu et al., 2012).

Later researchers recognized that sex hormones produce additional organizing effects at puberty (Schulz, Molenda-Figueira, & Sisk, 2009). The surge of hormones at puberty produces breast development in women, facial hair and penis growth in men, changes in voice, and male–female differences in the anatomy of certain parts of the hypothalamus (Ahmed et al., 2008). Some of the differences in brain anatomy between males and females increase during this time (Chung, de Vries, & Swaab, 2002). The changes developing at puberty persist throughout life, even after the concentration of sex hormones declines.

Activating effects are more temporary, continuing only while a hormone is present or shortly beyond. For example, current hormone levels influence the degree of sex drive. The burst of hormones during pregnancy produce complex, temporary effects on emotional arousal, aggressive behavior, learning, and cognition (Agrati, Fernández-Guasti, Ferreño, & Ferreira, 2011; Workman, Barha, & Galea, 2012). We shall encounter other examples later in this chapter. The organizing effects set the stage for activating effects. For example, organizing effects set up the female hypothalamus such that later hormones can activate the menstrual cycle. The distinction between organizing and activating effects is not absolute, as a hormone can produce a combination of temporary and longer-lasting effects (Arnold & Breedlove, 1985; C. L. Williams, 1986). Still, the distinction is generally useful.

Let's focus on the organizing effects during the early sensitive period, when hormones determine whether an embryo develops a male or female anatomy. You might imagine that testosterone produces male anatomy and estradiol produces female anatomy. No. In mammals, differentiation of the external genitals and several aspects of brain development depend mainly on the level of testosterone, not estradiol. A high level of testosterone, converted within cells to dihydrotestosterone, causes the external genitals to develop the male pattern, and a low level leads to the female pattern. Estradiol produces important effects on the internal organs, but it has little effect on the external genitals.

The human sensitive period for genital formation occurs during the first trimester of pregnancy (Money & Ehrhardt, 1972). At first, the external genitals of males and females look the same, as shown in Figure 10.4. As a male's developing

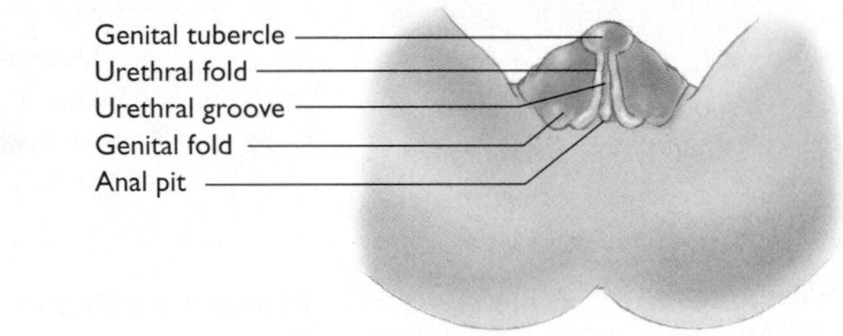

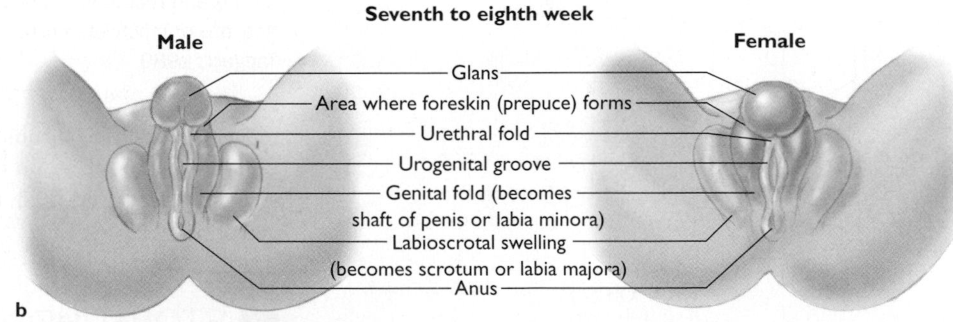

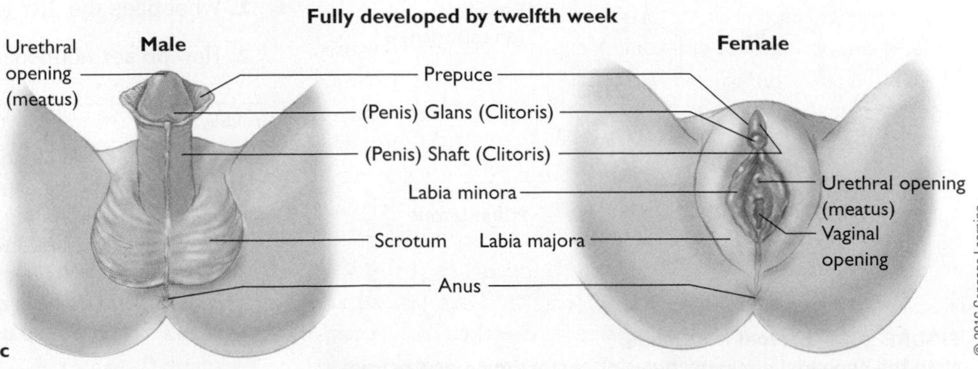

FIGURE 10.4 Development of the Human Genitals
The initial appearance is the same for all. Depending on the level of testosterone and its metabolite, dihydrotestosterone, the embryo develops either the male pattern or the female pattern.

testes secrete testosterone, certain enzymes convert it to dihydrotestosterone, which is far more effective at promoting growth of the penis. If levels of dihydrotesterone are high enough, the tiny genital tubercle grows and develops into a penis. If the levels are low, the tubercle develops into a clitoris. Similarly, depending on levels of testosterone and dihydrotestosterone, the embryo develops either a scrotum, characteristic of males, or labia, characteristic of females.

Most of the research exploring sexual development has been in rodents. In rats, testosterone begins masculinizing the external genitals during the last several days of pregnancy and first few days after birth and then continues masculinizing them at a declining rate for the next month (Bloch & Mills, 1995; Bloch, Mills, & Gale, 1995; E. C. Davis, Shryne, & Gorski, 1995; Rhees, Shryne, & Gorski, 1990). A female rat that is injected with testosterone during this period is partly masculinized, just as if her own body had produced the testosterone (I. L. Ward & Ward, 1985). Her clitoris grows larger than normal, and her behavior is partly masculinized. She approaches sexually receptive females (Woodson & Balleine, 2002), mounts them, and makes copulatory thrusting movements rather than arching her back and allowing males to mount her. In short, early testosterone promotes the male pattern and inhibits the female pattern (Gorski, 1985; J. D. Wilson, George, & Griffin, 1981).

Injecting a genetic male with estrogens produces little effect on his external anatomy. However, if he lacks androgens or androgen receptors, he develops the female-typical pattern of anatomy and behavior. That outcome could result from castration (removal of the testes), a genetic deficiency of androgen receptors, or prenatal exposure to drugs that interfere with androgen response, such as alcohol, marijuana, haloperidol (an antipsychotic drug), phthalates (chemicals common in many manufactured products), and cocaine (Ahmed, Shryne, Gorski, Branch, & Taylor, 1991; Dalterio & Bartke, 1979; Hull, Nishita, Bitran, & Dalterio, 1984; Raum, McGivern, Peterson, Shryne, & Gorski, 1990; Swan et al., 2010). Obviously, the amount of interference depends on the type of drug and the amount of exposure. To a slight extent, even aspirin interferes with the male pattern of development (Amateau & McCarthy, 2004). Although estradiol does not significantly alter a male's external anatomy, estradiol and several related compounds do produce abnormalities of the prostate gland—the gland that produces a fluid that accompanies and protects sperm cells when ejaculated during intercourse. Some of those estradiol-like compounds are now prevalent in the linings of plastic bottles and cans, so almost everyone is exposed to them (Timms, Howdeshell, Barton, Richter, & vom Saal, 2005). In short, male development is vulnerable to many sources of interference.

The overall mechanism of early sexual differentiation has been described by saying that nature's default setting is to make every mammal a female unless told to do otherwise. Add early testosterone and the individual becomes a male; without testosterone, it develops as a female, regardless of the amount of estradiol or other estrogens. That generalization is an overstatement. A genetic female that lacks estradiol during early life develops approximately normal female external anatomy but does not develop normal sexual behavior. Even if she is given estradiol injections as an adult, she shows little sexual response toward either male or female partners (Bakker, Honda, Harada, & Balthazart, 2002; Brock, Baum, & Bakker, 2011). So estradiol contributes to female development, including certain aspects of brain differentiation, even if it is not important for external anatomy.

STOP & CHECK

3. What would be the genital appearance of a mammal exposed to high levels of both androgens and estrogens during early development? What if it were exposed to low levels of both?

4. From the standpoint of protecting a male fetus's sexual development, what are some drugs that a pregnant woman should avoid?

ANSWERS

3. A mammal exposed to high levels of both male and female hormones will appear male. One exposed to low levels of both will appear female. Genital development depends mostly on the presence or absence of androgens, and is nearly independent of estradiol levels. **4.** Pregnant women should avoid alcohol, marijuana, haloperidol, phthalates, and cocaine because these drugs interfere with male sexual development. Even aspirin and the chemicals lining bottles and cans produce mild abnormalities. Obviously, the results depend on both quantities and timing of exposure to these chemicals.

Sex Differences in the Hypothalamus

In addition to controlling differences in the external genitals, sex hormones early in life influence development in parts of the hypothalamus, amygdala, and other brain areas (Shah et al., 2004). For example, one area in the anterior hypothalamus, known as the **sexually dimorphic nucleus**, is larger in males than in females and contributes to control of male sexual behavior, in ways that vary from one species to another. Parts of the female hypothalamus generate a cyclic pattern of hormone release, as in the human menstrual cycle. The male hypothalamus cannot produce such cycles, and neither can the hypothalamus of a female who was exposed to extra testosterone early in development.

In rodents, testosterone exerts much of its organizing effect through a surprising route: After it enters a neuron in early development, it is converted to estradiol! Testosterone and estradiol are chemically very similar, as you see in Figure 10.2. In organic chemistry, a ring of six carbon atoms containing three double bonds is an *aromatic* compound. An enzyme found in the brain can *aromatize* testosterone into estradiol. Drugs that prevent testosterone from being aromatized to estradiol block the organizing effects of testosterone on sexual development and thereby impair male sexual behavior and fertility (Gerardin & Pereira, 2002; Rochira et al., 2001).

Why, then, does a female rodent's own estradiol fail to masculinize her hypothalamus? During the early sensitive period, immature mammals have a protein called **alpha-fetoprotein** (Gorski, 1980; MacLusky & Naftolin, 1981). Alpha-fetoprotein in rodents binds with estradiol and prevents it from entering cells, where it could produce masculinizing effects. Because testosterone does not bind to alpha-fetoprotein, it enters neurons where enzymes convert it into estradiol. That is, testosterone is a way of getting estradiol to its receptors when estradiol circulating in the blood is inactivated.

This explanation of testosterone's effects makes sense of an otherwise puzzling fact: Injecting a large amount of estradiol actually masculinizes a female rodent's development. The reason is that normal amounts are bound to alpha-fetoprotein, but a larger amount exceeds the capacity of alpha-fetoprotein and therefore enters the cells and masculinizes them.

In primates such as humans, the mechanism is different. Testosterone enters neurons where it exerts its masculinizing effects directly, and it does not need to be aromatized to estradiol (Thornton, Zehr, & Loose, 2009). The similarity between primates and rodents is that in both cases, testosterone masculinizes the brain in one way or another.

STOP&CHECK

5. How would the external genitals appear on a genetic female rat that lacked alpha-fetoprotein?

ANSWER

5. A female that lacked alpha-fetoprotein would be masculinized by her own estradiol, as researchers have in fact demonstrated (Bakker et al., 2006).

Sex Differences in Childhood Behavior

As prenatal hormones influence the structure of the male or female brain, do they also contribute to differences in behavior? In the second module of this chapter, we shall consider influences on sexual behavior and sexual orientation, but at this point let's consider possible influences on childhood behavior.

Typically, many boys play mostly with toy cars and trains, balls, guns, and roughhouse activities. Girls are more likely than boys to spend time with dolls, toy tea sets, and calmer, cooperative play. Some children have a stronger preference for boys' or girls' activities than others do, and their preferences tend to be consistent over time. Those who show the greatest preference for typical boys' activities at age 3 usually show the greatest amount of typical boys' activities at age 13, and those with the greatest preference for girls' activities at 3 usually show the greatest preference for girls' activities at age 13 (Golombok, Rust, Zervoulis, Golding, & Hines, 2012).

Much of this pattern results from socialization, as most parents give their sons and daughters different sets of toys. However, socialization need not be the whole story. Indeed, it may be that parents give those toys because previous generations found that boys and girls typically differ in their interests from the start. In one study, infants 3 to 8 months old (too young to walk, crawl, or do much with a toy) sat in front of pairs of toys, where researchers could monitor eye movements. The girls looked at dolls more than they looked at toy trucks. The boys looked at both about equally (Alexander, Wilcox, & Woods, 2009). (Note that the children had not seen the trucks move, so at this point the trucks were simply unknown objects.) This study suggests a predisposition for boys and girls to prefer different types of toys, although we should consider an alternative explanation: Girls mature faster than boys, and perhaps it was harder for boys at this age to show a preference, whatever that preference may have been.

In two studies male monkeys played with balls and toy cars more than female monkeys did, whereas the females played more with dolls (Alexander & Hines, 2002; Hassett, Siebert, & Wallen, 2008). Figure 10.5 summarizes the results from one of those studies. Monkeys' preferences were not as strong as most children's, but it is noteworthy that the sexes differed at all in their first encounters with these toys. Other studies found that prenatal injections of testosterone to female monkey fetuses led to increased masculine-type play after they were born. In those cases the focus was on spontaneous, rough-and-tumble play rather than playing with toys, but the idea is similar (Wallen, 2005).

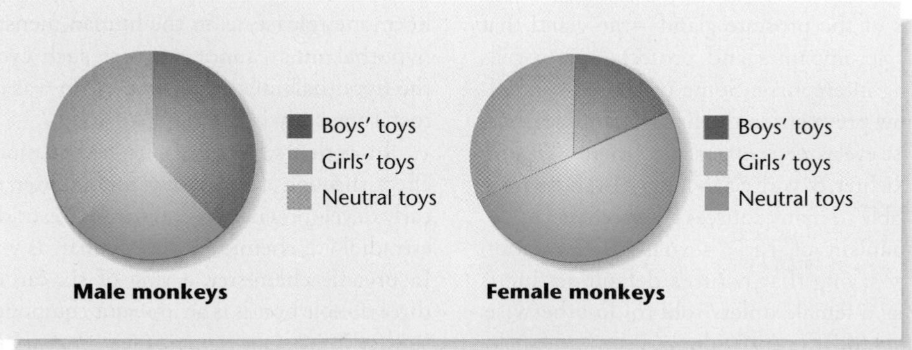

FIGURE 10.5 Toy choices by male and female monkeys
Male monkeys spent more time than female monkeys did with "boys' toys." *Source:* Based on data from G. M. Alexander & M. Hines (2002). Sex differences in response to children's toys in nonhuman primates (*Cercopithecus aethiops sabaeus*). *Evolution and Human Behavior*, *23*, pp. 467–479.

Two studies correlated chemicals in the mother's blood during pregnancy with their children's choices of toys years later. Researchers took blood samples from pregnant women, measuring testosterone (some of which would enter the fetus). When the daughters reached age 3½, researchers observed their toy play. The girls who had been exposed to higher testosterone levels in prenatal life showed slightly elevated preferences for boys' toys (Hines et al., 2002). These girls were anatomically normal, and we have no reason to believe that the parents treated girls differently based on how much testosterone had been present in prenatal life. Another study measured testosterone levels in infants over the first 6 months and compared results to their toy choices at age 14 months. Girls with higher testosterone levels in early infancy spent more time than average playing with toy trains, compared to other girls. Boys with higher testosterone levels spent less time than other boys did playing with dolls (Lamminmäki et al., 2012).

In another study, researchers measured phthalate levels in pregnant women. Phthalates inhibit testosterone production. U.S. law bans phthalates from children's toys, but pregnant women are exposed to phthalates from other sources, including perfumes, hair spray, food packaging, and others. Researchers measured phthalate levels in pregnant women's urine samples and compared results to the sons' toy use at ages 3 to 6. On average, sons of women with high phthalate levels showed less interest in typical boys' toys, and more interest in typical girls' toys (Swan et al., 2010). In summary, these studies suggest that prenatal hormones, especially testosterone, alter the brain in ways that influence differences between boys and girls in their activities and interests.

Do these studies imply that prenatal hormones determine toy preferences, regardless of rearing? No. Prenatal hormones combine forces with rearing experiences. When a child shows a preference for a certain kind of toy, even if it is just a small preference, parents tend to provide more of that kind of toy and more opportunities to strengthen that preference. Psychologists call this a "multiplier effect" (Dickens & Flynn, 2001). Furthermore, if most boys in the past have preferred one kind of toy and most girls preferred another, parents start with this presupposition and provide those toys from the start.

STOP&CHECK

6. What evidence most directly links children's toy play to prenatal hormones?

ANSWER

6. Girls whose mothers had higher testosterone levels during pregnancy tend to play with boys' toys more than the average for other girls. Boys whose mothers had higher phthalate exposure tend to play with boys' toys less than the average for other boys.

Activating Effects of Sex Hormones

At any time in life, not just during a sensitive period, current levels of testosterone or estradiol exert activating effects, temporarily modifying behavior. Changes in hormonal secretions influence sexual behavior within 15 minutes (Taziaux, Keller, Bakker, & Balthazart, 2007). Behaviors can also influence hormonal secretions. For example, when doves court each other, each stage of their behavior initiates hormonal changes that alter the birds' readiness for the next sequence of behaviors (C. Erickson & Lehrman, 1964; Lehrman, 1964; Martinez-Vargas & Erickson, 1973).

In addition to the sex hormones, the pituitary hormone **oxytocin** is also important for reproductive behavior. Oxytocin stimulates contractions of the uterus during delivery of a baby, and it stimulates the mammary gland to release milk. Sexual pleasure also releases oxytocin, especially at orgasm (M. R. Murphy, Checkley, Seckl, & Lightman, 1990). People typically experience a state of relaxation shortly after orgasm as a result of oxytocin release. Oxytocin is apparently responsible for the calmness and lack of anxiety after orgasm (Waldherr & Neumann, 2007).

Males

Testosterone, essential for male sexual arousal, acts partly by increasing touch sensitivity in the penis (Etgen, Chu, Fiber, Karkanias, & Morales, 1999). Sex hormones also bind to receptors that increase responses in parts of the hypothalamus, including the ventromedial nucleus, the medial preoptic area (MPOA), and the anterior hypothalamus.

Testosterone primes the MPOA and several other brain areas to release dopamine. MPOA neurons release dopamine strongly during sexual activity, and the more dopamine they release, the more likely the male is to copulate (Putnam, Du, Sato, & Hull, 2001). Castrated male rats produce normal amounts of dopamine in the MPOA, but they do not release it in the presence of a receptive female, and they do not attempt to copulate (Hull, Du, Lorrain, & Matuszewich, 1997).

In moderate concentrations, dopamine stimulates mostly type D_1 and D_5 receptors, which facilitate erection of the penis in the male (Hull et al., 1992) and sexually receptive postures in the female (Apostolakis et al., 1996). In higher concentrations, dopamine stimulates type D_2 receptors, which lead to orgasm (Giuliani & Ferrari, 1996; Hull et al., 1992). Whereas dopamine stimulates sexual activity, the neurotransmitter serotonin inhibits it by blocking dopamine release (Hull et al., 1999). Many popular antidepressant drugs increase serotonin activity, and one of their side effects is decreased sexual arousal.

Levels of testosterone correlate positively with men's sexual arousal and their drive to seek sexual partners. Researchers found that, on average, married men and men living with a woman in a committed relationship have lower testosterone levels than single, unpaired men of the same age (M. McIntyre et al., 2006). Two interpretations are likely: One is that marriage leads to decreased testosterone levels, because of decreased need to compete for a sexual partner. Consistent with this idea, one study found increased testosterone levels around the time of a divorce (Mazur & Michalek, 1998). The other interpretation is that men with lower testosterone levels are more likely than others to marry and remain married, and research clearly supports that idea as well (van Anders & Watson, 2006). Similar studies found that single women had higher testosterone levels than women with a long-term partner, either homosexual or heterosexual (van Anders & Goldey, 2010; van Anders & Watson, 2006). Also, both men and women with high testosterone levels are more likely than average to seek additional sex partners, even after they marry or establish a long-term relationship (M. McIntyre et al., 2006; van Anders, Hamilton, & Watson, 2007).

Decreases in testosterone levels generally decrease male sexual activity. For example, castration (removal of the testes) generally decreases a man's sexual interest and activity (Carter, 1992). However, low testosterone is not the usual basis for **impotence**, the inability to have an erection. The most common cause is impaired blood circulation, especially in older men. The drug sildenafil (Viagra) increases male sexual ability by prolonging the effects of nitric oxide, which increases blood flow to the penis (Rowland & Burnett, 2000). (As mentioned in Chapter 2, nitric oxide also increases blood flow in the brain.)

Testosterone reduction has sometimes been tried as a means of controlling sex offenders, including exhibitionists, rapists, child molesters, and those who commit incest. One major practical problem is getting sex offenders to continue taking drugs that block testosterone (Hughes, 2007). Another drawback is the side effects of testosterone deprivation, including weight gain, diabetes, and depression (Giltay & Gooren, 2009).

STOP&CHECK

7. By what mechanism does testosterone affect the hypothalamic areas responsible for sexual behavior?

8. Why do married men tend to have lower testosterone levels than single men of the same age?

ANSWERS

7. Testosterone primes hypothalamic cells to be ready to release dopamine. It also increases sensitivity in the genital area. **8.** Men with lower testosterone levels are more likely to get married than are men with higher testosterone levels. There may also be a tendency for testosterone levels to drop after marriage.

Females

A woman's hypothalamus and pituitary interact with the ovaries to produce the **menstrual cycle**, a periodic variation in hormones and fertility over the course of about 28 days (see Figure 10.6). After the end of a menstrual period, the anterior pituitary releases **follicle-stimulating hormone (FSH)**, which promotes the growth of a follicle in the ovary. The follicle nurtures the *ovum* (egg cell) and produces several types of estrogen, including estradiol. Toward the middle of the menstrual cycle, the follicle builds up more and more receptors

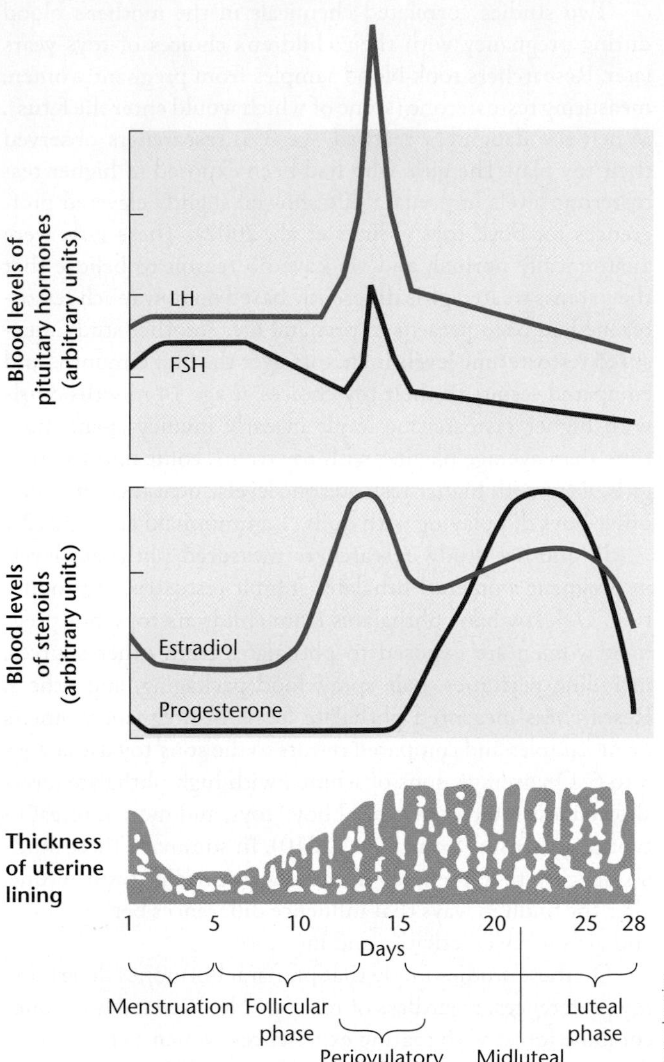

FIGURE 10.6 Blood levels of four hormones during the human menstrual cycle
Note that estrogen and progesterone are both at high levels during the midluteal phase but drop sharply at menstruation.

to FSH, so even though the actual concentration of FSH in the blood is decreasing, its effects on the follicle increase. As a result, the follicle produces increasing amounts of estradiol. The increased release of estradiol causes an increased release of FSH as well as a sudden surge in the release of **luteinizing hormone (LH)** from the anterior pituitary (see the top graph in Figure 10.6). FSH and LH combine to cause the follicle to release an ovum.

The remnant of the follicle (now called the *corpus luteum*) releases the hormone progesterone, which prepares the uterus for the implantation of a fertilized ovum. Progesterone also inhibits the further release of LH. If the woman is pregnant, estradiol and progesterone levels continue to increase. If she is not pregnant, both hormones decline (as shown in Figure 10.6), the lining of the uterus is cast off (menstruation), and the cycle begins again.

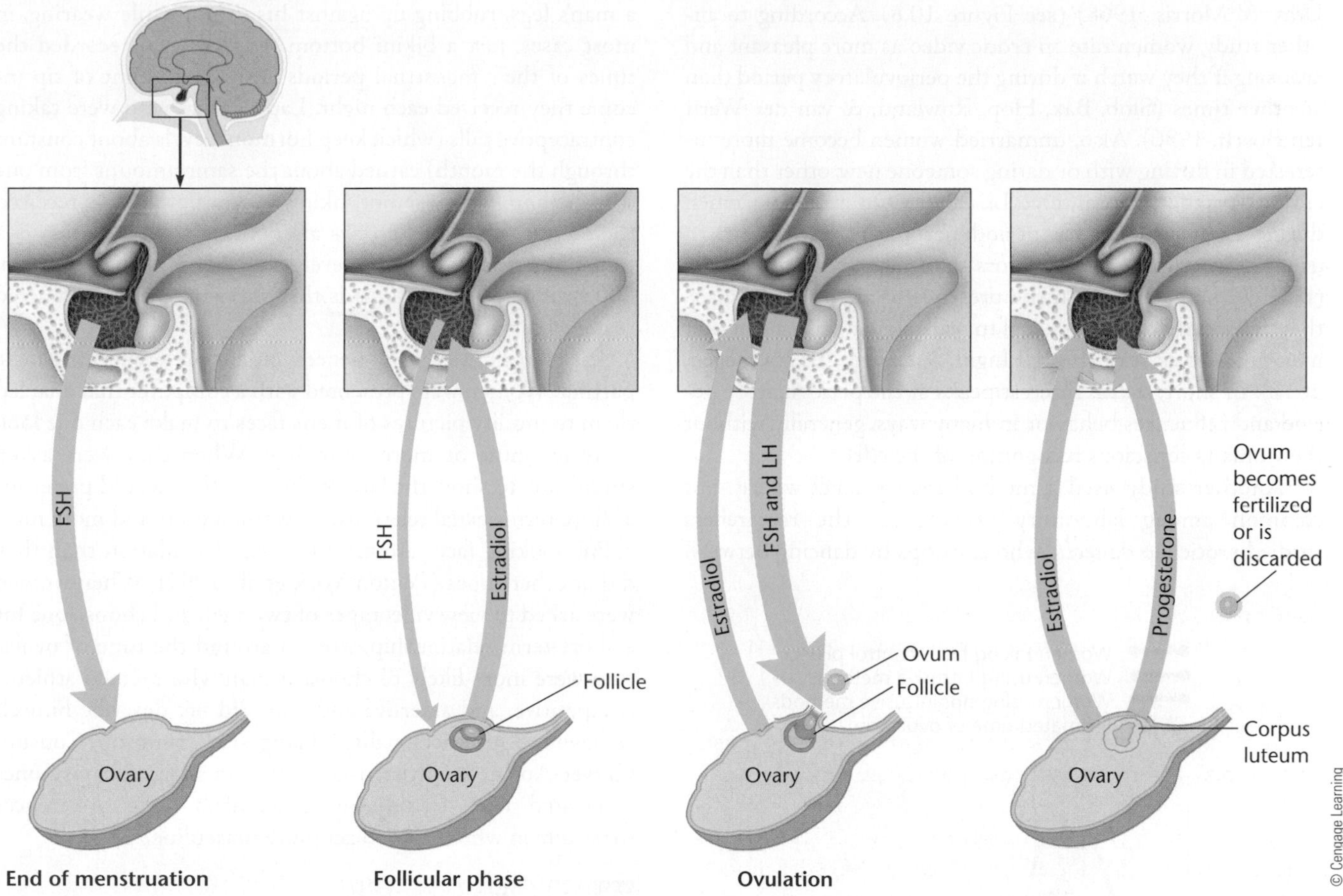

FIGURE 10.7 Interactions between the pituitary and the ovary
FSH from the pituitary stimulates a follicle of the ovary to develop and produce estradiol, releasing of a burst of FSH and LH from the pituitary. Those hormones cause the follicle to release its ovum and become a corpus luteum. The corpus luteum releases progesterone while the ovary releases estradiol.

One consequence of high estradiol and progesterone levels during pregnancy is fluctuating activity at the serotonin 3 ($5HT_3$) receptor, which is responsible for nausea (Rupprecht et al., 2001). Pregnant women often experience nausea because of the heightened activity of that receptor. Figure 10.7 summarizes the interactions between the pituitary and the ovary. Increased sensitivity to nausea may be an evolved adaptation to minimize the risk of eating something harmful to the fetus.

Birth-control pills prevent pregnancy by interfering with the usual feedback cycle between the ovaries and the pituitary. The most widely used birth-control pill, the *combination pill*, containing estrogen and progesterone, prevents the surge of FSH and LH that would otherwise release an ovum. The estrogen–progesterone combination also thickens the mucus of the cervix, making it harder for a sperm to reach the egg, and prevents an ovum, if released, from implanting in the uterus. Thus, the pill prevents pregnancy in many ways. Note, however, that it does not protect against sexually transmitted diseases such as AIDS or syphilis. "Safe sex" must go beyond the prevention of pregnancy.

In female rats, a combination of estradiol and progesterone is the most effective combination for enhancing sexual behavior (Matuszewich, Lorrain, & Hull, 2000). Estradiol increases the sensitivity of the *pudendal nerve*, which transmits tactile stimulation from the vagina and cervix to the brain (Komisaruk, Adler, & Hutchison, 1972).

For humans, the results concerning female sexual arousal are a bit more complex. When researchers compared young married women, they found that frequency of sexual intercourse correlated highly with the amount of testosterone that women produced at the **periovulatory period**, the days around the middle of the menstrual cycle, when fertility is highest (Morris, Udry, Khan-Dawood, & Dawood, 1987; Persky, Lief, Strauss, Miller, & O'Brien, 1978). However, a study comparing women's increases and decreases of sexual interest from day to day across one or two months found that sexual desire correlated strongly with changes in levels of estradiol, not testosterone (Roney & Simmons, 2013). Many women report a drop in sexual desire after surgical removal of their ovaries, resulting in lower estradiol levels (Graziottin, Koochaki, Rodenberg, & Dennerstein, 2009).

According to two studies, women not taking birth-control pills initiate sexual activity more often (either with a partner or by masturbation) during the periovulatory period than at other times of the month (D. B. Adams, Gold, & Burt, 1978;

Udry & Morris, 1968) (see Figure 10.8). According to another study, women rate an erotic video as more pleasant and arousing if they watch it during the periovulatory period than at other times (Slob, Bax, Hop, Rowland, & van der Werff ten Bosch, 1996). Also, unmarried women become more interested in flirting with or dating someone new, other than the current partner (Durante & Li, 2009). On average, women during the periovulatory period become more likely than usual to wear red or pink, colors that most men rate as sexy (Beall & Tracy, 2013). In the presence of an attractive male, they are more likely than usual to walk slowly, with a gait that men perceive as sexy (Fink, Hugill, & Lange, 2012; Guegen, 2012). In short, sexual interest peaks at the periovulatory period and influences behavior in many ways, generally without the woman's conscious recognition of the effect.

Another study used a method that is, shall we say, not common among laboratory researchers. The researchers studied erotic lap dancers, who earn tips by dancing between a man's legs, rubbing up against his groin, while wearing, in most cases, just a bikini bottom. Lap dancers recorded the times of their menstrual periods and the amount of tip income they received each night. Lap dancers who were taking contraceptive pills (which keep hormone levels about constant through the month) earned about the same amount from one day to another. Those not taking contraceptive pills received the largest tips 9 to 15 days after menstruation, which is a time of increasing estrogen levels (G. Miller, Tybur, & Jordan, 2007). A likely hypothesis is that the women felt and acted sexier at this time.

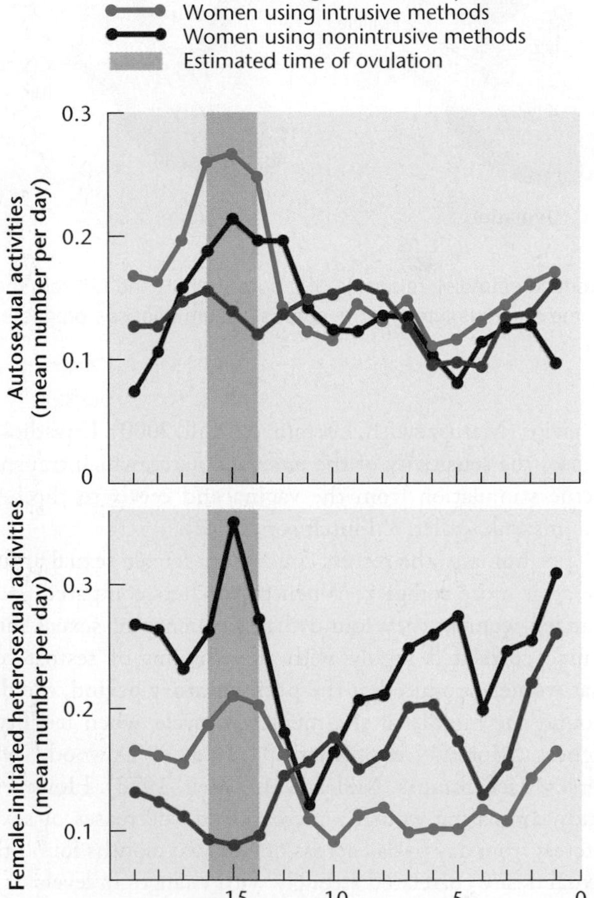

FIGURE 10.8 Female-initiated sexual activities
The top graph shows autosexual activities (masturbation and sexual fantasies); the bottom graph shows female-initiated activities with a male partner. "Intrusive" birth-control methods are diaphragm, foam, and condom; "nonintrusive" methods are IUD and vasectomy. Women other than pill users initiate sex more often when their estrogen levels peak. *Source:* Adams, Gold, & Burt, 1978

Sex hormones also influence women's preferences in a male partner. Women were presented with a computer that enabled them to modify pictures of men's faces to make each one look more feminine or more masculine. When they were asked specifically to show the face of the man they would prefer for a short-term sexual relationship, women preferred more masculine-looking faces around the time of ovulation than they did at other times (Penton-Voak et al., 1999). When women were asked to view videotapes of two men and choose one for a short-term relationship, women around the time of ovulation were more likely to choose a man who seemed athletic, competitive, and assertive and who did *not* describe himself as having a "nice personality" (Gangestad, Simpson, Cousins, Garver-Apgar, & Christensen, 2004). In short, the hormones associated with fertility move women's mate preferences toward men who look and act more masculine.

STOP & CHECK

9. At what time in a woman's menstrual cycle do her estradiol levels increase? When are they lowest?

ANSWER

9. Estrogen levels increase during the days leading up to the middle of the menstrual cycle. They are lowest during and just after menstruation.

Effects of Sex Hormones on Nonsexual Characteristics

Men and women differ in many ways other than their sexual behavior. Nearly all those differences vary at least somewhat according to culture, and it is easy to exaggerate the extent of difference (as in "Women are from Venus, Men are from Mars"). Still, some trends are moderately consistent.

Prenatal androgens and estrogens influence many aspects of brain development, including which neurons survive (Forger et al., 2004; Morris, Jordan, & Breedlove, 2004) and which synapses form (McEwen, Akama, Spencer-Segal, Milner, & Waters, 2012). Both androgens and estrogens stimulate brain areas important for memory (Bussiere, Beer, Neiss, & Janowsky, 2005; Wang, Hara, Janssen, Rapp, & Morrison, 2010). At least 85 identified genes are more active in the brains of one sex or the other (Reinius et al., 2008). Several brain areas are relatively larger in men on average, and others relatively larger in women, as Figure 10.9 shows

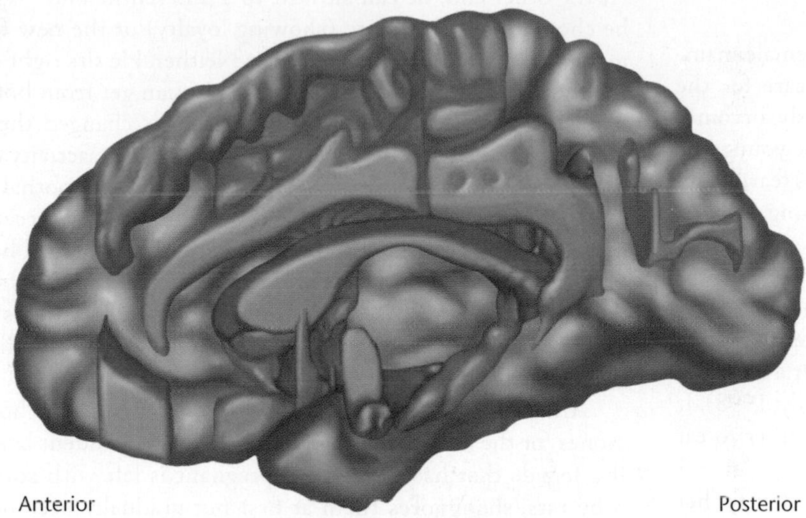

FIGURE 10.9 Men's and women's brains
Areas in pink are, on the average, larger in women relative to the total mass of the brain. Areas in blue are, on the average, larger in men relative to the total mass. *Source:* Based on Cahill, L. (2006). Why sex matters for neuroscience. *Nature Reviews Neuroscience*, 7, pp. 477–484, Cahill, L. (2006).

(Cahill, 2006; J. M. Goldstein et al., 2001). These differences are not simply a result of the fact that men are larger. When researchers compare men and women who have the same overall brain volume, many of the patterns shown in Figure 10.9 still emerge (Luders, Gaser, Narr, & Toga, 2009). However, remember that these are averages. Most individuals show male-typical patterns in some ways and female-typical patterns in others. Also, beware of uncritically relating brain differences to behavioral differences. You may hear someone remark that the male brain differs from the female brain in a particular way and that "this explains" why men and women behave differently in some regard. In most cases, the relationship between the brain differences and the behavioral differences is mere speculation (de Vries & Södersten, 2009).

One well-documented gender difference in behavior is that women tend to be better than men at recognizing facial expressions of emotion. Might sex hormones contribute to this difference? One way to approach the question experimentally is to administer extra testosterone to women. In one study, women's task was to examine photos of faces and try to identify the expressed emotions among six choices: anger, disgust, fear, happiness, sadness, and surprise. The photos were morphed from 0 percent (neutral expression) to 100 percent expression of an emotion. Figure 10.10 shows the example for anger. The result was that after women received testosterone, most became less accurate at recognizing facial expressions of anger (van Honk & Schutter, 2007). The effect was temporary, of course. The implication is that testosterone interferes with attention to emotional expressions. A similar study showed that testosterone decreased women's ability to infer people's mood from watching their eyes (van Honk et al., 2011).

STOP&CHECK

10. When someone demonstrates an anatomical difference between male and female brains, on average, what if anything can we conclude about its role in behavior?

ANSWER

10. Until we have further evidence, we should not conclude anything. It is easy to speculate about how brain differences produce behavioral differences between men and women, but it is harder to test those speculations with solid data.

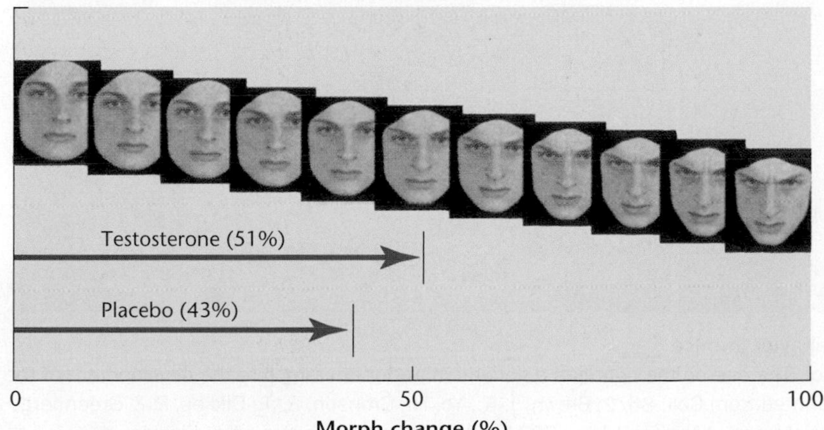

FIGURE 10.10 Stimuli to measure people's ability to identify emotion
For each of six emotions, researchers prepared views ranging from 0 percent to 100 percent expression of the emotion. In this case, the emotion is anger. Women identified the expression more quickly, on average, after a placebo injection than after a testosterone injection. *Source:* From van Honk, J., & Schutter, D. J. L. G., "Testosterone reduces conscious detection of signals serving social correction," *Psychological Science*, 18, pp. 663–667. Reprinted by Permission of SAGE Publications.

Parental Behavior

Hormonal changes during pregnancy prepare a female mammal to provide milk, and also prepare her to care for the young. Her behavior changes in many ways when she becomes a mother. In addition to nursing and caring for the young, she eats and drinks more than usual, and becomes less fearful and more aggressive, especially in defense of her young. After a mother rat delivers her babies, she increases her secretion of estradiol and prolactin, while decreasing production of progesterone (Numan & Woodside, 2010). Prolactin is necessary for milk production and for certain aspects of maternal behavior such as retrieving the young when they wander away from the nest (Lucas, Ormandy, Binart, Bridges, & Kelly, 1998). It also inhibits sensitivity to leptin, enabling the mother to eat far more than usual.

In addition to secreting hormones, the female changes her pattern of hormone receptors. Late in pregnancy, her brain increases its sensitivity to estradiol in the areas responsible for maternal behavior and attention to the young (Rosenblatt, Olufowobi, & Siegel, 1998), including the medial preoptic area and anterior hypothalamus (J. R. Brown, Ye, Bronson, Dikkes, & Greenberg, 1996; Featherstone, Fleming, & Ivy, 2000) (see Figure 10.11). We have already encountered the preoptic area/anterior hypothalamus, or POA/AH, because of its importance for temperature regulation, thirst, and sexual behavior. It's a busy little area.

Another key hormone is vasopressin, synthesized by the hypothalamus and secreted by the posterior pituitary gland. Vasopressin is important for social behavior in many species, partly by facilitating olfactory recognition of other individuals (Tobin et al., 2010). Male prairie voles, which secrete much vasopressin, establish long-term pair bonds with females and help rear their young. A male meadow vole, with much lower vasopressin levels, mates with a female and then ignores her (see Figure 10.12). Imagine a male meadow vole in a long, narrow cage. At one end, he can sit next to a female with which he has just mated. (She is confined there.) At the other end, he can sit next to a different female. Will he choose his recent mate (showing loyalty) or the new female (seeking variety)? The answer: Neither. He sits right in the middle, by himself, as far away as he can get from both females. However, these little social isolates changed their behavior after researchers found a way to increase activity of the genes responsible for vasopressin in the voles' hypothalamus. Suddenly, they showed a strong preference for a recent mate and, if placed into the same cage, they even helped her take care of her babies (M. M. Lim et al., 2004). Whether the female was surprised, we don't know. This result is a strong example of altering social behavior by manipulating the activity of a single gene.

Although rodent maternal behavior depends on hormones for the first few days, it becomes less dependent later. If a female that has never been pregnant is left with some baby rats, she ignores them at first but gradually becomes more attentive. (Because the babies cannot survive without parental care, the experimenter must periodically replace them with new, healthy babies.) After about 6 days, the adoptive mother builds a nest, assembles the babies in the nest, licks them, and does everything else that normal mothers do, except nurse them. This experience-dependent behavior does not require hormonal changes and occurs even in rats that had their ovaries removed (Mayer & Rosenblatt, 1979; Rosenblatt, 1967). That is, humans are not the only species in which a mother can adopt young without first going through pregnancy.

An important influence from being with babies is that the mother becomes accustomed to their odors. Infant rats release chemicals that stimulate the mother's vomeronasal organ, which responds to pheromones (see Chapter 6). We might imagine that evolution would have equipped infants with pheromones that elicit maternal behavior, but oddly, their pheromones stimulate aggressive behaviors that *interfere* with maternal behavior (Sheehan, Cirrito, Numan, & Numan, 2000). For a mother that has just gone through pregnancy, this interference does not matter because her hormones primed

FIGURE 10.11 Brain development and maternal behavior in mice
The mouse on the left shows normal maternal behavior. The one on the right has a genetic mutation that impairs the development of the preoptic area and anterior hypothalamus. *Source:* Reprinted from Cell, 86/2, Brown, J. R., Ye, H., Bronson, R. T., Dikkes, P., & Greenberg, M. E., "A defect in nurturing in mice lacking the immediate early gene fosB," pp. 297–309, 1996, with permission of Elsevier.

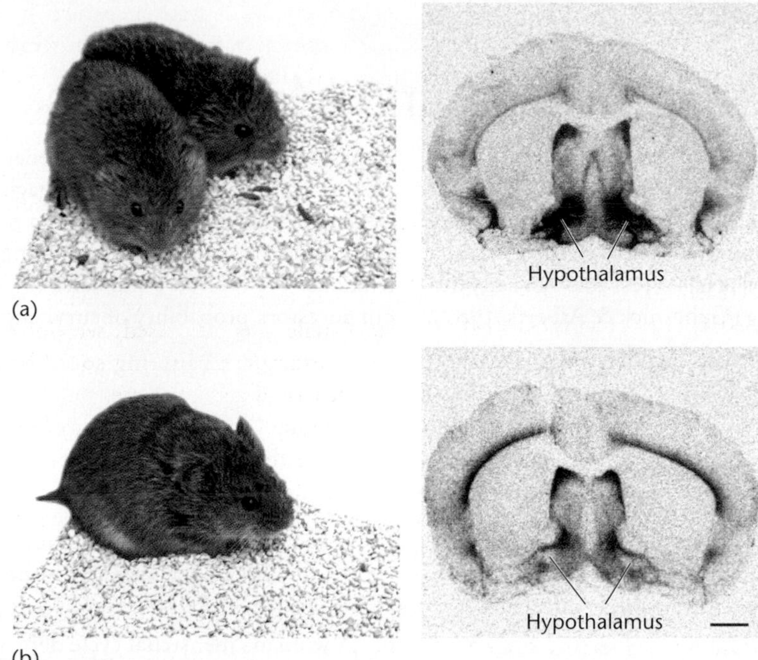

FIGURE 10.12 Effects of vasopressin on social and mating behaviors
Prairie voles (top) form long-term pair bonds. Staining of their brain shows much expression of the hormone vasopressin in the hypothalamus. A closely related species, meadow voles (bottom), show no social attachments. Their brains have lower vasopressin levels, as indicated by less staining in the hypothalamus. *Source:* Reprinted with permission from "Enhanced partner preference in a promiscuous species by manipulating the expression of a single gene," by Lim, M. M., Wang, Z., Olazabal, D. E., Ren, X., Terwillinger, E. F., & Young, L. J., *Nature, 429*, pp. 754–757. Copyright 2004 Nature Publishing Group/Macmillan Magazines Ltd.

her medial preoptic area so strongly that it overrides competing impulses. A female without hormonal priming, however, rejects the young until she has become familiar with their smell (Del Cerro et al., 1995).

Why do mammals need two mechanisms for maternal behavior—one hormone-dependent and one not? In the early phase, hormones compensate for the mother's lack of familiarity with the young. In the later phase, experience maintains the maternal behavior even though the hormones start to decline (Rosenblatt, 1970).

In humans, the hormonal changes during pregnancy and delivery enable a mother to produce milk, but otherwise hormones might seem unimportant for parental behavior. After all, both men and women who have never gone through pregnancy can adopt children and become excellent parents. However, it is possible that hormones influence the quality of parental care to some extent. In nonhuman mammals, mothers with a deficiency of the alpha type of estradiol receptor provide only poor maternal care—for example, not licking and grooming their offspring enough to provide normal stimulation. Humans show genetic variation in their alpha estrogen receptors, and one study (with admittedly a small sample) found that women with one of the genetic variants were more likely than average to treat their young children harshly, both physically and verbally (Lahey et al., 2012).

Several studies show a correlation between fathers' hormones and their behavior toward their infants and toddlers. On average, a man's testosterone level decreases and his prolactin level increases after a baby is born, especially if the man spends hours a day interacting with the child (Gettler, McDade, Feranil, & Kuzawa, 2011, 2012). On average, men with the lowest testosterone levels and highest prolactin levels spend the most time playing with and caring for their children (Gordon, Zagoory-Sharon, Leckman, & Feldman, 2010; Mascaro, Hackett, & Rilling, 2013). Because these are correlational data, we do not know to what extent the hormones are the cause of the men's behavior, and to what extent they are the result.

STOP & CHECK

11. What factors are responsible for maternal behavior shortly after rats give birth? What factors become more important in later days?

ANSWER

11. The early stage of rats' maternal behavior depends on a surge in the release of the hormones prolactin and estradiol. A few days later, her experience with the young decreases the vomeronasal responses that would tend to make her reject them. Experience with the young maintains maternal behavior after the hormone levels begin to drop.

MODULE 10.1 ■ IN CLOSING

Reproductive Behaviors and Motivations

A mother rat licks her babies all over shortly after their birth, and that stimulation is essential for their survival. Why does she do it? Presumably, she does not understand that licking will help them. She licks because they are covered with a salty fluid that tastes good to her. If she has access to other salty fluids, she stops licking her young (Gubernick & Alberts, 1983). Analogously, sexual behavior in general serves the function of passing on our genes, but we engage in sexual behavior just because it feels good. We evolved a tendency to enjoy the sex act. The same principle holds for hunger, thirst, and other motivations: We evolved tendencies to enjoy acts that increased our ancestors' probability of surviving and reproducing.

Summary

1. Male and female behaviors differ because of sex hormones that activate particular genes. Also, certain genes on the X and Y chromosomes exert direct effects on brain development. **326**
2. Organizing effects of a hormone, exerted during a sensitive period, produce relatively permanent alterations in anatomy and physiology. **328**
3. In the absence of sex hormones, an infant mammal develops female-looking external genitals. The addition of testosterone shifts development toward the male pattern. Extra estradiol, within normal limits, does not determine whether the individual looks male or female. **328**
4. During early development in rodents, testosterone is converted within certain brain cells to estradiol, which actually masculinizes their development. Estradiol in the blood does not masculinize development because it is bound to proteins in the blood. In primates, testosterone masculinizes brain development without being converted to estradiol. **329**
5. In adulthood, sex hormones activate sex behaviors, partly by facilitating activity in the medial preoptic area and anterior hypothalamus. The hormones prime cells to release dopamine in response to sexual arousal. **331**
6. A woman's menstrual cycle depends on a feedback cycle that controls the release of several hormones. Although women can respond sexually at any time in their cycle, on average, their sexual desire is greatest during the fertile period of the menstrual cycle, when estradiol levels are high. **332**
7. Sex hormones also influence behaviors not directly related to sexual reproduction, including brain development and the ability to recognize emotional expressions. **334**
8. Hormones released around the time of giving birth facilitate maternal behavior in females of many mammalian species. Prolonged exposure to young also induces parental behavior. In humans, the hormonal changes during pregnancy and delivery enable a woman to produce milk. Other aspects of human parental behavior do not require hormonal facilitation, although some influence of hormones is possible. **336**

Key Terms

Terms are defined in the module on the page number indicated. They're also presented in alphabetical order with definitions in the book's Subject Index/Glossary. Interactive flash cards, audio reviews, and crossword puzzles are among the online resources available to help you learn these terms and the concepts they represent.

activating effects **328**
alpha-fetoprotein **330**
androgens **326**
estradiol **327**
estrogens **326**
follicle-stimulating hormone (FSH) **332**
impotence **332**
luteinizing hormone (LH) **332**
menstrual cycle **332**
Müllerian ducts **326**
organizing effects **328**
ovaries **326**
oxytocin **331**
periovulatory period **333**
progesterone **327**
sensitive period **328**
sexually dimorphic nucleus **329**
SRY gene **326**
steroid hormones **327**
testes **326**
testosterone **327**
Wolffian ducts **326**

Thought Question

1. The pill RU-486 produces abortions by blocking the effects of progesterone. Why would blocking progesterone interfere with pregnancy?
2. The presence or absence of testosterone determines whether a mammal will differentiate as a male or a female. In birds, the story is the opposite: The presence or absence of estrogen is critical (Adkins & Adler, 1972). What problems would sex determination by estrogen create if that were the mechanism for mammals? Why do those problems not arise in birds? (Hint: Think about the difference between live birth and hatching from an egg.)
3. Antipsychotic drugs, such as haloperidol and chlorpromazine, block activity at dopamine synapses. What side effects might they have on sexual behavior?

MODULE 10.1: End of Module Quiz

1. At an early stage of embryological development, before the influence of sex hormones, what is the appearance of a fetus's external genitals?
   a. A male has a small penis and a female has a small clitoris.
   b. Both sexes have both a penis and a clitoris.
   c. Both sexes have small "unisex" structures that could develop into either a penis or a clitoris.
   d. Neither sex has any external genitals.
2. Sex hormones affect neurons in several ways. Which of the following is *not* one of those ways?
   a. They bind to membrane receptors.
   b. They activate certain proteins in the cell's cytoplasm.
   c. They attach to chromosomes and activate or inactivate genes.
   d. Brain enzymes convert them into dopamine and other neurotransmitters.
3. What is the main difference between organizing effects and activating effects of hormones?
   a. Organizing effects are long-lasting, whereas activating effects are temporary.
   b. Organizing effects alter brain activity, whereas activating effects alter other parts of the body.
   c. Organizing effects are excitatory, whereas activating effects are inhibitory.
   d. Organizing effects depend on estrogens, whereas activating effects depend on androgens.
4. If a developing mammal is exposed to high levels of both androgens and estrogens, its external anatomy will appear ______. If it is exposed to low levels of both, its external anatomy will appear ______.
   a. masculine . . . feminine
   b. feminine . . . masculine
   c. masculine . . . intermediate
   d. intermediate . . . feminine
5. How does sexual differentiation of the brain differ between rodents and primates?
   a. In rodents it depends on the level of testosterone. In primates it depends on the level of estradiol.
   b. In rodents it depends on the level of estradiol. In primates it depends on the level of testosterone.
   c. In rodents, testosterone must be aromatized to estradiol before it affects developing neurons.
   d. In primates, testosterone must be aromatized to estradiol before it affects developing neurons.
6. How much a child plays with boys' toys is apparently increased by prenatal exposure to ______ and decreased by prenatal exposure to ______.
   a. cortisol . . . estradiol
   b. testosterone . . . phthalates
   c. high temperatures . . . low temperatures
   d. cocaine . . . alcohol
7. In terms of neurotransmitter activity, how does the mechanism of erection differ from that of orgasm?
   a. Erection depends on acetylcholine, and orgasm depends on serotonin.
   b. Erection depends on increased dopamine release, and orgasm depends on decreased dopamine release.
   c. Erection depends on one set of dopamine receptors, and orgasm depends on different dopamine receptors.
   d. Erection depends on serotonin, and orgasm depends on nitric oxide.

8. Compared to other men, what are the testosterone levels of married men?
   a. Lower than average
   b. About the same as average
   c. Higher than average

9. At what time, if any, during the menstrual cycle do women's sexual desires tend to be highest, in women not taking birth-control pills?
   a. On average, sexual desire does not change over the cycle.
   b. Sexual desire is highest just after the menstrual period.
   c. Sexual desire is highest during the periovulatory period.
   d. Sexual desire is highest about a week after the periovulatory period.

10. What effect, if any, do sex hormones have on people's ability to recognize facial expressions of emotion?
   a. Estradiol impairs the ability to recognize emotional expressions.
   b. Testosterone improves the ability to recognize emotional expressions.
   c. Testosterone impairs the ability to recognize emotional expressions.
   d. No evidence suggests any effect of sex hormones on the ability to recognize emotional expressions.

11. What hormonal levels, if any, correlate with the amount of time and care that human fathers give their young children?
   a. High levels of prolactin and low levels of testosterone
   b. High levels of both testosterone and estradiol
   c. Low levels of both estradiol and prolactin
   d. Fathers' behavior does not correlate significantly with anything about hormones.

ANSWERS: 1c, 2d, 3a, 4a, 5c, 6b, 7c, 8a, 9c, 10c, 11a.

MODULE 10.2

Variations in Sexual Behavior

People vary in their frequency of sexual activity, preferred types of sexual activity, and sexual orientation. In this module, we explore some of that diversity, but first we consider a few differences between men and women in general. Do men's and women's mating behaviors make biological sense? If so, should we interpret these behaviors as products of evolution? These questions have proved to be difficult and controversial.

Evolutionary Interpretations of Mating Behavior

Part of Charles Darwin's theory of evolution by natural selection was that individuals whose genes help them survive will produce more offspring, and therefore the next generation will resemble those with these favorable genes. A second part of his theory, not so widely accepted at first, was **sexual selection**: Genes that make an individual more appealing to the other sex will increase the probability of reproduction, and therefore the next generation will resemble those who had these genes.

Sexual selection can go only so far, however, if it starts to interfere with survival. A male deer with large antlers attracts females, but being impressive wouldn't help if the weight became so great that it interfered with his movement. A bird's bright colors attract potential mates, but they also run the risk of attracting a predator's attention. In many bird species, the male is brightly colored, but the female is not, presumably because she sits on the nest and needs to be less conspicuous. In a few species, such as phalaropes, the female is more brightly colored, but in those species, the female lays the egg and deserts it, leaving the dull-colored male to sit on the nest. In species where the male and female share the nesting duties, such as pigeons and doves, the male and female look alike, and neither is especially gaudy.

In humans, too, some of the differences between men and women may be results of sexual selection. That is, to some extent women evolved based on what appeals to men, and men evolved based on what appeals to women. Certain aspects of behavior may also reflect different evolutionary pressures for men and women. Evolutionary psychologists cite several possible examples, although each has been controversial (Buss, 2000). Let's examine the evidence and reasoning.

Panu Ruengjan/Shutterstock.com

A female phalarope is brilliantly colored, and the male is drabber. The female lays eggs and deserts the nest, leaving the male to attend to it.

Interest in Multiple Mates

More men than women seek opportunities for casual sexual relationships with many partners. Why? From the evolutionary standpoint of spreading one's genes, men can succeed by either of two strategies (Gangestad & Simpson, 2000): Be loyal to one woman and devote your energies to helping her and her babies, or mate with many women and hope that some of them can raise your babies without your help. No one needs to be conscious of these strategies, of course. The idea is that men who acted these ways in the past propagated their genes, and today's men might have inherited genes that promote these behaviors. In contrast, a woman can have no more than one pregnancy per 9 months, regardless of her number of sex partners. So evolution may have predisposed men, or at least some men, to be more interested in multiple mates than women are.

One objection is that a woman does sometimes gain from having multiple sex partners (Hrdy, 2000). If her husband is infertile, mating with another man could be her only way of reproducing. Also, another sexual partner may provide aid of various sorts to her and her children. In addition, she has the possibility of "trading up," abandoning her first mate for a better one. So the prospect of multiple mates may be more appealing to men, but it has advantages for women, too.

Another objection is that researchers have no direct evidence that genes influence people's preferences for one mate or many. We shall return to this issue later.

What Men and Women Seek in a Mate

Almost all people prefer a romantic partner who is healthy, intelligent, honest, and physically attractive. Typically, women have some additional interests that are less common for men. In particular, women are more likely than men are to prefer a mate who is likely to be a good provider (Buss, 2000). According to evolutionary theorists, the reason is this: While a woman is pregnant or taking care of a small child, she needs help getting food and other requirements. Evolution would have favored any gene that caused women to seek good providers. Related to this tendency, most women tend to be cautious during courtship. Even if a man seems interested in her, a woman is generally cautious before concluding that he has a strong commitment to her (Buss, 2001). She would not want a man who acts interested and then leaves when she needs him.

Men tend to have a stronger preference for a young partner. An evolutionary explanation is that young women are likely to remain fertile longer than older women are, so a man can have more children by pairing with a young woman. Men remain fertile into old age, so a woman has less need to insist on youth. Women prefer young partners when possible, but in many societies, only older men have enough financial resources to get married.

Are these preferences rooted in genetics? Perhaps, but the variation from culture to culture suggests a strong learned component. In countries where women have good educational, economic, and employment opportunities, a woman is more likely to choose a partner close to her own age, and less likely to choose based on wealth (Zentner & Mitura, 2012).

Differences in Jealousy

Traditionally, in nearly all cultures, men have been more jealous of a wife's possible infidelity than women have been of a husband's infidelity. From an evolutionary standpoint, why? If a man is to pass on his genes—the key point in evolution—he needs to be sure that the children he supports are his own. An unfaithful wife threatens that certainty. A woman knows that any children she bears are her own, so she does not have the same worry. (She might, however, worry that her husband might start supporting some other woman's children, instead of her own children.) The degree of jealousy varies among cultures. Some cultures tolerate sexual infidelity by husbands, and some do not, and the intensity of prohibition against wives' infidelity varies, but no known society considers infidelity more acceptable for women than for men.

Which would upset you more: if your partner had a brief sexual affair with someone else, or if he or she became emotionally close to someone else? According to several studies, men say they would be more upset by the sexual infidelity, whereas women would be more upset by the emotional infidelity (Shakelford, Buss, & Bennett, 2002). However, those studies dealt with hypothetical situations. Most men and women who have actually dealt with an unfaithful partner say they were more upset by their partner's becoming emotionally close to someone else than by the sexual affair (C. H. Harris, 2002).

Evolved or Learned?

In many species of mammals and birds, a male defends his sexual access to one or more females and attacks any other approaching male. Meanwhile, the female shows little or no response if "her" male sexually approaches some other female. In such cases an interpretation in terms of evolutionary selection is generally noncontroversial. However, the interpretation is less clear for our own species. One reason is that when someone argues that evolutionary selection led men to be interested in multiple sex partners or to be more jealous than women are, it may sound like a justification for men to act that way. (It is not. Even if we have a biological predisposition to act a certain way, it does not force us to do so. We routinely override many impulses toward selfish behavior to maintain civilization.) But even if we leave aside the ethical implications, the scientific data are not conclusive on how much of our behavior is evolutionarily guided and how much is learned. Mating customs show some similarities across cultures, but also important differences. Yes, of course our behavioral tendencies are a product of evolution. But it is not clear to what extent evolution micromanages human behavior, down to such details as whether to look for a mate with high earning potential or how jealous to be of an unfaithful mate.

STOP & CHECK

12. What evolutionary advantage is suggested for why women are more interested in men's wealth and success than men are interested in women's wealth?

ANSWER

12. During pregnancy and early child care, a female is limited in her ability to get food and therefore prefers a male partner who can provide for her. A healthy male is not similarly dependent on a female.

Gender Identity and Gender-Differentiated Behaviors

In a species of fish called the coral goby, the male and female tend their eggs and young together. If one of them dies, the survivor looks for a new partner. But it does not look far. This is a very stay-at-home kind of fish. If it cannot easily find a partner of the opposite sex but does find an unmated member of its own sex—oh, well—it simply changes sex and mates with the neighbor. Male-to-female and female-to-male switches are equally common (Nakashima, Kuwamura, & Yogo, 1995).

People do not have the same flexibility as coral gobies, but we do have variations in sexual development. Sexual development is a sensitive issue, so let us specify from the start: "Different" does not mean "wrong." People differ naturally in their sexual development just as they do in anything else.

Gender identity is what we consider ourselves to be. The biological differences between males and females are *sex differences*, whereas the differences that result from people's thinking about themselves as male or female are *gender differences*. To maintain this useful distinction, we should resist the trend to speak of the "gender" of dogs, fruit flies, and so forth. Gender identity is a human characteristic.

In most cases, people accept the gender identity that matches their external appearance, which matches the way they were reared. However, some are dissatisfied with their assigned gender, and many people would describe themselves as being masculine in some ways and feminine in others. Psychologists have long assumed that gender depends mainly or entirely on the way people rear their children. However, several kinds of evidence suggest that biological factors, especially prenatal hormones, are important also.

Intersexes

Hermaphrodites (from Hermes and Aphrodite in Greek mythology) have anatomies intermediate between male and female, or show a mixture of male and female anatomies (Haqq & Donahoe, 1998). A *true hermaphrodite* has some testicular tissue and some ovarian tissue. One way for this to happen is for a woman to release two ova, each fertilized by a different sperm, which then unite instead of becoming twins. If one of the fertilized ova had an XX chromosome pattern and the other had XY, the resulting child has some XX cells and some XY cells. True hermaphrodites are rare. Some are fertile as either male or female, although no cases are known in which someone was fertile as both. Don't believe any report that some true hermaphrodite impregnated himself/herself.

More commonly, some people develop an intermediate appearance because of an atypical hormone pattern. Recall that testosterone masculinizes the genitals and the hypothalamus during early development. A genetic male with low levels of testosterone or a deficiency of testosterone receptors may develop a female or intermediate appearance (Misrahi et al., 1997). A genetic female who is exposed to more testosterone than the average female can be partly masculinized.

The most common cause of this condition is **congenital adrenal hyperplasia (CAH)**, meaning overdevelopment of the adrenal glands from birth. Ordinarily, the adrenal gland has a negative feedback relationship with the pituitary gland. The pituitary secretes adrenocorticotropic hormone (ACTH), which stimulates the adrenal gland. Cortisol, one of the hormones from the adrenal gland, feeds back to decrease the release of ACTH. Some people have a genetic limitation in their ability to produce cortisol. Because the pituitary fails to receive much cortisol as a feedback signal, it continues secreting more ACTH, causing the adrenal gland to secrete larger amounts of its other hormones, including testosterone. In a genetic male, the extra testosterone causes no apparent difficulty. However, genetic females with this condition develop various degrees of masculinization of their external genitals. (The ovaries and other internal organs are less affected.) Figure 10.13 shows a structure that appears intermediate between clitoris and penis and swellings that appear intermediate between labia and scrotum. After birth, these children are given medical treatments to bring their adrenal hormones within normal levels. Some are also given surgery to alter their external genital appearance, as we shall discuss later.

People whose sexual development is intermediate, as in Figure 10.13, are called **intersexes**. An alternative is to use the term *disorders of sexual development*. How common are intersexes? An estimated 1 child in 100 in the United States is born with some degree of genital ambiguity, and 1 in 2,000 has enough ambiguity to make its male or female status uncertain (Blackless et al., 2000). However, the accuracy of

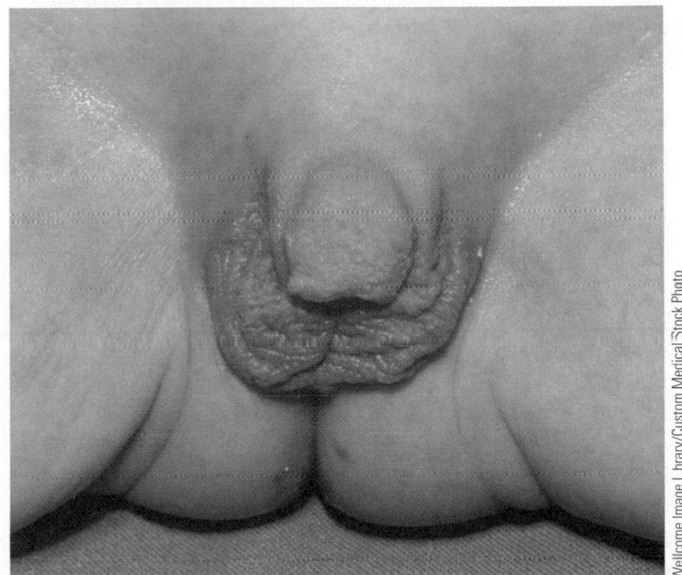

Wellcome Image Library/Custom Medical Stock Photo

FIGURE 10.13 External genitals of a genetic female, age 3 months
The genitals were masculinized by excess androgens from the adrenal gland before birth.

these estimates is doubtful, as hospitals and families keep the information private. Maintaining confidentiality is of course important, but an unfortunate consequence is that intersexed people have trouble finding others like themselves. For more information, consult the website of the Intersex Society of North America (ISNA).

STOP&CHECK

13. What is a common cause for a genetic female (XX) to develop a partly masculinized anatomy?

ANSWER

13. If a genetic female is genetically deficient in her ability to produce cortisol, the pituitary gland does not receive negative feedback signals and therefore continues stimulating the adrenal gland. The adrenal gland then produces large amounts of other hormones, including testosterone, which masculinizes development.

Interests and Preferences of CAH Girls

For many years, the policy was to raise most intersexes as girls, on the assumption that surgery could make them look like normal girls, and they would develop behaviors corresponding to the way they were reared. However, their brains were exposed to higher than normal testosterone levels during prenatal and early postnatal life compared to other girls. Was their behavior masculinized? As discussed in the first module of this chapter, prenatal levels of testosterone correlate with girls' toy choices. The same idea applies here. In several studies, girls with CAH were observed in a room full of toys—including some that were girl typical (dolls, plates and dishes, cosmetics kits), some that were boy typical (toy car, tool set, gun), and some that were neutral (puzzles, crayons, board games). The girls with CAH were intermediate between the preferences of boys and girls without CAH (Pasterski et al., 2005, 2011). That is, they played with boys' toys more than most other girls did, but less than the average for boys. When the children tested with a parent present, again the girls with CAH were intermediate between the other two groups. Other studies found that the girls exposed to the largest amount of testosterone in early development showed the largest preference for boys' toys (Berenbaum, Duck, & Bryk, 2000; Nordenström, Servin, Bohlin, Larsson, & Wedell, 2002). You might wonder whether the parents, knowing that these girls had been partly masculinized in appearance, might have encouraged tomboyish activities. Observations of the parents showed that they generally encouraged the girls to play with whatever they wanted to play with (Wong, Pasterski, Hindmarsh, Geffner, & Hines, 2013). On average, girls with CAH also perform slightly better than most other girls on spatial and mechanical skills, on which boys generally do better than girls (Berenbaum, Bryk, & Beltz, 2012). The girls' performance on these skills may reflect their interests rather than a true difference in abilities.

A study of CAH girls in adolescence found that, on average, their interests are intermediate between those of typical male and female adolescents. For example, they read more sports magazines and fewer style and glamour magazines than the average for other teenage girls (Berenbaum, 1999). In adulthood, they show more physical aggression than most other women do, and less interest in infants (Mathews, Fane, Conway, Brook, & Hines, 2009). They are more interested in rough sports and more likely than average to be in heavily male-dominated occupations such as auto mechanic and truck driver (Frisén et al., 2009). Together, the results imply that prenatal and early postnatal hormones influence people's interests as well as their physical development.

Testicular Feminization

Certain individuals with an XY chromosome pattern produce normal amounts of androgens (including testosterone) but lack the receptor that enables androgens to activate genes in a cell's nucleus. Consequently, the cells do not respond to androgens. This condition, known as **androgen insensitivity** or **testicular feminization**, occurs in various degrees resulting in anatomy that ranges from a smaller than average penis to genitals like those of a typical female, in which case no one has any reason to suspect the person is anything other than female, until puberty. Then, although her breasts develop and hips broaden she does not menstruate, because her body has internal testes instead of ovaries and a uterus. (The vagina is short and leads to nothing but skin.) Also, pubic hair is sparse or absent, because it depends on androgens in females as well as males. Psychologically, she develops as a typical female.

STOP&CHECK

14. If a genetic female is exposed to extra testosterone during prenatal development, what behavioral effect is likely?

15. What would cause a genetic male (XY) to develop a partly feminized external anatomy?

ANSWERS

14. A girl who is exposed to extra testosterone during prenatal development is more likely than most other girls to prefer boy-typical toys. **15.** A genetic male with a gene that prevents testosterone from binding to its receptors will develop an appearance that partly or completely resembles a female.

Issues of Gender Assignment and Rearing

Girls with CAH and related conditions are born with appearances ranging from almost typical female to something intermediate between female and male. Some genetic males are born with a very small penis because of a condition called *cloacal exstrophy*, a defect of pelvis development (Reiner &

Gearhart, 2004). Despite their genital anatomy, they had typical male levels of testosterone in prenatal development.

How should children with either of these conditions be reared? Beginning in the 1950s, medical doctors began recommending that anyone with an intermediate or ambiguous genital appearance should be reared as a girl, using surgery if necessary to make the genitals look more feminine (Dreger, 1998). The reason was that it is easier to reduce an enlarged clitoris to normal female size than expand it to penis size. If necessary, surgeons can build an artificial vagina or lengthen a short one. After the surgery, the child looks female. Physicians and psychologists assumed that any child who was consistently reared as a girl would fully accept that identity.

And she lives happily ever after, right? Not necessarily. Of the males with cloacal exstrophy who are reared as girls, all develop typical male interests, many or most eventually demand reassignment as males, and nearly all develop sexual attraction toward women, not men (Reiner & Gearhart, 2004).

Girls with the CAH history also have a difficult sexual adjustment, especially if they were subjected to clitoris-reduction surgery. A surgically created or lengthened vagina may be satisfactory to a male partner, but it provides no sensation to the woman and requires almost daily attention to prevent it from scarring over. Many such women have urinary incontinence. Most women with a history of CAH have significant sexual difficulties, including lack of orgasm. Many report no sexual partner ever, little pleasure in sex, and little or no romantic attraction to men (Frisén et al., 2009; Meyer-Bahlburg, Dolezal, Baker, & New, 2008; Minto, Liao, Woodhouse, Ransley, & Creighton, 2003; Nordenström et al., 2010; van der Zwan et al., 2013; Zucker et al., 1996). In one study, 25 percent said they had never had a love relationship of any type (Jürgensen et al., 2013).

Many intersexes wish they had their original "abnormal" enlarged clitoris instead of the mutilated, insensitive structure left to them by a surgeon. Moreover, intersexes resent being deceived. Historian Alice Dreger (1998) describes the case of one intersex:

> As a young person, [she] was told she had "twisted ovaries" that had to be removed; in fact, her testes were removed. At the age of twenty, "alone and scared in the stacks of a [medical] library," she discovered the truth of her condition. Then "the pieces finally fit together. But what fell apart was my relationship with both my family and physicians. It was not learning about chromosomes or testes that caused enduring trauma, it was discovering that I had been told lies. I avoided all medical care for the next 18 years.... [The] greatest source of anxiety is not our gonads or karyotype. It is shame and fear resulting from an environment in which our condition is so unacceptable that caretakers lie." (p. 192)

How *should* such a child be reared? A growing number of specialists follow these recommendations:

- Be completely honest with the intersexed person and the family, and do nothing without their informed consent.
- Identify the child as male or female based mainly on the predominant external appearance. That is, there should be no bias toward calling every intersex a female. Those born with masculinized external genitals seldom make a successful adaptation to a female gender assignment (Houk & Lee, 2010).
- Rear the child as consistently as possible, but be prepared that the person might later be sexually oriented toward males, females, both, or neither.
- Do *not* perform surgery to reduce the ambiguous penis/clitoris to the size of a normal clitoris. Such surgery impairs the person's erotic sensation and is at best premature, as no one knows how the child's sexual orientation will develop. If the intersexed person makes an informed request for such surgery in adulthood, then it is appropriate, but otherwise it should be avoided. (Diamond & Sigmundson, 1997)

Discrepancies of Sexual Appearance

To resolve the roles of rearing and hormones in determining gender identity, the most decisive observation would come from rearing a normal male baby as a female or rearing a normal female baby as a male. If the resulting adult was fully satisfied in the assigned role, we would know that upbringing determines gender identity. Although no one would perform such an experiment intentionally, we can learn from accidental events. In some cases, someone was exposed to a more-or-less normal pattern of male hormones before and shortly after birth but then reared as a girl.

One kind of case was reported first in the Dominican Republic and then in other places, usually in communities with much inbreeding. In each case, certain genetic males fail to produce *5α-reductase* 2, an enzyme that converts testosterone to *dihydrotestosterone*. Dihydrotestosterone is more effective than testosterone for masculinizing the external genitals. At birth, some of these individuals look almost like a typical female, while others have a swollen clitoris and somewhat "lumpy" labia. Nearly all are considered girls and reared as such. However, their brains had been exposed to male levels of testosterone during early development. At puberty, the testosterone levels increase sharply, and even without conversion to dihydrotestosterone, the result is growth of a penis and scrotum. Their size is generally less than average for other boys, but enough to be clearly male and not female.

Women: Imagine that at about age 12 years, your external genitals suddenly changed from female to male. Would you say, "Okay, I guess I'm a boy now"? Most of these people reacted exactly that way. The girl-turned-boy developed a male gender identity and directed his sexual interest toward females (Cohen-Kettenis, 2005; Imperato-McGinley, Guerrero, Gautier, & Peterson, 1974). Remember, these were not typical girls. Their brains had been exposed to male levels of testosterone from prenatal life onward.

A particularly upsetting case is that of one infant boy whose penis foreskin would not retract enough for easy urination. His parents took him to a physician to circumcise the foreskin, but the physician, using an electrical procedure, set the current too high and accidentally burned off the entire penis. On the advice of respected and well-meaning authorities, the parents elected to rear the child as a female, with the appropriate surgery. What makes this case especially interesting is that the child had a twin brother (whom the parents did not let the physician try to circumcise). If both twins developed satisfactory gender identities, one as a girl and the other as a boy, the results would say that rearing was decisive in gender identity.

Initial reports claimed that the child reared as a girl had a female gender identity, though she also had strong tomboyish tendencies (Money & Schwartz, 1978). However, by about age 10, she had figured out that something was wrong and that "she" was really a boy. She had preferred boys' activities and played only with boys' toys. She even tried urinating in a standing position, despite always making a mess. By age 14, she insisted that she wanted to live as a boy. At that time, her (now his) father tearfully explained the earlier events. The child changed names and became known as a boy. At age 25, he married a somewhat older woman and adopted her children. Clearly, a biological predisposition had won out over the family's attempts to rear the child as a girl (Colapinto, 1997; Diamond & Sigmundson, 1997). A few years later, the story ended tragically with this man's suicide.

We should not draw universal conclusions from a single case. However, the point is that it was a mistake to impose surgery and hormonal treatments to try to force this child to become female. When the prenatal hormone pattern of the brain is in conflict with a child's appearance, no one can be sure how that child will develop psychologically. Hormones don't have complete control, but rearing patterns don't, either.

STOP&CHECK

16. When children who had been reared as girls reached puberty and grew a penis and scrotum, what happened to their gender identity?

ANSWER

16. Most changed their gender identity from female to male.

Sexual Orientation

Contrary to what biologists once assumed, homosexual behavior occurs in many animal species, and not just in captive animals, those that cannot find a member of the opposite sex, or those with hormonal abnormalities (Bagemihl, 1999). If "natural" means "occurs in nature," then homosexuality is natural.

People discover their sexual orientation. They do not "choose" it, any more than people choose whether to be left-handed or right-handed. Whereas most men discover their sexual orientation early, many women are slower. Feminine-type behaviors in childhood and adolescence correlate strongly with homosexual orientation in adulthood for men (Cardoso, 2009; Alanko et al., 2010), but early masculine-type behaviors are poor predictors of sexual orientation in women (Alanko et al., 2010; Udry & Chantala, 2006).

A higher percentage of women than men experience at least some physical attraction to both males and females (Chivers, Rieger, Latty, & Bailey, 2004; Lippa, 2006), and some women switch—once or more—between homosexual and heterosexual orientations (Diamond, 2007). Men only rarely switch their sexual orientation. Although we shall note certain biological correlates of female homosexuality, the case for a biological predisposition seems stronger for men.

Behavioral and Anatomical Differences

On average, homosexual and heterosexual people differ anatomically in several ways. On average, heterosexual men are slightly taller and heavier than homosexual men (Bogaert, 2010). However, let's emphasize that term "slightly": The difference on average is only 1.5 cm (about half an inch). Contrary to the stereotype, a fair number of homosexual men are tall, athletic, and masculine in appearance.

On average, people who differ in sexual orientation also differ in several behaviors that are not directly related to sex. More men than women give directions in terms of distances and north, south, east, or west, whereas women are more likely to describe landmarks. Gay men also tend to use landmarks and are better than heterosexual men at remembering landmarks (Hassan & Rahman, 2007). Also consider this task: Experimenters repeatedly present a loud noise and measure the startle response. On some trials, they present a weaker noise just before the loud noise; the first noise decreases the startle response to the louder one. The decrease is called "prepulse inhibition." Prepulse inhibition is ordinarily stronger in men than in women. In this regard, homosexual women are slightly shifted in the male direction compared to heterosexual women (Rahman, Kumari, & Wilson, 2003).

Genetics

You will hear people argue about whether sexual orientation is a "genetic condition." The answer depends on what you mean by genetic condition. The evidence does point to a genetic contribution. However, the size of that contribution remains uncertain.

Studies of the genetics of sexual orientation have focused mainly on twins. Early studies of the genetics of human sexual orientation began by advertising in gay or lesbian publications for homosexual people with twins. Then they contacted the other twin to fill out a questionnaire. The questionnaire included diverse items to conceal the fact that the real interest was sexual orientation. The results showed a stronger concordance for monozygotic than dizygotic twins (Bailey & Pillard, 1991; Bailey, Pillard, Neale, & Agyei, 1993). That is, if one twin is homosexual, the probability for the other to be homosexual is fairly high for a monozygotic twin, and less high for a dizygotic twin. However, the kind of person who answers an ad in a gay or lesbian magazine may not be representative of others. A later study examined the data from all the twins in Sweden between

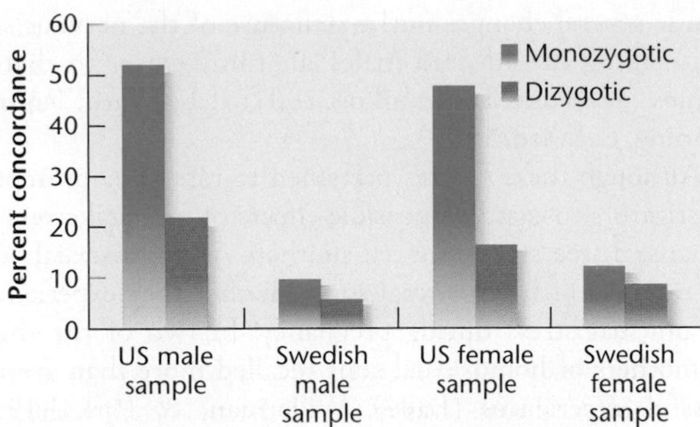

FIGURE 10.14 Twin concordance for homosexuality
The concordance for homosexual orientation (U.S. study) or homosexual activity (Swedish study) was higher for monozygotic twins than for dizygotic twins. *Source:* Based on the data of Bailey & Pillard, 1991; Bailey, Pillard, Neale, & Agyei, 1993; Långström, Rahman, Carlström, & Lichtenstein, 2010

ages 20 and 47 (Långström, Rahman, Carlström, & Lichtenstein, 2010). The Swedish study differed not only in the breadth of the sample, but also in the behavioral criterion. Instead of asking about sexual orientation, the researchers asked whether someone had ever had a same-sex partner. Figure 10.14 compares the data from the two studies. The results do not indicate number of people with homosexual activity or orientation. Rather, they indicate concordance—the probability of homosexual activity or orientation in one twin, given that the other twin had already indicated such activity. Although both sets of results show a higher concordance for monozygotic than dizygotic twins, note the huge difference between the studies. Other studies of twins in several countries also found higher concordance for sexual orientation in monozygotic than dizygotic twins, but the magnitude of the effect has varied considerably (Alanko et al., 2010; Burri, Cherkas, Spector, & Rahman, 2011).

Several studies have looked for a particular gene that might be linked to sexual orientation, but they failed to find anything with a significant effect (Ramagopalan, Dyment, Handunnetthi, Rice, & Ebers, 2010; Rice, Friberg, & Gavrilets, 2012). Two studies reported a higher incidence of homosexuality among the maternal than paternal relatives of homosexual men (Camperio-Ciani, Corna, & Capiluppi, 2004; Hamer, Hu, Magnuson, Hu, & Pattatucci, 1993). For example, uncles and cousins on the mother's side were more likely to be homosexual than uncles and cousins on the father's side. These results suggested a gene on the X chromosome, which a man necessarily receives from his mother. However, other studies have found no difference between relatives on the mother's and father's side (Bailey et al., 1999; Rice, Anderson, Risch, & Ebers, 1999; VanderLaan, Forrester, Petterson, & Vasey, 2008), and one study found more homosexual relatives on the father's side (Schwartz, Kim, Kolundzija, Rieger, & Sanders, 2010). Consequently, it seems unlikely that any gene on the X chromosome plays a major role.

An Evolutionary Question

A common estimate is that the average homosexual man has one-fifth as many children as the average heterosexual man. If a homosexual orientation depends on certain genes, why hasn't evolution selected strongly against those genes? Several possibilities are worth considering (Gavrilets & Rice, 2006). One is that genes for homosexuality are maintained by kin selection, as discussed in Chapter 4. That is, even if homosexual people do not have children themselves, they might do a wonderful job of helping their brothers and sisters rear children. Survey data in the United States indicate that homosexual men are no more likely, and perhaps less likely, than heterosexuals to help support their relatives (Bobrow & Bailey, 2001). However, observations in Samoa found that homosexual men are more helpful than average toward their nephews and nieces (Vasey & VanderLaan, 2010). It is difficult to know what might have been the usual pattern through human existence.

According to a second hypothesis, genes that produce male homosexuality might produce advantageous effects in their relatives, increasing their probability of reproducing and spreading the genes. What those advantages might be is a matter for speculation. One study found that homosexual men's mothers and aunts had a greater than average number of children (Camperio-Ciani et al., 2004). A study in a different country found that homosexual men had a greater than average number of relatives on the father's side (Schwartz et al., 2010).

A third idea is that homosexuality relates to epigenetics rather than changes in DNA sequence (Bocklandt, Horvath, Vilain, & Hamer, 2006). As mentioned in Chapter 4, it is possible for environmental events to attach an acetyl group or a methyl group (CH_3) to activate or inactivate a gene. Some epigenetic changes persist from one generation to the next. Perhaps epigenetic changes affect certain genes often enough to produce the observed prevalence of homosexuality.

STOP&CHECK

17. For which kind of twin pair is the concordance for sexual orientation greatest?

18. It seems difficult to explain how a gene could remain at a moderately high frequency in the population if most men with the gene do not reproduce. How would the hypothesis about epigenetics help with the explanation?

ANSWERS

17. Monozygotic twins have higher concordance than dizygotic twins. Be sure to state this point correctly: Do *not* say that homosexuality is more common in monozygotic than dizygotic twins. It is the *concordance* that is greater—that is, the probability that both twins have the *same* sexual orientation. **18.** According to this hypothesis, some unidentified event in the environment can attach an acetyl group or a methyl group to some gene, increasing or decreasing its activity. That gene modification could be passed to the next generation, producing evidence for a hereditary effect, even though there is no "gene for homosexuality." If events like this happen often enough, the result could be a moderately high prevalence of homosexuality, even if men with the inactivated gene seldom reproduce.

Prenatal Influences

Adult hormone levels do *not* explain sexual orientation. On average, homosexual and heterosexual men have nearly the same hormone levels, and most lesbian women have about the same hormone levels as heterosexual women. However, it is possible that sexual orientation depends on testosterone levels during a sensitive period of brain development (Ellis & Ames, 1987). Animal studies have shown that prenatal or early postnatal hormones can produce organizing effects on both external anatomy and brain development. External anatomy develops at a different time from the brain, and so it is possible for early hormones to alter the brain without changing external anatomy.

The mother's immune system may exert prenatal effects. Many studies report that the probability of a homosexual orientation is slightly higher among men who have older brothers (Blanchard, 2008; Schwartz et al., 2010). Younger brothers make no difference, nor do younger or older sisters (Bogaert, 2003b; Purcell, Blanchard, & Zucker, 2000). Furthermore, what matters is the number of *biological* older brothers. Growing up with older stepbrothers or adopted brothers has no apparent influence. Having a biological older brother has an influence, even if the brothers were reared separately (Bogaert, 2006). In short, the influence does not stem from social experiences. The key is how many previous times the mother gave birth to a son. The most prominent hypothesis is that a mother's immune system sometimes reacts against a protein in a son and then attacks subsequent sons enough to alter their development. That hypothesis fits with the observation that later-born homosexual men tend to be shorter than average (Bogaert, 2003a).

Another aspect of prenatal environment relates to stress on the mother during pregnancy. Research has shown that prenatal stress alters sexual development in laboratory animals. In several experiments, rats in the final week of pregnancy had the stressful experience of confinement in tight Plexiglas tubes for more than 2 hours each day under bright lights. In some cases, they were given alcohol as well. These rats' daughters looked and acted approximately normal. The sons, however, had normal male anatomy but, in adulthood, often responded to the presence of another male by arching their backs in the typical rat female posture for sex (I. L. Ward, Ward, Winn, & Bielawski, 1994). Most males that were subjected to either prenatal stress or alcohol developed male sexual behavior in addition to these female sexual behaviors, but those that were subjected to both stress and alcohol had decreased male sexual behaviors (I. L. Ward, Bennett, Ward, Hendricks, & French, 1999).

Prenatal stress and alcohol may alter brain development through several routes. Stress releases endorphins, which can antagonize the effects of testosterone on the hypothalamus (O. B. Ward, Monaghan, & Ward, 1986). Stress also elevates levels of certain adrenal hormones (corticosterone in rats, cortisol in human) that decrease testosterone release (O. B. Ward, Ward, Denning, French, & Hendricks, 2002; M. T. Williams, Davis, McCrea, Long, & Hennessy, 1999). The long-term effects of either prenatal stress or alcohol include several changes in the structure of the nervous system, making the affected males' anatomy closer to that of females (Nosenko & Reznikov, 2001; I. L. Ward, Romeo, Denning, & Ward, 1999).

Although these studies pertained to rats, they prompted investigators to examine possible effects of prenatal stress on humans. Three surveys asked mothers of homosexual sons and mothers of heterosexual sons whether they experienced any unusual stress during pregnancy. In two of the three, the mothers of homosexual sons recalled more than average stressful experiences (Bailey, Willerman, & Parks, 1991; Ellis, Ames, Peckham, & Burke, 1988; Ellis & Cole-Harding, 2001). However, these studies relied on women's memories of pregnancies more than 20 years earlier. A better but more difficult procedure would be to measure stress during pregnancy and examine the sexual orientation of the sons many years later. Not much research has addressed this question.

So, what influences account for differences in sexual orientation? The answer is probably not the same in all instances. Genetic or epigenetic factors contribute, as well as prenatal environment. Later experiences probably contribute too, although we know little about the types of experience that would be most decisive.

STOP&CHECK

19. By what route might having an older brother increase the probability of male homosexuality?

20. How might stress to a pregnant rat alter the sexual orientation of her male offspring?

ANSWERS

19. Having an older brother might increase the probability of male homosexuality by altering the mother's immune system in the prenatal environment. The effect of the older brother does not depend on growing up in the same home. **20.** Evidently, the stress increases the release of endorphins in the hypothalamus, and very high endorphin levels can block the effects of testosterone.

Brain Anatomy

Do brains also differ as a function of sexual orientation? The results are complex. On average, homosexual men are shifted partly in the female-typical direction for some brain structures but not others. Similarly, on average, homosexual women's brains are slightly shifted in the male direction in some ways but not others (Rahman & Wilson, 2003). Several of the reported differences have no clear relationship to sexuality itself, although they may relate to other behavioral differences between heterosexual and homosexual people.

On average, the left and right hemispheres of the cerebral cortex are of nearly equal size in heterosexual females, whereas

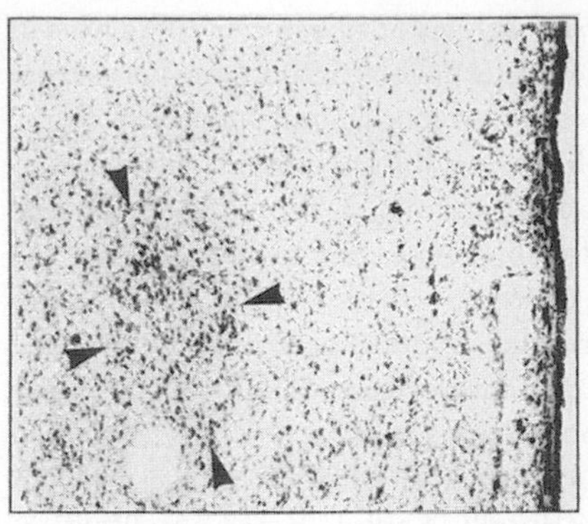

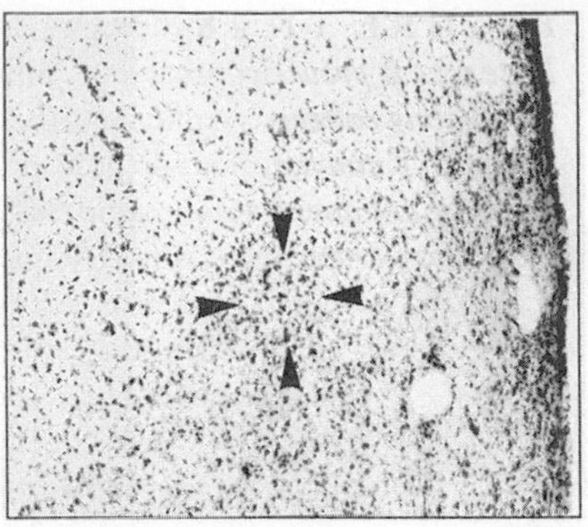

FIGURE 10.15 Typical sizes of interstitial nucleus 3 of the anterior hypothalamus
On the average, the volume of this structure was more than twice as large in a sample of heterosexual men (left) than in a sample of homosexual men (right), for whom it was about the same size as in women. *Source:* From "A difference in hypothalamic structure between heterosexual and homosexual men," by S. LeVay, *Science, 253*, pp. 1034–1037. Copyright 1991. Reprinted with permission from AAAS.

the right hemisphere is a few percent larger in heterosexual males. Homosexual males resemble heterosexual females in this regard, and homosexual females are intermediate between heterosexual females and males. Also, in heterosexual females, the left amygdala has more widespread connections than the right amygdala, whereas in heterosexual males, the right amygdala has more widespread connections. Again, homosexual males resemble heterosexual females in this regard, and homosexual females are intermediate (Savic & Lindström, 2008). The anterior commissure (see Figure 3.13) is, on average, larger in heterosexual women than in heterosexual men. In homosexual men, it is at least as large as in women, perhaps even slightly larger (Gorski & Allen, 1992). The suprachiasmatic nucleus (SCN) is also larger in homosexual men than in heterosexual men (Swaab & Hofman, 1990). However, when interpreting these and other reported differences, we should remember two cautions (Kaiser, Haller, Schmitz, & Nitsch, 2009): First, we don't know whether these brain differences are causes or effects of sexual orientation. Brain differences can predispose to different behaviors, but it is also true that persistent behaviors can change brain anatomy. Second, it is relatively easy to publish results showing a difference between two groups, such as homosexual and heterosexual people, even if the difference was unpredicted, small, and hard to explain. It is less easy to publish results showing no difference. Thus it is possible, even likely, that the published papers overstate certain anatomical differences.

The most widely cited research concerns the third interstitial nucleus of the anterior hypothalamus (INAH-3), which is generally more than twice as large in heterosexual men as in women. This area has more cells with androgen receptors in men than in women (Shah et al., 2004), and probably plays a role in sexual behavior, although the exact role is uncertain and probably varies among animal species. Simon LeVay (1991) examined INAH-3 in 41 people who had died between the ages of 26 and 59. Of these, 16 were heterosexual men, 6 were heterosexual women, and 19 were homosexual men. All of the homosexual men, 6 of the 16 heterosexual men, and 1 of the 6 women had died of AIDS. LeVay found that the mean volume of INAH-3 was larger in heterosexual men than in heterosexual women or homosexual men, who were about equal in this regard. Figure 10.15 shows typical cross-sections for a heterosexual man and a homosexual man. Figure 10.16 shows the distribution of volumes for the three groups. Note that the difference between heterosexual men and the other two groups is fairly large, on average, and that the cause of death (AIDS versus other) has no clear relationship to the results. LeVay (1993) later examined the hypothalamus of a homosexual man who died of lung cancer; he had a small INAH-3, like the homosexual men who died of AIDS. In Figure 10.16, note also the substantial amount of difference among individuals. If you could examine some man's INAH-3, you could make a reasonable guess about sexual orientation, but you could not be confident.

A later study partly replicated these trends. Researchers found that the INAH-3 nucleus was slightly larger in heterosexual than homosexual men, although in this study the homosexual men's INAH-3 nucleus was larger than

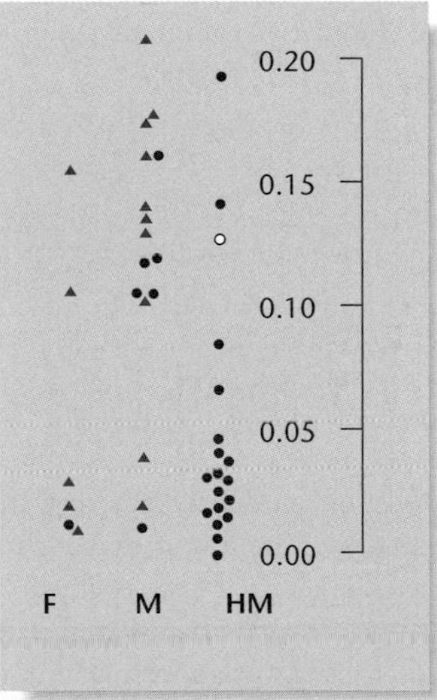

FIGURE 10.16 Volumes of the interstitial nucleus 3 of the anterior hypothalamus (INAH-3)
Samples are females (F), heterosexual males (M), and homosexual males (HM). Each filled circle represents a person who died of AIDS, and each triangle represents a person who died from other causes. The one open circle represents a bisexual man who died of AIDS. *Source:* Based on "A difference in hypothalamic structure between heterosexual and homosexual men," by S. LeVay, Science, 253, pp. 1034–1037. 1991, American Association for the Advancement of Science.

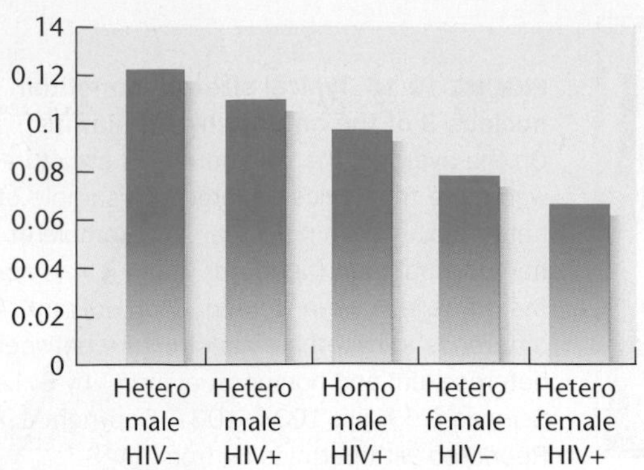

FIGURE 10.17 Another comparison of INAH-3
In this study, the mean volume for homosexual men was larger than that of women but smaller than that of men. *Source:* Based on data of Byne et al., 2001

that of heterosexual women (Byne et al., 2001). Among heterosexual men or women, the INAH-3 nucleus was larger in those who were HIV negative than those who were HIV positive, but even if we look only at HIV-positive men, we still find a difference in the hypothalamus between heterosexual and homosexual men. Figure 10.17 displays the means for the five groups. On microscopic examination of the INAH-3, researchers found that heterosexual men had larger neurons than homosexual men but about the same number. (Neither this study nor LeVay's earlier study included homosexual females.) Still another study found INAH-3 to be larger in heterosexual males than in male-to-female transsexuals—that is, people born as males who changed their identities to female (Garcia-Falgueras & Swaab, 2008).

The meaning of these results is not clear. Do differences in the hypothalamus influence sexual orientation, or does sexual activity influence the size of hypothalamic neurons? Some brain areas do grow or shrink in adults because of hormones or behavioral activities (Cooke, Tabibnia, & Breedlove, 1999). Although it would not be feasible to measure the size of INAH-3 before and after men's onset of sexual activity, a nonhuman study offers suggestive results. About 8 percent of rams (male sheep) direct their sexual behavior toward other males. One area of the anterior hypothalamus is larger in female-oriented rams than in male-oriented rams and larger in male-oriented rams than in females (Roselli, Larkin, Resko, Stellflug, & Stormshak, 2004). (Whether this area corresponds to human INAH-3 is uncertain.) This area becomes larger in male than female sheep before birth as a result of prenatal testosterone levels (Roselli, Stadelman, Reeve, Bishop, & Stormshak, 2007). In sheep, at least, an anatomical difference appears before any sexual behavior, and so it is more likely a cause than a result. The same may or may not be true in humans.

STOP&CHECK

21. In LeVay's study, what evidence argues against the idea that INAH-3 volume depends on AIDS rather than sexual orientation?

ANSWER

21. The average size of INAH-3 was about the same for heterosexual men who died of AIDS and those who died of other causes. One homosexual man who died of other causes had about the same size INAH-3 as heterosexual men who died of AIDS.

MODULE 10.2 ■ IN CLOSING

We Are Not All the Same

When Alfred Kinsey conducted the first massive surveys of human sexual behavior, he found that most of the people he interviewed considered their own behavior "normal," whatever it was. Many believed that sexual activity much more frequent than their own was abnormal and might even lead to insanity (Kinsey, Pomeroy, & Martin, 1948; Kinsey, Pomeroy, Martin, & Gebhard, 1953).

How far have we come since then? People today are more aware and generally more accepting of sexual diversity than they were in Kinsey's time. Still, intolerance remains common. Biological research will not tell us how to treat one another, but it can help us understand how we come to be so different.

Summary

1. In many species, males and females evolve different appearances and behaviors because of sexual selection. That is, they evolve in ways that make them more appealing to the other sex. **341**
2. Many of the mating habits of people can be interpreted in terms of increasing the probability of passing on our genes. However, it is hard to know to what extent the differences between men and women are evolutionary adaptations and to what extent they are learned. **341**

3. People can develop ambiguous genitals or genitals that don't match their chromosomal sex for several reasons. The most common is congenital adrenal hyperplasia, in which a genetic defect in cortisol production leads to overstimulation of the adrenal gland and therefore extra testosterone production. When that condition occurs in a female fetus, she becomes partly masculinized. **343**
4. On the average, girls with a history of congenital adrenal hyperplasia show more interest in boy-typical toys than other girls do, and during adolescence and young adulthood, they continue to show partly masculinized interests. **344**
5. Testicular feminization, or androgen insensitivity, is a condition in which someone with an XY chromosome pattern is partly or fully insensitive to androgens and therefore develops a female external appearance. **344**
6. People born with intermediate or ambiguous genitals are called intersexes. For many years, physicians recommended surgery to make these people look more feminine. However, many intersexes do not develop an unambiguous female identity, and many protest against the imposed surgery. **344**
7. Some children have a gene that decreases their early production of dihydrotestosterone. Such a child looks female at birth and is considered a girl but develops a penis at adolescence. Most of these people then accept a male gender identity. **345**
8. On average, homosexual people differ from heterosexual people in several anatomical and physiological regards, although the averages do not apply to every individual. **346**
9. Plausible biological explanations for homosexual orientation include genetics, prenatal hormones, and (in males) reactions to the mother's immune system. Hormone levels in adulthood are within the normal range. **346**
10. Several hypotheses have been offered for how genes promoting homosexuality could remain at moderate frequencies in the population although homosexual people are less likely than average to have children. **347**
11. On the average, certain aspects of brain anatomy differ between homosexual and heterosexual men, although it is not certain whether these differences are causes or effects of the behavior. **348**

Key Terms

Terms are defined in the module on the page number indicated. They're also presented in alphabetical order with definitions in the book's Subject Index/Glossary. Interactive flash cards, audio reviews, and crossword puzzles are among the online resources available to help you learn these terms and the concepts they represent.

androgen insensitivity **344**
congenital adrenal hyperplasia **343**
gender identity **343**
hermaphrodite **343**
intersex **343**
sexual selection **341**
testicular feminization **344**

Thought Question

1. On average, intersexes have IQ scores in the 110 to 125 range, well above the mean for the population (Dalton, 1968; Ehrhardt & Money, 1967; Lewis, Money, & Epstein, 1968). One possible interpretation is that a hormonal pattern intermediate between male and female promotes great intellectual development. Another possibility is that intersexuality may be more common in intelligent families than in less intelligent ones or that the more intelligent families are more likely to bring their intersexed children to an investigator's attention. What kind of study would be best for deciding among these hypotheses? (For one answer, see Money & Lewis, 1966.)
2. Recall LeVay's study of brain anatomy in heterosexual and homosexual men. Certain critics have suggested that one or more of the men classified as "heterosexual" might actually have been homosexual or bisexual. If so, would that fact strengthen or weaken the overall conclusions?

MODULE 10.2 End of Module Quiz

1. What is meant by "sexual selection"?
   a. Having an XX or XY chromosome pattern determines whether one develops as a female or a male.
   b. Hormones during a sensitive period produce long-lasting effects on anatomy and behavior.
   c. Some people choose to switch from one gender identity to another.
   d. Evolution favors characteristics that make an individual more appealing to the opposite sex.

2. In a fetus with congenital adrenal hypertrophy (CAH), the adrenal gland produces __________ cortisol, and as a result, the pituitary directs the adrenal gland to produce __________ testosterone.
   a. less than average . . . less than average
   b. less than average . . . more than average
   c. more than average . . . less than average
   d. more than average . . . more than average

3. A girl's interest in boys' toys correlates positively with which of the following?
   a. The size of her hippocampus
   b. Exposure to testosterone before birth
   c. Exposure to cortisol before birth
   d. Exposure to estradiol before birth

4. What condition occurs if a male lacks the receptor that enables androgens to activate genes in a cell's nucleus?
   a. Klinefelter's syndrome
   b. Congenital adrenal hyperplasia
   c. Testicular feminization
   d. Turner's syndrome

5. When genetic males lacked the enzyme that converts testosterone to dihydrotestosterone, what happened to their sexual development?
   a. They developed an exaggerated male anatomy.
   b. They looked female at birth but developed male structures at puberty.
   c. They looked male at birth but developed female structures at puberty.
   d. They developed as females, except without menstruation or pubic hair.

6. On average, how do heterosexual and homosexual men compare in height?
   a. On average, heterosexual men are several inches taller.
   b. On average, heterosexual men are only very slightly taller.
   c. On average, heterosexual and homosexual men are equal in height.
   d. On average, homosexual men are taller.

7. Of the following, which is *the least* plausible hypothesis for why natural selection has not eliminated genes for male homosexuality?
   a. Perhaps the relatives of a homosexual male have more than an average number of children.
   b. Homosexual people might spread their genes by helping their brothers and sisters rear their children.
   c. Maybe there is no gene for homosexuality. Instead, an environmental event produces an epigenetic effect that can be transmitted from one generation to the next.
   d. Some homosexual men have children.

8. Which of the following would increase the probability that a boy will develop a homosexual orientation?
   a. Living in a family with one or more older sisters
   b. Living in a family with an older, adopted brother
   c. Having a biological older brother, even if he did not live in the same house
   d. Having either an adopted or biological younger brother

9. How might stress to a pregnant rat alter the sexual orientation of her male offspring?
   a. Stress increases synthesis of the neurotransmitter acetylcholine.
   b. Stress decreases synthesis of alpha-fetoprotein.
   c. Stress increases the release of endorphins in the hypothalamus.
   d. Stress decreases the release of corticosterone or cortisol from the adrenal glands.

10. In what way was INAH-3 distinctive for most of the homosexual men in LeVay's study and the follow-up research?
   a. This nucleus had fewer than average neurons but only in men who died of AIDS.
   b. This nucleus had fewer than average neurons regardless of the cause of death.
   c. This nucleus had neurons with smaller than average volume.
   d. This nucleus had fewer neurons, but each of them had a larger than average volume.

ANSWERS: 1d, 2b, 3b, 4c, 5b, 6b, 7d, 8c, 9c, 10c.

Suggestions for Further Reading

Colapinto, J. (2000). *As nature made him: The boy who was raised as a girl.* New York: HarperCollins.

Describes the boy whose penis was accidentally removed, as presented on page **345**.

Diamond, J. (1997). *Why is sex fun?* New York: Basic Books.

Human sexual behavior differs from that of other species in many ways and therefore raises many evolutionary issues, which this book addresses. For example, why do humans have sex at times when the woman cannot become pregnant? Why do women have menopause? Why don't men breast-feed their babies? And what good are men, anyway? If you haven't thought about such questions before, you should read this book.

LeVay, S. (2011). *Gay, straight, and the reason why.* New York: Oxford University Press.

A scientific discussion of the research concerning the factors that influence sexual orientation.

kurhan/Shutterstock

Emotional Behaviors

11

CHAPTER OUTLINE

MODULE 11.1 What Is Emotion?
Emotions and Autonomic Arousal
Do People Have a Limited Number of Basic Emotions?
The Functions of Emotion
In Closing: Emotions and the Nervous System
MODULE 11.2 Attack and Escape Behaviors
Attack Behaviors
Fear and Anxiety
Anxiety Disorders
Relief From Anxiety
In Closing: Doing Something About Emotions
MODULE 11.3 Stress and Health
Stress and the General Adaptation Syndrome
Stress and the Hypothalamus-Pituitary-Adrenal Cortex Axis
Stress Control
In Closing: Emotions and Body Reactions

LEARNING OBJECTIVES

After studying this chapter, you should be able to:

1. Discuss the role of the autonomic nervous system in emotional feelings.
2. Explain why some psychologists are skeptical of the idea of a few basic emotions.
3. Describe some of the functions of emotions.
4. Describe what is known about the genetics of aggression and anxiety.
5. Discuss the role of the amygdala in emotional processing.
6. Comment on methods of relief from anxiety.
7. Define the general adaptation syndrome.
8. Describe the effects of stress on the immune system.

Unfortunately, one of the most significant things ever said about emotion may be that everyone knows what it is until they are asked to define it.

Joseph LeDoux (1996, p. 23)

Suppose researchers have discovered a new species—let's call it species X—and psychologists begin testing its abilities. They place food behind a green card and nothing behind a red card and find that after a few trials, X always goes to the green card. So we conclude that X shows learning, memory, and hunger. Then researchers offer X a green card and a variety of gray cards; X still goes to the green, so it must have color vision and not just brightness discrimination. Next they let X touch a blue triangle that is extremely hot. X makes a loud sound and backs away. Someone picks up the blue triangle (with padded gloves) and starts moving with it rapidly toward X. As soon as X sees this happening, it makes the same sound, turns, and starts moving rapidly away. Shall we conclude that it feels fear?

If you said yes, now let me add: I said this was a new species, and so it is, but it's a new species of robot, not animal. Do you still think X feels fear? Most people are willing to talk about artificial learning, memory, intelligence, and motivation, but not emotion.

If such behavior isn't adequate evidence for emotion in a robot, is it adequate evidence for an animal? When a dog runs away from a threat, you probably infer that it is afraid, but what about a butterfly that escapes as you approach? Was it afraid? How would we know? Emotion is a difficult topic because it implies conscious feelings that we cannot observe. Biological researchers therefore talk mostly about emotional *behaviors,* which are observable, even if the emotional feelings are not. Still, most of us hope eventually to learn something about the emotional experiences themselves.

OPPOSITE: People express emotion by facial expressions, gestures, and postures.

What Is Emotion?

By one definition, emotion includes "cognitive evaluations, subjective changes, autonomic and neural arousal, and impulses to action" (Plutchik, 1982, p. 551). That sounds okay, but by that definition, don't hunger and thirst count as emotions? One definition of motivation is "an internal process that modifies the way an organism responds to a certain class of external stimuli" (Numan & Woodside, 2010). By that definition, don't happiness, sadness, fear, and anger count as motivations? Distinguishing between motivation and emotion is difficult, and maybe there is no real difference.

Regardless of how we define emotion, or whether we define it at all, psychologists generally agree that emotion has components including cognitions ("This is a dangerous situation"), feelings ("I feel frightened"), and actions ("Run away now"). How do the components relate to one another?

Emotions and Autonomic Arousal

Emotional situations arouse the two branches of the autonomic nervous system—the sympathetic and the parasympathetic. Figure 11.1 reviews the anatomy. Researchers had long recognized that the sympathetic nervous system stimulates certain organs, such as the heart, while inhibiting others, such as the stomach and intestines. Walter Cannon (1945) was the

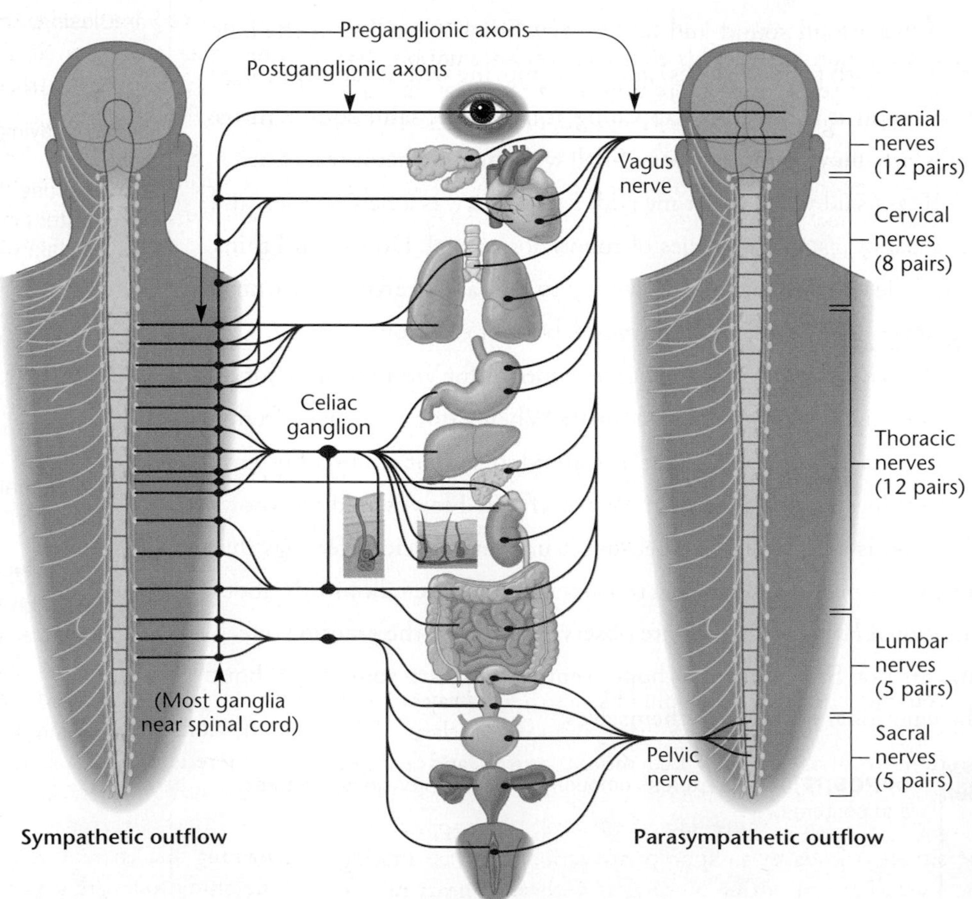

FIGURE 11.1 The sympathetic and parasympathetic nervous systems
Review Chapter 3 for more information.

first to recognize the pattern: It stimulates organs important for vigorous "fight-or-flight" activities while inhibiting vegetative activities that could wait until later. The parasympathetic nervous system increases digestion and other processes that save energy and prepare for later events. However, most situations evoke a combination of sympathetic and parasympathetic arousal (Wolf, 1995). For example, nausea is associated with sympathetic stimulation of the stomach (decreasing its contractions and secretions) and parasympathetic stimulation of the intestines and salivary glands.

National Library of Medicine

Walter B. Cannon
(1871–1945)

As a matter of routine I have long trusted unconscious processes to serve me. . . . [One] example I may cite was the interpretation of the significance of bodily changes which occur in great emotional excitement, such as fear and rage. These changes—the more rapid pulse, the deeper breathing, the increase of sugar in the blood, the secretion from the adrenal glands—were very diverse and seemed unrelated. Then, one wakeful night, after a considerable collection of these changes had been disclosed, the idea flashed through my mind that they could be nicely integrated if conceived as bodily preparations for supreme effort in flight or in fighting.

How does the autonomic nervous system relate to emotions? Common sense holds that you feel an emotion that changes your heart rate and prompts other responses. In contrast, according to the **James-Lange theory** (James, 1884), the autonomic arousal and skeletal actions come first. What you experience as an emotion is the label you give to your responses: You feel afraid *because* you run away, and you feel angry *because* you attack.

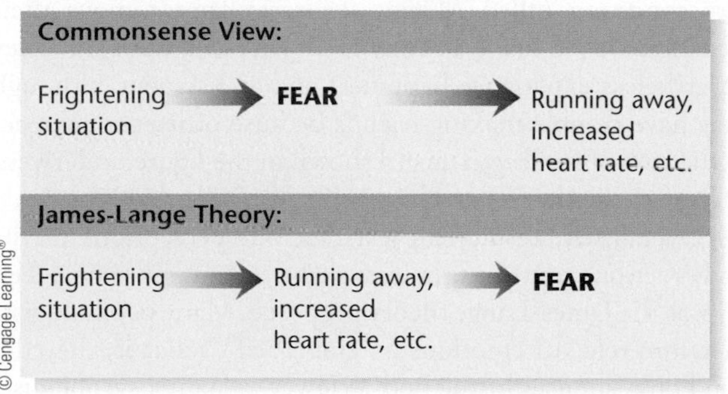

© Cengage Learning®

You might object, "How would I know to run away before I was scared?" In a later paper, William James (1894) clarified his position. An emotion includes cognitions, actions, and feelings. The cognitive aspect comes first. You quickly appraise something as good, bad, frightening, or whatever. Your appraisal of the situation leads to an appropriate action, such as running away, attacking, or sitting motionless with your heart racing. When James said that arousal and actions lead to emotions, he meant they lead to the *feeling* aspect of an emotion. That is,

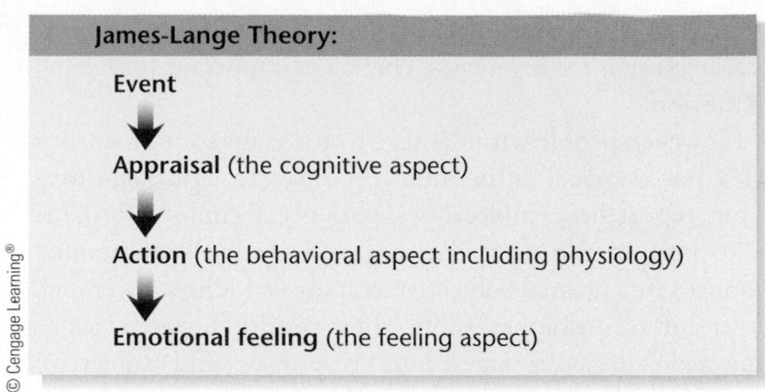

© Cengage Learning®

The James-Lange theory leads to two predictions: People with weak autonomic or skeletal responses should feel less emotion, and causing or increasing someone's responses should enhance an emotion. Let's consider the evidence.

Is Physiological Arousal *Necessary* for Emotional Feelings?

People with damage to the spinal cord have no sensations or voluntary movements from the level of the damage downward. (Reflexes remain.) Nevertheless, they generally report experiencing emotions about the same as before their injury (Cobos, Sánchez, Pérez, & Vila, 2004; Deady, North, Allan, Smith, & O'Carroll, 2010). That result might suggest that emotions don't depend on feedback from movement, but these people continue to have facial expressions and changes in heart rate, which they can detect. So although they are cut off from much of the usual sensation associated with an emotion, they continue to feel certain important aspects.

In people with an uncommon condition called **pure autonomic failure**, output from the autonomic nervous system to the body fails, either completely or almost completely. Heart beat and other organ activities continue, but the nervous system no longer regulates them. Someone with this condition does not react to stressful experiences with changes in heart rate, blood pressure, or sweating. According to the James-Lange theory, we would expect such people to report no emotions. In fact, they report having the same emotions as anyone else, and they have little difficulty identifying what emotion a character in a story would probably experience (Heims, Critchley, Dolan, Mathias, & Cipolotti, 2004). However, they say they feel their emotions much less intensely than before (Critchley, Mathias, & Dolan, 2001). Presumably, when they report that they experience emotions, they refer to the cognitive aspect: "Yes, I'm angry, because this is a situation that calls for anger." But if they *feel* the anger, they feel it weakly. Their decreased emotional feeling is consistent with predictions from the James-Lange theory.

Here is another example: Botulinum toxin ("BOTOX") blocks transmission at synapses and nerve–muscle junctions. Physicians sometimes use it to paralyze the muscles for frowning and thereby remove frown lines on people's faces. One study found that people with BOTOX injections that temporarily paralyzed all the facial muscles reported weaker than usual emotional responses when they watched short videos (Davis, Senghas, Brandt, & Ochsner, 2010). The implication is that feeling a body change is important for feeling an emotion.

However, people with damage to the right somatosensory cortex have normal autonomic responses to emotional music but report little subjective experience. People with damage to part of the prefrontal cortex have weak autonomic responses but normal subjective responses (Johnson, Tranel, Lutgendorf, & Adolphs, 2009). These results suggest a lack of connection between autonomic responses and subjective experience, although it remains possible that what they describe as a subjective experience may be more cognition than feeling.

Is Physiological Arousal *Sufficient* for Emotions?

According to the James-Lange theory, emotional feelings result from the body's actions. If your heart started racing and you started sweating and breathing rapidly, would you feel an emotion? Not necessarily. You might have those reactions from vigorous exercise, or they might accompany an illness with fever. However, if you had sudden intense arousal of the sympathetic nervous system without knowing the reason, you might experience it as an emotion. Such is the case with a **panic attack**, when people gasp for breath, worry that they are suffocating, and experience great anxiety (Klein, 1993).

Although physiological responses are seldom sufficient to produce emotional feelings, they do contribute. Increases in heart rate intensify ratings of both pleasant and unpleasant emotions, and they contribute most strongly in people who are most sensitive to their internal state, as measured by their ability to count their own heartbeats (Dunn et al., 2010). Also, several of the cortical areas that respond most strongly to the body's autonomic responses also respond strongly to emotional states, as indicated by fMRI recordings (Terasawa, Fukushima, & Umeda, 2013).

What about feedback from facial expressions? If you find yourself smiling, do you become happier? To test this hypothesis, how could we get people to smile? If we simply tell participants in an experiment to smile and then ask whether they are happy, they will surely say what they think we want to hear. Clever researchers found a way to get people to smile while concealing the purpose of the study. It is a method you could easily try yourself: Hold a pen in your mouth, with either your teeth or your lips, as shown in Figure 11.2. Now examine a page of newspaper comic strips. Mark each one + for very funny, ✓ for somewhat funny, or – for not funny. Most people rate cartoons funnier when holding a pen with their teeth, which forces a smile, than when holding it with their lips, which prevents a smile (Strack, Martin, & Stepper, 1988). Another study found that forcing a smile decreased a stressful experience, as measured by changes in heart rate (Kraft & Pressman, 2012). That is, the sensation caused by smiling increases happiness . . . slightly. (Telling people with severe depression to smile does not help. It just annoys them.)

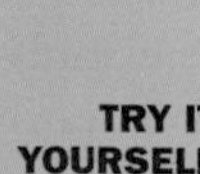

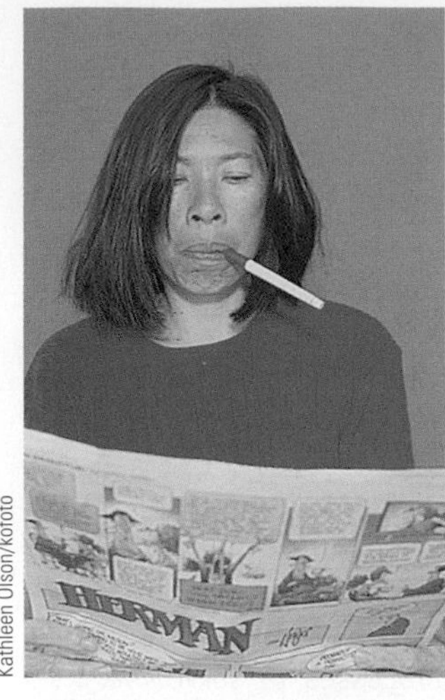

Kathleen Olson/kofoto

FIGURE 11.2 Effect of facial expression on emotion
People who hold a pen in their teeth, and who are therefore forced to smile, are more likely to report amusement than are people with a pen in their lips, who therefore cannot smile.

Researchers also found a clever way to ask people to frown without saying so. They said they wanted to test people's ability to do a cognitive task and a motor task at the same time. The cognitive task was to examine photographs and rate their pleasantness or unpleasantness. For the motor task, researchers attached golf tees to each of the person's eyebrows and said to try to keep the tips of the golf tees touching each other. The only way to do that was to frown. People given this instruction rated the photographs as more unpleasant than the average for people who were not induced to frown (Larsen, Kasimatis, & Frey, 1992). Another study found that changes in facial expression could alter the experiences of surprise and disgust (Lewis, 2012).

However, although facial expressions slightly alter emotions, smiles are not *necessary* for happiness. People with a rare condition called *Möbius syndrome* cannot move their facial muscles to make a smile, as shown in Figure 11.3. They nevertheless experience happiness and amusement, although they have trouble making friends because other people react to the lack of smiling. The girl shown in the figure underwent surgery to give her an artificial smile (G. Miller, 2007b).

Overall, the results suggest that our perceptions of the body's actions contribute at least slightly to our emotional feelings, as the James-Lange theory proposed. Many psychologists therefore refer to emotions as "embodied"—that is, they depend on responses of the body. However, many psychologists from the start have been dissatisfied with this theory. Walter Cannon (1927) objected that feedback from the viscera is neither necessary nor sufficient for emotion, that it does not distinguish one emotion from another, and that it is too slow to account for how fast we identify an event as happy, sad, or frightening. He and others have proposed additional theories, and no consensus has emerged (Moors, 2009). So here we are, well over a hundred years after William James proposed one of the first theories in psychology, and we still haven't decided whether it is correct. Shouldn't psychologists be embarrassed?

Courtesy of Lori Thomas

FIGURE 11.3 Möbius syndrome People with this condition cannot move their facial muscles to smile. This girl went through surgery to give her an artificial smile, as shown. The lack of a smile before surgery did not rob her of happiness or a sense of humor, although it interfered with her ability to make friends.

The problem may be that different theorists are talking about different questions, even when they use the same words. When James's defenders talk about "emotional feelings," they mean literally feelings—that is, sensations—and sensations come only from sense organs, such as those that detect body actions. Other theorists are talking about the complete emotional experience. Moreover, the debate about theories of emotion may be ultimately fruitless. Except for inspiring some interesting research studies of the types just described, theories of emotion don't have much application. In fact, several influential modern theorists question whether our whole concept of emotion is misguided.

Is Emotion a Useful Concept?

To talk about "an" emotion, such as anger or fear, implies that it is a coherent whole. Nearly all definitions of emotion include three or more aspects, such as cognition, feeling, and action. However, those aspects do not always stick together. You could have one aspect alone, or two aspects alone. For example, if you recognize that flu season is approaching (cognition) and you worry about getting sick (feeling), but you do nothing about it (no action), does that count as fear? What if you recognize flu season is coming (cognition), you don't really worry about it (no feeling), but you decide to get a vaccination anyway (action). Would that count as fear? What if you suddenly feel nervous (feeling), but you don't know why (no cognition), and you do nothing about it (no action). Is that an emotion? Perhaps emotion is not a coherent category.

Furthermore, if we have several emotions, wouldn't you expect that we could identify one from another physiologically? Traditionally, the **limbic system**—the forebrain areas surrounding the thalamus—has been regarded as critical for emotion (see Figure 11.4). We consider one part of it, the amygdala, in more detail later in this chapter. Much of the cerebral cortex also reacts to emotional situations.

Researchers have used PET or fMRI techniques to identify the brain areas that respond while people look at emotional pictures or listen to emotional stories. In Figure 11.5, each dot represents a research study that found significant activation of a

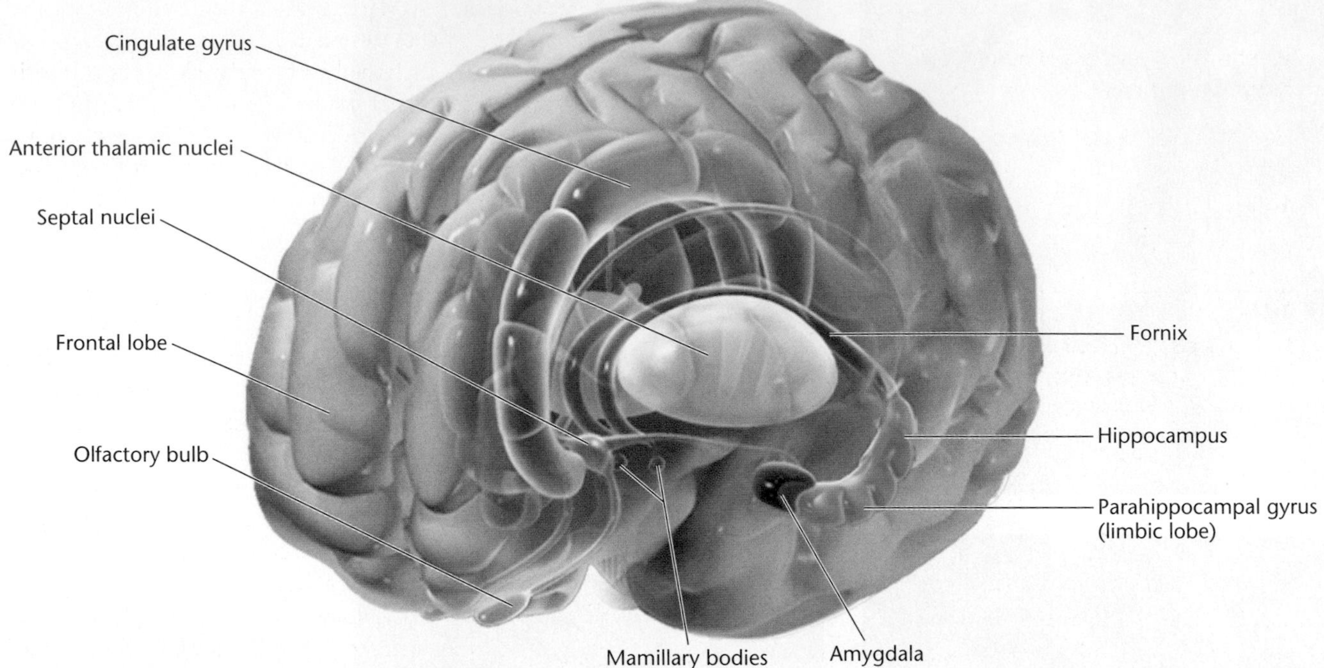

FIGURE 11.4 The limbic system
The limbic system is a group of structures in the interior of the brain. Here you see them as if the exterior of the brain were transparent.
Source: Based on MacLean, 1949

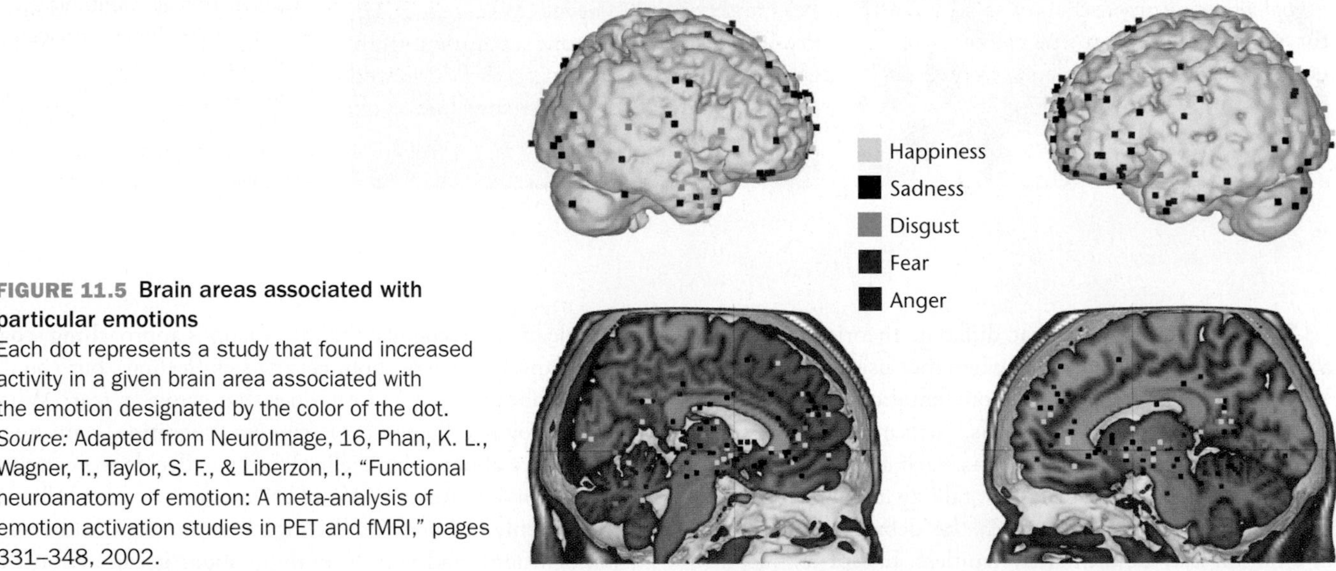

FIGURE 11.5 Brain areas associated with particular emotions
Each dot represents a study that found increased activity in a given brain area associated with the emotion designated by the color of the dot.
Source: Adapted from NeuroImage, 16, Phan, K. L., Wagner, T., Taylor, S. F., & Liberzon, I., "Functional neuroanatomy of emotion: A meta-analysis of emotion activation studies in PET and fMRI," pages 331–348, 2002.

particular cortical area associated with happiness, sadness, disgust, fear, or anger (Phan, Wager, Taylor, & Liberzon, 2002). The most salient point of this figure is the variability of locations for each emotion. The results apparently depend more on the details of procedure than on which emotion was targeted. A later extensive review of brain imaging studies found no strong evidence for localization of emotions. That is, no type of emotion consistently activates one brain area, and no brain area is associated with only one emotion. No brain area seems critical for emotion in general without contributing to other aspects of behavior (Lindquist, Wager, Kober, Bliss-Moreau, & Barrett, 2012).

Lisa Feldman Barrett (2012) has therefore argued that emotions are a real category only in the same sense that weeds are a real category. Nothing in nature makes weeds different from flowers. They differ only because people favor certain plants ("flowers") and disfavor other plants ("weeds"). Similarly, emotion is a socially constructed category that serves our purposes, but we shouldn't expect any scientific principle to explain what emotions "really are."

STOP&CHECK

1. What is the relevance of pure autonomic failure to the study of emotions?

2. How did researchers get people to smile or frown without using those words?

3. According to Lisa Barrett Feldman, why is it difficult to develop a scientific consensus about any theory of emotion?

ANSWERS

1. People with pure autonomic failure do not react to events with changes in heart rate or other autonomic functions. They report still having emotional experiences but they do not feel them as strongly. **2.** They got people to smile by telling them to hold a pen between their teeth. They got people to frown by attaching golf tees to their eyebrows and then telling them to keep the two tees touching each other. **3.** Emotion is a socially constructed category that people find useful, but it does not correspond to any category that exists in nature.

Do People Have a Limited Number of Basic Emotions?

In the early days of psychology (late 1800s and early 1900s), a goal of many researchers was to identify the elements of the mind, analogous to the elements of chemistry. They inquired whether the elements were thoughts, ideas, images, or something else. Before long, that quest seemed futile and the behaviorists, who rejected all reference to mind or mental experience, came to dominate academic psychology. Later, certain psychologists hoped to find the elements of motivation, offering lists of the basic motivations. That pursuit led to fascinating questions such as whether breathing counts as just one motivation or two (inhaling and exhaling). Today, emotion remains as virtually the only area in which many researchers still hope to identify elements of experience, to list a few "basic" emotions.

If we could identify brain areas, each associated with a particular emotion, we would count that as strong evidence for basic emotions, but as already mentioned, research has found no strong evidence for that conclusion. What is generally considered the main support for the idea of basic emotions is the existence of facial expressions for happiness, sadness, fear, anger, disgust, surprise, and perhaps other emotions. If shown a set of faces, such as those in Figure 11.6, and a list of emotion terms, most people in cultures throughout the world pair them up with greater-than-chance accuracy.

However, many psychologists find this evidence unconvincing. The faces used in most research, including those in Figure 11.6, were posed to try to maximize recognition. If we use photographs of spontaneous expressions in the real world, it is often difficult to distinguish sadness from disgust, or fear from surprise. Observers often see two or more emotions in a single face, and the emotion observers cite doesn't always match the self-report by the person in the photograph (Kayyal & Russell, 2013). Furthermore, we rarely identify someone's emotion from facial expression alone. Participants in one study viewed photos of pro tennis players who had just won or lost a point in a difficult, high-stakes match.

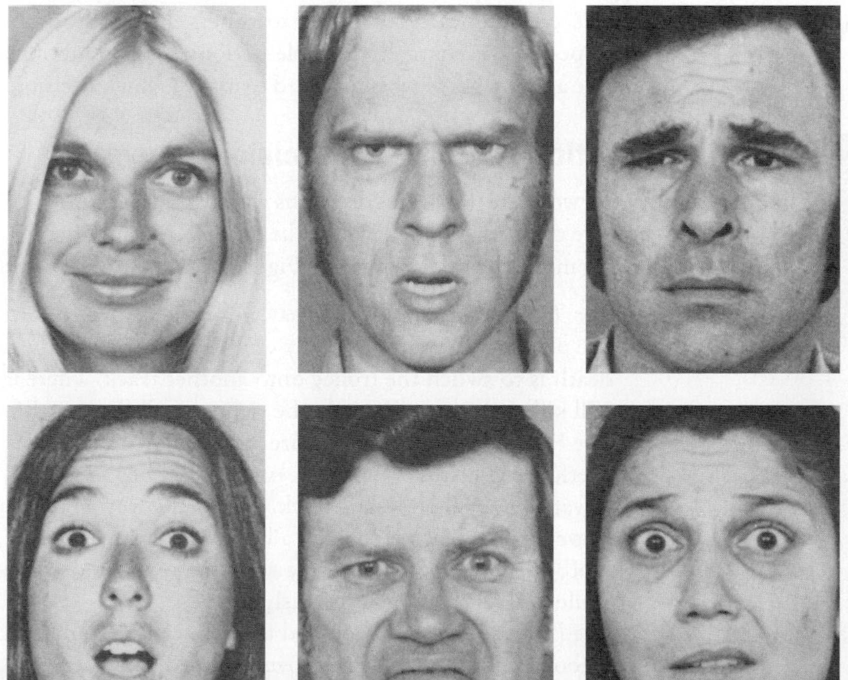

FIGURE 11.6 Facial Expressions of Emotion Can you identify which face corresponds to happiness, sadness, fear, anger, disgust, and surprise? Check answer A on page 366. *Source:* Reprinted from *Unmasking the face* (2nd ed.), by P. Ekman & W. V. Friesen, 1984. Palo Alto, CA: Consulting Psychologists Press.

From photos of body posture, the observers could usually guess whether the player was happy (having won the last point) or sad (having just lost it). But from facial expression alone, the observers could do no better than chance guessing (Aviezer, Trope, & Todorov, 2012). We also identify emotion by context and gestures (Figure 11.7). Tone of voice carries an enormous amount of emotional information (Iredale, Rushby, McDonald, Dimoska-Di Marco, & Swift, 2013). A simple expression such as "I see what you did" could convey pleasure, sadness, anger, fear, disgust, surprise, contempt . . . almost anything.

If we find the evidence for distinct basic emotions unconvincing, an alternative view is that emotional feelings vary along two or more continuous dimensions, such as weak versus strong, pleasant versus unpleasant, or approach versus avoid. Activity of the left hemisphere, especially its frontal and temporal lobes, relates to what Jeffrey Gray (1970) called the **behavioral activation system (BAS)**, marked by low to moderate autonomic arousal and a tendency to approach, which could characterize happiness or anger. Increased activity of the frontal and temporal lobes of the right hemisphere is associated with the **behavioral inhibition system (BIS)**, which increases attention and arousal, inhibits action, and stimulates emotions such as fear and disgust (Davidson & Fox, 1982; Davidson & Henriques, 2000; F. C. Murphy, Nimmo-Smith, & Lawrence, 2003; Reuter-Lorenz & Davidson, 1981).

People in one experiment viewed pictures flashed on one side or the other of the visual field, to prime one hemisphere or the other to process the information. People were quicker and more accurate at identifying happy faces when the information went to the left hemisphere. They had an advantage in processing sad or frightened information when the information went to the right hemisphere (Najt, Bayer, & Hausmann, 2013). Such results support an association between left hemisphere and approach, and between the right hemisphere and inhibition of action.

JONATHAN NACKSTRAND/AFP/Getty Images

Figure 11.7 Can you tell from this person's face whether she just won or lost? Or do you judge from the posture and context?

The difference between the hemispheres relates to personality: On the average, people with greater activity in the frontal cortex of the left hemisphere tend to be happier, more outgoing, and more fun-loving. People with greater right-hemisphere activity tend to be socially withdrawn, less satisfied with life, and prone to unpleasant emotions (Knyazev, Slobodskaya, & Wilson, 2002; Schmidt, 1999; Shackman, McMenamin, Maxwell, Greischar, & Davidson, 2009; Urry et al., 2004).

STOP&CHECK

4. What evidence challenges the idea that we identify people's emotions by their facial expressions?

ANSWER

4. Given a photo of a spontaneous facial expression, people usually see more than one emotion and often don't see the emotion described by the person whose face was shown. Also, in everyday life we identify someone's emotion by a combination of cues, including posture, context, gestures, and tone of voice.

The Functions of Emotion

If we evolved the capacity to experience and express emotions, emotions must have been adaptive for our ancestors, and probably for us as well. What good do emotions do?

For certain emotions, the answer is clear. Fear alerts us to escape from danger. Anger directs us to attack an intruder. Disgust tells us to avoid something that might cause illness. The adaptive value of happiness, sadness, embarrassment, and other emotions is less obvious, although researchers have suggested some plausible possibilities. Emotional expressions help us communicate our needs to others and understand other people's needs and probable actions. Also, emotions provide a useful guide when we need to make a quick decision.

Emotions and Moral Decisions

When we make important decisions we pay much attention to how we think an outcome will make us feel. Consider the following moral dilemmas, of which Figure 11.8 illustrates three:

> *The Trolley Dilemma.* A runaway trolley is headed toward five people on a track. The only way you can prevent their death is to switch the trolley onto another track, where it will kill one person. Would it be right to pull the switch?
>
> *The Footbridge Dilemma.* You are standing on a footbridge overlooking a trolley track. A runaway trolley is headed toward five people on a track. The only way you can prevent their death is to push a heavy-set stranger off the footbridge and onto the track so that he will block the trolley. Would it be right to push him?
>
> *The Lifeboat Dilemma.* You and five other people are on a lifeboat in icy waters, but it is overcrowded and starting to sink. If you push one of the people off the boat, the boat will stop sinking and the rest of you will survive. Would it be right to push someone off?

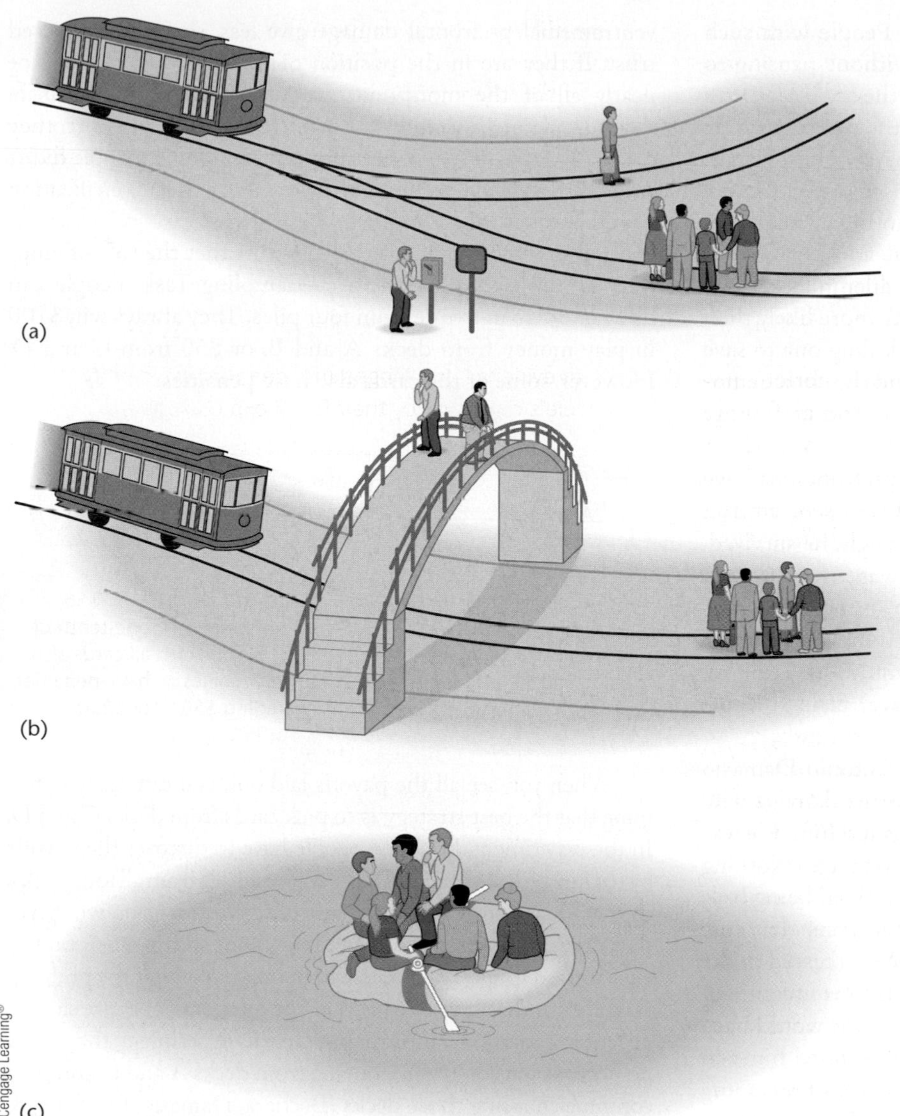

FIGURE 11.8 Three moral dilemmas (a) Would you divert a runaway train so it kills one person instead of five? (b) Would you push someone off a footbridge so a runaway train kills him instead of five others? (c) Would you push someone off a sinking lifeboat to save yourself and four others?

The Hospital Dilemma. You are a surgeon, and five of your patients will die soon unless they get organ transplants. Each needs the transplant of a different organ, and you haven't been able to find organ donors for any of them. A nurse bursts into your office: "Good news! A visitor to the hospital has just arrived, who has exactly the same tissue type as all five of your patients! We can kill this visitor and use the organs to save the five others!" Would it be right to do so?

In each of these dilemmas, you can save five people (including yourself in the lifeboat case) by killing one person. However, although that may be true logically, the decisions do not feel the same. Most people say it is right to pull the switch in the trolley dilemma, fewer say yes in the footbridge and lifeboat dilemmas, and almost no one endorses killing one person to save five others in the hospital dilemma. Brain scans show that contemplating the footbridge or lifeboat dilemma activates brain areas known to respond to emotions, including parts of the prefrontal cortex and cingulate gyrus (Greene, Sommerville, Nystrom, Darley, & Cohen, 2001). When you contemplate these situations, you react emotionally because you identify with the person whose suffering and death you might cause by your action, and that feeling is especially intense if you imagine putting your hands on someone rather than just flipping a switch. People with the strongest autonomic arousal are the least likely to make the "logical" decision to kill one and save five others (Cushman, Gray, Gaffey, & Mendes, 2012; Navarrete, McDonald, Mott, & Asher, 2012).

Is it right to make moral decisions emotionally? In the case of these dilemmas, certainly one can argue that sacrificing one person to save five others would benefit more people than it harms. However, a feeling that it is bad to push someone off a bridge is usually a good thing! In short, when we are making a decision about right and wrong, we seldom work it out rationally. One decision or the other just "feels" right. After we have already decided, we try to think of a logical justification (Haidt, 2001).

Decision Making after Brain Damage that Impairs Emotions

Damage to parts of the prefrontal cortex blunts people's emotions in most regards, except for an occasional outburst of anger. It also impairs decision making. People with such damage often make impulsive decisions without pausing to consider the consequences, including how they will feel after a possible mistake. When given a choice, they often make a quick decision and then sigh or wince, knowing that they have made the wrong choice (Berlin, Rolls, & Kischka, 2004). You might think of impulsive decisions as emotional, but these people's decisions often seem unemotional. For example, if confronted with the trolley car and other dilemmas we just discussed, people with prefrontal damage are more likely than average to choose the utilitarian option of killing one to save five, even in situations where most people find the choice emotionally unacceptable (Koenigs et al., 2007). And they make that utilitarian decision quickly and calmly.

The most famous case of a person with prefrontal damage is that of Phineas Gage. In 1848, an explosion sent an iron rod through Gage's prefrontal cortex. Amazingly, he survived. During the next few months, his behavior was impulsive and he made poor decisions. These are common symptoms of prefrontal damage. However, the reports about his behavior provide little detail. Over the years, with multiple retellings, people elaborated and exaggerated the meager facts available (Kotowicz, 2007).

We know more about a modern case. Antonio Damasio (1994) examined a man with prefrontal cortex damage who expressed almost no emotions. Nothing angered him. He was never very sad, even about his own brain damage. Nothing gave him much pleasure, not even music. Far from being brilliantly rational, he frequently made bad decisions that cost him his job, his marriage, and his savings. When tested in the laboratory, he successfully predicted the probable outcomes of various decisions. For example, when asked what would happen if he cashed a check and the bank teller handed him too much money, he knew the probable consequences of returning it or walking away with it. But he admitted, "I still wouldn't know what to do" (A. R. Damasio, 1994, p. 49). He knew that one action would win him approval and another would get him in trouble, but he apparently did not anticipate that approval would feel good and trouble would feel bad. Any choice requires consideration of values and emotions—how we think one outcome or another will make us feel. In Damasio's words, "Inevitably, emotions are inseparable from the idea of good and evil" (A. Damasio, 1999, p. 55).

After damage to a particular part of the prefrontal cortex—the ventromedial prefrontal cortex—people show inconsistent preferences, as if they aren't sure what they want or like (Camille, Griffiths, Vo, Fellows, & Kable, 2011). They also seem deficient in their sense of guilt, both in everyday life and in laboratory situations. Consider two economic games: In the one-shot Dictator game, you are the Dictator, and you are given some money to divide between yourself and another person, whatever way you choose. Most people split it evenly or almost evenly. People with ventromedial prefrontal damage keep about 90 percent, on average. In the Trust game, one person gets some money and has the option of giving some of it to a Trustee. If so, the amount given triples in value, and the Trustee can return any amount of it, such as half, to the first person. People with ventromedial prefrontal damage give less, showing decreased trust. If they are in the position of Trustee, they keep all or nearly all of the money instead of returning it (Krajbich, Adolphs, Tranel, Denburg, & Camerer, 2009). In short, they show less than normal concern for others. If most people didn't show a reasonable amount of concern for others, civilization would fall apart.

Here is an experiment to explore further the role of emotions in decisions. In the Iowa Gambling Task, people can draw one card at a time from four piles. They always win $100 in play money from decks A and B, or $50 from C and D. However, some of the cards also have penalties:

A	B	C	D
Gain $100; one-half of all cards also have penalties averaging $250	Gain $100; one-tenth of all cards also have penalties of $1250	Gain $50; one-half of all cards also have penalties averaging $50	Gain $50; one-tenth of all cards also have penalties of $250

When you see all the payoffs laid out, you can easily determine that the best strategy is to pick cards from decks C and D. In the experiment, however, people have to discover the payoffs by trial and error. Ordinarily, as people sample from all four decks, they gradually start showing signs of nervous tension whenever they draw a card from A or B, and they start shifting their preference toward C and D. People with damage to either the prefrontal cortex or the amygdala (part of the temporal lobe) are slow in processing emotional information. In this experiment, they show no nervous tension when drawing from decks A and B, and they continue choosing those decks (Bechara, Damasio, Damasio, & Lee, 1999). In short, failure to anticipate the unpleasantness of likely outcomes leads to bad decisions.

Of course, it is also true that emotions sometimes interfere with good decisions. If you were driving and suddenly started skidding on a patch of ice, what would you do? A patient with damage to his prefrontal cortex who faced this situation calmly followed the advice he had always heard: Take your foot off the accelerator and steer in the direction of the skid (Shiv, Loewenstein, Bechara, Damasio, & Damasio, 2005). Most people in this situation panic, hit the brakes, and steer away from the skid, making a bad situation worse.

STOP & CHECK

5. If brain damage impairs someone's emotions, what happens to the person's decision making?

ANSWER

5. After brain damage that impairs emotion, people make impulsive decisions, evidently because they do not quickly imagine how bad a poor decision might make them feel.

Emotions and the Nervous System

Although we regard emotions as nebulous internal states, they are fundamentally biological. As William James observed in the early days of psychology, emotions are "embodied"—an emotional feeling relates to the actions and sensations of the body.

Biological research sheds light on many of the central questions about the psychology of emotions. For example, one issue is whether people have a few basic emotions or continuous dimensions along which emotions vary. Biological research so far seems more consistent with the idea of dimensions. Studies of people with brain damage also shed light on the functions of emotion, particularly with relation to moral behavior and decision making. Far from being an impediment to intelligent behavior, emotional reactions are often a useful quick guide to appropriate actions. In short, understanding emotions and understanding their biology go hand in hand.

Summary

1. Most attempts to define emotion include several aspects including cognition, feelings, and action. **356**
2. The sympathetic nervous system readies the body for emergency fight-or-flight activities. **356**
3. According to the James-Lange theory, the feeling aspect of an emotion results from feedback from actions of the muscles and organs. **357**
4. People who have impaired autonomic responses continue to report emotional experiences, although the feeling aspect is weaker than before. **357**
5. Feedback from facial movements or other actions is not necessary for emotional experience, but it can strengthen emotional feelings. **358**
6. The various components of an emotion do not always occur together. Also, apparently no emotion corresponds to activity in a single brain area. For these and other reasons, many psychologists regard emotion as an arbitrary category, in which case we cannot expect to find any scientific answer to the question of what emotion is. **359**
7. We recognize other people's emotions by many cues, including facial expression, body posture, context, and tone of voice. Naturally occurring expressions do not fit neatly into a few distinct categories. **361**
8. Activation of the frontal and temporal areas of the left hemisphere is associated with approach and the behavioral activation system. The corresponding areas of the right hemisphere are associated with withdrawal, decreased activity, and the behavioral inhibition system. **362**
9. Brain damage that impairs emotional feelings and responses also impairs decision making. One interpretation is that people decide badly because they do not quickly imagine their emotional reactions to possible consequences. **363**
10. People with damage to the ventromedial prefrontal cortex show inconsistent preferences, as if they are unsure what they want or like. They also show little concern for other people. They apparently lack a normal sense of guilt. **364**

Key Terms

Terms are defined in the module on the page number indicated. They're also presented in alphabetical order with definitions in the book's Subject Index/Glossary. Interactive flash cards, audio reviews, and crossword puzzles are among the online resources available to help you learn these terms and the concepts they represent.

behavioral activation system (BAS) **362**
behavioral inhibition system (BIS) **362**
James-Lange theory **357**
limbic system **359**
panic attack **358**
pure autonomic failure **357**

Thought Question

According to the James-Lange theory, we should expect people with pure autonomic failure to experience weaker than average emotions. What kind of people might experience stronger than average emotions?

Answers to Questions in the Text

Question A, page 361: From left to right: happiness, anger, sadness, surprise, disgust, fear.

MODULE 11.1 End of Module Quiz

1. How do the functions of the sympathetic nervous system differ from those of the parasympathetic nervous system?
   a. The sympathetic system controls the left side of the body, and the parasympathetic system controls the right side.
   b. The parasympathetic system controls the left side of the body, and the sympathetic system controls the right side.
   c. The sympathetic system readies the body for emergency activities, and the parasympathetic activates digestive and other less urgent responses.
   d. The parasympathetic system readies the body for emergency activities, and the sympathetic activates digestive and other less urgent responses.
2. What is the contribution of the sympathetic nervous system to emotions?
   a. Sympathetic nervous system arousal is necessary and sufficient for an emotional experience.
   b. Sympathetic nervous system arousal is necessary but not sufficient for an emotional experience.
   c. Sympathetic nervous system arousal is sufficient but not necessary for an emotional experience.
   d. Sympathetic nervous system arousal is neither necessary nor sufficient for an emotional experience but it contributes to the feeling aspect of an emotion.
3. Which of the following causes a panic attack?
   a. Lack of feedback to the brain from heartbeat and other autonomic responses.
   b. Decreased heart rate in a situation that should call for heightened arousal.
   c. Equal, simultaneous arousal of the sympathetic and parasympathetic nervous systems.
   d. Intense, unexplained arousal of the sympathetic nervous system.
4. When researchers looked for brain areas associated with particular emotions, what did they find?
   a. Each emotion is centered in a different brain area.
   b. Anger is easy to localize in one brain area, but other emotions are not.
   c. Happiness and sadness each depends on one brain area, but other emotions do not.
   d. No brain area is responsible for one and only one emotion.
5. What brain area is associated with the behavioral activation system and a tendency to approach?
   a. The right hemisphere
   b. The left hemisphere
   c. The amygdala
   d. The hippocampus
6. When people consider a moral dilemma such as whether to push someone off a bridge to save five other people, which of the following correlates with a stronger tendency to agree to push the person?
   a. Weaker autonomic arousal
   b. Stronger autonomic arousal
   c. Lower intelligence
   d. Greater intelligence

ANSWERS:

1c, 2d, 3d, 4d, 5b, 6a.

Attack and Escape Behaviors

Have you ever watched a cat play with a rat or mouse before killing it? It might kick, bat, toss, pick up, shake, and carry the rodent. Is the cat sadistically tormenting its prey? No. A cat usually goes for a quick kill if the rodent is small and inactive or if the cat has been given drugs that lower its anxiety. The same cat withdraws altogether if confronted with a large, menacing rodent. In intermediate situations, the cat bats, tosses, and otherwise interacts with a mixture of attack and escape behaviors that might look to us like play (Adamec, Stark-Adamec, & Livingston, 1980; Biben, 1979; Pellis et al., 1988).

Most of the vigorous emotional behaviors we observe in animals fall into the categories of attack and escape, and it is no coincidence that we describe the sympathetic nervous system as the fight-or-flight system. These behaviors and their corresponding emotions—anger and fear—are closely related both behaviorally and physiologically.

Attack Behaviors

Attack behavior depends on the individual as well as the situation. If a hamster intrudes into another hamster's territory, the home hamster sniffs the intruder and eventually attacks, but usually not at once. Suppose the intruder leaves, and a little later, another hamster intrudes. The home hamster attacks faster and more vigorously than before. The first attack enhances home hamster's readiness to attack against any intruder for the next 30 minutes or more (Potegal, 1994). It is as if the first attack gets the hamster in the mood to fight. During that period, activity builds up in the corticomedial area of the amygdala (see Figure 11.9), and as it does so, it increases the hamster's probability of attacking (Potegal, Ferris, Hebert, Meyerhoff, & Skaredoff, 1996; Potegal, Hebert, DeCoster, & Meyerhoff, 1996). Something similar happens in people: If you hold a toddler's arm to prevent him or her from playing with a toy, the result is sometimes screaming and other signs of anger. If you do it again 30 seconds later, the anger is more rapid and more intense (Potegal, Robison, Anderson, Jordan, & Shapiro, 2007). (*Don't* try it yourself. It's unkind.)

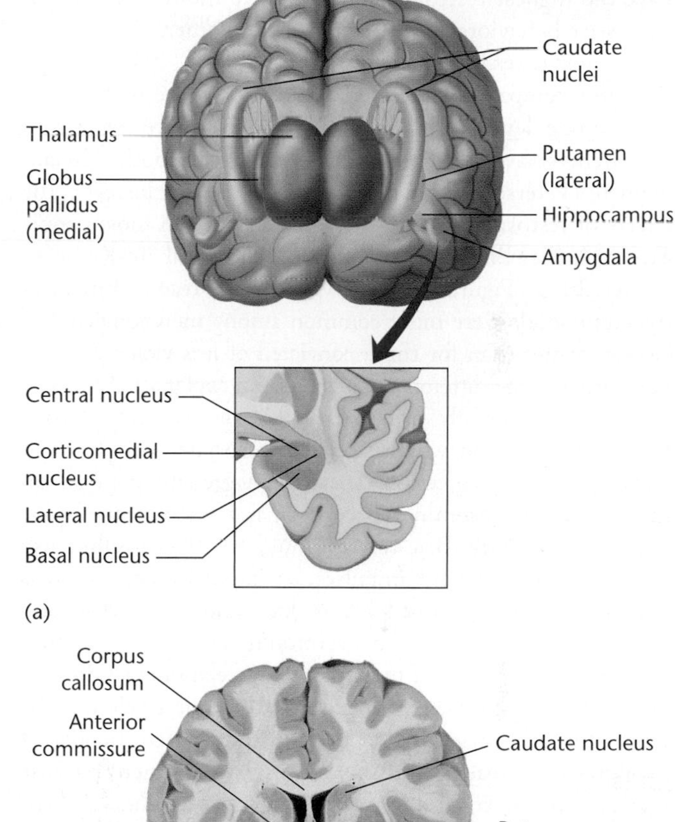

FIGURE 11.9 Location of amygdala in the human brain
The amygdala, located in the interior of the temporal lobe, receives input from many cortical and subcortical areas. Part (a) shows several nuclei of the amygdala. *Source:* (a) Based on Hanaway, Woolsey, Gado, & Roberts, 1998; Nieuwenhuys, Voogd, & vanHuijzen, 1988; (b) Photo courtesy of Dr. Dana Copeland

The same is true for adults. You may have noticed times when one person annoys you and a few minutes later you get angry with someone else. You have probably been told, "If you become angry, count to 10 before you act." Counting to a few thousand would work better, but the idea is correct. Lying on your back is another way to decrease anger. Research has shown that it is easier to feel angry while standing (and therefore in a position to attack) than while lying in a more helpless position (Harmon-Jones & Peterson, 2009). In other words, emotion is *embodied:* What you are doing affects how you feel.

Effects of Hormones

Most fighting in the animal kingdom is by males competing for mates or by females defending their young. Male aggressive behavior depends heavily on testosterone, which is highest for adult males in the reproductive season. Even in species that do not have a particular season for breeding, testosterone increases are linked with increased striving for social dominance (Beehner et al., 2009).

Similarly, throughout the world, men fight more often than women, commit more violent crimes, shout more insults at one another, and so forth. Moreover, young adult men, who have the highest testosterone levels, have the highest rate of aggressive behaviors and violent crimes. Women's violent acts are in most cases less severe (Archer, 2000).

If we compare people of the same age, those with higher testosterone levels tend on average to be more aggressive. Researchers have documented that tendency for both men and women (Peterson & Harmon-Jones, 2012). However, the effects of testosterone are generally smaller than most people expect (Archer, Birring, & Wu, 1998; Archer, Graham-Kevan, & Davies, 2005). Figure 11.10 shows one set of results. High testosterone levels were more common among men convicted of violent crimes than for those convicted of less violent crimes, but note that the differences are small. An explanation for why testosterone generally has small effects is that testosterone facilitates aggression, whereas cortisol (associated with fear and anxiety) inhibits aggression. Therefore, aggression depends on the ratio of testosterone to cortisol, not testosterone alone (Montoya, Terburg, Bos, & van Honk, 2012). Serotonin also tends to inhibit violent impulses, so impulsive aggression is highest when testosterone levels are high, and both cortisol and serotonin are low. We consider serotonin in more detail later.

To test the effects of testosterone, correlational studies are not ideal, because men with high testosterone levels may be unusual in other regards also. Several studies used the idea of temporarily increasing testosterone levels in women. Because most women start with low testosterone levels, the researchers can readily measure the effects of an increase. In one study, testosterone increased the amount of time women spent looking at angry faces (Terburg, Aarts, & van Honk, 2012). In another study, women were asked to make judgments about visual stimuli, either individually or in pairs. Testosterone did not alter accuracy of individuals' judgments, but it reduced the accuracy of pairs' decisions (Wright et al., 2012). The women became more likely to argue instead of collaborating, and one of them—not necessarily the more correct one—dominated the decision. This result fits with other research showing that committees work more harmoniously if they include a high percentage of women (presumably women who hadn't just been given testosterone) (Wooley, Chabris, Pentland, Hashmi, & Malone, 2010).

STOP&CHECK

6. What is one reason why testosterone levels correlate only weakly with human aggression levels?

ANSWER

6. Aggression depends on the ratio of testosterone to cortisol, not to testosterone alone.

Serotonin Synapses and Aggressive Behavior

Several lines of evidence link impulsiveness and aggressive behavior to low serotonin release. Let's examine some of this evidence.

Nonhuman Animals

Much of the earliest evidence came from studies on mice. Luigi Valzelli (1973) found that isolating male mice for 4 weeks increased their aggressive behavior and decreased their serotonin *turnover*. When neurons release serotonin, they reabsorb most of it and synthesize enough to replace the amount that washed away. Thus, the amount present in neurons remains fairly constant, but if we measure the serotonin metabolites in body

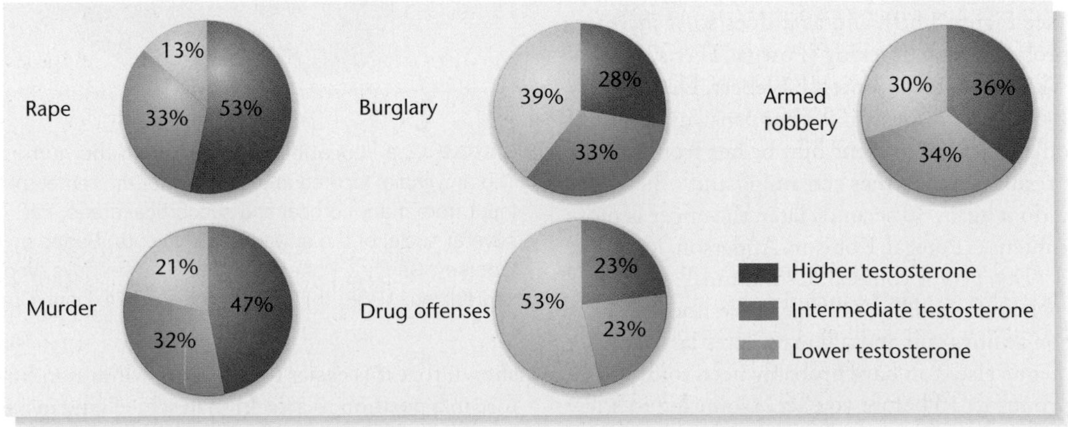

FIGURE 11.10 Testosterone levels for male prisoners
Testosterone levels are higher, on the average, for men convicted of murder or rape than for those convicted of burglary or drug offenses. *Source:* Based on Dabbs, Carr, Frady, & Riad, 1995

fluids, we gauge the **turnover**, the amount that neurons released and replaced. Researchers measure serotonin turnover by the concentration of **5-hydroxyindoleacetic acid (5-HIAA)**, serotonin's main metabolite, in the cerebrospinal fluid (CSF). Measuring the amount in the blood or urine is a simpler but less accurate alternative.

Comparing genetic strains of mice, Valzelli and his colleagues found that social isolation lowered serotonin turnover by the greatest amount in the strains that reacted with the greatest amount of fighting after social isolation (Valzelli & Bernasconi, 1979). Other methods of decreasing serotonin turnover also increase aggressive behavior (Audero et al, 2013). Serotonin activity is lower in juvenile rodents than in adults, and aggressive behavior is higher in the juveniles (Taravosh-Lahn, Bastida, & Delville, 2006). Serotonin release is also below average in highly aggressive hamsters (Cervantes & Delville, 2009).

In a fascinating study, investigators measured 5-HIAA levels in 2-year-old male monkeys living in a natural environment and then observed their behavior. The monkeys in the lowest quartile for 5-HIAA, and therefore the lowest serotonin turnover, were the most aggressive, had the greatest probability of attacking larger monkeys, and incurred the most injuries. Most of them died by age 6. In contrast, monkeys with high serotonin turnover survived (Higley et al., 1996). Female monkeys with low 5-HIAA levels were also likely to get injured and die young (Westergaard, Cleveland, Trenkle, Lussier, & Higley, 2003).

If most monkeys with low turnover die young, why hasn't natural selection eliminated the genes for low serotonin turnover? One possibility is that evolution selects for an intermediate amount of aggression and anxiety (Trefilov, Berard, Krawczak, & Schmidtke, 2000). The most fearless animals get into fights and die young, but those with too much fear have other problems. We could say the same about humans: People with too little fear take excessive risks, but those with too much fear are withdrawn and unlikely to succeed (Nettle, 2006).

We can also see aggressiveness as a high-risk, high-payoff strategy: A monkey with low 5-HIAA starts many fights and probably dies young. However, a monkey who wins enough of those fights survives and achieves a dominant status within the group (Howell et al., 2007). In female monkeys, too, those with low 5-HIAA levels tend to achieve higher status in the troop (Riddick et al., 2009). Under some circumstances, taking aggressive risks to achieve a dominant status might be a reasonable gamble.

Humans

Many studies have found low serotonin turnover in people with a history of violent behavior, including people convicted of arson and other violent crimes (Virkkunen, Nuutila, Goodwin, & Linnoila, 1987) and people who attempt suicide by violent means, as illustrated in Figure 11.11 (G. L. Brown et al., 1982; Edman, Åsberg, Levander, & Schalling, 1986; Mann, Arango, & Underwood, 1990; Pandey et al., 1995; Roy, DeJong, & Linnoila, 1989; Sher et al., 2006; Spreux-Varoquaux et al., 2001). Follow-up studies on people released

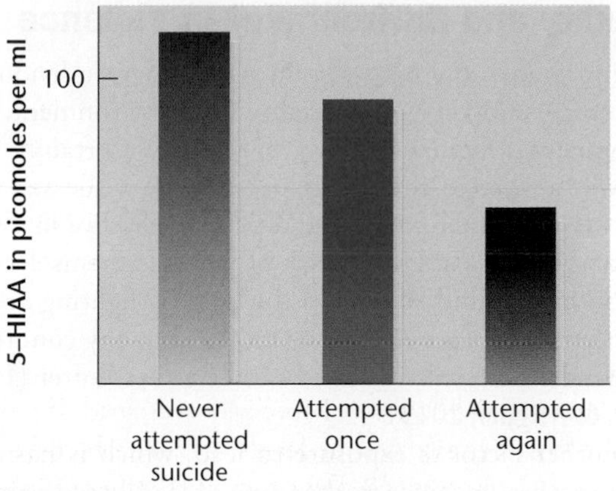

FIGURE 11.11 Levels of 5-HIAA in the CSF of people with depression
Measurements for the suicide-attempting groups were taken after the first attempt. Low levels of 5-HIAA indicate low serotonin turnover. *Source:* Based on results of Roy, DeJong, & Linnoila, 1989

from prison have found that those with lower serotonin turnover had a greater probability of further convictions for violent crimes (Virkkunen, DeJong, Bartko, Goodwin, & Linnoila, 1989; Virkkunen, Eggert, Rawlings, & Linnoila, 1996). Other studies have reported increased aggressive behavior after the use of drugs or diet to decrease serotonin activity (e.g., Moeller et al., 1996). However, although most studies show a relationship between low serotonin and increased aggressive behavior, not all do, and the relationship overall is a small one (Duke, Bègue, Bell, & Eisenlohr-Moul, 2013). Serotonin is evidently a contributor, but by itself not an important enough factor to enable us to make predictions about a given individual.

STOP & CHECK

7. If we want to know how much serotonin the brain has been releasing, what should we measure?

8. Given that monkeys with low serotonin turnover pick many fights and in most cases die young, what keeps natural selection from eliminating the genes for low serotonin turnover?

ANSWERS

7. We can measure the concentration of 5-HIAA, a serotonin metabolite, in the cerebrospinal fluid or other body fluids. The more 5-HIAA, the more serotonin has been released and presumably resynthesized. **8.** Although most monkeys with low serotonin turnover die young, many of the survivors achieve a dominant status that enables them to get more of the food and to reproduce more frequently. Monkeys with high serotonin turnover survive, but at the cost of accepting a low status.

Heredity and Environment in Violence

As with almost anything else in psychology, individual differences depend on both heredity and environment. Many environmental factors are easy to identify. Certainly people who were abused in childhood, people who witnessed violent abuse between their parents, and people who live in a violent neighborhood are at greater risk of violence themselves. People who have found success in the past by fighting are more likely than others are to fight again. Within any country, violence tends to increase as the weather grows hotter (Hsiang, Burke, & Miguel, 2013).

Another factor is exposure to lead, which is harmful to developing brains. Since the banning of lead-based paints and the rise of unleaded gasoline, the prevalence of violent crime has declined, possibly as a result of the decreased lead in the environment (Nevin, 2007).

What about heredity? Monozygotic twins resemble each other more closely than dizygotic twins do with regard to violent and criminal behaviors, and adopted children resemble their biological parents more closely than their adoptive parents (Rhee & Waldman, 2002). Genes influence violent behavior in many ways, including autonomic arousal. People with lower than average autonomic arousal tend, on average, to be more aggressive, probably because they react less strongly to fear of the consequences. Researchers found that 1-year-old infants with low autonomic arousal were more likely than average to show aggressive, antisocial behaviors when they reached age 3 (Baker, Shelton, Baibazarova, Hay, & van Goozen, 2013). However, various kinds of aggressive behavior occur under different circumstances, and we cannot expect to find a single gene or set of genes that will account for all the variations in all populations (Yeh, Coccaro, & Jacobson, 2010). For example, researchers found one gene linked to aggressive behavior that is common only among people of Finnish ancestry (Bevilacqua et al., 2010).

After researchers repeatedly failed to find a strong link between aggressive behavior and any single gene, they explored the possibility of interactions between heredity and environment. Particularly interesting is the gene controlling the enzyme *monoamine oxidase A* (MAO_A). After a neuron releases serotonin, dopamine, or norepinephrine, most of it returns to the neuron via reuptake. At that point the enzyme MAO_A breaks down some of it, preventing possible accumulation of an excessive amount. People vary in their genes for MAO_A, as some people have a less-active form of the gene. Considering the previous discussion of how low serotonin increases the probability of aggression, we might predict that the more active form of MAO_A would link to aggression, because it breaks down serotonin and leaves less available for release. Contrary to this prediction, the low-activity form shows more link to aggression. However, the effect of the gene depends on prior experience. A pioneering study reported that the low-activity form of the gene increased violent behavior *only* in people who had a seriously troubled childhood environment, such as being physically abused or watching parents fight (Caspi et al., 2002). This result is fascinating because of its apparent demonstration of an interaction between genetics and environment. Figure 11.12 illustrates this result.

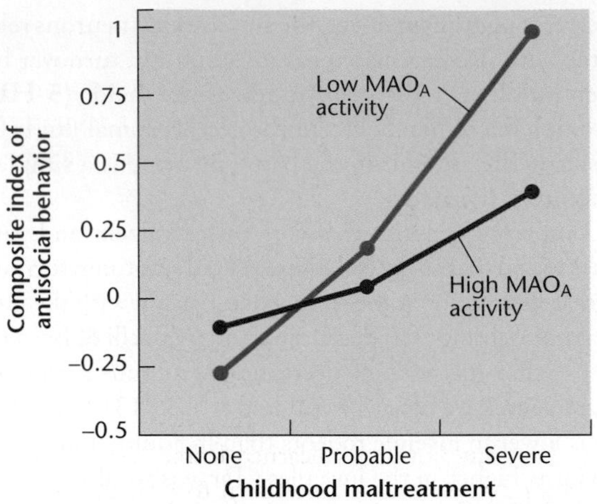

FIGURE 11.12 Genes, environment, and antisocial behavior in men
The *y* axis represents a complex score combining several types of measurement. Higher scores indicate more aggressive behaviors. *Source:* Based on "Role of genotype in the cycle of violence in maltreated children," from Caspi, A., et al., *Science*, 297, 851–854, 2002.

Since then, although some studies failed to replicate this finding, most studies did (e.g., Carver, Johnson, Joormann, Kim, & Nam, 2011; Fergusson, Boden, Horwood, Miller, & Kennedy, 2012; Gallardo-Pujol, Andrés-Pueyo, & Maydeu-Olivares, 2013; McDermott, Dawes, Prom-Wormley, Eaves, & Hatemi, 2013). The low-activity form of the gene is uncommon in most populations. Because it is an X-linked gene, far more men than women have just the low-activity form of the gene (Eme, 2013). It may, therefore, contribute to the greater prevalence of violent behavior in men than in women.

Overall, what can we say about the biological bases of aggressive behavior? At this point, not much is clear. Low serotonin activity is weakly associated with increased aggression, but the form of the MAO_A gene that strongly breaks down serotonin links to less aggression, and only for people with a history of childhood maltreatment. In any case, the effects are small. If we want to control human violence, biological interventions are probably not the most promising route.

STOP & CHECK

9. What relationship did Caspi et al. (2002) report between the enzyme MAO_A and antisocial behavior?

ANSWER

9. Overall, people with genes for high or low production of MAO_A do not differ significantly in their probability of antisocial behavior. However, among those who suffered serious maltreatment during childhood, people with lower levels of the enzyme showed higher rates of antisocial behavior.

Fear and Anxiety

What is the "right" amount of anxiety? It depends. Do you live in a quiet suburb or a war zone? Have you been attacked or witnessed an attack recently? Your life circumstances might justify great anxiety, or much less.

Nevertheless, even among people in the same situation, some show much more anxiety than others do. Both experiences and genetics modify activity in the amygdala, one of the main areas for regulating anxiety.

Role of the Amygdala

Do we have any built-in, unlearned fears? Yes, at least one: A sudden loud noise causes a newborn to arch the back, briefly extend the arms and legs, and cry. This reaction is called the *Moro reflex*. After infancy, a loud noise elicits the closely related **startle reflex**: Auditory information goes first to the cochlear nucleus in the medulla and from there directly to an area in the pons that commands tensing the muscles, especially the neck muscles. Tensing the neck muscles is important because the neck is so vulnerable to injury. Information reaches the pons within 3 to 8 ms after a loud noise, and the full startle reflex occurs in less than two-tenths of a second (Yeomans & Frankland, 1996).

Joe McBride/Stone/Getty Images

people's choices of activities depend in part on how easily they develop anxiety.

Although you don't have to learn to fear loud noises, your current mood or situation modifies your reaction. Your startle reflex is more vigorous if you are already tense. People with post-traumatic stress disorder, certainly known for their intense anxiety, show an enhanced startle reflex (Grillon, Morgan, Davis, & Southwick, 1998). So do people who report much anxiety, even if they don't qualify for a psychiatric diagnosis (McMillan, Asmundson, Zvolensky, & Carleton, 2012). In short, variations in the startle reflex correlate well enough with anxiety that we can measure the startle reflex to measure anxiety. Don't underestimate the power of that statement. Research on other types of emotion is hampered by the difficulty of measurement. For happiness, researchers rely almost entirely on self-reports, which are of questionable accuracy. Smiles are even less valid indicators of happiness, as people often smile without being happy or feel happy without smiling. We have no acceptable way to measure happiness in nonhuman animals. Researchers sometimes observe fighting to measure anger, but you could fight without being angry, or you could be angry without fighting. Again, facial expressions are only moderately valid measures of anger. The suitability of the startle reflex as a behavioral measure of anxiety means that we can use it with laboratory animals to explore the brain mechanisms.

Studies of Rodents

In research with nonhumans, psychologists first measure the startle response to a loud noise. Then they repeatedly pair a stimulus, such as a light or sound, with shock. Finally, they present the new stimulus just before the loud noise and determine how much it increases the startle response. A control group is tested with a stimulus that has not been paired with shock. Results of such studies consistently show that after animals have learned to associate a stimulus with shock, that stimulus becomes a fear signal, and presenting the fear signal just before a sudden loud noise enhances the startle response. Conversely, a stimulus previously associated with pleasant stimuli or the absence of danger becomes a safety signal that decreases the startle reflex (Schmid, Koch, & Schnitzler, 1995).

Investigators have determined that the amygdala (see Figures 11.9 and 11.13) is important for enhancing the startle reflex. Many cells in the amygdala, especially in the basolateral and central nuclei, get input from pain fibers as well as vision or hearing, so the circuitry is well suited to establishing conditioned fears (Uwano, Nishijo, Ono, & Tamura, 1995). By stimulating or damaging parts of laboratory animals' amygdala, researchers have found that one path through the amygdala is responsible for fear of pain, another for fear of predators, and another for fear of aggressive members of your own species (Gross & Canteras, 2012). Also, one part of the amygdala controls changes in breathing, another controls avoidance of potentially unsafe places, and another controls learning which particular places are safest (Kim et al., 2013). The path from the amygdala responsible for "freezing" in the presence of danger is separate from the path controlling changes in heart rate (Viviani et al., 2011). These findings are relevant to psychological theories about emotion, because they demonstrate that

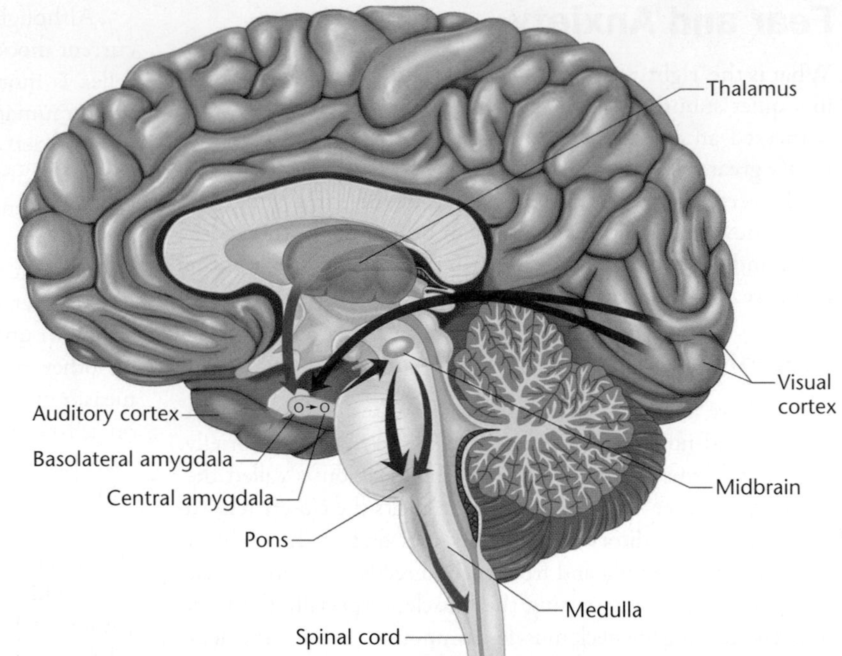

FIGURE 11.13 Amygdala and learned fears
The central amygdala receives sensory input from the lateral and basolateral amygdala. It sends output to the central gray area of the midbrain, which relays information to a nucleus in the pons responsible for the startle reflex. Damage anywhere along the route from the amygdala to the pons interferes with learned fears that modify the startle reflex.

what we call fear is a conglomerate of separate aspects, not a single indivisible state.

Output from the amygdala to the hypothalamus controls autonomic fear responses, such as increased blood pressure. The amygdala also has axons to areas of the prefrontal cortex that control approach and avoidance responses (Garcia, Vouimba, Baudry, & Thompson, 1999; Lacroix, Spinelli, Heidbreder, & Feldon, 2000). Its axons to the thalamus direct attention toward emotionally important stimuli (Zikopoulos & Barbas, 2012). It can heighten responses of the auditory cortex to a sound associated with danger (Headley & Weinberger, 2013). Additional axons extend from the amygdala to midbrain areas that relay information to the pons to control the startle reflex (LeDoux, Iwata, Cicchetti, & Reis, 1988; Zhao & Davis, 2004). Figure 11.13 shows the connections.

A rat with damage to the amygdala still shows a normal startle reflex, but signals before the noise do not modify the reflex. In one study, rats were repeatedly exposed to a light followed by shock and then tested for their responses to a loud noise. Intact rats showed a moderate startle reflex to the loud noise and an enhanced response if the light preceded the noise. In contrast, rats with damage in the path from the amygdala to the hindbrain showed the same startle reflex with or without the light (Hitchcock & Davis, 1991).

Do these results indicate that amygdala damage destroys fear? Not necessarily. An alternative explanation is that the rats have trouble interpreting or understanding stimuli with emotional consequences. The same issue arises with humans, as we shall see.

An odd parasite has evolved a way to exploit the consequences of amygdala damage (Berdoy, Webster, & Macdonald, 2000). *Toxoplasma gondii* is a protozoan that infects many mammals but reproduces only in cats. Cats excrete the parasite's eggs in their feces, thereby releasing them into the ground. Rats that burrow in the ground can become infected with the parasite. When the parasite enters a rat, it migrates to the brain where it apparently damages the amygdala. The rat then fearlessly approaches a cat, guaranteeing that the cat will eat the rat and that the parasite will find its way back into a cat!

The amygdala is important for learning what to fear, but that is not the only type of fear conditioning. If a rat has received shocks after a particular stimulus in a particular cage, it learns to fear the stimulus (by changes in the amygdala) but it also learns to fear the cage . . . and new cages . . . and new situations. The same is true for humans. If you are attacked or if you have other traumatic experiences, you become more fearful in a wide variety of situations. It is as if your brain has decided, "This is a dangerous world. I need to be alert for new threats." This long-term, generalized emotional arousal depends on a brain area called the **bed nucleus of the stria terminalis** (Duvarci, Bauer, & Paré, 2009; Toufexis, 2007). The stria terminalis is a set of axons that connect this nucleus to the amygdala, as shown in Figure 11.14. Axons from this nucleus to the ventral tegmental area also control increases and decreases in anxiety (Jennings et al., 2013).

STOP & CHECK

10. What brain mechanism enables the startle reflex to be so fast?

11. How could a researcher use the startle reflex to determine whether some stimulus causes fear?

ANSWERS

10. Loud noises activate a path from the cochlea to cells in the pons that trigger a tensing of neck muscles. **11.** Present the stimulus before giving a loud noise. If the stimulus increases the startle reflex beyond its usual level, then the stimulus produced fear.

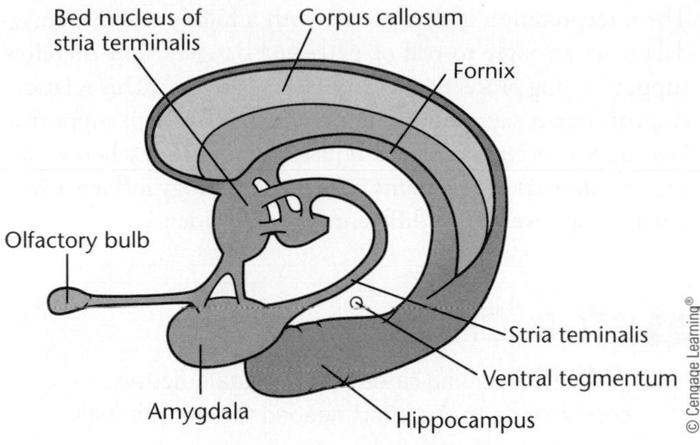

FIGURE 11.14 The bed nucleus of the stria terminalis
The bed nucleus is critical for long-term adjustments of anxiety, whereas the amygdala is responsible for fear of individual items. The stria terminalis is a set of axons connecting its bed nucleus to the amygdala.

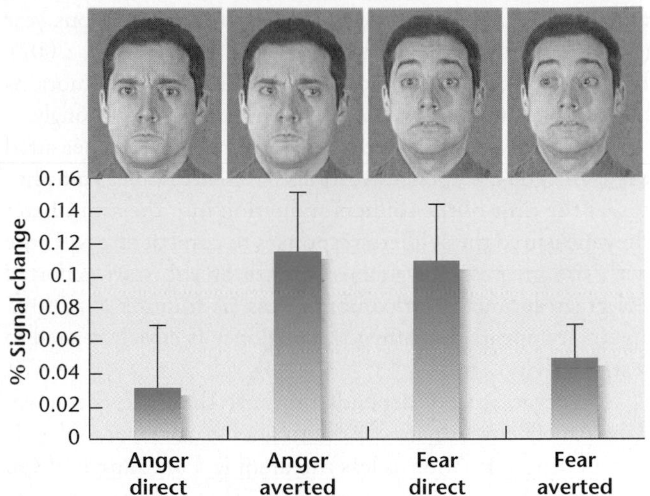

FIGURE 11.15 Amygdala response and direction of gaze
The amygdala responds more strongly to an angry face directed away from the viewer and to a frightened face directed toward the viewer.
Source: From R. B. Adams et al. "Effects of gaze on amygdala sensitivity to anger and fear faces," *Science*, 2003, 300:1536. Reprinted with permission from AAAS/Science Magazine.

Studies of Monkeys

The effect of amygdala damage in monkeys was described in classic studies early in the 1900s and is known as the *Klüver-Bucy syndrome*, from the names of the primary investigators. Monkeys showing this syndrome are tame and placid. They attempt to pick up lighted matches and other objects that they ordinarily avoid. They display less than the normal fear of snakes or of larger, more dominant monkeys (Kalin, Shelton, Davidson, & Kelley, 2001). They have impaired social behaviors, largely because they don't seem to learn which monkeys to approach with caution. Like rats with amygdala damage, monkeys with such damage are impaired at learning what to fear (Kazama, Heuer, Davis, & Bachevalier, 2012). Among intact monkeys, those with a more vigorously reactive amygdala tend to show the greatest fear in response to a noise or an intruder (Oler et al., 2010).

Response of the Human Amygdala to Visual Stimuli

Studies using fMRI show that the human amygdala responds strongly when people look at photos that arouse fear or photos of faces showing fear. To a lesser extent it also responds to faces showing happiness or sadness (Fusar-Poli et al., 2009). Instructing people to pay attention to pleasant stimuli increases the amygdala's responses to them (Cunningham, Van Bavel & Johnsen, 2008).

Contrary to what we might guess, the amygdala responds most strongly when a facial expression is a bit ambiguous or difficult to interpret. Consider angry and frightened faces. As a rule, it is easy to interpret an angry face looking straight at you, but a fearful face looking straight at you is more puzzling. Frightened people almost always stare at whatever is frightening them, and so you will almost never see someone stare at you with a fearful expression, unless the person is afraid of *you!* Consequently, you recognize an angry expression faster if it is directed toward you and a fearful expression faster if it is directed to the side (Adams & Kleck, 2005). The amygdala, however, responds more strongly to a fearful face directed toward you (Adams, Gordon, Baird, Ambady, & Kleck, 2003) (see Figure 11.15). That is, the amygdala responds more strongly to the expression that is harder to interpret. Apparently, the amygdala is active when it is working hard to interpret emotion-related information.

Individual Differences in Amygdala Response and Anxiety

Most people's tendency toward anxiety generally remains fairly consistent over time. Most infants with an "inhibited" temperament develop into shy, fearful children and then into shy adults who show an enhanced amygdala response to the sight of any unfamiliar face (Beaton et al., 2008; Schwartz, Wright, Shin, Kagan, & Rauch, 2003). Part of the variance in anxiety relates to genes controlling the serotonin transporter (the protein that produces reuptake of serotonin after its release). People with genes for reduced serotonin reuptake tend to have increased responses to threat and increased attention to threatening stimuli, especially in social situations. As a result, they are more likely than others to have anxiety disorders and difficult social interactions (Disner et al., 2013; Miu, Vulturar, Chis, Ungureanu, & Gross, 2013; Volman et al., 2013). Married people with those genes are more likely than average to react strongly to a marital conflict (Haase et al., 2013).

Individual differences in anxiety correlate strongly with amygdala activity. In one study, college students carried a device that beeped at unpredictable times each day for 28 days, asking the student to record his or her emotional state at the moment. A year later the students came into a laboratory for the second part of the study, in which an fMRI recorded their amygdala response to very brief presentations of frightening pictures. The amygdala responses correlated highly with the number of unpleasant emotions they had recorded the previous year (Barrett, Bliss-Moreau, Duncan, Rauch, & Wright, 2007). Presumably they recorded so many unpleasant emotions because they were biologically predisposed to react strongly.

In a study of Israeli soldiers, researchers first measured their amygdala responses to briefly flashed unpleasant photos, at the time of the soldiers' induction into the army. Later they measured the soldiers' responses to combat stress. Those with the greatest amygdala response at the start reported the greatest amount of combat stress (Admon et al., 2009). Again, it appears that amygdala response is closely related to fear reactivity.

However, anxiety depends on more than just the amygdala. An effective way to cope with anxiety is *reappraisal*—reinterpreting a situation as less threatening. For example, if you lose your job, you might tell yourself, "This will prompt me to look for a new job. It might turn out for the best." Or you hear what might be a gunshot, but you decide it might have been a car backfiring. Reappraisal and other methods of suppressing anxiety depend on top-down influences from the prefrontal cortex to inhibit activity in the amygdala (Marek, Strobel, Bredy, & Sah, 2013; Moscarello & LeDoux, 2013). People with depression or severe anxiety show below-average activity in the prefrontal cortex while viewing something frightening, and techniques that help people reduce their anxiety tend to increase activity in the prefrontal cortex (Britton et al., 2013; Holmes et al., 2012; J. S. Stevens et al., 2013; Zotev, Phillips, Young, Drevets, & Bodurka, 2013).

Anxiety reactivity affects much of life—even, according to one study, political attitudes. People were asked a series of questions about their support for use of military force, police powers, the death penalty, gun ownership, and so forth. Researchers also measured each person's responses to sudden loud noises, repeated numerous times. As shown in Figure 11.16, those showing high support for military and police action showed a greater startle response to the loud noises (Oxley et al., 2008).

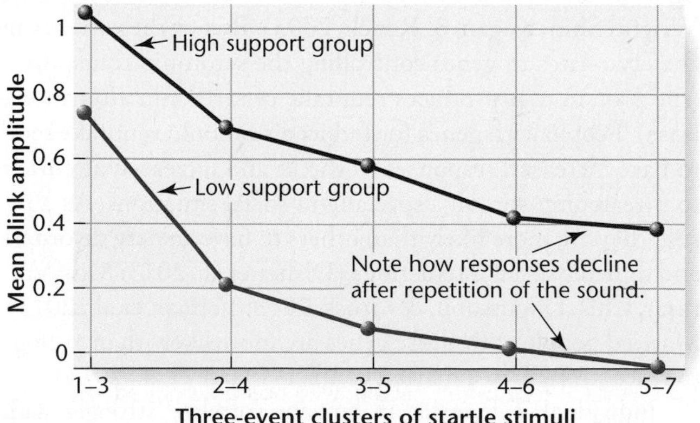

FIGURE 11.16 Fear responses and political attitudes
On the average, people who show a stronger startle response to loud noises tend to favor greater reliance on military and police powers. *Source:* Based on Oxley, D. R., Smith, K. B., Alford, J. R., Hibbing, M. V., Miller, J. L., Scalora, M., et al. (2008). Political attitudes vary with physiological traits. *Science*, 321, 1667–1670.

The interpretation is that people with a highly reactive amygdala react strongly to real or perceived dangers, and therefore support strong protection against those dangers. (This relationship, of course, says nothing about whether the high support or low support group is correct. It just indicates that when we are arguing about policy, variants in brain physiology influence how much weight we give to different types of evidence.)

STOP&CHECK

12. What evidence indicates that amygdala activity corresponds to the effort needed for interpreting emotional information?

13. What can we predict about someone if we know the strength of that person's amygdala responses to upsetting pictures or loud noises?

ANSWERS

12. The amygdala responds more strongly to a fearful face directed at the viewer, rather than a similar face looking to the side. People usually find it easier to understand a fearful face looking to the side. **13.** People with a highly reactive amygdala are likely to report many negative emotional experiences during a day, to show strong responses to stressful experiences, and to favor strong reliance on military and police power.

Damage to the Human Amygdala

With laboratory animals, researchers can intentionally damage the amygdala to see the effects. With humans, they have to rely on damage that occurs spontaneously. For example, some people suffer a stroke that damages the amygdala and surrounding areas, at least in one hemisphere. They are impaired in some ways and not others. When they examine emotional pictures, they can classify them as pleasant versus unpleasant about as well as anyone else. However, they experience little arousal from viewing unpleasant pictures (Berntson, Bechara, Damasio, Tranel, & Cacioppo, 2007). That is, they continue to experience the cognitive aspect of unpleasant emotions, but much less of the feeling aspect.

People with the rare genetic disorder *Urbach-Wiethe disease* accumulate calcium in the amygdala until it wastes away. Thus they have extensive damage to the amygdala without much damage to surrounding structures. Like the monkeys with Klüver-Bucy syndrome, they are impaired at processing emotional information and learning what to fear. Much of the research on this condition deals with a woman known by her initials, SM, who describes herself as fearless, and certainly acts that way. When she viewed 10 clips from the scariest movies the researchers could find, she reported feeling only excitement, no fear. Researchers took her to an exotic pet store. In spite of insisting that she hates snakes and spiders, she was happy to hold a snake (see Figure 11.17), and the staff repeatedly had to restrain her from touching or poking the tarantulas and venomous snakes. When the researchers took

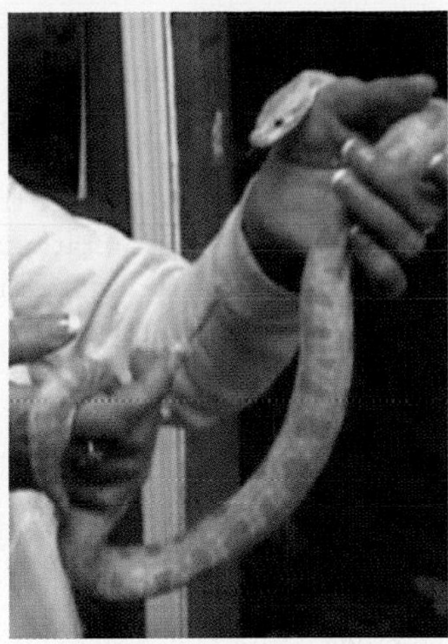

FIGURE 11.17 SM, a woman with amygdala damage, holds a snake at an exotic pet store
Although she said she hates snakes, she was curious to hold this one and wanted to touch the others, including venomous ones. *Source:* From Feinstein, J. S., Adolphs, R., Damasio, A., & Tranel, D. (2011). "The human amygdala and the induction and experience of fear." *Current Biology, 21,* 34–38 with permission from Elsevier.

her to a "haunted house," she led the way without hesitation, venturing down dark hallways. When people dressed as monsters jumped out, other people in the group screamed, but SM laughed, curiously poked one of the monsters, and scared the monster! Her fearlessness is dangerous to her. She has been held up at gunpoint and knifepoint and has been physically assaulted repeatedly. Evidently she plunges into dangerous situations without the caution other people would show. When she describes these events, she remembers feeling angry, but not afraid (Feinstein, Adolphs, Damasio, & Tranel, 2011).

Here is another example of her fearlessness: Suppose you are standing, and a person you don't know approaches you, face to face. How close could that person come before you began to feel uncomfortable? Most Americans stand about 0.7 m (2 ft) away from another person, but SM's preferred distance is about half that. When a man unknown to her, instructed by the experimenters, approached her so close that their noses touched, with eye-to-eye contact, she showed and reported no discomfort (Kennedy, Gläscher, Tyszka, & Adolphs, 2009). (She did say she wondered whether they were "up to something.")

The only event known to trigger her fear is breathing 35 percent carbon dioxide, which leaves a person gasping for breath. She and two others with Urbach-Wiethe disease reacted to concentrated CO_2 with a panic attack. The difference from other fear stimuli is that concentrated carbon dioxide affects the body directly, rather than by visual or auditory signals that the amygdala would have to interpret. However, although all three people said it was a terrible experience and they thought they were going to die, they all agreed to go through the experience again the following week, and did not think about the upcoming experience again during that delay (Feinstein et al., 2013). Apparently the amygdala is important for imagining the fear or thinking about the danger.

SM and other people with Urbach-Wiethe disease often fail to recognize the emotional expressions in faces, especially expressions of fear or disgust (Boucsein, Weniger, Mursch, Steinhoff, & Irle, 2001). Even when they recognize an expression as fear or disgust, they rate it as less intense than other people do, and they are less likely than average to remember a photo of an emotional expression if they see the same photo an hour later (Siebert, Markowitsch, & Bartel, 2003).

When SM was asked to draw faces showing certain emotions (see Figure 11.18), she made good drawings of most expressions but had trouble drawing a fearful expression, saying that she did not know what such a face would look like. When the researcher urged her to try, she drew someone crawling away with hair on end, as cartoonists often indicate fear (Adolphs, Tranel, Damasio, & Damasio, 1995).

Why do SM and others with amygdala damage have trouble identifying facial expressions of fear? At first, the assumption was that someone with amygdala damage doesn't feel fear and therefore cannot understand the expression. But then

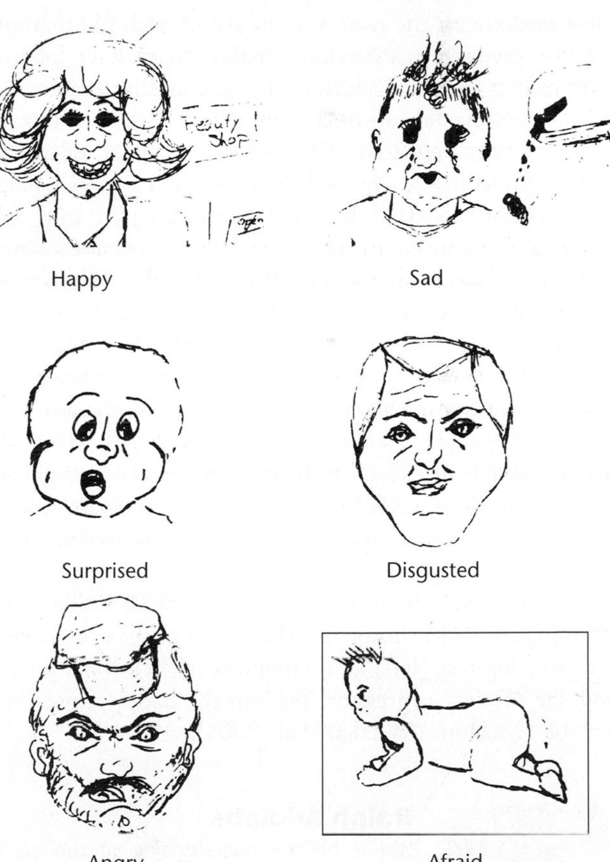

FIGURE 11.18 Drawings by SM, who has a damaged amygdala
She at first declined to draw a fearful expression because, she said, she could not imagine it. When urged to try, she remembered that frightened people are often depicted with their hair on end, at least in cartoons. *Source:* Based on "Fear and the human amygdala," by R. Adolphs, D. Tranel, H. Damasio, and A. Damasio, *Journal of Neuroscience*, 15, pp. 5879–5891. Oxford University Press, 1995.

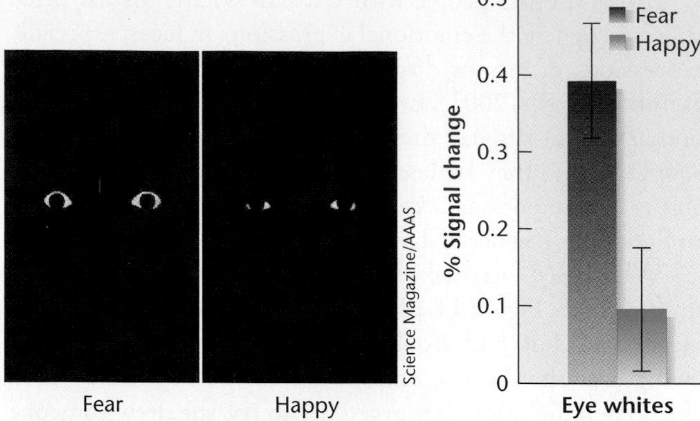

FIGURE 11.19 Eye expressions for fear and happiness
The eye whites alone enable most people to guess that the person on the left was feeling afraid. *Source:* From "Human amygdala responsivity to masked fearful eye whites," by P. J. Whalen et al., *Science, 2004,* 306, p. 2061. Reprinted by permission from AAAS/ Science magazine.

Ralph Adolphs and his colleagues observed that SM focuses almost entirely on the nose and mouth of each photograph. Also in everyday life, she seldom makes eye contact, looking at the mouth instead (Spezio, Huang, Castelli, & Adolphs, 2007). The amygdala automatically directs attention toward emotionally significant stimuli, even without your awareness (Amting, Greening, & Mitchell, 2010; Burra et al., 2013; Peck, Lau, & Salzman, 2013), but someone lacking an amygdala doesn't have this automatic tendency. Suppose you are looking at a computer screen, and a face is flashed briefly on the screen. Almost instantaneously, you would move your gaze to focus on the eyes, especially if the face was showing fear (Gamer & Büchel, 2009). SM has no reluctance to make eye contact, but someone's eyes simply don't attract her attention the way they do for other people (Kennedy & Adolphs, 2010). When researchers asked her to look at the eyes, she quickly recognized fearful expressions (Adolphs, Tranel, & Buchanan, 2005). Seeing the eyes is particularly important for recognizing fear. People express happiness with the mouth, but fear mainly with the eyes (Morris, deBonis, & Dolan, 2002; Vuilleumier, 2005). Figure 11.19 shows only the whites of the eyes of people expressing fear (left) and happiness (right). Most people recognize the fear expression, but not the happy expression, from the eyes alone (Whalen et al., 2004).

Ralph Adolphs

Will a better understanding of the social brain lead to a better understanding of social behavior? And can such knowledge ultimately be used to help our species negotiate and survive in the vastly complex social world it has helped create? To approach such questions, social neuroscientists will need to establish dialogues with other disciplines in the social and behavioral sciences, and to be highly sensitive to the public consequences of the data they generate. (Adolphs, personal communication)

These observations suggest an alternative interpretation of the function of the amygdala. Instead of being responsible for *feeling* fear or other emotions, perhaps it is responsible for detecting emotional information and directing other brain areas to pay attention to it in the proper way. The distinction between these interpretations is difficult to test. As is often the case, good research points the way for further research.

STOP&CHECK

14. Why do people with amygdala damage have trouble recognizing expressions of fear?

ANSWER

14. They focus their vision on the nose and mouth. Expressions of fear depend almost entirely on the eyes.

Anxiety Disorders

Most psychological disorders include increased anxiety as one of the symptoms. In generalized anxiety disorder, phobia, and panic disorder, the major symptom is increased anxiety. **Panic disorder** is characterized by frequent periods of anxiety and occasional attacks of rapid breathing, increased heart rate, sweating, and trembling—that is, extreme arousal of the sympathetic nervous system. It is more common in women than in men and far more common in adolescents and young adults than in older adults (Shen et al., 2007; Swoboda, Amering, Windhaber, & Katschnig, 2003). Twin studies suggest a genetic predisposition, although no single gene has been identified (Hettema, Neale, & Kendler, 2001; Kim, Lee, Yang, Hwang, & Yoon, 2009). Curiously, panic disorder occurs in about 15 percent of people with *joint laxity,* commonly known as being "double-jointed" (able to bend the fingers backward farther than usual). Even when people with joint laxity do not have panic disorder, they tend to have stronger fears than most other people do (Bulbena et al., 2004; Bulbena, Gago, Sperry, & Bergé, 2006).

The research so far links panic disorder to some abnormalities in the hypothalamus, and not necessarily the amygdala. Panic disorder is associated with decreased activity of the neurotransmitter GABA and increased levels of orexin. Orexin, as discussed in other chapters, is associated with maintaining wakefulness and activity. We might not have guessed that it would also be associated with anxiety, but apparently it is, and drugs that block orexin receptors block panic responses (Johnson et al., 2010).

People have long recognized that many soldiers returning from battle are prone to continuing anxieties and distress. In the past, people called this condition *battle fatigue* or *shell shock.* Today, they call it **post-traumatic stress disorder (PTSD)**, marked by frequent distressing recollections (flashbacks) and nightmares about the traumatic event, avoidance of reminders of it, and vigorous reactions to noises and other stimuli

(Yehuda, 2002). PTSD also occurs after other traumas, such as rape, beating, or watching someone get killed. For anyone living in dangerous circumstances, raising the anxiety level is understandable. We presumably evolved mechanisms to adjust our anxiety level up or down depending on the level of danger. The problem arises if someone fails to readjust the anxiety level back to a moderate level, long after returning to a safer environment.

Not all people who endure traumas develop PTSD, and we cannot predict who will get PTSD based on the severity of the trauma or the intensity of the person's initial reaction (Harvey & Bryant, 2002; Shalev et al., 2000). Evidently some people are more vulnerable than others, but why? Most PTSD victims have a smaller than average hippocampus (Stein, Hanna, Koverola, Torchia, & McClarty, 1997). To determine whether the small hippocampus was a cause or a result of PTSD, investigators examined men who developed PTSD during war. First, they confirmed earlier reports that most PTSD victims had a smaller than average hippocampus. Then they found cases in which the PTSD victim had a monozygotic twin who had not been in battle and who did not have PTSD. The results showed that the twin without PTSD *also* had a smaller than average hippocampus (Gilbertson et al., 2002). Presumably, both twins had a smaller than average hippocampus from the start, which increased their susceptibility to PTSD.

One further point about PTSD: A study compared Vietnam War veterans who suffered injuries that produced various kinds of brain damage. Of those whose damage included the amygdala, *none* suffered PTSD. Of those with damage elsewhere in the brain, 40 percent suffered PTSD (Koenigs et al., 2008). Apparently, the amygdala, which is so important for emotional processing, is essential for the extreme emotional impact that produces PTSD.

STOP&CHECK

15. What evidence indicates that a smaller than average hippocampus makes people more vulnerable to PTSD?

ANSWER

15. On the average, PTSD victims have a smaller than average hippocampus. For those who have a monozygotic twin, the twin also has a smaller than average hippocampus, even if he or she does not have PTSD.

Relief from Anxiety

People have many ways to cope with anxiety—social support, reappraisal of the situation, exercise, distraction, gaining a sense of control over the situation, and so forth. Here we examine the options for biological interventions.

Pharmacological Relief

People with excessive anxiety sometimes seek relief through medications. A variety of studies indicate that the transmitters orexin and CCK (cholecystokinin) increase anxiety by their actions in the amygdala and hippocampus (C. Becker et al., 2001; Frankland, Josselyn, Bradwejn, Vaccarino, & Yeomans, 1997). So far, no drugs based on orexin or CCK have been approved. However, many drugs are available to increase activity of the transmitter GABA, which inhibits anxiety.

The most common *anxiolytic* (anti-anxiety) drugs are the **benzodiazepines** (BEN-zo-die-AZ-uh-peens), such as diazepam (trade name Valium), chlordiazepoxide (Librium), and alprazolam (Xanax). Benzodiazepines bind to the **GABA$_A$ receptor**, which includes a site that binds GAB$_A$ as well as sites that modify the sensitivity of the GABA site (see Figure 11.20).

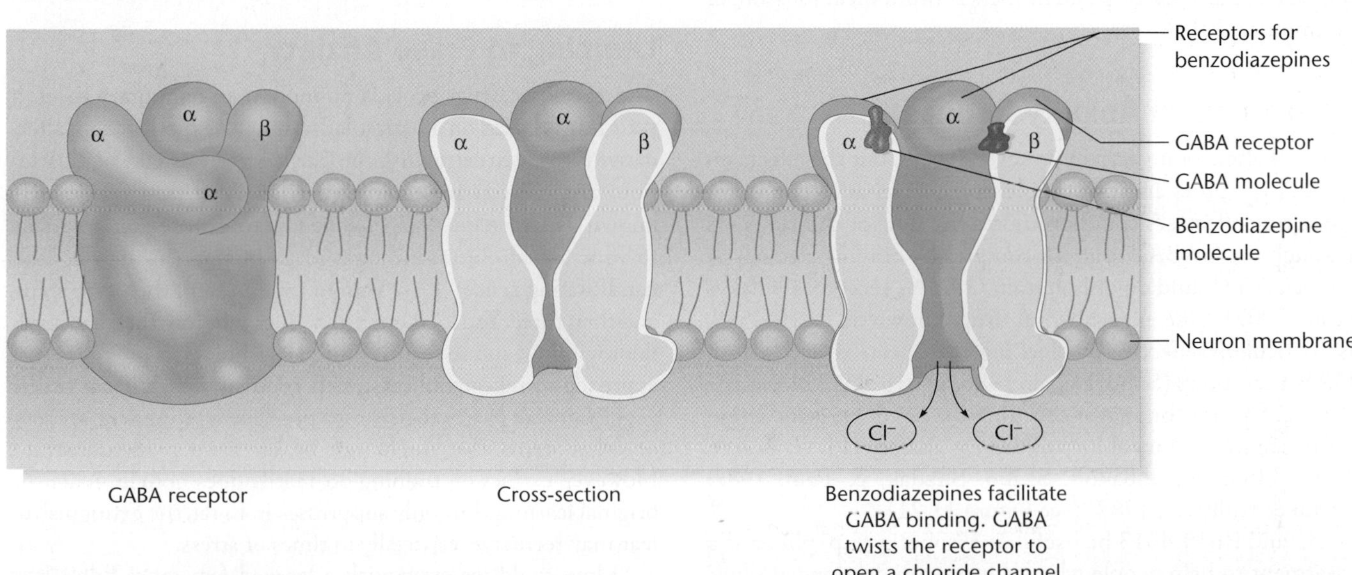

FIGURE 11.20 The GABA$_A$ receptor complex
Of its four receptor sites sensitive to GABA, the three α sites are also sensitive to benzodiazepines. *Source:* Based on Guidotti, Ferrero, Fujimoto, Santi, & Costa, 1986

(The brain also has other kinds of GABA receptors, such as $GABA_B$, with different behavioral effects.)

At the center of the $GABA_A$ receptor is a chloride channel. When open, it permits chloride ions (Cl^-) to cross the membrane into the neuron, hyperpolarizing the cell. (That is, the synapse is inhibitory.) Surrounding the chloride channel are four units, each containing one or more sites sensitive to GABA. Benzodiazepines bind to additional sites on three of those four units (labeled α in Figure 11.19). When a benzodiazepine molecule attaches, it neither opens nor closes the chloride channel but twists the receptor so that the GABA binds more easily (Macdonald, Weddle, & Gross, 1986). Benzodiazepines thus facilitate the effects of GABA.

Benzodiazepines exert their anti-anxiety effects in the amygdala, hypothalamus, midbrain, and several other areas. A minute amount of benzodiazepines injected directly into a rat's amygdala decreases learned shock-avoidance behaviors (Pesold & Treit, 1995), relaxes the muscles, and increases social approaches to other rats (S. K. Sanders & Shekhar, 1995). Benzodiazepines also decrease the responses in a rat's brain to the smell of a cat. Ordinarily, that smell triggers an apparently built-in fear (McGregor, Hargreaves, Apfelbach, & Hunt, 2004).

Benzodiazepines produce a variety of additional effects, including the possibility of addiction (Tan et al., 2010). When they reach the thalamus and cerebral cortex, they induce sleepiness, block epileptic convulsions, and impair memory (Rudolph et al., 1999). The mixture of effects is a problem. For example, you might want to reduce your anxiety without becoming sleepy, and presumably, you don't want to impair your memory. Researchers hope to develop drugs with more specific and limited effects (Korpi & Sinkkonen, 2006).

An unfortunate aspect of benzodiazepines is that they are extremely stable chemically. Typically they pass through the urine intact, pass through the waste treatment plant intact, and accumulate in lakes and rivers, where they alter the eating and social behavior of resident fish (Brodin, Fick, Jonsson, & Klaminder, 2013).

Alcohol as an Anxiety Reducer

Alcohol alters brain activity in several ways, but the effects on GABA receptors are responsible for the anti-anxiety and intoxicating effects. Alcohol promotes the flow of chloride ions through the $GABA_A$ receptor complex by binding strongly at a special site found on only certain $GABA_A$ receptors (Glykys et al., 2007). One experimental drug, known as Ro15-4513, is particularly effective in blocking the effects of alcohol on GABA receptors (Suzdak et al., 1986). Ro15-4513 blocks the effects of alcohol on motor coordination, its depressant action on the brain, and its ability to reduce anxiety (H. C. Becker, 1988; Hoffman, Tabakoff, Szabó, Suzdak, & Paul, 1987; Ticku & Kulkarni, 1988) (see Figure 11.21).

Could Ro15-4513 be useful as a "sobering-up" pill or as a treatment to help people who want to stop drinking alcohol? Hoffmann-La Roche, the company that discovered the drug, concluded that it would be too risky. People who relied on the pill might think they were sober enough to drive home when they were not. Also, giving such a pill to people with alcoholism would probably backfire. Because alcoholics drink to get drunk, a pill that decreased their feeling of intoxication would probably lead them to drink even more.

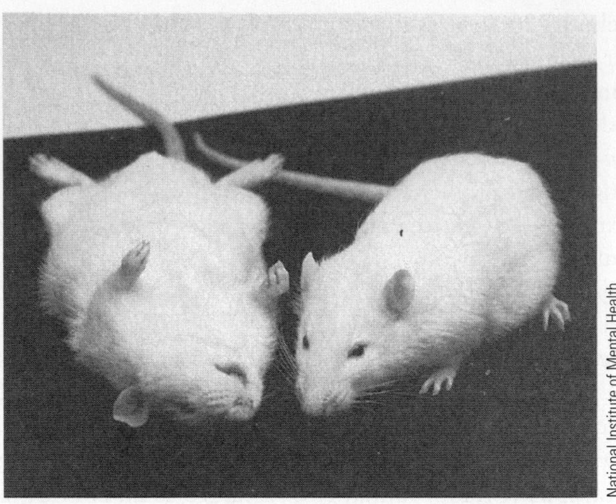

National Institute of Mental Health

FIGURE 11.21 Two rats that were given the same amount of alcohol
The rat on the right was later given the experimental drug Ro15-4513. Within 2 minutes, its performance and coordination improved significantly.

STOP&CHECK

16. What would be the effect of benzodiazepines on someone who had no GABA?

ANSWER

16. Benzodiazepines facilitate the effects of GABA, so a person without GABA would have no response to benzodiazepines.

Learning to Erase Anxiety

The anxiolytic drugs provide no more than temporary relief. If your fear is based on a particular traumatic experience, an alternative is to try to extinguish the learned fear. For sake of illustration, suppose you are afraid of heights. An effective approach, known as *systematic desensitization,* is to expose you gradually to your feared object, in hopes of extinction (in the classical-conditioning sense). First you go up one step, then two steps, and then three. You look out a first-floor window, then a second-floor window, and so forth. Clinical psychologists often use that approach to relieve phobias, with good success. Virtual reality goggles enable psychologists to expose clients to snakes, spiders, or other items that might not be on hand to demonstrate. However, extinction training ordinarily does not eliminate the original learning, but only suppresses it. Later, the extinguished fear may reemerge, especially in times of stress.

How could we extinguish a learned fear more fully? It is easier to extinguish a learned response immediately after original learning than it is later. After time has passed, the learning becomes stronger. Psychologists say it has **consolidated.**

Ordinarily, if you have a traumatic experience, no one is there to extinguish the learning in the next few minutes. However, a consolidated memory is not solid forever. A memory reawakened by a reminder becomes labile—that is, changeable or vulnerable. If a similar experience follows the reminder, the memory is **reconsolidated**—that is, strengthened again. During the time when reconsolidation might occur, a well-timed extinction experience can substantially weaken the memory. This process has been demonstrated for both rats (Monfils, Cowansage, Klann, & LeDoux, 2009) and humans. Here is a human study (Schiller et al., 2010): Imagine you watch as a series of red squares and blue squares appear. When you see a red square, nothing happens, but when you see a blue square, 38 percent of the time you receive a mildly painful shock. Before long, you show signs of anxiety at the sight of that blue square. A day later, you return to the laboratory and you see a blue square, just once, with no shock, just enough to give you a strong reminder of the experience. Later you undergo extinction training, with many presentations of both the red and blue squares, and no shock. If you get this extinction training about 10 minutes after the reminder, it is highly effective, and your learned fear virtually disappears, long term. If you receive the extinction training 6 hours after the reminder, or after no reminder, the extinction suppresses the fear temporarily, but it may return later. Unfortunately, the ability of a well-timed extinction experience to weaken the memory depends on many details of procedure. Some studies have replicated the effect (Oyarzun et al., 2012) and some have not (Kindt & Soeter, 2013). When it does occur, the decrease in fear correlates with a decreased response to the cue by the amygdala (Agren et al., 2012).

Because reconsolidation requires protein synthesis and altered synapses (Rao-Ruiz et al., 2011), a drug intervention could facilitate an extinction experience. The drug *propanolol* interferes with protein synthesis at certain synapses in the amygdala. Suppose you learn a fear of some stimulus. Later you are exposed to that stimulus, rendering it available for reconsolidation, under the influence of propanolol. By blocking protein synthesis, propanolol blocks the reconsolidation. The result is a much weaker emotional response to the stimulus, although you can still describe the experience in words (Kindt, Soeter, & Vervliet, 2009; Nader & Hardt, 2009; Sevenster, Beckers, & Kindt, 2013). Psychiatrists have applied this method to post-traumatic stress disorder, by asking people to describe their traumatic experience under the influence of propanolol. In many cases, patients reported a persisting decrease in fear intensity, although the research so far is not strong enough to be sure that the benefits outweigh the risk of side effects from the drug (Brunet et al., 2008; Kühlmeyer & Jox, 2013).

STOP & CHECK

17. Why is extinction more effective a few minutes after a brief reminder of the original learning?

ANSWER

17. The reminder brings the representation of the learning into a labile state from which it can be reconsolidated or extinguished.

MODULE 11.2 ■ IN CLOSING

Doing Something about Emotions

It is hard to foresee future developments, but suppose researchers make sudden advances in linking emotional behaviors to physiological measurements. Imagine if we could take a blood sample—measuring 5-HIAA or whatever—plus an fMRI scan and a few other measurements and then predict which people will commit violent crime. How accurate would those predictions have to be before we considered using them? And in what way, if any, would we use them?

And what about anxiety? Suppose research enables us to modulate people's anxiety precisely without undesirable side effects. What would be the consequences of chemically controlling everyone's anxiety? Future research will give us new options and opportunities. Deciding what to do with them is another matter.

Summary

1. An experience that gradually provokes an attack leaves an individual more ready than usual to attack again. 367
2. Differences in testosterone levels correlate weakly with variations in aggressive behavior. Aggressive behavior depends on a combination of chemicals, as testosterone increases the probability and cortisol decreases it. 368

3. Low serotonin turnover is associated with an increased likelihood of impulsive behavior, sometimes including violence. Monkeys with low serotonin turnover get into many fights and in most cases die young. However, those that survive have a high probability of achieving a dominant status. **368**
4. Aggressive behavior relates to both genetic and environmental influences. Several studies indicate that a gene decreasing the activity of monoamine oxidase A increases aggressive behavior mainly among people who had abusive experiences in childhood. **370**
5. Researchers measure enhancement of the startle reflex as an indication of anxiety or learned fears. **371**
6. The amygdala is critical for increasing or decreasing the startle reflex on the basis of learned information. **371**
7. According to studies using fMRI, the human amygdala responds strongly to fear stimuli and any other stimuli that evoke strong emotional processing. It responds most strongly when the processing is effortful. **373**
8. People with damage to the amygdala fail to focus their attention on stimuli with important emotional content. One woman with damage limited to the amygdala seems almost entirely fearless. **374**
9. Damage to the amygdala impairs recognition of fear expressions largely because of lack of attention to the eyes. **376**
10. Panic disorder is associated with increased orexin release and decreased GABA release in the hippocampus. **376**
11. Anti-anxiety drugs decrease fear by facilitating the binding of the neurotransmitter GABA to the $GABA_A$ receptors, especially in the amygdala. **377**
12. After a memory forms, it consolidates. A reminder brings an old memory into a labile state in which new experiences can reconsolidate it or weaken it. Administering the drug propranolol while a memory is in this labile state can substantially weaken it. **378**

Key Terms

Terms are defined in the module on the page number indicated. They're also presented in alphabetical order with definitions in the book's Subject Index/Glossary. Interactive flash cards, audio reviews, and crossword puzzles are among the online resources available to help you learn these terms and the concepts they represent.

bed nucleus of the stria terminalis **372**
benzodiazepines **377**
consolidation **378**
$GABA_A$ receptor **377**
5-hydroxyindoleacetic acid (5-HIAA) **369**
panic disorder **376**
post-traumatic stress disorder **376**
reconsolidation **379**
startle reflex **371**
turnover **369**

Thought Questions

1. Much of the play behavior of a cat can be analyzed into attack and escape components. Is the same true for children's play?
2. People with amygdala damage approach other people indiscriminately instead of trying to choose people who look friendly and trustworthy. What might be a possible explanation?

MODULE 11.2 End of Module Quiz

1. Aggressive behavior correlates with high levels of testosterone and low levels of what?
   a. Acetylcholine
   b. Epinephrine
   c. Cortisol
   d. Potassium
2. What does the level of 5-HIAA in the cerebrospinal fluid indicate?
   a. The amount of serotonin in the neurons
   b. The amount of turnover of serotonin in the brain
   c. The ratio of serotonin to dopamine
   d. The number of serotonin receptors

3. The less active form of the enzyme MAO_A correlates with an increased probability of antisocial behavior for what type of people, if any?

a. Those with a history of childhood maltreatment
b. Those who do not have a history of childhood maltreatment
c. Women
d. None

4. Why do we know more about the brain mechanisms of fear and anxiety than we do about other emotions?

a. Clinical psychologists have greater interest in anxiety than in other emotions.
b. Anxiety depends on brain areas that are easier to reach surgically.
c. Unlike other emotions, anxiety depends on only a single neurotransmitter.
d. Researchers can more satisfactorily measure anxiety than other emotions in laboratory animals.

5. After damage to the amygdala, what happens to the startle reflex?

a. It becomes stronger than before.
b. It becomes weaker than before.
c. It disappears altogether.
d. It becomes more consistent from one time or situation to another.

6. Suppose a researcher wants to determine whether someone is afraid of cats. Which of the following would be the most reasonable approach?

a. Present a photo of a cat and see whether it elicits a startle reflex.
b. Present a photo of a cat and then a loud sound. See whether the photo enhances the usual startle reflex.
c. Present a loud sound and then show a photo of a cat. See whether the photo calms the person after the startle reflex.
d. Present a loud sound to both a person and a cat and see which one shows the greater startle reflex.

7. Research on the amygdala supports which of these psychological conclusions?

a. People who experience great fear also tend to experience a great amount of anger.
b. Anxiety disorders are more common in women than in men, and more common in young people than in older people.
c. What we call fear is a combination of several components, not an indivisible entity.
d. People have six basic types of emotion.

8. The amygdala responds more strongly to a fearful face looking toward you than a similar face looking to the side. What is the likely interpretation?

a. The stronger the viewer's emotional response, the stronger the amygdala response.
b. The amygdala response is equally strong in the person making a fearful face and in the person viewing it.
c. Amygdala response indicates the effort needed to interpret emotional information.
d. The amygdala responds more strongly to familiar than to unfamiliar scenes.

9. Which brain area most strongly inhibits or modifies the response of the amygdala to a potentially threatening stimulus?

a. The prefrontal cortex
b. The cerebellum
c. The basal ganglia
d. The locus coeruleus

10. People with amygdala damage have trouble recognizing expressions of fear. If you wanted to help such people recognize fear, which of the following should you ask them to change?

a. The direction they focus their eyes
b. The amount of protein in their diet
c. Their time of waking and sleeping
d. Their ratio of talking to listening

11. Of the people who endure traumatic experiences, which of the following are the most likely to develop PTSD?

a. The people who suffered the most severe traumas
b. The people who reacted most intensely to the trauma at the time and shortly after it
c. People with a smaller than average hippocampus
d. People with a larger than average hippocampus

12. How does alcohol decrease anxiety?
   a. By shifting blood flow from the left hemisphere to the right hemisphere
   b. By increasing glutamate activity in the prefrontal cortex
   c. By facilitating the effects of GABA on certain receptors
   d. By inhibiting the reuptake of serotonin

13. Extinction of a learned response is most effective under which of these conditions?
   a. If extinction occurs at a different time of day from the original learning
   b. If extinction occurs a few minutes after a brief reminder of the original experience
   c. If extinction occurs under the influence of a drug that increases protein synthesis
   d. If extinction occurs in the presence of soft, soothing music

ANSWERS: 1c, 2b, 3a, 4d, 5d, 6b, 7c, 8c, 9a, 10a, 11c, 12c, 13b.

Stress and Health

In the early days of scientific medicine, physicians made little allowance for the relation of personality or emotions to health and disease. If someone became ill, the cause had to be structural, like a virus or bacterium. Today, **behavioral medicine** emphasizes the effects on health of diet, smoking, exercise, stressful experiences, and other behaviors. We accept the idea that emotions and other experiences influence people's illnesses and patterns of recovery. This view does not imply mind–body dualism. Stress and emotions are brain activities, after all.

Stress and the General Adaptation Syndrome

The term *stress*, like the term *emotion*, is hard to define or quantify. Hans Selye (1979) defined **stress** as the nonspecific response of the body to any demand made upon it. When Selye was in medical school, he noticed that patients with a wide variety of illnesses had much in common: They develop a fever, they lose their appetite, they become inactive, they are sleepy most of the day, their sex drive declines, and their immune systems become more active. Later, when doing laboratory research, he found that rats exposed to an injection of anything, as well as heat, cold, pain, confinement, or the sight of a cat responded with increased heart rate, breathing rate, and adrenal secretions. Selye inferred that any threat to the body, in addition to its specific effects, activated a generalized response to stress, which he called the **general adaptation syndrome**, due mainly to activity of the adrenal glands. In the initial stage, which he called *alarm*, the adrenal glands release the hormone epinephrine, thereby stimulating the sympathetic nervous system to ready the body for brief emergency activity. The adrenal glands also release the hormone **cortisol**, which increases blood glucose, providing the body with extra energy, and the hormone *aldosterone*, important for maintaining blood salt and blood volume. To maintain energy for emergency activity, the body temporarily suppresses less urgent activities, such as sexual arousal.

During the second stage, *resistance*, the sympathetic response declines, but the adrenal glands continue secreting cortisol and other hormones that enable the body to maintain prolonged alertness. The body adapts to the prolonged situation in whatever way it can, such as by decreasing activity to save energy. The body also has ways of adapting to prolonged cold or heat, low oxygen, and so forth.

After intense, prolonged stress, the body enters the third stage, *exhaustion*. During this stage, the individual is tired, inactive, and vulnerable because the nervous system and immune systems no longer have the energy to sustain their responses.

Stress-related illnesses and psychiatric problems are widespread in industrial societies, possibly because of changes in the type of stresses that we face. In our evolutionary past, the alarm stage readied our ancestors for fight or flight. Today, as Robert Sapolsky (1998) has argued, many of our crises are prolonged, such as working under a domineering boss, paying bills with inadequate income, or caring for a relative with a chronic health problem. Even watching televised coverage of a major disaster produces a stress response in many people (Silver et al., 2013). Married couples with *attachment anxiety* (insecurity about their relationship) experience stress and release much cortisol (Jaremka et al., 2013b). When stressful events produce prolonged activation of the general adaptation syndrome, the result can be exhaustion.

Stress is difficult to define or measure. Selye's concept of stress included any *change* in one's life, such as either getting fired from your job or getting promoted. Bruce McEwen (2000, p. 173) proposed an alternative definition that is better for most purposes: "events that are interpreted as threatening to an individual and which elicit physiological and behavioral responses." Although this definition differs from Selye's, the idea remains that many kinds of events can be stressful, and the body reacts to all kinds of stress in similar ways.

STOP&CHECK

18. Name three hormones that the adrenal glands release in the alarm stage of the body's response to stress.

ANSWER

18. Epinephrine, cortisol, and aldosterone.

Stress and the Hypothalamus-Pituitary-Adrenal Cortex Axis

Stress activates two body systems. One is the sympathetic nervous system, which prepares the body for brief fight-or-flight emergency responses. The other is the **HPA axis**—the hypothalamus, pituitary gland, and adrenal cortex. Activation of the hypothalamus induces the anterior pituitary gland to secrete **adrenocorticotropic hormone (ACTH)**, which in turn stimulates the human adrenal cortex to secrete cortisol, which enhances metabolic activity, elevates blood levels of sugar, and increases alertness (Akinola & Mendes, 2012) (see Figure 11.22). Many researchers refer to cortisol as a "stress hormone" and use measurements of cortisol level as an indication of someone's recent stress level. Compared to the autonomic nervous system, the HPA axis reacts more slowly, but it dominates the response to prolonged stressors such as living with an abusive parent or spouse.

Stress that releases cortisol mobilizes the body's energy to fight a difficult situation, but the effects depend on amount and duration. Brief or moderate stress improves attention and memory formation (Krugers, Hoogenraad, & Groc, 2010). It improves performance on relatively simple tasks, although it impairs performance that requires complex, flexible thinking (Arnsten, 2009). Stress also enhances activity of the immune system, helping it fight illnesses (Benschop et al., 1995). However, prolonged stress impairs immune activity and memory (Mika et al., 2012). To see why, we start with an overview of the immune system.

The Immune System

The **immune system** consists of cells that protect the body against viruses, bacteria, and other intruders. The immune system is like a police force: If it is too weak, the "criminals" (viruses and bacteria) run wild and create damage. If it becomes too strong and unselective, it starts attacking "law-abiding citizens" (the body's own cells). When the immune system attacks normal cells, we call the result an *autoimmune disease.* Myasthenia gravis and rheumatoid arthritis are examples of autoimmune diseases.

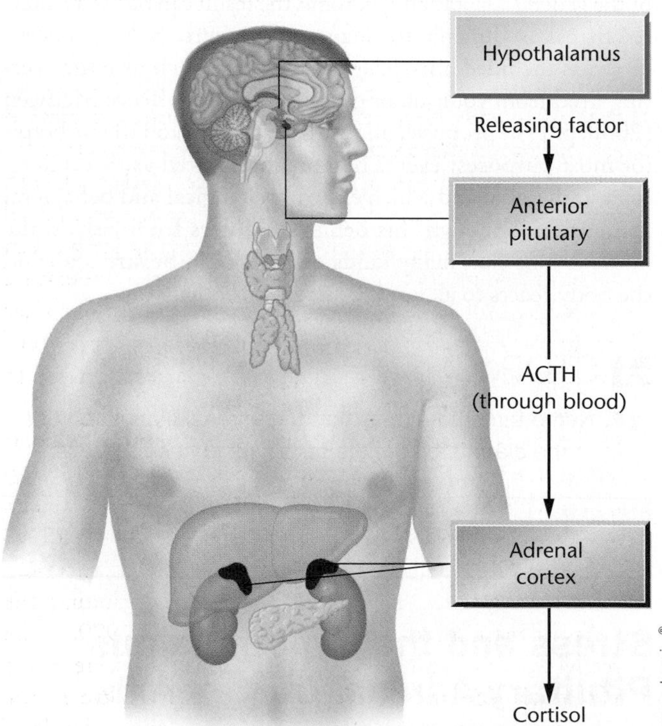

FIGURE 11.22 The hypothalamus-pituitary-adrenal cortex axis Prolonged stress increases secretion of the adrenal hormone cortisol, which elevates blood sugar and increases metabolism. These changes help the body sustain prolonged activity but at the expense of decreased immune system activity.

Leukocytes

The most important elements of the immune system are the **leukocytes**, commonly known as white blood cells (Kiecolt-Glaser & Glaser, 1993; O'Leary, 1990).

We distinguish several types of leukocytes, including B cells, T cells, and natural killer cells (see Figure 11.23):

- *B cells*, which mature mostly in the bone marrow, secrete **antibodies**, which are Y-shaped proteins that attach to particular antigens, just as a key fits a lock. Every cell has surface proteins called **antigens** (antibody-generator molecules), and your body's antigens are as unique as your fingerprints. The B cells recognize the "self" antigens, but when they find an unfamiliar antigen, they attack the cell. This kind of attack defends the body against viruses and bacteria, but it also causes rejection of organ transplants, unless physicians take special steps to minimize the attack. After the body has made antibodies against a particular intruder, it "remembers" the intruder and quickly builds more of the same kind of antibody if it encounters that intruder again.
- *T cells* mature in the thymus gland. Several kinds of T cells attack intruders directly (without secreting antibodies), and some help other T cells or B cells to multiply.
- *Natural killer cells*, another kind of leukocytes, attack tumor cells and cells that are infected with viruses. Whereas each B or T cell attacks a particular kind of foreign antigen, natural killer cells attack all intruders.

In response to an infection, leukocytes and other cells produce small proteins called **cytokines** (e.g., interleukin-1, or IL-1) that combat infections. Cytokines also stimulate the vagus nerve and trigger the release of **prostaglandins** that cross the blood–brain barrier and stimulate the hypothalamus to produce fever, sleepiness, lack of energy, lack of appetite, and loss of sex drive (Maier & Watkins, 1998; Saper, Romanovsky, & Scammell, 2012). Recall Selye's observation that most illnesses produce similar symptoms, such as fever, loss of energy, and so forth. Here we see the explanation. Aspirin and ibuprofen decrease fever and other signs of illness by inhibiting prostaglandins.

Note that these symptoms of illness are actually part of the body's way of fighting the illness. Most people think of fever and sleepiness as something the illness did to them, but in fact, fever and sleepiness are strategies that evolved for fighting the illness. As discussed in Chapter 9, a moderate fever helps fight many infections. Sleep and inactivity are ways of conserving energy so that the body can devote more energy to its immune attack against the intruders. Decreased appetite may be helpful in two ways—by decreasing the need for activity, and by reducing blood glucose, the preferred fuel for many microorganisms (Saper et al., 2012).

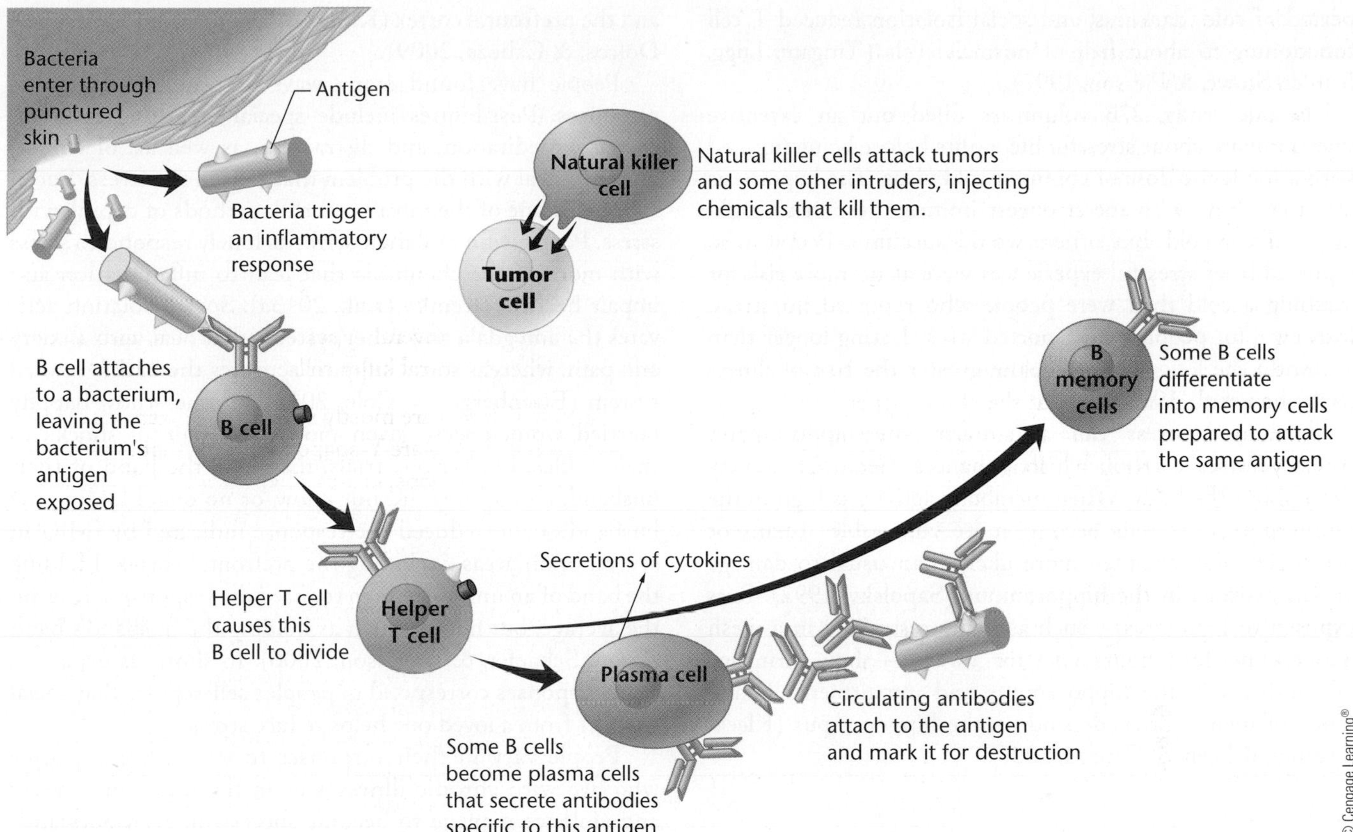

FIGURE 11.23 Immune system responses to a bacterial infection
B cells bind to bacteria and produce antibodies against the bacteria. When a helper T cell attaches to the B cell, it stimulates the B cell to generate copies of itself, called B memory cells, that immunize the body against future invasions by the same kind of bacteria.

STOP&CHECK

19. What kind of cell releases cytokines?

20. What changes do prostaglandins stimulate?

ANSWERS

19. Leukocytes, which are part of the immune system, release cytokines. **20.** Prostaglandins stimulate the hypothalamus to produce fever, decreased hunger, decreased sex drive, and increased sleepiness.

Effects of Stress on the Immune System

The nervous system has more control than we might have guessed over the immune system. The study of this relationship, called **psychoneuroimmunology**, deals with the ways experiences alter the immune system and how the immune system in turn influences the central nervous system.

Stress affects the immune system in several ways. In response to a brief stressful experience, the nervous system activates the immune system to increase its production of natural killer cells and the secretion of cytokines (Segerstrom & Miller, 2004). The elevated cytokine levels help combat infections, but they also trigger prostaglandins that reach the hypothalamus. Rats subjected to inescapable shocks show symptoms resembling illness, including sleepiness, decreased appetite, and elevated body temperature. The same is true for people who are under great stress (Maier & Watkins, 1998). People with PTSD have elevated cytokine levels (von Känel et al., 2007). Even viewing extremely disgusting images can activate the immune system and raise body temperature (Stevenson et al., 2012). In short, if you have been under much stress and start to feel lethargy or other symptoms of illness, one possibility is that your symptoms are reactions to the stress, acting through the immune system.

A prolonged stress response produces symptoms similar to depression and weakens the immune system (Lim, Huang, Grueter, Rothwell, & Malenka, 2012; Segerstrom & Miller, 2004). A likely hypothesis is that prolonged increase of cortisol directs energy toward increasing metabolism and therefore detracts energy from synthesizing proteins, including the proteins of the immune system. For example, in 1979, at the Three Mile Island nuclear power plant, a major accident was barely contained. The people who continued to live in the vicinity during the next year had lower than normal levels of B cells, T cells, and natural killer cells. They also complained of emotional distress and showed impaired performance on a proofreading task (A. Baum, Gatchel, & Schaeffer, 1983; McKinnon, Weisse, Reynolds, Bowles, & Baum, 1989). A study of research scientists in Antarctica found that a 9-month period of cold, darkness, and social isolation reduced T cell functioning to about half of normal levels (Tingate, Lugg, Muller, Stowe, & Pierson, 1997).

In one study, 276 volunteers filled out an extensive questionnaire about stressful life events before being injected with a moderate dose of common cold virus. The hypothesis was that those with the strongest immune responses could fight off the cold, but others would succumb. People who reported brief stressful experiences were at no more risk for catching a cold than were people who reported no stress. However, for people who reported stress lasting longer than a month, the longer it lasted, the greater the risk of illness (S. Cohen et al., 1998).

Prolonged stress can also harm the hippocampus. Stress releases cortisol, which enhances metabolic activity throughout the body. When metabolic activity is high in the hippocampus, its cells become more vulnerable. Toxins or overstimulation are then more likely than usual to damage or kill neurons in the hippocampus (Sapolsky, 1992). Rats exposed to high stress—such as being restrained in a mesh wire retainer for 6 hours a day for 3 weeks—show shrinkage of dendrites in the hippocampus and impairments in the kinds of memory that depend on the hippocampus (Kleen, Sitomer, Killeen, & Conrad, 2006).

STOP & CHECK

21. How do the effects of stress mimic the effects of illness?

22. How does prolonged stress damage the hippocampus?

ANSWERS

21. Stress increases release of cytokines, which communicate with the hypothalamus via the vagus nerve and prostaglandins. The hypothalamus reacts with the same responses it uses to combat illness, such as inactivity and loss of appetite. **22.** Stress increases the release of cortisol, which enhances metabolic activity throughout the body. When neurons in the hippocampus have high metabolic activity, they become more vulnerable to damage by toxins or overstimulation.

Stress Control

Individuals vary in their reactions to a stressful experience. Studies with mice have identified genes that relate to being more vulnerable or more resilient (Krishnan et al., 2007). Individual differences also relate to life circumstances. In baboon troops, the entry of a new adult male into a troop is stressful to females, because he may attack either them or their babies. However, a female who has a male "friend" to defend her (possibly the father of her babies) shows less stress response (Beehner, Bergman, Cheney, Seyfarth, & Whitten, 2005). In humans, resilience in the face of stress correlates with stronger connections between the amygdala and the prefrontal cortex (Kim & Whalen, 2009; St. Jacques, Dolcos, & Cabeza, 2009).

People have found many ways to control their stress responses. Possibilities include special breathing routines, exercise, meditation, and distraction, as well as, of course, trying to deal with the problem that caused the stress. Social support is one of the most powerful methods of coping with stress. People who rate themselves as lonely respond to stress with more of the chemicals that lead to inflammation and impair health (Jaremka et al., 2013a). Social isolation activates the amygdala and other systems that deal with anxiety and pain, whereas social support activates the brain's reward system (Eisenberger & Cole, 2012). In one study, happily married women were given moderately painful shocks to their ankles. On various trials, they held the hand of their husband, a man they did not know, or no one. Holding the husband's hand reduced the response indicated by fMRI in several brain areas, including the prefrontal cortex. Holding the hand of an unknown man reduced the response a little, on the average, but not as much as holding the husband's hand (Coan, Schaefer, & Davidson, 2006). In short, as expected, brain responses correspond to people's self-reports that social support from a loved one helps reduce stress.

People vary in their responses to stress. Some people who live with chronic illnesses or in the midst of poverty and violence manage to become successful, even outstanding. Others deteriorate badly in response to what would seem to be smaller problems. Psychologists describe these differences in terms of resilience, but what accounts for resilience? Part of the variation depends on genes that influence the amygdala and the vigor of the sympathetic nervous system (Lensvelt-Mulders & Hettema, 2001). Other influences include social support, physical health, and previous stressful experiences (Niwa et al., 2013; Russo, Murrough, Han, Charney, & Nestler, 2012; Southwick & Charney, 2012). Successfully coping with moderately stressful events prepares one to cope with later events, although a history of severely adverse events leaves one too exhausted to resist (Seery, Leo, Lupien, Kondrak, & Almonte, 2013). Research with rats finds that becoming a mother decreases later responses to stress (Maeng & Shors, 2012).

Resilience is not easy to investigate, because so many factors are probably important. Ideally, we would want to study a large number of physically and mentally healthy people before, during, and after a series of highly stressful experiences, and compare them to similar people who faced less stress. And we would want to be sure we could keep track of each person's whereabouts over several years. It sounds like an impossibly difficult task, and it would be, for anyone except for the military. In 2010, the U.S. Army began a five-year study of young people entering military service. All were healthy at the start, and many but not all would be exposed to various degrees of stress over the next few years. The army is superb at keeping track of where every soldier is at all times, and it can guarantee to do follow-up studies on each participant. The results, to be published in 2015, are likely to give us unprecedented information about stress and resilience.

MODULE 11.3 ■ IN CLOSING

Emotions and Body Reactions

Research on stress and health provides an interesting kind of closure. Decades ago, Hans Selye argued that any stressful event leads to the general adaptation syndrome, marked by fever and other signs of illness. We now see why: The body reacts to prolonged stress by activating the adrenal cortex and the immune system, and the resulting increase in cytokines produces the same reactions that an infection would. Research has also improved our understanding of the predispositions behind post-traumatic stress disorder and makes it possible to foresee a new era of advances in psychosomatic medicine. Emotional states, which once seemed too ephemeral for scientific study, are now part of mainstream biology.

Summary

1. Hans Selye introduced the idea of the general adaptation syndrome, which is the way the body responds to all kinds of illness and stress. **383**
2. Stress immediately activates the sympathetic nervous system and more slowly activates the hypothalamus-pituitary-adrenal cortex axis. The adrenal cortex releases cortisol, which increases metabolism. **383**
3. Although brief stress enhances the immune response and facilitates memory formation, prolonged stress drains the body of the resources it needs for other purposes. **383**
4. Stress activates the immune system, helping to fight viruses and bacteria. The immune system releases cytokines, which stimulate the hypothalamus via the vagus nerve and by releasing prostaglandins, which cross the blood–brain barrier. The hypothalamus reacts by activities to combat illness, including sleepiness, fever, and loss of appetite and energy. **384**
5. Because stress causes release of cytokines, it can also lead to lethargy and other symptoms that resemble those of illness. **385**
6. The high cortisol levels associated with prolonged stress damages cells in the hippocampus, thereby impairing memory. **386**
7. People vary in their resilience to stress, based on genetics, social support, previous experiences, and other factors. **386**

Key Terms

Terms are defined in the module on the page number indicated. They're also presented in alphabetical order with definitions in the book's Subject Index/Glossary. Interactive flash cards, audio reviews, and crossword puzzles are among the online resources available to help you learn these terms and the concepts they represent.

adrenocorticotropic hormone (ACTH) **384**
antibody **384**
antigen **384**
behavioral medicine **383**
cortisol **383**
cytokine **384**
general adaptation syndrome **383**
HPA axis **383**
immune system **384**
leukocyte **384**
prostaglandins **384**
psychoneuroimmunology **385**
stress **383**

Thought Question

If someone were unable to produce cytokines, what would be the consequences?

MODULE 11.3 End of Module Quiz

1. How does cortisol help the body deal with a stressful event?
   a. It maintains the salt in the blood and therefore maintains blood volume.
   b. It lowers body temperature.
   c. It activates the parasympathetic nervous system.
   d. It increases blood sugar, providing more energy.

2. How do the functions of the HPA axis compare to those of the sympathetic nervous system?
   a. The sympathetic nervous system readies the body for brief, vigorous action, and the HPA axis controls digestion and other vegetative activities.
   b. The sympathetic nervous system activates the brain, and the HPA axis activates the rest of the body.
   c. The sympathetic nervous system readies the body for brief, vigorous action, and the HPA axis prepares the body for prolonged coping with a persistent stressor.
   d. The sympathetic nervous system is active during a stressful situation, and the HPA axis becomes active at the end of the stressful situation.

3. Why do nearly all infections produce similar symptoms, such as fever, sleepiness, and loss of energy?
   a. Every infection damages the body's ability to maintain body temperature and overall activity.
   b. "Sickness behaviors" are an effective way for a sick person to gain sympathy and help.
   c. Infectious particles clog the arteries, making it difficult for other chemicals to reach their targets.
   d. The immune system sends prostaglandins to the brain, where they stimulate the hypothalamus to produce these effects.

4. What are the effects of stress on the immune system?
   a. All stressful experiences impair the immune system.
   b. Brief stress activates the immune system, but prolonged stress weakens it.
   c. Brief stress weakens the immune system, but prolonged stress strengthens it.
   d. All stressful experiences strengthen the immune system.

5. Prolonged stress is known to damage which brain area?
   a. The visual cortex
   b. The hippocampus
   c. The cerebellum
   d. The corpus callosum

ANSWERS:
1d, 2c, 3d, 4b, 5b.

Suggestions for Further Reading

Damasio, A. (1999). *The feeling of what happens.* New York: Harcourt Brace. A neurologist's account of the connection between emotion and consciousness, full of interesting examples.

Frazzetto, G.B. (2013). *Joy, guilt, anger, love.* New York: Penguin books. Insightful description of emotional experiences, with reference to relevant neurological studies.

McEwen, B. S., with Lasley, E. N. (2002). *The end of stress as we know it.* Washington, DC: Joseph Henry Press. Readable review by one of the leading researchers.

Pfaff, D. W. (2007). *The neuroscience of fair play.* New York: Dana Press. Exploration of how the physiology of emotions, especially the amygdala, relates to moral behavior.

Tim Davis/CORBIS

The Biology of Learning and Memory

12

CHAPTER OUTLINE

MODULE 12.1 Learning, Memory, and Amnesia
Localized Representations of Memory
Types of Memory
The Hippocampus
Other Types of Amnesia
The Basal Ganglia
Other Brain Areas and Memory
In Closing: Types of Memory
MODULE 12.2 Storing Information in the Nervous System
Blind Alleys and Abandoned Mines
Learning and the Hebbian Synapse
Single-Cell Mechanisms of Invertebrate Behavior Change
Long-Term Potentiation in Vertebrates
Improving Memory
In Closing: The Physiology of Memory

LEARNING OBJECTIVES

After studying this chapter, you should be able to:

1. Describe attempts to localize memory, beginning with Lashley's failed attempts and continuing to Thompson's successful research with the cerebellum.
2. Describe the memory losses experienced by patient H. M. and others.
3. Explain how the research on amnesia helped psychologists distinguish among types of memory.
4. Contrast the types of learning controlled by the basal ganglia to those controlled by the hippocampus and cerebral cortex.
5. Define Hebbian synapse.
6. Outline the major chemical steps responsible for long-term potentiation.

Suppose you type something on your computer and then save it. A year later, you come back, click the correct file name, and retrieve what you wrote. How did the computer remember what to do?

That question has two parts: First, how do the physical properties of silicon chips enable them to alter their properties when you type certain keys? Second, how does the wiring diagram take the changes in individual silicon chips and convert them into a useful activity?

Similarly, when we try to explain how you remember some experience, we deal with two questions: First, how does a pattern of sensory information alter the input–output properties of certain neurons? Second, after neurons change their properties, how does the nervous system produce the behavioral changes that we call learning or memory?

We begin this chapter by considering how the various brain areas interact to produce learning and memory. In the second module, we turn to the detailed physiology of how experience changes neurons and synapses.

OPPOSITE: Learning produces amazingly complex behaviors.

Learning, Memory, and Amnesia

Suppose you lost your ability to form memories. You are aware of the present but you forget your experience from even a few moments ago. You feel as if you awakened from a long sleep only a second ago. So you write on a sheet of paper, "Just now, for the first time, I have suddenly become conscious!" A little later, you forget this experience, too. As far as you can tell, you have just now emerged into consciousness after a long sleeplike period. You look at this sheet of paper on which you wrote about becoming conscious, but you don't remember writing it. How odd! You must have written it when in fact you were not conscious! Irritated, you cross off that statement and write anew, "*NOW* I am for the first time conscious!" And a minute later, you cross that one off and write it again. Eventually, someone finds this sheet of paper on which you have repeatedly written and crossed out statements about suddenly feeling conscious for the first time.

Sound far-fetched? It really happened to a patient who developed severe memory impairments after encephalitis damaged his temporal cortex (B. A. Wilson, Baddeley, & Kapur, 1995). Life without memory means no sense of existing across time. Your memory is almost synonymous with your sense of self.

Localized Representations of Memory

To study the physiology of learning, we must first characterize learning, and psychologists have traditionally distinguished two major categories, classical and instrumental conditioning. The Russian physiologist Ivan Pavlov pioneered the investigation of what we now call **classical conditioning** (see Figure 12.1a), in which pairing two stimuli changes the response to one of them (Pavlov, 1927). The experimenter starts by presenting a **conditioned stimulus (CS)**, which initially elicits no response of note, and then presents the **unconditioned stimulus (UCS)**, which automatically elicits the **unconditioned response (UCR)**. After some pairings of the CS and the UCS (perhaps just one or two, perhaps many), the individual begins making a new, learned response to the CS, called a **conditioned response (CR)**. In his original experiments, Pavlov presented a dog with a sound (CS) followed by meat (UCS), which stimulated the dog to salivate (UCR). After many such pairings, the sound alone (CS) stimulated the dog to salivate (CR). In that case and many others, the CR resembles the UCR, but in some cases, it does not. For example, if a rat experiences a CS paired with shock, the shock elicits screaming and jumping, but the CS elicits a freezing response.

In **instrumental conditioning** (also known as operant conditioning), an individual's response leads to a reinforcer or punishment (see Figure 12.1b). A **reinforcer** is any event that increases the future probability of the response. A **punishment** is an event that suppresses the frequency of the response. For example, when a rat enters one arm of a maze and finds Froot Loops cereal (a potent reinforcer for a rat), the rat increases its probability of entering that arm at future opportunities. If it receives a shock instead, the probability decreases. The primary difference between classical and instrumental conditioning is that in instrumental conditioning the individual's response determines the outcome (reinforcer or punishment), whereas in classical conditioning the CS and UCS occur at certain times regardless of the individual's behavior. (The behavior is useful, however, in preparing for the UCS.)

Some cases of learning are difficult to label as classical or instrumental. For example, after a male songbird hears the song of his own species during his first few months, he imitates it the following year. The song that he heard was not paired with any other stimulus, so it doesn't look like classical conditioning. He learned the song without reinforcers or punishments, so we cannot call it instrumental conditioning either. That is, animals have specialized methods of learning other than classical and instrumental conditioning. Also, the way animals (including people) learn varies from one situation to another. For example, in most situations, learning occurs only if the CS and UCS, or response and reinforcer, occur close together in time. But if you eat something, especially something unfamiliar, and get sick later, you learn a strong aversion to the taste of that food, even if taste and illness are separated by hours (Rozin & Kalat, 1971; Rozin & Schull, 1988).

Lashley's Search for the Engram

What happens in the brain when you learn something? Pavlov proposed the simple hypothesis that classical conditioning

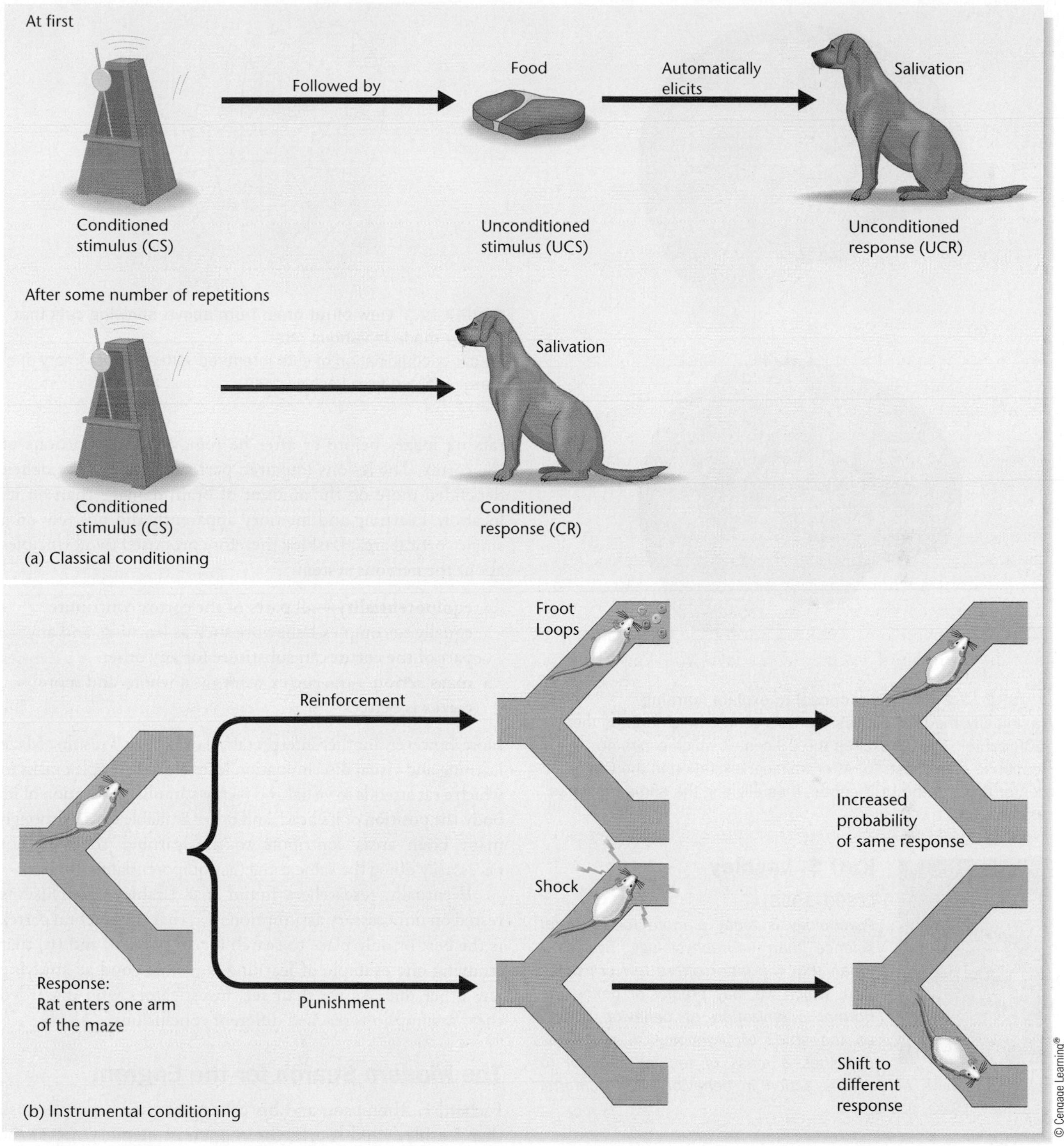

FIGURE 12.1 Classical conditioning and instrumental conditioning
(a) In classical conditioning, two stimuli (CS and UCS) are presented at certain times regardless of what the learner does.
(b) In instrumental conditioning, the learner's behavior controls the presentation of reinforcer or punishment.

reflects a strengthened connection between a CS center and a UCS center in the brain. That strengthened connection lets any excitation of the CS center flow to the UCS center, evoking the unconditioned response (see Figure 12.2). We now know that this hypothesis does not fit all behavioral observations. As mentioned, if a signal predicts shock, a rat does not react to the signal the way it reacts to a shock. However, psychologists of an earlier era were unaware of such observations and considered Pavlov's hypothesis plausible. Karl Lashley set out to test it. Lashley was searching for the **engram**—the physical representation of what has been learned. (A connection between two brain areas would be a possible example of an engram.)

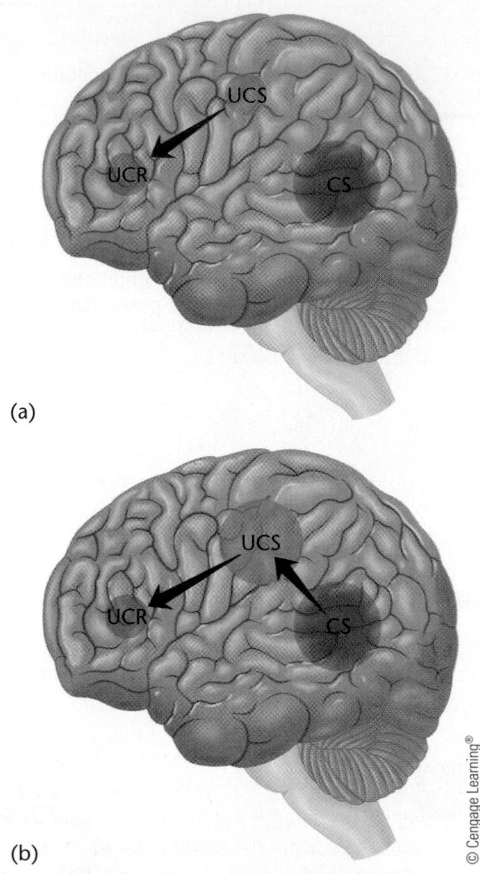

FIGURE 12.2 Pavlov's proposal to explain learning
(a) Initially, the UCS excites the UCS center, which excites the UCR center. The CS excites the CS center, which elicits no response of interest. (b) After training, excitation in the CS center flows to the UCS center, thus eliciting the same response as the UCS.

Karl S. Lashley

(1890–1958)

Psychology is today a more fundamental science than neurophysiology. By this I mean that the latter offers few principles from which we may predict or define the normal organization of behavior, whereas the study of psychological processes furnishes a mass of factual material to which the laws of nervous action in behavior must conform. (Lashley, 1930, p. 24)

Lashley reasoned that if learning depends on new or strengthened connections between two brain areas, a knife cut somewhere in the brain should interrupt that connection and abolish the learned response. He trained rats on mazes and a brightness discrimination task and then made deep cuts in varying locations in their cerebral cortices (Lashley, 1929, 1950) (see Figure 12.3). However, no knife cut significantly impaired the rats' performances. Evidently, the types of learning that he studied did not depend on connections across the cortex.

Lashley also tested whether any portion of the cerebral cortex is more important than others for learning. He trained rats on mazes before or after he removed large portions of the cortex. The lesions impaired performance, but the deficit depended more on the amount of brain damage than on its location. Learning and memory apparently did not rely on a single cortical area. Lashley therefore proposed two principles about the nervous system:

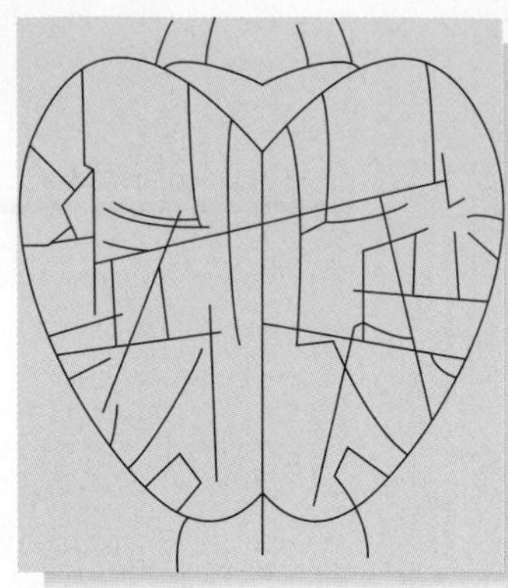

FIGURE 12.3 View of rat brain from above, showing cuts that Lashley made in various rats
No cut or combination of cuts interfered with a rat's memory of a maze. Adapted from Lashley, 1950

- **equipotentiality**—all parts of the cortex contribute equally to complex behaviors such as learning, and any part of the cortex can substitute for any other.
- **mass action**—the cortex works as a whole, and more cortex is better.

Note, however, another interpretation of Lashley's results: Maze learning and visual discrimination learning are complex tasks in which a rat attends to visual and tactile stimuli, the location of its body, the position of its head, and other available cues. Although many brain areas contribute to the learning, they are not necessarily doing the same thing (as equipotentiality implies).

Eventually, researchers found that Lashley's conclusions rested on unnecessary assumptions: (a) that the cerebral cortex is the best or only place to search for an engram, and (b) that studying one example of learning is just as good as studying any other one. As we shall see, investigators who discarded these assumptions reached different conclusions.

The Modern Search for the Engram

Richard F. Thompson and his colleagues used a simpler task than Lashley's and sought the engram of memory not in the cerebral cortex but in the cerebellum. Thompson and colleagues studied classical conditioning of eyelid responses in rabbits. They presented first a tone (CS) and then a puff of air (UCS) to the cornea of the rabbit's eye. At first, a rabbit blinked at the air puff but not at the tone. After repeated pairings, classical conditioning occurred and the rabbit blinked at the tone also. Investigators recorded the activity in various brain cells to determine which ones changed their responses during learning.

Thompson set out to determine the location of learning. Imagine a sequence of brain areas from the sensory receptors to the motor neurons controlling the muscles:

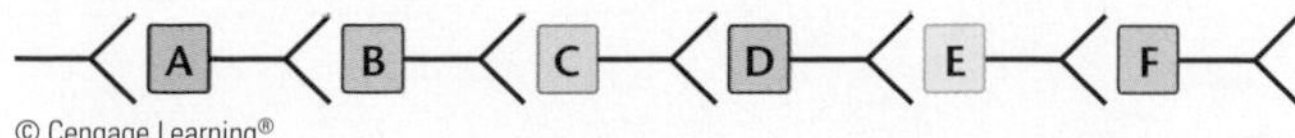

If we damage any one of those areas, learning will be impaired, but we cannot be sure that learning occurred in the damaged area. For example, if the learning occurs in area D, damage in A, B, or C will prevent learning by blocking the input to D. Damage in E or F will prevent learning by blocking the output from D. Thompson and colleagues reasoned as follows: Suppose the learning occurs in D. If so, then D has to be active at the time of the learning, and so do all the areas leading up to D (A, B, and C). However, learning should not require areas E and beyond. If area E were temporarily blocked, nothing would relay information to the muscles, so we would see no response, but learning could occur nevertheless, and we could see evidence of it later.

Thompson's research identified one nucleus of the cerebellum, the **lateral interpositus nucleus (LIP)**, as essential for learning. At the start of training, those cells showed little response to the tone, but as learning proceeded, their responses increased (R. F. Thompson, 1986). When the investigators temporarily suppressed that nucleus in an untrained rabbit, either by cooling the nucleus or by injecting a drug into it, and then presented the CSs and UCSs, the rabbit showed no responses during the training. Then they waited for the LIP to recover and continued training. At that point, the rabbit began to learn, but it learned *at the same speed as animals that had received no previous training.* Evidently, while the LIP was suppressed, the training had no effect.

But does learning actually occur *in* the LIP, or does this area just relay the information to a later area where learning occurs? In the next experiments, investigators suppressed activity in the red nucleus, a midbrain motor area that receives input from the cerebellum. When the red nucleus was suppressed, the rabbits again showed no responses during training. However, as soon as the red nucleus had recovered from the cooling or drugs, the rabbits showed strong learned responses to the tone (R. E. Clark & Lavond, 1993; Krupa, Thompson, & Thompson, 1993). In other words, suppressing the red nucleus temporarily prevented the response but did not prevent learning. Evidently, learning did not require activity in the red nucleus or any area after it, although later research found that the red nucleus does contribute to learning under certain circumstances (Pacheco-Calderón, Carretero-Guillén, Delgado-Garcia, & Gruart, 2012). Thompson and his colleagues concluded that the learning occurred in the LIP. How did they know that learning didn't depend on some area *before* the LIP? If it did, then suppressing the LIP would not have prevented learning. Figure 12.4 summarizes these experiments. This research made it possible for other researchers to explore the mechanisms in more detail, identifying the cells and neurotransmitters responsible for changes in the LIP (Freeman & Steinmetz, 2011).

The mechanisms for this type of conditioning are probably similar in humans. According to PET scans on young adults, developing a conditioned eyeblink causes increases in the cerebellum, red nucleus, and several other areas (Logan & Grafton, 1995). People who have damage in the cerebellum have weaker conditioned eyeblinks, and the blinks are less accurately timed relative to the onset of the air puff (Gerwig et al., 2005). The cerebellum is critical for many other instances of classical conditioning also, but only if the delay between the onset of the CS and the onset of the UCS is short (Pakaprot, Kim, & Thompson, 2009). As mentioned in Chapter 7, the cerebellum is specialized for timing brief intervals, on the order of a couple of seconds or less. Many instances of learning take place in other brain areas. For example, learning to avoid a taste because of subsequent illness depends on the amygdala (Hashikawa et al., 2013).

STOP&CHECK

1. Thompson found a localized engram, whereas Lashley did not. What key differences in procedures or assumptions were probably responsible for their different results?

2. What evidence indicates that the red nucleus is necessary for performance of a conditioned response but not for learning the response?

ANSWERS

1. Thompson studied a different, simpler type of learning. Also, he looked in the cerebellum instead of the cerebral cortex. **2.** If the red nucleus is inactivated during training, the animal makes no conditioned responses during the training, so the red nucleus is necessary for the response. However, as soon as the red nucleus recovers, the animal can show conditioned responses at once, without any further training, so learning occurred while the red nucleus was inactivated.

Types of Memory

Is memory just one thing, or do we have several types? If several, what are they? Studies of brain damage help us answer this question.

Short-Term and Long-Term Memory

Donald Hebb (1949) reasoned that no one mechanism could account for all the phenomena of learning. You can immediately repeat something you just heard, so it is clear that some memories form quickly. Old people can recall events from their childhood, so we also see that some memories last a lifetime. Hebb could not imagine a chemical process that is fast enough to account for immediate memory yet stable enough to provide permanent memory. He therefore proposed a distinction between **short-term memory** of events that have just occurred and **long-term memory** of events from further back. Several types of evidence supported this idea:

- Short-term memory and long-term memory differ in their capacity. If you hear a series of unrelated numbers or letters, such as DZLAUV, you can probably repeat no more than about seven of them, and with other kinds of

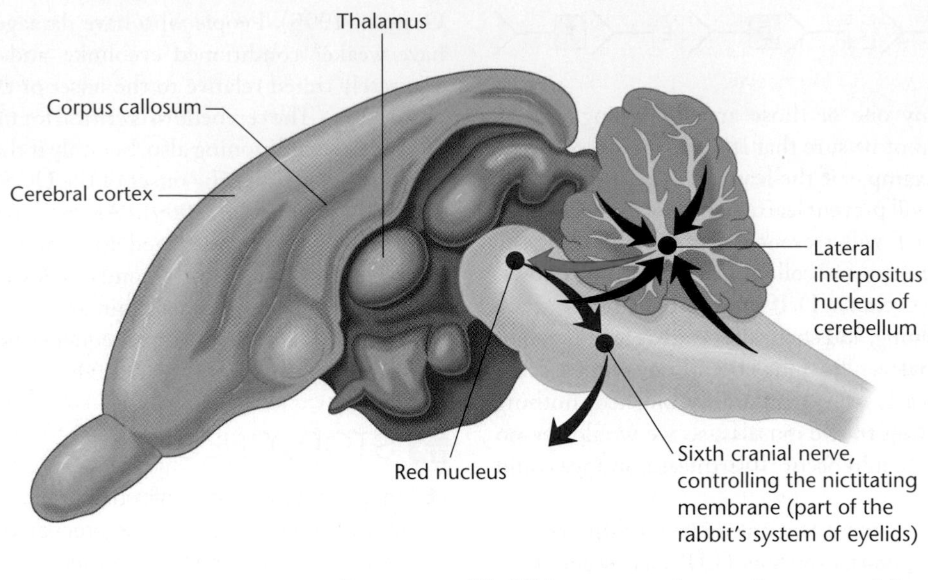

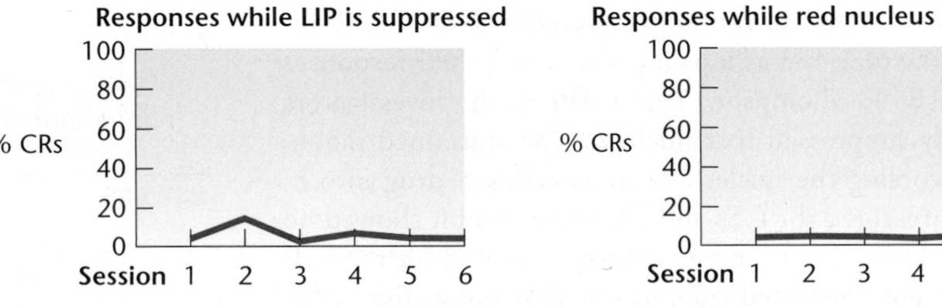

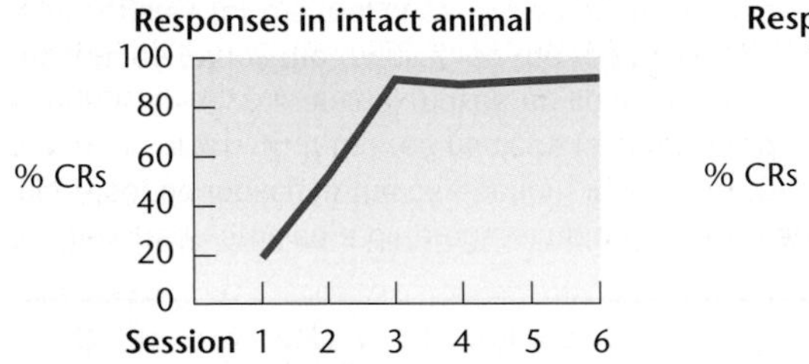

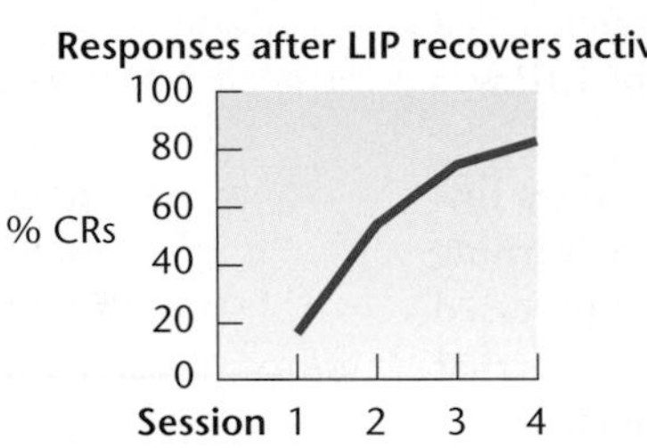

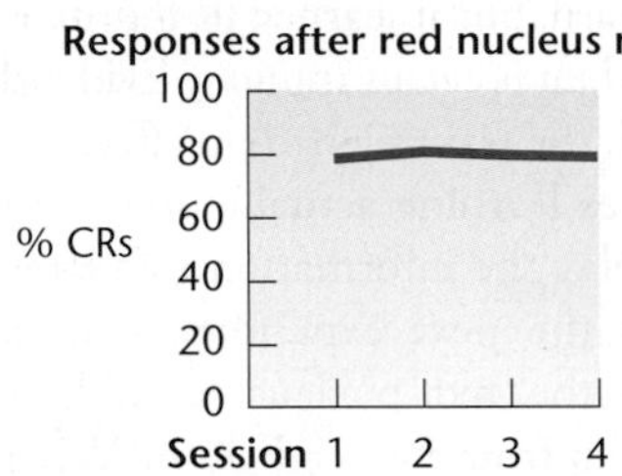

FIGURE 12.4 Localization of an engram
Temporarily inactivating the lateral interpositus nucleus blocked all indications of learning. After the inactivation wore off, the rabbits learned as slowly as rabbits with no previous training. Temporarily inactivating the red nucleus blocked responses during the period of inactivation, but the learned response appeared as soon as the red nucleus recovered. Based on the results of Clark & Lavond, 1993; Krupa, Thompson, & Thompson, 1993

material, your maximum is even less. You can hold a vast capacity of information in long-term memory.

- Short-term memory depends on rehearsal. For example, if you read the letter sequence DZLAUV and then something distracts you, your chance of repeating the letters declines rapidly (Peterson & Peterson, 1959). You can reconstruct long-term memories that you haven't thought about in years, although your recall might not be 100 percent accurate.
- With short-term memory, once you have forgotten something, it is lost. With long-term memory, a hint might help you reconstruct something you thought you had forgotten. For example, try naming all your high school teachers. After you have named all you can, you can name still more if someone shows you photos and tells you the teachers' initials.

Hebb suggested that we might store short-term memories by a reverberating circuit, in which neuron A excites neuron B, which excites neuron C, which then reexcites neuron A. As he predicted, some circuits do store information that way, although in some cases a neuron increases its excitability on its own (Dranias, Ju, Rajaram, & Van Dongen, 2013). Hebb further proposed that storing something in short-term memory for a sufficient period of time made it possible for the brain to **consolidate** it into long-term memory, presumably by building new synapses or other structural changes. If anything interrupted the rehearsal of short-term memory before consolidation completed its course, the information was simply lost.

Our Changing Views of Consolidation

Later studies made the distinction between short-term and long-term memory increasingly problematic. First, many short-term memories are not simply temporary stores on their way to being long-term memories. When you watch a soccer or hockey match, you remember the score until it changes, perhaps an hour later. Rehearsing that score for an hour doesn't turn it into a long-term memory.

Furthermore, consolidation isn't what we used to think it was. The original idea was that the brain held onto something in short-term memory for whatever time it needed to synthesize new proteins that establish a long-term memory (Canal & Gold, 2007). Once formed, the long-term memory was supposed to be permanent. Chapter 11 discussed one problem with that view: A reminder brings an old memory into a labile state from which it can be reconsolidated, altered, or weakened. Another problem is that the time needed for consolidation varies enormously. If you are trying to memorize facts that you consider boring, you might struggle for hours. But if someone warns you about the venomous snake that got loose in your dormitory, you won't have to repeat it over and over or write flash cards to remember it. Emotionally significant memories form quickly. Why? Stressful or emotionally exciting experiences increase the secretion of epinephrine (adrenaline) and cortisol. Small to moderate amounts of cortisol activate the amygdala and hippocampus, where they enhance the storage and consolidation of recent experiences (Cahill & McGaugh, 1998; Murty, LaBar, & Adcock, 2012). The amygdala in turn stimulates the hippocampus and cerebral cortex, which are both important for memory storage. However, prolonged stress, which releases even more cortisol, impairs memory (deQuervain, Roozendaal, & McGaugh, 1998; Newcomer et al., 1999). The main point here is that consolidation can be fast or slow, and it certainly depends on more than the time necessary to synthesize some new proteins.

James L. McGaugh

James L. McGaugh

Memory is perhaps the most critical capacity that we have as humans. Memory is not simply a record of experiences; it is the basis of our knowledge of the world, our skills, our hopes and dreams, and our ability to interact with others and thus influence our destinies. Investigation of how the brain enables us to bridge our present existence with our past and future is thus essential for understanding human nature. Clearly, the most exciting challenge of science is to determine how brain cells and systems create our memories.

STOP&CHECK

3. How do epinephrine and cortisol enhance memory storage?

ANSWER

3. Epinephrine and cortisol both enhance emotional memories by stimulating the amygdala and hippocampus.

Working Memory

To replace the concept of short-term memory, A. D. Baddeley and G. J. Hitch (1994) introduced the term **working memory** to refer to the way we store information while we are working with it. A common test of working memory is the **delayed response task**, in which you respond to something that you saw or heard a short while ago. Imagine that while you stare at a central fixation point, a light flashes briefly at some point toward the periphery. You have to continue staring at that central point for a few seconds until you hear a beep, and then look to where you remember seeing the light. This task can be modified for use with monkeys and other species. During the delay, the learner has to store a representation of the stimulus, and much research points to the prefrontal cortex as an important location for this storage. During the delay, certain cells in the prefrontal cortex as well as the parietal cortex increase their activity, and different cells become active depending on the direction the eye movement will need to take (Chafee & Goldman-Rakic, 1998). During visual working memory, the cells in the prefrontal cortex synchronize their activity with that of other cortical areas, implying that they work together (Liebe, Hoerzer, Logothetis, & Rainer, 2012; Salazar, Dotson, Bressler, & Gray, 2012).

Damage to the prefrontal cortex impairs performance, and the deficit can be amazingly precise, depending on the exact location of the damage. For example, after damage in a particular spot, a monkey might be unable to remember that the light had been directly to the left of fixation, despite being able to see that location and despite being able to remember a light in any other location. After damage in a different spot, a monkey might not be able to remember light in some other location (Sawaguchi & Iba, 2001).

Many older people have impairments of working memory, probably because of changes in the prefrontal cortex. Studies on aged monkeys find decreases in the number of neurons and the amount of input in certain parts of the prefrontal cortex (D. E. Smith, Rapp, McKay, Roberts, & Tuszynski, 2004). Older humans with declining memory show declining activity in the prefrontal cortex, but those with intact memory show *greater* activity than young adults (A. C. Rosen et al., 2002; Rossi et al., 2004). Presumably, the increased activity means that the prefrontal cortex is working harder to compensate for impairments elsewhere in the brain. Furthermore, stimulant drugs that enhance activity in the prefrontal cortex improve the memory of aged monkeys (Castner & Goldman-Rakic, 2004). Such treatments have potential for treating people with failing memory.

STOP&CHECK

4. What is a way to test working memory in both humans and nonhumans?

ANSWER

4. The delayed-response task, in which an individual sees a stimulus briefly and responds to it after a delay.

The Hippocampus

Amnesia is memory loss. One patient ate lunch and, 20 minutes later, ate a second lunch, apparently having forgotten the first meal. Another 20 minutes later, he started on a third lunch and ate most of it. A few minutes later, he said he would like to "go for a walk and get a good meal" (Rozin, Dow, Moscovitch, & Rajaram, 1998). Other patients with amnesia also forget that they have just eaten, although when they start to eat again, they remark on not enjoying the food as much as usual (Higgs, Williamson, Rotshtein, & Humphreys, 2008).

However, even in severe cases, no one loses all kinds of memory equally. A patient who forgets that he ate lunch a few minutes ago still remembers how to eat with a knife and fork, for example, and what different foods taste like, and how to cook them. Studies on amnesia help clarify the distinctions among different kinds of memory and enable us to explore the mechanisms of memory.

People with Hippocampal Damage

In 1953, Henry Molaison, known in most research reports as H. M., was suffering about 10 minor epileptic seizures per day and a major seizure about once a week, despite trying every available antiepileptic drug. Eventually, he agreed to a desperate measure. A surgeon who had experimented with various forms of lobotomy for mental illness was familiar with two cases in which removal of much of the medial temporal lobe had relieved epilepsy. Hoping that the same might work with H. M., the surgeon removed the hippocampus and some nearby structures of the medial temporal cortex from both of H. M.'s hemispheres. Researchers knew almost nothing about the hippocampus at the time, and no one knew what to expect after the surgery. We now know that parts of the hippocampus are active during the formation of memories and later recall (Eldridge, Engel, Zeineh, Bookheimer, & Knowlton, 2005). Although the operation reduced H. M.'s epilepsy to no more than two major seizures per year, he suffered a severe memory impairment (Milner, 1959; Penfield & Milner, 1958; Scoville & Milner, 1957). Figure 12.5 shows the normal anatomy of the hippocampus and the damage in H. M.

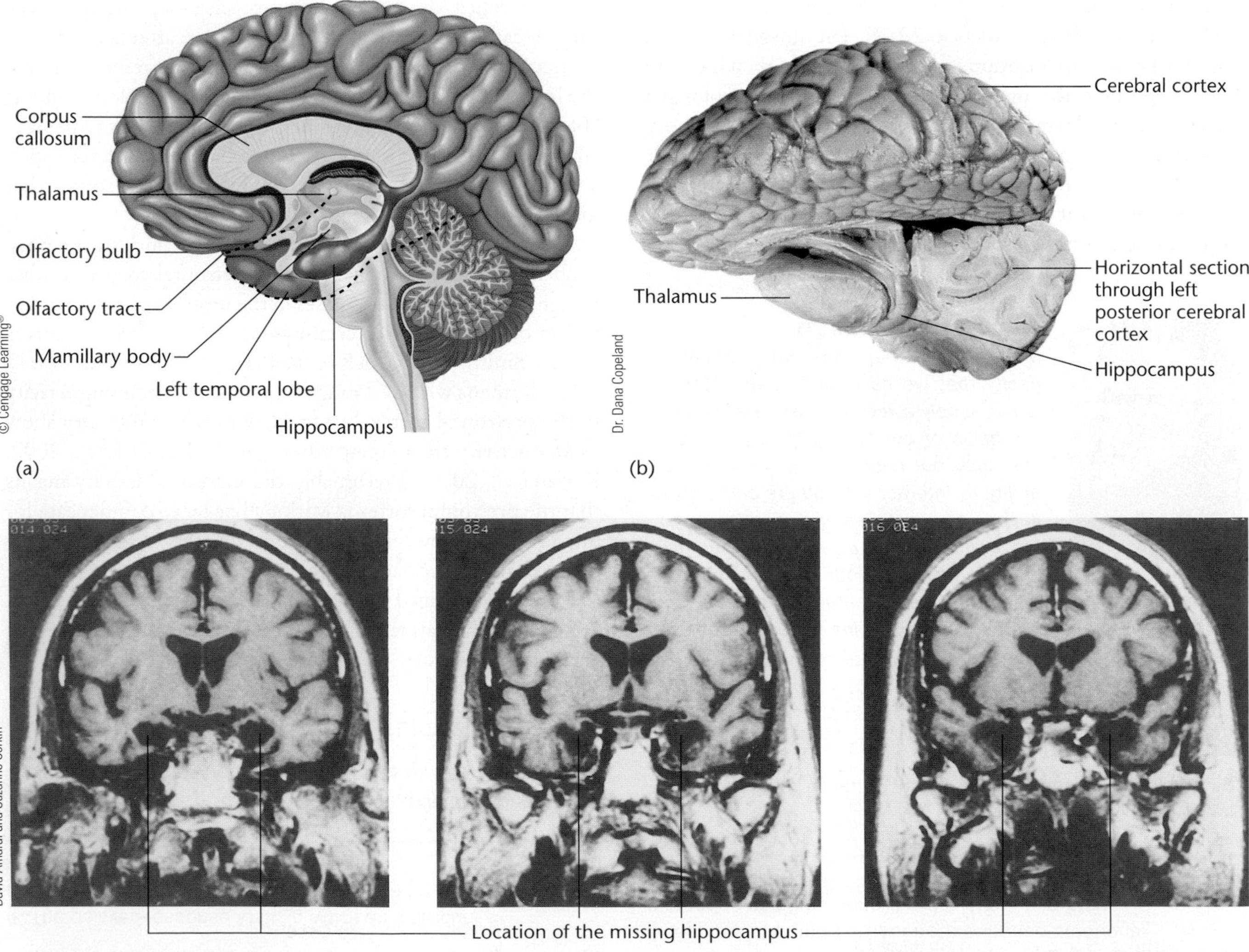

FIGURE 12.5 The hippocampus
(a) Location of the hippocampus in the interior of the temporal lobe. The left hippocampus is closer to the viewer than the rest of this plane; the right hippocampus is behind the plane. The dashed line marks the location of the temporal lobe, which is not visible in the midline. (b) Photo of a human brain from above. The top part of the left hemisphere has been cut away to show how the hippocampus loops over (dorsal to) the thalamus, posterior to it, and then below (ventral to) it. (c) MRI scan of H. M.'s brain, showing absence of the hippocampus. The three views show coronal planes at successive locations, anterior to posterior.

Anterograde and Retrograde Amnesia

After the surgery, H. M.'s intellect and language abilities remained intact, and his personality remained the same except for emotional placidity (Eichenbaum, 2002). However, he suffered massive **anterograde amnesia** (inability to form memories for events that happened after brain damage). He also suffered **retrograde amnesia** (loss of memory for events that occurred before the brain damage). Initially, researchers said his retrograde amnesia was confined to 1 to 3 years before the surgery. Later, they found it was more extensive. H. M. is representative of many people who have suffered amnesia after damage to the hippocampus and surrounding structures of the medial temporal lobe. All show both anterograde and retrograde amnesia, with the retrograde amnesia being most severe for the time leading up to the damage. For example, amnesic patients can usually tell where they lived as a child and where they lived as a teenager but might not be able to say where they lived 3 years ago (Bayley, Hopkins, & Squire, 2006).

Intact Working Memory

Despite H. M.'s huge deficits in forming long-term memories, his short-term or working memory remained intact. In one test, Brenda Milner (1959) asked him to remember the number 584. After a 15-minute delay without distractions, he recalled it correctly, explaining, "It's easy. You just remember 8. You see, 5, 8, and 4 add to 17. You remember 8, subtract it from 17, and it leaves 9. Divide 9 in half and you get 5 and 4, and there you are, 584. Easy." A moment later, after his attention had shifted to another subject, he had forgotten both the number and the complicated line of thought he had associated with it. Most other patients with severe amnesia also show normal working memory, given a lack of distraction (Shrager, Levy, Hopkins, & Squire, 2008).

Impaired Storage of Long-Term Memory

Although H. M. showed normal working memory, as soon as he was distracted, the memory was gone within seconds. For several years after his operation, whenever he was asked his age and the date, he answered "27" and "1953." After a few years, he started guessing wildly, generally underestimating his age by 10 years or more and missing the date by as many as 43 years (Corkin, 1984). He could read the same magazine repeatedly or work the same jigsaw puzzle repeatedly without losing interest. He could never remember that his favorite uncle had died (Corkin, 2013). Often, he told someone about a childhood incident and then, a minute or two later, told the same person the same story again (Eichenbaum, 2002). In 1980, he moved to a nursing home. Four years later, he could not say where he lived or who cared for him. Although he watched the news on television every night, he could recall only a few fragments of events since 1953. Over the years, many new words entered the English language, such as *Jacuzzi* and *granola*. H. M. regarded them as nonsense (Corkin, 2002).

You might wonder whether he was surprised at his own appearance in a photo or mirror. Yes and no. When asked his age or whether his hair turned gray, he replied that he did not know. When shown a photo of himself with his mother, taken long after his surgery, he recognized his mother but not himself. However, when he saw himself in the mirror, he showed no surprise (Corkin, 2002). He had, of course, seen himself daily in the mirror over all these years. He also had the context of knowing that the person in the mirror must be himself, whereas the person in the photo could be anyone.

H. M. formed a few new weak **semantic memories**—that is, memories of factual information (Corkin, 2002; O'Kane, Kensinger, & Corkin, 2004). For example, when he was given first names and asked to fill in appropriate last names, his replies included some who became famous after 1953, such as these:

	H. M.'s Answer
Elvis	Presley
Martin Luther	King
Billy	Graham
Fidel	Castro
Lyndon	Johnson

He provided even more names when he was given additional information:

	H. M.'s Answer
Famous artist, born in Spain . . .	Pablo Picasso

One study found an interesting qualification to the usual rule that patients with amnesia cannot learn new information. The investigators showed a series of shapes with unrelated labels, as shown in Figure 12.6. As expected, amnesic patients made no progress toward learning the labels for each shape. Then the researchers let the patients devise their own labels. Each patient had to look at one shape at a time and describe it so that another person, who was looking at the 12 shapes unlabeled, would know which one the patient was looking at. At first, the descriptions were slow and uninformative. For the shape at the upper right of Figure 12.6, one patient said, "The next one looks almost . . . the opposite of somebody kind uh . . . slumped down, on the ground, with the same type of . . ." Eventually, he said it looked like someone sleeping with his knees bent. By the fourth trial, he quickly labeled that shape as "the siesta guy," and he continued saying the same thing from then on, even in later sessions on later days (Duff, Hengst, Tranel, & Cohen, 2006).

Severe Impairment of Episodic Memory

H. M. had severe impairment of **episodic memories,** memories of single personal events. He could not describe any experience that he had after his surgery. His retrograde amnesia was also greatest for episodic memories. Although he could describe facts that he learned before his operation, he could describe clear memories for only two personal experiences (Corkin, 2013). Another patient, K. C., suffered widespread brain damage after a motorcycle accident, with scattered

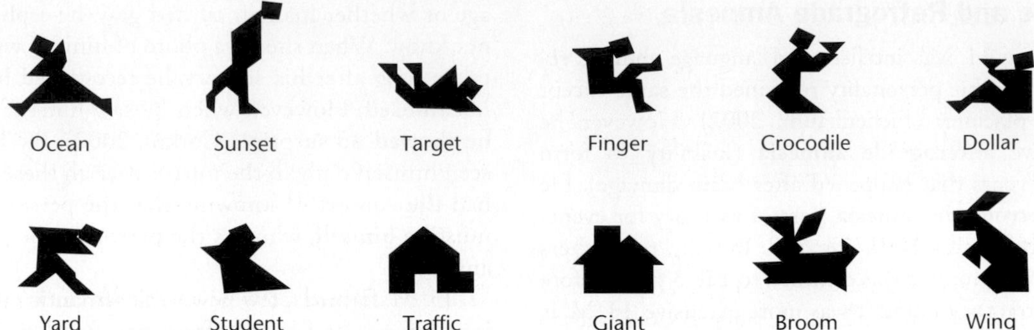

FIGURE 12.6 Displays for a Memory Test of Amnesic Patients
Although they could not remember the arbitrary labels that an experimenter gave to each object (as shown), they did remember the descriptions that they devised themselves. *Source:* From "Development of shared information in communication despite hippocampal amnesia," by M. C. Duff, J. Hengst, D. Tranel, & N. J. Cohen, 2006, *Nature Neuroscience*, 9, pp. 140–146. Used by permission, Macmillan Publishing Ltd.

damage in the hippocampus and other locations, leading to an apparently complete loss of episodic memories. He cannot describe a single event from any time of his life, although he remembers many facts. When he looks at old family pictures in a photo album, he identifies the people and sometimes the places, but he cannot remember anything about the events that happened in the photos (Rosenbaum et al., 2005). Although his brain damage is so diffuse that we cannot be sure which part of the damage is responsible for his memory loss, the observations do tell us that the brain treats episodic memories differently from other memories.

How would memory loss affect people's ability to imagine the future? If you try to imagine a future event, you call upon your memory of similar experiences and modify them. Studies using fMRI show that describing past events and imagining future events activate mostly the same areas, including the hippocampus (Addis, Wong, & Schacter, 2007). People with amnesia are just as impaired at imagining the future as they are at describing the past, although they have no trouble describing the present (Race, Keane, & Verfaellie, 2011). For example, here is part of one patient's attempt to imagine a visit to a museum (Hassabis, Kumaran, Vann, & Maguire, 2007, p. 1727):

> Patient: [pause] There's not a lot, as it happens.
> Psychologist: So what does it look like in your imagined scene?
> Patient: Well, there's big doors. The openings would be high, so the doors would be very big with brass handles, the ceiling would be made of glass, so there's plenty of light coming through. Huge room, exit on either side of the room, there's a pathway and map through the center and on either side there'd be the exhibits. [pause] I don't know what they are. There'd be people. [pause] To be honest there's not a lot coming. . . . My imagination isn't . . . well, I'm not imagining it, let's put it that way. . . . I'm not picturing anything at the moment.

The relationship between loss of episodic memory and difficulty imagining the future is theoretically interesting. Have you ever wondered what good is episodic memory? You can remember a great many events that happened to you years ago, some of them in detail. From an evolutionary standpoint, why did we evolve that ability? What good does it do to be able to remember details of an event that will never happen again? Now we see a possible answer: Remembering those details helps us imagine the future. And if we couldn't imagine the future in much detail, we couldn't plan for it.

Better Implicit than Explicit Memory

Nearly all patients with amnesia show better *implicit* than *explicit* memory. **Explicit memory** is deliberate recall of information that one recognizes as a memory, also known as **declarative memory**. If you have an explicit or declarative memory of something, you can state it in words. **Implicit memory** is an influence of experience on behavior, even if you do not recognize that influence. For example, H. M. became familiar with certain people, such as the psychologists who worked with him over the years, but he did not remember their names or where he had met them. Also, he would not remember what a recent conversation was about, but he would often spontaneously start talking about that same topic again (Corkin, 2013). To experience implicit memory, try the Online Try It Yourself exercise "Implicit Memories."

Another example of implicit memory: As an experiment, three hospital workers agreed to act in special ways toward a patient with amnesia. One was as pleasant as possible. The second was neutral. The third was stern, refused all requests, and made the patient perform boring tasks. After 5 days, the patient was asked to look at photos of the three workers and try to identify them or say anything he knew about them. He said he did not recognize any of them. Then he was asked which one he would approach as a possible friend or which one he would ask for help. He was asked this question repeatedly—it was possible to ask repeatedly because he never remembered being asked before—and he usually chose the photo of the "friendly" person and never chose the "unfriendly" person in spite of the fact that the unfriendly person was a beautiful woman, smiling in the photograph (Tranel & Damasio, 1993). He could not say why he chose to avoid her.

Intact Procedural Memory

Procedural memory, the development of motor skills and habits, is a special kind of implicit memory. As with other examples of implicit memory, you might not be able to describe a motor skill or habit in words, and you might not even recognize it as a memory. For example, H. M. learned to read words written backward, as they would be seen in a mirror, although he was surprised at this skill, as he did not remember having tried it before (Corkin, 2002). Patient K. C. has a part-time job at a library and has learned to use the Dewey decimal system in sorting books, although he does not remember when or where he learned it (Rosenbaum et al., 2005).

Here is another example of procedural memory: In the video game Tetris, geometrical forms such as ▭ and ⊞ fall from the top, and the player must move and rotate them to fill available spaces at the bottom of the screen. Normal people improve their skill over a few hours and readily describe the game and its strategy. After playing the same number of hours, patients with amnesia cannot describe the game and say they don't remember playing it. Nevertheless, they improve, slowly. Moreover, when they are about to fall asleep, they report seeing images of little piles of blocks falling and rotating (Stickgold, Malia, Maguire, Roddenberry, & O'Connor, 2000). They are puzzled and wonder what these images mean!

In summary, H. M. showed the following pattern, similar to several other amnesic patients:

- Normal working memory, unless distracted
- Severe anterograde amnesia for declarative memory—that is, difficulty forming new declarative memories, especially episodic memories.
- Severe loss of episodic memories, including most of those from before the damage
- Better implicit than explicit memory
- Nearly intact procedural memory

STOP&CHECK

5. Which types of memory were most impaired in H. M. and people with similar types of amnesia?

6. Which types of memory were least impaired in H. M. and people with similar types of amnesia?

ANSWERS

5. H. M. had severe anterograde amnesia (difficulty forming new long-term memories) and a severe loss of episodic memories. **6.** H. M. had nearly intact working memory, implicit memory, and procedural memory.

Theories of the Function of the Hippocampus

Exactly how does the hippocampus contribute to memory? Some of the research comes from patients with damage to the hippocampus, but to get better control over both the anatomy and the environment, researchers also conduct research on laboratory animals.

The Hippocampus and Declarative Memory

Although patients with hippocampal damage acquire new skills, they have great trouble learning new facts. Larry Squire (1992) proposed that the hippocampus is critical for declarative memory, especially episodic memory. How could we test this hypothesis with nonhumans, who cannot "declare" anything? What could they do that would be the equivalent of declarative or episodic memory? Here is one possible example: A rat digs food out of five piles of sand, each with a different odor. Then, it gets a choice between two of the odors and is rewarded if it goes toward the one it smelled first. Intact rats learn to respond correctly, apparently demonstrating memory of not only what they smelled but also when they smelled it. Because this task requires memory of a specific event, it seems to qualify as episodic. Rats with hippocampal damage do poorly on this task (Fortin, Agster, & Eichenbaum, 2002; Kesner, Gilbert, & Barua, 2002).

Larry Squire

Larry R. Squire

Memory is personal and evocative, intertwined with emotion, and it provides us with a sense of who we are. . . . There has been a revolution in our understanding of what memory is and what happens in the brain when we learn and remember. At the beginning of the 21st century, one has the sense that memory may be the first mental faculty that will be understandable in terms of molecules, cells, brain systems, and behavior. Yet, even with all the progress, there can be no doubt that the study of the brain is still a young science, rich with opportunity for the student and beginning scientist. This is a good time to hear about the promise and excitement of neuroscience. The best is yet to come. (Squire, personal communication)

In the **delayed matching-to-sample task,** an animal sees an object (the sample) and then, after a delay, gets a choice between two objects, from which it must choose the one that matches the sample. In the **delayed nonmatching-to-sample task,** the procedure is the same except that the animal must choose the object that is different from the sample (see Figure 12.7). In both cases, the animal must remember which object was present on this occasion, thereby showing what we might call a declarative memory, perhaps an episodic memory. Hippocampal damage strongly impairs performance in most cases (Heuer & Bachevalier, 2011; Moore, Schettler, Killiany, Rosene, & Moss, 2012; Zola et al., 2000).

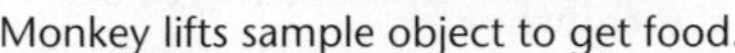

FIGURE 12.7 A delayed nonmatching-to-sample task

The Hippocampus and Spatial Memory

A second hypothesis focuses on spatial memories. Electrical recordings indicate that many neurons in a rat's hippocampus are tuned to particular spatial locations, responding best when an animal is in a particular place (O'Keefe & Burgess, 1996), looking in a particular direction (Dudchenko & Taube, 1997; Rolls, 1996), or getting ready to travel in a particular direction (Pfeiffer & Foster, 2013). When rats learn to perform certain tasks in a particular order at particular times, many hippocampal cells respond at a particular time (MacDonald, Lepage, Eden, & Eichenbaum, 2011). Evidently the hippocampus provides a map of both place and time.

Ordinarily, experimenters cannot implant electrodes into human brains, but an exception is made when a surgeon is exploring someone's brain to find the source from which severe epilepsy is originating. Such surgery is done under local anesthesia, keeping the patient awake. In two studies, patients with implanted electrodes performed virtual navigation through scenes on a computer. As with the rat studies, the results demonstrated cells in the hippocampus that respond to particular locations and directions of travel (Jacobs et al., 2013; J. F. Miller et al., 2013).

Researchers conducted PET scans on the brains of London taxi drivers as they answered navigation questions such as, "What's the shortest legal route from the Carlton Tower Hotel to the Sherlock Holmes Museum?" (London taxi drivers are well trained and answer with impressive accuracy.) Answering these questions activated their hippocampus much more than did answering nonspatial questions. MRI scans also revealed that the taxi drivers have a larger than average posterior hippocampus and that the longer they had been taxi drivers, the larger their posterior hippocampus (Maguire et al., 2000). This surprising result suggests actual growth of the adult human hippocampus in response to spatial learning experiences.

Consider a couple of ways to test spatial memory in nonhumans. From a central point, a **radial maze** has several arms—typically eight—some or all of which have a bit of food at the end (see Figure 12.8). A rat's best strategy is to explore each arm once and only once, remembering where it has already gone. In a variation of the task, a rat might have to learn that the arms with a rough floor never have food or that the arms pointing toward the window never have food. Thus, a rat can make a mistake either by entering a never-correct arm or by entering a correct arm twice.

Rats with damage to the hippocampus gradually learn not to enter the never-correct arms, but even after much training they often enter a correct arm twice. That is, they forget which arms they have already tried (Jarrard, Okaichi, Steward, & Goldschmidt, 1984; Olton & Papas, 1979; Olton, Walker, & Gage, 1978). With people, psychological researchers use a virtual radial maze that the person can navigate on a computer screen. On this task, people with damage to the hippocampus are slow to learn which arms are never correct, and they frequently visit one arm several times before trying all the others (Goodrich-Hunsaker & Hopkins, 2010). That is, the human data resemble those of rats.

Another test of spatial memory is the **Morris water maze,** in which a rat swims through murky water to find a rest platform that is just under the surface (see Figure 12.9). (Rats swim as little as they can. Humans are among the very few land mammals that swim recreationally.) A rat with hippocampal damage slowly learns to find the platform if it always starts from the same place and the rest platform is always in the same place. However, if it has to start from a different location or if the rest platform occasionally moves from one location to another, the rat is disoriented (Eichenbaum, 2000;

FIGURE 12.8 A radial maze
A rat that reenters one arm before trying other arms has made an error of spatial working memory.

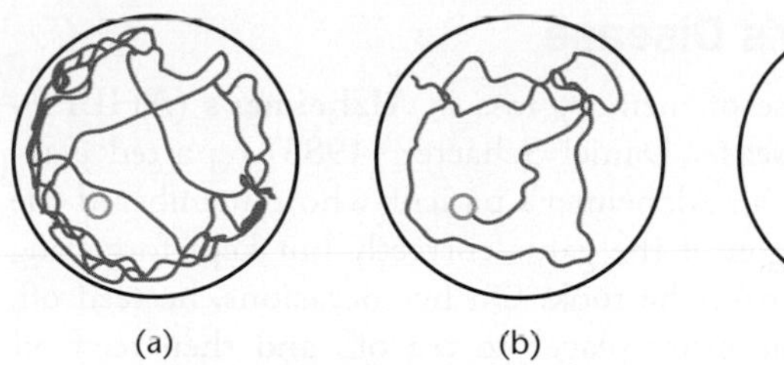

FIGURE 12.9 The Morris water maze
An intact rat learns by trial and error. In each case the line traces the path a rat took to the platform, marked by a circle. On the fifth trial (A), the rat stayed mainly near the edge and never found the platform. On the 34th trial (B), it found the platform in 35 seconds. On the 71st trial (C), it went directly to the platform in 6 seconds. *Source:* From "Response learning of rats in a Morris water maze: Involvement of the medial prefrontal cortex," by J. P. C. de Bruin, W. A. M. Winkels, & J. M. de Brabander, 1997, *Behavioral Brain Research, 85,* pp. 47–55.

P. Liu & Bilkey, 2001). Rodents with hippocampal damage also become disoriented if they see two identical landmarks in the water maze, even if less ambiguous markers are also present (Bannerman et al., 2012).

As with the radial maze, researchers sometimes test people with a virtual water maze that they navigate on a computer. People with a rare condition called *acute transient global amnesia* have a temporary dysfunction of the hippocampus. If they are tested soon after onset of the condition, they are slow to learn the correct route in a virtual water maze (Bartsch et al., 2010).

Hippocampus and Contextual Memory

A third hypothesis relates the hippocampus to memory for context. Research with patient H. M. showed the importance of the hippocampus for episodic memory. Think about one of your own episodic memories, any one of them. Presumably it includes a context—sights, sounds, one or more locations, and a series of events. Clearly, that memory could not be stored in a single location in the brain; it has to be spread over many locations. Perhaps the hippocampus is a coordinator, a director that brings together representations from various locations, in the correct order. In short, it reconstructs the context. When people successfully retrieve an episodic memory, activity in and around the hippocampus synchronizes with activity in several parts of the cortex, consistent with the idea that the hippocampus is providing the connections that are necessary for recall (Watrous, Tandon, Conner, Pieters, & Ekstrom, 2013).

Recent episodic memories generally include much contextual detail. Some older memories do also, but in most cases the details fade and we remember only the gist of the event. Memories with much contextual detail depend on the hippocampus, but older, less detailed memories depend mainly on the cerebral cortex with less contribution from the hippocampus (Takehara-Nishiuchi & McNaughton, 2008). The same is true of rats: When rats are trained to do something, and then tested again after a short delay, they remember the response best if they are tested in the same location. That is, their memory depends on the context. As time passes, the context matters less and less, and to the extent that rats remember the response, they remember it equally well in a different location. If rats with damage to the hippocampus learn something at all, they show no difference between testing in the familiar place and some other place. Their memory doesn't depend on context, presumably because they do not remember it (Winocur, Moscovitch, & Sekeres, 2007).

Single-cell recordings in rats confirm the idea that the hippocampus responds to context. In one study, rats learned that when they were in room A, they had to dig in flowerpot X instead of Y to find food, but in room B they had to dig in flowerpot Y instead of X, regardless of location of the flowerpots within each room. As already described, most cells in the hippocampus become active only in a particular location within a room or other setting. In this experiment, most of those "place" cells responded much more strongly to their preferred place if the correct kind of flowerpot was in that place (Komorowski, Manns, & Eichenbaum, 2009).

We have considered three hypotheses of the role of the hippocampus and found evidence to support each. The views are not necessarily in conflict, as the hippocampus probably contributes in more than one way. It is also possible that theorists will find a way to combine all three hypotheses into one.

STOP&CHECK

7. What type of memory do the radial maze and the Morris water maze test?

8. According to the context hypothesis, why does hippocampal damage impair recent memories more than distant memories?

ANSWERS

7. They test spatial memory. **8.** Recent memories include details of context, and the hippocampus is essential for memory of context. Most old memories include only the gist of the event, and the hippocampus is less important for memories of that type.

Other Types of Amnesia

Other kinds of brain damage produce other types of amnesia. Here we briefly consider two more examples: Korsakoff's syndrome and Alzheimer's disease.

Korsakoff's Syndrome

Korsakoff's syndrome, also known as *Wernicke-Korsakoff syndrome,* is brain damage caused by prolonged thiamine deficiency. Severe thiamine deficiency occurs mostly in chronic alcoholics who go for weeks at a time on a diet of nothing but alcoholic beverages, lacking in vitamins. The brain needs thiamine (vitamin B1) to metabolize glucose, its primary fuel. Prolonged thiamine deficiency leads to a loss or shrinkage of neurons throughout the brain. One of the areas most affected is the dorsomedial thalamus, the main source of input to the prefrontal cortex. The symptoms of Korsakoff's syndrome are similar to those of people with damage to the prefrontal cortex, including apathy, confusion, and memory loss. They also overlap those of hippocampal damage, with major impairment of episodic memory but sparing of implicit memory.

A distinctive symptom of Korsakoff's syndrome is **confabulation**, in which patients fill in memory gaps with guesses. (Some patients with other disorders also confabulate.) They seldom confabulate on semantic questions such as "What is the capital of Russia?" or nonsense questions such as "Who is Princess Lolita?" They confabulate mainly about their episodic memory, such as "What did you do last weekend?" (Borsutzky, Fujiwara, Brand, & Markowitsch, 2008; Schnider, 2003). Usually, the confabulated answer was true at some time in the past but not now, such as, "I went dancing," or "I visited with my children." Occasionally, patients try to act on their spontaneous confabulations, such as trying to leave the hospital to go to work, go to the airport, or prepare dinner for guests (Nahum, Bouzerda-Wahlen, Guggisberg, Ptak, & Schnider, 2012). Most confabulated answers are more pleasant than the currently true answers (Fotopoulou, Solms, & Turnbull, 2004). That tendency may reflect the patient's attempt to maintain pleasant emotions or merely the fact that the patient's past life was, on the whole, more pleasant than the present.

The tendency to confabulate produces a fascinating influence on the strategies for studying. Suppose you have to learn a long list of three-word sentences such as: "Medicine cured hiccups" and "Tourist desired photograph." Would you simply reread the list many times? Or would you alternate between reading the list and testing yourself?

Medicine cured ______________________.

Tourist desired ______________________.

Almost everyone learns better the second way. Completing the sentences forces you to be more active and calls your attention to the items you have not yet learned. Korsakoff's patients, however, learn much better the first way, by reading the list over and over. The reason is, when they test themselves, they confabulate. ("*Medicine cured headache. Tourist desired passport.*") Then they remember their confabulation instead of the correct answer (Hamann & Squire, 1995).

STOP & CHECK

9. On what kind of question is someone with Korsakoff's syndrome most likely to confabulate?

ANSWER

9. Patients with Korsakoff's syndrome confabulate on questions for which they would expect to know the answer, such as questions about themselves. Their confabulations are usually statements that were true at one time.

Alzheimer's Disease

Another cause of memory loss is **Alzheimer's** (AHLTZ-hime-ers) **disease.** Daniel Schacter (1983) reported playing golf with an Alzheimer's patient who remembered the rules and jargon of the game correctly but kept forgetting how many strokes he took. On five occasions, he teed off, waited for the other player to tee off, and then teed off again, having forgotten his first shot. As with other amnesic patients, patients with Alzheimer's have better procedural than declarative memory. They learn new skills but then surprise themselves with their good performance because they don't remember doing it before (Gabrieli, Corkin, Mickel, & Growdon, 1993). Their memory and alertness vary substantially from time to time, suggesting that many of their problems result from malfunctioning neurons and fluctuating levels of arousal, and not just the loss of neurons (Palop, Chin, & Mucke, 2006).

Alzheimer's disease gradually progresses to more serious memory loss, confusion, depression, restlessness, hallucinations, delusions, sleeplessness, and loss of appetite. It occasionally strikes people younger than age 40 but becomes more common with age, affecting almost 5 percent of people between ages 65 and 74 and almost 50 percent of people over 85 (Evans et al., 1989). Given that more people than ever are surviving into old age, Alzheimer's is an increasing problem.

The first major clue to the cause of Alzheimer's was the fact that people with *Down syndrome* (a type of mental retardation) almost invariably get Alzheimer's disease if they survive into middle age (Lott, 1982). People with Down syndrome have three copies of chromosome 21 rather than the usual two. That fact led investigators to examine chromosome 21, where they found a gene linked to many cases of early-onset Alzheimer's disease (Goate et al., 1991; Murrell, Farlow, Ghetti, & Benson, 1991). Later researchers found two more genes linked to early-onset Alzheimer's.

The genes controlling early-onset Alzheimer's disease cause a protein called **amyloid-β** to accumulate both inside and outside neurons (LaFerla, Green, & Oddo, 2007). The effect is to damage dendritic spines, decrease synaptic input, and decrease plasticity (Wei, Nguyen, Kessels, Hagiwara, Sisodia, & Malinow, 2010). As amyloid damages axons and dendrites, the damaged structures cluster into structures called *plaques* (Selkoe, 2000). As the plaques accumulate, the cerebral cortex, hippocampus, and other areas atrophy (waste away), as Figures 12.10 and 12.11 show.

In addition to amyloid-β, a second problem relates to the **tau protein** in the intracellular support structure of axons (Davies, 2000). High levels of amyloid-β cause more phosphate groups to attach to tau proteins. The altered tau cannot bind to its usual targets within axons, and so it starts spreading into the cell body and dendrites. The attack of tau from within dendrites adds to the attack by amyloid-β, magnifying the damage. Researchers hypothesize that altered tau also

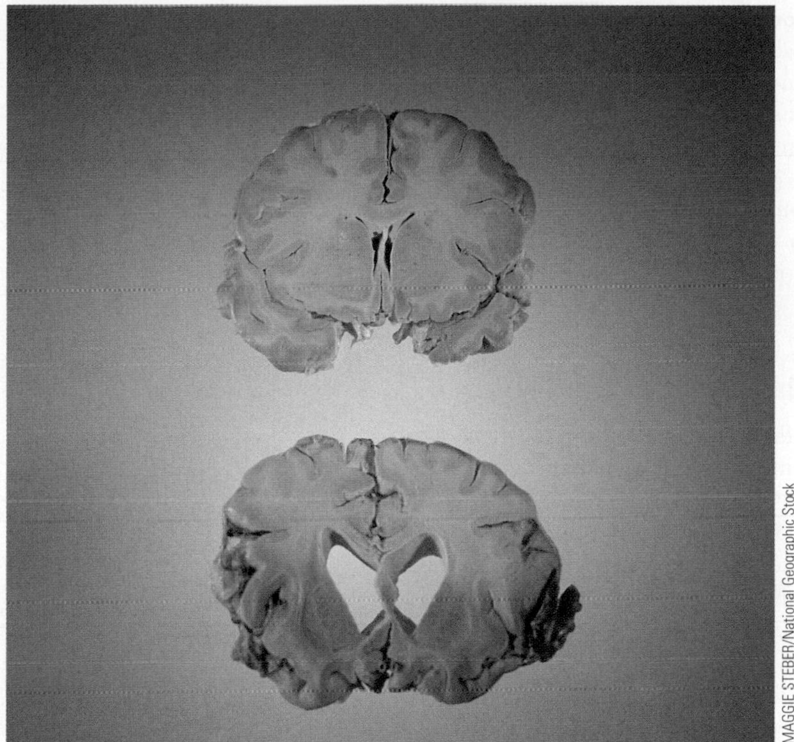

FIGURE 12.10 **Brain atrophy in Alzheimer's disease**
A patient with Alzheimer's (bottom photo) has gyri that are clearly shrunken in comparison with those of a normal person (top photo).

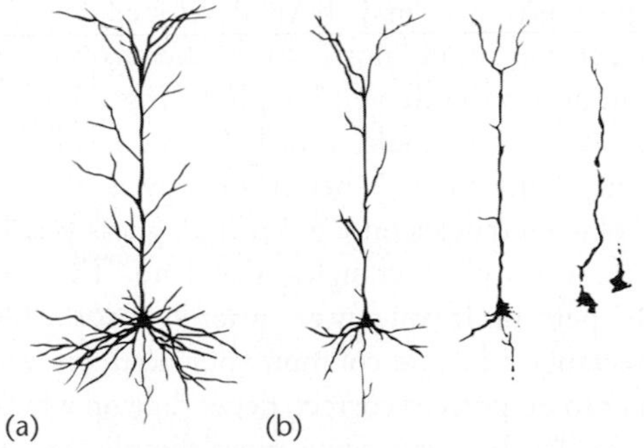

FIGURE 12.11 **Neuronal degeneration in Alzheimer's disease**
(a) A cell in the prefrontal cortex of a normal human; (b) cells from the same area of cortex in Alzheimer's disease patients at various stages of deterioration. *Source:* © Cengage Learning; Based on "Dendritic changes," by A. B. Scheibel, p. 70. In *Alzheimer's disease*, B. Reisberg, ed., 1983. Free Press.

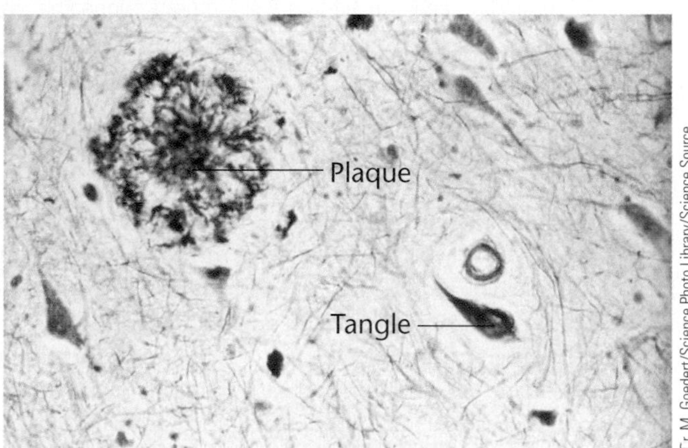

FIGURE 12.12 **Cerebral cortex of an Alzheimer's patient**
Plaques and tangles result from amyloid-β and abnormal tau protein. *Source:* From Taylor, Hardy, & Fischbeck, 2002

increases the production of amyloid-β, causing a vicious cycle (Ittner & Götz, 2011). The altered tau is principally responsible for *tangles*, structures formed from degeneration within neurons (see Figure 12.12). The pattern of chemicals varies from one patient to another, and controversy continues as to the relative importance of amyloid and tau in producing Alzheimer's disease.

For cases with onset of symptoms after age 60 to 65—vastly more common than early-onset cases—many genes increase or decrease the risk to varying degrees (Alagaikrishnan, Gill, & Fagarasanu, 2012). The most influential of these genes controls a chemical called apolipoprotein E, which helps remove β-amyloid from the brain (Cramer et al., 2012; Jonsson et al., 2012). However, about half of all patients with late-onset Alzheimer's disease have no known relatives with the disease (St. George-Hyslop, 2000).

At this point, no drug is highly effective for Alzheimer's disease, although researchers have tried many. The most common current treatment is to give drugs that stimulate acetylcholine receptors or prolong acetylcholine release, thereby increasing arousal. One hypothesis as to why so many drugs have proven ineffective is that by the time physicians recognize Alzheimer's disease, the damage may already be too extensive for any medication to help. An important research goal is to find ways to diagnose Alzheimer's at a very early stage, either from behavioral measures (Gamaldo, An, Allaire, Kitner-Triolo, & Zonderman, 2012) or perhaps from examination of the nerves in the retina (Frost et al., 2013).

What Patients with Amnesia Teach Us

The study of patients with amnesia reveals that people do not lose all aspects of memory equally. A patient with great difficulty establishing new memories may remember events from long ago, and someone with greatly impaired factual memory may learn new skills. Evidently, people have several somewhat independent kinds of memory that depend on different brain areas.

STOP&CHECK

10. Which type of memory is generally least impaired for people with Alzheimer's disease?

ANSWER

10. Procedural memory is generally the least impaired.

The Basal Ganglia

Episodic memory, dependent on the hippocampus, develops after a single experience. Many semantic memories also form after a single experience. That is, if someone tells you an interesting fact, you might remember it forever. However, we need a different mechanism for gradually learning what probably will or will not happen under certain circumstances. You take into account many types of information when you conclude that it will probably rain tomorrow, or that your mother probably wouldn't enjoy the movie you just saw, or that your favorite team will probably win its next game. You cannot trace any of those inferences to a single experience, and you may not even be aware of what cues you used or how you decided. Learning of this type depends on the basal ganglia (see Figure 7.16).

To illustrate, consider the following example. In each of 38 cases you have three pieces of information, here shown as blue or purple rectangles. Based on that information, guess whether it will rain tomorrow ("yes") or not ("no"). You are provided with the correct answer for the first 36. You will get the idea of the task best if you try the items one at a time. What do you guess for the final two items, and on what basis did you make that decision?

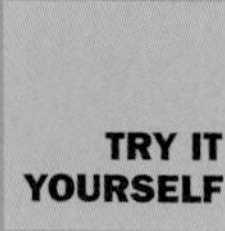

Δ	Δ	Δ	YES	Δ	▲	Δ	YES
▲	▲	▲	NO	▲	Δ	Δ	YES
Δ	▲	Δ	YES	Δ	Δ	▲	NO
Δ	▲	▲	YES	Δ	▲	Δ	YES
▲	Δ	▲	NO	▲	▲	Δ	YES
Δ	Δ	Δ	YES	Δ	Δ	Δ	YES
▲	Δ	Δ	YES	Δ	▲	Δ	YES
Δ	Δ	▲	NO	Δ	▲	▲	YES
Δ	Δ	Δ	YES	▲	Δ	Δ	YES
▲	Δ	Δ	YES	Δ	▲	Δ	YES
Δ	▲	Δ	YES	▲	Δ	▲	NO
Δ	▲	▲	NO	Δ	Δ	Δ	YES
▲	▲	▲	NO	▲	Δ	▲	NO
Δ	Δ	Δ	YES	▲	▲	Δ	NO
Δ	▲	Δ	YES	▲	▲	▲	NO
Δ	Δ	Δ	YES	Δ	Δ	Δ	YES
Δ	▲	▲	YES	▲	▲	Δ	NO
▲	▲	▲	NO	Δ	▲	Δ	?
▲	Δ	▲	NO	Δ	▲	▲	?

In this task, you may have developed any of several strategies. If you simply noticed that the answer is yes more often than no (evidently you are predicting the weather in a very rainy area), you could always answer yes, being correct 64 percent of the time. A better strategy is, if you see two or three blue rectangles on a given trial, guess yes. If you see two or three purple rectangles, guess no. That strategy is correct 83 percent. If you pay attention to just the blue versus purple rectangles in one column, your accuracy varies from 53 percent to 86 percent correct, depending on which column you choose. The best strategy is more complicated: If you see two or three blue rectangles, guess yes; if you see two or three purple rectangles, guess no; except that if it goes "blue-purple-purple," guess yes, and if it goes "blue-blue-purple," guess no. That strategy gives a correct answer 94 percent of the time with the material shown here. (So the answers for the final two items are YES, YES.)

You would not have figured out that last strategy from the small number of trials given here. But if you had the patience to continue for hundreds of trials, your accuracy would eventually, gradually climb up toward 94 percent correct. You might not be able to describe your strategy. You would just "know" somehow the right answer to guess each time. That gradual, probabilistic learning depends on the basal ganglia.

Suppose we run a test like this on people with Parkinson's disease, who have impairments of the basal ganglia. As a rule, they perform about the same as normal people at first, because they have an intact hippocampus and they can learn simple declarative facts such as "blue means yes and purple means no." However, even after many trials, they do not show the gradual improvement that requires the basal ganglia. On other kinds of complex learning tasks, if they don't form an explicit, declarative memory, they don't improve at all (Moody, Chang, Vanek, & Knowlton, 2010). That is, they don't acquire nonverbal habits.

People with amnesia after hippocampal damage perform randomly on the weather task for many trials, because they form no declarative memories and they cannot remember that any particular symbol is usually a signal for one outcome or another. However, if they continue for a very long time, they show gradual improvement, based on habits supported by the basal ganglia (Bayley, Frascino, & Squire, 2005; Shohamy, Myers, Kalanithi, & Gluck, 2008). If the signals switch, so that the signal that formerly predicted one outcome now predicts the other, they are very slow to switch their responses (Shohamy, Myers, Hopkins, Sage, & Gluck, 2009). When normal people try to learn a complex task under conditions of extreme distraction, they too learn slowly, like people with a damaged hippocampus. Their gradual learning under these conditions depends on the basal ganglia (Foerde, Knowlton, & Poldrack, 2006).

Together, these results suggest a division of labor between the basal ganglia and other brain areas (including the hippocampus and cerebral cortex), although it is not a complete separation. Nearly all tasks activate both systems to some extent (Albouy et al., 2008). Table 12.1 outlines the differences (Balleine, Delgado, & Hikosaka, 2007; Foerde, Race, Verfaellie, & Shohamy, 2013; Foerde & Shohamy, 2011; Koralek, Jin, Long, Costa, & Carmena, 2012; Shohamy, 2011; Wan et al., 2012).

STOP&CHECK

11. When you first learned to drive a car, you had to carefully think about everything you did. After much practice, your movements became smooth and automatic. What does this observation imply about the brain mechanisms of learning?

ANSWER

11. In the initial learning, you were relying on declarative knowledge that depends on the hippocampus and cerebral cortex. Later you gradually developed motor habits that depend on the basal ganglia.

Other Brain Areas and Memory

Most of this module has focused on the hippocampus and the basal ganglia. Chapter 11 mentioned the importance of the amygdala for fear memories. Other brain areas are important for learning and memory, too. In fact, most of the brain contributes. When mice learn an association between an odor and foot shock, even the responses of the olfactory receptors themselves change (Kass, Rosenthal, Pottackal, & McGann, 2013).

Investigators asked two patients with parietal lobe damage to describe various events from their past. When tested this way, their episodic memory appeared sparse, almost devoid of details. However, the investigators asked follow-up questions, such as, "Where were you?" and "Who else was there at the time?" Then these patients answered in reasonable detail, indicating that their episodic memories were intact, as well as their speech and their willingness to cooperate. What was lacking was their ability to elaborate on a memory spontaneously (Berryhill, Phuong, Picasso, Cabeza, & Olson, 2007). Ordinarily, when most of us recall an event, one thing reminds us of another, and we start adding one detail after another, until we have said all that we know. In people with parietal lobe damage, that process of associating one piece with another is impaired.

People with damage in the anterior temporal cortex suffer **semantic dementia**, a loss of semantic memory. One patient while riding down a road saw some sheep and asked what they were. The problem wasn't that he couldn't remember the word *sheep*. It was as if he had never seen a sheep before. When another person saw a picture of a zebra, she called it a horse but then pointed at the stripes and asked what "those funny things" were. She hadn't merely lost the word *zebra* but had lost the concept of zebra. Such patients cannot remember the typical color of common fruits and vegetables or the appearance of various animals. Don't imagine the anterior temporal cortex as the sole point of storage for semantic memory. It stores some of the information and serves as a hub for communicating with other brain areas to bring together a full concept (Patterson, Nestor, & Rogers, 2007). Serious deficits in semantic memory occur only after bilateral damage. People with damage to the temporal cortex in just one hemisphere perform almost normally (Ralph, Cipoloti, Manes, & Patterson, 2010).

TABLE 12.1 Brain Areas for Two Types of Learning

	Basal Ganglia	Hippocampus and Cerebral Cortex
One trial or many?	Integrates information over many trials	Can learn in a single trial
Produces:	Habits	More flexible responses
Learns based on what type of feedback?	Requires immediate feedback (reward or punishment)	Can connect information over time Can learn from delayed feedback
Explicit or implicit?	Generally implicit; often not possible to describe what's learned in words	Generally explicit; describable in words
Effect of damage	Loss of well-learned motor patterns, impaired learning of skills and habits	Impairs declarative memory, especially episodic memory

The prefrontal cortex contributes to learned behavior and decision making in many ways. In Figure 12.13, the areas shown in red are more important for inhibiting inappropriate responses and shifting to other behaviors. For example, in the Stroop task, people are supposed to look at words printed in colored ink (such as **green**) and say the color of the ink ("red") instead of the printed word ("green"). In another task, people sort objects for a while by one rule such as color, and then are supposed to ignore color and sort them by shape. Damage to the areas shown in red in Figure 12.13 causes impairments on both of these tasks (Gläscher et al., 2012). Immaturity of these areas helps explain why children and adolescents often have trouble inhibiting their impulses.

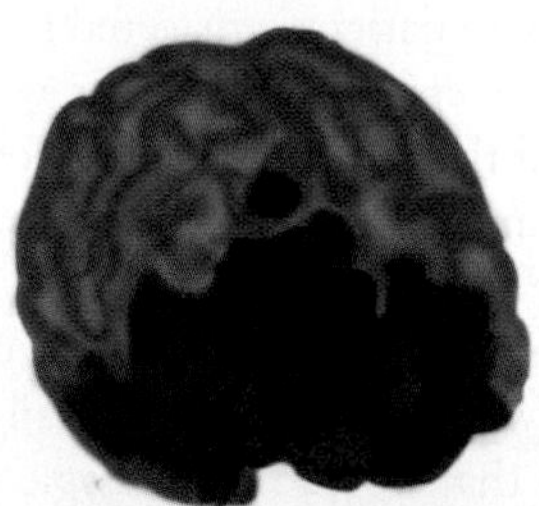

FIGURE 12.13 Two functions of the prefrontal cortex
The areas shown in red are more important for cognitive functions, especially inhibiting inappropriate behaviors. The areas shown in blue are more important for judging relative values of possible responses. *Source:* From "Lesion mapping of cognitive control and value-based decision making in the prefrontal cortex," by J. Gläscher et al., *Proceedings of the National Academy of Sciences, 109*, pp. 14681–14686.

The areas shown in blue, including the ventral prefrontal cortex, are more important for learning about rewards and punishments and making decisions based on them. For example, they are important for deciding which of two bets gives the better payoff (Gläscher et al., 2012). The basal ganglia also learn about the reward values of various actions, but they learn slowly, based on the average reward over a long period of time. The prefrontal cortex responds more quickly, based on the most recent events (Kovach et al., 2012). Therefore, it is important for responding flexibly, for altering or switching responses when the payoff rules change (Brigman et al., 2013). If you are confronted with an opportunity to make a response, cells in the ventromedial prefrontal cortex respond based on the reward to be expected. They relay that information to the nearby orbitofrontal cortex, which responds based on how a reward compares to other possible choices. For example, a $2 reward might be good or bad depending on whether other choices offer a $1 or $5 reward (Frank & Claus, 2006). You might prefer a pizza or a piece of cake, depending on what else you had just eaten and how recently (Rudebeck, Saunders, Prescott, Chau, & Murray, 2013).

STOP&CHECK

12. The basal ganglia and the prefrontal cortex contribute to learning a response based on rewards and punishments. How do these areas differ?

ANSWER

12. The prefrontal cortex learns faster and bases its decisions on the most recent events.

MODULE 12.1 ■ IN CLOSING

Types of Memory

"Overall intelligence," as measured by an IQ test, is a convenient fiction. It is convenient because, under most circumstances, people who are good at one kind of intellectual task are also good at other kinds, so an overall test score makes useful predictions. However, it is a fiction because different kinds of abilities rely on different brain processes, and it is possible to damage one but not another. Even memory is composed of separate abilities, and it is possible to lose one type or aspect of memory without impairing others. The study of amnesia shows how the brain operates as a series of partly independent mechanisms serving specific purposes.

Summary

1. Ivan Pavlov suggested that learning depends on the growth of a connection between two brain areas. Karl Lashley showed that learning does *not* depend on new connections across the cerebral cortex. **392**
2. Richard Thompson found that some instances of classical conditioning take place in small areas of the cerebellum. **394**
3. Psychologists distinguish between short-term memory and long-term memory. Short-term memory holds only a small amount of information and retains it only briefly unless it is constantly rehearsed. **395**
4. Working memory, a modern alternative to the concept of short-term memory, stores information that one is currently using. **397**

5. People with damage to the hippocampus have great trouble forming new long-term declarative memories, especially episodic memories. However, they still show implicit memory, they still store short-term memories, and they still form new procedural memories. **397**
6. Several theories about the hippocampus focus on its role in declarative memory, spatial memory, and memory for context. **401**
7. Patients with Korsakoff's syndrome often fill in their memory gaps with confabulations, which they then remember as if they were true. **403**
8. Alzheimer's disease is a progressive disease, most common in old age, characterized by impaired memory and attention. It is related to deposition of amyloid-β protein in the brain. The accumulating amyloid leads to abnormalities of the tau protein, causing additional difficulties. **404**
9. Whereas the hippocampus is important for rapid storage of an event, the basal ganglia learn gradually. Gradual learning is important for developing habits and for seeing complex patterns that may not be evident on a single trial. **406**
10. The parietal cortex is important for elaborating episodic memories. The anterior temporal cortex serves as a hub for semantic memories. The ventral prefrontal cortex remembers the reward or punishment values of various possible actions, and thereby contributes to decision making. **407**

Key Terms

Terms are defined in the module on the page number indicated. They're also presented in alphabetical order with definitions in the book's Subject Index/Glossary. Interactive flash cards, audio reviews, and crossword puzzles are among the online resources available to help you learn these terms and the concepts they represent.

Alzheimer's disease **404**
amnesia **397**
amyloid-β **404**
anterograde amnesia **399**
classical conditioning **392**
conditioned response (CR) **392**
conditioned stimulus (CS) **392**
confabulation **404**
consolidate **396**
declarative memory **400**
delayed matching-to-sample task **401**
delayed nonmatching-to-sample task **401**
delayed response task **397**
engram **393**
episodic memory **399**
equipotentiality **394**
explicit memory **400**
implicit memory **400**
instrumental conditioning **392**
Korsakoff's syndrome **403**
lateral interpositus nucleus (LIP) **395**
long-term memory **395**
mass action **394**
Morris water maze **402**
procedural memory **401**
punishment **392**
radial maze **402**
reinforcer **392**
retrograde amnesia **399**
semantic dementia **407**
semantic memory **399**
short-term memory **395**
tau protein **404**
unconditioned response (UCR) **392**
unconditioned stimulus (UCS) **392**
working memory **397**

Thought Question

Lashley sought to find the engram, the physiological representation of learning. In general terms, how would you recognize an engram if you saw one? That is, what would someone have to demonstrate before you could conclude that a particular change in the nervous system was really an engram?

MODULE 12.1 End of Module Quiz

1. What evidence led Lashley to draw his conclusions of equipotentiality and mass action?
   a. Learning depends on changes at synapses using all types of neurotransmitters.
   b. Electrical stimulation of the brain can produce either reward or punishment, depending on the intensity of stimulation.
   c. EEG studies show activation throughout the brain during an experiment on learning.
   d. Impairment of learning depended on the amount of cortical damage rather than the location.

2. What happened when Thompson temporarily inactivated the lateral interpositus nucleus of a rabbit's cerebellum during learning?
   a. The rabbit showed no responses during training but showed evidence of learning as soon as the lateral interpositus nucleus recovered.
   b. The rabbit showed no responses during training, and after the lateral interpositus nucleus recovered, the rabbit learned at the same pace as a rabbit with no previous training.
   c. The rabbit showed no evidence of learning during training and no ability to learn even after the lateral interpositus nucleus recovered.
   d. The rabbit showed normal responses during training but forgot them after the lateral interpositus nucleus recovered.

3. What happened when Thompson temporarily inactivated the red nucleus during learning?
   a. The rabbit showed no responses during training but showed evidence of learning as soon as the red nucleus recovered.
   b. The rabbit showed no responses during training, and after the red nucleus recovered, the rabbit learned at the same pace as a rabbit with no previous training.
   c. The rabbit showed no evidence of learning during training and no ability to learn even after the red nucleus recovered.
   d. The rabbit showed normal responses during training but forgot them after the red nucleus recovered.

4. Which of the following is an example of why the original idea of short-term and long-term memory is no longer considered adequate?
   a. Memory consolidation depends on more than just the time necessary to synthesize proteins.
   b. Short-term memory can hold as much information as long-term memory.
   c. Short-term memories are never really forgotten.
   d. Most emotional memories are quickly forgotten.

5. During visual working memory, which brain area synchronizes its activity with that of other areas of the cerebral cortex?
   a. Red nucleus
   b. Hypothalamus
   c. Substantia nigra
   d. Prefrontal cortex

6. Anterograde amnesia is loss of memory for ________, whereas retrograde amnesia is loss of memory for ________.
   a. personal experiences . . . factual information
   b. factual information . . . personal experiences
   c. events before the damage . . . events after the damage
   d. events after the damage . . . events before the damage

7. Research on amnesia suggests what explanation for the usefulness of episodic memory?
   a. Episodic memories keep the brain active so it can store more useful memories.
   b. Episodic memories give us something to talk about.
   c. Episodic memories help us plan for the future.
   d. Episodic memories help us reduce our fear.

8. Suppose a rat is in a radial maze in which six arms have food once per day, and two other arms never have food. What kind of mistake does a rat with hippocampal damage make?
   a. It enters the two arms that never have food.
   b. It avoids two other arms that sometimes do have food.
   c. It fails to enter any of the arms.
   d. It enters one arm more than once before trying all the other arms.

9. When researchers implanted electrodes into a person's hippocampus, they found cells sensitive to what?
   a. Color
   b. Temperature
   c. Location
   d. Rhyming

10. The basal ganglia are primarily responsible for which type of learning?
    a. Gradually learning habits, based on immediate feedback
    b. Acquiring and storing episodic memories
    c. Memories that people can easily describe in words
    d. Quickly adapting learned behaviors to new circumstances

11. Which of the following would probably prevent most cases of Korsakoff's syndrome?

a. Increase the availability of free exercise facilities

b. Decrease the prevalence of particulate matter in air pollution

c. Outlaw the possession of handguns in heavily populated areas

d. Require all alcoholic beverages to be fortified with vitamins

12. What is the relation of genetics to Alzheimer's disease?

a. Identified genes have a strong effect on early-onset Alzheimer's disease and a weaker effect on late-onset disease.

b. Identified genes have a weak effect on early-onset Alzheimer's disease and a stronger effect on late-onset disease.

c. Identified genes have a strong effect on both the early and late onset forms of Alzheimer's disease.

d. Identified genes have little or no effect on Alzheimer's disease, regardless of time of onset.

13. Which brain area records the expected gains and losses associated with possible actions?

a. Anterior temporal cortex

b. Amygdala

c. Parietal cortex

d. Ventral prefrontal cortex

14. How does the orbitofrontal cortex contribute to decision making?

a. It responds to the average value of each response over a long period of time.

b. It responds to how a reward compares to other possible outcomes.

c. It responds based on how soon the reward is likely to arrive.

d. It directly controls the muscle movements after a decision is made.

ANSWERS: 1d, 2b, 3a, 4a, 5d, 6d, 7c, 8d, 9c, 10a, 11d, 12a, 13d, 14b.

MODULE 12.2

Storing Information in the Nervous System

If you walk through a field, are the footprints that you leave "memories"? How about the mud that you pick up on your shoes? If the police wanted to know who walked across that field, a forensics expert could check your footprints or your shoes to answer the question. And yet we would not call these physical traces memories in the usual sense.

Similarly, when a pattern of activity passes through the brain, it leaves a path of physical changes, but not every change is a memory. The task of finding how the brain stores memories is a frustrating one, and researchers have explored many avenues that seemed promising for a while but now seem fruitless.

Blind Alleys and Abandoned Mines

Textbooks, including this one, concentrate mostly on successful research that led to our current understanding of a field. You may get the impression that science progresses smoothly, with each experiment contributing to the body of knowledge. However, if you look at old journals or textbooks, you will find discussions of many "promising" or "exciting" findings that we disregard today. Scientific research does not progress straight from ignorance to enlightenment. It explores one direction after another, a little like a rat in a complex maze, abandoning the dead ends and pursuing arms that lead further.

The problem with the maze analogy is that an investigator seldom runs into a wall that clearly identifies the end of a route. A better analogy is a prospector digging for gold, never certain whether to abandon an unprofitable spot or to keep digging just a little longer. Many previously exciting lines of research in the study of learning are now of little more than historical interest. Here are three examples:

1. Wilder Penfield sometimes performed brain surgery for severe epilepsy on conscious patients who had only scalp anesthesia. When he applied a brief, weak electrical stimulus to part of the brain, the patient could describe the experience that the stimulation evoked. Stimulation of the temporal cortex sometimes evoked vivid descriptions such as:

   I feel as though I were in the bathroom at school.
   I see myself at the corner of Jacob and Washington in South Bend, Indiana.
   I remember myself at the railroad station in Vanceburg, Kentucky; it is winter and the wind is blowing outside, and I am waiting for a train.

   Penfield (1955; Penfield & Perot, 1963) suggested that each neuron stores a particular memory, like a videotape of one's life. However, brain stimulation rarely elicited a memory of a specific event. Usually, it evoked vague sights and sounds, or recollections of common experiences such as "seeing a bed" or "hearing a choir sing 'White Christmas.'" Stimulation almost never elicited memories of doing anything—just of seeing and hearing. Also, some patients reported events that they had never actually experienced, such as being chased by a robber or seeing Christ descend from the sky. In short, the stimulation produced something more like a dream than a memory.

2. G. A. Horridge (1962) apparently demonstrated that decapitated cockroaches can learn. First he cut the connections between a cockroach's head and the rest of its body. Then he suspended the cockroach so that its legs dangled just above a surface of water. An electrical circuit was arranged as in Figure 12.14 so that the roach's leg received a shock whenever it touched the water. Each experimental roach was paired with a control roach that got a leg shock whenever the first roach did. Only the experimental roach had any control over the shock, however. This kind of experiment is known as a "yoked-control" design.

   Over 5 to 10 minutes, roaches in the experimental group increased a response of tucking the leg under the body to avoid shocks. Roaches in the control group did not, on average, change their leg position as a result of the shocks. Thus, the changed response apparently qualifies as learning and not as an accidental by-product of the shocks.

   These experiments initially seemed a promising way to study learning in a simple nervous system (Eisenstein & Cohen, 1965). Unfortunately, decapitated cockroaches learn slowly—wow, imagine that!—and the results vary sharply from one individual to another, limiting the usefulness of the results. After a handful of studies, interest in this line of research faded.

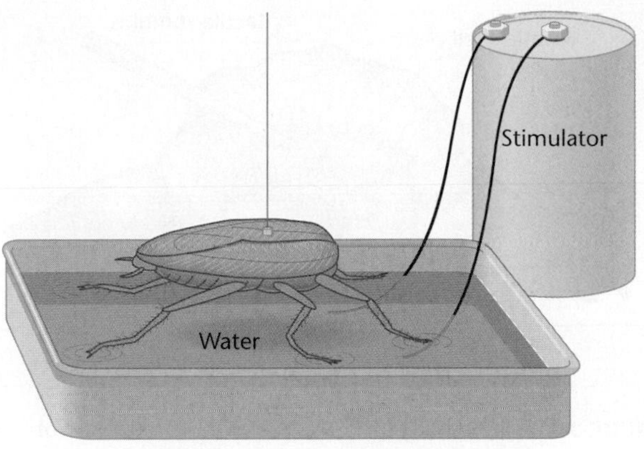

FIGURE 12.14 Learning in a headless cockroach? The decapitated cockroach, suspended just above the water, receives a shock whenever its hind leg touches the water. A cockroach in the control group gets a shock whenever the first roach does regardless of its own behavior. According to some reports, the experimental roach learned to keep its leg out of the water. *Source:* From "Learning of leg position by the ventral nerve cord in headless insects," by G. A. Horridge, *Proceedings of the Royal Society of London, B, 157,* 1962, pp. 33–52. Copyright © 1962 The Royal Society of London. Reprinted by permission of the Royal Society of London and G. A. Horridge.

3. In the 1960s and early 1970s, several investigators proposed that each memory is coded as a specific molecule, probably RNA or protein. The boldest test of that hypothesis was an attempt to transfer memories chemically from one individual to another. James McConnell (1962) reported that, when planaria (flatworms) cannibalized other planaria that had been classically conditioned to respond to a light, they apparently "remembered" what the cannibalized planaria had learned. At least they learned the response faster than planaria generally do.

   Inspired by that report, other investigators trained rats to approach a clicking sound for food (Babich, Jacobson, Bubash, & Jacobson, 1965). After the rats were well trained, the experimenters ground up their brains, extracted RNA, and injected it into untrained rats. The recipient rats learned to approach the clicking sound faster than rats in the control group did.

   That report led to a wealth of studies on the transfer of training by brain extracts. In *some* of these experiments, rats that received brain extracts from a trained group showed apparent memory of the task, whereas those that received extracts from an untrained group did not (Dyal, 1971; Fjerdingstad, 1973). The results were inconsistent and unreplicable, however, even within a single laboratory (L. T. Smith, 1975). Many laboratories failed to find any hint of a transfer effect. By the mid-1970s, most researchers saw no point in continuing this research.

Learning and the Hebbian Synapse

Research on the physiology of learning began with Ivan Pavlov's concept of classical conditioning. Although that theory led Karl Lashley to an unsuccessful search for connections in the cerebral cortex, it also stimulated Donald Hebb to propose a mechanism for change at a synapse.

Mary Ellen Hebb

Donald O. Hebb

(1904–1985)

Modern psychology takes completely for granted that behavior and neural function are perfectly correlated. . . . There is no separate soul or life force to stick a finger into the brain now and then and make neural cells do what they would not otherwise. . . . It is quite conceivable that some day the assumption will have to be rejected. But it is important also to see that we have not reached that day yet. . . . One cannot logically be a determinist in physics and chemistry and biology, and a mystic in psychology. (Hebb, 1949, p. xiii)

Hebb suggested that when the axon of neuron A "repeatedly or persistently takes part in firing [cell B], some growth process or metabolic change takes place in one or both cells" that increases the subsequent ability of axon A to excite cell B (Hebb, 1949, p. 62). In other words, an axon that has successfully stimulated cell B in the past becomes even more successful in the future. In still simpler words, "cells that fire together wire together."

Consider how this process relates to classical conditioning. Suppose axon A initially excites cell B slightly, and axon C excites B more strongly. If A and C fire together, their combined effect on B may produce an action potential. You might think of axon A as the conditioned stimulus and axon C as the unconditioned stimulus. Pairing activity in axons A and C increases the future effect of A on B.

A synapse that increases in effectiveness because of simultaneous activity in the presynaptic and postsynaptic neurons is called a **Hebbian synapse.** In Chapter 5, we encountered examples of this type of synapse. In the development of the visual system, if an axon from the left eye consistently fires at the same time as one from the right eye, a neuron in the visual cortex increases its response to both of them. Such synapses may also be critical for many kinds of associative learning. Neuroscientists have discovered much about the mechanisms of Hebbian synapses.

STOP&CHECK

13. How can a Hebbian synapse account for the basic phenomena of classical conditioning?

ANSWER

13. In a Hebbian synapse, pairing the activity of a weaker (CS) axon with a stronger (UCS) axon produces an action potential, and in the process strengthens the response of the cell to the CS axon. On later trials, it will produce a bigger depolarization of the post-synaptic cell, which we can regard as a conditioned response.

Single-Cell Mechanisms of Invertebrate Behavior Change

If we are going to look for a needle in a haystack, a good strategy is to look in a small haystack. Therefore, many researchers have turned to studies of invertebrates. Vertebrate and invertebrate nervous systems are organized differently, but the chemistry of the neuron, the principles of the action potential, and the neurotransmitters and their receptors are the same. If we identify the physical basis of learning and memory in an invertebrate, we have at least a hypothesis of what *might* work in vertebrates. Biologists have long used this strategy for studying genetics, embryology, and other biological processes.

Aplysia as an Experimental Animal

Aplysia, a marine invertebrate related to the slug, has been a popular animal for studies of the physiology of learning (see Figure 12.15). Compared to vertebrates, it has fewer neurons, many of which are large and easy to study. Moreover, unlike vertebrates, *Aplysia* neurons are virtually identical from one individual to another so that many investigators can study the properties of the same neuron.

One commonly studied behavior is the withdrawal response: If someone touches the siphon, mantle, or gill of an *Aplysia* (see Figure 12.16), the animal vigorously withdraws the irritated structure. Investigators have traced the neural path from the touch receptors through other neurons to the motor neurons that direct the response. Using this neural pathway, investigators have studied changes in behavior as a result of experience. In 2000, Eric Kandel won the Nobel Prize in Physiology or Medicine for this work.

FIGURE 12.15 *Aplysia*, a marine mollusk
A full-grown animal is a little larger than a human hand.

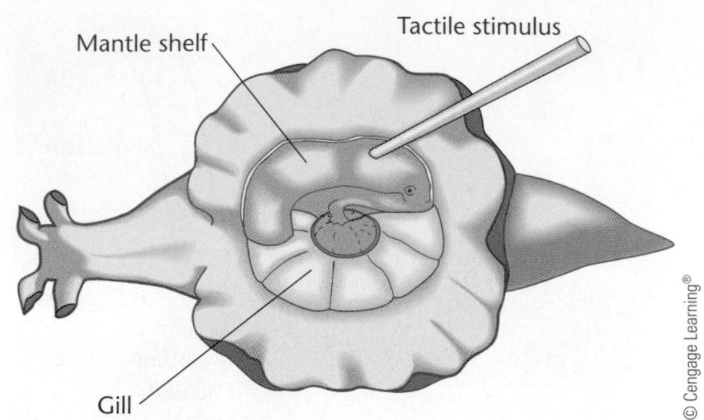

FIGURE 12.16 **Touching an *Aplysia* causes a withdrawal response**
The sensory and motor neurons controlling this reaction have been identified and studied.

Eric R. Kandel
The questions posed by higher cognitive processes such as learning and memory are formidable, and we have only begun to explore them. Although elementary aspects of simple forms of learning have been accessible to molecular analysis in invertebrates, we are only now beginning to know a bit about the genes and proteins involved in more complex, hippocampus-based learning processes of mammals.

Habituation in *Aplysia*

Habituation is a decrease in response to a stimulus that is presented repeatedly and accompanied by no change in other stimuli. For example, if your clock chimes every hour, you gradually respond less and less. If we repeatedly stimulate an *Aplysia*'s gills with a brief jet of seawater, it withdraws at first, but after many repetitions, it stops responding. The decline in response is not due to muscle fatigue because, even after habituation has occurred, direct stimulation of the motor neuron produces a full-size muscle contraction (Kupfermann, Castellucci, Pinsker, & Kandel, 1970). We can also rule out changes in the sensory neuron. The sensory neuron still gives a full, normal response to stimulation; it merely fails to excite the motor neuron as much as before (Kupfermann et al., 1970). We are therefore left with the conclusion that habituation in *Aplysia* depends on a change in the synapse between the sensory neuron and the motor neuron (see Figure 12.17).

Sensitization in *Aplysia*

If you experience an unexpected, intense pain, you temporarily react more strongly than usual to other strong, sudden stimuli. This phenomenon is **sensitization,** an increase in response to mild stimuli as a result of exposure to more intense stimuli. Similarly, a strong stimulus almost anywhere on *Aplysia*'s skin intensifies a later withdrawal response to a touch.

Researchers traced sensitization to changes at identified synapses (Cleary, Hammer, & Byrne, 1989;

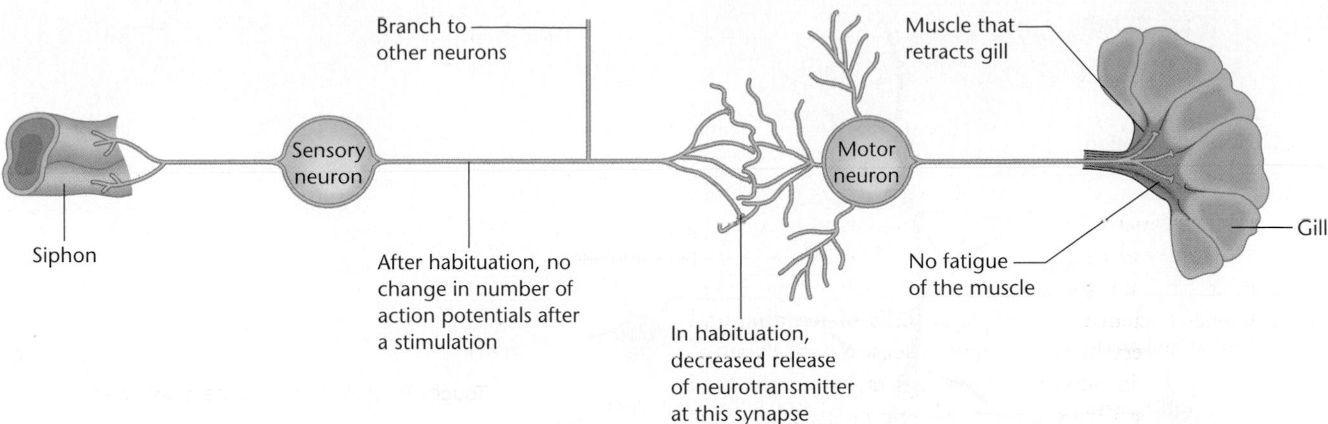

FIGURE 12.17 Habituation of the gill-withdrawal reflex in *Aplysia*
Touching the siphon causes gill withdrawal. After many repetitions, the response habituates (declines) because of decreased transmission at the synapse between the sensory neuron and the motor neuron. *Source:* Redrawn from "Neuronal mechanisms of habituation and dishabituation of the gill-withdrawal reflex in aplysia," by V. Castellucci, H. Pinsker, I. Kupfermann, and E. Kandel, *Science, 1970,* 167, pp. 1745–1748. Copyright © 1970 by AAAS. Used by permission of AAAS and V. Castellucci.

Dale, Schacher, & Kandel, 1988; Kandel & Schwartz, 1982). Strong stimulation on the skin excites a *facilitating interneuron* that releases serotonin (5-HT) onto the presynaptic terminals of many sensory neurons. Serotonin blocks potassium channels in these membranes. The result is that after later action potentials, the membrane takes longer than usual to repolarize (because potassium is slow to flow out of the cell). Therefore, the presynaptic neuron continues releasing its neurotransmitter for longer than usual. Repeating this process causes the sensory neuron to synthesize new proteins that produce long-term sensitization (C. H. Bailey, Giustetto, Huang, Hawkins, & Kandel, 2000). This research shows how it is possible to explain one example of behavioral plasticity in terms of molecular events. Later studies explored mechanisms of classical and instrumental conditioning in *Aplysia*.

STOP&CHECK

14. When serotonin blocks potassium channels on the presynaptic terminal, what is the effect on transmission?

ANSWER

14. Blocking potassium channels prolongs the action potential and therefore prolongs the release of neurotransmitters, producing an increased response.

Long-Term Potentiation in Vertebrates

Since the work of Charles Sherrington and Santiago Ramón y Cajal, most neuroscientists have assumed that learning depends on changes at synapses, and the work on *Aplysia* supports that idea. The first evidence for a similar process among vertebrates came from studies of neurons in the rat hippocampus (Bliss & Lømo, 1973). The phenomenon, known as **long-term potentiation (LTP),** is this: One or more axons connected to a dendrite bombard it with a rapid series of stimuli. The burst of intense stimulation leaves some of the synapses potentiated (more responsive to new input of the same type) for minutes, days, or weeks.

LTP shows three properties that make it an attractive candidate for a cellular basis of learning and memory:

- **specificity**—If some of the synapses onto a cell have been highly active and others have not, only the active ones become strengthened.
- **cooperativity**—Nearly simultaneous stimulation by two or more axons produces LTP much more strongly than does repeated stimulation by just one axon.
- **associativity**—Pairing a weak input with a strong input enhances later response to the weak input, as illustrated in Figure 12.18. In this regard, LTP matches what we would expect of Hebbian synapses. In some cases, a synapse that was almost completely inactive before LTP becomes effective afterward (Kerchner & Nicoll, 2008).

The opposite change, **long-term depression (LTD),** a prolonged decrease in response at a synapse, occurs for axons that have been less active than others, such as axon 3 in Figure 12.18 (Collingridge, Peineau, Howland, & Wang, 2010). You can think of this as a compensatory process. As one synapse strengthens, another weakens (Royer & Paré, 2003). If learning produced only a strengthening of synapses, then every time you learned something, your brain would get more and more active, burning more and more fuel!

Biochemical Mechanisms

Determining how LTP or LTD occurs has been a huge research challenge because each neuron has many tiny synapses, sometimes in the tens of thousands. Isolating the chemical changes at any one synapse takes an enormous amount of creative, patient research. We shall discuss LTP in the hippocampus, where it occurs most readily and where its mechanisms have been most extensively studied.

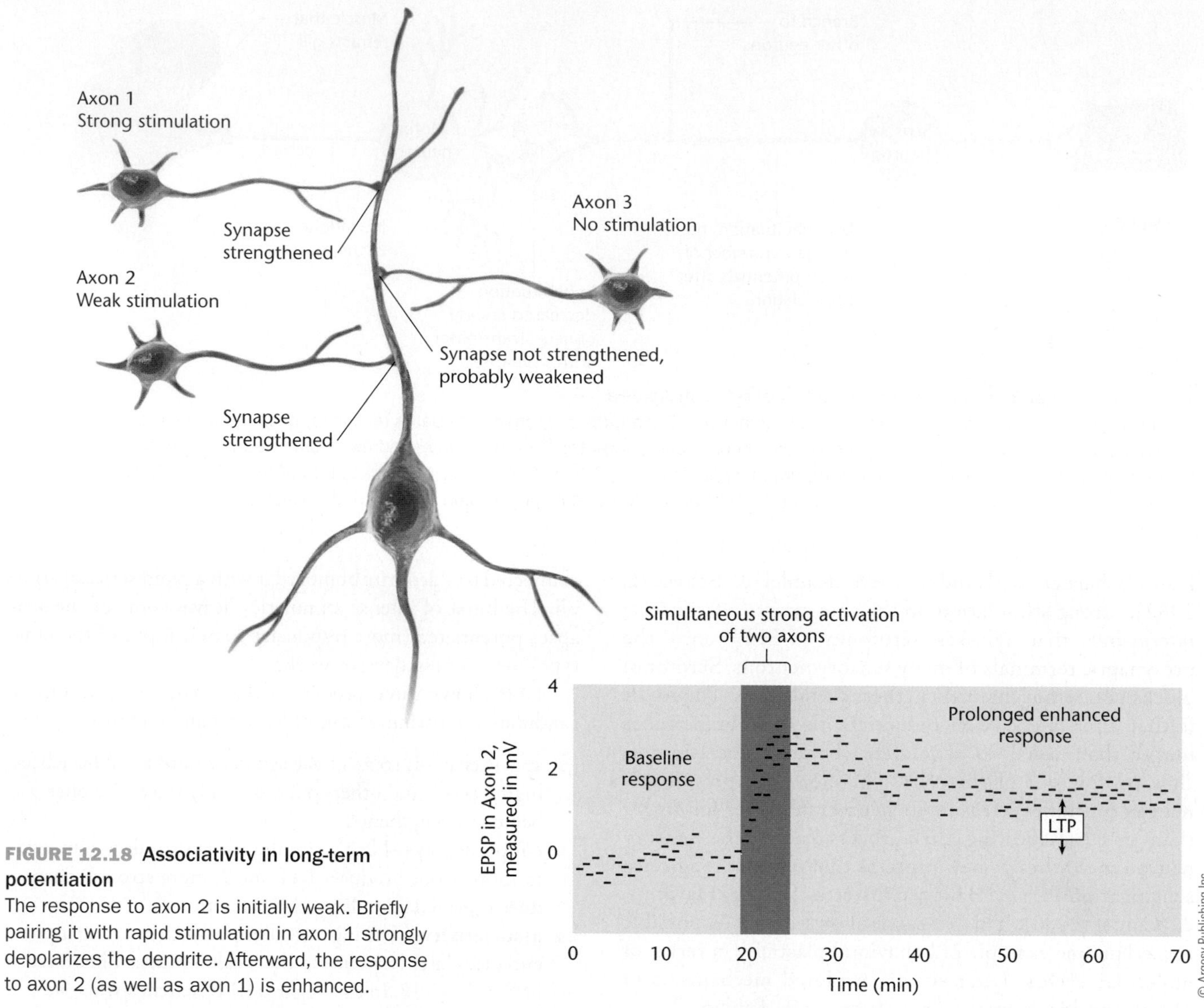

FIGURE 12.18 Associativity in long-term potentiation
The response to axon 2 is initially weak. Briefly pairing it with rapid stimulation in axon 1 strongly depolarizes the dendrite. Afterward, the response to axon 2 (as well as axon 1) is enhanced.

AMPA and NMDA Synapses

In a few cases, LTP depends on changes at GABA synapses (Nugent, Penick, & Kauer, 2007), but in most cases, it depends on changes at glutamate synapses. The brain has several types of receptors for glutamate, its most abundant transmitter. Neuroscientists identify different dopamine receptors by number, such as D_1 and D_2, and different GABA receptors by letter, such as $GABA_A$. They identify serotonin (5-hydroxytryptamine) synapses by both letter and number, such as $5HT_{2C}$. For glutamate, they named the receptors after certain drugs that stimulate them. Here we are interested in two types of glutamate receptors, called AMPA and NMDA. The **AMPA receptor** is excited by the neurotransmitter glutamate, but it can also respond to a drug called α-amino-3-hydroxy-5-methyl-4-isoxazolepropionic acid (abbreviated AMPA). The **NMDA receptor** is also ordinarily excited only by glutamate, but it can respond to a drug called N-methyl-D-aspartate (abbreviated NMDA).

Both are ionotropic receptors. That is, when they are stimulated, they open a channel to let ions enter the postsynaptic cell. The AMPA receptor is a typical ionotropic receptor that opens sodium channels. The NMDA receptor, however, is different: Its response to the transmitter glutamate depends on the degree of polarization across the membrane. When glutamate attaches to an NMDA receptor while the membrane is at its resting potential, the ion channel is usually blocked by magnesium ions. (Magnesium ions, positively charged, are attracted to the negative charge inside the cells but do not fit through the NMDA channel.) The NMDA channel permits ions to flow through it only if the magnesium leaves, and the surest way to detach the magnesium is to depolarize the membrane, decreasing the negative charge that attracts it (see Figure 12.19).

Suppose an axon releases glutamate repeatedly. Better yet, let's activate two axons repeatedly, side by side on the same dendrite. So many sodium ions enter through the AMPA channels that the dendrite becomes strongly depolarized. The depolarization displaces the magnesium molecules, enabling glutamate to open the NMDA channel. At that point, both sodium and calcium enter through the NMDA channel (see Figure 12.20).

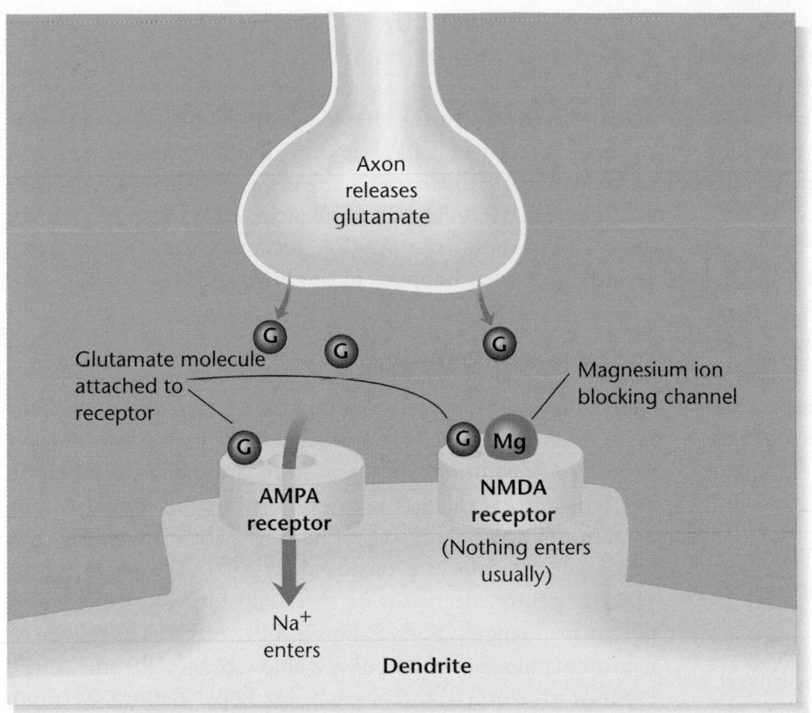

FIGURE 12.19 The AMPA and NMDA receptors before LTP
Glutamate attaches to both receptors. At the AMPA receptor, it opens a channel to let sodium ions enter. At the NMDA receptor, it binds but usually fails to open the channel, which is blocked by magnesium ions.

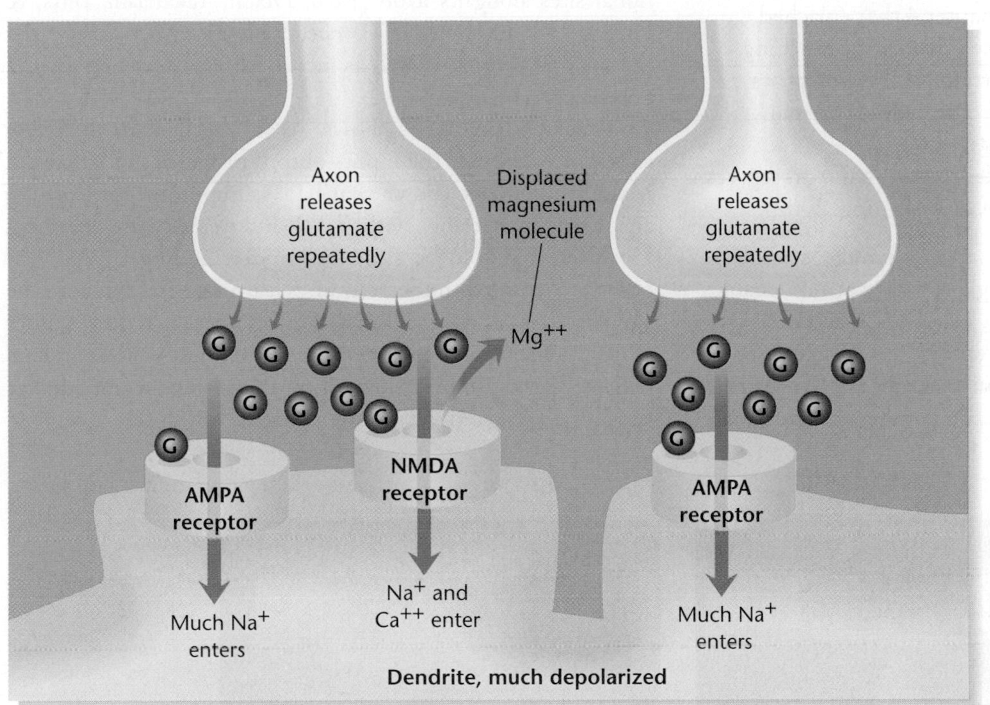

FIGURE 12.20 The AMPA and NMDA receptors during LTP
If one or more AMPA receptors have been repeatedly stimulated, enough sodium enters to largely depolarize the dendrite's membrane. Doing so displaces the magnesium ions and enables glutamate to open the NMDA receptor, through which sodium and calcium enter.

The entry of calcium is the key to maintaining LTP. When calcium enters through the NMDA channel, it activates a protein called CaMKII (α-calcium-calmodulin-dependent protein kinase II) (Lisman, Schulman, & Cline, 2002; Otmakhov et al., 2004). CaMKII sets in motion a series of reactions leading to release of a protein called CREB—cyclic adenosine monophosphate responsive element-binding protein. (You can see why it's almost always abbreviated.) CREB goes to the nucleus of the cell and regulates the expression of several genes. In some cases, the altered gene expression lasts for months or years, long enough to account for long-term memory (Miller et al., 2010). It is an example of an epigenetic change, as discussed in the chapter on development (Guo et al., 2011). The effects of CaMKII are necessary for LTP and for certain types of learning. Because activated CaMKII remains at the stimulated synapse and does not diffuse elsewhere, it is responsible for the specificity aspect of LTP—the fact that only the highly activated synapses become strengthened (Lisman, Yasuda, & Raghavachari, 2012; Redondo & Morris, 2011; Wang et al., 2009).

The effects of CaMKII and CREB are magnified by **BDNF**—brain-derived neurotrophic factor, a neurotrophin similar to nerve growth factor. Persisting activity at synapses leads to action potentials that start in axons but back-propagate into the dendrites, which then release BDNF. The formation and maintenance of LTP depends on all these chemicals—CaMKII, CREB, and BDNF (Kuczewski et al., 2008; Minichiello, 2009; Silva, Zhou, Rogerson, Shobe, & Balaji, 2009), as well as others. When neurons are repeatedly activated, only those with the greatest production of these chemicals will undergo LTP (Han et al., 2007). The final outcome varies, including these possibilities:

- The dendrite builds more AMPA receptors or moves old ones into better positions (Poncer & Malinow, 2001; Takahashi, Svoboda, & Malinow, 2003).
- The dendrite may make more branches and spines, thus forming additional synapses with the same axon (Engert & Bonhoeffer, 1999; Toni, Buchs, Nikonenko, Bron, & Muller, 1999; Ruediger et al., 2011; Xu et al., 2009) (Figure 12.21). Recall from Chapter 4 that enriched experience also leads to increased dendritic branching.
- Phosphate groups attach to certain AMPA receptors to make them more responsive than before (Lisman et al., 2012).
- In some cases, the neuron makes more NMDA receptors (Grosshans, Clayton, Coultrap, & Browning, 2002).

Let's summarize: When glutamate massively stimulates AMPA receptors, the resulting depolarization enables glutamate to stimulate nearby NMDA receptors also. Stimulation of the NMDA receptors lets calcium enter the cell, where it sets into motion a series of changes that potentiate the dendrite's future responsiveness to glutamate at AMPA receptors. After LTP occurs, NMDA receptors revert to their original condition.

Once LTP has been established, it no longer depends on NMDA synapses. Drugs that block NMDA synapses prevent the *establishment* of LTP, but they do not interfere with the *maintenance* of LTP that was already established (Gustafsson & Wigström, 1990; Uekita & Okaichi, 2005). In other words, once LTP occurs, the AMPA receptors stay potentiated, regardless of what happens to the NMDAs.

Presynaptic Changes

The changes just described occur in the postsynaptic neuron. In many cases, LTP depends on changes in the presynaptic neuron instead or in addition. Extensive stimulation of a postsynaptic cell causes it to release a **retrograde transmitter** that travels back to the presynaptic cell to modify it. In many cases, that retrograde transmitter is nitric oxide (NO). As a result, a presynaptic neuron decreases its threshold for producing action potentials (Ganguly, Kiss, & Poo, 2000), increases its release of neurotransmitter (Zakharenko, Zablow, & Siegelbaum, 2001), expands its axon (Routtenberg, Cantallops, Zaffuto, Serrano, & Namgung, 2000), and releases its transmitter from additional sites along its axon (Reid, Dixon, Takahashi, Bliss, & Fine, 2004). In short, LTP reflects increased activity by the presynaptic neuron as well as increased responsiveness by the postsynaptic neuron.

Research on LTP shows us a mechanism whereby experience can alter the input–output properties of a neuron. Many studies have shown that LTP is important for learning and that interfering with LTP interferes with learning. However, it should be clear that understanding LTP is just one step toward understanding learning. Except for the simplest cases of classical conditioning, learning requires more than just increasing the response to a stimulus. Researchers will need to continue exploring how the wiring diagram makes possible all the complexities of a learned response.

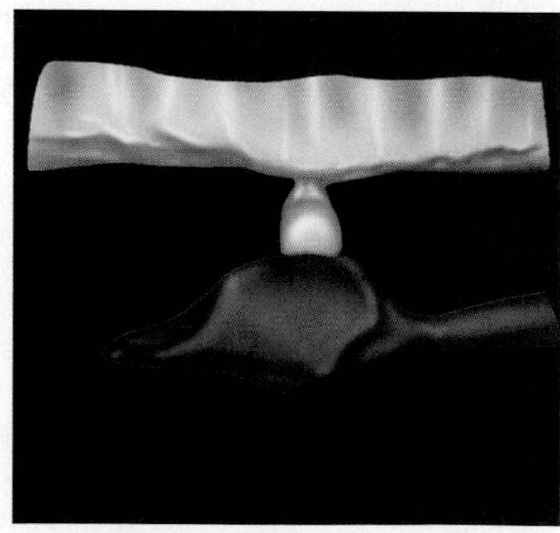
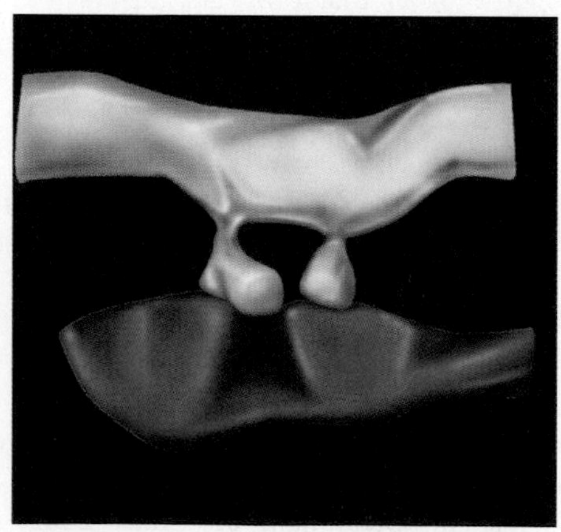

FIGURE 12.21 One way in which LTP occurs
In some cases, the dendrite makes new branches to the same axon, increasing the overall stimulation. *Source:* Based on Toni, Buchs, Nikonenko, Bron, & Muller, 1999

STOP&CHECK

15. Before LTP: In the normal state, what is the effect of glutamate at the AMPA receptors? At the NMDA receptors?

16. During the formation of LTP, when a burst of intense stimulation releases much more glutamate than usual at two or more incoming axons, what is the effect of the glutamate at the AMPA receptors? At the NMDA receptors?

17. After the neuron has gone through LTP, what is now the effect of glutamate at the AMPA receptors? At the NMDA receptors?

ANSWERS

15. Before LTP glutamate stimulates AMPA receptors but usually has little effect at the NMDA receptors because magnesium blocks them. **16.** During the formation of LTP the massive glutamate input strongly stimulates the AMPA receptors, thus depolarizing the dendrite. This depolarization enables glutamate to excite the NMDA receptors also. **17.** After LTP has been established, glutamate stimulates the AMPA receptors more than before, mainly because of an increased number of AMPA receptors. At the NMDA receptors, it is again usually ineffective.

Improving Memory

One reason for studying LTP and other biological mechanisms is the hope that it might lead to practical applications. LTP depends on production of several proteins, and enhancing production of these proteins enhances memory in rodents (Routtenberg et al., 2000; Shema et al., 2011). Drugs that inhibit their production weaken memory, even if the drugs are given days after the training (Shema, Sacktor, & Dudai, 2007). Several pharmaceutical companies are investigating drugs that might improve memory by enhancing LTP, but so far nothing is available. As in the rest of medicine, drugs that show promise in animal studies sometimes have unacceptable side effects when applied to humans.

The one type of medication that does aid memory—somewhat—is a drug such as caffeine, amphetamine, or methylphenidate (Ritalin). Moderate doses of stimulant drugs before or shortly after the time of original learning improve the storage of memory by increasing arousal. Emotionally stimulating experiences also help, by activating the amygdala. Cortisol just before testing sometimes helps people access memories (Roozendaal & McGaugh, 2011). Many patients with Alzheimer's disease take drugs that facilitate acetylcholine by blocking the enzyme that degrades it (Farah et al., 2004).

Other drugs recommended for memory improvement have more doubtful effects. You may have heard claims that the herb *Ginkgo biloba* improves memory. Drug companies face stiff regulation by the Food and Drug Administration before they can market a new drug, but a company marketing an herb or other naturally occurring substance does not have to do any research at all, provided that the label or advertisement does not claim medical benefits. You may see advertisements for vitamin pills or other supplements that brag of containing *Ginkgo biloba*. You may also notice that the ads generally leave it to your imagination what good, if any, this supplement does. Some early research on *Ginkgo biloba* suggested mild benefits to a small percentage of Alzheimer's patients or other older adults with impaired blood flow to the brain. However, a more extensive study of more than 3,000 people tested in many ways over six years found no benefits (Snitz et al., 2009).

Another herb, *Bacopa monnieri*, also known as water hyssop, has been used in India since the sixth century for several mental conditions. It works as an antioxidant and removes β-amyloids, so theoretically it seems a reasonable candidate for improving memory. However, in 17 controlled tests, only 9 found evidence of improved memory, and they found it in some memory tests and not others (Pase et al., 2012). Thus the herb may have benefits, but probably not large ones. (Increasing the dose leads to nausea.)

Researchers using biotechnological methods have found ways to alter gene expression in mice, enhancing memory in certain ways. However, so far the benefits come with a cost. Mice with increased expression of a gene that enhances NMDA receptors show faster learning, and also chronic pain. Mice with another variant gene learn complex mazes faster than usual, but are worse than average at learning simple mazes. Another type of mouse learns quickly, at the cost of learning fears quickly, and failing to unlearn the fears (Lehrer, 2009). Research with humans found that electrical stimulation to parts of the parietal or prefrontal cortex could improve certain types of memory, but always came at the cost of impairing a different type of memory (Iuculano & Kadosh, 2013). In short, biological methods to enhance memory probably have only limited potential.

Behavioral methods to improve memory are still the best bet. If you want to remember something later, study it well now, rehearse it later, and periodically test yourself. Supplements to these strategies are available, including computer programs that claim wonderful results. Be properly skeptical, as many of these claims have not been carefully tested. However, several types of computer software do enhance memory and cognition for many older people whose abilities might otherwise decline (Kueider, Parisi, Gross, & Rebok, 2012). Physical exercise also improves memory in old age, if it continues over a few weeks (Chapman et al., 2013).

STOP&CHECK

18. Researchers have found several ways of improving memory in rodents, including genetic modification. Why do we not apply these methods to humans?

ANSWER

18. So far, every such method comes with disadvantages. Although improving functioning in one way, it causes problems in another.

MODULE 12.2 ■ IN CLOSING

The Physiology of Memory

Why do we care about the physiology of memory? Some day our understanding may lead to practical applications, although so far nothing promising has emerged. The theoretical importance is clearer. Explaining memory in chemical terms underscores the idea of monism: Our experiences, our thoughts, and our memories are manifestations of chemical processes. All the researchers manipulating chemicals at tiny synapses are in a very real sense trying to help us understand human nature.

Summary

1. A Hebbian synapse is one that is strengthened by being repeatedly active when the postsynaptic neuron produces action potentials. **413**
2. Habituation of the gill-withdrawal reflex in *Aplysia* depends on a mechanism that decreases the release of transmitter from a particular presynaptic neuron. **414**
3. Sensitization of the gill-withdrawal reflex in *Aplysia* occurs when serotonin blocks potassium channels in a presynaptic neuron and thereby prolongs the release of transmitter from that neuron. **414**
4. Long-term potentiation (LTP) is an enhancement of response at certain synapses because of a brief but intense series of stimuli delivered to a neuron, generally by two or more axons delivering simultaneous inputs. **415**
5. If axons are active at a very slow rate, their synapses may decrease in responsiveness—a process known as long-term depression (LTD). **415**
6. LTP in hippocampal neurons occurs as follows: Repeated glutamate excitation of AMPA receptors depolarizes the membrane. The depolarization removes magnesium ions that had been blocking NMDA receptors. Glutamate is then able to excite the NMDA receptors, opening a channel for calcium ions to enter the neuron. **416**
7. When calcium enters through the NMDA-controlled channels, it activates a protein that sets in motion a series of events that build more AMPA receptors and increase the growth of dendritic branches. These changes increase the later responsiveness of the dendrite to incoming glutamate at AMPA receptors. **417**
8. At many synapses, LTP relates to increased release of transmitter from the presynaptic neuron, in addition to or instead of changes in the postsynaptic neuron. **418**
9. Although researchers hope to develop drugs or procedures to improve memory, at this point no such procedure is safe and effective, with the exception of mild stimulants such as caffeine. The best way to improve memory is to learn the material well and practice it. **419**

Key Terms

Terms are defined in the module on the page number indicated. They're also presented in alphabetical order with definitions in the book's Subject Index/Glossary. Interactive flash cards, audio reviews, and crossword puzzles are among the online resources available to help you learn these terms and the concepts they represent.

AMPA receptor **416**
associativity **415**
BDNF **418**
cooperativity **415**
habituation **414**
Hebbian synapse **413**
long-term depression (LTD) **415**
long-term potentiation (LTP) **415**
NMDA receptor **416**
retrograde transmitter **418**
sensitization **414**
specificity **415**

Thought Questions

1. If a synapse has already developed LTP once, should it be easier or more difficult to get it to develop LTP again? Why?
2. Dopamine facilitates activity at many AMPA synapses (Tye et al., 2010). How might this fact help explain how methylphenidate (Ritalin) improves learning?

MODULE 12.2 End of Module Quiz

1. Suppose axon A weakly excites cell C, and axon B strongly excites it. If these are Hebbian synapses, under what circumstance will axon A's synapse be strengthened?
   a. Whenever axon A's synapse is used
   b. Whenever axon B's synapse is used
   c. If axon A's synapse and axon B's synapse are active at the same time
   d. If axon A's synapse and axon B's synapse are active at different times

2. Why is *Aplysia* an appealing animal for studies of the physiology of learning?
   a. Its axon is thicker than that of mammals and therefore easier to study.
   b. Unlike mammals, it uses only one neurotransmitter and two types of receptors.
   c. Compared to other invertebrates, it learns faster and remembers longer.
   d. It has relatively few neurons, and they are the same from one individual to another.

3. What is meant by the "specificity" of LTP?
   a. LTP occurs in certain parts of the brain and not others.
   b. LTP occurs only at the synapses that have been activated.
   c. Nearly simultaneous stimulation by two or more axons produces LTP more strongly than does repeated stimulation by just one axon.
   d. LTP occurs only at glutamate synapses.

4. What is the difference between AMPA receptors and NMDA receptors?
   a. They respond to different neurotransmitters.
   b. AMPA receptors are excitatory, and NMDA receptors are inhibitory.
   c. AMPA receptors are ionotropic, and NMDA receptors are metabotropic.
   d. Although both respond to glutamate, different drugs activate them.

5. During the formation of LTP, which ions enter at the NMDA receptors?
   a. Calcium and magnesium
   b. Iron and magnesium
   c. Sodium and potassium
   d. Calcium and sodium

6. What does CaMKII do?
   a. It displaces magnesium and therefore permits glutamate to open calcium channels.
   b. It releases a protein that alters the expression of several genes.
   c. It diffuses from one synapse to another within the postsynaptic neuron.
   d. It sends a message back to the presynaptic neuron to alter its release of neurotransmitters.

7. At this point, what type of drug or chemical is most clearly shown to improve memory without unacceptable side effects?
   a. Drugs that enhance LTP
   b. *Ginkgo biloba*
   c. Caffeine and other stimulants
   d. The herb *Bacopa monnieri*

ANSWERS: 1c, 2d, 3b, 4d, 5d, 6b, 7c.

Suggestions for Further Reading

Corkin, S. (2013). *Permanent present tense*. New York: Basic Books. Thorough account of the life of amnesia patient Henry Molaison and psychologists' research on his memory.

Eichenbaum, H. (2002). *The cognitive neuroscience of memory*. New York: Oxford University Press. Thoughtful treatment of both the behavioral and physiological aspects of memory.

Schnider, A. (2008). *The confabulating mind: How the brain creates reality*. New York: Oxford. A study of people with Korsakoff's syndrome and other conditions that lead to confident but false memory reports.

Daly and Newton/Stone/Getty Images

Cognitive Functions

13

Biological explanations of vision, hearing, and movement are fairly detailed. Research progresses, mainly because researchers can measure the stimuli and behaviors reasonably well. Language, thought, and attention are harder to measure, and therefore harder to study. Nevertheless, they have been integral topics for neuroscience since its earliest days, beginning with Paul Broca's report in the 1860s that speech depends on part of the left frontal cortex.

Although research on the biology of cognition is difficult, many of the results are fascinating. After damage to the corpus callosum, which connects the two hemispheres, people act as if they have two fields of awareness—separate "minds," you might say. With damage to certain areas of the left hemisphere, people lose their language abilities, while remaining unimpaired in other ways. People with damage to parts of the right hemisphere ignore the left side of their body and the left side of the world. Studies of such people offer clues about how the brain operates and raise stimulating questions.

OPPOSITE: Language may have evolved from our tendency to make gestures.

CHAPTER OUTLINE

MODULE 13.1 **Lateralization of Function**
The Left and Right Hemispheres
Visual and Auditory Connections to the Hemispheres
The Corpus Callosum and the Split-Brain Operation
Development of Lateralization and Handedness
Avoiding Overstatements
In Closing: One Brain, Two Hemispheres

MODULE 13.2 **Evolution and Physiology of Language**
Nonhuman Precursors of Language
How Did Humans Evolve Language?
Brain Damage and Language
Music and Language
Dyslexia
In Closing: Language and the Brain

MODULE 13.3 **Conscious and Unconscious Processes and Attention**
The Mind–Brain Relationship
Consciousness of a Stimulus
Conscious and Unconscious People
Attention
In Closing: Attending to Attention and Being Conscious of Consciousness

MODULE 13.4 **Social Neuroscience**
The Biology of Love
Empathy and Altruism
In Closing: The Social Brain

LEARNING OBJECTIVES

After studying this chapter, you should be able to:

1. Identify the primary functions of the left and right hemispheres.
2. Describe the behavioral results from split-brain surgery
3. Describe the results of attempts to teach language to nonhumans.
4. Discuss hypotheses of how human language evolved.
5. Contrast Broca's aphasia with Wernicke's aphasia.
6. Discuss the biological basis for dyslexia.
7. Explain why nearly all neuroscientists and philosophers favor some version of monism with regard to the mind–brain relationship.
8. Describe what brain activities differentiate between conscious and unconscious processing, and the types of research leading to these conclusions.
9. List some key findings about biological influences on social behavior.

Lateralization of Function

Symmetry is common in nature. The sun, stars, and planets are nearly symmetrical, as are most animals and plants. When an atom undergoes radioactive decay, it emits identical rays in exactly opposite directions. However, the human brain is asymmetrical. The left hemisphere has somewhat different functions from the right hemisphere. Why? Presumably, assigning different functions to the two hemispheres provides some advantage. This module explores the distinctions between hemispheres.

The Left and Right Hemispheres

The left hemisphere of the cerebral cortex connects to skin receptors and muscles mainly on the right side of the body. The right hemisphere connects to skin receptors and muscles mainly on the left side. As an exception to this rule, both hemispheres control the trunk muscles and facial muscles. The left hemisphere sees only the right half of the world. The right hemisphere sees only the left half of the world. Each hemisphere gets auditory information from both ears but slightly stronger information from the contralateral ear. In insects, too, each side of the brain controls mostly the opposite side of the body (Crowner, Madden, Goeke, & Giniger, 2002). *Why* did brains evolve so that each hemisphere controls the contralateral (opposite) side of the body? No one knows. Taste and smell, however, are uncrossed. Each hemisphere gets taste information both sides of the tongue (Stevenson, Miller, & McGrillen, 2013) and smell information from the nostril on its own side (Herz, McCall, & Cahill, 1999; Homewood & Stevenson, 2001).

The left and right hemispheres exchange information through a set of axons called the **corpus callosum** and through the anterior commissure, the hippocampal commissure, and a couple of other small commissures (see Figure 13.1; see also Figures 3.10 and 3.13). The two hemispheres are not mirror images of each other. In most humans, the left hemisphere is specialized for language. The functions of the right hemisphere are more difficult to summarize, as we shall see later. Such division of labor between the two hemispheres is known as **lateralization.** If you had no corpus callosum, your left hemisphere could react only to information from the right side of your body, and your right hemisphere could react only to information from the left. Because of the corpus callosum, however, each hemisphere receives information from both sides. Only after damage to the corpus callosum (or to one hemisphere) do we see clear evidence of lateralization.

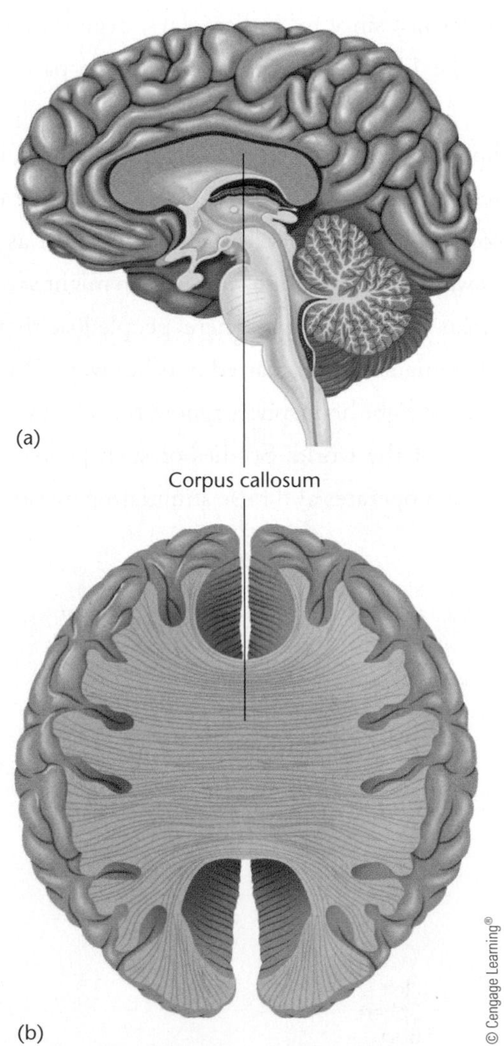

FIGURE 13.1 Two views of the corpus callosum
The corpus callosum is a large set of axons conveying information between the two hemispheres. (a) A sagittal section through the human brain. (b) A dissection (viewed from above) in which gray matter has been removed to expose the corpus callosum.

Visual and Auditory Connections to the Hemispheres

Before we can discuss lateralization of function in any detail, let's consider the sensory connections to the brain. The hemispheres connect to the eyes such that each hemisphere gets input from the opposite half of the visual world. That is, the left hemisphere sees the right side of the world, and the right hemisphere sees the left side. In rabbits and other species with eyes far to the side of the head, the left eye connects to the right hemisphere, and the right eye connects to the left. *Human eyes are not connected to the brain in this way.* Both of your eyes face forward. You see the left side of the world almost as well with your right eye as with your left eye.

Figure 13.2 illustrates the connections from the eyes to the human brain. Light from the right half of the **visual field** (what is visible at any moment) strikes the left half of each retina, and light from the left visual field strikes the right half of each retina. The left half of each retina connects to the left hemisphere, which therefore sees the right visual field. Similarly, the right half of each retina connects to the right hemisphere, which sees the left visual field. A small vertical strip down the center of each retina, covering about 5 degrees of visual arc, connects to both hemispheres (Innocenti, 1980; Lavidor & Walsh, 2004). In Figure 13.2, note how half of the axons from each eye cross to the opposite side of the brain at the **optic chiasm** (literally, the "optic cross").

Right visual field ⇒ left half of each retina ⇒ left hemisphere
Left visual field ⇒ right half of each retina ⇒ right hemisphere

The auditory system is organized differently. Each ear sends the information to both sides of the brain, because any brain area that contributes to localizing sounds must compare input from both ears. However, each hemisphere does pay more attention to the ear on the opposite side (Hugdahl, 1996).

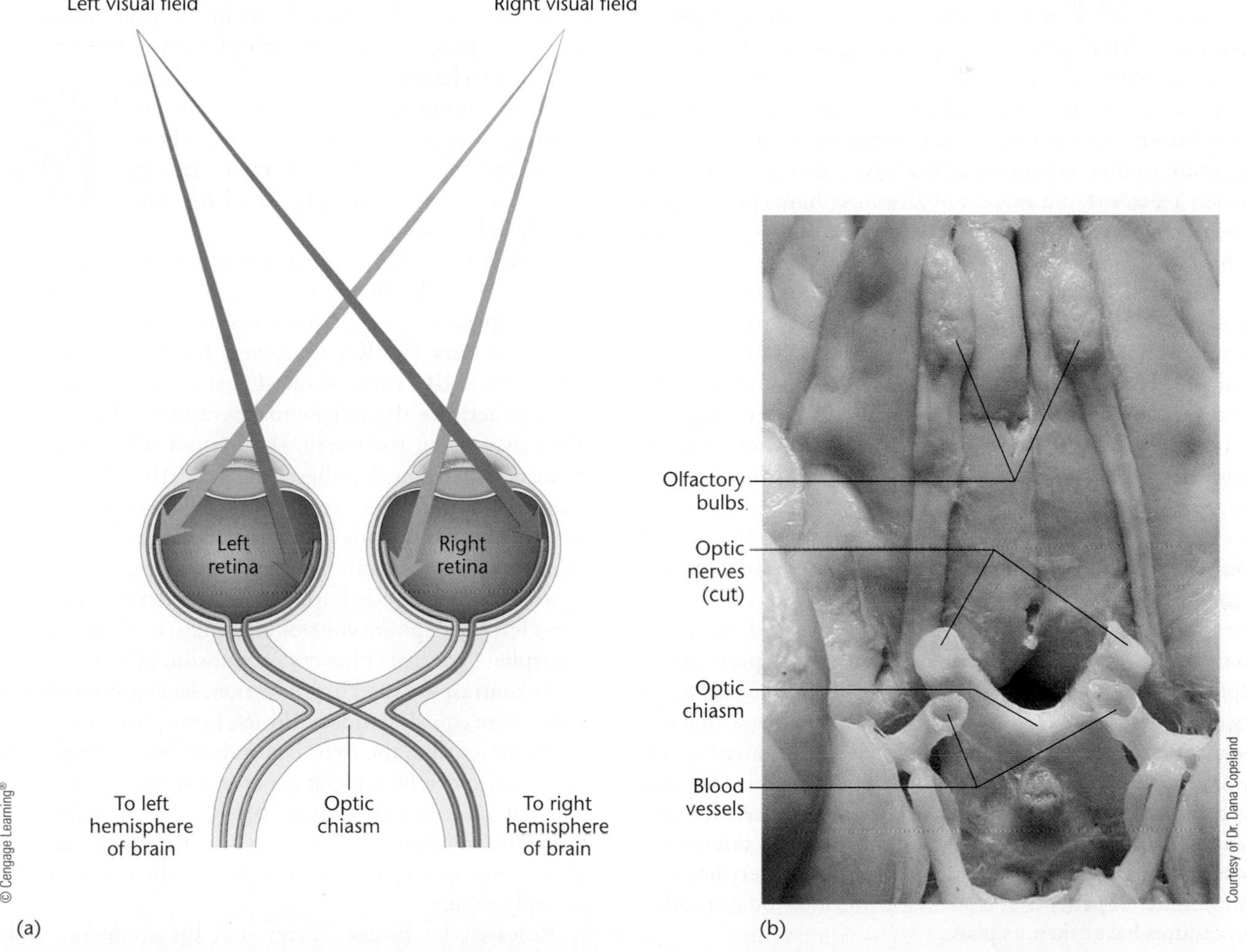

FIGURE 13.2 Connections from the eyes to the human brain
(a) The left hemisphere connects to the left half of each retina and thus gets visual input from the right half of the world. The opposite is true of the right hemisphere. (b) At the optic chiasm, axons from the right half of the left retina cross to the right hemisphere, and axons from the left half of the right retina cross to the left hemisphere.

STOP&CHECK

1. The left hemisphere of the brain is connected to the right eye in guinea pigs. In humans, the left hemisphere is connected to the left half of each retina. Explain the reason for this species difference.

2. In humans, the left half of the retina receives visual information from the ______ side of the visual field and sends its axons to the ______ hemisphere of the brain.

ANSWERS

1. In guinea pigs, the right eye is far to the side of the head and sees only the right visual field. In humans, the eyes point straight ahead and half of each eye sees the right visual field. 2. right . . . left

The Corpus Callosum and the Split-Brain Operation

Damage to the corpus callosum prevents the hemispheres from exchanging information. Occasionally, surgeons sever the corpus callosum as a treatment for severe **epilepsy**, a condition characterized by repeated episodes of excessive synchronized neural activity. Epilepsy can result from a mutation in a gene controlling the GABA receptor (Baulac et al., 2001), from trauma or infection in the brain, brain tumors, or exposure to toxic substances. Often, the cause is not known. About 1 percent to 2 percent of all people have epilepsy. The symptoms vary depending on the location and type of brain abnormality.

Antiepileptic drugs block sodium flow across the membrane or enhance the effects of GABA. More than 90 percent of epileptic patients respond well enough to live a normal life. However, if someone continues having frequent seizures despite medication, physicians consider surgically removing the **focus**, the point in the brain where the seizures begin. The location of the focus varies from one person to another.

Removing the focus is not an option if someone has several foci, or if the focus is in an area considered essential for language. Therefore, the idea arose to cut the corpus callosum to prevent epileptic seizures from crossing from one hemisphere to the other. One benefit is that, as predicted, the person's epileptic seizures affect only half the body. (The abnormal activity cannot cross the corpus callosum, so it remains within one hemisphere.) A surprising bonus is that the seizures become less frequent. Evidently, epileptic activity rebounds back and forth between the hemispheres and prolongs a seizure. If it cannot bounce back and forth across the corpus callosum, a seizure may not develop at all. Although this surgery helped a fair number of patients, it is seldom performed today, as other procedures have taken its place.

How does severing the corpus callosum affect other aspects of behavior? People who have undergone surgery to the corpus callosum, referred to as **split-brain people,** maintain their intellect and motivation, and they still walk without difficulty. They also use the two hands together on familiar tasks such as tying shoes. If they are asked to pretend they are hitting a golf ball, threading a needle, or attaching a fishhook to a line, they manage well enough on well-practiced tasks, but they struggle on unfamiliar tasks (Franz, Waldie, & Smith, 2000).

Split-brain people can use their two hands inependently in a way that other people cannot. For example, try drawing ⋃ with your left hand while simultaneously drawing ⊃ with your right hand. Most people find this task difficult, but split-brain people do it with ease. Or try drawing circles with both hands simultaneously, but one of them just a little faster than the other (not twice as fast). Most people find this task difficult; split-brain people spontaneously draw the circles at different speeds (Kennerley, Diedrichsen, Hazeltine, Semjen, & Ivry, 2002).

The difficulty of simultaneously moving your left hand one way and your right hand a different way reflects a cognitive difficulty more than a motor limitation. It is ordinarily hard to draw a ⋃ with one hand and a ⊃ with the other, but if you carefully draw both of them and then try to *trace over* the ⋃ with one hand and a ⊃ with the other, you will find it easier. Evidently, it is difficult to plan two actions at once unless you have clear targets to direct your movements. Split-brain people have no trouble planning different actions with the two hands. However, if the left hemisphere is concentrating on a difficult task, the drawings or other activities by the right hemisphere and left hand deteriorate (Gazzaniga, 2000). So the two hemispheres do not work entirely independently.

According to fMRI data and other methods, the left hemisphere is dominant for speech production in more than 95 percent of right-handers and nearly 80 percent of left-handers (McKeever, Seitz, Krutsch, & Van Eys, 1995). An fMRI study showed that even two-month-old children activate the left hemisphere more than the right when they listen to speech, though not when they listen to music (Dehaene-Lambertz et al., 2010). Evidently the brain treats speech as special from the start. Left-handers are more variable. Some strongly left-handed people have right hemisphere dominance for speech, but most people regarded as left-handed are partly ambidextrous and have either left hemisphere control or a mixture of left and right hemisphere control (Flowers & Hudson, 2013).

In contrast to speech production, language comprehension is more equally divided. The left hemisphere understands speech better than the right hemisphere, but the right hemisphere can generally understand speech if the vocabulary and grammar are relatively simple (Beeman & Chiarello, 1998). Therefore, an investigator can give instructions to both hemispheres of a split-brain person, but only the left hemisphere can reply vocally.

Research by Roger Sperry and his students (Nebes, 1974) revealed behavioral effects when stimuli were limited to one side of the body. In a typical experiment, a split-brain person stared straight ahead as the experimenter flashed words or pictures on either side of a screen, too briefly for

FIGURE 13.3 Effects of damage to the corpus callosum
(a) When the word *hatband* is flashed on a screen, (b) a woman with a split brain can report only what her left hemisphere saw, "band." (c) However, with her left hand, she can point to a hat, which is what the right hemisphere saw.

the person to move his or her eyes (see Figure 13.3). Information going to one hemisphere could not cross to the other, because of the damage to the corpus callosum. The person could then point with the left hand to what the right hemisphere saw and could point with the right hand to what the left hemisphere saw. The person could talk about anything the left hemisphere saw. However, when the right hemisphere saw something, the person would point to it correctly with the left hand, while saying, "I don't know what it was. I didn't see anything." The talking left hemisphere had no direct access to the information reaching the right hemisphere. (Of course, it could watch the left hand and infer what the right hemisphere had seen.)

Occasional exceptions arise to this rule. Because a small amount of information travels between the hemispheres through several smaller commissures, as shown in Figure 13.4,

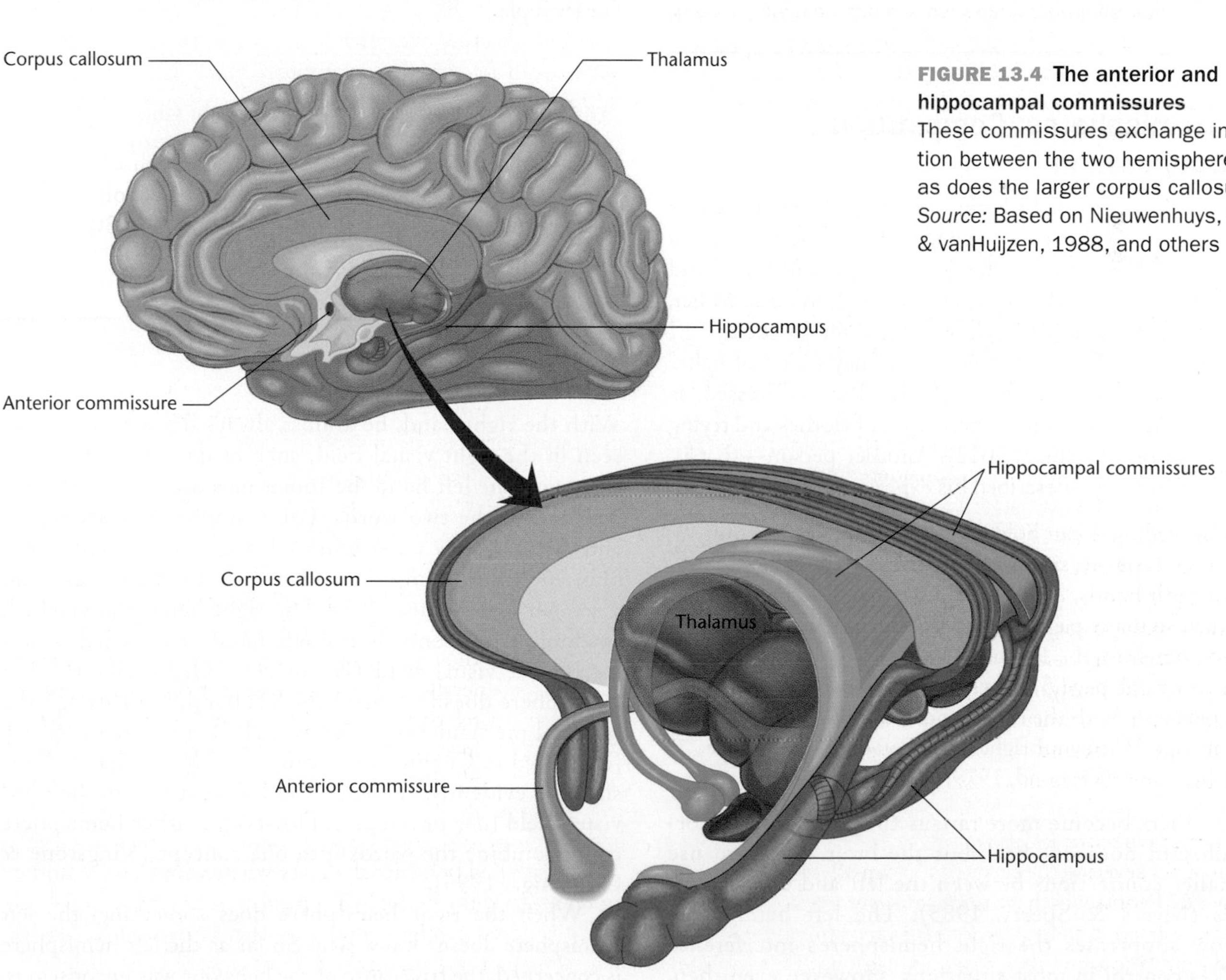

FIGURE 13.4 The anterior and hippocampal commissures
These commissures exchange information between the two hemispheres, as does the larger corpus callosum. *Source:* Based on Nieuwenhuys, Voogd, & vanHuijzen, 1988, and others

some split-brain people get enough information to give a partial description of what the right hemisphere saw (Berlucchi, Mangun, & Gazzaniga, 1997; Forster & Corballis, 2000).

Is it an advantage for just one hemisphere to control speech? Possibly. Many people who have bilateral control of speech stutter (Fox et al., 2000), although not all people who stutter have bilateral control of speech. Perhaps a conflict between two speech centers produces competing messages to the speech muscles.

STOP&CHECK

3. What can a split-brain person do that other people cannot do?

4. Can a split-brain person name an object after feeling it with the right hand? With the left hand? Explain.

ANSWERS

3. A split-brain person can draw different things with the two hands at the same time, or move the hands at different speeds at the same time. **4.** A split-brain person can describe something after feeling it with the right hand but not with the left. The right hand sends its information to the left hemisphere, which is dominant for language in most people. The left hand sends its information to the right hemisphere, which cannot speak.

Split Hemispheres: Competition and Cooperation

In the first weeks after split-brain surgery, the hemispheres act like separate people sharing one body. One split-brain person repeatedly took items from the grocery shelf with one hand and returned them with the other (Reuter-Lorenz & Miller, 1998). She explained, "I'd reach with my right for the thing I wanted, but the left would come in and they'd kind of fight." She had similar problems when she tried to get dressed, as each hand was picking out a different set of clothes and trying to put them on (Wolman, 2012). Another person—that is, his left hemisphere—described his experience as follows:

> If I'm reading, I can hold the book in my right hand; it's a lot easier to sit on my left hand, than to hold it with both hands. . . . You tell your hand—I'm going to turn so many pages in a book—turn three pages—then somehow the left hand will pick up two pages and you're at page 5, or whatever. It's better to let it go, pick it up with the right hand, and then turn to the right page. With your right hand, you correct what the left has done. (Dimond, 1979, p. 211)

Such conflicts become more rare as time passes. The corpus callosum does not heal, but the brain learns to use the smaller connections between the left and right hemispheres (Myers & Sperry, 1985). The left hemisphere somehow suppresses the right hemisphere's interference and takes control in most situations. However, even then, the hemispheres show differences of opinion if we test carefully enough. In one study, researchers asked a split-brain person to identify photos after viewing them briefly in one visual field or the other. They formed photos by morphing pictures of the split-brain person himself, and pictures of another familiar person. When he saw a picture in the right visual field (left hemisphere), he was more likely to say it was himself. When he saw it in the left visual field (right hemisphere), he usually thought it was the other person (Turk et al., 2002).

In other situations, the hemispheres learn to cooperate. A split-brain person who was tested with the apparatus shown in Figure 13.3 used an interesting strategy to answer a yes–no question about what he saw in the left visual field. Suppose an experimenter flashes a picture in the left visual field and asks, "Was it green?" The left (speaking) hemisphere takes a guess: "Yes." That guess might be correct. If not, the right hemisphere, knowing the correct answer, makes the face frown. (Both hemispheres control facial muscles on both sides of the face.) The left hemisphere, feeling the frown, says, "Oh, I'm sorry, I meant 'no.'"

In another experiment, a split-brain person saw two words flashed at once, one on each side. He was then asked to draw a picture of what he had read. Each hemisphere saw a full word, but the two words could combine to make a different word. For example,

Left Visual Field (Right Hemisphere)	Right Visual Field (Left Hemisphere)
hot	dog
honey	moon
sky	scraper
rain	bow

With the right hand, he almost always drew what he had seen in the right visual field, such as *dog* or *moon*. However, with the left hand, he sometimes drew a literal combination of the two words. For example, after seeing *hot* and *dog*, he drew an overheated dog, not a wiener on a bun, and after seeing *sky* and *scraper*, he drew a sky and a scraper (see Figure 13.5). The right hemisphere, which predominantly controls the left hand, drew what it saw in the left visual field (*hot* or *sky*). Ordinarily, the left hemisphere doesn't control the left hand, but through the bilateral mechanisms of the medial corticospinal pathway (described in Chapter 7), it can move the left hand clumsily and, evidently, enough to add what it saw in the right visual field (*dog* or *scraper*). However, neither hemisphere could combine the words into one concept (Kingstone & Gazzaniga, 1995).

When the right hemisphere does something, the left hemisphere doesn't know why. So far as the left hemisphere is concerned, the true cause of the behavior was unconscious.

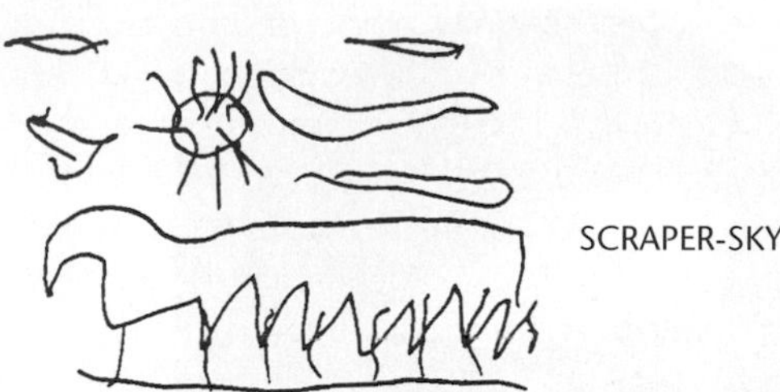

FIGURE 13.5 A split-brain person draws with the left hand
He saw the word *sky* in the left visual field and *scraper* in the right visual field. His left hemisphere controlled the left hand enough to draw a scraper, and his right hemisphere controlled it enough to draw a sky. *Source:* From "Subcortical transfer of higher order information: More illusory than real?" by A. Kingstone and M. S. Gazzaniga, 1995, *Neuropsychology*, 9, pp. 321–328. Copyright © 1995 American Psychological Association. Reprinted with permission.

```
B     B
B     B
B     B
B     B
BBBBBBB
B     B
B     B
B     B
B     B
```

FIGURE 13.6 Analytical versus holistic perception
When people are told to name the large composite letter, they have more activity in the right hemisphere. When told to name the small component letters, they have more activity in the left hemisphere. *Source:* Based on Fink, Halligan, et al., 1996

How does it react? Rather than acting surprised, it invents an explanation. For example, if the right hemisphere sees something pleasant or unpleasant, the left hemisphere feels the change of mood and might say, "What a beautiful wall that is!" or "Right now you are making me sad." In one study, experimenters flashed different pictures to the two hemispheres and asked the person to point to pictures associated with what he or she saw. In one case, the left hemisphere saw a chicken claw and the right hemisphere saw a snow scene. The right hand then pointed to a picture of a chicken and the left hand pointed to a shovel. When asked to explain why he pointed at a shovel, he replied that you would need a shovel to clean out the chicken shed. From observations like these, Michael Gazzaniga (2000) proposed the concept of the **interpreter**, the tendency of the left hemisphere to invent and defend explanations for actions, even when the true causes are unconscious. This feature is not limited to split-brain people. We all think we know why we are doing something, when in fact we might be wrong.

The Right Hemisphere

After researchers discovered the importance of the left hemisphere for speech, they at first imagined the right hemisphere as something like a vice president, helping in a subordinate role but initiating little except after damage to the other hemisphere. Gradually it became clear that the right hemisphere has important functions of its own.

The right hemisphere is more adept than the left at comprehending spatial relationships. For example, one young woman with damage to her posterior right hemisphere had trouble finding her way around, even in familiar areas. To reach a destination, she needed directions with specific visual details, such as, "Walk to the corner where you see a building with a statue in front of it. Then turn left and go to the corner that has a flagpole and turn right. . . ." Each of these directions had to include an unmistakable feature. If the instruction was "go to the city government building—that's the one with a tower," she might go to a different building that happened to have a tower (Clarke, Assal, & deTribolet, 1993).

According to Robert Ornstein (1997), the left hemisphere focuses more on details and the right hemisphere more on overall patterns. For example, in one study, people with intact brains examined visual stimuli such as the one in Figure 13.6, in which many repetitions of a small letter compose a different large letter. When they were asked to identify the small letters (in this case, B), activity increased in the left hemisphere, but when they were asked to identify the large overall letter (H), activity increased in the right hemisphere (G. R. Fink et al., 1996). The right hemisphere also helps see "the big picture" even in language comprehension, relating what one hears to the overall context (Vigneau et al., 2011; Wright, Stamatakis, & Tyler, 2012). Without help from the right hemisphere, the left hemisphere's understanding is sometimes overly literal.

Perhaps because of its tendency to focus on overall patterns, the right hemisphere is more responsive to emotional stimuli than the left. The right hemisphere is better than the left at perceiving the emotions in people's gestures and tone of voice, such as happiness or sadness (Adolphs, Damasio, & Tranel, 2002). People with damage to the right hemisphere speak in a monotone voice, do not recognize other people's emotional expressions, and usually fail to understand humor and sarcasm (Beeman & Chiarello, 1998; H. J. Rosen et al., 2002). Listening to either laughter or crying activates the right amygdala more than the left (Sander & Scheich, 2001).

In a split-brain person, the right hemisphere does better than the left at recognizing whether two photographs show the same or different emotions (Stone, Nisenson, Eliassen, & Gazzaniga, 1996). Jerre Levy and her colleagues showed faces like those in Figure 13.7 to people with intact brains. Which looks happier to you: face (a) or face (b)? Most people choose face (a), with the smile on the viewer's left (Heller & Levy, 1981; Hoptman & Levy, 1988; Levy, Heller, Banich, & Burton, 1983). Similarly, a frown on the viewer's left looks sadder than a frown on the viewer's right (Sackeim, Putz, Vingiano, Coleman, & McElhiney, 1988). Remember, what you see in your left visual field stimulates your right hemisphere first.

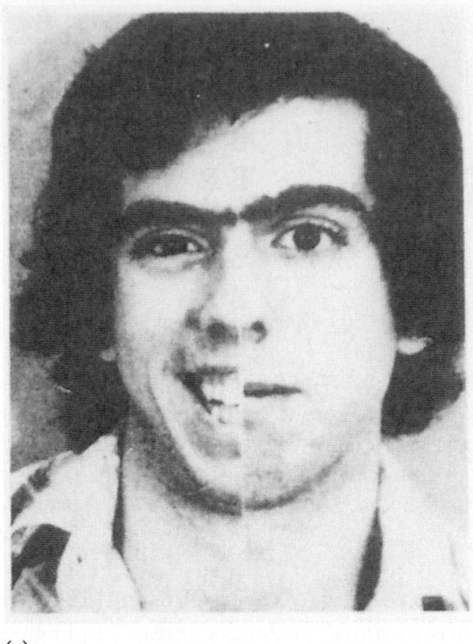
(a)

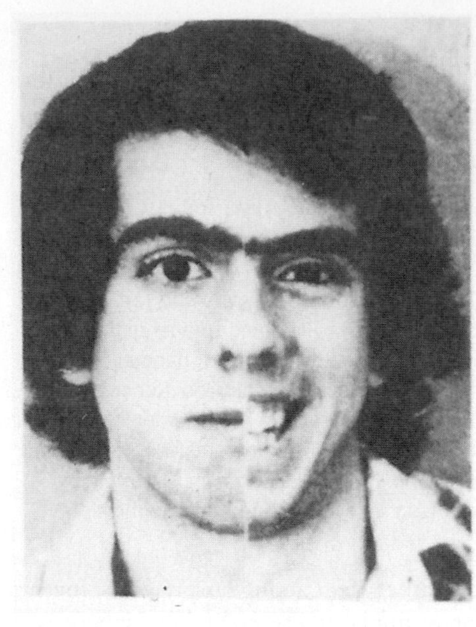
(b)

FIGURE 13.7 Half of a smiling face combined with half of a neutral face
Which looks happier to you—(a) the one with a smile on your left or (b) the one with a smile on your right? Your answer suggests which hemisphere of your brain is dominant for interpreting emotional expressions. *Source:* Reprinted from Brain and Cognition, 2/4, Levy, J., Heller, W., Banich, M.T., Burton, L.A., "Asymmetry of perception in free viewing of chimeric faces", pp. 404-19, 1983, with permission from Elsevier.

Jerre Levy

Jerre Levy

Despite the quite amazing progress of the last half century in neuroscientific understanding, we are still, in my view, as distant now as ever in knowing what questions to ask about how and why brains make minds. It is simply evading the issue to say, as some philosophers do, that our mental experiences are just the inside view of the stuff we measure on the outside. Why is the inside view so utterly different from our external measurements? Even if we specified all the critical spatiotemporal neural dynamics that were necessary and sufficient for a given mental experience, this would not tell us why those dynamics give rise to any experience at all. . . . Nature will answer if we ask the right questions. (Levy, personal communication)

In one fascinating study, people watched videotapes of 10 people. All 10 described themselves honestly during one speech and dishonestly during another. The task of the observers was to guess which of the two interviews was the honest one. The task is more difficult than it might sound, and most people are no more correct than chance (50 percent). The only group that performed best was a group of people with left-hemisphere brain damage (Etcoff, Ekman, Magee, & Frank, 2000). They got only 60 percent correct—not great, but at least better than chance. People with an intact left hemisphere relied on the left hemisphere's analysis of what people were saying. Those with left-hemisphere damage relied on the right hemisphere's more intuitive reactions to emotional expressions.

In another study, 11 patients went through a procedure in which one hemisphere at a time was anesthetized by drug injection into one of the carotid arteries, which provide blood to the head. (This procedure, called the Wada procedure, is sometimes used before certain kinds of brain surgery.) All 11 patients had left-hemisphere language, so they could not be interviewed with the left hemisphere inactivated. When they were tested with the right hemisphere inactivated, something fascinating happened: They could still describe any of the sad, frightening, or irritating events they had experienced in life, but they remembered only the facts, not the emotion. One patient remembered a car wreck, another remembered visiting his mother while she was dying, and another remembered a time his wife threatened to kill him. But they denied they had felt any significant fear, sadness, or anger. When they described the same events with both hemispheres active, they remembered strong emotions. So evidently, when the right hemisphere is inactive, people do not experience strong emotions and do not even remember feeling them (Ross, Homan, & Buck, 1994).

Hemispheric Specializations in Intact Brains

Even in people without brain damage, careful testing demonstrates differences between the hemispheres. Suppose you smell something with just one nostril, so the information goes primarily to one hemisphere (in this case, the ipsilateral one). Further suppose that it's an unfamiliar odor that you cannot name. Twelve seconds later you smell something again with

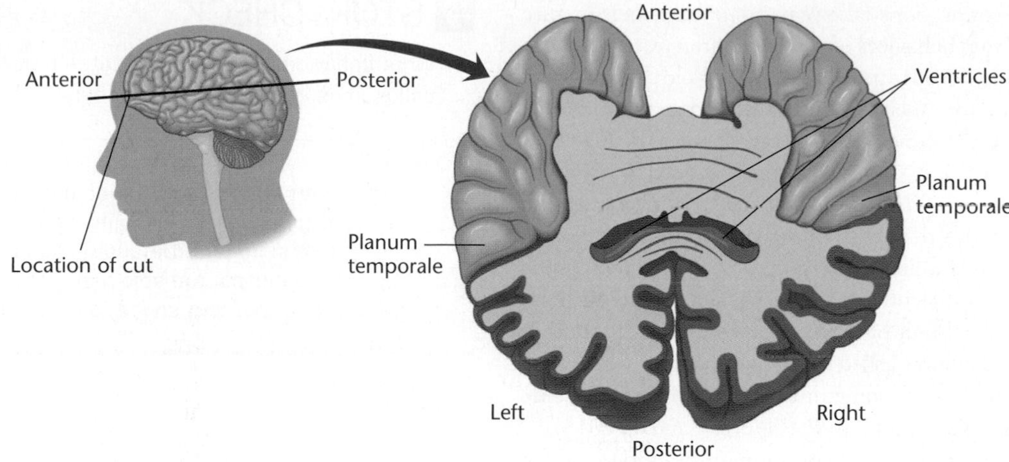

FIGURE 13.8 Horizontal section through a human brain
This cut, just above the surface of the temporal lobe, shows the planum temporale, an area critical for speech comprehension. It is larger in the left hemisphere than in the right hemisphere. *Source:* From "Human brain: Left-right asymmetries in temporal speech region," by N. Geschwind and W. Levitsky, 1968, *Science, 161,* pp. 186–187. Copyright © 1968 by AAAS and N. Geschwind. Reprinted with permission.

either the same nostril or the other one, and you have to say whether it is the same as the previous smell. You will be more accurate if you smelled the two substances with the same nostril, and therefore the same hemisphere (Yeshurun, Dudai, & Sobel, 2008). (Yes, you're right, this is the kind of thing that seldom happens in everyday life.)

Here is something you can try yourself: Tap with your right hand as many times as you can in a short period of time. Rest and repeat with your left hand. Then repeat with each hand while talking. The Online Try It Yourself activity "Hemisphere Control" will keep track of your totals. For most right-handers and many left-handers, talking decreases the tapping rate with the right hand more than with the left hand (Kinsbourne & McMurray, 1975). Evidently, it is more difficult to do two things at once when both activities depend on the same hemisphere.

STOP & CHECK

5. Which hemisphere is dominant for the following in most people: speech, emotional inflection of speech, interpreting other people's emotional expressions, spatial relationships?

ANSWER

5. The left hemisphere is dominant for speech. The right hemisphere is dominant for the other items listed.

Development of Lateralization and Handedness

Because most people's language depends primarily on the left hemisphere, it is natural to ask whether the hemispheres differ anatomically. If so, do they differ before speech develops? How does handedness relate to hemispheric dominance for speech?

Anatomical Differences between the Hemispheres

Norman Geschwind and Walter Levitsky (1968) found that one section of the temporal cortex, called the **planum temporale** (PLAY-num tem-poh-RAH-lee), is larger in the left hemisphere for 65 percent of people (see Figure 13.8). Sandra Witelson and Wazir Pallie (1973) examined the brains of infants who died before age 3 months and found that the left planum temporale was larger in 12 of 14. Later researchers demonstrated differences even in preterm infants (Hervé, Zago, Petit, Mazoyer, & Tzourio-Mazoyer, 2013). So the hemispheres differ from the start.

Smaller but still significant differences are found between left and right hemispheres of chimpanzees, bonobos, and gorillas (Hopkins, 2006). Chimpanzees with a larger left than right planum temporale generally show a preference for using their right hand, as most humans do (Hopkins, Russell, & Cantalupo, 2007). Evidently, the specialization we see in the human brain built on specializations already present in our apelike ancestors of long ago.

Maturation of the Corpus Callosum

The corpus callosum gradually grows and thickens as myelin increases around certain axons during childhood and adolescence (Luders, Thompson, & Toga, 2010). The corpus callosum also matures by discarding many axons. At an early stage, the brain generates far more axons than it will have at maturity (Ivy & Killackey, 1981; Killackey & Chalupa, 1986). The reason is that any two neurons connected by the corpus callosum need to have corresponding functions. A neuron in the left hemisphere that responds to light in the center of the fovea should be connected to a right-hemisphere neuron that responds to light in the same location. During early embryonic development, the genes cannot specify exactly where those two neurons will be. Therefore, many connections form across the corpus callosum, but only those axons that connect cells with similar functions survive (Innocenti & Caminiti, 1980).

Because the connections take years to develop their mature adult pattern, certain behaviors of young children resemble those of split-brain adults. In one study, 3- and 5-year-old children were asked to feel two fabrics, either with one hand at two times or with two hands at the same time, and say whether the materials felt the same or different. The 5-year-olds did equally well with one hand or with two. The 3-year-olds made 90 percent more errors with two hands than with one (Galin, Johnstone, Nakell, & Herron, 1979). The likely interpretation is that the corpus callosum matures sufficiently between ages 3 and 5 to facilitate the comparison of stimuli between the two hands. In another study, when experimenters asked children to point to where they had felt a touch, 4-year-olds sometimes pointed to the wrong side of the body (Yoshioka, Dillon, Beck, Rapp, & Landau, 2013).

Other kinds of tasks show continuing maturation of the corpus callosum in 5- and 6-year-olds. Did you ever play with an Etch A Sketch toy? You can rotate two wheels, one with each hand. One wheel moves a line up or down, and the other moves it left or right. Five- and 6-year-olds have great trouble with this toy, partly because their corpus callosum is not mature enough to integrate the actions of the two hands. In contrast, consider the task of tapping keys with one hand or two whenever a stimulus appears on the screen. Adults and older children are slower to respond with two hands than with one, presumably because the message to one hand interferes with the message to the other hand. Children younger than 6 years respond just as fast with two hands as with one, again suggesting that they do not yet have a mature corpus callosum (Franz & Fahey, 2007).

© Judith Collins/Alamy Limited

STOP&CHECK

6. What behavioral evidence indicates that the corpus callosum is immature in 3-year-olds?

ANSWER

6. When asked to compare fabrics that they feel with one hand or two, 3-year-olds are much more accurate with one hand. The interpretation is that immaturity of the corpus callosum makes it difficult for these children to compare input from the two sides of the body.

Avoiding Overstatements

The research on left-brain/right-brain differences is exciting, but it sometimes leads to unscientific assertions. Occasionally, you may hear a person say something like, "I don't do well in science because it is a left-brain subject and I am a right-brain person." That kind of statement is based on two reasonable premises and a doubtful one. The scientific ideas are that (1) the hemispheres are specialized for different functions, and (2) certain tasks evoke greater activity in one hemisphere or the other. The doubtful premise is that any individual habitually relies mostly on one hemisphere.

What evidence do you suppose someone has for believing, "I am a right-brain person"? Did he or she undergo an MRI or PET scan to determine which hemisphere was larger or more active? Not likely. Generally, when people say, "I am right-brained," their only evidence is that they perform well on creative tasks or poorly on logical tasks. (Saying, "I am right-brained" sometimes implies that *because* I do poorly on logical tasks, *therefore,* I am creative. Unfortunately, illogical is not the same as creative.) In fact, most tasks, especially difficult ones, require cooperation by both hemispheres.

MODULE 13.1 ■ IN CLOSING

One Brain, Two Hemispheres

Imagine you are a split-brain person. Someone asks you—that is, your left hemisphere, your talking side—a question to which you honestly reply that you do not know. Meanwhile, your left hand points to the correct answer. It sounds like an unsettling experience.

Now imagine life from the standpoint of that right hemisphere. You sit there mute, while that other hemisphere is jabbering away. Sometimes, you disagree with what that hemisphere is saying or wish it would just shut up. This must be an unsettling experience, too.

Do split-brain people really have two minds, two consciousnesses? At times, they seem to. The left hemisphere never says it "misses" its other half. We cannot get into someone else's head to know what it is like, but it is tempting to try to imagine.

Summary

1. The corpus callosum is a set of axons connecting the two hemispheres of the brain. **424**
2. The left hemisphere controls speech in most people, and each hemisphere controls mostly the hand on the opposite side, sees the opposite side of the world, and feels the opposite side of the body. **424**
3. In humans, the left visual field projects onto the right half of each retina, which sends axons to the right hemisphere. The right visual field projects onto the left half of each retina, which sends axons to the left hemisphere. **425**
4. After damage to the corpus callosum, each hemisphere can point or gesture to answer questions about the information that reaches it directly. However, because the left hemisphere controls speech in most people, only the left hemisphere of a split-brain person can give vocal answers about what it knows. **426**
5. Although the two hemispheres of a split-brain person are sometimes in conflict, they find ways to cooperate and cue each other. **428**
6. In split-brain people, the right hemisphere sometimes causes actions because of something the left hemisphere did not see. In such cases, the left hemisphere invents a logical-sounding explanation, even if it is, in fact, incorrect. **428**
7. The right hemisphere attends mostly to overall patterns in contrast to the left hemisphere, which is better for details. Also the right hemisphere is dominant for understanding and producing the emotional inflections of speech and for interpreting other people's emotional expressions. **429**
8. Young children have some trouble comparing information from the left and right hands because the corpus callosum is not fully mature. **431**

Key Terms

Terms are defined in the module on the page number indicated. They're also presented in alphabetical order with definitions in the book's Subject Index/Glossary. Interactive flash cards, audio reviews, and crossword puzzles are among the online resources available to help you learn these terms and the concepts they represent.

corpus callosum **424**
epilepsy **426**
focus **426**
interpreter **429**
lateralization **424**
optic chiasm **425**
planum temporale **431**
split-brain people **426**
visual field **425**

MODULE 13.1 End of Module Quiz

1. In humans, light from the right visual field strikes the _____ half of each retina, which sends its axons to the _____ hemisphere of the brain.

a. left . . . left
b. left . . . right
c. right . . . left
d. right . . . right

2. At the human optic chiasm, which axons cross to the opposite hemisphere?

a. Those from the nasal (inside) half of each retina.
b. Those from the temporal (outside) half of each retina.
c. Those from the center of each retina.
d. All the axons from each retina.

3. Under what circumstances, if any, can a split-brain person name an object?

a. After feeling it with the left hand
b. After feeling it with the right hand
c. Only after feeling it with both hands
d. Under no circumstances

4. After a split-brain person sees something in the left visual field, how can he or she identify the object, if at all?

a. By describing it in words
b. By pointing to it with the left hand
c. By pointing to it with the right hand
d. Not at all

5. When the right hemisphere reacts to something it sees, causing a behavior that the left hemisphere can feel, how does the left hemisphere react?
   a. It expresses surprise.
   b. It pretends the action did not occur.
   c. It tries to stop the action or do the opposite.
   d. It invents a logical-sounding explanation.

6. Of the following, which can people with left-hemisphere damage do better than the average for other people?
   a. Understand and describe a short story.
   b. Learn to speak a foreign language.
   c. Calculate statistics such as means and medians.
   d. Listen to people and guess whether they are lying.

7. At what age do anatomical differences emerge between the left and right hemispheres?
   a. In infancy
   b. When a child starts learning to talk
   c. In early adolescence
   d. In early adulthood

8. In one study, 3-year-old children were asked to feel fabrics and say whether they were the same or different. What evidence indicated that the corpus callosum was immature in these children?
   a. They made more errors at the start of a session than toward the end.
   b. They made more errors toward the end of a session than at the start.
   c. They made more errors when feeling with two hands than with one.
   d. They made more errors when feeling with one hand than with two.

ANSWERS:
1a, 2a, 3b, 4b, 5d, 6d, 7a, 8c.

Evolution and Physiology of Language

You spent some time as a child hearing, watching, and reading stories about animals—the three pigs, the three bears, various Disney and Warner Brothers cartoons, and others. In nearly all of them, the animals talked, right? In real life, *why don't they?*

Nonhuman animals do communicate through visual, auditory, tactile, or chemical (pheromonal) displays, but those signals don't have much flexibility. A monkey might have one alarm call to indicate eagle in the air and another for snake on the ground, but it has no way to indicate eagle on the ground or snake in the tree (Cheney & Seyfarth, 2005). Human language stands out from other forms of communication because of its **productivity,** its ability to improvise new combinations of signals to represent new ideas.

We probably didn't evolve language out of nothing. Evolution almost always develops something by modifying a previous structure. Bat wings are modified arms, porcupine quills are modified hairs, and skunk stench is modified sweat gland secretion. If our language evolved from some ability our ancient apelike ancestors had, what was it?

Nonhuman Precursors of Language

Our nearest living relatives, chimpanzees and other great apes, do not talk. But could they learn to speak or understand language, at least a little, if we taught them?

Common Chimpanzees

Several early attempts to teach chimpanzees to talk failed. One reason is that humans vocalize while breathing out, whereas chimpanzees vocalize while breathing in. Go ahead, try to say something while inhaling. You'll probably want to try it in private so that other people don't laugh at you.

However, chimpanzees in the wild do communicate with gestures, and investigators achieved better results by teaching them American Sign Language or other visual systems (B. T. Gardner & Gardner, 1975; Premack & Premack, 1972) (see Figure 13.9). In one version, chimps learned to press keys bearing symbols to type messages on a computer (Rumbaugh, 1977), such as "Please machine give apple" or to another chimpanzee, "Please share your chocolate."

Photo courtesy of Ann Premack

FIGURE 13.9 An attempt to teach chimpanzees language
Researcher Amy Samuels arranges colored chips to tell one of the Premacks' chimps, Elizabeth, "Not Elizabeth banana insert. Elizabeth apple wash."

Is the use of symbols really language? Not everything that we can translate as a series of words is really language. For example, when you insert your ATM card and enter your four-digit PIN, you don't really understand those four digits to mean, "Please machine give money." Similarly, when a chimpanzee presses four symbols on a machine, it may not understand them to mean, "Please machine give apple." The chimps' use of symbols had features that raised doubts about calling it language:

- The chimpanzees seldom used symbols in new, original combinations. That is, their symbol use was short on *productivity*.
- The chimpanzees used their symbols mainly to request, seldom to describe. (Rumbaugh, 1990; Terrace, Petitto, Sanders, & Bever, 1979)

Nevertheless, the chimpanzees showed at least moderate understanding. For example, the chimp Washoe, trained in sign language, usually answered "Who" questions with names, "What" questions with objects, and "Where" questions with places, even when she used the wrong symbol for a name, object, or place (Van Cantfort, Gardner, & Gardner, 1989).

Bonobos

Amid widespread skepticism about chimpanzee language, surprising results emerged from studies of an endangered species, *Pan paniscus,* known as the bonobo. Bonobos' social order resembles humans' in several regards. Males and females form strong, sometimes lasting, personal attachments. They often copulate face to face. The female is sexually responsive on almost any day and not just during her fertile period. The males contribute significantly to infant care. Adults often share food. They stand comfortably on their hind legs. In short, they resemble humans more than other primates do.

FIGURE 13.10 Language tests for Kanzi, a bonobo *(Pan paniscus)*
He listens to questions through earphones and points to answers on a board. The experimenter with him does not hear the questions. *Source:* From Georgia State University's Language Research Center, operated with the Yerkes Primate Center of Emory.

In the mid-1980s, Sue Savage-Rumbaugh, Duane Rumbaugh, and their associates tried to teach a female bonobo named Matata to press symbols that lit when touched. Each symbol represents a word (see Figure 13.10). Although Matata made little progress, her infant son Kanzi learned just by watching her. When given a chance to use the symbol board, he quickly excelled. Later, researchers noticed that Kanzi understood a fair amount of spoken language. For example, whenever anyone said the word *light,* Kanzi would flip the light switch. Kanzi and his younger sister developed language comprehension comparable to that of a typical 2- to 2½-year-old child:

- They understand more than they can produce.
- They follow unfamiliar, unlikely directions such as "Throw your ball in the river" or "Get the tomato in the microwave."
- They use symbols to name and describe objects even when they are not requesting them.
- They request items that they do not see, such as "bubbles" (I want to play with the bubble blower).
- They occasionally use the symbols to describe past events. Kanzi once pressed the symbols "Matata bite" to explain the cut that he had received on his hand an hour earlier.
- They frequently make original, creative requests, such as asking one person to chase another. (Hillix, Rumbaugh, & Savage-Rumbaugh, 2012; Savage-Rumbaugh, 1990; Savage-Rumbaugh, Sevcik, Brakke, & Rumbaugh, 1992; Savage-Rumbaugh et al., 1993)

Why have Kanzi and Mulika developed more impressive skills than other chimpanzees? Perhaps bonobos have more language

Photo courtesy of Duane Rumbaugh

Duane Rumbaugh, Sue Savage-Rumbaugh, and chimpanzee Austin

Chimpanzees and bonobos are outstanding teachers of psychology. They never presume that we, as their students, know a damn thing about who they are. And they certainly aren't impressed with our degrees. Consequently, they are able to teach all manner of important things about what it means to be human and to be ape—that is, if we as students are quiet, listen carefully, and let them tell us as only they can.

potential than common chimpanzees. A second explanation is that Kanzi and Mulika began language training when young. A third reason pertains to the method of training: Learning by observation and imitation (as humans do) promotes better language understanding than the formal training methods of previous studies (Savage-Rumbaugh et al., 1992).

STOP&CHECK

7. What are three likely explanations for why bonobos made more language progress than common chimpanzees?

ANSWER

7. Bonobos may be more predisposed to language than common chimpanzees. The bonobos started training at an earlier age. They learned by imitation instead of formal training techniques.

Nonprimates

What about nonprimate species? Spectacular results have been reported for Alex, an African gray parrot (see Figure 13.11). Parrots are, of course, famous for imitating sounds. Irene Pepperberg was the first to argue that parrots can use sounds meaningfully. She kept Alex in a stimulating environment and taught him by saying a word many times and offering rewards if Alex approximated the same sound. Gradually she moved on to more complex concepts (Pepperberg, 1981). Pepperberg generally used toys. For example, if Alex said "paper," "wood," or "key," she would give him what he asked for. In no case did she reward him with food for saying "paper" or "wood."

In one test, Alex viewed a tray of 12 objects and correctly answered 39 of 48 questions such as "What color is the key?" (answer: "green") and "What object is gray?" (answer: "circle"). Many of his incorrect answers were almost correct. In one case, he was asked the color of the block and he responded with the color of the rock (Pepperberg, 1993). He also answered questions of the form "How many blue keys?" in which he had to count the blue keys among objects of two shapes and two colors (Pepperberg, 1994).

Relying on language is not always helpful. Pepperberg put Alex and three other gray parrots on perches; each had a chain of large plastic links from the perch to an almond on the bottom. (Almonds are favorite foods for parrots.) The parrots untrained in language used their claws to pull up the chain until they reached the almond. Alex and another language-trained parrot repeatedly told the experimenter, "Want nut." When she declined to bring it to them, they gave up (Pepperberg, 2004).

What do we learn from studies of nonhuman language abilities? At a practical level, we gain insights into how best to teach language to those who do not learn it easily, such as people with brain damage or children with autism. At a more theoretical level, these studies indicate that human language evolved from precursors present in other species. These studies also point out the ambiguity of our concept: We cannot decide whether chimpanzees or parrots have language unless we define language more precisely.

How Did Humans Evolve Language?

When the early ancestors of humans first began to evolve language, language must have been a modification of some other capacity. But what? The great apes do make certain sounds, but their communication by sounds is limited and inflexible. An important step toward vocal communication was what

Rick Friedman/Corbis

FIGURE 13.11 Language tests for Alex Alex conversed about objects in simple English—for example, answering, "How many blue?" He received no food rewards.

cognitive psychologists call the **phonological loop**, the ability to hear something and remember it. Compared to other primates, the human brain has stronger connections between the auditory cortex and the prefrontal cortex, enabling much greater auditory memory (Aboitiz, Aboitiz, & García, 2010). Auditory working memory is not sufficient for language, but it is necessary.

Another possibility is that language evolved from communication by gestures (Corballis, 2012). All primates communicate by gestures, including humans. Children begin gesturing in the first year of life, and their ability to communicate by gestures predicts how soon they will develop spoken language (Iverson & Goldin-Meadow, 2005). Most adults also accompany most of their speech with gestures, even when talking on a telephone, when the listener cannot see the gestures.

A variant version of this hypothesis focuses specifically on mouth gestures. Monkeys use several mouth gestures to communicate, including a lip-smacking gesture, which has a rhythm similar to speech. Monkeys are known to watch one another's mouth movements, especially when another is vocalizing, and it is plausible that the combination of sound plus mouth gesture could have been a precursor to spoken language (Ghazanfar, 2013). Humans also watch each other's face during a conversation, when possible, and we do more lip-reading than we realize. Especially in a noisy room, watching the speaker's face facilitates understanding. Even young infants tend to look mostly toward the person whose lip movements synchronize with the sounds (Lickliter & Bahrick, 2000).

With regard to the brain, what changed to make language possible? Most theories fall into two categories: (1) We evolved it as a by-product of overall brain development, or (2) we evolved it as a specialization.

Language: By-product of Intelligence, or Specialized Adaptation?

One view is that humans evolved big brains for some other reason and language developed as an accidental by-product. In its simplest form, this hypothesis faces serious problems. One, of course, is that elephants, whales, and dolphins have larger brains than humans, but no language. But other problems exist even if we focus only on humans.

People with Normal Intelligence but Impaired Language

If language is a product of overall brain size, then anyone with a full-sized brain and normal overall intelligence should have normal language. However, not all do. In one family, 16 of 30 people over three generations show severe language deficits despite normal intelligence in other regards. Because of a particular dominant gene, the affected people have serious troubles in pronunciation and many other aspects of language (Fisher, Vargha-Khadem, Watkins, Monaco, & Pembrey, 1998; Gopnik & Crago, 1991; Lai, Fisher, Hurst, Vargha-Khadem, & Monaco, 2001). They have trouble with even simple grammatical rules, as shown in the following dialogue about making plurals:

Experimenter	**Respondent**
This is a wug; these are . . .	How should I know? *[Later]* These are wug.
This is a zat; these are . . .	These are zacko.
This is a sas; these are . . .	These are sasss. *[Not sasses]*

In another test, experimenters presented sentences and asked whether each sentence was correct and, if not, how to improve it. They made many errors and odd corrections. For example:

Original Item	**Attempted Correction**
The boy eats three cookie.	The boys eat four cookie.

Despite the language difficulties, these people behave normally and intelligently in most regards. Evidently, language requires more than just a large brain and overall intelligence.

People with Relatively Spared Language but Low Overall Intelligence

What about the reverse? Could someone with overall intellectual impairment, with an IQ of 50 to 60, have good language? Psychologists would have answered "no," until they discovered **Williams syndrome**, affecting about 1 person in 20,000. Affected people are poor at tasks related to numbers, visuomotor skills (e.g., copying a drawing), and spatial perception (e.g., finding their way home). When asked to estimate the length of a bus, three people with Williams syndrome answered "30 inches," "3 inches or 100 inches maybe," and "2 inches, 10 feet" (Bellugi, Lichtenberger, Jones, Lai, & St. George, 2000). They have frequent lapses of attention, poor planning, and difficulty inhibiting inappropriate responses (Greer, Riby, Hamilton, &

AP Photo/The Hutchinson News, Lindsey Bauman

People with Williams syndrome have a characteristic appearance, as well as a special set of behavioral strengths and weaknesses.

Riby, 2013). Throughout life, they require constant supervision and cannot hold even simple jobs. Nevertheless, many of them speak grammatically and fluently. Many also show good abilities at music, such as the ability to clap a complex rhythm and memorize songs (Levitin & Bellugi, 1998), and the ability to interpret facial expressions, such as relaxed or worried, serious or playful, flirtatious or uninterested (Tager-Flusberg, Boshart, & Baron-Cohen, 1998).

The cause of Williams syndrome is a deletion of several genes from chromosome 7 (Korenberg et al., 2000), leading to decreased gray matter, especially in visual processing areas (Kippenhan et al., 2005; Meyer-Lindenberg et al., 2004; Reiss et al., 2004).

Although their language abilities develop more slowly than average, some individuals have remarkably good language, considering their impairments in other regards. Figure 13.12 shows the result when a young woman with Williams syndrome was asked to draw an elephant and describe it. Contrast her almost poetic description to the unrecognizable drawing.

Let's not overstate the case. People with Williams syndrome do not handle language perfectly (Martens, Wilson, & Reutens, 2008; Meyer-Lindenberg, Mervis, & Berman, 2006). Their grammar is awkward, like that of someone who learned a second language late in life (Clahsen & Almazen, 1998; Karmiloff-Smith et al., 1998). They often use fancy words when a common word would work better, such as "I have to evacuate the glass" instead of "empty" or "pour out" the glass (Bellugi et al., 2000). Still, observations of Williams syndrome indicate that language is not simply a by-product of overall intelligence.

Language as a Specialization

If language is not just a by-product of overall intelligence, it must have evolved as a specialized brain mechanism. Noam Chomsky (1980) and Steven Pinker (1994) proposed that humans have a **language acquisition device,** a built-in mechanism for acquiring language. Most children develop language so quickly and easily that it seems they must have been biologically prepared for this learning. Also, deaf children quickly learn sign language, and if no one teaches them a sign language, they invent one and teach it to one another (Goldin-Meadow, McNeill, & Singleton, 1996; Goldin-Meadow & Mylander, 1998).

Researchers have begun to explore the genetic basis of this preparation for language. Remember that family whose members have such trouble with pronunciation and basic grammar? Their problem stems from a mutation in a gene designated *FOXP2*, which regulates a protein that promotes synapse formation in the cerebral cortex (Lai et al., 2001; Sia, Clem, & Huganir, 2013). Although both humans and chimpanzees have that gene, it differs in two places, resulting in proteins with different amino acids at two sites. That gene produces not only a multitude of effects, partly on brain development, but also on structures of the jaw and throat that are important for speech (Konopka et al., 2009). If researchers altered this gene in chimpanzees, what would happen? Language depends on more than just one gene, but the result would be interesting. That study hasn't been done, but researchers did alter the *FOXP2* gene in mice. The effects included changes in vocalizations and increased dendritic branching and synaptic plasticity in the basal ganglia (Enard et al., 2009).

For the moment, let's move beyond how humans evolved language and ask *why* we did. That is, why our species and not others? The fossil record cannot answer a question like this, and we are left with speculations. One is that language relates to the long period of dependency in childhood. Social interactions among people, including those between parents and children, favored the evolution of language. In that case, overall intelligence may be a by-product of language development more than language is a by-product of intelligence (Deacon, 1992, 1997).

STOP & CHECK

8. What evidence argues against the hypothesis that language evolution depended simply on the overall evolution of brain and intelligence?

9. Describe tasks that people with Williams syndrome do poorly and those that they do well.

ANSWERS

8. Some people have normal brain size but very poor language. Also, some people are mentally retarded but nevertheless develop nearly normal language. 9. Poor: self-care skills, attention, planning, numbers, visual-motor skills, and spatial perception. Relatively good: language, interpretation of facial expressions, some aspects of music.

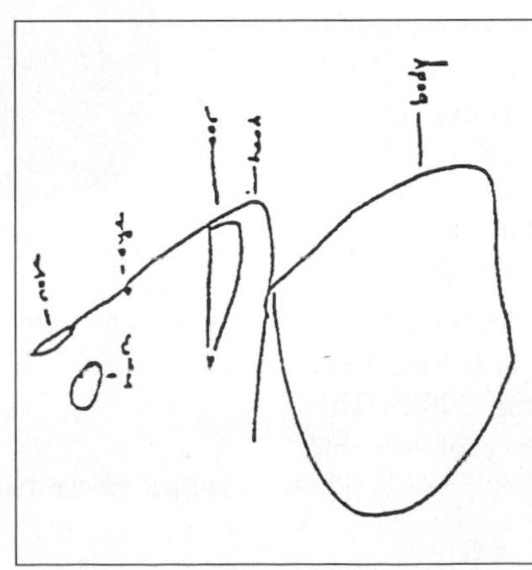

And what an elephant is, it is one of the animals. And what the elephant does, it lives in the jungle. It can also live in the zoo. And what it has, it has long gray ears, fan ears, ears that can blow in the wind. It has a long trunk that can pick up grass, or pick up hay . . . If they're in a bad mood it can be terrible . . . If the elephant gets mad it could stomp; it could charge, like a bull can charge. They have long big tusks. They can damage a car . . . it could be dangerous. When they're in a pinch, when they're in a bad mood it can be terrible. You don't want an elephant as a pet. You want a cat or a dog or a bird . . .

FIGURE 13.12 A young woman with Williams syndrome draws and describes an elephant

The investigator added the labels on the drawing based on what the woman said she was drawing. *Source:* Republished with permission of Taylor & Francis, from "Williams Syndrome: An Unusual Neuropsychological Profile," by U. Bellugi, P. O. Wang, and T. L. Jernigan, S. H. Broman and J. Grafman, Eds., *Atypical Cognitive Deficits in Developmental Disorders*. Copyright © 1994 Lawrence Erlbaum; permission conveyed through Copyright Clearance Center, Inc.

A Sensitive Period for Language Learning

If humans are specially adapted to learn language, perhaps we are adapted to learn best during a sensitive period early in life, just as sparrows learn their song best during an early period. One way to test this hypothesis is to see whether people learn a second language best if they start young. The consistent result is that adults are better than children at memorizing the vocabulary of a second language, but children have a great advantage on learning the pronunciation and grammar. There is no sharp cutoff for learning a second language; starting at age 2 is better than 4, 4 is better than 6, and 13 is better than 16 (Hakuta, Bialystok, & Wiley, 2003; Harley & Wang, 1997; Weber-Fox & Neville, 1996). However, people who start learning a second language beyond age 12 or so almost never reach the level of a true native speaker (Abrahamsson & Hyltenstam, 2009). Also, learning a second language from the start is very different from learning one later. The first module of this chapter noted that the left hemisphere is dominant for language. Many people guess that a bilingual person might rely on the left hemisphere for one language and the right hemisphere for the other. That guess is wrong. People who grow up in a bilingual home, speaking two languages from the start, show substantial bilateral activity during speech, for both languages (Peng & Wang, 2011). People who learn a second language after age 6 or so activate just the left hemisphere for both languages (Hull & Vaid, 2007; Peng & Wang, 2011). In bilingual people, especially those who learned both languages early, naming pictures or reading words aloud activates a larger area of the brain than the same activities do for other people. That is, being bilingual takes extra effort to find the right word and inhibit the incorrect word (Jones et al., 2012). However, don't feel sorry for bilinguals. In addition to the benefit of being able to communicate with more people, they learn to control their attention better than average, and they can shift their attention back and forth from one task to another with greater ease than most other people (Gold, Kim, Johnson, Kryscio, & Smith, 2013).

Another way to test the sensitive-period idea is to study people who learned no language during early childhood. The clearest data come from studies of deaf children whose parents concentrated unsuccessfully on teaching them spoken language and lip-reading, and then eventually gave up on this effort and introduced sign language. Children who began sign language while still young learned much better than those who started later (Harley & Wang, 1997). A child who learns a spoken language early can learn sign language later, and a deaf child who learns sign language early can learn a spoken language later (except for poor pronunciation), but a child who learns no language while young is permanently impaired at learning any kind of language (Mayberry, Lock, & Kazmi, 2002). This observation strongly supports the importance of learning language in early childhood.

STOP & CHECK

10. What is the strongest evidence in favor of a sensitive period for language learning?

ANSWER

10. Deaf children who are not exposed to sign language until later in life (and who did not learn spoken language either while they were young) do not become proficient at it.

Brain Damage and Language

Another way to study specializations for language is to examine the role of various brain areas. Much of our knowledge has come from studies of people with brain damage.

Broca's Aphasia (Nonfluent Aphasia)

In 1861, the French surgeon Paul Broca treated the gangrene of a patient who had been mute for 30 years. When the man died 5 days later, Broca did an autopsy and found a lesion in the left frontal cortex. Over the next few years, Broca examined the brains of additional patients with **aphasia** (language impairment). In nearly all cases, he found damage (usually stroke-related) that included this same area, which is now known as **Broca's area** (see Figure 13.13). When brain damage impairs language production, we call it **Broca's aphasia,** or **nonfluent aphasia**, regardless of the exact location of damage. Broca published his results in 1865, slightly later than reports by other French physicians, Marc and Gustave Dax, who also pointed to the left hemisphere as the seat of language abilities (Finger & Roe, 1996). Broca received the credit, however, because his description was more detailed and more convincing.

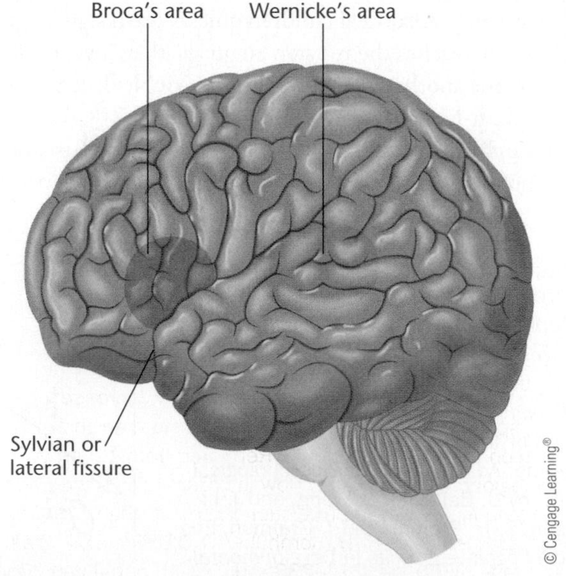

FIGURE 13.13 Two areas important for language

This discovery, the first demonstration of the function of a particular brain area, paved the way for modern neurology.

Modern methods have confirmed that Broca's area contributes to language production, and research has identified regions within Broca's area that contribute to language in distinct ways (Poeppel, Emmorey, Hickok, & Pylkkänen, 2012; Sahin, Pinker, Cash, Schomer, & Halgren, 2009). Nevertheless, damage limited to Broca's area produces only minor or brief language impairment. Speaking activates much of the brain, mostly in the left hemisphere, and not just Broca's area (Wallesch, Henriksen, Kornhuber, & Paulson, 1985) (see Figure 13.14). Every area that contributes to language contributes to other behaviors as well, and the role of each area can change over time, especially in response to damage of another area (Blumstein & Amso, 2013). Subcortical areas are important, too. Substantial aphasia can result from damage to areas of the basal ganglia that lie interior to Broca's area of the cortex (Damasio, Damasio, Rizzo, Varney, & Gersh, 1982; Fyndanis, 2012; Naeser et al., 1982). In fact, most cases of Broca's aphasia related to combined damage to parts of the cortex, thalamus, and basal ganglia.

Impaired Language Production

People with Broca's aphasia are slow and awkward with all forms of language communication, including speaking, writing, and gesturing, including the sign language of the deaf (Cicone, Wapner, Foldi, Zurif, & Gardner, 1979; Neville et al., 1998; Petitto et al., 2000). Broca's aphasia relates to language, not just the vocal muscles.

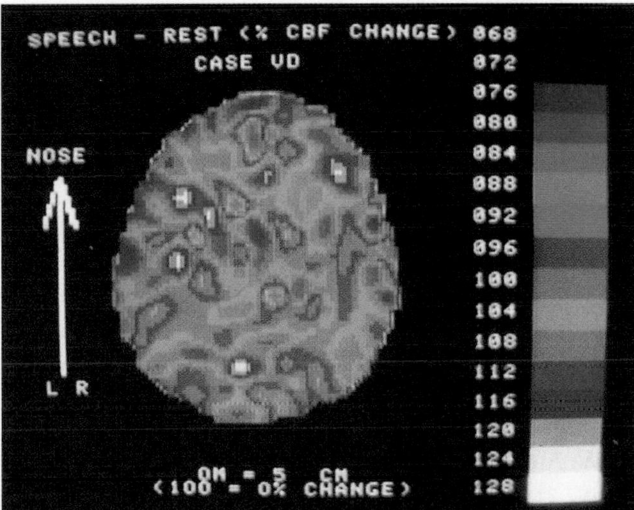

FIGURE 13.14 Brain activity during speech for a normal adult This study inferred brain activity from patterns of blood flow. Red indicates the highest level of activity, followed by yellow, green, and blue. The areas in red showed the greatest increase in activity during speech. Note the increased activity in many brain areas, especially on the left side. *Source:* Reprinted from "Observations on regional cerebral blood flow in cortical and subcortical structures during language production in normal man," by C.W. Wallesch, L. Henriksen, H. H. Kornhuber, & O.B. Paulson, *Brain and Language, 25*(2), pp. 224–233, 1985, with permission from Elsevier.

When people with Broca's aphasia speak, their speech is meaningful but sparse. For example, they might say, "Weather overcast" instead of "The weather is overcast." They generally omit pronouns, prepositions, conjunctions, auxiliary (helping) verbs, quantifiers, and tense and number endings. At least, that is the pattern for people speaking English. People with aphasia use more word endings if they speak German, Italian, or other languages in which word endings are more essential than they are in English (Blackwell & Bates, 1995). Prepositions, conjunctions, helping verbs, and so forth are known as the *closed class* of grammatical forms because a language rarely adds new prepositions, conjunctions, and the like. In contrast, new nouns and verbs (the *open class*) enter a language frequently. People with Broca's aphasia seldom use the closed-class words. They find it difficult or impossible to repeat a phrase such as "No ifs, ands, or buts." However, patients who cannot read aloud "To be or not to be" can read "Two bee oar knot two bee" (H. Gardner & Zurif, 1975). Clearly, the trouble is with the word meanings, not just pronunciation.

Why do people with Broca's aphasia omit the grammatical words and endings? Perhaps they have suffered damage to a "grammar area" in the brain, but here is another possibility: When speaking is a struggle, people leave out the weakest elements. Many people who are in pain speak as if they have Broca's aphasia (Dick et al., 2001).

Problems in Comprehending Grammatical Words and Devices

People with Broca's aphasia understand most speech, except when the meaning depends on prepositions, word endings, or complex grammar—the same items that they omit when speaking. If they hear a sentence with complex grammar, such as "The girl that the boy is chasing is tall," they know that someone is tall and someone is chasing, but they don't know which is which (Zurif, 1980). However, most English sentences are comprehensible even without the prepositions and conjunctions. You can demonstrate this for yourself by taking a paragraph and deleting its prepositions, conjunctions, articles, helping verbs, pronouns, and word endings to see how it might appear to someone with Broca's aphasia. Here is an example, taken from earlier in this section. Note how understandable it is despite the deletions:

> ~~In~~ 1861, ~~the~~ French surgeon Paul Broca treat~~ed~~ ~~the~~ gangrene ~~of a~~ patient ~~who had been~~ mute ~~for~~ 30 years. ~~When the~~ man die~~d~~ 5 day~~s~~ later, Broca ~~did an~~ autopsy ~~and~~ found ~~a~~ lesion ~~in the~~ left frontal cortex. ~~Over the~~ next few year~~s~~, Broca examine~~d~~ ~~the~~ brain~~s~~ ~~of~~ addition~~al~~ patient~~s~~ ~~with~~ aphasia (language impairment). ~~In~~ nearly all cases, ~~he~~ found damage (usual~~ly~~ stroke-relat~~ed~~) ~~that~~ include~~d~~ ~~this~~ same area, ~~which is~~ now know~~n~~ ~~as~~ Broca~~'s~~ area.

Still, people with Broca's aphasia have not totally lost their knowledge of grammar. For example, they generally recognize that something is wrong with the sentence "He written has songs," even if they cannot say how to improve it (Wulfeck & Bates, 1991). In many ways, their comprehension resembles that of intact people who are distracted. If you listen to someone speaking rapidly with a heavy accent in a noisy room, while you are trying to do something else at the same time, you catch bits and pieces of what the speaker says and try to guess the rest. Even when we hear a sentence clearly, we sometimes ignore the grammar. If you hear "The dog was bitten by the man," you might assume it was the dog that did the biting (Ferreira, Bailey, & Ferraro, 2002). Patients with Broca's aphasia just have to rely on inferences more often than others do.

STOP&CHECK

11. What kind of word are Broca's patients least likely to use?

12. What kind of word do Broca's patients have the most trouble understanding?

ANSWERS

11. They have the greatest trouble with "closed-class" words that are meaningful only in the context of a sentence, such as prepositions, conjunctions, and helping verbs. **12.** They have the most trouble understanding the same kind of words they have trouble producing—the closed-class words.

Wernicke's Aphasia (Fluent Aphasia)

In 1874, Carl Wernicke (pronounced WER-nih-kee by most English speakers, although the German pronunciation is VAYR-nih-keh), a 26-year-old junior assistant in a German hospital, discovered that damage in part of the left temporal cortex produced a different kind of language impairment. Although patients could speak and write, their language comprehension was poor. Damage in and around **Wernicke's area** (see Figure 13.13), located near the auditory cortex, produces **Wernicke's aphasia,** characterized by poor language comprehension and impaired ability to remember the names of objects. It is also known as **fluent aphasia** because the person can still speak smoothly. As with Broca's aphasia, the symptoms and brain damage vary, and the damage generally extends into the thalamus or basal ganglia. We use the term *Wernicke's aphasia,* or *fluent aphasia,* to describe a certain pattern of behavior, independent of the location of damage.

The typical characteristics of Wernicke's aphasia are as follows:

1. *Articulate speech.* In contrast to people with Broca's aphasia, those with Wernicke's aphasia speak fluently, except when pausing to try to think of the name of something.
2. *Difficulty finding the right word.* People with Wernicke's aphasia have **anomia** (ay-NOME-ee-uh), difficulty recalling the names of objects. They make up names (e.g., "thingamajig"), substitute one name for another, and use roundabout expressions such as "the thing that we used to do with the thing that was like the other one." When they do manage to find some of the right words, they often arrange them improperly, such as, "The Astros listened to the radio tonight" (instead of "I listened to the Astros on the radio tonight") (R. C. Martin & Blossom-Stach, 1986).
3. *Poor language comprehension.* People with Wernicke's aphasia have trouble understanding speech, writing, and sign language (Petitto et al., 2000). One study examined patients who had trouble understanding speech immediately after a stroke. Their recovery of speech comprehension correlated with increased blood flow to Wernicke's area (Hillis et al., 2006). Impaired comprehension relates closely to difficulty remembering the names of objects. Although many sentences are clear enough without the prepositions, word endings, and grammar that confuse Broca's aphasics, few sentences make sense without nouns and verbs (which trouble Wernicke's patients).

The following conversation is between a woman with Wernicke's aphasia and a speech therapist trying to teach her the names of some objects (the Duke University Department of Speech Pathology and Audiology provided this dialogue):

Therapist: *(Holding a picture of an apron)* Can you name that one?

Woman: Um . . . you see I can't, I can I can barely do; he would give me sort of umm . . .

T: A clue?

W: That's right . . . just a like, just a . . .

T: You mean, like, "You wear that when you wash dishes or when you cook a meal . . ."?

W: Yeah, something like that.

T: Okay, and what is it? You wear it around your waist, and you cook . . .

W: Cook. Umm, umm, see I can't remember.

T: It's an apron.

W: Apron, apron, that's it, apron.

T: *(Holding another picture)* That you wear when you're getting ready for bed after a shower.

W: Oh, I think that he put under different, something different. We had something, you know, umm, you know.

T: A different way of doing it?

W: No, umm . . . umm . . . *(Pause)*

T: It's actually a bathrobe.

W: Bathrobe. Uh, we didn't call it that, we called it something else.

T: Smoking jacket?

TABLE 13.1 | Broca's Aphasia and Wernicke's Aphasia

Type	Pronunciation	Content of Speech	Comprehension
Broca's aphasia	Poor	Mostly nouns and verbs; omits prepositions and other grammatical connectives	Impaired if the meaning depends on complex grammar
Wernicke's aphasia	Unimpaired	Grammatical but often nonsensical; has trouble finding the right word, especially names of objects	Seriously impaired

W: No, I think we called it, uh . . .

T: Lounging . . .?

W: No, no, something, in fact, we called it just . . . *(Pause)*

T: Robe?

W: Robe. Or something like that.

The patient still knows the names of objects and recognizes them when she hears them; she just has trouble finding them for herself. In some ways, her speech resembles that of a student called upon to speak in a foreign language class after poorly studying the vocabulary list.

Although Wernicke's area and surrounding areas are important, language comprehension also depends on the connections to other brain areas. For example, reading the word *lick* activates not only Wernicke's area but also the part of the motor cortex responsible for tongue movements. Reading *throw* activates the part of the premotor cortex controlling hand movements (Willems, Hagoort, & Casasanto, 2010). Apparently when you think about an action word, you imagine doing it. Table 13.1 contrasts Broca's aphasia and Wernicke's aphasia.

STOP&CHECK

13. Describe the speech production of people with Wernicke's aphasia.

14. Describe the speech comprehension of people with Wernicke's aphasia.

ANSWERS

13. People with Wernicke's aphasia speak fluently and grammatically but omit most nouns and verbs and therefore make little sense. **14.** People with Wernicke's aphasia understand little speech.

Music and Language

Language occurs in every human culture, and no other species develops language as we know it. Exactly the same could be said for music. Language and music have many parallels, including the fact that both rely on detecting small changes in sound, and that both can evoke strong emotions. Broca's area is strongly activated when orchestral musicians sight-read music (Sluming, Brooks, Howard, Downes, & Roberts, 2007). People's ability to detect small changes in the pitch of a musical note correlates strongly with their ability to detect small changes in tone of voice (Perrachione, Fedorenko, Vinke, Gibson, & Dilley, 2013). The parallels between language and music are sufficient to suggest that they arose together. That is, whatever evolutionary processes helped us develop language also enabled us to develop music.

Consider some of the parallels (Patel, 2008):

- Trained musicians and music students tend to be better than average at learning a second language.
- In both language and music, we alter the timing and volume to add emphasis or to express emotion.
- English speakers average about 0.5 to 0.7 seconds between one stressed syllable and another in speech and prefer music with about 0.5 to 0.7 seconds between beats.
- Greek and Balkan languages have less regular rhythms than English, and much of the music written by speakers of those languages has irregularly spaced beats.
- English usually stresses the first syllable of a word or phrase, whereas French more often stresses the final syllable. Similarly, French composers more often than English composers make the final note of a phrase longer than the others.
    - English vowels vary in duration more than French vowels do. For example, compare the vowels in *tourist* or *pirate*. English composers, on the average, have more variation in note length from one note to the next.

These similarities and others suggest that we use the language areas of the brain when we compose music, and we prefer music that resembles our language in rhythms and tones (Ross, Choi, & Purves, 2007). You could think of music as an alternative method of communication.

STOP&CHECK

15. In what way do musical compositions vary depending on the language spoken by the composer?

ANSWER

15. Musical compositions tend to follow the same rhythms that are common in the language spoken by the composer.

Dyslexia

Dyslexia is a specific impairment of reading in someone with adequate vision, motivation, and cognitive skills, and educational opportunity. It is more common in boys than girls and linked to several identified genes (Field et al., 2013). Dyslexia is especially common in English because it has so many words with odd spellings. (Consider *phlegm, bivouac, khaki, yacht, choir, physique,* and *gnat.*) However, dyslexia occurs in all languages and always pertains to a difficulty converting symbols into sounds (Ziegler & Goswami, 2005). A study comparing readers of English and Chinese found that normal readers activated somewhat different brain areas, presumably because English letters represent sounds, whereas a Chinese symbol represents a whole syllable or word. However, English-speaking and Chinese-speaking people with dyslexia were remarkably similar in showing decreased activation in several brain areas while reading (Hu, et al., 2010).

As a rule, people with dyslexia are more likely to have a bilaterally symmetrical cerebral cortex, whereas in other people, the planum temporale and certain other areas are larger in the left hemisphere (Galaburda, Sherman, Rosen, Aboitiz, & Geschwind, 1985; Hynd & Semrud-Clikeman, 1989; Jenner, Rosen, & Galaburda, 1999). Several brain areas in the parietal and temporal cortex have less than average gray matter in children with dyslexia, and show less arousal during reading (Hoeft et al., 2006; Gabrieli, 2009). Some of these differences are apparent in children with a family history of dyslexia, before they learn to read (Raschle, Zuk, & Gaab, 2012). However, it is known that learning to read induces changes in the brain (Dehaene et al., 2010), and the brains of 10-year-old dyslexic children resemble in several ways the brains of younger children who are just starting to learn to read (Krafnick, Flowers, Luetje, Napoliello, & Eden, 2014). Therefore, it is likely that when researchers compare the brains of dyslexic readers and normal readers, especially in late childhood or adulthood, some of the differences are causes of poor reading and some are results of less practice at reading.

In the often confusing literature about dyslexia, one point that stands out is that different people have different kinds of reading problems, and no one explanation works for all. Most (but not all) have auditory problems, a smaller number have impaired control of eye movements, and some have both (Judge, Caravolas, & Knox, 2006). Some researchers distinguish between *dysphonetic dyslexics* and *dyseidetic dyslexics* (Flynn & Boder, 1991), although many people with dyslexia do not fit neatly into either category (Farmer & Klein, 1995). Dysphonetic dyslexics have trouble sounding out words, so they try to memorize each word as a whole, and when they don't recognize a word, they guess based on context. For example, they might read the word *laugh* as "funny." Dyseidetic readers sound out words well enough, but they fail to recognize a word as a whole. They read slowly and have particular trouble with irregularly spelled words.

Most but not all people with dyslexia have problems related to hearing, although they are not simply matters of poor hearing, the kind of problem that could be corrected with hearing aids. Many deaf or partly deaf people can read, and people with dyslexia have no trouble carrying on a conversation (which would be difficult if their hearing were seriously impaired). In fact, occasionally even good musicians have dyslexia. Tests found that they had no trouble hearing whether a tone moved to a slightly higher or lower pitch, or whether a rhythm became slightly faster or slower. However, they had poor auditory memory. If they heard a sequences of tones and then after a short delay another sequence, they had trouble knowing whether it was the same as the first one (Weiss, Granot, & Ahissar, 2014). That result suggests a problem with how the brain handles auditory information, not a problem with the auditory information itself. Other studies found that people with dyslexia have weaker than normal connections between the auditory cortex and Broca's area (Boets et al., 2013).

Many people with dyslexia have particular trouble detecting the temporal order of sounds, such as noticing the difference between beep-click-buzz and beep-buzz-click (Farmer & Klein, 1995; Kujala et al., 2000; Nagarajan et al., 1999). They have also much difficulty making Spoonerisms—that is, trading the first consonants of two words, such as listening to "dear old queen" and saying "queer old dean" or hearing "way of life" and replying "lay of wife" (Paulesu et al., 1996). Doing so, of course, requires close attention to sounds and their order. Many people with dyslexia have trouble with other temporal order tasks as well, such as tapping a regular rhythm with the fingers (Wolff, 1993).

Many people with dyslexia also have abnormalities in their attention (Facoetti, Corradi, Ruffino, Gori, & Zorzi, 2010). Here is a demonstration. Fixate your eyes on the central dot in each display and, without moving your eyes left or right, try to read the middle letter of each three-letter display:

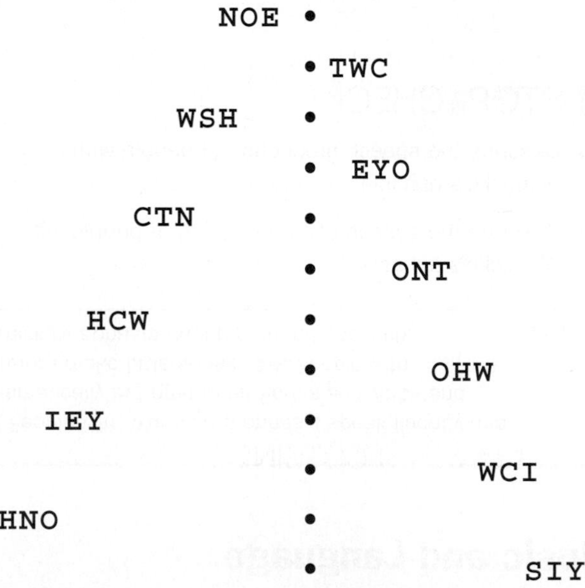

Most people find it easier to read the letters close to the fixation point, but some people with dyslexia are unusually adept at identifying letters well to the right of their fixation point. When they focus on a word, they are worse than average at

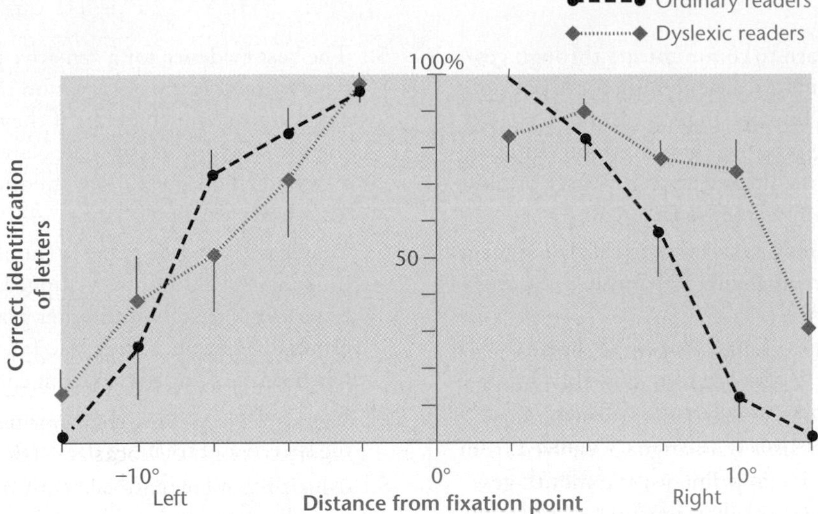

FIGURE 13.15 Identification of letters at various distances from the fixation point
Normal readers identify a letter most accurately when it is closest to the fixation point, and their accuracy drops for letters farther away. Many people with dyslexia are more accurate than normal readers are in identifying letters 5 to 10 degrees to the right of fixation.
Source: Reprinted from "Task-determined strategies of visual process," by G. Geiger, J. Y. Lettvin, & U. Zagarra-Moran, 1992, *Cognitive Brain Research, 1,* pp. 39–52, with kind permission of Elsevier Science-NL, Sara Burgerhartstraat 25, 1055 KV Amsterdam, the Netherlands.

reading it but better than average at perceiving letters 5 to 10 degrees to the right of it (Geiger, Lettvin, & Zegarra-Moran, 1992; Lorusso et al., 2004). That kind of attentional focus could certainly confuse attempts at reading (De Luca, Di Page, Judica, Spinelli, & Zoccolotti, 1999). Figure 13.15 shows the mean results for normal readers and for people with dyslexia.

For people with this abnormality, an effective treatment might be to teach them to attend to just one word at a time. Some children and adults with dyslexia have been told to place over the page that they are reading a sheet of paper with a window cut out of it that is large enough to expose just one word. In 3 months, 15 dyslexic children improved their reading skills by 1.22 grade levels (Geiger, Lettvin, & Fahle, 1994). Four dyslexic adults also made spectacular progress; one advanced from a third-grade to a tenth-grade reading level in 4 months (Geiger et al., 1992). After about the first 3 weeks of practice, they no longer needed the special cutout sheet of paper.

One final twist: Of the four adults with dyslexia who went through this process, three decided that they would rather return to being dyslexic! While dyslexic, they could attend to several tasks at once, such as talking to someone, listening to news on the radio, creating a work of art, and so forth. When they learned to read one word at a time, they found themselves able to perform only one task at a time, and they missed their old way of life. In short, their reading skills were tied to their overall attentional strategies.

STOP & CHECK

16. Why is dyslexia identified more frequently in children speaking English than in those speaking many other languages?

ANSWER

16. English has a large number of words with irregular, nonphonetic spellings.

MODULE 13.2 ■ IN CLOSING

Language and the Brain

Many of the earliest home computers had no speech capacity, but it was possible to plug in a device that would add speech, converting text output into sound. The evolution of human language was not like that. Our remote ancestors didn't just take a chimpanzee-type brain and add an independent module. Language required widespread modifications throughout the brain and made possible a great many additional changes in other functions. Trying to understand language is an important part of trying to understand what it means to be human.

Summary

1. Chimpanzees can learn to communicate through gestures or nonvocal symbols, although their output does not closely resemble human language. Bonobos have made more language progress than common chimpanzees because of species differences, early onset of training, and different training methods. **436**
2. An African gray parrot has shown surprising language abilities, with a brain organized differently from that of primates. **437**
3. Evolution of language may have begun with the vocalizations of primates, with the addition of the phonological loop that enables excellent auditory memory. A competing hypothesis is that language evolved from gestural communication in primates, and mouth gestures may have been especially important. **437**
4. The hypothesis that language emerged as a by-product of overall intelligence or brain size faces major problems: Some people have full-sized brains but impaired language, and people with Williams syndrome have nearly normal language despite mental retardation. **438**
5. The best evidence for a sensitive period for language development is the observation that deaf children learn sign language much better if they start early than if their first opportunity comes later in life. Also, learning a second language in early childhood differs in many ways from learning it later. **440**
6. People with Broca's aphasia (nonfluent aphasia) have difficulty speaking and writing. They find prepositions, conjunctions, and other grammatical connectives especially difficult. They also fail to understand speech when its meaning depends on complex grammar. **440**
7. People with Wernicke's aphasia have trouble understanding speech and recalling the names of objects. **442**
8. Music has many parallels with language. Composers usually write music with rhythm patterns that resemble the rhythm of speech in their own language. **443**
9. Dyslexia (reading impairment) has many forms. Typical people with dyslexia can hear well enough, but they show difficulties in remembering and processing sounds. Many also have abnormalities of attention. **444**

Key Terms

Terms are defined in the module on the page number indicated. They're also presented in alphabetical order with definitions in the book's Subject Index/Glossary. Interactive flash cards, audio reviews, and crossword puzzles are among the online resources available to help you learn these terms and the concepts they represent.

anomia **442**
aphasia **440**
Broca's aphasia (nonfluent aphasia) **440**
Broca's area **440**
dyslexia **444**
language acquisition device **439**
phonological loop **438**
productivity **435**
Wernicke's aphasia (fluent aphasia) **442**
Wernicke's area **442**
Williams syndrome **438**

Thought Questions

1. Most people with Broca's aphasia suffer from partial paralysis on the right side of the body. Most people with Wernicke's aphasia do not. Why?
2. In a syndrome called *word blindness*, a person loses the ability to read (even single letters), although the person can still see and speak. What is a possible neurological explanation? That is, can you imagine a pattern of brain damage that might produce this result?

MODULE 13.2 End of Module Quiz

1. What is meant by the "productivity" aspect of human language?
   a. The ability to convert a communication into action
   b. The ability to repeat something after hearing someone else say it
   c. The ability to read and write
   d. The ability to rearrange signals to represent new ideas

2. If human language did not evolve from other primates' vocalizations, what else is a likely hypothesis?
   a. Language evolved from nothing at all.
   b. Language evolved from dancing.
   c. Language evolved from gestures including mouth gestures.
   d. Language evolved from the ability to perceive objects in three dimensions.

3. What is the status of the hypothesis that language evolved as a by-product of overall intelligence?
   a. It is supported by findings that total brain mass correlates highly with language ability.
   b. It is supported by findings that teaching language to other primates causes an enormous amount of brain expansion.
   c. It is contradicted by findings that brain damage has no effect on language.
   d. It is contradicted by findings that some people have normal intelligence without language, and others have normal language despite mental retardation in many other regards.

4. If a child is bilingual from infancy, how are the two languages represented in the brain?
   a. The left hemisphere controls one language, and the right hemisphere controls the other language.
   b. The left hemisphere controls both languages.
   c. The right hemisphere controls both languages.
   d. Both hemispheres control both languages.

5. Which of the following is characteristic of Broca's aphasia?
   a. Difficulty forming new long-term memories, especially episodic memories
   b. Inability to describe anything seen in the left visual field or felt with the left hand
   c. Poor pronunciation and difficulty using and understanding grammar
   d. Good, fluent pronunciation but poor comprehension and difficulty remembering names of objects

6. Which of the following is most damaged in Broca's aphasia?
   a. The ability to control the muscles of the jaw and tongue
   b. The ability to hear the difference between one word and another
   c. The ability to produce certain aspects of language
   d. The ability to follow directions

7. Which of the following is characteristic of Wernicke's aphasia?
   a. Difficulty forming new long-term memories, especially episodic memories
   b. Inability to describe anything seen in the left visual field or felt with the left hand
   c. Poor pronunciation and difficulty using and understanding grammar
   d. Good, fluent pronunciation but poor comprehension and difficulty remembering names of objects

8. Which of the following activities strongly activates Broca's area?
   a. Folk dancing
   b. Driving a car
   c. Competitive swimming
   d. Sight-reading music

9. Which of the following is most seriously impaired in most people with dyslexia?
   a. Vision
   b. Ability to hear sounds
   c. Ability to remember sequences of sounds
   d. Motivation

ANSWERS:

1d, 2c, 3d, 4d, 5c, 6c, 7d, 8d, 9c.

MODULE 13.3

Conscious and Unconscious Processes and Attention

[W]e know the meaning [of consciousness] so long as no one asks us to define it.

William James (1892/1961, p. 19)

In Chapter 1, we introduced the mind–body problem: In a universe composed of matter and energy, why is there such a thing as consciousness? And how does it relate to the brain? Now armed with more understanding of the brain, it is time to return to those questions (even if we still cannot answer them).

The Mind–Brain Relationship

Suppose you say, "I became frightened because I saw a man with a gun." A neuroscientist says, "You became frightened because of increased electrochemical activity in the central amygdala of your brain." If both statements are right, what is the connection between them?

Biological explanations of behavior raise the **mind–body** or **mind–brain problem:** What is the relationship between the mind and the brain? The most widespread view among nonscientists is, no doubt, **dualism,** the belief that mind and body are different kinds of substance that exist independently. The French philosopher René Descartes defended dualism but recognized the vexing issue of how a mind that is not made of material could influence a physical brain. He proposed that mind and brain interact at a single point in space, which he suggested was the pineal gland, the smallest unpaired structure he could find in the brain (see Figure 13.16).

Although we credit Descartes with the first explicit defense of dualism, he hardly originated the idea. Our experiences seem so different from the physical actions of the brain that most people take it for granted that mind and brain are different. Even outstanding psychologists sometimes lapse into dualistic thinking. One psychologist commented, "we know little about . . . whether neural events drive psychological events, or the converse" (G. A. Miller, 2010, p. 716). In other words, we don't know whether brain activity causes thoughts or whether thoughts cause brain activity. But if thoughts and brain activity are the same thing, the question doesn't make sense.

Nearly all current philosophers and neuroscientists reject dualism. The decisive objection is that dualism conflicts with one of the cornerstones of physics, known as the law of the conservation of matter and energy: Matter can transform into energy or energy into matter, but neither one emerges from nothing, disappears into nothing, or changes without some action by other matter or energy. Because matter alters its course only when other matter or energy acts upon it, a mind that is not composed of matter or energy could not make anything happen, including muscle movements. If you use a term like *mind* to mean a ghostlike something that is neither matter nor energy, don't underestimate the scientific and philosophical arguments that can be marshaled against you (Dennett, 1991).

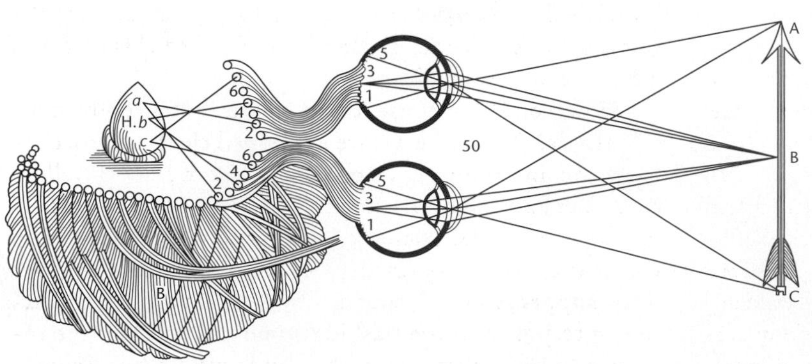

FIGURE 13.16 René Descartes's conception of brain and mind
Descartes understood how light from an object (the arrow) reached the retinas at the back of the eyes. The letters and numbers represent pathways that he imagined from the retinas to the pineal gland. (His guesses about those pathways were wrong.)
Source: From Descartes's *Treatise on Man*

The alternative to dualism is **monism,** the belief that the universe consists of only one kind of substance. Various forms of monism are possible, grouped into the following categories:

- **materialism:** the view that everything that exists is material, or physical. According to one version of this view, "eliminative materialism," mental events don't exist at all, and any folk psychology based on minds and mental activity is fundamentally mistaken. However, most of us find it difficult to believe that our minds are figments of our imagination! A more plausible version is that we will eventually find a way to explain all psychological experiences in purely physical terms.
- **mentalism:** the view that only minds really exist and that the physical world could not exist unless some mind were aware of it. The philosopher George Berkeley was the primary defender of this position. It is not easy to test this idea. (Go ahead and try!)
- **identity position:** the view that mental processes and certain kinds of brain processes are the same thing, described in different terms. By analogy, one could describe the *Mona Lisa* as an extraordinary painting, or one could list the exact color and brightness of each point on the painting. Although the two descriptions appear entirely different, they refer to the same object.

The identity position does not say that the mind is the brain. It says the mind is brain *activity*. Just as fire is not a "thing," but what happens to something, mental activity is what happens in the brain. Brain activity does not cause consciousness any more than consciousness causes brain activity. Each is the same as the other.

Can we be sure that monism is correct? No. However, researchers adopt it as the most reasonable working hypothesis, to see how much progress they can make on that assumption. As you have seen throughout this text, experiences and brain activities appear inseparable. Stimulation of any brain area provokes an experience, and any experience evokes brain activity, and damage to any brain area leads to loss of some mental function. As far as we can tell, you cannot have mental activity without brain activity, and you cannot have certain types of brain activity without mental activity.

(Does a belief in monism mean that we are lowering our evaluation of minds? Maybe not. Maybe we are elevating our concept of the material world.)

David Chalmers (1995) distinguished between what he calls the easy problems and the hard problem of consciousness. The easy problems pertain to such questions as the difference between wakefulness and sleep and what brain activity occurs during consciousness. These issues are difficult scientifically but not philosophically. In contrast, the **hard problem** concerns why consciousness exists at all. As Chalmers (1995, p. 203) put it, "Why doesn't all this information-processing go on 'in the dark,' free of any inner feel?" Why does brain activity *feel* like anything at all? Many scientists (Crick & Koch, 2004) and philosophers (Chalmers, 2004) agree that we cannot answer that question, at least at present. We don't even have a clear hypothesis to test. The best we can do is determine what brain activity is necessary or sufficient for consciousness. Maybe research on subordinate questions will some day lead us to a breakthrough on the hard question, or maybe not. But starting with the "easy" questions seems the best strategy.

STOP&CHECK

17. Why do nearly all scientists and philosophers reject the idea of dualism?

18. What is meant by the "hard problem"?

ANSWERS

17. Dualism contradicts the law of the conservation of matter and energy. According to that law, the only way to influence matter and energy, including that of your body, is to act on it with other matter and energy.
18. The hard problem is why minds exist at all in a physical world. Why is there such a thing as consciousness?

Consciousness of a Stimulus

We don't have even a good hypothesis about why consciousness exists at all. Nevertheless, we might be able to answer some lesser questions about consciousness. Perhaps answering some lesser questions might some day lead to insights about the deeper philosophical questions.

One of the main difficulties is that we cannot observe consciousness. Even defining it is treacherously difficult. For practical purposes, researchers use this operational definition: If a cooperative person reports awareness of one stimulus and not another, then he or she was **conscious** of the first and not the second. With individuals who cannot speak, including infants and nonhuman animals, this definition doesn't apply. Therefore, the research is limited to cooperative healthy adults.

Using this definition, the next step is to present a given stimulus under two conditions. In one condition we expect the observer to be conscious of it, and in the other condition we expect the observer to be unconscious of it. In both cases the stimulus excites receptors that send a message to the brain, but once the message reaches the brain, we can ask how the response differs depending on whether someone is or is not conscious of the stimulus.

How could we present a stimulus but prevent consciousness? Researchers have developed clever approaches based on interference. Suppose you clearly see a yellow dot. Then, although the dot remains on the screen, other dots around it flash on and off. While they are flashing, you cannot see the stationary dot. This procedure is called **flash suppression** (Kreiman, Fried, & Koch, 2002). The strong response to the flashing stimulus decreases the response to the steady stimulus, as if it were a fainter light (Yuval-Greenberg & Heeger, 2013). Similarly, suppose you see a yellow dot, and then some blue dots all around it start moving rapidly. They grab your attention so strongly that you have trouble seeing the yellow dot. In fact, it seems to disappear for a few seconds, reappear for a few seconds, disappear again, and so forth (Bonneh, Cooperman, & Sagi, 2001).

Experiments Using Masking

Many studies use **masking:** A brief visual stimulus is preceded and followed by longer interfering stimuli. In many cases, researchers present just the brief stimulus and a final stimulus, in which case the procedure is called **backward masking.** In one study, researchers flashed a word on a screen for 29 milliseconds (ms). On some trials, it was preceded and followed by a blank screen:

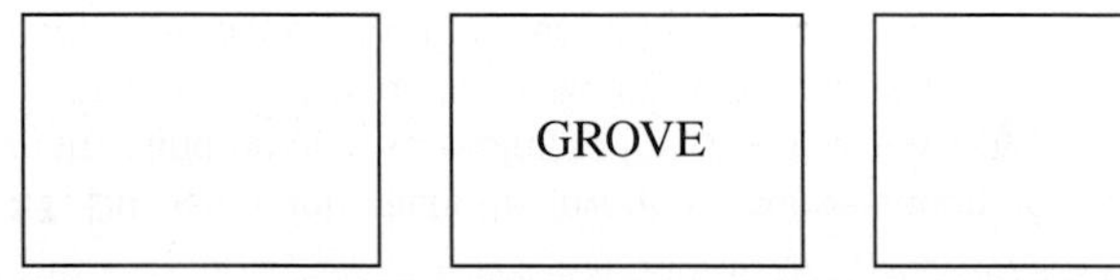

In these cases, people identified the word almost 90 percent of the time. On other trials, the researchers flashed a word for the same 29 ms but preceded and followed it with masking patterns:

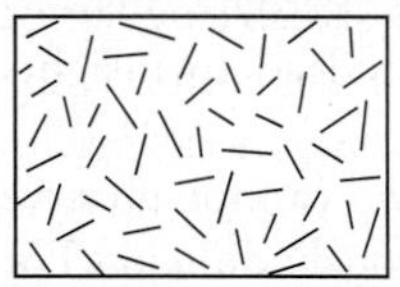

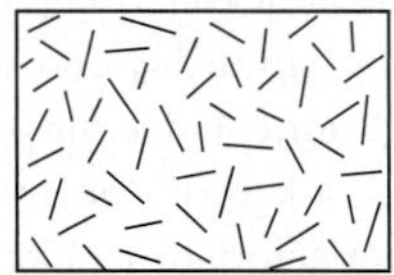

In the masking condition, people almost never identify it. They usually say they saw no word at all. Using fMRI and evoked potentials, the researchers found that the stimulus initially activates the primary visual cortex in both the conscious and unconscious conditions but activates it more strongly in the conscious condition, because of less interference. Also, in the conscious condition, the activity spreads to additional brain areas (Dehaene et al., 2001), including the prefrontal cortex and parietal cortex, which amplify the signal. For people with damage to the prefrontal cortex, a visual stimulus has to last longer before it becomes conscious, relative to other people (Del Cul, Dehaene, Reyes, Bravo, & Slachevsky, 2009).

A conscious stimulus also synchronizes responses for neurons in various brain areas (Eckhorn et al., 1988; Gray, König, Engel, & Singer, 1989; Melloni et al., 2007; Womelsdorf et al., 2007). When you see something and recognize it, it evokes activity precisely synchronized in several brain areas, in the frequency of about 30 to 50 Hz (cycles per second), known as *gamma waves* (Doesburg, Green, McDonald, & Ward, 2009; Fisch et al., 2009). One consequence of synchronized action potentials is that their synaptic inputs arrive simultaneously at their target cells, producing maximal summation (Fell & Axmacher, 2011).

Overall, the data imply that consciousness of a stimulus depends on the amount and spread of brain activity. Becoming conscious of something means that its information takes over more of your brain's activity.

STOP&CHECK

19. In the experiment by Dehaene et al., how were the conscious and unconscious stimuli similar? How were they different?

20. In this experiment, how did the brain's responses differ to the conscious and unconscious stimuli?

ANSWERS

19. The conscious and unconscious stimuli were physically the same (a word flashed on the screen for 29 ms). The difference was that a stimulus did not become conscious if it was preceded and followed by an interfering pattern. **20.** If a stimulus became conscious, it activated the same brain areas as an unconscious stimulus but more strongly, and then the activity spread to additional areas. Also, brain responses became synchronized when a pattern was conscious.

Experiments Using Binocular Rivalry

Here is another way to make a stimulus unconscious. Look at Figure 13.17, but hold it so close to your eyes that your nose touches the page, right between the two circles. Better yet, look at the two parts through a pair of tubes, such as the tubes inside rolls of paper towels or toilet paper, or roll up your hands like tubes. You should see red and black vertical stripes with your left eye and green and black horizontal stripes with your right eye. (Close one eye and then the other to make sure your eyes see completely different patterns.) Seeing something requires seeing *where* it is, and the red vertical stripes cannot be in the same place as the green horizontal stripes. Because your brain cannot perceive both patterns in the same location, your perception alternates. For a while, you see the red and black stripes, and then the green and black invade your consciousness. Then your perception shifts back to the red and black. For the average person, each perception lasts about 2 seconds before switching to the other, although some people switch faster or slower. These shifts, known as **binocular rivalry,** are gradual, sweeping from one side to another. You can voluntarily shift your attention to one or the other image, but only to a limited extent. Soon you see the other image anyway (Paffen & Alais, 2011). Instead of lines, the stimuli could be something else, such as a house versus a face.

The two images do not necessarily divide your attention time equally. Some people see with one eye longer than the other. Also, an emotionally charged image, such as a face with an emotional expression, generally holds attention longer than a neutral image (Yoon, Hong, Joormann, & Kang, 2009). A happy face holds attention longer for someone

FIGURE 13.17 Binocular rivalry
If possible, look at the two circles through tubes, such as those from inside rolls of toilet paper or paper towels. Otherwise, touch your nose to the paper between the two parts so that your left eye sees one pattern while your right eye sees the other. The two views will compete for your consciousness, and your perception will alternate between them.

in a happy mood, and a scowling face holds attention longer for someone in a sad mood (Anderson, Siegel, & Barrett, 2011; Anderson et al., 2013).

The stimulus seen by each eye evokes a brain response that researchers can measure with fMRI or similar methods. As the first perception fades and the stimulus seen by the other eye replaces it, the first pattern of brain activity fades also, and a different pattern replaces it. Each shift in perception is accompanied by a shift in the activity over a large portion of the brain (Lee, Blake, & Heeger, 2005).

Both the red–black and green–black patterns you just experienced were stationary. To make the brain responses easier to distinguish, researchers presented to one eye a stationary stimulus and to the other eye a pattern that pulsated in size and brightness, as shown in Figure 13.18. Then they recorded brain activity in several areas. At times when people reported consciousness of the pulsating stimulus, pulsating activity at the same rhythm was prominent in much of the brain, as shown in Figure 13.19. When people reported consciousness of the stationary stimulus, the pulsating activity was weak (Cosmelli et al., 2004). Again, the conclusion is that a conscious stimulus strongly activates much of the brain, virtually taking over brain activity. When the same stimulus is unconscious, it produces weaker and less widespread activity.

The Fate of an Unattended Stimulus

Let's further consider binocular rivalry. While you are attending to, say, the green and black stripes, your brain does not completely discard information from the red and black stripes in your other eye. Certainly, if a bright stimulus suddenly flashed in that eye, it would capture your attention. More interestingly, suppose a word fades onto the screen slowly, and you are to report the time when your attention shifts to the previously unattended eye. The word captures your attention, causing you to shift your attention faster than you would have otherwise. Moreover, if it is a word from your own language, or better yet your own name, it captures your attention faster

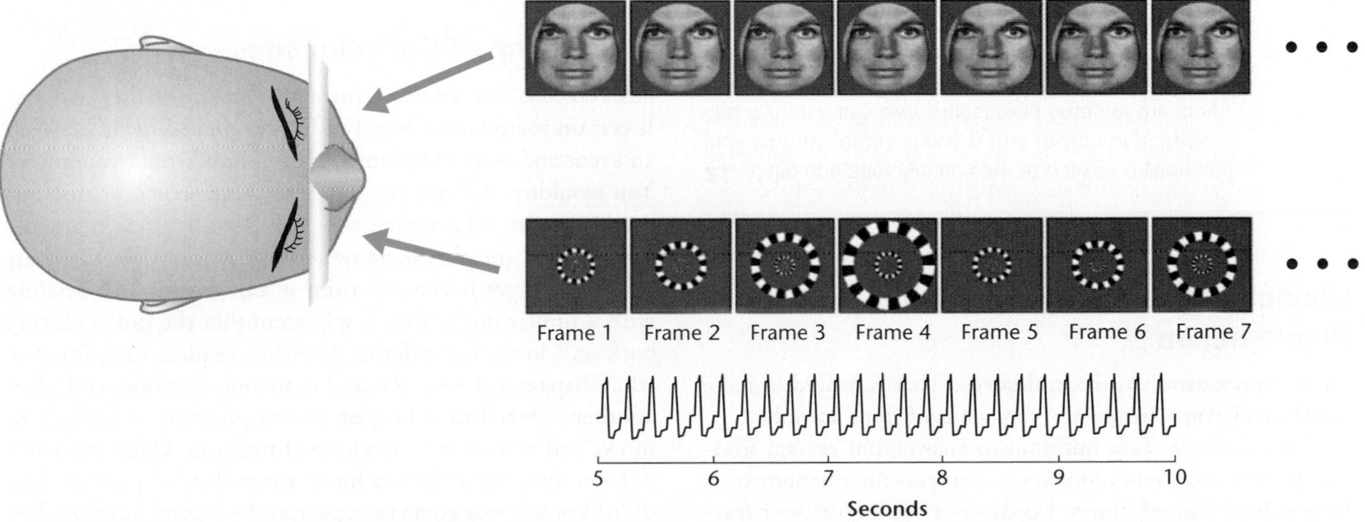

FIGURE 13.18 Stimuli for a study of binocular rivalry
The pattern in one eye was stationary. The one in the other eye pulsated a few times per second. Researchers could then examine brain activity to find cells that followed the rhythm of the pulsating stimulus. *Source:* Reprinted from "Waves of consciousness: Ongoing cortical patterns during binocular rivalry," by D. Cosmelli et al., 2004, *NeuroImage, 23*(1), pp. 128–140, with permission from Elsevier.

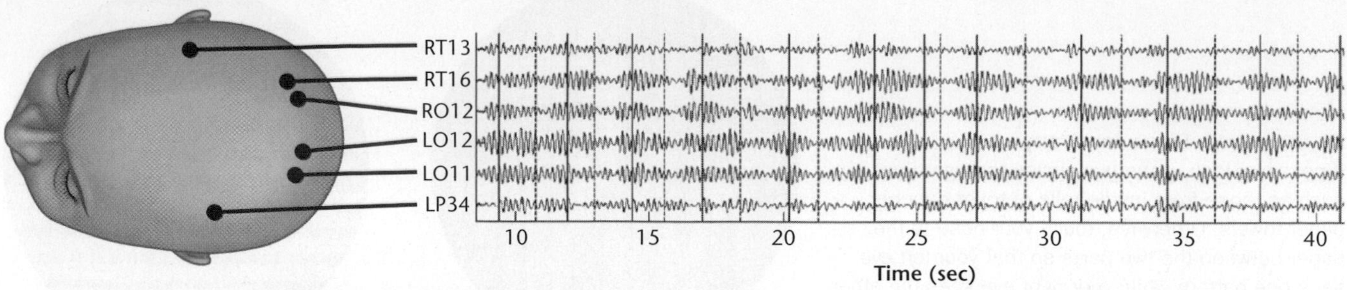

FIGURE 13.19 Brain activity during binocular rivalry
When the person reported seeing the pulsating stimulus, neurons throughout much of the brain responded vigorously at the same rhythm as the stimulus. When the person reported the stationary stimulus, the rhythmic activity subsided. *Source:* Reprinted from "Waves of consciousness: Ongoing cortical patterns during binocular rivalry," by D. Cosmelli et al., 2004, *NeuroImage, 23*(1), pp. 128–140, with permission from Elsevier.

than a word from a language you do not understand (Jiang, Costello, & He, 2007). If a meaningful stimulus captures your attention faster than a meaningless stimulus, somehow your brain had to know it was meaningful *before* it became conscious! The conclusion is that much of brain activity is unconscious, and even unconscious activity can influence behavior (Hassin, 2013).

STOP&CHECK

21. How could someone use fMRI to determine which of two patterns in binocular rivalry is conscious at a given moment?

22. If someone is aware of the stimulus on the right in a case of binocular rivalry, what evidence indicates that the brain is also processing the stimulus on the left?

ANSWERS

21. Make one stimulus pulsate at a given rhythm and look for brain areas showing that rhythm of activity. The rhythm takes over widespread areas of the brain when that pattern is conscious. **22.** If a stimulus gradually appears on the left side, attention shifts to the left faster if that stimulus is a meaningful word than if it is a word from an unfamiliar language.

Consciousness as a Threshold Phenomenon

Does consciousness come in degrees? That is, would it make sense to say you were "partly" conscious of some stimulus?

This is not an easy question to answer, but several studies suggest that consciousness is a yes–no phenomenon. Researchers flashed blurry words on a screen for brief fractions of a second and asked people to identify each word, if possible, and rate *how* conscious they were of the word on a scale from 0 to 100. People almost always rated a word either 0 or 100. They almost never said they were partly conscious of something (Sergent & Dehaene, 2004). These results suggest that consciousness is a threshold phenomenon. When a stimulus activates enough neurons to a sufficient extent, the activity reverberates, magnifies, and extends over much of the brain. If a stimulus fails to reach that level, the pattern fades away.

Studies using fMRI support the same conclusion. In studies using masking stimuli, the brain's response to a visual stimulus is the same in the first quarter of a second, regardless of whether the person will become aware of it. However, the later response is weak on trials when the person reports unawareness, but strong and widespread when the person reports being aware of the stimulus. With infants, the brain's response to a 50 ms visual stimulus is weak and brief, whereas the response to a 100 ms stimulus is stronger, longer, and more widespread (Kouider et al., 2013). We don't know for sure about consciousness in infants (because we cannot ask), but we see at least that the brain's response is either weak or strong, and not intermediate. Consciousness of a stimulus may indeed be an all-or-none phenomenon.

The Timing of Consciousness

Are you conscious of events instant by instant as they happen? It certainly seems that way, but if there were a delay between an event and your consciousness of it, how would you know? You wouldn't. Perhaps you sometimes construct a conscious experience after the event.

Consider the **phi phenomenon** that perceptual researchers noted long ago: If you see a dot in one position alternating with a similar dot nearby, it will seem that the dot is moving back and forth. Considering just the simplest case, imagine what happens if you see a dot in one position and then another: • ➞ •. You see a dot in one position, it appears to move, and you see it in the second position. Okay, but *when* did you see it move? When you saw it in the first position, you didn't know it was going to appear in the second position. You could not perceive it as moving until *after* it appeared in the second position. Evidently, you perceived it as moving from one position to the second after it appeared in the second position! In other words, the second position changed your perception of what occurred before it.

Another example: Suppose you hear a recorded word that is carefully engineered to sound halfway between *dent* and *tent*. We'll call it **ent*. If you hear it in the phrase "*ent in the fender," it sounds like *dent*. If you hear it in the phrase "*ent in the forest," it sounds like *tent*. That is, later words changed what you heard before them (Connine, Blasko, & Hall, 1991).

One more example: Suppose you are watching a screen on which at unpredictable times you see a very faint set of lines for 50 ms, and your task is to say the angle of the lines. Sometimes it appears on the left of the screen and sometimes on the right. The difficulty is adjusted so you get it right only some of the time and you often say you didn't see it at all. Now suppose that 400 ms *after* the stimulus, a cue flashes to tell you whether the stimulus was on the left or the right. That stimulus increases the chance you will say you saw the stimulus, and increases your accuracy of identifying its angle (Sergent et al., 2013). So you are capable of becoming conscious of something after it is gone. Somehow your brain held it in reserve, capable of activating it after the fact.

STOP&CHECK

23. In what way does the phi phenomenon imply that a new stimulus sometimes changes consciousness of what went before it?

ANSWER

23. Someone who sees a dot on the left and then a dot on the right perceives the dot as moving from left to right. The perceived movement would have occurred before the dot on the right, but the person had no reason to infer that movement until after the dot appeared on the right.

Conscious and Unconscious People

When we ask about the physiological basis for consciousness, we need to distinguish two questions. So far we have focused on what happens when a waking, alert, conscious person becomes conscious of a particular stimulus. The other question is what enables the person as a whole to be aware of anything at all. How do the brains of conscious people differ from those of people who are asleep, in a coma, or deeply anesthetized?

Two studies followed people as they lost consciousness under anesthesia and then regained it as the drug effects wore off. Loss of consciousness was marked by decreased overall activity and especially by decreased connectivity between the cerebral cortex and subcortical areas such as the thalamus, hypothalamus, and basal ganglia. Initial recovery of consciousness depended on increased connectivity between subcortical and cortical areas, and later increases in alertness depended on increased activity in the cortex (Långsjö et al, 2012; Schröter, 2012). Recall the earlier discussion that consciousness of a stimulus requires a spread of activity over much of the brain. With a loss of connectivity, no stimulus can spread its activity, and the person is conscious of nothing.

As discussed in the chapter on sleep, people in a minimally conscious state respond to at least a few stimuli, although they cannot talk. People in a vegetative state alternate between sleep and greater arousal, but even in their most aroused state they show no purposeful behaviors. Might they nevertheless be conscious? Researchers used fMRI to record brain activity in a young woman who was in a persistent vegetative state following a brain injury in a traffic accident. She had neither spoken nor made any other purposive movements. However, when she was told to imagine playing tennis, the fMRI showed increased activity in motor areas of her cortex, similar to what healthy volunteers showed. When she was told to imagine walking through her house, a different set of brain areas became active, again similar to those of healthy volunteers (Owen et al., 2006). Follow-up studies found similar results in 4 of 53 patients in a vegetative state. One patient used brain activity—imagining tennis versus imagining walking through a house—to answer yes/no questions such as "Do you have a brother?" (Monti et al., 2010).

Another approach shows promise without requiring any response at all. Researchers used brief magnetic stimulation to activate a localized brain area, and then used EEG to observe the spread of activity. The activity spread only locally in anesthetized people, sleeping people, and most people in a vegetative state. It spread more widely for people in a minimally conscious state (Casali et al, 2013; Rosanova et al., 2012). This method offers a potentially quick way to probe for consciousness in an unresponsive person.

STOP&CHECK

24. As people lost consciousness under anesthesia and later regained it, what changed most strikingly in the brain?

ANSWER

24. Connectivity between the cerebral cortex and subcortical areas including the thalamus, hypothalamus, and basal ganglia.

Attention

Attention isn't synonymous with consciousness, but it is closely related. You can be conscious without paying attention to anything, but you cannot pay attention to something without being conscious. At least that seems to be true for humans. Someone could no doubt build a robot that pays attention to some inputs more than others, but we wouldn't necessarily consider it conscious. Insects pay more attention to some stimuli than others, but it is hard to know whether they are conscious.

Of all that your eyes see at any instant, you are conscious of only those few to which you direct your attention (Huang, Treisman, & Pashler, 2007). For example, consider

inattentional blindness or *change blindness:* If something in a complex scene changes slowly, or changes while you blink your eyes, you probably will not notice it unless you are paying attention to the particular item that changes (Henderson & Hollingworth, 2003; Rensink, O'Regan, & Clark, 1997). You can experience this phenomenon with the Online Try It Yourself exercise "Change Blindness."

Brain Areas Controlling Attention

Psychologists distinguish bottom-up from top-down attention. A bottom-up process depends on the stimulus. If you are sitting on a park bench, gazing off into the distance, when suddenly a deer runs past you, it grabs your attention. A top-down process is intentional. You might be looking for someone you know in a crowd, and you have to check one face after another to find the one you want. Sometimes a top-down process overrules bottom-up processes. Suppose you are looking for a friend in a crowd, but it's a carnival crowd. Many people are dressed as clowns or wearing other gaudy attire, but your friend is wearing a plain shirt and blue jeans. You need to suppress the attention and activity that the unusual items would ordinarily attract (Mevorach, Hodsoll, Allen, Shalev, & Humphreys, 2010). Deliberate, top-down direction of attention depends on parts of the prefrontal cortex and parietal cortex (Buschman & Miller, 2007; Rossi, Bichot, Desimone, & Ungerleider, 2007).

You can control your attention (top-down) even without moving your eyes. To illustrate, keep your eyes fixated on the central *x* in the following display. Then attend to the G at the right and gradually shift your attention clockwise around the circle. Notice how you become aware of different parts of the circle without moving your eyes. As you deliberately shift your attention, you increase activity in one part after another of the visual cortex (Kamitani & Tong, 2005; Wegener, Freiwald, & Kreiter, 2004).

Another demonstration: What is the current sensation in your left foot? Chances are, before you read this question, you were not conscious of *any* sensation in your left foot. When you directed your attention to it, activity increased in the corresponding part of the somatosensory cortex (Lambie & Marcel, 2002).

One of psychologists' favorite ways to study attention is the **Stroop effect**, the difficulty of ignoring words and saying the color of ink. In the following display, say aloud the color of ink of each word, ignoring the words themselves:

RED BLUE GREEN GREEN BROWN BLUE
RED PURPLE GREEN RED

After all your years of learning to read words, it is hard to suppress that habit and respond to the color instead. However, when people successfully do so, they enhance the activity in the color-vision areas of the cortex and decrease the activity in the areas responsible for identifying words (Polk, Drake, Jonides, Smith, & Smith, 2008).

Your ability to resist distraction fluctuates. That is, you might pay close attention for a while, and then get distracted. In another experiment, people's task was to find one circle among an array of squares. On some trials, one of the squares was red instead of green. Anything that is different attracts attention, and on the average, people responded a bit more slowly on trials with a red square present. However, the speed of responding varied from trial to trial. On trials when activity was enhanced in the middle frontal gyrus (part of the prefrontal cortex) at the *start* of the trial (before seeing the stimuli), people did best at ignoring the red square and thereby resisting distraction (Leber, 2010). This result confirms the importance of the prefrontal cortex in directing attention.

The ability to resist distraction also varies among individuals. In general, people who habitually play action video games perform above average on many tests of attention, because of greatly enhanced top-down control (Mishra, Zinni, Bavelier, & Hillyard, 2011). However, we cannot draw cause-and-effect conclusions from correlational data. Perhaps people with better attention are more likely than others to spend many hours at video games. Controlled experiments find that certain types of video games enhance attention for people more than 60 years old, but produce only small to negligible effects for younger people (Anguera et al., 2013; Powers, Brooks, Aldrich, Palladino, & Alfieri, 2013). Intensive training at meditation also improves certain aspects of attention (Lutz et al., 2009).

STOP & CHECK

25. What brain response was related to people's ability to resist distraction from an irrelevant red square among the green squares and circle?

ANSWER

25. Resistance to distraction related to the amount of activity in part of the prefrontal cortex before the presentation of stimuli.

Spatial Neglect

Brain damage can produce special types of attention problems. Many people with damage to the right hemisphere show **spatial neglect**—a tendency to ignore the left side of the body, the left side of objects, much of what they hear in the left ear, and much of what they feel in the left hand, especially in the presence of any competing sensation from the right side. Some people have been known to put clothes on only the right side of the body. These effects are most pronounced early after a stroke or other damage, and most people show at least partial recovery over the next 10 to 20 weeks (Nijboer, Kollen, & Kwakkel, 2013). (Damage in the left hemisphere seldom produces significant neglect of the right side.)

If asked to point straight ahead, most patients with neglect point to the right of center. If a patient with neglect is shown a long horizontal line and asked to divide it in half, generally he or she picks a spot well to the right of center, as if part of the left side wasn't there (Richard, Honoré, Bernati, & Rousseaux, 2004).

People with intact brains generally do not hit the center of the line but veer 2 percent to 3 percent to the left of center. Also, if they are asked to indicate a rating of something along a scale from left to right, they show a slight tendency to prefer the left side (Nicholls, Orr, Okubo, & Loftus, 2006). For example, on the questions that follow, most people would rate their political views slightly more conservative on the first question than on the second:

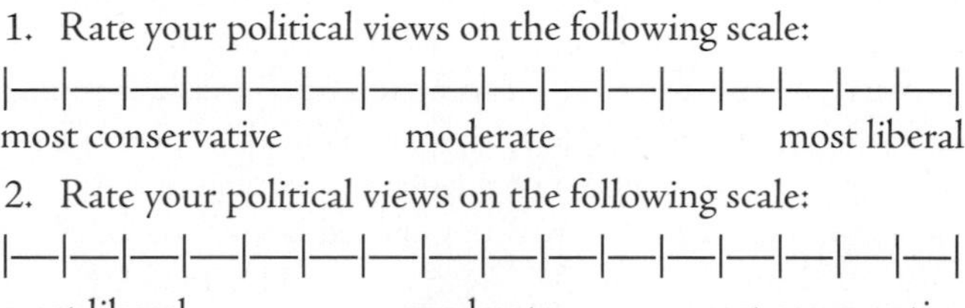

You might try the following demonstration. Try marking the center of the line below. Then measure it to see how close you came. Most people miss slightly to the left. Curiously, people with extensive musical training usually get within 1 percent of the exact center (Patston, Corballis, Hogg, & Tippett, 2006).

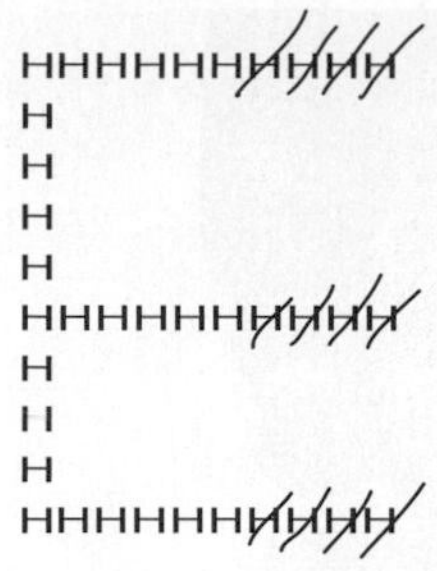

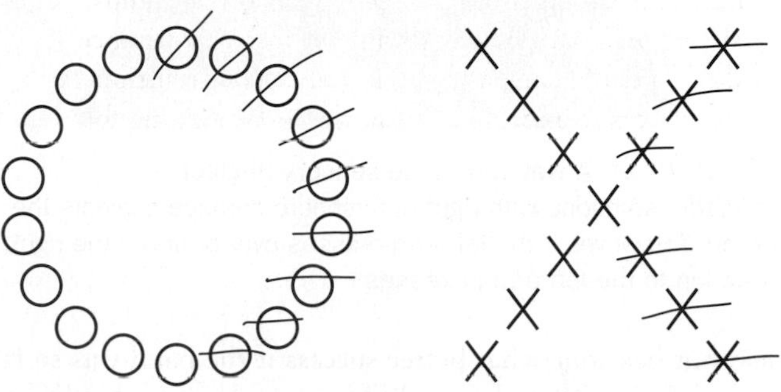

FIGURE 13.20 Spatial neglect
A patient with neglect identified the overall figures as E, O, and X, indicating that she saw the whole figures. However, when asked to cross off the elements that composed them, she crossed off only the parts on the right. *Source:* From "Seeing the forest but only half the trees?," by J. C. Marshall and P. W. Halligan, *Nature, 373,* pp. 521–523, Fig. 1 [parts C and E]. © 1995 Nature.

Some patients with neglect also show deviations when estimating the midpoint of a numerical range. For example, what is halfway between 11 and 19? The correct answer is, of course, 15, but some people with neglect say "17." Evidently, they discount the lower numbers as if they were on the left side (Doricchi, Guariglia, Gasparini, & Tomaiuolo, 2005; Zorzi, Priftis, & Umiltà, 2002). At least in Western society, many people visualize the numbers as a line stretching to the right, as in the *x* axis of a graph. All of these results vary, depending on the amount and location of right hemisphere damage (Buxbaum, 2006).

Although some neglect patients have sensory losses, in many cases, the main problem is loss of attention rather than impaired sensation. One patient was shown a letter E, composed of small Hs, as in Figure 13.20. She identified it as a big E composed of small Hs, indicating that she saw the whole figure. However, when she was then asked to cross off all the Hs, she crossed off only the ones on the right. When she was shown the figures in Figure 13.20, she identified them as an O composed of little Os and an X composed of little Xs. Again, she could see both halves of both figures, but when she was asked to cross off all the elements, she crossed off only the ones on the right. The researchers summarized by saying she saw the forest but only half the trees (Marshall & Halligan, 1995).

Several procedures increase attention to the neglected side. Simply telling the person to pay attention to the left side helps briefly. So does having the person look left while at the same time feeling an object with the left hand (Vaishnavi, Calhoun, & Chatterjee, 2001) or hearing a sound from the left side of the world (Frassinetti, Pavani, & Làdavas, 2002).

Other manipulations also shift the attention. For example, some patients with neglect usually report feeling nothing with the left hand, especially if the right hand feels something at the time. However, if you cross one hand over the other as shown in Figure 13.21, the person is more likely to report feeling the left hand, which is now on the right side of the body (Aglioti, Smania, & Peru, 1999). Also, the person ordinarily has trouble pointing to anything in the left visual

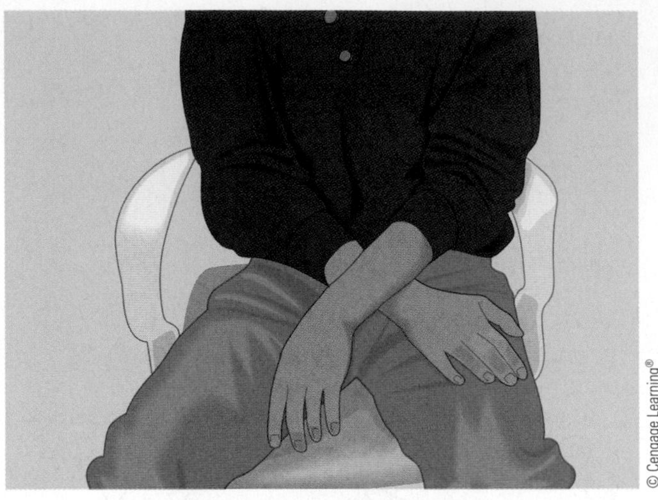

FIGURE 13.21 A way to reduce sensory neglect
Ordinarily, someone with right hemisphere damage neglects the left arm. However, if the left arm crosses over or under the right, attention to the left arm increases.

field but has somewhat better success if the hand was so far to the left that he or she would have to move it to the right to point to the object (Mattingley, Husain, Rorden, Kennard, & Driver, 1998). Again, the conclusion is that neglect is not due to a loss of sensation but a difficulty in directing attention to the left side.

STOP&CHECK

26. What is the evidence that spatial neglect is a problem in attention, not just sensation?

27. What are several procedures that increase attention to the left side in a person with spatial neglect?

ANSWERS

26. When a patient with neglect sees a large letter composed of small letters, he or she can identify the large letter but then neglects part of it when asked to cross off all the small letters. Also, someone who neglects the left hand pays attention to it when it is crossed over the right hand. **27.** Simply telling the person to attend to something on the left helps temporarily. Having the person look to the left while feeling something on the left side increases attention to the felt object. Crossing the left hand over the right increases attention to the left hand. Moving a hand far to the left makes it easier for the person to point to something in the left visual field because the hand will move toward the right to point at the object.

MODULE 13.3 ■ IN CLOSING

Attending to Attention and Being Conscious of Consciousness

Before the 1970s, many psychological researchers, especially those studying learning in rats, were not convinced that the concept of attention was useful at all. Today, the concept of attention is well established in cognitive psychology, although some still doubt that consciousness is a scientifically useful concept. Research in this area is difficult because we cannot observe consciousness itself, and we have no access to it beyond what people report. The hard problem of why consciousness exists at all remains deeply challenging. Still, progress continues at an encouraging rate on subordinate questions, such as finding the brain activities most important for consciousness and attention. How far we can go is uncertain, but the only way to find out is to try.

Summary

1. Dualism—the belief in a nonmaterial mind that exists separately from the body and influences it—conflicts with the conservation of matter and energy, one of the best-established principles of physics. Nearly all neuroscientists and philosophers accept some version of monism, the idea that mental activity is inseparable from brain activity. **448**
2. The hard problem is the question of why consciousness exists at all. Most researchers agree that we cannot answer this question, at least at present. **449**
3. To identify the brain activities associated with consciousness, researchers present the same stimulus under conditions when an observer probably will or probably will not identify it consciously. **449**
4. When someone is conscious of a stimulus, the representation of that stimulus spreads over a large portion of the brain. **450**
5. Many stimuli influence our behavior without being conscious. Even before a stimulus becomes conscious, the brain processes the information

enough to identify something as meaningful or meaningless. **451**

6. People almost never say they were partly conscious of something. It may be that consciousness is a threshold phenomenon: We become conscious of anything that exceeds a certain level of brain activity, and we are not conscious of other events. **452**
7. We are not always conscious of events instantaneously as they occur. Sometimes, a later event modifies our conscious perception of a stimulus that went before it. **452**
8. Researchers sometimes use brain recordings to infer whether someone is conscious. A few people diagnosed as being in a vegetative state have shown possible indications of consciousness. **453**
9. Attention to a stimulus requires increased brain responses to that stimulus and decreased responses to others. The prefrontal cortex is important for top-down control of attention. **454**
10. Attention and resistance to distraction vary across time and among individuals. **454**
11. Damage to parts of the right hemisphere produce spatial neglect for the left side of the body or the left side of objects. **454**
12. Neglect results from a deficit in attention, not sensation. For example, someone with neglect can see an entire letter enough to say what it is, even though that same person ignores the left half when asked to cross out all the elements that compose it. **455**

Key Terms

Terms are defined in the module on the page number indicated. They're also presented in alphabetical order with definitions in the book's Subject Index/Glossary. Interactive flash cards, audio reviews, and crossword puzzles are among the online resources available to help you learn these terms and the concepts they represent.

backward masking **450**
binocular rivalry **450**
conscious **449**
dualism **448**
flash suppression **449**
hard problem **449**
identity position **449**
inattentional blindness **454**
masking **450**
materialism **449**
mentalism **449**
mind–brain problem **448**
monism **449**
phi phenomenon **452**
spatial neglect **454**
Stroop effect **454**

Thought Questions

1. Could a computer be conscious? What evidence, if any, would convince you that it was conscious?
2. The operational definition of consciousness applies only to people willing and able to report that they are conscious of some events and not others. Research using this definition has determined certain brain correlates of consciousness. Could we now use those brain correlates to infer consciousness or its absence in newborn infants, people with brain damage, or nonhuman animals?

MODULE 13.3 End of Module Quiz

1. Which of the following best states the identity position regarding mind and brain?
   - **a.** The physical world could not exist unless some mind were aware of it.
   - **b.** Mental activity causes brain activity.
   - **c.** Brain activity causes mental activity.
   - **d.** Mental activity and brain activity are the same thing.
2. What is "hard" about the "hard problem"?
   - **a.** To solve it, we would need to conduct extremely expensive research.
   - **b.** The research to solve this problem would raise difficult ethical issues.
   - **c.** The question is philosophically challenging, and we don't know where to begin.
   - **d.** We already know the answer, but it is hard to get most people to accept it.
3. Which of the following questions, if any, can current research methods answer?
   - **a.** Why does consciousness exist at all?
   - **b.** What behaviors become possible because of consciousness that we could not do otherwise?

c. What types of brain activity occur during consciousness that don't occur otherwise?

d. Current methods do not enable us to answer any of these questions.

4. What procedure is used in backward masking?

a. A participant views a stationary dot surrounded by bright flashing dots.

b. Researchers present a brief visual stimulus followed by a longer stimulus.

c. A participant views one scene in the left eye and an incompatible scene in the right eye.

d. A participant views a dot in one position alternating with a similar dot nearby.

5. What is the purpose of experiments using flash suppression, backward masking, and binocular rivalry?

a. To measure how effectively a person can control attention

b. To find what happens in the brain during consciousness

c. To study the brain mechanisms responsible for consolidation of memory

d. To describe changes in the brain as someone recovers from a stroke

6. If your left eye views red vertical stripes and your right eye views green horizontal stripes, what do you perceive?

a. Red and green stripes superimposed

b. Yellow diagonal stripes

c. A white field without stripes

d. Alternation between seeing red stripes and seeing green stripes

7. What theoretical conclusion do the studies on binocular rivalry support?

a. Unconscious processes control much of human behavior.

b. A stimulus activates much of the brain when you are conscious of it.

c. Damage to the right hemisphere leads to a tendency to neglect the left side of space.

d. Certain people who appear to be in a vegetative state may nevertheless be conscious.

8. People are conscious of a prolonged stimulus, but not one with an extremely short presentation. What happens at an intermediate duration of presentation?

a. People report being partly conscious of it.

b. People are sometimes conscious of it and sometimes not, and the difference depends only on what happens at that moment.

c. People are sometimes conscious of it and sometimes not, and stimuli after the event can influence the outcome.

9. Certain people in a vegetative state gave possible indication of consciousness by doing what?

a. Laughing or crying in response to what someone said.

b. Moving their eyes to the left or right to answer yes/no questions.

c. Responding to directions to think about tennis or walking around a house.

d. Squeezing the hand of a loved one.

10. For people to do well on the Stroop task, activity must increase in the ______ areas of the brain and decrease in the ______ areas.

a. color-vision . . . word

b. word . . . attention

c. attention . . . auditory

d. auditory . . . color-vision

11. Suppose someone who is trying to divide a horizontal line in half picks a spot far to the right of center. This result suggests probable damage or malfunction in which part of the brain?

a. The left hemisphere

b. The right hemisphere

c. The prefrontal cortex

d. The primary visual cortex

12. If someone has spatial neglect of the left side, which of these procedures, if any, would increase attention to a touch sensation on the left side?

a. Ask the person to look to the left during the touch sensation.

b. Ask the person to look to the right during the touch sensation.

c. Ask the person to listen to music during the touch sensation.

d. None of these procedures would have any noticeable effect.

ANSWERS:

1d, 2c, 3c, 4b, 5b, 6d, 7b, 8c, 9c, 10a, 11b, 12a.

Social Neuroscience

One of the most distinguishing characteristics of humans is our social behavior. Chimpanzees do almost as well as humans on many cognitive tasks, but not on social cognitions such as inferring what someone else knows or intends to do. Humans make great efforts to teach one another (and even to teach chimpanzees!), but chimpanzees seldom make any intentional effort to teach one another (Tomasello & Herrmann, 2010).

Think of all the ways people act together. Many couples spend their whole adult lifetime together, helping each other, their children, and their grandchildren. Many people devote great efforts to helping people they don't know, occasionally even risking their own lives. Economic cooperation makes possible opportunities our ancestors could not have imagined. Tonight you might drive a car made in Europe and powered by fuel from the Middle East so you can eat food grown by farmers in Asia, cooked according to a recipe from South America, at a restaurant built by people in a previous century. And you are protected from disease by the combined efforts of medical researchers from many countries and many centuries.

What can neuroscience say about all of this? **Social neuroscience**, the study of how genes, chemicals, and brain areas contribute to social behavior, is a relatively new area of study, but one that excites growing enthusiasm.

The Biology of Love

Suppose you are deeply, passionately in love with someone. Researchers compare your brain activity (measured by fMRI) while you are looking at pictures of your beloved to pictures of other nice-looking people. Pictures of the person you love will produce increased activation of certain brain areas associated with reward, in ways similar to the high that people report from addictive drugs (Burkett & Young, 2012). Viewing a photo of your beloved also activates the hippocampus and other areas important for memory and cognition (Ortigue, Bianchi-Demicheli, Patel, Frum, & Lewis, 2010). (Naturally, thinking about someone you love evokes memories of what you have done together.) The point is that what we call love combines motivations, emotions, memories, and cognitions.

The role of **oxytocin** and the closely related hormone vasopressin has attracted much attention. Women release much oxytocin during and after childbirth. It stimulates contractions of the uterus, stimulates the breast to produce milk, and tends to promote maternal behavior and pair bonding in many mammalian species (McCall & Singer, 2012). Both men and women release it during sexual activity. It has been called the "love hormone," although a better term would be *love-enhancing* or *love-magnifying*.

A convenient way to study oxytocin's effects is to give it to people as a nasal spray and compare its effects to a placebo. Oxytocin passes directly from the nasal cavity to the brain and exerts effects about half an hour later. In one study, men who reported being passionately in love viewed photos of their female partner and other women, rating the attractiveness of each. They rated their partner higher when under the influence of oxytocin than that of a placebo. The oxytocin did not change their ratings of other women (Scheele et al., 2013). So oxytocin didn't increase attraction to everyone, but just to someone already loved.

In another study, heterosexual men received oxytocin or a placebo before meeting an attractive woman. The researchers simply measured how far away from her each man stood. Oxytocin had no effect for single men, but it caused those in a monogamous relationship to stand *farther* away (Scheele et al., 2012). That is, it apparently enhanced a man's fidelity to his partner, decreasing his willingness to face the temptation of another attractive woman.

Oxytocin helps people recognize facial expressions of emotion. It provides little benefit to people who are already good at recognizing expressions, because they have so little room for improvement. Oxytocin helps people who have trouble recognizing expressions, helping them mainly with fairly easy expressions (Guastella et al., 2010).

In many situations, oxytocin's effect on social relations depends on who the other people are. It increases conformity to the opinions of your in-group (people whom you perceive to be like yourself) but not to the opinions of an out-group (Stallen, De Dreu, Shalvi, Smidts, & Sanfey, 2012). In certain economic games, you can protect your initial money or invest it in a cooperative venture with someone else, trusting that the other person won't cheat you. In such situations, oxytocin increases trust toward your in-group members. It can increase, decrease, or have no effect on trust toward out-group members, depending on what you think of those people (van Ijzendoorn & Bakermans-Kranenburg, 2012).

The effects of oxytocin are not always pro-social. When people perceive themselves as being threatened, oxytocin increases their attention to possible dangers, increasing their anger, distress, and negative reactions to others, especially to strangers (Olff et al., 2013; Poulin, Holman, & Buffone, 2012). People who in general distrust others become even more distrustful under the influence of oxytocin (Bartz et al., 2011).

Here is a hypothesis to unify all these data: Oxytocin increases attention to important social cues (Olff et al., 2013). The result is greater attention to facial expressions and stronger positive responses to those whom you love or trust, but increased wariness when you have reason to doubt someone.

STOP&CHECK

28. Why is it misleading to call oxytocin the "love hormone"?

ANSWER

28. Oxytocin increases positive responses toward someone you already love or trust, but not toward everyone.

Empathy and Altruism

Civilized life depends on people helping one another. You might help explain something to a fellow student who is competing with you for a good grade in a course. You might contribute money to help victims of a natural disaster on the other side of the world. Helpfulness depends on **empathy**, the ability to identify with other people and feel their pain almost as if it were your own. Although empathy is not unique to humans, it is stronger in us than in other species. A monkey or chimpanzee with a choice between rewarding just itself, or rewarding both itself and another monkey or chimpanzee seems almost indifferent to the other, unless the other is a relative or long-term associate (Chang, Gariépy, & Platt, 2013; Silk et al., 2005). The ability to take someone else's perspective depends on an area where the temporal cortex meets the parietal cortex (Buckholtz & Marois, 2012; Morishima, Schunk, Bruhin, Ruff, & Fehr, 2012). However, no brain area concerns itself only with empathy and moral behavior, and many areas throughout the brain contribute (Young & Dungan, 2012).

Moral and religious leaders teach us that we should extend kindness to everyone, but in fact most people tend to be more generous toward those they see as similar to themselves. For example, if you watch someone who is feeling socially rejected by others, you will "feel the pain" and your brain will react accordingly, but you will react more strongly if the person feeling rejected is one of your relatives or close friends (Beeney, Franklin, Levy, & Adams, 2011).

From an evolutionary standpoint, it makes sense to be altruistic toward your relatives, and someone who seems similar is more likely to be related to you than someone very different. However, the strength of this in-group bias varies among individuals. Most people show brain responses that differ in several ways between viewing faces of their own race versus faces of another race, but the difference is greater in people with a strong bias toward their own race (Brosch, Bar-David, & Phelps, 2013; He, Johnson, Dovidio, & McCarthy, 2009).

Even rats show this in-group bias. Imagine a rat trapped in a plastic tube. A second rat outside the tube can open the door to let it escape. If they are from the same strain, such as two albino rats, the second rat opens the door. If they are from different strains, such as one albino rat and one hooded rat, the second rat ignores the trapped rat (see Figure 13.22). However, if an albino rat was reared throughout its life with other hooded rats, it helps a hooded rat but not another

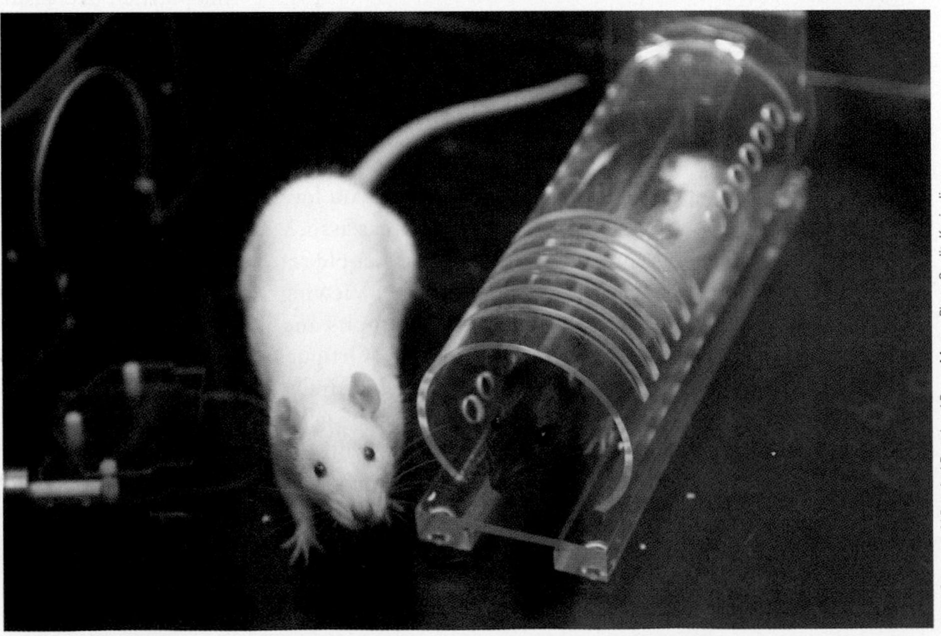

FIGURE 13.22 Out-group bias in rats A rat will open the door to help a member of its own strain escape from a plastic tube, but it will not help a member of a different strain.

Photo Courtesy of I.Ben-Ami Bartal and Peggy Mason. Photo Credit: Kevin Jiang albino rat (Ben-Ami Bartal et al., 2014). Rats don't look at themselves in mirrors, and therefore a rat reared with hooded rats assumes it is one too!

People vary in their degree of empathy and altruism, from generous to selfish. That variation correlates with brain activity. When people hear descriptions of someone else's distress, they vary in the arousal of their dorsomedial prefrontal cortex. Those with greater arousal report greater understanding of the distress, and they are more likely than average to devote time and money to helping others (Waytz, Zaki, & Mitchell, 2012).

People with psychopathic traits freely take actions that will harm others. Do they not understand that others will suffer? The research shows that they do understand . . . cognitively. However, the emotional areas of the brain show only weak activation when trying to imagine someone else's experience (Blair, 2013; Zaki & Ochsner, 2012). That is, they lack that empathic identification that would let them understand how the other person will feel.

STOP&CHECK

29. If a rat has an opportunity to help another rat in distress, under what circumstances will it or will it not help?

ANSWER

29. It helps the strain of rat with which it has grown up, regardless of whether it is genetically related to them.

MODULE 13.4 ■ IN CLOSING

The Social Brain

You may have noticed that this was a short module. Previous editions of this text did not include the topic at all. Why do neuroscientists have so much more to say about vision, for example, than social behavior? The reason certainly has nothing to do with a lack of interest in social behavior. The reason is that researchers prefer questions that they know how to answer. With vision or other senses, they can control the stimuli precisely and measure responses with reasonable accuracy. Social events are more difficult. With love, empathy, or cooperation, the stimulus is a long history of events, and the response is a complex combination of actions that varies from one person to another and one time to another. Research will continue on social neuroscience because of its great interest, but we need to be patient if the progress seems slow.

Summary

1. Passionate love excites the brain in ways that resemble those of addictive drugs. **459**
2. The hormone oxytocin magnifies feelings of love, but it does not create love where it did not exist. **459**
3. Oxytocin increases attention to important social cues, including emotional expressions. The result can be increased or decreased trust, depending on the circumstances. **460**
4. Humans show more empathy and altruism than other species do. **460**
5. Both humans and rats show a tendency to help those they perceive as similar to themselves, more than those they perceive as different. However, some show that tendency more strongly than others. **460**
6. People with psychopathic traits are aware that certain acts will harm others, but they have little tendency to feel other people's emotional pain. **461**

Key Terms

Terms are defined in the module on the page number indicated. They're also presented in alphabetical order with definitions in the book's Subject Index/Glossary. Interactive flash cards, audio reviews, and crossword puzzles are among the online resources available to help you learn these terms and the concepts they represent.

empathy **460**

oxytocin **459**

social neuroscience **459**

MODULE 13.4 End of Module Quiz

1. Which hypothesis best summarizes our current understanding about oxytocin?
   a. Oxytocin increases love and trust.
   b. Oxytocin helps people restrain their emotional responses.
   c. Oxytocin helps people overcome bad habits.
   d. Oxytocin increases attention toward social cues.
2. When people with psychopathic traits try to imagine someone else's suffering, how does their brain response compare to that of other people?
   a. People with psychopathic traits show less response in the cognitive areas of the brain.
   b. People with psychopathic traits show less response in the emotional areas of the brain.
   c. People with psychopathic traits show less response in both the cognitive and the emotional areas of the brain.
   d. People with psychopathic traits show the same responses in both the cognitive and the emotional areas of the brain.

ANSWERS:
1d, 2b.

Suggestions for Further Reading

Koch, C. (2012). *Consciousness: Confessions of a romantic reductionist.* Cambridge, MA: MIT Press. Thoughtful discussion of the mind–brain relationship.

Kellogg, R. T. (2013). *The making of the mind: The neuroscience of human nature.* Amherst, NY: Prometheus. Theoretical view of what must have changed in our brains and behavior as humans evolved from primate ancestors.

Ornstein, R. (1997). *The right mind.* New York: Harcourt Brace. Very readable description of split-brain research and the differences between the left and right hemispheres.

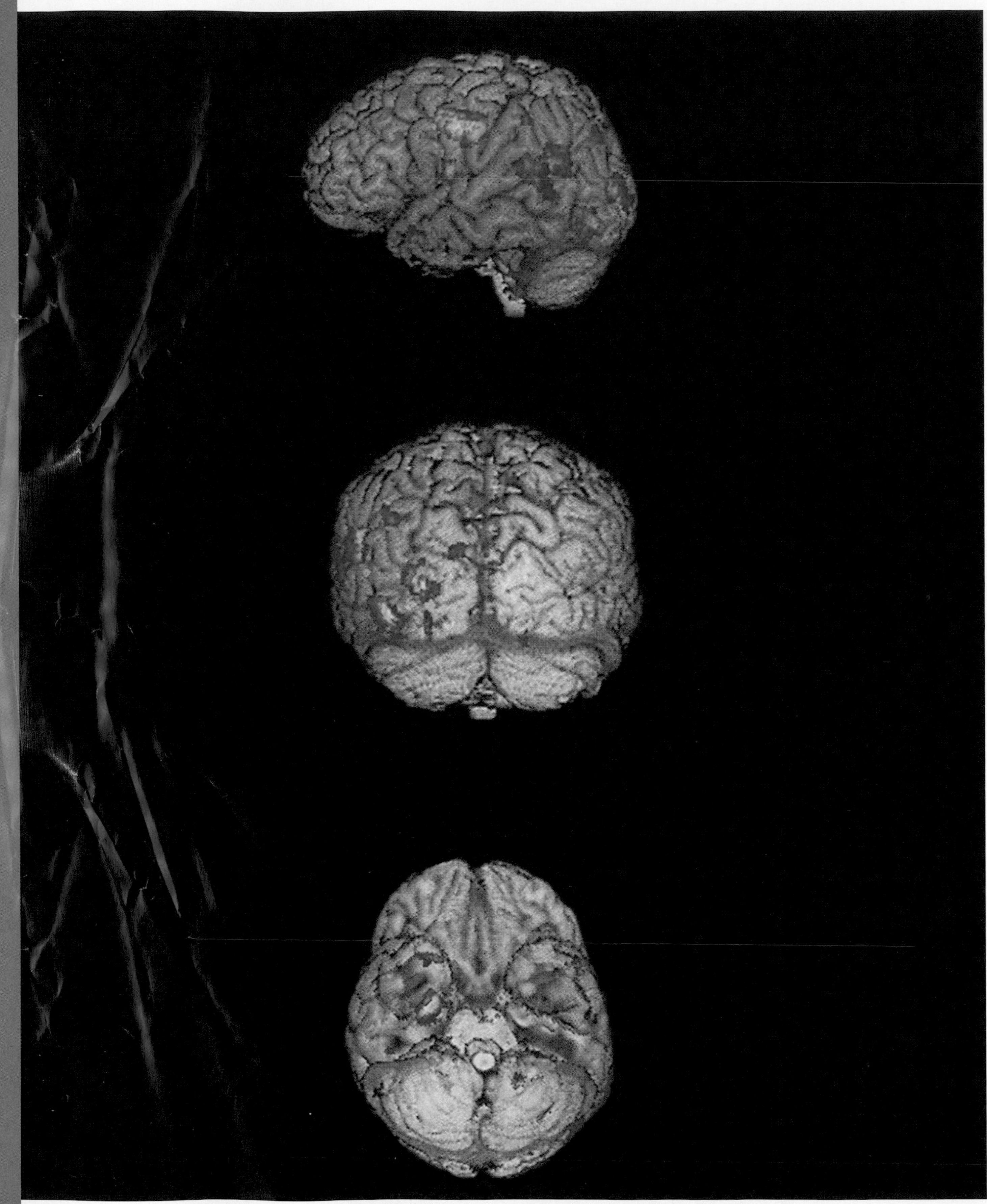

Psychological Disorders

14

CHAPTER OUTLINE

MODULE 14.1 Substance Abuse and Addiction
Drug Mechanisms
Predispositions
Treatments
In Closing: The Psychology and Biology of Addiction
MODULE 14.2 Mood Disorders
Major Depressive Disorder
Antidepressant Drugs
Bipolar Disorder
Seasonal Affective Disorder
In Closing: The Biology of Mood Swings
MODULE 14.3 Schizophrenia
Diagnosis
Genetics
The Neurodevelopmental Hypothesis
Treatments
In Closing: Many Remaining Mysteries
MODULE 14.4 Autism Spectrum Disorders
Symptoms and Characteristics
Genetics and Other Causes
Treatments
In Closing: Developmental Disorders

LEARNING OBJECTIVES

After studying this chapter, you should be able to:

1. Describe the role of the nucleus accumbens in reward.
2. Discuss cravings and their role in addiction.
3. Compare the role of genetics in substance abuse, depression, schizophrenia, and autism.
4. List important aspects of prenatal environment that may influence psychological disorders.
5. Describe medical and behavioral treatments for several psychological disorders.

A physician who wants to treat your cough will start by diagnosing the cause. Did the cough come from the flu, a cold, allergy, lung cancer, tuberculosis, or something else? A lab test can identify the correct diagnosis with reasonable certainty, and a diagnosis informs the physician what treatment options are best.

Does the same approach apply to psychological disorders? For many years most psychologists and psychiatrists assumed, and many still do assume, that a proper diagnosis is important. However, doubts have been growing. Because we have no accurate lab tests for psychological disorders, therapists make diagnoses based on behavior. The symptoms of schizophrenia or post-traumatic stress disorder are so variable that many patients with the same diagnosis have little in common (Galatzer-Levy & Bryant, 2013). Most of the genes that increase the risk of one disorder also increase the risk of a host of other disorders (Cross-Disorder Group of the Psychiatric Genomics Consortium, 2013). Drugs described as antidepressant or antipsychotic are sometimes effective for apparently unrelated disorders (Dean, 2011). Some patients with depression respond to both antidepressant drugs, which increase dopamine activity, and antipsychotic drugs, which block dopamine synapses (Dean, 2011). A growing number of researchers question the idea of distinct categories for psychological disorders.

This chapter is organized around traditional labels such as depression and schizophrenia, but the findings are valid even if we decide to abandon the categorical approach. Regardless of whether depression is or is not a useful diagnosis, depression is certainly an important symptom, and we can ask what causes it and what we can do about it. The same is true for addiction, thought disorder, and other problems.

OPPOSITE: PET scans show the brain areas that increase their activation during visual and auditory hallucinations by a patient with schizophrenia.

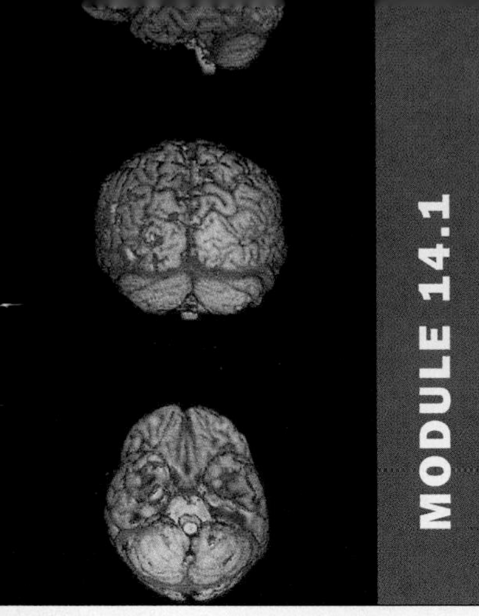

MODULE 14.1

Substance Abuse and Addiction

If you were doing something and you found that it did you more harm than good, you would stop doing it, right? That is why **addiction** (or *dependence*) is such a paradox. As an addiction progresses, the pleasures become weaker while the costs and risks increase. When we talk about addiction, we think mainly of alcohol and other drugs, but the same principles apply to gambling, overeating, excessive video game playing, and any other habit that dominates and harms someone's life.

Drug Mechanisms

Let's start with a brief description of how drugs work. Most of the commonly abused drugs derive from plants. For example, nicotine comes from tobacco, caffeine from coffee and tea, opiates from poppies, and cocaine from coca. We might wonder why our brains respond to plant chemicals. An explanation is more apparent if we put it the other way: Why do plants produce chemicals that affect our brains? Nearly all neurotransmitters and hormones are the same in humans as in other species (Cravchik & Goldman, 2000). So if a plant evolves a chemical to attract bees, repel caterpillars, or whatever, that chemical is likely to affect humans also.

Drugs either facilitate or inhibit transmission at synapses. A drug that blocks a neurotransmitter is an **antagonist**, whereas a drug that mimics or increases the effects is an **agonist.** (The term *agonist* is derived from a Greek word meaning "contestant." The term *agony* derives from the same root. An *antagonist* is an "anti-agonist," or member of the opposing team.) A *mixed agonist–antagonist* is an agonist for some effects of the neurotransmitter and an antagonist for others or an agonist at some doses and an antagonist at others.

Investigators say that a drug has an **affinity** for a receptor if it binds to it, like a key into a lock. Affinities vary from strong to weak. A drug's **efficacy** is its tendency to activate the receptor. A drug that binds to a receptor but fails to stimulate it has a high affinity but low efficacy.

The effectiveness and side effects of drugs vary from one person to another. Why? Most drugs affect several kinds of receptors. People vary in their abundance of each kind of receptor. For example, one person might have a relatively large number of dopamine type D_4 receptors and relatively few D_1 or D_2 receptors, whereas someone else has the reverse (Cravchik & Goldman, 2000).

STOP & CHECK

1. Is a drug with high affinity and low efficacy an agonist or an antagonist?

ANSWER

1. It is an antagonist because, by occupying the receptor, it blocks out the neurotransmitter.

Similarities and Differences among Addictive Substances

All or nearly all abused drugs increase activity at dopamine and norepinephrine synapses. The story behind the discovery of the brain mechanisms begins with a pair of young psychologists who were trying to answer a different question.

James Olds and Peter Milner (1954) wanted to test whether stimulation of a certain brain area might influence which direction a rat turns. When they implanted their electrode, they missed the intended target and instead hit an area called the septum. To their surprise, when the rat received the brain stimulation, it sat up, looked around, and sniffed, as if reacting to a favorable stimulus. Olds and Milner then gave rats the opportunity to press a lever to produce electrical **self-stimulation of the brain** (see Figure 14.1). With electrodes in the septum and certain other places, rats sometimes pressed as often as 2,000 times per hour (Olds, 1958). Later researchers found many brain areas that rats would work to stimulate. All those areas had axons that directly or indirectly increase the release of dopamine or norepinephrine in the **nucleus accumbens,** as illustrated in Figure 14.2 (Wise, 1996).

Science Source

FIGURE 14.1 A rat pressing a lever for self-stimulation of its brain

The nucleus accumbens is central to reinforcing experiences of all types. Addictive drugs strongly activate the nucleus accumbens by releasing dopamine or norepinephrine there (Caine et al., 2007; Weinshenker & Schroeder, 2007). Stimulant drugs such as cocaine and amphetamine block reuptake of released dopamine or reverse the dopamine transporter so that it releases dopamine instead of producing reuptake (Calipari & Ferris, 2013). Opiates inhibit neurons that release GABA, a transmitter that inhibits the firing of dopamine neurons (North, 1992). By inhibiting an inhibitor, the net effect is to increase dopamine release. Opiates also produce reward more directly by means independent of dopamine (Badiani, Belin, Epstein, Calu, & Shaham, 2011).

Sexual excitement also releases dopamine in the nucleus accumbens (Damsma, Pfaus, Wenkstern, Philips, & Fibiger, 1992; Lorrain, Riolo, Matuszewich, & Hull, 1999). So do music (Salimpoor et al., 2013), the taste of sugar (Roitman, Wheeler, Wightman, & Carelli, 2008), and simply imagining something pleasant (Costa, Lang, Sabatinelli, Versace, & Bradley, 2010). Gambling activates this area for habitual gamblers (Breiter, Aharon, Kahneman, Dale, & Shizgal, 2001), and video game playing activates it for habitual video game players (Ko et al., 2009; Koepp et al., 1998). People with major depression show less than normal response in the nucleus accumbens, corresponding to the fact that they report getting little joy out of life (Pizzagalli et al., 2009).

All abused drugs and even non-drug addictions such as gambling have much in common. Many people have more than one addiction, such as drinking, overeating, and gambling. A laboratory study found that after rats became binge eaters (because of the high-fat diet they were offered three times a week), they also developed a stronger than average cocaine habit when they had the opportunity (Puhl, Cason, Wojnicki, Corwin, & Grigson, 2011). However, addictions differ in important ways, too. For example, cocaine and amphetamine abuse lead to greater impulsiveness than opiate addiction does. Also, opiates impair learning more than stimulants do (Badiani et al., 2011).

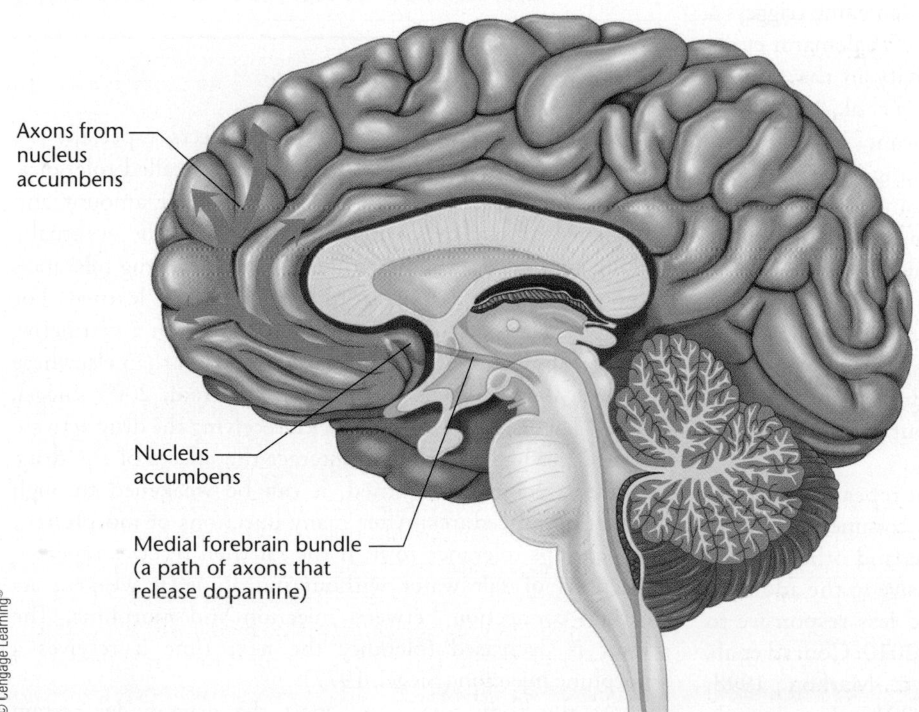

FIGURE 14.2 The nucleus accumbens in the human brain

Nearly all abused drugs, as well as a variety of other highly reinforcing or addictive activities increase dopamine release in the nucleus accumbens.

Stimulant drugs produce varied behavioral effects. Low doses of amphetamine are sometimes used as a treatment for attention deficit disorder (ADD), a condition marked by impulsiveness and poor control of attention. However, higher doses of stimulant drugs impair attention and learning (Stalnaker et al., 2007), and the attention problems that result from prolonged use continue for a year or more after someone quits taking the drugs (Toomey et al., 2003).

STOP&CHECK

2. How do opiates influence dopamine synapses?

3. What do drug use, sex, gambling, and video game playing have in common?

ANSWERS

2. Opiates stimulate endorphin synapses, which inhibit neurons that inhibit release of dopamine. By inhibiting an inhibitor, opiates increase the release of dopamine. **3.** They increase the release of dopamine in the nucleus accumbens.

Cravings

A distinguishing feature of any addiction is **craving**—an insistent search for the activity (Skinner & Aubin, 2010). Even after a long period of abstinence, exposure to cues associated with the substance triggers a renewed craving. For example, seeing a lit cigarette triggers a craving in smokers (Hutchison, LaChance, Niaura, Bryan, & Smolen, 2002), a video of cocaine use triggers cravings in cocaine users (Volkow et al., 2006), and the sight of a popular video game triggers a craving in an excessive video game player (Thalemann et al., 2007). A drug-related cue increases activity in the nucleus accumbens and several related areas (Gloria et al., 2009).

Someone with a craving has a strong "want." Psychologists distinguish between "wanting" and "liking" (Berridge & Robinson, 1995, 1998). Ordinarily, you want something that you like and like what you want, but not always. You might want medicine but not enjoy it. You know you would enjoy a fattening dessert, but you might not want it. Similarly, someone with an addiction strongly wants something and is preoccupied with thinking about it, but may or may not "like" it. Many people who excessively gamble, drink alcohol, or use drugs report more distress than pleasure, but they nevertheless find it difficult to stop.

Studies with laboratory rats show that repeated exposure to addictive substances such as nicotine, cocaine, or alcohol alters receptors in the nucleus accumbens and other reward areas such that they become more responsive to the addictive substance, or cues associated with it, and less responsive to other types of reinforcement (Changeux, 2010; Conrad et al., 2008; Epping-Jordan, Watkins, Koob, & Markou, 1998; Köpetz, Lejuez, Wiers, & Kruglanski, 2013; Koya et al., 2012; Mameli et al., 2009; Maze et al., 2010; J. Wang et al., 2012). Even sexual stimulation becomes less rewarding. You might say the addiction "highjacks" the reward system. After development of an addiction, a rat exposed to cues associated with the drug increases its efforts to obtain the drug, such as vigorous bar pressing (LeBlanc, Ostlund, & Maidment, 2012; Saunders, Yager, & Robinson, 2013). The rat's behavior resembles that of a person with a craving.

Repeated exposure to addictive drugs also disrupts activity in the prefrontal cortex and other areas responsible for restraining impulses (B. T. Chen et al., 2013; Goldstein & Volkow, 2011). Ordinarily a decision whether or not to do something is a matter of weighing the pros and cons, for rats just as for humans. However, after an addiction develops, the weakened prefrontal cortex fails to overrule the reward-seeking areas. After rats develop an alcohol habit—yes, rats as well as people are susceptible—they continue drinking alcohol even if it is adulterated with a bitter taste or if it is accompanied by foot shock (Saunders et al., 2013; Seif et al., 2013).

STOP&CHECK

4. How is the wanting versus liking distinction helpful in understanding addiction?

5. When addiction develops, how does the nucleus accumbens change its response to the addictive activity and to other reinforcements?

ANSWERS

4. Many people with an addiction say it provides them with more distress than pleasure. Therefore, they don't "like" it very much anymore. However, they continue to crave it (want it) strongly. **5.** The nucleus accumbens increases its response to the addictive activity and decreases its response to other reinforcers.

Tolerance and Withdrawal

As an addiction develops, many of its effects, especially the enjoyable effects, decrease. That decrease is called **tolerance**. Because of tolerance, heroin users raise their amount and frequency of use to greater and greater levels, eventually taking amounts that would kill other people. Drug tolerance, a complex phenomenon, is to a large extent learned. For example, rats that consistently receive drugs in a distinctive location show more tolerance in that location than elsewhere (Cepeda-Benito, Davis, Reynoso, & Harraid, 2005; Siegel, 1983). That is, cues associated with receiving the drug activate learned mechanisms that counteract the effects of the drug. Because tolerance is learned, it can be weakened through extinction procedures. After many injections of morphine, a rat develops tolerance to it. If the rat then receives repeated injections of salt water without morphine, it weakens its learned connection between injection and morphine. The result is decreased tolerance the next time it receives a morphine injection (Siegel, 1977).

As the body comes to expect the drug under certain circumstances, it reacts strongly when the drug is absent. That reaction is called **withdrawal**. The withdrawal symptoms after someone quits heroin or other opiates include anxiety, sweating, vomiting, and diarrhea. Symptoms of alcohol withdrawal include irritability, fatigue, shaking, sweating, and nausea. In severe cases, alcohol withdrawal progresses to hallucinations, convulsions, fever, and cardiovascular problems.

One theory is that addictive behavior is an attempt to avoid withdrawal symptoms. However, that cannot be the whole explanation. Ex-smokers sometimes report strong cravings months or years after quitting. Cocaine is addictive even though the withdrawal symptoms are mild. Gambling can be a powerful addiction, even though no substance is withdrawn.

A modified explanation is that someone with an addiction learns to use the substance (or gambling habit or whatever) to cope with stress. In one study, researchers gave rats an opportunity to press a lever to inject themselves with heroin. Then they withdrew the opportunity for the drug. Midway through the withdrawal period, some of the rats had an opportunity to self-administer heroin again, while others went through withdrawal without heroin. Later, when rats went through withdrawal a second time, all the rats had an opportunity to press a lever to try to get heroin, but this time, the lever was inoperative. Although both groups of rats pressed the lever, those that had self-administered heroin during the previous withdrawal state pressed far more frequently (Hutcheson, Everitt, Robbins, & Dickinson, 2001). Evidently, receiving an addictive drug during a withdrawal period is a powerful experience. In effect, the user—rat or human—learns that the drug relieves the distress caused by drug withdrawal. That learning can generalize to other situations, so that the user craves the drug during other kinds of distress.

STOP&CHECK

6. Someone who is quitting an addictive substance for the first time is strongly counseled not to try it again. Why?

ANSWER

6. Taking an addictive drug during the withdrawal period is likely to lead to a habit of using the drug to relieve other kinds of distress.

Predispositions

Most people drink alcohol in moderation, experiencing relaxation and decreased anxiety, whereas others develop a habit of alcohol abuse. The same pattern holds for other substances; some people try a drug a few times and then quit, whereas others develop an addiction, sometimes rapidly.

An important study examined brain and behavior in sibling pairs in which one had drug dependence and the other had no history of drug or alcohol abuse. Both the person with drug dependence and the brother or sister without it showed similar abnormalities of both gray matter and white matter, with certain brain areas larger than average and other areas smaller. Both also showed similar behavioral deficits on the Stop Signal task, in which the instruction is to respond quickly to a signal, but immediately inhibit the response if a second signal comes immediately after the first (Ersche et al., 2012). Evidently, certain aspects of brain and behavior are present from the start in people who have a familial predisposition to addiction, regardless of whether they do or do not actually develop a substance abuse problem.

Genetic Influences

One basis for predisposition is genetics. Studies of twins and adoptees confirm a strong influence of genetics on vulnerability to alcoholism and other drugs, especially cocaine (Kendler et al., 2012). However, attempts to identify individual genes associated with addiction have found many genes, each with a small effect (Hall, Drgonova, Jain, & Uhl, 2013). Few if any genes are specific to addiction. For example, the gene with the largest known contribution to alcoholism also increases the risk of bipolar disorder, and most of the genes related to addiction of any type also increase the probability of conduct disorder and antisocial personality (Kendler et al., 2012; J. C. Wang et al., 2013). Another gene is linked to alcoholism, cocaine abuse, obesity, and attention deficit disorder (Hess et al., 2013).

One gene controls variations in the dopamine type 4 receptor, one of the five types of dopamine receptor. The type 4 receptor has two common forms, *short* and *long*. The long form is less sensitive, and people with the long form report stronger than average cravings for additional alcohol after having one drink (Hutchison, McGeary, Smolen, & Bryan, 2002). Researchers speculate that people with less sensitive receptors seek more alcohol to compensate for receiving less than normal reinforcement.

Another key gene controls COMT, an enzyme that breaks down dopamine after its release. The more active form of this gene breaks down more dopamine and therefore tends to decrease reinforcement. People with that gene tend, on average, to be more impulsive—to choose immediate rewards, including alcohol, instead of bigger rewards later (Boettiger et al., 2007). Other genes influence alcohol use by their effects on risk-taking behavior (Fils-Aime et al., 1996; Virkkunen et al., 1994), responses to stress (Choi et al., 2004; Kreek, Nielsen, Butelman, & LaForge, 2005), and reactions to anxiety-provoking situations (Pandey et al., 2008).

Environmental Influences

Prenatal environment also contributes to the risk for alcoholism. A mother who drinks alcohol during pregnancy increases the probability that her child will develop alcoholism later, independently of how much she drinks as the child is growing up (Baer, Sampson, Barr, Connor, & Streissguth, 2003). Experiments with rats have also shown that prenatal exposure to alcohol increases alcohol consumption after birth (March, Abate, Spear, & Molina, 2009).

Childhood environment is critical also. People vary in a gene that controls GABA receptors. Those with a less sensitive form of the receptor tend to have difficulty inhibiting their impulses, including those leading to alcohol abuse or antisocial behavior. However, those who grew up in families with careful parental supervision are much less likely to develop these impulse problems (Dick et al., 2009).

Adult environment is especially important for late-onset alcoholism. Researchers distinguish two types of alcoholism, although not everyone fits neatly into one type or the other. People with **Type II** (or **Type B**) **alcoholism** have rapid onset, usually before age 25. Most are men with a family history of alcoholism. People with **Type I** (or **Type A**) **alcoholism** develop alcohol problems gradually, usually after age 25 (J. Brown, Babor, Litt, & Kranzler, 1994; Devor, Abell, Hoffman, Tabakoff, & Cloninger, 1994). The late-onset type depends more on a stressful life and less on genetics. It is generally less severe and more likely to respond well to treatment.

STOP&CHECK

7. What is the similarity between the long form of the dopamine type 4 receptor and the more active form of the COMT enzyme?

ANSWER

7. Both are linked to an increased risk of alcohol abuse, probably by making it harder to receive a normal amount of reinforcement. The long form of the dopamine type 4 receptor is less sensitive to dopamine. The more active form of the COMT enzyme breaks down dopamine more rapidly and therefore reduces the reinforcement it produces.

Behavioral Predictors of Abuse

If genes, early environment, or anything else predisposes certain people to drug or alcohol abuse, presumably the predisposition acts by altering behavioral reactions to the substance. If so, it should be possible to monitor behavior of young people and predict their risk for later problems. Doing so might be useful. By the time someone has developed a serious substance abuse problem, overcoming it is difficult. If we could identify people at risk before they develop a significant problem, could intervention be more successful? It is worth a try.

To identify people at risk, one strategy is to study huge numbers of people for years: Measure as many factors as possible for a group of children or adolescents, years later determine which of them developed alcohol problems, and then see which early factors predicted the onset of alcoholism. Such studies find that alcoholism is more likely among those who were described in childhood as impulsive, risk taking, easily bored, sensation seeking, and outgoing (Dick, Johnson, Viken, & Rose, 2000; Legrand, Iacono, & McGue, 2005).

Other research follows this design: First, identify young men who are not yet problem drinkers. Compare those whose fathers were alcoholics to those who have no close relative with an alcohol problem. Because of the strong familial tendency toward alcoholism, researchers expect that many of the sons of alcoholics are future alcoholics themselves. (Researchers focus on men instead of women because almost all Type II alcoholics are men. They study sons of fathers with alcoholism instead of mothers to focus on genetic instead of prenatal influences.) The idea is that any behavior more common in the sons of alcoholics is probably a predictor of future alcoholism (see Figure 14.3).

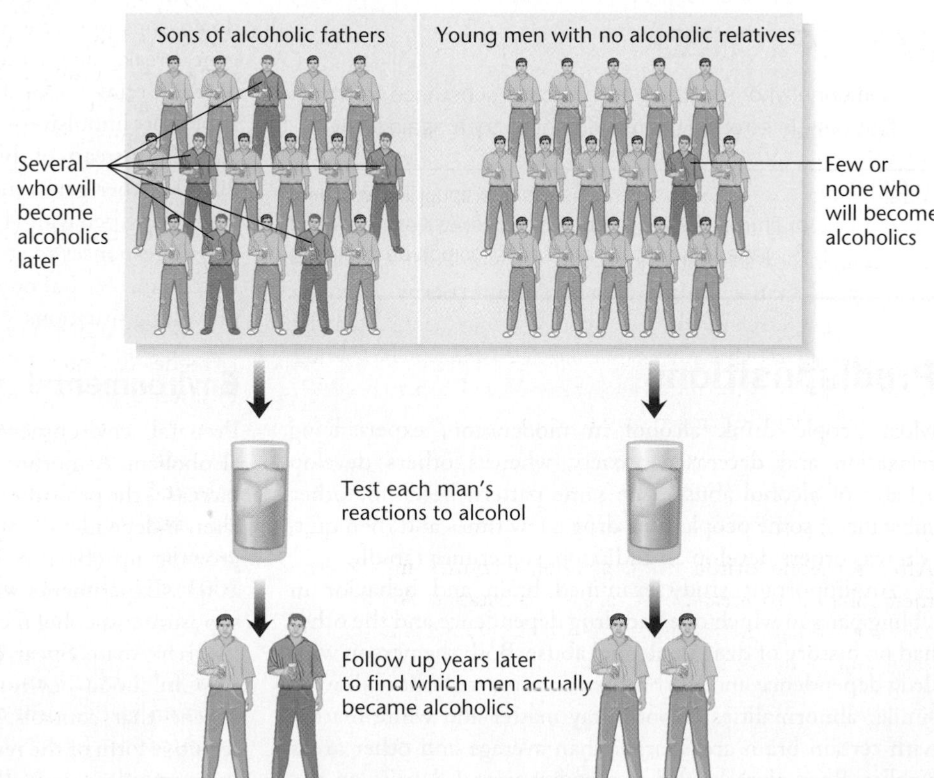

FIGURE 14.3 Design for studies of predisposition to alcoholism
Sons of alcoholic fathers are compared to other young men of the same age and same current drinking habits. Any behavior that is more common in the first group is presumably a predictor of later alcoholism.

Here are the findings:

- Sons of alcoholics show less than average intoxication after drinking a moderate amount of alcohol. They report feeling less drunk and show less body sway (Schuckit & Smith, 1996). Presumably, someone who starts feeling tipsy stops drinking at that point. People who "hold their liquor well" continue drinking, perhaps enough to impair their judgment. A follow-up study found that sons of alcoholics who report low intoxication after moderate drinking have a probability greater than 60 percent of developing alcoholism (Schuckit & Smith, 1997). Another follow-up found that men with low physical response to moderate drinking remain more likely to abuse alcohol throughout their lives (Schuckit & Smith, 2013). Similar results have been reported for women (Eng, Schuckit, & Smith, 2005). (So if you "hold your liquor well," it's not something to brag about. It's something to worry about.)
- Alcohol decreases stress for most people, but it decreases it even more for sons of alcoholics (Levenson, Oyama, & Meek, 1987).

James W. Kalat

FIGURE 14.4 Robin Kalat (the author's daughter) finds an alcohol vending machine in Tokyo in 1998
Restrictions against buying alcohol were traditionally weak in a country where most people cannot quickly metabolize acetaldehyde and therefore drink alcohol only in moderation. However, in 2000, Japan banned public alcohol vending machines.

STOP&CHECK

8. What are two ways sons of alcoholics differ behaviorally, on average, from sons of nonalcoholics?

ANSWER

8. Sons of alcoholics show less intoxication, including less body sway, after drinking a moderate amount of alcohol. They also show greater relief from stress after drinking alcohol.

Treatments

Some people who abuse alcohol or other substances as young adults manage to decrease their use without help. Those who discover that they cannot solve the problem on their own often try Alcoholics Anonymous, Narcotics Anonymous, or similar organizations, which are especially widespread in the United States. An alternative is to see a therapist, particularly a cognitive behavioral therapist. One version of therapy is *contingency management*, which includes rewards for remaining drug-free (Kaminer, 2000). Not many people turn to medications, but a few options are moderately helpful.

Medications to Combat Alcohol Abuse

After someone drinks ethyl alcohol, enzymes in the liver metabolize it to *acetaldehyde*, a toxic substance. An enzyme, acetaldehyde dehydrogenase, then converts acetaldehyde to *acetic acid*, a chemical that the body uses for energy:

$$\text{Ethyl alcohol} \longrightarrow \text{Acetaldehyde} \xrightarrow{\text{Acetaldehyde dehydrogenase}} \text{Acetic acid}$$

People with a gene for producing less acetaldehyde dehydrogenase metabolize acetaldehyde more slowly. If they drink much alcohol, they accumulate acetaldehyde, which produces flushing of the face, increased heart rate, nausea, headache, abdominal pain, impaired breathing, and tissue damage. More than a third of the people in China and Japan have a gene that slows acetaldehyde metabolism. Probably for that reason, alcohol abuse has historically been uncommon in those countries (Luczak, Glatt, & Wall, 2006) (see Figure 14.4).

The drug *disulfiram*, which goes by the trade name **Antabuse,** antagonizes the effects of acetaldehyde dehydrogenase by binding to its copper ion. Its effects were discovered by accident. The workers in one rubber-manufacturing plant found that when they got disulfiram on their skin, they developed a rash (L. Schwartz & Tulipan, 1933). If they inhaled it, they couldn't drink alcohol without getting sick. Soon therapists tried using disulfiram as a drug, hoping that alcoholics would associate alcohol with illness and stop drinking.

Most studies find that Antabuse is moderately effective (Hughes & Cook, 1997). When it works, it supplements the alcoholic's own commitment to stop drinking. By taking a daily pill and imagining the illness that could follow a drink of alcohol, the person reaffirms a decision to abstain. In that case, it doesn't matter whether or not the pill really contains Antabuse, because someone who never drinks does not experience the illness (Fuller & Roth, 1979). Those who drink in spite of taking the pill become ill, but often they quit taking the pill instead of quitting alcohol.

A related idea is to have people drink alcohol and then take a drug that produces nausea, thereby forming a learned aversion to the taste of the alcohol. That procedure usually produces quick and effective results, although its use has never become popular (Revusky, 2009).

Other medications are naloxone (trade name Revia) and naltrexone, which block opiate receptors and thereby decrease the pleasure from alcohol. On average these drugs are only moderately helpful, but the results vary considerably, partly because of variations in people's motivation to quit alcohol and partly because of genetic variation in responsiveness to the drugs (Heilig, Goldman, Berrettini, & O'Brien, 2011).

STOP&CHECK

9. How does Antabuse work?

ANSWER

9. Antabuse blocks the enzyme that converts acetaldehyde to acetic acid. It therefore makes people sick if they drink alcohol. Potentially, it could teach people an aversion to alcohol, but more often, it works as a way for the person to make a daily recommitment to abstain from drinking.

Medications to Combat Opiate Abuse

Heroin is an artificial substance invented in the 1800s as a supposedly safer alternative for people who were trying to quit morphine. Some physicians at the time recommended that people using alcohol switch to heroin (S. Siegel, 1987). They abandoned this idea when they discovered how addictive heroin is.

Still, the idea has persisted that people who cannot quit opiates might switch to a less harmful drug. **Methadone** (METH-uh-don), similar to heroin and morphine, activates the same brain receptors and produces the same effects. However, it has the advantage that it can be taken orally. (If heroin or morphine is taken orally, stomach acids break down most of it.) Methadone taken orally gradually enters the blood and then the brain, so its effects rise slowly, avoiding the "rush" experience that disrupts behavior. Because it is metabolized slowly and leaves the brain slowly, the withdrawal symptoms are also gradual. Furthermore, users avoid the risk of an injection with a possibly infected needle.

Buprenorphine and levomethadyl acetate (LAAM), similar to methadone, are also used to treat opiate addiction. LAAM has the advantage of producing a long-lasting effect so that the person visits a clinic three times a week instead of daily. People using any of these drugs live longer and healthier, on average, than heroin or morphine users, and they are far more likely to hold a job (Vocci, Acri, & Elkashef, 2005). However, these drugs do not end the addiction. They merely satisfy the craving in a less dangerous way.

STOP&CHECK

10. Methadone users who try taking heroin experience little effect from it. Why?

ANSWER

10. Because methadone is already occupying the endorphin receptors, heroin cannot add much stimulation to them.

In the Experimental Stage

Remember that an important aspect of addiction is craving, and a reminder of a drug can evoke a craving even after a long period of abstinence. Would it be possible to erase the connection between a drug and the cues associated with it?

As described in Chapter 11, a reawakened memory enters a labile, vulnerable period when it can be either reconsolidated or weakened. Reconsolidation requires protein synthesis, and certain drugs, including *propranolol,* interfere with protein synthesis and therefore prevent reconsolidation. In one study, cocaine users were shown several reminders of cocaine, including a 5-minute video, that typically evoke a cocaine craving. After 12 to 15 minutes, the reminders were repeated, followed by either propranolol or a placebo. A day later and a week later, these people were again shown the cocaine reminders. Those in the propranolol group reported weaker cravings than the placebo group (Saladin et al., 2013). Conceivably, this or a similar approach might become a useful treatment.

MODULE 14.1 ■ IN CLOSING

The Psychology and Biology of Addiction

Many people will tell you that alcoholism or other drug addiction is a disease. Is it? The medical profession has no firm definition of *disease*. Dis-ease is literally lack of ease, so in a sense anything that causes difficulty in life is a disease. However, the term is generally taken to imply that a disorder has a physiological basis and that medical intervention is the proper treatment.

As you have seen in this module, addiction does have a physiological basis, in part. Many genes increase the risk of addiction. Addiction alters the brain's reaction to the drug, cues for the drug, and other events. However, none of the physiology provides a full explanation. Addiction also reflects a history of experience from childhood to the present. Although medical treatments are helpful in many cases, behavioral interventions are still the most common and most reliable treatments. Addiction is a complex problem that requires attention to both the physiology and the social environment.

Summary

1. A drug that increases activity at a synapse is an agonist; one that decreases activity is an antagonist. Drugs act in many ways, varying in their affinity (tendency to bind to a receptor) and efficacy (tendency to activate it). **466**
2. Reinforcing brain stimulation, reinforcing experiences, and self-administered drugs increase the activity of axons that release dopamine in the nucleus accumbens. **466**
3. A key characteristic of addiction (or dependence) is craving. It is possible to crave something (want it) without "liking" it. **468**
4. As an addiction develops, synapses in the nucleus accumbens and elsewhere change to become more responsive to the drug and cues associated with it, but less responsive to other types of reinforcement. **468**
5. As an addiction develops, parts of the prefrontal cortex and other brain areas that ordinarily inhibit impulses become less active, leaving the individual more prone to impulsive behavior. **468**
6. Repeated use of a drug leads to tolerance (decreased response) and withdrawal (unpleasant sensations during abstention). **468**
7. Both genetic and environmental influences contribute to someone's predisposition toward substance abuse. **469**
8. Compared to Type I alcoholism, Type II alcoholism develops more rapidly and shows a stronger genetic contribution. **470**
9. People who can drink alcohol without loss of coordination (staggering or slurred speech) are more likely than other people to develop alcohol abuse. **470**
10. Several drugs including Antabuse and methadone help some people decrease their use of alcohol or opiates. **471**

Key Terms

Terms are defined in the module on the page number indicated. They're also presented in alphabetical order with definitions in the book's Subject Index/Glossary. Interactive flash cards, audio reviews, and crossword puzzles are among the online resources available to help you learn these terms and the concepts they represent.

addiction **466**
affinity **466**
agonist **466**
Antabuse **471**
antagonist **466**
craving **468**
efficacy **466**
methadone **472**
nucleus accumbens **466**
self-stimulation of the brain **466**
tolerance **468**
Type I (Type A) alcoholism **470**
Type II (Type B) alcoholism **470**
withdrawal **469**

Thought Question

The research on sensitization of the nucleus accumbens dealt with addictive drugs, mainly cocaine. Would you expect a gambling addiction to have similar effects? How could someone test this possibility?

MODULE 14.1 End of Module Quiz

1. Which of the following types of drug would be a strong agonist?

a. One with high affinity and high efficacy
b. One with high affinity and low efficacy
c. One with low affinity and high efficacy
d. One with low affinity and low efficacy

2. Addictive drugs and other activities producing reward increase the release of the neurotransmitter ______ in the ______.

a. glutamate . . . hippocampus
b. dopamine . . . nucleus accumbens
c. GABA . . . basal ganglia
d. acetylcholine . . . occipital cortex

3. Which of these drugs improves attention at low doses and impairs it at high doses?

a. Morphine
b. Amphetamine
c. Alcohol
d. Marijuana

4. Developing an addiction to a substance causes the nucleus accumbens to respond ______ strongly to that substance and ______ strongly to other rewards.
   a. less . . . more
   b. less . . . less
   c. more . . . more
   d. more . . . less

5. When addiction develops, why does the individual have less ability to inhibit undesirable impulses?
   a. Decreased activity in the nucleus accumbens
   b. Decreased activity in the prefrontal cortex
   c. Decreased release of dopamine
   d. Impairment of the blood–brain barrier

6. What evidence indicates that tolerance is to a large extent learned?
   a. Tolerance is greater in the location where one previously took the drug than elsewhere.
   b. Tolerance is greater in highly educated people than in poorly educated people.
   c. Tolerance is easily forgotten with the passage of time.
   d. Telling people about the effects of a drug can produce tolerance.

7. What evidence indicates that many people with drug addiction had a predisposition toward abuse?
   a. Brothers and sisters of the person with drug addiction show similar abnormalities of brain and behavior.
   b. People with drug addiction remember having a positive experience in their first encounter with the drug.
   c. Most young people can accurately predict whether they will eventually develop a drug addiction.
   d. An fMRI study on newborns accurately predicted which ones would later develop drug addiction.

8. Which type of alcoholism has a stronger genetic basis? Which type has earlier onset?
   a. Type I . . . Type I
   b. Type I . . . Type II
   c. Type II . . . Type I
   d. Type II . . . Type II

9. Which of the following predicts that a person is more likely than average to develop alcohol abuse?
   a. Failing to experience much relief from stress after drinking a moderate amount of alcohol
   b. Better than average scores on the Stop Signal task
   c. Being able to drink moderate amounts of alcohol without staggering or slurred speech
   d. Showing strong physical effects such as staggering or slurred speech after moderate drinking

10. If someone metabolizes acetaldehyde to acetic acid more slowly than normal, how (if at all) will this tendency affect the likelihood of alcohol abuse?
   a. It will increase the likelihood of alcohol abuse.
   b. It will have no significant effect on the likelihood of alcohol abuse.
   c. It will decrease the likelihood of alcohol abuse.

11. What is the advantage of taking methadone instead of morphine or heroin?
   a. Methadone is not addictive.
   b. Someone can gradually taper off methadone and become drug-free.
   c. Methadone is readily available without a prescription.
   d. Methadone satisfies the craving without seriously disrupting behavior.

ANSWERS:

1a, 2b, 3b, 4d, 5b, 6a, 7a, 8d, 9c, 10c, 11d.

Mood Disoders

Is it depressing to read about depression? It might be, but we shall spend much of this module considering how to relieve depression. People with depression look sad and act sad (see Figure 14.5), but most do recover.

Major Depressive Disorder

Everyone has times of feeling discouraged. Major depression is much more intense and prolonged. People with a **major depression** feel sad and helpless most of the day every day for weeks at a time. They don't enjoy anything and can hardly even imagine enjoying anything. They lack energy, feel worthless, contemplate suicide, have trouble sleeping, and cannot concentrate. When they have unpleasant thoughts, they have trouble getting rid of them (Foland-Ross et al., 2013). Changes in the synapses to the nucleus accumbens make it less responsive to reward (Russo & Nestler, 2013).

Absence of happiness is a more reliable symptom than increased sadness. In one study, people carried a beeper that sounded at unpredictable times to signal them to describe their emotional reactions at the moment. People with depression reported only an average number of unpleasant experiences but far below the average number of pleasant ones (Peters, Nicolson, Berkhof, Delespaul, & deVries, 2003). In other studies, people examined photographs or films as researchers recorded their reactions. Individuals with depression reacted normally to sad or frightening depictions but seldom smiled at the comedies or pleasant pictures (Rottenberg, Kasch, Gross, & Gotlib, 2002; Sloan, Strauss, & Wisner, 2001).

A survey reported that about 5 percent of adults in the United States have a "clinically significant" depression (i.e., serious enough to warrant attention) within a given year, and more than 10 percent do at some point in life (Narrow, Rae, Robins, & Regier, 2002). It is more common in adults than in children, but when it occurs in children it is likely to persist a long time (Rohde, Lewinsohn, Klein, Seeley, & Gau, 2013). After about age 14, depression is more common in females (Twenge & Nolen-Hoeksema, 2002).

Although some people suffer from long-term depression (Klein, 2010), it is more common to have episodes of depression separated by periods of normal mood. The first episode is special in certain regards. It is generally longer than most of the later episodes, and most patients can identify a highly stressful event that triggered the first episode. For later episodes, people are less and less likely to identify a triggering event (Post, 1992). It is as if the brain learns how to be depressed and gets better at it (Monroe & Harkness, 2005). In that regard it is like epilepsy and migraine headaches: The more often you have had an episode, the easier it is to start another one (Post & Silberstein, 1994).

Bruce Ayers/Getty Images

FIGURE 14.5 The face of depression
Depression shows in people's face, walk, voice, and mannerisms.

Genetics

Studies of twins and adopted children indicate a moderate degree of heritability for depression (Shih, Belmonte, & Zandi, 2004). However, although many studies have identified one or more genes as being linked to depression, the results vary from one study to another, with no one gene emerging as clearly important (Cohen-Woods, Craig, & McGuffin, 2013).

A possible explanation for why no gene shows a strong link to depression is that when we talk about depression, we may be combining separate syndromes. People with early-onset depression (before age 30) have a high probability of having other relatives with depression (Bierut et al., 1999; Kendler, Gardner, & Prescott, 1999; Lyons et al., 1998), as well as relatives with anxiety disorders, attention deficit disorder, alcohol or marijuana abuse, obsessive-compulsive disorder, bulimia, migraine headaches, and irritable bowel syndrome (Q. Fu et al., 2002; Hudson et al., 2003). People with late-onset depression (especially after age 45 to 50) have a high probability of relatives with circulatory problems (Kendler, Fiske, Gardner, & Gatz, 2009). Researchers have begun looking for genes that might be associated specifically with early-onset or late-onset depression (Power et al., 2012).

Given the difficulty so far in identifying any gene strongly linked to depression, another hypothesis arose: Perhaps the effect of a gene varies with the environment. Consider the gene that controls the serotonin transporter, a protein that regulates the ability of axons to reabsorb serotonin after its release. Investigators examined the serotonin transporter genes of 847 young adults, identifying two types: the *short* type and the *long* type. Each participant reported major stressful events over five years, such as financial setbacks, loss of job, and divorce. Figure 14.6 shows the results. For people with two short forms of the gene, increasing numbers of stressful experiences led to a major increase in the probability of depression. For those with two long forms, stressful events only slightly increased the risk of depression. Those with one short and one long gene were intermediate. In other words, the short form of the gene by itself did not lead to depression, but it magnified the reaction to stressful events (Caspi et al., 2003).

This is a fragile effect because of the difficulty of accurately measuring either stress or depression. Even measures of the short versus long form of the gene are sometimes inaccurate (Wray et al., 2009). Many studies have now confirmed that the short form of the serotonin transporter gene increases the risk of a depressive reaction to major stressors, especially the stress of early childhood maltreatment (Karg, Burmeister, Shedden, & Sen, 2011). However, many other studies failed to find this effect, and the conclusion remains uncertain.

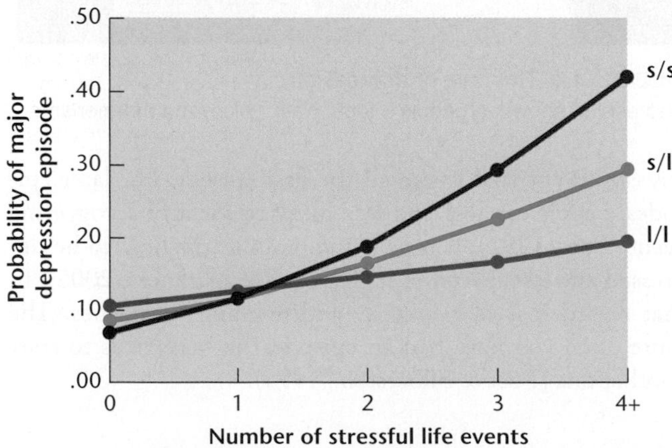

FIGURE 14.6 Genetics, stress, and depression
The effect of the serotonin transporter gene depended on the amount of stress. *Source:* From "Influence of life stress on depression: Moderation by a polymorphism in the 5-HTT gene," by A. Caspi, et al., *Science, 301,* pp. 386–389. Reprinted with permission. © 2003 AAAS.

STOP&CHECK

11. What evidence suggests two types of depression influenced by different genes?

12. What did Caspi and colleagues report to be the relationship between depression and the gene controlling the serotonin transporter protein?

ANSWERS

11. Relatives of people with early-onset depression have a high risk of depression and many other psychological disorders. Relatives of people with late-onset depression have a high probability of circulatory problems. **12.** People with the short form of the gene are more likely than other people to react to stressful experiences by becoming depressed. However, in the absence of stressful experiences, their probability is not increased.

Abnormalities of Hemispheric Dominance

Studies of normal people have found a fairly strong relationship between happy mood and increased activity in the left prefrontal cortex (Jacobs & Snyder, 1996). Most people with depression have decreased activity in the left prefrontal cortex and increased activity in the right prefrontal cortex, and this imbalance is stable over years despite changes in symptoms of depression (Davidson, 1984; Pizzagalli et al., 2002; Vuga et al., 2006). It probably represents a predisposition to depression rather than a reaction to it.

Here's something you can try: Ask someone to solve a verbal problem, such as, "See how many words you can think of that start with *sa-*," or "see how many words you can think of that end with -us." Unobtrusively watch the person's eye movements. Most people gaze to the right during verbal tasks, suggesting left hemisphere dominance, but most individuals with depression gaze to the left (Lenhart & Katkin, 1986).

STOP&CHECK

13. Some people offer to train you to use the right hemisphere of your brain more strongly, allegedly to increase creativity. If they were successful, can you see any disadvantage?

ANSWER

13. People with predominant right-hemisphere activity and decreased left-hemisphere activity show an increased tendency toward depression.

Antidepressant Drugs

You might assume that investigators first determine the causes of a psychological disorder and then develop medications based on the causes. The opposite order has been more common: First investigators find a drug that seems helpful, and then they try to figure out how it works. Nearly all of the earliest psychiatric drugs were discovered by accident. For example, someone who noticed that workers in a certain rubber factory avoided alcohol traced the cause to disulfiram, which altered the workers' metabolism so they became ill after drinking alcohol. Disulfiram became the drug Antabuse. The use of bromides to control epilepsy was originally based on a theory that was all wrong (Friedlander, 1986; Levitt, 1975). Many people in the 1800s believed that masturbation caused epilepsy and that bromides reduced sexual drive. Therefore, they reasoned, bromides should reduce epilepsy. That theory was all wrong, but bromides do sometimes relieve epilepsy.

Iproniazid, the first antidepressant drug, was originally marketed to treat tuberculosis, until physicians noticed that it relieved depression. Similarly, chlorpromazine was originally used for other purposes, until physicians noticed its ability to alleviate schizophrenia. For decades, researchers sought new drugs entirely by trial and error. Today, researchers evaluate new potential drugs in test tubes or tissue samples until they find one with a potential for stronger or more specific effects on neurotransmission. The result is the use of fewer laboratory animals.

Types of Antidepressants

Antidepressant drugs fall into several categories, including tricyclics, selective serotonin reuptake inhibitors, monoamine oxidase inhibitors, and atypical antidepressants. The **tricyclics** (e.g., imipramine, trade name Tofranil) operate by blocking the transporter proteins that reabsorb serotonin, dopamine, and norepinephrine into the presynaptic neuron after their release. Figure 14.7 shows how the serotonin transporter protein picks up a serotonin molecule outside the membrane and then flips into position to deliver the molecule to the inside of the neuron. A tricyclic drug locks the transporter into the initial position, as shown on the left of the figure (Penmatsa, Wang, & Gouaux, 2013; H. Wang et al., 2013). The result is to prolong the presence of the neurotransmitters in the synaptic cleft, where they continue stimulating the postsynaptic cell. Tricyclics also block histamine receptors, acetylcholine receptors, and certain sodium channels (Horst & Preskorn, 1998). Blocking histamine produces drowsiness. Blocking acetylcholine leads to dry mouth and difficulty urinating. Blocking sodium channels causes heart irregularities, among other problems. People have to limit their use of tricyclic drugs to minimize these side effects.

The **selective serotonin reuptake inhibitors (SSRIs)** are similar to tricyclics but specific to the neurotransmitter serotonin. For example, fluoxetine (trade name Prozac) blocks the reuptake of serotonin. SSRIs produce milder side effects than the tricyclics, but their effectiveness is about the same. Other common SSRIs include sertraline (Zoloft), fluvoxamine (Luvox), citalopram (Celexa), and paroxetine (Paxil or Seroxat). Several newer drugs are **serotonin norepinephrine reuptake inhibitors (SNRIs)**, such as duloxetine (Cymbalta) and venlafaxine (Effexor). As you might guess, these drugs block reuptake of serotonin and norepinephrine.

The **monoamine oxidase inhibitors (MAOIs)** (e.g., phenelzine, trade name Nardil) block the enzyme monoamine oxidase (MAO), a presynaptic enzyme that metabolizes catecholamines and serotonin into inactive forms. When MAOIs block this enzyme, the presynaptic terminal has more of its transmitter available for release. The MAOIs were the earliest antidepressants, but they are no longer the first choice for treatment. Generally, physicians prescribe tricyclics or SSRIs first and try MAOIs only with people who did not respond to the other drugs (Thase, Trivedi, & Rush, 1995). People taking MAOIs must avoid foods containing tyramine—including cheese, raisins, and many others—because a combination of tyramine and MAOIs increases blood pressure. Figure 14.8 summarizes the mechanisms of tricyclics, SSRIs, and MAOIs.

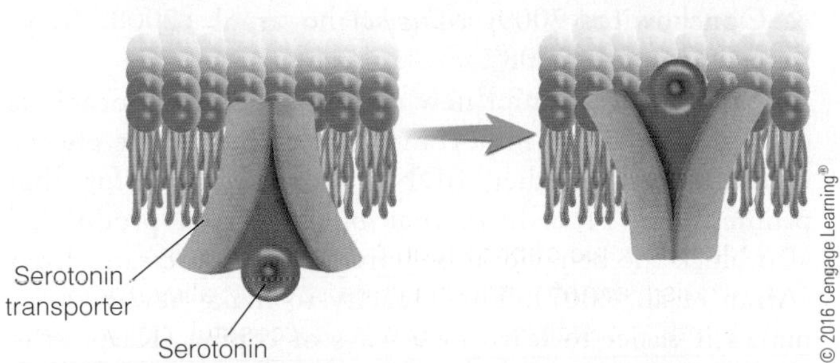

FIGURE 14.7 Reuptake of serotonin into the presynaptic neuron
The serotonin transporter protein is open to the outside of the neuron on the left. After it picks up a serotonin molecule, it flips position to deliver the serotonin to the inside of the presynaptic neuron. Tricyclic and SSRI antidepressants lock the transporter protein into the position shown at the left, preventing reuptake.

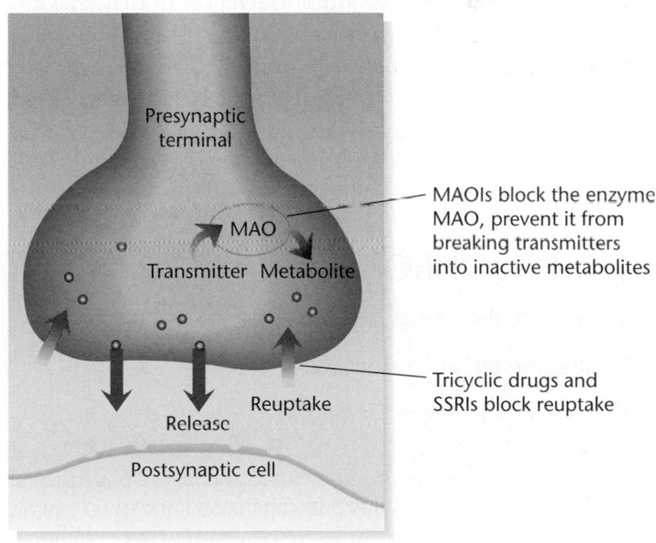

FIGURE 14.8 Routes of action of antidepressants
Tricyclics block the reuptake of dopamine, norepinephrine, and serotonin. SSRIs specifically block the reuptake of serotonin. SNRIs block reuptake of serotonin and norepinephrine. MAOIs block the enzyme MAO, which converts dopamine, norepinephrine, or serotonin into inactive chemicals.

The **atypical antidepressants** include everything other than the types just discussed (Horst & Preskorn, 1998). One example is bupropion (Wellbutrin), which inhibits reuptake of dopamine and to some extent norepinephrine but not serotonin. Although antidepressants vary in which neurotransmitter(s) they target—serotonin, dopamine, norepinephrine, or some combination—all appear to be nearly equal in their effectiveness (Montgomery et al., 2007).

Drug companies have not offered anything substantially new for depression in decades, but a couple of new possibilities are on the horizon. Ketamine, which antagonizes NMDA type glutamate receptors and also increases formation of new synapses, produces rapid antidepressant effects in patients who don't respond to other medications. However, it also sometimes produces hallucinations and delusions (Duman & Aghajanian, 2012). Ketamine itself would not be a suitable antidepressant, but perhaps something related to it might help. Another possibility is L-acetylcarnitine, which produces epigenetic changes on glutamate receptors. Preliminary studies with a small number of patients showed rapid antidepressant results with few side effects (Nasca et al., 2013).

Many people use St. John's wort, an herb, as an antidepressant. Because it is a nutritional supplement instead of a drug, the U.S. Food and Drug Administration does not regulate it, and its purity varies from one bottle to another. It has the advantage of being less expensive than antidepressant drugs. An advantage or disadvantage, depending on your point of view, is that it is available without prescription. People can get it easily but often take inappropriate amounts. Its effectiveness appears to be comparable to that of standard antidepressant drugs (Sarris, Panossian, Schweitzer, Stough, & Scholey, 2011). However, it has a potentially dangerous side effect: All mammals have a liver enzyme that breaks down plant toxins. St. John's wort increases the effectiveness of that enzyme. Increasing the breakdown of toxins sounds like a good thing, but the enzyme also breaks down most medicines. Therefore, taking St. John's wort decreases the effectiveness of other drugs you might be taking—including other antidepressant drugs, cancer drugs, and AIDS drugs (He, Yang, Li, Du, & Zhou, 2010; Moore et al., 2000).

STOP&CHECK

14. What are the effects of tricyclic drugs?

15. What are the effects of SSRIs?

16. What are the effects of MAOIs?

ANSWERS

14. Tricyclic drugs block reuptake of serotonin and catecholamines. They also block histamine receptors, acetylcholine receptors, and certain sodium channels, thereby producing unpleasant side effects. **15.** SSRIs selectively inhibit the reuptake of serotonin. **16.** MAOIs block the enzyme MAO, which breaks down catecholamines and serotonin. The result is increased availability of these transmitters.

Why Are Antidepressants Effective?

When researchers discovered that all the common antidepressants increase the availability of serotonin and other neurotransmitters, they at first assumed that the cause of depression was a lack of serotonin or other neurotransmitters. Gradually it became clear that this simple explanation couldn't work. So far as we can tell from blood metabolites, people with depression have approximately normal levels of neurotransmitters. In fact, some studies show that people with depression have *increased* serotonin release (Barton et al., 2008). Furthermore, it is possible to decrease serotonin levels suddenly by a diet with all the amino acids except tryptophan, the precursor to serotonin. For most people, this decrease in serotonin does not provoke any feelings of depression (Neumeister et al., 2004, 2006).

The biggest theoretical difficulty comes from the time course: Antidepressants produce their effects on neurotransmitters in the synapses within minutes to hours, depending on the drug, but people generally need to take the drugs for at least 2 weeks before they experience any mood elevation (Stewart et al., 1998). Clearly, increasing the levels of neurotransmitters at synapses is not sufficient to explain the benefits of the drugs.

How else might we explain the effects of antidepressant drugs? One hypothesis concerns neurotrophins. As discussed in Chapter 4, neurotrophins aid in the survival, growth, and connections of neurons. Most people with depression have lower than average levels of a neurotrophin called *brain-derived neurotrophic factor* (BDNF) that is important for synaptic plasticity, learning, and proliferation of new neurons in the hippocampus (Martinowich, Manji, & Lu, 2007; Sen, Duman, & Sanacora, 2008). As a result of low BDNF, most people with depression have a smaller than average hippocampus, impaired learning, and reduced production of new hippocampal neurons. Do antidepressant drugs increase BDNF levels? Many studies suggest that they do, over the course of weeks (consistent with the time course for antidepressants to take effect), although other studies found no BDNF increase, and several studies found that BDNF by itself does not relieve depression (Basterzi et al., 2008; Dean, 2011; Drzyzga, Marcinowska, & Obuchowicz, 2009; Matrisciano et al., 2008; Maya Vetencourt et al., 2008).

The proliferation of new neurons in the hippocampus does appear to be important for antidepressant effects, regardless of whether BDNF is responsible for that proliferation. Procedures that block neuron production also block the behavioral benefits of antidepressant drugs (Airan et al., 2007). The capacity to make new neurons makes it easier to learn new ways of coping (Karpova et al., 2011). The importance of new learning may explain why antidepressants don't elevate the mood of people who are not depressed: They aren't burdened with discouraging thoughts that they need to unlearn (Castrén & Rantamäki, 2010).

STOP&CHECK

17. In what way does the time course of antidepressants conflict with the idea that they improve mood by increasing neurotransmitter levels?

18. As opposed to an interpretation in terms of neurotransmitter levels, what is an alternative explanation for the benefits of antidepressant drugs?

ANSWERS

17. Antidepressants produce their effects on serotonin and other neurotransmitters quickly, but their behavioral benefits develop gradually over 2 to 3 weeks. **18.** Antidepressant drugs increase production of BDNF, which gradually promotes growth of new neurons in the hippocampus and new learning.

How Effective Are Antidepressants?

So far we have considered explanations of how antidepressants work. Ho w sure are we that they *do* work? Not everyone is convinced (Kirsch, 2010), and at least we have to say that the effectiveness is limited.

When people take antidepressants, many fail to show any benefit from the first drug they try. After 6 weeks or so, the physician prescribes a different drug, and then if necessary another one, and so forth. It is not possible to predict which drug will work best for a given patient, so it is strictly a trial and error process. Switching to a different type of drug (SSRI versus tricyclic, for example) is no more likely to be helpful than switching to a drug of the same type. Most patients eventually show a favorable response to one of the drugs (Keers & Uher, 2012). However, at that point, how can we be sure the drug was responsible for the improved mood? Depression occurs in episodes. That is, even without treatment, most people recover within a few months. Especially when someone goes through a series of drugs before one of them finally seems to work, we don't know whether the patient would have recovered just as fast without the drug. Unfortunately, many research studies have failed to include a placebo control group (e.g., Rush et al., 2006; Trivedi et al., 2006).

Figure 14.9 summarizes the results of many experiments in which people were randomly assigned to receive antidepressant drugs or placebos. The horizontal axis represents scores on the Hamilton Depression Rating Scale, where higher scores indicate more intense depression. The triangles represent patients receiving the drug in a study, and the circles represent patients receiving a placebo. The size of the triangle or circle is proportional to the number of patients in a group. Many people respond well on placebos, either because of spontaneous recovery over time or because of the expectation that comes from taking a pill. Younger patients are particularly likely to respond to placebos (Bridge, Birmaher, Iyengar, Barbe, & Brent, 2009). For patients with mild to moderate depression, the results for placebo groups overlap those for drug groups, and the differences between the groups appear too small to be meaningful. Only for people with severe depression did the drugs show a meaningful advantage (Kirsch et al., 2008).

However, a limitation of this analysis is that the Hamilton Depression Rating Scale is less reliable at lower levels of depression (Isaacson & Adler, 2012). That is, it measures improvement for patients with severe depression more accurately than for patients with mild or moderate depression. Therefore, we should not necessarily conclude that the drugs are useful only in severe depression (Fountoulakis, Veroniki, Siamouli, & Moller, 2013). Nevertheless, the point remains

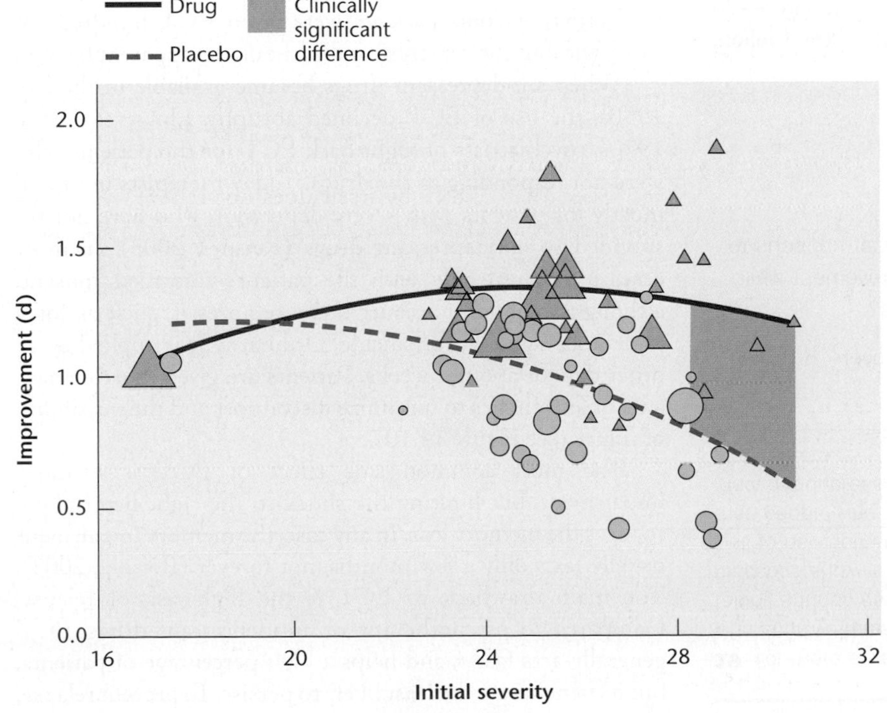

FIGURE 14.9 Mean improvement from depression by people taking antidepressants or placebos

Pink triangles represent people taking medications in a particular study. Gray circles represent people taking placebos. The size of the triangle or circle is proportional to the number of people in the study. *Source:* From Kirsch et al., 2008.

that antidepressant drugs are only moderately helpful for most patients with depression, and not helpful at all for many of them.

Alternatives to Antidepressant Drugs

Cognitive-behavioral therapy and other forms of psychotherapy are often helpful. Reviews of the research literature find that antidepressant drugs and psychotherapy are about equally effective for treating all levels of depression, from mild to severe (Bortolotti, Menchetti, Bellini, Montaguti, & Berardi, 2008). Of course, considering that much of the response to antidepressant drugs is a placebo effect, the same must be true for psychotherapy. The effects of antidepressants and those of psychotherapy overlap more than we might have guessed. Brain scans show that antidepressants and psychotherapy increase metabolism in the same brain areas (Brody et al., 2001; S. D. Martin et al., 2001). That similarity should not be terribly surprising if we accept mind–body monism. If mental activity is the same thing as brain activity, then changing someone's thoughts should indeed change brain chemistry.

Psychotherapy has an advantage because its effects are more likely to last. That is, a relapse into depression is more likely after antidepressant drug treatment than after psychotherapy (Vittengl, Clark, Dunn, & Jarrett, 2007).

Would a combination of antidepressant drugs and psychotherapy work better than either one alone? On average, people who improve while receiving both treatments show greater improvement than people receiving either one alone. However, the percentage of people showing improvement increases only slightly (de Maat et al., 2008; Hollon et al., 2005). That is, not many people respond to one treatment and not the other. Evidently, some people recover over time with no treatment or a placebo, another group improves with either antidepressants or psychotherapy, a few respond better to one than to the other, and the remainder—one-third to one-half, by most estimates—do not respond well to either one (Friedman et al., 2009; Hollon, Thase, & Markowitz, 2002; Thase et al., 1997).

STOP&CHECK

19. As depression becomes more severe, what happens to the percentage of patients showing improvement while taking antidepressant drugs or placebos?

20. What is an advantage of psychotherapy over antidepressant drugs?

ANSWERS

19. For more severe cases, the percentage of patients who improve remains about the same for patients taking antidepressant drugs, but fewer patients taking placebos show improvement. **20.** People who respond well to psychotherapy have a lower risk of later relapse than people who respond to antidepressant drugs. Also, antidepressant drugs produce unpleasant side effects.

Exercise

The simplest, least expensive antidepressant treatment is a program of regular, moderate-intensity exercise (Leppämäki, Partonen, & Lönnqvist, 2002). Controlled experiments have confirmed modest antidepressant benefits, especially for people over age 60 (Bridle, Spanjers, Patel, Atherton, & Lamb, 2012). Research with rats shows that exercise increases brain levels of serotonin and BDNF (Moon et al., 2012) and that it increases sensitivity to reward (Morris, Na, & Johnson, 2012). Exercise is best used as a supplement to other treatments rather than as a therapy by itself.

Electroconvulsive Therapy (ECT)

Another option, despite its stormy history, is treatment through an electrically induced seizure, known as **electroconvulsive therapy (ECT)**. ECT originated with the observation that for people with both epilepsy and schizophrenia, when symptoms of one disorder increase, symptoms of the other often decrease (Trimble & Thompson, 1986). In the 1930s, Ladislas Meduna and other physicians tried to relieve schizophrenia by inducing convulsions with a large dose of insulin. Insulin shock is a dreadful experience, however, and difficult to control. An Italian physician, Ugo Cerletti, after years of experimentation with animals, developed a method of inducing seizures with an electric shock through the head (Cerletti & Bini, 1938). Electroconvulsive therapy is quick, and most patients awaken calmly without remembering it.

Psychiatrists had only this shaky theoretical basis for expecting ECT to be helpful for schizophrenia. When it proved to be ineffective in most cases, you might guess that they would abandon it. Instead, they tried it for patients with other disorders, for whom they had no theoretical reason to expect it to work. Surprisingly, ECT did relieve depression in many cases. However, its misuse during the 1950s earned it a bad reputation, as some patients were given ECT hundreds of times without their consent and without any apparent benefit.

When antidepressant drugs became available in the late 1950s, the use of ECT declined abruptly. However, in the 1970s, psychiatrists brought back ECT for the patients who were not responding to the drugs. Today therapists use ECT mostly for patients with severe depression who have not responded to antidepressant drugs (Reisner, 2003). In most cases it is given only with the patient's informed consent, although sometimes a court order requires it, such as for a patient at high risk for suicide. Ordinarily it is applied every other day for about 2 weeks. Patients are given muscle relaxants or anesthetics to minimize discomfort and the possibility of injury (see Figure 14.10).

The most common side effect of ECT is memory impairment, but limiting the shock to the right hemisphere reduces the memory loss. In any case, the memory impairment usually lasts only a few months, not forever (Reisner, 2003). The main drawback to ECT is the high risk of relapse. Compared to psychotherapy or antidepressant drugs, ECT generally acts faster, and helps a high percentage of patients, but its benefits are the least likely to persist. To prevent relapse,

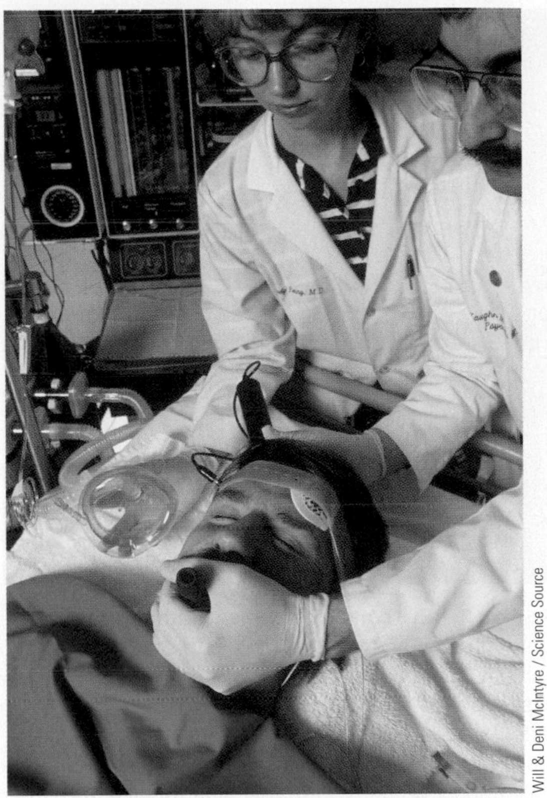

FIGURE 14.10 **Electroconvulsive therapy (ECT)**
In contrast to an earlier era, ECT today is administered with muscle relaxants or anesthetics to minimize discomfort.

a patient periodically returns for additional ECT treatments for at least several months, or follows ECT with other treatments (Petrides, Tobias, Kellner, & Rudorfer, 2011).

More than half a century after the introduction of ECT, no one is yet sure how it relieves depression, but like antidepressant drugs, ECT increases the proliferation of new neurons in the hippocampus (Perera et al., 2007). It also alters the expression of at least 120 genes in the hippocampus and frontal cortex alone (Altar et al., 2004).

A similar treatment is repetitive transcranial magnetic stimulation. An intense magnetic field is applied to the scalp, stimulating the axons near the surface of the brain. This procedure is moderately effective against depression, although its mechanism of behavioral effect is not known (Ridding & Rothwell, 2007).

Altered Sleep Patterns

Almost everyone with depression has sleep problems, and the sleep problems generally precede the mood changes. One study identified teenagers who reported almost daily problems in falling asleep or staying asleep. Within the next 6 to 7 years, more than half of these young people developed depression (Roane & Taylor, 2008). The usual sleep pattern for a person with depression resembles the sleep of healthy people who travel a couple of time zones west and have to go to bed later than usual: They fall asleep but awaken early, unable to get back to sleep, and they enter REM sleep within 45 minutes after going to sleep, as Figure 14.11 illustrates.

If you stay awake all night, how do you feel the next morning? Most people feel groggy, a bit grouchy, and definitely not good. Surprisingly, most people with depression feel substantially less depressed (Benedetti & Colombo, 2011). However, the benefit is brief, as depression usually returns after the next night's sleep. (Presumably someone discovered this therapy by accident. It's hard to imagine any other reason to have tried it.) Combining sleep deprivation with antidepressant drugs is sometimes helpful.

The mechanism by which sleep deprivation relieves depression is not well understood, but part of the explanation

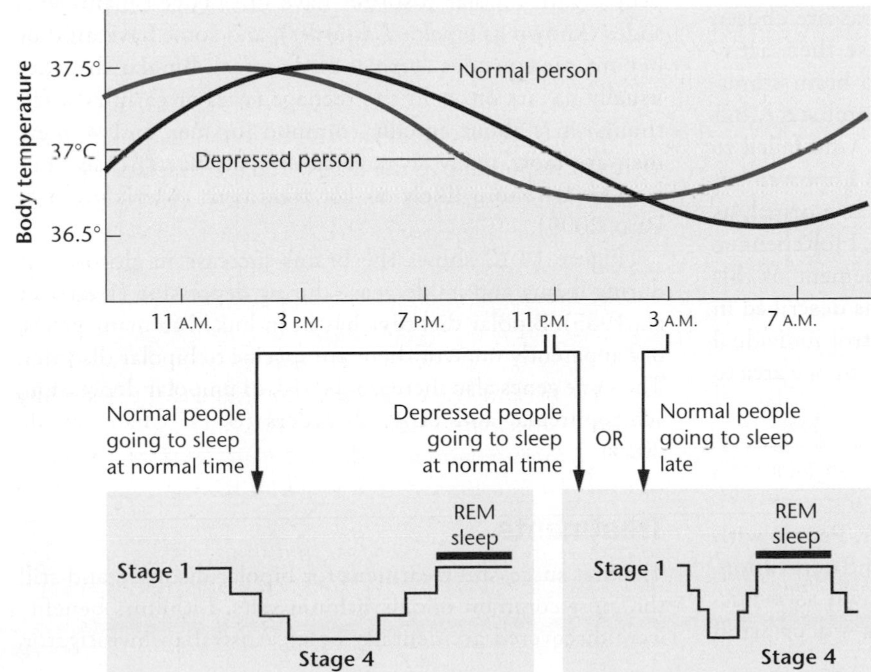

FIGURE 14.11 **Circadian rhythms and depression**
Most people with depression have their circadian rhythms advanced by several hours. They sleep as if they had gone to bed later than they actually did. *Source:* Bottom graphs from *Sleep*, by J. Allan Hobson, ©1989, 1995 by J. Allan Hobson. Reprinted by permission of Henry Holt and Company, LLC.

is that sleep deprivation causes astrocytes to release adenosine, which has antidepressant effects (Hines, Schmitt, Hines, Moss, & Haydon, 2013).

A more practical solution is to alter the sleep schedule, going to bed earlier than usual and awakening earlier than usual the next morning. The person then gets a normal amount of sleep with normal timing of REM sleep. For most patients, this procedure relieves depression for at least a week and often longer (Riemann et al., 1999). Eventually, however, their circadian rhythm shifts again, as if they had traveled a couple additional time zones west without adjusting.

STOP&CHECK

21. How can one decrease the memory loss associated with ECT?

22. What change in sleep habits sometimes relieves depression?

ANSWERS

21. ECT over just the right hemisphere produces less memory loss. **22.** Getting people with depression to go to bed earlier sometimes relieves depression.

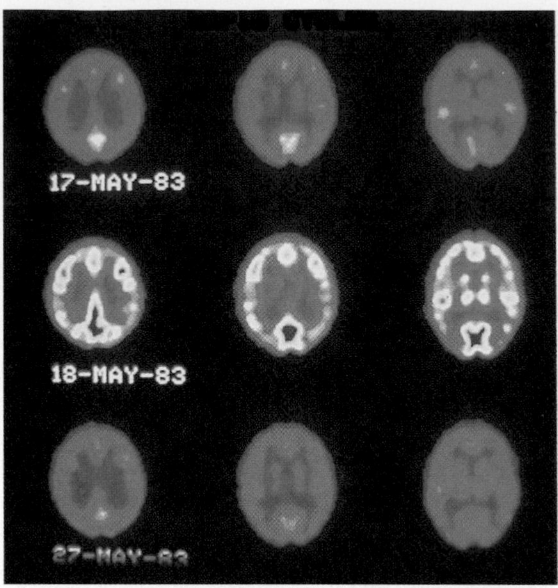

FIGURE 14.12 PET scans for a patient with bipolar disorder Horizontal planes through three levels of the brain are shown for each day. On May 17 and May 27, when the patient was depressed, brain metabolic rates were low. On May 18, when the patient was in a cheerful, hypomanic mood, the brain metabolic rate was high. Red indicates the highest metabolic rate, followed by yellow, green, and blue. *Source:* Reprinted by permission from Macmillan Publishers Ltd: Nature, A functional neuroanatomy of hallucinations in schizophrenia, Silbersweig et al., 1995.

Deep Brain Stimulation

Suppose you are getting desperate. You tried psychotherapy, you tried one antidepressant drug after another, you tried ECT, you exercised, and you changed your sleep schedule. Nothing worked, and you are still miserably depressed. Do you have any other hope?

Another option is certainly not the first thing you would try: With **deep brain stimulation**, a physician implants a battery-powered device into the brain to deliver periodic stimulation to certain brain areas. Those areas are chosen because of studies showing that they increase their activity as a result of antidepressant drugs. Deep brain stimulation for depression is still in the experimental stage, but results have been encouraging. Most patients who failed to respond to all other treatments show gradual improvement over months, and about half get fully back to normal, as long as the stimulation continues (Riva-Posse, Holtzheimer, Garlow, & Mayberg, 2013). A possible refinement of this procedure is to use optogenetic stimulation, as described in Chapter 3. Optogenetic stimulation can control individual connections, rather than all the axons going from one area to another (Deisseroth, 2014).

Bipolar Disorder

Depression can be either unipolar or bipolar. People with unipolar depression vary between normality and depression. People with **bipolar disorder**, formerly known as *manic-depressive disorder*, alternate between two poles—depression and its opposite, mania. **Mania** is characterized by restless activity, excitement, laughter, excessive self-confidence, rambling speech, and loss of inhibitions. People with mania become dangerous to themselves and others. Some people with bipolar disorder have full-fledged manic episodes (known as *bipolar I disorder*), and some have mild or hypomanic episodes (*bipolar II disorder*). Bipolar disorder usually has its onset in the teenage years or early 20s. Although it is about equally common for men and women, men are more likely to have severe (bipolar I) cases, but women are more likely to get treatment (Merikangas & Pato, 2009).

Figure 14.12 shows the brain's increase in glucose use during mania and its decrease during depression (Baxter et al., 1985). Bipolar disorder has been linked to many genes, but apparently none of them are specific to bipolar disorder. The same genes also increase the risk of unipolar depression, schizophrenia, and other disorders (S.-H. Chang et al., 2013).

Treatments

The first successful treatment for bipolar disorder, and still the most common one, is **lithium** salts. Lithium's benefits were discovered accidentally by an Australian investigator,

J. F. Cade, who believed uric acid might relieve mania and depression. Cade mixed uric acid (a component of urine) with a lithium salt to help it dissolve and then gave the solution to patients. It was indeed helpful, but investigators soon discovered that lithium was the effective agent, not uric acid.

Lithium stabilizes mood, preventing a relapse into either mania or depression. The dose must be regulated carefully, as a low dose is ineffective and a high dose is toxic (Schou, 1997). Two other effective drugs are valproate (trade names Depakene, Depakote, and others) and carbamazepine. If these drugs are not fully effective, physicians sometimes supplement them with antidepressant drugs or antipsychotic drugs—the ones also prescribed for schizophrenia. Antidepressant drugs are risky, as they sometimes provoke a switch from depression to mania. Antipsychotic drugs can be helpful, but they also produce unpleasant side effects.

Lithium, valproate, and carbamazepine have many effects on the brain. A good research strategy is to assume that they relieve bipolar disorder because of some effect they have in common. One effect they share is that they decrease the number of AMPA type glutamate receptors in the hippocampus (Du et al., 2008). Excessive glutamate activity is responsible for some aspects of mania. Also, the drugs that are effective against bipolar disorder block the synthesis of a brain chemical called *arachidonic acid,* which is produced during brain inflammation (S. I. Rapoport & Bosetti, 2002). Bipolar patients show an increased expression of genes associated with inflammation (Padmos et al., 2008). The effects of arachidonic acid are also counteracted by omega-3 fatty acids, such as those in seafood, and epidemiological studies suggest that people who eat at least a pound (0.45 kg) of seafood per week have a decreased risk of bipolar disorder (Noaghiul & Hibbeln, 2003).

Another possible treatment relates to sleep. Patients get little sleep during the manic phase; their sleep is more variable during the depressed phase. Sleep disturbance is often a warning sign of a renewed episode of mania or depression. Getting consistent, adequate sleep helps stabilize mood and decrease the risk of a new episode (Harvey, Talbot, & Gershon, 2009).

STOP & CHECK

23. What are two common treatments for bipolar disorder?

ANSWER

23. The common treatments for bipolar disorder are lithium salts and certain anticonvulsant drugs—valproate and carbamazepine.

Seasonal Affective Disorder

One more form of depression is **seasonal affective disorder (SAD)**—depression that recurs during a particular season, such as winter. SAD is most prevalent near the poles, where the winter nights are long (Haggarty et al., 2002).

SAD differs from other types of depression in many ways. For example, patients with SAD have phase-delayed sleep and temperature rhythms—becoming sleepy and wakeful later than normal—unlike most other patients with depression, whose rhythms are phase-advanced (Teicher et al., 1997) (see Figure 14.13). Also, SAD is seldom as severe as major depression. Many people with SAD have a mutation in one of the genes responsible for regulating the circadian rhythm, as discussed in Chapter 8 (Johansson et al., 2003).

It is possible to treat SAD with very bright lights (e.g., 2,500 lux) for an hour or more each day (Pail et al., 2011). Although its benefits are as yet unexplained, they are substantial. Bright light is less expensive than the other antidepressant therapies and produces its benefits more rapidly, often within 1 week (Kripke, 1998). It is sometimes helpful for other types of depression.

STOP & CHECK

24. What are the advantages of bright light treatment compared to antidepressant drugs?

ANSWER

24. It is cheaper, has no side effects, and produces its benefits more quickly.

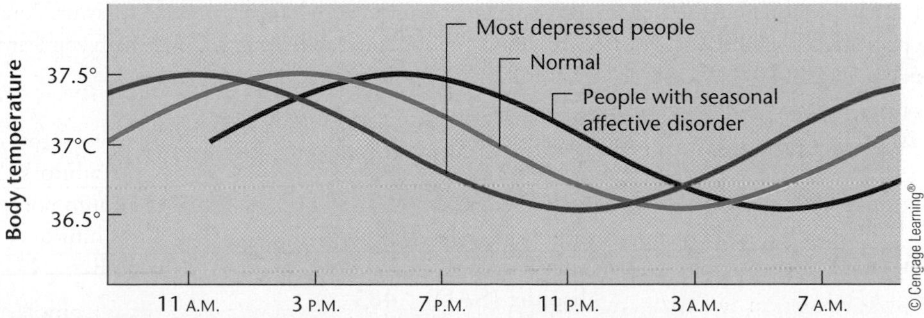

FIGURE 14.13 Circadian rhythms for major depression and seasonal affective disorder (SAD)
Patients with SAD are phase-delayed, whereas most other patients with depression are phase-advanced.

MODULE 14.2 ■ IN CLOSING

The Biology of Mood Swings

There is nothing abnormal about feeling sad or happy if something unusually bad or good has just happened to you. For people with major depression or bipolar disorder, mood becomes largely independent of events. A traumatic experience might trigger a bout of depression, but once someone has become depressed, the mood persists for months, and even the best of news provides little cheer. A bipolar patient in a manic state has boundless energy and self-confidence that no contradiction can deter. Studying these states has great potential to inform us about the brain states that correspond to moods.

Summary

1. People with major depression find that almost nothing makes them happy. In most cases, depression occurs as a series of episodes. 475
2. Depression has a genetic predisposition, but no one gene has a strong effect by itself. 475
3. Depression is associated with decreased activity in the left hemisphere of the cortex. 476
4. Several kinds of antidepressant drugs are in wide use. Tricyclics block reuptake of serotonin and catecholamines. SSRIs block reuptake of serotonin. SNRIs block reuptake of both serotonin and norepinephrine. MAOIs block an enzyme that breaks down catecholamines and serotonin. Atypical antidepressants are a miscellaneous group with diverse effects. Other options are in the experimental phase. 477
5. The effects of antidepressants on serotonin and other neurotransmitters may not be the main basis for their benefits. Ordinarily they affect synapses quickly but the mood benefits develop weeks later. 478
6. Alternative possibilities are that antidepressants exert their effects by increasing levels of BDNF or by promoting development of new neurons in the hippocampus. New neurons facilitate new learning that competes with old, unpleasant thoughts. 478
7. Most people do not respond quickly to antidepressant drugs, and much of the apparent benefit may be due to a placebo effect or the passage of time. 479
8. Psychotherapy is about as effective as antidepressant. Psychotherapy is more likely than antipsychotic drugs to produce long-lasting benefits that prevent or delay a relapse after the end of treatment. 480
9. Other therapies for depression include exercise, electroconvulsive therapy, altered sleep patterns, and deep brain stimulation. 480
10. People with bipolar disorder alternate between depression and mania. Effective therapies include lithium salts and certain anticonvulsant drugs. A consistent sleep schedule is also recommended. 482
11. Seasonal affective disorder is marked by recurrent depression during one season of the year. Exposure to bright lights is usually effective in treating it. 483

Key Terms

Terms are defined in the module on the page number indicated. They're also presented in alphabetical order with definitions in the book's Subject Index/Glossary. Interactive flash cards, audio reviews, and crossword puzzles are among the online resources available to help you learn these terms and the concepts they represent.

atypical antidepressants 478
bipolar disorder 482
deep brain stimulation 482
electroconvulsive therapy (ECT) 480
lithium 482
major depression 475
mania 482
monoamine oxidase inhibitors (MAOIs) 477
seasonal affective disorder (SAD) 483
selective serotonin reuptake inhibitors (SSRIs) 477
serotonin norepinephrine reuptake inhibitors (SNRIs) 477
tricyclics 477

Thought Questions

1. Some people have suggested that ECT relieves depression by causing people to forget the events that caused it. What evidence opposes this hypothesis?
2. Certain people suffer from what they describe as "post-Christmas depression," a feeling of letdown after all the excitement of the holiday season. What other explanation could you offer?

MODULE 14.2: End of Module Quiz

1. Which of the following is the most typical outcome after someone develops major depression?
   a. The person will remain seriously depressed for life.
   b. The depression will grow worse over time.
   c. The person will alternate between episodes of depression and periods of normal mood.
   d. The person will recover without any likelihood of returning to depression.
2. Relatives of people with late-onset depression have an increased probability of what type of disorder?
   a. Anxiety disorders
   b. Circulatory problems
   c. Alcohol abuse
   d. Migraine headaches
3. Which of the following is a likely reason why it has been difficult to identify a gene associated with depression?
   a. Depression does not have a genetic basis.
   b. Only early-onset depression has a genetic basis.
   c. Certain genes link to depression only in people who have undergone severe stress.
   d. Researchers have studied only animal models, not humans.
4. How do tricyclic drugs block the reuptake of serotonin and other neurotransmitters?
   a. They lock the transporter protein into one position.
   b. The transporter protein transports the tricyclic drug instead of the neurotransmitter.
   c. They chemically bond with the neurotransmitter, making a molecule that is too large to cross the membrane.
   d. They make the fluid in the synaptic cleft more viscous, inhibiting the motion of molecules.
5. What is the advantage of SSRIs compared to tricyclic drugs?
   a. They produce their antidepressant benefits more quickly.
   b. They help a larger percentage of people with depression.
   c. They produce milder side effects.
   d. They are less expensive.
6. What is the disadvantage of using St. John's wort as an antidepressant?
   a. St. John's wort is more expensive than standard antidepressant drugs.
   b. St. John's wort is less effective and produces benefits more slowly.
   c. St. John's wort decreases the effectiveness of other drugs someone might be taking.
   d. St. John's wort cannot be obtained legally.
7. Which of the following is evidence against the idea that antidepressant drugs relieve depression simply by elevating neurotransmitter levels?
   a. The dose of drug necessary for relieving depression is greater than the amount necessary to elevate neurotransmitter levels.
   b. The drugs quickly affect levels of serotonin and other neurotransmitters but take weeks to alter mood.
   c. The drugs become less and less effective in relieving depression after weeks of use.
   d. Several procedures other than antidepressant drugs are also effective in relieving depression.

8. If you are already in a normal mood, could you make yourself feel even better by taking antidepressant drugs? If not, why not?
   a. Yes, you could. Antidepressant drugs are equally effective for everyone.
   b. No, you could not. Laws prevent doctors from prescribing antidepressant drugs for anyone who is not depressed.
   c. No, you could not. Antidepressant drugs promote new learning that competes with depressed thoughts. Someone without depressed thoughts has little to gain.
   d. No, you could not. If people in a normal mood take antidepressants, they experience worse side effects than depressed people do.

9. Physicians prescribe drug A for a large group of depressed patients. Six weeks later they switch to drug B for every patient who did not respond to drug A. Many of these patients show improvement over the next few weeks. What conclusion, if any, follows?
   a. Drug B is more effective than drug A.
   b. Some people respond to drug B but not to drug A.
   c. Any switch in drugs increases patients' motivation and therefore helps them recover.
   d. None of these conclusions follows.

10. How does the effectiveness of psychotherapy compare to that of antidepressant drugs?
   a. Psychotherapy helps a higher percentage of depressed patients.
   b. Antidepressant drugs help a higher percentage of depressed patients.
   c. Patients who would respond to psychotherapy do not respond to antidepressant drugs, and vice versa.
   d. Psychotherapy and antidepressant drugs help about an equal percentage of patients, and mostly the same patients.

11. Which of these is a major disadvantage of ECT?
   a. Its benefits don't last long.
   b. Its benefits develop slowly.
   c. It helps only a small percentage of patients.
   d. It causes permanent memory damage.

12. What is the most common sleep problem of people with depression?
   a. They sleep without dreaming.
   b. They have trouble falling asleep.
   c. They awaken early and cannot get back to sleep.
   d. They fall asleep suddenly in the middle of the day.

13. Which of the following has been shown to decrease the probability of a renewed episode of bipolar disorder?
   a. Uric acid
   b. Avoidance of bright lights
   c. Consistent, adequate sleep
   d. A high carbohydrate diet

14. Where is seasonal affective disorder most common?
   a. Near the equator
   b. Nearer the poles
   c. Close to the ocean
   d. In the mountains

ANSWERS: 1c, 2b, 3c, 4a, 5c, 6c, 7b, 8c, 9d, 10d, 11a, 12c, 13c, 14b.

Schizophrenia

Here is a conversation between two people diagnosed with schizophrenia:

A: Do you work at the air base?

B: You know what I think of work. I'm 33 in June, do you mind?

A: June?

B: 33 years old in June. This stuff goes out the window after I live this, uh—leave this hospital. So I can't get my vocal cords back. So I lay off cigarettes. I'm in a spatial condition, from outer space myself. . . .

A: I'm a real spaceship from across.

B: A lot of people talk that way, like crazy, but "Believe It or Not," by Ripley, take it or leave it—alone—it's in the *Examiner*, it's in the comic section, "Believe It or Not," by Ripley, Robert E. Ripley. Believe it or not, but we don't have to believe anything, unless I feel like it. Every little rosette—too much alone.

A: Yeah, it could be possible.

B: I'm a civilian seaman.

A: Could be possible. I take my bath in the ocean.

B: Bathing stinks. You know why? 'Cause you can't quit when you feel like it. You're in the service. (Haley, 1959, p. 321)

People with schizophrenia say and do things that other people (including other people with schizophrenia) find difficult to understand. The causes of the disorder are not well understood, but both biological and environmental factors contribute.

Diagnosis

Schizophrenia was originally called *dementia praecox,* Latin for "premature mental deterioration." In 1911, Eugen Bleuler introduced the term *schizophrenia.* Although the term is Greek for "split mind," it is *not* related to *dissociative identity disorder* (previously known as *multiple personality disorder*), in which someone alternates among personalities. What Bleuler meant by *schizophrenia* was a split between the emotional and intellectual aspects of experience: The person's emotional expression or lack of it seems unconnected with current experiences. For example, someone might giggle or cry for no apparent reason or show no reaction to bad news. This detachment of emotion from intellect is no longer considered a defining feature, but the term lives on.

According to the *DSM-5* (American Psychiatric Association, 2013), to be diagnosed with schizophrenia, someone must have deteriorated in everyday functioning (work, interpersonal relations, self care, etc.) for at least 6 months for reasons not attributable to other disorders. The person must also have at least two symptoms from the following list, including at least one from the first three:

- **Delusions** (unjustifiable beliefs, such as "Beings from outer space are controlling my actions")
- **Hallucinations** (false sensory experiences, such as hearing voices when alone)
- Disorganized speech (rambling or incoherent)
- Grossly disorganized behavior
- Weak or absent signs of emotion, speech, and socialization

Each of these is a judgment call. Sometimes a statement that appears to be a delusion ("People are persecuting me") is actually true, or at least defensible. Many healthy people have heard a voice when they knew they were alone, most often when they were just waking up. The term "grossly disorganized behavior" encompasses a wide variety of possibilities. You could easily find several people diagnosed with schizophrenia who have almost nothing in common. As we shall see later in this module, the genetics vary among people diagnosed with schizophrenia, and so do the brain abnormalities. We are almost certainly dealing with a family of related conditions, not a single disorder.

The first four items on the list—delusions, hallucinations, disorganized speech, and disorganized behavior—are called **positive symptoms** (behaviors that are present that should be absent). Weak or absent emotion, speech, and socialization are **negative symptoms** (behaviors that are absent that should be present). Negative symptoms are usually stable over time and difficult to treat.

It is also useful to distinguish *cognitive* symptoms. The cognitive symptoms are limitations of thought and reasoning that are common in schizophrenia, even if they are not central to the diagnosis. People with schizophrenia typically have difficulty understanding and using abstract concepts. That is, they interpret sayings too literally. They also have trouble maintaining attention (Hahn et al., 2012). Even when they try to focus attention on something, they continue showing strong brain responses to irrelevant items (Lakatos, Schroeder, Leitman, & Javitt, 2013).

One hypothesis is that impairments of attention and working memory are the central problem. One way to test this idea is to see whether we could make normal, healthy people talk or behave in incoherent ways if we overtaxed their working memory. Imagine yourself in the following study. A researcher shows a series of pictures for 30 seconds each, and you are supposed to tell a short story about each one. If you see the same picture a second time, you should tell a new story about it, unlike your first one. Furthermore, sometimes you have an additional task to burden your memory while you are trying to tell a story: A series of letters appears on the screen, one at a time. You should pay attention to every second letter. Whenever it is the same as the last letter that you paid attention to, you should press a key. For example,

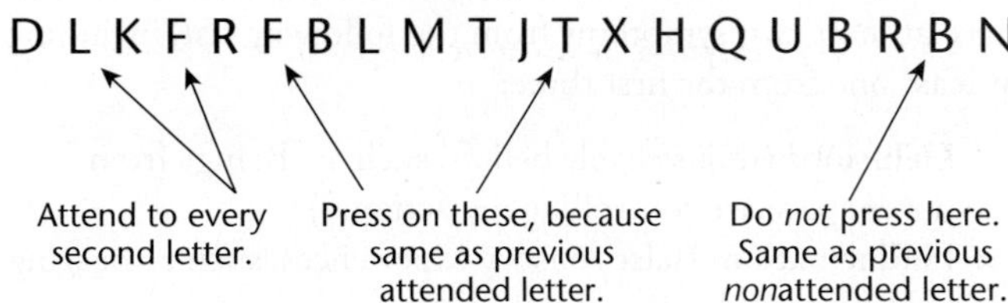

Most people's speech becomes less clear when they perform this memory task while trying to tell a story. If it is the second presentation of a picture, requiring them to avoid what they said the first time and tell a totally new story, the memory task causes even greater interference, and their speech becomes incoherent, much like schizophrenic speech (Kerns, 2007). The implication is that memory impairment could be the central symptom.

STOP&CHECK

25. Why are hallucinations considered a positive symptom?

ANSWER

25. Hallucinations are considered a positive symptom because they are present when they should be absent. A „positive" symptom is not a „good" symptom.

Differential Diagnosis of Schizophrenia

In the rules for diagnosing schizophrenia, did you notice the expression "not attributable to other disorders"? Even if someone's symptoms clearly match the description of schizophrenia, it is important to make a **differential diagnosis**—that is, one that rules out other conditions with similar symptoms. Here are a few conditions that sometimes resemble schizophrenia:

- *Substance abuse:* Prolonged use of amphetamine, methamphetamine, cocaine, LSD, or phencyclidine ("angel dust") can produce hallucinations or delusions. Someone who stops taking the drugs is likely, though not certain, to recover from these symptoms. Substance abuse is more likely than schizophrenia to produce visual hallucinations.
- *Brain damage:* Damage or tumors in the temporal or prefrontal cortex often produce some of the symptoms of schizophrenia.
- *Undetected hearing deficits:* Sometimes, someone who is starting to have trouble hearing thinks that everyone else is whispering and starts to worry, "They're whispering about me!" Delusions of persecution can develop.
- *Huntington's disease:* The symptoms of Huntington's disease include hallucinations, delusions, and disordered thinking, as well as motor symptoms. An uncommon type of schizophrenia, *catatonic schizophrenia,* includes motor abnormalities, so a mixture of psychological and motor symptoms could represent either schizophrenia or Huntington's disease.
- *Nutritional abnormalities:* Niacin deficiency can produce hallucinations and delusions (Hoffer, 1973), and so can a deficiency of vitamin C or an allergy to milk proteins (not the same as lactose intolerance). Some people who cannot tolerate wheat gluten or other proteins react with hallucinations and delusions (Reichelt, Seim, & Reichelt, 1996).

Demographic Data

Worldwide, about half of 1 percent of people suffer from schizophrenia at some point in life (Brown, 2011). The estimate rises or falls depending on how many mild cases we include. Although schizophrenia is less common than several other disorders, it often produces long-term debilitation. In terms of total loss of productive, pleasant years of life, it is a major health problem.

Since the mid-1900s, the reported prevalence of schizophrenia has been declining in many countries (Suvisaari, Haukka, Tanskanen, & Lönnqvist, 1999; Torrey & Miller, 2001). Is schizophrenia actually less common, or are psychiatrists just diagnosing it differently? This is not an easy question to answer.

Schizophrenia occurs in all ethnic groups and all parts of the world. However, it is significantly more common in cities than in rural areas (Kelly et al., 2010). Likely explanations include more exposure to toxic substances, less social support, and less exposure to the sun, resulting in less absorption of vitamin D.

Immigrants from third world countries, such as immigrants from Caribbean countries to Britain or the Netherlands, have an increased probability of developing schizophrenia, and so do their children (Cantor-Graae & Selten, 2005). One possible explanation is a loss of social support. Another is a change in diet. A diet high in sugar and saturated fat, as is common in prosperous countries, aggravates schizophrenia, whereas a diet rich in fish alleviates it (Peet, 2004).

Lifetime prevalence of schizophrenia is more common for men than women by a ratio of about 7:5. On average, it is also more severe in men and has an earlier onset—usually in the teens or early 20s for men, as compared to the mid- to late 20s for women (Aleman, Kahn, & Selten, 2003).

Researchers have documented several unexplained oddities about schizophrenia. The points that follow do not fit neatly into any currently prominent theory, illustrating how many mysteries remain:

- Schizophrenia is significantly less common than average among people with type 1 (juvenile-onset) diabetes, although it is more common than average in people with type 2 (adult-onset) diabetes (Juvonen et al., 2007).
- People with schizophrenia have an increased risk of colon cancer but a decreased risk of several other types of cancer, rheumatoid arthritis, and allergies (Goldman, 1999; Hippisley-Cox, Vinogradova, Coupland, & Parker, 2007; Roppel, 1978; Rubinstein, 1997; Tabarés-Seisdedos & Rubenstein, 2013).
- Women who have a schizophrenic breakdown during pregnancy usually give birth to daughters. However, those who have a breakdown shortly after giving birth usually gave birth to sons (M. A. Taylor, 1969).
- Many people with schizophrenia have a characteristic body odor, attributed to the chemical *trans*-3-methyl-2-hexenoic acid, and decreased ability to smell that chemical themselves (Brewer et al., 2007; K. Smith, Thompson, & Koster, 1969).
- Most people with schizophrenia and many of their unaffected relatives have deficits in pursuit eye movements—the ability to keep their eyes on a moving target (Keefe et al., 1997; Sereno & Holzman, 1993).

STOP & CHECK

26. Someone with the symptoms of schizophrenia might not qualify for the diagnosis. Why not?

ANSWER

26. Other conditions such as drug abuse or brain damage can produce similar symptoms.

Genetics

Huntington's disease (Chapter 7) can be called a genetic disease: By examining part of chromosome 4, one can predict with almost perfect accuracy who will develop the disease and who will not. At one time, many researchers believed that schizophrenia might be a genetic disease in the same sense. However, accumulating evidence indicates that although schizophrenia has a genetic basis, it does not depend on any single gene.

Family Studies

The more closely you are biologically related to someone with schizophrenia, the greater your own probability of schizophrenia, as shown in Figure 14.14 (Gottesman, 1991). Being closely related to someone with bipolar disorder also increases the risk of schizophrenia (Agerbo et al., 2012). Evidently the genetic predispositions of several disorders overlap.

One of the most important points in Figure 14.14, confirmed by other studies (Cardno et al., 1999), is that monozygotic twins have a much higher **concordance** (agreement) for schizophrenia than do dizygotic twins. Furthermore, twin pairs who are really monozygotic, but thought they weren't, are more concordant than twin pairs who thought they were, but really aren't (Kendler, 1983). That is, *being* monozygotic is more critical than *being treated as* monozygotic.

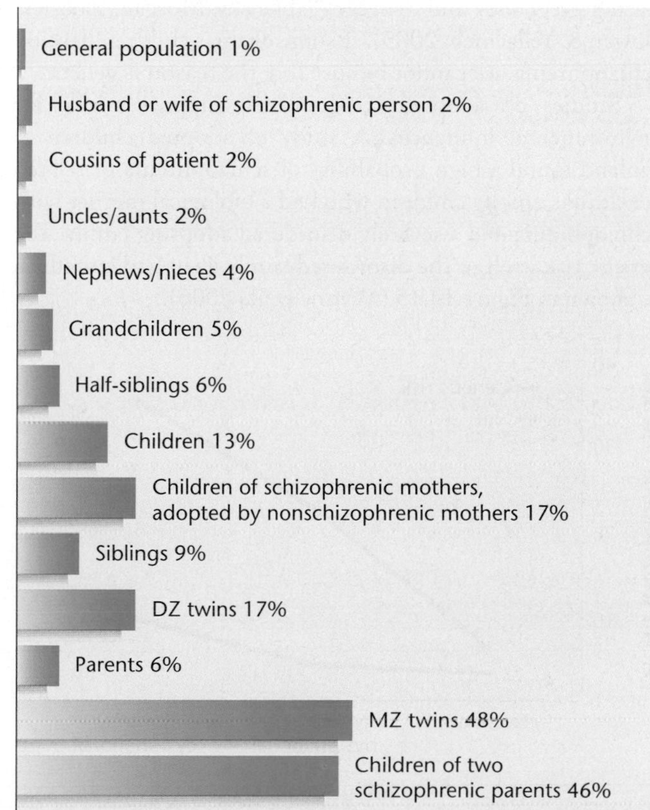

FIGURE 14.14 Probabilities of developing schizophrenia
People with a closer genetic relationship to someone with schizophrenia have a higher probability of developing it themselves. *Source:* Based on data from Gottesman, 1991

The high concordance for monozygotic twins has long been taken as strong evidence for a genetic influence. However, note two limitations:

- Monozygotic twins have only about 50 percent concordance, not 100 percent.
- In Figure 14.14, note the greater similarity between dizygotic twins than between siblings. Dizygotic twins have the same genetic resemblance as siblings but greater environmental similarity, including prenatal environment.

Adopted Children Who Develop Schizophrenia

For adopted children who develop schizophrenia, the disorder is more common in their biological relatives than their adopting relatives. A Danish study found schizophrenia in 12.5 percent of the immediate biological relatives and none of the adopting relatives (Kety et al., 1994). Note in Figure 14.14 that children of a mother with schizophrenia have a moderately high probability of schizophrenia, even if adopted by mentally healthy parents.

These results suggest a genetic basis, but they are also consistent with a prenatal influence. A pregnant woman with schizophrenia passes her genes to her child, but she also provides the prenatal environment. Many women with schizophrenia drink in excess, use other drugs, and eat a less than desirable diet. A disproportionate number have complications during pregnancy and delivery (Jablensky, Morgan, Zubrick, Bower, & Yellachich, 2005). If some of their children develop schizophrenia, we cannot be sure that the reason is genetic.

Studies on adopted children also support a role for environmental influences. A study of adopted children in Finland found a high probability of schizophrenia or related conditions among children who had a biological mother with schizophrenia *and* a severely disordered adopting family. The genetic risk itself or the disordered family itself had less effect, as shown in Figure 14.15 (Wynne et al., 2006).

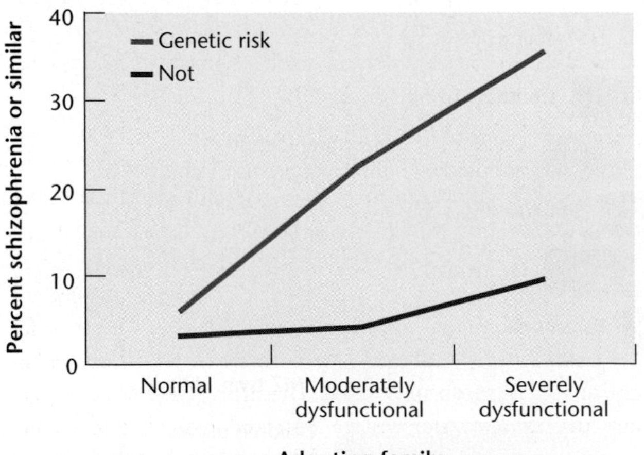

FIGURE 14.15 Probability of schizophrenia or similar conditions in adopted children
The probability was higher for children of a mother with schizophrenia, but growing up in a dysfunctional family magnified that risk. *Source:* Based on data from Wynne et al., 2006

Efforts to Locate a Gene

Researchers working with various populations have identified many genes that appear to be more common in people with schizophrenia—46 such genes in one study alone (Greenwood et al, 2011). However, many of the findings have been difficult to replicate. The apparent reason is that the genes that greatly increase the risk of schizophrenia are rare, whereas a large number of more common genes produce small effects that are difficult to see except in very large samples of the population (Giusti-Rodriguez & Sullivan, 2013).

One gene that has attracted much interest, called ***DISC1*** *(disrupted in schizophrenia 1)*, controls differentiation and migration of neurons in brain development (Ishizuka et al., 2011; Steinecke, Gampe, Valkova, Kaether, & Bolz, 2012), production of dendritic spines (Hayashi-Takagi et al., 2010), and the generation of new neurons in the hippocampus (Duan et al., 2007). Rare variants in the *DISC1* gene are more common in people with schizophrenia than in the rest of the population (Moens et al., 2011), although no common variant in that gene is convincingly linked to schizophrenia (Mathieson, Munafo, & Flint, 2012).

We should not be surprised that no single gene is responsible for schizophrenia. It would be hard for such a gene to remain in half of 1 percent of the population, given the selection pressures against it. On average, people with schizophrenia have fewer than half as many children as other people do, and their brothers and sisters do not compensate by having more children than average (Bundy, Stahl, & MacCabe, 2011). Any gene for schizophrenia should decline rapidly in prevalence, it seems.

If schizophrenia has a genetic basis but we cannot find any gene with a consistent link, and any gene that leads to schizophrenia cannot be passed down through many generations, what is going on? A prominent hypothesis is that many cases of schizophrenia arise from new mutations. Ordinarily, it would be ridiculous to suggest that a condition affecting so many people could depend on new mutations. Mutations just aren't that common. But proper brain development depends on hundreds of genes. A mutation in one gene is rare, but a mutation in any of several hundred is not so rare. An even more likely possibility is **microdeletion**, the deletion of a small part of a chromosome. Microdeletion is a fairly common error in reproduction (McConnell et al., 2013). Several studies have found that microdeletions are more common among people with schizophrenia than in other people (Buizer-Voskamp et al., 2011; Walsh et al., 2008). Those microdeletions were distributed over a great many genes. Thus, the hypothesis is that a new mutation or deletion of any of a large number of genes disrupts brain development and increases the probability of schizophrenia. As fast as natural selection weeds out those mutations or deletions, new ones arise to replace them.

An observation supporting this idea is that schizophrenia is somewhat more common among children of older fathers, especially those over age 55 (Byrne, Agerbo, Ewald, Eaton, & Mortensen, 2003; Malaspina et al., 2002; Torrey, Bartko, &

Yolken, 2012). Women are born with all the eggs they will ever have, but men continue making new sperm throughout life, and the possibility of mutations accumulates over time.

We need not assume that all cases of schizophrenia have a genetic predisposition. Others may depend on prenatal environment or other influences on brain development.

STOP&CHECK

27. The fact that adopted children who develop schizophrenia usually have biological relatives with schizophrenia implies a probable genetic basis. What other interpretation is possible?

28. Why would it be unlikely that a single gene was responsible for schizophrenia?

ANSWERS

27. A biological mother can influence her child's development through prenatal environment as well as genetics. **28.** People with schizophrenia have fewer children than other people do. Natural selection should steadily decrease the prevalence of any such gene.

The Neurodevelopmental Hypothesis

According to the **neurodevelopmental hypothesis** popular among researchers, prenatal or neonatal influences—genetic, environmental, or both—produce abnormalities that leave the developing brain vulnerable to other disturbances later in life, including but not limited to highly stressful experiences. The result is mild abnormalities in brain anatomy and major disorders of behavior (Fatemi & Folsom, 2009; Weinberger, 1996).

The supporting evidence is that (1) several kinds of prenatal or neonatal difficulties are linked to later schizophrenia; (2) people with schizophrenia have minor brain abnormalities that apparently originate early in life; and (3) it is plausible that abnormalities of early development could impair behavior in adulthood.

Prenatal and Neonatal Environment

E. F. Torrey and colleagues (2012) noted that one of the highest risk factors for schizophrenia is having a parent or sibling with schizophrenia. In contrast, having any one of the identified genes is only a small risk factor. If no gene by itself has a big effect, then either schizophrenia results from having many disordered genes or, more likely, it results from a combination of genetic and environmental influences. Torrey and colleagues distinguished between intermediate risk factors and low risk factors. (Nothing was strong enough to count as a high risk factor.)

Intermediate Risk Factors

Two intermediate risk factors have already been mentioned: Having a father over age 55 is a risk factor, presumably for genetic reasons. Living in a crowded city is another risk factor, presumably for environmental reasons.

Another intermediate risk factor is prenatal or childhood infection with the parasite *Toxoplasma gondii*. This parasite, already discussed in Chapter 11 in the context of anxiety and the amygdala, reproduces only in cats, but it can infect humans and other species also. People can be exposed to the parasite by handling infected cats or by playing in soil or sand where cats have defecated. If the parasite infects the brain of an infant or child, it impairs brain development. Antibodies against this parasite, indicating past exposure to it, are more common than average among people who have schizophrenia, as well as those who go on to develop it later (Yolken, Dickerson, & Torrey, 2009).

Low Risk Factors

The risk of schizophrenia is mildly elevated among people who had problems that could have affected their brain development, including poor nutrition of the mother during pregnancy, premature birth, low birth weight, and complications during delivery (Ballon, Dean, & Cadenhead, 2007). The risk is also elevated if the mother was exposed to extreme stress, such as the sudden death of a close relative, early in her pregnancy (Khashan, 2008) or if the mother had almost any prolonged illness during pregnancy (Brown, 2011). Schizophrenia has also been linked to head injuries in early childhood (Abdel Malik, Husted, Chow, & Bassett, 2003), although we do not know whether the head injuries led to schizophrenia or early symptoms of schizophrenia increased the risk of head injuries.

If a mother is Rh-negative and her baby is Rh-positive, the baby's Rh-positive blood factor may trigger an immunological rejection by the mother. The response is weak with the woman's first Rh-positive baby but stronger in later pregnancies, and it is more intense with boy than girl babies. Second- and later-born boy babies with Rh incompatibility have an increased risk of hearing deficits, mental retardation, and several other problems, and an increased probability of schizophrenia (Hollister, Laing, & Mednick, 1996).

Another suggestion of prenatal influences comes from the **season-of-birth effect:** the tendency for people born in winter to have a slightly greater probability of developing schizophrenia than people born at other times of the year. This tendency is particularly pronounced in latitudes far from the equator (Davies, Welham, Chant, Torrey, & McGrath, 2003; Torrey, Miller, et al., 1997). What might account for the season-of-birth effect? One possibility is viral infection. Influenza and other viral epidemics are common in the fall. Therefore, the reasoning goes, many pregnant women become infected in the fall with a virus that impairs a crucial stage of brain development in a baby who will be born in the winter. Researchers retrieved blood samples that hospitals had taken from pregnant women and stored for decades. They found increased incidence of influenza virus among mothers whose children eventually developed schizophrenia (A. S. Brown et al., 2004; Buka et al., 2001). A virus that affects the mother might or might not cross the placenta into the fetus's brain, but the mother's cytokines (part of the immune system) do cross, and excessive cytokines can impair brain development (Zuckerman, Rehavi, Nachman, & Weiner, 2003). Animal studies show that some of the effects of cytokines on brain development appear mild at first but gradually impair brain development as the individual approaches adulthood (Vuillermot, Weber, Feldon, & Meyer, 2010). The mother's infection also causes a fever, which can slow the division of fetal neurons (Laburn, 1996). (Exercise during pregnancy does not overheat the abdomen and is not dangerous to the fetus. Hot baths and saunas may be risky, however.)

The overall conclusion is that a wide variety of genetic and environmental influences can lead to schizophrenia. As stated before, schizophrenia is probably a family of related disorders, not a single entity.

STOP & CHECK

29. According to the neurodevelopmental hypothesis, when do the brain abnormalities associated with schizophrenia originate?

ANSWER

29. Before birth or in early childhood.

Mild Brain Abnormalities

In accord with the neurodevelopmental hypothesis, some (though not all) people with schizophrenia show mild abnormalities of brain anatomy that vary from one individual to another. On average, people with schizophrenia have less than average gray matter and white matter, and larger than average ventricles—the fluid-filled spaces within the brain (Meyer-Lindenberg, 2010; Wolkin et al., 1998; Wright et al., 2000) (see Figure 14.16). They also have a variety of minor abnormalities in subcortical areas (Spoletini et al., 2011).

On average, the hippocampus is smaller in people with schizophrenia than in other people. One study examined people with slight, preliminary symptoms and followed them over time as some of these people developed full symptoms of schizophrenia. At the start, they had areas of increased metabolism in the hippocampus. Later, the areas of increased metabolism showed atrophy (Schobel et al., 2013). Increased metabolism indicates increased glutamate release, and excessive glutamate can damage neurons.

The areas with consistent signs of abnormality include some that mature slowly, such as the dorsolateral prefrontal cortex (Berman, Torrey, Daniel, & Weinberger, 1992; Fletcher et al., 1998; Gur, Cowell, et al., 2000). The abnormalities include weaker than average connections from the dorsolateral prefrontal cortex to other brain areas, and less than normal activity in this area during tasks requiring attention and memory (Lynall et al., 2010; van den Heuvel, Mandl, Stam, Kahn, & Pol, 2010; Weiss et al., 2009). As you might predict, people with schizophrenia perform poorly at tasks that depend on the prefrontal cortex (Goldberg, Weinberger, Berman, Pliskin, & Podd, 1987; Spindler, Sullivan, Menon, Lim, & Pfefferbaum, 1997). Most patients with schizophrenia show deficits of memory and attention similar to those of people with damage to the temporal or prefrontal cortex (Park, Holzman, & Goldman-Rakic, 1995)

An example of a task that tests for damage to the prefrontal cortex is the Wisconsin Card Sorting Test. Someone is handed a shuffled deck of cards that differ in number, color, and shape of objects—for example, one card shows three red circles, another has five blue triangles, and another has four green squares. First the person might be asked to sort cards by color. Then the rule changes, and the person is supposed to sort them by number, and later by shape. Shifting to a new rule requires suppressing the old one and evokes activity in the prefrontal cortex (Konishi et al., 1998). People with damage to the prefrontal cortex can sort by whichever rule is first, but then they have trouble shifting to a new rule. People with schizophrenia have the same difficulty. (So do children.)

Lateralization also differs from the normal pattern. In most people, the left hemisphere is slightly larger than the right, especially in the planum temporale of the temporal lobe, but in people with schizophrenia, the right planum temporale is equal or larger (Kasai et al., 2003; Kwon et al., 1999). People with schizophrenia have lower than normal overall activity in the left hemisphere (Gur & Chin, 1999) and are more likely than other people to be left-handed (Satz & Green, 1999). All these results suggest a subtle change in brain development.

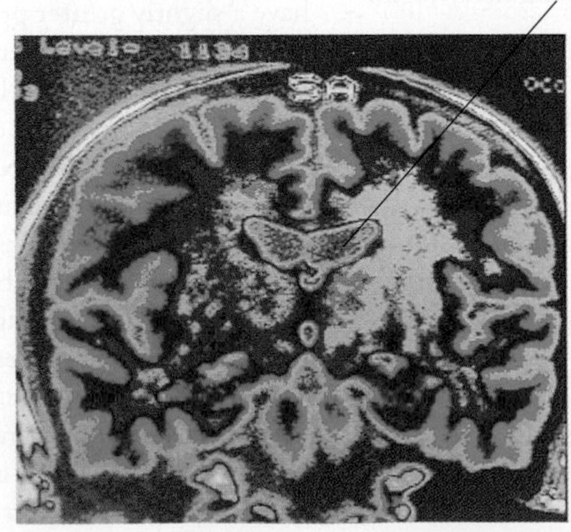

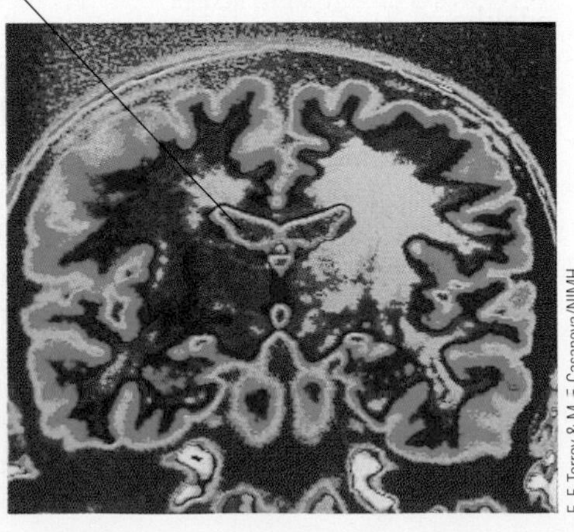

FIGURE 14.16 Coronal sections for identical twins
The twin on the left has schizophrenia; the twin on the right does not. The ventricles (near the center of each brain) are larger in the twin with schizophrenia.

E. F. Torrey & M. F. Casanova/NIMH

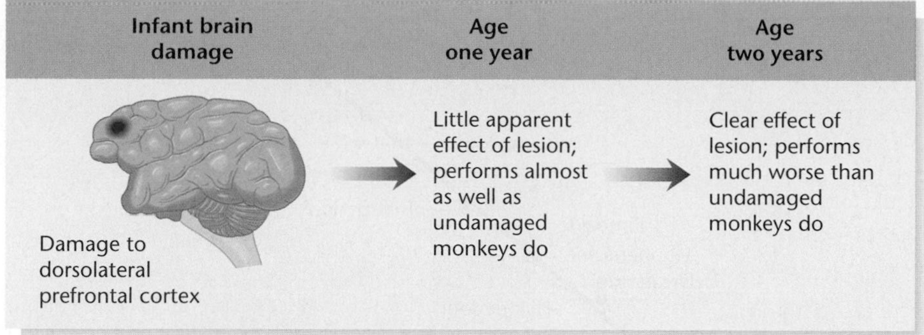

FIGURE 14.17 Delayed effects of brain damage in infant monkeys
After damage to the dorsolateral prefrontal cortex, monkeys are unimpaired at age 1 year but impaired later, when this area ordinarily matures. Researchers speculate that similar damage in humans might produce behavioral deficits not apparent until adulthood.
Source: Based on P. S. Goldman, 1976

Long-term Course

Decades ago, psychiatrists regarded schizophrenia as a *progressive* disorder—that is, one that progresses to worse and worse outcome over time, analogous to Parkinson's disease or Alzheimer's disease. However, that conclusion was based largely on experience from the era when patients with schizophrenia were confined to large, poorly staffed mental hospitals. It is understandable how someone who lived year after year in one of those grim places would deteriorate.

The more recent experience is that people diagnosed with schizophrenia vary in their outcome (Zipursky, Reilly, & Murray, 2013). Up to one-fourth show a serious disorder throughout life. Some of those do deteriorate, perhaps due to poverty, lack of social support, drug abuse, and poor care. A smaller number, perhaps 10 to 20 percent, recover from a first episode and remain recovered throughout life. The others have one or more remissions and one or more relapses.

MRI and other measures of brain anatomy show impairments at the start of the disorder and a moderate amount of additional loss during the first couple of years, but little or no further deterioration in most patients after that time (Andreasen et al., 2011; Chiapponi et al., 2013; Nesvag et al., 2012; Vita, De Peri, Deste, & Sacchetti, 2012). Whatever causes the brain abnormalities occurs before or during the first episode of schizophrenia, not progressively throughout life.

Early Development and Later Psychopathology

One question may have struck you. The neurodevelopmental hypothesis holds that schizophrenia results from factors that disrupt brain development before birth or during early childhood. How, then, can we explain the fact that most cases are not diagnosed until age 20 or later? The time course may be less puzzling than it seems at first (Weinberger, 1996). Most of the people who develop schizophrenia in adulthood had shown other problems since childhood, including deficits in attention, memory, and impulse control (Keshavan, Diwadkar, Montrose, Rajarethinam, & Sweeney, 2005). An analysis of home movies found that people who later developed schizophrenia showed movement abnormalities during infancy (Walker, Savoie, & Davis, 1994). These relatively minor problems developed into more serious problems later.

Furthermore, the dorsolateral prefrontal cortex, an area that shows consistent signs of deficit in schizophrenia, is one of the slowest brain areas to mature. Researchers damaged this area in infant monkeys and tested the monkeys later. At age 1 year, the monkeys' behavior was nearly normal, but by age 2 years, it had deteriorated markedly (P. S. Goldman, 1971, 1976). That is, the effects of the brain damage grew worse over age. Presumably, the effects of brain damage were minimal at age 1 year because the dorsolateral prefrontal cortex doesn't do much at that age anyway. Later, when it should begin assuming important functions, the damage begins to make a difference (see Figure 14.17).

STOP&CHECK

30. Now that we see that brain abnormalities do not continue to grow worse over time, what is the implication for the possibility of recovery?

ANSWER

30. The prospects for recovery are more encouraging than they would seem if the brain were continuing to deteriorate over time. With any type of brain damage, some degree of recovery over time is likely.

Treatments

Before antipsychotic drugs became available in the mid-1950s, most people with schizophrenia were confined to mental hospitals with little hope of recovery. Today, mental hospitals are far less crowded because of drugs and outpatient treatment.

Antipsychotic Drugs and Dopamine

In the 1950s, psychiatrists discovered that **chlorpromazine** (trade name Thorazine) relieves the positive symptoms of schizophrenia for most, though not all, patients. Researchers later discovered other **antipsychotic,** or **neuroleptic, drugs** (drugs that tend to relieve schizophrenia and similar conditions) in two chemical families: the **phenothiazines** (FEE-no-THI-uh-zeens), which include chlorpromazine, and the **butyrophenones** (BYOO-tir-oh-FEE-noans), which include haloperidol (trade name Haldol). Behavioral benefits of any

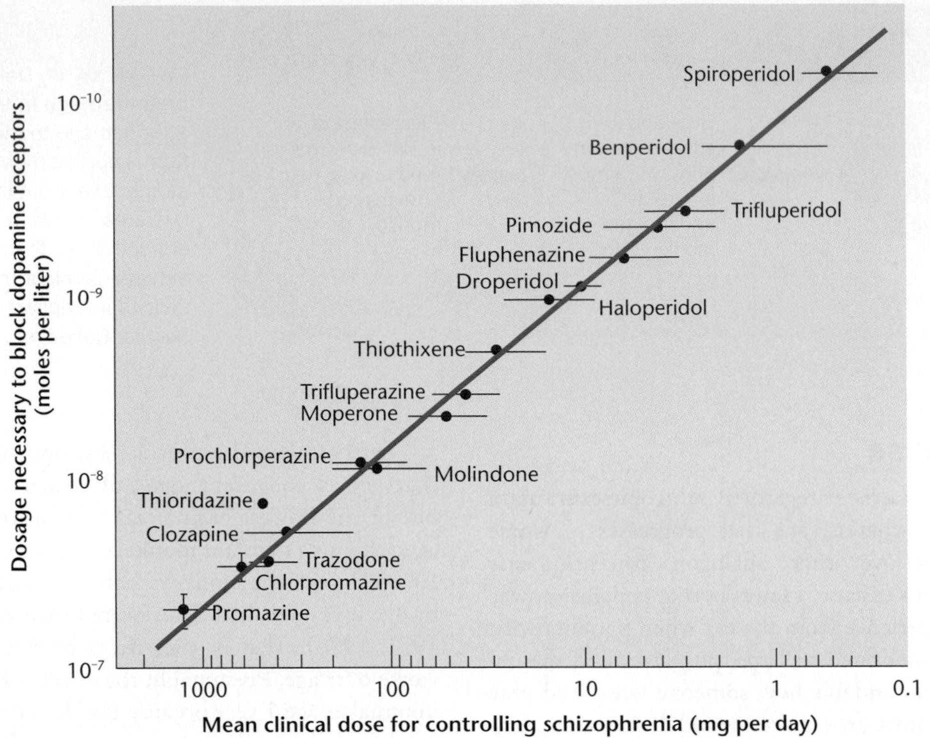

FIGURE 14.18 Dopamine-blocking effects of antipsychotic drugs
Drugs are arranged along the horizontal axis in terms of the average daily dose prescribed for patients with schizophrenia. (Horizontal lines indicate common ranges.) *Larger* doses are to the left, and *smaller* doses are to the right so that *more effective* drugs are to the right. Along the vertical axis is a measurement of the amount of each drug required to achieve a certain degree of blockage of postsynaptic dopamine receptors. *Larger* doses are toward the bottom, and *smaller* doses are toward the top so that the drugs on top are *more effective*. *Source:* From "Antipsychotic drug doses and neuroleptic/dopamine receptors," by P. Seeman, T. Lee, M. Chau-Wong, and K. Wong, 1976, *Nature, 261,* pp. 717–719. Copyright © 1976 Macmillan Magazines Limited. Reprinted by permission of Nature and Phillip Seeman.

of these drugs develop gradually over a month or more. Symptoms may or may not return after cessation of treatment.

As Figure 14.18 illustrates, each of these drugs blocks dopamine synapses. For each drug, researchers determined the mean dose prescribed for patients with schizophrenia (displayed along the horizontal axis) and the amount needed to block dopamine receptors (displayed along the vertical axis). As the figure shows, the drugs that are most effective against schizophrenia (and therefore used in the smallest doses) are the most effective at blocking dopamine receptors (Seeman, Lee, Chau-Wong, & Wong, 1976).

That finding inspired the **dopamine hypothesis of schizophrenia,** which holds that schizophrenia results from excess activity at dopamine synapses in certain brain areas. Although the concentration of dopamine in the brain as a whole is no higher than normal, dopamine release is increased in the basal ganglia (Simpson, Kellendonk, & Kandel, 2010). Further support for the dopamine hypothesis comes from the fact that extensive abuse of amphetamine, methamphetamine, or cocaine induces **substance-induced psychotic disorder,** characterized by hallucinations and delusions, the positive symptoms of schizophrenia. Each of these drugs increases or prolongs the activity at dopamine synapses. LSD, which also produces psychotic symptoms, is best known for its effects on serotonin synapses, but it also stimulates dopamine synapses.

In a clever study, researchers measured the number of dopamine receptors occupied at a given moment. They used a radioactively labeled drug, IBZM, that binds to type D_2 receptors. Because IBZM binds only to receptors that dopamine did not already bind, measuring the radioactivity counts the number of vacant dopamine receptors. Then the researchers used a second drug, AMPT, that blocks all synthesis of dopamine and again used IBZM to count the number of vacant D_2 receptors. Because AMPT had prevented production of dopamine, *all* D_2 receptors should be vacant at this time, so the researchers got a count of the total. Then they subtracted the first count from the second count, yielding the number of D_2 receptors occupied by dopamine at the first count. The people with schizophrenia had about twice as many D_2 receptors occupied as normal:

- First count: IBZM binds to all D_2 receptors not already attached to dopamine.
- Second count: IBZM binds to all D_2 receptors (because AMPT eliminated production of dopamine).
- Second count minus first count equals the number of D_2 receptors bound to dopamine at the first count.
(Abi-Dargham et al., 2000)

STOP&CHECK

31. The ability of traditional antipsychotic drugs to relieve schizophrenia correlates strongly with what effect on neurotransmitters?

ANSWER

31. Their ability to relieve schizophrenia correlates strongly with how well they block activity at dopamine synapses.

Role of Glutamate

Abnormalities of dopamine transmission need not be the whole story for schizophrenia. According to the **glutamate hypothesis of schizophrenia,** the problem relates in part to deficient activity at glutamate synapses in the prefrontal cortex. In many brain areas, dopamine inhibits glutamate release, or glutamate stimulates neurons that inhibit dopamine release. Therefore, increased dopamine would produce the same effects as decreased glutamate. The antipsychotic effects of drugs that block dopamine are compatible with either the excess-dopamine hypothesis or the deficient-glutamate hypothesis.

Studies have consistently found decreased glutamate release in the prefrontal cortex for people with schizophrenia (Marsman et al., 2013). Further support for the glutamate hypothesis comes from the effects of **phencyclidine (PCP)** ("angel dust"), a drug that inhibits the NMDA glutamate receptors. At low doses, it produces intoxication and slurred speech. At larger doses, it produces both positive and negative symptoms of schizophrenia, including hallucinations, thought disorder, loss of emotions, and memory loss. PCP is an interesting model for schizophrenia in other regards also:

- PCP and the related drug *ketamine* produce little if any psychotic response in preadolescents. Just as the symptoms of schizophrenia usually begin to emerge well after puberty, so do the psychotic effects of PCP and ketamine.
- LSD, amphetamine, and cocaine produce temporary schizophrenic symptoms in almost anyone, and the effects are not much worse in people with a history of schizophrenia than in anyone else. However, PCP produces a relapse for someone who has recovered from schizophrenia. (Farber, Newcomer, & Olney, 1999; Olney & Farber, 1995)

It might seem that the best test of the glutamate hypothesis would be to administer glutamate itself. However, recall from Chapter 4 that strokes kill neurons by overstimulating glutamate synapses. Increasing overall brain glutamate would be risky. However, drugs that stimulate particular kinds of metabotropic glutamate receptors have shown promise as treatments (González-Maeso et al., 2008; Patil et al., 2007).

Furthermore, the NMDA glutamate receptor has a primary site that is activated by glutamate and a secondary site that is activated by glycine. Glycine by itself does not activate the receptor, but it increases the effectiveness of glutamate. Thus, an increase in glycine can increase the activity at NMDA synapses without overstimulating glutamate throughout the brain. Although glycine is not an effective antipsychotic drug by itself, it increases the effects of other antipsychotic drugs, especially with regard to negative symptoms (Heresco-Levy et al., 1999; Heresco-Levy & Javitt, 2004).

STOP&CHECK

32. What drugs induce mainly the positive symptoms of schizophrenia? What drug can induce both positive and negative symptoms?

33. Why are the effects of antipsychotic drugs equally compatible with the dopamine hypothesis and the glutamate hypothesis?

ANSWERS

32. Abuse of amphetamine, cocaine, or LSD induces positive symptoms, such as hallucinations and delusions. Phencyclidine induces both positive and negative symptoms. **33.** Dopamine inhibits glutamate cells in many areas, and glutamate stimulates neurons that inhibit dopamine. Therefore, the effects of increasing dopamine are similar to those of decreasing glutamate.

Other Medications

The brain has several dopamine pathways with different functions. The drugs that block dopamine synapses produce their benefits by acting on neurons in the **mesolimbocortical system,** neurons that project from the midbrain tegmentum to the limbic system and prefrontal cortex. However, these drugs also block dopamine neurons in the *mesostriatal system* that projects to the basal ganglia (see Figure 14.19). The effect on the basal ganglia produces **tardive dyskinesia** (TARD-eev dis-kih-NEE-zhee-uh), characterized by tremors and other involuntary movements that develop gradually and to varying degrees among patients (Kiriakakis, Bhatia, Quinn, & Marsden, 1998).

Once tardive dyskinesia emerges, it can last long after someone quits the drug (Kiriakakis et al., 1998). Consequently, the best strategy is to prevent it from starting. Certain drugs called **second-generation antipsychotics,** or *atypical antipsychotics,* are regarded as less likely to produce movement problems, although opinions and results differ as to exactly how much they reduce the risk (see Figure 14.20). The most common of these drugs are clozapine, amisulpride, risperidone, olanzapine, and aripiprazole. Unfortunately, they produce other side effects, including weight gain and impairment of the immune system. All things considered, the atypical antipsychotics do not improve overall quality

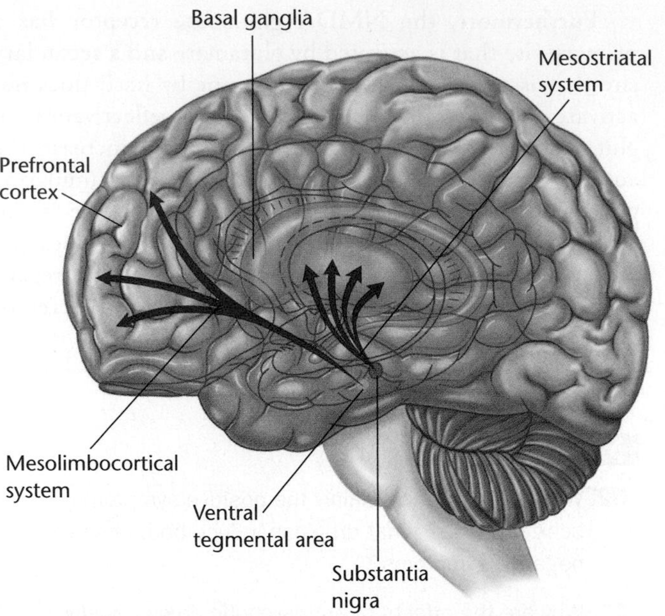

FIGURE 14.19 Two major dopamine pathways
Overactivity of the mesolimbocortical system is linked to the symptoms of schizophrenia. The path to the basal ganglia is associated with tardive dyskinesia, a movement disorder.
Source: Adapted from Valzelli, 1980

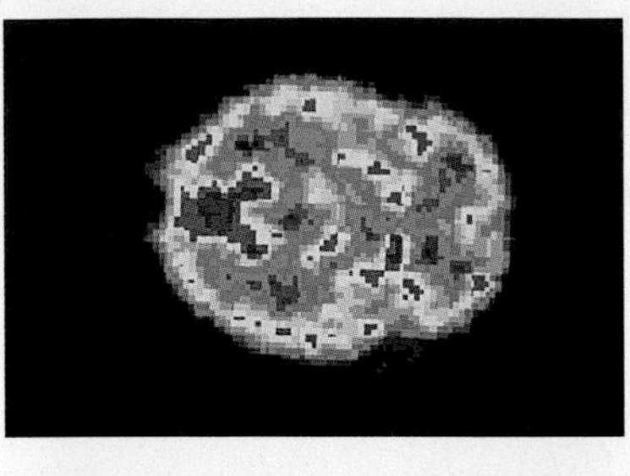

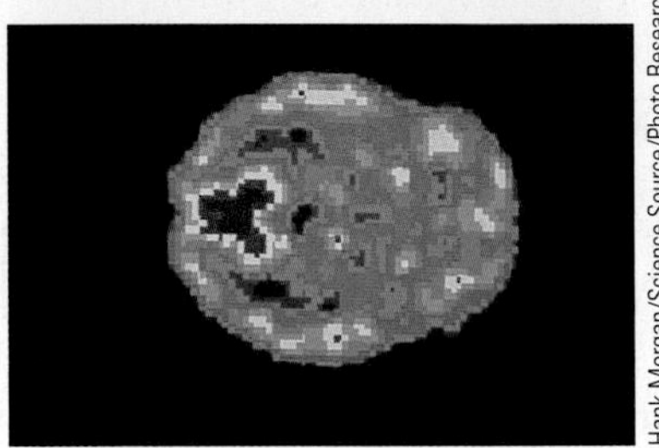

Hank Morgan/Science Source/Photo Researchers

FIGURE 14.20 PET scans of a patient with schizophrenia
These PET scans of a patient with schizophrenia (a) taking clozapine and (b) during a period off the drug demonstrate that clozapine increases brain activity in many brain areas. Red indicates the highest activity, followed by yellow, green, and blue.

of life more than the older drugs (P. B. Jones et al., 2006). Some drugs may be slightly more effective than others, but the deciding factor should be which one produces the most tolerable side effects for a given patient (Leucht et al., 2013).

Compared to drugs like haloperidol, the second-generation antipsychotics have less effect on dopamine type D_2 receptors but more strongly antagonize serotonin type 5-HT_2 receptors (Kapur et al., 2000; Meltzer, Matsubara, & Lee, 1989; Mrzljak et al., 1996; Roth, Willins, Kristiansen, & Kroeze, 1999). They also increase the release of glutamate (Melone et al., 2001). In short, schizophrenia is neither a one-gene disorder nor a one-neurotransmitter disorder.

MODULE 14.3 ■ IN CLOSING

Many Remaining Mysteries

Research is a little like reading a good mystery novel that presents a mixture of important clues and irrelevant information. In research on schizophrenia, we have an enormous amount of information, but also major gaps and occasional points that don't seem to fit. The final chapter of our mystery novel on schizophrenia isn't complete. However, although researchers have not yet solved the mystery, it should also be clear that they have made progress. It will be fascinating to see what develops in future research.

Summary

1. Positive symptoms of schizophrenia (behaviors that are not present in most other people) include hallucinations, delusions, inappropriate emotions, bizarre behaviors, and thought disorder. **487**
2. Negative symptoms (normal behaviors absent that should be present) include deficits of social interaction, emotional expression, and speech. **487**
3. Before diagnosing someone with schizophrenia, a therapist needs to rule out brain damage, drug abuse, and other conditions that could produce similar symptoms. **488**
4. Studies of twins and adopted children imply a genetic predisposition to schizophrenia. However, the adoption studies do not distinguish between the roles of genetics and prenatal environment. **489**

5. Researchers have identified many genes associated with schizophrenia, but no common gene increases the risk by much. A promising hypothesis is that schizophrenia results from new mutations or microdeletions of any of the hundreds of genes that are important for brain development. **490**
6. According to the neurodevelopmental hypothesis, either genes or difficulties early in life, often before birth, impair brain development in ways that increase vulnerability to later insults and predispose to behavioral abnormalities beginning in early adulthood. **491**
7. Many people with schizophrenia show mild abnormalities of brain development, especially in the temporal and frontal lobes. They also show cognitive deficits that make sense if their frontal and temporal lobes are less than fully functional. **492**
8. Contrary to what psychiatrists used to believe, most people with schizophrenia do not continue deteriorating throughout life. Some recover, some remain troubled throughout life, and some alternate between remission and relapse. Although the brain shows abnormalities during the first episode of schizophrenia, most people show little or no increase in those abnormalities as time passes. **493**
9. Parts of the prefrontal cortex are very slow to mature. It is plausible that early disruption of those areas might produce behavioral symptoms that become manifest as schizophrenia in young adults. **493**
10. According to the dopamine hypothesis, schizophrenia is due to excess dopamine activity. Drugs that block dopamine synapses reduce the positive symptoms of schizophrenia, and drugs that increase dopamine activity induce the positive symptoms. **493**
11. According to the glutamate hypothesis, part of the problem is deficient glutamate activity. Phencyclidine, which blocks NMDA glutamate synapses, produces both positive and negative symptoms of schizophrenia, especially in people predisposed to schizophrenia. **495**
12. Prolonged use of antipsychotic drugs may produce tardive dyskinesia, a movement disorder. Second-generation antipsychotic drugs apparently do not improve overall quality of life any better than the original drugs do. **495**

Key Terms

Terms are defined in the module on the page number indicated. They're also presented in alphabetical order with definitions in the book's Subject Index/Glossary. Interactive flash cards, audio reviews, and crossword puzzles are among the online resources available to help you learn these terms and the concepts they represent.

antipsychotic (neuroleptic) drugs **493**
butyrophenones **493**
chlorpromazine **493**
concordance **489**
delusions **487**
differential diagnosis **488**
DISC1 **490**
dopamine hypothesis of schizophrenia **494**
glutamate hypothesis of schizophrenia **495**
hallucinations **487**
mesolimbocortical system **495**
microdeletion **490**
negative symptoms **487**
neurodevelopmental hypothesis **491**
phencyclidine (PCP) **495**
phenothiazines **493**
positive symptoms **487**
schizophrenia **494**
season-of-birth effect **491**
second-generation antipsychotics **495**
substance-induced psychotic disorder **494**
tardive dyskinesia **495**

Thought Question

On average, people who use much marijuana are more likely than others to develop schizophrenia. However, over the last several decades, the use of marijuana has increased substantially while the prevalence of schizophrenia has remained steady or decreased. What would be a reasonable conclusion about the relationship between marijuana use and schizophrenia?

MODULE 14.3 End of Module Quiz

1. Keeping someone's working memory busy with an unrelated task causes normal, healthy people to produce which of these items that are characteristic of schizophrenia?
   a. Hallucinations
   b. Delusions
   c. Loss of emotion and social behavior
   d. Incoherent speech

2. Schizophrenia is more common than average in which of the following types of people?
   a. People with allergies
   b. People who live in cities
   c. People who move from Europe to one of the Caribbean countries
   d. People who eat a diet rich in fish

3. What is the conclusion from twin studies regarding schizophrenia?
   a. Monozygotic twins are more likely to develop schizophrenia than are dizygotic twins.
   b. Monozygotic twins are more likely to be concordant for schizophrenia than are dizygotic twins.
   c. Dizygotic twins are more likely to be concordant for schizophrenia than are monozygotic twins.
   d. Monozygotic and dizygotic twins are equally likely to be concordant for schizophrenia.

4. Which of the following is currently the most plausible statement about the role of genetics in schizophrenia?
   a. An aberrant form of the *DISC1* gene causes schizophrenia.
   b. One gene is responsible for schizophrenia, but investigators have not yet found that gene.
   c. Many mutations or microdeletions can increase the probability of schizophrenia.
   d. Schizophrenia is not related to genetics.

5. Which of the following has NOT been shown to increase the risk of schizophrenia?
   a. Being born during the winter
   b. Having a pet cat in childhood
   c. Having a father over age 55
   d. Living near the ocean

6. If schizophrenia is due to abnormal brain development in early life, how can we account for the fact that behavioral symptoms are not apparent until later in life?
   a. Schizophrenia impairs only social behavior, which is more important in adulthood.
   b. Other people do not notice the problems until the person is old enough to seek employment.
   c. A prime area of damage is the prefrontal cortex, which matures very slowly.
   d. Symptoms of brain abnormality do not emerge until the person encounters stress.

7. According to the dopamine hypothesis of schizophrenia, what is the chemical basis for schizophrenia?
   a. Deficient synthesis of dopamine
   b. Lack of sufficient dopamine type 1 receptors
   c. Lack of sufficient dopamine type 2 receptors
   d. Excessive activity at dopamine synapses

8. What is an alternative to the hypothesis that schizophrenia relates to excess dopamine activity?
   a. Increased reuptake of serotonin by the presynaptic neuron
   b. Decreased glutamate activity in the prefrontal cortex
   c. Decreased metabolism in the cerebellum
   d. Increased adenosine levels in the hypothalamus

9. What are the synaptic effects of glycine?
   a. It directly stimulates glutamate receptors.
   b. It facilitates the effects of glutamate.
   c. It directly stimulates acetylcholine receptors.
   d. It facilitates the effects of acetylcholine.

ANSWERS: 1d, 2b, 3b, 4c, 5d, 6c, 7d, 8b, 9b.

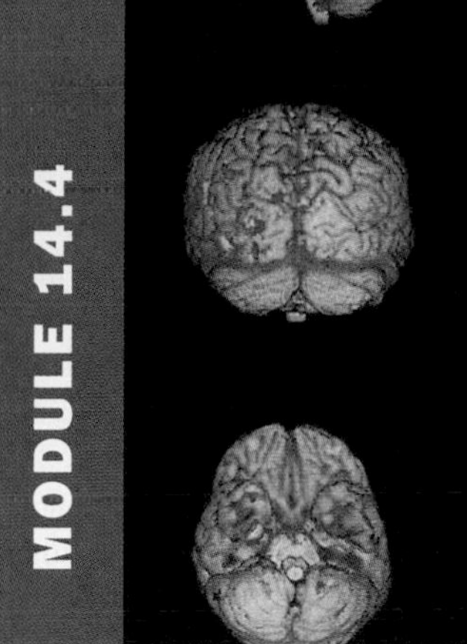

Autism Spectrum Disorders

Autism was once considered a rare condition. Today, estimates of its incidence vary substantially, with a worldwide median estimate of about one in 160 people (Elsabbagh et al., 2012). In any case, it is diagnosed far more frequently than in the past. Most of that change is due to greater awareness and greater likelihood of using the label *autism* instead of mental retardation or something else. However, it is also possible that this condition has become more common than it used to be.

Symptoms and Characteristics

Autism spectrum disorder includes a range of people with various degrees of difficulty. Therapists used to use the term *Asperger's syndrome* for people with a mild impairment, but the difference between Asperger's syndrome and autism is merely one of degree. Autism spectrum disorder encompasses both autism and what used to be called Asperger's syndrome. In this module, for simplicity we use just the term *autism*, but you should understand that the term applies to a range of disorders from severe to relatively mild. Other people have slight degrees of autistic tendencies, but not enough to qualify for a diagnosis.

Autism is much more common in boys than in girls. It occurs throughout the world, and we have no convincing evidence that its prevalence varies by geography, ethnic group, or socioeconomic status (Elsabbagh et al., 2012). According to the American Psychiatric Association (2013), the primary characteristics of autism spectrum disorder include these:

- Deficits in social and emotional exchange
- Deficits in gestures, facial expressions, and other nonverbal communication
- Stereotyped behaviors, such as repetitive movements (see Figure 14.21)
- Resistance to a change in routine
- Unusually weak or strong responses to stimuli, such as indifference to pain or a panicked reaction to a sound

Many people with autism have additional problems, especially attention deficit disorder. Many also have abnormalities in the cerebellum. Those who do show many of the deficits associated with cerebellar damage, including clumsiness and impaired voluntary eye movements (Fatemi et al., 2012).

M. Scott Brauer/Alamy

FIGURE 14.22 Stereotyped behaviors by an autistic child
Repetitive nonsocial behaviors are common in autism.

Parents of autistic children often notice a problem from the start, as an infant may not react comfortably to being held. Other problems increase over time. At age 2 months, children with autism make eye contact about as much as other children, but their eye contact gradually declines over the next two years (Jones & Klin, 2013).

In addition to the deficits characteristic of autism, certain strengths occur, too. A surprising one, not explained by any theory, is that children with autism tend to be substantially better than average at detecting motion by visual stimuli (Foss-Feig, Tadin, Schauder, & Cascio, 2013). Many develop narrow skills at which they excel.

Genetics and Other Causes

If you remember the information about genetics of schizophrenia, the genetic basis of autism will sound familiar: Many genes have been linked to autism, but no one of them is found in a high percentage of people with autism (O'Roak et al., 2012a; State & Levitt, 2011). Probably many or most cases result from new mutations or microdeletions in any of a number of genes. By examining a child's chromosomes, researchers can identify mutations and microdeletions that arose anew, because they are not present on the parents' chromosomes. Such mutations and deletions occur more often in children with autism than in their unaffected brothers and sisters (O'Roak et al., 2012b; Sanders et al., 2012). By examining the genes that surround the mutation or deletion, and then comparing the results to the parents' chromosomes, researchers can infer whether the mutation or deletion came from the mother or the father. Most of them occur on chromosomes inherited from the father, and—as in schizophrenia—the oldest fathers are more likely to have children with autism than younger fathers are (Kong et al., 2012; O'Roak et al., 2012b).

Several studies have focused on *topoisomerases*—enzymes that regulate the repair and replication of DNA and the production of certain types of RNA. Mutations that affect topoisomerases impair the expression of many genes that are important for brain development. Autism is a common result of mutation to topoisomerase genes (King et al., 2013; Xu et al., 2013).

Prenatal environment can also contribute to autism. (Again note the parallel to schizophrenia.) Some mothers of children with autism—measurements indicate about 12 percent—have antibodies that attack certain brain proteins. Few if any mothers of unaffected children have these antibodies. Identifying women with those antibodies might make it possible to intervene chemically to prevent autism (Braunschweig et al., 2013). As further evidence for the relevance of those antibodies, researchers injected pregnant monkeys with antibodies from mothers of children with autism or mothers of unaffected children. Those injected with antibodies from children with autism—and not the others—had offspring that avoided social contacts with other monkeys (Bauman et al., 2013).

One more contributing factor: Nutritionists recommend that pregnant women and women planning to become pregnant get adequate amounts of **folic acid** (vitamin B9), either from leafy green vegetables and orange juice, or from vitamin pills. Folic acid is important for development of the nervous system. Women who take folic acid pills during pregnancy have about half the probability of having a child with autism, compared to other women (Surén et al., 2013).

STOP & CHECK

34. How can researchers determine whether a mutation or microdeletion has arisen anew?

ANSWER

34. They compare the child's chromosome to those of the parents. If neither parent has that mutation or microdeletion, then it arose anew. They can also examine surrounding genes to determine whether the chromosome came from the father or the mother.

Treatments

No medical treatment helps with the central problems of decreased social behavior and communication. Risperidone, a second-generation antipsychotic drug, sometimes reduces the stereotyped behaviors, but at the risk of serious side effects. In rare cases autism is due to mutation of a gene whose effects could be reversed chemically (Han et al., 2012; Novarino et al., 2012). At least, that is true theoretically. No attempts to apply this approach have been reported.

Behavioral treatments address the deficits in social behavior and communication. Parents, teachers, and therapists focus on eliciting the child's attention and reinforcing favorable behaviors. This procedure is successful with many children but not all. Treatments for stereotyped behaviors include reinforcing other behaviors or competing behaviors. Not much solid research is available to evaluate the success of this approach (Reed, Hirst, & Hayman, 2012).

Parents who grow understandably disappointed with these treatments are vulnerable to anyone who promises something better. A huge number of fad treatments have arisen, including special diets, chelation, music, and therapeutic touch. A treatment can become popular despite a lack of evidence to support it, or even the presence of evidence that it is useless or harmful. Many fad treatments make the parents feel good that they are trying something, but otherwise they are a waste of time and money (Matson, Adams, Williams, & Rieske, 2013).

STOP & CHECK

35. For which aspect of autistic behavior is a medication sometimes prescribed?

ANSWER

35. Risperidone, an antipsychotic drug, is sometimes prescribed to control repetitive stereotyped behaviors, at the risk of serious side effects.

MODULE 14.4 ■ IN CLOSING

Developmental Disorders

All the disorders discussed in this chapter—alcoholism and substance abuse, depression, schizophrenia, and autism—relate to many genes, not just one. Many of the genes that increase the risk of one disorder increase the risk of others, too. Many people have more than one disorder. Certainly many people have both depression and alcohol abuse, both schizophrenia and alcohol or other substance abuse, or both autism and attention deficit disorder. In short, disorders that we discuss as if they were separate actually overlap. The early stages of brain development are complex and easily disrupted. Once the process goes off course, the risk increases for many undesirable outcomes.

Summary

1. Autism spectrum disorder remains uncommon, but the frequency of diagnosis has been increasing. The severity of symptoms varies greatly. **499**
2. Primary symptoms include a deficiency of social behavior and communication, including nonverbal communication. Many individuals also have repetitive stereotyped behaviors. **499**
3. No one gene is responsible for this condition. In most cases, it probably relates to new mutations or microdeletions. **500**
4. Some cases result because the mother during pregnancy produced certain antibodies that attack brain proteins. **500**
5. Behavioral treatments are the only effective approach to treating social and communicative deficits. Many parents try fad treatments of doubtful effectiveness. **501**

Key Terms

Terms are defined in the module on the page number indicated. They're also presented in alphabetical order with definitions in the book's Subject Index/Glossary. Interactive flash cards, audio reviews, and crossword puzzles are among the online resources available to help you learn these terms and the concepts they represent.

autism spectrum disorder **499**

folic acid **500**

Thought Question

Some people have their chromosomes examined to check for predispositions to various illnesses, such as breast cancer. What would be the pros and cons of checking for genes associated with psychological disorders?

MODULE 14.4 End of Module Quiz

1. In what way is the genetic basis of autism similar to that of schizophrenia?

a. In both, most cases can be traced to a mutation in the *DISC1* gene.

b. In both, most cases probably result from new mutations or microdeletions.

c. In both, a single dominant gene is responsible for the condition.

d. In both, the genes exert their effects by altering topoisomerases.

2. What dietary supplement during pregnancy decreases the probability of having an autistic child?
   a. Calcium
   b. Vitamin C
   c. Fish oil
   d. Folic acid

ANSWERS: 1b, 2d.

Suggestions for Further Reading

Andreasen, N. C. (2001). *Brave new brain*. New York: Oxford University Press. Excellent discussion of biological research on psychiatric disorders by one of the leading researchers dealing with schizophrenia.

Kirsch, I. (2010). *The Emperor's New Drugs*. New York: Basic Books. A highly skeptical discussion of the effectiveness or ineffectiveness of antidepressant drugs.

Brief, Basic Chemistry

MAIN IDEAS

1. All matter is composed of a limited number of elements that combine in endless ways.
2. Atoms, the component parts of an element, consist of protons, neutrons, and electrons. Most atoms can gain or lose electrons, or share them with other atoms.
3. The chemistry of life is predominantly the chemistry of carbon compounds.

Introduction

To understand certain aspects of biological psychology, particularly the action potential and the molecular mechanisms of synaptic transmission, you need to know a little about chemistry. If you have taken a high school or college course and remember the material reasonably well, you should have no trouble with the chemistry in this text. If your knowledge of chemistry is pretty hazy, this appendix will help. (If you plan to take other courses in biological psychology, you should study as much biology and chemistry as possible.)

Elements and Compounds

If you look around, you will see an enormous variety of materials—dirt, water, wood, plastic, metal, cloth, glass, your own body. Every object is composed of a small number of basic building blocks. If a piece of wood catches fire, it breaks down into ashes, gases, and water vapor. The same is true of your body. An investigator could take those ashes, gases, and water and break them down by chemical and electrical means into carbon, oxygen, hydrogen, nitrogen, and a few other materials. Eventually, however, the investigator arrives at a set of materials that cannot be broken down further: Pure carbon or pure oxygen, for example, cannot be converted into anything simpler, at least not by ordinary chemical means. (High-power bombardment with subatomic particles is another story.) The matter we see is composed of **elements** (materials that cannot be broken down into other materials) and **compounds** (materials made up by combining elements).

Chemists have found 92 elements in nature, and they have constructed more in the laboratory. (Actually, one of the 92—technetium—is so rare as to be virtually unknown in nature.) Figure A.1, the periodic table, lists each of these elements. Of these, only a few are important for life on Earth. Table A.1 shows the elements commonly found in the human body.

Note that each element has a one- or two-letter abbreviation, such as O for oxygen, H for hydrogen, and Ca for calcium. These are internationally accepted symbols that facilitate communication among chemists who speak different languages. For example, element number 19 is called potassium in English, potassio in Italian, kālijs in Latvian, and draslík in Czech. But chemists in all countries use the symbol K (from *kalium,* the Latin word for "potassium"). Similarly, the symbol for sodium is Na (from *natrium,* the Latin word for "sodium"), and the symbol for iron is Fe (from the Latin word *ferrum*).

A compound is represented by the symbols for the elements that compose it. For example, NaCl stands for sodium chloride (common table salt). H_2O, the symbol for water, indicates that water consists of two parts of hydrogen and one part of oxygen.

TABLE A.1 The Elements that Compose Almost All of the Human Body

Element	Symbol	Percentage by Weight in Human Body
Oxygen	O	65
Carbon	C	18
Hydrogen	H	10
Nitrogen	N	3
Calcium	Ca	2
Phosphorus	P	1.1
Potassium	K	0.35
Sulfur	S	0.25
Sodium	Na	0.15
Chlorine	Cl	0.15
Magnesium	Mg	0.05
Iron	Fe	Trace
Copper	Cu	Trace
Iodine	I	Trace
Fluorine	F	Trace
Manganese	Mn	Trace
Zinc	Zn	Trace
Selenium	Se	Trace
Molybdenum	Mo	Trace

Periodic Table of the Elements

Period	Alkali Metals 1 IA	Alkaline Earth Metals 2 IIA	3 IIIB	4 IVB	5 VB	6 VIB	7 VIIB	8 VIIIB	9 VIIIB	10 VIIIB	11 IB	12 IIB	13 IIIA	14 IVA	15 VA	16 VIA	Halogens 17 VIIA	Noble Gases 18 VIIA
			Transition Elements															
1	1 **H** hydrogen 1.008																	2 **He** helium 4.003
2	3 **Li** lithium 6.941	4 **Be** beryllium 9.012											5 **B** boron 10.81	6 **C** carbon 12.011	7 **N** nitrogen 14.007	8 **O** oxygen 16.0	9 **F** fluorine 18.999	10 **Ne** neon 20.179
3	11 **Na** sodium 22.99	12 **Mg** magnesium 24.305											13 **Al** aluminum 26.982	14 **Si** silicon 28.085	15 **P** phosphorous 30.974	16 **S** sulfur 32.060	17 **Cl** chlorine 35.453	18 **Ar** argon 39.948
4	19 **K** potassium 39.098	20 **Ca** calcium 40.08	21 **Sc** scandium 44.955	22 **Ti** titanium 47.90	23 **V** vanadium 50.941	24 **Cr** chromium 51.996	25 **Mn** manganese 54.938	26 **Fe** iron 55.847	27 **Co** cobalt 58.933	28 **Ni** nickel 58.70	29 **Cu** copper 63.546	30 **Zn** zinc 65.38	31 **Ga** gallium 69.72	32 **Ge** germanium 72.59	33 **As** arsenic 74.922	34 **Se** selenium 78.96	35 **Br** bromine 79.904	36 **Kr** krypton 83.80
5	37 **Rb** rubidium 85.468	38 **Sr** strontium 87.62	39 **Y** yttrium 88.906	40 **Zr** zirconium 91.22	41 **Nb** niobium 92.906	42 **Mo** molybdenum 95.940	43 **Tc** technetium (97)	44 **Ru** ruthenium 101.07	45 **Rh** rhodium 102.905	46 **Pd** palladium 106.40	47 **Ag** silver 107.868	48 **Cd** cadmium 112.41	49 **In** indium 114.82	50 **Sn** tin 118.69	51 **Sb** antimony 121.75	52 **Te** tellurium 127.60	53 **I** iodine 126.904	54 **Xe** xenon 131.30
6	55 **Cs** cesium 132.905	56 **Ba** barium 137.33	57 **La** lanthanum 138.906 †	72 **Hf** hafnium 178.49	73 **Ta** tantalum 180.948	74 **W** tungsten 183.85	75 **Re** rhenium 186.207	76 **Os** osmium 190.20	77 **Ir** iridum 192.22	78 **Pt** platinum 195.09	79 **Au** gold 196.967	80 **Hg** mercury 200.59	81 **Tl** thallium 204.37	82 **Pb** lead 207.20	83 **Bi** bismuth 208.980	84 **Po** polonium (209)	85 **At** astatine (210)	86 **Rn** radon (222)
7	87 **Fr** francium (223)	88 **Ra** radium 226.025	89 **Ac** actinium (227) ‡	104 **Rf** rutherfordium (261)	105 **Db** dubnium (262)	106 **Sg** seaborgium (266)	107 **Bh** bohrium (264)	108 **Hs** hassium (269)	109 **Mt** meitnerium (268)	110 **Ds** darmstadtium (271)	111 **Rg** roentgenium (272)	112 **Cn** copernicium (285)	113 **Uut** ununtrium (284)	114 **Uuq** ununquadium (289)	115 **Uup** ununpentium (288)	116 **Uuh** ununhexium (292)	117 **Uus** ununseptium (?)	118 **Uuo** ununoctium (?)

Inner Transition Elements

† Lanthanides 6	58 **Ce** cerium 140.12	59 **Pr** praseodymium 140.908	60 **Nd** neodymium 144.24	61 **Pm** prometheum (145)	62 **Sm** samarium 150.40	63 **Eu** europium 151.96	64 **Gd** gadolinium 157.25	65 **Tb** terbium 158.925	66 **Dy** dysprosium 162.50	67 **Ho** holmium 164.93	68 **Er** erbium 167.26	69 **Tm** thulium 168.934	70 **Yb** ytterbium 173.04	71 **Lu** lutetium 174.97
‡ Actinides 7	90 **Th** thorium 232.038	91 **Pa** protactinium 231.036	92 **U** uranium 238.029	93 **Np** neptunium (237)	94 **Pu** plutonium (244)	95 **Am** americium (243)	96 **Cm** curium (247)	97 **Bk** berkelium (247)	98 **Cf** californium (251)	99 **Es** einsteinium (254)	100 **Fm** fermium (257)	101 **Md** mendelevium (258)	102 **No** nobelium (255)	103 **Lr** lawrencium (260)

Key

atomic number — 1
symbol of element — **H**
element name — hydrogen
atomic weight — 1.008

FIGURE A.1 The periodic table of chemistry
It is called "periodic" because certain properties show up at periodic intervals. For example, the column from lithium down consists of metals that readily form salts. The column at the far right consists of gases that do not readily form compounds. Elements 113 to 118 have only tentative names and symbols.

Atoms and Molecules

A block of iron can be chopped finer and finer until it is divided into tiny pieces that cannot be broken down any further. These pieces are called **atoms.** Every element is composed of atoms. A compound, such as water, can also be divided into tinier and tinier pieces. The smallest possible piece of a compound is called a **molecule.** A molecule of water can be further decomposed into two atoms of hydrogen and one atom of oxygen, but when that happens the compound is broken and is no longer water. A molecule is the smallest piece of a compound that retains the properties of the compound.

An atom is composed of subatomic particles, including protons, neutrons, and electrons. A proton has a positive electrical charge, a neutron has a neutral charge, and an electron has a negative charge. The nucleus of an atom—its center—contains one or more protons plus a number of neutrons. Electrons are found in the space around the nucleus. Because an atom has the same number of protons as electrons, the electrical charges balance out. (Ions, which we will soon consider, have an imbalance of positive and negative charges.)

The difference between one element and another is in the number of protons in the nucleus of the atom. Hydrogen has just one proton, for example, and oxygen has eight. The number of protons is the **atomic number** of the element; in the periodic table it is recorded at the top of the square for each element. The number at the bottom is the element's **atomic weight,** which indicates the weight of an atom relative to the weight of one proton. A proton has a weight of one unit, a neutron has a weight just trivially greater than one, and an electron has a weight just trivially greater than zero. The atomic weight of the element is the number of protons in the atom plus the average number of neutrons. For example, most hydrogen atoms have one proton and no neutrons; a few atoms per thousand have one or two neutrons, giving an average atomic weight of 1.008. Sodium ions have 11 protons; most also have 12 neutrons, and the atomic weight is slightly less than 23. (Can you figure out the number of neutrons in the average potassium atom? Refer to Figure A.1.)

Ions and Chemical Bonds

An atom that has gained or lost one or more electrons is called an **ion.** For example, if sodium and chloride come together, the sodium atoms readily lose one electron each and the chloride atoms gain one each. The result is a set of positively charged sodium ions (indicated Na^+) and negatively charged chloride ions (Cl^-). Potassium atoms, like sodium atoms, tend to lose an electron and to become positively charged ions (K^+); calcium ions tend to lose two electrons and gain a double positive charge (Ca^{++}).

Because positive charges attract negative charges, sodium ions attract chloride ions. When dry, sodium and chloride form a crystal structure, as Figure A.2 shows. (In water solution, the two kinds of ions move about haphazardly, occasionally attracting one another but then pulling apart.) The attraction of positive ions for negative ions forms an **ionic bond.** In other cases, instead of transferring an electron from one atom to another, some pairs of atoms share electrons with each other, forming a **covalent bond.** For example, two hydrogen atoms bind, as shown in Figure A.3, and two hydrogen atoms bind with an oxygen atom, as shown in Figure A.4. Atoms that are attached by a covalent bond cannot move independently of one another.

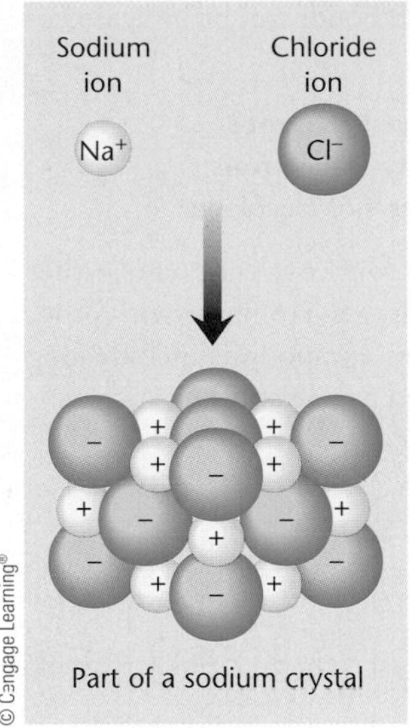

FIGURE A.2 The crystal structure of sodium
Each sodium ion is surrounded by chloride ions, and each chloride ion is surrounded by sodium ions; no ion is bound to any other single ion in particular.

Reactions of Carbon Atoms

Living organisms depend on the enormously versatile compounds of carbon. Because of the importance of these compounds for life, the chemistry of carbon is known as organic chemistry.

Carbon atoms form covalent bonds with hydrogen, oxygen, and a number of other elements. They also form covalent bonds with other carbon atoms. Two carbon atoms may share from

FIGURE A.3 Structure of a hydrogen molecule
A hydrogen atom has one electron; in the compound the two atoms share the two electrons equally.

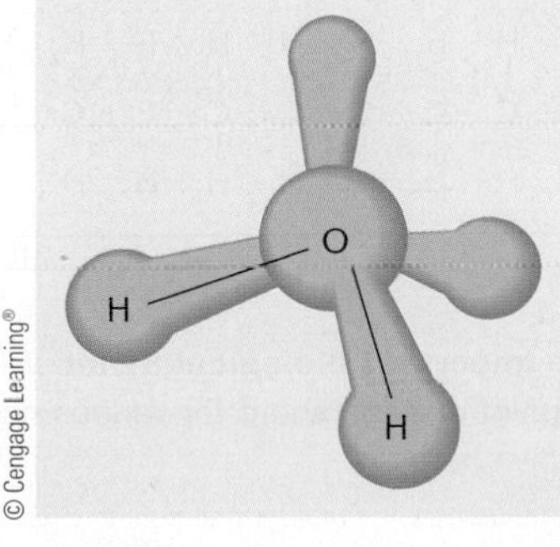

FIGURE A.4 Structure of a water molecule
The oxygen atom shares a pair of electrons with each hydrogen atom. Oxygen holds the electrons more tightly, making the oxygen part of the molecule more negatively charged than the hydrogen part of the molecule.

one to three pairs of electrons. Such bonds can be indicated as follows:

C−C Two atoms share one pair of electrons.
C=C Two atoms share two pairs of electrons.
C≡C Two atoms share three pairs of electrons.

Each carbon atom ordinarily forms four covalent bonds, either with other carbon atoms, with hydrogen atoms, or with other atoms. Many biologically important compounds include long chains of carbon compounds linked to one another, such as:

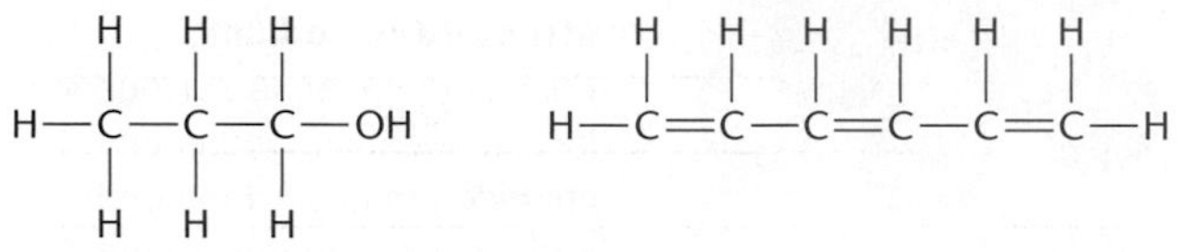

Note that each carbon atom has a total of four bonds, counting each double bond as two. In some molecules, the carbon chain loops around to form a ring:

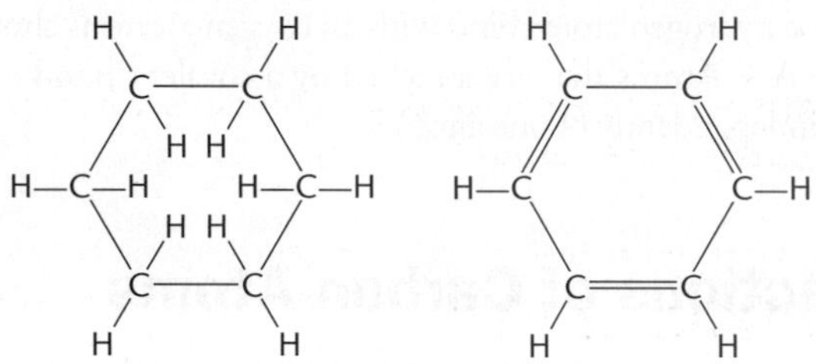

Ringed structures are common in organic chemistry. To simplify the diagrams, chemists often omit the hydrogen atoms. You can simply assume that each carbon atom in the diagram has four covalent bonds and that all the bonds not shown are with hydrogen atoms. To further simplify the diagrams, chemists often omit the carbon atoms themselves, showing only the carbon-to-carbon bonds. For example, the two molecules shown in the previous diagram might be rendered as follows:

If a particular carbon atom has a bond with some atom other than hydrogen, the diagram shows the exception. For example, in each of the two molecules diagrammed below, one carbon has a bond with an oxygen atom, which in turn has a bond with a hydrogen atom. All the bonds that are not shown are carbon–hydrogen bonds.

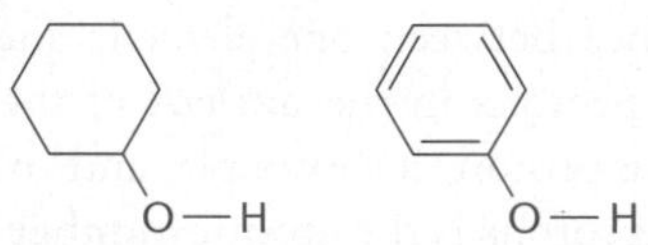

Figure A.5 illustrates some carbon compounds that are critical for animal life. Purines and pyrimidines form the central structure of DNA and RNA, the chemicals responsible for heredity. Proteins, fats, and carbohydrates are the primary

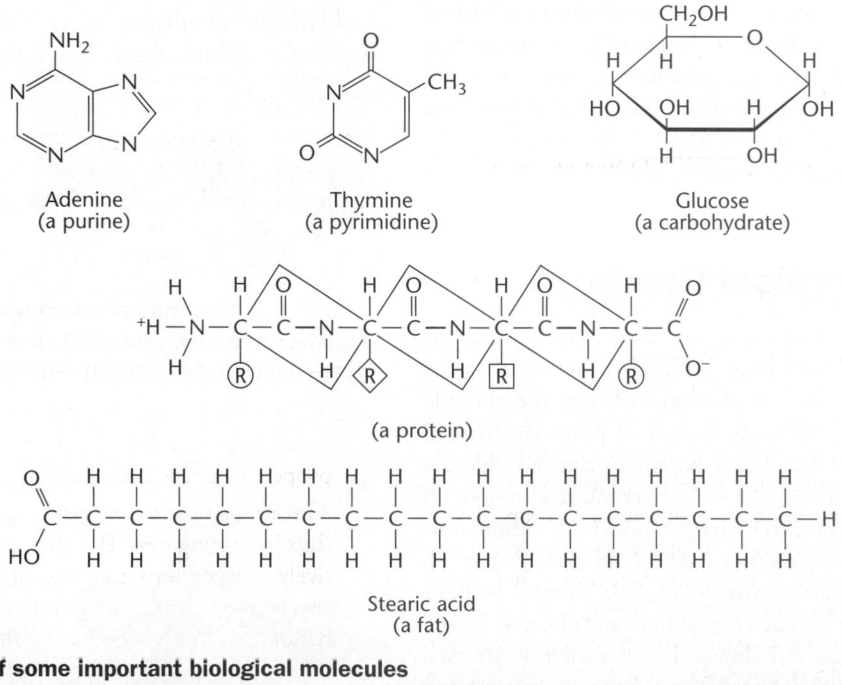

Adenine
(a purine)

Thymine
(a pyrimidine)

Glucose
(a carbohydrate)

(a protein)

Stearic acid
(a fat)

FIGURE A.5 Structures of some important biological molecules
The R in the protein represents a point of attachment for various chains that differ from one amino acid to another. Actual proteins are much longer than the chemical shown here.

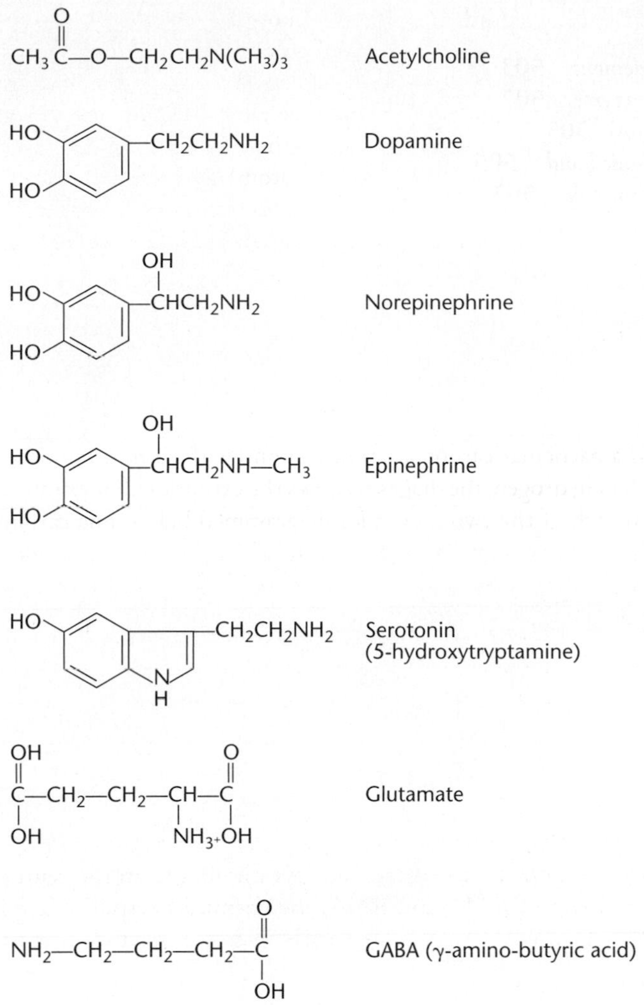

$CH_3C(=O)—O—CH_2CH_2N(CH_3)_3$ Acetylcholine

Dopamine

Norepinephrine

Epinephrine

Serotonin (5-hydroxytryptamine)

Glutamate

$NH_2—CH_2—CH_2—CH_2—C(=O)OH$ GABA (γ-amino-butyric acid)

FIGURE A.6 Chemical structures of seven abundant neurotransmitters

types of fuel that the body uses. Figure A.6 displays the chemical structures of seven neurotransmitters that are extensively discussed in this text.

Chemical Reactions in the Body

A living organism is an immensely complicated, coordinated set of chemical reactions. Life requires that the rate of each reaction be carefully regulated. In many cases one reaction produces a chemical that enters into another reaction, which produces another chemical that enters into another reaction, and so forth. If any one of those reactions is too rapid compared to the others, the chemical it produces will accumulate to possibly harmful levels. If a reaction is too slow, it will not produce enough product and the next reaction will be stalled.

Enzymes are proteins that control the rate of chemical reactions. Each reaction is controlled by a particular enzyme. Enzymes are a type of catalyst. A catalyst is any chemical that facilitates a reaction among other chemicals without being altered itself in the process.

Adenosine

Phosphates

Ribose

AMP

ADP

ATP

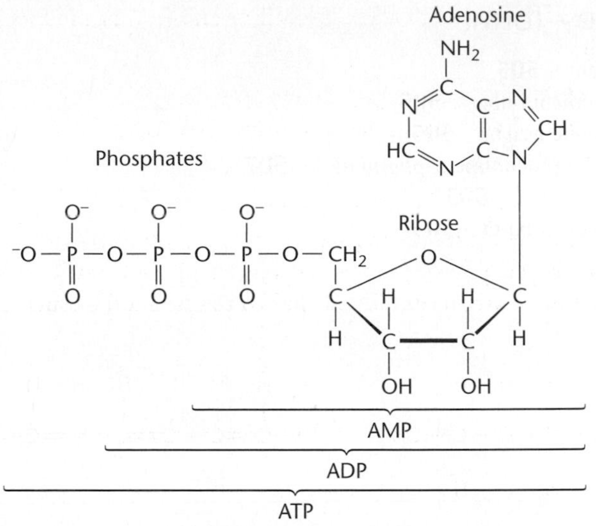

FIGURE A.7 ATP, composed of adenosine, ribose, and three phosphates

ATP can lose one phosphate group to form ADP (adenosine diphosphate) and then lose another one to form AMP (adenosine monophosphate). Each time it breaks off a phosphate group, it releases energy.

The Role of ATP

The body relies on **ATP (adenosine triphosphate)** as its main way of sending energy where it is needed (see Figure A.7). Much of the energy derived from food goes into forming ATP molecules that eventually provide energy for the muscles and other body parts.

ATP consists of adenosine bound to ribose and three phosphate groups (PO_3). Phosphates form high-energy covalent bonds. That is, a large amount of energy is required to form the bonds, and a large amount of energy is released when they break. ATP can break off one or two of its three phosphates to provide energy.

Summary

1. Matter is composed of 92 elements that combine to form an endless variety of compounds. **503**
2. An atom is the smallest piece of an element. A molecule is the smallest piece of a compound that maintains the properties of the compound. **505**
3. The atoms of some elements can gain or lose an electron, thus becoming ions. Positively charged ions attract negatively charged ions, forming an ionic bond. In some cases two or more atoms may share electrons, thus forming a covalent bond. **505**
4. The principal carrier of energy in the body is a chemical called ATP. **507**

Key Terms

atom **505**
atomic number **505**
atomic weight **505**
ATP (adenosine triphosphate) **507**
compound **503**
covalent bond **505**
element **503**
enzyme **507**
ion **505**
ionic bond **505**
molecule **505**

Society for Neuroscience Policies on the Use of Animals and Human Subjects in Research

Introduction

The Society for Neuroscience, as a professional society for basic and clinical researchers in neuroscience, endorses and supports the appropriate and responsible use of animals as experimental subjects. Knowledge generated by neuroscience research on animals has led to important advances in the understanding of diseases and disorders that affect the nervous system and in the development of better treatments that reduce suffering in humans and animals. This knowledge also makes a critical contribution to our understanding of ourselves, the complexities of our brains and what makes us human. Continued progress in understanding how the brain works and further advances in treating and curing disorders of the nervous system require investigation of complex functions at all levels in the living nervous system. Because no adequate alternatives exist, much of this research must be done on animal subjects. The Society takes the position that neuroscientists have an obligation to contribute to this progress through responsible and humane research on animals.

Several functions of the Society are related to the use of animals in research. A number of these involve decisions about research conducted by members of the Society, including the scheduling of scientific presentations at the Annual Meeting, the review and publication of original research papers in *The Journal of Neuroscience* and the defense of members whose ethical use of animals in research is questioned by animal rights activists. The Society's support for the research of individual members defines a relationship between the Society and its members. The purpose of this document is to outline the policy that guides that relationship. Compliance with the following policy will be an important factor in determining the suitability of research for presentation at the Annual Meeting or for publication in *The Journal of Neuroscience* and in situations where the Society is asked to provide public and active support for a member whose use of animals in research has been questioned.

The responsibility for implementing the policy in each of these areas rests with the relevant administrative body (Program Committee, Publications Committee, Editorial Board and Committee on Animals in Research, respectively) in consultation with Council.

Policy on the Use of Animals in Neuroscience Research

Neuroscience research uses complicated, often invasive methods, each of which is associated with different problems, risks, and specific technical considerations. An experimental method that would be deemed inappropriate for one kind of research may be the method of choice for another kind of research. It is therefore impossible for the Society to define specific policies and procedures for the care and use of all research animals and for the design and conduct of every neuroscience experiment.

The U.S. Public Health Service Policy on Humane Care and Use of Laboratory Animals (PHS Policy) and the *Guide for the Care and Use of Laboratory Animals* (the Guide) describe general policies and procedures designed to ensure the humane and appropriate use of live vertebrate animals in all forms of biomedical research. The Society finds the policies and procedures set forth in the PHS Policy and the Guide to be both necessary and sufficient to ensure a high standard of animal care and use and adopts them as its official Policy on the Use of Animals in Neuroscience Research (Society Policy). All Society members are expected to conduct their animal research in compliance with this policy. Members are required to verify that they have done so when submitting abstracts for presentation at the Annual Meeting or manuscripts for publication in *The Journal of Neuroscience*. Adherence to the Society policy is also an important step toward receiving help from the Society in responding to questions about a member's use of animals in research. A complete description of what to do if your research is questioned is included in this handbook. Also, a complete description of SfN's policy and procedures for defending members whose research comes under attack can be obtained by contacting the Society's Central Office.

Local Committee Review

An important element of the Society Policy is the establishment of a local committee that is charged with reviewing and approving all proposed animal care and use procedures. In addition to scientists experienced in research involving animals and a veterinarian, the membership of this local committee should include a person who is not affiliated with the member's institution in any other way. In reviewing a proposed use of animals, the committee should evaluate the adequacy of institutional policies, animal husbandry, veterinary care, and the physical plant. The committee should pay specific attention to proposed procedures for animal procurement, quarantine and stabilization, separation by species, disease diagnosis and treatment, anesthesia and analgesia, surgery and postsurgical care, and euthanasia. The review committee also should ensure that procedures involving live vertebrate animals are designed and performed with due consideration of their relevance to human or animal health, the advancement of knowledge or the good of society. This review and approval of a member's use of live vertebrate animals in research by a local committee is an essential component of the Society Policy. For assistance in developing appropriate animal care and use procedures and establishing a local review committee, call the Society and consult the documents recommended at the end of this section.

Other Laws, Regulations, and Policies

In addition to complying with the policy described above, Society members who reside in North America must also adhere to all relevant national, state, or local laws and/or regulations that govern their use of animals in neuroscience research. Thus, U.S. members must observe the U.S. Animal Welfare Act (as amended in 1985) and its implementing regulations from the U.S. Department of Agriculture. Canadian members must abide by the January 1993 Guide to the Care and Use of Experimental Animals. Members in Mexico must comply with the "Seventh Title of the Regulations of the General Law of Health Regarding Health Research." In addition to complying with the laws and regulations of their home countries, foreign members of the Society should adhere to the official Society Policy outlined here.

Recommended References

Canadian Council on Animal Care. Guide to the Care and Use of Experimental Animals Vol. 1. 2d ed. Ontario, Canada: CCAC, 1993.

Foundation for Biomedical Research. The Biomedical Investigator's Handbook for Researchers Using Animal Models. Washington, D.C.: FBR, 1987.

Laws and Codes of Mexico. "Seventh Title of the Regulations of the General Law of Health Regarding Health Research." 12th updated ed. Porrua Collection, 430-31. Mexico: Porrua Publishers, 1995.

National Academy of Sciences. Guide for the Care and Use of Laboratory Animals, 7th ed. Washington, D.C.: National Research Council, Institute for Laboratory Animal Research, NAS, 1996.

National Institutes of Health. OPRR Public Health Service Policy on Humane Care and Use of Laboratory Animals. Rockville, MD: NIH/Office for Protection from Research Risks, 1996.

National Institutes of Health. Preparation and Maintenance of Higher Mammals During Neuroscience Experiments. Report of a National Institutes of Health Workshop. NIH Publication No. 94-3207. Bethesda, MD: NIH/National Eye Institute, 1994.

Society for Neuroscience. Handbook for the Use of Animals in Neuroscience Research. Washington, D.C.: SfN, 1991.

Visual Neuroscience. 1 (4): 421-6. "Anesthesia and Paralysis in Experimental Animals." Report of a Workshop held in Bethesda, Md., Oct. 27, 1984. Organized by the Division of Research Grants, National Institutes of Health. England: VN, 1984.

General Principles

The following principles, based largely on the PHS Policy on Humane Care and Use of Laboratory Animals, can be a useful guide to designing and implementing experimental procedures involving laboratory animals.

Animals selected for a procedure should be of an appropriate species and quality and the minimum number required to obtain valid results.

Proper use of animals, including the avoidance or minimization of discomfort, distress, and pain, is imperative.

Procedures with animals that may cause more than momentary or slight pain or distress should be performed with appropriate sedation, analgesia, or anesthesia. Surgical or other painful procedures should not be performed on unanesthetized animals paralyzed by chemical agents.

Postoperative care of animals should minimize discomfort and pain and, in any case, should be equivalent to accepted practices in schools of veterinary medicine.

Animals that would otherwise suffer severe or chronic pain or distress that cannot be relieved should be painlessly killed at the end of the procedure or, if appropriate, during the procedure. If the study requires the death of the animal, the animal must be killed in a humane manner.

Living conditions should be appropriate for the species and contribute to the animals' well-being. Normally, the housing, feeding, and care of all animals used for biomedical purposes must be directed by a veterinarian or other scientist trained and experienced in the proper care, handling, and use of the species being maintained or studied. In any case, appropriate veterinary care shall be provided.

Exceptions to these principles require careful consideration and should only be made by an appropriate review group such as an institutional animal care and use committee.

Policy on the Use of Human Subjects in Neuroscience Research

Experimental procedures involving human subjects must have been conducted in conformance with the policies and principles contained in the Federal Policy for the Protection of Human Subjects (U. S. Office of Science and Technology Policy) and in the Declaration of Helsinki. When publishing a paper in *The Journal of Neuroscience* or submitting an abstract for presentation at the Annual Meeting, authors must sign a statement of compliance with this policy.

Recommended References

"Declaration of Helsinki." Adopted by 18th World Medical Assembly, Helsinki, 1964; revised by 29th World Medical Assembly, Tokyo, 1975; Venice, 1983; and Hong Kong, 1989.

"Federal Policy for the Protection of Human Subjects; Notices and Rules." Federal Register (June 18, 1991) 56: 28002–32.

Varga, Andrew C., Ed. The Main Issue in Bioethics Revised Edition. New York: Paulist Press, 1984.

References

Numbers in parentheses following entries indicate the chapter in which a reference is cited.

Abbott, N. J., Rönnback, L., & Hansson, E. (2006). Astrocyte-endothelial interactions at the blood–brain barrier. *Nature Reviews Neuroscience, 7,* 41–53. (1)

AbdelMalik, P., Husted, J, Chow, E. W. C., & Bassett, A. S. (2003). Childhood head injury and expression of schizophrenia in multiply affected families. *Archives of General Psychiatry, 60,* 231–236. (14)

Abi-Dargham, A., Rodenhiser, J., Printz, D., Zea-Ponce, Y., Gil, R., Kegeles, L. S., . . . Laruelle, M. (2000). Increased baseline occupancy of D2 receptors by dopamine in schizophrenia. *Proceedings of the National Academy of Sciences, USA, 97,* 8104–8109. (14)

Aboitiz, F., Aboitiz, S., & García, R. R. (2010). The phonological loop: A key innovation in human evolution. *Current Anthropology, 51* (Suppl. 1), S55–S65. (13)

Abrahamsen, B., Zhao, J., Asante, C. O., Cendan, C. M., Marsh, S., Martinez-Barbera, J. P., . . . Wood, J. N. (2008). The cell and molecular basis of mechanical, cold, and inflammatory pain. *Science, 321,* 702–705. (6)

Abrahamsson, N., & Hyltenstam, K. (2009). Age of onset and nativelikeness in a second language: Listener perception versus linguistic scrutiny. *Language Learning, 59,* 249–306. (13)

Ackman, J. B., Burbridge, T. J., & Crair, M. C. (2012). Retinal waves coordinate patterned activity throughout the developing visual system. *Nature, 490,* 219–225. (5)

Adamec, R. E., Stark-Adamec, C., & Livingston, K. E. (1980). The development of predatory aggression and defense in the domestic cat (*Felis catus*): 3. Effects on development of hunger between 180 and 365 days of age. *Behavioral and Neural Biology, 30,* 435–447. (11)

Adams, D. B., Gold, A. R., & Burt, A. D. (1978). Rise in female-initiated sexual activity at ovulation and its suppression by oral contraceptives. *New England Journal of Medicine, 299,* 1145–1150. (10)

Adams, R. B., Jr., Gordon, H. L., Baird, A. A., Ambady, N., & Kleck, R. E. (2003). Effects of gaze on amygdala sensitivity to anger and fear faces. *Science, 300,* 1536. (11)

Adams, R. B., Jr., & Kleck, R. E. (2005). Effects of direct and averted gaze on the perception of facially communicated emotion. *Emotion, 5,* 3–11. (11)

Addis, D. R., Wong, A. T., & Schacter, D. L. (2007). Remembering the past and imagining the future: Common and distinct neural substrates during event construction and elaboration. *Neuropsychologia, 45,* 1363–1377. (12)

Adkins, E. K., & Adler, N. T. (1972). Hormonal control of behavior in the Japanese quail. *Journal of Comparative and Physiological Psychology, 81,* 27–36. (10)

Adler, E., Hoon, M. A., Mueller, K. L., Chandrashekar, J., Ryba, N. J. P., & Zuker, C. S. (2000). A novel family of mammalian taste receptors. *Cell, 100,* 693–702. (6)

Admon, R., Lubin, G., Stern, O., Rosenberg, K., Sela, L., Ben-Ami, H., & Hendler, T. (2009). Human vulnerability to stress depends on amygdala's predisposition and hippocampal plasticity. *Proceedings of the National Academy of Sciences (U.S.A.), 106,* 14120–14125. (11)

Adolphs, R., Damasio, H., & Tranel, D. (2002). Neural systems for recognition of emotional prosody: A 3-D lesion study. *Emotion, 2,* 23–51. (13)

Adolphs, R., Tranel, D., & Buchanan, T. W. (2005). Amygdala damage impairs emotional memory for gist but not details of complex stimuli. *Nature Neuroscience, 8,* 512–518. (11)

Adolphs, R., Tranel, D., Damasio, H., & Damasio, A. (1995). Fear and the human amygdala. *Journal of Neuroscience, 15,* 5879–5891. (11)

Agarwal, N., Pacher, P., Tegeder, I., Amaya, F., Constantin, C. E., Brenner, G. J., . . . Kuner, R. (2007). Cannabinoids mediate analgesia largely via peripheral type 1 cannabinoid receptors in nociceptors. *Nature Neuroscience, 10,* 870–879. (6)

Agerbo, E., Mortensen, P. B., Wiuf, C., Pedersen, M. S., McGrath, J., Hollegaard, M. V., . . . Pedersen, C. B. (2012). Modelling the contribution of family history and variation in single nucleotide polymorphisms to risk of schizophrenia: A Danish national birth cohort-based study. *Schizophrenia Research, 134,* 246–252. (14)

Aglioti, S., Smania, N., Atzei, A., & Berlucchi, G. (1997). Spatio-temporal properties of the pattern of evoked phantom sensations in a left index amputee patient. *Behavioral Neuroscience, 111,* 867–872. (4)

Aglioti, S., Smania, N., & Peru, A. (1999). Frames of reference for mapping tactile stimuli in brain-damaged patients. *Journal of Cognitive Neuroscience, 11,* 67–79. (13)

Aglioti, S., Tassinari, G., Corballis, M. C., & Berlucchi, G. (2000). Incomplete gustatory localization as shown by analysis of taste discrimination after callosotomy. *Journal of Cognitive Neuroscience, 12,* 238–245. (13)

Agrati, D., Fernández-Guasti, A., Ferreño, M., & Ferreira, A. (2011). Coexpression of sexual behavior and maternal aggression: The ambivalence of sexually active mother rats toward male intruders. *Behavioral Neuroscience, 125,* 446–451. (10)

Agren, T., Engman, J., Frick, A., Björkstrand, J., Larsson, E.-M., Furmark, T., & Fredrikson, M. (2012). Disruption of reconsolidation erases a fear memory trace in the human amygdala. *Science, 337,* 1550–1552. (11)

Aguzzi, A., Barres, B. A., & Bennett, M. L. (2013). Microglia: Scapegoat, saboteur, or something else? *Science, 339,* 156–161. (1)

Ahlskog, J. E., & Hoebel, B. G. (1973). Overeating and obesity from damage to a noradrenergic system in the brain. *Science, 182,* 166–169. (9)

Ahlskog, J. E., Randall, P. K., & Hoebel, B. G. (1975). Hypothalamic hyperphagia: Dissociation from hyperphagia following destruction of noradrenergic neurons. *Science, 190,* 399–401. (9)

Ahmed, E. I., Zehr, J. L., Schulz, K. M., Lorenz, B. H., DonCarlos, L. L., & Sisk, C. L (2008). Pubertal hormones modulate the addition of new cells to sexually dimorphic brain regions. *Nature Neuroscience, 11,* 995–997. (10)

Ahmed, I. I., Shryne, J. E., Gorski, R. A., Branch, B. J., & Taylor, A. N. (1991). Prenatal ethanol and the prepubertal sexually dimorphic nucleus of the preoptic area. *Physiology & Behavior, 49,* 427–432. (10)

Airaksinen, M. S., & Saarma, M. (2002). The GDNF family: Signalling, biological functions and therapeutic value. *Nature Reviews Neuroscience, 3,* 383–394. (4)

Airan, R. D., Meltzer, L. A., Roy, M., Gong, Y., Chen, H., & Deisseroth, K. (2007). High-speed imaging reveals neurophysiological links to behavior in an animal model of depression. *Science, 317,* 819–823. (14)

Airavaara, M., Harvey, B. K., Voutilainen, M. H., Shen, H., Chou, J., Lindholm, P., . . . Wang, Y. (2012). CDNF protects the nigrostriatal dopamine system and promotes recovery after MPTP treatment in mice. *Cell Transplantation, 21,* 1213–1223. (7)

Akinola, M., & Mendes, W. B. (2012). Stress-induced cortisol facilitates threat-related decision making among police officers. *Behavioral Neuroscience, 126,* 167–174. (11)

Alanko, K., Santtila, P., Harlaar, N., Witting, K., Varjonen, M., Jern, P., . . . Sandnabba, N. K. (2010). Common genetic effects of gender atypical behavior in childhood and sexual orientation in adulthood: A study of Finnish twins. *Archives of Sexual Behavior, 39,* 81–92. (10)

Albanese, M.-C., Duerden, E. G., Rainville, P., & Duncan, G. H. (2007). Memory traces of pain in human cortex. *Journal of Neuroscience, 27,* 4612–4620. (6)

Albouy, G., Sterpenich, V., Balteau, E., Vandewalle, G., Desseilles, M., Dang-Vu, T., . . . Maquet, P. (2008). Both the hippocampus and striatum are involved in consolidation of motor sequence memory. *Neuron, 58,* 261–272. (12)

Albright, T. D., Jessell, T. M., Kandel, E. R., & Posner, M. I. (2001). Progress in the neural sciences in the century after Cajal (and the mysteries that remain). *Annals of the New York Academy of Sciences, 929,* 11–40. (1)

Aleman, A., Kahn, R. S., & Selten, J. P. (2003). Sex differences in the risk of schizophrenia. *Archives of General Psychiatry, 60,* 565–571. (14)

Alexander, G. M., & Hines, M. (2002). Sex differences in response to children's toys in nonhuman primates (*Cercopithecus aethiops sebaeus*). *Evolution and Human Behavior, 23,* 467–479. (10)

Alexander, G. M., Wilcox, T., & Woods, R. (2009). Sex differences in infants' visual interest in toys. *Archives of Sexual Behavior, 38,* 427–433. (10)

Alexander, W. H., & Brown, J. W. (2011). Medial prefrontal cortex as an action-outcome predictor. *Nature Neuroscience, 14,* 1338–1344. (3)

Alagiakrishnan, K., Gill, S. S., & Fagarasanu, A. (2012). Genetics and epigenetics of Alzheimer's disease. *Postgraduate Medical Journal, 88,* 522–529. (12)

Allen, H. L., Estrada, K., Lettre, G., Berndt, S. I., Weedon, M. N., Rivadeneira, F., . . . Hirschhorn, J. N. (2010). Hundreds of variants clustered in genomic loci and biological pathways affect human height. *Nature, 467,* 832–838. (4)

Allen, J. S., Damasio, H., Grabowski, T. J., Bruss, J., & Zhang, W. (2003). Sexual dimorphism and asymmetries in the gray-white composition of the human cerebrum. *NeuroImage, 18,* 880–894. (3)

Alleva, E., & Francia, N. (2009). Psychiatric vulnerability: Suggestions from animal models and role of neurotrophins. *Neuroscience and Biobehavioral Reviews, 33,* 525–536. (4)

Allison, T., & Cicchetti, D. V. (1976). Sleep in mammals: Ecological and constitutional correlates. *Science, 194,* 732–734. (8)

Almli, C. R., Fisher, R. S., & Hill, D. L. (1979). Lateral hypothalamus destruction in infant rats produces consummatory deficits without sensory neglect or attenuated arousal. *Experimental Neurology, 66,* 146–157. (9)

Alonso, M., Lepousez, G., Wagner, S., Bardy, C., Gabellec, M.-M., Torquet, N., & Lledo, P.-M. (2012). Activation of adult-born neurons facilitates learning and memory. *Nature Neuroscience, 15,* 897–904. (4)

Al-Rashid, R. A. (1971). Hypothalamic syndrome in acute childhood leukemia. *Clinical Pediatrics, 10,* 53–54. (9)

Altar, C. A., Laeng, P., Jurata, L. W., Brockman, J. A., Lemire, A., Bullard, J., . . . Palfreyman, M. G. (2004). Electroconvulsive seizures regulate gene expression of distinct neurotrophic signaling pathways. *Journal of Neuroscience, 24,* 2667–2677. (14)

Amateau, S. K., & McCarthy, M. M. (2004). Induction of PGE2 by estradiol mediates developmental masculinization of sex behavior. *Nature Neuroscience, 7,* 643–650. (10)

American Psychiatric Association (2013). *Diagnostic and statistical manual of mental disorders.* Washington, DC: American Psychiatric Publishing. (14)

Amiry-Moghaddam, M., & Ottersen, O. P. (2003). The molecular basis of water transport in the brain. *Nature Reviews Neuroscience, 4,* 991–1001. (1)

Amting, J. M., Greening, S. G., & Mitchell, D. G. V. (2010). Multiple mechanisms of consciousness: The neural correlates of emotional awareness. *Journal of Neuroscience, 30,* 10039–10047. (11)

Anaclet, C., Parmentier, R., Ouk, K., Guidon, G., Buda, C., Sastre, J.-P., . . . Ohtsu, H. (2009). Orexin/hypocretin and histamine: Distinct roles in the control of wakefulness demonstrated using knock-out mouse models. *Journal of Neuroscience, 29,* 14423–14438. (8)

Anand, P., & Bley, K. (2011). Topical capsaicin for pain management: Therapeutic potential and mechanisms of action of the new high-concentration capsaicin 8% patch. *British Journal of Anaesthesia, 107,* 490–502. (6)

Andersen, J. L., Klitgaard, H., & Saltin, B. (1994). Myosin heavy chain isoforms in single fibres from m. vastus lateralis of sprinters: Influence of training. *Acta Physiologica Scandinavica, 151,* 135–142. (7)

Andersen, T. S., Tiippana, K., & Sams, M. (2004). Factors influencing audiovisual fission and fusion illusions. *Cognitive Brain Research, 21,* 301–308. (3)

Anderson, E., Dryman, M. T., Worthington, J., Hoge, E. A., Fischer, L. E., Pollack, M. H., . . . Simon, N. M. (2013). Smiles may go unseen in generalized social anxiety disorder: Evidence from binocular rivalry for reduced visual consciousness of positive facial expressions. *Journal of Anxiety Disorders, 27,* 619–626. (13)

Anderson, E., Siegel, E. H., & Barrett, L. F. (2011). What you feel influences what you see. The role of affective feelings in resolving binocular rivalry. *Journal of Experimental Social Psychology, 47,* 856–860. (13)

Anderson, S., Parbery-Clark, A., White-Schwoch, T., & Kraus, N. (2012). Aging affects neural precision of speech encoding. *Journal of Neuroscience, 32,* 14156–14164. (6)

Andreasen, N. C. (1988). Brain imaging: Applications in psychiatry. *Science, 239,* 1381–1388. (3)

Andreasen, N. C., Nopoulos, P., Magnotta, V., Pierson, R., Ziebell, S., & Ho, B-C. (2011). Progressive brain change in schizophrenia: A prospective longitudinal study of first-episode schizophrenia. *Biological Psychiatry, 70,* 672–679. (14)

Andrew, D., & Craig, A. D. (2001). Spinothalamic lamina I neurons selectively sensitive to histamine: A central neural pathway for itch. *Nature Neuroscience, 4,* 72–77. (6)

Andrews, T. J., Halpern, S. D., & Purves, D. (1997). Correlated size variations in human visual cortex, lateral geniculate nucleus, and optic tract. *Journal of Neuroscience, 17,* 2859–2868. (5)

Anguera, J. A., Boccanfuso, J., Rintoul, J. L., Al-Hashimi, O., Faraji, F., Janowich, J., . . . Gazzaley, A. (2013). Video game training enhances cognitive control in older adults. *Nature, 501,* 97–101. (13)

Angulo, M. C., Kozlov, A. S., Charpak, S., & Audinat, E. (2004). Glutamate released from glial cells synchronizes neuronal activity in the hippocampus. *Journal of Neuroscience, 24,* 6920–6927. (1)

Ankney, C. D. (1992). Sex differences in relative brain size: The mismeasure of women, too? *Intelligence, 16,* 329–336. (3)

Antanitus, D. S. (1998). A theory of cortical neuron-astrocyte interaction. *Neuroscientist, 4,* 154–159. (1)

Apostolakis, E. M., Garai, J., Fox, C., Smith, C. L., Watson, S. J., Clark, J. H., & O'Malley, B. W. (1996). Dopaminergic regulation of progesterone receptors: Brain D5 dopamine receptors mediate induction of lordosis by D1-like agonists in rats. *Journal of Neuroscience, 16,* 4823–4834. (10)

Araneda, R. C., Kini, A. D., & Firestein, S. (2000). The molecular receptive range of an odorant receptor. *Nature Neuroscience, 3,* 1248–1255. (6)

Archer, J. (2000). Sex differences in aggression between heterosexual partners: A meta-analytic review. *Psychological Bulletin, 126,* 651–680. (11)

Archer, J., Birring, S. S., & Wu, F. C. W. (1998). The association between testosterone and aggression in young men: Empirical findings and a meta-analysis. *Aggressive Behavior, 24,* 411–420. (11)

Archer, J., Graham-Kevan, N., & Davies, M. (2005). Testosterone and aggression: A reanalysis of Book, Starzyk, and Quinsey's (2001) study. *Aggression and Violent Behavior, 10,* 241–261. (11)

Arcurio, L. R., Gold, J. M., & James, T. W. (2012). The response of face-selective cortex with single face parts and part combinations. *Neuropsychologia, 50,* 2454–2459. (5)

Armstrong, J. B., & Schindler, D. E. (2011). Excess digestive capacity in predators reflects a life of feast and famine. *Nature, 476,* 84–87. (9)

Arnold, A. P. (2004). Sex chromosomes and brain gender. *Nature Reviews Neuroscience, 5,* 701–708. (10)

Arnold, A. P. (2009). The organizational-activational hypothesis as the foundation for a unified theory of sexual differentiation of all mammalian tissues. *Hormones and Behavior, 55,* 570–578. (10)

Arnold, A. P., & Breedlove, S. M. (1985). Organizational and activational effects of sex steroids on brain and behavior: A reanalysis. *Hormones and Behavior, 19,* 469–498. (10)

Arnsten, A. F. T. (2009). Stress signaling pathways that impair prefrontal cortex structure and function. *Nature Reviews Neuroscience, 10,* 410–422. (11)

Arvidson, K., & Friberg, U. (1980). Human taste: Response and taste bud number in fungiform papillae. *Science, 209,* 807–808. (6)

Asai, M., Ramachandrappa, S., Joachim, M., Shen, Y., Zhang, R., Nuthalapati, N., . . . Majzoub, J. A. (2013). Loss of function of the melanocortin 2 receptor accessory protein 2 is associated with mammalian obesity. *Science, 341,* 275–278. (9)

Asari, H., & Meister, M. (2012). Divergence of visual channels in the inner retina. *Nature Neuroscience, 15,* 1581–1589. (5)

Aserinsky, E., & Kleitman, N. (1955). Two types of ocular motility occurring in sleep. *Journal of Applied Physiology, 8,* 1–10. (8)

Ashmore, L. J., & Sehgal, A. (2003). A fly's eye view of circadian entrainment. *Journal of Biological Rhythms, 18,* 206–216. (8)

Aston-Jones, G., Chen, S., Zhu, Y., & Oshinsky, M. L. (2001). A neural circuit for circadian regulation of arousal. *Nature Neuroscience, 4,* 732–738. (8)

Athos, E. A., Levinson, B., Kistler, A., Zemansky, J., Bostrom, A., Freimer, N., & Gitschier, J. (2007). Dichotomy and perceptual distortions in absolute pitch ability. *Proceedings of the National Academy of Sciences, USA, 104,* 14795–14800. (6)

Audero, E., Mlinar, B., Baccini, G., Skachokova, Z. K., Corradetti, R., & Gross, C. (2013). Suppression of serotonin neuron firing increases aggression in mice. *Journal of Neuroscience, 33,* 8678–8688. (11)

Avena, N. M., Rada, P., & Hoebel, B. G. (2008). Evidence for sugar addiction: Behavioral and neurochemical effects of intermittent, excessive sugar intake. *Neuroscience and Biobehavioral Reviews, 32,* 20–39. (9)

Aviezer, H., Trope, Y., & Todorov, A. (2012). Body cues, not facial expressions, discriminate between intense positive and negative emotions. *Science, 338,* 1225–1229. (11)

Babich, F. R., Jacobson, A. L., Bubash, S., & Jacobson, A. (1965). Transfer of a response to naive rats by injection of ribonucleic acid extracted from trained rats. *Science, 149,* 656–657. (12)

Babiloni, C., Brancucci, A., Pizzella, V., Romani, G. L., Tecchio, F., Torquati, K., . . . Rossini, P. M. (2005). Contingent negative variation in the parasylvian cortex increases during expectancy of painful sensorimotor events: A magnetoencephalographic study. *Behavioral Neuroscience, 119,* 491–502. (6)

Babkoff, H., Caspy, T., Mikulincer, M., & Sing, H. C. (1991). Monotonic and rhythmic influences: A challenge for sleep deprivation research. *Psychological Bulletin, 109,* 411–428. (8)

Backlund, E.-O., Granberg, P.-O., Hamberger, B., Sedvall, G., Seiger, A., & Olson, L. (1985). Transplantation of adrenal medullary tissue to striatum in Parkinsonism. In A. Björklund & U. Stenevi (Eds.), *Neural grafting in the mammalian CNS* (pp. 551–556). Amsterdam: Elsevier. (7)

Bäckman, J., & Alerstam, T. (2001). Confronting the winds: Orientation and flight behavior of roosting swifts, *Apus apus. Proceedings of the Royal Society of London. Series B—Biological Sciences, 268,* 1081–1087. (8)

Baddeley, A. D., & Hitch, G. J. (1994). Developments in the concept of working memory. *Neuropsychology, 8,* 485–493. (12)

Badiani, A., Belin, D., Epstein, D., Calu, D., & Shaham, Y. (2011). Opiate versus psychostimulant addiction: The differences do matter. *Nature Reviews Neuroscience, 12,* 685–698. (14)

Baer, J. S., Sampson, P. D., Barr, H. M., Connor, P. D., & Streissguth, A. P. (2003). A 21-year longitudinal analysis of the effects of prenatal alcohol exposure on young adult drinking. *Archives of General Psychiatry, 60,* 377–385. (14)

Bagemihl, B. (1999). *Biological exuberance.* New York: St. Martin's Press. (10)

Baghdoyan, H. A., Spotts, J. L., & Snyder, S. G. (1993). Simultaneous pontine and basal fore brain microinjections of carbachol suppress REM sleep. *Journal of Neuroscience, 13,* 229–242. (8)

Bailey, C. H., Giustetto, M., Huang, Y.-Y., Hawkins, R. D., & Kandel, E. R. (2000). Is heterosynaptic modulation essential for stabilizing Hebbian plasticity and memory? *Nature Reviews Neuroscience, 1,* 11–20. (12)

Bailey, J. M., & Pillard, R. C. (1991). A genetic study of male sexual orientation. *Archives of General Psychiatry, 48,* 1089–1096. (10)

Bailey, J. M., Pillard, R. C., Dawood, K., Miller, M. B., Farrer, L. A., Trivedi, S., & Murphy, R. L. (1999). A family history study of male sexual orientation using three independent samples. *Behavior Genetics, 29,* 79–86. (10)

Bailey, J. M., Pillard, R. C., Neale, M. C., & Agyei, Y. (1993). Heritable factors influence sexual orientation in women. *Archives of General Psychiatry, 50,* 217–223. (10)

Bailey, J. M., Willerman, L., & Parks, C. (1991). A test of the maternal stress theory of human male homosexuality. *Archives of Sexual Behavior, 20,* 277–293. (10)

Baker, E., Shelton, K. H., Baibazarova, E., Hay, D. F., & van Goozen, S. H. M. (2013). Low skin conductance in infancy predicts aggression in toddlers 2 years later. *Psychological Science, 24,* 1051–1056. (11)

Bakken, T. E., Roddey, J. C., Djurovic, S., Akshoomoff, N., Amaral, D. G., Bloss, C. S., . . . Dale, A. M. (2012). Association of common genetic variants in GPCPD1 with scaling of visual cortical surface in humans. *Proceedings of the National Academy of Sciences (U.S.A.), 109,* 3985–3990. (5)

Bakker, J., De Mees, C., Douhard, Q., Balthazart, J., Gabant, P., Szpirer, J., & Szpirer, C. (2006). Alpha-fetoprotein protects the developing female mouse brain from masculinization and defeminization by estrogens. *Nature Neuroscience, 9,* 220–226. (10)

Bakker, J., Honda, S.-I., Harada, N., & Balthazart, J. (2002). The aromatase knock-out mouse provides new evidence that estradiol is required during development in the female for the expression of sociosexual behaviors in adulthood. *Journal of Neuroscience, 22,* 9104–9112. (10)

Ballard, P. A., Tetrud, J. W., & Langston, J. W. (1985). Permanent human Parkinsonism due to 1-methyl-4-phenyl-1,2,3,6-tetrahydropyridine (MPTP). *Neurology, 35,* 949–956. (7)

Balleine, B. W., Delgado, M. R., & Hikosaka, O. (2007). The role of the dorsal striatum in reward and decision-making. *Journal of Neuroscience, 27,* 8161–8165. (12)

Ballon, J. S., Dean, K. A., & Cadenhead, K. S. (2007). Obstetrical complications in people at risk for developing schizophrenia. *Schizophrenia Research, 98,* 307–311. (14)

Banks, W. P., & Isham, E. A. (2009). We infer rather than perceive the moment we decided to act. *Psychological Science, 20,* 17–21. (7)

Bannerman, D. M., Bus, T., Taylor, A. M., Sanderson, D. J., Schwarz, I., . . . Sprengel, R. (2012). Dissecting spatial knowledge from spatial choice by hippocampal NMDA receptor deletion. *Nature Neuroscience, 15,* 1153–1159. (12)

Barbour, D. L., & Wang, X. (2003). Contrast tuning in auditory cortex. *Science, 299,* 1073–1075. (6)

Bargary, G., Barnett, K. J., Mitchell, K. J., & Newell, F. N. (2009). Colored-speech synaesthesia is triggered by multisensory, not unisensory, perception. *Psychological Science, 20,* 529–533. (6)

Barinaga, M. (1996). Finding new drugs to treat stroke. *Science, 272,* 664–664. (4)

Barnea, G., O'Donnell, S., Mancia, F., Sun, X., Nemes, A., Mendelsohn, M., & Axel, R. (2004). Odorant receptors on axon termini in the brain. *Science, 304,* 1468. (6)

Barnes, B. M. (1996, September/October). Sang froid. *The Sciences, 36*(5), 13–14. (8)

Barnett, K. J., Finucane, C., Asher, J. E., Bargary, G., Corvin, A. P., Newell, F. N., & Mitchell, K. J. (2008). Familial patterns and the origins of individual differences in synaesthesia. *Cognition, 106,* 871–893. (6)

Barrett, L. F. (2012). Emotions are real. *Emotion, 12,* 413–429. (11)

Barrett, L. F., Bliss-Moreau, E., Duncan, S. L., Rauch, S. L., & Wright, C. I. (2007). The amygdala and the experience of affect. *Social Cognitive & Affective Neuroscience, 2,* 73–83. (11)

Barrientos, R. M., Frank, M. G., Crysdale, N. Y., Chapman, T. R., Ahrendsen, J. T., Day, H. E. W., . . . Maier, S. F. (2011). Little exercise, big effects: Reversing aging and infection-induced memory deficits, and underlying processes. *Journal of Neuroscience, 31,* 115778–11586. (4)

Barton, D. A., Esler, M. D., Dawood, T., Lambert, E. A., Haikerwal, D., Brenchley, C., . . . Lambert, G. W. (2008). Elevated brain serotonin turnover in patients with depression. *Archives of General Psychiatry, 65,* 38–46. (14)

Barton, R. A., & Harvey, P. H. (2000). Mosaic evolution of brain structure in mammals. *Nature, 405,* 1055–1058. (3)

Bartoshuk, L. M. (1991). Taste, smell, and pleasure. In R. C. Bolles (Ed.), *The hedonics of taste* (pp. 15–28). Hillsdale, NJ: Erlbaum. (6)

Bartoshuk, L. M., Gentile, R. L., Moskowitz, H. R., & Meiselman, H. L. (1974). Sweet taste induced by miracle fruit (*Synsephalum dulcificum*). *Physiology & Behavior, 12,* 449–456. (6)

Bartsch, T., Schönfeld, R., Müller, F. J., Alfke, K., Leplow, B., Aldenhoff, J., . . . Koch, J. M. (2010). Focal lesions of human hippocampal CA1 neurons in transient global amnesia impair place memory. *Science, 328,* 1412–1415. (12)

Bartz, J. A., Simeon, D., Hamilton, H., Kim, S., Crystal, S., Braun, A., Vicens, V., & Hollander, E. (2011). Oxytocin can hinder trust and cooperation in borderline personality disorder. *Social, Cognitive, and Affective Neuroscience, 6,* 556–563. (13)

Barzilai, N., Alzmon, G., Derby, C. A., Bauman, J. M., & Lipton, R. B. (2006). A genotype of exceptional longevity is associated with preservation of cognitive function. *Neurology, 67,* 2170–2175. (4)

Bashford, J. A., Warren, R. M., & Lenz, P. W. (2013). Maintaining intelligibility at high speech intensities: Evidence of lateral inhibition in the lower auditory pathway. *Journal of the Acoustical Society of America, 134,* EL119–EL125. (5)

Basterzi, A. D., Yazici, K., Aslan, E., Delialioglu, B. T., Acar, S. T., & Yazici, A. (2008). Effects of fluoxetine and venlafaxine on serum brain derived neurotrophic factor levels in depressed patients. *Progress in Neuro-psychopharmacology & biological psychiatry,* 33, 281–285. (14)

Battersby, S. (1997). Plus c'est le même chews. *Nature, 385,* 679. (9)

Baulac, S., Huberfeld, G., Gourfinkel-An, I., Mitropoulou, G., Beranger, A., Prud'homme, J.-F., . . . LeGuern, E. (2001). First genetic evidence of GABAA receptor dysfunction in epilepsy: A mutation in the g2-subunit gene. *Nature Genetics, 28,* 46–48. (13)

Baum, A., Gatchel, R. J., & Schaeffer, M. A. (1983). Emotional, behavioral, and physiological effects of chronic stress at Three Mile Island. *Journal of Consulting and Clinical Psychology, 51,* 565–582. (11)

Bauman, M. D., Iosif, A.-M., Ashwood, P., Braunschweig, D., Lee, A., Schumann, C. M., . . . Amaral, D. G. (2013). Maternal antibodies from mothers of children with autism alter brain growth and social behavior development in the rhesus monkey. *Translational Psychiatry, 3,* e278. (14)

Bautista, D. M., Sigal, Y. M., Milstein, A. D., Garrison, J. L., Zorn, J. A., Tsuruda, P. R., . . . Julius, D. (2008). Pungent agents from Szechuan peppers excite sensory neurons by inhibiting two-pore potassium channels. *Nature Neuroscience, 11,* 772–779. (6)

Baxter, L. R., Phelps, M. E., Mazziotta, J. C., Schwartz, J. M., Gerner, R. H., Selin, C. E., & Sumida, R. M. (1985). Cerebral metabolic rates for glucose in mood disorders. *Archives of General Psychiatry, 42,* 441–447. (14)

Bayley, P. J., Frascino, J. C., & Squire, L. R. (2005). Robust habit learning in the absence of awareness and independent of the medial temporal lobe. *Nature, 436,* 550–553. (12)

Bayley, P. J., Hopkins, R. O., & Squire, L. R. (2006). The fate of old memories after medial temporal lobe damage. *Journal of Neuroscience, 26,* 13311–13317. (12)

Baylis, G. C., & Driver, J. (2001). Shape-coding in IT cells generalizes over contrast and mirror reversal but not figure-ground reversal. *Nature Neuroscience, 4,* 937–942. (5)

Beall, A. T., & Tracy, J. L. (2013). Women are more likely to wear red or pink at peak fertility. *Psychological Science, 24,* 1837–1841. (10)

Beaton, E. A., Schmidt, L. A., Schulkin, J., Antony, M. M., Swinson, R. P., & Hall, G. B. (2008). Different neural responses to stranger and personally familiar faces in shy and bold adults. *Behavioral Neuroscience, 122,* 704–709. (11)

Beauchamp, M. S., & Ro, T. (2008). Neural substrates of sound-touch synesthesia after a thalamic lesion. *Journal of Neuroscience, 28,* 13696–13702. (6)

Bechara, A., Damasio, H., Damasio, A. R., & Lee, G. P. (1999). Different contributions of the human amygdala and ventromedial prefrontal cortex to decision-making. *Journal of Neuroscience, 19,* 5473–5481. (11)

Beck, S., Richardson, S. P., Shamin, E. A., Dang, N., Schubert, M., & Hallett, M. (2008). Short intracortical and surround inhibition are selectively reduced during movement initiation in focal hand dystonia. *Journal of Neuroscience, 28,* 10363–10369. (4)

Becker, C., Thiébot, M.-H., Touitou, Y., Hamon, M., Cesselin, F., & Benoliel, J.-J. (2001). Enhanced cortical extracellular levels of cholecystokinin-like material in a model of anticipation of social defeat in the rat. *Journal of Neuroscience, 21,* 262–269. (11)

Becker, H. C. (1988). Effects of the imidazobenzodiazepine Ro15-4513 on the stimulant and depressant actions of ethanol on spontaneous locomotor activity. *Life Sciences, 43,* 643–650. (11)

Becks, L., & Agrawal, A. F. (2010). Higher rates of sex evolve in spatially heterogeneous environments. *Nature, 468,* 89–92. (10)

Bedny, M., Pascual-Leone, A., Dodell-Feder, D., Fedorenko, E., & Saxe, R. (2011). Language processing in the occipital cortex of congenitally blind adults. *Proceedings of the National Academy of Sciences (U.S.A.), 108,* 4429–4434. (4)

Beebe, D. W., & Gozal, D. (2002). Obstructive sleep apnea and the prefrontal cortex: Towards a comprehensive model linking nocturnal upper airway obstruction to daytime cognitive and behavioral deficits. *Journal of Sleep Research, 11,* 1–16. (8)

Beehner, J. C., Bergman, T. J., Cheney, D. L., Seyfarth, R. M., & Whitten, P. L. (2005). The effect of new alpha males on female stress in free-ranging baboons. *Animal Behaviour, 69,* 1211–1221. (11)

Beehner, J. C., Gesquirere, L., Seyfarth, R. M., Cheney, D. L., Alberts, S. C., & Altmann, J. (2009). Testosterone related to age and life-history stages in male baboons and geladas. *Hormones and Behavior, 56,* 472–480. (11)

Beeman, M. J., & Chiarello, C. (1998). Complementary right- and left-hemisphere language comprehension. *Current Directions in Psychological Science, 7,* 2–8. (13)

Beeney, J. E., Franklin, R. G. Jr., Levy, K. N., & Adams, R. B. Jr. (2011). I feel your pain: Emotional closeness modulates neural responses to empathically experienced rejection. *Social Neuroscience, 6,* 369–376. (13)

Behrens, M., Foerster, S., Staehler, F., Raguse, J.-D., & Meyerhof, W. (2007). Gustatory expression pattern of the human TAS2R bitter receptor gene family reveals a heterogenous population of bitter responsive taste receptor cells. *Journal of Neuroscience, 27,* 12630–12640. (6)

Bellugi, U., Lichtenberger, L., Jones, W., Lai, Z., & St. George, M. (2000). I. The neurocognitive profile of Williams syndrome: A complex pattern of strengths and weaknesses. *Journal of Cognitive Neuroscience, 12*(Suppl.), 7–29. (13)

Ben Achour, S., & Pascual, O. (2012). Astrocyte-neuron communication: Functional consequences. *Neurochemical Research, 37,* 2464–2473. (1)

Ben-Ami Bartal, I., Rodgers, D. A., Sarria, M. S. B., Decety, J., & Mason, P. (2014). Pro-social behavior in rats is modulated by social experience. *eLife, 3,* e01385. (13)

Benedetti, F., Arduino, C., & Amanzio, M. (1999). Somatotopic activation of opioid systems by target-directed expectations of analgesia. *Journal of Neuroscience, 19,* 3639–3648. (6)

Benedetti, F., & Colombo, C. (2011). Sleep deprivation in mood disorders. *Neuropsychobiology, 64,* 141–151. (14)

Benes, F. M., Turtle, M., Khan, Y., & Farol, P. (1994). Myelination of a key relay zone in the hippocampal formation occurs in the human brain during childhood, adolescence, and adulthood. *Archives of General Psychiatry, 51,* 477–484. (4)

Benschop, R. J., Godaert, G. L. R., Geenen, R., Brosschot, J. F., DeSmet, M. B. M., Olff, M., . . . Ballieux, R. E. (1995). Relationships between cardiovascular and immunologic changes in an experimental stress model. *Psychological Medicine, 25,* 323–327. (11)

Berdoy, M., Webster, J. P., & Macdonald, D. W. (2000). Fatal attraction in rats infected with *Toxoplasma gondii*. *Proceedings of the Royal Society of London, B, 267,* 1591–1594. (11)

Berenbaum, S. A. (1999). Effects of early androgens on sex-typed activities and interests in adolescents with congenital adrenal hyperplasia. *Hormones and Behavior, 35,* 102–110. (10)

Berenbaum, S. A., Bryk, K. L. K., & Beltz, A. M. (2012). Early androgen effects on spatial and mechanical abilities: Evidence from congenital adrenal hyperplasia. *Behavioral Neuroscience, 126,* 86–96. (10)

Berenbaum, S. A., Duck, S. C., & Bryk, K. (2002). Behavioral effects of prenatal versus postnatal androgen excess in children with 21-hydroxylase-deficient congenital adrenal hyperplasia. *Journal of Clinical Endocrinology & Metabolism, 85,* 727–733. (10)

Berger, R. J., & Phillips, N. H. (1995). Energy conservation and sleep. *Behavioural Brain Research, 69,* 65–73. (8)

Berger-Sweeney, J., & Hohmann, C. F. (1997). Behavioral consequences of abnormal cortical development: Insights into developmental disabilities. *Behavioural Brain Research, 86,* 121–142. (4)

Bergmann, O., Bhardwaj, R. D., Bernard, S., Zdunek, S., Barnabé-Heider, F., Walsh, S., . . . Druid, H. (2009). Evidence for cardiomyocyte renewal in humans. *Science, 324,* 98–102. (4)

Bergmann, O., Liebl, J., Bernard, S., Alkass, K., Yeung, M. S. Y., Steier, P., . . . Frisén, J. (2012). The age of olfactory bulb neurons in humans. *Neuron, 74,* 634–639. (4)

Berlin, H. A., Rolls, E. T., & Kischka, U. (2004). Impulsivity, time perception, emotion and reinforcement sensitivity in patients with orbitofrontal cortex lesions. *Brain, 127,* 1108–1126. (11)

Berlucchi, G., Mangun, G. R., & Gazzaniga, M. S. (1997). Visuospatial attention and the split brain. *News in Physiological Sciences, 12,* 226–231. (13)

Berman, K. F., Torrey, E. F., Daniel, D. G., & Weinberger, D. R. (1992). Regional cerebral blood flow in monozygotic twins discordant and concordant for schizophrenia. *Archives of General Psychiatry, 49,* 927–934. (14)

Bernal, D., Donley, J. M., Shadwick, R. E., & Syme, D. A. (2005). Mammal-like muscles power swimming in a cold-water shark. *Nature, 437,* 1349–1352. (9)

Bernstein, J. J., & Gelderd, J. B. (1970). Regeneration of the long spinal tracts in the goldfish. *Brain Research, 20,* 33–38. (4)

Berntson, G. G., Bechara, A., Damasio, H., Tranel, D., & Cacioppo, J. T. (2007). Amygdala contribution to selective dimensions of emotion. *Social Cognitive & Affective Neuroscience, 2,* 123–129. (11)

Berridge, K. C., & Robinson, T. E. (1995). The mind of an addicted brain: Neural sensitization of wanting versus liking. *Current Directions in Psychological Science, 4,* 71–76. (14)

Berridge, K. C., & Robinson, T. E. (1998). What is the role of dopamine in reward: Hedonic impact, reward learning, or incentive salience? *Brain Research Reviews, 28,* 309–369. (14)

Berryhill, M. E., Phuong, L., Picasso, L., Cabeza, R., & Olson, I. R. (2007). Parietal lobe and episodic memory: Bilateral damage causes impaired free recall of autobiographical memory. *Journal of Neuroscience, 27,* 14415–14423. (12)

Berson, D. M., Dunn, F. A., & Takao, M. (2002). Phototransduction by retinal ganglion cells that set the circadian clock. *Science, 295,* 1070–1073. (8)

Beuming, T., Kniazeff, J., Bergmann, M. L., Shi, L., Gracia, L., Raniszewska, K., . . . Loland, C. J. (2008). The binding sites for cocaine and dopamine in the dopamine transporter overlap. *Nature Neuroscience, 11,* 780–789. (2)

Bevilacqua, L., Doly, S., Kaprio, J., Yuan, Q., Tikkanen, R., Paunio, T., . . . Goldman, D. (2010). A population-specific *HTR2B* stop codon predisposes to severe impulsivity. *Nature, 468,* 1061–1066. (11)

Bezzola, L., Mérillat, S., Gaser, C., & Jäncke, L. (2011). Training-induced neural plasticity in golf novices. *Journal of Neuroscience, 31,* 12444–12448. (4)

Bian, L., Hanson, R. L., Ossowski, V., Wiedrich, K., Mason, C. C., Traurig, M., . . . Bogardus, C. (2010). Variants in ASK1 are associated with skeletal muscle ASK1 expression, *in vivo* insulin resistance, and Type 2 diabetes in Pima Indians. *Diabetes, 59,* 1276–1282. (9)

Biben, M. (1979). Predation and predatory play behaviour of domestic cats. *Animal Behaviour, 27,* 81–94. (11)

Bickart, K. C., Wright, C. I., Dautoff, R. J., Dickerson, B. C., & Barrett, L. F. (2011). Amygdala volume and social network size in humans. *Nature Neuroscience, 14,* 163–164. (3)

Bierut, L. J., Heath, A. C., Bucholz, K. K., Dinwiddie, S. H., Madden, P. A. F., Statham, D. J., . . . Martin, N. G. (1999). Major depressive disorder in a community-based twin sample. *Archives of General Psychiatry, 56,* 557–563. (14)

Bilalic, M., Langner, R., Ulrich, R., & Grodd, W. (2011). Many faces of expertise: Fusiform face area in chess experts and novices. *Journal of Neuroscience, 31,* 10206–10214. (5)

Billington, C. J., & Levine, A. S. (1992). Hypothalamic neuropeptide Y regulation of feeding and energy metabolism. *Current Opinion in Neurobiology, 2,* 847–851. (9)

Bimler, D., & Kirkland, J. (2009). Colour-space distortion in women who are heterozygous for colour deficiency. *Vision Research, 49,* 536–543. (5)

Bird, A. (2007). Perceptions of epigenetics. *Nature, 447,* 396–398. (4)

Biss, R. K., & Hasher, L. (2012). Happy as a lark: Morning-type younger and older people are higher in positive affect. *Emotion, 12,* 437–441. (8)

Bjorklund, A., & Kordower, J. H. (2013). Cell therapy for Parkinson's disease: What next? *Movement Disorders, 28,* 110–115. (7)

Björnsdotter, M., Löken, L., Olausson, H., Vallbo, Å., & Wessberg, J. (2009). Somatotopic organization of gentle touch processing in the posterior insular cortex. *Journal of Neuroscience, 29,* 9314–9320. (6)

Blackless, M., Charuvastra, A., Derryck, A., Fausto-Sterling, A., Lauzanne, K., & Lee, E. (2000). How sexually dimorphic are we? Review and synthesis. *American Journal of Human Biology, 12,* 151–166. (10)

Blackwell, A., & Bates, E. (1995). Inducing agrammatic profiles in normals: Evidence for the selective vulnerability of morphology under cognitive resource limitation. *Journal of Cognitive Neuroscience, 7,* 228–257. (13)

Blair, R. J. R. (2013). The neurobiology of psychopathic traits in youths. *Nature Reviews Neuroscience, 14,* 786–799. (13)

Blake, R., & Hirsch, H. V. B. (1975). Deficits in binocular depth perception in cats after alternating monocular deprivation. *Science, 190,* 1114–1116. (5)

Blake, R., Palmeri, T. J., Marois, R., & Kim, C.-Y. (2005). On the perceptual reality of synesthetic color. In L. C. Robertson & N. Sagiv (Eds.), *Synesthesia* (pp. 47–73). Oxford, England: Oxford University Press. (6)

Blakemore, S.-J., Wolpert, D. M., & Frith, C. D. (1998). Central cancellation of self-produced tickle sensation. *Nature Neuroscience, 1,* 635–640. (6)

Blanchard, R. (2008). Review and theory of handedness, birth, order, and homosexuality in men. *Laterality, 13,* 51–70. (10)

Blanke, O. (2012). Multisensory brain mechanisms of bodily self-consciousness. *Nature Reviews Neuroscience, 13,* 556–571. (3)

Bliss, T. V. P., & Lømo, T. (1973). Long-lasting potentiation of synaptic transmission in the dentate area of the anaesthetized rabbit following stimulation of the perforant path. *Journal of Physiology (London), 232,* 331–356. (12)

Bloch, G. J., & Mills, R. (1995). Prepubertal testosterone treatment of neonatally gonadectomized male rats: Defeminization and masculinization of behavioral and endocrine function in adulthood. *Neuroscience and Biobehavioral Reviews, 59,* 187–200. (10)

Bloch, G. J., Mills, R., & Gale, S. (1995). Prepubertal testosterone treatment of female rats: Defeminization of behavioral and endocrine function in adulthood. *Neuroscience and Biobehavioral Reviews, 19,* 177–186. (10)

Blumstein, S. E., & Amso, D. (2013). Dynamic functional organization of language: Insights from functional neuroimaging. *Perspectives on Psychological Science, 8,* 44–48. (13)

Bobrow, D., & Bailey, J. M. (2001). Is male homosexuality maintained via kin selection? *Evolution and Human Behavior, 22,* 361–368. (10)

Bocklandt, S., Horvath, S., Vilain, E., & Hamer, D. H. (2006). Extreme skewing of X chromosome inactivation in mothers of homosexual men. *Human Genetics, 118,* 691–694. (10)

Boettiger, C. A., Mitchell, J. M., Tavares, V. C., Robertson, M., Joslyn, G., D'Esposito, M., & Fields, H. L. (2007). Immediate reward bias in humans: Fronto-parietal networks and a role for the catechol-O-methyltransferase $158^{val/val}$ genotype. *Journal of Neuroscience, 27,* 14383–14391. (14)

Boets, B., Op de Beeck, H. P., Vandermosten, M., Scott, S. K., Gillebert, C. R., Mantini, D., . . . Ghesquière, P. (2013). Intact but less accessible phonetic representations in adults with dyslexia. *Science, 342,* 1251–1254. (13)

Bogaert, A. F. (2003a). The interaction of fraternal birth order and body size in male sexual orientation. *Behavioral Neuroscience, 117,* 381–384. (10)

Bogaert, A. F. (2003b). Number of older brothers and sexual orientation: New tests and the attraction/behavior distinction in two national probability samples. *Journal of Personality and Social Psychology, 84,* 644–652. (10)

Bogaert, A. F. (2006). Biological versus nonbiological older brothers and men's sexual orientation. *Proceedings of the National Academy of Sciences, USA, 103,* 10771–10774. (10)

Bogaert, A. F. (2010). Physical development and sexual orientation in men and women: An analysis of NATSAL-2000. *Archives of Sexual Behavior, 39,* 110–116. (10)

Boivin, D. B., Duffy, J. F., Kronauer, R. E., & Czeisler, C. A. (1996). Dose-response relationships for resetting of human circadian clock by light. *Nature, 379,* 540–542. (8)

Boly, M., Perlbarg, V., Marrelec, G., Schabus, M., Laureys, S., Doyon, J., . . . Benali, H. (2012). Hierarchical clustering of brain activity during human nonrapid eye movement sleep. *Proceedings of the National Academy of Sciences (U.S.A.), 109,* 5856–5861. (8)

Bonath, B., Noesselt, T., Martinez, A., Mishra, J., Schwiecker, K., Heinze, H.-J., & Hillyard, S. A. (2007). Neural basis of the ventriloquist illusion. *Current Biology, 17,* 1697–1703. (3)

Bonneh, Y. S., Cooperman, A., & Sagi, D. (2001). Motion-induced blindness in normal observers. *Nature, 411,* 798–801. (13)

Booth, D. A., Higgs, S., Schneider, J., & Klinkenberg, I. (2010). Learned liking versus inborn delight: Can sweetness give sensual pleasure or is it just motivating? *Psychological Science, 21,* 1656–1663. (6)

Booth, F. W., & Neufer, P. D. (2005, January/February). Exercise controls gene expression. *American Scientist, 93,* 28–35. (7)

Booth, W., Johnson, D. H., Moore, S., Schal, C., & Vargo, E. L. (2011). Evidence for viable, nonclonal but fatherless Boa constrictors. *Biology Letters, 7,* 253–256. (10)

Borgland, S. L., Chang, S.-J., Bowers, M. S., Thompson, J. L., Vittoz, N., Floresco, S. B., . . . Bonci, A. (2009). Orexin A/hypocretin-1 selectively promotes motivation for positive reinforcers. *Journal of Neuroscience, 29,* 11215–11225. (9)

Borisovska, M., Bensen, A. L., Chong, G., & Westbrook, G. L. (2013). Distinct modes of dopamine and GABA release in a dual transmitter neuron. *Journal of Neuroscience, 33,* 1790–1796. (2)

Born, S., Levit, A., Niv, M. Y., Meyerhof, W., & Belvens, M. (2013). The human bitter taste receptor TAS2R10 is tailored to accommodate numerous diverse ligands. *Journal of Neuroscience, 33,* 201–213. (6)

Borodinsky, L. N., Root, C. M., Cronin, J. A., Sann, S. B., Gu, X., & Spitzer, N. C. (2004). Activity-dependent homeostatic specification of transmitter expression in embryonic neurons. *Nature, 429,* 523–530. (2)

Borsutzky, S., Fujiwara, E., Brand, M., & Markowitsch, H. J. (2008). Confabulations in alcoholic Korsakoff patients. *Neuropsychologia, 46,* 3133–3143. (12)

Bortolotti, B., Menchetti, M., Bellini, F., Montaguti, M. B., & Berardi, D. (2008). Psychological interventions for major depression in primary care: A meta-analytic review of randomized controlled trials. *General Hospital Psychiatry, 30,* 293–302. (14)

Boucsein, K., Weniger, G., Mursch, K., Steinhoff, B. J., & Irle, E. (2001). Amygdala lesion in temporal lobe epilepsy subjects impairs associative learning of emotional facial expressions. *Neuropsychologia, 39,* 231–236. (11)

Bourque, C. W. (2008). Central mechanisms of osmosensation and systemic osmoregulation. *Nature Reviews Neuroscience, 9,* 519–531. (9)

Boutrel, B., Franc, B., Hen, R., Hamon, M., & Adrien, J. (1999). Key role of 5-HT1B receptors in the regulation of paradoxical sleep as evidenced in 5-HT1B knock-out mice. *Journal of Neuroscience, 19,* 3204–3212. (8)

Bowles, S. (2006). Group competition, reproductive leveling, and the evolution of human altruism. *Science, 314,* 1569–1572. (4)

Bowles, S., & Posel, B. (2005). Genetic relatedness predicts South African migrant workers' remittances to their families. *Nature, 434,* 380–383. (1)

Bowmaker, J. K. (1998). Visual pigments and molecular genetics of color blindness. *News in Physiological Sciences, 13,* 63–69. (5)

Bowmaker, J. K., & Dartnall, H. J. A. (1980). Visual pigments of rods and cones in a human retina. *Journal of Physiology (London), 298,* 501–511. (5)

Branco, T., Clark, B. A., & Häusser, M. (2010). Dendritic discrimination of temporal input sequences in cortical neurons. *Science, 329,* 1671–1675. (2)

Brandt, T. (1991). Man in motion: Historical and clinical aspects of vestibular function. *Brain, 114,* 2159–2174. (6)

Brans, R. G. H., Kahn, R. S., Schnack, H. G., van Baal, G. C. M., Posthuma, D., van Haren, N. E. M., . . . Pol, H. E. H. (2010). Brain plasticity and intellectual ability are influenced by shared genes. *Journal of Neuroscience, 30,* 5519–5524. (4)

Braun, A. R., Balkin, T. J., Wesensten, N. J., Guadry, F., Carson, R. E., Varga, M., . . . Herscovitch, P. (1998). Dissociated pattern of activity in visual cortices and their projections during human rapid eye movement sleep. *Science, 279,* 91–95. (7, 8)

Braunschweig, D., Krakowiak, P., Duncanson, P., Boyce, R., Hansen, R. L., Ashwood, P., . . . Van de Water, J. (2013). Autism-specific maternal autoantibodies recognize critical proteins in developing brain. *Translational Psychiatry, 3,* e277. (14)

Braus, H. (1960). Anatomie des Menschen, 3. Band: Periphere Leistungsbahnen II. Centrales Nervensystem, Sinnesorgane. 2. Auflage [Human anatomy: Vol. 3. Peripheral pathways II. Central nervous system, sensory organs (2nd ed.)]. Berlin: Springer-Verlag. (3)

Bray, G. A., Nielsen, S. J., & Popkin, B. M. (2004). Consumption of high-fructose corn syrup in beverages may play a role in the epidemic of obesity. *American Journal of Clinical Nutrition, 79,* 537–543. (9)

Breiter, H. C., Aharon, I., Kahneman, D., Dale, A., & Shizgal, P. (2001). Functional imaging of neural responses to expectancy and experience of monetary gains and losses. *Neuron, 30,* 619–639. (14)

Bremmer, F., Kubischik, M., Hoffmann, K.-P., & Krekelberg, B. (2009). Neural dynamics of saccadic suppression. *Journal of Neuroscience, 29,* 12374–12383. (5)

Brewer, W. J., Wood, S. J., Pantelis, C., Berger, G. E., Copolov, D. L., & McGorry, P. D. (2007). Olfactory sensitivity through the course of psychosis: Relationships to olfactory identification, symptomatology and the schizophrenia odour. *Psychiatry Research, 149,* 97–104. (14)

Breysse, N., Carlsson, T., Winkler, C., Björklund, A., & Kirik, D. (2007). The functional impact of the intrastriatal dopamine neuron grafts in Parkinsonian rats is reduced with advancing disease. *Journal of Neuroscience, 27,* 5849–5856. (7)

Bridge, H., Thomas, O., Jbabdi, S., & Cowey, A. (2008). Changes in connectivity after visual cortical brain damage underlie altered visual function. *Brain, 131,* 1433–1444. (5)

Bridge, H., Thomas, O. M., Minini, L., Cavina-Pratesi, C., Milner, A. D., & Parker, A. J. (2013). Structural and functional changes across the visual cortex of a patient with visual form agnosia. *Journal of Neuroscience, 33,* 12779–12791. (5)

Bridge, J. A., Birmaher, B., Iyengar, S., Barbe, R. P., & Brent, D. A. (2009). Placebo response in randomized controlled trials of antidepressants for pediatric major depressive disorder. *American Journal of Psychiatry, 166,* 42–49. (14)

Bridgeman, B., & Staggs, D. (1982). Plasticity in human blindsight. *Vision Research, 22,* 1199–1203. (5)

Bridle, C., Spanjers, K., Patel, S., Atherton, N. M., & Lamb, S. E. (2012). Effect of exercise on depression severity in older people: Systematic review and meta-analysis of randomised controlled trials. *British Journal of Psychiatry, 201,* 180–185. (14)

Brigman, J. L., Daut, R. A., Wright, T., Gunduz-Cinar, O., Graybeal, C., Davis, M. I., . . . Holmes, A. (2013). GluN2B in corticostriatal circuits governs choice learning and choice shifting. *Nature Neuroscience, 16,* 1101–1110. (12)

Britton, J. C., Grillon, C., Lissek, S., Norcross, M. A., Szuhany, K. L., Chen, G., . . . Pine, D. S. (2013). Response to learned threat: An fMRI study in adolescent and adult anxiety. *American Journal of Psychiatry, 170,* 1195–1204. (11)

Brock, O., Baum, M. J., & Bakker, J. (2011). The development of female sexual behavior requires prepubertal estradiol. *Journal of Neuroscience, 31,* 5574–5578. (10)

Brodin, T., Fick, J., Jonsson, M., & Klaminder, J. (2013). Dilute concentrations of a psychiatric drug alter behavior of fish from natural populations. *Science, 339,* 814–815. (11)

Brody, A. L., Saxena, S., Stoessel, P., Gillies, L. A., Fairbanks, L. A., Alborzian, S., .. Baxter, L. R. (2001). Regional brain metabolic changes in patients with major depression treated with either paroxetine or interpersonal therapy. *Archives of General Psychiatry, 58,* 631–640. (14)

Brooks, P. L., & Peever, J. H. (2011). Impaired GABA and glycine transmission triggers cardinal features of rapid eye movement sleep behavior disorder in mice. *Journal of Neuroscience, 31,* 7111–7121. (8)

Brooks, P. L., & Peever, J. H. (2012). Identification of the transmitter and receptor mechanisms responsible for REM sleep paralysis. *Journal of Neuroscience, 32,* 9785–9795. (8)

Brooks, D. C., & Bizzi, E. (1963). Brain stem electrical activity during deep sleep. *Archives Italiennes de Biologie, 101,* 648–665. (8)

Brosch, T., Bar-David, E., & Phelps, E. A. (2013). Implicit race bias decreases the similarity of neural representations of Black and White faces. *Psychological Science, 24,* 160–166. (13)

Brouwer, G. J., & Heeger, D. J. (2009). Decoding and reconstructing color from responses in human visual cortex. *Journal of Neuroscience, 29,* 13992–14003. (5)

Brown, A. S. (2011). The environment and susceptibility to schizophrenia. *Progress in Neurobiology, 93,* 23–58. (14)

Brown, A. S., Begg, M. D., Gravenstein, S., Schaefer, C. A., Wyatt, R. J., Bresnahan, M., . . . Susser, E. S. (2004). Serologic evidence of prenatal influenza in the etiology of schizophrenia. *Archives of General Psychiatry, 61,* 774–780. (14)

Brown, C. E., Li, P., Boyd, J. D., Delaney, K. R., & Murphy, T. H. (2007). Extensive turnover of dendritic spines and vascular remodeling in cortical tissues recovering from stroke. *Journal of Neuroscience, 27,* 4101–4109. (4)

Brown, G. L., Ebert, M. H., Goyer, P. F., Jimerson, D. C., Klein, W. J., Bunney, W. E., & Goodwin, F. K. (1982). Aggression, suicide, and serotonin: Relationships of CSF amine metabolites. *American Journal of Psychiatry, 139,* 741–746. (11)

Brown, J., Babor, T. F., Litt, M. D., & Kranzler, H. R. (1994). The type A/type B distinction. *Annals of the New York Academy of Sciences, 708,* 23–33. (14)

Brown, J. R., Ye, H., Bronson, R. T., Dikkes, P., & Greenberg, M. E. (1996). A defect in nurturing in mice lacking the immediate early gene *fos B. Cell, 86,* 297–309. (10)

Bruck, M., Cavanagh, P., & Ceci, S. J. (1991). Fortysomething: Recognizing faces at one's 25th reunion. *Memory & Cognition, 19,* 221–228. (5)

Brumpton, B., Langhammer, A., Romundstad, P., Chen, Y., & Mai, X. M. (2013). The associations of anxiety and depression symptoms with weight change and incident obesity: The HUNT study. *International Journal of Obesity, 37,* 1268–1274. (9)

Brunet, A., Orr, S. P., Tremblay, J., Robertson, K., Nader, K., & Pitman, R. K. (2008). Effect of post-retrieval propanolol on psychophysiologic responding during subsequent script-driven traumatic imagery in post-traumatic stress disorder. *Journal of Psychiatric Research, 42,* 503–506. (11)

Bruno, R. M., & Sakmann, B. (2006). Cortex is driven by weak but synchronously active thalamocortical synapses. *Science, 312,* 1622–1627. (2)

Bruns, P. Liebnau, R., & Röder, B. (2011). Cross-modal training induces changes in spatial representations early in the auditory processing pathway. *Psychological Science, 22,* 1120–1126. (3)

Bucci, M. P., & Seessau, M. (2012). Saccadic eye movements in children: a developmental study *Experimental Brain Research, 222,* 21–30. (7)

Buck, L., & Axel, R. (1991). A novel multigene family may encode odorant receptors: A molecular basis for odor recognition. *Cell, 65,* 175–187. (6)

Buckholtz, J. W., & Marois, R. (2012). The roots of modern justice: Cognitive and neural foundations of social norms and their enforcement. *Nature Neuroscience, 15,* 655–661, (13)

Buell, S. J., & Coleman, P. D. (1981). Quantitative evidence for selective dendritic growth in normal human aging but not in senile dementia. *Brain Research, 214,* 23–41. (4)

Buhle, J. T., Stevens, B. L., Friedman, J. J., & Wager, T. D. (2012). Distraction and placebo: Two separate routes to pain control. *Psychological Science, 23,* 246–253. (6)

Buizer-Voskamp, J. E., Muntjewerff, J. W., Strengman, E., Sabatti, C., Stefansson, H., Vorstman, J. A. S., & Ophoff, R. A. (2011). Genome-wide analysis shows increased frequency of copy number variations deletions in Dutch schizophrenia patients. *Biological Psychiatry, 70,* 655–662. (14)

Buka, S. L., Tsuang, M. T., Torrey, E. F., Klebanoff, M. A., Bernstein, D., & Yolken, R. H. (2001). Maternal infections and subsequent psychosis among offspring. *Archives of General Psychiatry, 58,* 1032–1037. (14)

Bulbena, A., Gago, J., Martin-Santos, R., Porta, M., Dasquens, J., & Berrios, G. E. (2004). Anxiety disorder & joint laxity: A definitive link. *Neurology, Psychiatry and Brain Research, 11,* 137–140. (11)

Bulbena, A., Gago, J., Sperry, L., & Bergé, D. (2006). The relationship between frequency and intensity of fears and a collagen condition. *Depression and Anxiety, 23,* 412–417. (11)

Bundgaard, M. (1986). Pathways across the vertebrate blood–brain barrier: Morphological viewpoints. *Annals of the New York Academy of Sciences, 481,* 7–19. (1)

Bundy, H., Stahl, B. H., & MacCabe, J. H. (2011). A systematic review and meta-analysis of the fertility of patients with schizophrenia and their unaffected relatives. *Acta Psychiatrica Scandinavica, 123,* 98–106. (14)

Burgaleta, M., Head, K., Álvarez-Linera, J., Martinez, K., Escorial, S., Haier, R., & Colom, R. (2012). Sex differences in brain volume are related to specific skills, not general intelligence. *Intelligence, 40,* 60–68. (3)

Burke, S. M., Veltman, D. J., Gerber, J., Hummel, T., & Bakker, J. (2012). Heterosexual men and women both show a hypothalamic response to the chemo-signal androstadienone. *PLoS One, 7,* e40993. (6)

Burkett, J. P., & Young, L. J. (2012). The behavioral, anatomical, and pharmacological parallels between social attachment, love, and addiction. *Psychopharmacology, 224,* 1–26. (13)

Burman, D. D., Lie-Nemeth, T., Brandfonbrener, A. G., Parisi, T., & Meyer, J. R. (2009). Altered finger representations in sensorimotor cortex of musicians with focal dystonia: Precentral cortex. *Brain Imaging and Behavior, 3,* 10–23. (4)

Burr, D. C., Morrone, M. C., & Ross, J. (1994). Selective suppression of the magnocellular visual pathway during saccadic eye movements. *Nature, 371,* 511–513. (5)

Burra, N., Hervais-Adelman, A., Kerzel, D., Tamietto, M., de Gelder, B., & Pegna, A. J. (2013). Amygdala activation for eye contact despite complete cortical blindness. *Journal of Neuroscience, 33,* 10483–10489. (11)

Burrell, B. (2004). *Postcards from the brain museum.* New York: Broadway Books. (3)

Burri, A., Cherkas, L., Spector, T., & Rahman, Q. (2011). Genetic and environmental influences on female sexual orientation, childhood gender typicality and adult gender identity. *PLoS One, 6,* e21982. (10)

Burt, S. A. (2009). Rethinking environmental contributions to child and adolescent psychopathology: A meta-analysis of shared environmental influences. *Psychological Bulletin, 135,* 608–637. (4)

Burton, H., Snyder, A. Z., Conturo, T. E., Akbudak, E., Ollinger, J. M., & Raichle, M. E. (2002). Adaptive changes in early and late blind: A fMRI study of Braille reading. *Journal of Neurophysiology, 87,* 589–607. (4)

Burton, R. F. (1994). *Physiology by numbers.* Cambridge, England: Cambridge University Press. (9)

Buschman, T. J., & Miller, E. K. (2007). Top-down versus bottom-up control of attention in the prefrontal and posterior parietal cortices. *Science, 315,* 1860–1862. (13)

Buss, D. M. (1994). The strategies of human mating. *American Scientist, 82,* 238–249. (4)

Buss, D. M. (2000). Desires in human mating. *Annals of the New York Academy of Sciences, 907,* 39–49. (10)

Buss, D. M. (2001). Cognitive biases and emotional wisdom in the evolution of conflict between the sexes. *Current Directions in Psychological Science, 10,* 219–223. (10)

Bussiere, J. R., Beer, T. M., Neiss, M. B., & Janowsky, J. S. (2005). Androgen deprivation impairs memory in older men. *Behavioral Neuroscience, 119,* 1429–1437. (10)

Butler, M. P., Turner, K. W., Park, J. H., Schoomer, E. E., Zucker, I., & Gorman, M. R. (2010). Seasonal regulation of reproduction: Altered role of melatonin under naturalistic conditions in hamsters. *Proceedings of the Royal Society B, 277,* 2867–2874. (8)

Buxbaum, L. J. (2006). On the right (and left) track: Twenty years of progress in studying hemispatial neglect. *Cognitive Neuropsychology, 23,* 184–201. (13)

Byars, J. A., Beglinger, L. J., Moser, D. J., Gonzalez-Alegre, P., & Nopoulos, P. (2012). Substance abuse may be a risk factor for earlier onset of Huntington's disease. *Journal of Neurology, 259,* 1824–1831. (7)

Byl, N. N., McKenzie, A., & Nagarajan, S. S. (2000). Differences in somatosensory hand organization in a healthy flutist and a flutist with focal hand dystonia: A case report. *Journal of Hand Therapy, 13,* 302–309. (4)

Byne, W., Tobet, S., Mattiace, L. A., Lasco, M. S., Kemether, E., Edgar, M. A., . . . Jones, L. B. (2001). The interstitial nuclei of the human anterior hypothalamus: An investigation of variation with sex, sexual orientation, and HIV status. *Hormones and Behavior, 40,* 86–92. (10)

Byrne, M., Agerbo, E., Ewald, H., Eaton, W. W., & Mortensen, P. B. (2003). Parental age and risk of schizophrenia. *Archives of General Psychiatry, 60,* 673–678. (14)

Cabeza, R., & Moscovitch, M. (2013). Memory systems, processing modes, and components: Functional neuroimaging evidence. *Perspectives on Psychological Science, 8,* 49–55. (3)

Cahill, L. (2006). Why sex matters for neuroscience. *Nature Reviews Neuroscience, 7,* 477–484. (10)

Cahill, L., & McGaugh, J. L. (1998). Mechanisms of emotional arousal and lasting declarative memory. *Trends in Neurosciences, 21,* 294–299. (12)

Cai, D. J., Mednick, S. A., Harrison, E. M., Kanady, J. C., & Mednick, S. C. (2009). REM, not incubation, improves creativity by priming associative networks. *Proceedings of the National Academy of Sciences (U.S.A.), 106,* 10130–10134. (8)

Cai, D. J., & Rickard, T. C. (2009). Reconsidering the role of sleep for motor memory. *Behavioral Neuroscience, 123,* 1153–1157. (8)

Cai, D. J., Shuman, T., Gorman, M. R., Sage, J. R., & Anagnostaras, S. G. (2009). Sleep selectively enhances hippocampus-dependent memory in mice. *Behavioral Neuroscience, 123,* 713–719. (8)

Caine, S. B., Thomsen, M., Gabriel, K. I., Berkowitz, J. S., Gold, L. H., Koob, G. F., . . . Xu, M. (2007). Lack of self-administration of cocaine in dopamine D_1 receptor knock-out mice. *Journal of Neuroscience, 27,* 13140–13150. (14)

Cajal, S. R. (1937). Recollections of my life. *Memoirs of the American Philosophical Society, 8.* (Original work published 1901–1917) (1)

Caldara, R., & Seghier, M. L. (2009). The fusiform face area responds automatically to statistical regularities optimal for face categorization. *Human Brain Mapping, 30,* 1615–1625. (5)

Calipari, E. S., & Ferris, M. J. (2013). Amphetamine mechanisms and actions at the dopamine terminal revisited.. *Journal of Neuroscience, 33,* 8923–8925. (14)

Cameron, N. M., Champagne, F. A., Parent, C., Fish, E. W., Ozaki-Kuroda, K., & Meaney, M. J. (2005). The programming of individual differences in defensive responses and reproductive strategies in the rat through variations in maternal care. *Neuroscience and Biobehavioral Reviews, 29,* 843–865. (4)

Camille, N., Griffiths, C. A., Vo, K., Fellows, L. K., & Kable, J. W. (2011). Ventromedial frontal lobe damage disrupts value maximization in humans. *Journal of Neuroscience, 31,* 7527–7532. (8)

Campbell, S. S., & Tobler, I. (1984). Animal sleep: A review of sleep duration across phylogeny. *Neuroscience and Biobehavioral Reviews, 8,* 269–300. (8)

Camperio-Ciani, A., Corna, F., & Capiluppi, C. (2004). Evidence for maternally inherited factors favouring male homosexuality and promoting female fecundity. *Proceedings of the Royal Society of London, B, 271,* 2217–2221. (10)

Campfield, L. A., Smith, F. J., Guisez, Y., Devos, R., & Burn, P. (1995). Recombinant mouse OB protein: Evidence for a peripheral signal linking adiposity and central neural networks. *Science, 269,* 546–552. (9)

Canal, C. E., & Gold, P. E. (2007). Different temporal profiles of amnesia after intra-hippocampus and intra-amygdala infusions of anisomycin. *Behavioral Neuroscience, 121,* 732–741. (12)

Canepari, M., Rossi, R., Pellegrino, M. A., Orell, R. W., Cobbold, M., Harridge, S., & Bottinelli, R. (2005). Effects of resistance training on myosin function studies by the in vitro motility assay in young and older men. *Journal of Applied Physiology, 98,* 2390–2395. (7)

Cannon, J. R., & Greenamyre, J. T. (2013). Gene-environment interactions in Parkinson's disease: Specific evidence in humans and mammalian models. *Neurobiology of Disease, 57,* 38–46. (7)

Cannon, W. B. (1927). The James-Lange theory of emotions: Critical examinations and an alternative theory. *American Journal of Psychology, 39,* 106–124. (11)

Cannon, W. B. (1929). Organization for physiological homeostasis. *Physiological Reviews, 9,* 399–431. (9)

Cannon, W. B. (1945). *The way of an investigator.* New York: Norton. (11)

Cantor-Graae, E., & Selten, J. P. (2005). Schizophrenia and migration: A meta-analysis and review. *American Journal of Psychiatry, 162,* 12–24. (14)

Cao, M., & Guilleminault, C. (2010). Families with sleepwalking. *Sleep Medicine, 11,* 726–734. (8)

Capettini, L. S. A., Savergnini, S. Q., da Silva, R. F., Stergiopulos, N., Santos, R. A. S., Mach, F., & Montecucco, F. (2012). Update on the role of cannabinoid receptors after ischemic stroke. *Mediators of Inflammation,* Article 824093. (4)

Cardno, A. G., Marshall, E. J., Coid, B., Macdonald, A. M., Ribchester, T. R., Davies, N. J., ... Murray, R. M. (1999). Heritability estimates for psychotic disorders. *Archives of General Psychiatry, 56,* 162–168. (14)

Cardoso, F. L. (2009). Recalled sex-typed behavior in childhood and sports' preferences in adulthood of heterosexual, bisexual, and homosexual men from Brazil, Turkey, and Thailand. *Archives of Sexual Behavior, 38,* 726–736. (10)

Carlsson, A. (2001). A paradigm shift in brain research. *Science, 294,* 1021–1024. (2)

Carpenter, G. A., & Grossberg, S. (1984). A neural theory of circadian rhythms: Aschoff's rule in diurnal and nocturnal mammals. *American Journal of Physiology, 247,* R1067–R1082. (8)

Carruth, L. L., Reisert, I., & Arnold, A. P. (2002). Sex chromosome genes directly affect brain sexual differentiation. *Nature Neuroscience, 5,* 933–934. (10)

Carter, C. S. (1992). Hormonal influences on human sexual behavior. In J. B. Becker, S. M. Breedlove, & D. Crews (Eds.), *Behavioral endocrinology* (pp. 131–142). Cambridge, MA: MIT Press. (10)

Carter, M. E., Soden, M. E., Zweifel, L. S., & Palmiter, R. D. (2013). Genetic identification of a neural circuit that suppresses appetite. *Nature,* ...

Carver, C. S., Johnson, S. L., Joormann, J., Kim, Y., & Nam, J. Y. (2011). Serotonin transporter polymorphism interacts with childhood adversity to predict aspects of impulsivity. *Psychological Science, 22,* 589–595. (11)

Casali, A. G., Gosseries, O., Rosanova, M., Boly, M., Sarasso, S., Casali, K. R., ... Massimini, M. (2013). A theoretically based index of consciousness independent of sensory processes and behavior. *Science Translational Medicine, 5,* 198ra105. (13)

Casey, B. J., & Caudle, K. (2013). The teenage brain: Self control. *Current Directions in Psychological Science, 22,* 82–87. (4)

Cash, S. S., Halgren, E., Dehghani, N., Rosssetti, A. O., Thesen, T., Wang, C. M., ... Ulbert, I. (2009). The human K-complex represents an isolated cortical down-state. *Science, 324,* 1084–1087. (8)

Caspi, A., McClay, J., Moffitt, T. E., Mill, J., Martin, J., Craig, I. W., . . . Poulton, R. (2002). Role of genotype in the cycle of violence in maltreated children. *Science, 297,* 851–854. (11)

Caspi, A., Sugden, K., Moffitt, T. E., Taylor, A., Craig, I. W., Harrington, H., . . . Poulton, R. (2003). Influence of life stress on depression: Moderation by a polymorphism in the 5-HTT gene. *Science, 301,* 386–389. (14)

Cassia, V. M., Turati, C., & Simion, F. (2004). Can a nonspecific bias toward top-heavy patterns explain newborns' face preference? *Psychological Science, 15,* 379–383. (5)

Castellucci, V. F., Pinsker, H., Kupfermann, I., & Kandel, E. (1970). Neuronal mechanisms of habituation and dishabituation of the gill-withdrawal reflex in *Aplysia. Science, 167,* 1745–1748. (12)

Castner, S. A., & Goldman-Rakic, P. S. (2004). Enhancement of working memory in aged monkeys by a sensitizing regimen of dopamine D1 receptor stimulation. *Journal of Neuroscience, 24,* 1446–1450. (12)

Castrén, E., & Rantamäki, T. (2010). The role of BDNF and its receptors in depression and antidepressant drug action: Reactivation of developmental plasticity. *Developmental Neurobiology, 70,* 289–296. (14)

Castro-Alvarez, J. F., Gutierrez-Vargas, J., Darnaudéry, M., & Cardona-Gómez, G. P. (2011). ROCK inhibition prevents tau hyperphosphorylation and p25/CDK5 increase after global cerebral ischemia. *Behavioral Neuroscience, 125,* 465–472. (4)

Catalano, S. M., & Shatz, C. J. (1998). Activity-dependent cortical target selection by thalamic axons. *Science, 281,* 559–562. (4)

Catania, K. C. (2006). Underwater "sniffing" by semi-aquatic mammals. *Nature, 444,* 1024–1025. (6)

Catchpole, C. K., & Slater, P. J. B. (1995). *Bird song: Biological themes and variations.* Cambridge, England: Cambridge University Press. (0)

Catmur, C., Walsh, V., & Heyes, C. (2007). Sensorimotor learning configures the human mirror system. *Current Biology, 17,* 1527–1531. (7)

Catterall, W. A. (1984). The molecular basis of neuronal excitability. *Science, 223,* 653–661. (1)

Cavina-Pratesi, C., Connolly, J. D., & Milner, A. D. (2013). Optic ataxia as a model to investigate the role of the posterior parietal cortex in visually guided action: Evidence from studies of patient M. H. *Frontiers in Human Neuroscience, 7,* Article 336. (5)

Cepeda-Benito, A., Davis, K. W., Reynoso, J. T., & Harraid, J. H. (2005). Associative and behavioral tolerance to the analgesic effects of nicotine in rats: Tail-flick and paw-lick assays. *Psychopharmacology, 180,* 224–233. (14)

Cerletti, U., & Bini, L. (1938). L'Elettro-shock. *Archivio Generale di Neurologia e Psichiatria e Psicoanalisi, 19,* 266–268. (14)

Cervantes, M. C., & Delville, Y. (2009). Serotonin 5-HT_{1A} and 5-HT_3 receptors in an impulsive-aggressive phenotype. *Behavioral Neuroscience, 123,* 589–598. (11)

Chablis, C. F., Hebert, B. M., Benjamin, D. J., Beauchamp, J., Cesarini, D., van der Loos, M., . . . Laibson, D. (2012). Most reported genetic associations with general intelligence are probably false positives. *Psychological Science, 23,* 1314–1323. (4)

Chabris, C. F., & Glickman, M. E. (2006). Sex differences in intellectual performance: Analysis of a large cohort of competitive chess players. *Psychological Science, 17,* 1040–1046. (3)

Chafee, M. V., & Goldman-Rakic, P. S. (1998). Matching patterns of activity in primate prefrontal area 8a and parietal area 7ip neurons during a spatial working memory task. *Journal of Neurophysiology, 79,* 2919–2940. (12)

Chalmers, D. J. (1995). Facing up to the problem of consciousness. *Journal of Consciousness Studies, 2,* 200–219. (13)

Chalmers, D. L. (2004). How can we construct a science of consciousness? In M. S. Gazzaniga (Ed.), *The cognitive neurosciences* (3rd ed.) (pp. 1111–1119). Cambridge, MA: MIT Press. (13)

Chalmers, D. (2007). Naturalistic dualism. In M. Velmans & S. Schneider (Eds.), *The Blackwell companion to consciousness* (pp. 359–368). Malden, MA: Blackwell. (0)

Chang, E. F., & Merzenich, M. M. (2003). Environmental noise retards auditory cortical development. *Science, 300,* 498–502. (6)

Chang, G.-Q., Gaysinskaya, V., Karatayev, O., & Leibowitz, S. F. (2008). Maternal high-fat diet and fetal programming: Increased proliferation of hypothalamic peptide-producing neurons that increase risk for overeating and obesity. *Journal of Neuroscience, 28,* 12107–12119. (9)

Chang, S.-H., Gao, L., Li, Z., Zhang, W.-N., Du, Y., & Wang, J. (2013). BDgene: A genetic database for bipolar disorder and its overlap with schizophrenia and major depressive disorder. *Biological Psychiatry, 74,* 727–733. (14)

Chang, S. W. C., Gariépy, J.-F., & Platt, M. L. (2013). Neuronal reference frames for social decisions in primate frontal cortex. *Nature Neuroscience, 16,* 243–250. (13)

Changeux, J.-P. (2010). Nicotine addiction and nicotinic receptors: Lessons from genetically modified mice. *Nature Reviews Neuroscience, 11,* 389–401. (14)

Chao, M. V. (2010). A conversation with Rita Levi-Montalcini. *Annual Review of Physiology, 72,* 1–13. (4)

Chapman, S. B., Aslan, S., Spence, J. S., DeFina, L. F., Keebler, M. W., Didehbani, N., & Lu, H. (2013). Shorter term aerobic exercise improves brain, cognition, and cardiovascular fitness in aging. *Frontiers in Aging Neuroscience, 5,* Article 75. (12)

Chaudhari, N., Landin, A. M., & Roper, S. D. (2000). A metabotropic glutamate receptor variant functions as a taste receptor. *Nature Neuroscience, 3,* 113–119. (6)

Chee, M. J. S., Myers, M. G. Jr., Price, C. J., & Colmers, W. F. (2010). Neuropeptide Y suppresses anorexigenic output from the ventromedial nucleus of the hypothalamus. *Journal of Neuroscience, 30,* 3380–3390. (9)

Chen, B. T., Yau, H.-J., Hatch, C., Kusumoto-Yoshida, I., Cho, S. L., & Hopf, F. W. (2013). Rescuing cocaine-induced prefrontal cortex hypoactivity prevents compulsive cocaine seeking. *Nature, 496,* 359–362. (14)

Chen, L. M., Friedman, R. M., & Roe, A. W. (2003). Optical imaging of a tactile illusion in area 3b of the primary somatosensory cortex. *Science, 302,* 881–885. (6)

Chen, X., Gabitto, M., Peng, Y., Ryba, N. J. P., & Zuker, C. S. (2011). A gustotopic map of taste qualities in the mammalian brain. *Science, 333,* 1262–1266. (6)

Chen, X., Leischner, U., Rochefort, N. L., Nelken, I., & Konnerth, A. (2011). Functional mapping of single spines in cortical neurons in vivo. *Nature, 475,* 501–505. (6)

Cheney, D. L. (2011). Cooperation in nonhuman primates. In R. Menzel & J. Fischer (Eds.), *Animal thinking* (pp. 239–252). Cambridge, MA: MIT Press. (4)

Cheney, D. L., & Seyfarth, R. M. (2005). Constraints and adaptations in the earliest stages of language evolution. *Linguistic Review, 22,* 135–159. (13)

Cheour-Luhtanen, M., Alho, K., Sainio, K., Rinne, T., Reinikainen, K., Pohjavuoir, M., . . . Naatanen, R. (1996). The ontogenetically earliest discriminative response of the human brain. *Psychophysiology, 33,* 478–481. (13)

Cheyne, J. A., & Pennycook, G. (2013). Sleep paralysis postepisode distress: Modeling potential effects of episode characteristics, general psychological distress, beliefs, and cognitive style. *Clinical Psychological Science, 1,* 135–148. (8)

Chiapponi, C., Piras, F., Fagioli, S., Piras, F., Caltagirone, C., & Spalletta, G. (2013). Age-related brain trajectories in schizophrenia: A systematic review of structural MRI studies. *Psychiatry Research—Neuroimaging, 214,* 83–93. (14)

Chiarreotto-Ropelle, E. C., Pauli, L. S. S., Katashima, C. K., Pimentel, G. D., Picardi, P. K., Silva, V. R. R., . . . Pauli, J. R. (2013). Acute exercise suppresses hypothalamic PTP1B protein level and improves insulin and leptin signaling in obese rats. *American Journal of Physiology: Endocrinology and Metabolism, 305,* E649–E659. (9)

Chiang, M.-C., Barysheva, M., Shattuck, D. W., Lee, A. D., Madsen, S. K., Avedissian, C., . . . Thompson, P. M. (2009). Genetics of brain fiber architecture and intellectual performance. *Journal of Neuroscience, 29,* 2212–2224. (3)

Chiu, I. M., von Hehn, C. A., & Woolf, C. J. (2012). Neurogenic inflammation and the peripheral nervous system in host defense and immunopathology. *Nature Neuroscience, 15,* 1063–1067. (6)

Chiueh, C. C. (1988). Dopamine in the extrapyramidal motor function: A study based upon the MPTP-induced primate model of Parkinsonism. *Annals of the New York Academy of Sciences, 515,* 226–248. (7)

Chivers, M. L., Rieger, G., Latty, E., & Bailey, J. M. (2004). A sex difference in the specificity of sexual arousal. *Psychological Science, 15,* 736–744. (10)

Cho, K. (2001). Chronic "jet lag" produces temporal lobe atrophy and spatial cognitive deficits. *Nature Neuroscience, 4,* 567–568. (8)

Choi, D.-S., Cascini, M.-G., Mailliard, W., Young, H., Paredes, P., McMahon, T., . . . Messing, R. O. (2004). The type I equilibrative nucleoside transporter regulates ethanol intoxication and preference. *Nature Neuroscience, 7,* 855–861. (14)

Chomsky, N. (1980). *Rules and representations.* New York: Columbia University Press. (13)

Chong, S. Y. C., Ptácek, L. J., & Fu, Y. H. (2012). Genetic insights on sleep schedules: This time it's PERsonal. *Trends in Genetics, 28,* 598–605. (8)

Chong, S. C., Jo, S., Park, K. M., Joo, E. Y., Lee, M.-J., Hong, S. C., & Hong, S. B. (2013). Interaction between the electrical stimulation of a face-selective area and the perception of face stimuli. *NeuroImage, 77,* 70–76. (5)

Chuang, H., Prescott, E. D., Kong, H., Shields, S., Jordt, S.-E., Basbaum, A. I., . . . Julius, D. (2001). Bradykinin and nerve growth factor release the capsaicin receptor from PtdIns(4, 5)P2-mediated inhibition. *Nature, 411,* 957–962. (6)

Chung, W. C. J., de Vries, G. J., & Swaab, D. F. (2002). Sexual differentiation of the bed nucleus of the stria terminalis in humans may extend into adulthood. *Journal of Neuroscience, 22,* 1027–1033. (10)

Chung, Y. C., Bok, E., Huh, S. H., Park, J.-Y., Yoon, S.-H., Kim, S. R., . . . Jin, B. K. (2011). Cannabinoid receptor type 1 protects nigrostriatal dopaminergic neurons against MPTP neurotoxicity by inhibiting microglial activation. *Journal of Immunology, 187,* 6508–6517. (4)

Churchland, P. S. (1986). *Neurophilosophy.* Cambridge, Massachusetts: MIT Press. (0)

Cicone, N., Wapner, W., Foldi, N. S., Zurif, E., & Gardner, H. (1979). The relation between gesture and language in aphasic communication. *Brain and Language, 8,* 342–349. (13)

Clahsen, H., & Almazen, M. (1998). Syntax and morphology in Williams syndrome. *Cognition, 68,* 167–198. (13)

Clark, D. A., Mitra, P. P., & Wang, S. S.-H. (2001). Scalable architecture in mammalian brains. *Nature, 411,* 189–193. (3)

Clark, R. E., & Lavond, D. G. (1993). Reversible lesions of the red nucleus during acquisition and retention of a classically conditioned behavior in rabbits. *Behavioral Neuroscience, 107,* 264–270. (12)

Clark, W. S. (2004). Is the zone-tailed hawk a mimic? *Birding, 36,* 494–498. (0)

Clarke, L. E., & Barres, B. A. (2013). Emerging roles of astrocytes in neural circuit development. *Nature Reviews Neuroscience, 14,* 311–321. (1)

Clarke, S., Assal, G., & deTribolet, N. (1993). Left hemisphere strategies in visual recognition, topographical orientation and time planning. *Neuropsychologia, 31,* 99–113. (13)

Cleary, L. J., Hammer, M., & Byrne, J. H. (1989). Insights into the cellular mechanisms of short-term sensitization in *Aplysia.* In T. J. Carew & D. B. Kelley (Eds.), *Perspectives in neural systems and behavior* (pp. 105–119). New York: Liss. (12)

Cleary, M., Moody, A. D., Buchanan, A., Stewart, H., & Dutton, G. N. (2009). Assessment of a computer-based treatment for older amblyopes: The Glasgow Pilot Study. *Eye, 23,* 124–131. (5)

Clelland, C. D., Choi, M., Romberg, C., Clemenson, G. D. Jr., Fragniere, A., Tyers, P., . . . Bussey, T. J. (2009). A functional role for adult hippocampal neurogenesis in spatial pattern separation. *Science, 325,* 210–213. (4)

Clements, K. M., Smith, L. M., Reynolds, J. N. J., Overton, P. G., Thomas, J. D., & Napper, R. M. (2012). Early postnatal ethanol exposure: Glutamatergic excitotoxic cell death during acute withdrawal. *Neurophysiology, 44,* 376–386. (4)

Clutton-Brock, T. H., O'Riain, M. J., Brotherton, P. N. M., Gaynor, D., Kansky, R., Griffin, A. S., & Manser, M. (1999). Selfish sentinels in cooperative mammals. *Science, 284,* 1640–1644. (4)

Coan, J. A., Schaefer, H. S., & Davidson, R. J. (2006). Lending a hand: Social regulation of the neural response to threat. *Psychological Science, 17,* 1032–1039. (11)

Cobos, P., Sánchez, M., Pérez, N., & Vila, J. (2004). Effects of spinal cord injuries on the subjective component of emotions. *Cognition and Emotion, 18,* 281–287. (11)

Coderre, T. J., Katz, J., Vaccarino, A. L., & Melzack, R. (1993). Contribution of central neuroplasticity to pathological pain: Review of clinical and experimental evidence. *Pain, 52,* 259–285. (6)

Coenen, A. M. L. (1995). Neuronal activities underlying the electroencephalogram and evoked potentials of sleeping and waking: Implications for information-processing. *Neuroscience and Biobehavioral Reviews, 19,* 447–463. (8)

Cohen, D., & Nicolelis, M. A. L. (2004). Reduction of single-neuron firing uncertainty by cortical ensembles during motor skill learning. *Journal of Neuroscience, 24,* 3574–3582. (7)

Cohen, L. G., Celnik, P., Pascual-Leone, A., Corwell, B., Faiz, L., Dambrosia, J., . . . Hallett, M. (1997). Functional relevance of cross-modal plasticity in blind humans. *Nature, 389,* 180–183. (4)

Cohen, S., Frank, E., Doyle, W. J., Skoner, D. P., Rabin, B. S., & Swaltney, J. M., Jr. (1998). Types of stressors that increase susceptibility to the common cold in healthy adults. *Health Psychology, 17,* 214–223. (11)

Cohen-Kettenis, P. T. (2005). Gender change in 46, XY persons with 5a-reductase-2 deficiency and 17b-hydroxysteroid dehydrogenase-3 deficiency. *Archives of Sexual Behavior, 34,* 399–410. (10)

Cohen-Tannoudji, M., Babinet, C., & Wassef, M. (1994). Early determination of a mouse somatosensory cortex marker. *Nature, 368,* 460–463. (4)

Cohen-Woods, S., Craig, I. W., & McGuffin, P. (2013). The current state of play on the molecular genetics of depression. *Psychological Medicine, 43,* 673–687. (14)

Colantuoni, C., Rada, P., McCarthy, J., Patten, C., Avena, N. M., Chadeayne, A., & Hoebel, B. G. (2002). Evidence that intermittent, excessive sugar intake causes endogenous opioid dependence. *Obesity Research, 10,* 478–488. (9)

Colantuoni, C., Schwenker, J., McCarthy, J., Rada, P., Ladenheim, B., Cadet, J.-L., . . . Hoebel, B. G. (2001). Excessive sugar intake alters binding to dopamine and mu-opioid receptors in the brain. *NeuroReport, 12,* 3549–3552. (9)

Colapinto, J. (1997, December 11). The true story of John/Joan. *Rolling Stone,* pp. 54–97. (10)

Collinger, J. L., Wodlinger, B., Downey, J. E., Wang, W., Tyler-Kabara, E., Weber, D. J., . . . Schwartz, A. B. (2013). High-performance neuroprosthetic control by an individual with tetraplegia. *Lancet, 381,* 557–564. (7)

Collingridge, G. L., Peineau, S., Howland, J. G., & Wang, Y. T. (2010). Long-term depression in the CNS. *Nature Reviews Neuroscience, 11,* 459–473. (12)

Collins, C. E. (2011). Variability in neuron densities across the cortical sheet in primates. *Brain, Behavior and Evolution, 78,* 37–50. (3)

Colom, R., Haier, R. J., Head, K., Álvarez-Linera, J., Quiroga, M. A., Shih, P. C., & Jung, R. E. (2009). Gray matter correlates of fluid, crystallized, and spatial intelligence: Testing the P-FIT model. *Intelligence, 37,* 124–135. (3)

Colom, R., Quiroga, M. A., Solana, A. B., Burgaleta, M., Román, F. J., Privado, J., . . . Karama, S. (2012). Structural changes after videogame practice related to a brain network associated with intelligence. *Intelligence, 40,* 479–489. (4)

Conn, P. M., & Parker, J. V. (2008). Winners and losers in the animal-research war. *American Scientist, 96,* 184–186. (0)

Connine, C. M., Blasko, D. G., & Hall, M. (1991). Effects of subsequent sentence context in auditory word recognition: Temporal and linguistic constraints. *Journal of Memory and Language, 30,* 234–250. (13)

Conrad, K. L., Tseng, K. Y., Uejima, J. L., Reimers, J. M., Heng, L.-J., Shaham, Y., . . . Wolf, M. E. (2008). Formation of accumbens GluR2-lacking AMPA receptors mediates incubation of cocaine seeking. *Nature, 454,* 118–121. (14)

Considine, R. V., Sinha, M. K., Heiman, M. L., Kriauciunas, A., Stephens, T. W., Nyce, M.R., . . . Caro, J. F. (1996). Serum immunoreactive-leptin concentrations in normal-weight and obese humans. *New England Journal of Medicine, 334,* 292–295. (9)

Conti, V., Marini, C., Gana, S., Sudi, J., Dobyns, W. B., & Guerrini, R. (2011). Corpus callosum agenesis, severe mental retardation, epilepsy, and dyskinetic quadriparesis due to a novel mutation in the homeodomain of ARX. *American Journal of Medical Genetics Part A, 155A,* 892–897. (4)

Contreras, J. M., Banaji, M. R., & Mitchell, J. P. (2013). Multivoxel patterns in fusiform face area differentiate faces by sex and race. *PLoS One, 8,* e69684. (5)

Cooke, B. M., Tabibnia, G., & Breedlove, S. M. (1999). A brain sexual dimorphism controlled by adult circulating androgens. *Proceedings of the National Academy of Sciences, USA, 96,* 7538–7540. (10)

Coppola, D. M., Purves, H. R., McCoy, A. N., & Purves, D. (1998). The distribution of oriented contours in the real world. *Proceedings of the National Academy of Sciences, USA, 95,* 4002–4006. (5)

Corballis, M. C. (2012a). How language evolved from manual gestures. *Gesture, 12,* 200-226. (13)

Corballis, M. C. (May–June, 2012b). Mind wandering. *American Scientist, 100(3),* 210–217. (3)

Corcoran, A. J., Barber, J. R., & Conner, W. E. (2009). Tiger moth jams bat sonar. *Science, 325,* 325–327. (6)

Corkin, S. (1984). Lasting consequences of bilateral medial temporal lobectomy: Clinical course and experimental findings in H. M. *Seminars in Neurology, 4,* 249–259. (12)

Corkin, S. (2002). What's new with the amnesic patient H. M.? *Nature Reviews Neuroscience, 3,* 153–159. (12)

Corkin, S. (2013). *Permanent present tense.* New York: Basic books. (12)

Corkin, S., Rosen, T. J., Sullivan, E. V., & Clegg, R. A. (1989). Penetrating head injury in young adulthood exacerbates cognitive decline in later years. *Journal of Neuroscience, 9,* 3876–3883. (4)

Corradi-Dell'Acqua, C., Hofstetter, C., & Vuilleumier, P. (2011). Felt and seen pain evoke the same local patterns of cortical activity in insular and cingulate cortex. *Journal of Neuroscience, 31,* 17996–18006. (6)

Cosmelli, D., David, O., Lachaux, J.-P., Martinerie, J., Garnero, L., Renault, B., & Varela, F. (2004). Waves of consciousness: Ongoing cortical patterns during binocular rivalry. *NeuroImage, 23,* 128–140. (13)

Coss, R. G., Brandon, J. G., & Globus, A. (1980). Changes in morphology of dendritic spines on honeybee calycal interneurons associated with cumulative nursing and foraging experiences. *Brain Research, 192,* 49–59. (4)

Costa, V. D., Lang, P. J., Sabatinelli, D., Versace, F., & Bradley, M. M. (2010). Emotional imagery: Assessing pleasure and arousal in the brain's reward circuitry. *Human Brain Mapping, 31,* 1446–1457. (14)

Courchesne, E., Townsend, J., Akshoomoff, N. A., Saitoh, O., Yeung-Courchesne, R., Lincoln, A. J., . . . Lau, L. (1994). Impairment in shifting attention in autistic and cerebellar patients. *Behavioral Neuroscience, 108,* 848–865. (3)

Cowart, B. J. (2005, Spring). Taste, our body's gustatory gatekeeper. *Cerebrum, 7*(2), 7–22. (6)

Cowey, A., & Stoerig, P. (1995). Blindsight in monkeys. *Nature, 373,* 247–249. (5)

Cox, J. J., Reimann, F., Nicholas, A. K., Thornton, G., Roberts, E., Springell, K., . . . Woods, C. G. (2006). An *SCN9A* channelopathy causes congenital inability to experience pain. *Nature, 304,* 115–117. (6)

Craig, A. D., Krout, K., & Andrew, D. (2001). Quantitative response characteristics of thermoreceptive and nociceptive lamina I spinothalamic neurons in the cat. *Journal of Neurophysiology, 86,* 1459–1480. (6)

Craig, A. M., & Boudin, H. (2001). Molecular heterogeneity of central synapses: Afferent and target regulation. *Nature Neuroscience, 4,* 569–578. (2)

Crair, M. C., Gillespie, D. C., & Stryker, M. P. (1998). The role of visual experience in the development of columns in cat visual cortex. *Science, 279,* 566–570. (5)

Crair, M. C., & Malenka, R. C. (1995). A critical period for long-term potentiation at thalamocortical synapses. *Nature, 375,* 325–328. (5)

Cramer, P. E., Cirrito, J. R., Wesson, D. W., Lee, C. Y. D., Karlo, J. C., . . . Landreth, G. E. (2012). Apo E-directed therapeutics rapidly clear β-amyloid and reverse deficits in AD mouse models. *Science, 335,* 1503–1506. (12)

Cravchik, A., & Goldman, D. (2000). Neurochemical individuality. *Archives of General Psychiatry, 57,* 1105–1114. (14)

Crick, F. C., & Koch, C. (2004). A framework for consciousness. In M. S. Gazzaniga (Ed.), *The cognitive neurosciences* (3rd ed., pp. 1133–1143). Cambridge, MA: MIT Press. (13)

Crick, F., & Mitchison, G. (1983). The function of dream sleep. *Nature, 304,* 111–114. (8)

Critchley, H. D., Mathias, C. J., & Dolan, R. J. (2001). Neuroanatomical basis for first- and second-order representations of bodily states. *Nature Neuroscience, 4,* 207–212. (11)

Critchley, H. D., & Rolls, E. T. (1996). Hunger and satiety modify the responses of olfactory and visual neurons in the primate orbitofrontal cortex. *Journal of Neurophysiology, 75,* 1673–1686. (9)

Cromwell, H. C., & Schultz, W. (2003). Effects of expectations for different reward magnitudes on neuronal activity in primate striatum. *Journal of Neurophysiology, 89,* 2823–2838. (7)

Crone, E. A., & Dahl, R. E. (2012). Understanding adolescence as a period of social-affective engagement and goal flexibility. *Nature Reviews Neuroscience, 13,* 636–650. (4)

Cross-Disorder Group of the Psychiatric Genomic Consortium. (2013). Identification of risk loci with shared effects on five major psychiatric disorders: A genome-wide analysis. *Lancet, 381,* 1371–1379. (14)

Crossin, K. L., & Krushel, L. A. (2000). Cellular signaling by neural cell adhesion molecules of the immunoglobulin family. *Developmental Dynamics, 218,* 260–279. (4)

Crowley, S. J., & Eastman, C. I. (2013). Melatonin in the afternoons of a gradually advancing sleep schedule enhances the circadian phase advance. *Psychopharmacology, 225,* 825–837. (8)

Crowner, D., Madden, K., Goeke, S., & Giniger, E. (2002). Lola regulates midline crossing of CNS axons in *Drosophila. Development, 129,* 1317–1325. (13)

Cryan, J. F., & Dinan, T. G. (2012). Mind-altering microorganisms: The impact of the gut microbiota on brain and behavior. *Nature Reviews Neuroscience, 13,* 701–712. (9)

Cui, G., Jun, S. B., Jin, X., Pham, M. D., Vogel, S. S., Lovinger, D. M., & Costa, R. M. (2013). Concurrent activation of striatal direct and indirect pathways during action initiation. *Nature, 494,* 238–242. (7)

Cummings, D. E., Clement, K., Purnell, J. Q., Vaisse, C., Foster, K. E., Frayo, R. S., . . . Weigle, D. S. (2002). Elevated plasma ghrelin levels in Prader-Willi syndrome. *Nature Medicine, 8,* 643–644. (9)

Cummings, D. E., & Overduin, J. (2007). Gastrointestinal regulation of food intake. *Journal of Clinical Investigation, 117,* 13–23. (9)

Cunningham, W. A., Van Bavel, J. J., & Johnsen, I. R. (2008). Adaptive flexibility: Evaluative processing goals shape amygdala activity. *Psychological Science, 19*, 152–160. (11)

Curry, A. (2013). The milk revolution. *Nature, 500*, 20–22. (9)

Cushman, F., Gray, K., Gaffey, A., & Mendes, M. B. (2012). Simulating murder: The aversion to harmful action. *Emotion, 12*, 2–7. (11)

Cutler, W. B., Preti, G., Krieger, A., Huggins, G. R., Garcia, C. R., & Lawley, H. J. (1986). Human axillary secretions influence women's menstrual cycles: The role of donor extract from men. *Hormones and Behavior, 20*, 463–473. (6)

Czeisler, C. (2013). Casting light on sleep deficiency. *Nature, 497*, S13. (8)

Czeisler, C. A., Johnson, M. P., Duffy, J. F., Brown, E. N., Ronda, J. M., & Kronauer, R. E. (1990). Exposure to bright light and darkness to treat physiologic maladaptation to night work. *New England Journal of Medicine, 322*, 1253–1259. (8)

Czeisler, C. A., Weitzman, E. D., Moore-Ede, M. C., Zimmerman, J. C., & Knauer, R. S. (1980). Human sleep: Its duration and organization depend on its circadian phase. *Science, 210*, 1264–1267. (8)

Dabbs, J. M., Jr., Carr, T. S., Frady, R. L., & Riad, J. K. (1995). Testosterone, crime, and misbehavior among 692 male prison inmates. *Personality and Individual Differences, 18*, 627–633. (11)

Dale, N., Schacher, S., & Kandel, E. R. (1988). Long-term facilitation in *Aplysia* involves increase in transmitter release. *Science, 239*, 282–285. (12)

Dale, P. S., Harlaar, N., Haworth, C. M. A., & Plomin, R. (2010). Two by two: A twin study of second-language acquisition. *Psychological Science, 21*, 635–640. (4)

Dalterio, S., & Bartke, A. (1979). Perinatal exposure to cannabinoids alters male reproductive function in mice. *Science, 205*, 1420–1422. (10)

Dalton, K. (1968). Ante-natal progesterone and intelligence. *British Journal of Psychiatry, 114*, 1377–1382. (10)

Dalton, P., Doolittle, N., & Breslin, P. A. (2002). Gender-specific induction of enhanced sensitivity to odors. *Nature Neuroscience, 5*, 199–200. (6)

Damasio, A. (1999). *The feeling of what happens*. New York: Harcourt Brace. (11)

Damasio, A. R. (1994). *Descartes' error*. New York: Putnam's Sons. (11)

Damasio, A. R., Damasio, H., Rizzo, M., Varney, N., & Gersh, F. (1982). Aphasia with nonhemorrhagic lesions in the basal ganglia and internal capsule. *Archives of Neurology, 39*, 15–20. (13)

Damsma, G., Pfaus, J. G., Wenkstern, D., Phillips, A. G., & Fibiger, H. C. (1992). Sexual behavior increases dopamine transmission in the nucleus accumbens and striatum of male rats: A comparison with novelty and locomotion. *Behavioral Neuroscience, 106*, 181–191. (14)

Darwin, C. (1859). *The origin of species*. New York: D. Appleton. (4)

Davidson, R. J. (1984). Affect, cognition, and hemispheric specialization. In C. E. Izard, J. Kagan, & R. B. Zajonc (Eds.), *Emotions, cognition, & behavior* (pp. 320–365). Cambridge, England: Cambridge University Press. (14)

Davidson, R. J., & Fox, N. A. (1982). Asymmetrical brain activity discriminates between positive and negative affective stimuli in human infants. *Science, 218*, 1235–1237. (11)

Davidson, R. J., & Henriques, J. (2000). Regional brain function in sadness and depression. In J. C. Borod (Ed.), *The neuropsychology of emotion* (pp. 269–297). London: Oxford University Press. (11)

Davidson, S., Zhang, X., Khasabov, S. G., Simone, D. A., & Giesler, G. J. Jr. (2009). Relief of itch by scratching: State-dependent inhibition of primate spinothalamic tract neurons. *Nature Neuroscience, 12*, 544–546. (6)

Davies, G., Welham, J., Chant, D., Torrey, E. F., & McGrath, J. (2003). A systematic review and meta-analysis of Northern hemisphere season of birth effects in schizophrenia. *Schizophrenia Bulletin, 29*, 587–593. (14)

Davies, P. (2000). A very incomplete comprehensive theory of Alzheimer's disease. *Annals of the New York Academy of Sciences, 924*, 8–16. (12)

Davies, P. (2006). *The Goldilocks enigma*. Boston, MA: Houghton Mifflin. (0)

Davis, E. C., Shryne, J. E., & Gorski, R. A. (1995). A revised critical period for the sexual differentiation of the sexually dimorphic nucleus of the preoptic area in the rat. *Neuroendocrinology, 62*, 579–585. (10)

Davis, J. I., Senghas, A., Brandt, F., & Ochsner, K. N. (2010). The effects of BOTOX injections on emotional experience. *Emotion, 10*, 433–440. (11)

Davis, J. M., Chen, N., & Glick, I. D. (2003). A meta-analysis of the efficacy of second-generation antipsychotics. *Archives of General Psychiatry, 60*, 553–564. (14)

Davis, K. D., Kiss, Z. H. T., Luo, L., Tasker, R. R., Lozano, A. M., & Dostrovsky, J. O. (1998). Phantom sensations generated by thalamic microstimulation. *Nature, 391*, 385–387. (4)

Dawkins, R. (1989). *The selfish gene* (new ed.). Oxford, England: Oxford University Press. (4)

Dawson, T. M., Gonzalez-Zulueta, M., Kusel, J., & Dawson, V. L. (1998). Nitric oxide: Diverse actions in the central and peripheral nervous system. *The Neuroscientist, 4*, 96–112. (2)

Day, S. (2005). Some demographic and socio-cultural aspects of synesthesia. In L. C. Robertson & N. Sagiv (Eds.), *Synesthesis* (pp. 11–33). Oxford, England: Oxford University Press. (6)

de Bruin, J. P. C., Winkels, W. A. M., & de Brabander, J. M. (1997). Response learning of rats in a Morris water maze: Involvement of the medial prefrontal cortex. *Behavioral Brain Research, 85*, 47–55. (12)

Dayan, E., Censor, N., Buch, E. R., Sandrini, M., & Cohen, L. G. (2013). Noninvasive brain stimulation: From physiology to network dynamics and back. *Nature Neuroscience, 16*, 838–844. (3)

de Castro, J. M. (2000). Eating behavior: Lessons from the real world of humans. *Nutrition, 16*, 800–813. (9)

de Jong, W. W., Hendriks, W., Sanyal, S., & Nevo, E. (1990). The eye of the blind mole rat (*Spalax ehrenbergi*): Regressive evolution at the molecular level. In E. Nevo & O. A. Reig (Eds.), *Evolution of subterranean mammals at the organismal and molecular levels* (pp. 383–395). New York: Liss. (8)

De Luca, M., Di Page, E., Judica, A., Spinelli, D., & Zoccolotti, P. (1999). Eye movement patterns in linguistic and non-linguistic tasks in developmental surface dyslexia. *Neuropsychologia, 37*, 1407–1420. (13)

de Maat, S., Dekker, J., Schoevers, R., van Aalst, G., Gijsbers-van Wijk, C., Hendriksen, M., . . . de Jonghe, F. (2008). Short psychodynamic supportive psychotherapy, antidepressants, and their combination in the treatment of major depression: A mega-analysis based on three randomized clinical trials. *Depression and Anxiety, 25*, 565–574. (14)

De Wall, C. N., Mac Donald, G., Webster, G. D., Masten, C. L., Baumeister, R. F., Powell, C., . . . Eisenberger, N. I. (2010). Acetaminophen reduces social pain: Behavioral and neural evidence. *Psychological Science, 21*, 931–937. (6)

Deacon, T. W. (1990). Problems of ontogeny and phylogeny in brain-size evolution. *International Journal of Primatology, 11*, 237–282. (3)

Deacon, T. W. (1992). Brain-language coevolution. In J. A. Hawkins & M. Gell-Mann (Eds.), *The evolution of human languages* (pp. 49–83). Reading, MA: Addison-Wesley. (13)

Deacon, T. W. (1997). *The symbolic species*. New York: Norton. (3, 13)

Deady, D. K., North, N. T., Allan, D., Smith, M J. L., & O'Carroll, R. E. (2010). Examining the effect of spinal cord injury on emotional awareness, expressivity and memory for emotional material. *Psychology, Health and Medicine, 15*, 406–419. (11)

Dean, C. E. (2011). Psychopharmacology: A house divided. *Progress in Neuro-Psychopharmacology & Biological Psychiatry, 35*, 1–10. (14)

DeArmond, S. J., Fusco, M. M., & Dewey, M. M. (1974). *Structure of the human brain*. New York: Oxford University Press. (9)

DeCoursey, P. (1960). Phase control of activity in a rodent. *Cold Spring Harbor symposia on quantitative biology, 25*, 49–55. (8)

de Groot, J. H. B., Smeets, M. A. M., Kaldewaij, A., Duijndam, M. J. A., & Semin, G. R. (2012). Chemosignals communicate human emotions. *Psychological Science, 23*, 1417–1424. (6)

Dehaene-Lambertz, G., Montavont, A., Jobert, A., Allirol, L., Dubois, J., Hertz-Pannier, L., & Dehaene, S. (2010). Language or music, mother or Mozart? Structural and environmental influences on infants' language networks. *Brain & Language, 114*, 53–65. (13)

Dehaene, S., Naccache, L., Cohen, L., LeBihan, D., Mangin, J.-F., Poline, J.-B., & Riviere, D. (2001). Cerebral mechanisms of word masking and unconscious repetition priming. *Nature Neuroscience, 4*, 752–758. (13)

Dehaene, S., Pegado, F., Braga, L. W., Ventura, P., Filho, G. N., Jobert, A., . . . Cohen, L. (2010). How learning to read changes the cortical networks for vision and language. *Science, 330*, 1359–1364. (13)

Deisseroth, K. (2014). Circuit dynamics of adaptive and maladaptive behaviour. *Nature, 505*, 309–317. (14)

Del Cerro, M. C. R., Perez Izquierdo, M. A., Rosenblatt, J. S., Johnson, B. M., Pacheco, P., & Komisaruk, B. R. (1995). Brain 2-deoxyglucose levels related to maternal behavior-inducing stimuli in the rat. *Brain Research, 696*, 213–220. (10)

Del Cul, A., Dehaene, S., Reyes, P., Bravo, E., & Slachevsky, A. (2009). Causal role of prefrontal cortex in the threshold for access to consciousness. *Brain, 132,* 2531–2540. (13)

Deliagina, T. G., Orlovsky, G. N., & Pavlova, G. A. (1983). The capacity for generation of rhythmic oscillations is distributed in the lumbosacral spinal cord of the cat. *Experimental Brain Research, 53,* 81–90. (7)

Dement, W. (1972). *Some must watch while some must sleep.* San Francisco: Freeman. (8)

Dement, W., & Kleitman, N. (1957a). Cyclic variations in EEG during sleep and their relation to eye movements, body motility, and dreaming. *Electroencephalography and Clinical Neurophysiology, 9,* 673–690. (8)

Dement, W., & Kleitman, N. (1957b). The relation of eye movements during sleep to dream activity: An objective method for the study of dreaming. *Journal of Experimental Psychology, 53,* 339–346. (8)

Dement, W. C. (1990). A personal history of sleep disorders medicine. *Journal of Clinical Neurophysiology, 7,* 17–47. (8)

Dennett, D. C. (1991). *Consciousness explained.* Boston, MA: Little, Brown. (0, 13)

deQuervain, D. J.-F., Roozendaal, B., & McGaugh, J. L. (1998). Stress and glucocorticoids impair retrieval of long-term spatial memory. *Nature, 394,* 787–790. (12)

Derégnaucourt, S., Mitra, P. P., Fehér, O., Pytte, C., & Tchernichovski, O. (2005). How sleep affects the developmental learning of bird song. *Nature, 433,* 710–716. (8)

DeSimone, J. A., Heck, G. L., & Bartoshuk, L. M. (1980). Surface active taste modifiers: A comparison of the physical and psycho-physical properties of gymnemic acid and sodium lauryl sulfate. *Chemical Senses, 5,* 317–330. (6)

DeSimone, J. A., Heck, G. L., Mierson, S., & DeSimone, S. K. (1984). The active ion transport properties of canine lingual epithelia in vitro. *Journal of General Physiology, 83,* 633–656. (6)

Desmurget, M., Reilly, K. T., Richard, N., Szathmari, A., Mottolese, C., & Sirigu, A. (2009). Movement intention after parietal cortex stimulation in humans. *Science, 324,* 811–813. (7)

Detre, J. A., & Floyd, T. F. (2001). Functional MRI and its applications to the clinical neurosciences. *Neuroscientist, 7,* 64–79. (3)

Deutsch, D., Henthorn, T., Marvin, E., & Xu, H. S. (2006). Absolute pitch among American and Chinese conservatory students: Prevalence differences, and evidence for a speech-related critical period. *Journal of the Acoustical Society of America, 119,* 719–722. (6)

Deutsch, J. A., & Ahn, S. J. (1986). The splanchnic nerve and food intake regulation. *Behavioral and Neural Biology, 45,* 43–47. (9)

Deutsch, J. A., Young, W. G., & Kalogeris, T. J. (1978). The stomach signals satiety. *Science, 201,* 165–167. (9)

DeValois, R. L., Albrecht, D. G., & Thorell, L. G. (1982). Spatial frequency selectivity of cells in macaque visual cortex. *Vision Research, 22,* 545–559. (5)

Devor, E. J., Abell, C. W., Hoffman, P. L., Tabakoff, B., & Cloninger, C. R. (1994). Platelet MAO activity in Type I and Type II alcoholism. *Annals of the New York Academy of Sciences, 708,* 119–128. (14)

Devor, M. (1996). Pain mechanisms. *The Neuroscientist, 2,* 233–244. (6)

de Vries, G. J., & Södersten, P. (2009). Sex differences in the brain: The relation between structure and function. *Hormones and Behavior, 55,* 589–596. (10)

Dewan, A., Pacifico, R., Zhan, R., Rinberg, D., & Bozza, T. (2013). Non-redundant coding of aversive odours in the main olfactory pathway. *Nature, 497,* 486–489. (6)

DeYoe, E. A., Felleman, D. J., Van Essen, D. C., & McClendon, E. (1994). Multiple processing streams in occipitotemporal visual cortex. *Nature, 371,* 151–154. (5)

De Young, C. G., Hirsch, J. B., Shane, M. S., Papadenaetris, X., Rajeevan, N., & Gray, J. R. (2010). Testing predictions from personality neuroscience: Brain structure and the big five. *Psychological Science, 21,* 820–828. (3)

Dhingra, R., Sullivan, L., Jacques, P. F., Wang, T. J., Fox, C. S., Meigs, J. B., . . . Vasan, R. S. (2007). Soft drink consumption and risk of developing cardiometabolic risk factors and the metabolic syndrome in middle-aged adults in the community. *Circulation, 116,* 480–488. (9)

Di Lorenzo, P. M., Chen, J.-Y., & Victor, J. D. (2009). Quality time: Representation of a multidimensional sensory domain through temporal coding. *Journal of Neuroscience, 29,* 9227–9238. (6)

Di Lorenzo, P. M., Leshchinskiy, S., Moroney, D. N., & Ozdoba, J. M. (2009). Making time count: Functional evidence for temporal coding of taste sensation. *Behavioral Neuroscience, 123,* 14–25. (1, 6)

Diamond, L. M. (2007). A dynamical systems approach to the development and expression of female same-sex sexuality. *Perspectives on Psychological Science, 2,* 142–161. (10)

Diamond, M., & Sigmundson, H. K. (1997). Management of intersexuality: Guidelines for dealing with persons with ambiguous genitalia. *Archives of Pediatrics and Adolescent Medicine, 151,* 1046–1050. (10)

Dichgans, J. (1984). Clinical symptoms of cerebellar dysfunction and their topodiagnostic significance. *Human Neurobiology, 2,* 269–279. (7)

Dick, D. M., Johnson, J. K., Viken, R. J., & Rose, R. J. (2000). Testing between-family associations in within-family comparisons. *Psychological Science, 11,* 409–413. (14)

Dick, D. M., Latendresse, S. J., Lansford, J. E., Budde, J. P., Goate, A., Dodge, K. A., . . . Bates, J. E. (2009). Role of *GABRA2* in trajectories of externalizing behavior across development and evidence of moderation by parental monitoring. *Archives of General Psychiatry, 66,* 649–657. (14)

Dick, F., Bates, E., Wulfeck, B., Utman, J. A., Dronkers, N., & Gernsbacher, M. A. (2001). Language deficits, localization, and grammar: Evidence for a distributive model of language breakdown in aphasic patients and neurologically intact individuals. *Psychological Review, 108,* 759–788. (13)

Dickens, W. T., & Flynn, J. R. (2001). Heritability estimates versus large environmental effects: The IQ paradox resolved. *Psychological Review, 108,* 346–369. (10)

Diéguez, C., Vazquez, M. J., Romero, A., López, M., & Nogueiras, R. (2011). Hypothalamic control of lipid metabolism: Focus on leptin, ghrelin and melanocortins. *Neuroendocrinology, 94,* 1–11. (9)

Dierks, T., Linden, D. E. J., Jandl, M., Formisano, E., Goebel, R., Lanfermann, H., . (1999). Activation of Heschl's gyrus during auditory hallucinations. *Neuron, 22,* 615–621. (3)

Dijk, D.-J., & Archer, S. N. (2010). *PERIOD3,* circadian phenotypes, and sleep homeostasis. *Sleep Medicine Reviews, 14,* 151–160. (8)

Dijk, D.-J., & Cajochen, C. (1997). Melatonin and the circadian regulation of sleep initiation, consolidation, structure, and the sleep EEG. *Journal of Biological Rhythms, 12,* 627–635. (8)

Dijk, D.-J., Neri, D. F., Wyatt, J. K., Ronda, J. M., Riel, E., Ritz-deCecco, A., . . . Czeisler, C. A. (2001). Sleep, performance, circadian rhythms, and light-dark cycles during two space shuttle flights. *American Journal of Physiology: Regulatory, Integrative, and Comparative Physiology, 281,* R1647–R1664. (8)

Diller, L., Packer, O. S., Verweij, J., McMahon, M. J., Williams, D. R., & Dacey, D. M. (2004). L and M cone contributions to the midget and parasol ganglion cell receptive fields of macaque monkey retina. *Journal of Neuroscience, 24,* 1079–1088. (5)

Dimond, S. J. (1979). Symmetry and asymmetry in the vertebrate brain. In D. A. Oakley & H. C. Plotkin (Eds.), *Brain, behaviour, and evolution* (pp. 189–218). London: Methuen. (13)

Dinstein, I., Hasson, U., Rubin, N., & Heeger, D. J. (2007). Brain areas selective for both observed and executed movements. *Journal of Neurophysiology, 98,* 1415–1427. (7)

Dinstein, I., Thomas, C., Humphreys, K., Minshew, N., Behrmann, M., & Heeger, D. J. (2010). Normal movement selectivity in autism. *Neuron, 66,* 461–469. (7)

Disner, S. G., Beevers, C. G., Lee, H.-J., Ferrell, R. E., Hariri, A. R., & Telch, M. J. (2013). War zone stress interacts with the 5-HTTLPR polymorphism to predict the development of sustained attention for negative emotion stimuli in soldiers returning from Iraq. *Clinical Psychological Science, 1,* 413–425. (11)

Do, C. B., Tung, J. Y., Dorfman, E., Kiefer, A. K., Drabant, E. M., Francke, U., . . . Eriksson, N. (2011). Web-based genome-wide association study identifies two novel loci and a substantial genetic component for Parkinson's disease. *PLoS Genetics, 7,* e1002141. (7)

Doesburg, S. M., Green, J. J., McDonald, J. J., & Ward, L. M. (2009). Rhythms of consciousness: Binocular rivalry reveals large-scale oscillatory network dynamics mediating visual perception. *PLoS One, 4,* e6142. (13)

Doremus-Fitzwater, T. L., Barretto, M., & Spear, L. P. (2012). Age-related differences in impulsivity among adolescent and adult Sprague-Dawley rats. *Behavioral Neuroscience, 126,* 735–741. (4)

Doricchi, F., Guariglia, P., Gasparini, M., & Tomaiuolo, F. (2005). Dissociation between physical and mental number line bisection in right hemisphere brain damage. *Nature Neuroscience, 8,* 1663–1665. (13)

Dormal, G., Lepore, F., & Collignon, O. (2012). Plasticity of the dorsal "spatial" stream in visually deprived individuals. *Neural Plasticity,* Article 687659. (5)

Doty, R. L., Applebaum, S., Zusho, H., & Settle, R. G. (1985). Sex differences in odor identification ability: A cross-cultural analysis. *Neuropsychologia, 23,* 667–672. (6)

Dowling, J. E. (1987). *The retina.* Cambridge, MA: Harvard University Press. (5)

Dowling, J. E., & Boycott, B. B. (1966). Organization of the primate retina. *Proceedings of the Royal Society of London, B, 166,* 80–111. (5)

Downar, J., Mikulis, D. J., & Davis, K. D. (2003). Neural correlates of the prolonged salience of painful stimulation. *NeuroImage, 20,* 1540–1551. (6)

Downing, P. E., Chan, A. W.-Y., Peelen, M. V., Dodds, C. M., & Kanwisher, N. (2005). Domain specificity in visual cortex. *Cerebral Cortex, 16,* 1453–1461. (5)

Doyon, J., Korman, M., Morin, A., Dostie, V., Tahar, A. H., Benali, H., Carrier, J. (2009). Contribution of night and day sleep vs. simple passage of time to the consolidation of motor sequence and visuomotor adaptation learning. *Experimental Brain Research, 195,* 15–26. (8)

Draganski, B., Gaser, C., Busch, V., Schuierer, G., Bogdahn, U., & May, A. (2004). Changes in grey matter induced by training. *Nature, 427,* 311–312. (4)

Dranias, M. R., Ju, H., Rajaram, E., & Van Dongen, A. M. J. (2013). Short-term memory in networks of dissociated cortical neurons. *Journal of Neuroscience, 33,* 1940–1953. (12)

Drdla-Schutting, R., Benrath, J., Wunderbaldinger, G., & Sandkühler, J. (2012). Erasure of a spinal memory trace of pain by a brief, high-dose opioid administration. *Science, 335,* 235–238. (6)

Dreger, A. D. (1998). *Hermaphrodites and the medical invention of sex.* Cambridge, MA: Harvard University Press. (10)

Drewnowski, A., Henderson, S. A., Shore, A. B., & Barratt-Fornell, A. (1998). Sensory responses to 6-*n*-propylthiouracil (PROP) or sucrose solutions and food preferences in young women. *Annals of the New York Academy of Sciences, 855,* 797–801. (6)

Drzyzga, L. R., Marcinowska, A., & Obuchowicz, E. (2009). Antiapoptotic and neurotrophic effects of antidepressants: A review of clinical and experimental studies. *Brain Research Bulletin, 79,* 248–257. (14)

Du, J., Creson, T. K., Wu, L.-J., Ren, M., Gray, N. A., Falke, C., Manji, H. K. (2008). The role of hippocampal GluR1 and GluR2 receptors in manic-like behavior. *Journal of Neuroscience, 28,* 68–79. (14)

Duan, X., Chang, J. H., Ge, S., Faulkner, R. L., Kim, J. Y., Kitabatake, Y., . . . Song, H. (2007). Disrupted-in-schizophrenia 1 regulated integration of newly generated neurons in the adult brain. *Cell, 130,* 1146–1158. (14)

Ducommun, C. Y., Michel, C. M., Clarke, S., Adriani, M., Seeck, M., Landis, T., & Blanke, O. (2004). Cortical motion deafness. *Neuron, 43,* 765–777. (6)

Dudchenko, P. A., & Taube, J. S. (1997). Correlation between head direction cell activity and spatial behavior on a radial arm maze. *Behavioral Neuroscience, 111,* 3–19. (12)

Duff, M. C., Hengst, J., Tranel, D., & Cohen, N. J. (2006). Development of shared information in communication despite hippocampal amnesia. *Nature Neuroscience, 9,* 140–146. (12)

Duke, A. A., Bègue, L., Bell, R., & Eisenlohr-Moul, T. (2013). Revisiting the serotonin-aggression relation in humans: A meta-analysis. *Psychological Bulletin, 139,* 1148–1172. (11)

Dulcis, D., Jamshidi, P., Leutgeb, S., & Spitzer, N. C. (2013). Neurotransmitter switching in the adult brain regulates behavior. *Science, 340,*449–553. (2)

Duman, R. S., & Aghajanian, G. K. (2012). Synaptic dysfunction in depression: Potential therapeutic targets. *Science, 338,* 68–72. (14)

Dunn, B. D., Galton, H. C., Morgan, R., Evans, D., Olliver, C., Meyer, M., . . . Dalgeish, T. (2010). Listening to your heart: How interoception shapes emotion experience and intuitive decision making. *Psychological Science, 21,* 1835–1844. (11)

Durante, K. M., & Li, N. P. (2009). Oestradiol level and opportunistic mating in women. *Biology Letters, 5,* 179–182. (10)

Duvarci, S., Bauer, E. P., & Paré, D. (2009). The bed nucleus of the stria terminalis mediates inter-individual variations in anxiety and fear. *Journal of Neuroscience, 29,* 10357–10361. (11)

Dyal, J. A. (1971). Transfer of behavioral bias: Reality and specificity. In E. J. Fjerdingstad (Ed.), *Chemical transfer of learned information* (pp. 219–263). New York: American Elsevier. (12)

Earnest, D. J., Liang, F.-Q., Ratcliff, M., & Cassone, V. M. (1999). Immortal time: Circadian clock properties of rat suprachiasmatic cell lines. *Science, 283,* 693–695. (8)

Eastman, C. I., Hoese, E. K., Youngstedt, S. D., & Liu, L. (1995). Phase-shifting human circadian rhythms with exercise during the night shift. *Physiology & Behavior, 58,* 1287–1291. (8)

Eaves, L. J., Martin, N. G., & Heath, A. C. (1990). Religious affiliation in twins and their parents: Testing a model of cultural inheritance. *Behavior Genetics, 20,* 1–22. (4)

Eccles, J. C. (1964). *The physiology of synapses.* Berlin: Springer-Verlag. (2)

Eckhorn, R., Bauer, R., Jordan, W., Brosch, M., Kruse, W., Munk, M., & Reitboeck, H. J. (1988). Coherent oscillations: A mechanism of feature linking in the visual cortex? *Biological Cybernetics, 60,* 121–130. (13)

Eckstrand, K. L., Ding, Z. H., Dodge, N. C., Cowan, R. L., Jacobson, J. L., Jacobson, S. W., & Avison, M. J. (2012). Persistent dose-dependent changes in brain structure in young adults with low-to-moderate alcohol exposure *in utero. Alcoholism—Clinical & Experimental Research, 36,* 1892–1902. (4)

Edelman, G. M. (1987). *Neural Darwinism.* New York: Basic Books. (4)

Edinger, J. D., McCall, W. V., Marsh, G. R., Radtke, R. A., Erwin, C. W., & Lininger, A. (1992). Periodic limb movement variability in older DIMS patients across consecutive nights of home monitoring. *Sleep, 15,* 156–161. (8)

Edlinger, M., Hausmann, A., Kemmler, G., Kurz, M., Kurzhaler, I., Walch, T., . . . Fleischhacker, W. W. (2005). Trends in the pharmacological treatment of patients with schizophrenia over a 12 year observation period. *Schizophrenia Research, 77,* 25–34. (14)

Edman, G., Åsberg, M., Levander, S., & Schalling, D. (1986). Skin conductance habituation and cerebrospinal fluid 5-hydroxy-indoleacetic acid in suicidal patients. *Archives of General Psychiatry, 43,* 586–592. (11)

Ehrhardt, A. A., & Money, J. (1967). Progestin-induced hermaphroditism: IQ and psychosexual identity in a study of ten girls. *Journal of Sex Research, 3,* 83–100. (10)

Ehrlich, P. R., Dobkin, D. S., & Wheye, D. (1988). *The birder's handbook.* New York: Simon & Schuster. (9)

Eichenbaum, H. (2000). A cortical-hippocampal system for declarative memory. *Nature Reviews Neuroscience, 1,* 41–50. (12)

Eichenbaum, H. (2002). *The cognitive neuroscience of memory.* New York: Oxford University Press. (12)

Eidelberg, E., & Stein, D. G. (1974). Functional recovery after lesions of the nervous system. *Neurosciences Research Program Bulletin, 12,* 191–303. (4)

Eippert, F., Finsterbusch, J., Binget, U., & Büchel, C. (2009). Direct evidence for spinal cord involvement in placebo analgesia. *Science, 326,* 404. (6)

Eisenberger, N. I., & Cole, S. W. (2012). Social neuroscience and health: Neurophysiological mechanisms linking social ties with physical health. *Nature Neuroscience, 15,* 669–674. (11)

Eisenberger, N. I., Lieberman, M. D., & Williams, K. D. (2003). Does rejection hurt? An fMRI study of social exclusion. *Science, 302,* 290–292. (6)

Eisenstein, E. M., & Cohen, M. J. (1965). Learning in an isolated prothoracic insect ganglion. *Animal Behaviour, 13,* 104–108. (12)

Ek, M., Engblom, D., Saha, S., Blomqvist, A., Jakobsson, P.-J., & Ericsson-Dahlstrand, A. (2001). Pathway across the blood–brain barrier. *Nature, 410,* 430–431. (9)

Ekman, P., & Friesen, W. V. (1984). *Unmasking the face* (2nd ed.). Palo Alto, CA: Consulting Psychologists Press. (11)

Elbert, T., Candia, V., Altenmüller, E., Rau, H., Sterr, A., Rockstroh, B., . . . Taub, E. (1998). Alteration of digital representations in somatosensory cortex in focal hand dystonia. *Neuroreport, 9,* 3571–3575. (4)

Elbert, T., Pantev, C., Wienbruch, C., Rockstroh, B., & Taub, E. (1995). Increased cortical representation of the fingers of the left hand in string players. *Science, 270,* 305–307. (4)

Eldar, E., Cohen, J. D., & Niv, Y. (2013). The effects of neural gain on attention and learning. *Nature Neuroscience, 16,* 1146–1153. (8)

Eldridge, L. L., Engel, S. A., Zeineh, M. M., Bookheimer, S. Y., & Knowlton, B. J. (2005). A dissociation of encoding and retrieval processes in the human hippocampus. *Journal of Neuroscience, 25,* 3280–3286. (12)

Elias, C. F., Lee, C., Kelly, J., Aschkenazi, C., Ahima, R. S., Couceyro, P. R., . . . Elmquist, J. K.

(1998). Leptin activates hypothalamic CART neurons projecting to the spinal cord. *Neuron, 21,* 1375–1385. (9)

Ellacott, K. L. J., & Cone, R. D. (2004). The central melanocortin system and the integration of short- and long-term regulators of energy homeostasis. *Recent Progress in Hormone Research, 59,* 395–408. (9)

Ellemberg, D., Lewis, T. L., Maurer, D., Brar, S., & Brent, H. P. (2002). Better perception of global motion after monocular than after binocular deprivation. *Vision Research, 42,* 169–179. (5)

Elliott, T. R. (1905). The action of adrenalin. *Journal of Physiology (London), 32,* 401–467. (2)

Ellis, L., & Ames, M. A. (1987). Neurohormonal functioning and sexual orientation: A theory of homosexuality–heterosexuality. *Psychological Bulletin, 101,* 233–258. (10)

Ellis, L., Ames, M. A., Peckham, W., & Burke, D. (1988). Sexual orientation of human offspring may be altered by severe maternal stress during pregnancy. *Journal of Sex Research, 25,* 152–157. (10)

Ellis, L., & Cole-Harding, S. (2001). The effects of prenatal stress, and of prenatal alcohol and nicotine exposure, on human sexual orientation. *Physiology & Behavior, 74,* 213–226. (10)

Ellis-Behnke, R. G., Liang, Y.-X., You, S.-W., Tay, D. K. C., Zhang, S., So, K.-F., & Schneider, G. E. (2006). Nano neuro knitting: Peptide nanofiber scaffold for brain repair and axon regeneration with functional return of vision. *Proceedings of the National Academy of Sciences, USA, 103,* 5054–5059. (4)

Ells, L. J., Hillier, F. C., Shucksmith, J., Crawley, H., Harbige, L., Shield, J., . . . Summerbell, C. D. (2008). A systematic review of the effect of dietary exposure that could be achieved through normal dietary intake on learning and performance of school-aged children of relevance to UK schools. *British Journal of Nutrition, 100,* 927–936. (9)

Elsabbagh, M., Divan, G., Koh, Y. J., Kim, Y. S., Kauchali, S., Marcin, C., . . . Fombonne, E. (2012). Global prevalence of autism and other pervasive developmental disorders. *Autism Research, 5,* 160–179. (14)

Elston, G. N. (2000). Pyramidal cells of the frontal lobe: All the more spinous to think with. *Journal of Neuroscience, 20,* RC95: 1–4. (3)

Eme, R. (2013). MAOA and male antisocial behavior: A review. *Aggression and Violent Behavior, 18,* 395–398. (11)

Emmorey, K., Allen, J. S., Bruss, J., Schenker, N., & Damasio, H. (2003). A morphometric analysis of auditory brain regions in congenitally deaf adults. *Proceedings of the National Academy of Sciences, USA, 100,* 10049–10054. (6)

Enard, W., Gehre, S., Hammerschmidt, K., Hölter, S. M., Blass, T., Somel, M., . . . Paabo, S. (2009). A humanized version of Foxp2 affects cortico-basal ganglia circuits in mice. *Cell, 137,* 961–971. (13)

Eng, M. Y., Schuckit, M. A., & Smith, T. L. (2005). The level of response to alcohol in daughters of alcoholics and controls. *Drug and Alcohol Dependence, 79,* 83–93. (14)

Engert, F., & Bonhoeffer, T. (1999). Dendritic spine changes associated with hippocampal long-term synaptic plasticity. *Nature, 399,* 66–70. (12)

Epping-Jordan, M. P., Watkins, S. S., Koob, G. F., & Markou, A. (1998). Dramatic decreases in brain reward function during nicotine withdrawal. *Nature, 393,* 76–79. (14)

Erickson, C., & Lehrman, D. (1964). Effect of castration of male ring doves upon ovarian activity of females. *Journal of Comparative and Physiological Psychology, 58,* 164–166. (10)

Erickson, K. I., Prakash, R. S., Voss, M. W., Chaddock, L., Heo, S., McLaren, M., . . . Kramer, A. F. (2010). Brain-derived neurotrophic factor is associated with age-related decline in hippocampal volume. *Journal of Neuroscience, 30,* 5368–5375. (4)

Erickson, R. P. (1982). The across-fiber pattern theory: An organizing principle for molar neural function. *Contributions to Sensory Physiology, 6,* 79–110. (6)

Ernst, M. B., Wunderlich, C. M., Hess, S., Paehler, M., Mesaros, A., Koralov, S. B., . . . Wunderlich, F. T. (2009). Enhanced stat3 activation in POMC neurons provokes negative feedback inhibition of leptin and insulin signaling in obesity. *Journal of Neuroscience, 29,* 11582–11593. (9)

Ersche, K. D., Jones, P. S., Williams, G. B., Turton, A. J., Robbins, T. W., & Bullmore, E. T. (2012). Abnormal brain structure implicated in stimulant drug addiction. *Science, 335,* 601–604. (14)

Eschenko, O., Mölle, M., Born, J., & Sara, S. J. (2006). Elevated sleep spindle density after learning or after retrieval in rats. *Journal of Neurophysiology, 26,* 12914–12920. (8)

Esser, S. K., Hill, S., & Tononi, G. (2009). Breakdown of effective connectivity during slow wave sleep: Investigating the mechanism underlying a cortical gate using large-scale modeling. *Journal of Neurophysiology, 102,* 2096–2111. (8)

Etcoff, N. L., Ekman, P., Magee, J. J., & Frank, M. G. (2000). Lie detection and language comprehension. *Nature, 405,* 139. (13)

Etgen, A. M., Chu, H.-P., Fiber, J. M., Karkanias, G. B., & Morales, J. M. (1999). Hormonal integration of neurochemical and sensory signals governing female reproductive behavior. *Behavioural Brain Research, 105,* 93–103. (10)

Euston, D. R., Tatsuno, M., & McNaughton, B. L. (2007). Fast-forward playback of recent memory sequences in prefrontal cortex during sleep. *Science, 318,* 1147–1150. (8)

Evans, D. A., Funkenstein, H. H., Albert, M. S., Scherr, P. A., Cook, N. R., Chown, M. J., . . . Taylor, J. O. (1989). Prevalence of Alzheimer's disease in a community population of older persons. *Journal of the American Medical Association, 262,* 2551–2556. (12)

Evarts, E. V. (1979). Brain mechanisms of movement. *Scientific American, 241*(3), 164–179. (7)

Evenson, K. R., Foraker, R. E., Morris, D. L., & Rosamond, W. D. (2009). A comprehensive review of prehospital and in-hospital delay times in acute stroke care. *International Journal of Stroke, 4,* 187–199. (4)

Eyre, J. A., Taylor, J. P., Villagra, F., Smith, M., & Miller, S. (2001). Evidence of activity-dependent withdrawal of corticospinal projections during human development. *Neurology, 57,* 1543–1554. (7)

Facoetti, A., Corradi, N., Ruffino, M., Gori, S., & Zorzi, M. (2010). Visual spatial attention and speech segmentation are both impaired in preschoolers at familial risk for developmental dyslexia. *Dyslexia, 16,* 22–239. (13)

Fadda, F. (2000). Tryptophan-free diets: A physiological tool to study brain serotonin function. *News in Physiological Sciences, 15,* 260–264. (2)

Fadool, D. A., Tucker, K., Perkins, R., Fasciani, G., Thompson, R. N., Parsons, A. D.. . . . Kaczmarek, L. K. (2004). Kv1.3 channel gene-targeted deletion produces "super-smeller mice" with altered glomeruli, interacting scaffolding proteins, and biophysics. *Neuron, 41,* 389–404. (6)

Falk, D., Lepore, F. E., & Noe, A. (2013). The cerebral cortex of Albert Einstein: A description and preliminary analysis of unpublished photographs. *Brain, 136,* 1304–1327. (3)

Falleti, M. G., Maruff, P., Collie, A., Darby, D. G., & McStephen, M. (2003). Qualitative similarities in cognitive impairment associated with 24 h of sustained wakefulness and a blood alcohol concentration of 0.05%. *Journal of Sleep Research, 12,* 265–274. (8)

Fan, W., Ellacott, K. L. J., Halatchev, I. G., Takahashi, K., Yu, P., & Cone, R. D. (2004). Cholecystokinin-mediated suppression of feeding involves the brainstem melanocortin system. *Nature Neuroscience, 7,* 335–336. (9)

Fantz, R. L. (1963). Pattern vision in newborn infants. *Science, 140,* 296–297. (5)

Farah, M. J. (1990). *Visual agnosia.* Cambridge, MA: MIT Press. (5)

Farah, M. J., Illes, J., Cook-Deegan, R., Gardner, H., Kandel, E., King, P., . . . Wolpe, P. R. (2004). Neurocognitive enhancement: What can we do and what should we do? *Nature Reviews Neuroscience, 5,* 421–425. (12)

Farah, M. J., Wilson, K. D., Drain, M., & Tanaka, J. N. (1998). What is "special" about face perception? *Psychological Review, 105,* 482–498. (5)

Farber, N. B., Newcomer, J. W., & Olney, J. W. (1999). Glycine agonists: What can they teach us about schizophrenia? *Archives of General Psychiatry, 56,* 13–17. (14)

Farivar, R. (2009). Dorsal-ventral integration in object recognition. *Brain Research Reviews, 61,* 144–153. (5)

Farmer, M. E., & Klein, R. M. (1995). The evidence for a temporal processing deficit linked to dyslexia: A review. *Psychonomic Bulletin & Review, 2,* 460–493. (13)

Fatemi, S. H., Aldinger, K. A., Ashwood, P., Bauman, M. L., Blaha, C. D., Blatt, G. J., . . . Welsh, J. P. (2012). Consensus paper: Pathological role of the cerebellum in autism. *Cerebellum, 11,* 777–807. (14)

Fatemi, S. H., & Folsom, T. D. (2009). The neurodevelopmental hypothesis of schizophrenia, revisited. *Schizophrenia Bulletin, 35,* 528–548. (14)

Featherstone, R. E., Fleming, A. S., & Ivy, G. O. (2000). Plasticity in the maternal circuit: Effects of experience and partum condition on brain astrocyte number in female rats. *Behavioral Neuroscience, 114,* 158–172. (10)

Fedrigo, O., Pfefferle, A. D., Babbitt, C. C., Haygood, R., Wall, C. E., & Wray, G. A. (2011). A potential role for glucose transporters in the evolution of human brain size. *Brain, Behavior and Evolution, 78,* 315–326. (4)

Feeney, D. M., & Sutton, R. L. (1988). Catecholamines and recovery of function after brain damage. In D. G. Stein & B. A. Sabel (Eds.), *Pharmacological approaches to the treatment of brain and spinal cord injury* (pp. 121–142). New York: Plenum Press. (4)

Feeney, D. M., Sutton, R. L., Boyeson, M. G., Hovda, D. A., & Dail, W. G. (1985). The locus coeruleus and cerebral metabolism: Recovery of function after cerebral injury. *Physiological Psychology, 13,* 197–203. (4)

Feinstein, J. S., Adolphs, R., Damasio, A., & Tranel, D. (2011). The human amygdala and the induction and experience of fear. *Current Biology, 21,* 34–38. (11)

Feinstein, J. S., Buzza, C., Hurlemann, R., Follmer, R. L., Dahdaleh, N. S., Coryell, W. H., . . . Wemmie, J. A. (2013). Fear and panic in humans with bilateral amygdala damage. *Nature Neuroscience, 16,* 270–272. (11)

Fell, J., & Axmacher, N. (2011). The role of phase synchronization in memory processes. *Nature Reviews Neuroscience, 12,* 105–118. (13)

Feller, G. (2010). Protein stability and enzyme activity at extreme biological temperatures. *Journal of Physics—Condensed Matter, 22,* article 323101. (9)

Fendrich, R., Wessinger, C. M., & Gazzaniga, M. S. (1992). Residual vision in a scotoma: Implications for blindsight. *Science, 258,* 1489–1491. (5)

Feng, J., Fouse, S., & Fan, G. (2007). Epigenetic regulation of neural gene expression and neuronal function. *Pediatric Research, 61 (5), Part 2,* 58R–63R. (4)

Feng, J., Spence, I., & Pratt, J. (2007). Playing an action video game reduces gender differences in spatial cognition. *Psychological Science, 18,* 850–855. (3)

Fentress, J. C. (1973). Development of grooming in mice with amputated forelimbs. *Science, 179,* 704–705. (7)

Fergusson, D. M., Boden, J. M., Horwood, L. J., Miller, A., & Kennedy, M. A. (2012). Moderating role of the *MAOA* genotype in antisocial behavior. *British Journal of Psychiatry, 200,* 116–123. (11)

Ferreira, F., Bailey, K. G. D., & Ferraro, V. (2002). Good-enough representations in language comprehension. *Current Directions in Psychological Science, 11,* 11–15. (13)

Fettiplace, R. (1990). Transduction and tuning in auditory hair cells. *Seminars in the Neurosciences, 2,* 33–40. (6)

Field, L. L., Shumansky, K., Ryan, J., Truong, D, Swiergala, E., & Kaplan, B. J. (2013). Dense-map genome scan for dyslexia supports loci at 4q13, 16p12, 17q22; suggests novel locus at 7q36. *Genes, Brain and Behavior, 12,* 56–69. (13)

Filosa, J. A., Bonev, A. D., Straub, S. V., Meredith, A. L., Wilkerson, M. K., Aldrich, R. W., & Nelson, M. T. (2006). Local potassium signaling couples neuronal activity to vasodilation in the brain. *Nature Neuroscience, 9,* 1397–1403. (1)

Fils-Aime, M.-L., Eckardt, M. J., George, D. T., Brown, G. L., Mefford, I., & Linnoila, M. (1996). Early-onset alcoholics have lower cerebrospinal fluid 5-hydroxyindoleacetic acid levels than late-onset alcoholics. *Archives of General Psychiatry, 53,* 211–216. (14)

Finch, C. E. (2009). Update on slow aging and negligible senescence—A mini-review. *Gerontology, 55,* 307–313. (4)

Fine, I., Smallman, H. S., Doyle, P., & MacLeod, D. I. A. (2002). Visual function before and after the removal of bilateral congenital cataracts in adulthood. *Vision Research, 42,* 191–210. (5)

Fine, I. Wade, A. R., Brewer, A. A., May, M. G., Goodman, D. F., Boynton, G. M., . . . McLeod, D. I. A. (2003). Long-term deprivation affects visual perception and cortex. *Nature Neuroscience, 6,* 915–916. (5)

Finger, S., & Roe, D. (1996). Gustave Dax and the early history of cerebral dominance. *Archives of Neurology, 53,* 806–813. (13)

Fink, B., Hugill, N., & Lange, B. P. (2012). Women's body movements are a potential cue to ovulation. *Personality and Individual Differences, 53,* 759–763. (10)

Fink, G., Sumner, B. E. H., Rosie, R., Grace, O., & Quinn, J. P. (1996). Estrogen control of central neurotransmission: Effect on mood, mental state, and memory. *Cellular and Molecular Neurobiology, 16,* 325–344. (13)

Fink, G. R., Halligan, P. W., Marshall, J. C., Frith, C. D., Frackowiak, R. S. J., & Dolan, R. J. (1996). Where in the brain does visual attention select the forest and the trees? *Nature, 382,* 626–628. (13)

Fisch, L, Privman, E., Ramot, M., Harel, M., Nir, Y., Kipervasser, S., . . . Malach, R. (2009). Neural "ignition": Enhanced activation linked to perceptual awareness in human ventral stream visual cortex. *Neuron, 64,* 562–574. (13)

Fisher, S. E., Vargha-Khadem, F., Watkins, K. E., Monaco, A. P., & Pembrey, M. E. (1998). Localisation of a gene implicated in a severe speech and language disorder. *Nature Genetics, 18,* 168–170. (13)

Fitts, D. A., Starbuck, E. M., & Ruhf, A. (2000). Circumventricular organs and ANGII-induced salt appetite: Blood pressure and connectivity. *American Journal of Physiology, 279,* R2277–R2286. (9)

Fjell, A. M., Walhovd, K. B., Fennema-Notestine, C., McEvoy, L. K., Hagler, D. J., Holland, D., . . . Dale, A. M. (2009). One-year brain atrophy evident in healthy aging. *Journal of Neuroscience, 29,* 15223–15231. (4)

Fjerdingstad, E. J. (1973). Transfer of learning in rodents and fish. In W. B. Essman & S. Nakajima (Eds.), *Current biochemical approaches to learning and memory* (pp. 73–98). Flushing, NY: Spectrum. (12)

Flatz, G. (1987). Genetics of lactose digestion in humans. *Advances in Human Genetics, 16,* 1–77. (9)

Fleet, W. S., & Heilman, K. M. (1986). The fatigue effect in hemispatial neglect. *Neurology, 36*(Suppl. 1), 258. (4)

Fletcher, P. C., McKenna, P. J., Frith, C. D., Grasby, P. M., Friston, K. J., & Dolan, R. J. (1998). Brain activations in schizophrenia during a graded memory task studied with functional neuroimaging. *Archives of General Psychiatry, 55,* 1001–1008. (14)

Fletcher, R., & Voke, J. (1985). *Defective colour vision.* Bristol, England: Hilger. (5)

Flöel, A., Knecht, S., Lohmann, H., Deppe, M., Sommer, J., Dräger, B., . . . Henningsen, H. (2001). Language and spatial attention can lateralize to the same hemisphere in healthy humans. *Neurology, 57,* 1018–1024. (13)

Flor, H., Elbert, T., Knecht, S., Wienbruch, C., Pantev, C., Birbaumer, N., . . . Taub, E. (1995). Phantom-limb pain as a perceptual correlate of cortical reorganization following arm amputation. *Nature, 375,* 482–484. (4)

Florence, S. L., & Kaas, J. H. (1995). Large-scale reorganization at multiple levels of the somatosensory pathway follows therapeutic amputation of the hand in monkeys. *Journal of Neuroscience, 15,* 8083–8095. (4)

Flowers, K. A., & Hudson, J. M. (2013). Motor laterality as an indicator of speech laterality. *Neuropsychology, 27,* 256–265. (13)

Flynn, J. M., & Boder, E. (1991). Clinical and electrophysiological correlates of dysphonetic and dyseidetic dyslexia. In J. F. Stein (Ed.), *Vision and visual dyslexia* (pp. 121–131). Vol. 13 of J. R. Cronly-Dillon (Ed.), *Vision and visual dysfunction.* Boca Raton, FL: CRC Press. (13)

Foerde, K., Knowlton, B. J., & Poldrack, R. A. (2006). Modulation of competing memory systems by distraction. *Proceedings of the National Academy of Sciences, USA, 103,* 11778–11783. (12)

Foerde, K., Race, E., Verfaellie, M., & Shohamy, D. (2013). A role for the medial temporal lobe in feedback-driven learning: Evidence from amnesia. *Journal of Neuroscience, 33,* 5698–5704. (12)

Foerde, K., & Shohamy, D. (2011). Feedback timing modulates brain systems for learning in humans. *Journal of Neuroscience, 31,* 13157–13167. (12)

Fogel, S. M., Nader, R., Cote, K. A., & Smith, C. T. (2007). Sleep spindles and learning potential. *Behavioral Neuroscience, 121,* 1–10. (8)

Foland-Ross, L. C., Hamilton, J. P., Joormann, J., Berman, M. G., Jonides, J., & Gotlib, I. H. (2013). The neural basis of difficulties disengaging from negative irrelevant material in major depression. *Psychological Science, 24,* 334–344. (14)

Földy, C., Neu, A., Jones, M. V., & Soltesz, I. (2006). Presynaptic activity-dependent modulation of cannabinoid type 1 receptor-mediated inhibition of GABA release. *Journal of Neuroscience, 26,* 1465–1469. (2)

Foltynie, T., & Kahan, J. (2013). Parkinson's disease: An update on pathogenesis and treatment. *Journal of Neurology, 260,* 1433–1440. (7)

Foltz, E. I., & White, L. E. Jr. (1962). Pain "relief" by frontal cingulumotomy. *Journal of Neurosurgery, 19,* 89–100. (6)

Foo, H., & Mason, P. (2009). Analgesia accompanying food consumption requires ingestion of hedonic foods. *Journal of Neuroscience, 29,* 13053–13062. (6)

Forger, N. G., & Breedlove, S. M. (1987). Motoneuronal death during human fetal development. *Journal of Comparative Neurology, 234,* 118–122. (4)

Forger, N. G., Rosen, G. J., Waters, E. M., Jacob, D., Simerly, R. B., & de Vries, G. J. (2004). Deletion of *Bax* eliminates sex differences in the mouse forebrain. *Proceedings of the National Academy of Sciences, USA, 101,* 13666–13671. (10)

Foroni, F., & Semin, G. R. (2009). Language that puts you in touch with your bodily feelings. *Psychological Science, 20,* 974–980. (7)

Forster, B., & Corballis, M. C. (2000). Interhemispheric transfer of colour and shape information in the presence and absence of the corpus callosum. *Neuropsychologia, 38,* 32–45. (13)

Forsyth, R. J., Salorio, C. F., & Christensen, J. R. (2010). Modeling early recovery patterns after paediatric traumatic brain injury. *Archives of Disease in Childhood, 95,* 266–270. (4)

Fortin, N. J., Agster, K. L., & Eichenbaum, H. B. (2002). Critical role of the hippocampus in memory for sequences of events. *Nature Neuroscience, 5,* 458–462. (12)

Foss, A. J., Gregson, R. M., MacKeith, D., Herbison, N., Ash, I. M., Cobb, S. V., . . . Haworth, S. M. (2013). Evaluation and development of a novel binocular treatment (I-BiT™) system using video clips and interactive games to improve vision in children with amblyopia ("lazy eye"): Study protocol for a randomized controlled trial. *Trials, 14,* Article 145. (5)

Foss-Feig, J. H., Tadin, D., Schauder, K. B., & Cascio, C. J. (2013). A substantial and unexpected enhancement of motion perception in autism. *Journal of Neuroscience, 33,* 8243–8249. (14)

Fotopoulou, A., Solms, M., & Turnbull, O. (2004). Wishful reality distortions in confabulation: A case report. *Neuropsychologia, 47,* 727–744. (12)

Fountoulakis, K. N., Veroniki, A. A., Siamouli, M., & Moller, H. J. (2013). No role for initial severity on the efficacy of antidepressants: Results of a multi-meta-analysis. *Archives of General Psychiatry, 12,* Article 26. (14)

Fox, P. T., Ingham, R. J., Ingham, J. C., Zamarripa, F., Xiong, J.-H., & Lancaster, J. L. (2000). Brain correlates of stuttering and syllable production: A PET performance-correlation analysis. *Brain, 123,* 1985–2004. (13)

Frangou, S., Chitins, X., & Williams, S. C. R. (2004). Mapping IQ and gray matter density in healthy young people. *NeuroImage, 23,* 800–805. (3)

Frank, M. J., & Claus, E. D. (2006). Anatomy of a decision: Striato-orbitofrontal interactions in reinforcement learning, decision making, and reversal. *Psychological Review, 113,* 300–326. (12)

Frank, R. A., Mize, S. J. S., Kennedy, L. M., de los Santos, H. C., & Green, S. J. (1992). The effect of *Gymnema sylvestre* extracts on the sweetness of eight sweeteners. *Chemical Senses, 17,* 461–479. (6)

Frankland, P. W., Josselyn, S. A., Bradwejn, J., Vaccarino, F. J., & Yeomans, J. S. (1997). Activation of amygdala cholecystokinin B receptors potentiates the acoustic startle response in the rat. *Journal of Neuroscience, 17,* 1838–1847. (11)

Franz, E. A., & Fahey, S. (2007). Developmental change in interhemispheric communication. *Psychological Science, 18,* 1030–1031. (13)

Franz, E. A., Waldie, K. E., & Smith, M. J. (2000). The effect of callosotomy on novel versus familiar bimanual actions: A neural dissociation between controlled and automatic processes? *Psychological Science, 11,* 82–85. (13)

Frassinetti, F., Pavani, F., & Làdavas, E. (2002). Acoustical vision of neglected stimuli: Interaction among spatially converging audiovisual inputs in neglect patients. *Journal of Cognitive Neuroscience, 14,* 62–69. (13)

Frayling, T. M., Timpson, N. J., Weedon, M. N., Zeggini, E., Freathy, R. M., Lindgren, C. M., . . . McCarthy, M. I. (2007). A common variant in the *FTO* gene is associated with body mass index and predisposes to childhood and adult obesity. *Science, 316,* 889–894. (9)

Freed, C. R., Greene, P. E., Breeze, R. E., Tsai, W.-Y., DuMouchel, W., Kao, R., . . . Fahn, S. (2001). Transplantation of embryonic dopamine neurons for severe Parkinson's disease. *New England Journal of Medicine, 344,* 710–719. (7)

Freedman, M. S., Lucas, R. J., Soni, B., von Schantz, M., Muñoz, M., David-Gray, Z., & Foster, R. (1999). Regulation of mammalian circadian behavior by non-rod, non-cone, ocular photoreceptors. *Science, 284,* 502–504. (8)

Freeman, J., Ziemba, C. M., Heeger, D. J., Simoncelli, E. P., & Movshon, J. A. (2013). A functional and perceptual signature of the second visual area in primates. *Nature Neuroscience, 16,* 974–981. (5)

Freeman, J. H., & Steinmetz, A. B. (2011). Neural circuitry and plasticity mechanisms underlying delay eyeblink conditioning. *Learning & Memory, 18,* 666–677. (12)

Freire, C., & Koifman, S. (2012). Pesticide exposure and Parkinson's disease: Epidemiological evidence of association. *Neurotoxicology, 33,* 947–971. (7)

Frese, M., & Harwich, C. (1984). Shiftwork and the length and quality of sleep. *Journal of Occupational Medicine, 26,* 561–566. (8)

Freund, J., Brandmaier, A. M., Lewejohann, L., Kirste, I., Kritzler, M., Krüger, A., . . . Kempermann, G. (2013). Emergence of individuality in genetically identical mice. *Science, 340,* 756–759. (4)

Frey, S. H., Bogdanov, S., Smith, J. C., Watrous, S., & Breidenbach, W. C. (2008). Chronically deafferented sensory cortex recovers a grossly typical organization after allogenic hand transplantation. *Current Biology, 18,* 1530–1534. (4)

Friedlander, W. J. (1986). Who was "the father of bromide treatment of epilepsy"? *Archives of Neurology, 43,* 505–507. (14)

Friedman, E. S., Thase, M. E., Wisniewski, S. R., Trivedi, M. H., Biggs, M. M., Fava, M., . . . Rush, A. J. (2009). Cognitive therapy augmentation versus CT switch treatment: A STAR*D report. *International Journal of Cognitive Therapy, 2,* 66–87. (14)

Friedman, M. I., & Stricker, E. M. (1976). The physiological psychology of hunger: A physiological perspective. *Psychological Review, 83,* 409–431. (9)

Frisén, L., Nordenström, A., Falhammar, H., Filipsson, H., Holmdahl, G., Janson, P. O., . . . Nordenskjold, A. (2009). Gender role behavior, sexuality, and psychosocial adaptation in women with congenital adrenal hyperplasia due to CYP21A2 deficiency. *Journal of Clinical Endocrinology & Metabolism, 94,* 3432–3439. (10)

Fritsch, G., & Hitzig, E. (1870). Über die elektrische Erregbarkeit des Grosshirns [Concerning the electrical stimulability of the cerebrum]. *Archiv für Anatomie Physiologie und Wissenschaftliche Medicin, 300*–332. (7)

Frost, S., Kanagasingam, Y., Sohrabi, H., Bourgeat, P., Villemagne, V., Rowe, C. C., . . . Martins, R. N. (2013). Pupil response biomarkers for early detection and monitoring of Alzheimer's disease. *Current Alzheimer Research, 10,* 931–939. (12)

Fu, L.-Y., Acuna-Goycolea, C., & van den Pol, A. N. (2004). Neuropeptide Y inhibits hypocretin/orexin neurons by multiple presynaptic and postsynaptic mechanisms: Tonic depression of the hypothalamic arousal system. *Journal of Neuroscience, 24,* 8741–8751. (9)

Fu, Q. A., Heath, A. C., Bucholz, K. K., Nelson, E., Goldberg, J., Lyons, M. J., . . . Eisen, S. A. (2002). Shared genetic risk of major depression, alcohol dependence, and marijuana dependence. *Archives of General Psychiatry, 59,* 1125–1132. (14)

Fu, W., Sugai, T., Yoshimura, H., & Onoda, N. (2004). Convergence of olfactory and gustatory connections onto the endopiriform nucleus in the rat. *Neuroscience, 126,* 1033–1041. (6)

Fuchs, T., Haney, A., Jechura, T. J., Moore, F. R., & Bingman, V. P. (2006). Daytime naps in night-migrating birds: Behavioural adaptation to seasonal sleep deprivation in the Swainson's thrush, *Catharus ustulatus*. *Animal Behaviour, 72,* 951–958. (8)

Fuller, R. K., & Roth, H. P. (1979). Disulfiram for the treatment of alcoholism: An evaluation in 128 men. *Annals of Internal Medicine, 90,* 901–904. (14)

Fusar-Poli, P., Placentino, A., Carletti, F., Landi, P., Allen, P., Surguladze, S., . . . Politi, P. (2009). Functional atlas of emotional faces processing: A voxel-based meta-analysis of 105 functional magnetic resonance imaging studies. *Journal of Psychiatry & Neuroscience, 34,* 418–432. (11)

Fuster, J. M. (1989). *The prefrontal cortex* (2nd ed.). New York: Raven Press. (3)

Fyndanis, V. (2012). Basal ganglia and linguistic performance: A case study. *Procedia—Social and Behavioral Sciences, 61,* 252–254. (13)

Gabrieli, J. D. E. (2009). Dyslexia: A new synergy between education and cognitive neuroscience. *Science, 325,* 280–283. (13)

Gabrieli, J. D. E., Corkin, S., Mickel, S. F., & Growdon, J. H. (1993). Intact acquisition of mirror-tracing skill in Alzheimer's disease and in global amnesia. *Behavioral Neuroscience, 107,* 899–910. (12)

Gaetani, S., Fu, J., Cassano, T., Dipasquale, P., Romano, A., Righetti, L., . . . Piomelli, D. (2010). The fat-induced satiety factor oleoylethanolamide suppresses feeding through central release of oxytocin. *Journal of Neuroscience, 30,* 8096–8101. (9)

Gage, F. H. (2000). Mammalian neural stem cells. *Science, 287,* 1433–1438. (4)

Gais, S., Plihal, W., Wagner, U., & Born, J. (2000). Early sleep triggers memory for early visual discrimination skills. *Nature Neuroscience, 3,* 1335–1339. (8)

Galaburda, A. M., Sherman, G. F., Rosen, G. D., Aboitiz, F., & Geschwind, N. (1985). Developmental dyslexia: Four consecutive patients with cortical anomalies. *Annals of Neurology, 18,* 222–233. (13)

Galatzer-Levy, I. R., & Bryant, R. A. (2013). 636,120 ways to have posttraumatic stress disorder. *Perspectives on Psychological Science, 8,* 651–662. (14)

Galin, D., Johnstone, J., Nakell, L., & Herron, J. (1979). Development of the capacity for tactile information transfer between hemispheres in normal children. *Science, 204,* 1330–1332. (13)

Gallardo-Pujol, D., Andrés-Pueyo, A., Maydeu-Olivares, A. (2013). *MAOA* genotype, social exclusion and aggression: An experimental test of a gene-enviornmental interaction. *Genes, Brain and Behavior, 12,* 140–145. (11)

Gallese, V., Fadiga, L., Fogassi, L., & Rizzolatti, G. (1996). Action recognition in the premotor cortex. *Brain, 119,* 593–609. (7)

Gamaldo, A. A., An, Y., Allaire, J. C., Kitner-Triolo, M. H., & Zonderman, A. B. (2012). Variability in performance: Identifying early signs of future cognitive impairment. *Neuropsychology, 26,* 534–540. (12)

Gamer, M., & Büchel, C. (2009). Amygdala activation predicts gaze toward fearful eyes. *Journal of Neuroscience, 29,* 9123–9126. (11)

Gan, W.-B., Kwon, E., Feng, G., Sanes, J. R., & Lichtman, J. W. (2003). Synaptic dynamism measured over minutes to months: Age-dependent decline in an autonomic ganglion. *Nature Neuroscience, 6,* 956–960. (4)

Gangestad, S. W., & Simpson, J. A. (2000). The evolution of human mating: Trade-offs and strategic pluralism. *Behavioral and Brain Sciences, 23,* 573–644. (10)

Gangestad, S. W., Simpson, J. A., Cousins, A. J., Garver-Apgar, C. E., & Christensen, P. N. (2004). Women's preferences for male behavioral displays change across the menstrual cycle. *Psychological Science, 15,* 203–207. (10)

Ganguly, K., Kiss, L., & Poo, M. (2000). Enhancement of presynaptic neuronal excitability by correlated presynaptic and postsynaptic spiking. *Nature Neuroscience, 3, 1018*–1026. (12)

Ganis, G., Keenan, J. P., Kosslyn, S. M., & Pascual-Leone, A. (2000). Transcranial magnetic stimulation of primary motor cortex affects mental rotation. *Cerebral Cortex, 10,* 175–180. (3)

Gao, J.-H., Parsons, L. M., Bower, J. M., Xiong, J., Li, J., & Fox, P. T. (1996). Cerebellum implicated in sensory acquisition and discrimination rather than motor control. *Science, 272,* 545–547. (7)

Garcia, R., Vouimba, R.-M., Baudry, M., & Thompson, R. F. (1999). The amygdala modulates prefrontal cortex activity relative to conditioned fear. *Nature, 402,* 294–296. (11)

Garcia-Falgueras, A., & Swaab, D. F. (2008). A sex difference in the hypothalamic uncinate nucleus: Relationship to gender identity. *Brain, 131,* 3132–3146. (10)

Gardner, B. T., & Gardner, R. A. (1975). Evidence for sentence constituents in the early utterances of child and chimpanzee. *Journal of Experimental Psychology: General, 104,* 244–267. (13)

Gardner, H., & Zurif, E. B. (1975). Bee but not be: Oral reading of single words in aphasia and alexia. *Neuropsychologia, 13,* 181–190. (13)

Gaser, C., & Schlaug, G. (2003). Brain structures differ between musicians and non-musicians. *Journal of Neuroscience, 23,* 9240–9245. (4)

Gavrilets, S., & Rice, W. R. (2006). Genetic models of homosexuality: Generating testable predictions. *Proceedings of the Royal Society, B, 273,* 3031–3038. (10)

Gazzaniga, M. S. (2000). Cerebral specialization and interhemispheric communication: Does the corpus callosum enable the human condition? *Brain, 123,* 1293–1326. (13)

Ge, S., Yang, C.-H., Hsu, K.-S., Ming, G.-L., & Song, H. (2007). A critical period for enhanced synaptic plasticity in newly generated neurons of the adult brain. *Neuron, 54,* 559–566. (4)

Geerling, J. C., & Loewy, A. D. (2008). Central regulation of sodium appetite. *Experimental Physiology, 93,* 177–209. (9)

Geier, C. F., Terwilliger, R., Teslovich, T., Velanova, K., & Luna, B. (2010). Immaturities in reward processing and its influence on inhibitory control in adolescence. *Cerebral Cortex, 20,* 1613–1629. (4)

Geiger, B. M., Haburcak, M., Avena, N. M., Moyer, M. C., Hoebel, B. G., & Pothos, E. N. (2009). Deficits of mesolimbic dopamine neurotransmission in rat dietary obesity. *Neuroscience, 159,* 1193–1199. (9)

Geiger, G., Lettvin, J. Y., & Fahle, M. (1994). Dyslexic children learn a new visual strategy for reading: A controlled experiment. *Vision Research, 34,* 1223–1233. (13)

Geiger, G., Lettvin, J. Y., & Zegarra-Moran, O. (1992). Task-determined strategies of visual process. *Cognitive Brain Research, 1,* 39–52. (13)

Gerardin, D. C. C., & Pereira, O. C. M. (2002). Reproductive changes in male rats treated perinatally with an aromatase inhibitor. *Pharmacology Biochemistry and Behavior, 71,* 309–313. (10)

Gerwig, M., Hajjar, K., Dimitrova, A., Maschke, M., Kolb, F. P., Frings, M., . . . Timmann, D. (2005). Timing of conditioned eyeblink responses is impaired in cerebellar patients. *Journal of Neuroscience, 25,* 3919–3931. (12)

Geschwind, N., & Levitsky, W. (1968). Human brain: Left–right asymmetries in temporal speech region. *Science, 161,* 186–187. (13)

Gettler, L. T., McDade, T. W., Feranil, A. B., & Kuzawa, C. W. (2011). Longitudinal evidence that fatherhood decreases testosterone in human males. *Proceedings of the National Academy of Sciences (U.S.A.), 108,* 16194–16199. (10)

Gettler, L. T., McDade, T. W., Feranil, A. B., & Kuzawa, C. W. (2012). Prolactin, fatherhood, and reproductive behavior in human males. *American Journal of Physical Anthropology, 148,* 362–370. (10)

Geuter, S., & Büchel, C. (2013). Facilitation of pain in the human spinal cord by nocebo treatment. *Journal of Neuroscience, 33,* 13784–13790. (6)

Ghashghaei, H. T., Lai, C., & Anton, E. S. (2007). Neuronal migration in the adult brain: Are we there yet? *Nature Reviews Neuroscience, 8,* 141–151. (4)

Ghazanfar, A. A. (2013). Multisensory vocal communication in primates and the evolution of rhythmic speech. *Behavioral Ecology and Sociobiology, 67,* 1441–1448. (13)

Ghosh, A., Sydekum, E., Haiss, F., Peduzzi, S., Zorner, B., Schneider, R., . . . Schwab, M. E. (2009). Functional and anatomical reorganization of the sensory-motor cortex after incomplete spinal cord injury in adult rats. *Journal of Neuroscience, 29,* 12210–12219. (4)

Gibbs, F. P. (1983). Temperature dependence of the hamster circadian pacemaker. *American Journal of Physiology, 244,* R607–R610. (8)

Gibbs, J., Young, R. C., & Smith, G. P. (1973). Cholecystokinin decreases food intake in rats. *Journal of Comparative and Physiological Psychology, 84,* 488–495. (9)

Gilbertson, M. W., Shenton, M. E., Ciszewski, A., Kasai, K., Lasko, N. B., Orr, S. P., & Pitman, R. K. (2002). Smaller hippocampal volume predicts pathological vulnerability to psychological trauma. *Nature Neuroscience, 5,* 1242–1247. (11)

Gilmore, J. H., Lin, W., Prastawa, M. W., Looney, C. B., Vetsa, Y. S. K., Knickmeyer, R. C., . . . Gerig, G. (2007). Regional gray matter growth, sexual dimorphism, and cerebral asymmetry in the neonatal brain. *Journal of Neuroscience, 27,* 1255–1260. (3)

Gilmour, D., Knaut, H., Maischein, H.-M., & Nüsslein-Volhard, C. (2004). Towing of sensory axons by their migrating target cells *in vivo*. *Nature Neuroscience, 7,* 491–492. (4)

Giltay, E. J., & Gooren, L. J. G. (2009). Potential side effects of androgen deprivation treatment in sex offenders. *Journal of the American Academy of Psychiatry and the Law, 37,* 53–58. (10)

Giuliani, D., & Ferrari, F. (1996). Differential behavioral response to dopamine D2 agonists by sexually naive, sexually active, and sexually inactive male rats. *Behavioral Neuroscience, 110,* 802–808. (10)

Giummarra, M. J., Georgiou-Karistianis, N., Nicholls, M. E. R., Gibson, S. J., Chou, M., & Bradshaw, J. L. (2010). Corporeal awareness and proprioceptive sense of the phantom. *British Journal of Psychology, 101,* 791–808. (4)

Giusti-Rodriguez, P., & Sullivan, P. F. (2013). The genomics of schizophrenia: Update and implications. *Journal of Clinical Investigation, 123,* 4557–4563. (14)

Gläscher, J., Adolphs, R., Damasio, H., Behara, A., Rudrauf, D., Calamia, M., . . . Tranel, D. (2012). Lesion mapping of cognitive control and value-based decision making in the prefrontal cortex. *Proceedings of the National Academy of Sciences (U.S.A.), 109,* 14681–14686. (12)

Glendenning, K. K., Baker, B. N., Hutson, K. A., & Masterton, R. B. (1992). Acoustic chiasm V: Inhibition and excitation in the ipsilateral and contralateral projections of LSO. *Journal of Comparative Neurology, 319,* 100–122. (6)

Gloria, R., Angelos, L., Schaefer, H. S., Davis, J. M., Majeskie, M., Richmond, B. S., . . . Baker, T. B. (2009). An fMRI investigation of the impact of withdrawal on regional brain activity during nicotine anticipation. *Psychophysiology, 46,* 681–693. (14)

Glykys, J., Peng, Z., Chandra, D., Homanics, G. E., Houser, C. R., & Mody, I. (2007). A new naturally occurring GABAA receptor subunit partnership with high sensitivity to ethanol. *Nature Neuroscience, 10,* 40–48. (11)

Goard, M., & Dan, Y. (2009). Basal forebrain activation enhances cortical coding of natural scenes. *Nature Neuroscience, 12,* 1444–1449. (8)

Goate, A., Chartier-Harlin, M. C., Mullan, M., Brown, J., Crawford, F., Fidani, L., . . . Owen, M. (1991). Segregation of a missense mutation in the amyloid precursor protein gene with familial Alzheimer's disease. *Nature, 349,* 704–706. (12)

Godfrey, K. M., Lillycrop, K. A., Burdge, G. C., Gluckman, P. D., & Hanson, M. A. (2007). Epigenetic mechanisms and the mismatch concept of the developmental origins of health and disease. *Pediatric Research, 61 (5), Part 2,* 5R–10R. (4)

Gogos, J. A., Osborne, J., Nemes, A., Mendelsohn, M., & Axel, R. (2000). Genetic ablation and restoration of the olfactory topographic map. *Cell, 103,* 609–620. (4)

Gold, B. T., Kim, C., Johnson, N. F., Kryscio, R. J., & Smith, C. D. (2013). Lifelong bilingualism maintains neural efficiency for cognitive control in aging. *Journal of Neuroscience, 33,* 387–396. (13)

Gold, R. M. (1973). Hypothalamic obesity: The myth of the ventromedial hypothalamus. *Science, 182,* 488–490. (9)

Goldberg, T. E., Weinberger, D. R., Berman, K. F., Pliskin, N. H., & Podd, M. H. (1987). Further evidence for dementia of the prefrontal type in schizophrenia? *Archives of General Psychiatry, 44,* 1008–1014. (14)

Goldin-Meadow, S., McNeill, D., & Singleton, J. (1996). Silence is liberating: Removing the handcuffs on grammatical expression in the manual modality. *Psychological Review, 103,* 34–55. (13)

Goldin-Meadow, S., & Mylander, C. (1998). Spontaneous sign systems created by deaf children in two cultures. *Nature, 391,* 279–281. (13)

Goldman, L. S. (1999). Medical illness in patients with schizophrenia. *Journal of Clinical Psychiatry, 60*(Suppl 21), 10–15. (14)

Goldman, P. S. (1971). Functional development of the prefrontal cortex in early life and the problem of neuronal plasticity. *Experimental Neurology, 32,* 366–387. (14)

Goldman, P. S. (1976). The role of experience in recovery of function following orbital prefrontal lesions in infant monkeys. *Neuropsychologia, 14,* 401–412. (14)

Goldstein, A. (1980). Thrills in response to music and other stimuli. *Physiological Psychology, 8,* 126–129. (6)

Goldstein, J. M., Seidman, L. J., Horton, N. J., Makris, N., Kennedy, D. N., Caviness, V. S., Jr., . . . Tsuang, M. T. (2001). Normal sexual dimorphism of the adult human brain assessed by in vivo magnetic resonance imaging. *Cerebral Cortex, 11,* 490–497. (10)

Goldstein, R. Z., & Volkow, N. D. (2011). Dysfunction of the prefrontal cortex in addiction: Neuroimaging findings and clinical implications. *Nature Reviews Neuroscience, 12,* 652–669. (14)

Golestani, N., Molko, N., Dehaene, S., LeBihan, D., & Pallier, C. (2007). Brain structure predicts the learning of foreign speech sounds. *Cerebral Cortex, 17,* 575–582. (4)

Golestani, N., Price, C. J., & Scott, S. K. (2011). Born with an ear for dialects? Structural plasticity in the expert phonetician brain. *Journal of Neuroscience, 31,* 4213–4220. (4)

Goller, A. I., Richards, K., Novak, S., & Ward, J. (2013). Mirror-touch synaesthesia in the phantom limbs of amputees. *Cortex, 49,* 243–251. (4)

Golombok, S., Rust, J., Zervoulis, K., Golding, J., & Hines, M. (2012). Continuity in sex-typed behavior from preschool to adolescence: A longitudinal population study of boys and girls aged 3-13 year. *Archives of Sexual Behavior, 41,* 591–597. (10)

Golumbic, E. Z., Cogan, G. B., Schroeder, C. E., & Poeppel, D. (2013). Visual input enhances selective speech envelope tracking in auditory cortex at a "cocktail party." *Journal of Neuroscience, 33,* 1417–1426. (6)

Gong, G., He, Y., & Evans, A. C. (2011). Brain connectivity: Gender makes a difference. *Neuroscientist, 17,* 575–591. (3)

Gonzalez Andino, S. L., de Peralta Menendez, R. G., Khateb, A., Landis, T., & Pegna, A. J. (2009). Electrophysiological correlates of affective blindsight. *NeuroImage, 44,* 581–589. (5)

González-Maeso, J., Ang, R. L., Yuen, T., Chan, P., Weisstaub, N. V., López-Giménez, J. F., . . . Sealfon, S. C. (2008). Identification of a serotonin/glutamate receptor complex implicated in psychosis. *Nature, 452,* 93–97. (14)

Goodale, M. A. (1996). Visuomotor modules in the vertebrate brain. *Canadian Journal of Physiology and Pharmacology, 74,* 390–400. (7)

Goodale, M. A., Milner, A. D., Jakobson, L. S., & Carey, D. P. (1991). A neurological dissociation between perceiving objects and grasping them. *Nature, 349,* 154–156. (7)

Goodrich-Hunsaker, N. J., & Hopkins, R. O. (2010). Spatial memory deficits in a virtual radial arm maze in amnesic participants with hippocampal damage. *Behavioral Neuroscience, 124,* 405–413. (12)

Gooley, J. J., Rajaratnam, S. M. W., Brainard, G. C., Kronauer, R. E., Czeisler, C. A., & Lockley, S. W. (2010). Spectral responses of the human circadian system depend on the irradiance and duration of exposure to light. *Science Translational Medicine, 2,* 31ra33. (8)

Gopnik, M., & Crago, M. B. (1991). Familial aggregation of a developmental language disorder. *Cognition, 39,* 1–50. (13)

Gordon, I., Zagoory-Sharon, O., Leckman, J. F., & Feldman, R. (2010). Prolactin, oxytocin, and the development of paternal behavior across the first six months of fatherhood. *Hormones and Behavior, 58,* 513–518. (10)

Gorski, R. A. (1980). Sexual differentiation of the brain. In D. T. Krieger & J. C. Hughes (Eds.), *Neuroendocrinology* (pp. 215–222). Sunderland, MA: Sinauer. (10)

Gorski, R. A. (1985). The 13th J. A. F. Stevenson memorial lecture. Sexual differentiation of the brain: Possible mechanisms and implications. *Canadian Journal of Physiology and Pharmacology, 63,* 577–594. (10)

Gorski, R. A., & Allen, L. S. (1992). Sexual orientation and the size of the anterior commissure in the human brain. *Proceedings of the National Academy of Sciences, USA, 89,* 7199–7202. (10)

Gottesman, I. I. (1991). *Schizophrenia genesis.* New York: Freeman. (14)

Gougoux, F., Belin, P., Voss, P., Lepore, F., Lassonde, M., & Zatorre, R. J. (2009). Voice perception in blind persons: A functional magnetic resonance imaging study. *Neuropsychologia, 47,* 2967–2974. (4)

Gradisar, M., Gardner, G., & Dohnt, H. (2011). Recent worldwide sleep patterns and problems during adolescence: A review and meta-analysis of age, region, and sleep. *Sleep Medicine, 12,* 110–118. (8)

Granger, N., Blamires, H., Franklin, R. J. M., & Jeffery, N. D. (2012). Autologous olfactory mucosal cell transplants in clinical spinal cord injury: A randomized double-blinded trial in a canine translational model. *Brain, 135,* 3227–3237. (4)

Gray, C. M., König, P., Engel, A. K., & Singer, W. (1989). Oscillatory responses in cat visual cortex exhibit inter-columnar synchronization which reflects global stimulus properties. *Nature, 338,* 334–337. (13)

Gray, J. A. (1970). The psychophysiological basis of introversion–extraversion. *Behavioural Research Therapy, 8,* 249–266. (11)

Graziadei, P. P. C., & deHan, R. S. (1973). Neuronal regeneration in frog olfactory system. *Journal of Cell Biology, 59,* 525–530. (4)

Graziano, M. S. A., Taylor, C. S. R., & Moore, T. (2002). Complex movements evoked by microstimulation of precentral cortex. *Neuron, 34,* 841–851. (3, 7)

Graziottin, A., Koochaki, P. E., Rodenberg, C. A., & Dennerstein, L. (2009). The prevalence of hypoactive sexual desire disorder in surgically menopausal women: An epidemiological study of women in four European countries. *Journal of Sexual Medicine, 6,* 2143–2153. (10)

Greene, J. D., Sommerville, R. B., Nystrom, L. E., Darley, J. M., & Cohen, J. D. (2001). An fMRI investigation of emotional engagement in moral judgment. *Science, 293,* 2105–2108. (11)

Greengard, P. (2001). The neurobiology of slow synaptic transmission. *Science, 294,* 1024–1030. (2)

Greenough, W. T. (1975). Experiential modification of the developing brain. *American Scientist, 63,* 37–46. (4)

Greenwood, T. A., Lazzeroni, L. C., Murray, S. S., Cadenhead, K. S., Calkins, M. E., Dobie, D. J., . . . Braff, D. L. (2011). Analysis of 94 candidate genes and 12 endophenotypes for schizophrenia from the Consortium on the Genetics of Schizophrenia. *American Journal of Psychiatry, 168,* 930–946. (14)

Greer, J., Riby, D. M., Hamiliton, C., & Riby, L. M. (2013). Attentional lapse and inhibition control in adults with Williams syndrome. *Research in Developmental Disabilities, 34,* 4170–4177. (13)

Gregerson, P. K., Kowalsky, E., Lee, A., Baron-Cohen, S., Fisher, S. E., Asher, J. E., . . . Li, W. T. (2013). Absolute pitch exhibits phenotypic and genetic overlap with synesthesia. *Human Molecular Genetics, 22,* 2097–2104. (6)

Griffin, D. R., Webster, F. A., & Michael, C. R. (1960). The echolocation of flying insects by bats. *Animal Behaviour, 8,* 141–154. (6)

Griffiths, T. D., Uppenkamp, S., Johnsrude, I., Josephs, O., & Patterson, R. D. (2001). Encoding of the temporal regularity of sound in the human brainstem. *Nature Neuroscience, 4,* 633–637. (6)

Grillon, C., Morgan, C. A., III, Davis, M., & Southwick, S. M. (1998). Effect of darkness on acoustic startle in Vietnam veterans with PTSD. *American Journal of Psychiatry, 155,* 812–817. (11)

Gritton, H. J., Sutton, B. C., Martinez, V., Sarter, M., & Lee, T. M. (2009). Interactions between cognition and circadian rhythms: Attentional demands modify circadian entrainment. *Behavioral Neuroscience, 123,* 937–948. (8)

Groeger, J. A., Lo, J. C. Y., Burns, C. G., & Dijk, D.-J. (2011). Effects of sleep inertia after daytime naps vary with executive load and time of day. *Behavioral Neuroscience, 125,* 252–260. (8)

Gross, C. G. (1999). The fire that comes from the eye. *The Neuroscientist, 5,* 58–64. (5)

Gross, C. G., & Graziano, M. S. A. (1995). Multiple representations of space in the brain. *The Neuroscientist, 1,* 43–50. (3)

Gross, C. T., & Canteras, N. S. (2012). The many paths to fear. *Nature Reviews Neuroscience, 13,* 651–658. (11)

Grosshans, D. R., Clayton, D. A., Coultrap, S. J., & Browning, M. D. (2002). LTP leads to rapid surface expression of NMDA but not AMPA receptors in adult rat CA1. *Nature Neuroscience, 5,* 27–33. (12)

Grossman, S. P., Dacey, D., Halaris, A. E., Collier, T., & Routtenberg, A. (1978). Aphagia and adipsia after preferential destruction of nerve cell bodies in hypothalamus. *Science, 202,* 537–539. (9)

Grueter, M., Grueter, T., Bell, V., Horst, J., Laskowki, W., Sperling, K., Kennerknecht, I. (2007). Hereditary prosopagnosia: The first case series. *Cortex, 43,* 734–749. (5)

Grutzendler, J., Kasthuri, N., & Gan, W.-B. (2002). Long-term dendritic spine stability in the adult cortex. *Nature, 420,* 812–816. (4)

Guastella, A. J., Einfeld, S. L., Gray, K. M., Rinehart, N. J., Tonge, B. J., Lambert, T. J., & Hickie, I. B. (2010). Intranasal oxytocin improves emotion recognition for youth with autism spectrum disorders. *Biological Psychology, 67,* 692–694. (13)

Gubernick, D. J., & Alberts, J. R. (1983). Maternal licking of young: Resource exchange and proximate controls. *Physiology & Behavior, 31,* 593–601. (10)

Gueguen, N. (2012). Gait and menstrual cycle: Ovulating women use sexier gaits and walk slowly ahead of men. *Gait & Posture, 35,* 621–624. (10)

Guggisberg, A. G., & Mottaz, A. (2013). Timing and awareness of movement decisions: Does consciousness really come too late? *Frontiers in Human Neuroscience, 7,* Article 385. (7)

Guidotti, A., Ferrero, P., Fujimoto, M., Santi, R. M., & Costa, E. (1986). Studies on endogenous ligands (endocoids) for the benzodiazepine/beta carboline binding sites. *Advances in Biochemical Pharmacology, 41,* 137–148. (11)

Guillery, R. W., Feig, S. L., & Lozsádi, D. A. (1998). Paying attention to the thalamic reticular nucleus. *Trends in Neurosciences, 21,* 28–32. (9)

Guillery, R. W., Feig, S. L., & van Lieshout, D. P. (2001). Connections of higher order visual relays in the thalamus: A study of corticothalamic pathways in cats. *Journal of Comparative Neurology, 438,* 66–85. (5)

Guiso, L., Monte, F., Sapienza, P., & Zingales, L. (2008). Culture, gender, and math. *Science, 320,* 1164–1165. (3)

Güler, A. D., Ecker, J. L., Lall, G. S., Haq, S., Altimus, C. M., Liao, H.-W., . . . Hattar, S. (2008). Melanopsin cells are the principal conduits for rod-cone input to non-image-forming vision. *Nature, 453,* 102–105. (8)

Gunn, S. R., & Gunn, W. S. (2007). Are we in the dark about sleepwalking's dangers? In C. A. Read (Ed.), *Cerebrum 2007: Emerging ideas in brain science* (pp. 71–84). New York: Dana Press. (8)

Guo, J. U., Ma, D. K., Mo, H., Ball, M. P., Jang, M.-H., . . . Song, H. (2011) Neuronal activity modifies the DNA methylation landscape in the adult brain. *Nature Neuroscience, 14,* 1345–1351. (12)

Guo, S.-W., & Reed, D. R. (2001). The genetics of phenylthiocarbamide perception. *Annals of Human Biology, 28,* 111–142. (6)

Gupta, A. S., van der Meer, M. A. A., Touretzky, D. S., & Redish, A. D. (2010). Hippocampal replay is not a simple function of experience. *Neuron, 65,* 695–705. (8)

Gur, R. E., & Chin, S. (1999). Laterality in functional brain imaging studies of schizophrenia. *Schizophrenia Bulletin, 25,* 141–156. (14)

Gur, R. E., Cowell, P. E., Latshaw, A., Turetsky, B. I., Grossman, R. I., Arnold, S. E., . . . Gur, R. C. (2000). Reduced dorsal and orbital prefrontal gray matter volumes in schizophrenia. *Archives of General Psychiatry, 57,* 761–768. (14)

Gusella, J. F., & MacDonald, M. E. (2000). Molecular genetics: Unmasking polyglutamine triggers in neurodegenerative disease. *Nature Reviews Neuroscience, 1,* 109–115. (7)

Gustafsson, B., & Wigström, H. (1990). Basic features of long-term potentiation in the hippocampus. *Seminars in the Neurosciences, 2,* 321–333. (12)

Guterstam, A., Petkova, V. I., & Ehrsson, H. H. (2011). The illusion of owning a third arm. *PLoS One, 6,* e17208. (3)

Gutschalk, A., Patterson, R. D., Scherg, M., Uppenkamp, S., & Rupp, A. (2004). Temporal dynamics of pitch in human auditory cortex. *NeuroImage, 22,* 755–766. (6)

Gvilia, I., Turner, A., McGinty, D., & Szymusiak, R. (2006). Preoptic area neurons and the homeostatic regulation of rapid eye movement sleep. *Journal of Neuroscience, 26,* 3037–3044. (8)

Gwinner, E. (1986). Circannual rhythms in the control of avian rhythms. *Advances in the Study of Behavior, 16,* 191–228. (8)

Haase, C. M., Saslow, L. R., Bloch, L., Saturn, S. R., Casey, J. J., Seider, B. H., . . . Levenson, R. W. (2013). The 5-HTTLPR polymorphism in the serotonin transporter gene moderates the association between emotional behavior and changes in marital satisfaction over time. *Emotion, 13,* 1068–1079. (11)

Hadjikhani, N., Liu, A. K., Dale, A. M., Cavanagh, P., & Tootell, R. B. H. (1998). Retinotopy and color sensitivity in human visual cortical area V8. *Nature Neuroscience, 1,* 235–241. (5)

Hagenauer, M. H., & Lee, T. M. (2012). The neuroendocrine control of the circadian system: Adolescent chronotype. *Frontiers in Neuroendocrinology, 33,* 211–229. (8)

Hagenbuch, B., Gao, B., & Meier, P. J. (2002). Transport of xenobiotics across the blood-brain barrier. *News in Physiological Sciences, 17,* 231–234. (1)

Haggarty, J. M., Cernovsky, Z., Husni, M., Minor, K., Kermean, P., & Merskey, H. (2002). Seasonal affective disorder in an Arctic community. *Acta Psychiatrica Scandinavica, 105,* 378–384. (14)

Hägglund, M., Dougherty, K. J., Borgius, L., Itohara, S., Iwasato, T., & Kiehn, O. (2013). Optogenetic dissection reveals multiple rhythmogenic modules underlying locomotion. *Proceedings of the National Academy of Sciences, 110,* 11589–11594. (7)

Hahn, B., Robinson, B. M., Kaiser, S. T., Matveeva, T. M., Harvey, A. N., Luck, S. J., & Gold, J. M. (2012). Kraepelin and Bleuler had it right: People with schizophrenia have deficits sustaining attention over time. *Journal of Abnormal Psychology, 121,* 641–648. (14)

Haider, B., Häusser, M., & Carandini, M. (2013). Inhibition dominates sensory responses in the awake cortex. *Nature, 493,* 97–100. (5)

Haidt, J. (2001). The emotional dog and its rational tail: A social intuitionist approach to moral judgment. *Psychological Review, 108,* 814–834. (11)

Haier, R. J., Colom, R., Schroeder, D. H., Condon, C. A., Tang, C., Eaves, E., & Head, K. (2009). Gray matter and intelligence factors: Is there a neuro-*g*? *Intelligence, 37,* 136–144. (3)

Haier, R. J., Jung, R. E., Yeo, R. A., Head, K., & Alkire, M. T. (2004). Structural brain variation and general intelligence. *NeuroImage, 23,* 425–433. (3)

Haimov, I., & Arendt, J. (1999). The prevention and treatment of jet lag. *Sleep Medicine Reviews, 3,* 229–240. (8)

Haimov, I., & Lavie, P. (1996). Melatonin—A soporific hormone. *Current Directions in Psychological Science, 5,* 106–111. (8)

Hains, B. C., Everhart, A. W., Fullwood, S. D., & Hulsebosch, C. E. (2002). Changes in serotonin, serotonin transporter expression and serotonin denervation supersensitivity: Involvement in chronic central pain after spinal hemisection in the rat. *Experimental Neurology, 175,* 347–362. (4)

Hakuta, K., Bialystok, E., & Wiley, E. (2003). Critical evidence: A test of the critical-period hypothesis for second-language acquisition. *Psychological Science, 14,* 31–38. (13)

Halaas, J. L, Gajiwala, K. S., Maffei, M., Cohen, S. L., Chait, B. T., Rabinowitz, D., . . . Friedman, J. M. (1995). Weight-reducing effects of the plasma protein encoded by the obese gene. *Science, 269,* 543–546. (9)

Halaschek-Wiener, J., Amirabbasi-Beik, M., Monfared, N., Pieczyk, M., Sailer, C., Kollar, A., . . . Brooks-Wilson, A. R. (2009). Genetic variation in healthy oldest-old. *PLoS ONE, 4,* e6641. (4)

Haley, J. (1959). An interactional description of schizophrenia. *Psychiatry, 22,* 321–332. (14)

Hall, F. S., Drgonova, J., Jain, S., & Uhl, G. R. (2013). Implications of genome wide association studies for addiction: Are our *a priori* assumptions all wrong? *Pharmacology & Therapeutics, 140,* 267–279. (14)

Hallem, E. A., Fox, A. N., Zwiebel, L. J., & Carlson, J. R. (2004). Mosquito receptor for human-sweat odorant. *Nature, 427,* 212–213. (6)

Hallmayer, J., Faraco, J., Lin, L., Hesselson, S., Winkelmann, J., Kawashima, M., . . . Mignot, E.

(2009). Narcolepsy is strongly associated with the T-cell receptor alpha locus. *Nature Genetics, 41*, 708–711. (8)

Halpern, S. D., Andrews, T. J., & Purves, D. (1999). Interindividual variation in human visual performance. *Journal of Cognitive Neuroscience, 11*, 521–534. (5)

Hamann, K., Warneken, F., Greenberg, J. R., & Tomasello, M. (2011). Collaboration encourages equal sharing in children but not in chimpanzees. *Nature, 476*, 328–331. (4)

Hamann, S. B., & Squire, L. R. (1995). On the acquisition of new declarative knowledge in amnesia. *Behavioral Neuroscience, 109*, 1027–1044. (12)

Hamer, D. H., Hu, S., Magnuson, V. L., Hu, N., & Pattatucci, A. M. L. (1993). A linkage between DNA markers on the X chromosome and male sexual orientation. *Science, 261*, 321–327. (10)

Hamilton, W. D. (1964). The genetical evolution of social behavior (I and II). *Journal of Theoretical Biology, 7*, 1–16, 17–52. (4)

Han, J.-H., Kushner, S. A., Yiu, A. P., Cole, C. J., Matynia, A., Brown, R. A., . . . Josselyn, S. A. (2007). Neuronal competition and selection during memory formation. *Science, 316*, 457–460. (12)

Han, S., Tai, C., Westenbroek, R. E., Yu, F. H., Cheah, C. S., Potter, G. B., . . . Catterall, W. A. (2012). Autistic-like behaviour in *Scn1a+/-* mice and rescue by enhanced GABA-mediated neurotransmission. *Nature, 489*, 385–390. (14)

Hanada, R., Leibbrandt, A., Hanada, T., Kitaoka, S., Furuyashiki, T., Fujihara, H., . . . Penninger, J. M. (2009). Central control of fever and female body temperature by RANKL/RANK. *Nature, 462*, 515–509. (9)

Hanaway, J., Woolsey, T. A., Gado, M. H., & Roberts, M. P., Jr. (1998). *The brain atlas*. Bethesda, MD: Fitzgerald Science Press. (11)

Hannibal, J., Hindersson, P., Knudsen, S. M., Georg, B., & Fahrenkrug, J. (2001). The photopigment melanopsin is exclusively present in pituitary adenylate cyclase-activating polypeptide-containing retinal ganglion cells of the retinohypothalamic tract. *Journal of Neuroscience, 21*, RC191: 1–7. (8)

Haqq, C. M., & Donahoe, P. K. (1998). Regulation of sexual dimorphism in mammals. *Physiological Reviews, 78*, 1–33. (10)

Hara, J., Beuckmann, C. T., Nambu, T., Willie, J. T., Chemelli, R. M., Sinton, C. M., . . . Sakurai, T. (2001). Genetic ablation of orexin neurons in mice results in narcolepsy, hypophagia, and obesity. *Neuron, 30*, 345–354. (8)

Hargreaves, R. (2007). New migraine and pain research. *Headache, 47*(Suppl 1), S26–S43. (3)

Hari, R. (1994). Human cortical functions revealed by magnetoencephalography. *Progress in Brain Research, 100*, 163–168. (3)

Harley, B., & Wang, W. (1997). The critical period hypothesis: Where are we now? In A. M. B. deGroot & J. F. Knoll (Eds.), *Tutorials in bilingualism* (pp. 19–51). Mahwah, NJ: Erlbaum. (13)

Harmon-Jones, E., & Gable, P. A. (2009). Neural activity underlying the effect of approach-motivated positive affect on narrowed attention. *Psychological Science, 20*, 406–49. (9)

Harmon-Jones, E., & Peterson, C. K. (2009). Supine body position reduces neural response to anger evocation. *Psychological Science, 20*, 1209–1210. (11)

Hárosi, F. I., & Hashimoto, Y. (1983). Ultraviolet visual pigment in a vertebrate: A tetrachromatic cone system in the dace. *Science, 222*, 1021–1023. (5)

Harper, L. V. (2005). Epigenetic inheritance and the intergenerational transfer of experience. *Psychological Bulletin, 131*, 340–360. (4)

Harris, C. H. (2002). Sexual and romantic jealousy in heterosexual and homosexual adults. *Psychological Science, 13*, 7–12. (10)

Harris, C. R. (1999, July/August). The mystery of ticklish laughter. *American Scientist, 87*(4), 344–351. (6)

Harris, K. M., & Stevens, J. K. (1989). Dendritic spines of CA1 pyramidal cells in the rat hippocampus: Serial electron microscopy with reference to their biophysical characteristics. *Journal of Neuroscience, 9*, 2982–2997. (1)

Harrison, G. H. (2008, January). How chickadees weather winter. *National Wildlife, 46*(1), 14–15. (9)

Hart, B. L. (Ed.). (1976). *Experimental psychobiology*. San Francisco: Freeman. (9)

Hartline, H. K. (1949). Inhibition of activity of visual receptors by illuminating nearby retinal areas in the limulus eye. *Federation Proceedings, 8*, 69. (5)

Harvey, A. G., & Bryant, R. A. (2002). Acute stress disorder: A synthesis and critique. *Psychological Bulletin, 128*, 886–902. (11)

Harvey, A. G., Talbot, L. S., & Gershon, A. (2009). Sleep disturbance in bipolar disorder across the lifespan. *Clinical Psychology: Science & Practice, 16*, 256–277. (14)

Hashikawa, K., Naka, M., Nakayama, D., Matsumoto, N., Neve, R., & Matsuki, N. (2013). Blockade of stimulus convergence in amygdala neurons disrupts taste associative learning. *Journal of Neuroscience, 33*, 4958–4963. (12)

Hasler, B. P., & Clark, D. B. (2013). Circadian misalignment, reward-related brain function, and adolescent alcohol involvement. *Alcoholism: Clinical and Experimental Research, 37*, 558–565. (8)

Hassabis, D., Kumaran, D., Vann, S. D., & Maguire, E. A. (2007). Patients with hippocampal amnesia cannot imagine new experiences. *Proceedings of the National Academy of Sciences, USA, 104*, 1726–1731. (12)

Hassan, B., & Rahman, Q. (2007). Selective sexual orientation-related differences in object location memory. *Behavioral Neuroscience, 121*, 625–633. (10)

Hassani, O. K., Lee, M. G., Henny, P., & Jones, B. E. (2009). Discharge profiles of identified GABAergic in comparison to cholinergic and putative glutamatergic basal forebrain neurons across the sleep-wake cycle. *Journal of Neuroscience, 29*, 11828–11840. (8)

Hassett, J. M., Siebert, E. R., & Wallen, K. (2008). Sex differences in rhesus monkey toy preferences parallel those of children. *Hormones and Behavior, 54*, 359–364. (10)

Hassin, R. R. (2013). Yes, it can: On the functional abilities of the human unconscious. *Perspectives on Psychological Science, 8*, 195–207. (13)

Haueisen, J., & Knösche, T. R. (2001). Involuntary motor activity in pianists evoked by music perception. *Journal of Cognitive Neuroscience, 13*, 786–792. (7)

Havlicek, J., & Roberts, S. C. (2009). MHC-correlated mate choice in humans: A review. *Psychoneuroendocrinology, 34*, 497–512. (6)

Hayashi-Takagi, A., Takaki, M., Graziane, N., Seshadri, S., Murdoch, H., Dunlop, A. J., . . . Sawa, A. (2010). Disrupted-in-schizophrenia 1(*DISC-1*) regulates spines of the glutamate synapse via Rac1. *Nature Neuroscience, 13*, 327–332. (14)

Haydon, P. G. (2001). Glia: Listening and talking to the synapse. *Nature Reviews Neuroscience, 2*, 185 193. (1)

Hayes, J. E., Bartoshuk, L. M., Kidd, J. R., & Duffy, V. B. (2008). Supertasting and PROP bitterness depends on more than the *TAS2R38* gene. *Chemical Senses, 33*, 255–265. (6)

He, S. M., Yang, A. K., Li, X. T., Du, Y. M., & Zhou, S. F. (2010). Effects of herbal products on the metabolism and transport of anticancer agents. *Expert Opinion on Drug Metabolism & Toxicity, 6*, 1195–1213. (14)

He, W., Yasumatsu, K., Varadarajan, V., Yamada, A., Lem, J., Ninomiya, Y., . . . Damak, S. (2004). Umami taste receptors are mediated by alpha-transducin and alpha-gustducin. *Journal of Neuroscience, 24*, 7674–7680. (6)

He, Y., Johnson, M. K., Dovidio, J. F., & McCarthy, G. (2009). The relation between race-related implicit associations and scalp-recorded neural activity evoked by faces from different races. *Social Neuroscience, 4*, 426–442. (13)

Headley, D. B., & Weinberger, N. M. (2013). Fear conditioning enhances gamma oscillations and their entrainment of neurons representing the conditioned stimulus. *Journal of Neuroscience, 33*, 5705–5717. (11)

Hebb, D. O. (1949). *Organization of behavior*. New York: Wiley. (12)

Heuer, E., & Bachevalier, J. (2011). Neonatal hippocampal lesions in rhesus macaques alter the monitoring, but not maintenance, of information in working memory. *Behavioral Neuroscience, 125*, 859–870. (12)

Hegdé, J., & Van Essen, D. C. (2000). Selectivity for complex shapes in primate visual area V2. *Journal of Neuroscience, 20*, RC61: 1–6. (5)

Heilig, M., Goldman, D., Berrettini, W., & O'Brien, C. P. (2011). Pharmacogenetic approaches to the treatment of alcohol addiction. *Nature Reviews Neuroscience, 12*, 670–684. (14)

Heims, H. C., Critchley, H. D., Dolan, R., Mathias, C. J., & Cipolotti, L. (2004). Social and motivational functioning is not critically dependent on feedback of autonomic responses: Neuropsychological evidence from patients with pure autonomic failure. *Neuropsychologia, 42*, 1979–1988. (11)

Held, R., Ostrovsky, Y., deGelder, B., Gandhi, T., Ganesh, S., Mathur, U., & Sinha, P. (2011). The newly sighted fail to match seen with felt. *Nature Neuroscience, 14*, 551–553. (5)

Hellal, F., Hurtado, A., Ruschel, J., Flynn, K. C., Laskowski, C. J., Umlauf, M., . . . Bradke, F. (2011). Microtubule stabilization reduces scarring and causes axon regeneration after spinal cord injury. *Science, 331*, 928–931. (4)

Heller, W., & Levy, J. (1981). Perception and expression of emotion in right-handers and left-handers. *Neuropsychologia, 19,* 263–272. (13)

Henderson, J. M., & Hollingworth, A. (2003). Global transsaccadic change blindness during scene perception. *Psychological Science, 14,* 493–497. (13)

Henderson, L. A., Peck, C. C., Petersen, E. T., Rae, C. D., Youssef, A. M., Reeves, J. M., . . . Gustin, S. M. (2013). *Journal of Neuroscience, 33,* 7574–7582. (6)

Hendry, S. H. C., & Reid, R. C. (2000). The koniocellular pathway in primate vision. *Annual Review of Neuroscience, 23,* 127–153. (5)

Hennig, R., & Lømo, T. (1985). Firing patterns of motor units in normal rats. *Nature, 314,* 164–166. (7)

Herb, B. R., Wolschin, F., Hansen, K. D., Aryee, M. J., Langmead, B., Irizarry, R., . . . Feinberg, A. P. (2012). Reversible switching between epigenetic states in honeybee behavioral subcastes. *Nature Neuroscience, 15,* 1371–1373. (4)

Herculano-Houzel, S. (2011). Not all brains are made the same: New views on brain scaling in evolution. *Brain, Behavior and Evolution, 78,* 22–36. (3)

Herdener, M., Esposito, F., di Salle, F., Boller, C., Hilti, C. C., Habermeyer, B., . . . Cattapan-Ludewig, K. (2010). Musical training induces functional plasticity in human hippocampus. *Journal of Neuroscience, 30,* 1377–1384. (4)

Heresco-Levy, U., & Javitt, D. C. (2004). Comparative effects of glycine and D-cycloserine on persistent negative symptoms in schizophrenia: A retrospective analysis. *Schizophrenia Research, 66,* 89–96. (14)

Heresco-Levy, U., Javitt, D. C., Ermilov, M., Mordel, C., Silipo, G., & Lichtenstein, M. (1999). Efficacy of high-dose glycine in the treatment of enduring negative symptoms of schizophrenia. *Archives of General Psychiatry, 56,* 29–36. (14)

Herrero, S. (1985). *Bear attacks: Their causes and avoidance.* Piscataway, NJ: Winchester. (6)

Hertzog, C., Kramer, A. F., Wilson, R. S., & Lindenberger, U. (2009). Enrichment effects on adult cognitive development. *Psychological Science in the Public Interest, 9,* 1–65. (4)

Hervé, P. Y., Zago, L., Petit, L., Mazoyer, B., & Tzourio-Mazoyer, N. (2013). Revisiting human hemispheric specialization with neuroimaging. *Trends in Cognitive Sciences, 17,* 69–80. (13)

Herz, R. S., McCall, C., & Cahill, L. (1999). Hemispheric lateralization in the processing of odor pleasantness versus odor names. *Chemical Senses, 24,* 691–695. (13)

Hess, B. J. M. (2001). Vestibular signals in self-orientation and eye movement control. *News in Physiological Sciences, 16,* 234–238. (6)

Hesse, M. D., Thiel, C. M., Stephan, K. E., & Fink, G. R. (2006). The left parietal cortex and motor intention: An event-related functional magnetic resonance imaging study. *Neuroscience, 140,* 1209–1221. (7)

Hess, M. E., Hess, S., Meyer, K. D., Verhagen, L.A. W., Koch, L., Brönneke, H. S., . . . Brüning, J. C. (2013). The fat mass and obesity associated gene (*Fto*) regulates activity of the dopaminergic midbrain circuitry. *Nature Neuroscience, 16,* 1042–1048. (14)

Hesselmann, G., Hebart, M., & Malach, R. (2011). Differential BOLD activity associated with subjective and objective reports during "blindsight" in normal observers. *Journal of Neuroscience, 31,* 12936–12944. (5)

Hettema, J. M., Neale, M. C., & Kendler, K. S. (2001). A review and meta-analysis of the genetic epidemiology of anxiety disorders. *American Journal of Psychiatry, 158,* 1568–1578. (11)

Heyes, C. (2010). Where do mirror neurons come from? *Neuroscience and Biobehavioral Reviews, 34,* 575–583. (7)

Higgs, S., Williamson, A. C., Rotshtein, P., & Humphreys, G. W. (2008). Sensory-specific satiety is intake in amnesics who eat multiple meals. *Psychological Science, 19,* 623–628. (12)

Higley, J. D., Mehlman, P. T., Higley, S. B., Fernald, B., Vickers, J., Lindell, S. G., . . . Linnoila, M. (1996). Excessive mortality in young free-ranging male nonhuman primates with low cerebrospinal fluid 5-hydroxyindoleacetic acid concentrations. *Archives of General Psychiatry, 53,* 537–543. (11)

Hillis, A. E., Kleinman, J. T., Newhart, M., Heidler-Gary, J., Gottesman, R., Barker, P. B., . . . Chaudhry, P. (2006). Restoring cerebral blood flow reveals neural regions critical for naming. *Journal of Neuroscience, 26,* 8069–8073. (13)

Hillix, W. A., Rumbaugh, D. M., & Savage-Rumbaugh, E. S. (2012). The emergence of reason, intelligence, and language in humans and animals. In L. L'Abate (Ed.), *Paradigms in Theory Construction* (pp. 397–420). New York: Springer. (13)

Himmelbach, M., Boehme, R., & Karnath, H.-O. (2012). 20 years later: A second look on DF's motor behavior. *Neuropsychologia, 50,* 139–144. (5)

Hines, D. J., Schmitt, L. I., Hines, R. M., Moss, S. J., & Haydon, P. G. (2013). Antidepressant effects of sleep deprivation require astrocyte-dependent adenosine mediated signaling. *Translational Psychiatry, 3,* e212. (14)

Hines, M., Golombok, S., Rust, J., Johnston, K. J., Golding, J., & the Avon Longitudinal Study of Parents and Children Study Team. (2002). Testosterone during pregnancy and gender role behavior of preschool children: A longitudinal, population study. *Child Development, 73,* 1678–1687. (10)

Hippisley-Cox, J., Vinogradova, Y., Coupland, C., & Parker, C. (2007). Risk of malignancy in patients with schizophrenia or bipolar disorder. *Archives of General Psychiatry, 64,* 1368–1376. (14)

Hitchcock, J. M., & Davis, M. (1991). Efferent pathway of the amygdala involved in conditioned fear as measured with the fear-potentiated startle paradigm. *Behavioral Neuroscience, 105,* 826–842. (11)

Hiyama, T. Y., Watanabe, E., Okado, H., & Noda, M. (2004). The subfornical organ is the primary locus of sodium-level sensing by Nax sodium channels for the control of salt-intake behavior. *Journal of Neuroscience, 24,* 9276–9281. (9)

Hobson, J. A. (1989). *Sleep.* New York: Scientific American Library. (14)

Hobson, J. A. (2009). REM sleep and dreaming: Towards a theory of protoconsciousness. *Nature Reviews Neuroscience, 10,* 803–813. (8)

Hobson, J. A., & McCarley, R. W. (1977). The brain as a dream state generator: An activation-synthesis hypothesis of the dream process. *American Journal of Psychiatry, 134,* 1335–1348. (8)

Hobson, J. A., Pace-Schott, E. F., & Stickgold, R. (2000). Dreaming and the brain: Toward a cognitive neuroscience of conscious states. *Behavioral and Brain Sciences, 23,* 793–1121. (8)

Hochberg, L. R., Bacher, D., Jarosiewicz, B., Masse, N. Y., Simeral, J. D., Vogel, J., . . . Donoghue, J. P. (2012). Reach and grasp by people with tetraplegia using a neurally controlled robotic arm. *Nature, 485,* 372–375. (7)

Hoebel, B. G., & Hernandez, L. (1993). Basic neural mechanisms of feeding and weight regulation. In A. J. Stunkard & T. A. Wadden (Eds.), *Obesity: Theory and therapy* (2nd ed., pp. 43–62). New York: Raven Press. (9)

Hoebel, B. G., Rada, P. V., Mark, G. P., & Pothos, E. (1999). Neural systems for reinforcement and inhibition of behavior: Relevance to eating, addiction, and depression. In D. Kahneman, E. Diener, & N. Schwartz (Eds.), *Well-being: Foundations of hedonic psychology* (pp. 560–574). New York: Russell Sage Foundation. (9)

Hoeft, F., Hernandez, A., McMillon, G., Taylor-Hill, H., Martindale, J. L., Meyler, A., . . . Gabrieli, J. D. E. (2006). Neural basis of dyslexia: A comparison between dyslexic and nondyslexic children equated for reading ability. *Journal of Neuroscience, 26,* 10700–10708. (13)

Hoffer, A. (1973). Mechanism of action of nicotinic acid and nicotinamide in the treatment of schizophrenia. In D. Hawkins & L. Pauling (Eds.), *Orthomolecular psychiatry* (pp. 202–262). San Francisco: Freeman. (14)

Hoffman, P. L., Tabakoff, B., Szabó, G., Suzdak, P. D., & Paul, S. M. (1987). Effect of an imidazobenzodiazepine, Ro15-4513, on the incoordination and hypothermia produced by ethanol and pento-barbital. *Life Sciences, 41,* 611–619. (11)

Hoffmann, F., & Curio, G. (2003). REM-Schlaf und rezidivierende Erosio corneae—eine Hypothese. [REM sleep and recurrent corneal erosion—A hypothesis.] *Klinische Monatsblatter für Augenheilkunde, 220,* 51–53. (8)

Hökfelt, T., Johansson, O., & Goldstein, M. (1984). Chemical anatomy of the brain. *Science, 225,* 1326–1334. (2)

Holcombe, A. O., & Cavanagh, P. (2001). Early binding of feature pairs for visual perception. *Nature Neuroscience, 4,* 127–128. (3)

Hollister, J. M., Laing, P., & Mednick, S. A. (1996). Rhesus incompatibility as a risk factor for schizophrenia in male adults. *Archives of General Psychiatry, 53,* 19–24. (14)

Hollon, S. D., Jarrett, R. B., Nierenberg, A. A., Thase, M. E., Trivedi, M., & Rush, A. J. (2005). Psychotherapy and medication in the treatment of adult and geriatric depression: Which monotherapy or combined treatment? *Journal of Clinical Psychiatry, 66,* 455–468. (14)

Hollon, S. D., Thase, M. E., & Markowitz, J. C. (2002). Treatment and prevention of depression. *Psychological Science in the Public Interest, 3,* 39–77. (14)

Holmes, A. J., Lee, P. H., Hollinshead, M. O., Bakst, L., Roffman, J. L., Smoller, J. W., &

Buckner, R. L. (2012). Individual differences in amygdala-medial prefrontal anatomy link negative affect, impaired social functioning, and polygenic depression risk. *Journal of Neuroscience, 32,* 18087–18100. (11)

Holy, T. E., Dulac, C., & Meister, M. (2000). Responses of vomeronasal neurons to natural stimuli. *Science, 289,* 1569–1572. (6)

Homewood, J., & Stevenson, R. J. (2001). Differences in naming accuracy of odors presented to the left and right nostrils. *Biological Psychology, 58,* 65–73. (13)

Honea, R., Crow, T. J., Passingham, D., & Mackay, C. E. (2005). Regional deficits in brain volume in schizophrenia: A meta-analysis of voxel-based morphometry studies. *American Journal of Psychiatry, 162,* 2233–2245. (14)

Hopkins, W. D. (2006). Comparative and familial analysis of handedness in great apes. *Psychological Bulletin, 132,* 538–559. (13)

Hopkins, W. D., Russell, J. L., & Cantalupo, C. (2007). Neuroanatomical correlates of handedness for tool use in chimpanzees (*Pan troglodytes*). *Psychological Science, 18,* 971–977. (13)

Hoptman, M. J., & Levy, J. (1988). Perceptual asymmetries in left- and right-handers for cartoon and real faces. *Brain and Cognition, 8,* 178–188. (13)

Horikawa, T., Tamaki, M., Miyawaki, Y., & Kamitani, Y. (2013). Neural decoding of visual imagery during sleep. *Science, 340,* 639–642. (3)

Horne, J. A. (1992). Sleep and its disorders in children. *Journal of Child Psychology & Psychiatry & Allied Disciplines, 33,* 473–487. (8)

Horne, J. A., & Minard, A. (1985). Sleep and sleepiness following a behaviourally "active" day. *Ergonomics, 28,* 567–575. (8)

Horridge, G. A. (1962). Learning of leg position by the ventral nerve cord in headless insects. *Proceedings of the Royal Society of London, B, 157,* 33–52. (12)

Horst, W. D., & Preskorn, S. H. (1998). Mechanisms of action and clinical characteristics of three atypical antidepressants: Venlafaxine, nefazodone, bupropion. *Journal of Affective Disorders, 51,* 237–254. (14)

Horvath, T. L. (2005). The hardship of obesity: A soft-wired hypothalamus. *Nature Neuroscience, 8,* 561–565. (9)

Hoshi, E., & Tanji, J. (2000). Integration of target and body-part information in the premotor cortex when planning action. *Nature, 408,* 466–470. (7)

Houk, C. P., & Lee, P. A. (2010). Approach to assigning gender in 46,XX congenital adrenal hyperplasia with male external genitalia: Replacing dogmatism with pragmatism. *Journal of Clinical Endocrinology & Metabolism, 95,* 4501–4508. (10)

Hourai, A., & Miyata, S. (2013). Neurogenesis in the circumventricular organs of adult mouse brains. *Journal of Neuroscience Research, 91,* 757–770. (9)

Hovda, D. A., & Feeney, D. M. (1989). Amphetamine-induced recovery of visual cliff performance after bilateral visual cortex ablation in cats: Measurements of depth perception thresholds. *Behavioral Neuroscience, 103,* 574–584. (4)

Howard, J. D., Plailly, J., Grueschow, M., Haynes, J.-D., & Gottfried, J. A. (2009). Odor quality coding and categorization in human posterior piriform cortex. *Nature Neuroscience, 12,* 932–938. (6)

Howell, S., Westergaard, G., Hoos, B., Chavanne, T. J., Shoaf, S. E., Cleveland, A., . . . Higley, J. D. (2007). Serotonergic influences on life-history outcomes in free-ranging male rhesus macaques. *American Journal of Primatology, 69,* 851–865. (11)

Hrdy, S. B. (2000). The optimal number of fathers. *Annals of the New York Academy of Sciences, 907,* 75–96. (10)

Hróbjartsson, A., & Gøtzsche, P. C. (2001). Is the placebo powerless? *New England Journal of Medicine, 344,* 1594–1602. (6)

Hsiang, S. M., Burke, M., & Miguel, E. (2011). Quantifying the influence of climate on human conflict. *Science, 341,* 1212. (11)

Hsieh, P.-J., Vul, E., & Kanwisher, N. (2010). Recognition alters the spatial pattern of fMRI activation in early retinotopic cortex. *Journal of Neurophysiology, 103,* 1501–1507. (5)

Hu, P., Stylos-Allan, M., & Walker, M. P. (2006). Sleep facilitates consolidation of emotional declarative memory. *Psychological Science, 17,* 891–898. (8)

Hu, W., Lee, H. L., Zhang, Q., Liu, T., Geng, L. B., Seghier, M. L., . . . Price, C. J. (2010). Developmental dyslexia in Chinese and English populations: Dissociating the effect of dyslexia from language differences. *Brain, 133,* 1694–1706. (13)

Hua, J. Y., & Smith, S. J. (2004). Neural activity and the dynamics of central nervous system development. *Nature Neuroscience, 7,* 327–332. (4)

Huang, A. L., Chen, X., Hoon, M. A., Chandrashekar, J., Guo, W., Tränker, D., . . . Zuker, C. S. (2006). The cells and logic for mammalian sour taste detection. *Nature, 442,* 934–938. (6)

Huang, L., Treisman, A., & Pashler, H. (2007). Characterizing the limits of human visual awareness. *Science, 317,* 823–825. (13)

Huang, Y.-J., Maruyama, Y., Lu, K.-S., Pereira, E., Plonsky, I., Baur, J. E., . . . Roper, S. D. (2005). Mouse taste buds use serotonin as a neurotransmitter. *Journal of Neuroscience, 25,* 843–847. (2)

Hubbard, E. M., Piazza, M., Pinel, P., & Dehaene, S. (2005). Interactions between number and space in parietal cortex. *Nature Reviews Neuroscience, 6,* 435–448. (3)

Hubel, D. H. (1963, November). The visual cortex of the brain. *Scientific American, 209*(5), 54–62. (5)

Hubel, D. H., & Wiesel, T. N. (1959). Receptive fields of single neurons in the cat's striate cortex. *Journal of Physiology, 148,* 574–591. (5)

Hubel, D. H., & Wiesel, T. N. (1965). Binocular interaction in striate cortex of kittens reared with artificial squint. *Journal of Neurophysiology, 28,* 1041–1059. (5)

Hubel, D. H., & Wiesel, T. N. (1977). Functional architecture of macaque monkey visual cortex. *Proceedings of the Royal Society of London, B, 198,* 1–59. (5)

Hubel, D. H., & Wiesel, T. N. (1998). Early exploration of the visual cortex. *Neuron, 20,* 401–412. (5)

Huber, R., Ghilardi, M. F., Massimini, M., & Tononi, G. (2004). Local sleep and learning. *Nature, 430,* 78–81. (8)

Hudson, J. I., Hiripi, E., Pope, H. G., Jr., & Kessler, R. C. (2007). The prevalence and correlates of eating disorders in the National Comorbidity Survey Replication. *Biological Psychiatry, 61,* 348–358. (9)

Hudson, J. I., Mangweth, B., Pope, H. G., Jr., De Col, C., Hausmann, A., Gutweniger, S., . . . Tsuang, M. T. (2003). Family study of affective spectrum disorder. *Archives of General Psychiatry, 60,* 170–177. (14)

Hudspeth, A. J. (1985). The cellular basis of hearing: The biophysics of hair cells. *Science, 230,* 745–752. (6)

Hugdahl, K. (1996). Brain laterality—Beyond the basics. *European Psychologist, 1,* 206–220. (13)

Hughes, J. C., & Cook, C. C. H. (1997). The efficacy of disulfiram: A review of outcome studies. *Addiction, 92,* 381–395. (14)

Hughes, J. R. (2007). Review of medical reports on pedophilia. *Clinical Pediatrics, 46,* 667–682. (10)

Hull, E. M., Du, J., Lorrain, D. S., & Matuszewich, L. (1997). Testosterone, preoptic dopamine, and copulation in male rats. *Brain Research Bulletin, 44,* 327–333. (10)

Hull, E. M., Eaton, R. C., Markowski, V. P., Moses, J., Lumley, L. A., & Loucks, J. A. (1992). Opposite influence of medial preoptic D_1 and D_2 receptors on genital reflexes: Implications for copulation. *Life Sciences, 51,* 1705–1713. (10)

Hull, E. M., Lorrain, D. S., Du, J., Matuszewich, L., Lumley, L. A., Putnam, S. K., & Moses, J. (1999). Hormone-neurotransmitter interactions in the control of sexual behavior. *Behavioural Brain Research, 105,* 105–116. (10)

Hull, E. M., Nishita, J. K., Bitran, D., & Dalterio, S. (1984). Perinatal dopamine-related drugs demasculinize rats. *Science, 224,* 1011–1013. (10)

Hull, R., & Vaid, J. (2007). Bilingual language lateralization: A meta-analytic tale of two hemispheres. *Neuropsychologia, 45,* 1987–2008. (13)

Hunt, L. T., Kolling, N., Soltani, A., Woolrich, M. W., Rushworth, M. F. S., & Behrens, T. E. J. (2012). Mechanisms underlying cortical activity during value-guided choice. *Nature Neuroscience, 15,* 470–476. (3)

Hunt, S. P., & Mantyh, P. W. (2001). The molecular dynamics of pain control. *Nature Reviews Neuroscience, 2,* 83–91. (6)

Huntington's Disease Collaborative Research Group. (1993). A novel gene containing a trinucleotide repeat that is expanded and unstable on Huntington's disease chromosomes. *Cell, 72,* 971–983. (7)

Hurovitz, C. S., Dunn, S., Domhoff, G. W., & Fiss, H. (1999). The dreams of blind men and women: A replication and extension of previous findings. *Dreaming, 9,* 183–193. (5)

Hurvich, L. M., & Jameson, D. (1957). An opponent-process theory of color vision. *Psychological Review, 64,* 384–404. (5)

Huszar, D., Lynch, C. A., Fairchild-Huntress, V., Dunmore, J. H., Fang, Q., Berkemeier, L. R., . . . Lee, F. (1997). Targeted disruption of the melanocortin-4 receptor results in obesity in mice. *Cell, 88,* 131–141. (9)

Hutcheson, D. M., Everitt, B. J., Robbins, T. W., & Dickinson, A. (2001). The role of withdrawal in heroin addiction: Enhances reward or promotes avoidance? *Nature Neuroscience, 4,* 943–947. (14)

Hutchins, S., & Peretz, I. (2012). Amusics can imitate what they cannot discriminate. *Brain & Language, 123,* 234–239. (6)

Hutchison, K. E., LaChance, H., Niaura, R., Bryan, A., & Smolen, A. (2002). The DRD4 VNTR polymorphism influences reactivity to smoking cues. *Journal of Abnormal Psychology, 111,* 134–143. (14)

Hutchison, K. E., McGeary, J., Smolen, A., & Bryan, A. (2002). The DRD4 VNTR polymorphism moderates craving after alcohol consumption. *Health Psychology, 21,* 139–146. (14)

Hyde, J. (2005). The gender similarities hypothesis. *American Psychologist, 60,* 581–592. (3)

Hyde, J. S., Lindberg, S. M., Linn, M. C., Ellis, A. B., & Williams, C. C. (2008). Gender similarities characterize math performance. *Science, 321,* 494–495. (3)

Hyde, K. L., Lerch, J., Norton, A., Forgeard, M., Winner, E., Evans, A. C., & Schlaug, G. (2009a). Musical training shapes structural brain development. *Journal of Neuroscience, 29,* 3019–3025. (4)

Hyde, K. L., Lerch, J., Norton, A., Forgeard, M., Winner, E., Evans, A. C., . . . Schlaug, G. (2009b). The effects of musical training on structural brain development: A longitudinal study. *Annals of the New York Academy of Sciences, 1169,*182–186. (4)

Hyde, K. L., Lerch, J. P., Zatorre, R. J., Griffiths, T. D., Evans, A. C., & Peretz, I. (2007). Cortical thickness in congenital amusia: When less is better than more. *Journal of Neuroscience, 27,* 13028–13032. (6)

Hyde, K. L., & Peretz, I. (2004). Brains that are out of tune but in time. *Psychological Science, 15,* 356–360. (6)

Hynd, G. W., & Semrud-Clikeman, M. (1989). Dyslexia and brain morphology. *Psychological Bulletin, 106,* 447–482. (13)

Iggo, A., & Andres, K. H. (1982). Morphology of cutaneous receptors. *Annual Review of Neuroscience, 5,* 1–31. (6)

Ikeda, H., Stark, J., Fischer, H., Wagner, M., Drdla, R., Jäger, T., & Sandkuler, J.. (2006). Synaptic amplifier of inflammatory pain in the spinal dorsal horn. *Science, 312,* 1659–1662. (6)

Ikonomidou, C., Bittigau, P. Ishimaru, M. J., Wozniak, D. F., Koch, C., Genz, K., . . . Olney, J. W. (2000). Ethanol-induced apoptotic neurodegeneration and fetal alcohol syndrome. *Science, 287,* 1056–1060. (4)

Imamura, K., Mataga, N., & Mori, K. (1992). Coding of odor molecules by mitral/tufted cells in rabbit olfactory bulb: I. Aliphatic compounds. *Journal of Neurophysiology, 68,* 1986–2002. (6)

Immordino-Yang, M. H., Christodoulou, J. A., & Singh, V. (2012). Rest is not idleness: Implications of the brain's default mode for human development and education. *Perspectives on Psychological Science, 7,* 352–364. (3)

Imperato-McGinley, J., Guerrero, L., Gautier, T., & Peterson, R. E. (1974). Steroid 5 alpha-reductase deficiency in man: An inherited form of male pseudohermaphroditism. *Science, 186,* 1213–1215. (10)

Ingram, C. J. E., Mulcare, C. A., Itan, Y., Thomas, M. G., & Swallow, D. M. (2009). Lactose digestion and the evolutionary genetics of lactase persistence. *Human Genetics, 124,* 579–591. (9)

Innocenti, G. M. (1980). The primary visual pathway through the corpus callosum: Morphological and functional aspects in the cat. *Archives Italiennes de Biologie, 118,* 124–188. (13)

Innocenti, G. M., & Caminiti, R. (1980). Postnatal shaping of callosal connections from sensory areas. *Experimental Brain Research, 38,* 381–394. (13)

Inouye, S. T., & Kawamura, H. (1979). Persistence of circadian rhythmicity in a mammalian hypothalamic "island" containing the suprachiasmatic nucleus. *Proceedings of the National Academy of Sciences, USA, 76,* 5962–5966. (8)

International Schizophrenia Consortium. (2009). Common polygenic variation contributes to risk of schizophenia and bipolar disorder. *Nature, 460,* 748–752. (4, 15)

Iredale, J. M., Rushby, J. A., McDonald, S., Dimoska-Di Marco, A., & Swift, J. (2013). Emotion in voice matters: Neural correlates of emotional prosody perception. *International Journal of Psychophysiology, 89,* 483–490. (11)

Isaacson, G., & Adler, M. (2012). Randomized clinical trials underestimate the efficacy of antidepressants in less severe depression. *Acta Psychiatrica Scandinavica, 125,* 453–459. (14)

Ishizuka, K., Kamiya, A., Oh, E. C., Kanki, H., Seshadri, S., Robinson, J. F., . . . Sawa, A. (2011). DISC-1-dependent switch from progenitor proliferation to migration in the developing cortex. *Nature, 473,* 92–96. (14)

Isoda, M., & Hikosaka, O. (2007). Switching from automatic to controlled action by monkey medial frontal cortex. *Nature Neuroscience, 10,* 240–248. (7)

Ito, M. (1984). *The cerebellum and neural control.* New York: Raven Press. (7)

Ittner, L. M., & Götz, J. (2011). Amyloid-beta and tau—alpha toxic *pas de deux* in Alzheimer's disease. *Nature Reviews Neuroscience, 12,* 67–72. (12)

Iuculano, T., & Kadosh, R. C. (2013). The mental cost of cognitive enhancement. *Journal of Neuroscience, 33,* 4482–4486. (12)

Iverson, J. M., & Goldin-Meadow, S. (2005). Gesture paves the way for language development. *Psychological Science, 16,* 367–371. (13)

Ivry, R. B., & Diener, H. C. (1991). Impaired velocity perception in patients with lesions of the cerebellum. *Journal of Cognitive Neuroscience, 3,* 355–366. (7)

Ivy, G. O., & Killackey, H. P. (1981). The ontogeny of the distribution of callosal projection neurons in the rat parietal cortex. *Journal of Comparative Neurology, 195,* 367–389. (13)

Iwema, C. L., Fang, H., Kurtz, D. B., Youngentob, S. L., & Schwob, J. E. (2004). Odorant receptor expression patterns are restored in lesion-recovered rat olfactory epithelium. *Journal of Neuroscience, 24,* 356–369. (6)

Jablensky, A. V., Morgan, V., Zubrick, S. R., Bower, C., & Yellachich, L.-A. (2005). Pregnancy, delivery, and neonatal complications in a population cohort of women with schizophrenia and major affective disorders. *American Journal of Psychiatry, 162,* 79–91. (14)

Jacobs, B., & Scheibel, A. B. (1993). A quantitative dendritic analysis of Wernicke's area in humans: I. Lifespan changes. *Journal of Comparative Neurology, 327,* 83–96. (4)

Jacobs, G. D., & Snyder, D. (1996). Frontal brain asymmetry predicts affective style in men. *Behavioral Neuroscience, 110,* 3-6. (14)

Jacobs, G. H., Williams, G. A., Cahill, H., & Nathans, J. (2007). Emergence of novel color vision in mice engineered to express a human cone photopigment. *Science, 315,* 1723–1725. (5)

Jacobs, J., Weidemann, C. T., Miller, J. F., Solway, A., Burke, J. F., Wei, X.-X., . . . Kahana, M. J. (2013). Direct recordings of grid-like neuronal activity in human spatial navigation. *Nature Neuroscience, 16,* 1188–1190. (12)

James, R. S. (2013). A review of the thermal sensitivity of the mechanics of vertebrate skeletal muscle. *Journal of Comparative Physiology B: Biochemical, Systemic, and Environmental Physiology, 183,* 723–733. (9)

James, T. W., & James, K. H. (2013). Expert individuation of objects increases activation in the fusiform face area of children. *NeuroImage, 67,* 182–192. (5)

James, W. (1884). What is an emotion? *Mind, 9,* 188–205. (11)

James, W. (1894). The physical basis of emotion. *Psychological Review, 1,* 516–529. (11)

James, W. (1961). *Psychology: The briefer course.* New York: Harper. (Original work published 1892) (13)

Jäncke, L., Beeli, G., Eulig, C., & Hänggi, J. (2009). The neuroanatomy of grapheme-color synesthesia. *European Journal of Neuroscience, 29,* 1287–1293. (6)

Jaremka, L. M., Fagundes, C. P., Peng, J., Bennett, J. M., Glaser, R., Malarkey, W. B., & Kiecolt-Glaser, J. K. (2013a). Loneliness promotes inflammation during acute stress. *Psychological Science, 24,* 1089–1097. (11)

Jaremka, L.M., Glaser, R., Loving, T. J., Malarkey, W. B., Stowell, J. R., & Kiecolt-Glaser, J. K. (2013b). Attachment anxiety is linked to alterations in cortisol production and cellular immunity. *Psychological Science, 24,* 272–279. (11)

Jarrard, L. E., Okaichi, H., Steward, O., & Goldschmidt, R. B. (1984). On the role of hippocampal connections in the performance of place and cue tasks: Comparisons with damage to hippocampus. *Behavioral Neuroscience, 98,* 946–954. (12)

Jenner, A. R., Rosen, G. D., & Galaburda, A. M. (1999). Neuronal asymmetries in primary visual cortex of dyslexic and nondyslexic brains. *Annals of Neurology, 46,* 189–196. (13)

Jennings, J. H., Rizzi, G., Stamatakis, A. M., Ung, R. L., & Stuber, G. D. (2013). The inhibitory circuit architecture of the lateral hypothalamus orchestrates feeding. *Science, 341,* 1517–1521. (9)

Jennings, J. H., Sparta, D. R., Stamatakis, A. M., Ung, R. L., Pleil, K. E., Kash, T. L., & Stuber, G. D. (2013). Distinct extended amygdala circuits for divergent motivational states. *Nature, 496,* 224–228. (11)

Jerison, H. J. (1985). Animal intelligence as encephalization. *Philosophical Transactions of the Royal Society of London, B, 308*, 21–35. (3)

Ji, D., & Wilson, M. A. (2007). Coordinated memory replay in the visual cortex and hippocampus during sleep. *Nature Neuroscience, 10*, 100–107. (8)

Jiang, P., Josue, J., Li, X., Glaser, D., Li, W., Brand, J. G., . . . Beauchamp, G. K. (2012). Major taste loss in carnivorous mammals. *Proceedings of the National Academy of Sciences (U.S.A.), 109*, 4956–4961. (6)

Jiang, Y., Costello, P., & He, S. (2007). Processing of invisible stimuli. *Psychological Science, 18*, 349–355. (13)

Johanek, L. M., Meyer, R. A., Hartke, T., Hobelmann, J. G., Maine, D. N., LaMotte, R. H., & Ringkamp, M. (2007). Psychophysical and physiological evidence for parallel afferent pathways mediating the sensation of itch. *Journal of Neuroscience, 27*, 7490–7497. (6)

Johansson, C., Willeit, M., Smedh, C., Ekholm, J., Paunio, T., Kieseppä, T., . . . Partonen, T. (2003). Circadian clock-related polymorphisms in seasonal affective disorder and their relevance to diurnal preference. *Neuropsychopharmacology, 28*, 734–739. (14)

Johnson, E. L., Tranel, D., Lutgendorf, S., & Adolphs, R. (2009). A neuroanatomical dissociation for emotion induced by music. *International Journal of Psychophysiology, 72*, 24–33. (11)

Johnson, P. M., & Kenny, P. J. (2010). Dopamine D2 receptors in addiction-like reward dysfunction and compulsive eating in obese rats. *Nature Neuroscience, 13*, 635–641. (9, 10)

Jones, A. R., & Shusta, E. V. (2007). Blood–brain barrier transport of therapeutics via receptor-mediation. *Pharmaceutical Research, 24*, 1759–1771. (1)

Jones, C. R., Campbell, S. S., Zone, S. E., Cooper, F., DeSano, A., Murphy, P. J., . . . Ptacek, L. J. (1999). Familial advanced sleep-phase syndrome: A short-period circadian rhythm variant in humans. *Nature Medicine, 5*, 1062–1065. (8)

Jones, C. R., Huang, A. L., Ptácek, L. J., & Fu, Y.-H. (2013). Genetic basis of human circadian rhythm disorders. *Experimental Neurology, 243*, 28–33. (8)

Jones, E. G., & Pons, T. P. (1998). Thalamic and brainstem contributions to large-scale plasticity of primate somatosensory cortex. *Science, 282*, 1121–1125. (4)

Jones, H. S., & Oswald, I. (1968). Two cases of healthy insomnia. *Electroencephalography and Clinical Neurophysiology, 24*, 378–380. (8)

Jones, O. P., Green, D. W., Grogan, A., Pliatsikas, C., Filippopolitis, K., Ali, N., . . . Price, C. J. (2012). Where, when and why brain activation differs for bilinguals and monolinguals during picture naming and reading aloud. *Cerebral Cortex, 22*, 892–902. (13)

Jones, P. B., Barnes, T. R. E., Davies, L., Dunn, G., Lloyd, H., Hayhurst, K. P., . . . Lewis, S. W. (2006). Randomized controlled trial of the effect on quality of life of second- vs. first-generation antipsychotic drugs in schizophrenia. *Archives of General Psychiatry, 63*, 1079–1087. (14)

Jones, W., & Klin, A. (2013). Attention to eyes is present but in decline in 2-6-month-old infants later diagnosed with autism. *Nature, 504*, 427–431. (14)

Jonsson, T., Atwal, J. K., Steinberg, S., Snaedal, J., Jonsson, P. V., . . . Stefansson, K. (2012). A mutation in APP protects against Alzheimer's disease and age-related cognitive decline. *Nature, 488*, 96–99. (12)

Jordan, H. A. (1969). Voluntary intragastric feeding. *Journal of Comparative and Physiological Psychology, 62*, 237–244. (9)

Jouvet, M. (1960). Telencephalic and rhombencephalic sleep in the cat. In G. E. W. Wolstenholme & M. O'Connor (Eds.), *CIBA Foundation symposium on the nature of sleep* (pp. 188–208). Boston: Little, Brown. (8)

Joyner, A. L., & Guillemot, F. (1994). Gene targeting and development of the nervous system. *Current Opinion in Neurobiology, 4*, 37–42. (3)

Juda, M., Vetter, C., & Roenneberg, T. (2013). Chronotype modulates sleep duration, sleep quality, and social jet lag in shift-workers. *Journal of Biological Rhythms, 28*, 141–151. (8)

Judge, J., Caravolas, M., & Knox, P. C. (2006). Smooth pursuit eye movements and phonological processing in adults with dyslexia. *Cognitive Neuropsychology, 23*, 1174–1189. (13)

Jueptner, M., & Weiller, C. (1998). A review of differences between basal ganglia and cerebellar control of movements as revealed by functional imaging studies. *Brain, 121*, 1437–1449. (7)

Jürgensen, M., Kleinemeier, E., Lux, A., Steensma, T. D., Cohen-Kettenis, P. T., Hiort, O., . . . DSD Network Working Group. (2013). Psychosexual development in adolescents and adults with disorders of sexual development—Results from the German Clinical Evaluation Study. *Journal of Sexual Medicine, 10*, 2703–2714. (10)

Juvonen, H., Reunanen, A., Haukka, J., Muhonen, M., Suvisari, J., Arajärvi, R., . . . Lönnqvist, J. (2007). Incidence of schizophrenia in a nationwide cohort of patients with type 1 diabetes mellitus. *Archives of General Psychiatry, 64*, 894–899. (14)

Kaas, J. H. (1983). What, if anything, is SI? Organization of first somatosensory area of cortex. *Physiological Reviews, 63*, 206–231. (6)

Kaas, J. H., Merzenich, M. M., & Killackey, H. P. (1983). The reorganization of somatosensory cortex following peripheral nerve damage in adult and developing mammals. *Annual Review of Neuroscience, 6*, 325–356. (4)

Kaas, J. H., Nelson, R. J., Sur, M., Lin, C.-S., & Merzenich, M. M. (1979). Multiple representations of the body within the primary somatosensory cortex of primates. *Science, 204*, 521–523. (3)

Kaiser, A., Haller, S., Schmitz, S., & Nitsch, C. (2009). On sex/gender related similarities and differences in fMRI language research. *Brain Research Reviews, 61*, 49-59. (10)

Kales, A., Scharf, M. B., & Kales, J. D. (1978). Rebound insomnia: A new clinical syndrome. *Science, 201*, 1039–1041. (8)

Kalin, N. H., Shelton, S. E., Davidson, R. J., & Kelley, A. E. (2001). The primate amygdala mediates acute fear but not the behavioral and physiological components of anxious temperament. *Journal of Neuroscience, 21*, 2067–2074. (11)

Kaminer, Y. (2000). Contingency management reinforcement procedures for adolescent substance abuse. *Journal of the American Academy of Child and Adolescent Psychiatry, 39*, 1324–1326. (14)

Kamitani, Y., & Tong, F. (2005). Decoding the visual and subjective contents of the human brain. *Nature Neuroscience, 8*, 679–685. (13)

Kandel, E. R., & Schwartz, J. H. (1982). Molecular biology of learning: Modulation of transmitter release. *Science, 218*, 433–443. (12)

Kanwisher, N. (2010). Functional specificity in the human brain: A window into the functional architecture of the mind. *Proceedings of the National Academy of Sciences, 107*, 11163–11170. (5)

Kanwisher, N., & Yovel, G. (2006). The fusiform face area: A cortical region specialized for the perception of faces. *Philosophical Transactions of the Royal Society, B, 361*, 2109–2128. (5)

Kapur, S., Zipusky, R., Jones, C., Shammi, C. S., Remington, G., & Seeman, P. (2000). A positron emission tomography study of quetiapine in schizophrenia. *Archives of General Psychiatry, 57*, 553–559. (14)

Karama, S., Ad-Dab'bagh, Y., Haier, R. J., Deary, I. J., Lyttelton, O. C., Lepage, C., & Evans, A. C. (2009). Positive association between cognitive ability and cortical thickness in a representative US sample of healthy 6 to 18 year olds. *Intelligence, 37*, 145–155. (3)

Karg, K., Burmeister, M., Shedden, K., & Sen, S. (2011). The serotonin transporter promoter variant (5-HTTLPR), stress, and depression meta-analysis revisited. *Archives of General Psychiatry, 68*, 444–454. (14)

Kargo, W. J., & Nitz, D. A. (2004). Improvements in the signal-to-noise ratio of motor cortex cells distinguish early versus late phases of motor skill learning. *Journal of Neuroscience, 24*, 5560–5569. (7)

Karlsson, M., & Frank, L. M. (2009). Awake replay of remote experiences in the hippocampus. *Nature Neuroscience, 12*, 913–918. (8)

Karmiloff-Smith, A., Tyler, L. K., Voice, K., Sims, K., Udwin, O., Howlin, P., & Davises, M.. (1998). Linguistic dissociations in Williams syndrome: Evaluating receptive syntax in on-line and off-line tasks. *Neuropsychologia, 36*, 343–351. (13)

Karnath, H. O., Rüter, J., Mandler, A., & Himmelbach, M. (2009). The anatomy of object recognition: Visual form agnosia caused by nedial occipitotemporal stroke. *Journal of Neuroscience, 29*, 5854–5862. (5)

Karns, C. M., Dow, M. W., & Neville, H. J. (2012). Altered cross-modal processing in the primary auditory cortex of congenitally deaf adults: A visual-somatosensory fMRI study with a double-flash illusion. *Journal of Neuroscience, 32*, 9626–638. (4)

Karpova, N. N., Pickenhagen, A., Lindhom, J., Tiraboschi, E., Kulesskaya, N., . . . Castrén, E. (2011). Fear erasure in mice requires synergy between antidepressant drugs and extinction training. *Science, 334*, 1731–1734. (14)

Karra, E., O'Daly, O. G., Choudhury, A. I., Yousseif, A., Millership, S., Neary, M. T., . . . Batterham, R. L. (2013). A link between FTO, ghrelin, and impaired brain food-cue responsivity. *Journal of Clinical Investigation, 123*, 3539–3551. (9)

Karrer, T., & Bartoshuk, L. (1991). Capsaicin desensitization and recovery on the human tongue. *Physiology & Behavior, 49*, 757–764. (6)

Kas, M. J. H., Tiesjema, B., van Dijk, G., Garner, K. M., Barsh, G. S., Ter Brake, O., . . . Adan, R. A. H. (2004). Induction of brain region-specific forms of obesity by agouti. *Journal of Neuroscience, 24*, 10176–10181. (9)

Kasai, K., Shenton, M. E., Salisbury, D. F., Hirayasu, Y., Onitsuka, T., Spencer, M. H., McCarley, R. W. (2003). Progressive decrease of left Heschl gyrus and planum temporale gray matter volume in first-episode schizophrenia. *Archives of General Psychiatry, 60*, 766–775. (14)

Kass, M. D., Rosenthal, M. C., Pottackal, J., & McGann, J. P. (2013). Fear learning enhances neural responses to threat-predictive sensory stimuli. *Science, 342*, 1389–1392. (12)

Kavanau, J. L. (1998). Vertebrates that never sleep: Implications for sleep's basic function. *Brain Research Bulletin, 46*, 269–279. (8)

Kayyal, M. H., & Russell, J. A. (2013). Americans and Palestinians judge spontaneous facial expressions of emotion. *Emotion, 13*, 891–904. (11)

Kazama, A. M., Heurer, E., Davis, M., & Bachevalier, J. (2012). Effects of neonatal amygdala lesions on fear learning, conditioned inhibition, and extinction in adult macaques. *Behavioral Neuroscience, 126*, 392–403. (11)

Keefe, R. S. E., Silverman, J. M., Mohs, R. C., Siever, L. J., Harvey, P. D., Friedman, L., . . . Davis, K. L. (1997). Eye tracking, attention, and schizotypal symptoms in nonpsychotic relatives of patients with schizophrenia. *Archives of General Psychiatry, 54*, 169–176. (14)

Keele, S. W., & Ivry, R. (1990). Does the cerebellum provide a common computation for diverse tasks? *Annals of the New York Academy of Sciences, 608*, 179–207. (7)

Keers, R., & Uher, R. (2012). Gene-environment interaction in major depression and antidepressant treatment response. *Current Psychiatry Reports, 14*, 129–137. (14)

Kelly, B. D., O'Callaghan, E., Waddington, J. L., Feeney, L., Browne, S., Scully, P. J., Larkin, C. (2010). Schizophrenia and the city: A review of literature and prospective study of psychosis and urbanicity in Ireland. *Schizophrenia Research, 116*, 75–89. (14)

Kelly, T. L., Neri, D. F., Grill, J. T., Ryman, D., Hunt, P. D., Dijk, D.-J., . . . Czeisler, C. A. (1999). Nonentrained circadian rhythms of melatonin in submariners scheduled to an 18-hour day. *Journal of Biological Rhythms, 14*, 190–196. (8)

Kendler, K. S. (1983). Overview: A current perspective on twin studies of schizophrenia. *American Journal of Psychiatry, 140*, 1413–1425. (14)

Kendler, K. S., Chen, X., Dick, D., Maes, H., Gillespie, N., Neale, M. C., & Riley, B. (2012). Recent advances in the genetic epidemiology and molecular genetics of substance use disorders. *Nature Neuroscience, 15*, 181–189. (14)

Kendler, K. S., Fiske, A., Gardner, C. O., & Gatz, M. (2009). Delineation of two genetic pathways to major depression. *Biological Psychiatry, 65*, 808–811. (14)

Kendler, K. S., Gardner, C. O., & Prescott, C. A. (1999). Clinical characteristics of major depression that predict risk of depression in relatives. *Archives of General Psychiatry, 56*, 322–327. (14)

Kennard, C., Lawden, M., Morland, A. B., & Ruddock, K. H. (1995). Colour identification and colour constancy are impaired in a patient with incomplete achromatopsia associated with prestriate cortical lesions. *Proceedings of the Royal Society of London, B, 260*, 169–175. (5)

Kennaway, D. J., & Van Dorp, C. F. (1991). Free-running rhythms of melatonin, cortisol, electrolytes, and sleep in humans in Antarctica. *American Journal of Physiology, 260*, R1137–R1144. (8)

Kennedy, D. P., & Adolphs, R. (2010). Impaired fixation to eyes following amygdala damage arises from abnormal bottom-up attention. *Neuropsychologia, 48*, 3392–3398. (11)

Kennedy, D. P., Gläscher, J., Tyszka, J. M., & Adolphs, R. (2009). Personal space regulation by the human amygdala. *Nature Neuroscience, 12*, 1226–1227. (11)

Kennerley, S. W., Diedrichsen, J., Hazeltine, E., Semjen, A., & Ivry, R. B. (2002). Callosotomy patients exhibit temporal uncoupling during continuous bimanual movements. *Nature Neuroscience, 5*, 376–381. (13)

Kerchner, G. A., & Nicoll, R. A. (2008). Silent synapses and the emergence of a postsynaptic mechanism for LTP. *Nature Reviews Neuroscience, 9*, 813–825. (12)

Kerns, J. G. (2007). Experimental manipulation of cognitive control processes causes an increase in communication disturbances in healthy volunteers. *Psychological Medicine, 37*, 995–1004. (14)

Kerr, A. L., & Swain, R. A. (2011). Rapid cellular genesis and apoptosis: Effects of exercise in the adult rat. *Behavioral Neuroscience, 125*, 1–9. (4)

Keshavan, M. S., Diwadkar, V. A., Montrose, D. M., Rajarethinam, R., & Sweeney, J. A. (2005). Premorbid indicators and risk for schizophrenia: A selective review and update. *Schizophrenia Research, 79*, 45–57. (14)

Kesner, R. P., Gilbert, P. E., & Barua, L. A. (2002). The role of the hippocampus in meaning for the temporal order of a sequence of odors. *Behavioral Neuroscience, 116*, 286–290. (12)

Kety, S. S., Wender, P. H., Jacobson, B., Ingraham, L. J., Jansson, L., Faber, B., & Kinney, D. K . (1994). Mental illness in the biological and adoptive relatives of schizophrenic adoptees. *Archives of General Psychiatry, 51*, 442–455. (14)

Keverne, E. B. (1999). The vomeronasal organ. *Science, 286*, 716–720. (6)

Khashan, A. S., Abel, K. M., McNamee, R., Pedersen, M. G., Webb, R. T., Baker, P. N., . . . Mortensen, P. B. (2008). Higher risk of offspring schizophrenia following antenatal maternal exposure to severe adverse life events. *Archives of General Psychiatry, 65*, 146–152. (14)

Kiecolt-Glaser, J. K., & Glaser, R. (1993). Mind and immunity. In D. Goleman & J. Gurin (Eds.), *Mind/body medicine* (pp. 39–61). Yonkers, NY: Consumer Reports Books. (11)

Kilgour, A. R., de Gelder, B., & Lederman, S. J. (2004). Haptic face recognition and prosopagnosia. *Neuropsychologia, 42*, 707–712. (5)

Killackey, H. P., & Chalupa, L. M. (1986). Ontogenetic change in the distribution of callosal projection neurons in the postcentral gyrus of the fetal rhesus monkey. *Journal of Comparative Neurology, 244*, 331–348. (13)

Killeffer, F. A., & Stern, W. E. (1970). Chronic effects of hypothalamic injury. *Archives of Neurology, 22*, 419–429. (9)

Kilner, J. M., Neal, A., Weiskopf, N., Friston, K. J., & Frith, C. D. (2009). Evidence of mirror neurons in human inferior frontal gyrus. *Journal of Neuroscience, 29*, 10153–10159. (7)

Kim, M. J., & Whalen, P. J. (2009). The structural integrity of an amygdala-prefrontal pathway predicts trait anxiety. *Journal of Neuroscience, 29*, 11614–11618. (11)

Kim, S.-Y., Adhikari, A., Lee, S. Y., Marshel, J. H., Kim, C. K., Mallory, C. S., . . . Deisseroth, K. (2013). Diverging neural pathways assemble a behavioural state from separable features in anxiety. *Nature, 496*, 219–223. (11)

Kim, U., Jorgenson, E., Coon, H., Leppert, M., Risch, N., & Drayna, D. (2003). Positional cloning of the human quantitative trait locus underlying taste sensitivity to phenylthiocarbamide. *Science, 299*, 1221–1225. (6)

Kim, Y.-K., Lee, H.-J., Yang, J.-C., Hwang, J.-A., & Yoon, H.-K. (2009). A tryptophan hydroxylase 2 gene polymorphism is associated with panic disorder. *Behavior Genetics, 39*, 170–175. (11)

Kim-Han, J. S., Antenor-Dorsey, J. A., & O'Malley, K. L. (2011). The Parkinsonian mimetic, MPP^+, specifically impairs mitochondrial transport in dopamine axons. *Journal of Neuroscience, 31*, 7212–7221. (7)

Kindt, M., & Soeter, M. (2013). Reconsolidation in a human fear conditioning study: A test of extinction as updating mechanism. *Biological Psychology, 92*, 43–50. (11)

Kindt, M., Soeter, M., & Vervliet, B. (2009). Beyond extinction: Erasing human fear responses and preventing the return of fear. *Nature Neuroscience, 12*, 256–258. (11)

King, B. M. (2006). The rise, fall, and resurrection of the ventromedial hypothalamus in the regulation of feeding behavior and body weight. *Physiology & Behavior, 87*, 221–244. (9)

King, B. M. (2013). The modern obesity epidemic, ancestral hunter-gatherers, and the sensory/reward control of food intake. *American Psychologist, 68*, 88–96. (9)

King, B. M., Smith, R. L., & Frohman, L. A. (1984). Hyperinsulinemia in rats with ventromedial hypothalamic lesions: Role of hyperphagia. *Behavioral Neuroscience, 98*, 152–155. (9)

King, I. F., Yandava, C. N., Mabb, A. M., Hsiao, J. S., Huang, H. S., Pearson, B. L., . . . Philpot, B. D. (2013). Topoisomerases facilitate transcription of long genes linked to autism. *Nature, 501*, 58–62. (14)

Kingstone, A., & Gazzaniga, M. S. (1995). Subcortical transfer of higher order information: More illusory than real? *Neuropsychology, 9*, 321–328. (13)

Kinnamon, J. C. (1987). Organization and innervation of taste buds. In T. E. Finger & W. L. Silver (Eds.), *Neurobiology of taste and smell* (pp. 277–297). New York: Wiley. (6)

Kinomura, S., Larsson, J., Gulyás, B., & Roland, P. E. (1996). Activation by attention of the human reticular formation and thalamic intralaminar nuclei. *Science, 271*, 512–515. (8)

Kinoshita, M., Matsui, R., Kato, S., Hasegawa, T., Kasahara, H., . . . Isa, T. (2012). Genetic dissection of the circuit for hand dexterity in primates. *Nature, 487*, 235–238. (7)

Kinsbourne, M., & McMurray, J. (1975). The effect of cerebral dominance on time sharing between speaking and tapping by preschool children. *Child Development, 46*, 240–242. (13)

Kinsey, A. C., Pomeroy, W. B., & Martin, C. E. (1948). *Sexual behavior in the human male*. Philadelphia: Saunders. (10)

Kinsey, A. C., Pomeroy, W. B., Martin, C. E., & Gebhard, P. H. (1953). *Sexual behavior in the human female*. Philadelphia: Saunders. (10)

Kippenhan, J. S., Olsen, R. K., Mervis, C. B., Morris, C. A., Kohn, P., Meyer-Lindenberg, A., & Berman, K. F. (2005). Genetic contributions to human gyrification: Sulcal morphometry in Williams syndrome. *Journal of Neuroscience, 25*, 7840–7846. (13)

Kiriakakis, V., Bhatia, K. P., Quinn, N. P., & Marsden, C. D. (1998). The natural history of tardive dyskinesia: A long-term follow-up study of 107 cases. *Brain, 121*, 2053–2066. (14)

Kirkpatrick, P. J., Smielewski, P., Czosnyka, M., Menon, D. K., & Pickard, J. D. (1995). Near-infrared spectroscopy in patients with head injury. *Journal of Neurosurgery, 83*, 963–970. (4)

Kirsch, I. (2010). *The Emperor's New Drugs*. New York: Basic Books. (14)

Kirsch, I., Deacon, B. J., Huedo-Medina, T. B., Scoboria, A., Moore, T. J., & Johnson, B. T. (2008). Initial severity and antidepressant benefits: A meta-analysis of data submitted to the Food and Drug Administration. *PLoS Medicine, 5*, e45. (14)

Kleen, J. K., Sitomer, M. T., Killeen, P. R., & Conrad, C. D. (2006). Chronic stress impairs spatial memory and motivation for reward without disrupting motor ability and motivation to explore. *Behavioral Neuroscience, 120*, 842–851. (11)

Kleiber, M. L., Mantha, K., Stringer, R. L., & Singh, S. M. (2013). Neurodevelopmental alcohol exposure elicits long-term changes to gene expression that alter distinct molecular pathways dependent on timing of exposure. *Journal of Neurodevelopmental Disorders, 5*, article 6. (4)

Klein, D. F. (1993). False suffocation alarms, spontaneous panics, and related conditions. *Archives of General Psychiatry, 50*, 306–317. (11)

Klein, D. N. (2010). Chronic depression: Diagnosis and classification. *Current Directions in Psychological Science, 19*, 96–100. (14)

Kleitman, N. (1963). *Sleep and wakefulness* (Rev. ed.). Chicago: University of Chicago Press. (8)

Klengel, T., Mehta, D., Anacker, C., Rex-Haffner, M., Pruessner, J. C., Pariante, C. M., . . . Binder, E. B. (2013). Allele-specific *FKBP5* DNA demethylation mediates gene-childhood trauma interactions. *Nature Neuroscience, 16*, 33–41. (4)

Klinge, C., Eippert, F., Roder, B., & Büchel, C. (2010). Corticocortical connections mediate primary visual cortex responses to auditory stimulation in the blind. *Journal of Neuroscience, 30*, 12798–12805. (4)

Kluger, M. J. (1991). Fever: Role of pyrogens and cryogens. *Physiological Reviews, 71*, 93–127. (9)

Klüver, H., & Bucy, P. C. (1939). Preliminary analysis of functions of the temporal lobes in monkeys. *Archives of Neurology and Psychiatry, 42*, 979–1000. (3)

Knyazev, G. G., Slobodskaya, H. R., & Wilson, G. D. (2002). Psychophysiological correlates of behavioural inhibition and activation. *Personality and Individual Differences, 33*, 647–660. (11)

Ko, C.-H., Liu, G.-C., Hsiao, S., Yen, J.-Y., Yang, M.-J., Lin, W.-C., . . . Chen, C. S. (2009). Brain activities associated with gaming urge of online gaming addiction. *Journal of Psychiatric Research, 43*, 739–747. (14)

Kobayakawa, K., Kobayakawa, R., Matsumoto, H., Oka, Y., Imai, T., Ikawa, M., . . . Sakano, H. (2007). Innate versus learned odour processing in the mouse olfactory bulb. *Nature, 450*, 503–508. (6)

Kobelt, P., Paulitsch, S., Goebel, M., Stengel, A., Schmidtmann, M., van der Voort, I. R., . . . Monnikes, H. (2006). Peripheral injection of CCK-8S induces Fos expression in the dorsomedial hypothalamic nucleus in rats. *Brain Research, 1117*, 109–117. (9)

Koenigs, M., Huey, E. D., Raymont, V., Cheon, B., Solomon, J., Wassermann, E. M., & Grafman, J. (2008). Focal brain damage protects against post-traumatic stress disorder in combat veterans. *Nature Neuroscience, 11*, 232–237. (11)

Koenigs, M., Young, L., Adolphs, R., Tranel, D., Cushman, F., Hauser, M., & Damasio, A. (2007). Damage to the prefrontal cortex increases utilitarian moral judgments. *Nature, 446*, 908–911. (11)

Koepp, M. J., Gunn, R. N., Lawrence, A. D., Cunningham, V. J., Dagher, A., Jones, T., . . . Grasby, P. M. (1998). Evidence for striatal dopamine release during a video game. *Nature, 393*, 266–268. (14)

Kohler, E., Keysers, C., Umiltà, M. A., Fogassi, L., Gallese, V., & Rizzolatti, G. (2002). Hearing sounds, understanding actions: Action representation in mirror neurons. *Science, 297*, 846–848. (7)

Kohn, M. (2008). The needs of the many. *Nature, 456*, 296–299. (4)

Koleske, A. J. (2013). Molecular mechanisms of dendrite stability. *Nature Reviews Neuroscience, 14*, 536–550. (4)

Komisaruk, B. R., Adler, N. T., & Hutchison, J. (1972). Genital sensory field: Enlargement by estrogen treatment in female rats. *Science, 178*, 1295–1298. (10)

Komorowski, R. W., Manns, J. R., & Eichenbaum, H. (2009). Robust conjunctive item-lace coding by hippocampal neurons parallels learning what happens where. *Journal of Neuroscience, 29*, 9918–9929. (12)

Komura, Y., Tamura, R., Uwano, T., Nishijo, H., Kaga, K., & Ono, T. (2001). Retrospective and prospective coding for predicted reward in the sensory thalamus. *Nature, 412*, 546–549. (3)

Kong, A., Frigge, M. L., Masson, G., Besenbacher, S., Sulem, P., Magnusson, G., . . . Stefansson, K. (2012). Rate of *de novo* mutations and the importance of father's age to disease risk. *Nature, 488*, 471–475. (14)

Konishi, S., Nakajima, K., Uchida, I., Kameyama, M., Nakahara, K., Sekihara, K., & Miyashita, Y. (1998). Transient activation of inferior prefrontal cortex during cognitive set shifting. *Nature Neuroscience, 1*, 80–84. (14)

Konopka, G., Bomar, J. M., Winden, K., Coppola, G., Jonsson, Z. O., Gao, F., . . . Geschwind, D. H. (2009). Human specific transcriptional regulation of CNS development genes by *FOXP2*. *Nature, 462*, 213–217. (4, 13)

Köpetz, C. E., Lejuez, C. W., Wiers, R. W., & Kruglanski, A. W. (2013). Motivation and self-regulation in addiction: A call for convergence. *Perspectives on Psychological Science, 8*, 3–24. (14)

Koralek, A. C., Jin, X., Long, J. D. II, Costa, R. M., & Carmena, J. M. (2012). Corticostriatal plasticity is necessary for learning intentional neuroprosthetic skills. *Nature, 483*, 331–335. (12)

Kordasiewicz, H. B., Stanek, L. M., Wancewicz, E. V., Mazur, C., McAlonis, M. M., Pytel, K. A, . . . Cleveland, D. W. (2012). Sustained therapeutic reversal of Huntington's disease by transient repression of Huntingtin synthesis. *Neuron, 74*, 1031–1044. (7)

Korenberg, J. R., Chen, X.-N., Hirota, H., Lai, Z., Bellugi, U., Burian, D., . . . Matsuoka, R. (2000). VI. Genome structure and cognitive map of Williams syndrome. *Journal of Cognitive Neuroscience, 12*(Suppl.), 89–107. (13)

Korman, M., Doyon, J., Doljansky, J., Carrier, J., Dagan, Y., & Karni, A. (2007). Daytime sleep condenses the time course of motor memory consolidation. *Nature Neuroscience, 10*, 1206–1213. (8)

Körner, A., Kiess, W., Stumvoll, M., & Kovacs, P. (2008). Polygenic contribution to obesity: Genome-wide strategies reveal new targets. *Obesity and Metabolism, 36*, 12–36. (9)

Kornhuber, H. H. (1974). Cerebral cortex, cerebellum, and basal ganglia: An introduction to their motor functions. In F. O. Schmitt & F. G. Worden (Eds.), *The neurosciences: Third study program* (pp. 267–280). Cambridge, MA: MIT Press. (7)

Korpi, E. R., & Sinkkonen, S. T. (2006). GABAA receptor subtypes as targets for neuropsychiatric drug development. *Pharmacology & Therapeutics, 109*, 12–32. (11)

Kosslyn, S. M., Ganis, G., & Thompson, W. L. (2001). Neural foundations of imagery. *Nature Reviews Neuroscience, 2*, 635–642. (5)

Kosslyn, S. M., & Thompson, W. L. (2003). When is early visual cortex activated during visual mental imagery? *Psychological Bulletin, 129*, 723–746. (5)

Kostrzewa, R. M., Kostrzewa, J. P., Brown, R. W., Nowak, P., & Brus, R. (2008). Dopamine receptor supersensitivity: Development, mechanisms, presentation, and clinical applicability. *Neurotoxicity Research, 14*, 121–128. (4)

Kotowicz, Z. (2007). The strange case of Phineas Gage. *History of the Human Sciences, 20*, 115–131. (11)

Kotrschal, A., Rogell, B., Bundsen, A., Svensson, B., Zajitschek, S., Brännström, I., . . . Kolm, N. (2013). Artificial selection on relative brain size in the guppy reveals costs and benefits of evolving a larger brain. *Current Biology, 23*, 168–171. (4)

Kouider, S., Stahlhut, C., Gelskov, S. V., Barbosa, L. S., Dutat, M., de Gardelle, V., . . . Dehaene-

Lambertz, G. (2013). A neural marker of perceptual consciousness in infants. *Science, 340,* 376–380. (13)

Kourtzi, Z., & Kanwisher, N. (2000). Activation in human MT/MST by static images with implied motion. *Journal of Cognitive Neuroscience, 12,* 48–55. (5)

Kovach, C. K., Daw, N. D., Rudrauf, D., Tranel, D., & O'Doherty, J. P. (2012). Anterior prefrontal cortex contributes to action selection through tracking of recent reward trends. *Journal of Neuroscience, 32,* 8434–8442. (12)

Koya, E., Cruz, F. C., Ator, R., Golden, S. A., Hoffman, A. F., Lupica, C. R., & Hope, B. T. (2012). Silent synapses in selectively activated nucleus accumbens neurons following cocaine sensitization. *Nature Neuroscience, 15,* 1556–1562. (14)

Kraemer, D. J. M., Macrae, C. N., Green, A. E., & Kelley, W. M. (2005). Sound of silence activates auditory cortex. *Nature, 434,* 158. (6)

Kindt, M., & Soeter, M. (2013). Reconsolidation in a human fear conditioning study: A test of extinction as updating mechanism. *Biological Psychology, 92,* 43–50. (11)

Krafnick, A. J., Flowers, D. L., Luetje, M., Napoliello, E. M., & Eden, G. F. (2014). An investigation into the origin of anatomical differences in dyslexia. *Journal of Neuroscience, 34,* 901–908. (13)

Kraft, T. L., & Pressman, S. D. (2012). Grin and bear it: The influence of manipulated facial expression on the stress response. *Psychological Science, 23,* 1372–1378. (11)

Krajbich, I., Adolphs, R., Tranel, D., Denburg, N. L., & Camerer, C. F. (2009). Economic games quantify diminished sense of guilt in patients with damage to the prefrontal cortex. *Journal of Neuroscience, 29,* 2188–2192. (11)

Krakauer, A. H. (2005). Kin selection and cooperative courtship in wild turkeys. *Nature, 434,* 69–72. (4)

Krause, E. G., de Kloet, A. D., Flak, J. N., Smeltzer, M. D., Solomon, M. B., Evanson, N. K., . . . Herman, J. P. (2011). Hydration state controls stress responsiveness and social behavior. *Journal of Neuroscience, 31,* 5470–5476. (9)

Krause, E. G., & Sakal, R. R. (2007). Richter and sodium appetite: From adrenalectomy to molecular biology. *Appetite, 49,* 353–367. (9)

Kravitz, A. V., Tye, L. D., & Kreitzer, A. C. (2012). Distinct roles for direct and indirect pathway striatal neurons in reinforcement. *Nature Neuroscience, 15,* 816–818. (7)

Kreek, M. J., Nielsen, D. A., Butelman, H. R., & LaForge, K. S. (2005). Genetic influences on impulsivity, risk taking, stress responsivity and vulnerability to drug abuse and addiction. *Nature Neuroscience, 8,* 1450–1457. (14)

Kreiman, G., Fried, I., & Koch, C. (2002). Single-neuron correlates of subjective vision in the human medial temporal lobe. *Proceedings of the National Academy of Sciences (U.S.A.), 99,* 8378–8383. (13)

Kreitzer, A. C., & Regehr, W. G. (2001). Retrograde inhibition of presynaptic calcium influx by endogenous cannabinoids at excitatory synapses onto Purkinje cells. *Neuron, 29,* 717–727. (2)

Kripke, D. F. (1998). Light treatment for nonseasonal depression: Speed, efficacy, and combined treatment. *Journal of Affective Disorders, 49,* 109–117. (14)

Krishnan, V., Han, M.-H., Graham, D. L., Berton, O., Renthal, W., Russo, S. J., . . . Nestler, E. J. (2007). Molecular adaptations underlying susceptibility and resistance to social defeat in brain reward regions. *Cell, 131,* 391–404. (11)

Kristensson, K. (2011). Microbes' roadmap to neurons. *Nature Reviews Neuroscience, 12,* 345–357. (1)

Kross, E., Berman, M. G., Mischel, W., Smith, E. E., & Wager, T. D. (2011). Social rejection shares somatosensory representations with physical pain. *Proceedings of the National Academy of Sciences (U.S.A.), 108,* 6270–6275. (6)

Krueger, J. M., Rector, D. M., Roy, S., Van Dongen, H. P. A., Belenky, G., & Panksepp, J. (2008). Sleep as a fundamental property of neuronal assemblies. *Nature Reviews Neuroscience, 9,* 910–919. (8)

Krugers, H. J., Hoogenraad, C. C., & Groc, L. (2010). Stress hormones and AMPA receptor trafficking in synaptic plasticity and memory. *Nature Reviews Neuroscience, 11,* 675–681. (11)

Krupa, D. J., Thompson, J. K., & Thompson, R. F. (1993). Localization of a memory trace in the mammalian brain. *Science, 260,* 989–991. (12)

Kuba, H., Ishii, T. M., & Ohmori, H. (2006). Axonal site of spike initiation enhances auditory coincidence detection. *Nature, 444,* 1069–1072. (1)

Kubista, H., & Boehm, S. (2006). Molecular mechanisms underlying the modulation of exocytotic noradrenaline release via presynaptic receptors. *Pharmacology & Therapeutics, 112,* 213–242. (2)

Kuczewski, N., Porcer, C., Ferrand, N., Fiorentino, H., Pellegrino, C., Kolarow, R., . . . Gaiarsa, J. L. (2008). Backpropagating action potentials trigger dendritic release of BDNF during spontaneous network activity. *Journal of Neuroscience, 28,* 7013–7023. (12)

Kueider, A. M., Parisi, J. M., Gross, A. L., & Rebok, G. W. (2012). Computerized cognitive training with older adults: A systematic review. *PLoS One, 7,* e40588. (12)

Kujala, T., Myllyviita, K., Tervaniemi, M., Alho, K., Kallio, J., & Näätänen, R. (2000). Basic auditory dysfunction in dyslexia as demonstrated by brain activity measurements. *Psychophysiology, 37,* 262–266. (13)

Kujawa, S. G., & Liberman, M. C. (2009). Adding insult to injury: Cochlear nerve degeneration after "temporary" noise-induced hearing loss. *Journal of Neuroscience, 29,* 14077–14085. (6)

Kukkonen, J. P. (2013). Physiology of the orexinergic/hypocretinergic system: A revisit in 2012. *American Journal of Physiology, 304,* C2–C32. (8)

Kullmann, D. M., & Lamsa, K. P. (2007). Long-term synaptic plasticity in hippocampal interneurons. *Nature Reviews Neuroscience, 8,* 687–699. (2)

Kühlmeyer, K., & Jox, R. J. (2013). Prophylaxe und Therapie der posttraumatischen Belastungsstörung mit Propanolol (Prophylaxis and therapy of posttraumatic stress disorder with propranolol). *Nervenarzt, 84,* 1183–1189. (11)

Kumpik, D. P., Kacelnik, O., & King, A. J. (2010). Adaptive reweighting of auditory localization cues in response to chronic unilateral earplugging in humans. *Journal of Neuroscience, 30,* 4883–4894. (6)

Kupfermann, I., Castellucci, V., Pinsker, H., & Kandel, E. (1970). Neuronal correlates of habituation and dishabituation of the gill withdrawal reflex in *Aplysia. Science, 167,* 1743–1745. (12)

Kusunoki, M., Moutoussis, K., & Zeki, S. (2006). Effect of background colors on the tuning of color-selective cells in monkey area V4. *Journal of Neurophysiology, 95,* 3047–3059. (5)

Kuypers, H. G. J. M. (1989). Motor system organization. In G. Adelman (Ed.), *Neuroscience year* (pp. 107–110). Boston: Birkhäuser. (7)

Kwon, J. S., McCarley, R. W., Hirayasu, Y., Anderson, J. E., Fischer, I. A., Kikinis, R., . . . Shenton, M. E. (1999). Left planum temporale volume reduction in schizophrenia. *Archives of General Psychiatry, 56,* 142–148. (14)

Laburn, H. P. (1996). How does the fetus cope with thermal challenges? *News in Physiological Sciences, 11,* 96–100. (4, 14)

Lacroix, L., Spinelli, S., Heidbreder, C. A., & Feldon, J. (2000). Differential role of the medial and lateral prefrontal cortices in fear and anxiety. *Behavioral Neuroscience, 114,* 1119–1130. (11)

Laeng, B., & Caviness, V. S. (2001). Prosopagnosia as a deficit in encoding curved surfaces. *Journal of Cognitive Neuroscience, 13,* 556–576. (5)

Laeng, B., Svartdal, F., & Oelmann, H. (2004). Does color synesthesia pose a paradox for early-selection theories of attention? *Psychological Science, 15,* 277–281. (6)

LaFerla, F. M., Green, K. N., & Oddo, S. (2007). Intracellular amyloid-β in Alzheimer's disease. *Nature Reviews Neuroscience, 8,* 499–509. (12)

Lahey, B. B., Michalska, K. J., Liu, C. Y., Chen, Q., Hipwell, A. E., Chronis-Tuscano, A., . . . Decety, J. (2012). Preliminary genetic imaging study of the association between estrogen receptor-alpha gene polymorphisms and harsh human maternal parenting. *Neuroscience Letters, 525,* 17–22. (10)

Lahti, T. A., Leppämäki, S., Ojanen, S.-M., Haukka, J., Tuulio-Henriksson, A., Lönnqvist, J., .& Partonen, T. (2006). Transition into daylight saving time influences the fragmentation of the rest–activity cycle. *Journal of Circadian Rhythms, 4,* 1. (8)

Lai, C. S. L., Fisher, S. E., Hurst, J. A., Vargha-Khadem, F., & Monaco, A. P. (2001). A forkhead-domain gene is mutated in a severe speech and language disorder. *Nature, 413,* 519–523. (13)

Lake, R. I. E., Eaves, L. J., Maes, H. H. M., Heath, A. C., & Martin, N. G. (2000). Further evidence against the environmental transmission of individual differences in neuroticism from a collaborative study of 45,850 twins and relatives on two continents. *Behavior Genetics, 30,* 223–233. (4)

Lakatos, P., Schroeder, C. E., Leitman, D. I., & Javitt, D. C. (2013). Predictive suppression of cortical excitability and its deficit in schizophrenia. *Journal of Neuroscience, 33,* 11692–11702. (14)

Lalancette-Hébert, M., Gowing, G., Simard, A., Weng, Y. C., & Kriz, J. (2007). Selective ablation of proliferating microglial cells exacerbates ischemic injury in the brain. *Journal of Neuroscience, 30,* 2596–2605. (4)

Lambie, J. A., & Marcel, A. J. (2002). Consciousness and the varieties of emotion experience: A theoretical framework. *Psychological Review, 109,* 219–259. (13)

Lamminmäki, A., Hines, M., Kuiri-Hänninen, T., Kilpeläinen, L., Dunkel, L., & Sankilampi, U. (2012). Testosterone measured in infancy predicts subsequent sex-typed behavior in boys and girls. *Hormones and Behavior, 61,* 611–616. (10)

Land, E. H., Hubel, D. H., Livingstone, M. S., Perry, S. H., & Burns, M. M. (1983). Colour-generating interactions across the corpus callosum. *Nature, 303,* 616–618. (5)

Landis, D. M. D. (1987). Initial junctions between developing parallel fibers and Purkinje cells are different from mature synaptic junctions. *Journal of Comparative Neurology, 260,* 513–525. (2)

Långsjö, J. W., Alkire, M. T., Kaskinoro, K., Hayama, H., Maksimow, A., Kaisti, K. K., . . . Scheinin, H. (2012). Returning from oblivion: Imagining the neural core of consciousness. *Journal of Neuroscience, 32,* 4935–4943. (13)

Långström, N., Rahman, Q., Carlström, E., & Lichtenstein, P. (2010). Genetic and environmental effects on same-sex sexual behavior: A population study of twins in Sweden. *Archives of Sexual Behavior, 39,* 75–80. (10)

Lapid, H., Shushan, S., Plotkin, A., Voet, H., Roth, Y., Hummel, T., . . . Sobel, N. (2011). Neural activity at the human olfactory epithelium reflects olfactory perception. *Nature Neuroscience, 14,* 1455–461. (6)

Larsen, R. J., Kasimatis, M., & Frey, K. (1992). Facilitating the furrowed brow—An unobtrusive test of the facial feedback hypothesis applied to unpleasant affect. *Cognition & Emotion, 6,* 321–338. (11)

Lashley, K. S. (1929). *Brain mechanisms and intelligence.* Chicago: University of Chicago Press. (12)

Lashley, K. S. (1930). Basic neural mechanisms in behavior. *Psychological Review, 37,* 1–24. (12)

Lashley, K. S. (1950). In search of the engram. *Symposia of the Society for Experimental Biology, 4,* 454–482. (12)

Lassonde, M., Bryden, M. P., & Demers, P. (1990). The corpus callosum and cerebral speech lateralization. *Brain and Language, 38,* 195–206. (13)

Lau, H. C., Rogers, R. D., Haggard, P., & Passingham, R. E. (2004). Attention to intention. *Science, 303,* 1208–1210. (7)

Lau, B., & Glimcher, P. W. (2008). Value representations in the primate striatum during matching behavior. *Neuron, 58,* 451–463. (7)

Laurent, J.-P., Cespuglio, R., & Jouvet, M. (1974). Dèlimitation des voies ascendantes de l'activité ponto-géniculo-occipitale chez le chat [Demarcation of the ascending paths of ponto-geniculo-occipital activity in the cat]. *Brain Research, 65,* 29–52. (8)

Lavidor, M., & Walsh, V. (2004). The nature of foveal representation. *Nature Reviews Neuroscience, 5,* 729–735. (13)

Lavzin, M., Rapoport, S., Polsky, A., Garion, L., & Schiller, J. (2012). Nonlinear dendritic processing determines angular tuning of barrel cortex neurons in vivo. *Nature, 490,* 397–401. (2)

Lebel, C., & Beaulieu, C. (2011). Longitudinal development of human brain wiring continues from childhood into adulthood. *Journal of Neuroscience, 31,* 10937–10947. (4)

Leber, A. B. (2010). Neural predictors of within-subject fluctuations in attentional control. *Journal of Neuroscience, 30,* 11458–11465. (13)

LeBlanc, K. H., Ostlund, S. B., & Maidment, N. T. (2012). Pavlovian-to-instrumental transfer in cocaine seeking rats. *Behavioral Neuroscience, 126,* 681–689. (14)

LeDoux, J. (1996). *The emotional brain.* New York: Simon & Schuster. (11)

LeDoux, J. E., Iwata, J., Cicchetti, P., & Reis, D. J. (1988). Different projections of the central amygdaloid nucleus mediate autonomic and behavioral correlates of conditioned fear. *Journal of Neuroscience, 8,* 2517–2529. (11)

Lee, P.-C., Bordelon, Y., Bronstein, J., & Ritz, B. (2012). Traumatic brain injury, paraquat exposure, and their relationship to Parkinson disease. *Neurology, 79,* 2061–2066. (7)

Lee, H. L., Devlin, J. T., Shakeshaft, C., Stewart, L. H., Brennan, A., Glensman, J., . . . Price, C. J. (2007). Anatomical traces of vocabulary acquisition in the adolescent brain. *Journal of Neuroscience, 27,* 1184–1189. (3)

Lee, K. M., Skoe, E., Kraus, N., & Ashley, R. (2009). Selective subcortical enhancement of musical intervals in musicians. *Journal of Neuroscience, 29,* 5832–5840. (4)

Lee, M. G., Hassani, O. K., & Jones, B. E. (2005). Discharge of identified orexin/hypocretin neurons across the sleep-waking cycle. *Journal of Neuroscience, 25,* 6716–6720. (8)

Lee, S.-H., Blake, R., & Heeger, D. J. (2005). Traveling waves of activity in primary visual cortex during binocular rivalry. *Nature Neuroscience, 8,* 22–23. (13)

Lee, S. J., Verma, S., Simonds, S. E., Kirigiti, M. A., Kievit, P., Lindsley, S. R., . . . Grove, K. L. (2013). Leptin stimulates neuropeptide Y and cocaine amphetamine-regulated transcript coexpressing neuronal activity in the dorsomedial hypothalamus in diet-induced obese mice. *Journal of Neuroscience, 33,* 15306–15317. (9)

Lee, Y., Morrison, B. M., Li, Y., Lengacher, S., Farah, M. H., . . . Rothstein, J. D. (2012). Oligodendroglia metabolically support axons and contribute to neurodegeneration. *Nature, 487,* 443–448. (1)

Legrand, L. N., Iacono, W. G., & McGue, M. (2005, March/April). Predicting addiction. *American Scientist, 93,* 140–147. (14)

Lehky, S. R. (2000). Deficits in visual feature binding under isoluminant conditions. *Journal of Cognitive Neuroscience, 12,* 383–392. (3)

Lehrman, D. S. (1964). The reproductive behavior of ring doves. *Scientific American, 211*(5), 48–54. (10)

Lehrer, J. (2009). Small, furry . . . and smart. *Nature, 461,* 862–864. (12)

Leibniz, G. (1989). *The Principles of Nature and Grace, Based on Reason.* Dordrecht, Netherlands: Kluwer Publishers. (Original work published 1714) (0)

Leibowitz, S. F., & Alexander, J. T. (1991). Analysis of neuropeptide Y-induced feeding: Dissociation of Y_1 and Y_2 receptor effects on natural meal patterns. *Peptides, 12,* 1251–1260. (9)

Leibowitz, S. F., & Hoebel, B. G. (1998). Behavioral neuroscience of obesity. In G. A. Bray, C. Bouchard, & P. T. James (Eds.), *Handbook of obesity* (pp. 313–358). New York: Dekker. (9)

Lein, E. S., & Shatz, C. J. (2001). Neurotrophins and refinement of visual circuitry. In W. M. Cowan, T. C. Südhof, & C. F. Stevens (Eds.), *Synapses* (pp. 613–649). Baltimore: Johns Hopkins University Press. (5)

Leinders-Zufall, T., Lane, A. P., Puche, A. C., Ma, W., Novotny, M. V., Shipley, M. T., & Zufall, F. (2000). Ultrasensitive pheromone detection by mammalian vomeronasal neurons. *Nature, 405,* 792–796. (6)

Le Magueresse, C., Alfonso, J., Khodesovich, K., Martin, A. A. A., Bark, C., & Monyer, H. (2011). "Small axonless neurons": Postnatally generated neocortical interneurons with delayed functional maturation. *Journal of Neuroscience, 31,* 16731–16747. (1)

Lemos, B., Araripe, L. O., & Hartl, D. L. (2008). Polymorphic Y chromosomes harbor cryptic variation with manifold functional consequences. *Science, 319,* 91–93. (10)

Lenggenhager, B., Tadi, T., Metzinger, T., & Blanke, O. (2007). Video ergo sum: Manipulating bodily self-consciousness. *Science, 317,* 1096–1099. (3)

Lenhart, R. E., & Katkin, E. S. (1986). Psychophysiological evidence for cerebral laterality effects in a high-risk sample of students with subsyndromal bipolar depressive disorder. *American Journal of Psychiatry, 143,* 602–607. (14)

Lensvelt-Mulders, G., & Hettema, J. (2001). Genetic analysis of autonomic reactivity to psychologically stressful situations. *Biological Psychiatry, 58,* 25–40. (11)

Lenz, F. A., & Byl, N. N. (1999). Reorganization in the cutaneous core of the human thalamic principal somatic sensory nucleus (ventral caudal) in patients with dystonia. *Journal of Neurophysiology, 82,* 3204–3212. (4)

Leon, L. R. (2002). Invited review: Cytokine regulation of fever: Studies using gene knockout mice. *Journal of Applied Physiology, 92,* 2648–2655. (9)

Leppämäki, S., Partonen, T., & Lönnqvist, J. (2002). Bright-light exposure combined with physical exercise elevates mood. *Journal of Affective Disorders, 72,* 572–575. (14)

Lesku, J. A., Rattenborg, N. C., Valcu, M., Vyssotski, A. L., Kuhn, S., Kuemmeth, F., . . . Kempenaers, B. (2012). Adaptive sleep loss in polygynous pectoral sandpipers. *Science, 337,* 1654–1658. (8)

Leucht, S., Cipriani, A., Spineli, L., Marridis, D., Örey, D., Richter, F., . . . Davis, J. M. (2013). Comparative efficacy and tolerability of 15 antipsychotic drugs in schizophrenia: A multiple-treatments meta-analysis. *Lancet, 382,* 951–962. (14)

LeVay, S. (1991). A difference in hypothalamic structure between heterosexual and homosexual men. *Science, 253,* pp. 1034–1037. (10)

LeVay, S. (1993). *The sexual brain.* Cambridge, MA: MIT Press. (10)

Levenson, R. W., Oyama, O. N., & Meek, P. S. (1987). Greater reinforcement from alcohol for those at risk: Parental risk, personality risk, and sex. *Journal of Abnormal Psychology, 96,* 242–253. (14)

Levi-Montalcini, R. (1987). The nerve growth factor 35 years later. *Science, 237,* 1154–1162. (4)

Levi-Montalcini, R. (1988). *In praise of imperfection.* New York: Basic Books. (4)

Levin, E. D., & Rose, J. E. (1995). Acute and chronic nicotine interactions with dopamine systems and working memory performance. *Annals of the New York Academy of Sciences, 757,* 245–252. (2)

Levine, J. A., Lanningham-Foster, L. M., McCrady, S. K., Krizan, A. C., Olson, L. R., Kane, P. H., . . . Clark, M. M. (2005). Interindividual variation in posture allocation: Possible role in human obesity. *Science, 307,* 584–586. (9)

Levine, J. D., Fields, H. L., & Basbaum, A. I. (1993). Peptides and the primary afferent nociceptor. *Journal of Neuroscience, 13,* 2273–2286. (2)

Levitin, D. J., & Bellugi, U. (1998). Musical abilities in individuals with Williams syndrome. *Music Perception, 15,* 357–389. (13)

Levitt, R. A. (1975). *Psychopharmacology.* Washington, DC: Hemisphere. (14)

Levitzki, A. (1988). From epinephrine to cyclic AMP. *Science, 241,* 800–806. (2)

Levy, J., Heller, W., Banich, M. T., & Burton, L. A. (1983). Asymmetry of perception in free viewing of chimeric faces. *Brain and Cognition, 2,* 404–419. (13)

Lewis, E. R., Everhart, T. E., & Zeevi, Y. Y. (1969). Studying neural organization in *Aplysia* with the scanning electron microscope. *Science, 165,* 1140–1143. (2)

Lewis, M. B. (2012). Exploring the positive and negative implications of facial feedback. *Emotion, 12,* 852–859. (11)

Lewis, T. L., & Maurer, D. (2005). Multiple sensitive periods in human visual development: Evidence from visually deprived children. *Developmental Psychobiology, 46,* 163–183. (5)

Lewis, V. G., Money, J., & Epstein, R. (1968). Concordance of verbal and nonverbal ability in the adrenogenital syndrome. *Johns Hopkins Medical Journal, 122,* 192–195. (10)

Li, N., & DiCarlo, J. J. (2008). Unsupervised natural experience rapidly alters invariant object representation in visual cortex. *Science, 321,* 1502–1507. (5)

Liberles, S. D., & Buck, L. B. (2006). A second class of chemosensory receptors in the olfactory epithelium. *Nature, 442,* 645–650. (6)

Libet, B., Gleason, C. A., Wright, E. W., & Pearl, D. K. (1983). Time of conscious intention to act in relation to onset of cerebral activities (readiness potential): The unconscious initiation of a freely voluntary act. *Brain, 106,* 623–642. (7)

Lickliter, R., & Bahrick, L. E. (2000). The development of infant intersensory perception: Advantages of a comparative convergent-operations approach. *Psychological Bulletin, 126,* 260–280. (13)

Liebe, S., Hoerzer, G. M., Logothetis, N. K., & Rainer, G. (2012). Theta coupling between V4 and prefrontal cortex predicts visual short-term memory performance. *Nature Neuroscience, 15,* 456–462. (12)

Liebman, M., Pelican, S., Moore, S. A., Holmes, B., Wardlaw, M. K., Melcher, L. M., . . . Haynes, G. W. (2006). Dietary intake-, eating behavior-, and physical activity-related determinants of high body mass index in the 2003 Wellness IN the Rockies cross-sectional study. *Nutrition Research, 26,* 111–117. (9)

Lim, B. K., Huang, K. W., Grueter, B. A., Rothwell, P. E., & Malenka, R. C. (2012). Anhedonia requires MC4R-mediated synaptic adaptations in nucleus accumbens. *Nature, 487,* 183–189. (11)

Lim, M. M., Wang, Z., Olazábal, D. E., Ren, X., Terwilliger, E. F., & Young, L. J. (2004). Enhanced partner preference in a promiscuous species by manipulating the expression of a single gene. *Nature, 429,* 754–757. (10)

Lin, D. Y., Shea, S. D., & Katz, L. C. (2006). Representation of natural stimuli in the rodent main olfactory bulb. *Neuron, 50,* 937–949. (6)

Lin, J.-S., Hou, Y., Sakai, K., & Jouvet, M. (1996). Histaminergic descending inputs to the mesopontine tegmentum and their role in the control of cortical activation and wakefulness in the cat. *Journal of Neuroscience, 16,* 1523–1537. (8)

Lin, L., Faraco, J., Li, R., Kadotani, H., Rogers, W., Lin, X., . . . Mignot, E. (1999). The sleep disorder canine narcolepsy is caused by a mutation in the hypocretin (orexin) receptor 2 gene. *Cell, 98,* 365–376. (8)

Lindberg, N. O., Coburn, C., & Stricker, E. M. (1984). Increased feeding by rats after subdiabetogenic streptozotocin treatment: A role for insulin in satiety. *Behavioral Neuroscience, 98,* 138–145. (9)

Lindemann, B. (1996). Taste reception. *Physiological Reviews, 76,* 719–766. (6)

Lindner, A., Iyer, A., Kagan, I., & Andersen, R. A. (2010). Human posterior parietal cortex plans where to reach and what to avoid. *Journal of Neuroscience, 30,* 11715–11725. (7)

Lindquist, K. A., Wager, T. D., Kober, H., Bliss-Moreau, E., & Barrett, L. F. (2012). The brain basis of emotion: A meta-analytic review. *Behavioral and Brain Sciences, 35,* 121–202. (11)

Lindsay, P. H., & Norman, D. A. (1972). *Human information processing.* New York: Academic Press. (6)

Liou, Y.-C., Tocilj, A., Davies, P. L., & Jia, Z. (2000). Mimicry of ice structure by surface hydroxyls and water of a beta-helix antifreeze protein. *Nature, 406,* 322–324. (9)

Lippa, R. A. (2006). Is high sex drive associated with increased sexual attraction to both sexes? *Psychological Science, 17,* 46–52. (10)

Lisman, J., Schulman, H., & Cline, H. (2002). The molecular basis of CaMKII function in synaptic and behavioural memory. *Nature Reviews Neuroscience, 3,* 175–190. (12)

Lisman, J., Yasuda, R., & Raghavachari, S. (2012). Mechanisms of CaMKII action in long-term potentiation. *Nature Reviews Neuroscience, 13,* 169–182. (12)

Lisman, J. E., Raghavachari, S., & Tsien, R. W. (2007). The sequence of events that underlie quantal transmission at central glutamatergic synapses. *Nature Reviews Neuroscience, 8,* 597–609. (2)

Liu, F., Wollstein, A., Hysi, P. G., Ankra-Badu, G. A., Spector, T. D., Park, D, . . . Kayser, M. (2010). Digital quantification of human eye color highlights genetic association of three new loci. *PLoS Genetics, 6,* e1000934. (4)

Liu, G., & Tsien, R. W. (1995). Properties of synaptic transmission at single hippocampal synaptic boutons. *Nature, 375,* 404–408. (2)

Liu, J., Dietz, K., DeLoyht, J. M., Pedre, X., Kelkar, D., Kaur, J., . . . Casaccia, P. (2012). Impaired adult myelination in the prefrontal cortex of socially isolated mice. *Nature Neuroscience, 15,* 1621–1623. (4)

Liu, K., Lu, Y., Lee, J. K., Samara, R., Willenberg, R., Sears-Kraxberger, I., . . . He, Z. G. (2010). PTEN deletion enhances the regenerative ability of adult corticospinal neurons. *Nature Neuroscience, 13,* 1075–1081. (5)

Liu, P., & Bilkey, D. K. (2001). The effect of excitotoxic lesions centered on the hippocampus or perirhinal cortex in object recognition and spatial memory tasks. *Behavioral Neuroscience, 115,* 94–111. (12)

Liu, X., Zwiebel, L. J., Hinton, D., Benzer, S., Hall, J. C., & Rosbash, M. (1992). The period gene encodes a predominantly nuclear protein in adult Drosophila. *Journal of Neuroscience, 12,* 2735–2744. (8)

Liu, Y., Rutlin, M., Huang, S., Barrick, C. A., Wang, F., Jones, K. R., . . . Ginty, D. D. (2012). Sexually dimorphic BDNF signaling directs sensory innervation of the mammary gland. *Science, 338,* 1357–1360. (10)

Liu, Y., Samad, O. A., Zhang, L., Duan, B., Tong, Q., Lopes, C., . . . Ma, Q. (2010). VGLUT2-dependent glutamate release from nociceptors is required to sense pain and suppress itch. *Neuron, 68,* 543–556. (6)

Liu, Z.-W., Faraguna, U., Cirelli, C., Tononi, G., & Gao, X.-B. (2010). Direct evidence for wake-related increases and sleep-related decreases in synaptic strength in rodent cortex. *Journal of Neuroscience, 30,* 8671–8675. (8)

Livingstone, M. S. (1988, January). Art, illusion and the visual system. *Scientific American, 258*(1), 78–85. (5)

Livingstone, M. S., & Hubel, D. (1988). Segregation of form, color, movement, and depth: Anatomy, physiology, and perception. *Science, 240,* 740–749. (5)

Lockwood, A. H., Salvi, R. J., Coad, M. L., Towsley, M. L., Wack, D. S., & Murphy, B. W. (1998). The functional neuroanatomy of tinnitus: Evidence for limbic system links and neural plasticity. *Neurology, 50,* 114–120. (6)

Loe, I. M., Feldman, H. M., Yasui, E., & Luna, B. (2009). Oculomotor performance identifies underlying cognitive deficits in attention-deficit/hyperactivity disorder. *Journal of the American Academy of Child and Adolescent Psychiatry, 48,* 431–440. (7)

Loewenstein, W. R. (1960, August). Biological transducers. *Scientific American, 203*(2), 98–108. (6)

Loewi, O. (1960). An autobiographic sketch. *Perspectives in Biology, 4,* 3–25. (2)

Logan, C. G., & Grafton, S. T. (1995). Functional anatomy of human eyeblink conditioning determined with regional cerebral glucose metabolism and positron-emission tomography. *Proceedings of the National Academy of Sciences, USA, 92,* 7500–7504. (12)

Löken, L. S., Wessberg, J., Morrison, I., McGlone, F., & Olausson, H. (2009). Coding of pleasant touch by unmyelinated afferents in humans. *Nature Neuroscience, 12*, 547–548. (6)

Lomber, S. G., & Malhotra, S. (2008). Double dissociation of "what" and "where" processing in auditory cortex. *Nature Neuroscience, 11*, 609–617. (6)

Lomniczi, A., Loche, A., Castellano, J. M., Ronnekleiv, O. K., Bosch, M., Kaidar, G., . . . Ojeda, S. R. (2013). Epigenetic control of female puberty. *Nature Neuroscience, 16*, 281–289. (4)

Long, M. A., Jutras, M. J., Connors, B. W., & Burwell, R. D. (2005). Electrical synapses coordinate activity in the suprachiasmatic nucleus. *Nature Neuroscience, 8*, 61–66. (8)

Lord, G. M., Matarese, G., Howard, J. K., Baker, R. J., Bloom, S. R., & Lechler, R. I. (1998). Leptin modulates the T-cell immune response and reverses starvation-induced immunosuppression. *Nature, 394*, 897–901. (9)

Lorincz, A., & Nusser, Z. (2010). Molecular identity of dendritic voltage-gated sodium channels. *Science, 328*, 906–909. (1)

Lorrain, D. S., Riolo, J. V., Matuszewich, L., & Hull, E. M. (1999). Lateral hypothalamic serotonin inhibits nucleus accumbens dopamine: Implications for sexual refractoriness. *Journal of Neuroscience, 19*, 7648–7652. (14)

Lorusso, M. L., Facoetti, A., Pesenti, S., Cattaneo, C., Molteni, M., & Geiger, G. (2004). Wider recognition in peripheral vision common to different subtypes of dyslexia. *Vision Research, 44*, 2413–2424. (13)

Lott, I. T. (1982). Down's syndrome, aging, and Alzheimer's disease: A clinical review. *Annals of the New York Academy of Sciences, 396*, 15–27. (12)

Lotto, R. B., & Purves, D. (2002). The empirical basis of color perception. *Consciousness and Cognition, 11*, 609–629. (5)

Lotze, M., Grodd, W., Birbaumer, N., Erb, M., Huse, E., & Flor, H. (1999). Does use of a myoelectric prosthesis prevent cortical reorganization and phantom limb pain? *Nature Neuroscience, 2*, 501–502. (4)

Loui, P., Alsop, D., & Schlaug, G. (2009). Tone deafness: A new disconnection syndrome? *Journal of Neuroscience, 29*, 10215–10220. (6)

Lu, B., Al-Ramahi, I., Valencia, A., Wang, Q., Berenshteyn, F., Yang, H., . . . Palacino, J. (2013). Identification of *NUB1* as a suppressor of mutant huntingtin toxicity via enhanced protein clearance. *Nature Neuroscience, 16*, 562–570. (7)

Lu, S., Das, P., Fadool, D. A., & Kaczmarek, L. K. (2010). The Slack sodium-activated potassium channel provides a major outward current in olfactory neurons of Kv 1.3-/- super-smeller mice. *Journal of Neurophysiology, 103*, 3311–3319. (6)

Lucas, B. K., Ormandy, C. J., Binart, N., Bridges, R. S. & Kelly, P. A. (1998). Null mutation of the prolactin receptor gene produces a defect in maternal behavior. *Endocrinology, 139*, 4102–4107. (10)

Lucas, R. J., Douglas, R. H., & Foster, R. G. (2001). Characterization of an ocular photopigment capable of driving pupillary constriction in mice. *Nature Neuroscience, 4*, 621–626. (8)

Lucas, R. J., Freedman, M. S., Muñoz, M., Garcia-Fernández, J.-M., & Foster, R. G. (1999). Regulation of the mammalian pineal by non-rod, non-cone ocular photoreceptors. *Science, 284*, 505–507. (8)

Luczak, S. E., Glatt, S. J., & Wall, T. L. (2006). Meta-analysis of *ALDHx* and *ADHIB* with alcohol dependence in Asians. *Psychological Bulletin, 132*, 607–621. (14)

Luders, E., Gaser, C., Narr, K. L., & Toga, A. W. (2009). Why sex matters: Brain size independent differences in gray matter distributions between men and women. *Journal of Neuroscience, 29*, 14265–14270. (10)

Luders, E., Narr, K. I., Thompson, P. M., Rex, D. E., Jancke, L., Steinmetz, H., & Toga, A. W. (2004). Gender differences in cortical complexity. *Nature Neuroscience, 7*, 799–800. (3)

Luders, E., Thompson, P. M., & Toga, A. W. (2010). The development of the corpus callosum in the healthy human brain. *Journal of Neuroscience, 30*, 10985–10990. (13)

Ludwig, M., & Leng, G. (2006). Dendritic peptides release and peptide-dependent behaviours. *Nature Reviews Neuroscience, 7*, 126–136. (2)

Luna, B., Padmanabhan, A., & O'Hearn, K. (2010). What has fMRI told us about the development of cognitive control through adolescence? *Brain and Cognition, 72*, 101–113. (4)

Lund, R. D., Lund, J. S., & Wise, R. P. (1974). The organization of the retinal projection to the dorsal lateral geniculate nucleus in pigmented and albino rats. *Journal of Comparative Neurology, 158*, 383–404. (5)

Lutz, A., Slagter, H. A., Rawlings, N. B., Francis, A. D., Greischar, L. L., & Davidson, R. J. (2009). Mental training enhances attentional stability: Neural and behavioral evidence. *Journal of Neuroscience, 29*, 13418–13427. (13)

Lyman, C. P., O'Brien, R. C., Greene, G. C., & Papafrangos, E. D. (1981). Hibernation and longevity in the Turkish hamster *Mesocricetus brandti*. *Science, 212*, 668–670. (8)

Lynall, M.-E., Bassett, D. S., Kerwin, R., McKenna, P. J., Kitzbichler, M., Muller, U., & Bullmore, E. (2010). Functional connectivity and brain networks in schizophrenia. *Journal of Neuroscience, 30*, 9477–9487. (14)

Lyons, M. J., Eisen, S. A., Goldberg, J., True, W., Lin, N., Meyer, J. M., . . . Tsuang, M. T. (1998). A registry-based twin study of depression in men. *Archives of General Psychiatry, 55*, 468–472. (14)

MacDonald, C. J., Lepage, K. Q., Eden, U. T., & Eichenbaum, H. (2011). Hippocampal "time cells" bridge the gap in memory for discontinuous events. *Neuron, 71*, 737–749. (12)

Macdonald, R. L., Weddle, M. G., & Gross, R. A. (1986). Benzodiazepine, beta-carboline, and barbiturate actions on GABA responses. *Advances in Biochemical Psychopharmacology, 41*, 67–78. (11)

Macey, P. M., Henderson, L. A., Macey, K. E., Alger, J. R., Frysinger, R. C., Woo, M. A., . . . Harper, R. M. (2002). Brain morphology associated with obstructive sleep apnea. *American Journal of Respiratory & Critical Care Medicine, 166*, 1382–1387. (8)

MacFarlane, J. G., Cleghorn, J. M., & Brown, G. M. (1985a, September). *Circadian rhythms in chronic insomnia*. Paper presented at the World Congress of Biological Psychiatry, Philadelphia. (8)

MacFarlane, J. G., Cleghorn, J. M., & Brown, G. M. (1985b). Melatonin and core temperature rhythms in chronic insomnia. In G. M. Brown & S. D. Wainwright (Eds.), *The pineal gland: Endocrine aspects* (pp. 301–306). New York: Pergamon Press. (8)

MacFarquhar, L. (2009, July 27). The kindest cut. *The New Yorker, 85*(22), 38–51. (4)

MacLean, P. D. (1949). Psychosomatic disease and the "visceral brain": Recent developments bearing on the Papez theory of emotion. *Psychosomatic Medicine, 11*, 338–353. (11)

MacLusky, N. J., & Naftolin, F. (1981). Sexual differentiation of the central nervous system. *Science, 211*, 1294–1303. (10)

Macphail, E. M. (1985). Vertebrate intelligence: The null hypothesis. *Philosophical Transactions of the Royal Society of London, B, 308*, 37–51. (3)

Maeng, L. Y., & Shors, T. J. (2012). Once a mother, always a mother: Maternal experience protects females from the negative effects of stress on learning. *Behavioral Neuroscience, 126*, 137–141. (11)

Maffei, A., Nataraj, K., Nelson, S. B., & Turrigiano, G. G. (2006). Potentiation of cortical inhibition by visual deprivation. *Nature, 443*, 81–84. (5)

Maguire, E. A., Gadian, D. G., Johnsrude, I. S., Good, C. D., Ashburner, J., Frackowiak, R. S. J., & Frith, C. D. (2000). Navigation-related structural change in the hippocampi of taxi drivers. *Proceedings of the National Academy of Sciences, USA, 97*, 4398–4403. (12)

Maier, S. F., & Watkins, L. R. (1998). Cytokines for psychologists: Implications of bidirectional immune-to-brain communication for understanding behavior, mood, and cognition. *Psychological Review, 105*, 83–107. (11)

Malaspina, D., Corcoran, C., Fahim, C., Berman, A., Harkavy-Friedman, J., Yale, S., . . . Gorman, J. (2002). Paternal age and sporadic schizophrenia: Evidence for de novo mutations. *American Journal of Medical Genetics, 114*, 299–303. (14)

Malik, S., Vinukonda, G., Vose, L. R., Diamond, D., Bhimavarapu, B. B.R., Hu, F., . . . Ballabh, P. (2013). Neurogenesis continues in the third trimester of pregnancy and is suppressed by premature birth. *Journal of Neuroscience, 33*, 411–423. (4)

Mallis, M. M., & DeRoshia, C. W. (2005). Circadian rhythms, sleep, and performance in space. *Aviation, Space, and Environmental Medicine, 76*(Suppl. 6), B94–B107. (8)

Malmberg, A. B., Chen, C., Tonegawa, S., & Basbaum, A. I. (1997). Preserved acute pain and reduced neuropathic pain in mice lacking PKCg. *Science, 278*, 279–283. (6)

Mameli, M., Halbout, B., Creton, C., Engblom, D., Parkitna, J. R., Spanagel, R., & Luscher, C. (2009). Cocaine-evoked synaptic plasticity: Persistence in the VTA triggers adaptations in the NAc. *Nature Neuroscience, 12*, 1036–1041. (14)

Mancuso, K., Hauswirth, W. W., Li, Q., Connor, T. B., Kuchenbecker, J. A., Mauck, M. C., . . . Neitz, M. (2009). Gene therapy for red-green colour blindness. *Nature, 461*, 784–787. (5)

Mangan, M. A. (2004). A phenomenology of problematic sexual behavior. *Archives of Sexual Behavior, 33*, 287–293. (8)

Mangiapane, M. L., & Simpson, J. B. (1980). Subfornical organ: Forebrain site of pressor and dipsogenic action of angiotensin II. *American Journal of Physiology, 239,* R382–R389. (9)

Mann, J. J., Arango, V., & Underwood, M. D. (1990). Serotonin and suicidal behavior. *Annals of the New York Academy of Sciences, 600,* 476–485. (11)

Mann, T., Tomiyama, A. J., Westling, E., Lew, A.-M., Samuels, B., & Chatman, J. (2007). Medicare's search for effective obesity treatments. *American Psychologist, 62,* 220–233. (9)

Maquet, P., Laureys, S., Peigneux, P., Fuchs, S., Petiau, C., Phillips, C., . . . Cleermans, A. (2000). Experience-dependent changes in cerebral activation during human REM sleep. *Nature Neuroscience, 3,* 831–836. (8)

Maquet, P., Peters, J.-M., Aerts, J., Delfiore, G., Degueldre, C., Luxen, A., & Franck, G. (1996). Functional neuroanatomy of human rapid-eye-movement sleep and dreaming. *Nature, 383,* 163–166. (7, 8)

Marcar, V. L., Zihl, J., & Cowey, A. (1997). Comparing the visual deficits of a motion blind patient with the visual deficits of monkeys with area MT removed. *Neuropsychologia, 35,* 1459–1465. (5)

March, S. M., Abate, P., Spear, N. E., & Molina, J. C. (2009). Fetal exposure to moderate ethanol doses: Heightened operant responsiveness elicited by ethanol-related reinforcers. *Alcoholism: Clinical and Experimental Research,* 33, 1981–1993. (14)

Marek, R., Strobel, C., Bredy, T. W., & Sah, P. (2013). Partners in the fear circuit. *Journal of Physiology, 591,* 2381–2391. (11)

Maret, S., Faraguna, U., Nelson, A. B., Cirelli, C., & Tononi, G. (2011). Sleep and waking modulate spine turnover in the adolescent mouse cortex. *Nature Neuroscience, 14,* 1418–1420. (8)

Maricich, S. M., Wellnitz, S. A., Nelson, A. M., Lesniak, D. R., Gerling, G. J., Lumpkin, E. A., . . . Zoghbi, H.. Y. (2009). Merkel cells are essential for light-touch responses. *Science, 324,* 1580–1582. (6)

Mariño, G., Fernández, A. F., Cabrera, S., Lundberg, Y. W., Cabanillas, R., Rodríguez, F., Lopez-Otin, C. (2010). Autophagy is essential for mouse sense of balance. *Journal of Clinical Investigation, 120,* 2331–2344. (6)

Mark, A. L. (2013). Selective leptin resistance revisited. *American Journal of Physiology: Regulatory, Integrative, and Comparative Physiology, 305,* R566–R581. (9)

Marlatt, M. W., Potter, M. C., Lucassen, P. J., & van Praage, H. (2012). Running throughout middle-age improves memory function, hippocampal neurogenesis, and BDNF levels in female C57B1/6J mice. *Developmental Neurobiology,* 72(S1), 943–952. (4)

Marris, E. (2006). Grey matters. *Nature, 444,* 808–810. (0)

Marshall, J. C., & Halligan, P. W. (1995). Seeing the forest but only half the trees? *Nature, 373,* 521–523. (13)

Marshall, J. F. (1985). Neural plasticity and recovery of function after brain injury. *International Review of Neurobiology, 26,* 201–247. (4)

Marsman, A., van den Heuvel, M. P., Klomp, D. W. J., Kahn, R. S., Luijten, P. R., & Pol, H. E. H. (2013). Glutamate in schizophrenia: A focused review and meta-analysis of H-1-MRS studies. *Schizophrenia Bulletin, 39,* 120–129. (14)

Martens, M. A., Wilson, S. J., & Reutens, D. C. (2008). Research review: Williams syndrome: A critical review of the cognitive, behavioral, and neuroanatomical phenotype. *Journal of Child Psychology and Psychiatry, 49,* 576–608. (13)

Martin, G., Rojas, L. M., Ramírez, Y., & McNeil, R. (2004). The eyes of oilbirds (*Steatornis caripensis*): Pushing at the limits of sensitivity. *Naturwissenschaften, 91,* 26–29. (5)

Martin, P. R., Lee, B. B., White, A. J. R., Solomon, S. G., & Rütiger, L. (2001). Chromatic sensitivity of ganglion cells in the peripheral primate retina. *Nature, 410,* 933–936. (5)

Martin, R. C., & Blossom-Stach, C. (1986). Evidence of syntactic deficits in a fluent aphasic. *Brain and Language, 28,* 196–234. (13)

Martin, S. D., Martin, E., Rai, S. S., Richardson, M. A., Royall, R., & Eng, C. (2001). Brain blood flow changes in depressed patients treated with interpersonal psychotherapy or venlafaxine hydrochloride. *Archives of General Psychiatry, 58,* 641–648. (14)

Martindale, C. (2001). Oscillations and analogies: Thomas Young, MD, FRS, genius. *American Psychologist, 56,* 342–345. (5)

Martinez-Vargas, M. C., & Erickson, C. J. (1973). Some social and hormonal determinants of nest-building behaviour in the ring dove (*Streptopelia risoria*). *Behaviour, 45,* 12–37. (10)

Martinowich, K., Manji, H., & Lu, B. (2007). New insights into BDNF function in depression and anxiety. *Nature Neuroscience, 10,* 1089–1093. (14)

Mascaro, J. S., Hackett, P. D., & Rilling, J. K. (2013). Testicular volume is inversely correlated with nurturing-related brain activity in human fathers. *Proceedings of the National Academy of Sciences, 110,* 15746–15751. (10)

Masland, R. H. (2012). The tasks of amacrine cells. *Visual Neuroscience, 29,* 3–9. (5)

Masland, R. H. (2001). The fundamental plan of the retina. *Nature Neuroscience, 4,* 877–886. (5)

Mason, M. F., Norton, M. I., Van Horn, J. D., Wegner, D. M., Grafton, S. T., & Macrae, C. N. (2007). Wandering minds: The default network and stimulus-independent thought. *Science, 315,* 393–395. (4)

Massimini, M., Ferrarelli, F., Huber, R., Esser, S. K., Singh, H., & Tononi, G. (2005). Breakdown of cortical effective connectivity during sleep. *Science, 309,* 2228–2232. (8)

Mathews, G. A., Fane, B. A., Conway, G. S., Brook, C. G. D., & Hines, M. (2009). Personality and congenital adrenal androgen exposure. *Hormones and Behavior, 55,* 285–291. (10)

Mathieson, I., Munafo, M. R., & Flint, J. (2012). Meta-analysis indicates that common variants at the *DISC1* locus are not associated with schizophrenia. *Molecular Psychiatry, 17,* 634–641. (14)

Matrisciano, F., Bonaccorso, S., Ricciardi, A., Scaccianoce, S., Panaccione, I., Wang, L., . . . Shelton, R. C. (2008). Changes in BDNF serum levels in patients with major depression disorder (MDD) after 6 months treatment with sertraline, escitalopram, or venlafaxine. *Journal of Psychiatric Research, 43,* 247–254. (14)

Matson, J. L., Adams, H. L., Williams, L. W., & Rieske, R. D. (2013). Why are there so many unsubstantiated treatments in autism? *Research in Autism Spectrum Disorders, 7,* 466–474. (14)

Matsumoto, Y., Mishima, K., Satoh, K., Tozawa, T., Mishima, Y., Shimizu, T., & Hishikawa, Y. (2001). Total sleep deprivation induces an acute and transient increase in NK cell activity in healthy young volunteers. *Sleep, 24,* 804–809. (8)

Matsunami, H., Montmayeur, J.-P., & Buck, L. B. (2000). A family of candidate taste receptors in human and mouse. *Nature, 404,* 601–604. (6)

Mattingley, J. B., Husain, M., Rorden, C., Kennard, C., & Driver, J. (1998). Motor role of human inferior parietal lobe revealed in unilateral neglect patients. *Nature, 392,* 179–182. (13)

Matuszewich, L., Lorrain, D. S., & Hull, E. M. (2000). Dopamine release in the medial preoptic area of female rats in response to hormonal manipulation and sexual activity. *Behavioral Neuroscience, 114,* 772–782. (10)

Maurice, D. M. (1998). The Von Sallmann lecture of 1996: An ophthalmological explanation of REM sleep. *Experimental Eye Research, 66,* 139–145. (8)

May, P. R. A., Fuster, J. M., Haber, J., & Hirschman, A. (1979). Woodpecker drilling behavior: An endorsement of the rotational theory of impact brain injury. *Archives of Neurology, 36,* 370–373. (4)

Maya Vetencourt, J. F., Sale, A., Viegi, A., Baroncelli, L., DePasquale, R., O'Leary, O. F., . . . Maffei, L. (2008). The antidepressant fluoxetine restores plasticity in the adult visual cortex. *Science, 320,* 385–388. (14)

Mayberry, R. I., Lock, E., & Kazmi, H. (2002). Linguistic ability and early language exposure. *Nature, 417,* 38. (13)

Mayer, A. D., & Rosenblatt, J. S. (1979). Hormonal influences during the ontogeny of maternal behavior in female rats. *Journal of Comparative and Physiological Psychology, 93,* 879–898. (10)

Maze, I., Covington, H. E. III, Dietz, D. M., La Plant, Q., Renthal, W., Russo, S. J., . . . Nestler, E. J. (2010). Essential role of the histone methyltransferase G9a in cocaine-induced plasticity. *Science, 327,* 213–216. (14)

Mazur, A., & Michalek, J. (1998). Marriage, divorce, and male testosterone. *Social Forces, 77,* 315–330. (10)

McBurney, D. H., & Bartoshuk, L. M. (1973). Interactions between stimuli with different taste qualities. *Physiology & Behavior,* 10, 1101–1106. (6)

McCall, C., & Singer, T. (2012). The animal and human neuroendocrinology of social cognition, motivation and behavior. *Nature Neuroscience, 15,* 681–688. (13)

McCarley, R. W., & Hoffman, E. (1981). REM sleep, dreams, and the activation-synthesis hypothesis. *American Journal of Psychiatry, 138,* 904–912. (8)

McClintock, M. K. (1971). Menstrual synchrony and suppression. *Nature, 229,* 244–245. (6)

McConnell, J. V. (1962). Memory transfer through cannibalism in planarians. *Journal of Neuropsychiatry,* 3(Suppl. 1), 42–48. (12)

McConnell, M. J., Lindberg, M. R., Brennand, K. J., Piper, J. C., Voet, T., Cowing-Zitron, C., . . . Gage, F. H. (2013). Mosaic copy number variation in human neurons. *Science, 342,* 632–637. (14)

McConnell, S. K. (1992). The genesis of neuronal diversity during development of cerebral cortex. *Seminars in the Neurosciences, 4,* 347–356. (4)

McDaniel, M. A. (2005). Big-brained people are smarter: A meta-analysis of the relationship between *in vivo* brain volume and intelligence. *Intelligence, 33,* 337–346. (3)

McDermott, R., Dawes, C., Prom-Wormley, E., Eaves, L., & Hatemi, P. K. (2013). MAOS and aggression: A gene-environment interaction in two populations. *Journal of Conflict Resolution, 57,* 1043–1064. (11)

McEwen, B. S. (2000). The neurobiology of stress: From serendipity to clinical relevance. *Brain Research, 886,* 172–189. (9, 11)

McEwen, B. S., Akama, K. T., Spencer-Segal, J. L., Milner, T. A., & Waters, E. M. (2012). Estrogen effects on the brain: Actions beyond the hypothalamus via novel mechanisms. *Behavioral Neuroscience, 126,* 4–16. (10)

McGregor, I. S., Hargreaves, G. A., Apfelbach, R., & Hunt, G. E. (2004). Neural correlates of cat odor-induced anxiety in rats: Region-specific effects of the benzodiazepine midazolam. *Journal of Neuroscience, 24,* 4134–4144. (11)

McGuire, S., & Clifford, J. (2000). Genetic and environmental contributions to loneliness in children. *Psychological Science, 11,* 487–491. (4)

McHugh, P. R., & Moran, T. H. (1985). The stomach: A conception of its dynamic role in satiety. *Progress in Psychobiology and Physiological Psychology, 11,* 197–232. (9)

McIntyre, M., Gangestad, S. W., Gray, P. B., Chapman, J. F., Burnham, T. C., O'Rourke, M. T., & Thornhill, R. (2006). Romantic involvement often reduces men's testosterone levels—but not always: The moderating effect of extrapair sexual interest. *Journal of Personality and Social Psychology, 91,* 642–651. (10)

McIntyre, R. S., Konarski, J. Z., Wilkins, K., Soczynska, J. K., & Kennedy, S. H. (2006). Obesity in bipolar disorder and major depressive disorder: Results from a National Community Health Survey on Mental Health and Well-Being. *Canadian Journal of Psychiatry, 51,* 274–280. (9)

McKeever, W. F., Seitz, K. S., Krutsch, A. J., & Van Eys, P. L. (1995). On language laterality in normal dextrals and sinistrals: Results from the bilateral object naming latency task. *Neuropsychologia, 33,* 1627–1635. (13)

McKemy, D. D., Neuhausser, W. M., & Julius, D. (2002). Identification of a cold receptor reveals a general role for TRP channels in thermosensation. *Nature, 416,* 52–58. (6)

McKinnon, W., Weisse, C. S., Reynolds, C. P., Bowles, C. A., & Baum, A. (1989). Chronic stress, leukocyte-subpopulations, and humoral response to latent viruses. *Health Psychology, 8,* 839–402. (11)

McMillan, K. A., Asmundson, G. J. G., Zvolensky, M. J., & Carleton, R. N. (2012). Startle response and anxiety sensitivity: Subcortical indices of physiologic arousal and fear responding. *Emotion, 12,* 1264–1272. (11)

Meddis, R., Pearson, A. J. D., & Langford, G. (1973). An extreme case of healthy insomnia. *EEG and Clinical Neurophysiology, 35,* 213–214. (8)

Mednick, S.C., McDevitt, E. A., Walsh, J. K., Wamsley, E., Paulus, M., Kanady, J. C., & Drummond, S. P. A. (2013). The critical role of sleep spindles in hippocampal-dependent memory: A pharmacological study. *Journal of Neuroscience, 13,* 4494–4504. (8)

Meister, M., Wong, R. O. L., Baylor, D. A., & Shatz, C. J. (1991). Synchronous bursts of action potentials in ganglion cells of the developing mammalian retina. *Science, 252,* 939–943. (4)

Melloni, L., Molina, C., Pena, M., Torres, D., Singer, W., & Rodriguez, E. (2007). Synchronization of neural activity across cortical areas correlates with conscious perception. *Journal of Neuroscience, 27,* 2858–2865. (13)

Melone, M., Vitellaro-Zuccarello, L., Vallejo-Illarramendi, A., Pérez-Samartin, A., Matute, C., Cozzi, A., . . . Conti, F. (2001). The expression of glutamate transporter GLT-1 in the rat cerebral cortex is down-regulated by the antipsychotic drug clozapine. *Molecular Psychiatry, 6,* 380–386. (14)

Meltzer, H. Y., Matsubara, S., & Lee, J.-C. (1989). Classification of typical and atypical antipsychotic drugs on the basis of dopamine D-1, D-2 and serotonin2 pKi values. *Journal of Pharmacology and Experimental Therapeutics, 251,* 238–246. (14)

Meltzoff, A. N., & Moore, M. K. (1977). Imitation of facial and manual gestures by human neonates. *Science, 198,* 75–78. (7)

Melzack, R., & Wall, P. D. (1965). Pain mechanisms: A new theory. *Science, 150,* 971–979. (6)

Mendieta-Zéron, H., López, M., & Diéguez, C. (2008). Gastrointestinal peptides controlling body weight homeostasis. *General and Comparative Endocrinology, 155,* 481–495. (9)

Mergen, M., Mergen, H., Ozata, M., Oner, R., & Oner, C. (2001). A novel melanocortin 4 receptor (MC4R) gene mutation associated with morbid obesity. *Journal of Clinical Endocrinology & Metabolism, 86,* 3448–3451. (9)

Merikangas, K. P., & Pato, M. (2009). Recent developments in the epidemiology of bipolar disorder in adults and children: Magnitude, correlates, and future directions. *Clinical Psychology: Science and Practice, 16,* 121–133. (14)

Merzenich, M. M., Nelson, R. J., Stryker, M. P., Cynader, M. S., Schoppman, A., & Zook, J. M. (1984). Somatosensory cortical map changes following digit amputation in adult monkeys. *Journal of Comparative Neurology, 224,* 591–605. (4)

Mesgarani, N., & Chang, E. F. (2013). Selective cortical representation of attended speaker in multi-talker speech perception. *Nature, 485,* 233–236. (6)

Meshi, D., Drew, M. R., Saxe, M., Ansorge, M. S., David, D., Santarelli, L., . . . Hen, R. (2006). Hippocampal neurogenesis is not required for behavioral effects of environmental enrichment. *Nature Neuroscience, 9,* 729–731. (4)

Mesulam, M.-M. (1995). Cholinergic pathways and the ascending reticular activating system of the human brain. *Annals of the New York Academy of Sciences, 757,* 169–179. (8)

Mevorach, C., Hodsoll, J., Allen, H., Shalev, L., & Humphreys, G. (2010). Ignoring the elephant in the room: A neural circuit to downregulate salience. *Journal of Neuroscience, 30,* 6072–6079. (13)

Meyer, K., Kaplan, J. T., Essex, R., Webber, C., Damasio, H., & Damasio, A. (2010). Predicting visual stimuli on the basis of activity in auditory cortices. *Nature Neuroscience, 13,* 667–671. (6)

Meyer-Bahlburg, H. F. L., Dolezal, C., Baker, S. W., & New, M. I. (2008). Sexual orientation in women with classical or non-classical congenital adrenal hyperplasia as a function of degree of prenatal androgen excess. *Archives of Sexual Behavior, 37,* 85–99. (10)

Meyer-Lindenberg, A. (2010). From maps to mechanisms through neuroimaging of schizophrenia. *Nature, 468,* 194–202. (14)

Meyer-Lindenberg, A., Kohn, P., Mervis, C. B., Kippenhan, J. S., Olsen, R. K., Morris, C. A., & Berman, K. F. (2004). Neural basis of genetically determined visuospatial construction deficit in Williams syndrome. *Neuron, 43,* 623–631. (13)

Meyer-Lindenberg, A., Mervis, C. B., & Berman, K. F. (2006). Neural mechanisms in Williams syndrome: A unique window to genetic influences on cognition and behaviour. *Nature Reviews Neuroscience, 7,* 380–393. (13)

Mezzanotte, W. S., Tangel, D. J., & White, D. P. (1992). Waking genioglossal electromyogram in sleep apnea patients versus normal controls (a neuromuscular compensatory mechanism). *Journal of Clinical Investigation, 89,* 1571–1579. (8)

Mihalcescu, I., Hsing, W., & Leibler, S. (2004). Resilient circadian oscillator revealed in individual cyanobacteria. *Nature, 430,* 81–85. (8)

Mika, A., Mazur, G. J., Hoffman, A. N., Talboom, J. S., Bimonte-Nelson, H. A., Sanabria, F., & Conrad, C. D. (2012). Chronic sgress impairs prefrontal cortex-dependent response inhibition and spatial working memory. *Behavioral Neuroscience, 126,* 605–619. (11)

Milich, R., & Pelham, W. E. (1986). Effects of sugar ingestion on the classroom and playgroup behavior of attention deficit disordered boys. *Journal of Consulting and Clinical Psychology, 54,* 714–718. (9)

Miller, C. A., Gavin, C. F., White, J. A., Parrish, R. R, Honasoge, A., Yancey, C. R., . . . Sweatt, J. D. (2010). Cortical DNA methylation maintains remote memory. *Nature Neuroscience, 13,* 664–666. (12)

Miller, G. (2007a). Animal extremists get personal. *Science, 318,* 1856–1585. (0)

Miller, G. (2007b). The mystery of the missing smile. *Science, 316,* 826–827. (11)

Miller, G. A. (2010). Mistreating psychology in the decades of the brain. *Perspectives on Psychological Science, 5,* 716–743. (13)

Miller, G., Tybur, J. M., & Jordan, B. D. (2007). Ovulatory cycle effects on tip earnings by lap dancers: Economic evidence for human estrus? *Evolution and Human Behavior, 28,* 375–381. (10)

Miller, I. N., Neargarder, S., Risi, M. M., & Cronin-Golomb, A. (2013). Frontal and posterior subtypes of neuropsychological deficit in Parkinson's disease. *Behavioral Neuroscience, 127,* 175–183. (7)

Miller, J. F., Neufang, M., Solway, A., Brandt, A., Trippel, M., Mader, I., . . . Schulze-Bonhage, A. (2013). Neural activity in human hippocampal formation reveals the spatial context of retrieved memories. *Science, 342,* 1111–1114. (12)

Miller, S. L., & Maner, J. K. (2010). Scent of a woman: Men's testosterone responses to olfactory ovulation cues. *Psychological Science, 21,* 276–283. (6)

Milner, B. (1959). The memory defect in bilateral hippocampal lesions. *Psychiatric Research Reports, 11,* 43–58. (12)

Milner, A. D. (2012). Is visual processing in the dorsal stream accessible to consciousness? *Proceedings of the National Academy of Sciences (U.S.A.), 279,* 2289–2298. (5)

Mineur, Y. S., Abizaid, A., Rao, Y., Salas, R., DiLeone, R. J., Gündisch, D., . . . Picciotto, M. R. (2011). Nicotine decreases food intake through activation of POMC neurons. *Science, 332,* 1330–1332. (9)

Minichiello, L. (2009). TrkB signaling pathways in LTP and learning. *Nature Reviews Neuroscience, 10,* 850–860. (12)

Minkel, J. D., Banks, S., Htaik, O., Moreta, M. C., Jones, C. W., McGlinchey, E. L., . . . Dinges, D. F. (2012). Sleep deprivation and stressors: Evidence for elevated negative affect in response to mild stressors when sleep deprived. *Emotion, 12,* 1015–1020. (8)

Minnerup, J., Sutherland, B. A., Buchan, A. M., & Kleinschnitz, C. (2012). Neuroprotection for stroke: Current status and future prospects. *International Journal of Molecular Sciences, 13,* 11753–11772. (4)

Minokoshi, Y., Alquier, T., Furukawa, N., Kim, Y.-B., Lee, A., Xue, B., . . . Kahn, B. B. (2004). AMP-kinase regulates food intake by responding to hormonal and nutrient signals in the hypothalamus. *Nature, 428,* 569–574. (9)

Minto, C. L., Liao, L.-M., Woodhouse, C. R. J., Ransley, P. G., & Creighton, S. M. (2003). The effect of clitoral surgery in individuals who have intersex conditions with ambiguous genitalia: A cross-sectional study. *Lancet, 361,* 1252–1257. (10)

Mishra, J., Zinni, M., Bavelier, D., & Hillyard, S. A. (2011). Neural basis of superior performance of action videogame players in an attention-demanding task. *Journal of Neuroscience, 31,* 992–998. (13)

Misrahi, M., Meduri, G., Pissard, S., Bouvattier, C., Beau, I., Loosfelt, H., . . . Bougneres, P. (1997). Comparison of immunocytochemical and molecular features with the phenotype in a case of incomplete male pseudohermaphroditism associated with a mutation of the luteinizing hormone receptor. *Journal of Clinical Endocrinology & Metabolism, 82,* 2159–2165. (10)

Mistlberger, R. E., & Skene, D. J. (2004). Social influences on mammalian circadian rhythms: Animal and human studies. *Biological Rhythms, 79,* 533–556. (8)

Mitchell, D. E. (1980). The influence of early visual experience on visual perception. In C. S. Harris (Ed.), *Visual coding and adaptability* (pp. 1–50). Hillsdale, NJ: Erlbaum. (5)

Miu, A. C., Vulturar, R., Chis, A., Ungureanu, L., & Gross, J. J. (2013). Reappraisal as a mediator in the link between 5-HTTLPR and social anxiety symptoms. *Emotion, 13,* 1012–1022. (11)

Miyazawa, A., Fujiyoshi, Y., & Unwin, N. (2003). Structure and gating mechanism of the acetylcholine receptor pore. *Nature, 423,* 949–955. (2)

Mochizuki, T., Crocker, A., McCormack, S., Yanagisawa, M., Sakurai, T., & Scammell, T. E. (2004). Behavioral state instability in orexin knock-out mice. *Journal of Neuroscience, 24,* 6291–6300. (8)

Moeller, F. G., Dougherty, D. M., Swann, A. C., Collins, D., Davis, C. M., & Cherek, D. R. (1996). Tryptophan depletion and aggressive responding in healthy males. *Psychopharmacology, 126,* 97–103. (11)

Moens, L. N., De Rijk, P., Reumers, J., Van den Bossche, M. J. A., Glassee, W., De Zutter, S., . . . Del-Favero, J. (2011). Sequencing of *DISC1* pathway genes reveals increased burden of rare missense variants in schizophrenia patients from a northern Swedish population. *PLoS One, 6,* e23450. (14)

Mohr, C., Landis, T., Bracha, H. S., & Brugger, P. (2003). Opposite turning behavior in right-handers and non-right-handers suggests a link between handedness and cerebral dopamine asymmetries. *Behavioral Neuroscience, 117,* 1448–1452. (13)

Money, J. (1967). Sexual problems of the chronically ill. In C. W. Wahl (Ed.), *Sexual problems: Diagnosis and treatment in medical practice* (pp. 266–287). New York: Free Press. (7)

Money, J., & Ehrhardt, A. A. (1972). *Man & woman, boy & girl.* Baltimore: Johns Hopkins University Press. (10)

Money, J., & Lewis, V. (1966). IQ, genetics and accelerated growth: Adrenogenital syndrome. *Bulletin of the Johns Hopkins Hospital, 118,* 365–373. (10)

Money, J., & Schwartz, M. (1978). Biosocial determinants of gender identity differentiation and development. In J. B. Hutchison (Ed.), *Biological determinants of sexual behaviour* (pp. 765–784). Chichester, England: Wiley. (10)

Monfils, M.-H., Cowansage, K. K., Klann, E., & LeDoux, J. E. (2009). Extinction-reconsolidation boundaries: Key to persistent attenuation of fear memories. *Science, 324,* 951–955. (11)

Monk, T. H., & Aplin, L. C. (1980). Spring and autumn daylight time changes: Studies of adjustment in sleep timings, mood, and efficiency. *Ergonomics, 23,* 167–178. (8)

Monroe, S. M., & Harkness, K. L. (2005). Life stress, the "kindling" hypothesis, and the recurrence of depression. *Psychological Review, 112,* 417–445. (14)

Monteleone, P., Serritella, C., Scognamiglio, P., & Maj, M. (2010). Enhanced ghrelin secretion in the cephalic phase of food ingestion in women with bulimia nervosa. *Psychoneuroendocrinology, 35,* 284–288. (9)

Montgomery, K. J., Seeherman, K. R., & Haxby, J. V. (2009). The well-tempered social brain. *Psychological Science, 20,* 1211–1213. (7)

Montgomery, S. A., Baldwin, D. S., Blier, P., Fineberg, N. A., Kasper, S., Lader, M., . . . Thase, M. E. (2007). Which antidepressants have demonstrated superior efficacy? A review of the evidence. *International Clinical Psychopharmacology, 22,* 323–329. (14)

Monti, M. M., Vanhaudenhuyse, A., Coleman, M. R., Boly, M., Pickard, J. D., Tshibanda, L., . . . Laureys, S. (2010). Willful modulation of brain activity in disorders of consciousness. *New England Journal of Medicine, 362,* 579–589. (13)

Monti-Bloch, L., Jennings-White, C., Dolberg, D. S., & Berliner, D. L. (1994). The human vomeronasal system. *Psychoneuroendocrinology, 19,* 673–686. (6)

Montoya, E. R., Terburg, D., Bos, P. A., & van Honk, J. (2012). Testosterone, cortisol, and serotonin as key regulators of social aggression: A review. *Motivation & Emotion, 36,* 65–73. (11)

Moody, T. D., Chang, G. Y., Vanek, Z. F., & Knowlton, B. J. (2010). Concurrent discrimination learning in Parkinson's disease. *Behavioral Neuroscience, 124,* 1–8. (12)

Moon, H. Y., Kim, S. H., Yang, Y. R., Song, P., Yu, H. S., Park, H. G., . . . Suh, P.-G. (2012). Macrophage migration inhibitory factor mediates the antidepressant actions of voluntary exercise. *Proceedings of the National Academy of Sciences (U.S.A.), 109,* 13094–13099. (14)

Moore, L. B., Goodwin, B., Jones, S. A., Wisely, G. B., Serabjit-Singh, C. J., Willson, T. M., . . . Kliewer, S. A. (2000). St. John's wort induces hepatic drug metabolism through activation of the pregnane X receptor. *Proceedings of the National Academy of Sciences, USA, 97,* 7500–7502. (14)

Moore, T., Rodman, H. R., Repp, A. B., & Gross, C. G. (1995). Localization of visual stimuli after striate cortex damage in monkeys: Parallels with human blindsight. *Proceedings of the National Academy of Sciences, USA, 92,* 8215–8218. (5)

Moore, T. L., Schetter, S. P., Killiany, R. J., Rosene, D. L., & Moss, M. B. (2012). Impairment in delayed nonmatching to sample following lesions of dorsal prefrontal cortex. *Behavioral Neuroscience, 126,* 772–780. (12)

Moore-Ede, M. C., Czeisler, C. A., & Richardson, G. S. (1983). Circadian timekeeping in health and disease. *New England Journal of Medicine, 309,* 469–476. (8)

Moors, A. (2009). Theories of emotion causation: A review. *Cognition & Emotion, 23,* 625–662. (11)

Moreau, P., Jolicoeur, P., & Peretz, I. (2013). Pitch discrimination without awareness in congenital amusia: Evidence from event-related potentials. *Brain and Cognition, 81,* 337–344. (6)

Morfini, G. A., You, Y-M., Pollema, S. L., Kaminska, A., Liu, K., Yoshioka, K., . . . Brady, S. T. (2009). Pathogenic huntingtin inhibits fast axonal transport by activating JNK3 and phosphorylating kinesin. *Nature Neuroscience, 12,* 864–871. (7)

Mori, K., Mataga, N., & Imamura, K. (1992). Differential specificities of single mitral cells in rabbit olfactory bulb for a homologous series of fatty acid odor molecules. *Journal of Neurophysiology, 67,* 786–789. (6)

Morishima, Y., Schunk, D., Bruhin, A., Ruff, C. C., & Fehr, E. (2012). Linking brain structure and activation in temporoparietal junction to explain the neurobiology of human altruism. *Neuron, 75,* 73–79. (13)

Morley, J. E., Levine, A. S., Grace, M., & Kneip, J. (1985). Peptide YY (PYY), a potent orexigenic agent. *Brain Research, 341,* 200–203. (9)

Morran, L. T., Schmidt, O. G., Gelarden, I. A., Parrish, R. C. II, & Lively, C. M. (2011). Running with the red queen: Host-parasite coevolution selects for biparental sex. *Science, 333,* 216–218. (10)

Morris, J. A., Jordan, C. L., & Breedlove, S. M. (2004). Sexual differentiation of the vertebrate nervous system. *Nature Neuroscience, 7,* 1034–1039. (10)

Morris, J. S., deBonis, M., & Dolan, R. J. (2002). Human amygdala responses to fearful eyes. *NeuroImage, 17,* 214–222. (11)

Morris, M., Lack, L., & Dawson, D. (1990). Sleep-onset insomniacs have delayed temperature rhythms. *Sleep, 13,* 1–14. (8)

Morris, M. J., Na, E. S., & Johnson, A. K. (2012). Voluntary running-wheel exercise decreases the threshold for rewarding intracranial self-stimulation. *Behavioral Neuroscience, 126,* 582–587. (14)

Morris, N. M., Udry, J. R., Khan-Dawood, F., & Dawood, M. Y. (1987). Marital sex frequency and midcycle female testosterone. *Archives of Sexual Behavior, 16,* 27–37. (10)

Morrison, A. R., Sanford, L. D., Ball, W. A., Mann, G. L., & Ross, R. J. (1995). Stimulus-elicited behavior in rapid eye movement sleep without atonia. *Behavioral Neuroscience, 109,* 972–979. (8)

Morrison, J. H., & Baxter, M. G. (2012). The ageing cortical synapse: Hallmarks and implications for cognitive decline. *Nature Reviews Neuroscience, 13,* 240–250. (4)

Morton, A. J., Wood, N. I., Hastings, M. H., Hurelbink, C., Barker, R. A., & Maywood, E. S. (2005). Disintegration of the sleep–wake cycle and circadian timing in Huntington's disease. *Journal of Neuroscience, 25,* 157–163. (8)

Morton, G. J., Cummings, D. E., Baskin, D. G., Barsh, G. S., & Schwartz, M. W. (2006). Central nervous system control of food intake and body weight. *Nature, 443,* 289–295. (9)

Moruzzi, G., & Magoun, H. W. (1949). Brain stem reticular formation and activation of the EEG. *Electroencephalography and Clinical Neurophysiology, 1,* 455–473. (8)

Moscarello, J. M., & LeDoux, J. E. (2013). Active avoidance learning requires prefrontal suppression of amygdala-mediated defensive reactions. *Journal of Neuroscience, 33,* 3815–3823. (11)

Moser, H. R., & Giesler, G. J. Jr. (2013). Itch and analgesia resulting from intrathecal application of morphine: Contrasting effects on different populations of trigeminothalamic tract neurons. *Journal of Neuroscience, 33,* 6093–6101. (6)

Moss, C. F., & Simmons, A. M. (1986). Frequency selectivity of hearing in the green treefrog, *Hyla cinerea. Journal of Comparative Physiology, A, 159,* 257–266. (6)

Moss, S. J., & Smart, T. G. (2001). Constructing inhibitory synapses. *Nature Reviews Neuroscience, 2,* 240–250. (2)

Mrzljak, L., Bergson, C., Pappy, M., Huff, R., Levenson, R., & Goldman-Rakic, P. S. (1996). Localization of dopamine D4 receptors in GABAergic neurons of the primate brain. *Nature, 381,* 245–248. (14)

Mueller, K. L. O., Marion, S. D., Paul, L. K., & Brown, W. S. (2009). Bimanual motor coordination in agenesis of the corpus callosum. *Behavioral Neuroscience, 123,* 1000–1011. (13)

Muller, Y. L., Hanson, R. L., Bian, L., Mack, J., Shi, X. L., Pakyz, R., . . . Baier, L. J. (2010). Functional variants in MBL2 are associated with Type 2 diabetes and pre-diabetes traits in Pima Indians and the Old Order Amish. *Diabetes, 59,* 2080–2085. (9)

Mulligan, S. J., & MacVicar, B. A. (2004). Calcium transients in astrocyte end feet cause cerebrovascular constrictions. *Nature, 431,* 195–199. (1)

Munk, M. H. J., Roelfsema, P. R., König, P., Engel, A. K., & Singer, W. (1996). Role of reticular activation in the modulation of intracortical synchronization. *Science, 272,* 271–274. (8)

Munoz, D. P., & Everling, S. (2004). Look away: The anti-saccade task and the voluntary control of eye movement. *Nature Reviews Neuroscience, 5,* 218–228. (7)

Murphy, F. C., Nimmo-Smith, I., & Lawrence, A. D. (2003). Functional neuroanatomy of emotions: A meta-analysis. *Cognitive, Affective, & Behavioral Neuroscience, 3,* 207–233. (11)

Murphy, M. R., Checkley, S. A., Seckl, J. R., & Lightman, S. L. (1990). Naloxone inhibits oxytocin release at orgasm in man. *Journal of Clinical Endocrinology & Metabolism, 71,* 1056–1058. (10)

Murray, G., Carrington, M. J., Nicholas, C. L., Kleiman, J., Dwyer, R., Allen, N. B., & Trinder, J. (2009). Nature's clocks and human mood: The circadian system modulates reward motivation. *Emotion, 9,* 705–716. (8)

Murrell, J., Farlow, M., Ghetti, B., & Benson, M. D. (1991). A mutation in the amyloid precursor protein associated with hereditary Alzheimer's disease. *Science, 254,* 97–99. (12)

Murty, V. P., LaBar, K. S., & Adcock, R. A. (2012). Threat of punishment motivates memory encoding via amygdala, not midbrain, interactions with the medial temporal lobe. *Journal of Neuroscience, 32,* 8969–8976. (12)

Musacchia, G., Sams, M., Skoe, E., & Kraus, N. (2007). Musicians have enhanced subcortical auditory and audiovisual processing of speech and music. *Proceedings of the National Academy of Sciences, USA, 104,* 15894–15898. (4)

Muto, A., Ohkura, M., Abe, G., Nakai, J., & Kawakami, K. (2013). Real-time visualization of neuronal activity during perception. *Current Biology, 23,* 1–5. (3)

Myers, J. J., & Sperry, R. W. (1985). Interhemispheric communication after section of the forebrain commissures. *Cortex, 21,* 249–260. (13)

Nadal, A., Díaz, M., & Valverde, M. A. (2001). The estrogen trinity: Membrane, cytosolic, and nuclear effects. *News in Physiological Sciences, 16,* 251–255. (10)

Nadarajah, B., & Parnavelas, J. G. (2002). Modes of neuronal migration in the developing cerebral cortex. *Nature Reviews Neuroscience, 3,* 423–432. (4)

Nader, K., & Hardt, O. (2009). A single standard for memory: The case for reconsolidation. *Nature Reviews Neuroscience, 10,* 224–241. (11)

Naeser, M. A., Alexander, M. P., Helm-Estabrooks, N., Levine, H. L., Laughlin, S. A., & Geschwind, N. (1982). Aphasia with predominantly subcortical lesion sites: Description of three capsular/putaminal aphasia syndromes. *Archives of Neurology, 39,* 2–14. (13)

Nagarajan, S., Mahncke, H., Salz, T., Tallal, P., Roberts, T., & Merzenich, M. M. (1999). Cortical auditory signal processing in poor readers. *Proceedings of the National Academy of Sciences, USA, 96,* 6483–6488. (13)

Nagy, E. (2011). Sharing the moment: The duration of embraces in humans. *Journal of Ethology, 29,* 389–393. (7)

Nahum, L., Bouzerda-Wahlen, A., Guggisberg, A., Ptak, R., & Schnider, A. (2012). Forms of confabulation: Dissociations and associations. *Neuropsychologia, 50,* 2224–2234. (12)

Najt, P., Bayer, U., & Hausmann, M. (2013). Models of hemispheric specialization in facial emotion perception—A reevaluation. *Emotion, 13,* 159–167. (11)

Nakamura, K. (2011). Central circuitries for body temperature regulation and fever. *American Journal of Physiology—Regulatory, Integrative, and Comparative Physiology, 301,* R1207–R1228. (9)

Nakashima, Y., Kuwamura, T., & Yogo, Y. (1995). Why be a both-ways sex changer? *Ethology, 101,* 301–307. (10)

Nakata, H., Yoshie, M., Miura, A., & Kudo, K. (2010). Characteristics of the athletes' brain: Evidence from neurophysiology and neuroimaging. *Brain Research Reviews, 62,* 197–211. (5)

Nara, K., Saraiva, L. R., Ye, X., & Buck, L.B. (2011). A large-scale analysis of odor coding in the olfactory epithelium. *Journal of Neuroscience, 31,* 9179–9191. (6)

Narr, K. L., Woods, R. P., Thompson, P. M., Szeszko, P., Robinson, D., Dimtcheva, T., . . . Bilder, R. M. (2007). Relationships between IQ and regional cortical gray matter thickness in healthy adults. *Cerebral Cortex, 17,* 2163–2171. (3)

Narrow, W. E., Rae, D. S., Robins, L. N., & Regier, D. A. (2002). Revised prevalence estimates of mental disorders in the United States. *Archives of General Psychiatry, 59,* 115–123. (14)

Nasca, C., Xenos, D., Barone, Y., Caruso, A., Scaccianoce, S., Matrisciano, F., . . . Nicoletti, F. (2013). L-acetylcarnitine causes rapid antidepressant effects through the epigenetic induction of mGlu2 receptors. *Proceedings of the National Academy of Sciences, 110,* 4804–4809. (14)

Nassi, J. J., & Callaway, E. M. (2006). Multiple circuits relaying primate parallel visual pathways to the middle temporal cortex. *Journal of Neuroscience, 26,* 12789–12798. (5)

Nassi, J. J., & Callaway, E. M. (2009). Parallel processing strategies of the primate visual system. *Nature Reviews Neuroscience, 10,* 360–372. (5)

Nathans, J., Davenport, C. M., Maumenee, I. H., Lewis, R. A., Hejtmancik, J. F., Litt, M., . . . Fishman, G. (1989). Molecular genetics of human blue cone monochromacy. *Science, 245,* 831–838. (5)

Naumer, M. J., & van den Bosch, J. J. F. (2009). Touching sounds: Thalamocortical plasticity and the neural basis of multisensory integration. *Journal of Neurophysiology, 102,* 7–8. (6)

Navarrete, C. D., McDonald, M. M., Mott, M. L., & Asher, B. (2012). Virtual morality: Emotion and action in a simulated three-dimensional "trolley problem." *Emotion, 12*, 364–370. (11)

Nebes, R. D. (1974). Hemispheric specialization in commissurotomized man. *Psychological Bulletin, 81*, 1–14. (13)

Nedergaard, M., & Verkhatsky, A. (2012). Artifact versus reality: How astrocytes contribute to synaptic events. *Glia, 60*, 1013–1023. (1)

Nef, P. (1998). How we smell: The molecular and cellular bases of olfaction. *News in Physiological Sciences, 13*, 1–5. (6)

Nelson, D. L., Orr, H. T., & Warren, S. T. (2013). The unstable repeats—three evolving faces of neurological disease. *Neuron, 77*, 825–843. (7)

Nelson, C. A., Wewerka, S., Thomas, K. M., Tribby-Walbridge, S., deRegnier, R., & Georgieff, M. (2000). Neurocognitive sequelae of infants of diabetic mothers. *Behavioral Neuroscience, 114*, 950–956. (4)

Nesvag, R., Bergmann, O., Rimol, L. M., Lange, E. H., Haukvik, U. K., Hartberg, C. B.., . . . Agartz, I. (2012). A 5-year follow-up study of brain cortical and subcortical abnormalities in a schizophrenia cohort. *Schizophrenia Research, 142*, 209–216. (14)

Netter, F. H. (1983). *CIBA collection of medical illustrations: Vol. 1. Nervous system.* New York: CIBA. (10)

Nettle, D. (2006). The evolution of personality variation in humans and other animals. *American Psychologist, 61*, 622–631. (11)

Neugebauer, H., Kollmar, R., Niesen, W. D., Bosel, J., Schneider, H., Hobohm, C., . . . Juttler, E. (2013). DEcompressive surgery Plus hypoTHermia for Space-Occupying Stroke (DEPTH-SOS): A protocol of a multicenter randomized controlled clinical trial and a literature review. *International Journal of Stroke, 8*, 383–387. (4)

Neumeister, A., Hu, X.-Z., Luckenbaugh, D. A., Schwarz, M., Nugent, A. C., Bonne, O., . . . Charney, D. S. (2006). Differential effects of *5-HTTLPR* genotypes on the behavioral and neural responses to tryptophan depletion in patients with major depression and controls. *Archives of General Psychiatry, 63*, 978–986. (14)

Neumeister, A., Nugent, A. C., Waldeck, T., Geraci, M., Schwarz, M., Bonne, O., . . . Drevets, W. C. (2004). Neural and behavioral responses to tryptophan depletion in unmedicated patients with remitted major depressive disorder and controls. *Archives of General Psychiatry, 61*, 765–773. (14)

Neville, H. J., Bavelier, D., Corina, D., Rauschecker, J., Karni, A., Lalwani, A., . . . Turner, R. (1998). Cerebral organization for language in deaf and hearing subjects: Biological constraints and effects of experience. *Proceedings of the National Academy of Sciences, USA*, 95, 922–929. (13)

Nevin, R. (2007). Understanding international crime trends: The legacy of preschool lead exposure. *Environmental Research, 104*, 315–336. (11)

Newcomer, J. W., Selke, G., Melson, A. K., Hershey, T., Craft, S., Richards, K., & Alderson, A. L. (1999). Decreased memory performance in healthy humans induced by stress-level cortisol treatment. *Archives of General Psychiatry, 56*, 527–533. (12)

Nicholls, M. E. R., Orr, C. A., Okubo, M., & Loftus, A. (2006). Satisfaction guaranteed: The effect of spatial biases on responses to Likert scales. *Psychological Science, 17*, 1027–1028. (13)

Nicklas, W. J., Saporito, M., Basma, A., Geller, H. M., & Heikkila, R. E. (1992). Mitochondrial mechanisms of neurotoxicity. *Annals of the New York Academy of Sciences, 648*, 28–36. (7)

Nicolelis, M. A. L., Ghazanfar, A. A., Stambaugh, C. R., Oliveira, L. M. O., Laubach, M., Chapin, J. K., . . . Kaas, J. H. (1998). Simultaneous encoding of tactile information by three primate cortical areas. *Nature Neuroscience, 1*, 621–630. (3)

Nieuwenhuys, R., Voogd, J., & vanHuijzen, C. (1988). *The human central nervous system* (3rd rev. ed.). Berlin: Springer-Verlag. (3, 9, 11, 13)

Nijboer, T. C. W., Kollen, B. J., & Kwakkel, G. (2013). Time course of visuospatial neglect early after stroke: A longitudinal cohort study. *Cortex, 59*, 2021–2027. (13)

Nilsson, G. E. (1999, December). The cost of a brain. *Natural History, 108*, 66–73. (3)

Nir, Y., & Tononi, G. (2010). Dreaming and the brain: From phenomenology to neurophysiology. *Trends in Cognitive Sciences, 14*, 88–100. (8)

Nishimaru, H., Restrepo, C. E., Ryge, J., Yanagawa, Y., & Kiehn, O. (2005). Mammalian motor neurons corelease glutamate and acetylcholine at central synapses. *Proceedings of the National Academy of Sciences, USA, 102*, 5245–5249. (2)

Nishimura, Y., Onoe, H., Morichika, Y., Perfiliev, S., Tsukada, H., & Isa, T. (2007). Time-dependent central compensatory mechanisms of finger dexterity after spinal cord injury. *Science, 318*, 1150–1155. (4)

Nishizawa, K., Fukabori, R., Okada, K., Kai, N., Uchigashima, M., Watanabe, M., . . . Kobayashi, K. (2012). Striatal indirect pathway contributes to selection accuracy of learned motor actions. *Journal of Neuroscience, 32*, 13421–13432. (7)

Nitabach, M. N., & Taghert, P. H. (2008). Organization of the *Drosophila* circadian control circuit. *Current Biology, 18*, R84–R93. (8)

Niwa, M., Jaaro-Peled, H., Tankou, S., Seshadri, S., Hikida, T., Matsumoto, Y., . . . Sawa, A. (2013). Adolescent stress-induced epigenetic control of dopaminergic neurons via glucocorticoids. *Science, 339*, 335–339. (11)

Noaghiul, S., & Hibbeln, J. R. (2003). Cross-national comparisons of seafood consumption and rates of bipolar disorders. *American Journal of Psychiatry, 160*, 2222–2227. (14)

Nordenström, A., Frisén, L., Falhammar, H., Filipsson, H., Holmdahl, G., Janson, P. O., . . . Nordenskjold, A. (2010). Sexual function and surgical outcome in women with congenital adrenal hyperplasia due to CYP21A2 deficiency: Clinical perspective and the patients' perception. *Journal of Clinical Endocrinology & Metabolism, 95*, 3633–3640. (10)

Nordenström, A., Servin, A., Bohlin, G., Larsson, A., & Wedell, A. (2002). Sex-typed toy play behavior correlates with the degree of prenatal androgen exposure assessed by *CYP21* genotype in girls with congenital adrenal hyperplasia. *Journal of Clinical Endocrinology & Metabolism, 87*, 5119–5124. (10)

North, R. A. (1989). Neurotransmitters and their receptors: From the clone to the clinic. *Seminars in the Neurosciences, 1*, 81–90. (2)

North, R. A. (1992). Cellular actions of opiates and cocaine. *Annals of the New York Academy of Sciences, 654*, 1–6. (14)

Noseda, R., Kainz, V., Jakubowki, M., Gooley, J. J., Saper, C. B., Digre, K., & Burstein, R. (2010). A neural mechanism for exacerbation of headache by light. *Nature Neuroscience, 13*, 239–245. (8)

Nosenko, N. D., & Reznikov, A. G. (2001). Prenatal stress and sexual differentiation of monoaminergic brain systems. *Neurophysiology, 33*, 197–206. (10)

Nottebohm, F. (2002). Why are some neurons replaced in adult brain? *Journal of Neuroscience, 22*, 624–628. (4)

Novarino, G., El-Fishawy, P., Kayserili, H., Meguid, N. A., Scott, E. M., Schroth, J., . . . Gleeson, J. G. (2012). Mutations in *BCKD-kinase* lead to a potentially treatable form of autism with epilepsy. *Science, 338*, 394–397. (14)

Nowak, M. A., & Sigmund, K. (2005). Evolution of indirect reciprocity. *Science, 437*, 1291–1298. (4)

Nugent, F. S., Penick, S. C., & Kauer, J. A. (2007). Opioids block long-term potentiation of inhibitory synapses. *Nature, 446*, 1086–1090. (12)

Numan, M., & Woodside, B. (2010). Maternity: Neural mechanisms, motivational processes, and physiological adaptations. *Behavioral Neuroscience, 124*, 715–741. (10, 11)

Obeso, J. A., Marin, C., Rodriguez-Oroz, C., Blesa, J., Benitez-Temiño, B., Mena-Segovia, J., . . . Olanow, C. W. (2008). The basal ganglia in Parkinson's disease: Current concepts and unexplained observations. *Annals of Neurology, 64* (Suppl.), S30–S46. (7)

O'Dowd, B. F., Lefkowitz, R. J., & Caron, M. G. (1989). Structure of the adrenergic and related receptors. *Annual Review of Neuroscience, 12*, 67–83. (2)

Ohira, K., Furuta, T., Hioki, H., Nakamura, K. C., Kuramoto, E., Tanaka, Y., . . . Nakamura, S. (2010). Ischemia-induced neurogenesis of neocortical layer 1 progenitor cells. *Nature Neuroscience, 13*, 173–179. (4)

Oka, Y., Butnaru, M., von Buchholtz, L., Ryba, N. J. P., & Zuker, C. S. (2013). High salt recruits aversive taste pathways. *Nature, 494*, 472–475. (6)

O'Kane, G., Kensinger, E. A., & Corkin, S. (2004). Evidence for semantic learning in profound amnesia: An investigation with patient H. M. *Hippocampus, 14*, 417–425. (12)

O'Keefe, J., & Burgess, N. (1996). Geometric determinants of the place fields of hippocampal neurons. *Nature, 381*, 425–434. (12)

Olanow, C. W., Goetz, C. G., Kordower, J. H., Stoessl, A. J., Sossi, V., Brin, M. F., . . . Freeman, T. B. (2003). A double-blind controlled trial of bilateral fetal nigral transplantation in Parkinson's disease. *Annals of Neurology, 54*, 403–414. (7)

Olds, J. (1958). Satiation effects in self-stimulation of the brain. *Journal of Comparative and Physiological Psychology, 51*, 675–678. (14)

Olds, J., & Milner, P. (1954). Positive reinforcement produced by electrical stimulation of the septal area and other regions of the rat brain. *Journal of Comparative and Physiological Psychology, 47, 419–428. (14)

O'Leary, A. (1990). Stress, emotion, and human immune function. *Psychological Bulletin, 108,* 363–382. (11)

Oler, J. A., Fox, A. S., Shelton, S. E., Rogers, J., Dyer, T. D., Davidson, R. J., . . . Kalin, N. H. (2010). Amygdalar and hippocampal substrates of anxious temperament differ in their heritability. *Nature, 466,* 864–868. (11)

Olff, M., Frijling, J. L., Kubzansky, L. D., Bradley, B., Ellenbogen, M. A., Cardoso, C., . . . van Zuiden, M. (2013). The role of oxytocin in social bonding, stress regulation and mental health: An update on the moderating effects of context and individual differences. *Psychoneuroendocrinology, 38,* 1883–1894. (13)

Oliet, S. H. R., Baimouknametova, D. V., Piet, R., & Bains, J. S. (2007). Retrograde regulation of GABA transmission by the tonic release of oxytocin and endocannabinoids governs postsynaptic firing. *Journal of Neuroscience, 27,* 1325–1333. (2)

Olney, J. W., & Farber, N. B. (1995). Glutamate receptor dysfunction and schizophrenia. *Archives of General Psychiatry, 52,* 998–1007. (14)

Olson, E. J., Boeve, B. F., & Silber, M. H. (2000). Rapid eye movement sleep behaviour disorder: Demographic, clinical and laboratory findings in 93 cases. *Brain, 123,* 331–339. (8)

Olton, D. S., & Papas, B. C. (1979). Spatial memory and hippocampal function. *Neuropsychologia, 17,* 669–682. (12)

Olton, D. S., Walker, J. A., & Gage, F. H. (1978). Hippocampal connections and spatial discrimination. *Brain Research, 139,* 295–308. (12)

Ono, M., Igarashi, T., Ohno, E., & Sasaki, M. (1995). Unusual thermal defence by a honeybee against mass attack by hornets. *Nature, 377,* 334–336. (9)

O'Roak, B. J., Vives, L., Fu, W., Egertson, J. D., Stanaway, I. B., Phelps, I. G., . . . Shendure, J., (2012a). Multiplex targeted sequencing identifies recurrently mutated genes in autism spectrum disorders. *Science, 338,* 1619–1622. (14)

O'Roak, B. J., Vives, L., Girirajan, S., Karakoc, E., Krumm, N., . . . Eichler, E. E. (2012b). Sporadic autism exomes reveal a highly interconnected protein network of *de novo* mutations. *Nature, 485,* 246–250. (14)

Ornstein, R. (1997). *The right mind.* New York: Harcourt Brace. (13)

O'Rourke, N. A., Weiler, N. C., Micheva, K. D., & Smith, S. J. (2012). Deep molecular diversity of mammalian synapses: Why it matters and how to measure it. *Nature Reviews Neuroscience, 13,* 365–379. (2)

Ortigue, S., Bianchi-Demicheli, F., Patel, N., Frum, C., & Lewis, J. W. (2010). Neuroimaging of love: fMRI meta-analysis evidence towards new perspectives in sexual medicine. *Journal of Sexual Medicine, 7,* 3541–3552. (13)

Osman, A. M., Porritt, M. J., Nilsson, M., & Kuhn, H. G. (2011). Long-term stimulation of neural progenitor cell migration after cortical ischemia in mice. *Stroke, 42,* 3559–3565. (4)

Ostrovsky, Y., Meyers, E., Ganesh, S., Mathur, U., & Sinha, P. (2009). Visual parsing after recovery from blindness. *Psychological Science, 20,* 1484–1491. (5)

Otmakhov, N., Tao-Cheng, J.-H., Carpenter, S., Asrican, B., Dosemici, A., & Reese, T. S. (2004). Persistent accumulation of calcium/calmodulin-dependent protein kinase II in dendritic spines after induction of NMDA receptor-dependent chemical long-term potentiation. *Journal of Neuroscience, 25,* 9324–9331. (12)

Ouchi, Y., Yoshikawa, E., Okada, H., Futatsubashi, M., Sekine, Y., Iyo, M., & Sakamoto, M. (1999). Alterations in binding site density of dopamine transporter in the striatum, orbitofrontal cortex, and amygdala in early Parkinson's disease: Compartment analysis for ß-CFT binding with positron emission tomography. *Annals of Neurology, 45,* 601–610. (7)

Ousman, S. S., & Kubes, P. (2012). Immune surveillance in the central nervous system. *Nature Neuroscience, 15,* 1096–1101. (1)

Owen, A. M., Coleman, M. R., Boly, M., Davis, M. H., Laureys, S., & Pickard, J. D. (2006). Detecting awareness in the vegetative state. *Science, 313,* 1402. (13)

Oyarzun, J. P., Lopez-Barroso, D., Fuentemilla, L., Cucurell, D., Pedraza, C., Rodriguez-Fornells, A., & de Diego-Balaguer, R. (2012). Updating fearful memories with extinction training during reconsolidation: A human study using auditory aversive stimuli. *PLoS One, 7,* e38849. (11)

Oxley, D. R., Smith, K. B., Alford, J. R., Hibbing, M. V., Miller, J. L., Scalora, M., . . . Hibbing, J. R. (2008). Political attitudes vary with physiological traits. *Science, 321,* 1667–1670. (11)

Pacheco-Calderón, R., Carretero-Guillén, A., Delgado-Garcia, J. M., & Gruart, A. (2012). Red nucleus neurons actively contribute to the acquisition of classically conditioned eyelid responses in rabbits. *Journal of Neuroscience, 32,* 12129–12143. (12)

Packer, A. M., Roska, B., & Häusser, M. (2013). Targeting neurons and photons for optogenetics. *Nature Neuroscience, 16,* 805–815. (3)

Padmos, R. C., Hillegers, M. H. J., Knijff, E. M., Vonk, R., Bouvy, A., Staal, F. J. T., . . . Drexhage, H. A. (2008). A discriminating messenger RNA signature for bipolar disorder formed by an aberrant expression of inflammatory genes in monocytes. *Archives of General Psychiatry, 65,* 395–407. (14)

Paffen, C. L. E., & Alais, D. (2011). Attentional modulation of binocular rivalry. *Frontiers in Human Neuroscience, 5,* Article 105. (13)

Pail, G., Huf, W., Pjrek, E., Winkler, D., Willeit, M., Praschak-Rider, N., & Kasper, S. (2011). Bright-light therapy in the treatment of mood disorders. *Neuropsychobiology, 64,* 152–162. (14)

Pakaprot, N., Kim, S., & Thompson, R. F. (2009). The role of the cerebellar interpositus nucleus in short and long term memory for trace eyeblink conditioning. *Behavioral Neuroscience, 123,* 54–61. (12)

Palop, J. J., Chin, J., & Mucke, L. (2006). A network dysfunction perspective on neurodegenerative diseases. *Nature, 443,* 768–773. (12)

Palva, S., Linkenkaer-Hansen, K., Näätänen, R., & Palva, J. M. (2005). Early neural correlates of conscious somatosensory perception. *Journal of Neuroscience, 25,* 5248–5258. (6)

Pan, A. H., Li, M., Gao, J. Y., Xue, Z. Q., Li, Z. Y., Yuan, X. Y., . . . Yan, X. X. (2013). Experimental epidural hematoma causes cerebral infarction and activates neocortical glial and neuronal genesis in adult guinea pigs. *Journal of Neuroscience Research, 92,* 249–261. (4)

Pandey, G. N., Pandey, S. C., Dwivedi, Y., Sharma, R. P., Janicak, P. G., & Davis, J. M. (1995). Platelet serotonin-2A receptors: A potential biological marker for suicidal behavior. *American Journal of Psychiatry, 152,* 850–855. (11)

Pandey, S. C., Zhang, H., Ugale, R., Prakash, A., Xu, T., & Misra, K. (2008). Effector intermediate-early gene Arc in the amygdala plays a critical role in alcoholism. *Journal of Neuroscience, 28,* 2589–2600. (14)

Panegyres, P. K., & Goh, J. G. S. (2011). The neurology and natural history of patients with indeterminate CAG repeat length mutations of the Huntington disease gene. *Journal of the Neurological Sciences, 301,* 14–20. (7)

Panov, A. V., Gutekunst, C.-A., Leavitt, B. R., Hayden, M. R, Burke, J. R., Strittmatter, W. J., & Greenamyre, J. T. (2002). Early mitochondrial calcium defects in Huntington's disease are a direct effect of polyglutamines. *Nature Neuroscience, 5,* 731–736. (7)

Panula, P., & Nuutinen, S. (2013). The histaminergic network in the brain: Basic organization and role in disease. *Nature Reviews Neuroscience, 14,* 472–487. (8)

Pardal, R., & López-Barneo, J. (2002). Low glucose-sensing cells in the carotid body. *Nature Neuroscience, 5,* 197–198. (9)

Paré, M., Smith, A. M., & Rice, F. L. (2002). Distribution and terminal arborizations of cutaneous mechanoreceptors in the glabrous finger pads of the monkey. *Journal of Comparative Neurology, 445,* 347–359. (6)

Parent, M. B., Habib, M. K., & Baker, G. B. (1999). Task-dependent effects of the antidepressant/antipanic drug phenelzine on memory. *Psychopharmacology, 142,* 280–288. (8)

Parise, E., & Csibra, G. (2012). Electrophysiological evidence for the understanding of maternal speech by 9-month-old infants. *Psychological Science, 23,* 728–733. (3)

Park, D. C., & McDonough, I. M. (2013). The dynamic aging mind: Revelations from functional neuroimaging research. *Perspectives on Psychological Science, 8,* 62–67. (4)

Park, I. S., Lee, K. J., Han, J. W., Lee, N. J., Lee, W. T., Park, K. A., & Rhyu, I. J. (2009). Experience-dependent plasticity of cerebellar vermis in basketball players. *Cerebellum, 8,* 334–339. (7)

Park, I. S., Lee, N. J., Kim, T.-Y., Park, J.-H., Won, Y.-M., Jung, Y.-J., . . . Rhyu, I. J. (2012). Volumetric analysis of cerebellum in short-track speed skating players. *Cerebellum, 11,* 925–930. (7)

Park, S., Holzman, P. S., & Goldman-Rakic, P. S. (1995). Spatial working memory deficits in the relatives of schizophrenic patients. *Archives of General Psychiatry, 52,* 821–828. (14)

Parker, G. H. (1922). *Smell, taste, and allied senses in the vertebrates.* Philadelphia: Lippincott. (6)

Parton, L. E., Ye, C. P., Coppari, R., Enriori, P. J., Choi, B., Zhang, C.-Y., . . . Lowell, B. B. (2007). Glucose sensing by POMC neurons regulates glucose homeostasis and is impaired in obesity. *Nature, 449,* 228–232. (9)

Parvizi, J., Jacques, C., Foster, B. L., Withoft, N., Rangarajan, V., Weiner, K. S., & Grill-Spector, K. (2012). Electrical stimulation of human fusiform face-selective regions distorts face perception. *Journal of Neuroscience, 32,* 14915–14920. (5)

Pascual, A., Hidalgo-Figueroa, M., Piruat, J. I., Pintado, C. O., Gómez-Díaz, R., & López-Barneo, J. (2008). Absolute requirement of GDNF for adult catecholaminergic neuron survival. *Nature Neuroscience, 11,* 755–761. (4)

Pase, M. P., Kean, J., Sarris, J., Neale, C., Scholey, A. B., & Stough, C. (2012). The cognitive-enhancing effects of *Bacopa monnieri*: A systematic review of randomized, controlled human trials. *Journal of Alternative and Complementary Medicine, 18,* 647–652. (12)

Pasterski, V. L., Geffner, M. E., Brain, C., Hindmarsh, P., Brook, C., & Hines, M. (2005). Prenatal hormones and postnatal socialization by parents as determinants of male-typical toy play in girls with congenital adrenal hyperplasia. *Child Development, 76,* 264–278. (10)

Pasterski, V., Geffner, M. E., Brain, C., Hindmarsh, P., Brook, C., & Hines, M. (2011). Prenatal hormones and childhood sexual selection: Playmate and play style preferences in girls with congenital adrenal hyperplasia. *Hormones and Behavior, 59,* 549–555. (10)

Patel, A. D. (2008). *Music, language, and the brain.* New York: Oxford University Press. (13)

Patil, S. T., Zhang, L., Martenyi, F., Lowe, S. L., Jackson, K. A., Andreev, B. V., . . . Morozova, M. A. (2007). Activation of mGlu 2/3 receptors as a new approach to treat schizophrenia: A randomized phase 2 clinical trial. *Nature Medicine,* 1102–1107. (14)

Patston, L L. M., Corballis, M. C., Hogg, S. L., & Tippet, L. J. (2006). The neglect of musicians: Line bisection reveals an opposite bias. *Psychological Science, 17,* 1029–1031. (13)

Patterson, K., Nestor, P. J., & Rogers, T. T. (2007). Where do you know what you know? The representation of semantic knowledge in the human brain. *Nature Reviews Neuroscience, 8,* 976–987. (12)

Paul, L. K., Brown, W. S., Adolphs, R., Tyszka, J. M., Richards, L. J., Mukherjee, P., & Sherr, E. H. (2007). Agenesis of the corpus callosum: Genetic, developmental and functional aspects of connectivity. *Nature Reviews Neuroscience, 8,* 287–299. (13)

Paulesu, E., Frith, U., Snowling, M., Gallagher, A., Morton, J., Frackowiak, R. S. J., & Frith, C. D. (1996). Is developmental dyslexia a disconnection syndrome? *Brain, 119,* 143–157. (13)

Paus, T., Marrett, S., Worsley, K. J., & Evans, A. C. (1995). Extraretinal modulation of cerebral blood flow in the human visual cortex: Implications for saccadic suppression. *Journal of Neurophysiology, 74,* 2179–2183. (5)

Pavlov, I. P. (1927). *Conditioned reflexes.* Oxford, England: Oxford University Press. (12)

Pearson, H. (2006). Freaks of nature? *Nature, 444,* 1000–1001. (7)

Peciña, M., Azhar, H., Love, T. M., Lu, T., Fredrickson, B. L., Stohler, C. S., & Zubieta, J.-K. (2013). Personality trait predictors of placebo analgesia and neurobiological correlates. *Neuropsychopharmacology, 38,* 639–646. (6)

Peck, C. J., Lau, B., & Salzman, C. D. (2013). The primate amygdala combines information about space and value. *Nature Neuroscience, 16,* 340–348. (11)

Peelle, J. E., Troiani, V., Grossman, M., & Wingfield, A. (2011). Hearing loss in older adults affects neural systems supporting speech comprehension. *Journal of Neuroscience, 31,* 12638–12643. (6)

Peet, M. (2004). Nutrition and schizophrenia: Beyond omega-3 fatty acids. *Prostaglandins, Leukotrienes and Essential Fatty Acids, 70,* 417–422. (14)

Peeters, R., Simone, L., Nelissen, K., Fabbri-Desstro, M., Vanduffel, W., Rizzolatti, G., & Orban, G. A. (2009). The representation of tool use in humans and monkeys: Common and uniquely human features. *Journal of Neuroscience, 29,* 11523–11539. (0)

Peigneux, P., Laureys, S., Fuchs, S., Collette, F., Perrin, F., Reggers, J., . . . Maquet, P. (2004). Are spatial memories strengthened in the human hippocampus during slow wave sleep? *Neuron, 44,* 535–545. (8)

Peleg, G., Katzir, G., Peleg, O., Kamara, M., Brodsky, L., Hel-or, H., . . . Nevo, E. (2006). Hereditary family signature of facial expression. *Proceedings of the National Academy of Sciences, USA, 103,* 15921–15926. (4)

Pelli, D. G., & Tillman, K. A. (2008). The uncrowded window of object recognition. *Nature Neuroscience, 11,* 1129–1135. (5)

Pellis, S. M., O'Brien, D. P., Pellis, V. C., Teitelbaum, P., Wolgin, D. L., & Kennedy, S. (1988). Escalation of feline predation along a gradient from avoidance through "play" to killing. *Behavioral Neuroscience, 102,* 760–777. (11)

Pelleymounter, M. A., Cullen, M. J., Baker, M. B., Hecht, R., Winters, D., Boone, T., & Collins, F. (1995). Effects of the obese gene product on body weight regulation in *ob/ob* mice. *Science, 269,* 540–543. (9)

Penagos, H., Melcher, J. R., & Oxenham, A. J. (2004). A neural representation of pitch salience in nonprimary human auditory cortex revealed with functional magnetic resonance imaging. *Journal of Neuroscience, 24,* 6810–6815. (6)

Penfield, W. (1955). The permanent record of the stream of consciousness. *Acta Psychologica, 11,* 47–69. (12)

Penfield, W., & Milner, B. (1958). Memory deficit produced by bilateral lesions in the hippocampal zone. *Archives of Neurology and Psychiatry, 79,* 475–497. (12)

Penfield, W., & Perot, P. (1963). The brain's record of auditory and visual experience. *Brain, 86,* 595–696. (12)

Penfield, W., & Rasmussen, T. (1950). *The cerebral cortex of man.* New York: Macmillan. (3, 7)

Peng, G., & Wang, W. S.-Y. (2011). Hemisphere lateralization is influenced by bilingual status and composition of words. *Neuropsychologia, 49,* 1981–1986. (13)

Penmatsa, A., Wang, K. H., & Gouaux, E. (2013). X-ray structure of dopamine transporter elucidates antidepressant mechanism. *Nature, 503,* 85–90. (14)

Penton-Voak, I. S., Perrett, D. I., Castles, D. L., Kobayashi, T., Burt, D. M., Murray, L. K., & Minamisawa, R. (1999). Menstrual cycle alters face preference. *Nature, 399,* 741–742. (10)

Pepperberg, I. M. (1981). Functional vocalizations by an African grey parrot. *Zeitschrift für Tierpsychologie, 55,* 139–160. (13)

Pepperberg, I. M. (1993). Cognition and communication in an African grey parrot (*Psittacus erithacus*): Studies on a nonhuman, nonprimate, nonmammalian subject. In H. L. Roitblat, L. M. Herman, & P. E. Nachtigall (Eds.), *Language and communication: Comparative perspectives* (pp. 221–248). Hillsdale, NJ: Erlbaum. (13)

Pepperberg, I. M. (1994). Numerical competence in an African gray parrot (*Psittacus erithacus*). *Journal of Comparative Psychology, 108,* 36–44. (13)

Pepperberg, I. M. (2004). "Insightful" string-pulling in grey parrots (*Psittacus erithacus*) is affected by vocal competence. *Animal Cognition, 7,* 263–266. (13)

Perera, T. D., Coplan, J. D., Lisanby, S. H., Lipira, C. M., Arif, M., Carpio, C., . . . Dwork, A. J. (2007). Antidepressant-induced neurogenesis in the hippocampus of adult nonhuman primates. *Journal of Neuroscience, 27,* 4894–4901. (14)

Peretz, I., Cummings, S., & Dube, M. P. (2007). The genetics of congenital amusia (tone deafness): A family-aggregation study. *American Journal of Human Genetics, 81,* 582–588. (6)

Perge, J. A., Niven, J. E., Mugnaini, E., Balasubramanian, V., & Sterling, P. (2012). Why do axons differ in caliber? *Journal of Neuroscience, 32,* 626–638. (1)

Perlow, M. J., Freed, W. J., Hoffer, B. J., Seiger, A., Olson, L., & Wyatt, R. J. (1979). Brain grafts reduce motor abnormalities produced by destruction of nigrostriatal dopamine system. *Science, 204,* 643–647. (7)

Perrachione, T. K., Fedorenko, E. G., Vinke, L., Gibson, E., & Dilley, L. C. (2013). Evidence for shared cognitive processing of pitch in music and language. *PLoS One, 8,* e73372. (13)

Perrone, J. A., & Thiele, A. (2001). Speed skills: Measuring the visual speed analyzing properties of primate MT neurons. *Nature Neuroscience, 4,* 526–532. (5)

Persky, H., Lief, H. I., Strauss, D., Miller, W. R., & O'Brien, C. P. (1978). Plasma testosterone level and sexual behavior of couples. *Archives of Sexual Behavior, 7,* 157–173. (10)

Pert, C. B., & Snyder, S. H. (1973). The opiate receptor: Demonstration in nervous tissue. *Science, 179,* 1011–1014. (2, 6)

Pesold, C., & Treit, D. (1995). The central and basolateral amygdala differentially mediate the anxiolytic effect of benzodiazepines. *Brain Research, 671,* 213–221. (11)

Peters, F., Nicolson, N. A., Berkhof, J., Delespaul, P., & deVries, M. (2003). Effects of daily events on mood states in major depressive disorder. *Journal of Abnormal Psychology, 112,* 203–211. (14)

Peters, R. H., Sensenig, L. D., & Reich, M. J. (1973). Fixed-ratio performance following ventromedial hypothalamic lesions in rats. *Physiological Psychology, 1,* 136–138. (9)

Peters, R. M., Hackeman, E., & Goldreich, D. (2009). Diminutive digits discern delicate details: Fingertip size and the sex difference in tactile spatial acuity. *Journal of Neuroscience, 29,* 15756–15761. (6)

Peterson, C. K., & Harmon-Jones, E. (2012). Anger and testosterone: Evidence that situationally-induced anger relates to situationally-induce testosterone. *Emotion, 12,* 899–902. (11)

Peterson, L. R., & Peterson, M. J. (1959). Short-term retention of individual verbal items. *Journal of Experimental Psychology, 58,* 193–198. (12)

Petitto, L. A., Zatorre, R. J., Gauna, K., Nikelski, E. J., Dostie, D., & Evans, A. C. (2000). Speech-like cerebral activity in profoundly deaf people processing signed languages: Implications for the neural basis of human language. *Proceedings of the National Academy of Sciences, USA, 97,* 13961–13966. (13)

Petrides, G., Tobias, K. G., Kellner, C. H., & Rudorfer, M. V. (2011). Continuation and maintenance electroconvulsive therapy for mood disorders: Review of the literature. *Neuropsychobiology, 64,* 129–140. (14)

Petrovic, P., Kalso, E., Petersson, K. M., & Ingvar, M. (2002). Placebo and opioid analgesia—Imaging a shared neuronal network. *Science, 295,* 1737–1740. (6)

Pezzoli, G., & Cereda, E. (2013). Exposure to pesticides or solvents and risk of Parkinson's disease. *Neurology, 80,* 2035–2041. (7)

Pfaff, D. W. (2007). *The neuropsychology of fair play.* New York: Dana Press. (11)

Pfeiffer, B. E., & Foster, D. J. (2013). Hippocampal place-cell sequences depict future paths to remembered goals. *Nature, 497,* 74–79. (12)

Phan, K. L., Wager, T., Taylor, S. F., & Liberzon, I. (2002). Functional neuroanatomy of emotion: A meta-analysis of emotion activation studies in PET and fMRI. *NeuroImage, 16,* 331–348. (11)

Phelps, M. E., & Mazziotta, J. C. (1985). Positron emission tomography: Human brain function and biochemistry. *Science, 228,* 799–809. (3)

Pietropaolo, S., Feldon, J., Alleva, E., Cirulli, F., & Yee, B. K. (2006). The role of voluntary exercise in enriched rearing: A behavioral analysis. *Behavioral Neuroscience, 120,* 787–803. (4)

Pihlstrom, L., Axelsson, G., Bjornara, K. A., Dizdar, N., Fardell, C., Forsgren, L., . . . Toft, M. (2013). Supportive evidence for 11 loci from genome-wide association studies in Parkinson's disease. *Neurobiology of Aging, 34,* 1708e.7–1708.e13. (7)

Pinker, S. (1994). *The language instinct.* New York: HarperCollins. (13)

Pinkston, J. W., & Lamb, R. J. (2011). Delay discounting in C57BL/6J and DBA/2J mice: Adolescent-limited and life-persistent patterns of impulsivity. *Behavioral Neuroscience, 125,* 194–201. (4)

Pinto, L., & Götz, M. (2007). Radial glial cell heterogeneity: The source of diverse progeny in the CNS. *Progress in Neurobiology, 83,* 2–23. (1)

Pizzagalli, D. A., Holmes, A. J., Dillon, D. G., Goetz, E. L., Birk, J. L., Bogdan, R., . . . Fava, M. (2009). Reduced caudate and nucleus accumbens response to rewards in unmedicated individuals with major depressive disorder. *American Journal of Psychiatry, 166,* 702–710. (14)

Pizzagalli, D. A., Nitschke, J. B., Oakes, T. R., Hendrick, A. M., Horras, K. A., Larson, C. L., . . . Davidson, R. J. (2002). Brain electrical tomography in depression: The importance of symptom severity, anxiety, and melancholic features. *Biological Psychiatry, 52,* 73–85. (14)

Pizzorusso, T., Medini, P., Berardi, N., Chierzi, S., Fawcett, J. W., & Maffei, L. (2002). Reactivation of ocular dominance plasticity in the adult visual cortex. *Science, 298,* 1248–1251. (5)

Plihal, W., & Born, J. (1997). Effects of early and late nocturnal sleep on declarative and procedural memory. *Journal of Cognitive Neuroscience, 9,* 534–547. (8)

Plomin, R., Corley, R., DeFries, J. C., & Fulker, D. (1990). Individual differences in television viewing in early childhood: Nature as well as nurture. *Psychological Science, 1,* 371–377. (4)

Plomin, R., Haworth, C. M. A., Meaburn, E. L., Price, T. S., Wellcome Trust Case Control Consortium 2, & Davis, O. S. P. (2013). Common DNA markers can account for more than half of the genetic influence on cognitive abilities. *Psychological Science, 24,* 562–568. (4)

Ploner, M., Gross, J., Timmerman, L., & Schnitzler, A. (2006). Pain processing is faster than tactile processing in the human brain. *Journal of Neuroscience, 26,* 10879–10882. (6)

Plutchik, R. (1982). A psychoevolutionary theory of emotions. *Social Science Information, 21,* 529–553. (11)

Poduslo, S. E., Huang, R., & Spiro, A. III (2009). A genome screen of successful aging without cognitive decline identifies LRP1B by haplotype analysis. *American Journal of Medical Genetics, B, 153B,* 114–119. (4)

Poeppel, D., Emmorey, K., Hickok, G., & Pylkkännen, L. (2012). Towards a new neurobiology of language. *Journal of Neuroscience, 32,* 14125–14131. (13)

Pogorzala, L. A., Mishra, S. K., & Hoon, M. A. (2013). The cellular code for mammalian thermosensation. *Journal of Neuroscience, 33,* 5533–5541. (6)

Poldrack, R. A., Sabb, F. W., Foerde, K., Tom, S. M., Asarnow, R. F., Bookheimer, S. Y., & Knowlton, B. J. (2005). The neural correlates of motor skill automaticity. *Journal of Neuroscience, 25,* 5356–5364. (7)

Polk, T. A., Drake, R. M., Jonides, J. J., Smith, M. R., & Smith, E. E. (2008). Attention enhances the neural processing of relevant features and suppresses the processing of irrelevant features in humans: A functional magnetic resonance imaging study of the Stroop task. *Journal of Neuroscience, 28,* 13786–13792. (13)

Poncer, J. C., & Malinow, R. (2001). Postsynaptic conversion of silent synapses during LTP affects synaptic gain and transmission dynamics. *Nature Neuroscience, 4,* 989–996. (12)

Pons, T. P., Garraghty, P. E., Ommaya, A. K., Kaas, J. H., Taub, E., & Mishkin, M. (1991). Massive cortical reorganization after sensory deafferentation in adult macaques. *Science, 252,* 1857–1860. (4)

Pontieri, F. E., Tanda, G., Orzi, F., & DiChiara, G. (1996). Effects of nicotine on the nucleus accumbens and similarity to those of addictive drugs. *Nature, 382,* 255–257. (3)

Poremba, A., Saunders, R. C., Crane, A. M., Cook, M., Sokoloff, L., & Mishkin, M. (2003). Functional mapping of the primate auditory system. *Science, 299,* 568–572. (6)

Porter, J., Craven, B., Khan, R. M., Chang, S.-J., Kang, I., Judkewicz, B., . . . Sobel, N. (2007). Mechanisms of scent-tracking in humans. *Nature Neuroscience, 10,* 27–29. (6)

Posner, S. F., Baker, L., Heath, A., & Martin, N. G. (1996). Social contact, social attitudes, and twin similarity. *Behavior Genetics, 26,* 123–133. (4)

Post, R. M. (1992). Transduction of psychological stress into the neurobiology of recurrent affective disorder. *American Journal of Psychiatry, 149,* 999–1010. (14)

Post, R. M., & Silberstein, S. D. (1994). Shared mechanisms in affective illness, epilepsy, and migraine. *Neurology, 44*(Suppl 7), S37–S47. (14)

Potegal, M. (1994). Aggressive arousal: The amygdala connection. In M. Potegal & J. F. Knutson (Eds.), *The dynamics of aggression* (pp. 73–111). Hillsdale, NJ: Erlbaum. (11)

Potegal, M., Ferris, C., Hebert, M., Meyerhoff, J. M., & Skaredoff, L. (1996). Attack priming in female Syrian golden hamsters is associated with a *c-fos* coupled process within the corticomedial amygdala. *Neuroscience, 75,* 869–880. (11)

Potegal, M., Hebert, M., DeCoster, M., & Meyerhoff, J. L. (1996). Brief, high-frequency stimulation of the corticomedial amygdala induces a delayed and prolonged increase of aggressiveness in male Syrian golden hamsters. *Behavioral Neuroscience, 110,* 401–412. (11)

Potegal, M., Robison, S., Anderson, F., Jordan, C., & Shapiro, E. (2007). Sequence and priming in 15 month-olds' reactions to brief arm restraint: Evidence for a hierarchy of anger responses. *Aggressive Behavior, 33,* 508–518. (11)

Poulin, M. J., Holman, E. A., & Buffone, A. (2012). The neruogenetics of nice: Oxytocin and vasopressin receptor genes and prosocial behavior. *Psychological Science, 23,* 446–452. (13)

Powell, L. H., Calvin, J. E., III, & Calvin, J. E., Jr. (2007). Effective obesity treatments. *American Psychologist, 62,* 234–246. (9)

Power, R. A., Keers, R., Ng, M. Y., Butler, A. W., Uher, R., Cohen-Woods, S., . . . Lewis, C. M. (2012). Dissecting the genetic heterogeneity of depression through age at onset. *American Journal of Medical Genetics, 159B,* 859–868. (14)

Powers, K. L., Brooks, P. J., Aldrich, N. J., Palladino, M. A., & Alfieri, L. (2013). Effects of video-game play on information processing: A meta-analytic investigation. *Psychonomic Bulletin & Review, 20,* 1055–1074. (13)

Preckel, F., Lipnevich, A. A., Anastasiya, A., Schneider, S., & Roberts, R. D. (2011). Chronotype, cognitive abilities, and academic achievement: A meta-analytic investigation. *Learning and Individual Differences, 21,* 483–492. (8)

Preckel, F., Lipnevich, A. A., Boehme, K., Brandner, L., Georgi, K., Könen, T., . . . Roberts, R. D. (2013). Morningness-eveningness and educational outcomes: The lark has an advantage over the owl at high school. *British Journal of Educational Psychology, 83,* 114–134. (8)

Premack, A. J., & Premack, D. (1972). Teaching language to an ape. *Scientific American, 227*(4), 92–99. (13)

Preti, G., Cutler, W. B., Garcia, C. R., Huggins, G. R., & Lawley, H. J. (1986). Human axillary secretions influence women's menstrual cycles: The role of donor extract of females. *Hormones and Behavior, 20*, 474–482. (6)

Price, M. P., Lewin, G. R., McIlwrath, S. L., Cheng, C., Xie, J., Heppenstall, P. A., . . . Welsh, M. J. (2000). The mammalian sodium channel BNC1 is required for normal touch sensation. *Nature, 407*, 1007–1011. (6)

Pritchard, T. C., Hamilton, R. B., Morse, J. R., & Norgren, R. (1986). Projections of thalamic gustatory and lingual areas in the monkey, *Macaca fascicularis*. *Journal of Comparative Neurology, 244*, 213–228. (6)

Pritchard, T. C., Macaluso, D. A., & Eslinger, P. J. (1999). Taste perception in patients with insular cortex lesions. *Behavioral Neuroscience, 113*, 663–671. (13)

Provine, R. R. (1979). "Wing-flapping" develops in wingless chicks. *Behavioral and Neural Biology, 27*, 233–237. (7)

Provine, R. R. (1981). Wing-flapping develops in chickens made flightless by feather mutations. *Developmental Psychobiology, 14*, 48 B 1–486. (7)

Provine, R. R. (1984). Wing-flapping during development and evolution. *American Scientist, 72*, 448–455. (7)

Provine, R. R. (1986). Yawning as a stereotyped action pattern and releasing stimulus. *Ethology, 72*, 109–122. (7)

Provine, R. R. (1972). Ontogeny of bioelectric activity in the spinal cord of the chick embryo and its behavioral implications. *Brain Research, 41*, 365–378. (4)

Prutkin, J., Duffy, V. B., Etter, L., Fast, K., Gardner, E., Lucchina, L. A., . . . Bartoshuk, L. M. (2000). Genetic variation and inferences about perceived taste intensity in mice and men. *Physiology & Behavior, 69*, 161–173. (6)

Puca, A. A., Daly, M. J., Brewster, S. J., Matise, T. C., Barrett, J., Shea-Drinkwater, M., . . . Perls, T. (2001). A genome-wide scan for linkage to human exceptional longevity identifies a locus on chromosome 4. *Proceedings of the National Academy of Sciences (U.S.A.), 98*, 10505–10508. (4)

Pudas, S., Persson, J., Josefsson, M., de Luna, X., Nilsson, L.-G., & Nyberg, L. (2013). Brain characteristics of individuals resisting age-related cognitive decline over two decades. *Journal of Neuroscience, 33*, 8668–8677. (4)

Puhl, M. D., Cason, A. M., Wojnicki, F. H. E., Corwin, R. L., & Grigson, P. S. (2011). A history of bingeing on fat enhances cocaine seeking and taking. *Behavioral Neuroscience, 125*, 930–942. (14)

Purcell, D. W., Blanchard, R., & Zucker, K. J. (2000). Birth order in a contemporary sample of gay men. *Archives of Sexual Behavior, 29*, 349–356. (10)

Purves, D., & Hadley, R. D. (1985). Changes in the dendritic branching of adult mammalian neurones revealed by repeated imaging *in situ*. *Nature, 315*, 404–406. (4)

Purves, D., & Lotto, R. B. (2003). *Why we see what we do: An empirical theory of vision*. Sunderland, MA: Sinauer Associates. (5)

Purves, D., Shimpi, A., & Lotto, R. B. (1999). An empirical explanation of the Cornsweet effect. *Journal of Neuroscience, 19*, 8542–8551. (5)

Putnam, S. K., Du, J., Sato, S., & Hull, E. M. (2001). Testosterone restoration of copulatory behavior correlates with medial preoptic dopamine release in castrated male rats. *Hormones and Behavior, 39*, 216–224. (10)

Queen, T. L., & Hess, T. M. (2010). Age differences in the effects of conscious and unconscious thought in decision making. *Psychology and Aging, 25*, 251–261. (4)

Race, E., Keane, M. M., & Verfaellie, M. (2011). Medial temporal lobe damage causes deficits in episodic memory and episodic future thinking not attributable to deficits in narrative construction. *Journal of Neuroscience, 31*, 10262–10269. (12)

Radoeva, P. D., Prasad, S., Brainard, D. H., & Aguirre, G. K. (2008). Neural activity within area V1 reflects unconscious visual performance in a case of blindsight. *Journal of Cognitive Neuroscience, 20*, 1927–1939. (5)

Ragsdale, D. S., McPhee, J. C., Scheuer, T., & Catterall, W. A. (1994). Molecular determinants of state-dependent block of Na1 channels by local anesthetics. *Science, 265*, 1724–1728. (1)

Rahman, Q., Kumari, V., & Wilson, G. D. (2003). Sexual orientation-related differences in prepulse inhibition of the human startle response. *Behavioral Neuroscience, 117*, 1096–1102. (10)

Rahman, Q., & Wilson, G. D. (2003). Born gay? The psychobiology of human sexual orientation. *Personality and Individual Differences, 34*, 1337–1382. (10)

Rainville, P., Duncan, G. H., Price, D. D., Carrier, B., & Bushnell, M. C. (1997). Pain affect encoded in human anterior cingulate but not somatosensory cortex. *Science, 277*, 968–971. (6)

Raj, A., Rifkin, S. A., Andersen, E., & van Oudenaarden, A. (2010). Variability in gene expression underlies incomplete penetrance. *Nature, 463*, 913–918. (4)

Rakic, P. (1998). Cortical development and evolution. In M. S. Gazzaniga & J. S. Altman (Eds.), *Brain and mind: Evolutionary perspectives* (pp. 34–40). Strasbourg, France: Human Frontier Science Program. (4)

Rakic, P., & Lidow, M. S. (1995). Distribution and density of monoamine receptors in the primate visual cortex devoid of retinal input from early embryonic stages. *Journal of Neuroscience, 15*, 2561–2574. (5)

Ralph, M. A. L., Cipolotti, L., Manes, F., & Patterson, K. (2010). Taking both sides: Do unilateral anterior temporal lobe lesions disrupt semantic memory? *Brain, 133*, 3243–3255. (12)

Ralph, M. R., Foster, R. G., Davis, F. C., & Menaker, M. (1990). Transplanted suprachiasmatic nucleus determines circadian period. *Science, 247*, 975–978. (8)

Ralph, M. R., & Menaker, M. (1988). A mutation of the circadian system in golden hamsters. *Science, 241*, 1225–1227. (8)

Ramachandran, V. S. (2003, May). Hearing colors, tasting shapes. *Scientific American, 288*(5), 52–59. (6)

Ramachandran, V. S., & Blakeslee, S. (1998). *Phantoms in the brain*. New York: Morrow. (4)

Ramachandran, V. S., & Hirstein, W. (1998). The perception of phantom limbs: The D. O. Hebb lecture. *Brain, 121*, 1603–1630. (4)

Ramagopalan, S. V., Dyment, D. A., Handunnetthi, L., Rice, G. P., & Ebers, G. C. (2010). A genome-wide scan of male sexual orientation. *Journal of Human Genetics, 55*, 131–132. (10)

Ramirez, J. J. (2001). The role of axonal sprouting in functional reorganization after CNS injury: Lessons from the hippocampal formation. *Restorative Neurology and Neuroscience, 19*, 237–262. (4)

Ramirez, J. J., Bulsara, K. R., Moore, S. C., Ruch, K., & Abrams, W. (1999). Progressive unilateral damage of the entorhinal cortex enhances synaptic efficacy of the crossed entorhinal afferent to dentate granule cells. *Journal of Neuroscience, 19*: RC42, 1–6. (4)

Ramirez, J. J., Campbell, D., Poulton, W., Barton, C., Swails, J., Geghman, K., . . . Courchesne, S. L. (2007). Bilateral entorhinal cortex lesions impair acquisition of delayed spatial alternation in rats. *Neurobiology of Learning and Memory, 87*, 264–268. (4)

Ramirez, J. J., McQuilkin, M., Carrigan, T., MacDonald, K., & Kelley, M. S. (1996). Progressive entorhinal cortex lesions accelerate hippocampal sprouting and spare spatial memory in rats. *Proceedings of the National Academy of Sciences, USA, 93*, 15512–15517. (4)

Ramón y Cajal, S. *see* Cajal, S. R.

Randler, C., Ebenhöh, N., Fischer, A., Höchel, S., Schroff, C., Stoll, J. C., & Vollmer, C. (2012). Chronotype but not sleep length is related to salivary testosterone in young men. *Psychoneuroendocrinology, 37*, 1740–1744. (8)

Ranson, S. W., & Clark, S. L. (1959). *The anatomy of the nervous system: Its development and function* (10th ed.). Philadelphia: Saunders. (3)

Rao-Ruiz, P., Rotaru, D. C., van der Loo, R. J., Mansvelder, H. D., Stiedl, O., Smith, A. B., & Spijker, S. (2011). Retrieval-specific endocytosis of GluA2-AMPARs underlies adaptive reconsolidation of contextual fear. *Nature Neuroscience, 14*, 1302–1308. (11)

Rapoport, S. I., & Bosetti, F. (2002). Do lithium and anticonvulsants target the brain arachidonic acid cascade in bipolar patients? *Archives of General Psychiatry, 59*, 592–596. (14)

Rapoport, S. I., & Robinson, P. J. (1986). Tight-junctional modification as the basis of osmotic opening of the blood–brain barrier. *Annals of the New York Academy of Sciences, 481*, 250–267. (1)

Rasch, B., Pommer, J., Diekelmann, & Born, J. (2009). Pharmacological REM sleep suppression paradoxically improves rather than impairs skill memory. *Nature Neuroscience, 12*, 396–397. (8)

Raschle, N. M., Zuk, J., & Gaab, N. (2012). Functional characteristics of developmental dyslexia in left-hemispheric posterior brain regions predate reading onset. *Proceedings of the National Academy of Sciences (U.S.A.), 109*, 2156–2161. (13)

Rattenborg, N. C., Amlaner, C. J., & Lima, S. L. (2000). Behavioral, neurophysiological and evolutionary perspectives on unihemispheric sleep. *Neuroscience and Biobehavioral Reviews, 24,* 817–842. (8)

Rattenborg, N. C., Mandt, B. H., Obermeyer, W. H., Winsauer, P. J., Huber, R., Wikelski, M., & Benca, R. M. (2004). Migratory sleeplessness in the white-crowned sparrow (*Zonotrichia leucophrys gambelii*). *PLoS Biology, 2,* 924–936. (8)

Raum, W. J., McGivern, R. F., Peterson, M. A., Shryne, J. H., & Gorski, R. A. (1990). Prenatal inhibition of hypothalamic sex steroid uptake by cocaine: Effects on neurobehavioral sexual differentiation in male rats. *Developmental Brain Research, 53,* 230–236. (10)

Rauschecker, A. M., Dastjerdi, M., Weiner, K. S., Witthoft, N., Chen, J., Selimbeyoglu, A., & Parvizi, J. (2011). Illusions of visual motion elicited by electrical stimulation of human MT complex. *PLoS One, 6,* e21798. (5)

Rauskolb, S., Zagrebelsky, M., Dreznjak, A., Deogracias, R., Matsumoto, T., Wiese, S., . . . Barde, Y. A. (2010). Global deprivation of brain-derived neurotrophic factor in the CNS reveals an area-specific requirement for dendritic growth. *Journal of Neuroscience, 30,* 1739–1749. (4)

Redmond, D. E., Jr., Bjugstad, K. B., Teng, Y. D., Ourednik, V., Ourednik, J., Wakeman, D. R., ... Snyder, E. Y. (2007). Behavioral improvement in a primate Parkinson's model is associated with multiple homeostatic effects of human neural stem cells. *Proceedings of the National Academy of Sciences, USA, 104,* 12175–12180. (7)

Redondo, R. L., & Morris, R. G. M. (2011). Making memories last: The synaptic tagging and capture hypothesis. *Nature Reviews Neuroscience, 12,* 17–30. (12)

Reed, F. D. D., Hirst, J. M., & Hayman, S. R. (2012). Assessment and treatment of stereotypic behavior in children with autism and other developmental disabilities: A thirty year review. *Research in Autism Spectrum Disorders, 6,* 422–430. (14)

Reeves, A. G., & Plum, F. (1969). Hyperphagia, rage, and dementia accompanying a ventromedial hypothalamic neoplasm. *Archives of Neurology, 20,* 616–624. (9)

Refinetti, R. (2000). *Circadian physiology.* Boca Raton, FL: CRC Press. (8)

Refinetti, R., & Carlisle, H. J. (1986). Complementary nature of heat production and heat intake during behavioral thermoregulation in the rat. *Behavioral and Neural Biology, 46,* 64–70. (9)

Refinetti, R., & Menaker, M. (1992). The circadian rhythm of body temperature. *Physiology & Behavior, 51,* 613–637. (8)

Regan, T. (1986). The rights of humans and other animals. *Acta Physiologica Scandinavica, 128*(Suppl. 554), 33–40. (0)

Reichelt, K. L., Seim, A. R., & Reichelt, W. H. (1996). Could schizophrenia be reasonably explained by Dohan's hypothesis on genetic interaction with a dietary peptide overload? *Progress in Neuro-Psychopharmacology & Biological Psychiatry, 20,* 1083–1114. (14)

Reick, M., Garcia, J. A., Dudley, C., & McKnight, S. L. (2001). NPAS2: An analog of clock operative in the mammalian forebrain. *Science, 293,* 506–509. (8)

Reid, C. A., Dixon, D. B., Takahashi, M., Bliss, T. V. P., & Fine, A. (2004). Optical quantal analysis indicates that long-term potentiation at single hippocampal mossy fiber synapses is expressed through increased release probability, recruitment of new release sites, and activation of silent synapses. *Journal of Neuroscience, 24,* 3618–3626. (12)

Reiner, W. G., & Gearhart, J. P. (2004). Discordant sexual identity in some genetic males with cloacal exstrophy assigned to female sex at birth. *New England Journal of Medicine, 350,* 333–341. (10)

Reinius, B., Saetre, P., Leonard, J. A., Blekhman, R., Merino-Martinez, R., Gilad, Y., & Jazin, E. (2008). An evolutionarily conserved sexual signature in the primate brain. *PLoS Genetics,* e1000100. (10)

Reisner, A. D. (2003). The electroconvulsive therapy controversy: Evidence and ethics. *Neuropsychology Review, 13,* 199–219. (14)

Reiss, A. L., Eckert, M. A., Rose, F. E., Karchemskiy, A., Kesler, S., Chang, M., . . . Galaburda, A. (2004). An experiment of nature: Brain anatomy parallels cognition and behavior in Williams syndrome. *Journal of Neuroscience, 24,* 5009–5015. (13)

Rennaker, R. L., Chen, C.-F. F., Ruyle, A. M., Sloan, A. M., & Wilson, D. A. (2007). Spatial and temporal distribution of odorant-evoked activity in the piriform cortex. *Journal of Neuroscience, 27,* 1534–1542. (6)

Rensch, B. (1977). Panpsychic identism and its meaning for a universal evolutionary picture. *Scientia, 112,* 337–349. (0)

Rensink, R. A., O'Regan, J. K., & Clark, J. J. (1997). To see or not to see: The need for attention to perceive changes in scenes. *Psychological Science, 8,* 368–373. (13)

Reuter-Lorenz, P., & Davidson, R. J. (1981). Differential contributions of the two cerebral hemispheres to the perception of happy and sad faces. *Neuropsychologia, 19,* 609–613. (11)

Reuter-Lorenz, P. A., & Miller, A. C. (1998). The cognitive neuroscience of human laterality: Lessons from the bisected brain. *Current Directions in Psychological Science, 7,* 15–20. (13)

Revusky, S. (2009). Chemical aversion treatment of alcoholism. In S. Reilly & T. R. Schachtman (Eds.), *Conditioned taste aversion* (pp. 445–472). New York: Oxford University Press. (14)

Reyna, V. F., & Farley, F. (2006). Risk and rationality in adolescent decision making. *Psychological Science in the Public Interest, 7,* 1–44. (4)

Rhee, S. H., & Waldman, I. D. (2002). Genetic and environmental influences on antisocial behavior: A meta-analysis of twin and adoption studies. *Psychological Bulletin, 128,* 490–529. (11)

Rhees, R. W., Shryne, J. E., & Gorski, R. A. (1990). Onset of the hormone-sensitive perinatal period for sexual differentiation of the sexually dimorphic nucleus of the preoptic area in female rats. *Journal of Neurobiology, 21,* 781–786. (10)

Rhodes, J. S., van Praag, H., Jeffrey, S., Girard, I., Mitchell, G. S., Garland, T., Jr., & Gage, F. H. (2003). Exercise increases hippocampal neurogenesis to high levels but does not improve spatial learning in mice bred for increased voluntary wheel running. *Behavioral Neuroscience, 117,* 1006–1016. (4)

Ricciardi, E., Bonino, D., Sani, L., Vecchi, T., Guazzelli, M., Haxby, J. V., . . . Pietrini, P. (2009). Do we really need vision? How blind people "see" the actions of others. *Journal of Neuroscience, 29,* 9719–9724. (7)

Rice, G., Anderson, C., Risch, N., & Ebers, G. (1999). Male homosexuality: Absence of linkage to microsatellite markers at Xq28. *Science, 284,* 665–667. (10)

Rice, W. R., Friberg, U., & Gavrilets, S. (2012). Homosexuality as a consequence of epigenetically canalized sexual development. *Quarterly Review of Biology, 87,* 343–368. (10)

Richard, C., Honoré, J., Bernati, T., & Rousseaux, M. (2004). Straight-ahead pointing correlates with long-line bisection in neglect patients. *Cortex, 40,* 75–83. (13)

Richter, C. P. (1922). A behavioristic study of the activity of the rat. *Comparative Psychology Monographs, 1,* 1–55. (8)

Richter, C. P. (1936). Increased salt appetite in adrenalectomized rats. *American Journal of Physiology, 115,* 155–161. (9)

Richter, C. P. (1950). Taste and solubility of toxic compounds in poisoning of rats and humans. *Journal of Comparative and Physiological Psychology, 43,* 358–374. (6)

Richter, C. P. (1967). Psychopathology of periodic behavior in animals and man. In J. Zubin & H. F. Hunt (Eds.), *Comparative psychopathology* (pp. 205–227). New York: Grune & Stratton. (8)

Richter, C. P. (1975). Deep hypothermia and its effect on the 24-hour clock of rats and hamsters. *Johns Hopkins Medical Journal, 136,* 1–10. (8)

Ridaura, V. K., Faith, J. J., Rey, F. E., Cheng, J., Duncan, A. E., Kau, A. L., . . . Gordon, J. I. (2013). Gut microbiota from twins discordant for obesity modulate metabolism in mice. *Science, 341,* 1079. (9)

Riddick, N. V., Czoty, P. W., Gage, H. D., Kaplan, J. R., Nader, S. H., Icenhower, M., . . . Nader, M. A. (2009). Behavioral and neurobiological characteristics influencing social hierarchy formation in female cynomolgus monkeys. *Neuroscience, 158,* 1257–1265. (11)

Ridding, M. C., & Rothwell, J. C. (2007). Is there a future for therapeutic use of transcranial magnetic stimulation? *Nature Reviews Neuroscience, 8,* 559–567. (14)

Riemann, D., König, A., Hohagen, F., Kiemen, A., Voderholzer, U., Backhaus, J., . . . Berger, M. (1999). How to preserve the antidepressive effect of sleep deprivation: A comparison of sleep phase advance and sleep phase delay. *European Archives of Psychiatry and Clinical Neuroscience, 249,* 231–237. (14)

Rietveld, C. A., Medland, S. E., Derringer, J., Yang, J., Esko, T., Martin, N. W., . . . Koellinger, P. D. (2013). GWAS of 126,559 individuals identifies genetic variants associated with educational attainment. *Science, 340,* 1467–1471. (4)

Rigoni, D., Brass, M., & Sartori, G. (2010). Post-action determinants of the reported time of conscious intentions. *Frontiers in Human Neuroscience, 4,* article 38. (7)

Rinn, W. E. (1984). The neuropsychology of facial expression: A review of the neurological and psychological mechanisms for producing facial expressions. *Psychological Bulletin, 95,* 52–77. (7)

Rittenhouse, C. D., Shouval, H. Z., Paradiso, M. A., & Bear, M. F. (1999). Monocular deprivation induces homosynaptic long-term depression in visual cortex. *Nature, 397,* 347–350. (5)

Ritz, B., Ascherio, A., Checkoway, H., Marder, K. S., Nelson, L. M., Rocca, W. A., . . . Gorell, J. (2007). Pooled analysis of tobacco use and risk of Parkinson's disease. *Archives of Neurology, 64,* 990–997. (7)

Riva-Posse, P., Holtzheimer, P. E., Garlow, S. J., & Mayberg, H. S. (2013). Practical considerations in the development and refinement of subcallosal cingulate white matter deep brain stimulation for treatment-resistant depression. *World Neurosurgery, 80,* S27.E25–S27.E34. (14)

Rizzolatti, G., & Sinigaglia, C. (2010). The functional role of the parieto-frontal mirror circuit: Interpretations and misinterpretations. *Nature Reviews Neuroscience, 11,* 264–274. (7)

Roane, B. M., & Taylor, D. J. (2008). Adolescent insomnia as a risk factor for early adult depression and substance abuse. *Sleep, 31,* 1351–1356. (14)

Robbins, T. W., & Everitt, B. J. (1995). Arousal systems and attention. In M. S. Gazzaniga (Ed.), *The cognitive neurosciences* (pp. 703–720). Cambridge, MA: MIT Press. (8)

Roberson, D. P., Gudes, S., Sprague, J. M., Patoski, H. A. W., Robson, V. K., Blasl, F., . . . Woolf, C. J. (2013). Activity-dependent silencing reveals functionally distinct itch-generating sensory neurons. *Nature Neuroscience, 16,* 910–918. (6)

Roberts, L. E., Eggermont, J. J., Caspary, D. M., Shore, S. E., Melcher, J. R., & Kaltenbach, J. A. (2010). Ringing ears: The neuroscience of tinnitus. *Journal of Neuroscience, 30,* 14972–14979. (6)

Roberts, S. C., Gosling, L. M., Carter, V., & Petrie, M. (2008). MHC-correlated odour preferences in humans and the use of oral contraceptives. *Proceedings of the Royal Society B, 275,* 2715–2722. (6)

Robertson, I. H. (2005, Winter). The deceptive world of subjective awareness. *Cerebrum, 7*(1), 74–83. (3)

Robinson, M. J. F., & Berridge, K. C. (2013). Instant transformation of learned repulsion into motivational "wanting." *Current Biology, 23,* 282–289. (9)

Rochira, V., Balestrieri, A., Madeo, B., Baraldi, E., Faustini-Fustini, M., Granata, A. R. M., & Carani, C. (2001). Congenital estrogen deficiency: In search of the estrogen role in human male reproduction. *Molecular and Cellular Endocrinology, 178,* 107–115. (10)

Rodriguez, I., Greer, C. A., Mok, M. Y., & Mombaerts, P. A. (2000). A putative pheromone receptor gene expressed in human olfactory mucosa. *Nature Genetics, 26,* 18–19. (6)

Roenneberg, T., Allebrandt, K. V., Merrow, M., & Vetter, C. (2012). Social jetlag and obesity. *Current Biology, 22,* 939–943. (8)

Roenneberg, T., Kuehnle, T., Pramstaller, P. P., Ricken, J., Havel, M., Guth, A., & Merrow, M. (2004). A marker for the end of adolescence. *Current Biology, 14,* R1038–R1039. (8)

Roenneberg, T., Kumar, C. J., & Merrow, M. (2007). The human circadian clock entrains to sun time. *Current Biology, 17,* R44–R45. (8)

Roeser, K., Scharb, A. A., & Kübler, A. (2013). The chronotype-academic performance model (CAM): Daytime sleepiness and learning motivation link chronotype and school performance in adolescents. *Personality and Individual Differences, 54,* 836–840. (8)

Roffwarg, H. P., Muzio, J. N., & Dement, W. C. (1966). Ontogenetic development of human sleep-dream cycle. *Science, 152,* 604–609. (8)

Rohde, P., Lewinsohn, P. M., Klein, D. N., Seeley, J. R., & Gau, J. M. (2013). Key characteristics of major depression disorder occurring in childhood, adolescence, emerging adulthood, and adulthood. *Clinical Psychological Science, 1,* 41–53. (14)

Roitman, M. F., Wheeler, R. A., Wightman, R. M., & Carelli, R. M. (2008). Real-time chemical responses in the nucleus accumbens differentiate rewarding and aversive stimuli. *Nature Neuroscience, 11,* 1376–1377. (14)

Rokers, B., Cormack, L. K., & Huk, A. C. (2009). Disparity- and velocity-based signals for three-dimensional motion perception in human MT1. *Nature Neuroscience, 12,* 1050–1055. (5)

Rolls, A., Shechter, R., & Schwartz, M. (2009). The bright side of the glial scar in CNS repair. *Nature Reviews Neuroscience, 10,* 235–241. (4)

Rolls, E. T. (1995). Central taste anatomy and neurophysiology. In R. L. Doty (Ed.), *Handbook of olfaction and gustation* (pp. 549–573). New York: Dekker. (6)

Rolls, E. T. (1996) The representation of space in the primate hippocampus, and its relation to memory. In K. Ishikawa, J. L. McGaugh, & H. Sakata (Eds.), *Brain processes and memory* (pp. 203–227). Amsterdam: Elsevier. (12)

Rolls, E. T., & McCabe, C. (2007). Enhanced affective brain representations of chocolate in cravers vs. non-cravers. *European Journal of Neuroscience, 26,* 1067–1076. (3)

Rome, L. C., Loughna, P. T., & Goldspink, G. (1984). Muscle fiber activity in carp as a function of swimming speed and muscle temperature. *American Journal of Psychiatry, 247,* R272–R279. (7)

Romer, A. S. (1962). *The vertebrate body.* Philadelphia: Saunders. (4)

Romero, E., Cha, G.-H., Verstreken, P., Ly, C. V., Hughes, R. E., Bellen, H. J., & Botas, J. (2008). Suppression of neurodegeneration and increased neurotransmission caused by expanded full-length huntingtin accumulating in the cytoplasm. *Neuron, 57,* 27–40. (7)

Rommel, S. A., Pabst, D. A., & McLellan, W. A. (1998). Reproductive thermoregulation in marine mammals. *American Scientist, 86,* 440–448. (9)

Roney, J. R., & Simmons, Z. L. (2013). Hormonal predictors of sexual motivation in natural menstrual cycles. *Hormones and Behavior, 63,* 636–645. (10)

Roorda, A., & Williams, D. R. (1999). The arrangement of the three cone classes in the living human eye. *Nature, 397,* 520–522. (5)

Roozendaal, B., & McGaugh, J. L. (2011). Memory modulation. *Behavioral Neuroscience, 125,* 797–824. (12)

Roppel, R. M. (1978). Cancer and mental illness. *Science, 201,* 398. (14)

Rosano, C., Venkatraman, V. K., Guralnik, J., Newman, A. B., Glynn, N. W., Launer, L., . . . Aizenstein, H. (2010). Psychomotor speed and functional brain MRI 2 years after completing a physical activity treatment. *Journals of Gerontology Series A-Biological Sciences and Medical Sciences, 65,* 639–647. (4)

Rosanova, M., Gosseries, O., Casarotto, S., Boly, M., Casali, A. G., Bruno, M.-A., . . . Massimini, M. (2012). Recovery of cortical effective connectivity and recovery of consciousness in vegetative patients. *Brain, 135,* 1308–1320. (13)

Rose, J. E., Brugge, J. F., Anderson, D. J., & Hind, J. E. (1967). Phase-locked response to low-frequency tones in single auditory nerve fibers of the squirrel monkey. *Journal of Neurophysiology, 30,* 769–793. (6)

Roselli, C. E., Larkin, K., Resko, J. A., Stellflug, J. N., & Stormshak, F. (2004). The volume of a sexually dimorphic nucleus in the ovine medial preoptic area/anterior hypothalamus varies with sexual partner preference. *Endocrinology, 145,* 478–483. (10)

Roselli, C. E., Stadelman, H., Reeve, R., Bishop, C. V., & Stormshak, F. (2007). The ovine sexually dimorphic nucleus of the medial preoptic area is organized prenatally by testosterone. *Endocrinology, 148,* 4450–4457. (10)

Rosen, A. C., Prull, M. W., O'Hara, R., Race, E. A., Desmond, J. E., Glover, G. H., . . . Gabrieli, J. D. E. (2002). Variable effects of aging on frontal lobe contributions to memory. *NeuroReport, 13,* 2425–2428. (12)

Rosen, H. J., Perry, R. J., Murphy, J., Kramer, J. H., Mychack, P., Schuff, N., . . . Miller, B. L. (2002). Emotion comprehension in the temporal variant of frontotemporal dementia. *Brain, 125,* 2286–2295. (13)

Rosenbaum, R. S., Köhler, S., Schacter, D. L., Moscovitch, M., Westmacott, R., Black, S. E., . . . Tulving, E. (2005). The case of K. C.: Contributions of a memory-impaired person to memory theory. *Neuropsychologia, 43,* 989–1021. (12)

Rosenblatt, J. S. (1967). Nonhormonal basis of maternal behavior in the rat. *Science, 156,* 1512–1514. (10)

Rosenblatt, J. S. (1970). Views on the onset and maintenance of maternal behavior in the rat. In L. R. Aronson, E. Tobach, D. S. Lehrman, & J. S. Rosenblatt (Eds.), *Development and evolution of behavior* (pp. 489–515). San Francisco: Freeman. (10)

Rosenblatt, J. S., Olufowobi, A., & Siegel, H. I. (1998). Effects of pregnancy hormones on maternal responsiveness, responsiveness to estrogen stimulation of maternal behavior, and the lordosis response to estrogen stimulation. *Hormones and Behavior, 33,* 104–114. (10)

Rosenkranz, K., Butler, K., Williamson, A., & Rothwell, J. C. (2009). Regaining motor control in musician's dystonia by restoring sensorimotor organization. *Journal of Neuroscience, 29,* 14627–14636. (4)

Rosenzweig, M. R., & Bennett, E. L. (1996). Psychobiology of plasticity: Effects of training and experience on brain and behavior. *Behavioural Brain Research, 78*, 57–65. (4)

Ross, D., Choi, J., & Purves, D. (2007). Musical intervals in speech. *Proceedings of the National Academy of Sciences, USA, 104*, 9852–9857. (13)

Ross, E. D., Homan, R. W., & Buck, R. (1994). Differential hemispheric lateralization of primary and social emotions. *Neuropsychiatry, Neuropsychology, and Behavioral Neurology, 7*, 1–19. (13)

Rossi, A. F., Bichot, N. P., Desimone, R., & Ungerleider, L. G. (2007). Top-down attentional deficits in macaques with lesions of lateral prefrontal cortex. *Journal of Neuroscience, 27*, 11306–11314. (13)

Rossi, D. J., Oshima, T., & Attwell, D. (2000). Glutamate release in severe brain ischaemia is mainly by reversed uptake. *Nature, 403*, 316–321. (4)

Rossi, E. A., & Roorda, A. (2010). The relationship between visual resolution and cone spacing in the human fovea. *Nature Neuroscience, 13*, 156–157. (5)

Rossi, S., Miniussi, C., Pasqualetti, P., Babiloni, C., Rossini, P. M., & Cappa, S. F. (2004). Age-related functional changes of prefrontal cortex in long-term memory: A repetitive transcranial magnetic stimulation study. *Journal of Neuroscience, 24*, 7939–7944. (12)

Rossion, B., Hanseeuw, B., & Dricot, L. (2012). Defining face perception areas in the human brain: A large-scale factorial fMRI face localizer analysis. *Brain and Cognition, 79*, 138–157. (5)

Roth, B. L., Willins, D. L., Kristiansen, K., & Kroeze, W. K. (1999). Activation is hallucinogenic and antagonism is therapeutic: Role of 5-HT2A receptors in atypical antipsychotic drug actions. *Neuroscientist, 5*, 254–262. (14)

Rottenberg, J., Kasch, K. L., Gross, J. J., & Gotlib, I. H. (2002). Sadness and amusement reactivity differentially predict concurrent and prospective functioning in major depressive disorder. *Emotion, 2*, 135–146. (14)

Roussin, A. T., D'Agostino, A. E., Fooden, A. M., Victor, J. D., & DiLorenzo, P. M. (2012). Taste coding in the nucleus of the solitary tract of the awake, freely licking rat. *Journal of Neuroscience, 32*, 10494–10506. (6)

Routtenberg, A., Cantallops, I., Zaffuto, S., Serrano, P., & Namgung, U. (2000). Enhanced learning after genetic overexpression of a brain growth protein. *Proceedings of the National Academy of Sciences, USA, 97*, 7657–7662. (12)

Rouw, R., & Scholte, H. S. (2007). Increased structural connectivity in grapheme-color synesthesia. *Nature Neuroscience, 10*, 792–797. (6)

Rovainen, C. M. (1976). Regeneration of Müller and Mauthner axons after spinal transection in larval lampreys. *Journal of Comparative Neurology, 168*, 545–554. (4)

Rowland, D. L., & Burnett, A. L. (2000). Pharmacotherapy in the treatment of male sexual dysfunction. *Journal of Sex Research, 37*, 226–243. (10)

Roy, A., DeJong, J., & Linnoila, M. (1989). Cerebrospinal fluid monoamine metabolites and suicidal behavior in depressed patients. *Archives of General Psychiatry, 46*, 609–612. (11)

Royer, S., & Paré, D. (2003). Conservation of total synaptic weight through balanced synaptic depression and potentiation. *Nature, 422*, 518–522. (12)

Rozin, P., Dow, S., Moscovitch, M., & Rajaram, S. (1998). What causes humans to begin and end a meal? A role for memory for what has been eaten, as evidenced by a study of multiple meal eating in amnesic patients. *Psychological Science, 9*, 392–396. (12)

Rozin, P., & Kalat, J. W. (1971). Specific hungers and poison avoidance as adaptive specializations of learning. *Psychological Review, 78*, 459–486. (9, 12)

Rozin, P., & Pelchat, M. L. (1988). Memories of mammaries: Adaptations to weaning from milk. *Progress in Psychobiology and Physiological Psychology, 13*, 1–29. (9)

Rozin, P., & Schull, J. (1988). The adaptive-evolutionary point of view in experimental psychology. In R. C. Atkinson, R. J. Herrnstein, G. Lindzey, & R. D. Luce (Eds.), *Stevens' handbook of experimental psychology* (2nd ed.): Vol. 1. *Perception and motivation* (pp. 503–546). New York: Wiley. (12)

Rubens, A. B., & Benson, D. F. (1971). Associative visual agnosia. *Archives of Neurology, 24*, 305–316. (5)

Rubin, B. D., & Katz, L. C. (2001). Spatial coding of enantiomers in the rat olfactory bulb. *Nature Neuroscience, 4*, 355–356. (6)

Rubinow, M. J., Arseneau, L. M., Beverly, J. L., & Juraska, J. M. (2004). Effect of the estrous cycle on water maze acquisition depends on the temperature of the water. *Behavioral Neuroscience, 118*, 863–868. (9)

Rubinstein, G. (1997). Schizophrenia, rheumatoid arthritis and natural resistance genes. *Schizophrenia Research, 25*, 177–181. (14)

Rudebeck, P. H., Saunders, R. C., Prescott, A. T., Chau, L. S., & Murray, E. A. (2013). Prefrontal mechanisms of behavioral flexibility, emotion regulation and value updating. *Nature Neuroscience, 16*, 1140–1145. (3, 12)

Rudolph, U., Crestani, F., Benke, D., Brünig, I., Benson, J. A., Fritschy, J.-M., . . . Mohler, H. (1999). Benzodiazepine actions mediated by specific gamma-aminobutyric acid(A) receptor subtypes. *Nature, 401*, 796–800. (11)

Rudoy, J. D., Voss, J. L., Westerberg, C. E., & Paller, K. A. (2009). Strengthening individual memories by reactivating them during sleep. *Science, 326*, 1079. (8)

Ruediger, S., Vittori, C., Bednarek, E., Genoud, C., Strata, P., Sacchetti, B., . . . Caroni, P. (2011). Learning-related feedforward inhibitory connectivity growth required for memory precision. *Nature, 473*, 514–518. (12)

Rugg, M. D., & Thompson-Schill, S. L. (2013). Moving forward with fMRI data. *Perspectives on Psychological Science, 8*, 84–87. (3)

Rumbaugh, D. M. (Ed.). (1977). *Language learning by a chimpanzee: The Lana Project*. New York: Academic Press. (13)

Rumbaugh, D. M. (1990). Comparative psychology and the great apes: Their competency in learning, language, and numbers. *Psychological Record, 40*, 15–39. (13)

Rumbaugh, D. M., Savage-Rumbaugh, E. S., King, J. E., & Tagliatela, J. P. (2010). The foundations of primate intelligence and language skills. In D. Broadbent, M. Yuan, K. Schick, & N. Toth (Eds.), *The human brain evolving* (pp. 283–292). Gosport, IN: Stone Age Institute Press. (4)

Rupprecht, R., di Michele, F., Hermann, B., Ströhle, A., Lancel, M., Romeo, E., & Holsboer, F. (2001). Neuroactive steroids: Molecular mechanisms of action and implications for neuropsychopharmacology. *Brain Research Reviews, 37*, 59–67. (10)

Rusak, B., & Zucker, I. (1979). Neural regulation of circadian rhythms. *Physiological Reviews, 59*, 449–526. (8)

Rush, A. J., Trivedi, M. H., Wisniewski, S. R., Stewart, J. W., Nierenberg, A. A., Thase, M. E., . . . Fava, M. (2006). Bupropion-SR, sertraline, or venlaxine-XR after failure of SSRIs for depression. *New England Journal of Medicine, 354*, 1231–1242. (14)

Russell, M. J., Switz, G. M., & Thompson, K. (1980). Olfactory influences on the human menstrual cycle. *Pharmacology, Biochemistry, and Behavior, 13*, 737–738. (6)

Russo, S. J., Murrough, J. W., Han, M.-H., Charney, D. S., & Nestler, E. J. (2012). Neurobiology of resilience. *Nature Neuroscience, 15*, 1475–1484. (11)

Russo, S. J., & Nestler, E. J. (2013). The brain reward circuitry in mood disorders. *Nature Reviews Neuroscience, 14*, 609–625. (14)

Rüttiger, L., Braun, D. I., Gegenfurtner, K. R., Petersen, D., Schönle, P., & Sharpe, L. T. (1999). Selective color constancy deficits after circumscribed unilateral brain lesions. *Journal of Neuroscience, 19*, 3094–3106. (5)

Saad, W. A., Luiz, A. C., Camargo, L. A. A., Renzi, A., & Manani, J. V. (1996). The lateral preoptic area plays a dual role in the regulation of thirst in the rat. *Brain Research Bulletin, 39*, 171–176. (9)

Sääksjärvi, K., Knekt, P., Rissanen, H., Laaksonen, M. A., Reunanen, A., & Männistö, S. (2008). Prospective study of coffee consumption and risk of Parkinson's disease. *European Journal of Clinical Nutrition, 62*, 908–915. (7)

Sabel, B. A. (1997). Unrecognized potential of surviving neurons: Within-systems plasticity, recovery of function, and the hypothesis of minimal residual structure. *The Neuroscientist, 3*, 366–370. (4)

Sabo, K. T., & Kirtley, D. D. (1982). Objects and activities in the dreams of the blind. *International Journal of Rehabilitation Research, 5*, 241–242. (3)

Sack, R. L., & Lewy, A. J. (2001). Circadian rhythm sleep disorders: Lessons from the blind. *Sleep Medicine Reviews, 5*, 189–206. (8)

Sackeim, H. A., Putz, E., Vingiano, W., Coleman, E., & McElhiney, M. (1988). Lateralization in the processing of emotionally laden information: I. Normal functioning. *Neuropsychiatry, Neuropsychology, and Behavioral Neurology, 1*, 97–110. (13)

Sacks, O. (2010, August 30). Face-blind. *The New Yorker, 86(31)*, 36–43. (5)

Sadato, N., Pascual-Leone, A., Grafman, J., Deiber, M.-P., Ibañez, V., & Hallett, M. (1998). Neural networks for Braille reading by the blind. *Brain, 121*, 1213–1229. (4)

Sadato, N., Pascual-Leone, A., Grafman, J., Ibañez, V., Deiber, M.-P., Dold, G., & Hallett, M. (1996). Activation of the primary visual cortex by Braille reading in blind subjects. *Nature, 380*, 526–528. (4)

Sadri-Vakili, G., Kumaresan, V., Schmidt, H. D., Famous, K. R., Chawla, P., Vassoler, F. M., . . . Cha, J. H. J. (2010). Cocaine-induced chromatin remodeling increases brain-derived neurotrophic factor transcription in the rat medial prefrontal cortex, which alters the reinforcing efficacy of cocaine. *Journal of Neuroscience, 30,* 11735–11744. (4)

Sahin, N. T., Pinker, S., Cash, S. S., Schomer, D., & Halgren, E. (2009). Sequential processing of lexical, grammatical, and phonological information within Broca's area. *Science, 326,* 445–449. (13)

Sia, G. M., Clem, R. L., & Huganir, R. L. (2013). The human language-associated gene *SRPX2* regulates synapse formation and vocalization in mice. *Science, 342,* 987–991. (13)

Sakurai, T. (2007). The neural circuit of orexin (hypocretin): Maintaining sleep and wakefulness. *Nature Reviews Neuroscience, 8,* 171–181. (8)

Saladin, M. E., Gray, K. M., McRae-Clark, A. L., LaRowe, S. D., Yeatts, S. D., Baker, N. L., . . . Brady, K. T. (2013). A double blind, placebo-controlled study of the effects of post-retrieval propranolol on reconsolidation of memory for craving and cue reactivity in cocaine dependent humans. *Psychopharmacology, 226,* 721–737. (14)

Salazar, R. F., Dotson, N. M., Bressler, S. L., & Gray, C. M. (2012). Content-specific fronto-parietal synchronization during visual working memory. *Science, 338,* 1097–1100. (12)

Salimpoor, V. N., van den Bosch, I., Kovacevic, N., McIntosh, A. R., Dagher, A., & Zatorre, R. J. (2013). Interactions between the nucleus accumbens and auditory cortices predict music reward value. *Science, 340,* 216–219. (14)

Salmelin, R., Hari, R., Lounasmaa, O. V., & Sams, M. (1994). Dynamics of brain activation during picture naming. *Nature, 368,* 463–465. (3)

Salthouse, T. A. (2006). Mental exercise and mental aging. *Perspectives on Psychological Science, 1,* 68–87. (4)

Samejima, K., Ueda, Y., Doya, K., & Kimura, M. (2005). Representation of action-specific reward values in the striatum. *Science, 310,* 1337–1340. (7)

Sander, K., & Scheich, H. (2001). Auditory perception of laughing and crying activates human amygdala regardless of attentional state. *Cognitive Brain Research, 12,* 181–198. (13)

Sanders, R. D., Hassell, J., Davidson, A. J., Robertson, N. J., & Ma, D. (2013). Impact of anaesthetics and surgery on neurodevelopment: An update. *British Journal of Anaesthesia, 110* (Suppl. 1), 53–72. (4)

Sanders, S. J., Murtha, M. T., Gupta, A. R., Murdoch, J. D., Raubeson, M. J., . . . State, M. W. (2012). *De novo* mutations revealed by whole-exome sequencing are strongly associated with autism. *Nature, 485,* 237–241. (14)

Sanders, S. K., & Shekhar, A. (1995). Anxiolytic effects of chlordiazepoxide blocked by injection of $GABA_A$ and benzodiazepine receptor antagonists in the region of the anterior basolateral amygdala of rats. *Biological Psychiatry, 37,* 473–476. (11)

Sanes, J. N., Donoghue, J. P., Thangaraj, V., Edelman, R. R., & Warach, S. (1995). Shared neural substrates controlling hand movements in human motor cortex. *Science, 268,* 1775–1777. (7)

Sanes, J. R. (1993). Topographic maps and molecular gradients. *Current Opinion in Neurobiology, 3,* 67–74. (4)

Sanger, T. D., Pascual-Leone, A., Tarsy, D., & Schlaug, G. (2001). Nonlinear sensory cortex response to simultaneous tactile stimuli in writer's cramp. *Movement Disorders, 17,* 105–111. (4)

Sanger, T. D., Tarsy, D., & Pascual-Leone, A. (2001). Abnormalities of spatial and temporal sensory discrimination in writer's cramp. *Movement Disorders, 16,* 94–99. (4)

Saper, C. B., Romanovsky, A. A., & Scammell, T. E. (2012). Neural circuitry engaged by prostaglandins during the sickness syndrome. *Nature Neuroscience, 15,* 1088–1095. (11)

Sapolsky, R. M. (1992). *Stress, the aging brain, and the mechanisms of neuron death.* Cambridge, MA: MIT Press. (11)

Sapolsky, R. M. (1998). *Why zebras don't get ulcers.* New York: Freeman. (11)

Sarris, J., Panossian, A., Schweitzer, I., Stough, C., & Scholey, A. (2011). Herbal medicine for depression, anxiety and insomnia: A review of psychopharmacology and clinical evidence. *European Neuropsychopharmacology, 21,* 841–860. (14)

Satinoff, E. (1991). Developmental aspects of behavioral and reflexive thermoregulation. In H. N. Shanir, G. A. Barr, & M. A. Hofer (Eds.), *Developmental psychobiology: New methods and changing concepts* (pp. 169–188). New York: Oxford University Press. (9)

Satinoff, E., McEwen, G. N., Jr., & Williams, B. A. (1976). Behavioral fever in newborn rabbits. *Science, 193,* 1139–1140. (9)

Satinoff, E., & Rutstein, J. (1970). Behavioral thermoregulation in rats with anterior hypothalamic lesions. *Journal of Comparative and Physiological Psychology, 71,* 77–82. (9)

Sato, M., & Stryker, M. P. (2008). Distinctive features of adult ocular dominance plasticity. *Journal of Neuroscience, 28,* 10278–10286. (5)

Satz, P., & Green, M. F. (1999). Atypical handedness in schizophrenia: Some methodological and theoretical issues. *Schizophrenia Bulletin, 25,* 63–78. (14)

Saunders, B. T., Yager, L. M., & Robinson, T. E. (2013). Cue-evoked cocaine "craving": Role of dopamine in the accumbens cores. *Journal of Neuroscience, 33,* 13989–14000. (14)

Savage-Rumbaugh, E. S. (1990). Language acquisition in a nonhuman species: Implications for the innateness debate. *Developmental Psychobiology, 23,* 599–620. (13)

Savage-Rumbaugh, E. S., Murphy, J., Sevcik, R. A., Brakke, K. E., Williams, S. L., & Rumbaugh, D. M. (1993). Language comprehension in ape and child. *Monographs of the Society for Research in Child Development, 58*(Serial no. 233). (13)

Savage-Rumbaugh, E. S., Sevcik, R. A., Brakke, K. E., & Rumbaugh, D. M. (1992). Symbols: Their communicative use, communication, and combination by bonobos (*Pan paniscus*). In L. P. Lipsitt & C. Rovee-Collier (Eds.), *Advances in infancy research* (Vol. 7, pp. 221–278). Norwood, NJ: Ablex. (13)

Savic, I., Berglund, H., & Lindström, P. (2005). Brain response to putative pheromones in homosexual men. *Proceedings of the National Academy of Sciences (U.S.A.), 102,* 7356–7361. (6)

Savic, I., & Lindström, P. (2008). PET and MRI show differences in cerebral asymmetry and functional connectivity between homo- and heterosexual subjects. *Proceedings of the National Academy of Sciences, USA, 105,* 9403–9408. (10)

Sawaguchi, T., & Iba, M. (2001). Prefrontal cortical representation of visuospatial working memory in monkeys examined by local inactivation with muscimol. *Journal of Neurophysiology, 86,* 2041–2053. (12)

Schacter, D. L. (1983). Amnesia observed: Remembering and forgetting in a natural environment. *Journal of Abnormal Psychology, 92,* 236–242. (12)

Scheele, D., Striepens, N., Güntürkün, O., Deutschländer, S., Maier, W., Kendrick, K. M., & Hurlemann, R. (2012). Oxytocin modulates social distance between males and females. *Journal of Neuroscience, 32,* 16074–16079. (13)

Scheele, D., Wille, A., Kendrick, K. M., Stoffel-Wagner, B., Becker, B., Güntürkün, O., . . . Hurlemann, R. (2013). Oxytocin enhances brain reward system responses in men viewing the face of their female partner. *Proceedings of the National Academy of Sciences (U.S.A.), 110,* 20308–20313. (13)

Scheer, F. A. J. L., Wright, K. P., Jr., Kronauer, R. E., & Czeisler, C. A. (2007). Plasticity of the intrinsic period of the human circadian timing system. *PLoS ONE, 8,* e721. (8)

Scheibel, A. B. (1983). Dendritic changes. In B. Reisberg (Ed.), *Alzheimer's Disease* (pp. 69–73). New York: Free Press. (12)

Schenk, T. (2006). An allocentric rather than perceptual deficit in patient D. F. *Nature Neuroscience, 9,* 1369–1370. (5)

Schenk, T., Mai, N., Ditterich, J., & Zihl, J. (2000). Can a motion-blind patient reach for moving objects? *European Journal of Neuroscience, 12,* 3351–3360. (5)

Scherer, S. S. (1986). Reinnervation of the extraocular muscles in goldfish is nonselective. *Journal of Neuroscience, 6,* 764–773. (4)

Scherrer, G., Imamachi, N., Cao, Y.-Q., Contet, C., Mennicken, F., O'Donnell, D., . . . Basbaum, A. I. (2009). Dissociation of the opioid receptor mechanisms that control mechanical and heat pain. *Cell, 137,* 1148–1159. (6)

Schiffman, S. S. (1983). Taste and smell in disease. *New England Journal of Medicine, 308,* 1275–1279, 1337–1343. (6)

Schiffman, S. S., & Erickson, R. P. (1971). A psychophysical model for gustatory quality. *Physiology & Behavior, 7,* 617–633. (6)

Schiffman, S. S., & Erickson, R. P. (1980). The issue of primary tastes versus a taste continuum. *Neuroscience and Biobehavioral Reviews, 4,* 109–117. (6)

Schiffman, S. S., Lockhead, E., & Maes, F. W. (1983). Amiloride reduces the taste intensity of Na^+ and Li^+ salts and sweeteners. *Proceedings of the National Academy of Sciences, USA, 80,* 6136–6140. (6)

Schiffman, S. S., McElroy, A. E., & Erickson, R. P. (1980). The range of taste quality of sodium salts. *Physiology & Behavior, 24,* 217–224. (6)

Schiller, D., Monfils, M.-H., Raio, C. M., Johnson, D. C., LeDoux, J. E., & Phelps, E. A. (2010). Preventing the return of fear in humans using reconsolidation update mechanisms. *Nature, 463,* 49–53. (11)

Schlack, A., Krekelberg, B., & Albright, T. D. (2007). Recent history of stimulus speeds affects the speed tuning of neurons in area MT. *Journal of Neuroscience, 27,* 11009–11018. (5)

Schlerf, J., Ivry, R. B., & Diedrichsen, J. (2012). Encoding of sensory prediction errors in the human cerebellum. *Journal of Neuroscience, 32,* 4913–4922. (7)

Schlinger, H. D., Jr. (1996). How the human got its spots. *Skeptic, 4,* 68–76. (4)

Schmid, A., Koch, M., & Schnitzler, H.-U. (1995). Conditioned pleasure attenuates the startle response in rats. *Neurobiology of Learning and Memory, 64,* 1–3. (11)

Schmid, M. C., Mrowka, S. W., Turchi, J., Saunders, R. C., Wilke, M., Peters, A. J., . . . Leopold, D. A. (2010). Blindsight depends on the lateral geniculate nucleus. *Nature, 466,* 373–377. (5)

Schmidt, L. A. (1999). Frontal brain electrical activity in shyness and sociability. *Psychological Science, 10,* 316–320. (11)

Schmidt, R., Leventhal, D. K., Mallet, N., Chen, F., & Berke, J. D. (2013). Canceling actions involves a race between basal ganglia pathways. *Nature Neuroscience, 16,* 1118–1124. (7)

Schmidt-Hieber, C, Jonas, P., & Bischofberger, J. (2004). Enhanced synaptic plasticity in newly generated granule cells of the adult hippocampus. *Nature, 429,* 184–187. (4)

Schmitt, K. C., & Reith, M. E. A. (2010). Regulation of the dopamine transporter. *Annals of the New York Academy of Sciences, 1187,* 316–340. (2)

Schneider, B. A., Trehub, S. E., Morrongiello, B. A., & Thorpe, L. A. (1986). Auditory sensitivity in preschool children. *Journal of the Acoustical Society of America, 79,* 447–452. (6)

Schneider, P., Scherg, M., Dosch, G., Specht, H. J., Gutschalk, A., & Rupp, A. (2002). Morphology of Heschl's gyrus reflects enhanced activation in the auditory cortex of musicians. *Nature Neuroscience, 5,* 688–694. (4)

Schnider, A. (2003). Spontaneous confabulation and the adaptation of thought to ongoing reality. *Nature Reviews Neuroscience, 4,* 662–671. (12)

Schobel, S. A., Chaudhury, N. H., Khan, U. A., Paniagua, B., Styner, M. A., Asllani, I., . . . Small, S. A. (2013). Imaging patients with psychosis and a mouse model establishes a spreading pattern of hippocampal dysfunction and implicates glutamate as a driver. *Neuron, 78,* 81–93. (14)

Schomacher, M., Müller, H. D., Sommer, C., Schwab, S., & Schäbitz, W.-R. (2008). Endocannabinoids mediate neuroprotection after transient focal cerebral ischemia. *Brain Research, 1240,* 213–220. (4)

Schou, M. (1997). Forty years of lithium treatment. *Archives of General Psychiatry, 54,* 9–13. (14)

Schroeder, J. A., & Flannery-Schroeder, E. (2005). Use of herb *Gymnema sylvestre* to illustrate the principles of gustatory sensation: An undergraduate neuroscience laboratory exercise. *Journal of Undergraduate Neuroscience Education, 3,* A59–A62. (6)

Schröter, M. S., Spoormaker, V. I., Schorer, A., Wohlschläger, A., Czisch, M., Kochs, E. F., . . . Ilg, R. (2012). Spatiotemporal reconfiguration of large-scale brain functional networks during propofol-induced loss of consciousness. *Journal of Neuroscience, 32,* 12832–12840. (13)

Schuckit, M. A., & Smith, T. L. (1996). An 8-year follow-up of 450 sons of alcoholic and control subjects. *Archives of General Psychiatry, 53,* 202–210. (14)

Schuckit, M. A., & Smith, T. L. (1997). Assessing the risk for alcoholism among sons of alcoholics. *Journal of Studies on Alcohol, 58,* 141–145. (14)

Schuckit, M. A., & Smith, T. L. (2013). Stability of scores and correlations with drinking behaviors over 15 years for the self-report of the effects of alcohol questionnaire. *Drug and Alcohol Dependence, 128,* 194–199. (14)

Schulkin, J. (1991). *Sodium hunger: The search for a salty taste.* Cambridge, England: Cambridge University Press. (9)

Schulz, K. M., Molenda-Figueira, H. A., & Sisk, C. L. (2009). Back to the future: The organizational-activational hypothesis adapted to puberty and adolescence. *Hormones and Behavior, 55,* 597–604. (10)

Schwab, M. E. (1998). Regenerative nerve fiber growth in the adult central nervous system. *News in Physiological Sciences, 13,* 294–298. (4)

Schwartz, C. E., Wright, C. I., Shin, L. M., Kagan, J., & Rauch, S. L. (2003). Inhibited and uninhibited infants "grown up": Adult amygdalar response to novelty. *Science, 300,* 1952–1953. (11)

Schwartz, G., Kim, R. M., Kolundzija, A. B., Rieger, G., & Sanders, A. R. (2010). Biodemographic and physical correlates of sexual orientation in men. *Archives of Sexual Behavior, 39,* 93–109. (10)

Schwartz, G. J. (2000). The role of gastrointestinal vagal afferents in the control of food intake: Current prospects. *Nutrition, 16,* 866–873. (9)

Schwartz, L., & Tulipan, L. (1933). An outbreak of dermatitis among workers in a rubber manufacturing plant. *Public Health Reports, 48,* 809–814. (14)

Schwartz, M. F. (1995). Re-examining the role of executive functions in routine action production. *Annals of the New York Academy of Sciences, 769,* 321–335. (7)

Schwartz, W. J., & Gainer, H. (1977). Suprachiasmatic nucleus: Use of ^{14}C-labeled deoxyglucose uptake as a functional marker. *Science, 197,* 1089–1091. (8)

Schweinhardt, P., Seminowicz, D. A., Jaeger, E., Duncan, G. H., & Bushnell, M. C. (2009). The anatomy of the mesolimbic reward system: A link between personality and the placebo analgesic response. *Journal of Neuroscience, 29,* 4882–4887. (6)

Scott, S. H. (2004). Optimal feedback control and the neural basis of volitional motor control. *Nature Reviews Neuroscience, 5,* 532–544. (7)

Scoville, W. B., & Milner, B. (1957). Loss of recent memory after bilateral hippocampal lesions. *Journal of Neurology, Neurosurgery, and Psychiatry, 20,* 11–21. (12)

Seal, R. P., Wang, X., Guan, Y., Raja, S., Woodbury, C. J., Basbaum, A. I., & Edwards, R. H. (2009). Injury-induced mechanical hypersensitivity requires C-low threshold mechanoreceptors. *Nature, 462,* 651–655. (6)

Seeley, R. J., Kaplan, J. M., & Grill, H. J. (1995). Effect of occluding the pylorus on intraoral intake: A test of the gastric hypothesis of meal termination. *Physiology & Behavior, 58,* 245–249. (9)

Seeman, P., Lee, T., Chau-Wong, M., & Wong, K. (1976). Antipsychotic drug doses and neuroleptic/dopamine receptors. *Nature, 261,* 717–719. (14)

Seery, M. D., Leo, R. J., Lupien, S. P., Kondrak, C. L., & Almonte, J. L. (2013). An upside to adversity? Moderate cumulative lifetime adversity is associated with resilient responses in the face of controlled stressors. *Psychological Science, 24,* 1181–1189. (11)

Segal, N. L. (2000). Virtual twins: New findings on within-family environmental influences on intelligence. *Journal of Educational Psychology, 92,* 442–448. (4)

Segerstrom, S. C., & Miller, G. E. (2004). Psychological stress and the human immune system: A meta-analytic study of 30 years of inquiry. *Psychological Bulletin, 130,* 601–630. (11)

Sehgal, A., Ousley, A., Yang, Z., Chen, Y., & Schotland, P. (1999). What makes the circadian clock tick: Genes that keep time? *Recent Progress in Hormone Research, 54,* 61–85. (8)

Seid, M. A., Castillo, A, & Wcislo, W. T. (2011). The allometry of brain miniaturization in ants. *Brain, Behavior and Evolution, 77,* 5–13. (3)

Seif, T., Chang, S.-J., Simms, J. A., Gibb, S. L., Dodgar, J., Chen, B. T., . . . Hopf, F. W. (2013). Cortical activation of accumbens hyperpolarization-active NMDARs mediates aversion-resistant alcohol intake. *Nature Neuroscience, 16,* 1094–1100. (14)

Sejnowski, T. J., & Destexhe, A. (2000). Why do we sleep? *Brain Research, 886,* 208–223. (8)

Selkoe, D. J. (2000). Toward a comprehensive theory for Alzheimer's disease. *Annals of the New York Academy of Sciences, 924,* 17–25. (12)

Selye, H. (1979). Stress, cancer, and the mind. In J. Taché, H. Selye, & S. B. Day (Eds.), *Cancer, stress, and death* (pp. 11–27). New York: Plenum Press. (11)

Selzer, M. E. (1978). Mechanisms of functional recovery and regeneration after spinal cord transection in larval sea lamprey. *Journal of Physiology, 277,* 395–408. (4)

Semendeferi, K., Lu, A., Schenker, N., & Damasio, H. (2002). Humans and great apes share a large frontal cortex. *Nature Neuroscience, 5,* 272–276. (3)

Seminowicz, D. A., Wideman, T. H., Naso, L., Hatami-Khoroushahi, Z., Fallatah, S., Ware, M. A., . . . Stone, L. S. (2011). Effective treatment of chronic low back pain in humans reverses abnormal brain anatomy and function. *Journal of Neuroscience, 31,* 7540–7550. (6)

Sen, S., Duman, R., & Sanacora, G. (2008). Serum brain-derived neurotrophic factor, depression, and antidepressant medications: Meta-analyses and implications. *Biological Psychiatry, 64,* 527–532. (14)

Sens, E., Teschner, U., Meissner, W., Preul, C., Huonker, R., Witte, O. W., . . . Weiss, T. (2012).

Effects of temporary functional deafferentation on the brain, sensation, and behavior of stroke patients. *Journal of Neuroscience, 32,* 11773–11779. (4)

Sereno, A. B., & Holzman, P. S. (1993). Express saccades and smooth pursuit eye movement function in schizophrenic, affective disorder, and normal subjects. *Journal of Cognitive Neuroscience, 5,* 303–316. (14)

Sergent, C., & Dehaene, S. (2004). Is consciousness a gradual phenomenon? *Psychological Science, 15,* 720–728. (13)

Sergent, C., Wyart, V., Babo-Rebelo, M., Cohen, L., Naccache, L., & Tallon-Baudry, C. (2013). Cueing attention after the stimulus is gone can retrospectively trigger conscious perception. *Current Biology, 23,* 150–155. (13)

Serino, A., Pizzoferrato, F., & Làdavas, E. (2008). Viewing a face (especially one's own face) being touched enhances tactile perception on the face. *Psychological Science, 19,* 434–438. (6)

Severens, M., Farquhar, J., Desain, P., Duysens, J., & Gielen, C. (2010). Transient and steady-state responses to mechanical stimulation of different fingers reveal interactions based on lateral inhibition. *Clinical Neurophysiology, 121,* 2090–2096. (5)

Sevenster, D., Beckers, T., & Kindt, M. (2013). Prediction error governs pharmacologically induced amnesia for learned fear. *Science, 339,* 830–833. (11)

Shackman, A. J., McMenamin, B. W., Maxwell, J. S., Greischar, L. L., & Davidson, R. J. (2009). Right dorsolateral prefrontal cortical activity and behavioral inhibition. *Psychological Science, 20,* 1500–1506. (11)

Shah, B., Shine, R., Hudson, S., & Kearney, M. (2003). Sociality in lizards: Why do thick-tailed geckos (*Nephrurus milii*) aggregate? *Behaviour, 140,* 1039–1052. (9)

Shah, N. M., Pisapia, D. J., Maniatis, S., Mendelsohn, M. M., Nemes, A., & Axel, R. (2004). Visualizing sexual dimorphism in the brain. *Neuron, 43,* 313–319. (10)

Shakelford, T. K., Buss, D. M., & Bennett, K. (2002). Forgiveness or breakup: Sex differences in responses to a partner's infidelity. *Cognition and Emotion, 16,* 299–307. (10)

Shalev, A. Y., Peri, T., Brandes, D., Freedman, S., Orr, S. P., & Pitman, R. K. (2000). Auditory startle response in trauma survivors with posttraumatic stress disorder: A prospective study. *American Journal of Psychiatry, 157,* 255–261. (11)

Shapiro, C. M., Bortz, R., Mitchell, D., Bartel, P., & Jooste, P. (1981). Slow-wave sleep: A recovery period after exercise. *Science, 214,* 1253–1254. (8)

Sharbaugh, S. M. (2001). Seasonal acclimatization to extreme climatic conditions by black-capped chickadees (*Poecile atricapilla*) in interior Alaska (64° N). *Physiological and Biochemical Zoology, 74,* 568–575. (9)

Sharma, J., Angelucci, A., & Sur, M. (2000). Induction of visual orientation modules in auditory cortex. *Nature, 404,* 841–847. (4)

Shatz, C. J. (1992, September). The developing brain. *Scientific American, 267*(9), 60–67. (4)

Shatz, C. J. (1996). Emergence of order in visual-system development. *Proceedings of the National Academy of Sciences, USA, 93,* 602–608. (5)

Shaughnessy, M. F. (2009). An interview with Christian Ambler: Traumatic brain injury in sports. *North American Journal of Psychology, 11,* 297–308. (4)

Shaw, D. J., & Czekóová, K. (2013). Exploring the development of the mirror neuron system: Finding the right paradigm. *Developmental Neuropsychology, 38,* 256–271. (7)

Sheehan, T. P., Cirrito, J., Numan, M. J., & Numan, M. (2000). Using *c-Fos* immunocytochemistry to identify forebrain regions that may inhibit maternal behavior in rats. *Behavioral Neuroscience, 114,* 337–352. (10)

Shema, R., Haramati, S., Ron, S., Hazvi, S., Chen, A., Sacktor, T. C., . . . Dudai, Y. (2011). Enhancement of consolidated long-term memory by overexpression of protein kinase Mζ in the neocortex. *Science, 331,* 1207–1210. (12)

Shema, R., Sacktor, T. C., & Dudai, Y. (2007). Rapid erasure of long-term memory associations in the cortex by an inhibitor of PKMζ. *Science, 317,* 951–953. (12)

Shen, H., Gong, Q. H., Aoki, C., Yuan, M., Ruderman, Y., Dattilo, M., . . . Smith, S. S. (2007). Reversal of neurosteroid effects at alpha 4 beta 2 delta $GABA_A$ receptors triggers anxiety at puberty. *Nature Neuroscience, 10,* 469–477. (11)

Sher, L., Carballo, J. J., Grunebaum, M. F., Burke, A. K., Zalsman, G., Huang, Y.-Y., . . . Oquendo, M. A. (2006). A prospective study of the association of cerebrospinal fluid monoamine metabolite levels with lethality of suicide attempts in patients with bipolar disorder. *Bipolar Disorders, 8,* 543–550. (11)

Sherrington, C. S. (1906). *The integrative action of the nervous system* (2nd ed.). New York: Scribner's. New Haven, CT: Yale University Press, 1947. (2)

Sherrington, C. S. (1941). *Man on his nature.* New York: Macmillan. (2)

Shih, R. A., Belmonte, P. L., & Zandi, P. P. (2004). A review of the evidence from family, twin and adoption studies for a genetic contribution to adult psychiatric disorders. *International Review of Psychiatry, 16,* 260–283. (14)

Shima, K., Isoda, M., Mushiake, H., & Tanji, J. (2007). Categorization of behavioural sequences in the prefrontal cortex. *Nature, 445,* 315–318. (7)

Shimojo, S., Kamitani, Y., & Nishida, S. (2001). Afterimage of perceptually filled-in surface. *Science, 293,* 1677–1680. (5)

Shine, R., Phillips, B., Waye, H., LeMaster, M., & Mason, R. T. (2001). Benefits of female mimicry in snakes. *Nature, 414,* 267. (9)

Shiv, B., Loewenstein, G., Bechara, A., Damasio, H., & Damasio, A. R. (2005). Investment behavior and the negative side of emotion. *Psychological Science, 16,* 435–439. (11)

Shohamy, D. (2011). Learning and motivation in the human striatum. *Current Opinion in Neurobiology, 21,* 408–414. (12)

Shohamy, D., Myers, C. E., Hopkins, R. O., Sage, J., & Gluck, M. A. (2009). Distinct hippocampal and basal ganglia contributions to probabilistic learning and reversal. *Journal of Cognitive Neuroscience, 21,* 1821–1833. (12)

Shohamy, D., Myers, C. E., Kalanithi, J., & Gluck, M. A. (2008). Basal ganglia and dopamine contributions to probabilistic category learning. *Neuroscience and Biobehavioral Reviews, 32,* 219–236. (12)

Shoulson, I. (1990). Huntington's disease: Cognitive and psychiatric features. *Neuropsychiatry, Neuropsychology, and Behavioral Neurology, 3,* 15–22. (7)

Shrager, Y., Levy, D. A., Hopkins, R. O., & Squire, L. R. (2008). Working memory and the organization of brain systems. *Journal of Neuroscience, 28,* 4818–4822. (12)

Shubin, N., Tabin, C., & Carroll, S. (2009). Deep homology and the origins of evolutionary novelty. *Nature, 457,* 818–823. (0)

Shutts, D. (1982). *Lobotomy: Resort to the knife.* New York: Van Nostrand Reinhold. (3)

Siebert, M., Markowitsch, H. J., & Bartel, P. (2003). Amygdala, affect and cognition: Evidence from 10 patients with Urbach-Wiethe disease. *Brain, 126,* 2627–2637. (11)

Siegel, J. M. (1995). Phylogeny and the function of REM sleep. *Behavioural Brain Research, 69,* 29–34. (8)

Siegel, J. M. (2009). Sleep viewed as a state of adaptive inactivity. *Nature Reviews Neuroscience, 10,* 747–753. (8)

Siegel, J. M. (2012). Suppression of sleep for mating. *Science, 337,* 1610–1611. (8)

Siegel, S. (1977). Morphine tolerance as an associative process. *Journal of Experimental Psychology: Animal Behavior Processes, 3,* 1–13. (14)

Siegel, S. (1983). Classical conditioning, drug tolerance, and drug dependence. *Research Advances in Alcohol and Drug Problems, 9,* 279–314. (14)

Siegel, S. (1987). Alcohol and opiate dependence: Reevaluation of the Victorian perspective. *Research Advances in Alcohol and Drug Problems, 9,* 279–314. (14)

Silber, B. Y., & Schmitt, J. A. J. (2010). Effects of tryptophan loading on human cognition, mood, and sleep. *Neuroscience and Biobehavioral Reviews, 34,* 387–407. (9)

Silbersweig, D. A., Stern, E., Frith, C., Cahill, C., Holmes, A., Grootoonk, S., . . . Frackowiak, R. S. J. (1995). A functional neuroanatomy of hallucinations in schizophrenia. *Nature, 378,* 176–179. (14)

Silk, J. B., Brosnan, S. F., Vonk, J., Henrich, J., Povinelli, D. J., Richardson, A. S., . . . Schapiro, S. J. (2005). Chimpanzees are indifferent to the welfare of unrelated group members. *Nature, 437,* 1357–1359. (1, 13)

Silva, A. J., Zhou, Y., Rogerson, T., Shobe, J., & Balaji, J. (2009). Molecular and cellular approaches to memory allocation in neural circuits. *Science, 326,* 391–395. (12)

Silver, R. A. (2010). Neuronal arithmetic. *Nature Reviews Neuroscience, 11,* 474–489. (2)

Silver, R. C., Holman, E. A., Anderson, J. P., Poulin, M., McIntosh, D. N., & Gil-Rivas, V. (2013). Mental- and physical-health effects of acute exposure to media images of the September

11, 2001, attacks and the Iraq war. *Psychological Science, 24*, 1623–1634. (11)

Simner, J., & Ward, J. (2006). The taste of words on the tip of the tongue. *Nature, 444*, 438. (6)

Simon, B., Fletcher, J. A., & Doebeli, M. (2013). Towards a general theory of group selection. *Evolution, 67*, 1561–1572. (4)

Simpson, E. H., Kellendonk, C., & Kandel, E. (2010). A possible role for the striatum in the pathogenesis of the cognitive symptoms of schizophrenia. *Neuron, 65*, 585–596. (14)

Sincich, L. C., Park, K. F., Wohlgemuth, M. J., & Horton, J. C. (2004). Bypassing V1: A direct geniculate input to area MT. *Nature Neuroscience, 7*, 1123–1128. (5)

Singer, T., Seymour, B., O'Doherty, J., Kaube, H., Dolan, R. J., & Frith, C. D. (2004). Empathy for pain involves the affective but not sensory components of pain. *Science, 303*, 1157–1162. (6)

Singh, S., & Mallick, B. N. (1996). Mild electrical stimulation of pontine tegmentum around locus coeruleus reduces rapid eye movement sleep in rats. *Neuroscience Research, 24*, 227–235. (8)

Sirigu, A., Grafman, J., Bressler, K., & Sunderland, T. (1991). Multiple representations contribute to body knowledge processing. Evidence from a case of autopagnosia. *Brain, 114*, 629–642. (6)

Sirotin, Y. B., Hillman, E. M. C., Bordier, C., & Das, A. (2009). Spatiotemporal precision and hemodynamic mechanism of optical point spreads in alert primates. *Proceedings of the National Academy of Sciences, 106*, 18390–18395. (3)

Sjöström, M., Friden, J., & Ekblom, B. (1987). Endurance, what is it? Muscle morphology after an extremely long distance run. *Acta Physiologica Scandinavica, 130*, 513–520. (7)

Skinner, M. D., & Aubin, H.-J. (2010). Craving's place in addiction theory: Contributions of the major models. *Neuroscience and Biobehavioral Reviews, 34*, 606–623. (14)

Skitzki, J. J., Chen, Q., Wang, W. C., & Evans, S. S. (2007). Primary immune surveillance: Some like it hot. *Journal of Molecular Medicine, 85*, 1361–1367. (9)

Skoe, E., & Kraus, N. (2012). A little goes a long way: How the adult brain is shaped by musical training in childhood. *Journal of Neuroscience, 32*, 11507–11510. (4)

Slavich, G. M., & Cole, S. W. (2013). The emerging field of human social genomics. *Clinical Psychological Science, 1*, 331–348. (4)

Sloan, D. M., Strauss, M. E., & Wisner, K. L. (2001). Diminished response to pleasant stimuli by depressed women. *Journal of Abnormal Psychology, 110*, 488–493. (14)

Slob, A. K., Bax, C. M., Hop, W. C. J., Rowland, D. L., & van der Werff ten Bosch, J. J. (1996). Sexual arousability and the menstrual cycle. *Psychoneuroendocrinology, 21*, 545–558. (10)

Sluming, V., Brooks, J., Howard, M., Downes, J. J., & Roberts, N. (2007). Broca's area supports enhanced visuospatial cognition in orchestral musicians. *Journal of Neuroscience, 27*, 3799–3806. (13)

Smith, D. E., Rapp, P. R., McKay, H. M., Roberts, J. A., & Tuszynski, M. H. (2004). Memory impairment in aged primates is associated with focal death of cortical neurons and atrophy of subcortical neurons. *Journal of Neuroscience, 24*, 4373–4381. (12)

Smith, G. P. (1998). Pregastric and gastric satiety. In G. P. Smith (Ed.), *Satiation: From gut to brain* (pp. 10–39). New York: Oxford University Press. (9)

Smith, G. P., & Gibbs, J. (1998). The satiating effects of cholecystokinin and bombesin-like peptides. In G. P. Smith (Ed.), *Satiation: From gut to brain* (pp. 97–125). New York: Oxford University Press. (9)

Smith, K., Thompson, G. F., & Koster, H. D. (1969). Sweat in schizophrenic patients: Identification of the odorous substance. *Science, 166*, 398–399. (14)

Smith, L. T. (1975). The interanimal transfer phenomenon: A review. *Psychological Bulletin, 81*, 1078–1095. (12)

Smith, M. A., Brandt, J., & Shadmehr, R. (2000). Motor disorder in Huntington's disease begins as a dysfunction in error feedback control. *Nature, 403*, 544–549. (7)

Smith, P. J., Blumenthal, J. A., Hoffman, B. M., Cooper, H., Strauman, T. A., Welsh-Bohmer, K., . . . Sherwood, A. (2010). Aerobic exercise and neurocognitive performance: A meta-analytic review of randomized controlled trials. *Psychosomatic Medicine, 72*, 239–252. (4)

Smulders, T. V., Shiflett, M. W., Sperling, A. J., & DeVoogd, T. J. (2000). Seasonal changes in neuron numbers in the hippocampal formation of a food-hoarding bird: The black-capped chickadee. *Journal of Neurobiology, 44*, 414–422. (4)

Snitz, B. E., O'Meara, E. S., Carlson, M. C., Arnold, A. M., Ives, D. G., Rapp, S. R., . . . DeKosky, S. T. (2009). *Ginkgo biloba* for preventing cognitive decline in older adults: A randomized trial. *Journal of the American Medical Association, 302*, 2663–2670. (12)

Snyder, L. H., Grieve, K. L., Brotchie, P., & Andersen, R. A. (1998). Separate body- and world-referenced representations of visual space in parietal cortex. *Nature, 394*, 887–891. (7)

Solms, M. (1997). *The neuropsychology of dreams*. Mahwah, NJ: Erlbaum. (8)

Solms, M. (2000). Dreaming and REM sleep are controlled by different brain mechanisms. *Behavioral and Brain Sciences, 23*, 843–850. (8)

Solomon, S. G., & Lennie, P. (2007). The machinery of colour vision. *Nature Reviews Neuroscience, 8*, 276–286. (5)

Somjen, G. G. (1988). Nervenkitt: Notes on the history of the concept of neuroglia. *Glia, 1*, 2–9. (1)

Song, H., Stevens, C. F., & Gage, F. H. (2002). Neural stem cells from adult hippocampus develop essential properties of functional CNS neurons. *Nature Neuroscience, 5*, 438–445. (4)

Song, J. H., Skoe, E., Banai, K., & Kraus, N. (2012). Training to improve hearing speech in noise: Biological mechanisms. *Cerebral Cortex, 22*, 1180–1190. (6)

Soon, C. S., Brass, M., Heinze, H.-J., & Haynes, J.-D. (2008). Unconscious determinants of free decisions in the human brain. *Nature Neuroscience, 11*, 543–545. (7)

Southwell, D. G., Paaredes, M. F., Galvao, R. P., Jones, D. L., Froemke, R. C., Sebe, J. Y., . . . Alvarez-Buylla, A. A. (2012). Intrinsically determined cell death of developing cortical interneurons. *Nature, 491*, 109–113. (4)

Southwick, S. M., & Charney, D. S. (2012). The science of resilience: Implications for the prevention and treatment of depression. *Science, 338*, 79–82. (11)

Sowell, E. R., Thompson, P. M., Holmes, C. J., Jernigan, T. L., & Toga, A. W. (1999). In vivo evidence for post-adolescent brain maturation in frontal and striatal regions. *Nature Neuroscience, 6*, 309–315. (4)

Spalding, K. L., Bergmann, O., Alkass, K., Bernard, S., Salehpour, M., Huttner, H. B., . . . Frisén, J. (2013). Dynamics of hippocampal neurogenesis in adult humans. *Cell, 153*, 1219–1227. (4)

Spalding, K. L., Bhardwaj, R. D., Buchholz, B. A., Druid, H., & Frisén, J. (2005). Retrospective birth dating of cells in humans. *Cell, 122*, 133–143. (4)

Spangler, R., Wittkowski, K. M., Goddard, N. L., Avena, N. M., Hoebel, B. G., & Leibowitz, S. F. (2004). Opiate-like effects of sugar on gene expression in reward areas of the rat brain. *Molecular Brain Research, 124*, 134–142. (9)

Speer, N. K., Reynolds, J. R., Swallow, K. M., & Zacks, J. M. (2009). Reading stories activates neural representations of visual and motor experiences. *Psychological Science, 20*, 989–999. (7)

Spelke, E. S. (2005). Sex differences in intrinsic aptitude for mathematics and science? *American Psychologist, 60*, 950–958. (3)

Spencer, R. M. C., Zelaznik, H. N., Diedrichsen, J., & Ivry, R. B. (2003). Disrupted timing of discontinuous but not continuous movements by cerebellar lesions. *Science, 300*, 1437–1439. (7)

Sperandie, I., Chouinard, P. A., & Goodale, M. A. (2012). Retinotopic activity in V1 reflects the perceived and not the retinal size of an afterimage. *Nature Neuroscience, 15*, 540–542. (5)

Sperry, R. W. (1943). Visuomotor coordination in the newt (*Triturus viridescens*) after regeneration of the optic nerve. *Journal of Comparative Neurology, 79*, 33–55. (4)

Sperry, R. W. (1975). In search of psyche. In F. G. Worden, J. P. Swazey, & G. Adelman (Eds.), *The neurosciences: Paths of discovery* (pp. 425–434). Cambridge, MA: MIT Press. (4)

Spezio, M. L., Huang, P.-Y. S., Castelli, F., & Adolphs, R. (2007). Amygdala damage impairs eye contact during conversations with real people. *Journal of Neuroscience, 27*, 3994–3997. (11)

Spiegel, T. A. (1973). Caloric regulation of food intake in man. *Journal of Comparative and Physiological Psychology, 84*, 24–37. (9)

Spindler, K. A., Sullivan, E. V., Menon, V., Lim, K. O., & Pfefferbaum, A. (1997). Deficits in multiple systems of working memory in schizophrenia. *Schizophrenia Research, 27*, 1–10. (14)

Spitzer, N. C. (2012). Activity-dependent neurotransmitter respecification. *Nature Reviews Neuroscience, 13*, 94–106. (2)

Spoletini, I., Cherubini, A., Banfi, G., Rubino, I. A., Peran, P., Caltagirone, C., & Spalletta, G. (2011). Hippocampi, thalami, and accumbens microstructural damage in schizophrenia: A volumetry, diffusivity, and neuropsychological study. *Schizophrenia Bulletin, 37*, 118–130. (14)

Spreux-Varoquaux, O., Alvarez, J.-C., Berlin, I., Batista, G., Despierre, P.-G., Gilton, A., & Cremniter, D. (2001). Differential abnormalities in plasma 5-HIAA and platelet serotonin concentrations in violent suicide attempters. *Life Sciences, 69*, 647–657. (11)

Spurzheim, J. G. (1908). *Phrenology* (rev. ed.) Philadelphia: Lippincott. (3)

Squire, L. R. (1992). Memory and the hippocampus: A synthesis from findings with rats, monkeys, and humans. *Psychological Review, 99*, 195–231. (12)

Squires, T. M. (2004). Optimizing the vertebrate vestibular semicircular canal: Could we balance any better? *Physical Review Letters, 93*, 198106. (6)

St. George-Hyslop, P. H. (2000). Genetic factors in the genesis of Alzheimer's disease. *Annals of the New York Academy of Sciences, 924*, 1–7. (12)

St. Jacques, P. L., Dolcos, F., & Cabeza, R. (2009). Effects of aging on functional connectivity of the amygdala for subsequent memory of negative pictures. *Psychological Science, 20*, 74–84. (11)

Stallen, M., De Dreu, C. K. W., Shalvi, S., Smidts, A., & Sanfey, A. G. (2012). The herding hormone: Oxytocin stimulates in-group conformity. *Psychological Science, 23*, 1288–1292. (13)

Stalnaker, T. A., Roesch, M. R., Franz, T. M., Calu, D. J., Singh, T., & Schoenbaum, G. (2007). Cocaine-induced decision-making deficits are mediated by miscoding in basolateral amygdala. *Nature Neuroscience, 10*, 949–951. (14)

Stanford, L. R. (1987). Conduction velocity variations minimize conduction time differences among retinal ganglion cell axons. *Science, 238*, 358–360. (1)

Starr, C., & Taggart, R. (1989). *Biology: The unity and diversity of life.* Pacific Grove, CA: Brooks/Cole. (2, 3, 7, 10)

State, M. W., & Levitt, P. (2011). The conundrums of understanding genetic risks for autism spectrum disorders. *Nature Neuroscience, 14*, 1499–1506. (14)

Steele, C. J., Bailey, J. A., Zatorre, R. J., & Penhune, V. B. (2013). Early musical training and white-matter plasticity in the corpus callosum: Evidence for a sensitive period. *Journal of Neuroscience, 33*, 1282–1290. (4)

Stefansson, H., Rujescu, D., Cichon, S., Pietiläinen, O. P. H., Ingason, A., Steinberg, S., . . . Stefansson, K. (2008). Large recurrent microdeletions associated with schizophrenia. *Nature, 455*, 232–236. (4)

Steffens, B. (2007). *Ibn al-Haytham: First Scientist.* Greensboro, NC: Morgan Reynolds Publishing. (5)

Stein, M. B., Hanna, C., Koverola, C., Torchia, M., & McClarty, B. (1997). Structural brain changes in PTSD. *Annals of the New York Academy of Sciences, 821*, 76–82. (11)

Steinberg, L. (2013). The influence of neuroscience on US Supreme Court decisions about adolescents' criminal culpability. *Nature Reviews Neuroscience, 14*, 513–518. (4)

Steinberg, L., Graham, S., O'Brien, L., Woolard, J., Cauffman, E., & Banich, M. (2009). Age differences in future orientation and delay discounting. *Child Development, 80*, 28–44. (4)

Steinecke, A., Gampe, C., Valkova, C., Kaether, C., & Bolz, J. (2012). Disrupted-in-schizophrenia 1 (DISC1) is necessary for the correct migration of cortical interneurons. *Journal of Neuroscience, 32*, 738–745. (14)

Stephens, T. W., Basinski, M., Bristow, P. K., Bue-Valleskey, J. M., Burgett, S. G., Craft, L., . . . Heiman, M. (1995). The role of neuropeptide Y in the antiobesity action of the obese gene product. *Nature, 377*, 530–532. (9)

Sterling, P. (2012). Allostasis: A model of predictive regulation. *Physiology & Behavior, 106*, 5–15. (9)

Sterpenich, V., D'Argembeau, A., Desseiles, M., Balteau, E., Albouy, G., Vandewalle, G., . . . Maquet, P. (2006). The locus ceruleus is involved in the successful retrieval of emotional memories in humans. *Journal of Neuroscience, 26*, 7416–7423. (8)

Stevens, C. F. (2001). An evolutionary scaling law for the primate visual system and its basis in cortical function. *Nature, 411*, 193–195. (5)

Stevens, J. S., Jovanovic, T., Fani, N., Ely, T. D., Glover, E. M., Bradley, B., & Ressler, K. J. (2013). Disrupted amygdala-prefrontal connectivity in civilian women with posttraumatic stress disorder. *Journal of Psychiatric Research, 47*, 1469–1478. (11)

Stevens, M., & Cuthill, I. C. (2007). Hidden messages: Are ultraviolet signals a special channel in avian communication? *Bioscience, 57*, 501–507. (5)

Stevenson, R. J., Hodgson, D., Oaten, M. J., Moussavi, M., Langberg, R., Case, T. I., & Barouei, J. (2012). Disgust elevates core body temperature and up-regulates certain oral immune markers. *Brain Behavior and Immunity, 26*, 1160–1168. (11)

Stevenson, R. J., Miller, L. A., & McGrillen, K. (2013). The lateralization of gustatory function and the flow of information from tongue to cortex. *Neuropsychologia, 51*, 1408–1416. (6, 13)

Stewart, J. W., Quitkin, F. M., McGrath, P. J., Amsterdam, J., Fava, M., Fawcett, J., . . . Roback, P. (1998). Use of pattern analysis to predict differential relapse of remitted patients with major depression during 1 year of treatment with fluoxetine or placebo. *Archives of General Psychiatry, 55*, 334–343. (14)

Stickgold, R., Malia, A., Maguire, D., Roddenberry, D., & O'Connor, M. (2000). Replaying the game: Hypnagogic images in normals and amnesics. *Science, 290*, 350–353. (12)

Stokes, M., Thompson, R., Cusack, R., & Duncan, J. (2009). Top-down activation of shape-specific population codes in visual cortex during mental imagery. *Journal of Neuroscience, 29*, 1565–1572. (5)

Stone, V. E., Nisenson, L., Eliassen, J. C., & Gazzaniga, M. S. (1996). Left hemisphere representations of emotional facial expressions. *Neuropsychologia, 34*, 23–29. (13)

Storey, K. B., & Storey, J. M. (1999, May/June). Lifestyles of the cold and frozen. *The Sciences, 39*(3), 33–37. (9)

Strack, F., Martin, L. L., & Stepper, S. (1988). Inhibiting and facilitating conditions of the human smile: A nonobtrusive test of the facial feedback hypothesis. *Journal of Personality and Social Psychology, 54*, 768–777. (11)

Strausfeld, N. J., & Hirth, F. (2013). Deep homology of arthropod central complex and vertebrate basal ganglia. *Science, 340*, 157–161. (3)

Stricker, E. M. (1969). Osmoregulation and volume regulation in rats: Inhibition of hypovolemic thirst by water. *American Journal of Physiology, 217*, 98–105. (9)

Stricker, E. M., & Hoffmann, M. L. (2007). Presystemic signals in the control of thirst, salt appetite, and vasopressin secretion. *Physiology & Behavior, 91*, 404–412. (9)

Stricker, E. M., Swerdloff, A. F., & Zigmond, M. J. (1978). Intrahypothalamic injections of kainic acid produce feeding and drinking deficits in rats. *Brain Research, 158*, 470–473. (9)

Striemer, C. L., Chapman, C. S., & Goodale, M. A. (2009). "Real-time" obstacle avoidance in the absence of primary visual cortex. *Proceedings of the National Academy of Sciences (U.S.A.), 106*, 15996–16001. (5)

Stroebele, N., de Castro, J. M., Stuht, J., Catenacci, V., Wyatt, H. R., & Hill, J. O. (2008). A small-changes approach reduces energy intake in free-living humans. *Journal of the American College of Nutrition, 28*, 63–68. (9)

Strotmann, J., Levai, O., Fleischer, J., Schwarzenbacher, K., & Breer, H. (2004). Olfactory receptor proteins in axonal processes of chemosensory neurons. *Journal of Neuroscience, 224*, 7754–7761. (6)

Stryker, M. P., & Sherk, H. (1975). Modification of cortical orientation selectivity in the cat by restricted visual experience: A reexamination. *Science, 190*, 904–906. (5)

Stryker, M. P., Sherk, H., Leventhal, A. G., & Hirsch, H. V. B. (1978). Physiological consequences for the cat's visual cortex of effectively restricting early visual experience with oriented contours. *Journal of Neurophysiology, 41*, 896–909. (5)

Stunkard, A. J., Sorensen, T. I. A., Hanis, C., Teasdale, T. W., Chakraborty, R., Schull, W. J., & Schulsinger, F. (1986). An adoption study of human obesity. *New England Journal of Medicine, 314*, 193–198. (9)

Stuss, D. T., & Benson, D. F. (1984). Neuropsychological studies of the frontal lobes. *Psychological Bulletin, 95*, 3–28. (3)

Sun, Y.-G., & Chen, Z.-F. (2007). A gastrin-releasing peptide receptor mediates the itch sensation in the spinal cord. *Nature, 448*, 700–703. (6)

Sun, Y.-G., Zhao, Z.-Q., Meng, X.-L., Yin, J., Liu, X.-Y., & Chen, Z. F. (2009). Cellular basis of itch sensation. *Science, 325*, 1531–1534. (6)

Sunaert, S., Van Hecke, P., Marchal, G., & Orban, G. A. (1999). Motion-responsive regions of the human brain. *Experimental Brain Research, 127*, 355–370. (5)

Sur, M., & Leamey, C. A. (2001). Development and plasticity of cortical areas and networks. *Nature Reviews Neuroscience, 2*, 251–262. (5)

Surén, P., Roth, C., Bresnahan, M., Haugen, M., Hornig, M., Hirtz, D., . . . Stoltenberg, C., (2013). Association between maternal use of folic acid supplements and risk of autism spectrum disorders in children. *Journal of the American Medical Association, 309*, 570–577. (14)

Sutton, L. C., Lea, E., Will, M. J., Schwartz, B. A., Hartley, C. E., Poole, J. C., . . . Maier, S. F. (1997). Inescapable shock-induced potentiation of morphine analgesia. *Behavioral Neuroscience, 111*, 1105–1113. (6)

Sutton, R. L., Hovda, D. A., & Feeney, D. M. (1989). Amphetamine accelerates recovery of locomotor function following bilateral frontal cortex ablation in rats. *Behavioral Neuroscience, 103,* 837–841. (4)

Suvisaari, J. M., Haukka, J. K., Tanskanen, A. J., & Lönnqvist, J. K. (1999). Decline in the incidence of schizophrenia in Finnish cohorts born from 1954 to 1965. *Archives of General Psychiatry, 56,* 733–740. (14)

Suzdak, P. D., Glowa, J. R., Crawley, J. N., Schwartz, R. D., Skolnick, P., & Paul, S. M. (1986). A selective imidazobenzodiazepine antagonist of ethanol in the rat. *Science, 234,* 1243–1247. (11)

Swaab, D. F., & Hofman, M. A. (1990). An enlarged suprachiasmatic nucleus in homosexual men. *Brain Research, 537,* 141–148. (10)

Swan, S. H., Liu, F., Hines, M., Kruse, R. L., Wang, C., Redmon, J. B., . . . Weiss, B. (2010). Prenatal phthalate exposure and reduced masculine play in boys. *International Journal of Andrology, 33,* 259-269. (10)

Swithers, S. E., & Davidson, T. L. (2008). A role for sweet taste: Calorie predictive relations in energy regulation by rats. *Behavioral Neuroscience, 122,* 161–173. (9)

Swithers, S. E., Ogden, S. B., & Davidson, T. L. (2011). Fat substitutes promote weight gain in rats consuming high-fat diets. *Behavioral Neuroscience, 125,* 512–518. (9)

Swoboda, H., Amering, M., Windhaber, J., & Katschnig, H. (2003). The long-term course of panic disorder—an 11 year follow-up. *Journal of Anxiety Disorders, 17,* 223–232. (11)

Syken, J., GrandPre, T., Kanold, P. O., & Shatz, C. J. (2006). PirB restricts ocular-dominance plasticity in visual cortex. *Science, 313,* 1795–1800. (5)

Szymusiak, R. (1995). Magnocellular nuclei of the basal forebrain: Substrates of sleep and arousal regulation. *Sleep, 18,* 478–500. (8)

Tabarean, I. V., Sanchez-Alavez, M., & Sethi, J. (2012). Mechanisms of H-2 histamine receptor dependent modulation of body temperature and neuronal activity in the medial preoptic nucleus. *Neuropharmacology, 63,* 171–180. (9)

Tabarés-Seisdedos, R., & Rubenstein, J. L. (2013). Inverse cancer comorbidity: A serendipitous opportunity to gain insight into CNS disorders. *Nature Reviews Neuroscience, 14,* 293–304. (14)

Tabrizi, S. J., Cleeter, M. W. J., Xuereb, J., Taanman, J.-W., Cooper, J. M., & Schapira, A. H. V. (1999). Biochemical abnormalities and excitotoxicity in Huntington's disease brain. *Annals of Neurology, 45,* 25–32. (7)

Taddese, A., Nah, S. Y., & McCleskey, E. W. (1995). Selective opioid inhibition of small nociceptive neurons. *Science, 270,* 1366–1369. (6)

Tagawa, Y., Kanold, P. O., Majdan, M., & Shatz, C. J. (2005). Multiple periods of functional ocular dominance plasticity in mouse visual cortex. *Nature Neuroscience, 8,* 380–388. (5)

Tager-Flusberg, H., Boshart, J., & Baron-Cohen, S. (1998). Reading the windows to the soul: Evidence of domain-specific sparing in Williams syndrome. *Journal of Cognitive Neuroscience, 10,* 631–639. (13)

Tai, L.-H., Lee, A. M., Benavidez, N., Bonci, A., & Wilbrecht, L. (2012). Transient stimulation of distinct subpopulations of striatal neurons mimics changes in action value. *Nature Neuroscience, 15,* 1281–1289. (7)

Taillard, J., Philip, P., Coste, O., Sagaspe, P., & Bioulac, B. (2003). The circadian and homeostatic modulation of sleep pressure during wakefulness differs between morning and evening chronotypes. *Journal of Sleep Research, 12,* 275–282. (8)

Takahashi, T., Svoboda, K., & Malinow, R. (2003). Experience strengthening transmission by driving AMPA receptors into synapses. *Science, 299,* 1585–1588. (12)

Takano, T., Tian, G.-F., Peng, W., Lou, N., Libionka, W., Han, X., & Nedergaard, M. (2006). Astrocyte-mediated control of cerebral blood flow. *Nature Neuroscience, 9,* 260–267. (1)

Takatsuru, Y., Fukumoto, D., Yoshitomo, M., Nemoto, T., Tsukada, H., & Nabekura, J. (2009). Neuronal circuit remodeling in the contralateral cortical hemisphere during functional recovery from cerebral infarction. *Journal of Neuroscience, 29,* 10081–10086. (4)

Takehara-Nishiuchi, K., & McNaughton, B. L. (2008). Spontaneous changes of neocortical code for associative memory during consolidation. *Science, 322,* 960–963. (12)

Takemura, H., Ashida, H., Amano, K., Kitaoka, A., & Murakami, I. (2012). Neural correlates of induced motion perception in the human brain. *Journal of Neuroscience, 32,* 14344–14354. (5)

Tamietto, M., Castelli, L., Vighetti, S., Perozzo, P., Geminiani, G., Weiskrantz, L., & de Gelder, B. (2009). Unseen facial and bodily expressions trigger fast emotional reactions. *Proceedings of the National Academy of Sciences (U.S.A.), 106,* 17661–17666. (5)

Tan, K. R., Brown, M., Laboèbe, G., Yvon, C., Creton, C., Fritschy, J.-M., . . . Luscher, C. (2010). Neural bases for addictive properties of benzodiazepines. *Nature, 463,* 769–774. (11)

Tanaka, J., Hayashi, Y., Nomura, S., Miyakubo, H., Okumura, T., & Sakamaki, K. (2001). Angiotensinergic and noradrenergic mechanisms in the hypothalamic paraventricular nucleus participate in the drinking response induced by activation of the subfornical organ in rats. *Behavioural Brain Research, 118,* 117–122. (9)

Tanaka, J., Hori, K., & Nomura, M. (2001). Dipsogenic response induced by angiotensinergic pathways from the lateral hypothalamic area to the subfornical organ in rats. *Behavioural Brain Research, 118,* 111–116. (9)

Tanaka, M., Nakahara, T., Muranaga, T., Kojima, S., Yasuhara, D., Ueno, H., . . . Inui, A. (2006). Ghrelin concentrations and cardiac vagal tone are decreased after pharmacologic and cognitive-behavioral treatment in patients with bulimia nervosa. *Hormones and Behavior, 50,* 261–265. (9)

Tanaka, Y., Kamo, T., Yoshida, M., & Yamadori, A. (1991). "So-called" cortical deafness. *Brain, 114,* 2385–2401. (6)

Tandon, S., Simon, S. A., & Nicolelis, M. A. L. (2012). Appetitive changes during salt deprivation are paralleled by widespread neuronal adaptations in nucleus accumbens, lateral hypothalamus, and central amygdala. *Journal of Neurophysiology, 108,* 1089–1105. (9)

Tanigawa, H., Lu, H. D., & Roe, R. W. (2010). Functional organization for color and orientation in macaque V4. *Nature Neuroscience, 13,* 1542–1548. (5)

Tanji, J., & Shima, K. (1994). Role for supplementary motor area cells in planning several movements ahead. *Nature, 371,* 413–416. (7)

Tanner, C. M., Kamel, F., Ross, G. W., Hoppin, J. A., Goldman, S. M., Korell, M., . . . Langston, J. W. (2011). Rotenone, paraquat, and Parkinson's disease. *Environmental Health Perspectives, 119,* 866–872. (7)

Tanner, C. M., Ottman, R., Goldman, S. M., Ellenberg, J., Chan, P., Mayeux, R., & Langston, J. W. (1999). Parkinson disease in twins: An etiologic study. *Journal of the American Medical Association, 281,* 341–346. (7)

Tappy, L., & Lê, K.-A. (2010). Metabolic effects of fructose and the worldwide increase in obesity. *Physiological Reviews, 90,* 23–46. (9)

Taravosh-Lahn, K., Bastida, C., & Delville, Y. (2006). Differential responsiveness to fluoxetine during puberty. *Behavioral Neuroscience, 120,* 1084–1092. (11)

Tarr, M. J., & Gauthier, I. (2000). FFA: A flexible fusiform area for subordinate-level visual processing automatized by experience. *Nature Neuroscience, 3,* 764–769. (5)

Taruno, A., Vingtdeux, V., Ohmoto, M., Ma, Z., Dvoryanchikov, G., Li. A., . . . Foskett, J. K. (2013). CALHM1 ion channel mediates purinergic neurotransmission of sweet, bitter, and umami tastes. *Nature, 495,* 223–226. (6)

Tattersall, G. J., Andrade, D. V., & Abe, A. S. (2009). Heat exchange from the toucan bill reveals a controllable vascular thermal radiator. *Science, 325,* 468–470. (9)

Taub, E., & Berman, A. J. (1968). Movement and learning in the absence of sensory feedback. In S. J. Freedman (Ed.), *The neuropsychology of spatially oriented behavior* (pp. 173–192). Homewood, IL: Dorsey. (4)

Taylor, J. P., Hardy, J., & Fischbeck, K H. (2002). Toxic proteins in neurodegenerative disease. *Science, 296,* 1991–1995. (12)

Taylor, M. A. (1969). Sex ratios of newborns: Associated with prepartum and postpartum schizophrenia. *Science, 164,* 723–721. (14)

Taziaux, M., Keller, M., Bakker, J., & Balthazart, J. (2007). Sexual behavior activity tracks rapid changes in brain estrogen concentrations. *Journal of Neuroscience, 27,* 6563–6572. (10)

Teff, K. L., Elliott, S. S., Tschöp, M., Kieffer, T. J., Rader, D., Heiman, M., . . . Havel, P. J. (2004). Dietary fructose reduces circulating insulin and leptin, attenuates postprandial suppression of ghrelin, and increases triglycerides in women. *Journal of Clinical Endocrinology & Metabolism, 89,* 2963–2972. (9)

Teicher, M. H., Glod, C. A., Magnus, E., Harper, D., Benson, G., Krueger, K., & McGreenery, C. E. (1997). Circadian rest–activity disturbances in seasonal affective disorder. *Archives of General Psychiatry, 54,* 124–130. (14)

Teitelbaum, P. (1961). Disturbances in feeding and drinking behavior after hypothalamic lesions. In M. R. Jones (Ed.), *Nebraska Symposia on Motivation 1961* (pp. 39–69). Lincoln: University of Nebraska Press. (9)

Teitelbaum, P., & Epstein, A. N. (1962). The lateral hypothalamic syndrome. *Psychological Review, 69,* 74–90. (9)

Teitelbaum, P., Pellis, V. C., & Pellis, S. M. (1991). Can allied reflexes promote the integration of a robot's behavior? In J. A. Meyer & S. W. Wilson (Eds.), *From animals to animats: Simulation of animal behavior* (pp. 97–104). Cambridge, MA: MIT Press/Bradford Books. (7)

Terawawa, Y., Fukushima, H., & Umeda, S. (2013). How does interoceptive awareness interact with the subjective experience of emotion? An fMRI study. *Human Brain Mapping, 34,* 598–612. (11)

Terburg, D., Aarts, H., & van Honk, J. (2012). Testosterone affects gaze aversion from angry faces outside of conscious awareness. *Psychological Science, 23,* 459–463. (11)

Terzaghi, M., Sartori, I., Tassi, L., Rustioni, V., Proserpio, P., Lorusso, G. . . . Nobili, L. (2012). Dissociated local arousal states underlying essential features of non-rapid eye movement arousal parasomnia: An intracerebral stereo-electroencephalographic study. *Journal of Sleep Research, 21,* 502–506. (8)

Terrace, H. S., Petitto, L. A., Sanders, R. J., & Bever, T. G. (1979). Can an ape create a sentence? *Science, 206,* 891–902. (13)

Tetrud, J. W., Langston, J. W., Garbe, P. L., & Ruttenber, A. J. (1989). Mild Parkinsonism in persons exposed to 1-methyl-4-phenyl-1,2,3,6-tetrahydropyridine (MPTP). *Neurology, 39,* 1483–1487. (7)

Thacker, E. L., & Ascherio, A. (2008). Familial aggregation of Parkinson's disease: A meta-analysis. *Movement Disorders, 23,* 1174–1183. (7)

Thalemann, R., Wölfling, K., & Grüsser, S. M. (2007). Specific cue reactivity on computer game-related cues in excessive gamers. *Behavioral Neuroscience, 121,* 614–618. (14)

Thannickal, T. C., Moore, R. Y., Nienhuis, R., Ramanathan, L., Gulyani, S., Aldrich, M., . . . Siegel, J. M. (2000). Reduced number of hypocretin neurons in human narcolepsy. *Neuron, 27,* 469–474. (8)

Thase, M. E., Greenhouse, J. B., Frank, E., Reynolds, C. F., III, Pilkonis, P. A., Hurley, K., . . . Kupfer, D. J. (1997). Treatment of major depression with psychotherapy or psychotherapy-psychopharmacology combinations. *Archives of General Psychiatry, 54,* 1009–1015. (14)

Thase, M. E., Trivedi, M. H., & Rush, A. J. (1995). MAOIs in the contemporary treatment of depression. *Neuropsychopharmacology, 12,* 185–219. (14)

Theusch, E., Basu, A., & Gitschier, J. (2009). Genome-wide study of families with absolute pitch reveals linkage to 8q24.21 and locus heterogeneity. *American Journal of Human Genetics, 85,* 112–119. (6)

Thier, P., Dicke, P. W., Haas, R., & Barash, S. (2000). Encoding of movement time by populations of cerebellar Purkinje cells. *Nature, 405,* 72–76. (7)

Thomas, C., Avidan, G., Humphreys, K., Jung, K., Gao, F., & Behrmann, M. (2009). Reduced structural connectivity in ventral visual cortex in congenital prosopagnosia. *Nature Neuroscience, 12,* 29–31. (5)

Thomas, C., & Baker, C. I. (2013). Teaching an adult brain new tricks: A critical review of evidence for training-dependent structural plasticity in humans. *NeuroImage, 73,* 225–236. (4)

Thompson, R. F. (1986). The neurobiology of learning and memory. *Science, 233,* 941–947. (12)

Thompson, W. F., Marin, M. M., & Stewart, L. (2012). Reduced sensitivity to emotional prosody in congenital amusia rekindles the musical protolanguage hypothesis. *Proceedings of the National Academy of Sciences (U.S.A.), 109,* 19027–19032. (6)

Thornton, J., Zehr, J. L., & Loose, M. D. (2009). Effects of prenatal androgens on rhesus monkeys: A model system to explore the organizational hypothesis in primates. *Hormones and Behavior, 55,* 633–644. (10)

Ticku, M. K., & Kulkarni, S. K. (1988). Molecular interactions of ethanol with GABAergic system and potential of Ro15-4513 as an ethanol antagonist. *Pharmacology Biochemistry and Behavior, 30,* 501–510. (11)

Timms, B. G., Howdeshell, K. L., Barton, L., Richter, C. A., & vom Saal, F. S. (2005). Estrogenic chemicals in plastic and oral contraceptives disrupt development of the fetal mouse prostate and urethra. *Proceedings of the National Academy of Sciences, USA, 102,* 7014–7019. (10)

Tinbergen, N. (1951). *The study of instinct.* Oxford, England: Oxford University Press. (0)

Tinbergen, N. (1973). The search for animal roots of human behavior. In N. Tinbergen (Ed.), *The animal in its world* (Vol. 2, pp. 161–174). Cambridge, MA: Harvard University Press. (0)

Tingate, T. R., Lugg, D. J., Muller, H. K., Stowe, R. P., & Pierson, D. L. (1997). Antarctic isolation: Immune and viral studies. *Immunology and Cell Biology, 75,* 275–283. (11)

Tiruneh, M. A., Huang, B. S., & Leenen, F. H. H. (2013). Role of angiotensin II type 1 receptors in the pressor responses to central sodium in rats. *Brain Research, 1527,* 79–86. (9)

Tishkoff, S. A., Reed, F. A., Ranciaro, A., Voight, B. F., Babbitt, C. C., Silverman, J. S., Deloukas, P. (2007). Convergent adaptation of human lactase persistence in Africa and Europe. *Nature Genetics, 39,* 31–40. (9)

Tizzano, M., Gulbransen, B. D., Vandenbeuch, A., Clapp, T. R., Herman, J. P., Sibhatu, H. M., . . . Finger, T. E. (2010). Nasal chemosensory cells use bitter taste signaling to detect irritants and bacterial signals. *Proceedings of the National Academy of Sciences (U.S.A.), 107,* 3210–3215. (6)

Tobin, V. A., Hashimoto, H., Wacker, D. W., Takayanagi, Y., Langnaese, K., Caquíneau, C., . . . Ludwig, M. (2010). An intrinsic vasopressin system in the olfactory bulb is involved in social recognition. *Nature, 464,* 413–417. (10)

Toh, K. L., Jones, C. R., He, Y., Eide, E. J., Hinz, W. A., Virshup, D. M., . . . Fu, Y. H. (2001). An h*Per2* phosphorylation site mutation in familial advanced sleep phase syndrome. *Science, 291,* 1040–1043. (8)

Tøien, Ø., Blake, J., Edgar, D. M., Grahn, D. A., Heller, H. C., & Barnes, B. M. (2011). Hibernation in black bears: Independence of metabolic suppression from body temperature. *Science, 331,* 906–909. (8)

Tokizawa, K., Yasuhara, S., Nakamura, M., Uchida, Y., Crawshaw, L. I., & Nagashma, K. (2010). Mild hypohydration induced by exercise in the heat attenuates autonomic thermoregulatory responses to the heat, but not thermal pleasantness in humans. *Physiology & Behavior, 100,* 340–345. (9)

Tomasello, M., & Herrmann, E. (2010). Ape and human cognition: What's the difference? *Current Directions in Psychological Science, 19,* 3–8. (13)

Tominaga, M., Caterina, M. J., Malmberg, A. B., Rosen, T. A., Gilbert, H., Skinner, K., . . . Julius, D. (1998). The cloned capsaicin receptor integrates multiple pain-producing stimuli. *Neuron, 21,* 531–543. (6)

Tomo, I., de Monvel, J. B., & Fridberger, A. (2007). Sound-evoked radial strain in the hearing organ. *Biophysical Journal, 93,* 3279–3284. (6)

Tomson, S. N., Narayan, M., Allen, G. I., & Eagleman, D. M. (2013). Neural networks of colored sequence synesthesia. *Journal of Neuroscience, 33,* 14098–14106. (6)

Tong, Q., Ye, C.-P., Jones, J. E., Elmquist, J. K., & Lowell, B. B. (2008). Synaptic release of GABA by AgRP neurons is required for normal regulation of energy balance. *Nature Neuroscience, 11,* 998–1000. (9)

Toni, N., Buchs, P.-A., Nikonenko, I., Bron, C. R., & Muller, D. (1999). LTP promotes formation of multiple spine synapses between a single axon terminal and a dendrite. *Nature, 402,* 421–425. (12)

Toomey, R., Lyons, M. J., Eisen, S. A., Xian, H., Chantarujikapong, S., Seidman, L. J., . . . Tsuang, M. T. (2003). A twin study of the neuropsychological consequences of stimulant abuse. *Archives of General Psychiatry, 60,* 303–310. (14)

Torrey, E. F., Bartko, J. J., & Yolken, R. H. (2012). *Toxoplasma gondii* and other risk factors for schizophrenia: An update. *Schizophrenia Bulletin, 38,* 642–647. (14)

Torrey, E. F., & Miller, J. (2001). *The invisible plague: The rise of mental illness from 1750 to the present.* New Brunswick, NJ: Rutgers University Press. (14)

Torrey, E. F., Miller, J., Rawlings, R., & Yolken, R. H. (1997). Seasonality of births in schizophrenia and bipolar disorder: A review of the literature. *Schizophrenia Research, 28,* 1–38. (14)

Toufexis, D. (2007). Region- and sex-specific modulation of anxiety behaviours in the rat. *Journal of Neuroendocrinology, 19,* 461–473. (11)

Townsend, J., Courchesne, E., Covington, J., Westerfield, M., Harris, N. S., Lyden, P., . . . Press, G. A. (1999). Spatial attention deficits in patients with acquired or developmental cerebellar abnormality. *Journal of Neuroscience, 19,* 5632–5643. (7)

Tran, P. B., & Miller, R. J. (2003). Chemokine receptors: Signposts to brain development and disease. *Nature Reviews Neuroscience, 4,* 444–455. (4)

Tranel, D., & Damasio, A. (1993). The covert learning of affective valence does not require structures in hippocampal system or amygdala. *Journal of Cognitive Neuroscience, 5,* 79–88. (12)

Travers, S. P., Pfaffmann, C., & Norgren, R. (1986). Convergence of lingual and palatal gustatory neural activity in the nucleus of the solitary tract. *Brain Research, 365,* 305–320. (6)

Trefilov, A., Berard, J., Krawczak, M., & Schmidtke, J. (2000). Natal dispersal in rhesus macaques is related to serotonin transporter gene promoter variation. *Behavior Genetics, 30,* 295–301. (11)

Trevena, J. A., & Miller, J. (2002). Cortical movement preparation before and after a conscious decision to move. *Consciousness and Cognition, 11,* 162–190. (7)

Trimble, M. R., & Thompson, P. J. (1986). Neuropsychological and behavioral sequelae of spontaneous seizures. *Annals of the New York Academy of Sciences, 462,* 284–292. (14)

Tritsch, N. X., Ding, J. B., & Sabatini, B. L. (2012). Dopaminergic neurons inhibit striatal output through non-canonical release of GABA. *Nature, 490,* 262–266. (2, 7)

Trivedi, M. H., Fava, M., Wisniewski, S. R., Thase, M. E., Quitlein, F., Warden, D., . . . Rush, A. J. (2006). Medication augmentation after failure of SSRIs for depression. *New England Journal of Medicine, 354,* 1243–1252. (14)

Trivers, R. L. (1985). *Social evolution.* Menlo Park, CA: Benjamin/Cummings. (4)

Trudel, E., & Bourque, C. W. (2010). Central clock excites vasopressin neurons by waking osmosensory afferents during late sleep. *Nature Neuroscience, 13,* 467–474. (9)

Tsankova, N., Renthal, W., Kumar, A., & Nestler, E. J. (2007). Epigenetic regulation in psychiatric disorders. *Nature Reviews Neuroscience, 8,* 355–367. (4)

Ts'o, D. Y., & Roe, A. W. (1995). Functional compartments in visual cortex: Segregation and interaction. In M. S. Gazzaniga (Ed.), *The cognitive neurosciences* (pp. 325–337). Cambridge, MA: MIT Press. (5)

Tsunematsu, T., Kilduff, T. S., Boyden, E. S. Takahashi, S., & Yamanaka, A. (2011). Acute optogenetic silencing of orexin/hypocretin neurons induces slow-wave sleep in mice. *Journal of Neuroscience, 31,* 10529–10539. (8)

Tucker, D. M., Luu, P., & Pribram, K. H. (1995). Social and emotional self-regulation. *Annals of the New York Academy of Sciences, 769,* 213–239. (7)

Tups, A. (2009). Physiological models of leptin resistance. *Journal of Neuroendocrinology, 21,* 961–971. (9)

Turk, D. J., Heatherton, T. F., Kelley, W. M., Funnell, M. G., Gazzaniga, M. S., & Macrae, C. N. (2002). Mike or me? Self-recognition in a split-brain patient. *Nature Neuroscience, 5,* 841–842. (13)

Turner, R. S., & Anderson, M. E. (2005). Context-dependent modulation of movement-related discharge in the primate globus pallidus. *Journal of Neuroscience, 25,* 2965–2976. (7)

Turner, R. S., & Desmurget, M. (2010). Basal ganglia contributions to motor control: A vigorous tutor. *Current Opinion in Neurobiology, 20,* 704–716. (7)

Twenge, J. M., & Nolen-Hoeksema, S. (2002). Age, gender, race, socioeconomic status, and birth cohort differences on the children's depression inventory: A meta-analysis. *Journal of Abnormal Psychology, 111,* 578–588. (14)

Tye, K. M., Tye, L. D., Cone, J. J., Hekkelman, E. F., Janak, P. H., & Bonci, A. (2010). Methylphenidate facilitates learning-induced amygdala plasticity. *Nature Neuroscience, 13,* 475–481. (12)

Uchida, N., Takahashi, Y. K., Tanifuji, M., & Mori, K., (2000). Odor maps in the mammalian olfactory bulb: Domain organization and odorant structural features. *Nature Neuroscience, 3,* 1035–1043. (6)

Udry, J. R., & Chantala, K. (2006). Masculinity–femininity predicts sexual orientation in men but not in women. *Journal of Biosocial Science, 38,* 797–809. (10)

Udry, J. R., & Morris, N. M. (1968). Distribution of coitus in the menstrual cycle. *Nature, 220,* 593–596. (10)

Uekita, T., & Okaichi, H. (2005). NMDA antagonist MK-801 does not interfere with the use of spatial representation in a familiar environment. *Behavioral Neuroscience, 119,* 548–556. (12)

Ueno, M., Fujita, Y., Tanaka, T., Nakamura, Y., Kikuta, J., Ishii, M., & Yamashita, T. (2013). Layer V cortical neurons require microglial support for survival during postnatal development. *Nature Neuroscience, 16,* 543–551. (1)

Unterberg, A. W., Stover, J., Kress, B., & Kiening, K. L. (2004). Edema and brain trauma. *Neuroscience, 129,* 1021–1029. (4)

Urry, H. L., Nitschke, J. B., Dolski, I., Jackson, D. C., Dalton, K. M., Mueller, C. J., . . . Davidson, R. J. (2004). Making a life worth living: Neural correlates of well-being. *Psychological Science, 15,* 367–372. (11)

Uslaner, J. M., Tye, S. J., Eddins, D. M., Wang, X. H., Fox, S. V., Savitz, A. T. . . . Renger, J. J. (2013). Orexin receptor anatgonists differ from standard sleep drugs by promoting sleep at doses that do not disrupt cognition. *Science Translational Medicine, 5,* 179ra44. (8)

U.S.–Venezuela Collaborative Research Project. (2004). Venezuelan kindreds reveal that genetic and environmental factors modulate Huntington's disease age of onset. *Proceedings of the National Academy of Sciences, USA, 101,* 3498–3503. (7)

Uwano, T., Nishijo, H., Ono, T., & Tamura, R. (1995). Neuronal responsiveness to various sensory stimuli, and associative learning in the rat amygdala. *Neuroscience, 68,* 339–361. (11)

Vaishnavi, S., Calhoun, J., & Chatterjee, A. (2001). Binding personal and peripersonal space: Evidence from tactile extinction. *Journal of Cognitive Neuroscience, 13,* 181–189. (13)

Vallines, I., & Greenlee, M. W. (2006). Saccadic suppression of retinotopically localized blood oxygen level-dependent responses in human primary visual area V1. *Journal of Neuroscience, 26,* 5965–5969. (5)

Valzelli, L. (1973). The "isolation syndrome" in mice. *Psychopharmacologia, 31,* 305–320. (11)

Valzelli, L. (1980). *An approach to neuroanatomical and neurochemical psychophysiology.* Torino, Italy: C. G. Edizioni Medico Scientifiche. (14)

Valzelli, L., & Bernasconi, S. (1979). Aggressiveness by isolation and brain serotonin turnover changes in different strains of mice. *Neuropsychobiology, 5,* 129–135. (11)

van Anders, S. M., & Goldey, K. L. (2010). Testosterone and parnering are linked via relationship status for women and "relationship orientation" for men. *Hormones and Behavior, 58,* 820–826. (10)

van Anders, S. M., Hamilton, L. D., & Watson, N. V. (2007). Multiple partners are associated with higher testosterone in North American men and women. *Hormones and Behavior, 51,* 454–459. (10)

van Anders, S. M., & Watson, N. V. (2006). Relationship status and testosterone in North American heterosexual and non-heterosexual men and women: Cross-sectional and longitudinal data. *Psychoneuroendocrinology, 31,* 715–723. (10)

Van Cantfort, T. E., Gardner, B. T., & Gardner, R. A. (1989). Developmental trends in replies to Wh-questions by children and chimpanzees. In R. A. Gardner, B. T. Gardner, & T. E. Van Cantfort (Eds.), *Teaching sign language to chimpanzees* (pp. 198–239). Albany: State University of New York Press. (13)

van den Heuvel, M. P., Mandl, R. C. W., Stam, C. J., Kahn, R. S., & Pol, H. E. H. (2010). Aberrant frontal and temporal complex network structure in schizophrenia: A graph theoretical analysis. *Journal of Neuroscience, 30,* 15915–15926. (14)

van den Pol, A. N. (1999). Hypothalamic hypocretin (orexin): Robust innervation of the spinal cord. *Journal of Neuroscience, 19,* 3171–3182. (9)

Van der Borght, K., Havekes, R., Bos, T., Eggen, B. J. L., & Van der Zee, E. A. (2007). Exercise improves memory acquisition and retrieval in the Y-maze task: Relationship with hippocampal neurogenesis. *Behavioral Neuroscience, 121,* 324–334. (4)

van der Kloet, D., Merckelbach, H., Giesbrecht, T., & Lynn, S. J. (2012). Fragmented sleep, fragmented mind: The role of sleep in dissociative symptoms. *Perspectives on Psychological Science, 7,* 159–175. (8)

VanderLaan, D. P., Forrester, D. L., Petterson, L. J., & Vasey, P. L. (2013). The prevalence of Fa'afafine relatives among Samoan gynephilic men and fa'afafine. *Archives of Sexual Behavior, 42,* 353–359. (10)

van der Zwan, Y. G., Janssen, E. H. C. C., Callens, N., Wolffenbuttel, K. P., Cohen-Kettenis, P. T., van den Berg, M., . . . Beerendonk, C. (2013). Severity of virilization is associated with cosmetic appearance and sexual function in women with congenital adrenal hyperplasia: A cross-sectional study. *Journal of Sexual Medicine, 10,* 866–875. (10)

Van Essen, D. C., & DeYoe, E. A. (1995). Concurrent processing in the primate visual cortex. In M. S. Gazzaniga (Ed.), *The cognitive neurosciences* (pp. 383–400). Cambridge, MA: MIT Press. (5)

van Honk, J., & Schutter, D. J. L. G. (2007). Testosterone reduces conscious detection of signals serving social correction. *Psychological Science, 18,* 663–667. (10)

van Honk, J., Schutter, D. J., Bos, P. A., Kruijt, A. W., Lentjes, E. G., & Baron-Cohen, S. (2011). Testosterone administration impairs cognitive empathy in women depending on second-to-fourth digit ratio. *Proceedings of the National Academy of Sciences (U.S.A.), 108,* 3448–3452. (10)

van Ijzendoorn, M. H., & Bakermans-Kranenburg, M. J. (2012). A sniff of trust: Meta-analysis of the effects of intranasal oxytocin administration on face recognition, trust to in-group, and trust to out-group. *Psychoneuroendocrinology, 37,* 438–443. (13)

van Leeuwen, M., Peper, J. S., van den Berg, S. M., Brouwer, R. M., Pol, H. E. H., Kahn, R. S., & Boomsma, D. I. (2009). A genetic analysis of brain volumes and IQ in children. *Intelligence, 37,* 181–191. (3)

van Meer, M. P. A., van der Marel, K., Wang, K., Otte, W. M., el Bouazati, S., Roeling, T. A. P., . . . Dijkhuizen, R. M. (2010). Recovery of sensorimotor function after experimental stroke correlates with restoration of resting-state interhemispheric functional activity. *Journal of Neuroscience, 30,* 3964–3972. (4)

van Praag, H., Kempermann, G., & Gage, F. H. (1999). Running increases cell proliferation and neurogenesis in the adult mouse dentate gyrus. *Nature Neuroscience, 2,* 266–270. (4)

van Praag, H., Schinder, A. F., Christie, B. R., Toni, N., Palmer, T. D., & Gage, F. H. (2002). Functional neurogenesis in the adult hippocampus. *Nature, 415,* 1030–1034. (4)

Van Wanrooij, M. M., & Van Opstal, A. J. (2004). Contribution of head shadow and pinna cues to chronic monaural sound localization. *Journal of Neuroscience, 24,* 4163–4171. (6)

Van Wanrooij, M. M., & Van Opstal, A. J. (2005). Relearning sound localization with a new ear. *Journal of Neuroscience, 25,* 5413–5424. (6)

Van Zoeren, J. G., & Stricker, E. M. (1977). Effects of preoptic, lateral hypothalamic, or dopamine-depleting lesions on behavioral thermoregulation in rats exposed to the cold. *Journal of Comparative and Physiological Psychology, 91,* 989–999. (9)

Vanduffel, W., Fize, D., Mandeville, J. B., Nelissen, K., Van Hecke, P., Rosen, B. R., . . . Orban, G. A. (2001). Visual motion processing investigated using contrast agent-enhanced fMRI in awake behaving monkeys. *Neuron, 32,* 565–577. (5)

Vargas-Irwin, C. E., Shakhnarovich, G., Yadollahpour, P., Mislow, J. M. K., Black, M. J., & Donoghue, J. P. (2010). Decoding complete reach and grasp actions from local primary motor cortex populations. *Journal of Neuroscience, 30,* 9659–9669. (7)

Vasey, P. L., & VanderLaan, D. P. (2010). An adaptive cognitive dissociation between willingness to help kin and nonkin in Samoan *Fa'afafine. Psychological Science, 21,* 292–297. (10)

Vawter, M. P., Evans, S., Choudary, P., Tomita, H., Meador-Woodruff, J., Molnar, M., . . . Bunney, W. E. (2004). Gender-specific gene expression in post-mortem human brain. Localization to sex chromosomes. *Neuropsychopharmacology, 29,* 373–384. (10)

Velanova, K., Wheeler, M. E., & Luna, B. (2009). The maturation of task set-related activation supports late developmental improvements in inhibitory control. *Journal of Neuroscience, 29,* 12558–12567. (7)

Verhage, M., Maia, A. S., Plomp, J. J., Brussard, A. B., Heeroma, J. H., Vermeer, H., . . . Sudhof, T. C. (2000). Synaptic assembly of the brain in the absence of neurotransmitter secretion. *Science, 287,* 864–869. (4)

Verrey, F., & Beron, J. (1996). Activation and supply of channels and pumps by aldosterone. *News in Physiological Sciences, 11,* 126–133. (9)

Vessal, M., & Darian-Smith, C. (2010). Adult neurogenesis occurs in primate sensorimotor cortex following cervical dorsal rhizotomy. *Journal of Neuroscience, 30,* 8613–8623. (4)

Vigneau, M., Beaucousin, V., Hervé, P.-Y., Jobard, G., Petit, L., Crivello, F., . . . Tzourio-Mazoyer, N. (2011). What is right-hemisphere contribution to phonological, lexico-semantic, and sentence processing? Insights from a meta-analysis. *NeuroImage, 54,* 577–593. (13)

Villeda, S. A., Luo, J., Mosher, K. I., Zou, B., Britshgi, M., Bieri, G., . . . Rando, T. A. (2011). The ageing systemic milieu negatively regulates neurogenesis and cognitive function. *Nature, 477,* 90–94. (4)

Virkkunen, M., DeJong, J., Bartko, J., Goodwin, F. K., & Linnoila, M. (1989). Relationship of psychobiological variables to recidivism in violent offenders and impulsive fire setters. *Archives of General Psychiatry, 46,* 600–603. (11)

Virkkunen, M., Eggert, M., Rawlings, R., & Linnoila, M. (1996). A prospective follow-up study of alcoholic violent offenders and fire setters. *Archives of General Psychiatry, 53,* 523–529. (11)

Virkkunen, M., Nuutila, A., Goodwin, F. K., & Linnoila, M. (1987). Cerebrospinal fluid monoamine metabolite levels in male arsonists. *Archives of General Psychiatry, 44,* 241–247. (11)

Virkkunen, M., Rawlings, R., Tokola, R., Poland, R. E., Guidotti, A., Nemeroff, C., . . . Linnoila, M. (1994). CSF biochemistries, glucose metabolism, and diurnal activity rhythms in alcoholic, violent offenders, fire setters, and healthy volunteers. *Archives of General Psychiatry, 51,* 20–27. (14)

Visser, E. K., Beersma, G. M., & Daan, S. (1999). Melatonin suppression by light in humans is maximal when the nasal part of the retina is illuminated. *Journal of Biological Rhythms, 14,* 116–121. (8)

Viswanathan, A., & Freeman, R. D. (2007). Neurometabolic coupling in cerebral cortex reflects synaptic more than spiking activity. *Nature Neuroscience, 10,* 1308–1312. (3)

Vita, A., De Peri, L., Deste, G., & Sacchetti, E. (2012). Progressive loss of cortical gray matter in schizophrenia: A meta-analysis and meta-regression of longitudinal MRI studies. *Translational Psychiatry, 2,* Article e190. (14)

Vittengl, J. R., Clark, L. A., Dunn, T. W., & Jarrett, R. B. (2007). Reducing relapse and recurrence in unipolar depression: A comparative meta-analysis of cognitive-behavioral therapy's effects. *Journal of Consulting and Clinical Psychology, 75,* 475–488. (14)

Viviani, D., Charlet, A., van den Burg, E., Robinet, C., Hurni, N., Abatis, M., . . . Stoop, R. (2011). Oxytocin selectively gates fear responses through distinct outputs from the central amygdala. *Science, 333,* 104–107. (11)

Vliegen, J., Van Grootel, T. J., & Van Opstal, A. J. (2004). Dynamic sound localization during rapid eye–head gaze shifts. *Journal of Neuroscience, 24,* 9291–9302. (6)

Vocci, F. J., Acri, J., & Elkashef, A. (2005). Medication development for addictive disorders: The state of the science. *American Journal of Psychiatry, 162,* 1432–1440. (14)

Volkow, N. D., Wang, G.-J., Telang, F., Fowler, J. S., Logan, J., Childress, A.-R., . . . Wong, C. (2006). Cocaine cues and dopamine in dorsal striatum: Mechanism of craving in cocaine addiction. *Journal of Neuroscience, 26,* 6583–6588. (14)

Volman, I., Verlagen, L., den Ouden, H. E. M., Fernández, G., Rijpkema, M., Franke, B., Toni, I., & Roelofs, K. (2013). Reduced serotonin transporter availability decreases prefrontal control of the amygdala. *Journal of Neuroscience, 33,* 8974–8979. (11)

von der Ohe, C. G., Darian-Smith, C., Garner, C. C., & Heller, H. C. (2006). Ubiquitous and temperature-dependent neural plasticity in hibernators. *Journal of Neuroscience, 26,* 10590–10598. (8)

von Gall, C., Garabette, M. L., Kell, C. A., Frenzel, S., Dehghani, F., Schumm-Draeger, P. M., . . . Stehle, J. H. (2002). Rhythmic gene expression in pituitary depends on heterologous sensitization by the neurohormone melatonin. *Nature Neuroscience, 5,* 234–238. (8)

von Känel, R., Hepp, U., Kraemer, B., Traber, R., Keel, M., Mica, L., & Schnyder, U. (2007). Evidence for low-grade systemic proinflammatory activity in patients with posttraumatic stress disorder. *Journal of Psychiatric Research, 41,* 744–752. (11)

von Melchner, L., Pallas, S. L., & Sur, M. (2000). Visual behaviour mediated by retinal projections directed to the visual pathway. *Nature, 404,* 871–876. (4)

Vrba, E. S. (1998). Multiphasic growth models and the evolution of prolonged growth exemplified by human brain evolution. *Journal of Theoretical Biology, 190,* 227–239. (4)

Vuga, M., Fox, N. A., Cohn, J. F., George, C. J., Levenstein, R. M., & Kovacs, M. (2006). Long-term stability of frontal electroencephalographic asymmetry in adults with a history of depression and controls. *International Journal of Psychophysiology, 59,* 107–115. (14)

Vuillermot, S., Weber, L., Feldon, J., & Meyer, U. (2010). A longitudinal examination of the neurodevelopmental impact of prenatal immune activation in mice reveals primary defects in dopaminergic development relevant to schizophrenia. *Journal of Neuroscience, 30,* 1270–1287. (14)

Vuilleumier, P. (2005). Cognitive science: Staring fear in the face. *Nature, 433,* 22–23. (11)

Vyadyslav, V. V., & Harris, K. D. (2013). Sleep and the single neuron: The role of global slow oscillations in individual cell rest. *Nature Reviews Neuroscience, 14,* 443–451. (8)

Vyazovskiy, V. V., Cirelli, C., Pfister-Genskow, M., Faraguna, U., & Tononi, G. (2008). Molecular and electrophysiological evidence for net synaptic potentiation in wake and depression in sleep. *Nature Neuroscience, 11,* 200–208. (8)

Wager, T. D., & Atlas, L. Y. (2013). How is pain influenced by cognition? Neuroimaging weighs in. *Perspectives on Psychological Science, 8,* 91–97. (3)

Wager, T. D., Scott, D. J., & Zubieta, J.-K. (2007). Placebo effects on human μ-opioid activity during pain. *Proceedings of the National Academy of Sciences, USA, 104,* 11056–11061. (6)

Wagner, A. D., Schacter, D. L., Rotte, M., Koutstaal, W., Maril, A., Dale, A. M., . . . Buckner, R. L. (1998). Building memories: Remembering and forgetting of verbal experiences as predicted by brain activity. *Science, 281,* 1188–1191. (3)

Wagner, D. D., Boswell, R. G., Kelley, W. M., & Heatherton, T. F. (2012). Inducing negative affect increases the reward value of appetizing foods in dieters. *Journal of Cognitive Neuroscience, 24,* 1625–1633. (9)

Wagner, E. L., & Gleeson, T. T. (1997). Postexercise thermoregulatory behavior and recovery from exercise in desert iguanas. *Physiology & Behavior, 61,* 175–180. (9)

Wagner, U., Gais, S., Haider, H., Verleger, R., & Born, J. (2004). Sleep inspires insight. *Nature, 427,* 352–355. (8)

Waisbren, S. R., Brown, M. J., de Sonneville, L. M. J., & Levy, H. L. (1994). Review of neuropsychological functioning in treated phenylketonuria: An information-processing approach. *Acta Paediatrica, 83*(Suppl. 407), 98–103. (4)

Waldherr, M., & Neumann, I. D. (2007). Centrally released oxytocin mediates mating-induced anxiolysis in male rats. *Proceedings of the National Academy of Sciences, USA, 104,* 16681–16684. (10)

Waldvogel, J. A. (1990). The bird's eye view. *American Scientist, 78,* 342–353. (5)

Walker, E. F., Savoie, T., & Davis, D. (1994). Neuromotor precursors of schizophrenia. *Schizophrenia Bulletin, 20,* 441–451. (14)

Wallen, K. (2005). Hormonal influences on sexually differentiated behavior in nonhuman primates. *Frontiers in Neuroendocrinology, 26,* 7–26. (10)

Wallesch, C.-W., Henriksen, L., Kornhuber, H. H., & Paulson, O. B. (1985). Observations on regional cerebral blood flow in cortical and subcortical structures during language production in normal man. *Brain and Language, 25,* 224–233. (13)

Wallis, J. D. (2012). Cross-species studies of orbitofrontal cortex and value-based decision-making. *Nature Neuroscience, 15,* 13–19. (3)

Wallman, J., & Pettigrew, J. D. (1985). Conjugate and disjunctive saccades in two avian species with contrasting oculomotor strategies. *Journal of Neuroscience, 5,* 1418–1428. (5)

Walsh, T., McClellan, J. M., McCarthy, S. E., Addington, A. M., Pierce, S. B., & Cooper, G. M. (2008). Rare structural variants disrupt multiple genes in neurodevelopmental pathways in schizophrenia. *Science, 320,* 539–543. (14)

Walters, E. T., (2009). Chronic pain, memory, and injury: Evolutionary clues from snail and rat nociceptors. *International Journal of Comparative Psychology, 22,* 127–140. (6)

Wan, C. Y., Wood, A. G., Reutens, D. C., & Wilson, S. J. (2010). Early but not late-blindness leads to enhanced auditory perception. *Neuropsychologia, 48,* 344–348. (4)

Wan, X., Takano, D., Asamizuya, T., Suzuki, C., Ueno, K., Cheng, K., . . . Tanaka, K. (2012). Developing intuition: Neural correlates of cognitive-skill learning in caudate nucleus. *Journal of Neuroscience, 32,* 17492–17501. (12)

Wang, A., Costello, S., Cockburn, M., Zhang, X., Bronstein, J., & Ritz, B. (2011). Parkinson's disease risk from ambient exposure to pesticides. *European Journal of Epidemiology, 26,* 547–555. (7)

Wang, A. C. J., Hara, Y., Janssen, W. G. M., Rapp, P. R., & Morrison, J. H. (2010). Synaptic estrogen receptor-alpha levels in prefrontal cortex in female rhesus monkeys and their correlation with cognitive performance. *Journal of Neuroscience, 30,* 12770–12776. (10)

Wang, A. Y., Miura, K., & Uchida, N. (2013). The dorsomedial striatum encodes net expected return, critical for energizing performance vigor. *Nature Neuroscience, 16,* 639–647. (7)

Wang, C., Jiang, Y., Ma, J., Wu, H., Wacker, D., Katritch, V., . . . Xu, H. E. (2013). Structural basis for molecular recognition at serotonin receptors. *Science, 340,* 610–614. (2)

Wang, D. O., Kim, S. M., Zhao, Y., Hwang, H., Miura, S. K., Sossin, W. S., & Martin, K. C. (2009). Synapse- and stimulus-specific local translation during long-term neuronal plasticity. *Science, 324,* 1536–1540. (12)

Wang, H., Goehring, A., Wang, K. H., Penmatsa, A., Ressler, R., & Gouaux, E. (2013). Structural basis for action by diverse antidepressants on biogenic amine transporters. *Nature, 503,* 141–145. (14)

Wang, J., Hamida, S. B., Darcq, E., Zhu, W., Gibb, S. L., Lanfranco, M. F., . . . Ron, D. (2012). Ethanol-mediated facilitation of AMPA receptor function in the dorsomedial striatum: Implications for alcohol drinking behavior. *Journal of Neuroscience, 32,* 15124–15132. (14)

Wang, J. C., Foroud, T., Hinrichs, A. L., Le, N. X. H., Bertelsen, S., Budde, J. P., . . . Goae, A. M. (2013). A genome-wide association study of alcohol-dependence symptom counts in extended pedigrees identifies C15orf53. *Molecular Psychiatry, 18,* 1218–1224. (14)

Wang, M., Gamo, N. J., Yang, Y., Jin, L. E., Wang, X.-J., Laubach, M., . . . Arnsten, A. F. T. (2011). Neuronal basis of age-related working memory decline. *Nature, 476,* 210–213. (4)

Wang, Q., Schoenlein, R. W., Peteanu, L. A., Mathies, R. A., & Shank, C. V. (1994). Vibrationally coherent photochemistry in the femtosecond primary event of vision. *Science, 266,* 422–424. (5)

Wang, T., Okano, Y., Eisensmith, R., Huang, S. Z., Zeng, Y. T., Lo, W. H. Y., & Woo, S. L. C. (1989). Molecular genetics of phenylketonuria in Orientals: Linkage disequilibrium between a termination mutation and haplotype 4 of the phenylalanine hydroxylase gene. *American Journal of Human Genetics, 45,* 675–680. (4)

Warach, S. (1995). Mapping brain pathophysiology and higher cortical function with magnetic resonance imaging. *The Neuroscientist, 1,* 221–235. (3)

Ward, I. L., Bennett, A. L., Ward, O. B., Hendricks, S. E., & French, J. A. (1999). Androgen threshold to activate copulation differs in male rats prenatally exposed to alcohol, stress, or both factors. *Hormones and Behavior, 36,* 129–140. (10)

Ward, I. L., Romeo, R. D., Denning, J. H., & Ward, O. B. (1999). Fetal alcohol exposure blocks full masculinization of the dorsolateral nucleus in rat spinal cord. *Physiology & Behavior, 66,* 571–575. (10)

Ward, I. L., Ward, B., Winn, R. J., & Bielawski, D. (1994). Male and female sexual behavior potential of male rats prenatally exposed to the influence of alcohol, stress, or both factors. *Behavioral Neuroscience, 108,* 1188–1195. (10)

Ward, I. L., & Ward, O. B. (1985). Sexual behavior differentiation: Effects of prenatal manipulations in rats. In N. Adler, D. Pfaff, & R. W. Goy (Eds.), *Handbook of behavioral neurobiology* (Vol. 7, pp. 77–98). New York: Plenum Press. (10)

Ward, O. B., Monaghan, E. P., & Ward, I. L. (1986). Naltrexone blocks the effects of prenatal stress on sexual behavior differentiation in male rats. *Pharmacology Biochemistry and Behavior, 25,* 573–576. (10)

Ward, O. B., Ward, I. L., Denning, J. H., French, J. A., & Hendricks, S. E. (2002). Postparturitional testosterone surge in male offspring of rats stressed and/or fed ethanol during late pregnancy. *Hormones and Behavior, 41,* 229–235. (10)

Warman, G. R., Pawley, M. D. M., Bolton, C., Cheeseman, J. F., Fernando, A. T., Arendt, J., & Wirz-Justice, A. (2011). Circadian-related sleep disorders and sleep medication use in the New Zealand blind population: An observational prevalence study. *PLoS One,* 322073. (8)

Warren, R. M. (1999). *Auditory perception.* Cambridge, England: Cambridge University Press. (6)

Watanabe, D., Savion-Lemieux, T., & Penhune, V. B. (2007). The effect of early musical training on adult motor performance: Evidence for a sensitive period in motor learning. *Experimental Brain Research, 176,* 332–340. (4)

Watanabe, M., & Munoz, D. P. (2010). Presetting basal ganglia for volitional actions. *Journal of Neuroscience, 30,* 10144–10157. (7)

Watrous, A. J., Tandon, N., Conner, C. R., Pieters, T., & Ekstrom, A. D. (2013). Frequency-specific network connectivity increases underlie accurate spatiotemporal memory retrieval. *Nature Neuroscience, 16,* 349–356. (12)

Wattendorf, E., Welge-Lüssen, A., Fiedler, K., Bilecen, D., Wolfensberger, M., Fuhr, P., . . . Westermann, B. (2009). Olfactory impairment predicts brain atrophy in Parkinson's disease. *Journal of Neuroscience, 29,* 15410–15413. (7)

Waxman, S. G., & Ritchie, J. M. (1985). Organization of ion channels in the myelinated nerve fiber. *Science, 228,* 1502–1507. (1)

Waytz, A., Zaki, J., & Mitchell, J. P. (2012). Response of dorsomedial prefrontal cortex predicts altruistic behavior. *Journal of Neuroscience, 32,* 7646–7650. (13)

Weaver, I. C. G., Cervoni, N., Champagne, F. A., D'Alessio, A. C., Sharma, S., Seckl, J. R., . . . Meaney, M. J. (2004). Epigenetic programming by maternal behavior. *Nature Neuroscience, 7,* 847–854. (4)

Weber-Fox, C. M., & Neville, H. J. (1996). Maturational constraints on functional specializations for language processing: ERP and behavioral evidence in bilingual speakers. *Journal of Cognitive Neuroscience, 8,* 231–256. (13)

Wegener, D., Freiwald, W. A., & Kreiter, A. K. (2004). The influence of sustained selective attention on stimulus selectivity in macaque visual area MT. *Journal of Neuroscience, 24,* 6106–6114. (13)

Wei, W., Nguyen, L. N., Kessels, H. W., Hagiwara, H., Sisodia, S., & Malinow, R. (2010). Amyloid beta from axons and dendrites reduces local spine number and plasticity. *Nature Neuroscience, 13,* 190–196. (12)

Weidensaul, S. (1999). *Living on the wind.* New York: North Point Press. (9)

Weinberger, D. R. (1996). On the plausibility of "the neurodevelopmental hypothesis" of schizophrenia. *Neuropsychopharmacology, 14,* 1S–11S. (14)

Weindl, A. (1973). Neuroendocrine aspects of circumventricular organs. In W. F. Ganong & L. Martini (Eds.), *Frontiers in neuroendocrinology 1973* (pp. 3–32). New York: Oxford University Press. (9)

Weinshenker, D., & Schroeder, J. P. (2007). There and back again: A tale of norepinephrine and drug addiction. *Neuropsychopharmacology, 32,* 1433–1451. (14)

Weiskrantz, L., Warrington, E. K., Sanders, M. D., & Marshall, J. (1974). Visual capacity in the hemianopic field following a restricted occipital ablation. *Brain, 97,* 709–728. (5)

Weiss, A. H., Granot, R. Y., & Ahissar, M. (2014). The enigma of dyslexic musicians. *Neuropsychologia, 54,* 28–40. (13)

Weiss, A. P., Ellis, C. B., Roffman, J. L., Stufflebeam, S., Hamalainen, M. S., Duff, M., . . . Schacter, D. L. (2009). Aberrant frontoparietal function during recognition memory in schizophrenia: A multimodal neuroimaging investigation. *Journal of Neuroscience, 29,* 11347–11359. (14)

Weiss, P. (1924). Die funktion transplantierter amphibienextremitäten. Aufstellung einer resonanztheorie der motorischen nerventätigkeit auf grund abstimmter endorgane [The function of transplanted amphibian limbs. Presentation of a resonance theory of motor nerve action upon tuned end organs]. *Archiv für Mikroskopische Anatomie und Entwicklungsmechanik, 102,* 635–672. (4)

Weiss, P. H., & Fink, G. R. (2009). Grapheme-colour synaesthetes show increased grey matter volumes of parietal and fusiform cortex. *Brain, 132,* 65–70. (6)

Weissman, D. H., Roberts, K. C., Visscher, K. M., & Woldorff, M. G. (2006). The neural bases of momentary lapses in attention. *Nature Neuroscience, 9,* 971–978. (4)

Welchman, A. E., Stanley, J., Schomers, M. R., Miall, C., & Bülthoff, H. H. (2010). The quick and the dead: When reaction beats intention. *Proceedings of the Royal Society, B, 277,* 1667–1674. (7)

Weller, L., Weller, A., Koresh-Kamin, H., & Ben-Shoshan, R. (1999). Menstrual synchrony in a sample of working women. *Psychoneuroendocrinology, 24,* 449–459. (6)

Weller, L., Weller, A., & Roizman, S. (1999). Human menstrual synchrony in families and among close friends: Examining the importance of mutual exposure. *Journal of Comparative Psychology, 113,* 261–268. (6)

Wessinger, C. M., VanMeter, J., Tian, B., Van Lare, J., Pekar, J., & Rauschecker, J. P. (2001). Hierarchical organization of the human auditory cortex revealed by functional magnetic resonance imaging. *Journal of Cognitive Neuroscience, 13,* 1–7. (6)

Westergaard, G. C., Cleveland, A., Trenkle, M. K., Lussier, I. D., & Higley, J. D. (2003). CSF 5-HIAA concentration as an early screening tool for predicting significant life history outcomes in female specific-pathogen-free (SPF) rhesus macaques (*Macaca mulatta*) maintained in captive breeding groups. *Journal of Medical Primatology, 32,* 95–104. (11)

Whalen, P. J., Kagan, J., Cook, R. G., Davis, F. C., Kim, H., Polis, S., . . . Johnstone, T. (2004). Human amygdala responsivity to masked fearful eye whites. *Science, 306,* 2061. (11)

White, L. E., Coppola, D. M., & Fitzpatrick, D. (2001). The contribution of sensory experience to the maturation of orientation selectivity in ferret visual cortex. *Nature, 411,* 1049–1052. (5)

Whitesell, J. D., Sorensen, K. A., Jarvie, B. C., Hentges, S. T., & Schoppa, N. E. (2013). Interglomerular lateral inhibition targeted on external tufted cells in the olfactory bulb. *Journal of Neuroscience, 33,* 1552–1563. (5)

Whyte, J., Katz, D., Long, D., DiPasquale, M. C., Polansky, M., Kalmar, K., . . . Eifert, B. (2005). Predictors of outcome in prolonged posttraumatic disorders of consciousness and assessment of medication effects: A multicenter study. *Archives of Physical Medicine and Rehabilitation, 86,* 453–462. (4)

Wiesel, T. N. (1982). Postnatal development of the visual cortex and the influence of environment. *Nature, 299,* 583–591. (5)

Wiesel, T. N., & Hubel, D. H. (1963). Single-cell responses in striate cortex of kittens deprived of vision in one eye. *Journal of Neurophysiology, 26,* 1003–1017. (5)

Wild, H. M., Butler, S. R., Carden, D., & Kulikowski, J. J. (1985). Primate cortical area V4 important for colour constancy but not wavelength discrimination. *Nature, 313,* 133–135. (5)

Willems, R. M., Hagoort, P., & Casasanto, D. (2010). Body-specific representations of action verbs: Neural evidence from right- and left-handers. *Psychological Science, 21,* 67–74. (13)

Willerman, L., Schultz, R., Rutledge, J. N., & Bigler, E. D. (1991). In vivo brain size and intelligence. *Intelligence, 15,* 223–228. (3)

Williams, C. L. (1986). A reevaluation of the concept of separable periods of organizational and activational actions of estrogens in development of brain and behavior. *Annals of the New York Academy of Sciences, 474,* 282–292. (10)

Williams, G., Cai, X. J., Elliott, J. C., & Harrold, J. A. (2004). Anabolic neuropeptides. *Physiology & Behavior, 81,* 211–222. (9)

Williams, M. T., Davis, H. N., McCrea, A. E., Long, S. J., & Hennessy, M. B. (1999). Changes in the hormonal concentrations of pregnant rats and their fetuses following multiple exposures to a stressor during the third trimester. *Neurotoxicology and Teratology, 21,* 403–414. (10)

Williams, R. W., & Herrup, K. (1988). The control of neuron number. *Annual Review of Neuroscience, 11,* 423–453. (1, 7)

Willingham, D. B., Koroshetz, W. J., & Peterson, E. W. (1996). Motor skills have diverse neural bases: Spared and impaired skill acquisition in Huntington's disease. *Neuropsychology, 10,* 315–321. (7)

Wilson, B. A., Baddeley, A. D., & Kapur, N. (1995). Dense amnesia in a professional musician following herpes simplex virus encephalitis. *Journal of Clinical and Experimental Neuropsychology, 17,* 668–681. (12)

Wilson, J. D., George, F. W., & Griffin, J. E. (1981). The hormonal control of sexual development. *Science, 211,* 1278–1284. (10)

Wilson, R. I., & Nicoll, R. A. (2002). Endocannabinoid signaling in the brain. *Science, 296,* 678–682. (2)

Winer, G. A., Cottrell, J. F., Gregg, V., Fournier, J. S., & Bica. L. A. (2002). Fundamentally misunderstanding visual perception: Adults' belief in visual emissions. *American Psychologist, 57,* 417–424. (5)

Winfree, A. T. (1983). Impact of a circadian clock on the timing of human sleep. *American Journal of Physiology, 245,* R497–R504. (8)

Winocur, G., & Hasher, L. (1999). Aging and time-of-day effects on cognition in rats. *Behavioral Neuroscience, 113,* 991–997. (8)

Winocur, G., & Hasher, L. (2004). Age and time-of-day effects on learning and memory in a non-matching-to-sample test. *Neurobiology of Aging, 25,* 1107–1115. (8)

Winocur, G., Moscovitch, M., & Sekeres, M. (2007). Memory consolidation or transformation: Context manipulation and hippocampal representations of memory. *Nature Neuroscience, 10,* 555–557. (12)

Wirdefeldt, K., Gatz, M., Pawitan, Y., & Pedersen, N. L. (2005). Risk and protective factors for Parkinson's disease: A study in Swedish twins. *Annals of Neurology, 57,* 27–33. (7)

Wise, R. A. (1996). Addictive drugs and brain stimulation reward. *Annual Review of Neuroscience, 19,* 319–340. (14)

Wissman, A. M., & Brenowitz, E. A. (2009). The role of neurotrophins in the seasonal-like growth of the avian song control system. *Journal of Neuroscience, 29,* 6461–6471. (4)

Witelson, S. F., Beresh, H., & Kigar, D. L. (2006). Intelligence and brain size in 100 postmortem brains: Sex, lateralization and age factors. *Brain, 129,* 386–398. (3)

Witelson, S. F., & Pallie, W. (1973). Left hemisphere specialization for language in the newborn: Neuroanatomical evidence of asymmetry. *Brain, 96,* 641–646. (13)

Witthoft, N., & Winawer, J. (2013). Learning, memory, and synesthesia. *Psychological Science, 24,* 258–263. (6)

Wokke, M. E., Vandenbroucke, A. R. E., Scholte, H. S., & Lamme, V. A. F. (2013). Confuse your illusion: Feedback to early visual cortex contributes to perceptual completion. *Psychological Science, 24,* 63–71. (5)

Wolf, S. (1995). Dogmas that have hindered understanding. *Integrative Physiological and Behavioral Science, 30,* 3–4. (11)

Wolff, P. H. (1993). Impaired temporal resolution in developmental dyslexia. *Annals of the New York Academy of Sciences, 682,* 87–103. (13)

Wolkin, A., Rusinek, H., Vaid, G., Arena, L., Lafargue, T., Sanfilipo, M., . . . Rotrosen, J. (1998). Structural magnetic resonance image averaging in schizophrenia. *American Journal of Psychiatry, 155,* 1064–1073. (14)

Wolman, D. (2012). A tale of two halves. *Nature, 483*, 260–263. (13)

Wolpert, L. (1991). *The triumph of the embryo.* Oxford, England: Oxford University Press. (4)

Womelsdorf, T., Schoffelen, J.-M., Oostenveld, R., Singer, W., Desimone, R., Engel, A. K., & Fries, P.. (2007). Modulation of neuronal interactions through neuronal synchronization. *Science, 316*, 1609–1612. (13)

Wong, M., Gnanakumaran, V., & Goldreich, D. (2011). Tactile spatial acuity enhancement in blindness: Evidence for experience-dependent mechanisms. *Journal of Neuroscience, 31*, 7028–7037. (4)

Wong, P. C. M., Skoe, E., Russo, N. M., Dees, T., & Kraus, N. (2007). Musical experience shapes human brainstem encoding of linguistic pitch perception. *Nature Neuroscience, 10*, 420–422. (4)

Wong, W. I., Pasterski, V., Hindmarsh, P. C., Geffner, M. E., & Hines, M. (2013). Are there parental socialization effects on the sex-typed behavior of individuals with congenital adrenal hyperplasia? *Archives of Sexual Behavior, 42*, 381–391. (10)

Wooding, S., Kim, U., Bamshad, M J., Larsen, J., Jorde, L. B., & Drayna, D. (2004). Natural selection and molecular evolution in *PTC*, a bitter-taste receptor gene. *American Journal of Human Genetics, 74*, 637–646. (4)

Woodson, J. C., & Balleine, B. W. (2002). An assessment of factors contributing to instrumental performance for sexual reward in the rat. *Quarterly Journal of Experimental Psychology, 55B*, 75–88. (10)

Woodworth, R. S. (1934). *Psychology* (3rd ed.). New York: Holt. (1)

Wooley, A. W., Chabris, C. F., Pentland, A., Hashmi, N., & Malone, T. W. (2010). Evidence for a collective intelligence factor in the performance of human groups. *Science, 330*, 686–688. (11)

Woolf, N. J. (1991). Cholinergic systems in mammalian brain and spinal cord. *Progress in Neurobiology, 37*, 475–524. (3)

Woolf, N. J. (1996). Global and serial neurons form a hierarchically arranged interface proposed to underlie memory and cognition. *Neuroscience, 74*, 625–651. (8)

Workman, J. L., Barha, C. K., & Galea, L. A. M. (2012). Endocrine substrates of cognitive and affective changes during pregnancy and postpartum. *Behavioral Neuroscience, 126*, 54–72. (10)

Wray, N. R., James, M. R., Gordon, S. D., Dumenil, T., Ryan, L., Coventry, W. L., . . . Martin, N. G. (2009). Accurate, large-scale genotyping of 5HTTLPR and flanking single nucleotide polymorphisms in an association study of depression, anxiety, and personality measures. *Biological Psychiatry, 66*, 468–476. (14)

Wright, I. C., Rabe-Hesketh, S., Woodruff, P. W. R., David, A. S., Murray, R. M., & Bullmore, E. T. (2000). Meta-analysis of regional brain volumes in schizophrenia. *American Journal of Psychiatry, 157*, 16–25. (14)

Wright, N. D., Bahrami, B., Johnson, E., DiMalta, G., Rees, G., Frith, C. D., & Dolan, R. J. (2012). Testosterone disrupts human collaboraton by increasing egocentric choices. *Proceedings of the Royal Society B, 279*, 2275–2280. (11)

Wright, P., Stamatakis, E. A., & Tyler, L. K. (2012). Differentiating hemispheric contributions to syntax and semantics in patients with left-hemisphere lesions. *Journal of Neuroscience, 32*, 8149–8157. (13)

Wu, L.-Q., & Dickman, J. D. (2012). Neural correlates of a magnetic sense. *Science, 336*, 1054–1057. (6)

Wu, Q., Clark, M. S., & Palmiter, R. D. (2012). Deciphering a neuronal circuit that mediates appetite. *Natue, 483*, 594–597. (9)

Wulfeck, B., & Bates, E. (1991). Differential sensitivity to errors of agreement and word order in Broca's aphasia. *Journal of Cognitive Neuroscience, 3*, 258–272. (13)

Wurtman, J. J. (1985). Neurotransmitter control of carbohydrate consumption. *Annals of the New York Academy of Sciences, 443*, 145–151. (2)

Wyart, C., Webster, W. W., Chen, J. H., Wilson, S. R., McClary, A., Khan, R. M., & Sobel, N. (2007). Smelling a single component of male sweat alters levels of cortisol in women. *Journal of Neuroscience, 27*, 1261–1265. (6)

Wyatt, H. R. (2013). Update on treatment strategies for obesity. *Journal of Clinical Endocrinology and Metabolism, 98*, 1299–1306. (9)

Wynne, C. D. L. (2004). The perils of anthropomorphism. *Nature, 428*, 606. (0)

Wynne, L. C., Tienari, P., Nieminen, P., Sorri, A., Lahti, I., Moring, J., . . . Miettunen, J. (2006). Genotype-environment interaction in the schizophrenia spectrum: Genetic liability and global family ratings in the Finnish adoption study. *Family Process, 45*, 419–434. (14)

Wyss, M. T., Jolivet, R., Buck, A., Magistretti, P. J., & Weber, B. (2011). *In vivo* evidence for lactate as a neuronal energy source. *Journal of Neuroscience, 31*, 7477–7485. (1)

Xu, D., Shen, W., Guo, R., Xue, Y., Peng, W., Sima, J., . . . Wang, W. (2013). Top3β is an RNA topoisomerase that works with fragile X syndrome protein to promote synapse formation. *Nature Neuroscience, 16*, 1238–1247. (14)

Xu, H.-T., Pan, F., Yang, G., & Gan, W.-B. (2007). Choice of cranial window type for *in vivo* imaging affects dendritic spine turnover in the cortex. *Nature Neuroscience, 10*, 549–551. (4)

Xu, T. H., Yu, X. Z., Perlik, A. J., Tobin, W. F., Zweig, J. A., Tennant, K., . . . Zuo, Y. (2009). Rapid formation and selective stabilization of synapses for enduring motor memories. *Nature, 462*, 915–919. (12)

Xu, X., You, H., & Han, F. (2011). An *Archaeopteryx*-lie theropod from China and the origin of Avialae. *Nature, 475*, 465–470. (4)

Xu, Y., Padiath, Q. S., Shapiro, R. E., Jones, C. R., Wu, S. C., Saigoh, N., . . . Fu, Y. H. (2005). Functional consequences of a *CKI delta* mutation causing familial advanced sleep phase syndrome. *Nature, 434*, 640–644. (8)

Yamaguchi, S., Isejima, H., Matsuo, T., Okura, R., Yagita, K., Kobayashi, M., . . . Okamura, H. (2003). Synchronization of cellular clocks in the suprachiasmatic nucleus. *Science, 302*, 1408–1412. (8)

Yamamoto, T. (1984). Taste responses of cortical neurons. *Progress in Neurobiology, 23*, 273–315. (6)

Yanagisawa, K., Bartoshuk, L. M., Catalanotto, F. A., Karrer, T. A., & Kveton, J. F. (1998). Anesthesia of the chorda tympani nerve and taste phantoms. *Physiology & Behavior, 63*, 329–335. (6)

Yang, G., Pan, F., & Gan, W.-B. (2009). Stably maintained dendritic spines are associated with lifelong memories. *Nature, 462*, 920–924. (4)

Yarmolinsky, D. A., Zuker, C. S., & Ryba, N. J. P. (2009). Common sense about taste: From mammals to insects. *Cell, 139*, 234–244. (6)

Yeh, M. T., Coccaro, E. F., & Jacobson, K. C. (2010). Multivariate behavior genetic analyses of aggressive behavior subtypes. *Behavior Genetics, 40*, 603–617. (11)

Yehuda, R. (2002). Post-traumatic stress disorder. *New England Journal of Medicine, 346*, 108–114. (11)

Yenari, M. A., & Han, H. S. (2012). Neuroprotective mechanisms of hypothermia in brain ischaemia. *Nature Reviews Neuroscience, 13*, 267–278. (4)

Yeo, G. S. H., & Heisler, L. K. (2012). Unraveling the brain regulation of appetite: Lessons from genetics. *Nature Neuroscience, 15*, 1343–1349. (9)

Yeomans, J. S., & Frankland, P. W. (1996). The acoustic startle reflex: Neurons and connections. *Brain Research Reviews*, 21, 301–314. (11)

Yeshurun, Y., Dudai, Y., & Sobel, N. (2008). Working memory across nostrils. *Behavioral Neuroscience, 122*, 1031–1037. (13)

Yin, H. H., & Knowlton, B. J. (2006). The role of the basal ganglia in habit formation. *Nature Reviews Neuroscience, 7*, 464–476. (7)

Yiu, G., & He, Z. (2006). Glial inhibition of CNS axon regeneration. *Nature Reviews Neuroscience, 7*, 617–627. (4)

Yolken, R. H., Dickerson, F. B., & Torrey, E. F. (2009). Toxoplasma and schizophrenia. *Parasite Immunology, 31*, 706–715. (14)

Yoo, S.-S., Hu, P. T., Gujar, N., Jolesz, F. A., & Walker, M. P. (2007). A deficit in the ability to form new human memories without sleep. *Nature Neuroscience, 10*, 385–392. (8)

Yoon, K. L., Hong, S. W., Joormann, J., & Kang, P. (2009). Perception of facial expressions of emotion during binocular rivalry. *Emotion, 9*, 172–182. (13)

Yoon, S.-H., & Park, S. (2011). A mechanical analysis of woodpecker drumming and its application to shock-absorbing systems. *Bioinspiration and Biomimetics, 6*: 016003. (4)

Yoshida, J., & Mori, K. (2007). Odorant category profile selectivity of olfactory cortex neurons. *Journal of Neuroscience, 27*, 9105–9114. (6)

Yoshida, K., Li, X., Cano, G., Lazarus, M., & Saper, C. B. (2009). Parallel preoptic pathways for thermoregulation. *Journal of Neuroscience, 29*, 11954–11964. (9)

Yoshida, W., Seymour, B., Koltzenburg, M., & Dolan, R. J. (2013). Uncertainty increases pain: Evidence for a novel mechanism of pain modulation involving the periaqueductal gray. *Journal of Neuroscience, 33*, 5638–5646. (6)

Yoshioka, T., Dillon, M. R., Beck, G. C., Rapp, B., & Landau, B. (2013). Tactile localization on digits and hand: Structure and development. *Psychological Science, 24*, 1653–1663. (13)

Young, A. B. (1995). Huntington's disease: Lessons from and for molecular neuroscience. *The Neuroscientist, 1*, 51–58. (7)

Young, C., Jevtovic-Todorovic, V., Qin, Y. Q., Tenkova, T., Wang, H., Labruyere, J., & Olney, J. W. (2005). Potential of ketamine and midazolam, individually or in combination, to induce apoptotic neurodegeneration in the infant mouse brain. *British Journal of Pharmacology, 146,* 189–197. (4)

Young, L., & Dungan, J. (2012). Where in the brain is morality? Everywhere and maybe nowhere. *Social Neuroscience, 7,* 1–10. (13)

Yousem, D. M., Maldjian, J. A., Siddiqi, F., Hummel, T., Alsop, D. C., Geckle, R. J., . . . Doty, R. L. (1999). Gender effects on odor-stimulated functional magnetic resonance imaging. *Brain Research, 818,* 480–487. (6)

Yu, T. W., & Bargmann, C. I. (2001). Dynamic regulation of axon guidance. *Nature Neuroscience Supplement, 4,* 1169–1176. (4)

Yuval-Greenberg, S., & Heeger, D. J. (2013). Continuous flash suppression modulates cortical activity in early visual cortex. *Journal of Neuroscience, 33,* 9635–9643. (13)

Zadra, A., Desautels, A., Petit, D., & Montplaisir, J. (2013). Somnambulism: Clinical aspects and pathophysiological hypotheses. *Lancet Neurology, 12,* 285–294. (8)

Zadra, A., & Pilon, M. (2008). Polysomnographic diagnosis of sleepwalking: Effects of sleep deprivation. *Annals of Neurology, 63,* 513–519. (8)

Zakharenko, S. S., Zablow, L., & Siegelbaum, S. A. (2001). Visualization of changes in presynaptic function during long-term synaptic plasticity. *Nature Neuroscience, 4,* 711–717. (12)

Zaki, J., & Ochsner, K. (2012). The neuroscience of empathy: Progress, pitfalls, and promise. *Nature Neuroscience, 15,* 675–680. (13)

Zanto, T. P., Rubens, M. T., Thangavel, A., & Gazzaley, A. (2011). Causal role of the prefrontal cortex in top-down modulation of visual processing and working memory. *Nature Neuroscience, 14,* 656–661. (3)

Zatorre, R. J., Bouffard, M., & Belin, P. (2004). Sensitivity to auditory object features in human temporal neocortex. *Journal of Neuroscience, 24,* 3637–3642. (6)

Zatorre, R. J., Fields, R. D., & Johansen-Berg, H. (2012). Plasticity in gray and white: Neuroimaging changes in brain structure during learning. *Nature Neuroscience, 4,* 528–536. (4)

Zeki, S. (1980). The representation of colours in the cerebral cortex. *Nature, 284,* 412–418. (5)

Zeki, S. (1983). Colour coding in the cerebral cortex: The responses of wavelength-selective and colour-coded cells in monkey visual cortex to changes in wavelength composition. *Neuroscience, 9,* 767–781. (5)

Zeki, S., McKeefry, D. J., Bartels, A., & Frackowiak, R. S. J. (1998). Has a new color area been discovered? *Nature Neuroscience, 1,* 335. (5)

Zeki, S., & Shipp, S. (1988). The functional logic of cortical connections. *Nature, 335,* 311–317. (5)

Zentner, M., & Mitura, K. (2012). Stepping out of the caveman's shadow: Nations' gender gap predicts degree of sex differentiation in mate preferences. *Psychological Science, 23,* 1176–1185. (10)

Zhang, J., Ackman, J. B., Xu, H.-P., & Crair, M. C. (2012). Visual map development depends on the temporal pattern of binocular activity in mice. *Nature Neuroscience, 15,* 298–307. (5)

Zhang, M., Wang, H., Zhao, J., Chen, C., Leak, R. K., Xu, Y., . . . Zhang, F. (2013). Drug-induced hypothermia in stroke models: Does it always protect? *CNS & Neurological Disorders-Drug Targets, 12,* 371–380. (4)

Zhang, T. Y., Hellstron, I. C., Bagot, R. C., Wen, X. L., Dioro, J., & Meaney, M. J. (2010). Maternal care and DNA methylation of a glutamic acid decarboxylase 1 promoter in rat hippocampus. *Journal of Neuroscience, 30,* 13130–13137. (4)

Zhang, X., & Firestein, S. (2002). The olfactory receptor gene superfamily of the mouse. *Nature Neuroscience, 5,* 124–133. (6)

Zhang, Y., Proenca, R., Maffei, M., Barone, M., Leopold, L., & Friedman, J. M. (1994). Positional cloning of the mouse obese gene and its human homologue. *Nature, 372,* 425–432. (9)

Zhang, Y. E., Landback, P., Vibranovski, M. D., & Long, M. (2011). Accelerated recruitment of new brain development genes into the human genome. *PLoS Biology,* e1001179. (4)

Zhao, Y., Terry, D., Shi, L., Weinstein, H., Blanchard, S. C., & Javitch, J. A. (2010). Single-molecule dynamics of gating in a neurotransmitter transporter homologue. *Nature, 465,* 188–193. (2)

Zhao, Z., & Davis, M. (2004). Fear-potentiated startle in rats is mediated by neurons in the deep layers of the superior colliculus/deep mesencephalic nucleus of the rostral midbrain through the glutamate non-NMDA receptors. *Journal of Neuroscience, 24,* 10326–10334. (11)

Zheng, B., Larkin, D. W., Albrecht, U., Sun, Z. S., Sage, M., Eichele, G., . . . Bradley, A. (1999). The *mPer2* gene encodes a functional component of the mammalian circadian clock. *Nature, 400,* 169–173. (8)

Zhou, D., Lebel, C., Lepage, C., Rasmussen, C., Evans, A., Wyper, K., . . . Beaulieu, C. (2011). Developmental cortical thinning in fetal alcohol spectrum disorders. *NeuroImage, 58,* 16–25. (4)

Zhou, F., Zhu, X. W., Castellani, R. J., Stimmelmayr, R., Perry, G., Smith, M. A., & Drew, K. L. (2001). Hibernation, a model of neuroprotection. *American Journal of Pathology, 158,* 2145–2151. (8)

Zhu, Q., Zhang, J., Luo, Y. L. L., Dilks, D. D., & Liu, J. (2011). Resting-state neural activity across face-selective cortical regions is behaviorally relevant. *Journal of Neuroscience, 31,* 10323–10330. (5)

Zhu, Y., Fenik, P., Zhan, G. X., Mazza, E., Kelz, M., Aston-Jones, G., & Veasey, S. C. (2007). Selective loss of catecholaminergic wake-active neurons in a murine sleep apnea model. *Journal of Neuroscience, 27,* 10060–10071. (8)

Ziegler, J. C., & Goswami, U. (2005). Reading acquisition, developmental dyslexia, and skilled reading across languages: A psycholinguistic grain size theory. *Psychological Bulletin, 131,* 3–29. (13)

Zihl, J., von Cramon, D., & Mai, N. (1983). Selective disturbance of movement vision after bilateral brain damage. *Brain, 106,* 313–340. (5)

Zikopoulos, B., & Barbas, H. (2012). Pathways for emotions and attention converge on the thalamic reticular nucleus in primates. *Journal of Neuroscience, 32,* 5338–5350. (11)

Zipursky, R. B., Reilly, T. J., & Murray, R. M. (2013). The myth of schizophrenia as a progressive brain disease. *Schizophrenia Bulletin, 39,* 1363–1372. (14)

Zipser, B. D., Johanson, C. E., Gonzalez, L., Berzin, T. M., Tavares, R., Hulette, C. M., . . . Stopa, E. G. (2007). Microvascular injury and blood–brain barrier leakage in Alzheimer's disease. *Neurobiology of Aging, 28,* 977–986. (1)

Zola, S. M., Squire, L. R., Teng, E., Stefanacci, L., Buffalo, E. A., & Clark, R. E. (2000). Impaired recognition memory in monkeys after damage limited to the hippocampal region. *Journal of Neuroscience, 20,* 451–463. (12)

Zorzi, M., Priftis, K., & Umiltà, C. (2002). Neglect disrupts the mental number line. *Nature, 417,* 138. (13)

Zotev, V., Phillips, R., Young, K. D., Drevets, W. C., & Bodurka, J. (2013). Prefrontal control of the amygdala during real-time fMRI neurofeedback training of emotion regulation. *PLoS One, 8,* e79184. (11)

Zucker, K. J., Bradley, S. J., Oliver, G., Blake, J., Fleming, S., & Hood, J. (1996). Psychosexual development of women with congenital adrenal hyperplasia. *Hormones and Behavior, 30,* 300–318. (10)

Zuckerman, L, Rehavi, M., Nachman, R., & Weiner, I. (2003). Immune activation during pregnancy in rats leads to a post-pubertal emergence of disrupted latent inhibition, dopaminergic hyperfunction, and altered limbic morphology in the offspring: A novel neurodevelopmental model of schizophrenia. *Neuropsychopharmacology, 28,* 1778–1789. (14)

Zurif, E. B. (1980). Language mechanisms: A neuropsychological perspective. *American Scientist, 68,* 305–311. (13)

Name Index

Aarts, H., 368
Abate, P., 469
Abatis, M., 371
Abbott, N.J., 22
Abdel Malik, P., 491
Abe, A. S., 294
Abe, G., 91
Abel, K. M., 491
Abell, C. W., 470
Abi-Dargham, A., 494
Abizaid, A., 314
Aboitiz, F., 438, 444
Aboitiz, S., 438
Abrahamsen, B., 201
Abrahamsson, N., 440
Abrams, W., 139
Acar, S.T., 478
Ackman, J.B., 171
Acri, J., 472
Acuna-Goycolea, C., 314
Adamec, R.E., 367
Adams, D.B., 333, 334
Adams, H. L., 500
Adams, R.B., Jr., 373, 460
Adan, R. A. H., 314
Adcock, R. A., 397
Ad-Dab'bagh, Y., 97
Addington, A. M., 490
Addis, D.R., 400
Adhikari, A., 371
Adler, E., 214
Adler, M., 479
Adler, N. T., 333
Admon, R., 374
Adolphs, R., 358, 364, 375, 376, 408, 429
Adriani, M., 192
Adrien, J., 279
Aerts, J., 238, 278
Agartz, I., 493
Agarwal, N., 206
Agerbo, E., 489, 490
Aghajanian, G. K., 478
Aglioti, S., 141, 455
Agrati, D., 328
Agrawal, A.F., 326
Agren, T., 379
Agster, K. L., 401
Aguirre G. K., 166
Aguzzi, A., 20
Agyei, Y., 346, 347
Aharon, I., 467
Ahima, R. S., 312
Ahissar, M., 444
Ahlskog, J.E., 316
Ahmed, E.I., 328
Ahmed, I.I., 329
Ahn, S. J., 310
Ahrendsen, J.T., 132
Airaksinen, M.S., 123
Airan, R.D., 478
Airavaara, M., 254
Aizenstein, H., 127
Akama, K. T., 334
Akbudak, E., 127
Akinola, M., 384
Akshoomoff, N., 153
Akshoomoff, N. A., 71
Alagiakrishnan, K., 405
Alais, D., 450
Alanko, K., 346, 347
Albanese, M.-C., 203
Albert, M. S., 404
Alberts, S.C., 368
Alborzian, S., 480
Albouy, G., 275, 407
Albrecht, D. G., 170
Albrecht, U., 269
Albright, T. D., 16, 181
Aldenhoff, J., 403
Aldinger, K. A., 499
Aldrich, M., 280
Aldrich, N. J., 454
Aldrich, R. W., 20
Aleman, A., 489
Alerstam, T., 285
Alexander, G.M., 330
Alexander, J. T., 314
Alexander, M. P., 441
Alexander, W.H., 85
Alfieri, L., 454
Alfke, K., 403
Alfonso, J., 34
Alford, J.R., 374
Alger, J. R., 279
Al-Hashimi, O., 454
Alho, K., 444
Ali, N., 440
Alkass, K., 119
Alkire, M. T., 97, 453
Allaire, J. C., 406
Allan, D., 357
Allebrandt, K. V., 266
Allen, G. I., 221
Allen, H., 454
Allen, H.L., 105
Allen, J. S., 98, 192
Allen, L. S., 349
Allen, N.B., 263
Allen, P., 373
Alleva, E., 123, 126
Allirol, L., 426, 444
Allison, T., 285
Almazen, M., 439
Almli, C.R., 315
Almonte, J. L., 386
Alonso, M., 119
Alquier, T., 313
Al-Ramahi, I., 256
Al-Rashid, R.A., 316
Alsop, D., 191
Alsop, D. C., 220
Altar, C.A., 481
Altenmüller, E., 130
Altimus, C. M., 268
Altmann, J., 368
Alvarez, J.-C., 369
Alvarez-Buylla, A. A., 123
Álvarez-Linera, J., 97, 98
Alzmon, G., 132
Amano, K., 182
Amanzio, M., 206
Amaral, D.G., 153, 500
Amateau, S.K., 329
Amaya, F., 206
Ambady, N., 373
American Psychiatric Association, 499
Amering, M., 376
Ames, M. A., 348
Amirabbasi-Beik, M., 112
Amiry-Moghaddam, M., 22
Amlaner, C. J., 277
Amso, D., 441
Amsterdam, J., 478
Amting, J.M., 376
An, Y., 406
Anacker, C., 107
Anaclet, C., 275
Anagnostaras, S. G., 286
Anand, P., 206
Anastasiya, A., 266
Andersen, E., 108
Andersen, J.L., 230
Andersen, R. A., 237
Anderson, C., 347
Anderson, D. J., 190
Anderson, E., 451
Anderson, F., 367
Anderson, J. E., 492
Anderson, J. P., 383
Anderson, M. E., 244
Anderson, S., 193
Anderson, T.S., 86
Andrade, D. V., 294
Andreasen, N.C., 94, 493
Andreev, B. V., 495
Andres, K. H., 199
Andrés-Pueyo, A., 370
Andrew, D., 201, 207, 208
Andrews, T. J., 153
Ang, R. L., 495
Angelos, L., 468
Angelucci, A., 124
Anguera, J.A., 454
Angulo, M.C., 20
Ankney, C.D., 98
Ankra-Badu, G. A., 105
Ansorge, M. S., 119
Antanitus, D.S., 20, 21
Antenor-Dorsey, J. A., 253
Anton, E. S., 118
Antony, M.M., 373
Aoki, C., 376
Apfelbach, R., 378
Aplin, L. C., 264
Apostaolakis, E.M., 331
Applebaum, S., 220
Arajärvi, R., 489
Araneda, R.C., 219
Arango, V., 369
Araripe, L. O., 327
Archer, J., 368
Archer, S. N., 269
Arcurio, L.R., 180
Arduino, C., 206
Arena, L., 492
Arendt, J., 264, 265
Armstrong, J.B., 307
Arnold, A. M., 419
Arnold, A. P., 327, 328
Arnold, S. E., 492
Arnsten, A. F. T., 132, 384
Arseneau, L. M., 295
Arvidson, K., 212
Aryee, M. J., 107
Asai, M., 314
Asante, C.O., 201
Asari, H., 149
Asarnow, R. F., 246
Åsberg, M., 369
Ascherio, A., 253
Aschkenazi, C., 312
Aserinsky, E., 273
Ash, I. M., 172
Ashburner, J., 402
Asher, B., 363
Asher, J. E., 221
Ashida, H., 182
Ashley, R., 128
Ashmore, L.J., 269
Ashwood, P., 499, 500
Aslan, E., 478
Aslan, S., 419
Asllani, I., 492
Asmundson, G. J. G., 371
Asrican, B., 417
Assal, G., 429
Aston-Jones, G., 269, 279
Atherton, N. M., 480
Athos, E.A., 191
Atlas, L. Y., 93
Ator, R., 468
Attwell, D., 136
Atwal, J. K., 405
Atzei, A., 141
Aubin, H.-J., 468
Audero, E., 369
Audinat, E., 20
Avedissian, C., 98
Avena, N. M., 317, 320
Avidan, G., 180
Aviezer, H., 362
Avison, M. J., 124
Avon Longitudinal Study of Parents and Children Study Team, 331
Axel, R., 119, 218, 219, 220, 329, 349
Axelsson, G., 253
Axmacher, N, 450
Azhar, H., 206

Babbitt, C. C., 111, 308
Babich, F.R., 413
Babiloni, C., 203, 397
Babinet, C., 124
Babkoff, H., 262
Babor, T. F., 470
Babo-Rebelo, M., 453
Baccini, G., 369
Bacher, D., 235
Bachevalier, J., 373, 401
Backhaus, J., 482
Backlund, E.-O., 254
Bäckman, J., 285
Baddeley, A. D., 392, 397
Badiani, A., 467
Baer, J.S., 469
Bagemihl, B., 346
Baghdoyan, H.A., 279
Bagot, R. C., 107
Bahrami, B., 368
Bahrick, L. E., 438
Baibazarova, E., 370
Baier, L. J., 318
Bailey, C.H., 415
Bailey, J. A., 128
Bailey, J. M., 346, 347, 348
Bailey, K. G. D., 442
Baimouknametova, D. V., 56
Bains, J. S., 56
Baird, A.A., 373

Baker, B. N., 192
Baker, C. I., 129
Baker, E., 370
Baker, G. B., 288
Baker, L., 109
Baker, M. B., 313
Baker, N. L., 472
Baker, P. N., 491
Baker, R. J., 312
Baker, S. W., 345
Baker, T. B., 468
Bakermans-Kranenburg, M. J., 460
Bakken, T.E., 153
Bakker, J., 220, 329, 331
Bakst, L., 374
Balaji, J., 418
Balasubramanian, V., 31
Baldwin, D. S., 478
Balestrieri, A., 329
Balkin, T. J., 238, 278
Ball, M. P., 417
Ball, W. A., 277
Ballabh, P., 118
Ballard, P.A., 253
Balleine, B.W., 329, 407
Ballieux, R.E., 384
Ballon, J.S., 491
Balteau, E., 275, 407
Balthazart, J., 329, 331
Bamshad, M J., 105
Banai, K., 193
Banaji, M. R., 180
Banfi, G., 492
Banich, M., 131
Banich, M. T., 429, 430
Banks, S., 284
Banks, W.P., 248
Bannerman, D.M., 403
Baraldi, E., 329
Barash, S., 243
Barbas, H., 372
Barbe, R. P., 479
Barber, J. R., 187
Barbosa, L. S., 452
Barbour, D.L., 192
Bar-David, E., 460
Barde, Y. A., 123
Bardy, C., 119
Bargary, G., 221
Bargmann, C. I., 120
Barha, C. K., 328
Barinaga, M., 137
Bark, C., 34
Barker, P. B., 442
Barker, R. A., 280
Barnabé-Heider, F., 119
Barnea, G., 220
Barnes, B.M., 284, 285
Barnes, T. R. E., 496
Barnett, K.J., 221
Baroncelli, L., 478
Baron-Cohen, S., 221, 335, 439
Barone, M., 312
Barone, Y., 478
Barouei, J., 385
Barr, H.M., 469
Barratt-Fornell, A., 215
Barres, B.A., 20
Barrett, J., 112
Barrett, L. F., 95, 360, 374, 451
Barretto, M., 131
Barrientos, R.M., 132
Barsh, G. S., 312, 314
Bartel, P., 284, 375
Bartels, A., 181
Bartke, A., 329
Bartko, J., 369
Bartko, J. J., 490–491
Barton, C., 139
Barton, D.A., 478
Barton, L., 329
Barton, R. A., 80, 81
Bartoshuk, L., 207
Bartoshuk, L. M., 213, 214, 215
Bartsch, T., 403
Bartz, J.A., 460
Barua, L. A., 401
Barysheva, M., 98
Barzilai, N., 132
Basbaum, A. I., 53, 205, 207
Basinski, M., 314
Baskin, D. G., 312
Basma, A., 253
Bassett, A.S., 491
Bassett, D. S., 492
Basterzi, A.D., 478
Bastida, C., 369
Basu, A., 191
Bates, E., 441, 442
Bates, J. E., 470
Batista, G., 369
Batterham, R. L., 314
Battersby, S., 309
Baudry, M., 372
Bauer, E. P., 372
Bauer, R., 450
Baulac, S., 426
Baum, A., 385
Baum, M. J., 329
Bauman, J.M., 132
Bauman, M. L., 499
Bauman, M.D., 500
Baumeister, R. F., 204
Baur, J. E., 53
Bautista, D.M., 199
Bavelier, D., 441, 454
Bax, C. M., 334
Baxter, L. R., 480
Baxter, L.R., 482
Baxter, M. G., 132
Bayer, U., 362
Bayley, P.J., 399, 407
Baylis, G.C., 178, 179
Baylor, D. A., 122
Beall, A.T., 334
Bear, M. F., 171
Beaton, E.A., 373
Beau, I., 343
Beauchamp, G. K., 215
Beauchamp, J., 109
Beauchamp, M.S., 222
Beaucousin, V., 429
Beaulieu, C., 118, 124
Bechara, A., 364, 374
Beck, G. C., 432
Beck, S., 130
Becker, B., 459
Becker, C., 377
Becker, H.C., 378
Beckers, T., 379
Becks, L., 326
Bednarek, E., 418
Bedny, M., 127
Beebe, D.W., 279
Beehner, J.C., 368, 386
Beeli, G., 221
Beeman, M.J., 426, 429
Beeney, J.E., 460
Beer, T. M., 334
Beerendonk, C., 345
Beersma, G. M., 268
Beevers, C. G., 373
Begg, M. D., 491
Beglinger, L. J., 256
Bègue, L., 369
Behara, A., 408
Behrens, M., 214
Behrens, T. E. J., 85
Behrmann, M., 180, 238
Belenky, G., 277
Belin, D., 467
Belin, P., 127, 192
Bell, R., 369
Bell, V., 180
Bellen, H. J., 256
Bellini, F., 480
Bellugi, U., 438, 439
Belmonte, P. L., 475
Beltz, A.M., 344
Belvens, M., 214
Ben Achour, S., 20
Benali, H., 277, 286
Ben-Ami, H., 374
Ben-Ami Bartal, I., 461
Benavidez, N., 246
Benca, R. M., 285
Benedetti, F., 206, 481
Benes, F.M., 118
Benitez-Temiño, B., 253
Benjamin, D. J., 109
Benke, D., 378
Bennett, A. L., 348
Bennett, E. L., 125
Bennett, J. M., 386
Bennett, K., 342
Bennett, M.L., 20
Benoliel, J.-J., 377
Benrath, J., 207
Benschop, R.J., 384
Bensen, A.L., 51
Ben-Shoshan, R., 220
Benson, D. F., 85, 179
Benson, G., 483
Benson, J. A., 378
Benson, M. D., 404
Benzer, S., 268
Beranger, A., 426
Berard, J., 369
Berardi, D., 480
Berardi, N., 171
Berdoy, M., 372
Berenbaum, S.A., 344
Berenshteyn, F., 256
Beresh, H., 98
Bergé, D., 376
Berger, G. E., 489
Berger, M., 482
Berger, R.J., 284
Berger-Sweeney, J., 118
Berglund, H., 220
Bergman, T.J., 386
Bergmann, M.L., 55
Bergmann, O., 119, 493
Bergson, C., 496
Berke, J. D., 238
Berkeley, G., 449
Berkemeier, L. R., 314
Berkhof, J., 475
Berkowitz, J. S., 467
Berlin, H.A., 364
Berlin, I., 369
Berliner, D. L., 220
Berlucchi, G., 141, 428
Berman, A., 490
Berman, A. J., 142
Berman, K. F., 439, 492
Berman, M. G., 204, 475
Bernal, D., 296
Bernard, S., 119
Bernasconi, S., 369
Bernati, T., 455
Berndt, S.I., 105
Bernstein, D., 491
Bernstein, J.J., 139
Berntson, G.G., 374
Beron, J., 304
Berrettini, W., 472
Berridge, K. C., 304, 468
Berrios, G. E., 376
Berryhill, M.E., 407
Berson, D.M., 268
Bertelsen, S., 469
Berton, O., 386
Berzin, T. M., 22
Besenbacher, S., 500
Beuckmann, C. T., 280
Beuming, T., 55
Bever, T. G., 435
Beverly, J. L., 295
Bevilacqua, L., 370
Bezzola, L., 129
Bhardwaj, R.D., 119
Bhatia, K. P., 495
Bhimavarapu, B. B.R., 118
Bialystok, E., 440
Bian, L., 318
Bianchi-Demicheli, F., 459
Biben, M., 367
Bica. L. A., 148
Bichot, N. P., 454
Bickhart, K.C., 95
Bielawski, D., 348
Bieri, G., 132
Bierut, L.J., 476
Biggs, M. M., 480
Bigler, E. D., 98
Bilalic, M., 181
Bilder, R. M., 98
Bilecen, D., 252
Bilkey, D. K., 403
Billington, C.J., 314
Bimler, D., 158
Bimonte-Nelson, H. A., 384
Binart, N., 336
Binder, E. B., 107
Binget, U., 206
Bingman, V. P., 285
Bini, L., 480
Bioulac, B., 265
Birbaumer, N., 141
Bird, A., 104
Birk, J. L., 467
Birmaher, B., 479
Birring, S.S., 368
Bischofberger, J., 119
Bishop, C. V., 350
Biss, R.K., 266
Bitran, D., 329
Bittigau, P., 124
Bizzi, E., 278
Björklund, A., 254
Björkstrand, J., 379
Bjornara, K. A., 253
Björnsdotter, M., 201
Bjugstad, K. B., 254
Black, M. J., 235
Black, S. E., 400, 401
Blackless, M., 343
Blackwell, A., 441
Blaha, C. D., 499
Blair, R.J.R., 461
Blake, J., 284, 345
Blake, R., 171, 221, 451
Blakemore, S.-J., 201
Blakeslee, S., 141
Blamires, H., 139
Blanchard, R., 348
Blanchard, S. C., 55
Blanke, O., 86, 192
Blasko, D. G., 453
Blasl, F., 208
Blass, T., 439

Blatt, G. J., 499
Blekhman, R., 334
Blesa, J., 253
Bleuler, E., 487
Bley, K., 206
Blier, P., 478
Bliss, T. V. P., 415, 418
Bliss-Moreau, E., 360, 374
Bloch, G.J., 329
Bloch, L., 373
Blomqvist, A., 299
Bloom, S. R., 312
Bloss, C.S., 153
Blossom-Stach, C., 442
Blumstein, S.E., 441
Bobrow, D., 347
Boccanfuso, J., 454
Bocklandt, S., 347
Boden, J. M., 370
Boder, E., 444
Bodurka, J., 374
Boehm, S., 56
Boehme, K., 266
Boehme, R., 178
Boets, B., 444
Boettiger, C.A., 469
Boeve, B. F., 281
Bogaert, A.F., 346, 348
Bogardus, C., 318
Bogdahn, U., 129
Bogdan, R., 467
Bogdanov, S., 141
Bohlin, G., 344
Boivin, D.B., 265
Bok, E., 137
Boller, C., 128
Bolton, C., 264
Boly, M., 277, 453
Bolz, J., 490
Bomar, J. M., 107, 439
Bonaccorso, S., 478
Bonath, B., 86
Bonci, A., 246, 314
Bonev, A. D., 20
Bonhoeffer, T., 418
Bonino, D., 239
Bonne, O., 478
Bonneh, Y.S., 450
Bookheimer, S. Y., 246, 398
Boomsma, D. I., 98
Boone, T., 313
Booth, D.A., 212
Booth, F.W., 230
Booth, W., 325
Bordelon, Y., 253
Bordier, C., 92
Borgius, L., 232
Borgland, S.L., 314
Borisovska, M., 51
Born, J., 286, 287, 288
Born, S., 214
Borodinsky, L.N., 50
Borsutzky, S., 404
Bortolotti, B., 480
Bortz, R., 284
Bos, P. A., 335, 368
Bosch, M., 107
Bosel, J., 137
Bosetti, F., 483
Boshart, J., 439
Bostrom, A., 191
Boswell, R. G., 318
Botas, J., 256
Bottinelli, R., 230
Boucsein, K., 375
Boudin, H., 51
Bouffard, M., 192
Bougneres, P., 343
Bourgeat, P., 406
Bourque, C. W., 302
Boutrel, B., 279
Bouvattier, C., 343
Bouvy, A., 483
Bouzerda-Wahlen, A., 404
Bower, C., 490
Bower, J. M., 242
Bowers, M.S., 314
Bowles, C. A., 385
Bowles, S., 113, 114
Bowmaker, J.K., 154, 158
Boyce, R., 500
Boycott, B.B., 163
Boyd, J. D., 139
Boyden, E. S., 275
Boyeson, M. G., 138
Boynton, G. M., 173
Bozza, T., 216
Bradke, F., 139
Bradley, A., 269
Bradley, B., 374, 460
Bradley, M. M., 467
Bradley, S. J., 345
Bradshaw, J. L., 141
Bradwejn, J., 377
Brady, K. T., 472
Brady, S. T., 256
Braff, D. L., 490
Brain, C., 344
Brainard, D. H., 166
Brainard, G. C., 268
Brakke, K. E., 436, 437
Branch, B.J., 329
Branco, T., 43
Brancucci, A., 203
Brand, J. G., 215
Brand, M., 404
Brandes, D., 377
Brandfonbrener, A. G., 130
Brandmaier, A. M., 107
Brandner, L., 266
Brandon, J. G., 125
Brandt, A., 402
Brandt, F., 358
Brandt, J., 254
Brandt, T., 198
Brännström, I., 111
Brans, R.G.H., 132
Brar, S., 173
Brass, M., 248
Braun, A., 460
Braun, A. R., 238, 278
Braun, D. I., 181
Braunschweig, D., 500
Braunschweig, D., 500
Braus, H., 72
Bravo, E., 450
Bray, G. A., 319
Bredy, T. W., 374
Breedlove, S. M., 123, 328, 334, 350
Breer, H., 220
Breeze, R. E., 254
Breidenbach, W. C., 141
Breiter, H. C., 467
Bremmer, F., 182–183
Brenchley, C., 478
Brennan, A., 95
Brennand, K. J., 490
Brenner, G. J., 206
Brenowitz, E. A., 119
Brent, D. A., 479
Brent, H. P., 173
Breslin, P. A., 220
Bresnahan, M., 491, 500
Bressler, K., 202
Bressler, S. L., 397
Brewer, A. A., 173
Brewer, W. J., 489
Brewster, S. J., 112
Breysse, N., 254
Bridge, H., 167
Bridge, H., Thomas, 178
Bridge, J. A., 479
Bridgeman, B., 166
Bridges, R. S., 336
Bridle, C., 480
Brigman, J. L., 408
Brin, M. F., 254
Bristow, P. K., 314
Britshgi, M., 132
Britton, J. C., 374
Broca, P., 88, 440–441
Brock, O., 329
Brockman, J.A., 481
Brodin, T., 378
Brodsky, L., 104
Brody, A. L., 480
Bron, C. R., 418
Brönneke, H. S., 469
Bronson, R.T., 336
Bronstein, J., 253
Brook, C., 344
Brook, C. G. D., 344
Brooks, D.C., 278
Brooks, J., 443
Brooks, P. J., 454
Brooks, P.L., 277, 281
Brooks-Wilson, A. R., 112
Brosch, M., 450
Brosch, T., 460
Brosnan, S. F., 113, 460
Brosschot, J.F., 384
Brotchie, P., 237
Brotherton, P. N. M., 113
Brouwer, G. J., 181
Brouwer, R. M., 98
Brown, A. S., 488, 491
Brown, C. E., 139
Brown, E. N., 265
Brown, G. L., 369, 469
Brown, G. M., 279
Brown, J., 404, 470
Brown, J.R., 336
Brown, J.W., 85
Brown, M., 378
Brown, M. J., 109
Brown, R. A., 418
Brown, R. W., 140
Browne, S., 488
Browning, M. D., 418
Bruck, M., 179
Brugge, J. F., 190
Bruhin, A., 460
Brumpton, B., 318
Brunet, A., 379
Brünig, I., 378
Brüning, J. C., 469
Bruno, M. A., 453
Bruno, R. M., 42
Bruns, P., 86
Brus, R., 140
Bruss, J., 98, 192
Brussard, A. B., 123
Bryan, A., 468, 469
Bryant, R. A., 377, 465
Bryk, K., 344
Bryk, K.L.K., 344
Bubash, S., 413
Bucci, M. P., 238
Buch, E. R., 90
Buchan, A. M., 137
Buchanan, A., 172
Buchanan, T.W., 376
Büchel, C., 127, 206, 376
Bucholz, K. K., 476
Buchs, P. A., 418
Buck, A., 23
Buck, L., 218, 219
Buck, L. B., 214, 219, 220
Buck, R., 430
Buckholtz, J. W., 460
Buckner, R. L., 374
Bucy, P. C., 84
Buda, C., 275
Budde, J. P., 469, 470
Buell, S. J., 118
Bue-Valleskey, J. M., 314
Buffalo, E. A., 401
Buffone, A., 460
Buhle, J. T., 206
Buizer-Voskamp, J. E., 490
Buka, S. L., 491
Bulbena, A., 376
Bullard, J., 481
Bullmore, E., 492
Bullmore, E. T., 469, 492
Bulsara, K. R., 139
Bülthoff, H. H., 246
Bundgaard, M., 22
Bundsen, A., 111
Bundy, H., 490
Bunney, W. E., 327, 369
Burbridge, T.J., 171
Burdge, G. C., 107
Burgaleta, M., 98, 129
Burgess, N., 402
Burgett, S. G., 314
Burian, D., 439
Burke, A. K., 369
Burke, D., 348
Burke, J. F., 402
Burke, J. R., 256
Burke, M., 370
Burke, S. M., 220
Burkett, J. P., 459
Burman, D. D., 130
Burmeister, M., 476
Burn, P., 312
Burnett, A. L., 332
Burns, C. G., 286
Burns, M. M., 158
Burr, D. C., 183
Burra, N., 376
Burrell, B., 96
Burri, A., 347
Burstein, R., 268
Burt, A.D., 333, 334
Burt, D. M., 334
Burt, S.A., 109
Burton, H., 127
Burton, L. A., 429, 430
Burton, R.F., 296
Burwell, R. D., 267
Bus, T., 403
Busch, V., 129
Buschman, T. J., 454
Bushnell, M. C., 203, 205
Buss, D. M., 112, 341, 342
Bussey, T. J., 119
Bussiere, J. R., 334
Butelman, H. R., 469
Butler, A. W., 476
Butler, K., 130
Butler, M. P., 269
Butler, S. R., 181
Butnaru, M., 212
Buxbaum, L.J., 455
Buzza, C., 375
Byars, J. A., 256
Byl, N. N., 130
Byne, W., 350
Byrne, J. H., 414
Byrne, M., 490

Cabanillas, R., 198
Cabeza, R., 93, 386, 407
Cabrera, S., 198
Cacioppo, J.T., 374
Cade, J.F., 483
Cadenhead, K. S., 490, 491
Cadet, J.-L., 320
Cahill, H., 158
Cahill, L., 335, 397, 424
Cai, D. J., 286
Cai, X. J., 314
Caine, S. B., 467
Cajal, S., 16–17, 40
Cajochen, C., 269
Calamia, M., 408
Caldara, R., 180
Calhoun, J., 455
Calipari, E. S., 467
Calkins, M. E., 490
Callaway, E. M., 150, 165, 177, 181
Callens, N., 345
Caltagirone, C., 492, 493
Calu, D., 467
Calu, D. J., 468
Calvin, J. E., III, 319
Calvin, J. E., Jr., 319
Camargo, L. A. A., 303
Camerer, C. F., 364
Cameron, N. M., 124
Camille, N., 364
Caminiti, R., 431
Campbell, D., 139
Campbell, S. S., 269, 285
Camperio-Ciani, A., 347
Campfield, L. A., 312
Canal, C. E., 397
Candia, V., 130
Canepari, M., 230
Cannon, J. R., 253
Cannon, W.B., 295, 356–357, 358
Cano, G., 298
Cantallops, I., 418, 419
Cantalupo, C., 431
Canteras, N. S., 371
Cantor-Graae, E., 489
Cao, M., 281
Cao, Y.-Q., 205
Capettini, L. S. A., 137
Capiluppi, C., 347
Cappa, S. F., 397
Caquíneau, C., 336
Carani, C., 329
Caravolas, M., 444
Carballo, J. J., 369
Carden, D., 181
Cardno, A. G., 489
Cardona-Gómez, G. P., 136
Cardoso, C., 460
Cardoso, F.L., 346
Carelli, R. M., 467
Carey, D. P., 237
Carleton, R. N., 371
Carletti, F., 373
Carlisle, H. J., 296
Carlson, J. R., 187
Carlson, M. C., 419
Carlsson, A., 48
Carlsson, T., 254
Carlström, E., 347
Carmena, J. M., 407
Caro, J. F., 313
Caron, M. G., 53
Caroni, P., 418
Carpenter, G. A., 262
Carpenter, S., 417
Carr, T. S., 368
Carretero-Guillén, A., 395
Carrier, B., 203
Carrier, J., 286
Carrigan, T., 139
Carrington, M.J., 263
Carroll, S., 7
Carruth, L. L., 327
Carson, R. E., 238, 278
Carter, C.S., 332
Carter, M. E., 314
Carter, V., 218
Caruso, A., 478
Carver, C. S., 370
Casaccia, P., 118, 328
Casali, A. G., 453
Casali, K. R., 453
Casarotto, S., 453
Casasanto, D., 443
Cascini, M.-G., 469
Cascio, C. J., 500
Case, T. I., 385
Casey, B. J., 131
Casey, J. J., 373
Cash, S. S., 273, 441
Cason, A. M., 467
Caspary, D. M., 193
Caspi, A., 370, 476
Caspy, T., 262
Cassano, T., 310
Cassia, V.M., 180
Cassone, V. M., 267
Castellani, R. J., 285
Castellano, J. M., 107
Castelli, F., 376
Castelli, L., 166
Castellucci, V., 414, 415
Castillo, A, 97
Castles, D. L., 334
Castner, S. A., 397
Castrén, E., 478
Castro-Alvarez, J. F., 136
Catalano, S. M., 121
Catalanotto, F. A., 214
Catania, K.C., 217
Catchpole, C. K., 7
Catenacci, V., 319
Caterina, M. J., 207
Catmur, C., 239
Cattaneo, C., 445
Cattapan-Ludewig, K., 128
Catterall, W. A., 31, 32, 500
Caudle, K., 131
Cauffman, E., 131
Cavanagh, P., 86, 179, 181
Cavina-Pratesi, C., 178
Caviness, V. S., 181
Caviness, V. S., Jr., 335
Ceci, S. J., 179
Celnik, P., 127
Cendan, C.M., 201
Censor, N., 90
Cepeda-Benito, A., 468
Cereda, E., 253
Cerletti, U., 480
Cernovsky, Z., 483
Cervantes, M. C., 369
Cervoni, N., 107
Cesarini, D., 109
Cespuglio, R., 278
Cesselin, F., 377
Cha, G.-H., 256
Cha, J. H. J., 107
Chablis, C. F., 109
Chabris, C. F., 98, 368
Chaddock, L., 132
Chafee, M. V., 397
Chait, B. T., 312
Chakraborty, R., 318
Chalmers, D., 4
Chalmers, D.J., 449
Chalmers, D.L., 449
Chalupa, L. M., 431
Champagne, F. A., 107, 124
Chan, A. W.-Y., 179
Chan, P., 253, 495
Chandra, D., 378
Chandrashekar, J., 214
Chang, E. F., 192, 193
Chang, G. Y., 407
Chang, G. Q., 318
Chang, J. H., 490
Chang, M., 439
Chang, S. W. C., 460
Chang, S.-H., 482
Chang, S. J., 217, 314, 468
Changeux, J. P., 468
Chant, D., 491
Chantala, K., 346
Chantarujikapong, S., 468
Chao, M., 122
Chapin, J. K., 83
Chapman, C. S., 166
Chapman, S. B., 419
Chapman, T.R., 132
Charlet, A., 371
Charney, D. S., 386
Charpak, S., 20
Chartier-Harlin, M. C., 404
Charuvastra, A., 343
Chatman, J., 319
Chatterjee, A., 455
Chau, L. S., 90, 408
Chaudhari, N., 213
Chaudhry, P., 442
Chaudhury, N. H., 492
Chau-Wong, M., 494
Chavanne, T. J., 369
Chawla, P., 107
Che, J.-Y., 214
Cheah, C. S., 500
Checkley, S. A., 331
Checkoway, H., 253
Chee, M. J. S., 316
Cheeseman, J. F., 264
Chemelli, R. M., 280
Chen, A., 419
Chen, B. T., 468
Chen, C., 137, 207
Chen, C. S., 467
Chen, C.-F. F., 219
Chen, F., 238
Chen, G., 374
Chen, H., 478
Chen, J., 182
Chen, J. H., 220
Chen, J.-Y., 213
Chen, L. M., 202
Chen, Q., 299, 337
Chen, S., 269
Chen, X., 192, 214, 215, 469
Chen, X.-N., 439
Chen, Y., 268, 318
Chen, Z. F., 207
Cheney, D. L., 113, 368, 386, 435
Cheng, C., 199
Cheng, J., 319
Cheon, B., 377
Cherek, D.R., 369
Cherkas, L., 347
Cherubini, A., 492
Cheyne, J. A., 278
Chiang, M. C., 98
Chiapponi, C., 493
Chiarello, C., 426, 429
Chiarreotto-Ropelle, E. C., 313
Chierzi, S., 171
Childress, A.-R., 468
Chin, J., 404
Chin, S., 492
Chis, A., 373
Chitins, X., 97
Chiu, I. M., 207
Chiueh, C.C., 253
Chivers, M. L., 346
Cho, K., 265
Cho, S. L., 468
Choi, B., 314
Choi, D.-S., 469
Choi, J., 443
Choi, M., 119
Chomsky, N., 439
Chong, G., 51
Chong, S. C., 180
Chong, S. Y. C., 269
Chou, J., 254
Chou, M., 141
Choudary, P., 327
Choudhury, A. I., 314
Chouinard, P. A., 166
Chow, E.W.C., 491
Chown, M. J., 404
Christensen, J. R., 136
Christensen, P. N., 334
Christie, B. R., 119
Christodoulou, J. A., 93
Chronis-Tuscano, A., 337
Chu, H.-P., 331
Chuang, H., 207
Chung, W. C. J., 328
Chung, Y. C., 137
Churchland, P.S., 4
Cicchetti, D.V., 285
Cicchetti, P., 372
Cichon, S., 107
Cicone, N., 441
Cipolotti, L., 357, 407
Cipriani, A., 496
Cirelli, C., 287
Cirrito, J. R., 405
Cirulli, F., 126
Ciszewski, A., 377
Clahsen, H., 439
Clapp, T. R., 214
Clark, B.A., 43
Clark, D. A., 80, 81
Clark, D. B., 266
Clark, J. J., 454
Clark, J. H., 331
Clark, L. A., 480
Clark, M. M., 318
Clark, M. S., 313
Clark, R. E., 395, 396, 401
Clark, S. L., 81
Clark, W. S., 7
Clarke, L. E., 20
Clarke, S., 192, 429
Claus, E. D., 408
Clayton, D. A., 418
Cleary, L. J., 414
Cleary, M., 172
Cleermans, A., 286
Cleeter, M. W. J., 255
Clegg, R. A., 142
Cleghorn, J. M., 279
Clelland, C. D., 119
Clem, R. L., 439
Clemenson, G. D. Jr., 119
Clement, K., 318
Clements, K. M., 124
Cleveland, A., 369
Cleveland, D. W., 256
Clifford, J., 109
Cline, H., 417, 418
Cloninger, C. R., 470
Clutton-Brock, T. H., 113
Coad, M. L., 193

Coan, J. A., 386
Cobb, S. V., 172
Cobbold, M., 230
Cobos, P., 357
Coburn, C., 312
Coccaro, E. F., 370
Cockburn, M., 253
Coderre, T. J., 207
Coenen, A. M. L., 276
Cogan, G. B., 193
Cohen, D., 246
Cohen, J. D., 363
Cohen, J. D.,, 275
Cohen, L., 450, 453
Cohen, L. G., 90, 127
Cohen, M. J., 412
Cohen, N. J., 399
Cohen, N.J., 400
Cohen, S., 386
Cohen, S. L., 312
Cohen-Kettenis, P. T., 345
Cohen-Kettenis, P.T., 345
Cohen-Tannoudji, M., 124
Cohen-Woods, S., 476
Cohn, J. F., 476
Coid, B., 489
Colantuoni, C., 320
Colapinto, J., 346
Cole, C. J., 418
Cole, S. W., 107, 386
Cole-Harding, S., 348
Coleman, E., 429
Coleman, M. R., 453
Coleman, P. D., 118
Collette, F., 286
Collie, A., 284
Collier, T., 315
Collignon, O., 173
Collinger, J. L., 235
Collingridge, G. L., 415
Collins, C.E., 80
Collins, D., 369
Collins, F., 313
Colmers, W. F., 316
Colom, R., 97, 98, 129
Colombo, C., 481
Condon, C. A., 97
Cone, R. D., 314
Conn, M., 11
Conner, C. R., 403
Conner, W. E., 187
Connine, C. M., 453
Connolly, J. D., 178
Connor, P.D., 469
Connor, T. B., 158
Connors, B. W., 267
Conrad, C. D., 384, 386
Conrad, K. L., 468
Considine, R. V., 313
Constantin, C. E., 206
Contet, C., 205
Conti, F., 496
Conti, V., 123
Contreras, J. M., 180
Conturo, T. E., 127
Conway, G. S., 344
Cook, C. C. H., 471
Cook, M., 192
Cook, N. R., 404
Cook, R. G., 376
Cook-Deegan, R., 419
Cooke, B. M., 350
Coon, H., 215
Cooper, F., 269
Cooper, G. M., 490
Cooper, J. M., 255
Cooperman, A., 450
Copeland, D., 367
Copolov, D. L., 489
Coppari, R., 314
Coppola, D. M., 167, 171
Coppola, G., 107, 439
Corballis, M. C., 93, 428, 438, 455
Corcoran, A. J., 187
Corcoran, C., 490
Corina, D., 441
Corkin, S., 142, 399, 400, 401, 404
Corley, R., 109
Cormack, L. K., 181
Corna, F., 347
Corradetti, R., 369
Corradi, N., 444
Corradi-Dell'Acqua, C., 203
Corvin, A.P., 221
Corwell, B., 127
Corwin, R. L., 467
Coryell, W. H., 375
Cosmelli, D., 451, 452
Coss, R., 126
Coss, R. G., 125
Costa, E., 377
Costa, R. M., 243, 407
Costa, V. D., 467
Coste, O., 265
Costello, P., 452
Costello, S., 253
Cote, K. A., 287
Cottrell, J. F., 148
Couceyro, P. R., 312
Coultrap, S. J., 418
Coupland, C., 489
Courchesne, E., 71, 243
Courchesne, S. L., 139
Cousins, A. J., 334
Coventry, W. L., 476
Covington, H. E. III, 468
Covington, J., 243
Cowan, R. L., 124
Cowansage, K. K., 379
Cowell, P. E., 492
Cowey, A., 167, 182
Cowing-Zitron, C., 490
Cox, J. J., 204
Cozzi, A., 496
Craft, L., 314
Crago, M. B., 438
Craig, A. M., 51
Craig, A. D., 201, 207, 208
Craig, I. W., 370, 476
Crair, M. C., 171
Crair, M.C., 171
Cramer, P. E., 405
Crane, A. M., 192
Cravchik, A., 466
Craven, B., 217
Crawford, F., 404
Crawley, H., 308, 309
Crawley, J. N., 378
Crawshaw, L. I., 296
Creighton, S. M., 345
Cremniter, D., 369
Creson, T. K., 483
Crestani, F., 378
Creton, C., 378, 468
Crick, F., 287
Crick, F. C., 449
Critchley, H. D., 316, 357
Crivello, F., 429
Crocker, A., 280
Cromwell, H. C., 246
Crone, E. A., 131
Cronin, J.A., 50
Cronin-Golomb, A., 252
Cross-Disorder Group of the Psychiatric Genomics Consortium, 465
Crossin, K. L., 118
Crowley, S. J., 269
Crowner, D., 424
Cruz, F. C., 468
Cryan, J. F., 319
Crysdale, N.Y., 132
Crystal, S., 460
Csibra, G., 91
Cucurell, D., 379
Cui, G., 243
Cullen, M. J., 313
Cummings, D. E., 310, 312, 318
Cummings, S., 191
Cunningham, V. J., 467
Cunningham, W. A., 373
Curio, G., 288
Curry, A., 308, 309
Cusack, R., 166
Cushman, F., 363, 364
Cuthill, I. C., 154
Cutler, W. B., 220
Cutler, W.B., 221
Cynader, M. S., 140
Czeisler, C., 268
Czeisler, C. A., 263, 264, 265, 268, 274
Czeisler, C.A., 265
Czekóová, K., 239
Czisch, M., 453
Czosnyka, M., 136
Czoty, P. W., 369

da Silva, R. F., 137
Daan, S., 268
Dabbs, J. M., Jr., 368
Dacey, D., 315
Dacey, D. M., 155
Dagan, Y., 286
Dagher, A., 467
D'Agostino, A. E., 215
Dahdaleh, N. S., 375
Dahl, R. E., 131
Dail, W. G., 138
Dale, A., 467
Dale, A. M., 132, 153, 181
Dale, N., 415
Dale, P. S., 109
D'Alessio, A. C., 107
Dalgeish, T., 358
Dalterio, S., 329
Dalton, K. M., 362
Dalton, P., 220
Daly, M. J., 112
Damak, S., 214
Damasio, A., 192, 364, 401
Damasio, A. R., 364, 375, 441
Damasio, H., 84, 98, 192, 364, 374, 375, 408, 429, 441
Dambrosia, J., 127
Damsma, G., 467
Dan, Y., 275
Dang, N., 130
Dang-Vu, T., 407
Daniel, D.G., 492
Darby, D. G., 284
Darcq, E., 468
D'Argembeau, A., 275
Darian-Smith, C., 119, 284
Darley, J. M., 363
Darnaudéry, M., 136
Dartnall, H.J.A., 154
Darwin, C., 110, 341
Das, A., 92
Das, P., 220
Dasquens, J., 376
Dastjerdi, M., 182
Dattilo, M., 376
Daut, R. A., 408
Dautoff, R.J., 95
Davenport, C. M., 158
David, A. S., 492
David, D., 119
David, O., 451, 452
David-Gray, Z., 268
Davidson, R. J., 362, 373, 386, 454, 476
Davidson, S., 208
Davidson, T. L., 319
Davies, G., 491
Davies, L., 496
Davies, M., 368
Davies, N. J., 489
Davies, P., 4, 404
Davies, P. L., 297
Davis, C. M., 369
Davis, D., 493
Davis, E. C., 329
Davis, F. C., 267, 376
Davis, H. N., 348
Davis, J. I., 358
Davis, J. M., 369, 468, 496
Davis, K. D., 140, 202
Davis, K. L., 489
Davis, K. W., 468
Davis, M., 371, 372, 373
Davis, M. H., 453
Davis, M. I.;Holmes, A., 408
Davis, O. S. P., 109
Davises, M., 439
Daw, N. D., 408
Dawes, C., 370
Dawkins, R., 111, 113
Dawood, K., 347
Dawood, M. Y., 333
Dawood, T., 478
Dawson, D., 263, 279
Dawson, T. M., 50
Dawson, V. L., 50
Dax, G., 440
Dax, M., 440
Day, H.E.W., 132
Day, S., 221
Dayan, E., 90
De Brabander, J.M., 403
De Bruin, J.P.C., 403
de Castro, J. M., 319
De Castro, J.M., 311, 313
De Col, C., 476
de Diego-Balaguer, R., 379
De Dreu, C. K. W., 459
de Gardelle, V., 452
de Gelder, B., 166, 180, 376
de Groot, J. H. B., 217
de Jong, W. W., 268
de Jonghe, F., 480
de Kloet, A. D., 303
de los Santos, H. C., 213
De Luca, M., 445
de Luna, X., 132
de Maat, S., 480
de Monvel, J. B., 191
de Peralta Menendez, R. G., 166, 167
De Peri, L., 493
De Rijk, P., 490
de Sonneville, L. M. J., 109
de Vries, G. J., 328, 334, 335
De Wall, C. N., 204
De Young, C. G., 95
De Zutter, S., 490
Deacon, B. J., 479
Deacon, T. W., 82, 97, 439
Deady, D. K., 357
Dean, C.E., 465, 478
Dean, K.A., 491
DeArmond, S. J., 303
Deary, I. J., 97
deBonis, M., 376
Decety, J., 337, 461

DeCoster, M., 367
DeCoursey, P.J., 262
Dees, T., 128
DeFina, L. F., 419
DeFries, J. C., 109
deGelder, B., 173
Degueldre, C., 238, 278
Dehaene, S., 83, 128, 426, 444, 450, 452
Dehaene-Lambertz, G., 426, 444, 452
deHan, R. S., 119
Dehghani, F., 269
Dehghani, N., 273
Deiber, M. P., 127
Deisseroth, K., 90, 371, 478, 482
DeJong, J., 369
Dekker, J., 480
DeKosky, S. T., 419
Del Cerro, M. C. R., 337
Del Cul, A., 450
Delaney, K. R., 139
Delespaul, P., 475
Del-Favero, J., 490
Delfiore, G., 238, 278
Delgado, M.R., 407
Delgado-Garcia, J. M., 395
Deliagina, T. G., 232
Delialioglu, B.T., 478
Deloukas, P., 308
DeLoyht, J. M., 118, 328
Delville, Y., 369
Dement, W., 274
Dement, W.C., 273, 287
den Ouden, H. E. M., 373
Denburg, N. L., 364
Dennerstein, L., 333
Dennett, D.C., 4, 448
Denning, J. H., 348
Deogracias, R., 123
DePasquale, R., 478
deQuervain, D. J.-F., 397
Derby, C.A., 132
Derégnaucourt, S., 286
deRegnier, R., 123
DeRoshia, C. W., 264
Derringer, J., 109
Derryck, A., 343
DeSano, A., 269
Desautels, A., 277
Descartes, R., 148, 448
DeSimone, J. A., 213, 214
Desimone, R., 450, 454
DeSimone, S. K., 214
DeSmet, M.B.M., 384
Desmond, J. E., 397
Desmurget, M., 237, 246
Despierre, P. G., 369
D'Esposito, M., 469
Desseiles, M., 275
Desseilles, M., 407
Deste, G., 493
Destexhe, A., 284
Detre, J. A., 92
deTribolet, N., 429
Deutsch, D., 191
Deutsch, J. A., 310
Deutschländer, S., 459
DeValois, R. L., 170
Devlin, J. T., 95
DeVoogd, T. J., 119
Devor, E. J., 470
Devor, M., 207
Devos, R., 312
deVries, M., 475
Dewan, A., 216
Dewey, M. M., 303
DeYoe, E. A., 177
Dhingra, R., 319
Di Lorenzo, P. M., 31, 213, 214
di Michele, F., 333
Di Page, E., 445
di Salle, F., 128
Diamond, D., 118
Diamond, L.M., 346
Diamond, M., 345, 346
Díaz, M., 327
DiCarlo, J. J., 179
Dichgans, J., 242
DiChiara, G., 54
Dick, D., 469
Dick, D. M., 470
Dick, F., 441
Dicke, P. W., 243
Dickens, W. T., 331
Dickerson, B.C., 95
Dickerson, F. B., 491
Dickinson, A, 469
Dickman, J. D., 187
Didehbani, N., 419
Diedrichsen, J., 241, 242, 426
Diéguez, C., 313, 314
Diener, H. C., 243
Dierks, T., 84
Dietz, D. M., 468
Dietz, K., 118, 328
Digre, K., 268
Dijk, D.-J., 263, 264, 269, 286
Dijkhuizenn, R. M., 138
Dikkes, P., 336
DiLeone, R. J., 314
Dilks, D. D., 180
Diller, L., 155
Dilley, L. C., 443
Dillon, D. G., 467
Dillon, M. R., 432
DiLorenzo, P. M., 215
DiMalta, G., 368
Dimitrova, A., 395
Dimond, S.J., 428
Dimoska-Di Marco, A., 362
Dimtcheva, T., 98
Dinan, T. G., 319
Ding, J. B., 51, 253
Ding, Z. H., 124
Dinges, D. F., 284
Dinstein, I., 238
Dinwiddie, S.H., 476
Dioro, J., 107
DiPasquale, M. C., 138
Dipasquale, P., 310
Disner, S. G., 373
Ditterich, J., 182
Divan, G., 499
Diwadkar, V. A., 493
Dixon, D. B., 418
Dizdar, N., 253
Djurovic, S., 153
Do, C. B., 253
Dobie, D. J., 490
Dobkin, D. S., 294
Dobyns, W. B., 123
Dodds, C. M., 179
Dodell-Feder, D., 127
Dodgar, J., 468
Dodge, K. A., 470
Dodge, N. C., 124
Doebeli, M., 114
Doesburg, S. M., 450
Dohnt, H., 266
Dolan, R., 357
Dolan, R. J., 203, 206, 357, 368, 376, 429, 492
Dolberg, D. S., 220
Dolcos, F., 386
Dolezal, C., 345
Doljansky, J., 286
Dolski, I., 362
Doly, S., 370
Domhoff, G. W., 166
Donahoe, P. K., 343
DonCarlos, L.L., 328
Donley, J.M., 296
Donoghue, J. P., 235
Donoghue, J.P., 235
Doolittle, N., 220
Doremus-Fitzwater, T. L., 131
Dorfman, E., 253
Doricchi, F., 455
Dormal, G., 173
Dosch, G., 127
Dosemici, A., 417
Dostie, D., 441, 442
Dostie, V., 286
Dostrovsky, J. O., 140
Dotson, N. M., 397
Doty, R. L., 220
Dougherty, D. M., 369
Dougherty, K. J., 232
Douglas, R. H., 268
Dovidio, J. F., 460
Dow, M. W., 127
Dow, S., 398
Dowling, J.E., 163
Downar, J., 202
Downes, J. J., 443
Downey, J. E., 235
Downing, P. E., 179
Doya, K., 246
Doyle, P., 173
Doyle, W. J., 386
Doyon, J., 277, 286
Drabant, E. M., 253
Draganski, B., 129
Drain, M., 180
Drake, R. M., 454
Dranias, M. R., 396
Drayna, D., 105, 215
Drdla, R., 207
Drdla-Schutting, R., 207
Dreger, A.D., 345
Drevets, W. C., 374, 478
Drew, K. L., 285
Drew, M. R., 119
Drewnowski, A., 215
Drexhage, H. A., 483
Dreznjak, A., 123
Drgonova, J., 469
Dricot, L., 180
Driver, J., 178, 179, 456
Dronkers, N., 441
Druid, H., 119
Drummond, S. P. A., 287
Dryman, M.T., 451
Drzyzga, L. R., 478
DSD Network Working Group, 345
Du, J., 331, 483
Du, Y., 482
Du, Y. M., 478
Duan, B., 208
Duan, X., 490
Dube, M. P., 191
Dubois, J., 426, 444
Duck, S.C., 344
Ducommun, C. Y., 192
Dudai, Y., 419, 431
Dudchenko, P. A., 402
Dudley, C., 269
Duerden, E.G., 203
Duff, M., 492
Duff, M. C., 399, 400
Duffy, J. F., 265
Duffy, V. B., 215
Duijndam, M. J. A., 217
Duke, A. A., 369
Dulac, C., 220
Dulcis, D., 52
Duman, R., 478
Duman, R. S., 478
Dumenil, T., 476
DuMouchel, W., 254
Duncan, A. E., 319
Duncan, G. H., 203, 205
Duncan, J., 166
Duncan, S.L, 374
Duncanson, P., 500
Dungan, J., 460
Dunkel, L., 331
Dunlop, A. J., 490
Dunmore, J. H., 314
Dunn, B. D., 358
Dunn, F.A., 268
Dunn, G., 496
Dunn, S., 166
Dunn, T. W., 480
Durante, K. M., 334
Dutat, M., 452
Dutton, G. N., 172
Duvarci, S., 372
Dvoryanchikov, G., 214
Dwivedi, Y., 369
Dwyer, R., 263
Dyal, J.A., 413
Dyer, T. D., 373
Dyment, D. A., 347

Eagleman, D. M., 221
Earnest, D. J., 267
Eastman, C. I., 264, 269
Eaton, R. C., 331
Eaton, W. W., 490
Eaves, E., 97
Eaves, L., 370
Eaves, L. J., 109
Ebenhöh, N., 266
Ebers, G., 347
Ebers, G. C., 347
Ebert, M. H., 369
Eccles, J., 41–42, 52
Eckardt, M. J., 469
Ecker, J. L., 268
Eckert, M. A., 439
Eckhorn, R., 450
Eckstrand, K. L., 124
Eddins, D. M., 275
Edelman, G.M., 122
Edelman, R. R., 235
Eden, G. F., 444
Eden, U. T., 402
Edgar, D. M., 284
Edgar, M. A.,, 350
Edinger, J. D., 280
Edman, G., 369
Edwards, R. H., 207
EEldridge, L. L., 398
Egertson, J. D., 500
Eggen, B. J. L., 126
Eggermont, J. J., 193
Eggert, M., 369
Ehrhardt, A. A., 328
Ehrlich, P. R., 294
Ehrsson, H. H., 87
Eichele, G., 269
Eichenbaum, H., 399, 402, 403
Eichenbaum, H. B., 401
Eichler, E. E., 500
Eide, E. J., 269
Eidelberg, E., 136
Eifert, B., 138
Einfeld, S. L., 459
Eippert, F., 127, 206
Eisen, S. A., 468, 476
Eisenberger, N. I., 204, 386

Eisenlohr-Moul, T., 369
Eisensmith, R., 109
Eisenstein, E. M., 412
Ek, M., 299
Ekblom, B, 230
Ekholm, J., 483
Ekman, P., 361, 430
Ekstrom, A. D., 403
el Bouzati, S., 138
Elbert, T., 128, 130, 141
Eldar, E., 275
El-Fishawy, P., 500
Elias, C. F., 312
Eliassen, J. C., 429
Elkashef, A., 472
Ellacott, K. L. J., 314
Ellemberg, D., 173
Ellenberg, J., 253
Ellenbogen, M. A., 460
Elliott, J. C., 314
Elliott, S. S., 319
Elliott, T.R., 48
Ellis, A. B., 98
Ellis, C. B., 492
Ellis, L., 348
Ellis-Behnke, R. G., 139
Ells, L. J., 308, 309
Elmquist, J. K., 312, 314
Elsabbagh, M., 499
Elston, G.N., 84
Ely, T. D., 374
Eme, R., 370
Emmorey, K., 192, 441
Enard, W., 439
Eng, C., 480
Eng, M. Y., 471
Engblom, D., 299, 468
Engel, A. K., 275, 450
Engel, S. A., 398
Engert, F., 418
Engman, J., 379
Enriori, P. J., 314
Epping-Jordan, M. P., 468
Epstein, A. N., 315
Epstein, D., 467
Erb, M., 141
Erickson, C., 331
Erickson, C. J., 331
Erickson, K. I., 132
Erickson, R. P., 187, 211, 213
Ericsson-Dahlstrand, A., 299
Eriksson, N., 253
Ermilov, M., 495
Ernst, M. B., 313
Ersche, K. D., 469
Erwin, C. W., 280
Eschenko, O., 287
Escorial, S., 98
Esko, T., 109
Esler, M.D., 478
Esposito, F., 128
Esser, S. K., 277
Essex, R., 192
Estrada, K., 105
Etcoff, N. L., 430
Etgen, A. M., 331
Etter, L., 215
Eulig, C., 221
Euston, D. R., 286
Evans, A., 124
Evans, A. C., 97, 98, 128, 183, 191, 441, 442
Evans, D., 358
Evans, D. A., Funkenstein, H. H., 404
Evans, S., 327
Evans, S. S., 299
Evanson, N. K., 303
Evarts, E.V., 228
Evenson, K. R., 137
Everhart, A. W., 140
Everitt, B. J., 276, 469
Everling, S., 238
Ewald, H., 490
Eyre, J. A., 241

F., 316
Fabbri-Desstro, M., 7
Faber, B., 490
Facoetti, A., 444, 445
Fadda, F., 51
Fadiga, L., 238
Fadool, D. A., 220
Fagarasanu, A., 405
Fagioli, S., 493
Fagundes, C. P., 386
Fahey, S., 432
Fahim, C., 490
Fahn, S., 254
Fahrenkrug, J., 268
Fairbanks, L. A., 480
Fairchild-Huntress, V., 314
Faith, J. J., 319
Faiz, L., 127
Falhammar, H., 344, 345
Falke, C., 483
Fallatah, S., 207
Falleti, M. G., 284
Famous, K. R., 107
Fan, G., 98, 107
Fan, W., 314
Fane, B. A., 344
Fang, H., 220
Fang, Q., 314
Fani, N., 374
Fantz, R.L., 179
Faraco, J., 280
Faraguna, U., 287
Farah, M. J., 180, 181, 419
Faraji, F., 454
Farber, N. B., 495
Fardell, C., 253
Farivar, R., 178
Farley, F., 131
Farlow, M., 404
Farmer, M. E., 444
Farol, P., 118
Farrer, L.A., 347
Fasciani, G., 220
Fast, K., 215
Fatemi, S. H., 491, 499
Faulkner, R. L., 490
Faustini-Fustini, M., 329
Fausto-Sterling, A., 343
Fava, M., 467, 478, 479, 480
Fawcett, J., 478
Fawcett, J. W., 171
Featherstone, R. E., 336
Fedorenko, E., 127
Fedorenko, E. G., 443
Fedrigo, O., 111
Feeney, D. M., 138
Feeney, L., 488
Fehér, O., 286
Fehr, E., 460
Feig, S. L., 162, 275
Feinberg, A. P., 107
Feinstein, J. S., 375
Feldman, H. M., 238
Feldman, R., 337
Feldon, J., 126, 372, 492
Fell, J., 450
Felleman, D. J., 177
Feller, G., 297
Fellows, L. K., 364
Fendrich, R., 166
Feng, G., 132
Feng, J., 98, 107
Fenik, P., 279
Fennema-Notestine, C., 132
Fentress, J.C., 232
Feranil, A. B., 337
Fergusson, D. M., 370
Fernald, B., 369
Fernández, A. F., 198
Fernández, G., 373
Fernández-Guasti, A., 328
Fernando, A. T., 264
Ferrand, N., 418
Ferrarelli, F., 277
Ferrari, F., 331
Ferraro, V., 442
Ferreira, A., 328
Ferreira, F., 442
Ferrell, R. E., 373
Ferreño, M., 328
Ferrero, P., 377
Ferris, C., 367
Ferris, M. J., 467
Fettriplace, R., 190
Fiber, J. M., 331
Fibiger, H. C., 467
Fick, J., 378
Fidani, L., 404
Fiedler, K., 252
Field, L. L., 444
Fields, H. L., 53, 469
Fields, R. D., 129
Filippopolitis, K., 440
Filipsson, H., 344, 345
Filosa, J. A., 20
Fils-Aime, M.-L., 469
Finch, C.E., 113
Fine, A., 418
Fine, I., 173
Fineberg, N. A., 478
Finger, S., 440
Finger, T. E., 214
Fink, B., 334
Fink, G. R., 221, 237, 429
Finsterbusch, J., 206
Finucane, C., 221
Fiorentino, H., 418
Firestein, S., 218, 219
Fisch, L., 450
Fischer, A., 266
Fischer, H., 207
Fischer, I. A., 492
Fischer, L.E., 451
Fish, E. W., 124
Fisher, R.S., 315
Fisher, S. E., 221, 438, 439
Fishman, G., 158
Fiske, A., 476
Fiss, H., 166
Fitts, D. A., 304
Fitzpatrick, D., 171
Fize, D., 181
Fjell, A. M., 132
Fjerdingstad, E.J., 413
Flak, J. N., 303
Flannery-Schroeder, E, 213
Flatz, G., 308
Fleet, W. S., 142
Fleischer, J., 220
Fleming, A. S., 336
Fleming, S., 345
Fletcher, J. A., 114
Fletcher, P. C., 492
Fletcher, R., 158
Flint, J., 490
Flor, H., 141
Florence, S. L., 140
Floresco, S.B., 314
Flowers, D. L., 444
Flowers, K. A., 426
Floyd, T. F., 92
Flynn, J. M., 444
Flynn, J. R., 331
Flynn, K. C., 139
Foerde, K., 246, 407
Foerster, S., 214
Fogassi, L., 238, 238–239
Fogel, S. M., 287
Foland-Ross, L. C., 475
Foldi, N. S., 441
Földy, C., 56
Follmer, R. L., 375
Folsom, T. D., 491
Foltynie, T., 254
Foltz, E. I., 203
Fombonne, E., 499
Foo, H., 205
Fooden, A. M., 215
Foraker, R. E., 137
Forgeard, M., 128
Forger, N. G., 123, 334
Formisano, E., 84
Foroni, F., 239
Foroud, T., 469
Forrester, D. L., 347
Forsgren, L., 253
Forster, B., 428
Forsyth, R. J., 136
Fortin, N. J., 401
Foskett, J. K., 214
Foss, A. J., 172
Foss-Feig, J. H., 500
Foster, B. L., 180
Foster, D. J., 402
Foster, K. E., 318
Foster, R., 268
Foster, R. G., 267, 268
Fotopoulou, A., 404
Fountoulakis, K. N., 479
Fournier, J. S., 148
Fouse, S., 98, 107
Fowler, J. S., 468
Fox, A. N., 187
Fox, A. S., 373
Fox, C., 331
Fox, C. S., 319
Fox, N. A., 362, 476
Fox, P. T., 242, 428
Fox, S. V., 275
Frackowiak, R. S. J., 181, 402, 429, 444
Frady, R. L., 368
Fragniere, A., 119
Franc, B., 279
Francia, N., 123
Francis, A. D., 454
Franck, G., 238, 278
Francke, U., 253
Frangou, S., 97
Frank, E., 386, 480
Frank, L. M., 287
Frank, M. G., 430
Frank, M. J., 408
Frank, M.G., 132
Frank, R. A., 213
Franke, B., 373
Frankland, P. W., 371, 377
Franklin, R. J. M., 139
Franklin, R.G., Jr., 460
Franz, E. A., 426, 432
Franz, T. M., 468
Frascino, J.C., 407
Frassinetti, F., 455
Frayling, T. M., 318
Frayo, R. S., 318
Freathy, R. M., 318
Fredrickson, B. L., 206
Fredrickson, M., 379

Freed, C. R., 254
Freed, W. J., 254
Freedman, M. S., 268
Freedman, S., 377
Freeman, J., 178
Freeman, J. H., 395
Freeman, R. D., 92
Freeman, T. B., 254
Freeman, W., 85
Freimer, N., 191
Freire, C., 253
Freiwald, W. A., 454
French, J. A., 348
Frenzel, S., 269
Frese, M., 265
Freund, J., 107
Frey, K., 358
Frey, S. H., 141
Friberg, U., 212, 347
Frick, A., 379
Fridberger, A., 191
Friden, J., 230
Fried, I., 449
Friedlander, W.J., 477
Friedman, E. S., 480
Friedman, J. J., 206
Friedman, J. M., 312
Friedman, L., 489
Friedman, M., 316
Friedman, R. M., 202
Fries, P., 450
Friesen, W. V., 361
Frigge, M. L., 500
Frijling, J. L., 460
Frings, M., 395
Frisén, J., 119
Frisén, L., 344, 345
Friston, K. J., 238, 492
Frith, C. D., 203, 238, 368, 402, 429, 444, 492
Frith, C.D., 201
Frith, U., 444
Fritsch, G., 235
Fritschy, J.-M., 378
Froemke, R. C., 123
Frohman, L. A., 316
Frost, S., 406
Frum, C., 459
Frysinger, R. C., 279
Fu, J., 310
Fu, L.-Y., 314
Fu, Q. A., 476
Fu, W., 212, 500
Fu, Y. H., 269
Fu, Y.-H., 269
Fuchs, S., 286
Fuchs, T., 285
Fuentemilla, L., 379
Fuhr, P., 252
Fujihara, H., 299
Fujimoto, M., 377
Fujita, Y., 20
Fujiwara, E., 404
Fujiyoshi, Y., 52
Fukabori, R., 243
Fukumoto, D., 138
Fukushima, H., 358
Fulker, D., 109
Fuller, R. K.,, 471
Fullwood, S. D., 140
Funnell, M. G., 428
Furmark, T., 379
Furukawa, N., 313
Furuta, T., 119
Furuyashiki, T., 299
Fusar-Poli, P., 373
Fusco, M. M., 303
Fuster, J. M., 136
Fuster, J.M., 84
Futatsubashi, M., 252
Fyndanis, V., 441

Gaab, N., 444
Gabellec, M.-M., 119
Gabitto, M., 215
Gable, P. A., 313
Gabriel, K. I., 467
Gabrieli, J. D. E., 397, 404, 444
Gabrieli, J.D.E., 444
Gadian, D. G., 402
Gado, M. H., 367
Gaetani, S., 310
Gaffey, A., 363
Gage, F. H., 119, 126, 402, 490
Gage, F.H., 119
Gage, H. D., 369
Gage, P., 364
Gago, J., 376
Gaiarsa, J. L., 418
Gainer, H., 267
Gais, S., 286, 288
Gajiwala, K. S., 312
Galaburda, A., 439
Galaburda, A. M., 444
Galatzer-Levy, I. R., 465
Gale, S., 329
Galea, L. A. M., 328
Galin, D., 432
Gall, F., 94
Gallagher, A., 444
Gallardo-Pujol, D., 370
Gallese, V., 238, 238–239
Galton, H. C., 358
Galvao, R. P., 123
Gamaldo, A. A., 406
Gamer, M., 376
Gamo, N. J., 132
Gampe, C., 490
Gan, W.-B., 125, 132
Gana, S., 123
Gandhi, T., 173
Ganesh, S., 173
Gangestad, S. W., 334, 341
Ganguly, K., 418
Ganis, G., 90, 178
Gao, B., 21
Gao, F., 107, 180, 439
Gao, J. Y., 119
Gao, J.-H., 242
Gao, L., 482
Gao, X.-B., 287
Garabette, M. L., 269
Garai, J., 331
Garbe, P. L., 253
Garcia, C. R., 220
Garcia, J. A., 269
Garcia, R., 372
García, R.R., 438
Garcia-Falgueras, A., 350
Garcia-Fernández, J.-M., 268
Gardner, B. T., 435
Gardner, C. O., 476
Gardner, E., 215
Gardner, G., 266
Gardner, H., 419, 441
Gardner, R. A., 435
Gariépy, J.-F., 460
Garion, L., 45
Garland, T., Jr., 126
Garlow, S. J., 482
Garner, C. C., 284
Garner, K. M., 314
Garnero, L., 451, 452
Garraghty, P. E., 140
Garrison, J.L., 199
Garver-Apgar, C. E., 334
Gaser, C., 128, 129, 335
Gasparini, M., 455
Gatz, M., 253, 476
Gau, J. M., 475
Gauna, K., 441, 442
Gauthier, I, 181
Gautier, T., 345
Gavin, C. F., 417
Gavrilets, S., 347
Gaynor, D., 113
Gaysinskaya, V., 318
Gazzaley, A., 85, 454
Gazzaniga, M. S., 166, 426, 428, 429
Gazzaniga, M.S., 428
Ge, S., 119, 490
Gearhart, J. P., 344–345
Geckle, R. J., 220
Geenen, R., 384
Geerling, J. C., 304
Geffner, M. E., 344
Gegenfurtner, K. R., 181
Geghman, K., 139
Gehre, S., 439
Geier, C. F., 131
Geiger, B. M., 317
Geiger, G., 445
Gelarden, I. A., 326
Gelderd, J.B., 139
Geller, H. M., 253
Gelskov, S. V., 452
Geminiani, G., 166
Geng, L. B., 444
Genoud, C., 418
Gentile, R.L., 213
Genz, K., 124
Georg, B., 268
George, C. J., 476
George, D. T., 469
George, F. W., 329
Georgi, K., 266
Georgieff, M., 123
Georgiou-Karistianis, N., 141
Geraci, M., 478
Gerardin, D. C. C., 329
Gerber, J., 220
Gerig, G., 98
Gerling, G. J., 199
Gerner, R.H., 482
Gernsbacher, M. A., 441
Gersh, F., 441
Gershon, A., 483
Gerwig, M., 395
Geschwind, D. H., 107, 439
Geschwind, N., 431, 441, 444
Gesquirere, L., 368
Gettler, L. T., 337
Geuter, S., 206
Ghashghaei, H. T., 118
Ghazanfar, A. A., 83
Ghazanfar, A.A., 438
Ghesquière, P., 444
Ghetti, B., 404
Ghilardi, M. F., 286
Ghosh, A., 138
Gibb, S. L., 468
Gibbs, F.P., 266
Gibbs, J., 310
Gibson, E., 443
Gibson, S. J., 141
Giesbrecht, T., 284
Giesler, G. J. Jr., 208
Gijsbers-van Wijk, C., 480
Gil, R., 494
Gilad, Y., 334
Gilbert, H., 207
Gilbert, P. E., 401
Gilbertson, M. W., 377
Gill, S. S., 405
Gillebert, C.R., 444
Gillespie, D. C., 171
Gillespie, N., 469
Gillies, L. A., 480
Gilmore, J. H., 98
Gilmour, D., 118
Gil-Rivas, V., 383
Giltay, E. J., 332
Gilton, A., 369
Giniger, E., 424
Girard, I., 126
Girirajan, S., 500
Gitschier, J., 191
Giuliani, D., 331
Giummarra, M. J., 141
Giustetto, M., 415
Giusti-Rodriguez, P., 490
Gläscher, J., 375, 408
Glaser, D., 215
Glaser, R., 383, 384, 386
Glassee, W., 490
Glatt, S. J., 471
Gleason, C. A., 246, 247, 248
Gleeson, J. G., 500
Gleeson, T. T., 297
Glendenning, K. K., 192
Glensman, J., 95
Glickman, M. E., 98
Glimcher, P. W., 246
Globus, A., 125
Glod, C. A., 483
Gloria, R., 468
Glover, E. M., 374
Glover, G. H., 397
Glowa, J. R., 378
Gluck, M. A., 407
Gluckman, P. D., 107
Glykys, J., 378
Glynn, N. W., 127
Gnanakumaran, V., 127
Goae, A. M., 469
Goard, M., 275
Goate, A., 404, 470
Godaert, G.L.R., 384
Goddard, N. L., 320
Godfrey, K. M., 107
Goebel, M., 310
Goebel, R., 84
Goehring, A., 477
Goeke, S., 424
Goetz, C. G., 254
Goetz, E. L., 467
Gogos, J. A., 119
Goh, J. G. S., 255
Gold, A.R., 333, 334
Gold, B. T., 440
Gold, J. M., 488
Gold, J.M., 180
Gold, L. H., 467
Gold, P. E., 397
Gold, R.M., 316
Goldberg, J., 476
Goldberg, R., 189
Goldberg, T. E., 492
Golden, S. A., 468
Goldey, K. L., 332
Golding, J., 330, 331
Goldin-Meadow, S., 438, 439
Goldman, D., 370, 466, 472
Goldman, L.S., 489
Goldman, P.S., 493
Goldman, S. M., 253
Goldman-Rakic, P. S., 397, 492, 496
Goldreich, D., 127, 199
Goldschmidt, R. B., 402
Goldspink, G., 230
Goldstein, A., 205
Goldstein, J. M., 335

Goldstein, M., 51
Goldstein, R. Z., 468
Golestani, N., 128
Golgi, C., 17
Goller, A. I., 141
Golombok, S., 330, 331
Golumbic, E. Z., 193
Gómez-Díaz, R., 123
Gong, G., 98
Gong, Q. H., 376
Gong, Y., 478
Gonzalez, L., 22
Gonzalez Andino, S. L., 166, 167
Gonzalez-Alegre, P., 256
González-Maeso, J., 495
Gonzalez-Zulueta, M., 50
Good, C. D., 402
Goodale, M. A., 166, 237
Goodale, M.A., 237
Goodman, D. F., 173
Goodrich-Hunsaker, N. J., 402
Goodwin, B., 478
Goodwin, F. K., 369
Gooley, J. J., 268
Gooren, L. J. G., 332
Gopnik, M., 438
Gordon, H.L., 373
Gordon, I., 337
Gordon, J. I., 319
Gordon, S. D., 476
Gorell, J., 253
Gori, S., 444
Gorman, J., 490
Gorman, M. R., 269, 286
Gorski, R. A., 329, 349
Gorski, R.A., 329, 330
Gosling, L. M., 218
Goss, R.G., 20
Gosseries, O., 453
Goswami, U., 444
Gotlib, I. H., 475
Gottesman, I.I., 489
Gottesman, R., 442
Gottfried, J. A., 219
Götz, J., 405
Götz, M., 20
Gøtzsche, P. C., 205
Gouaux, E., 477
Gougoux, F., 127
Gourfinkel-An, I., 426
Gowing, G., 137
Goyer, P. F., 369
Gozal, D., 279
Grabowski, T.J., 98
Grace, M., 314
Gracia, L., 55
Gradisar, M., 266
Grafman, J., 127, 202, 377
Grafton, S. T., 93, 395
Graham, D. L., 386
Graham, S., 131
Graham-Kevan, N., 368
Grahn, D. A., 284
Granata, A. R. M., 329
Granberg, P.-O., 254
GrandPre, T., 171
Granger, N., 139
Granot, R. Y., 444
Grasby, P. M., 467, 492
Gratchel, R.J., 385
Gravenstein, S., 491
Gray, C. M., 397, 450
Gray, J., 362
Gray, J. R., 95
Gray, K., 363
Gray, K. M., 459, 472
Gray, N. A., 483
Graybeal, C., 408
Graziadei, P. P. C., 119
Graziane, N., 490
Graziano, M. S. A., 83, 84, 237
Graziottin, A., 333
Green, A. E., 192
Green, D. W., 440
Green, J. J., 450
Green, K. N., 404
Green, M. F., 492
Green, S. J., 213
Greenamyre, J. T, 253
Greenamyre, J. T., 256
Greenberg, J. R., 113
Greenberg, M.E., 336
Greene, G. C., 285
Greene, J. D., 363
Greene, P. E., 254
Greengard, P., 53
Greenhouse, J. B., 480
Greening, S.G., 376
Greenlee, M. W., 183
Greenough, W.T., 125
Greenwood, T. A., 490
Greer, C. A., 220
Greer, J., 438–439
Gregerson, P. K., 221
Gregg, V., 148
Gregson, R. M., 172
Greischar, L. L., 362, 454
Grieve, K. L., 237
Griffin, A. S., 113
Griffin, D. R., 187
Griffin, J. E., 329
Griffiths, C. A., 364
Griffiths, T. D., 191, 192
Grigson, P. S., 467
Grill, H. J., 310
Grill, J. T., 263
Grillon, C., 371, 374
Grill-Spector, K., 180
Gritton, H. J., 264
Groc, L., 384
Grodd, W., 141, 181
Groeger, J. A., 286
Grogan, A., 440
Gross, A. L., 419
Gross, C. G, 167
Gross, C. G., 83
Gross, C. T., 371
Gross, C.G., 148, 369
Gross, J., 202
Gross, J. J., 373, 475
Gross, R. A., 378
Grossberg, S., 262
Grosshans, D. R., 418
Grossman, M., 193
Grossman, R. I., 492
Grossman, S. P., 315
Grove, K. L., 313
Growdon, J. H., 404
Gruart, A., 395
Grueschow, M., 219
Grueter, B. A., 385
Grueter, M., 180
Grueter, T., 180
Grunebaum, M. F., 369
Grüsser, S. M., 468
Grutzendler, J., 132
Gu, X., 50
Guadry, F., 238, 278
Guan, Y., 207
Guariglia, P., 455
Guastella, A. J., 459
Guazzelli, M., 239
Gudes, S., 208
Guegen, N., 334
Guerrero, L., 345
Guerrini, R., 123
Guggisberg, A., 404
Guggisberg, A. G., 248
Guidon, G., 275
Guidotti, A., 377, 469
Guilleminault, C., 281
Guillemot, F., 90
Guillery, R. W., 162, 275
Guisez, Y., 312
Guiso, L., 98
Gujar, N., 286
Gulbransen, B. D., 214
Güler, A. D., 268
Gulyani, S., 280
Gulyás, B., 275
Gündisch, D., 314
Gunduz-Cinar, O., 408
Gunn, R. N., 467
Gunn, S. R., 281
Gunn, W. S., 281
Güntürkün, O., 459
Guo, J. U., 417
Guo, R., 500
Guo, S.-W., 215, 216
Guo, W., 214
Gupta, A. R., 500
Gupta, A. S., 287
Gur, R. C., 492
Gur, R. E., 492
Guralnik, J., 127
Gusella, J.F., 256
Gustafsson, B., 418
Gustin, S. M., 207
Gutekunst, C.-A., 256
Guterstam, A., 87
Guth, A., 266
Gutierrez-Vargas, J., 136
Gutschalk, A., 127, 192
Gutweniger, S., 476
Gvilia, I., 289
Gwinner, E., 262

Haas, R., 243
Haase, C. M., 373
Haber, J., 136
Habermeyer, B., 128
Habib, M. K., 288
Haburcak, M., 317
Hackeman, E., 199
Hackett, P. D., 337
Hadjikhani, N., 181
Hadley, R.D., 125, 126
Hagenauer, M. H., 266
Hagenbuch, B., 21
Haggard, P., 247, 248
Haggarty, J. M., 483
Hägglund, M., 232
Hagiwara, H., 404
Hagler, D. J., 132
Hagoort, P., 443
Hahn, B., 488
Haider, H., 286
Haidt, J., 363
Haier, R. J., 97
Haier, R.J., 97, 98
Haikerwal, D., 478
Haimov, I., 265, 269
Hains, B. C., 140
Haiss, F., 138
Hajjar, K., 395
Hakuta, K., 440
Halaas, J. L., 312
Halaris, A. E., 315
Halaschek-Wiener, J., 112
Halatchev, I. G., 314
Halbout, B., 168
Haley, J., 487
Halgren, E., 273, 441
Hall, F. S., 469
Hall, G.B., 373
Hall, J. C., 268
Hall, M., 453
Hallem, E. A., 187
Haller, S., 349
Hallett, M., 127, 130
Halligan, P. W., 429, 455
Halligan, P.W., 455
Hallmayer, J., 280
Halpern, S. D., 153
Halpern, S.D., 153
Hamalainen, M. S., 492
Hamann, K., 113
Hamann, S. B., 404
Hamberger, B., 251
Hamer, D. H., 347
Hamer, D.H., 347
Hamida, S. B., 468
Hamiliton, C., 438–439
Hamilton, H., 460
Hamilton, J. P., 475
Hamilton, L. D., 332
Hamilton, R. B., 214
Hamilton, W.D., 113
Hammer, M., 414
Hammerschmidt, K., 439
Hamon, M., 279, 377
Han, F., 110
Han, H. S., 137
Han, J. W., 241
Han, J.-H., 418
Han, M.-H., 386
Han, S., 500
Han, X., 20
Hanada, R., 299
Hanada, T., 299
Hanaway, J., 367
Handunnetthi, L., 347
Haney, A., 285
Hänggi, J., 221
Hanis, C., 318
Hanna, C., 377
Hannibal, J., 268
Hanseeuw, B., 180
Hansen, K. D., 107
Hanson, M. A., 107
Hanson, R. L., 318
Hanson, R.L., 318, 500
Hansson, E., 22
Haq, S., 268
Haqq, C. M., 343
Hara, J., 280
Hara, Y., 334
Harada, N., 329
Haramati, S., 419
Harbige, L., 308, 309
Hardt, O., 379
Harel, M., 450
Hargreaves, G. A., 378
Hargreaves, R., 77
Hari, R., 91
Hariri, A. R., 373
Harkavy-Friedman, J., 490
Harkness, K. L., 475
Harlaar, N., 109, 346, 347
Harley, B., 440
Harmon-Jones, E., 313, 367, 368
Hárosi, F. I., 158
Harper, D., 483
Harper, L.V., 107
Harper, R. M., 279
Harraid, J. H., 468
Harridge, S., 230
Harrington, H., 476
Harris, C.H., 342
Harris, C.R., 201
Harris, K. D., 284
Harris, K.M., 19

Harris, N. S., 243
Harrison, E. M., 286
Harrison, G.H., 307
Harrold, J. A., 314
Hart, B.L., 315
Hartberg, C. B., 493
Hartke, T., 207
Hartl, D. L., 327
Hartley, C. E., 205
Hartline, H.K., 164
Harvey, A. G., 377, 483
Harvey, A. N., 488
Harvey, B.K., 254
Harvey, P. D., 489
Harvey, P.H., 80
Harvey, R. H., 81
Harwich, C., 265
Hasegawa, T., 235
Hasher, L., 266
Hashikawa, K., 395
Hashimoto, H., 336
Hashimoto, Y., 158
Hashmi, N., 368
Hasler, B. P., 266
Hassabis, D., 400
Hassan, B., 346
Hassani, O. K., 275
Hassett, J. M., 330
Hassin, R.R., 452
Hasson, U., 238
Hastings, M. H., 280
Hatami-Khoroushahi, Z., 207
Hatch, C., 468
Hatemi, P. K., 370
Hattar, S., 268
Haugen, M., 500
Haukka, J., 264, 489
Haukka, J. K., 488
Haukvik, U. K., 493
Hauser, M., 364
Hausmann, A., 476
Hausmann, M., 362
Häusser, M., 43, 90
Hauswirth, W. W., 158
Havekes, R., Bos, T., 126
Havel, M., 266
Havel, P. J., 319
Havlicek, J., 217
Hawkins, R.D., 415
Haworth, C. M. A., 109
Haworth, S. M., 172
Haxby, J. V., 238, 239
Hay, D.F, 370
Hayama, H., 453
Hayashi, Y., 304
Hayashi-Takagi, A., 490
Hayden, M. R., 256
Haydon, P. G., 482
Haydon, P.G., 20
Hayes, J. E., 215
Haygood, R., 111
Hayhurst, K. P., 496
Hayman, S. R., 500
Haynes, G. W, 319
Haynes, J.-D., 219, 248
Haytham, I., 148
Hazeltine, E., 426
Hazvi, S., 419
He, S., 452
He, S. M., 478
He, W., 214
He, Y., 98, 269, 460
He, Z., 139
Head, K., 97, 98
Headley, D. B., 372
Heath, A., 109
Heath, A. C., 109, 476
Heath, A.C., 476
Heatherton, T. F., 318, 428
Hebart, M., 167
Hebb, D.O., 395–396, 413
Hebert, B. M., 109
Hebert, M., 367
Hecht, R., 313
Heck, G. L., 213, 214
Heeger, D. J., 178, 181, 238, 449, 451
Heeroma, J. H., 123
Hegdé, J., 178
Heidbreder, C. A., 372
Heidler-Gary, J., 442
Heikkila, R. E., 253
Heilig, M., 472
Heilman, K. M., 142
Heiman, M., 314, 319
Heiman, M. L., 313
Heims, H. C., 357
Heinze, H.-J., 86, 248
Heisler, L. K., 318
Hejtmancik, J. F., 158
Held, R., 173
Hellal, F., 139
Heller, H. C., 284
Heller, W., 429, 430
Hellstron, I. C., 107
Helm-Estabrooks, N., 441
Helmholtz, H., 154
Hel-or, H., 104
Hen, R., 119, 279
Henderson, J. M., 454
Henderson, L. A., 207, 279
Henderson, S. A., 215
Hendler, T., 374
Hendrick, A. M., 476
Hendricks, S. E., 348
Hendriks, W., 268
Hendriksen, M., 480
Hendry, S. H. C., 166
Heng, L.-J., 468
Hengst, J., 399, 400
Hennessy, M. B., 348
Hennig, R., 230
Henny, P., 275
Henrich, J., 113, 460
Henriksen, L., 441
Henriques, J., 362
Henthorn, T., 191
Heo, S., 132
Hepp, U., 385
Heppenstall, P. A., 199
Herb, B. R., 107
Herbison, N., 172
Herculano-Houzel, S., 80, 97
Herdener, M., 128
Heresco-Levy, U., 495
Hering, E., 155
Herman, J. P., 214, 303
Hermann, B., 333
Hernandez, A., 444
Hernandez, L., 316
Herrero, S., 187
Herrmann, E., 459
Herron, J., 432
Herrup, K., 16, 241
Herscovitch, P., 238, 278
Hertzog, C., 126
Hertz-Pannier, L., 426, 444
Hervais-Adelman, A., 376
Hervé, P. Y., 431
Hervé, P.-Y., 429
Herz, R. S., 424
Hess, B.J.M., 198
Hess, M. E., 469
Hess, S., 313, 469
Hess, T. M., 132
Hesse, M. D., 237
Hesselmann, G., 167
Hesselson, S., 280
Hettema, J., 386
Hettema, J. M., 167
Heuer, E., 401
Heurer, E., 373
Heyes, C., 239
Hibbeln, J. R., 483
Hibbing, M.V., 374
Hickie, I. B., 459
Hickok, G., 441
Hidalgo-Figueroa, M., 123
Higgs, S., 212, 398
Higley, J. D., 369
Higley, S. B., 369
Hikida, T., 386
Hikosaka, O., 238, 407
Hill, D.L., 315
Hill, J. O., 319
Hill, S., 277
Hillegers, M. H. J., 483
Hillier, F. C., 308, 309
Hillis, A. E., 442
Hillix, W. A., 436
Hillman, E. M. C., 92
Hillyard, S. A., 454
Hillyard, S.A., 86
Hilti, C. C., 128
Himmelbach, M., 178
Hind, J. E., 190
Hindersson, P., 268
Hindmarsh, P., 344
Hindmarsh, P. C., 344
Hines, D. J., 482
Hines, M., 329, 330, 331, 344
Hines, R. M., 482
Hinrichs, A. L., 469
Hinton, D., 268
Hinz, W. A., 269
Hioki, H., 119
Hiort, O., 345
Hippisley-Cox, J., 489
Hipwell, A. E., 337
Hirayasu, Y., 492
Hiripi, E., 319
Hirota, H., 439
Hirsch, H. V. B., 172
Hirsch, H.V.B., 171
Hirsch, J. B., 95
Hirschhorn, J.N., 105
Hirschman, A., 136
Hirst, J. M., 500
Hirstein, W., 141
Hirth, F., 80
Hirtz, D., 500
Hishikawa, Y., 284
Hitch, G.J., 397
Hitchcock, J. M., 372
Hiyama, T. Y., 235, 303
Ho, B.-C., 493
Hobelmann, J. G., 207
Hobohm, C., 137
Hobson, J. A., 288
Hobson, J.A., 288, 481
Hochberg, L.R., 235
Höchel, S., 266
Hodgson, D., 385
Hodsoll, J., 454
Hoebel, B. G., 315, 316, 317, 320
Hoebel, B.G., 316, 320
Hoeft, F., 444
Hoerzer, G. M., 397
Hoese, E. K., 264
Hoffer, A., 488
Hoffer, B. J., 254
Hoffman, A. F., 468
Hoffman, A. N., 384
Hoffman, E., 288
Hoffman, P. L., 378, 470
Hoffmann, F., 288
Hoffmann, K.-P., 182–183
Hoffmann, M. L., 303
Hofman, M. A., 349
Hofstetter, C., 203
Hoge, E.A., 451
Hogg, S. L., 455
Hohagen, F., 482
Hohmann, C.F., 118
Hökfelt, T., 51
Holcombe, A. O., 86
Holland, D., 132
Hollander, E., 460
Hollegaard, M.V., 489
Hollingworth, A., 454
Hollinshead, M. O., 374
Hollister, J. M., 491
Hollon, S. D., 480
Holman, E. A., 383, 460
Holmdahl, G., 344, 345
Holmes, A. J., 374, 467
Holmes, B., 319
Holmes, C. J., 123
Holsboer, F., 333
Hölter, S. M., 439
Holtzheimer, P. E., 482
Holy, T. E., 220
Holzman, P. S., 489, 492
Homan, R. W., 430
Homanics, G. E., 378
Homewood, J., 424
Honasoge, A., 417
Honda, S.-I., 329
Hong, S. B., 180
Hong, S. C., 180
Hong, S. W., 450
Honoré, J., 455
Hood, J., 345
Hoogenraad, C. C., 384
Hoon, M. A., 199, 214
Hoon, M.A., 214
Hoos, B., 369
Hop, W. C. J., 334
Hope, B. T., 468
Hopf, F. W., 468
Hopkins, R. O., 399, 402, 407
Hopkins, R.O., 399
Hopkins, W. D., 431
Hopkins, W.D., 431
Hoppin, J. A., 253
Hoptman, M. J., 429
Hori, K., 304
Horikawa, T., 93
Horne, J. A., 284
Horne, J.A., 279
Hornig, M., 500
Horras, K. A., 476
Horridge, G.A., 412, 413
Horst, J., 180
Horst, W. D., 477, 478
Horton, J. C., 183
Horton, N. J., 335
Horvath, S., 347
Horvath, T.L., 313
Horwood, L. J., 370
Hoshi, E., 238
Hou, Y., 275, 276
Houk, C. P., 345
Hourai, A., 303
Houser, C. R., 378
Hovda, D. A., 138
Howard, J. D., 219
Howard, J. K., 312
Howard, M., 113
Howdeshell, K. L., 329
Howell, S., 369
Howland, J. G., 415
Howlin, P., 439

Hrdy, S.B., 342
Hróbjartsson, A., 205
Hsiang, S. M., 370
Hsiao, J. S., 500
Hsiao, S., 467
Hsieh, P.-J., 169
Hsing, W., 284
Hsu, K.-S., 119
Htaik, O., 284
Hu, F., 118
Hu, N., 347
Hu, P., 286
Hu, P. T., 286
Hu, S., 347
Hu, W., 444
Hua, J. Y., 121
Huang, A. L., 214, 269
Huang, B. S., 303
Huang, H. S., 500
Huang, K. W., 385
Huang, L., 453
Huang, P.-Y. S., 376
Huang, R., 112
Huang, S. Z., 109
Huang, Y.-J., 53
Huang, Y.-Y., 369, 415
Hubbard, E. M., 83
Hubel, D., 177
Hubel, D. H., 158, 171
Hubel, D.H., 167, 168, 169
Huber, R., 277, 285, 286
Huberfeld, G., 426
Hudson, J. I., 319, 476
Hudson, J. M., 426
Hudson, S., 294
Hudspeth, A.J., 190
Huedo-Medina, T. B., 479
Huey, E. D., 377
Huf, W., 483
Huff, R., 496
Huganir, R. L., 439
Hugdahl, K., 425
Huggins, G. R., 220
Hughes, J. C., 471
Hughes, J.R., 332
Hughes, R. E., 256
Hugill, N., 334
Huh, S. H., 137
Huk, A. C., 181
Hulette, C. M., 22
Hull, E. M., 329, 331, 333, 467
Hull, R., 440
Hulsebosch, C. E., 140
Hummel, T., 219, 220
Humphreys, G., 454
Humphreys, G. W, 398
Humphreys, K., 180, 238
Hunt, G. E., 378
Hunt, L. T., 85
Hunt, P. D., 263
Hunt, S. P., 203, 204, 207
Huntington's Disease Collaborative Research Group, 255
Huonker, R., 142
Hurelbink, C., 280
Hurlemann, R., 375, 459
Hurley, K., 480
Hurni, N., 371
Hurovitz, C. S., 166
Hurst, J. A., 438, 439
Hurtado, A., 139
Hurvich, L. M., 155
Husain, M., 456
Huse, E., 141
Husni, M., 483
Husted, J., 491
Huszar, D., 314
Hutcheson, D. M., 469
Hutchins, S., 191
Hutchison, J., 333
Hutchison, K. E., 468, 469
Hutson, K. A., 192
Huttner, H. B., 119
Hwang, H., 418
Hwang, J.-A., 376
Hyde, J., 98
Hyde, J. S., 98
Hyde, K. L., 128, 191
Hyltenstam, K., 440
Hynd, G. W., 444
Hysi, P. G., 105

Iacono, W. G., 470
Iba, M., 397
Ibañez, V., 127
Icenhower, M., 369
Igarashi, T., 294
Iggo, A., 199
Ikawa, M., 216, 217
Ikeda, H., 207
Ikonomidou, C., 124
Ilg, R., 453
Illes, J., 419
Imai, T., 216, 217
Imamachi, N., 205
Imamura, K., 219
Immordino-Yang, M. H., 93
Imperato-McGinley, J., 345
Ingason, A., 107
Ingham, J. C., 428
Ingham, R. J., 428
Ingraham, L. J., 490
Ingram, C. J. E., 308
Ingvar, M., 206
Innocenti, G. M., 431
Innocenti, G.M., 425
Inouye, S. T., 267
International Schizophrenia Consortium, 107
Inui, A., 320
Iosif, A.-M., 500
Iredale, J. M., 362
Irizarry, R., 107
Irle, E., 375
Isa, T., 138, 235
Isaacson, G., 479
Isejima, H., 267
Isham, E.A., 248
Ishii, M., 20
Ishii, T. M., 32
Ishimaru, M. J., 124
Ishizuka, K., 490
Isoda, M., 238
Itan, Y., 308
Ito, M., 242
Itohara, S., 232
Ittner, L. M., 405
Iuculano, T., 419
Iverson, J. M., 438
Ives, D. G., 419
Ivry, R., 243
Ivry, R. B., 241, 242, 243, 426
Ivy, G. O., 336, 431
Iwasato, T., 232
Iwata, J., 372
Iwema, C. L., 220
Iyengar, S., 479
Iyer, A., 237
Iyo, M., 252

J., Diekelmann, 288
Jaaro-Peled, H., 386
Jablensky, A. V., 490
Jackson, D. C., 362
Jackson, K. A., 495
Jacob, D., 334
Jacobs, B., 118
Jacobs, G. D., 476
Jacobs, G. H., 158
Jacobs, J., 402
Jacobson, A., 413
Jacobson, A.L., 413
Jacobson, B., 490
Jacobson, J. L., 124
Jacobson, K. C., 370
Jacobson, S. W., 124
Jacques, C., 180
Jacques, P. F., 319
Jaeger, E., 205
Jäger, T., 207
Jain, S., 469
Jakobson, L. S., 237
Jakobsson, P.-J., 299
Jakubowki, M., 268
James, K. H., 181
James, M. R., 476
James, R.S., 297
James, T. W., 181
James, T.W., 180
James, W., 357, 448
Jameson, D., 155
Jamshidi, P., 52
Jancke, L., 98
Jäncke, L., 129, 221
Jandl, M., 84
Jang, M.-H., 417
Janicak, P. G., 369
Janowich, J., 454
Janowsky, J. S., 334
Janson, P. O., 344, 345
Janssen, E. H. C. C., 345
Janssen, W. G. M., 334
Jansson, L., 490
Jaremka, L. M., 386
Jaremka, L.M., 383
Järlaker, B., 230
Jarosiewicz, B., 235
Jarrard, L. E., 402
Jarrett, R. B., 480
Javitch, J. A., 55
Javitt, D. C., 488, 495
Jazin, E., 334
Jbabdi, S., 167
Jechura, T. J., 285
Jeffery, N. D., 139
Jeffrey, S., 126
Jenner, A. R., 444
Jennings, J. H., 314, 372
Jennings-White, C., 220
Jerison, H.J., 96
Jern, P., 346, 347
Jernigan, T. L., 123
Jernigan, T.L., 439
Jessell, T.M., 16
Ji, D., 286
Jia, Z., 297
Jiang, P., 215
Jiang, Y., 54, 452
Jimerson, D. C., 369
Jin, B. K., 137
Jin, L. E., 132
Jin, X., 243, 407
Jo, S., 180
Joachim, M., 314
Jobard, G., 429
Jobert, A., 426, 444
Johanek, L. M., 207
Johansen-Berg, H., 129
Johanson, C. E., 22
Johansson, C., 483
Johansson, O., 51
Johnsen, I. R., 373
Johnson, A. K., 480
Johnson, B. M., 337
Johnson, B. T., 479
Johnson, D. C., 379
Johnson, D.H., 325
Johnson, E., 368
Johnson, E. L., 358
Johnson, J. K., 470
Johnson, M. K., 460
Johnson, M. P., 265
Johnson, N. F., 440
Johnson, P. M., 317, 376
Johnson, S. L., 370
Johnsrude, I., 192
Johnsrude, I. S., 402
Johnston, K. J., 331
Johnstone, J., 432
Johnstone, T., 376
Jolesz, F. A., 286
Jolicoeur, P., 191
Jolivet, R., 23
Jonas, P., 119
Jones, A. R., 22
Jones, B. E., 275
Jones, C., 496
Jones, C. R., 269
Jones, C. W., 284
Jones, D. L., 123
Jones, E. G., 140
Jones, H. S., 279
Jones, J. E., 314
Jones, L. B., 350
Jones, M. V., 56
Jones, O. P., 440
Jones, P. B., 496
Jones, P. S., 469
Jones, S. A., 478
Jones, T., 467
Jones, W., 438, 439, 500
Jonides, J., 475
Jonides, J. J., 454
Jonsson, M., 378
Jonsson, P. V., 405
Jonsson, T., 405
Jonsson, Z. O., 107, 439
Joo, E. Y., 180
Joormann, J., 370, 450, 475
Jooste, P., 284
Jordan, B. D., 334
Jordan, C., 367
Jordan, C. L., 334
Jordan, H.A., 310
Jordan, W., 450
Jorde, L. B., 105
Jordt, S.-E., 207
Jorgenson, E., 215
Josefsson, M., 132
Josephs, O., 192
Joslyn, G., 469
Josselyn, S. A., 377, 418
Josue, J., 215
Jouvet, M., 273, 275, 276, 278
Jovanovic, T., 374
Jox, R. J., 379
Joyner, A. L., 90
Ju, H., 396
Juda, M., 265
Judge, J., 444
Judica, A., 445
Judkewicz, B., 217
Jueptner, M., 246
Julius, D., 199, 207
Jun, S. B., 243
Jung, K., 180
Jung, R. E., 97
Jung, R.E., 97
Jung, Y.-J., 241
Juraska, J. M., 295
Jurata, L.W., 481
Jürgensen, M., 345

Jutras, M. J., 267
Juttler, E., 137
Juvonen, H., 489

Kaas, J. H., 83, 140
Kaas, J.H., 202
Kable, J. W., 364
Kacelnik, O., 195
Kaczmarek, L. K., 220
Kadosh, R. C., 419
Kadotani, H., 280
Kaether, C., 490
Kaga, K., 75
Kagan, I., 237
Kagan, J., 373, 376
Kahan, J., 254
Kahana, M. J., 402
Kahn, B. B., 313
Kahn, R. S., 98, 492, 495
Kahn, R.A., 489
Kahn, R.S., 132
Kahneman, D., 467
Kai, N., 243
Kaidar, G., 107
Kainz, V., 268
Kaiser, A., 349
Kaiser, S. T., 488
Kaisti, K. K., 453
Kalat, J. W., 304, 392
Kalat, R., 471
Kaldewaij, A., 217
Kales, A., 279
Kales, J. D., 279
Kalin, N. H., 373
Kallio, J., 444
Kalmar, K., 138
Kalogeris, T. J., 310
Kalso, E., 206
Kaltenbach, J. A., 193
Kamara, M., 104
Kamel, F., 253
Kameyama, M., 492
Kaminer, Y., 471
Kaminska, A., 256
Kamitani, Y., 93, 156, 454
Kamiya, A., 490
Kamo, T., 192
Kanady, J. C., 286, 287
Kanagasingam, Y., 406
Kandel, E., 414, 419, 494
Kandel, E.R., 16, 414, 415
Kane, P. H., 318
Kang, I., 217
Kang, P., 450
Kanki, H., 490
Kanold, P. O., 171
Kansky, R., 113
Kanwisher, N., 169, 179, 180, 181
Kao, R., 254
Kaplan, B. J., 444
Kaplan, J. M., 310
Kaplan, J. R., 369
Kaplan, J. T., 192
Kaprio, J., 370
Kapur, N., 392
Kapur, S., 496
Karakoc, E., 500
Karama, S., 97, 129
Karatayev, O., 318
Karchemskiy, A., 439
Karg, K., 476
Kargo, W. J., 246
Karkanias, G. B., 331
Karlo, J. C., 405
Karlsson, M., 287
Karmiloff-Smith, A., 439
Karnath, H. O., 178
Karni, A., 286, 441
Karns, C. M., 127
Karpova, N. N., 478
Karra, E., 314
Karrer, T., 207
Karrer, T. A., 214
Kas, M. J. H., 314
Kasahara, H., 235
Kasai, K., 377, 492
Kasch, K. L., 475
Kasimatis, M., 358
Kaskinoro, K., 453
Kasper, S., 478, 483
Kass, M. D., 407
Kasthuri, N., 132
Katashima, C. K., 313
Katkin, E. S., 476
Kato, S., 235
Katritch, V., 54
Katschnig, H., 376
Katz, D., 138
Katz, J., 207
Katz, L. C., 218, 219
Katzir, G., 104
Kau, A. L., 319
Kaube, H., 203
Kauchali, S., 499
Kauer, J. A., 416
Kaur, J., 118, 328
Kavanau, J. L., 285
Kawakami, K., 91
Kawamura, H., 267
Kawashima, M., 280
Kayser, M., 105
Kayserili, H., 500
Kayyal, M. H., 361
Kazama, A. M., 373
Kazmi, H., 440
Kean, J., 419
Keane, M. M., 400
Kearney, M., 294
Keebler, M. W., 419
Keefe, R. S. E., 489
Keel, M., 385
Keele, S. W., 243
Keenan, J. P., 90
Keers, R., 476, 479
Kegeles, L.S., 494
Kelkar, D., 118, 328
Kell, C. A., 269
Kellendonk, C., 494
Keller, M., 331
Kelley, A. E., 373
Kelley, M. S., 139
Kelley, W. M., 192, 318, 428
Kellner, C. H., 481
Kelly, B. D., 488
Kelly, J., 312
Kelly, P. A., 336
Kelly, T. L., 263
Kelz, M., 279
Kemether, E., 350
Kempenaers, B., 285
Kempermann, G., 107, 126
Kendler, K. S., 376, 469, 476, 489
Kendrick, K. M., 459
Kennard, C., 156, 456
Kennaway, D. J., 264
Kennedy, D. N., 335
Kennedy, D. P., 375, 376
Kennedy, L. M., 213
Kennedy, M. A., 370
Kennedy, S., 367
Kennedy, S. H., 318, 331, 332
Kennerknecht, I., 180
Kennerley, S. W., 426
Kenny, P. J., 317, 376
Kensinger, E. A., 399
Kerchner, G. A., 415
Kermean, P., 483
Kerns, J. G., 488
Kerr, A. L., 126
Kerwin, R., 492
Kerzel, D., 376
Keshavan, M. S., 493
Kesler, S., 439
Kesner, R. P., 401
Kessels, H. W., 404
Kessler, R. C., 319
Kety, S. S., 490
Keverne, E. B., 220
Keysers, C., 238–239
Khan, R. M., 217, 220
Khan, U. A., 492
Khan, Y., 118
Khan-Dawood, F., 333
Khasabov, S. G., 208
Khashan, A. S., 491
Khateb, A., 166, 167
Khodesovich, K., 34
Kidd, J. R., 215
Kiecolt-Glaser, J. K., 383, 384, 386
Kiefer, A. K., 253
Kieffer, T. J., 319
Kiehn, O., 51–52, 232
Kiemen, A., 482
Kiening, K. L., 136
Kieseppä, T., 483
Kiess, W., 318
Kievit, P., 313
Kigar, D. L., 98
Kikinis, R., 492
Kikuta, J., 20
Kilduff, T. S., 275
Kilgour, A. R., 180
Killackey, H. P., 140, 431
Killeen, P. R., 386
Killeffer, F. A., 316
Killiany, R. J., 401
Kilner, J. M., 238
Kilpeläinen, L., 331
Kim, C., 440
Kim, C. K., 371
Kim, C.-Y., 221
Kim, H., 376
Kim, J. Y., 490
Kim, M. J., 386
Kim, R. M., 347, 348
Kim, S., 395, 460
Kim, S. H., 480
Kim, S. M., 418
Kim, S. R., 137
Kim, S.-Y., 371
Kim, T.-Y., 241
Kim, U., 105, 215
Kim, Y., 370
Kim, Y. S., 499
Kim, Y.-B., 313
Kim, Y.-K., 376
Kim-Han, J. S., 253
Kimura, M., 246
Kindt, M., 379
King, A. J., 195
King, B. M., 307, 316
King, I. F., 500
King, J. E., 111
King, P., 419
Kingstone, A., 428, 429
Kini, A. D., 219
Kinnamon, J. C., 212
Kinney, D. K., 490
Kinomura, S., 275
Kinoshita, M., 235
Kinsbourne, M., 431
Kipervasser, S., 450
Kippenhan, J. S., 439
Kiriakakis, V., 495
Kirigiti, M. A., 313
Kirik, D., 254
Kirkland, J., 158
Kirkpatrick, P. J., 136
Kirsch, I., 479
Kirste, I., 107
Kirtley, D. D., 83
Kischka, U., 364
Kiss, L., 418
Kiss, Z. H. T., 140
Kistler, A., 191
Kitabatake, Y., 490
Kitaoka, A., 182
Kitaoka, S., 299
Kitner-Triolo, M. H., 406
Kitzbichler, M., 492
Klaminder, J., 378
Klann, E., 379
Klebanoff, M. A., 491
Kleck, R.E., 373
Kleen, J. K., 386
Kleiber, M. L., 124
Kleiman, J., 263
Klein, D. F., 358
Klein, D. N., 475
Klein, R. M., 444
Klein, W. J., 369
Kleinemeier, E., 345
Kleinman, J. T., 442
Kleinschnitz, C., 137
Kleitman, N., 273, 274, 284
Klengel, T., 107
Kliewer, S. A., 478
Klin, A., 500
Klinge, C., 127
Klinkenberg, I., 212
Klitgaard, H., 230
Klomp, D. W. J., 495
Kluger, M. J., 299
Klüver, H., 84
Knauer, R. S., 274
Knaut, H., 118
Knecht, S., 141
Kneip, J., 314
Knekt, P., 253
Kniazeff, J., 55
Knickmeyer, R. C., 98
Knijff, E. M., 483
Knowlton, B. J., 246, 252, 398, 407
Knox, P. C., 444
Knudsen, S. M., 268
Knyazev, G. G., 362
Ko, C.-H., 467
Kobayakawa, K., 216, 217
Kobayakawa, R., 216, 217
Kobayashi, K, 243
Kobayashi, M., 267
Kobayashi, T., 334
Kobelt, P., 310
Kober, H., 360
Koch, C., 124, 449
Koch, J.M., 403
Koch, L., 469
Koch, M., 371
Kochs, E. F., 453
Koellinger, P. D., 109
Koenigs, M., 364, 377
Koepp, M. J., 467
Koh, Y. J., 499
Kohler, E., 238–239
Köhler, S., 400, 401
Kohn, M., 114
Kohn, P., 439
Koifman, S., 253
Kojima, S., 320
Kolarow, R., 418
Kolb, F. P., 395
Koleske, A. J., 125

Kollar, A., 112
Kollen, B. J., 455
Kolling, N., 85
Kollmar, R., 137
Kolm, N., 111
Koltzenburg, M., 206
Kolundzija, A. B., 347, 348
Komisaruk, B. R., 333, 337
Komorowski, R. W., 403
Komura, Y., 75
Konarski, J. Z., 318, 331, 332
Kondrak, C. L., 386
Könen, T., 266
Kong, A., 500
Kong, H., 207
König, A., 482
König, P., 275, 450
Konishi, S., 492
Konnerth, A., 192
Konopka, G., 107, 439
Koob, G. F., 467, 468
Koochaki, P. E., 333
Köpetz, C. E., 468
Koralek, A. C., 407
Koralov, S. B., 313
Kordasiewicz, H. B., 256
Kordower, J. H., 254
Kordower, J.H., 254
Korell, M., 253
Korenberg, J. R., 439
Koresh-Kamin, H., 220
Korman, M., 286
Körner, A., 318
Kornhuber, H. H., 242, 441
Koroshetz, W. J., 246, 255
Korpi, E. R., 378
Kosslyn, S. M., 90, 166, 178
Koster, H. D, 489
Kostrzewa, J. P., 140
Kostrzewa, R. M., 140
Kotowicz, Z., 364
Kotrschal, A., 111
Kouider, S., 452
Kourtzi, Z., 181
Kovacevic, N., 467
Kovach, C. K., 408
Kovacs, M., 476
Kovacs, P., 318
Koverola, C., 377
Kowalsky, E., 221
Koya, E., 468
Kozlov, A. S., 20
Kraemer, B., 385
Kraemer, D. J. M., 192
Krafnick, A. J., 444
Kraft, T. L., 358
Krajbich, I., 364
Krakauer, A. H., 113
Krakowiak, P., 500
Kramer, A. F., 126, 132
Kramer, J. H., 429
Kranzler, H. R., 470
Kraus, N., 128, 193
Krause, E. G., 303, 304
Kravitz, A. V., 243
Krawczak, M., 369
Kreek, M. J., 469
Kreiman, G., 449
Kreiter, A. K., 454
Kreitzer, A. C., 56, 243
Krekelberg, B., 181, 182–183
Kress, B., 136
Kriauciunas, A., 313
Kripke, D. F., 483
Krishnan, V., 386
Kristensson, K., 22
Kristiansen, K., 496
Kritzler, M., 107
Kriz, J., 137
Krizan, A. C., 318
Kroeze, W. K., 496
Kronauer, R. E., 263, 265, 268
Kronauer, R.E., 265
Kross, E., 204
Krout, K., 201
Krueger, J. M., 277
Krueger, K., 483
Krüger, A., 107
Krugers, H. J., 384
Kruglanski, A. W., 468
Kruijt, A. W., 335
Krumm, N., 500
Krupa, D. J., 395, 396
Kruse, R. L., 329, 331
Kruse, W., 450
Krushel, L. A., 118
Krutsch, A. J., 426
Kryscio, R. J., 440
Kuba, H., 32
Kubes, P., 22
Kubischik, M., 182–183
Kubista, H., 56
Kübler, A., 266
Kubzansky, L. D., 460
Kuchenbecker, J. A., 158
Kuczewski, N., 418
Kudo, K., 153
Kuehnle, T., 266
Kueider, A. M., 419
Kuemmeth, F., 285
Kühlmeyer, K., 379
Kuhn, H. G., 119
Kuhn, S., 285
Kuiri-Hänninen, T., 331
Kujala, T., 444
Kujawa, S. G., 193
Kukkonen, J. P., 275
Kulesskaya, N., 478
Kulikow-ski, J. J., 181
Kulkarni, S. K., 378
Kullmann, D. M., 45
Kumar, A., 107
Kumar, C. J., 264, 266
Kumaran, D., 400
Kumaresan, V., 107
Kumari, V., 346
Kumpik, D. P., 195
Kuner, R., 206
Kupfer, D. J., 480
Kupfermann, I., 414, 415
Kuramoto, E., 119
Kurtz, D. B., 220
Kusel, J., 50
Kushner, S. A., 418
Kusumoto-Yoshida, I., 468
Kusunoki, M., 181
Kuwamura, T., 343
Kuypers, H. G. J. M., 241
Kuzawa, C. W., 337
Kveton, J. F., 214
Kwakkel, G., 455
Kwon, E., 132
Kwon, J. S., 492

La Plant, Q., 468
Laaksonen, M. A., 253
LaBar, K. S., 397
Laboèbe, G., 378
Laburn, H. P., 123, 492
LaChance, H., 468
Lachaux, J.-P., 451, 452
Lack, L., 263, 279
Lacroix, L., 372
Làdavas, E., 455
Ladenheim, B., 320
Lader, M., 478
Laeng, B., 181, 221
Laeng, P., 481
Lafargue, T., 492
LaFerla, F. M., 404
LaForge, K. S., 469
Lahey, B. B., 337
Lahti, I., 490
Lahti, T. A., 264
Lai, C., 118
Lai, C. S. L., 438, 439
Lai, Z., 438, 439
Laibson, D., 109
Laing, P., 491
Lakatos, P., 488
Lake, R. I. E., 109
Lalancette-Hébert, M., 137
Lall, G. S., 268
Lalwani, A., 441
Lamarck, J., 110
Lamb, R. J., 131
Lamb, S. E., 480
Lambert, E. A., 478
Lambert, G. W., 478
Lambert, T. J., 459
Lambie, J. A., 454
Lamme, V. A. F., 170
Lamminmäki, A., 331
LaMotte, R. H., 207
Lamsa, K. P., 45
Lancaster, J. L., 428
Lancel, M., 333
Land, E., 158
Land, E. H., 158
Landau, B., 432
Landback, P., 111
Landi, P., 373
Landin, A. M., 213
Landis, D. M. D., 17
Landis, T., 166, 167, 192
Landreth, G. E., 405
Lane, A. P., 220
Lanfermann, H., 84
Lanfranco, M. F., 468
Lang, P. J., 467
Langberg, R., 385
Lange, B. P., 334
Lange, E. H., 493
Langford, G., 279
Langhammer, A., 318
Langmead, B., 107
Langnaese, K., 336
Langner, R., 181
Långsjö, J. W., 453
Langston, J. W., 253
Långström, N., 347
Lanningham-Foster, L. M., 318
Lansford, J. E., 470
Lapid, H., 219
Larkin, C., 488
Larkin, D. W., 269
Larkin, K., 350
LaRowe, S. D., 472
Larsen, J., 105
Larsen, R. J., 358
Larson, C. L., 476
Larsson, A., 344
Larsson, E.-M., 379
Larsson, J., 275
Laruelle, M., 494
Lasco, M. S., 350
Lashley, K., 393–394, 413
Lasko, N. B., 377
Laskowki, W., 180
Laskowski, C. J., 139
Lassonde, M., 127
Latendresse, S. J., 470
Latshaw, A., 492
Latty, E., 346
Lau, B., 246, 376
Lau, H. C., 247, 248
Lau, L., 71
Laubach, M., 83, 132
Laughlin, S. A., 441
Launer, L., 127
Laurent, J.-P., 278
Laureys, S., 277, 286, 453
Lauzanne, K., 343
Lavidor, M., 425
Lavie, P., 269
Lavond, D. G., 395, 396
Lavzin, M., 45
Lawden, M., 156
Lawley, H. J., 220
Lawrence, A. D., 362, 467
Lazarus, M., 298
Lazzeroni, L. C., 490
Lê, K.-A., 319
Le, N. X. H., 469
Le Magueresse, C., 34
Lea, E., 205
Leak, R. K., 137
Leamey, C. A., 153
Leavitt, B. R., 256
Lebel, C., 118, 124
Leber, A. B., 454
LeBihan, D., 128, 450
LeBlanc, K. H., 468
Lechler, R. I., 312
Leckman, J. F., 337
Lederman, S. J., 180
LeDoux, J., 355
LeDoux, J. E., 372, 374, 379
Lee, A., 221, 313, 500
Lee, A. D., 98
Lee, A. M., 246
Lee, B. B., 155
Lee, C., 312
Lee, C. Y. D., 405
Lee, E., 343
Lee, F., 314
Lee, G.P., 364
Lee, H. L., 95, 444
Lee, H.-J., 373, 376
Lee, J.-C., 496
Lee, K. J., 241
Lee, K. M., 128
Lee, M. G., 275
Lee, M.-J., 180
Lee, N. J., 241
Lee, P. A., 345
Lee, P. H., 374
Lee, P.-C., 253
Lee, S. J., 313
Lee, S. Y., 371
Lee, S.-H., 451
Lee, T., 494
Lee, T. M., 264, 266
Lee, W. T., 241
Lee, Y., 20
Leenen, F. H. H., 303
Lefkowitz, R. J., 53
Legrand, L. N., 470
LeGuern, E., 426
Lehky, S. R., 86
Lehrer, J., 419
Lehrman, D., 331
Lehrman, D. S., 331
Leibbrandt, A., 299
Leibler, S., 284
Leibniz, G., 4
Leibowitz, S. F., 314, 315, 318, 320
Lein, E. S., 171
Leinders-Zufall, T., 220
Leischner, U., 192
Leitman, D. I., 488
Lejuez, C. W., 468

Lem, J., 214
LeMaster, M., 294
Lemire, A., 481
Lemos, B., 327
Leng, G., 53
Lenggenhager, B., 86
Lenhart, R. E., 476
Lennie, P., 155
Lensvelt-Mulders, G., 386
Lentjes, E. G., 335
Lenz, F. A., 130
Leo, R. J., 386
Leon, L. R., 299
Leonard, J. A., 334
Leopold, D. A., 167
Leopold, L., 312
Lepage, C., 97, 124
Lepage, K. Q., 402
Leplow, B., 403
Lepore, F., 127, 173
Lepousez, G., 119
Leppämäki, S., 264, 480
Leppert, M., 215
Lerch, J., 128
Lerch, J. P., 191
Leshchinskiy, S., 31, 213
Lesku, J. A., 285
Lesniak, D. R., 199
Lettre, G., 105
Lettvin, J. Y., 445
Leucht, S., 496
Leutgeb, S., 52
Levai, O., 220
Levander, S., 369
LeVay, S., 349
Levenson, R., 496
Levenson, R. W., 373, 471
Levenstein, R. M., 476
Leventhal, A. G., 172
Leventhal, D. K., 238
LeVere, T. E., 273
Levi-Montalcini, R., 122
Levin, E. D., 54
Levine, A. S., 314
Levine, A.S., 314
Levine, H. L., 441
Levine, J. A., 318
Levine, J. D., 53
Levinson, B., 191
Levit, A., 214
Levitin, D. J., 439
Levitsky, W., 431
Levitt, P., 500
Levitt, R. A., 477
Levitzki, A., 53
Levy, D. A., 399
Levy, H. L., 109
Levy, J., 429, 430
Levy, K.N., 460
Lew, A.-M., 319
Lewejohann, L., 107
Lewin, G. R., 199
Lewinsohn, P. M., 475
Lewis, C. M., 476
Lewis, E. R., 152
Lewis, J. W., 459
Lewis, M. B., 358
Lewis, R. A., 158
Lewis, S. W., 496
Lewis, T. L., 171, 173
Lewy, A. J., 264
Li, J., 242
Li, M., 119
Li, N., 179
Li, N. P., 334
Li, P., 139
Li, Q., 158
Li, R., 280
Li, W., 215
Li, W. T., 221
Li, X., 215, 298
Li, X. T., 478
Li, Z., 482
Li, Z. Y., 119
Li. A., 214
Liang, F.-Q., 267
Liang, Y.-X., 139
Liao, H.-W., 268
Liao, L.-M., 345
Liberles, S. D., 220
Liberman, M. C., 193
Liberzon, I., 360
Libet, B., 246, 247, 248
Libionka, W., 20
Lichtenberger, L., 438, 439
Lichtenstein, M., 495
Lichtenstein, P., 347
Lichtman, J. W., 132
Lickliter, R., 438
Lidow, M. S., 171
Liebe, S., 397
Lieberman, M. D., 204
Liebl, J., 119
Liebman, M., 319
Liebnau, R., 86
Lief, H. I., 333
Lie-Nemeth, T., 130
Lightman, S. L., 331
Lillycrop, K. A., 107
Lim, B. K., 385
Lim, K. O., 492
Lim, M. M., 336, 337
Lima, S. L., 277
Lin, C.-S., 83
Lin, D. Y., 219
Lin, J.-S., 275, 276
Lin, L., 280
Lin, N., 476
Lin, W., 98
Lin, W.-C., 467
Lin, X., 280
Lincoln, A. J., 71
Lindberg, M. R., 490
Lindberg, N. O., 312
Lindberg, S. M., 98
Lindell, S. G., 369
Lindemann, B., 214
Linden, D. E. J., 84
Lindenberger, U., 126
Lindgren, C. M., 318
Lindholm, P., 254
Lindhom, J., 478
Lindner, A., 237
Lindquist, K. A., 360
Lindsay, P. H., 193
Lindsley, S. R., 313
Lindström, P., 220, 349
Lininger, A., 280
Linkenkaer-Hansen, K., 202
Linn, M. C., 98
Linnoila, M., 369, 469
Liou, Y.-C., 297
Lipnevich, A. A., 266
Lippa, R. A., 346
Lipton, R. B., 132
Lisman, J., 417, 418
Lisman, J. E., 52
Lissek, S., 374
Litt, M., 158
Litt, M. D., 470
Liu, A. K., 181
Liu, C. Y., 337
Liu, F., 105, 329, 331
Liu, G., 55
Liu, G.-C., 467
Liu, J., 118, 180, 328
Liu, K., 256
Liu, L., 264
Liu, P., 403
Liu, T., 444
Liu, X., 268
Liu, X.-Y., 207
Liu, Y., 208
Liu, Z.-W., 287
Lively, C. M., 326
Livingston, K. E., 367
Livingstone, M. S., 158, 177
Lledo, P.-M., 119
Lloyd, H., 496
Lo, J. C. Y., 286
Lo, W. H. Y., 109
Loche, A., 107
Lock, E., 440
Lockhead, E., 214
Lockley, S. W., 268
Lockwood, A. H., 193
Loe, I. M., 238
Loewenstein, G., 364
Loewenstein, W. R., 199
Loewi, O., 48
Loewy, A. D, 304
Loftus, A., 455
Logan, C. G., 395
Logan, J., 468
Logothetis, N. K., 397
Löken, L., 201
Löken, L. S., 201
Loland, C. J., 55
Lomber, S. G., 192
Lomniczi, A., 107
Lømo, T., 230, 415
Long, D., 138
Long, J. D. II, 407
Long, M., 111
Long, M. A., 267
Long, S. J., 348
Lönnqvist, J., 264, 480, 489
Lönnqvist, J. K., 488
Looney, C. B., 98
Loose, M. D., 330
Loosfelt, H., 343
Lopes, C., 208
López, M., 313, 314
López-Barneo, J., 123, 311
Lopez-Barroso, D., 379
López-Giménez, J. F., 495
Lopez-Otin, C., 198
Lord, G. M., 312
Lorenz, B. H., 328
Lorincz, A., 31
Lorrain, D. S., 331, 333, 467
Lorusso, G., 277
Lorusso, M. L., 445
Lott, I. T., 404
Lotto, R. B., 156, 157, 158
Lotze, M., 141
Lou, N., 20
Loucks, J. A., 331
Loughna, P. T., 230
Loui, P., 191
Lounasmaa, O. V., 91
Love, T. M., 206
Loving, T. J., 383
Lovinger, D. M., 243
Lowe, S. L., 495
Lowell, B. B., 314
Lozano, A. M., 140
Lozsádi, D. A., 275
Lu, A., 84
Lu, B., 256, 478
Lu, H., 419
Lu, H. D., 181
Lu, K.-S., 53
Lu, S., 220
Lu, T., 206
Lubin, G., 374
Lucas, B. K., 336
Lucas, R. J., 268
Lucassen, P. J., 126
Lucchina, L. A., 215
Luck, S. J., 488
Luczak, S. E., 471
Luders, E., 98, 335, 431
Ludwig, M., 53, 336
Luetje, M., 444
Lugg, D. J., 386
Luijten, P. R., 495
Luiz, A. C., 303
Lumley, L. A., 331
Lumpkin, E. A., 199
Luna, B, 131
Luna, B., 131, 238
Lund, J. S., 150
Lund, R. D., 150
Lundberg, Y. W., 198
Luo, J., 132
Luo, L., 140
Luo, Y. L. L., 180
Lupica, C. R., 468
Lupien, S. P., 386
Luscher, C., 378, 468
Lussier, I. D., 369
Lutgendorf, S., 358
Lutz, A., 454
Luu, P., 238
Lux, A., 345
Luxen, A., 238, 278
Ly, C. V., 256
Lyden, P., 243
Lyman, C. P., 285
Lynall, M.-E., 492
Lynch, C. A., 314
Lynn, S. J., 284
Lyons, M. J., 468, 476
Lyttelton, O. C., 97

Ma, D. K., 417
Ma, J., 54
Ma, Q., 208
Ma, W., 220
Ma, Z., 214
Mabb, A. M., 500
Mac Donald, G., 204
MacCabe, J. H., 490
Macdonald, A. M., 489
MacDonald, C. J., 402
Macdonald, D.W., 372
MacDonald, K., 139
MacDonald, M. E., 256
Macdonald, R. L., 378
Macey, K. E., 279
Macey, P. M., 279
MacFarlane, J. G., 279
MacFarquhar, L., 113
Mach, F., 137
Mack, J., 318
MacKeith, D., 172
MacLean, P. D., 360
MacLeod, D. I. A., 173
MacLusky, N. J., 330
Macphail, E. M., 97
Macrae, C. N., 93, 192, 428
MacVicar, B. A., 20
Madden, K., 424
Madden, P. A. F., 476
Madeo, B., 329
Mader, I., 402
Madsen, S. K., 98
Maeng, L. Y., 386
Maes, F. W., 214
Maes, H., 469
Maes, H. H. M., 109

Maffei, A., 171
Maffei, L., 171, 478
Maffei, M., 312
Magee, J. J., 430
Magistretti, P. J., 23
Magnotta, V., 493
Magnus, E., 483
Magnuson, V. L., 347
Magnusson, G., 500
Magoun, H. W., 275
Maguire, D., 401
Maguire, E. A., 400, 402
Mahncke, H., 444
Mai, N., 182
Mai, X. M., 318
Maia, A. S., 123
Maidment, N. T., 468
Maier, S. F., 132, 205, 384, 385
Maier, W., 459
Mailliard, W., 469
Maine, D. N., 207
Maischein, H.-M., 118
Maj, M., 320
Majdan, M., 171
Majeskie, M., 468
Majzoub, J. A., 314
Makris, N., 335
Maksimow, A., 453
Malach, R., 167, 450
Malarkey, W. B., 383, 386
Malaspina, D., 490
Maldjian, J. A., 220
Malenka, R. C., 171, 385
Malhotra, S., 192
Malia, A., 401
Malik, S., 118
Malinow, R., 404, 418
Mallet, N., 238
Mallick, B. N., 279
Mallis, M. M., 264
Mallory, C. S., 371
Malmberg, A. B., 207
Malone, T. W., 368
Mameli, M., 468
Manani, J. V., 303
Mancia, F., 220
Mancuso, K., 158
Mandeville, J. B., 181
Mandl, R. C. W., 492
Mandler, A., 178
Mandt, B. H., 285
Maner, J. K, 220
Manes, F., 407
Mangan, M. A., 281
Mangiapane, M. L., 304
Mangin, J.-F., 450
Mangun, G. R., 428
Mangweth, B., 476
Maniatis, S., 329, 349
Manji, H., 478
Manji, H. K., 483
Mann, G. L., 277
Mann, J. J., 369
Mann, T., 319
Männistö, S., 253
Manns, J. R., 403
Manser, M., 113
Mansvelder, H. D., 379
Mantha, K., 124
Mantini, D., 444
Mantyh, P. W., 203, 204, 207
Maquet, P., 238, 275, 278, 286, 407
Marcar, V. L., 182
Marcel, A. J., 454
March, S. M., 469
Marchal, G., 181
Marcin, C., 499
Marcinowska, A., 478
Marder, K. S., 253
Marek, R., 374
Maret, S., 287
Maricich, S. M., 199
Marin, C., 253
Marin, M. M., 191
Marini, C., 123
Mariño, G., 198
Mark, A. L., 312
Mark, G. P., 320
Markou, A., 468
Markowitsch, H. J., 375, 404
Markowitz, J. C., 480
Markowski, V. P., 331
Marlatt, M. W., 126
Marois, R., 221, 460
Marrelec, G., 277
Marrett, S., 183
Marridis, D., 496
Marris, E., 11
Marsden, C. D., 495
Marsh, G. R., 280
Marsh, S., 201
Marshall, E. J., 489
Marshall, J., 166
Marshall, J. C., 429, 455
Marshall, J. F., 142
Marshel, J. H., 371
Marsman, A., 495
Martens, M. A., 439
Martenyi, F., 495
Martin, A. A. A., 34
Martin, E., 480
Martin, G., 153
Martin, J., 370
Martin, K. C., 418
Martin, L. L., 358
Martin, N. G., 109, 476
Martin, N. W., 109
Martin, P. R., 155
Martin, R. C., 442
Martin, S. D., 480
Martindale, C., 154
Martindale, J. L., 444
Martinerie, J., 451, 452
Martinez, A., 86
Martinez, K., 98
Martinez, V., 264
Martinez-Barbera, J. P., 201
Martinez-Vargas, M. C., 331
Martinowich, K., 478
Martins, R. N., 406
Martin-Santos, R., 376
Maruff, P., 284
Maruyama, Y., 53
Marvin, E., 191
Mascaro, J. S., 337
Maschke, M., 395
Masland, R. H., 149, 153
Mason, C. C., 318
Mason, M. F., 93
Mason, P., 205, 461
Mason, R. T., 294
Masse, N. Y., 235
Massimini, M., 277, 286, 453
Masson, G., 500
Masten, C. L., 204
Masterton, R. B., 192
Mataga, N., 219
Matarese, G., 312
Mathews, G. A., 344
Mathias, C. J., 357
Mathies, R. A., 153
Mathieson, I., 490
Mathur, U., 173
Matise, T. C., 112
Matrisciano, F., 478
Matson, J. L., 500
Matsubara, S., 496
Matsui, R., 235
Matsuki, N., 395
Matsumoto, H., 216, 217
Matsumoto, N., 395
Matsumoto, T., 123
Matsumoto, Y., 284, 386
Matsunami, H., 214
Matsuo, T., 267
Matsuoka, R., 439
Mattiace, L. A., 350
Mattingley, J. B., 456
Matuszewich, L., 331, 333, 467
Matute, C., 496
Matveeva, T. M., 488
Matynia, A., 418
Mauck, M. C., 158
Maumenee, I. H., 158
Maurer, D., 171, 173
Maurice, D., 288
Maxwell, J. S., 362
May, A., 129
May, M. G., 173
May, P. R. A., 136
Maya Vetencourt, J. F., 478
Mayberg, H. S., 482
Mayberry, R. I., 440
Maydeu-Olivares, A., 370
Mayer, A. D., 336
Mayeux, R., 253
Maywood, E. S., 280
Maze, I., 468
Mazoyer, B., 431
Mazur, A., 331
Mazur, C., 256
Mazur, G. J., 384
Mazza, E., 279
Mazziotta, J. C., 92, 482
McAlonis, M. M., 256
McBurney, D. H., 213
McCabe, C., 92
McCall, C., 424, 459
McCall, W. V., 280
McCarley, R. W., 288, 492
McCarthy, G., 460
McCarthy, J., 320
McCarthy, M. I., 318
McCarthy, M.M., 329
McCarthy, S. E., 490
McClarty, B., 377
McClary, A., 220
McClay, J., 370
McClellan, J. M., 490
McClendon, E., 177
McCleskey, E. W., 205
McClintock, M. K., 220
McConnell, J. V., 413
McConnell, M. J., 490
McConnell, S.K., 124
McCormack, S., 280
McCoy, A. N., 167
McCrady, S. K., 318
McCrea, A. E., 348
McDade, T. W., 337
McDaniel, M. A., 97
McDermott, R., 370
McDevitt, E. A., 287
McDonald, J. J., 450
McDonald, M. M., 363
McDonald, S., 362
McDonough, I. M., 132
McElhiney, M., 429
McElroy, A. E., 213
McEvoy, L. K., 132
McEwen, B., 383
McEwen, B. S., 295, 334
McEwen, G. N., Jr., 299
McGann, J. P., 407
McGaugh, J. L., 397, 419
McGeary, J., 469
McGinty, D., 289
McGivern, R. F., 329
McGlinchey, E. L., 284
McGlone, F., 201
McGorry, P. D., 489
McGrath, J., 489, 491
McGrath, P. J., 478
McGreenery, C. E., 483
McGregor, I. S., 378
McGrillen, K., 214, 424
McGue, M., 470
McGuffin, P., 476
McGuire, S., 109
McHugh, P. R., 310
McIlwrath, S. L., 199
McIntosh, A. R., 467
McIntosh, D. N., 383
McIntyre, R. S., 318, 331, 332
McKay, H. M., 397
McKeefry, D. J., 181
McKeever, W. F., 426
McKemy, D. D., 199
McKenna, P. J., 492
McKenzie, A., 130
McKinnon, W., 385
McKnight, S. L., 269
McLaren, M., 132
McLellan, W. A., 297, 299
McLeod, D. I. A., 173
McMahon, M. J., 155
McMahon, T., 469
McMenamin, B. W., 362
McMillan, K. A., 371
McMillon, G., 444
McMurray, J., 431
McNamee, R., 491
McNaughton, B. L., 286, 403
McNeil, R., 153
McNeill, D., 439
McPhee, J. C., 31
McQuilkin, M., 139
McRae-Clark, A. L., 472
McStephen, M., 284
Meaburn, E. L., 109
Meador-Woodruff, J., 327
Meaney, M. J., 107, 124
Meddis, R., 279
Medini, P., 171
Medland, S. E., 109
Mednick, S. A., 286, 491
Mednick, S. C., 286
Mednick, S.C., 287
Meduna, L., 480
Meduri, G., 343
Meek, P. S., 471
Mefford, I., 469
Meguid, N. A., 500
Mehlman, P. T., 369
Mehta, D., 107
Meier, P. J., 21
Meigs, J. B., 319
Meiselman, H. L., 213
Meissner, W., 142
Meister, M., 122, 149, 220
Melcher, J. R., 192, 193
Melcher, L. M., 319
Melloni, L., 450
Melone, M., 496
Meltzer, H. Y., 496
Meltzer, L. A., 478
Meltzoff, A. N., 239
Melzack, R., 205, 207
Menaker, M., 267
Mena-Segovia, J., 253
Menchetti, M., 480
Mendel, G., 104

Mendelsohn, M., 119, 220
Mendelsohn, M. M., 329, 349
Mendes, M. B., 363
Mendes, W. B., 384
Mendieta-Zéron, H., 313
Meng, X.-L., 207
Mennicken, F., 205
Menon, D. K., 136
Menon, V., 492
Merckelbach, H., 284
Meredith, A. L., 20
Mergen, H., 318
Mergen, M., 318
Merikangas, K. P., 482
Mérillat, S., 129
Merino-Martinez, R., 334
Merrow, M., 264, 266
Merskey, H., 483
Mervis, C. B., 439
Merzenich, M. M., 83, 140, 192, 444
Mesaros, A., 313
Mesgarani, N., 193
Meshi, D., 119
Messing, R. O., 469
Mesulam, M.-M., 275
Metzinger, T., 86
Mevorach, C., 454
Meyer, J. M., 476
Meyer, J. R., 130
Meyer, K., 192
Meyer, K. D., 469
Meyer, M., 358
Meyer, R. A., 207
Meyer, U., 492
Meyer-Bahlburg, H. F. L., 345
Meyerhof, W., 214
Meyerhoff, J. L., 367
Meyerhoff, J. M., 367
Meyer-Lindenberg, A., 439, 492
Meyers, E., 173
Meyler, A., 444
Mezzanotte, W. S., 279
Miall, C., 246
Mica, L., 385
Michael, C. R., 187
Michalek, J., 331
Michalska, K. J., 337
Michel, C. M., 192
Micheva, K. D., 54
Mickel, S. F., 404
Mierson, S., 214
Miettunen, J., 490
Mignot, E., 280
Miguel, E., 370
Mihalcescu, I., 284
Mika, A., 384
Mikulincer, M., 262
Mikulis, D. J., 202
Milich, R., 308
Mill, J., 370
Miller, A., 370
Miller, A. C., 428
Miller, B. L., 429
Miller, C. A., 417
Miller, E. K., 454
Miller, G., 11, 334, 358
Miller, G. A., 448
Miller, G. E., 385
Miller, I. N., 252
Miller, J., 247, 488, 491
Miller, J. F., 402
Miller, J. L., 374
Miller, L. A., 214, 424
Miller, M. B., 347
Miller, R. J., 118
Miller, S., 241
Miller, S. L., 220
Miller, W. R., 333
Millership, S., 314
Mills, R., 329
Milner, A. D., 178, 237
Milner, B., 398, 399
Milner, P., 466
Milner, T. A., 334
Milstein, A. D., 199
Minamisawa, R., 334
Minard, A., 284
Mineur, Y. S., 314
Ming, G.-L., 119
Minichiello, L., 418
Miniussi, C., 397
Minkel, J. D., 284
Minnerup, J., 137
Minokoshi, Y., 313
Minor, K., 483
Minshew, N., 238
Minto, C. L., 345
Mischel, W., 204
Mishima, K., 284
Mishima, Y., 284
Mishkin, M., 140, 192
Mishra, J., 86, 454
Mishra, S. K., 199
Mislow, J. M. K., 235
Misra, K., 469
Misrahi, M., 343
Mistlberger, R. E., 264
Mitchell, D., 284
Mitchell, D. E., 172
Mitchell, D. G. V., 376
Mitchell, G. S., 126
Mitchell, J. M., 469
Mitchell, J. P., 180, 461
Mitchell, K. J., 221
Mitchison, G., 287
Mitra, P. P., 80, 81, 286
Mitropoulou, G., 426
Mitura, K., 342
Miu, A. C., 373
Miura, A., 153
Miura, K., 246
Miura, S. K., 418
Miyakubo, H., 304
Miyashita, Y., 492
Miyata, S., 303
Miyawaki, Y., 93
Miyazawa, A., 52
Mize, S. J. S., 213
Mlinar, B., 369
Mo, H., 417
Mochizuki, T., 280
Mody, I., 378
Moeller, F. G., 369
Moens, L. N., 490
Moffitt, T. E., 370, 476
Mohler, H., 378
Mohs, R. C., 489
Mok, M. Y., 220
Molaison, H., 398–399, 400, 401, 403
Molenda-Figueira, H. A., 328
Molina, C., 450
Molina, J. C., 469
Molko, N., 128
Mölle, M., 287
Moller, H. J., 479
Molnar, M., 327
Molteni, M., 445
Mombaerts, P. A., 220
Monaco, A. P., 438, 439
Monaghan, E. P., 348
Money, J., 328, 346
Monfared, N., 112
Monfils, M.-H., 379
Monk, T. H., 264
Monnikes, H., 310
Monroe, S. M., 475
Montaguti, M. B., 480
Montavont, A., 426, 444
Monte, F., 98
Montecucco, F., 137
Monteleone, P., 320
Montgomery, K. J., 238
Montgomery, S. A., 478
Monti, M. M., 453
Monti-Bloch, L., 220
Montmayeur, J.-P., 214
Montoya, E. R., 368
Montplaisir, J., 277
Montrose, D. M., 493
Monyer, H, 34
Moody, A. D., 172
Moody, T. D., 407
Moon, H. Y., 480
Moore, F. R., 285
Moore, L. B., 478
Moore, M. K., 239
Moore, R. Y., 280
Moore, S., 325
Moore, S. A., 319
Moore, S. C., 139
Moore, T., 84, 167, 237
Moore, T. J., 479
Moore, T. L., 401
Moore-Ede, M. C., 264, 274
Moors, A., 358
Morales, J. M., 331
Moran, T. H., 310
Mordel, C., 495
Moreau, P., 191
Moreta, M. C., 284
Morfini, G. A., 256
Morgan, C. A., III, 371
Morgan, R., 358
Morgan, V., 490
Mori, K., 219
Morichika, Y., 138
Morin, A., 286
Moring, J., 490
Morishima, Y., 460
Morland, A. B., 156
Morley, J. E., 314
Moroney, D. N., 31, 213
Morozova, M. A., 495
Morran, L. T., 326
Morris, C. A., 439
Morris, D. L., 137
Morris, J. A., 334
Morris, J. S., 376
Morris, M., 263, 279
Morris, M. J., 480
Morris, N. M., 333, 334
Morris, R. G. M., 418
Morrison, A. R., 277
Morrison, I., 201
Morrison, J. H., 132, 334
Morrone, M. C., 183
Morrongiello, B. A., 188
Morse, J. R., 214
Mortensen, P. B., 489, 490, 491
Morton, A. J., 280
Morton, G. J., 312
Morton, J., 444
Moruzzi, G., 275
Moscarello, J. M., 374
Moscovitch, M., 93, 398, 400, 401, 403
Moser, D. J., 256
Moser, H. R., 208
Moses, J., 331
Mosher, K. I., 132
Moskowitz, H. R., 213
Moss, C. F., 187
Moss, M. B., 401
Moss, S. J., 52, 482
Mott, M. L., 363
Mottaz, A., 248
Mottolese, C., 237
Moussavi, M., 385
Moutoussis, K., 181
Movshon, J. A., 178
Moyer, M. C., 317
Mrowka, S. W., 167
Mrzljak, L., 496
Mucke, L., 404
Mueller, C. J., 362
Mueller, K. L., 214
Mugnaini, E., 31
Muhonen, M., 489
Mulcare, C. A., 308
Mullan, M., 404
Muller, D., 418
Müller, F. J., 403
Müller, H. D., 137, 138
Muller, H. K., 386
Müller, J., 148
Muller, U., 492
Muller, Y. L., 318
Mulligan, S. J., 20
Munafo, M. R., 490
Munk, M., 450
Munk, M. H. J., 275
Munoz, D. P., 238
Muñoz, M., 268
Muntjewerff, J. W., 490
Murakami, I., 182
Muranaga, T., 320
Murdoch, H., 490
Murdoch, J. D., 500
Murphy, B. W., 193
Murphy, F. C., 362
Murphy, J., 429, 436
Murphy, M. R., 331
Murphy, P. J., 269
Murphy, R. L., 347
Murphy, T. H., 139
Murray, E. A., 90, 408
Murray, G., 263
Murray, L. K., 334
Murray, R. M., 489, 492, 493
Murray, S. S., 490
Murrell, J., 404
Murrough, J. W., 386
Mursch, K., 375
Murtha, M. T., 500
Murty, V. P., 397
Musacchia, G., 128
Mushiake, H., 238
Muto, A., 91
Muzio, J. N., 287
Mychack, P., 429
Myers, C. E., 407
Myers, J. J., 428
Myers, M. G. Jr., 316
Myllyviita, K., 444

Na, E. S., 480
Näätänen, R., 202, 444
Nabekura, J., 138
Naccache, L., 450, 453
Nachman, R., 492
Nadal, A., 327
Nadarajah, B., 118
Nader, K., 379
Nader, M. A., 369
Nader, R., 287
Nader, S. H., 369
Naeser, M. A., 441
Naftolin, F., 330
Nagarajan, S., 444
Nagarajan, S. S., 130
Nagashma, K., 296
Nagy, E., 233
Nah, S. Y., 205

Nahum, L., 404
Najt, P., 362
Naka, M., 395
Nakahara, K., 492
Nakahara, T., 320
Nakai, J., 91
Nakajima, K., 492
Nakamura, K. C., 119
Nakamura, M., 296
Nakamura, S., 119
Nakamura, Y., 20
Nakashima, Y., 343
Nakata, H., 153
Nakayama, D., 395
Nakell, L., 432
Nam, J. Y., 370
Nambu, T., 280
Namgung, U., 418, 419
Napoliello, E. M., 444
Napper, R. M., 124
Nara, K., 219
Narayan, M., 221
Narr, K. L., 98
Narr, K. L., 98, 335
Narrow, W. E., 475
Nasca, C., 478
Naso, L., 207
Nassi, J. J., 150, 165, 177, 181
Nataraj, K., 171
Nathans, J., 158
Naumer, M. J., 222
Navarrete, C. D., 363
Neal, A., 238
Neale, C., 419
Neale, M. C., 346, 347, 376, 469
Neargarder, S., 252
Neary, M. T., 314
Nebes, R. D., 426
Nedergaard, M., 20
Nef, P., 219
Neiss, M. B., 334
Neitz, M., 158
Nelissen, K., 7, 181
Nelken, I., 192
Nelson, A. B., 287
Nelson, A. M., 199
Nelson, C. A., 123
Nelson, D. L., 256
Nelson, E., 476
Nelson, L. M., 253
Nelson, M. T., 20
Nelson, R. J., 83, 140
Nelson, S. B., 171
Nemeroff, C., 469
Nemes, A., 119, 220, 329, 349
Nemoto, T., 138
Neri, D. F., 263, 264
Nestler, E. J., 107, 386, 468, 475
Nestor, P. J., 407
Nesvag, R., 493
Netter, F. H., 326
Nettle, D., 369
Neu, A., 56
Neufang, M., 402
Neufer, P. D., 230
Neugebauer, H., 137
Neuhausser, W. M., 199
Neumann, I. D., 331
Neumeister, A., 478
Neve, R., 395
Neville, H. J., 127, 440, 441
Nevin, R., 370
Nevo, E., 104, 268
New, M. I., 345
Newcomer, J. W., 495
Newell, F. N., 221
Newhart, M., 442
Newman, A. B., 127
Ng, M. Y., 476
Nguyen, L. N., 404
Niaura, R., 468
Nicholas, A. K., 204
Nicholas, C. L., 263
Nicholls, M. E. R., 141, 455
Nicklas, W. J., 253
Nicolelis, M. A. L., 83, 246, 304
Nicoletti, F., 478
Nicoll, R. A., 56, 415
Nicolson, N. A., 475
Nielsen, D. A., 469
Nielsen, S. J., 319
Nieminen, P., 490
Nienhuis, R., 280
Nierenberg, A. A., 479, 480
Niesen, W. D., 137
Nieuwenhuys, R., 73, 75, 76, 298, 367, 427
Nijboer, T. C. W., 455
Nikelski, E. J., 441, 442
Nikonenko, I., 418
Nilsson, G. E., 97
Nilsson, L.-G., 132
Nilsson, M., 119
Nimmo-Smith, I., 362
Ninomiya, Y., 214
Nir, Y., 288, 450
Nisenson, L., 429
Nishida, S., 156
Nishijo, H., 75, 371
Nishimaru, H., 51–52
Nishimura, Y., 138
Nishita, J. K., 329
Nishizawa, K., 243
Nitabach, M. N., 269
Nitsch, C., 349
Nitschke, J. B., 362, 476
Nitz, D. A., 246
Niv, M. Y., 214
Niv, Y., 275
Niven, J. E., 31
Niwa, M., 386
Noaghiul, S., 483
Nobili, L., 277
Noda, M, 235, 303
Noesselt, T., 86
Nogueiras, R., 314
Nolen-Hoeksema, S., 475
Nomura, M., 304
Nomura, S., 304
Nopoulos, P., 256, 493
Norcross, M. A., 374
Nordenskjold, A., 344, 345
Nordenström, A., 344, 345
Norgren, R., 214
Norman, D. A., 193
North, N. T., 357
North, R. A., 53, 467
Norton, A., 128
Norton, M. I., 93
Noseda, R., 268
Nosenko, N. D., 348
Nottebohm, F., 119
Novak, S., 141
Novarino, G., 500
Novotny, M. V., 220
Nowak, M. A., 113
Nowak, P., 140
Nugent, A. C., 478
Nugent, F. S., 416
Numan, M., 336, 356
Nusser, Z., 31
Nüsslein-Volhard, C., 118
Nuthalapati, N., 314
Nuutila, A., 369
Nuutinen, S., 275
Nyberg, L., 132
Nyce, M. R., 313
Nystrom, L. E., 363

O. M., Minini, L., 178
Oakes, T. R., 476
Oaten, M. J., 385
Obermeyer, W. H., 285
Obeso, J. A., 253
O'Brien, C. P., 333, 472
O'Brien, D. P., 367
O'Brien, L., 131
O'Brien, R. C., 285
Obuchowicz, E., 478
O'Callaghan, E., 488
O'Carroll, R. E., 357
Ochsner, K., 461
Ochsner, K. N., 358
O'Connor, M., 401
O'Daly, O. G., 314
Oddo, S., 404
O'Doherty, J., 203
O'Doherty, J. P., 408
O'Donnell, D., 205
O'Donnell, S., 220
O'Dowd, B. F., 53
Oelmann, H., 221
Ogden, S. B., 319
Oh, E. C., 490
O'Hara, R., 397
O'Hearn, K., 131
Ohira, K., 119
Ohkura, M., 91
Ohmori, H., 32
Ohmoto, M., 214
Ohno, E., 294
Ohtsu, H., 275
Ojanen, S.-M., 264
Ojeda, S. R., 107
Oka, Y., 212, 216, 217
Okada, H., 252
Okada, K., 243
Okado, H., 235, 303
Okaichi, H., 402, 418
Okamura, H., 267
O'Kane, G., 399
Okano, Y., 109
O'Keefe, J., 402
Okubo, M., 455
Okumura, T., 304
Okura, R., 267
Olanow, C. W., 253, 254
Olausson, H., 201
Olazabal, D. E., 337
Olazábal, D. E., 336
Olds, J., 466
O'Leary, A., 384
O'Leary, O. F., 478
Oler, J. A., 373
Olff, M., 384, 460
Oliet, S. H. R., 56
Oliveira, L. M. O., 83
Oliver, G., 345
Ollinger, J. M., 127
Olliver, C., 358
Olney, J. W., 124, 495
Olsen, R. K., 439
Olson, E. J., 281
Olson, I. R., 407
Olson, L., 254
Olson, L. R., 318
Olton, D. S., 402
Olufowobi, A., 336
O'Malley, B. W., 331
O'Malley, K. L., 253
O'Meara, E. S., 419
Ommaya, A. K., 140
Oner, C., 318
Oner, R., 318
Onitsuka, T., 492
Ono, M., 294
Ono, T., 75, 371
Onoda, N., 212
Onoe, H., 138
Oostenveld, R., 450
Op de Beeck, H. P., 444
Ophoff, R. A., 490
Oquendo, M. A., 369
Orban, G. A., 7, 181
O'Regan, J. K., 454
Orell, R. W., 230
Örey, D., 496
O'Riain, M. J., 113
Orlovsky, G. N., 232
Ormandy, C. J., 336
Ornstein, R., 429
O'Roak, B. J., 500
O'Rourke, N. A., 54
Orr, C. A., 455
Orr, H. T., 256
Orr, S. P., 377, 379
Ortigue, S., 459
Orzi, F., 54
Osborne, J., 119
Oshima, T., 136
Oshinsky, M. L., 269
Osman, A. M., 119
Ossowski, V., 318
Ostlund, S. B., 468
Ostrovsky, Y., 173
Oswald, I., 279
Otmakhov, N., 417
Otte, W. M., 138
Ottersen, O. P., 22
Ottman, R., 253
Ouchi, Y., 252
Ouk, K., 275
Ourednik, J., 254
Ourednik, V., 254
Ousley, A., 268
Ousman, S. S., 22
Overduin, J., 310
Overton, P. G., 124
Owen, A. M., 453
Owen, M., 404
Oxenham, A. J., 192
Oxley, D. R., 374
Oyama, O. N., 471
Oyarzun, J. P., 379
Ozaki-Kuroda, K., 124
Ozata, M., 318
Ozdoba, J. M., 31, 213

Paabo, S., 439
Paaredes, M. F., 123
Pabst, D. A., 297, 299
Pace-Schott, E. F., 288
Pacheco, P., 337
Pacheco-Calderón, R., 395
Pacher, P., 206
Pacifico, R., 216
Packer, A. M., 90
Packer, O. S., 155
Padiath, Q. S., 269
Padmanabhan, A., 131
Padmos, R. C., 483
Paehler, M., 313
Paffen, C. L. E., 450
Pail, G., 483
Pakaprot, N., 395
Pakyz, R., 318
Palacino, J., 256
Palfreyman, M. G., 481
Palladino, M. A., 454
Pallas, S. L., 125
Paller, K. A., 286
Pallie, W., 431

Pallier, C., 128
Palmer, T. D., 119
Palmeri, T. J., 221
Palmiter, R. D., 313, 314
Palop, J. J., 404
Palva, J. M., 202
Palva, S., 202
Pan, A. H., 119
Pan, F., 125
Panaccione, I., 478
Pandey, G. N., 369
Pandey, S. C., 369, 469
Panegyres, P. K., 255
Paniagua, B., 492
Panksepp, J., 277
Panossian, A., 478
Panov, A. V., 256
Pantelis, C., 489
Pantev, C., 128, 141
Panula, P., 275
Papadenaetris, X., 95
Papafrangos, E. D., 285
Papas, B. C., 402
Pappy, M., 496
Paradiso, M. A., 171
Parbery-Clark, A., 193
Pardal, R., 311
Paré, D., 372, 415
Paré, M., 199
Paredes, P., 469
Parent, C., 124
Parent, M. B., 288
Pariante, C. M., 107
Parise, E., 91
Parisi, J. M., 419
Parisi, T., 130
Park, D., 105
Park, D. C., 132
Park, H. G., 480
Park, I. S., 241
Park, J. H., 269
Park, J.-H., 241
Park, J.-Y., 137
Park, K. A., 241
Park, K. F., 183
Park, K. M., 180
Park, S., 136, 492
Parker, A. J., 178
Parker, C., 489
Parker, G. H., 211
Parker, J., 11
Parkitna, J. R., 468
Parks, C., 348
Parmentier, R., 275
Parnavelas, J. G., 118
Parrish, R. C. II, 326
Parrish, R. R., 417
Parsons, A. D., 220
Parsons, L. M., 242
Parton, L. E., 314
Partonen, T, 264
Partonen, T., 480, 483
Parvizi, J., 180, 182
Pascual, A., 123
Pascual, O., 20
Pascual-Leone, A., 90, 127, 130
Pase, M. P., 419
Pashler, H., 453
Pasqualetti, P., 397
Passingham, R. E., 247, 248
Pasterski, V., 344
Pasterski, V. L., 344
Patel, A. D., 443
Patel, N., 459
Patel, S., 480
Patil, S. T., 495
Pato, M., 482
Patoski, H. A. W., 208
Patston, L. L. M., 455
Pattatucci, A. M. L., 347
Patterson, K., 407
Patterson, R. D., 192
Paul, S. M., 378
Paulesu, E., 444
Pauli, J. R., 313
Pauli, L. S. S., 313
Paulitsch, S., 310
Paulson, O. B., 441
Paulus, M., 287
Paunio, T., 370, 483
Paus, T., 183
Pavani, F., 455
Pavlov, I. P., 392–393, 413
Pavlova, G. A., 232
Pawitan, Y., 253
Pawley, M. D. M., 264
Pearl, D. K., 246, 247, 248
Pearson, A. J. D., 279
Pearson, B. L., 500
Pearson, H., 230
Peciña, M., 206
Peck, C. C., 207
Peck, C. J., 376
Peckham, W., 348
Pedersen, C. B., 489
Pedersen, M. G., 491
Pedersen, M. S., 489
Pedersen, N. L., 253
Pedraza, C., 379
Pedre, X., 118, 328
Peduzzi, S., 138
Peelen, M. V., 179
Peelle, J. E., 193
Peet, M., 489
Peeters, R., 7
Peever, J. H., 277, 281
Pegna, A. J., 166, 167, 376
Peigneux, P., 286
Peineau, S., 415
Pekar, J., 192
Pelchat, M. L., 308
Peleg, G., 104
Peleg, O., 104
Pelham, W. E., 308
Pelican, S., 319
Pellegrino, C., 418
Pellegrino, M. A., 230
Pelleymounter, M. A., 313
Pelli, D. G., 152
Pellis, S. M., 252, 367
Pellis, V. C., 252, 367
Pembrey, M. E., 438
Pena, M., 450
Penagos, H., 192
Penfield, W., 83, 237, 398, 412
Peng, G., 440
Peng, J., 386
Peng, W., 20, 500
Peng, Y., 215
Peng, Z., 378
Penhune, V. B., 128
Penick, S. C., 416
Penmatsa, A., 477
Penninger, J. M., 299
Pennycook, G., 278
Pentland, A., 368
Penton-Voak, I. S., 334
Peper, J. S., 98
Pepperberg, I. M., 437
Peran, P., 492
Pereira, E., 53
Pereira, O. C. M., 329
Perera, et al, 2007, 481
Peretz, I., 191
Pérez, N., 357
Perez Izquierdo, M. A., 337
Pérez-Samartin, A., 496
Perfiliev, S., 138
Perge, J. A., 31
Peri, T., 377
Perkins, R., 220
Perlbarg, V., 277
Perlik, A. J., 418
Perlow, M. J., 254
Perls, T., 112
Perot, P., 412
Perozzo, P., 166
Perrachione, T. K., 443
Perrett, D. I., 334
Perrin, F., 286
Perrone, J. A., 181
Perry, G., 285
Perry, R. J., 429
Perry, S. H., 158
Persky, H., 333
Persson, J., 132
Pert, C., 205
Pert, C. B., 55
Peru, A., 455
Pesenti, S., 445
Pesold, C., 378
Peteanu, L. A., 153
Peters, A. J., 167
Peters, F., 475
Peters, J.-M., 238, 278
Peters, R. H., 316
Peters, R. M., 199
Petersen, D., 181
Petersen, E. T., 207
Peterson, C. K., 367, 368
Peterson, E. W., 246, 255
Peterson, L. R., 396
Peterson, M. A., 329
Peterson, M. J., 396
Peterson, R. E., 345
Petersson, K. M., 206
Petiau, C., 286
Petit, D., 277
Petit, L., 429, 431
Petitto, L. A., 435, 441, 442
Petkova, V. I., 87
Petrides, G., 481
Petrie, M., 218
Petrovic, P., 206
Petterson, L. J., 347
Pettigrew, J. D., 150
Pezzoli, G., 253
Pfaffmann, C., 214
Pfaus, J. G., 467
Pfefferbaum, A., 492
Pfefferle, A. D., 111
Pfeiffer, B. E., 402
Pfister-Genskow, M., 287
Pham, M. D., 243
Phan, K.L., 360
Phelps, E. A., 379, 460
Phelps, I. G., 500
Phelps, M. E., 92, 482
Philip, P., 265
Phillips, A. G., 467
Phillips, B., 294
Phillips, C., 286
Phillips, N. H., 284
Phillips, R., 374
Philpot, B. D., 500
Phuong, L., 407
Piazza, M., 83
Picardi, P. K., 313
Picasso, L., 407
Picciotto, M. R., 311
Pickard, J. D., 136, 453
Pickenhagen, A., 478
Pieczyk, M., 112
Pierce, S. B., 490
Pierson, D. L., 386
Pierson, R., 493
Piet, R., 56
Pieters, T., 403
Pietiläinen, O. P. H., 107
Pietrini, P., 239
Pietropaolo, S., 126
Pihlstrom, L., 253
Pilkonis, P. A., 480
Pillard, R. C., 346, 347
Pilon, M., 281
Pimentel, G. D., 313
Pine, D. S., 374
Pinel, P., 83
Pinker, S., 439, 441
Pinkston, J. W., 131
Pinsker, H., 414, 415
Pintado, C. O., 123
Pinto, L., 20
Piomelli, D., 310
Piper, J. C., 490
Piras, F., 493
Piruat, J. I., 123
Pisapia, D. J., 329, 349
Pissard, S., 343
Pitman, R. K., 377, 379
Pizzagalli, D. A., 467, 476
Pizzella, V., 203
Pizzorusso, T., 171
Pjrek, E., 483
Placentino, A., 373
Plailly, J., 219
Platt, M. L., 460
Pliatsikas, C., 440
Plihal, W., 288
Pliskin, N. H., 492
Plomin, R, 109
Plomin, R., 109
Plomp, J. J., 123
Ploner, M., 202
Plonsky, I., 53
Plotkin, A., 219
Plutchik, R., 356
Podd, M. H., 492
Poduslo, S. E., 112
Poeppel, D., 193, 441
Pogorzala, L. A., 199
Pol, H. E. H., 98, 132, 492, 495
Poland, R. E., 469
Polansky, M., 138
Poldrack, R. A., 246, 407
Poline, J.-B., 450
Polis, S., 376
Politi, P., 373
Polk, T. A., 454
Pollack, M. H., 451
Pollema, S. L., 256
Polsky, A., 45
Pommer, 288
Poncer, J. C., 418
Pons, T. P., 140
Pontieri, F. E., 54
Poo, M., 418
Poole, J. C., 205
Pope, H. G., Jr., 319, 476
Popkin, B. M., 319
Porcer, C., 418
Poremba, A., 192
Porritt, M. J., 119
Porta, M., 376
Porter, J., 217
Posel, B., 113
Posner, M. I., 16
Posner, S. F., 109
Post, R. M., 475
Posthuma, D., 132
Potegal, M., 367
Pothos, E., 320

Pothos, E. N., 317
Pottackal, J., 407
Potter, G. B., 500
Potter, M. C., 126
Poulin, M., 383
Poulin, M. J., 460
Poulton, R., 370, 476
Poulton, W., 139
Povinelli, D. J., 113, 460
Powell, C., 204
Powell, L. H., 319
Power, R. A., 476
Powers, K. L., 454
Prakash, A., 469
Prakash, R. S., 132
Pramstaller, P. P., 266
Prasad, S., 166
Praschak-Rider, N., 483
Prastawa, M. W., 98
Preckel, F., 266
Premack, A. J., 435
Premack, D., 435
Prescott, A. T., 90, 408
Prescott, C. A., 476
Prescott, E. D., 207
Preskorn, S. H., 477, 478
Press, G. A., 243
Pressman, S. D., 358
Preti, G., 220
Preul, C., 142
Pribram, K. H., 238
Price, C. J., 95, 128, 316, 440, 444
Price, D. D., 203
Price, M. P., 199
Price, T. S., 109
Priftis, K., 455
Printz, D., 494
Pritchard, T. C., 214
Privado, J., 129
Privman, E., 450
Proenca, R., 312
Prom-Wormley, E., 370
Proserpio, P., 277
Provine, R. R., 117, 232, 233
Prud'homme, J.-F., 426
Pruessner, J. C., 107
Prull, M. W., 397
Prutkin, J., 215
Ptacek, L. J., 269
Ptácek, L. J., 269
Ptak, R., 404
Puca, A. A., 112
Puche, A. C., 220
Pudas, S., 132
Puhl, M. D., 467
Purcell, D. W., 348
Purnell, J. Q., 318
Purves, D., 125, 126, 153, 156, 157, 158, 167, 443
Purves, H. R., 167
Putnam, S. K., 331
Putz, E., 429
Pylkkännen, L., 441
Pytel, K. A., 256
Pytte, C., 286

Queen, T. L., 132
Quinn, N. P., 495
Quiroga, M. A., 97, 129
Quitkin, F. M., 478
Quitlein, F., 479

Rabe-Hesketh, S., 492
Rabin, B. S., 386
Rabinowitz, D., 312
Race, E., 400, 407
Race, E. A., 397
Rada, P., 320
Rada, P. V., 320
Rader, D., 319
Radoeva, P. D., 166
Radtke, R. A., 280
Rae, C. D., 207
Rae, D. S., 475
Raghavachari, S., 52, 418
Ragsdale, D. S., 31
Raguse, J.-D., 214
Rahman, Q., 346, 347, 348
Rai, S. S., 480
Raichle, M. E., 127
Rainer, G., 397
Rainville, P., 203
Raio, C. M., 379
Raj, A., 108
Raja, S., 207
Rajaram, E., 396
Rajaram, S., 398
Rajaratnam, S. M. W., 268
Rajarethinam, R., 493
Rajeevan, N., 95
Rakic, P., 118, 171
Ralph, M. A. L., 407
Ralph, M. R., 267
Ramachandran, V. S., 141, 221
Ramachandrappa, S., 314
Ramagopalan, S. V., 347
Ramanathan, L., 280
Ramirez, J. J., 139
Ramírez, Y., 153
Ramot, M., 450
Ranciaro, A., 308
Randall, P. K., 316
Randler, C., 266
Rando, T. A., 132
Rangarajan, V., 180
Raniszewska, K., 55
Ransley, P. G., 345
Ranson, S. W., 81
Rantamäki, T., 478
Rao, Y., 314
Rao-Ruiz, P., 379
Rapoport, S., 45
Rapoport, S. I., 22, 483
Rapp, B., 432
Rapp, P. R., 334, 397
Rapp, S. R., 419
Rasch, B., 288
Raschle, N. M., 444
Rasmussen, C., 124
Rasmussen, T., 83, 237
Ratcliff, M., 267
Rattenborg, N. C., 277, 285
Rau, H., 130
Raubeson, M. J., 500
Rauch, S. L., 373, 374
Raum, W. J., 329
Rauschecker, A. M., 182
Rauschecker, J., 441
Rauschecker, J. P., 192
Rauskolb, S., 123
Rawlings, N. B., 454
Rawlings, R., 369, 469, 491
Raymont, V., 377
Rebok, G. W., 419
Rector, D. M., 277
Redish, A. D., 287
Redmon, J. B., 329, 331
Redmond, D. E., Jr., 254
Redondo, R. L., 418
Reed, D. R., 215, 216
Reed, F. A., 308
Reed, F. D. D., 500
Rees, G., 368
Reese, T. S., 417
Reeve, R., 350
Reeves, A. G.; Plum, 316
Reeves, J. M., 207
Refinetti, R., 264, 267, 296
Regan, T., 10
Regehr, W. G., 56
Reggers, J., 286
Regier, D. A., 475
Rehavi, M., 492
Reich, M. J., 316
Reichelt, K. L., 488
Reichelt, W. H., 488
Reick, M., 269
Reid, C. A., 418
Reid, R. C., 166
Reilly, K. T., 237
Reilly, T. J., 493
Reimann, F., 204
Reimers, J. M., 468
Reiner, W. G., 344–345
Reinius, B., 334
Reis, D. J., 372
Reisert, I., 327
Reisner, A. D., 480
Reiss, A. L., 439
Reitboeck, H. J., 450
Reith, M. E. A., 55
Remington, G., 496
Ren, M., 483
Ren, X., 336, 337
Renault, B., 451, 452
Renger, J. J., 275
Rennaker, R. L., 219
Rensch, B., 4
Rensink, R. A., 454
Renthal, W., 107, 386, 468
Renzi, A., 303
Repp, A. B., 167
Resko, J. A., 350
Ressler, K. J., 374
Ressler, R., 477
Restrepo, C. E., 51–52
Reumers, J., 490
Reunanen, A., 253, 489
Reutens, D. C., 127, 407, 439
Reuter-Lorenz, P., 362
Reuter-Lorenz, P. A., 428
Revusky, S., 471
Rex, D. E., 98
Rex-Haffner, M., 107
Rey, F. E., 319
Reyes, P., 450
Reyna, V. F., 131
Reynolds, C. F., III, 480
Reynolds, C. P., 385
Reynolds, J. N. J., 124
Reynolds, J. R., 239
Reynoso, J. T., 468
Reznikov, A. G., 348
Rhee, S. H., 370
Rhees, R. W., 329
Rhodes, J. S., 126
Rhyu, I. J., 241
Riad, J. K., 368
Ribchester, T. R., 489
Riby, D. M., 438–439
Riby, L. M., 438–439
Ricciardi, A., 478
Ricciardi, E., 239
Rice, F. L., 199
Rice, G., 347
Rice, G. P., 347
Rice, W. R., 347
Richard, C., 455
Richard, N., 237
Richards, K., 141
Richardson, A. S., 113, 460
Richardson, G. S., 264
Richardson, M. A., 480
Richardson, S. P., 130
Richmond, B. S., 468
Richter, C., 262, 266, 267
Richter, C. A., 329
Richter, C. P., 187, 304
Richter, F., 496
Rickard, T. C., 286
Ricken, J., 266
Ridaura, V. K., 319
Riddick, N. V., 369
Ridding, M. C., 481
Rieger, G., 346, 347, 348
Riel, E., 264
Riemann, D., 482
Rieske, R. D., 500
Rietveld, C. A., 109
Rifkin, S. A., 108
Righetti, L., 310
Rigoni, D., 248
Rijpkema, M., 373
Riley, B., 469
Rilling, J. K., 337
Rimol, L. M., 493
Rinberg, D., 216
Rinehart, N. J., 459
Ringach, D., 11
Ringkamp, M., 207
Rinn, W. E., 235
Rintoul, J. L., 454
Riolo, J. V., 467
Risch, N., 215, 347
Risi, M. M., 252
Rissanen, H., 253
Ritchie, J. M., 34
Rittenhouse, C. D., 171
Ritz, B., 253
Ritz-deCecco, A., 264
Rivadeneira, F., 105
Riva-Posse, P., 482
Riviere, D., 450
Rizzi, G., 314, 372
Rizzo, M., 441
Rizzolatti, G., 7, 238, 238–239
Ro, T., 222
Roane, B. M., 481
Roback, P., 478
Robbins, T. W., 276, 469
Roberson, D. P., 208
Roberts, E., 204
Roberts, J. A., 397
Roberts, K. C., 93
Roberts, L. E., 193
Roberts, M. P., Jr., 367
Roberts, N., 443
Roberts, R. D., 266
Roberts, S. C., 217, 218
Roberts, T., 444
Robertson, I. H., 86
Robertson, K., 379
Robertson, M., 469
Robinet, C., 371
Robins, L. N., 475
Robinson, B. M., 488
Robinson, D., 98
Robinson, J. F., 490
Robinson, M. J. F., 304
Robinson, P. J., 22
Robinson, T. E., 468
Robison, S., 367
Robson, V. K., 208
Rocca, W. A., 253
Rochefort, N. L., 192
Rochira, V., 329
Rockstroh, B., 128, 130
Roddenberry, D., 401
Roddey, J. C., 153
Rodenberg, C. A., 333
Rodenhiser, J., 494
Roder, B., 127

Röder, B., 86
Rodgers, D. A., 461
Rodman, H. R., 167
Rodriguez, E., 450
Rodríguez, F., 198
Rodriguez, I., 220
Rodriguez-Fornells, A., 379
Rodriguez-Oroz, C., 253
Roe, A. W., 177, 202
Roe, D., 440
Roe, R. W., 181
Roelfsema, P. R., 275
Roeling, T. A. P., 138
Roelofs, K., 373
Roenneberg, T., 264, 265, 266
Roesch, M. R., 468
Roeser, K., 266
Roffman, J. L., 374, 492
Roffwarg, H. P., 287
Rogell, B., 111
Rogers, J., 373
Rogers, R. D., 247, 248
Rogers, T. T., 407
Rogers, W., 280
Rogerson, T., 418
Rohde, P., 475
Roitman, M. F., 467
Roizman, S., 220
Rojas, L. M., 153
Rokers, B., 181
Roland, P. E., 275
Rolls, A., 139
Rolls, E. T., 92, 215, 316, 364, 402
Román, F. J., 129
Romani, G. L., 203
Romano, A., 310
Romanovsky, A. A., 384
Romberg, C., 119
Rome, L. C., 230
Romeo, E., 333
Romeo, R. D., 348
Romer, A. S., 120
Romero, A., 314
Romero, E., 256
Rommel, S. A., 297, 299
Romundstad, P., 318
Ron, D., 468
Ron, S., 419
Ronda, J. M., 264, 265
Roney, J. R., 333
Rönnback, L., 22
Ronnekleiv, O. K., 107
Roorda, A., 152, 154, 155
Root, C. M., 50
Roozendaal, B., 397, 419
Roper, S. D., 53, 213
Roppel, R. M., 489
Rorden, C., 456
Rosamond, W. D., 137
Rosano, C., 127
Rosanova, M., 453
Rosbash, M., 268
Rose, F. E., 439
Rose, J. E., 54, 190
Rose, R. J., 470
Roselli, C. E., 350
Rosen, A. C., 397
Rosen, B. R., 181
Rosen, G. D., 444
Rosen, G. J., 334
Rosen, H. J., 429
Rosen, T. A., 207
Rosen, T. J., 142
Rosenbaum, R. S., 400, 401
Rosenberg, K., 374
Rosenblatt, J. S., 336, 337
Rosene, D. L., 401
Rosenkranz, K., 130
Rosenthal, M. C., 407
Rosenzweig, M. R., 125
Roska, B., 90
Ross, D., 443
Ross, E. D., 430
Ross, G. W., 253
Ross, J., 183
Ross, R.J., 277
Rossi, A. F., 454
Rossi, D. J., 136
Rossi, E. A., 152
Rossi, R., 230
Rossi, S., 397
Rossini, P. M., 203, 397
Rossion, B., 180
Rosssetti, A. O., 273
Rotaru, D. C., 379
Roth, B. L., 496
Roth, C., 500
Roth, H. P., 471
Roth, Y., 219
Rothwell, J. C., 130, 481
Rothwell, P. E., 385
Rotrosen, J., 492
Rotshtein, P., 398
Rottenberg, J., 475
Rousseaux, M., 455
Roussin, A. T., 215
Routtenberg, A., 315, 418, 419
Rouw, R., 221
Rovainen, C. M., 139
Rowe, C. C., 406
Rowland, D. L., 332, 334
Roy, A., 369
Roy, M., 478
Roy, S., 277
Royall, R., 480
Royer, S., 415
Rozin, P., 304, 308, 392, 398
Rubens, A. B., 179
Rubens, M. T., 85
Rubenstein, J. L., 489
Rubin, B. D., 218
Rubin, N., 238
Rubino, I. A., 492
Rubinow, M. J., 295
Rubinstein, G., 489
Ruch, K., 139
Ruddock, K. H, 156
Rudebeck, P. H., 90, 408
Ruderman, Y., 376
Rudolph, U., 378
Rudorfer, M. V., 481
Rudoy, J. D., 286
Rudrauf, D., 408
Ruediger, S., 418
Ruff, C. C., 460
Ruffino, M., 444
Rugg, M. D., 92
Ruhf, A., 304
Rujescu, D., 107
Rumbaugh, D. M., 111, 435, 436, 437
Rupp, A., 127, 192
Rupprecht, R., 333
Rusak, B., 264
Ruschel, J., 139
Rush, A. J, 477
Rush, A. J., 479, 480
Rushby, J. A., 362
Rushworth, M. F. S., 85
Rusinek, H., 492
Russell, J. A., 361
Russell, J. L., 431
Russell, M. J., 220
Russo, N. M., 128
Russo, S. J., 386, 468, 475
Rust, J., 330, 331
Rustioni, V., 277
Rüter, J., 178
Rütiger, L., 155
Rutledge, J. N., 98
Rutstein, J., 299
Ruttenber, A. J., 253
Rüttiger, L., 181
Ruyle, A. M., 219
Ryan, J., 444
Ryan, L., 476
Ryba, N. J. P., 212, 214, 215
Ryge, J., 51–52
Ryman, D., 263

Saad, W. A., 303
Sääksjärvi, K., 253
Saarma, M., 123
Sabatinelli, D., 467
Sabatini, B. L., 51, 253
Sabatti, C., 490
Sabb, F. W., 246
Sabel, B. A., 140
Sabo, K. T., 83
Sacchetti, B., 418
Sacchetti, E., 493
Sack, R. L., 264
Sackeim, H. A., 429
Sacks, O., 180
Sacktor, T. C., 419
Sadato, N., 127
Sadri-Vakili, G., 107
Saetre, P., 334
Sagaspe, P., 265
Sage, J., 407
Sage, J. R., 286
Sage, M., 269
Sagi, D., 450
Sah, P., 374
Saha, S., 299
Sahin, N. T., 441
Saigoh, N., 269
Sailer, C., 112
Saitoh, O., 71
Sakai, K., 275, 276
Sakal, R. R., 304
Sakamaki, K., 304
Sakamoto, M., 252
Sakano, H., 216, 217
Sakmann, B., 42
Sakurai, T., 275, 280
Saladin, M. E., 472
Salas, R., 314
Salazar, R. F., 397
Sale, A., 478
Salehpour, M., 119
Salimpoor, V. N., 467
Salisbury, D. F., 492
Salmelin, R., 91
Salorio, C. F., 136
Salthouse, T. A., 126
Saltin, B., 230
Salvi, R. J., 193
Salz, T., 444
Salzman, C. D., 376
Samad, O. A., 208
Samejima, K., 246
Sampson, P. D., 469
Sams, M., 86, 91, 128
Samuels, A., 435
Samuels, B., 319
Sanabria, F., 384
Sanacora, G., 478
Sánchez, M., 357
Sanchez-Alavez, M., 299
Sander, K., 429
Sanders, A. R., 347, 348
Sanders, M. D., 166
Sanders, R. J., 435
Sanders, S. J., 500
Sanders, S. K., 378
Sanderson, D. J., 403
Sandkühler, J., 207
Sandkuler, J., 207
Sandnabba, N. K., 346, 347
Sandrini, M., 90
Sanes, J. N., 235
Sanes, J. R., 120, 132
Sanfey, A. G., 459
Sanfilipo, M., 492
Sanford, L. D., 277
Sanger, T. D., 130
Sani, L., 239
Sankilampi, U., 331
Sann, S. B., 50
Santarelli, L., 119
Santi, R. M., 377
Santos, R. A. S., 137
Santtila, P., 346, 347
Sanyal, S., 268
Saper, C. B., 268, 298, 384
Sapienza, P., 98
Sapolsky, R., 383
Sapolsky, R. M., 386
Saporito, M., 253
Sara, S. J., 287
Saraiva, L. R., 219
Sarasso, S., 453
Sarria, M. S. B., 461
Sarris, J., 419, 478
Sarter, M., 264
Sartori, G., 248
Sartori, I., 277
Sasaki, M., 294
Saslow, L. R., 373
Sastre, J.-P., 275
Satinoff, E., 295, 299
Sato, M., 171
Sato, S., 331
Satoh, K., 284
Saturn, S. R., 373
Satz, P., 492
Saunders, B. T., 468
Saunders, R. C., 90, 167, 192, 408
Savage-Rumbaugh, E. S., 111, 436, 437
Savergnini, S. Q., 137
Savic, I., 220, 349
Savion-Lemieux, T., 128
Savitz, A. T., 275
Savoie, T., 493
Sawa, A., 386, 490
Sawaguchi, T., 397
Saxe, M., 119
Saxe, R., 127
Saxena, S., 480
Scaccianoce, S., 478
Scalora, M., 374
Scammell, T. E., 280, 384
Schäbitz, W. R., 138
Schäbitz, W.-R., 137
Schabus, M., 277
Schacher, S., 415
Schacter, D. L., 400, 401, 404, 492
Schaefer, C. A., 491
Schaefer, H. S., 386, 468
Schaeffer, M.A., 385
Schal, C., 325
Schalling, D., 369
Schapira, A. H. V., 255
Schapiro, S. J., 113, 460
Scharb, A. A., 266
Scharf, M. B., 279
Schauder, K. B., 500
Scheele, D., 159
Scheer, F. A. J. L., 263
Scheibel, A. B., 118, 405
Scheich, H., 429
Scheinin, H., 453

Schenk, T., 178, 182
Schenker, N., 84, 192
Scherer, S. S., 139
Scherg, M., 127, 192
Scherr, P. A., 404
Scherrer, G., 205
Schetter, S. P., 401
Scheuer, T., 31
Schiffman, S. S., 187, 213, 214
Schiller, D., 379
Schiller, J., 45
Schinder, A. F., 119
Schindler, D. E., 307
Schlack, A., 181
Schlaug, G., 128, 130, 191
Schlerf, J., 242
Schlinger, H. D., Jr., 114
Schmid, A., 371
Schmid, M. C., 167
Schmidt, H. D., 107
Schmidt, L. A., 362, 373
Schmidt, O. G., 326
Schmidt, R., 238
Schmidt-Hieber, C., 119
Schmidtke, J., 369
Schmidtmann, M., 310
Schmitt, J. A. J., 309
Schmitt, K. C., 55
Schmitt, L. I., 482
Schmitz, S., 349
Schnack, H. G., 132
Schneider, B. A., 188
Schneider, G. E., 139
Schneider, H., 137
Schneider, J., 212
Schneider, P., 127
Schneider, R., 138
Schneider, S., 266
Schnider, A., 404
Schnitzler, A., 202
Schnitzler, H.-U., 371
Schnyder, U., 385
Schobel, S. A., 492
Schoenbaum, G., 468
Schoenlein, R. W., 153
Schoevers, R., 480
Schoffelen, J.-M., 450
Scholey, A., 478
Scholey, A. B., 419
Scholte, H. S., 170, 221
Schomacher, M., 137, 138
Schomer, D., 441
Schomers, M. R., 246
Schönfeld, R., 403
Schönle, P., 181
Schoomer, E. E., 269
Schoppman, A., 140
Schorer, A., 453
Schotland, P., 268
Schou, M., 483
Schroeder, C. E., 193, 488
Schroeder, D. H., 97
Schroeder, J. A., 213
Schroeder, J. P., 467
Schroff, C., 266
Schröter, M. S., 453
Schroth, J., 500
Schubert, M., 130
Schuckit, M. A., 471
Schuff, N., 429
Schuierer, G., 129
Schulkin, J., 304, 373
Schull, J., 392
Schull, W. J., 318
Schulman, H., 417, 418
Schulsinger, F., 318
Schultz, R., 98
Schultz, W., 246
Schulz, K. M., 328
Schulze-Bonhage, A., 402
Schumann, C. M., 500
Schumm-Draeger, P. M., 269
Schunk, D., 460
Schutter, D. J., 335
Schutter, D. J. L. G., 335
Schwab, M. E., 138, 139
Schwab, S., 137, 138
Schwartz, A. B., 235
Schwartz, B. A., 205
Schwartz, C. E., 373
Schwartz, G., 347, 348
Schwartz, G. J., 310
Schwartz, J. H., 415
Schwartz, J. M., 482
Schwartz, L., 471
Schwartz, M., 139, 312, 346
Schwartz, M. F., 238
Schwartz, R. D., 378
Schwartz, W. J., 267
Schwarz, I., 403
Schwarz, M., 478
Schwarzenbacher, K., 220
Schweinhardt, P., 205
Schweitzer, I., 478
Schwenker, J., 320
Schwiecker, K., 86
Schwob, J. E., 220
Scoboria, A., 479
Scognamiglio, P., 320
Scott, D. J., 206
Scott, E. M., 500
Scott, S H., 237
Scott, S. K., 128, 444
Scoville, W. B., 398
Scully, P. J., 488
Seal, R. P., 207
Sealfon, S. C., 495
Sebe, J. Y., 123
Seckl, J. R., 107, 331
Sedvall, G., 254
Seeck, M., 192
Seeherman, K. R., 238
Seeley, J. R., 475
Seeley, R. J., 310
Seeman, P., 494, 496
Seery, M. D., 386
Seessau, M., 238
Segal, N. L., 108
Segerstrom, S. C., 385
Seghier, M. L., 180, 444
Sehgal, A., 268, 269
Seid, M. A., 97
Seider, B. H., 373
Seidman, L. J., 335, 468
Seif, T., 468
Seiger, A., 254
Seim, A. R., 488
Seitz, K. S., 426
Sejnowski, T. J., 284
Sekeres, M., 403
Sekihara, K., 492
Sekine, Y., 252
Sela, L., 374
Selimbeyoglu, A., 182
Selin, C. E., 482
Selkoe, D. J., 404
Selten, J. P., 489
Selye, H., 383
Selzer, M. E., 139
Semendeferi, K., 84
Semin, G. R., 217, 239
Seminowicz, D. A., 205, 207
Semjen, A., 426
Semrud-Clikeman, M, 444
Sen, S., 476, 478
Senghas, A., 358
Sens, E., 142
Sensenig, L. D., 316
Serabjit-Singh, C. J., 478
Sereno, A. B., 489
Sergent, C., 452, 453
Serrano, P., 418, 419
Serritella, C., 320
Servin, A., 344
Seshadri, S., 386, 490
Sethi, J., 299
Settle, R. G., 220
Sevcik, R. A., 436, 437
Sevenster, D., 379
Seyfarth, R. M., 368, 386, 435
Seymour, B., 203, 206
Shackman, A. J., 362
Shadmehr, R., 254
Shadwick, R. E., 296
Shah, B., 294
Shah, N. M., 329, 349
Shaham, Y., 467, 468
Shakelford, T. K., 342
Shakeshaft, C., 95
Shakhnarovich, G., 235
Shalev, A. Y., 377
Shalev, L., 454
Shalvi, S., 459
Shamin, E. A., 130
Shammi, C. S., 496
Shane, M. S., 95
Shank, C. V., 153
Shapiro, C. M., 284
Shapiro, E., 367
Shapiro, R. E., 269
Sharbaugh, S. M., 307
Sharma, J., 124
Sharma, R. P., 369
Sharma, S., 107
Sharpe, L. T., 181
Shattuck, D. W., 98
Shatz, C. J., 121, 122, 125, 171
Shaughnessy, M. F., 136
Shaw, D. J., 239
Shea, S. D., 219
Shea-Drinkwater, M., 112
Shechter, R., 139
Shedden, K., 476
Shekhar, A., 378
Shelton, K. H., 370
Shelton, R. C., 478
Shelton, S. E., 373
Shema, R., 419
Shen, H., 254, 376
Shen, W., 500
Shen, Y., 314
Shendure, J., 500
Shenton, M. E., 377, 492
Sher, L., 369
Sherk, H., 172
Sherman, G. F., 444
Sherrington, C., 16, 40–42, 43–44, 48, 51, 52
Shi, L., 55
Shi, X. L., 318
Shield, J., 308, 309
Shields, S., 207
Shiflett, M. W., 119
Shih, P. C., 97
Shih, R. A., 475
Shima, K., 238
Shimizu, T., 284
Shimojo, S., 156
Shimpi, A., 156, 157
Shin, L. M., 373
Shine, R., 294
Shipley, M. T., 220
Shipp, S., 177
Shiv, B., 364
Shizgal, P., 467
Shoaf, S. E., 369
Shobe, J., 418
Shohamy, D., 407
Shore, A. B., 215
Shore, S. E., 193
Shors, T. J., 386
Shoulson, I., 255
Shouval, H. Z., 171
Shrager, Y., 399
Shryne, J. E., 329
Shryne, J. H., 329
Shubin, N., 7
Shucksmith, J., 308, 309
Shuman, T., 286
Shumansky, K., 444
Shushan, S., 219
Shusta, E. V., 22
Shutts, D., 85
Sia, G. M., 439
Siamouli, M., 479
Sibhatu, H. M., 214
Siddiqi, F., 220
Siebert, E. R., 330
Siebert, M., 375
Siegel, E.H., 451
Siegel, H. I., 336
Siegel, J. M., 280, 284, 285, 287
Siegel, S., 468, 472
Siegelbaum, S. A., 418
Siever, L. J., 489
Sigal, Y. M., 199
Sigmund, K., 113
Sigmundson, H. K., 345, 346
Silber, B. Y., 309
Silber, M. H., 281
Silberstein, S. D, 475
Silipo, G., 495
Silk, J. B., 113, 460
Silva, A. J., 418
Silva, V. R. R., 313
Silver, R. A., 45
Silver, R. C., 383
Silverman, J. M., 489
Silverman, J. S., 308
Sima, J., 500
Simard, A., 137
Simeon, D., 460
Simeral, J. D., 235
Simerly, R. B., 334
Simion, F., 180
Simmons, A. M., 187
Simmons, Z. L., 333
Simms, J. A., 468
Simner, J., 221
Simon, B., 114
Simon, N. M., 451
Simon, S. A., 304
Simoncelli, E. P., 178
Simonds, S. E., 313
Simone, D. A., 208
Simone, L., 7
Simpson, E. H., 494
Simpson, J. A., 334, 341
Simpson, J. B., 304
Sims, K., 439
Sincich, L. C., 183
Sing, H. C., 262
Singer, T., 203, 459
Singer, W., 275, 450
Singh, H., 277
Singh, S., 279
Singh, S. M., 124
Singh, T., 468
Singh, V., 93
Singleton, J., 439
Sinha, M. K., 313
Sinha, P., 173

Sinigaglia, C., 238
Sinkkonen, S. T., 378
Sinton, C. M., 280
Sirigu, A., 202, 237
Sirotin, Y. B., 92
Sisk, C. L., 328
Sisodia, S., 404
Sitomer, M. T., 386
Sjöström, M., 230
Skachokova, Z. K., 369
Skaredoff, L., 367
Skene, D. J., 264
Skinner, K., 207
Skinner, M. D., 468
Skitzki, J. J., 299
Skoe, E., 128, 193
Skolnick, P., 378
Skoner, D. P., 386
Slachevsky, A., 450
Slagter, H. A., 454
Slater, P. J. B., 7
Slavich, G. M., 107
Sloan, A. M., 219
Sloan, D. M., 475
Slob, A. K., 334
Slobodskaya, H. R., 362
Sluming, V., 443
Small, S. A., 492
Smallman, H. S., 173
Smania, N., 141, 455
Smart, T. G., 52
Smedh, C., 483
Smeets, M. A. M., 217
Smeltzer, M. D., 303
Smidts, A., 459
Smielewski, P., 136
Smith, A. B., 379
Smith, A. M., 199
Smith, C. D., 440
Smith, C. L., 331
Smith, C. T., 287
Smith, D. E., 397
Smith, E. E., 204, 454
Smith, F. J., 312
Smith, G. P., 310
Smith, J. C., 141
Smith, K., 489
Smith, K. B., 374
Smith, L. M., 124
Smith, L. T., 413
Smith, M., 241
Smith, M. A., 254, 285
Smith, M. J., 426
Smith, M .J. L., 357
Smith, M. R., 454
Smith, P. J., 127
Smith, R. L., 316
Smith, S. J., 54, 121
Smith, S. S., 376
Smith, T. L., 471
Smolen, A., 468, 469
Smoller, J. W., 374
Smulders, T. V., 119
Snaedal, J., 405
Snitz, B. E., 419
Snowling, M., 444
Snyder, A. Z., 127
Snyder, D., 476
Snyder, E. Y., 254
Snyder, L. H., 237
Snyder, S., 205
Snyder, S. G., 279
Snyder, S. H., 55
So, K.-F., 139
Sobel, N., 217, 219, 220, 431
Soczynska, J. K., 318, 331, 332
Soden, M. E., 314
Södersten, P., 335
Soeter, M., 379
Sohrabi, H., 406
Sokoloff, L., 192
Solana, A. B., 129
Solms, M., 274, 288, 404
Solomon, J., 377
Solomon, M. B., 303
Solomon, S. G., 155
Soltani, A., 85
Soltesz, I., 56
Solway, A., 402
Somel, M., 439
Somjen, G. G., 19
Sommer, C., 137, 138
Sommerville, R. B., 363
Song, H., 119, 417, 490
Song, J. H., 193
Song, P., 480
Soni, B., 268
Soon, C. S., 248
Sorensen, T. I. A., 318
Sorri, A., 490
Sossi, V., 254
Sossin, W. S., 418
Southwell, D. G., 123
Southwick, S. M., 371, 386
Sowell, E. R., 123
Spalding, K. L., 119
Spalletta, G., 492, 493
Spanagel, R., 468
Spangler, R., 320
Spanjers, K., 480
Spear, L. P., 131
Spear, N. E., 469
Specht, H. J., 127
Spector, T., 347
Spector, T. D., 105
Speer, N. K., 239
Spelke, E. S., 98
Spence, J. S., 419
Spencer, M. H., 492
Spencer, R. M. C., 241
Spencer-Segal, J. L., 334
Sperandie, I., 166
Sperling, A. J., 119
Sperling, K., 180
Sperry, L., 376
Sperry, R., 120, 426
Sperry, R. W., 428
Spezio, M. L., 376
Spiegel, T. A., 310
Spijker, S., 379
Spindler, K. A., 492
Spineli, L., 496
Spinelli, D., 445
Spinelli, S., 372
Spiro, A. III, 112
Spitzer, N. C., 50, 52
Spoletini, I., 492
Spoormaker, V. I., 453
Spotts, J. L., 279
Sprague, J. M., 208
Sprengel, R., 403
Spreux-Varoquaux, O., 369
Springell, K., 204
Spurzheim, J. G., 94
Squire, L. R., 399, 401, 404, 407
Squires, T. M., 198
St. George, M., 438, 439
St. George-Hyslop, P. H., 405
St. Jacques, P. L., 386
Staal, F. J. T., 483
Stadelman, H., 350
Staehler, F., 214
Staggs, D., 166
Stahl, B. H., 490
Stahlhut, C., 452
Stallen, M., 459
Stalnaker, T. A., 468
Stam, C. J., 492
Stamatakis, A. M., 314, 372
Stamatakis, E. A., 429
Stambaugh, C. R., 83
Stanaway, I. B., 500
Stanek, L. M., 256
Stanford, L. R., 26
Stanley, J., 246
Starbuck, E. M., 304
Stark, J., 207
Stark-Adamec, C., 367
Starr, C., 58, 59, 229, 327
State, M. W., 500
Statham, D. J., 476
Steele, C. J., 128
Steensma, T. D., 345
Stefanacci, L., 401
Stefansson, H., 107, 490
Stefansson, K., 107, 405, 500
Steffens, B., 148
Stehle, J. H., 269
Steier, P., 119
Stein, D. G., 136
Stein, M. B., 377
Steinberg, L., 131
Steinberg, S., 107, 405
Steinecke, A., 490
Steinhoff, B. J., 375
Steinmetz, A. B., 395
Steinmetz, H., 98
Stellflug, J. N., 350
Stengel, A., 310
Stephan, K. E., 237
Stephens, T. W., 313, 314
Stepper, S., 358
Stergiopulos, N., 137
Sterling, P., 31, 295
Stern, O., 374
Stern, W. E., 316
Sterpenich, V., 275, 407
Sterr, A., 130
Stevens, B. L., 206
Stevens, C. F., 119, 153
Stevens, J. K., 19
Stevens, J. S., 374
Stevens, M., 154
Stevenson, R. J., 214, 385, 424
Steward, O., 402
Stewart, H., 172
Stewart, J. W., 478, 479
Stewart, L., 191
Stewart, L. H., 95
Stickgold, R., 288, 401
Stiedl, O., 379
Stimmelmayr, R., 285
Stoerig, P., 167
Stoessl, A. J., 254
Stoesssel, P., 480
Stoffel-Wagner, B., 459
Stohler, C. S., 206
Stokes, M., 166
Stoll, J. C., 266
Stoltenberg, C.,, 500
Stone, L. S., 207
Stone, V. E., 429
Stoop, R., 371
Stopa, E. G., 22
Storey, J. M., 297
Storey, K. B., 297
Stormshak, F., 350
Stough, C., 419, 478
Stover, J., 136
Stowe, R. P., 386
Stowell, J. R., 383
Strack, F., 358
Strata, P., 418
Straub, S. V., 20
Strausfeld, N. J., 80
Strauss, D., 333
Strauss, M. E., 475
Streissguth, A. P., 469
Strengman, E., 490
Stricker, E., 316
Stricker, E. M., 299, 303, 304, 312, 315
Striemer, C. L., 166
Striepens, N., 459
Stringer, R. L., 124
Strittmatter, W. J., 256
Strobel, C., 374
Stroebele, N., 319
Ströhle, A., 333
Strotmann, J., 220
Stryker, M. P., 140, 171, 172
Stuber, G. D., 314, 372
Stufflebeam, S., 492
Stuht, J., 319
Stumvoll, M., 318
Stunkard, A. J., 318
Stuss, D. T., 85
Stylos-Allan, M., 286
Styner, M. A., 492
Sudhof, T. C., 123
Sudi, J., 123
Sugai, T., 212
Sugden, K., 476
Suh, P.-G., 480
Sulem, P., 500
Sullivan, E. V., 142, 492
Sullivan, L., 319
Sullivan, P. F., 490
Sumida, R. M., 482
Summerbell, C. D., 308, 309
Sun, X., 220
Sun, Y.-G., 207
Sun, Z. S., 269
Sunaert, S., 181
Sunderland, T., 202
Sur, M., 83, 124, 125, 153
Surén, P., 500
Surguladze, S., 373
Susser, E. S., 491
Sutherland, B. A., 137
Sutton, B. C., 264
Sutton, L. C., 205
Sutton, R. L., 138
Suvisaari, J. M., 488
Suvisari, J., 489
Suzdak, P. D., 378
Svartdal, F., 221
Svensson, B., 111
Svoboda, K., 418
Swaab, D. F., 328, 349, 350
Swails, J., 139
Swain, R. A., 126
Swallow, D. M., 308
Swallow, K. M., 239
Swaltney, J. M., Jr., 386
Swan, S. H., 329, 331
Swann, A. C., 369
Sweatt, J. D., 417
Sweeney, J. A., 493
Swerdloff, A. F., 315
Swiergala, E., 444
Swift, J., 362
Swinson, R. P., 373
Swithers, S. E., 319
Switz, G. M., 220
Swoboda, H., 376
Sydekum, E., 138
Syken, J., 171
Syme, D.A., 296
Szabó, G., 378
Szathmari, A., 237
Szeszko, P., 98
Szuhany, K. L., 374

Szymusiak, R., 275, 276, 289

Taanman, J.-W., 255
Tabakoff, B., 378, 470
Tabarean, I. V., 299
Tabarés-Seisdedos, R., 489
Tabibnia, G., 350
Tabin, C., 7
Tabrizi, S. J., 255
Taddese, A., 205
Tadi, T., 86
Tadin, D., 500
Tagawa, Y., 171
Tager-Flusberg, H., 439
Taggart, R., 58, 59, 229, 327
Taghert, P. H., 269
Tagliatela, J. P., 111
Tahar, A. H., 286
Tai, C., 500
Tai, L.-H., 246
Taillard, J., 265
Takahashi, K., 314
Takahashi, M., 418
Takahashi, S., 275
Takahashi, T., 418
Takahashi, Y. K., 219
Takaki, M., 490
Takano, T., 20
Takao, M., 268
Takatsuru, Y., 138
Takayanagi, Y., 336
Takehara-Nishiuchi, K., 403
Takemura, H., 182
Talboom, J. S., 384
Talbot, L. S., 483
Tallal, P., 444
Tallon-Baudry, C., 453
Tamaki, M., 93
Tamietto, M., 166, 376
Tamura, R., 75, 371
Tan, K. R., 378
Tanaka, J., 304
Tanaka, J. N., 180
Tanaka, M., 320
Tanaka, T., 20
Tanaka, Y., 119, 192
Tanda, G., 54
Tandon, N., 403
Tandon, S., 304
Tang, C., 97
Tangel, D. J., 279
Tanifuji, M., 219
Tanigawa, H., 181
Tanji, J, 238
Tanji, J., 238
Tankou, S., 386
Tanner, C. M., 253
Tanskanen, A. J., 488
Tao-Cheng, J.-H., 417
Tappy, L., 319
Taravosh-Lahn, K., 369
Tarr, M. J., 181
Tarsy, D., 130
Taruno, A., 214
Tasker, R. R., 140
Tassi, L., 277
Tatsuno, M., 286
Tattersall, G. J., 294
Taub, E., 128, 130, 140, 141, 142
Taube, J. S., 402
Tavares, R., 22
Tavares, V. C., 469
Tay, D. K. C., 139
Taylor, A., 476
Taylor, A. M., 403
Taylor, A. N., 329
Taylor, C. S. R., 84, 237
Taylor, D. J., 481
Taylor, J. O., 404
Taylor, J. P., 241
Taylor, M. A., 489
Taylor, S. F., 360
Taylor-Hill, H., 444
Taziaux, M., 331
Tchernichovski, O., 286
Teasdale, T. W., 318
Tecchio, F., 203
Teff, K. L., 319
Tegeder, I., 206
Teicher, M. H., 483
Teitelbaum, P., 252, 315, 317, 367
Telang, F., 468
Telch, M. J., 373
Teng, E., 401
Teng, Y. D., 254
Tennant, K., 418
Ter Brake, O., 314
Terawawa, Y., 358
Terburg, D., 368
Terrace, H. S., 435
Terry, D., 55
Tervaniemi, M., 444
Terwilliger, E. F., 336, 337
Terwilliger, R., 131
Terzaghi, M., 277
Teschner, U., 142
Teslovich, T., 131
Tetrud, J. W., 253
Thacker, E. L., 253
Thalemann, R., 468
Thangaraj, V., 235
Thangavel, A., 85
Thannickal, T. C., 280
Thase, M. E., 477, 478, 479, 480
Thesen, T., 273
Theusch, E., 191
Thiébot, M.-H., 377
Thiel, C. M., 237
Thiele, A., 181
Thier, P., 243
Thomas, C., 129, 180, 238
Thomas, J. D., 124
Thomas, K. M., 123
Thomas, M. G., 308
Thomas, O., 167
Thompson, G. F., 489
Thompson, J. K., 395, 396
Thompson, J. L., 314
Thompson, K., 220
Thompson, P. J., 480
Thompson, P. M., 98, 123, 431
Thompson, R., 166
Thompson, R. F., 372, 394, 395, 396
Thompson, R. N., 220
Thompson, W. F., 191
Thompson, W. L., 166, 178
Thompson-Schill, S. L., 92
Thomsen, M., 467
Thorell, L. G., 170
Thornton, G., 204
Thornton, J., 330
Thorpe, L. A., 188
Tian, B., 192
Tian, G.-F., 20
Ticku, M. K., 378
Tienari, P., 490
Tiesjema, B., 314
Tiippana, K., 86
Tikkanen, R., 370
Tillman, K. A., 152
Timmann, D., 395
Timmerman, L., 202
Timms, B. G., 329
Timpson, N. J., 318
Tingate, T. R., 386
Tingergen, N., 3, 6, 11
Tippet, L. J., 455
Tiraboschi, E., 478
Tiruneh, M. A., 303
Tishkoff, S. A., 308
Tizzano, M., 214
Tobet, S., 350
Tobias, K. G., 481
Tobin, V. A., 336
Tobin, W. F., 418
Tobler, I., 285
Tocilj, A., 297
Todorov, A., 362
Toft, M., 253
Toga, A. W., 98, 123, 335, 431
Toh, K. L., 269
Toien, Ø., 284
Tokizawa, K., 296
Tokola, R., 469
Tom, S. M., 246
Tomaiuolo, F., 455
Tomasello, M., 113, 459
Tominaga, M., 207
Tomita, H., 327
Tomiyama, A. J., 319
Tomo, I., 191
Tomson, S. N., 221
Tonegawa, S., 207
Tong, F., 454
Tong, Q., 208, 314
Tonge, B. J., 459
Toni, I., 373
Toni, N., 119, 418
Tononi, G., 277, 286, 287, 288
Toomey, R., 468
Tootell, R. B. H., 181
Torchia, M., 377
Torquati, K., 203
Torquet, N., 119
Torres, D., 450
Torrey, E. F., 488, 490–491, 491
Torrey, E.F., 492
Toufexis, D., 372
Touitou, Y., 377
Touretzky, D. S., 287
Townsend, J., 71, 243
Towsley, M. L., 193
Tozawa, T., 284
Traber, R., 385
Tracy, J. L., 334
Tran, P. B., 118
Tranel, D., 358, 364, 374, 375, 376, 399, 401, 408, 429
Tränker, D., 214
Tranvel, D., 375, 400
Traurig, M., 318
Travers, S. P., 214
Trefilov, A., 369
Trehub, S. E., 188
Treisman, A., 453
Treit, D., 378
Tremblay, J., 379
Trenkle, M. K., 369
Trevena, J. A., 247
Tribby-Walbridge, S., 123
Trimble, M. R., 480
Trippel, M., 402
Tritsch, N. X., 51, 253
Trivedi, M., 480
Trivedi, M. H., 477, 479, 480
Trivedi, S., 347
Trivers, R. L., 113
Troiani, V., 193
Trope, Y,, 362
Trudel, E., 302
True, W., 476
Truong, D., 444
Tsai, W.-Y., 254
Tsankova, N., 107
Tschöp, M., 319
Tseng, K. Y., 468
Tshibanda, L., 453
Tsien, R. W., 52, 55
Ts'o, D. Y., 177
Tsuang, M. T., 335, 468, 476, 491
Tsukada, H., 138
Tsunematsu, T., 275
Tsuruda, P. R., 199
Tucker, D. M., 238
Tucker, K., 220
Tulipan, L., 471
Tulving, E., 400, 401
Tung, J. Y., 253
Tups, A., 313
Turati, C., 180
Turchi, J., 167
Turetsky, B. I., 492
Turk, D. J., 428
Turnbull, O., 404
Turner, A., 289
Turner, K. W., 269
Turner, R., 441
Turner, R. S., 244, 246
Turrigiano, G. G., 171
Turtle, M., 118
Turton, A. J., 469
Tuszynski, M. H., 397
Tuulio-Henriksson, A., 264
Twenge, J. M., 475
Tybur, J. M., 334
Tye, L. D., 243
Tye, S. J., 275
Tyers, P., 119
Tyler, L. K., 429, 439
Tyler-Kabara, E., 235
Tyszka, J. M., 375
Tzourio-Mazoyer, N., 429, 431

Uchida, I., 492
Uchida, N., 219, 246
Uchida, Y., 296
Uchigashima, M., 243
Udry, J. R., 333, 334, 346
Udwin, O., 439
Ueda, Y., 246
Uejima, J. L., 468
Uekita, T., 418
Ueno, H., 320
Ueno, M., 20
Ugale, R., 469
Uher, R., 476, 479
Uhl, G. R., 469
Ulbert, I., 273
Ulrich, R., 181
Umeda, S., 358
Umiltà, C., 455
Umiltà, M. A., 238–239
Umlauf, M., 139
Underwood, M. D., 369
Ung, R. L., 314, 372
Ungerleider, L. G., 454
Ungureanu, L., 373
Unterberg, A. W., 136
Unwin, N., 52
Uppenkamp, S., 192
Urry, H. L., 362
Uslaner, J. M., 275
U.S.–Venezuela Collaborative Research Project, 255
Utman, J. A., 441
Uwano, T., 75, 371

Vaccarino, A. L., 207
Vaccarino, F. J., 377
Vaid, G., 492
Vaid, J., 440
Vaishnavi, S., 455

Vaisse, C., 318
Valcu, M., 285
Valencia, A., 256
Valkova, C., 490
Vallbo, Å., 201
Vallejo-Illarramendi, A., 496
Vallines, I., 183
Valverde, M. A., 327
Valzelli, L., 368–369, 369, 496
van Aalst, G., 480
van Anders, S. M., 332
van Baal, G. C. M., 132
Van Bavel, J. J., 373
Van Cantfort, T. E., 435
Van de Water, J., 500
van den Berg, M., 345
van den Berg, S. M., 98
van den Bosch, I., 467
van den Bosch, J. J. F., 222
Van den Bossche, M. J. A., 490
van den Burg, E., 371
van den Heuvel, M. P., 492, 495
van den Pol, A. N., 314, 316
Van der Borght, K., 126
van der Kloet, D., 284
van der Loo, R. J., 379
van der Loos, M., 109
van der Marel, K., 138
van der Meer, M. A. A., 287
van der Voort, I. R., 310
van der Werff ten Bosch, J. J., 334
Van der Zee, E. A., 126
van der Zwan, Y. G., 345
van Dijk, G., 314
Van Dongen, A. M. J., 396
Van Dongen, H. P. A., 277
Van Dorp, C. F., 264
Van Essen, D. C., 177, 178
Van Eys, P. L., 426
van Goozen, S. H. M., 370
Van Grootel, T. J., 193
van Haren, N.E.M., 132
Van Hecke, P., 181
Van Honk, J., 335
van Honk, J., 335, 368
Van Horn, J. D., 93
van Ijzendoorn, M. H., 460
Van Lare, J., 192
van Leeuwen, M., 98
van Lieshout, D. P., 162
van Meer, M. P. A., 138
Van Opstal, A. J, 189, 195
Van Opstal, A. J., 193
van Oudenaarden, A., 108
van Praag, H., 119, 126
van Praage, H., 126
Van Wanrooij, M. M., 189, 195
Van Zoeren, J. G., 299
van Zuiden, M., 460
Vandenbeuch, A., 214
Vandenbroucke, A. R. E., 170
VanderLaan, D. P., 347
Vandermosten, M., 444
Vandewalle, G., 275, 407
Vanduffel, W., 7, 181
Vanek, Z. F., 407
Vanhaudenhuyse, A., 453
vanHuijzen, C., 73, 75, 76, 298, 367, 427
VanMeter, J., 192
Vann, S. D., 400
Varadarajan, V., 214
Varela, F., 451, 452
Varga, M., 238, 278
Vargas-Irwin, C. E., 235
Vargha-Khadem, F., 438, 439
Vargo, E.L., 325
Varjonen, N., 346, 347
Varney, N., 441
Vasan, R. S, 319
Vasey, P. L., 347
Vassoler, F. M., 107
Vawter, M. P., 327
Vazquez, M. J., 314
Veasey, S. C., 279
Vecchi, T., 239
Velanova, K., 131, 238
Veltman, D. J., 220
Venkatraman, V. K., 127
Verfaellie, M., 400, 407
Verhage, M., 123
Verhagen, L. A. W., 469
Verkhatsky, A., 20
Verlagen, L., 373
Verleger, R., 286
Verma, S., 313
Vermeer, H., 123
Veroniki, A. A., 479
Verrey, F., 304
Versace, F., 467
Verstreken, P., 256
Vervliet, B., 379
Verweij, J., 155
Vessal, M., 119
Vetsa, Y. S. K., 98
Vetter, C., 265, 266
Vibranovski, M. D., 111
Vicens, V., 460
Vickers, J., 369
Victor, J. D., 213, 215
Victor, J.D., 214
Viegi, A., 478
Vighetti, S., 166
Vigneau, M., 429
Viken, R. J., 470
Vila, J., 357
Vilain, E., 347
Villagra, F., 241
Villeda, S. A., 132
Villemagne, V., 406
Vingiano, W., 429
Vingtdeux, V., 214
Vinke, L., 443
Vinogradova, Y., 489
Vinukonda, G., 118
Virkkunen, M., 369, 469
Virshup, D. M., 269
Visscher, K. M., 93
Visser, E. K., 268
Viswanathan, A., 92
Vita, A., 493
Vitellaro-Zuccarello, L., 496
Vittengl, J. R., 480
Vittori, C., 418
Vittoz, N., 314
Vives, L., 500
Viviani, D., 371
Vliegen, J., 193
Vo, K., 364
Vocci, F. J., 472
Voderholzer, U., 482
Voet, H., 219
Voet, T., 490
Vogel, J., 235
Vogel, S. S., 243
Voice, K., 439
Voight, B. F., 308
Voke, J., 158
Volkow, N. D., 468
Vollmer, C., 266
Volman, I., 373
vom Saal, F. S., 329
von Buchholtz, L., 212
von Cramon, D., 182
von der Ohe, C. G., 284
von Gall, C., 269
von Hehn, C. A., 207
von Känel, R., 385
von Melchner, L., 125
von Schantz, M., 268
Vonk, J., 113, 460
Vonk, R., 483
Voogd, J., 73, 75, 76, 298, 367, 427
Vorstman, J. A. S., 490
Vose, L. R., 118
Voss, J. L., 286
Voss, M. W., 132
Voss, P., 127
Vouimba, R.-M., 372
Voutilainen, M. H., 254
Vrba, E. S., 118
Vuga, M., 476
Vuillermot, S., 492
Vuilleumier, P., 203, 376
Vul, E., 169
Vulturar, R., 373
Vyadyslav, V. V., 284
Vyazovskiy, V. V., 287
Vyssotski, A. L., 285

Wack, D. S., 193
Wacker, D., 54
Wacker, D. W., 336
Waddington, J. L., 488
Wade, A. R., 173
Wager, T. D., 93, 204, 206, 360
Wagner, D. D., 318
Wagner, E. L., 297
Wagner, M., 207
Wagner, S., 119
Wagner, T., 360
Wagner, U., 286, 288
Waisbren, S. R., 109
Wakeman, D. R., 254
Waldeck, T., 478
Waldherr, M., 331
Waldie, K. E., 426
Waldman, I. D., 370
Waldvogel, J. A., 150
Walhovd, K. B., 132
Walker, E. F., 493
Walker, J. A., 402
Walker, M. P., 286
Wall, C. E., 111
Wall, P. D., 205
Wall, T. L., 471
Wallen, K., 330
Wallesch, C. W., 441
Wallesch, C.-W., 441
Wallis, J. D., 85
Wallman, J., 150
Walsh, J. K., 287
Walsh, S., 119
Walsh, T., 490
Walsh, V., 239, 425
Walters, E. T., 207
Wamsley, E., 287
Wan, C. Y., 127, 407
Wancewicz, E. V., 256
Wang, A., 253
Wang, A. C. J., 334
Wang, A. Y., 246
Wang, C., 54, 329, 331
Wang, C. M., 273
Wang, D. O., 418
Wang, G.-J., 468
Wang, H., 137, 477
Wang, J., 468, 482
Wang, J. C., 469
Wang, K., 138
Wang, K. H., 477
Wang, L., 478
Wang, M., 132
Wang, P. O., 439
Wang, Q., 153, 256
Wang, S. S.-H., 80
Wang, T., 109
Wang, T. J., 319
Wang, W, 440
Wang, W., 235, 500
Wang, W. C., 299
Wang, W. S.-Y., 440
Wang, X., 192, 207
Wang, X. H., 275
Wang, X.-J., 132
Wang, Y., 254
Wang, Y. T., 415
Wang, Z., 336, 337
Wapner, W., 441
Warach, S., 94, 235
Ward, B., 348
Ward, I. L., 329, 348
Ward, J., 141, 221
Ward, L. M., 450
Ward, O. B., 329, 348
Warden, D., 479
Wardlaw, M. K., 319
Ware, M. A., 207
Warman, G. R., 264
Warneken, F., 113
Warren, R. M., 191
Warren, S. T., 256
Warrington, E. K., 166
Wassef, M., 124
Wassermann, E. M., 377
Watanabe, D., 128
Watanabe, E., 235, 303
Watanabe, M., 238, 243
Waters, E. M., 334
Watkins, K. E., 438
Watkins, L. R., 384, 385
Watkins, S. S., 468
Watrous, A. J., 403
Watrous, S., 141
Watson, N. V., 332
Watson, S. J., 331
Wattendorf, E., 252
Waxman, S. G., 34
Waye, H., 294
Waytz, A., 461
Wcislo, W. T., 97
Weaver, I. C. G., 107
Webb, R. T., 491
Webber, C., 192
Weber, B., 23
Weber, D. J., 235
Weber, L., 492
Weber-Fox, C. M., 440
Webster, F. A., 187
Webster, G. D., 204
Webster, J. P., 372
Webster, W. W., 220
Weddle, M. G., 378
Wedell, A., 344
Weedon, M. N., 105, 318
Wegener, D., 454
Wegner, D. M., 93
Wei, W., 404
Wei, X.-X., 402
Weidemann, C. T., 402
Weidensaul, S., 297
Weigle, D. S., 318
Weiler, N. C., 54
Weiller, C., 246
Weinberger, D. R., 491, 492, 493
Weinberger, N. M., 372
Weindl, A., 303
Weiner, I., 492
Weiner, K. S., 180, 182
Weinshenker, D., 467
Weinstein, H., 55
Weiskopf, N., 238

Weiskrantz, L., 166
Weiss, A. H., 444
Weiss, A. P., 492
Weiss, B., 329, 331
Weiss, P., 119
Weiss, P. H., 221
Weiss, T., 142
Weisse, C. S., 385
Weissman, D. H., 93
Weisstaub, N. V., 495
Weitzman, E. D., 274
Welchman, A. E., 246
Welge-Lüssen, A., 252
Welham, J., 491
Wellcome Trust Case Control Consortium 2, 109
Weller, A., 220
Weller, L., 220
Wellnitz, S. A., 199
Welsh, J. P., 499
Welsh, M. J., 199
Wemmie, J. A., 375
Wen, X. L., 107
Wender, P. H., 490
Weng, Y. C., 137
Weniger, G., 375
Wenkstern, D., 467
Werblin, F. S., 152
Wernicke, C., 442
Wesensten, N. J., 238, 278
Wessberg, J., 201
Wessinger, C. M., 166, 192
Wesson, D. W., 405
Westbrook, G. L., 51
Westenbroek, R. E., 500
Westerberg, C. E., 286
Westerfield, M., 243
Westergaard, G., 369
Westergaard, G. C., 369
Westermann, B., 252
Westling, E., 319
Westmacott, R., 400, 401
Wewerka, S., 123
Whalen, P. J., 376, 386
Wheeler, M. E., 238
Wheeler, R. A., 467
Wheye, D., 294
White, A. J. R., 155
White, D. P., 279
White, J. A., 417
White, L. E., 171
White, L. E. Jr., 203
White-Schwoch, T., 193
Whitten, P. L., 386
Whyte, J., 138
Wideman, T. H., 207
Wiedrich, K., 318
Wienbruch, C., 128, 141
Wiers, R. W., 468
Wiese, S., 123
Wiesel, T. N., 167, 168, 169, 171
Wightman, R. M., 467
Wigström, H., 418
Wikelski, M., 285
Wilbrecht, L., 246
Wilcox, T., 330
Wild, H. M., 181
Wiley, E., 440
Wilke, M., 167
Wilkerson, M. K., 20
Wilkins, K., 318, 331, 332
Will, M. J., 205
Wille, A., 459
Willeit, M., 483
Willems, R. M., 443
Willerman, L., 98, 348
Williams, B. A., 299
Williams, C. C., 98
Williams, C. L., 328
Williams, D. R., 154, 155
Williams, G., 314
Williams, G. A., 158
Williams, G. B., 469
Williams, K. D., 204
Williams, L. W., 500
Williams, M. T., 348
Williams, R. W., 16, 241
Williams, S. C. R., 97
Williams, S. L., 436
Williamson, A., 130
Williamson, A. C., 398
Willie, J. T., 280
Willingham, D. B., 246, 255
Willins, D. L., 496
Willson, T. M., 478
Wilson, B. A., 392
Wilson, D. A., 219
Wilson, G. D., 346, 348, 362
Wilson, J. D., 329
Wilson, K. D., 180
Wilson, M. A., 286
Wilson, R. I., 56
Wilson, R. S., 126
Wilson, S. J., 127, 407, 439
Wilson, S. R., 220
Winawer, J., 221
Winden, K., 107, 439
Windhaber, J., 376
Winer, G. A., 148
Winfree, A. T., 265
Wingfield, A., 193
Winkelmann, J., 280
Winkels, W. A. M., 403
Winkler, C., 254
Winkler, D., 483
Winn, R. J., 348
Winner, E., 128
Winocur, G., 266, 403
Winsauer, P. J., 285
Winters, D., 313
Wirdefeldt, K., 253
Wirz-Justice, A., 264
Wise, R. A., 466
Wise, R. P., 150
Wisely, G. B., 478
Wisner, K. L., 475
Wisniewski, S. R., 479, 480
Wissman, A. M., 119
Witelson, S. F., 98, 431
Withoft, N., 180
Witte, O. W., 142
Witthoft, N., 182, 221
Witting, K., 346, 347
Wittkowski, K. M., 320
Wiuf, C., 489
Wodlinger, B., 235
Wohlgemuth, M. J., 183
Wohlschläger, A., 453
Wojnicki, F. H. E., 467
Wokke, M. E., 170
Woldorff, M. G., 93
Wolf, M. E., 468
Wolf, S., 357
Wolfensberger, M., 252
Wolff, P. H., 444
Wolffenbuttel, K. P., 345
Wölfling, K., 468
Wolgin, D. L., 367
Wolkin, A., 492
Wollstein, A., 105
Wolman, D., 428
Wolpe, P. R., 419
Wolpert, D. M., 201
Wolpert, L., 123
Wolschin, F., 107
Womelsdorf, T., 450
Won, Y.-M., 241
Wong, A. T., 400
Wong, C., 468
Wong, K., 494
Wong, M., 127
Wong, P. C. M., 128
Wong, R. O. L., 122
Wong, S. S.-H., 81
Wong, W. I., 344
Woo, M. A., 279
Woo, S. L. C., 109
Wood, A. G., 127, 407
Wood, J. N., 201
Wood, N. I., 280
Wood, S. J., 489
Woodbury, C. J., 207
Woodhouse, C. R. J., 345
Wooding, S., 105
Woodruff, P. W. R., 492
Woods, C. G., 204
Woods, R., 330
Woods, R. P., 98
Woodside, B., 336, 356
Woodson, J. C., 329
Woodworth, R. S., 34
Woolard, J., 131
Wooley, A. W., 368
Woolf, C. J., 207, 208
Woolf, N. J., 76, 275
Woolrich, M. W., 85
Woolsey, T. A., 367
Workman, J. L., 328
Worsley, K. J., 183
Worthington, J., 451
Wozniak, D. F., 124
Wray, G. A., 111
Wray, N. R., 476
Wright, C. I., 95, 373, 374
Wright, E. W., 246, 247, 248
Wright, I. C., 492
Wright, K. P., Jr., 263
Wright, N. D., 368
Wright, P., 429
Wright, T., 408
Wu, F. C. W., 368
Wu, H., 54
Wu, L.-J., 483
Wu, L.-Q., 187
Wu, Q., 313
Wu, S. C., 269
Wulfeck, B., 441, 442
Wunderbaldinger, G., 207
Wunderlich, C. M., 313
Wunderlich, F. T., 313
Wurtman, J. J., 51
Wyart, C., 220
Wyart, V., 453
Wyatt, H. R., 318, 319
Wyatt, J. K., 264
Wyatt, R. J., 254, 491
Wynne, L. C., 490
Wyper, K., 124
Wyss, M. T., 23

Xenos, D., 478
Xian, H., 468
Xie, J., 199
Xiong, J., 242
Xiong, J.-H., 428
Xu, D., 500
Xu, H. E., 54
Xu, H. S., 191
Xu, H.-T., 125
Xu, M., 467
Xu, T., 469
Xu, T. H., 418
Xu, X., 110
Xu, Y., 137, 269
Xue, B., 313
Xue, Y., 500
Xue, Z. Q., 119
Xuereb, J., 255

Yadollahpour, P., 235
Yager, L. M., 468
Yagita, K., 267
Yale, S., 490
Yamada, A., 214
Yamadori, A., 192
Yamaguchi, S., 267
Yamamoto, T., 214
Yamanaka, A., 275
Yamashita, T., 20
Yan, X. X., 119
Yanagawa, Y., 51–52
Yanagisawa, K., 214
Yanagisawa, M., 280
Yancey, C. R., 417
Yandava, C. N., 500
Yang, A. K., 478
Yang, C.-H., 119
Yang, G., 125
Yang, H., 256
Yang, J., 109
Yang, J.-C., 376
Yang, M.-J., 467
Yang, Y., 132
Yang, Y. R., 480
Yang, Z., 268
Yarmolinsky, D. A., 215
Yasuda, R., 418
Yasuhara, D., 320
Yasuhara, S., 296
Yasui, E., 238
Yasumatsu, K., 214
Yau, H.-J., 468
Yazici, A., 478
Yazici, K., 478
Ye, C. P., 314
Ye, H., 336
Ye, X., 219
Yeatts, S. D., 472
Yee, B. K., 126
Yeh, M. T., 370
Yehuda, R., 377
Yellachich, L.-A., 490
Yen, J.-Y., 467
Yenari, M. A., 137
Yeo, G. S. H., 318
Yeo, R. A., 97
Yeomans, J. S., 371, 377
Yeshurun, Y., 431
Yeung, M. S. Y., 119
Yeung-Courchesne, R., 71
Yin, H. H., 246, 252
Yin, J., 207
Yiu, A. P., 418
Yiu, G., 139
Yogo, Y., 343
Yolken, R. H., 490–491, 491
Yoo, S.-S., 286
Yoon, H.-K, 376
Yoon, K. L., 450
Yoon, S.-H., 136, 137
Yoshida, J., 219
Yoshida, K., 298
Yoshida, M., 192
Yoshida, W., 206
Yoshie, M., 153
Yoshikawa, E., 252
Yoshimura, H., 212
Yoshioka, K., 256
Yoshioka, T., 432
Yoshitomo, M., 138
You, H., 110

You, S. W., 139
You, Y.-M., 256
Young, A. B., 254
Young, H., 469
Young, K. D., 374
Young, L., 364, 460
Young, L. J., 336, 337, 459
Young, R. C., 310
Young, T., 154
Young, W. G., 310
Youngentob, S. L., 220
Youngstedt, S. D., 264
Yousem, D. M., 220
Youssef, A. M., 207
Yousseif, A., 314
Yovel, G., 180, 181
Yu, F. H., 500
Yu, H. S., 480
Yu, P., 314
Yu, T. W., 120
Yu, X. Z., 418
Yuan, M., 376
Yuan, Q., 370
Yuan, X. Y., 119
Yuen, T., 495
Yuval-Greenberg, S., 449
Yvon, C., 378

Zablow, L., 418
Zacks, J. M., 239
Zadra, A., 277, 281
Zaffuto, S., 418, 419
Zagarra-Moran, U., 445
Zago, L., 431
Zagoory-Sharon, O., 337
Zagrebelsky, M., 123
Zajitschek, S., 111
Zakharenko, S. S., 418
Zaki, J., 461
Zalsman, G., 369
Zamarripa, F., 428
Zandi, P. P., 475
Zanto, T. P., 85
Zatorre, R. J., 127, 128, 129, 191, 192, 441, 442, 467
Zdunek, S., 119
Zea-Ponce, Y., 494
Zeevi, Y. Y., 152
Zegarra-Moran, O., 445
Zeggini, E., 318
Zehr, J. L., 328, 330
Zeineh, M. M., 398
Zeki, S., 156, 177, 181
Zelaznik, H. N., 241
Zemansky, J., 191
Zeng, Y. T., 109
Zentner, M., 342
Zervoulis, K., 330
Zhan, G. X., 279
Zhan, R., 216
Zhang, C. Y., 314
Zhang, F., 137
Zhang, H., 469
Zhang, J., 180
Zhang, L., 208, 495
Zhang, M., 137
Zhang, Q., 444
Zhang, R., 314
Zhang, S., 139
Zhang, T. Y., 107
Zhang, W., 98
Zhang, W. N., 482
Zhang, X., 208, 218, 253
Zhang, Y., 312
Zhang, Y. E., 111
Zhao, J., 137, 201
Zhao, Y., 55, 418
Zhao, Z., 372
Zhao, Z.-Q., 207
Zheng, B., 269
Zhou, D., 124
Zhou, F., 285
Zhou, S. F., 478
Zhou, Y., 418
Zhu, Q., 180
Zhu, W., 468
Zhu, X. W., 285
Zhu, Y., 269, 279
Ziebell, S., 493
Ziegler, J. C., 444
Ziemba, C. M., 178
Zigmond, M. J., 315
Zihl, J., 182
Zikopoulos, B., 372
Zimmerman, J. C., 274
Zingales, L., 98
Zinni, M., 454
Zipser, B. D., 22
Zipursky, R. B., 493
Zipusky, R., 496
Zoccolotti, P., 445
Zoghbi, H. Y., 199
Zola, S. M., 401
Zonderman, A. B., 406
Zone, S. E., 269
Zook, J. M., 140
Zorn, J. A., 199
Zorner, B., 138
Zorzi, M., 444, 455
Zotev, V., 374
Zou, B., 132
Zubieta, J.-K., 206
Zubrick, S. R., 490
Zucker, I., 264, 269
Zucker, K. J., 345, 348
Zuckerman, L., 492
Zufall, F., 220
Zuk, J., 444
Zuker, C. S., 212, 214, 215
Zuo, Y., 418
Zurif, E., 441
Zurif, E. B., 441
Zusho, H., 220
Zvolensky, M. J., 371
Zweifel, L. S., 314
Zweig, J. A., 418
Zwiebel, L. J., 187, 268

Subject Index/Glossary

Note: Italicized page numbers refer to figures, illustrations, and tables.

Ablation removal of a brain area, generally with a surgical knife, 89, *96*
Absolute pitch, 191
Absolute refractory period a time when the membrane is unable to produce an action potential, 31
Acetaldehyde, 471
Acetic acid, 471
Acetylcholine a chemical similar to an amino acid, except that it includes an $N(CH_3)_3$ group instead of an NH_2, group
  and Alzheimer's disease, 406, 419
  ionotropic effects, 52
  parasympathetic nervous system, 69–70
  receptor, 52
  and sleep, 275, *277*
  synthesis of, 50–51, *50*
Acetylcholinesterase a chemical similar to an amino acid, except that it includes an $N(CH_3)_3$ group instead of an NH_2, group, 55
Across-fiber pattern principle idea that each receptor responds to a wide range of stimuli and contributes to the perception of every stimulus in its system, 211
ACTH. *See* **Adrenocorticotropic hormone**
Action potential messages sent by axons
  all-or-none law, 31
  in chemical events at the synapse, 49, *49*
  definition of, 29
  molecular basis of, 29–31
  and myelin, 32–33
  of parallel fibers, 243
  propagation of, 32, *33*
  refractory period, 31–32
  relationship between EPSP and IPSP, 44–45
  in release and diffusion of transmitters, 51
Activating effects temporary effect of a hormone, which occurs at any time in life while the hormone is present, 328, 331–335
Activation-synthesis hypothesis idea that a dream represents the brain's effort to make sense of sparse and distorted information, 288
Active transport a protein-mediated process that expends energy to enable a molecule to cross a membrane, 22
Acuity, 152
Acute transient global amnesia, 403
Adaptation decreased response to a stimulus as a result of recent exposure to it, 213
ADD (attention deficit disorder), 468
Addiction condition marked by repetitive craving and the potential to harm one's life
  cravings, 468
  drug mechanisms, 466–469
  predispositions, 469–471
  tolerance and withdrawal, 468–469
  treatments, 471–472
Adenine, 105
adenosine triphosphate (ATP) a molecule composed of adenosine, ribose, and three phosphate groups, which the body uses to store and release energy, 507, *507*
ADH. *See* **Antidiuretic hormone**
Adolescence, brain and behavioral development, 131–132
Adopted children, 108, *490*
Adrenal cortex, *58*, 383–386
Adrenal gland, 343
Adrenaline, 48
Adrenal medulla, *58*
Adrenocorticotropic hormone (ACTH) chemical released from the anterior pituitary gland, which enhances metabolic activity and elevates blood levels of sugar, 343, 384
Aerobic requiring the use of oxygen during movements, 230
Afferent axon axon that brings information into a structure, 19
Affinity tendency of a drug to bind to a receptor, 466
Age
  and circadian rhythms, 266, *266*
  hearing and attention, 194
  and sleep, 286–287
Aggressive behaviors, 368–370
Agonist a drug that mimics or increases the effects of a neurotransmitter, 466
Agouti-related peptide (AgRP) inhibitory transmitter that blocks the satiety actions of the paraventricular nucleus, 314
Alcohol
  as an anxiety reducer, 378
  fetal alcohol syndrome, 124
  predisposition for addiction to, 469–471, *470*
Alcohol abuse, medications for, 471–472
Aldosterone adrenal hormone that causes the body to retain salt, 304, 383
Allied medical field, 8
All-or-none law principle that the amplitude and velocity of an action potential are independent of the stimulus that initiated it, 31
Allostasis the adaptive way in which the body changes its set points depending on the situation, 295
Alpha-fetoprotein protein that binds with estradiol in the bloodstream of immature mammals, 330
Alpha waves a steady series of brain waves at a frequency of 8 to 12 per second that are characteristic of relaxation, 272
Altered sleep patterns, 481–482
Altruism, 460–461
Altruistic behavior an action that benefits someone other than the actor, 113
Alzheimer's disease condition characterized by memory loss, confusion, depression, restlessness, hallucinations, delusions, sleeplessness, and loss of appetite, 404–406, *405*
Amacrine cells, 149, *151*, 162, *163*
American Sign Language, 435
Amino acids acids containing an amine group (NH_2), 50, *50*
Amnesia memory loss
  anterograde and retrograde amnesia, 399
  hippocampal damage, 398–401, *398*
  impaired storage of long-term memory, 399
  impairment of episodic memory, 399–400
  implicity and explicit memory, 400–401
  intact procedural memory, 401
  intact working memory, 399
  other types of, 403–406
AMPA receptor a glutamate receptor that can respond to α-amino-3-hydrozy-5-methyl-4-isoxazolepropionic acid (AMPA), 416–418, *417*
Amphetamine a drug that blocks reuptake of dopamine and other neurotransmitters, 55, *57*
Amplitude the intensity of a sound wave, 31, 188
Amputation, 140–142, *140*
Amusia, 191
Amygdala
  damage to, 374–376, *375*
  fear and anxiety, 371, *372*, 373–376, *373*, 379
  and limbic system, *360*
  location of, *76*, *367*
  and pain, 203, *204*
  as part of the limbic system, 74, *74*
  and post-traumatic stress disorder, 377
Amyloid-β a protein that accumulates to higher than normal levels in the brains of people with Alzheimer's disease, 404–405
Amyotrophic lateral sclerosis, *240*
Anaerobic proceeding without using oxygen at the time of a reaction, 230
Analytical perception, 429
Anandamide chemical that binds to cannabinoid receptors, 56, *56*
Anatomical differences, and sexual orientation, 346
Androgen insensitivity condition in which individuals with an XY chromosome pattern have the genital appearance of a female, 344
Androgens testes-produced hormones that are more abundant in males, 326, *327*, 329, 334–335
Angel dust. *See* **Phencyclidine (PCP)**
Angiotensin II hormone that constricts the blood vessels, compensating for the drop in blood pressure; triggers thirst, 304
Animal cells, structures of, 17
Animals. *See also* **Primates**
  aggressive behaviors, 368–369
  hunger, 307–308, *307*
  and language, 435–437, *437*
  parental behavior, 336–337, *336*, *337*
  and sleep, 262, *262*, 285, *286*
  temperature regulation, 294–295, 296–297
  use of in research, 9–11, 509–511
Anomia difficulty recalling the names of objects, 442
Antabuse drug that antagonizes the effects of acetaldehyde dehydrogenase by binding to its copper ion, 471, 477
Antagonist a drug that blocks a neurotransmitter, 466
Antagonistic muscles opposing sets of muscles that are required to move a leg or arm back and forth, 43, 228, *229*
Anterior, *68*
Anterior commissure bundle of axons that connects the two hemispheres of the cerebral cortex, 74, 80
Anterior pituitary portion of the pituitary gland, composed of glandular tissue, 58, *58*, *59*
Anterior temporal cortex, 407
Anterior thalmic nuclei, *360*
Anterograde amnesia inability to form memories for events that happened after brain damage, 399
Antibodies Y-shaped proteins that attach to particular kinds of antigens, 384
Antidepressant drugs
  alternatives to, 480–482
  and dopamine, 56
  effectiveness of, 478–480, *479*
  types of, 477–478

Antidiuretic hormone (**ADH**) hormone that enables the kidneys to reabsorb water from urine; also known as vasopressin, 302
Antigens surface proteins on a cell that identify the cell as your own, 384
Antipsychotic drugs drugs that tend to relieve schizophrenia and similar conditions, 56, 493–495, *494*
Antisaccade task a voluntary eye movement away from the normal direction, 238
Antisocial behavior, *370*. *See also* Aggressive behaviors
Anvil, *189*, 190
Anxiety
  and the amygdala, 6, 371
  monkey studies, 373
  and political attitudes, *374*
  rodent studies, 371–372
Anxiety disorders, 376–377
  and alcohol, 378
  learning to erase anxiety, 378–379
  pharmacological relief, 377–378
  relief from, 377–379
Anxiolytic drugs, 377–378
Aphasia language impairment, 440–442
Aplysia, 414–415, *414*, *415*
Apoptosis a programmed mechanism of cell death, 122, 124, 126
Arcuate nucleus hypothalamic area with sets of neurons for hunger and satiety, 313–315
Area A1. *See* **Primary auditory cortex**
Area MT (**middle temporal cortex**), 181–183, 192
Area V1. *See* **Primary visual cortex**
Area V2. *See* **Secondary visual cortex**
Area V4, 181
Arousal, brain mechanisms of, 275–276
Artificial selection a process of selecting plants/animals for desired traits, 110
Asperger's syndrome, 499
Associativity property that a weak input paired with a stronger input enhances its later response, 415, *416*
Astigmatism a decreased responsiveness to one kind of line or another, caused by an asymmetric curvature of the eyes, 172, *172*
Astrocytes star-shaped glia that synchronize the activity of the axons, 20, *21*
Atomic number identification of an element determined by its number of protons, 505
Atomic weight weight of an element in proportion to the weight of a proton, 505
Atoms tiny building blocks of matter, 505
ATP (**adenosine triphosphate**) molecule that provides the energy for muscles and other body activities, 507, *507*
Attachment anxiety, 383
Attack and escape behaviors
  anxiety disorders, 376–377
  fear and anxiety, 371–376
  heredity and environment in violence, 370
  hormones, 368
  serotonin synapses and aggressive behavior, 368–369
Attention, 194, 453–456, 488
Attention, brain mechanisms of, 275–276
Attention deficit disorder (ADD), 468
Atypical antidepressants miscellaneous group of drugs with antidepressant effects but only mild side effects, 478
Atypical antipsychotics, 495–496
Audition
  auditory cortex, 192–193
  hearing loss, 193–194
  pitch perception, 190–191
  sound and the ear, 188–190
  sound localization, 194–195
Auditory connections in the brain hemispheres, 425–426
Auditory cortex, 192–193, 438
Autism spectrum disorders family of psychological disorders marked by impaired social and emotional exchange and other symptoms, 499–500, *499*
Autoimmune disease, 384
Autonomic arousal, 357–359
Autonomic nervous system, 69–71
Autonomic nervous system part of the PNS that controls the heart, intestines, and other organs, *66*, *67*
Autoreceptor receptor on a presynaptic neuron that responds to the released transmitter by inhibiting further release of it, 56
Autosomal genes all chromosomes other than X and Y, 106
Axon thin fiber of constant diameter; the neuron's information sender, 18, *19*
  chemical gradients, 120–121
  competition among, 121–122
  connections, 120, *120*, *121*
  and muscle fibers, *229*
  pathfinding by, 119–122
  regrowth of, 139
  sprouting, 139

Backward masking a brief visual stimulus after another brief visual stimulus that leads to failure to remember the first, 450
Bacopa monnieri, 419
Ballistic movement motion that proceeds as a single organized unit that cannot be redirected once it begins, 232
BAS. *See* **Behavioral activation system**
Basal forebrain, 76, *76*
Basal forebrain forebrain area anterior and dorsal to the hypothalamus; includes cell clusters that promote wakefulness and sleep, 275, *277*
Basal ganglia a group of subcortical forebrain structures lateral to the thalamus, 243–246
  learning and memory, 406–407, *407*
  location of, *74*, *245*
  overview of, *75*, *76*
Basal metabolism energy used to maintain a constant body temperature while at rest, 296, 297
Basilar membrane, 190–191, *191*
Battle fatigue. *See* **Post-traumatic stress disorder (PTSD)**
B cells, 384, 385
BDNF. *See* **Brain-derived neurotrophic factor**
Bed nucleus of the stria terminalis a set of neurons that connect to the amygdala, 372, *373*
Behavior
  biological approach to, 4–6
  biological explanations of, 6–7
  correlated with brain anatomy, 94–96
  effect of genetics on, 109–110
  evolution of, 110–114
  and food selection, 308–309
  genetics and, 104–114
  predictors of substance abuse, 470–471
  sequences of, 232–233
Behavioral activation system (**BAS**) left brain hemispheric activity marked by low to moderate autonomic arousal and a tendency to approach, which could characterize either happiness or anger, 362
Behavioral development, and brain development, 131–132
Behavioral inhibition system (**BIS**) right brain hemispheric activity, which increases attention and arousal, inhibits action, and stimulates emotions such as fear and disgust, 362
Behavioral medicine field that includes the effects of diet, smoking, exercise, stressful experiences, and other behaviors on health, 383
Behavioral regulation of temperature, 296–297, *297*
Behavior differences, and sexual orientation, 346
Benzodiazepines anti-anxiety drugs, 377–378, *377*
Bilingual people, 440
Binding problem question of how various brain areas produce a perception of a single object, 85–87, *86*, *87*
Binocular input stimulation from both eyes, 171
Binocular rivalry alternating conscious perceptions that occur when one views incompatible displays with the two eyes, 450–451, *451*, *452*
Biological clock
  mechanisms of, 266–269
  rhythms of waking and sleeping, 264–266
Biological psychology the study of the physiological, evolutionary, and developmental mechanisms of behavior and experience
  career opportunities, 8–9
  definition of, 5
  fields of specialization, 8
  use of animals in research, 9–11
Bipolar cells type of neuron in the retina that receives input directly from the receptors, 149, *150*, *151*, *152*, 162, *163*, 164
Bipolar disorder a condition that alternates between depression and mania, 482–483, *482*
Birdsong, *7*
Birth-control pills, 333–334
BIS. *See* **Behavioral inhibition system**
Blindness, 82–83, *104*, 127
Blindsight the ability to respond in limited ways to visual information without perceiving it consciously, 166–167
Blind spot area at the back of the retina where the optic nerve exits; it is devoid of receptors, 149, *151*, *163*
Blood–brain barrier mechanism that excludes most chemicals from the brain, 21–23, *22*
Blood volume, *303*
Body, chemical reactions in, 507
Body temperature control
  advantages of, 297–298
  brain mechanisms, 298–299
  extreme cold, survival in, 297
  fever, 299
Body weight, and eating disorders, 318
Bonobos, 436–437
Botulinum toxin, 357–358
Brain. *See also* Lateralization
  abnormalities and schizophrenia, 492, *493*
  abnormalities of hemispheric dominance, 476
  activity during speech, *441*
  areas for learning, *407*
  and attention, 454
  connection to eyes, 149–152
  connection to spinal cord, 239–241
  coronal section, *74*
  correlated with behavior, 94–96
  development of, 118, *118*
  dorsal view, 5, *73*
  and emotions, 359–360, *360*
  evolution of, 111
  formation of, 117, *117*
  horizontal section, *431*
  insectivores vs. primates, *81*
  major divisions of, 71, *71*
  mammalian brains, comparison of, *80*
  mind-brain relationship, 448–449
  nucleus accumbens, *467*
  olfaction and, 219–220
  as part of the central nervous system, 66
  sagittal section of, *73*

and schizophrenia, 492
of several species, *9*
sex differences, 335
and sexual orientation, 348–350
split-brain operation, 426–431
stimulation of, 412
structures for arousal and sleep, *277*
taste coding, 214–215
ventral view, *5*
volume of cortex vs. volume of rest, *81*
Brain activity, recording, 91–94
Brain actvity, sleep and, 276–278
Brain damage
and decision making, 363–364
effects of, 89–90, *96*
images of, *137*
and language, 440–443
later mechanisms of, 138–142
plasticity after, 136–142
research methods and, 88–89
and schizophrenia, 488
short-term recovery, 136–138
Brain death condition with no sign of brain activity and no response to any stimulus, 272
Brain-derived neurotrophic factor (BDNF) a neurotrophin similar to nerve growth factor, 123, 418, 478
Brain development
and behavioral development, 131–132
determinants of neuronal survival, 122–123
differentiation of the cortex, 124–125
fine-tuning by experience, 125–131
maturation of the vertebrate brain, 117–119
pathfinding by axons, 119–122
vulnerability of, 123–124
Brain function in REM sleep, 278–279
Brain mechanisms
and body temperature control, 298–299
and hunger, 313–317
of movement, 235–248
and stages of sleep, 272–281
of wakefulness, arousal, and sleep, 275–278
Brain reorganization, 129–130
Brain size and intelligence
comparisons across species, 96–97
comparisons among humans, 97
comparisons of men and women, 98
Brainstem the medulla, pons, midbrain, and central structure of the forebrain, 71, *71*
Brain stimulation, 90–91, 138
Brain-to-body ratio, 96–97, *96*
Brightness constancy, *157*
Broca's aphasia brain damage that causes impaired language, 440–442, *443*
Broca's area portion of the brain that is associated with language production, 88, 440, *440*
Bulimia nervosa a condition in which people alternate between binges of overeating and periods of strict dieting, 319–320
Bupropion, 478
Butyrophenones a chemical family that includes antipsychotic drugs (haloperidol) that relieve the positive symptoms of schizophrenia, 493

CAH. *See* **Congenital adrenal hyperplasia**
Cajal, Santiago Ramón y, 16–17
CaMKII, 417–418
Cannabinoids chemicals related to D[9]-THC, 56, *56*, *57*, 137, *138*, 206–207
Capsaicin a chemical, found in hot peppers, that produces a painful burning sensation by releasing substance P; high dosages damage pain receptors, 199, 206–207
Carbamazepine, 483
Carbon atoms, reactions of, 505–507
Cardiac muscles muscles of the heart that have properties intermediate between those of smooth and skeletal muscles, 228, *229*
Cataplexy, 280
Cataracts, 173
Catecholamines compounds that contain a catechol and an amine group, 50, 55
Catechol-o-methyltransferase (COMT), 55, 469
CAT scan method of visualizing a living brain by injecting a dye into the blood and placing a person's head into a CT scanner; x-rays are passed through the head and recorded by detectors on the opposite side, 94, *95*, *96*
Caudate nucleus, *76*
Caudate nucleus large subcortical structure, part of the basal ganglia, 243
CCK. *See* **Cholecystokinin**
Cell body structure containing the nucleus, ribosomes, and mitochondria, 18
Cell structures, *19*
Cellular organization, 243
Central canal a fluid-filled channel in the center of the spinal cord, 77
Central nervous system (CNS) the brain and the spinal cord
anatomical directions in, 67, *67*, *68*
formation of, 117, *117*
overview of, 66, *66*
somatosensation in, 201–202, *201*
Central pattern generators neural mechanisms in the spinal cord that generate rhythmic patterns of motor output, 232
Central sulcus one of the deepest grooves in the surface of the cerebral cortex, *5*, 83
Cerebellar cortex the surface of the cerebellum, *242*, 243
Cerebellar nuclei, *242*
Cerebellum highly folded hindbrain structure that is important for behaviors that depend on accurate timing, *5*
celluar organization of, *244*
classical conditioning, 395
location of, *74*
and movement, 241–243
overview of, 71
in sagittal section of the brain, *73*
Cerebral cortex layers of cells on the outer surface of the cerebral hemisphere of the forebrain
Alzheimer's disease, *405*
areas of and columns, *82*
frontal lobe, 84–85
laminae, *81*
learning and memory, *407*
location of, *74*
and movement, 235–241
occipital lobe, 82–83
organization of, 80–82
parietal lobe, 83
parts work together, 85–87
pathways for touch and pain, *203*
in sagittal section of the brain, *73*
taste, *215*
temporal lobe, 83–84
Cerebrospinal fluid (CSF) a clear fluid similar to blood plasma produced by choroid plexus in the brain ventricles, 77
Cerebrovascular accident result of interrupted blood flow to the brain resulting from either a blood clot or a ruptured artery, 136
Change blindness, 454
Chemical bonds, 505
Chemical coding, 211
Chemical events at the synapse, 48–49, 57–59
Chemical gradients, 120–121
Chemical pathfinding by axons, 119–121
Chemical senses
chemical coding, 211
olfaction, 216–220
pheromones, 220–221
sequence of, 49–57
synesthesia, 221–222
taste, 212–216
Chemistry
atoms and molecules, 505
ATP, role of, 507
chemical reactions in the body, 507
elements and compounds, 503
ions and chemical bonds, 505
reactions of carbon atoms, 505–507
Chemokines, 118
Chewing gum, *309*
Childhood behavior, sex diffferences in, 330–331
China, *110*
Chloride ions, 28
Chlorpromazine, 477
Chlorpromazine antipsychotic drug that relieves the positive symptoms of schizophrenia for most, though not all, patients, 493
Cholecystokinin (CCK) hormone released from the duodenum that constricts the sphincter muscle between the stomach and duodenum, limiting the meal size, 310, 314, 377
Choroid plexus, 77
Chromosomes strands of genes, 104, 327, 343, 347
Cingulate cortex, 203, *204*
Cingulate gyrus, 74, *74*, *360*
Circadian rhythm, 262–264, 265, *266*, 268–269, 279, *481*, *483*. *See also* Biological clock
Classical conditioning type of conditioning produced by the pairing of two simuli, one of which evokes an automatic response, 392, *393*
Clinico-anatomical hypothesis idea that considers dreams as a type of thinking that occurs under unusual conditions, 288–289
Cloacal exstrophy, 344–345
Closed class of grammatical forms, 441
Closed head injury a result of a sharp blow to the head that does not puncture the brain, 136
CNS. *See* **Central nervous system**
Cocaine a drug that blocks reuptake of dopamine, 55, *56*, *57*
Cochlea structure in the inner ear containing auditory receptors, *189*, 190–191, *190*, *191*, 193–194
Cochlear nucleus, *192*
Cognitive-behavioral therapy, 480
Cognitive functions
attention, 453–456
conscious and unconscious processes, 448–453
language, 435–445
lateralization of function, 421–432
social neuroscience, 459–461
Collateral sprouts newly formed branches of an axon, 139, *139*
Color constancy the ability to recognize colors despite changes in lighting, 156
Color perception, *157*, 181, 211
Color vision, 153–158
Color vision deficiency inability to perceive color differences, 158
Columnar organization of the visual cortex, 169–170
Columns collection of cells having similar properties, arranged perpendicular to the laminae, *68*, 81
Coma an extended period of unconsciousness with a low level of brain activity, 272
Combination pill, 333
Commissures, *427*

Complex cells type of visual cortex cell located in areas V1 and V2 that responds to a pattern of light in a particular orientation anywhere within its large receptive field, 167, *168*
Complex receptive fields, 167–169
Compound material composed of two or more types of element bound together, 503
Computerized axial tomograpy (CT or CAT scan) method of visualizing a living brain by injecting a dye into the blood and placing a person's head into a CT scanner; x-rays are passed through the head and recorded by detectors on the opposite side, 94, *95*, *96*
COMT (catechol-o-methyltransferase) enzyme that breaks down excess dopamine into inactive chemicals that cannot stimulate the dopamine receptors, 55, 469
Concentration gradient difference in distribution of ions across the neuron's membrane, 27–28
Conditioned response (CR) response evoked by a conditioned stimulus after it has been paired with an unconditioned stimulus, 392
Conditioned stimulus (CS) stimulus that evokes a particular response only after it has been paired with an unconditioned stimulus, 392, *393*, 394–395, *394*
Conductive deafness hearing loss that occurs if the bones of the middle ear fail to transmit sound waves properly to the cochlea, 193
Cones type of retinal receptor that contributes to color perception, 152–153, *152*, *153*, *154*, 155, *155*, 162, *163*, 164
Confabulation a distinctive symptom of Korsakoff's syndrome in which patients fill in memory gaps with guesses, 404
Congenital adrenal hyperplasia (CAH) the overdevelopment of the adrenal glands from birth, 343, 344–345
Conscious capable of reporting the presence of a stimulus, 449–450
Conscious and unconscious processes
  conscious and unconscious people, 453
  consciousness as a threshold phenomenon, 452
  consciousness of stimulus, 449–453
  mind-brain relationship, 448–449
  timing of consciousness, 452–453
Conscious decisions, and movement, 246–248, *247*
Consciousness awareness of an experience, ordinarily indicated in people by their ability to describe something in words 4–5, 272, 453
Consolidate to strengthen a memory and make it more long-lasting, 378–379, 396–397
Contextual memory, 403
Contingency management, 471
Continuous flash suppression, 167
Continuous positive airway pressure (CPAP) mask, *280*
Contralateral, *68*
Control, of movement, 228–233
Cooperation, 113
Cooperativity tendency for nearly simultaneous stimulation by two or more axons to produce long-term potentiation much more effectively than stimulation by just one, 415
Corical thinning, 124, *124*
Coronal plane, *68*
Corpus callosum bundle of axons that connects the two hemispheres of the cerebral cortex
  damage to, *427*
  lateralization, 424, *424*
  maturation of, 431–432
  overview of, *74*, *80*
  in sagittal section of the brain, *73*
  and split-brain operation, 426–431, *428*
Corpus luteum, 332, *333*
Cortex, differentiation of, 124–125
Cortial blindness, 82–83
Corticospinal tracts paths from the cerebral cortex to the spinal cord, 239
Cortisol hormone secreted by the adrenal cortex that elevates blood sugar and enhances metabolism, 265, 343, 383, *384*, 397, 419
Covalent bonds connections in which atoms share electrons with each other, 505–506
CPAP (continuous positive airway pressure) mask, *280*
CR. *See* **Conditioned response**
Cranial nerves nerves that control sensations from the head, muscle movements in the head, and much of the parasympathetic output to the organs, 71, *72*
Craniosacral system, 69
Cravings, 468, 472
CREB, 417–418
Cross-adaptation reduced response to one taste after exposure to another, 213
CS. *See* **Conditioned stimulus**
CSF. *See* **Cerebrospinal fluid**
CT scan method of visualizing a living brain by injecting a dye into the blood and placing a person's head into a CT scanner; x-rays are passed through the head and recorded by detectors on the opposite side, 94, *95*, *96*
Cyclotron, 92
Cytokines small proteins that combat infections and communicate with the brain to elicit appropriate behaviors, 384
Cytosine, 105

Dairy products, 308
Deafferent to remove or disable the sensory nerves from a body part, 142
Deafness, 193–194, 440
Decapitate cockroaches, 412, *413*
Decision making
  after brain damage, 363–364
  and emotions, 363–364
  prefronal cortex and, 85
Declarative memory deliberate recall of information that one recognizes as a memory, 400, 401, 407
Deep brain stimulation use of a battery-powered device implanted into a brain to deliver stimulation to certain areas, 482
Delayed matching-to-sample task task in which an animal sees a sample object and then after a delay must choose an objet that matches the sample, 401
Delayed nonmatching-to-sample task task in which an animal sees an object and then after a delay must choose an object that does not match the sample, 401, *402*
Delayed response task, 397
Delayed-response task assignment in which an animal must respond on the basis of a signal that it remembers but that is no longer present, 85
Delayed transmission, 41
Delusions unjustifiable beliefs, 487
Dendrites branching fibers from a neuron that receive information from other neurons, 18, 125–126, *126*
Dendritic branching, 125–127
Dendritic spines short outgrowths that increase the surface area available for synapses, 18, *19*
Denervation supersensitivity (receptor supersensitivity) increased sensitivity to neurotransmitters by a postsynaptic neron after loss of input, 139–140
Deoxyribonucleic acid (DNA) double-stranded molecule that is part of the chromosomes, 104–105, *105*, 107, *108*
Dependence. *See* **Addiction**
Depolarize (depolarization) to reduce polarization toward zero across a membrane, 29–30
Depression. *See* **Antidepressant drugs; Major depression**
Deprived experience in one or both eyes, 171
Dermatome area of the body connected to a particular spinal nerve, 201, *202*
Diabetes, *312*
Diaschisis decreased activity of surviving brain neurons after damage to other neurons, 138
Diet beverages, 319
Differential diagnosis one that rules out other conditions with similar symptoms, 488
Differentiate to develop the axon and dendrites that give a neuron its distinctive properties, 118, 124
Digestion, 307–309
Digestive system, *308*
Dihydrotestosterone, 345
DISC1 (disrupted in schizophrenia 1) gene that controls production of dendritic spines and the generation of new neurons in the hippocampus, 490
Disorders of sexual development, 343
Disorganized speech, 487
Disrupted in schizophrenia 1 (*DISC1*), 490
Dissociative identity disorder, 487
Distal, *68*
Distraction, 454
Disulfiram, 471, 477
Dizygotic twins fraternal (non-identical) twins derived from two eggs, 108, 346–347
DNA. *See* **Deoxyribonucleic acid (DNA)**
Dominant gene gene that shows a strong effect in either the homozygous or heterozygous condition, 105
Dopamine
  and addiction, 469
  and antipsychotic drugs, 493–495, *494*
  effect of drugs on, 56, *56*
  and lateral hypothalamus, 315
  and L-dopa, 253–254
  in men, 331
  reuptake of, 55
  and stimulant drugs, 55
  synthesis of, 50–51, *50*
Dopamine hypothesis of schizophrenia idea that schizophrenia results from excess activity at dopamine synapses in certain brain areas, 494
Dorsal located toward the back, 5, *5*, 67, *68*
Dorsal path, 177–178
Dorsal raphe and pons hindbrain areas that release the neurotransmitter serotonin, interrupting REM sleep, *277*
Dorsal root ganglia clusters of sensory neurons outside the spinal cord, 69
Dorsal stream visual path in the parietal cortex that helps the motor system locate objects; the "where" path, 178
Dorsal striatum brainstem areas that include serotonin pathways that interrupt sleep, 243
Dorsomedial nucleus, *75*
Down syndrome, 404
Dreaming, biological perspectives on, 288–289
Drug mechanisms, 466–469
Dualism belief that mind and body are different kinds of substance that exist independently, 6, 448
Duodenum part of the small intestine adjoining the stomach; first digestive site that absorbs nutrients, 310
Dyseidetic dyslexics, 444
Dyslexia a specific impairment of reading in someone with adequate vision, adequate motivation, and adequate overall cognitive skills, 444–445
Dysphonetic dyslexics, 444

Eardrum, 189
Early exposure to a limited array of patterns, 172–173
Ears, 188–190, *189*
Eating disorders
bulimia nervosa, 319–320
genetics and body weight, 318
and weight loss, 318–319
"Ecstasy" (MDMA), *57*
ECT. *See* **Electroconvulsive therapy**
Ectothermic, 296
Edema accumulation of fluid, 136
EEG. *See* **Electroencephalograph**
Efferent axon neuron that carries information away from a structure, 19
Efficacy a drug's tendency to activate the receptor, 466
Electrical gradient difference in electrical charges between the inside and outside of the cell, 26
Electrical synapses, 57
Electroconvulsive therapy (ECT) a treatment for depression by electrically inducing a seizure, 480–481, *481*
Electroencephalograph (EEG) a device that records electrical activity of the brain through electrodes attached to the scalp, 91, *91*, *96*, 272–273, 274
Elements materials that cannot be broken down into other types of materials, 503, *503*
Emotional behaviors, 383–386. *See also* attack and escape behaviors; emotion/emotions
Emotional pain, 203–204
Emotion/emotions
ability to identify, *335*
autonomic arousal, 356–361
definition of, 356
functions of, 362–364
possibly basic, 361–362
usefulness of the concept, 359–361
Empathy the ability to identify with other people and share their experience almost as if it were one's own, 460–461
Endocrine glands hormone-producing glands, 57–58, *58*
Endogenous circadian rhythm self-generated rhythm that lasts about a day, 262
Endogenous circannual rhythm self-generated rhythm that lasts about a year, 262
Endogenous morphines, 55
Endogenous rhythms, 262–263
Endoplasmic reticulum network of thin tubes that transport newly synthesized proteins to other locations, 17
Endorphins transmitters that attach to the same receptors as morphine, 55, 205
Endothelial cells, 22
Endothermic, 296
End-stopped cell type of visual cortex cell that resembles complex cells; responds best to stimuli of a precisely limited type, anywhere in a large receptive field, with a strong inhibitory field at one end of its field, 167, *168*
Energy conservation, and sleep, 284
Engram physical representation of what has been learned, 393, 394–395, *396*
Environment, and heredity, 108–110
Environmental influences, 469–470
Environmental modification, 109, 370
Enzymes biological catalysts that regulate chemical reactions in the body, 507
Epigenetics, 107–108, 347
Epigenetics a field that deals with changes in gene expression without modification of the DNA sequence, 107–108
Epilepsy a condition characterized by repeated episodes of excessive synchronized neutral activity, 426
Epinephrine, 50–51, *50*, 55
Episodic memory memories of single personal events, 399–400, 401, 403, 406
EPSP. *See* **Excitatory postsynaptic potential**
Equipotentiality concept that all parts of the cortex contribute equally to complex behaviors; any part of the cortex can substitute for any other, 394
Escape behaviors. *See* Attack and escape behaviors
Estradiol a hormone in the estrogen family, 327, *327*, *329*, 333, *333*, *336*
Estrogens family of hormones that are more abundant in females, 326, *327*, *329*, 332, 333, 334–335
Evaporation, 296
Evening people and morning people, 265–266
Evoked potentials electrical recordings on the scalp from brain activity in response to a stimulus, 91, *96*
Evoked reponses electrical recordings on the scalp from brain activity in response to a stimulus, 91
Evolution a change over generations in the frequencies of various genes in a population
of behavior, 110–114
of the brain, 111
of language, 437–440
Evolutionary explanation understanding in terms of the evolutionary history of a structure or behavior, 7
Evolutionary interpretations, of mating behavior, 341–342
Evolutionary psychology field that deals with how behaviors evolved, 7, 112–114
Excitatory postsynaptic potential (EPSP) graded depolarization, 41, 44–45
Excitatory synapses, *252*, *276*
Exercise, 480
Exhaustion, 383
Exocytosis a release of neurotransmitter from the presynaptic neuron into the synaptic cleft that separates one neuron from another, 51
Experience, and fine-tuning brain development, 125–131
Experimental treatments for substance abuse, 472
Explicit memory deliberate recall of information that one recognizes as a memory, 400–401
Extensor muscle that straightens the limb, 228
Extracellular fluid, 302
Extreme cold, survival in, 297
Eye expressions, 376, *376*
Eyes, 149–152, *150*, *151*

Facial expressions
and amygdala, 373
and blindness, *104*
and emotions, 358, *358*, 361–362, *361*
and infants, *239*
and oxytocin, 459
and Urbach-Wiethe disease, 375–376, *375*
Facial recognition, 179–181
Facilitating interneuron, 415
Family studies, and schizophrenia, 489–490
Far transfer, 126
Fast muscles, 230
Fast-twitch fibers muscle fibers that produce fast contractions but fatigue rapidly, 230
Fat cells, *58*
Fear and anxiety, 371–376
and the amygdala, 6, 371
monkey studies, 373
and political attitudes, *374*
rodent studies, 371–372
Feature detectors neurons whose responses indicate the presence of a particular feature, 169–170
Feedback, movements varying in sensitivity to, 232
Feeding, regulation of
glucose, insulin, and glucagon, 310–312
leptin, 312–313
oral factors, 309–310
stomach and intestines, 310
Fetal alcohol syndrome a condition resulting from prenatal exposure to alcohol and marked by hyperactivity, impulsiveness, decreased alertness, varying degrees of mental retardation, motor problems, heart defects, and facial abnormalities, 124
Fetal neurons, 254
Fever, 299
Finger-to-nose test, 242
Fissure, *68*
Fitness the spreading of genes; number of copies of one's genes that endure in later generations, 111
5α-reductase 2, 345
5-hydroxyindoleacetic acid (5-HIAA) serotonin's main metabolite, 369, *369*
Fixation point, 444–445, *445*
Flash suppression procedure of making a stationary object impossible to see consciously by surrounding it with flashing objects, 449–450
Flexor muscle that flexes the limb, 228
Fluent aphasia condition characterized by poor language comprehension and impaired ability to remember the name of objects, 442–443
fMRI. *See* **Functional magnetic resonance imaging**
Focal hand dystonia (musician's cramp) a disorder where one or more fingers is in constant contraction or where moving one finger independently of others is difficult, 130
Focus point in the brain where an epileptic seizure begins, 426
Foliate papilla, *212*
Folic acid vitamin that is important for development of the nervous system, 500
Follicle-stimulating hormone (FSH) chemical released from the anterior pituitary; promotes the growth of a follicle in the ovary, 332, *333*
Food selection, 307–309
Footbridge dilemma, 362, *363*
Forebrain most anterior part of the brain; consists of two cerebral hemispheres, *71*, 72–77
Fornix, *360*
Fovea a tiny area of the retina specialized for acute, detailed vision, 149–152, 153
Frequency the number of cycles per second, measured in Hz, 188
Frequency theory concept that the basilar membrane vibrates in synchrony with a sound, causing auditory nerve axons to produce action potentials at the same frequency, 190–191
Frontal cortex, *75*
Frontal lobe section of cerebral cortex that extends from the central sulcus to the anterior limit of the brain, *5*, *73*, *74*, *82*, 84–85, *360*
FSH. *See* **Follicle-stimulating hormone**
Functional explanation understanding why a structure or behavior evolved as it did, 7, *7*, 112
Functional magnetic resonance imaging (fMRI) a modified version of MRI that measures energies based on hemoglobin instead of water; determines the brain areas receiving the greatest supply of blood and using the most oxygen, 92–93, *92*, *96*, 359–360, 373, 400
Fungiform papilla, *212*, 215, *216*

Fusiform gyrus brain area of the inferior temporal cortex that recognizes faces, 179, *179*, 181

GABA (gamma-aminobutyric acid), 52, 54, 277, *277*, 281
GABA$_A$ receptor receptor complex structure that includes a site that binds GABA as well as sites that modify the sensitivity of the GABA site, 376, 377–378, *377*, 416, 426, 469–470
Ganglion/Ganglia, 68, 69
Ganglion cells type of neuron in the retina that receives input from the bipolar cells, 149–150, *151*, 162, *163*, 166, *166*, 268
Gap junction a direct contact of one neuron with another, enabling electrical transmission, 57, *57*
Gases one of the categories of neurotransmitters, including nitric oxide and possibly others, 50, *50*
Gastric bypass surgery, 319
Gastrin-releasing peptide, 207
Gate theory idea that stimulation of certain axons can close the "gates" for pain messages, 205
Gender differences, 343
Gender-differentiated behaviors, 343–346
Gender identity, sex with which a person identifies, 343–346
General adaptation syndrome a generalized response to stress, 383
Genes units of heredity that maintain their structural identity from one generation to another, 104, 326
Genetic drift, 7
Genetics. *See also* **Heritability**
  autism spectrum disorders, 500
  and body weight, 318
  and eating disorders, 318
  effect on behavior, 109–110
  and the environment, 108–110
  and the evolution of behavior, 104–114
  and Huntington's disease, 255–256, *255*, *256*
  and major depression, 475–476, *476*
  Mendelian genetics, 104–108
  and predispositions, 469
  and schizophrenia, 489–491, *489*
  sex-linked and sex-limited genes, 106–107
  and sexual orientation, 346–347
  and violence, 370
Genitals, 326, 328–329, *328*
Germany, 264, *264*
Gestures, 438
Ghrelin chemical released by the stomach during a period of food deprivation; also released as a neurotransmitter in the brain, where it stimulates eating, 314, 318
GHRH (growth-hormone releaseing hormone), 314
Ginkgo biloba, 419
Glia type of cell in the nervous system that, in contrast to neurons, does not conduct impulses over long distances, 5, 19–21, *21*
Globus pallidus large subcortical structure; part of the basal ganglia, *76*, 243
Glucagon pancreatic hormone that stimulates the liver to convert stored glycogen to glucose, 310–312, *311*
Glucose a simple sugar, 23, 92, 111, 310–312
Glutamate, 52, 124, 137, 213, *277*, 416, 492, 495
Glutamate hypothesis of schizophrenia proposal that schizophrenia relates in part to deficient activity at glutamate synapses, especially in the prefrontal cortex, 495
Glutamine, 105
Glymnema sylvestre, 213
Golgi tendon organs receptors that respond to increases in muscle tension; inhibit further contractions, 231
Goose bumps, 112
G protein a protein coupled to guanosine triphosphate (GTP), an energy-storing molecule, 53, 218, *219*
Graded potential a membrane potential that varies in magnitude in proportion to the intensity of the stimulus, 34
Grasp reflex, 112, *112*
Gray matter areas of the nervous system that are densely packed with cell bodies and dendrites, 69, *69*, 128, *169*
Group selection, 114
Growth-hormone releasing hormone (GHRH), 314
Guanine, 105
Gyrus, 68

Habituation a decrease in response to a stimulus that is presented repeatedly and accompanied by no change in other stimuli, 414, *415*
Hair cells the auditory receptors that lie along the basilar membrane in the cochlea, 190
Hair-follicle receptors, *200*
Hallucinations false sensory experiences, 487
Hallucinogenic drugs drugs that distort perception, 54, *57*
Hamilton Depression Rating Scale, 479
Hammer, *189*, 190
Handedness, 113, 431–432
Hard problem philosophical question as to why and how brain activity becomes conscious, 449
Hawks, 150
Head injuries. *See* Brain damage
Hearing aids, 194
Hearing deficits, undetected, 488
Hearing loss, 193–194
Hebbian synapse a synapse that increases in effectiveness because of simultaneous activity in the presynaptic and postsynaptic neurons, 413
Hemiplegia, *240*
Hemoglobin, 92
Hemorrhage type of stroke resulting from a ruptured artery, 136
Heritability estimate of the degree to which variation in a characteristic depends on genetic variations in a given population, 108–109. *See also* Genetics
Hermaphrodites individual who appears to be a mixture of male and female anatomies, 343
Heroin, 55
Heterozygous having two unlike genes for a given trait, 105, *106*
Hibernation, 284–285
High-fructose corn syrup, 319
Hindbrain the posterior part of the brain, 71, *71*
Hippocampus a large structure located toward the posterior of the forebrain, between the thalamus and the cerebral cortex
  and amnesia, 397–403, *398*, 407
  commissures, *427*
  damage to, 398–401
  development of, 119
  and epigenetics, 107
  learning and memory, 407, *407*
  and limbic system, *360*
  old age and, 131
  overview of, 76–77
  and pain, 203, *204*
  as part of the limbic system, 74, *74*
  and schizophrenia, 492
  and stress, 386
  theories of the function of, 401–403
Histamine, 275, 277
Histones proteins that bind DNA into a shape that resembles a string wound around a ball, 107, *108*
Hold function, 242
Holistic perception, *429*
Homeobox genes, 123
Homeostasis tendency to maintain a variable, such as temperature, within a fixed range, 295
Homeothermic using physiological mechanisms to maintain a nearly constant body temperature despite changes in the environment's temperature, 296
Homosexuality. *See* Sexual orientation
Homozygous having two identical genes for a given characteristic, 105
Horizontal cells type of cell that receives input from receptors and delivers inhibitory input to bipolar cells, 162, *163*, 164
Horizontal plane, 68
Hormone chemical that is secreted by cells in one part of the body and conveyed by the blood to influence other cells
  activating effects of, 331–335
  and attack behaviors, 368
  and genital differentiation, 326–327
  list of, 58
  organizing effects of, 328–331
  overview of, 57–59
  parental behavior, 336–337
  sex hormones, 328–331
Hospital dilemma, 363
HPA axis the hypothalamus, pituitary gland, and adrenal cortex, 383–386, *384*
Human subjects, use of in research, 509–511
Hunger
  brain mechanisms, 313–317
  digestion and food selection, 307–309
  eating disorders, 317–320
  short- and long-term regulation of feeding, 309–313
Hunger signals, *313*
Huntingtin protein produced by the gene whose mutation leads to Huntington's disease, 256
Huntington's disease a severe neurological disorder characterized by jerky arm movements and facial twitches and later by tremors, writhing movements, and psychological symptoms, 254–256, *255*, *256*, 280, 488, 489
Hydrocephalus, 77
Hydrogen molecule, 505
Hypercomplex cells visual cortex cells that respond to a bar-shaped pattern of light in a particular orientation, but only if it does not extend beyond a certain point, 167
Hyperpolarization increased polarization across a membrane, 29
Hypnagogic hallucinations, 280
Hypocretin neurotransmitter that increases wakefulness and arousal, 275
Hypothalamic lesions, *317*
Hypothalamus small area near the base of the brain, ventral to the thalamus
  arousal and sleep, *277*
  fear and anxiety, 372
  hormone release, 329
  and hormones, 58, *58*
  HPA axis, 383–386
  and hunger, 314, *314*
  hunger, 313
  hunger signals, *313*
  location of, *59*
  major subdivisions of, *298*
  medial areas of, 316 *317*
  overview of, 75
  and pain, *204*
  and panic disorder, 376
  as part of the limbic system, 74, *74*

in sagittal section of the brain, *73*
sex diffferences in, 329–330
Hypothalamus-pituitary-adrenal cortex axis, 383–386
Hypovolemia, *304*
Hypovolemic thirst thirst provoked by low blood volume, 302, 304, *304*

Identity position view that mental processes and certain kinds of brain processes are the same thing, described in different terms, 449
Immune system, 384–386, *385*
Immune system structures that protect the body against viruses, bacteria, and other intruders, 384–385
Immunoglobulins, 118
Impaired infant vision, 173
Implicit memory an influence of experience on behavior, even if the influence is not recognized, 400–401
Impotence the inability to have an erection, 332
Impulsiveness, 364
Inattention blindness tendency not to notice a visible change in an object to which one was not paying attention, 454
Infant vision, 173, 179–180, *179*, *180*
Inferior, *68*
Inferior colliculus swelling on the surface of the tectum that contributes to hearing, *73*
Inferior temporal cortex portion of the cortex where neurons are highly sensitive to complex aspects of the shape of visual stimuli within very large receptive fields, 178–179
In-group bias, 460–461
Inhibition, of movement, 238
Inhibitory postsynaptic potential (IPSP) temporary hyperpolarization of a membrane, 43, *44*
Inhibitory synapses, 43–44, 164, *252*, *276*
Inner ear, 189
Inner-ear deafness hearing loss that results from damage to the cochlea, the hair cells, or the auditory nerve, 193
Insomnia, 279, *279*
Instrumental conditioning a type of condition in which reinforcement or punishment changes the future probabilities of a given behavior, 392, *393*
Insulin pancreatic hormone that enables glucose to enter the cells, 51, 310–312, *311*
Intact procedural memory, 401
Intelligence
and brain size, 97, *97*
and the environment, 126–127
and language, 438–439
Interior colliculus, 72
Internal regulation
hunger, 307–320
temperature, 294–299
thirst, 302–304
Interneuron neuron whose axons and dendrites are all confined within a given structure, 19, 43, *44*
Interpreter tendency of the left hemisphere to invent an explanation for an action when the true cause was unconscious, 429
Intersexes people whose sexual development is intermediate or ambiguous, 343–345, *343*
Interstitial nucleus 3 of the anterior hypothalamus (INAH-3), 349–350, *349*
Intertebrate behavior change, 414–415
Intestines, in regulation of feeding, 310
Intracellular fluid, 302
Intrinsic neuron neuron whose axons and dendrites are all confined within a given structure, 19, *40*
Involuntary movements, 232
Ion channels, *27*
Ionic bond attraction between a positively charged ion and a negatively charged ion, 505
Ionotropic effects synaptic effects that depend on the rapid opening of some kind of gate in the membrane, 52, *53*
Ions atoms that have gained or lost one or more electrons, 505
Iowa Gambling Task, 364
Iproniazid, 477
Ipsilateral, *68*
Ipsilateral ear, *192*
IPSP. *See* **Inhibitory postsynaptic potential**
Ischemia type of stroke resulting from a blood clot or other obstruction in an artery, 136–137
Itch, 207–208

James-Lange theory theory proposal that an event first provokes the autonomic arousal and skeletal responses and that the feeling aspect of emotion is the perception of those responses, 357, 358–359
Jealousy, 342
Jet lag a disruption of circadian rhythms due to crossing time zones, 265, *265*
Joint laxity, 376
The Journal of Neuroscience, 507

K-complex a sharp brain wave associated with temporary inhibition of neuronal firing, 273
Ketamine, 478, 495
Kidney, *58*
Kin selection selection for a gene that benefits the individual's relatives, 113
Klüver-Bucy syndrome, 373
Klüver-Bucy syndrome a behavioral disorder caused by temporal lobe damage, 84
Knee-jerk reflex, *231*
Koniocellular neurons small ganglion cells that occur throughout the retina, 165–166
Korsakoff's syndrome brain damage caused by prolonged thiamine deficiency, 22, 403–404
Krause end bulbs, *200*

Labeled-line principle concept that each receptor responds to a limited range of stimuli and has a direct line to the brain, 211
Lactase intestinal enzyme that metabolizes lactose, 308
Lactose sugar in milk, 308, *309*
Laminae layer of cell bodies that are parallel to the surface of the cerebral cortex and separated from each other by layers of fibers, 68, 80–81, *81*
Language
and brain damage, 440–443
dyslexia, 444–445
evolution of, 437–440
learning, sensitive period for, 440
and music, 443
nonhuman precursors of, 435–437
by-product of intelligence vs. specialized adaptation, 438–439
Wernicke's aphasia, 442–443
Language acquisition device a built-in mechanism for acquiring language, 439
Large-scale integration, 85–86
Lateral, *68*
Lateral corticospinal tract a set of axons from the primary motor cortex, surrounding areas, and midbrain area that is primarily responsible for controlling the peripheral muscles, 240, *240*, *241*
Lateral fissure, *440*
Lateral geniculate body, *75*
Lateral geniculate nucleus thalamic nucleus that receives incoming visual information, 162, 166
Lateral hypothalamus area of the hypothalamus that controls insulin secretion, alters taste responsiveness, and facilitates feeding in other ways, 314, 315–316, *315*, *316*
Lateral inhibition the reduction of activity in one neurons by activity in neighboring neurons, 162, 164, *165*
Lateral interpositus nucleus (LIP) a nucleus of the cerebellum that is essential for learning, 395, *396*
Lateralization divisions of labor between the two brain hemispheres, 424, 492
Lateralization of function
corpus callosum and split-brain operation, 426–431
development of, 431–432
and handedness, 431–432
hemispheric specializations in intact brains, 430–431
left and right hemispheres, 424
visual and auditory connections, 425–426
Lateral preoptic area part of the hypothalamus that controls drinking, 303
Law of specific nerve energies statement that whatever excites a particular nerve always sends the same kind of information to the brain, 148
Lazy eye, 171–172
L-dopa chemical precursor to dopamine, 51, 253–254
L-dopa treatment, 253–254
Learned adjustments in behavior, 142
Learned fears, 372
Learning and memory
basal ganglia, 406–407
Hebbian synapse, 413
and the hippocampus, 397–403
information storage in the nervous system, 412–419
localized representations of memory, 392–395
memory consolidation, 396–397
memory improvement, 419
and other brain areas, 407–408
and sleep, 286–287
types of memory, 395–397
Left hemisphere, 424
Leg flexion, 40–41
Leptin, 312–313
Lesion damage to a structure, 89–90, *96*, *317*
Leukocytes white blood cells, 384
LH. *See* **Luteinizing hormone**
Lifeboat dilemma, 362, *363*
Ligand, 52
Ligand-gated channels channel that opens when a neurotransmitter attaches, 52
Limbic system interlinked structures that form a border around the brainstem, 74, *74*, 359–360, *360*
Lithium element whose salts are often used as therapy for bipolar disorder, 482–483
Lobotomies. *See* **Prefrontal lobotomies**
Local anesthetic drugs that attach to the sodium channels of the membrane, stopping action potentials, 31
Local committee review, 509–510
Localized representations of memory, 392–395
Local neurons neurons without an axon, 34
Locus coeruleus a small structure in the pons that emits bursts of impulses in response to meaningful events, especially those that produce emotional arousal, 275, *277*
Longitudinal fissure, 5
Long-term depression (LTD) a prolonged decrease in response at a synapse where the axons have been less active than certain other axons afferent to that neuron, 415

Long-term memory memory of events that occurred further back in time, 395–396, 399
Long-term potentiation (**LTP**) phenomenon that when one or more axons connected to a dendrite bombard it with a rapid series of stimuli, some of the synapses become more responsive to new input of the same type for minutes, days, or weeks, 415–419, *416*, *417*, *418*
Loudness, 194, *194*
Love, biology of, 459–460
LSD (lysergic acid diathylamide), 54, *54*
LTD. *See* **Long-term depression**
LTP. *See* **Long-term potentiation**
Lucid dreaming, 277
Luteinizing hormone (**LH**) hormone released from the anterior pituitary that causes the follicle to release an ovum, 332, *333*

Magnetic resonance imaging (**MRI**) method of imaging a living brain by using a magnetic field and a radio frequency field to make atoms with odd atomic weights all rotate in the same direction and then removing those fields and measuring the energy that the atoms release, 94–95, *95*, *96*, 127–128
Magnetoencephalograph (**MEG**) a device that measures the faint magnetic fields generated by brain activity, 91, *91*, *96*, 127
Magnocellular neurons large cell bodies with large receptive fields that are distributed evenly throughout the retina, 165–166
Major depression a condition in which people feel sad and helpless every day for weeks at a time, 475–476, *476*, 481–482, *481*, *483*. *See also* **Antidepressant drugs**
Mamillary body, *74*, *360*
Mammalian visual system, 162
Mania a condition characterized by restless activity, excitement, laughter, self-confidence, rambling speech, and loss of inhibitions, 482
Manic-depressive disorder. *See* **Bipolar disorder**
MAO (**monoamine oxidase**) enzyme that converts catecholamines and serotonin into synaptically inactive forms, 51
MAO_A (monoamine oxidase A), 370
MAOIs. *See* **Monoamine oxidase inhibitors**
Masking use of one stimulus to block perception of another, 450
Mass action concept that the cortex works as a whole and the more cortex, the better, 394
Materialism view that everything that exists is material or physical, 449
Mates, characteristics sought in, 342
Mating behavior, evolutionary interpretations, 341–342
MDMA ("Ecstasy"), 57
Mechanical senses
  itch, 207–208
  pain, 202–207
  somatosensation, 198–202
  vestibular sensation, 198
Medial, *68*
Medial areas of the hypothalamus, 316–317
Medial corticospinal tract set of axons from many parts of the cerebral cortex, midbrain, and medulla; responsible for control of bilateral muscles of the neck, shoulders, and trunk, *240*, 241
Medial preoptic area (MPOA), 331
Medical fields, 8
Medulla hindbrain structure located just above the spinal cord; could be regarded as an enlarged extension of the spinal cord, 5, 71, *73*, *74*, 203, *203*
MEG. *See* **Magnetoencephalograph**
Meissner's corpuscles, 199, *200*
Melanocortin type of chemical that promotes satiety, 314
Melatonin hormone that influences both circadian and circannual rhythms, 269
Membrane structure that separates the inside of the cell from the outside environment, 17, *26*, *27*
Memory and learning
  basal ganglia, 406–407
  Hebbian synapse, 413
  and the hippocampus, 397–403
  information storage in the nervous system, 412–419
  localized representations of memory, 392–395
  memory consolidation, 396–397
  memory improvement, 419
  and other brain areas, 407–408
  and sleep, 286–287
  types of memory, 395–397
Men
  activating effects, 331–332
  aggressive behaviors, 368, *368*, 370, *370*
  brain size compared to women, 98
  brains of, 335
  characteristcs sought in mates, 342
  discrepancies of sexual appearance, 345–346
  effects of sex hormones on nonsexual characteristics, 334–335
  gender assignment and rearing, 344–345
  genitals, *326*, *328*
  interest in multiple mates, 341–342
  and jealousy, 342
  and oxytocin, 459
  parental behavior, 337
  and pheromones, 220–221
  and schizophrenia, 489
  sex hormones, 328–331
  sexual orientation, 346–347
Mendelian genetics, 104–108
Meninges membranes that surround the brain and spinal cord, 77
Menstrual cycle a periodic variation in hormones and fertility over the course of about 28 days, 332, *332*
Mentalism view that only the mind really exists and that the physical world could not exist unless some mind were aware of it, 449
Merkel disks, 199, *200*
Mesolimbocortical system a set of neurons that project from the midbrain tegmentum to the limbic system, 495, *496*
Mesostriatal system, 495
Messenger RNA, 269, *269*
Metabotropic effects a sequence of metabolic reactions that produce slow and long-lasting effects at a synapse, 53, *53*
Methadone drug similar to heroin and morphine that is taken orally, 55, 472
Methylphenidate stimulant drug prescribed for ADHD that increases the stimulation of dopamine synapses by blocking the reuptake of dopamine by the presynaptic neuron, 55, *57*, 419
Microdeletion deletion of a small part of a chromosome, 490
Microelectrodes, 27
Microglia cells that remove waste material and other microorganisms from the nervous system, 20, *21*
Midbrain middle part of the brain, 71–72, *71*, *73*
Middle ear, 189
Middle-ear deafness hearing loss that occurs if the bones of the middle ear fail to transmit sound waves properly to the cochlea, 193
Middle temporal cortex, 181–182
Middle temporal cortex (area MT), 181–183, 192
Midget ganglion cells ganglion cells in the fovea of humans and other primates, 150
Migrate movement of brain neurons or glia, 118, 124
Mind-body problem or **mind-brain problem** question about the relationship between mental experience and brain activity, 4, 448–449, *448*
Minimally conscious state condition of decreased brain activity with occasional, brief periods of purposeful actions and limited speech comprehension, 272, 453
Miracle berries, 213
Mirror neurons cells that are active during a movement and while watching someone else perform the same movement, 238–239
Mitochondrion structure that performs metabolic activities, 17
Möbius syndrome, 358, *359*
Molecular basis of action potential, 29–31
Molecule two or more atoms bound together, 505, *506*
Monism belief that the universe consists of only one kind of substance, 6, 449
Monoamine oxidase A (MAO_A), 370
Monoamine oxidase inhibitors (**MAOIs**) drugs that block the enzyme monoamine oxidase (MAO), a presynaptic terminal enzyme that metabolizes catecholamines and serotonin into inactive forms, 477, *477*
Monoamines chemicals formed by a change in certain amino acids, 50, *50*
Monosodium glutamate (MSG), 213
Monozygotic twins twins derived from one egg, 108, 347, 490
Mood disorders
  antidepressant drugs, 477–482
  bipolar disorder, 482–483
  major depressive disorder, 475–476
  seasonal affective disorder, 483
Moods, and sleep, 263, *263*
Mooney faces, *170*
Moral decisions, and emotions, 362–363
Morning people and evening people, 265–266
Moro reflex, 371
Morphine, 55, 205
Morris water maze a procedure used to test for spatial memory in nonhumans, 402–403, *403*
Motion blindness an impaired ability to perceive movement, 182–183
Motion perception, 181–183
Motor control, *236*
Motor information in the cortex, *83*
Motor learning, 246
Motor neuron neuron that receives excitation from other neurons and conducts impulses to a muscle, 17, *18*, *40*, *44*, *123*, *236*
Motor program a fixed sequence of movements, 232–233
Move function, 242
Movement
  basal ganglia and, 243–246
  brain mechanisms, 235–248
  cerebellum and, 241–243
  cerebral cortex and, 235–241
  and conscious decisions, 246–248
  control of, 228–233
  disorders, 252–256
  inhibition of, 237–238
  and muscles, 228–232
  planning of, 237–238
  and temperature, 230
  units of, 232–233
MPOA (medial preoptic area), 331

MPP⁺ a chemical that accumulates in, and then destroys, neurons that release dopamine, 253
MPTP a chemical that the body converts to MPP⁺, 253
MRI. *See* **Magnetic resonance imaging**
MST (medial superior temporal cortex), temporal cortex area that responds best to the expansion, contraction, or rotation of a visual display, 181–182, *182*
Müllerian ducts embryonic structures that can develop into a female's oviducts, uterus, and upper vagina, 326, *326*
Müllerian-inhibiting hormone (MIH), 326
Multiple mates, interest in, 341–342
Multiple sclerosis, 33–34
Muscles
  control of by propioceptors, 231–232
  fast vs. slow, 230
  and movement, 228–232
Muscle spindle a receptor parallel to the muscle that responds to a stretch, 231
Music, and language, 443
Music training, 127–128, *128*, 129–130
Mutation a heritable change in a DNA molecule, 107
Myelin an insulating material composed of fats and proteins, 32, 118
Myelinated axons axons covered with myelin sheaths, 32
Myelination process by which glia produce the insulating fatty sheaths that accelerate transmission in many vertebrate axons, 118
Myelin sheath insulating material that covers vertebrate axon, 18–19, 32–34, *34*

Naloxone, 472
Naltrexone, 472
Narcolepsy a condition characterized by frequent periods of sleepiness during the day, 280
Natural killer cells, 384
Near transfer, 126
Necrosis, 122
Negative color afterimage result of staring at a colored object for a prolonged length of time and then looking at a white surface, the image is seen as a negative image, with a replacement of red with green, green with red, yellow and blue with each other, and black and white with each other, 155–156, *155*, *156*
Negative feedback homeostatic processes that reduce discrepancies from the set point, 56–57, *59*, 295
Negative symptoms absence of behaviors ordinarily seen in normal people (e.g., lack of emotional expression), 487
Nerve, *68*
Nerve cells
  blood–brain barrier, 21–23
  cells of the nervous system, 16–23
Nerve deafness hearing loss that results from damage to the cochlea, the hair cells, or the auditory nerve, 193
Nerve growth factor (NGF) a protein that promotes the survival and growth of axons in the sympathetic nervous system and certain axons in the brain, 122–123
Nerve impulses
  action potential, 29–32
  local neurons, 34
  myelin sheath and saltatory conduction, 32–34
  propagation of the action potential, 32
  resting potential, 26–29
Nervous system, cells of, 16–23
Nervous system, information storage in
  Hebbian synapse, 413
  maze analogy, 412–413
  memory improvement, 419
  single-cell mechanisms of invertebrate behavior change, 414–415
Neural Darwinism principle of competition among axons, 122
Neuroanatomy the anatomy of the nervous system, 65
Neurodevelopmental hypothesis proposal that schizophrenia begins with abnormalities in the prenatal or neonatal development of the nervous system, based on either genetics or other influences, 491–493
Neuroleptic drug drug that tends to relieve schizophrenia and similar conditions, 493
Neuromodulators chains of amino acids, 53
Neuromuscular junction a synapse between a motor neuron axon and a muscle fiber, 228
Neurons cells that receive information and transmit it to other cells
  and the brain, 5
  definition of, 16
  degeneration of, *405*
  determinants of neuronal survival, 122–123
  development of, 118–119
  growth and development of, 117–119
  in the human body, *16*
  image of, *5*, *17*, *18*
  membrane of, *26*
  methods for recording activity, *27*
  structure of, 17–19
  variations in, 19
Neuropeptides chains of amino acids, 50, *50*, 53–54, *54*, 55, 203
Neuropeptide Y (NPY) peptide that blocks the satiety actions of the paraventricular nucleus, 314
Neurotransmitters chemicals released by neurons that affect other neurons
  in events at the synapse, *49*
  inactivation and reuptake of, 55
  list of, *50*
  release and diffusion of, 51–52
  structures of, *507*
  synthesis of, 50–51
  types of, 50–51
Neurotrophin a chemical that promotes the survival and activity of neurons, 123
NGF. *See* **Nerve growth factor**
Niacin, 488
Nicotine a stimulant drug that stimulates certain acetylcholine receptors, 54, 57, 314
Nicotine receptors, 54
Night terrors experiences of intense anxiety from which a person awakens screaming in terror; more severe than a nightmare, 281
Nitric oxide a gas released by many small local neurons, 50, 418
NMDA receptor a glutamate receptor that can respond to the drug N-methyl-D-aspartate (NMDA), 416–418, *417*, 419, 495
NO. *See* **Nitric oxide**
Nodes of Ranvier interruptions in the myelin sheath of vertebrate axons, 19, 32, *34*
Nonfluent aphasia brain damage that causes impaired language, 440–442
Non-REM (NREM) sleep stages of sleep other than REM, 274, 281
Nonsexual characteristics, effects of sex hormones on, 334–335
Nontasters, 215, *216*
Norepinephrine, 50–51, *50*, 55, 69–70, *277*
Nourishment, of vertebrate neurons, 23
NPY. *See* **Neuropeptide Y**
NREM sleep. *See* **Non-REM sleep**
NTS. *See* **Nucleus of the tractus solitarius**
Nuclei of the cerebellum clusters of cell bodies in the interior of the cerebellum, 243
Nucleus structure that contains the chromosomes, 17, *68*
Nucleus accumbens brain area that is rich in dopamine and is central to the brain's reinforcement system, 466–467, *467*
Nucleus basalis a forebrain structure that lies on the ventral surface; receives input from the hypothalamus and basal ganglia; sends axons to areas in the cerebral cortex, 76
Nucleus of the tractus solitarius (NTS) structure in the medulla that receives input from taste receptors, 214–215
Nutritional abnormalities, and schizophrenia, 488

Obesity, 311–313, *312*, 317, 318–319
Occipital lobe posterior section of the cerebral cortex, 5, *73*, 82–83, *82*
Occipital cortex, *75*
OEA (oleoylethanolamide), 310
Old age, 112–113, 132
Oleoylethanolamide (OEA), 310
Olfaction the sense of smell, which is the response to chemicals that contact the membranes inside the nose, 216–220
Olfactory bulb, 5, *74*, *74*, 119, 219, *360*
Olfactory cells neurons responsible for smell, located on the olfactory epithelium in the rear of the nasal air passages, 218
Olfactory receptors, 119, 218–219, *218*, *219*
Oligodendrocytes glia cells that build myelin sheaths, 20, *21*
Ondansetron, 54
One child policy, *110*
Ontogenetic explanation understanding in terms of how a structure or behavior develops, 6, *7*
Open class of grammatical forms, 441
Opiate abuse, medications for, 472
Opiate drugs drugs derived from the opium poppy, 54–55, *57*, 467
Opioids, 205
Opioid mechanisms systems that respond to opiate drugs and similar chemicals, 205
Opponent-process theory idea that we perceive color in terms of opposites, 155–156
Optic chiasm area where axons from each eye cross to the opposite side of the brain, 424, *424*
Optic nerve ganglion cell axons that exit through the back of the eye and continue to the brain, 5, 149
Optic tract, *75*
Optogenetics method of controlling a neuron's activity by implanting a light-sensitive protein in the cell and then shining light onto it, 90
Oral factors in regulation of feeding, 309–310
Orexin neurotransmitter that increases wakefulness and arousal, 275, *277*, 280, 376, 377
Organizing effects long-lasting effects of a hormone that are present during a sensitive period early in development, 328–331
Organum vasculosum laminae terminalis (OVLT), 303
Osmotic pressure tendency of water to flow across a semipermeable membrane from the area of low solute concentration to the area of high solute concentration, 302, *303*
Osmotic thirst thirst triggered by certain neurons that detect the loss of their own water, 302–303, *304*
Outer ear, 189
Out-group bias, *460*
Oval window a membrane of the inner ear, 190
Ovaries the female's egg-producing organs, 58, 326, *326*, 333

OVLT (organum vasculosum laminae terminalis) brain area that detects osmotic pressure and salt content of the blood, 303
Oxygen debt, 230
Oxytocin hormone released by posterior pituitary; important for sexual and parental behaviors, 58, *59*, 331, 459–460

Pacinian corpuscle receptor that responds to a sudden displacement of the skin or high-frequency vibrations on the skin, 199, *200*
Pain
- emotional, 203–204
- relief of, 204–207
- sensitization of, 207
- spinal pathways for, *203*
- stimuli and spinal cord path, 202–203
- synapses for, *205*

Pancreas, *58*
Panic attack period marked by extreme sympathetic nervous system arousal, 358, 375
Panic disorder condition marked by frequent periods of anxiety and rapid breathing, increased heart rate, sweating, and trembling, 376
Papillae structures on a tongue's surface that contain taste buds, 212
Paradoxical sleep sleep that is deep in some ways and light in others, 273–274
Parahippocampsl gyrus, *360*
Parallel fibers axons in the cerebellum, parallel to one another and perpendicular to the planes of Purkinje cells, 243, *244*
Paralysis, *240*
Paraplegia, *240*
Parasympathetic nervous system system of nerves that facilitate vegetative, nonemergency responses by the body's organs, 69–70, *70*, 356–357, *356*
Paraventricular hypothalamus, 313–315, *315*
Paraventricular nucleus (PVN) part of the hypothalamus in which activity tends to limit meal size and damage leads to excessively large meals, 303, 314, *314*
Parental behavior, 336–337
Parietal lobe section of the cerebral cortex between the occipital lobe and the central sulcus, 5, *73*, *82*, *83*, 407
Parkinson's disease malady caused by damage to a dopamine pathway, resulting in slow movements, difficulty initiating movements, rigidity of the muscles, and tremors, 51, 246, 252–254, 406–407
Parvocellular neurons small cell bodies with small receptive fields in or near the fovea, 165–166
Pathfinding by axons, 119–122
PCP. *See* **Phencyclidine**
Peacocks, *111*
Peptide hormones hormones composed of short chains of amino acids, 58
Perceptions, 6, 148–149
Perfect pitch, 191
Periaqueductal gray area area of the brainstem that is rich in endorphin synapses, 205, *206*
Period (PER), 268–269, *269*
Periodic limb movement disorder a sleep disorder characterized by repeated involuntary movement of the legs and sometimes the arms, 280
Periodic table of elements, *504*
Periovulatory period time around the middle of the menstrual cycle of maximum fertility and high estrogen levels, 333–334
Peripheral nervous system (PNS) nerves outside the brain and spinal cord, 66, *67*
Peripheral vision, 153
PET **(positron-emission tomography)** method of mapping activity in a living brain by recording the emission of radioactivity from injected chemicals, 92, *92*, *96*, 359–360, 402, *482*, *496*
PGO waves a distinctive pattern of high-amplitude electrical potentials that occur first in the pons, then in the lateral geniculate, and then in the occipital cortex, 278, *278*, 288
Phantom limb a continuing sensation of an amputated body part, 141, *141*
Phase-advance, 265, 279
Phase-delay, 265, 279
Phase difference, 195, *195*
Phencyclidine (PCP) drug that inhibits the NMDA glutamate receptors, 495
Phenothiazines a chemical family that includes antipsychotic drugs (chlorpromazine) that relieve the positive symptoms of schizophrenia, 493
Phenylketonuria (PKU) a genetic inability to metabolize the amino acid phenylalanine, 109
Phenylthiocarbamide (PTC), 105
Pheromones chemicals released by an animal that affect the behavior of other members of the same species, 220–221, 294
Phi phenomenon tendency to see something as moving back and forth between positions when in fact it is alternately blinking on and off in those positions, 452
Phonological loop mechanism that enables someone to hear something and remember it, 438
Photopigments chemicals contained in rods and cones that release energy when struck by light, 153
Phrenology a process of relating skull anatomy to behavior, 94, *94*
Phthalates, 331
Physiological arousal, and emotions, 357–359
Physiological explanation understanding in terms of the activity of the brain and other organs, 6, *7*
Pima people, 318
Pineal gland an endocrine gland located just posterior to the thalamus that releases the hormone melatonin, 58, 269
Pinna the outer ear structure of flesh and cartilage that sticks out from each side of the head, 189
Pitch perception, 190–191
Pitch the aspect of auditory perception related to the frequency of a sound, 188
Pituitary gland an endocrine gland attached to the base of the hypothalamus
- and hormones, 58, 59
- HPA axis, 383–386
- interaction with ovary, 333
- and intersexes, 343
- major subdivisions of, *298*
- overview of, 75
- in sagittal section of the brain, *73*

PKU (phenylketonuria) a genetic inability to metabolize the amino acid phenylalanine, 109
Placebo effect, 480
Placebos a drug or other procedure with no pharmacological effects, 205–206, 479, *479*
Place theory concept that pitch perception depends on which part of the inner ear has cells with the greatest activity level, 190
Planning, of movement, 237–238
Planum temprale section of the temporal cortex that is larger in the left hemisphere, 431
Plaques, 404, *405*
Plasticity after brain damage, 136–142
PNS. *See* **Peripheral nervous system**
POA/AH (preoptic area/anterior hypothalamus) brain area important for temperature regulation, thirst, and sexual behavior, 298–299, *299*, 336
Poikilothermic maintaining the body at the same temperature as the environment, 296
Polarization difference in electrical charges between the inside and outside of the cell, 26
Poliomyelitis, *240*
Political attitudes and fear responses, *374*
Polysomnograph a combination of EEG and eye-movement records, 272, *273*
Pons hindbrain structure that lies anterior and ventral to the medulla, 71, *73*
Pontomesencephalon part of the reticular formation that contributes to cortical arousal, 275, *277*
Positive symptoms presence of behaviors not seen in normal people, 487
Positron-emission tomography (PET) method of mapping activity in a living brain by recording the emission of radioactivity from injected chemicals, 92, *92*, *96*, 359–360, 402, *482*, *496*
Postcentral gyrus area just posterior to the central gyrus; primary receptor site for touch and other body sensations, 5, *83*
Posterial parietal cortex area with a mixture of visual, somatosensory, and movement functions, particularly in monitoring the position of the body relative to objects in the world, 237
Posterior, *68*
Posterior pituitary portion of the pituitary gland, which releases hormones synthesized by the hypothalamus, 58, *58*, *59*
Postganglionic fibers, 69
Postsynaptic cells, 52, 56–57
Postsynaptic neuron neuron that receives transmission from another neuron, 41, *42*, 42, 49, *49*, 52, *53*, 53
Post-traumatic stress disorder (PTSD) a condition resulting from a severe traumatic experience, leading to a long-lasting state of frequent distressing recollections (flashbacks) and nightmares about the traumatic event, avoidance of reminders of it, and exaggerated arousal in response to noises and other stimuli, 376–377
Potassium channels, 30, 32
Potassium gradients, 28, *28*
Potassium ions, 27–28, *30*
Practitioner fields of psychology, 8
Prader-Willi syndrome, 318
Precentral gyrus, 5, 84
Predispositions
- behavioral predictors of abuse, 470–471
- environmental influences, 469–470
- genetic influences, 469

Prefrontal cortex anterior portion of the frontal lobe, which responds mostly to the sensory stimuli that signal the need for a movement
- and addiction, 468
- in adolescents, 131
- damage to, 358, 363–364, 397
- functions of, 85
- and language, 438
- learning and memory, 408, *408*
- and movement, 238
- overview of, 84
- and pain, 203
- and schizophrenia, 492
- species differences in, *84*

Prefrontal lobotomies surgical disconnection of the prefrontal cortex from the rest of the brain, 85
Preganglionic axons, 69
Premotor cortex area of the frontal cortex, active during the planning of a movement, 236, 238

Prenatal environment
alcoholism, 469
autism spectrum disorders, 500
schizophrenia, 490–491
sexual orientation, 348
Preoptic area/anterior hypothalamus (POA/AH) brain area important for temperature regulation, thirst, and sexual behavior, 298–299, *299*, 336
Presymptomatic testing, for Huntington's disease, 255–256
Presynaptic changes, 418–419
Presynaptic neuron neuron that delivers transmission to another neuron, 41, 51, *477*
Presynaptic terminal (end bulb or bouton) point where an axon releases chemicals, 19
Primary auditory cortex (area A1) area in the superior temporal cortex in which cells respond best to tones of a particular frequency, 192–193, *192*, *193*
Primary motor cortex area of the prefrontal cortex just anterior to the central sulcus; a primary point of origin for axons conveying messages to the spinal cord, *75*, 235, *237*
Primary somatosensory cortex, *75*, 83, 201–202, *237*
Primary visual cortex (area V1) area of the cortex responsible for the first stage of visual processing, 82, 166–170, *169*, *177*, 178, 289, 373
Primates order of mammals that includes monkeys, apes, and humans, 80
aggressive behaviors, 369
bonobos, 436–437
fear and anxiety, 373
and language, 435, *435*, *436*
sex differences, 330, *330*
Procedural memory the development of motor skills and habits; a special kind of implicit memory, 401
Productivity ability of language to produce new signals to represent new ideas, 435
Progesterone steroid hormone that prepares the uterus for the implantation of a fertilized ovum and promotes the maintenance of pregnancy, 327, *332*, 333, *333*
Prolactin, 336
Proliferation production of new cells, 117–118, 124
Propagation of the action potential transmission of an action potential down an axon, 32
Propranolol, 379, 472
Proprioceptor a receptor that detects the position or movement of a part of the body, 231–232, *231*
Prosody, 188
Prosopagnosia the inability to recognize faces due to damage of several brain areas, 180–181
Prostaglandins chemicals the immune system delivers to the hypothalamus, causing a fever, 384
Protein hormones hormones composed of long chains of amino acids, 58
Proximal, *68*
Psychological disorders
autism spectrum disorders, 499–500
mood disorders, 475–483
schizophrenia, 487–496
substance abuse and addiction, 466–472
Psychoneuroimmunology study of the ways in which experiences, especially stressful ones, alter the immune system and how the immune system influences the central nervous system, 385
Psychotherapy, 480
PTC (phenylthiocarbamide), 105
PTSD. *See* **Post-traumatic stress disorder**
Pudendal nerve, 333
Punishment an event that suppresses the frequency of the preceding response, 392, *393*
Pupil an opening in the center of the iris where light enters, 149
Pure autonomic failure condition when output from the autonomic nervous system to the body fails, 357
Purines a category of chemicals including adenosine and several of its derivatives, 50, *50*
Purkinje cells flat cells in sequential planes, in the cerebellar cortex, parallel to one another, 243, *244*
Putamen large subcortical structure, part of the basal ganglia, *76*, 243
PVN. *See* **Paraventricular nucleus**
Pyramids, 240

Quadriplegia, *240*

Radial glia cells that guide the migration of neurons and the growth of axons and dendrites during embryological development, 20, *21*
Radial maze an apparatus used to test spatial memory in nonhumans, 402, *402*, 403
Rapid eye movement (REM) sleep sleep stage with rapid eye movements, high brain activity, and relaxation of the large muscles, 273–274, 278–279, 287–288
Readiness potential recordable activity in the motor cortex prior to voluntary movement, 247, *247*
Reappraisal, 374
Receptive fields the area in visual space that excites or inhibits any neuron, 165, *165*
Receptors
drugs that bind to, 54–55
olfactory, 218–219
for osmotic pressure and blood volume, *303*
taste, 212–214
variations in, 54
visual, 152–153
Receptor supersensitivity, 139–140
Recessive gene one that shows effects only in the homozygous condition, 105
Reciprocal altruism helping others who may be helpful in return, 113–114
Reconsolidation restrengthening of a memory by a similar later experience, 379
Red-green color deficiency, *106*
Red nucleus, 240
Reflex arc a circuit from sensory neuron to muscle response, 40, *40*
Reflexes automatic muscular responses to stimuli, 40–41, 231, 232
Refractory period time when the cell resists the production of further action potentials, 31–32
Reinforcer any event that increases the future probability of the preceding response, 392, *393*
Relative refractory period time after the absolute refractory period that requires a stronger stimulus to initiate an action potential, 31
Releasing hormones hormone released by the hypothalamus that flows through the blood to the anterior pituitary, 58
REM behavior disorder a condition in which people move around vigorously during REM sleep, 280–281
REM sleep. *See* **Rapid eye movement (REM) sleep**
Renin, 304
Reorganized sensory representations, 140–142
Repetitive transcranial magnetic stimulation, 481
Reproduction, 111
Reproductive behaviours
sex and hormones, 326–337
variations in sexual behavior, 341–350
Research fields, 8
Research methods
brain anatomy correlated with behavior, 94–96, *96*
brain size and intelligence, 96–98
effects of brain damage, 89–90, *96*
effects of brain stimulation, 90–91, *96*
recording brain activity, 91–94, *96*
Resilience, 386
Resistance, 383
Resting membrane, *28*
Resting potential condition of a neuron's membrane when it has not been stimulated or inhibited
definition of, 27
of the neuron, 26–29
sodium and potassium channels, 30
sodium and potassium ions, 27–28
Reticular formation a structure that extends from the medulla into the forebrain; controls motor areas of the spinal cord and selectively increases arousal and attention in various forebrain areas, 275
Retina the rear surface of the eye, which is lined with visual receptors, 149–152, *151*, *155*, 162–165, *163*
Retinal axons, *121*
Retinal disparity the discrepancy between what the left and right eyes see, 171
Retinex theory concept that the cortex compares information from various parts of the retina to determine the brightness and color for each area, 156–158
Retinohypothalamic path, 268
Retinotopic organization, *163*
Retrograde amnesia loss of memory for events that occurred before brain damage, 399
Retrograde transmitter a transmitter released by a postsynaptic cell that travels back to the presynaptic cell to modify it, 418
Reuptake reabsorption of a neurotransmitter by the presynaptic terminal, 55
Rhythms of waking and sleeping
biological clock, 264–266
endogenous rhythms, 262–263
Ribonucleic acid (RNA) a single-strand chemical, 105, *105*, 269, 413
Ribosomes sites for cell synthesization of new protein molecules, 17
Right hemisphere, 424, 429–430
Ritalin. *See* **Methylphenidate**
RNA. *See* **Ribonucleic acid**
Ro15-4513, 378
Rodent studies, 371–372, 393–394
Rods type of retinal receptor that detects brightness of light, 152–153, *152*, *154*, 162, *163*, 164
Ruffini endings, 199, *200*

Saccades voluntary eye movements, 182–183
Saccule, 198
SAD. *See* **Seasonal affective disorder (SAD)**
Sagittal plane, *68*
Saltatory conduction the jumping of action potentials from node to node, 33, *34*
Schizophrenia, 85
demographic data, 488–489
diagnosis, 487–489
differential diagnosis, 488
early development and later psychopathology, 493
family studies, 489–490
genetics, 107, 489–491

Schizophrenia, *(continued)*
long-term course, 493
mild brain abnormalities, 492
neurodevelopmental hypothesis, 491–493
prenatal and neonatal environment, 491–492
treatments, 493–496
Schwann cells glia cells that build myelin sheaths, 20, *21*
SCN. *See* **Suprachiasmatic nucleus**
Seasonal affective disorder (SAD) depression that recurs during a particular season, such as winter, 483, *483*
Season-of-birth effect tendency for people born in winter to have a slightly greater probability of developing schizophrenia than people born at other times of the year, 491
Secondary visual cortex (area V2) area of the brain that processes information from the primary visual cortex and transmits it to additional areas, 177, *177*, 178
Second-generation antipsychotics drugs that alleviate schizophrenia with less likelihood of movement problems, 495–496
Second messenger a chemical that, when activated by a neurotransmitter, initiates communication to many areas within the neuron, 53, *53*
Selective permeability ability of some chemicals to pass more freely than others through a membrane, 27
Selective serotonin reuptake inhibitors (SSRIs) drugs that block the reuptake of serotonin in the presynaptic terminal, 477
Self-stimulation of the brain behavior that is reinforced by electrical stimulation of a brain area, 466
Semantic dementia a loss of semantic memory, 407
Semantic memories memories of factual information, 399, 406, *407*
Semicircular canals structures located in the vestibular organ, oriented in three planes and lined with hair cells; sensitive to the directional tilt of the head, 198
Seminal vesicles, 326, *326*
Sensitive period time early in development when experiences have a particularly strong and enduring influence, 171, 328
Sensitization an increase in response to mild stimuli as a result of exposure to more intense stimuli, 414–415
Sensory information in the cortex, *83*
Sensory neglect, *456*
Sensory neuron neuron that is highly sensitive to a specific type of stimulation, 17, *18*, *40*
Sensory systems
audition, 188–195
chemical senses, 211–222
mechanical senses, 198–208
pain, 202–207
Sentinel behavior, *113*
Septal nuclei, *360*
Sequence of chemical events at the synapse
activation of receptors of the postsynaptic cell, 52
drugs that bind to receptors, 54–55
electrical synapses, 57
inactivation and reuptake of neurotransmitters, 55
ionotropic effects, 52
metabotropic effects and second messenger systems, 53
negative feedback from the postsynaptic cell, 56–57
neuropeptides, 53–54
release and diffusion of transmitters, 51–52
storage of transmitters, 51
synthesis of transmitters, 50–51
types of neurotransmitters, 50–51
variations in receptors, 54
Serotonin
arousal and sleep, 277
and depression, 476, *476*
fear and anxiety, 373
and LSD, *54*
receptors, 54
reuptake of, 55, 477
and stimulant drugs, 55
synthesis of, 50–51, *50*
Serotonin norepinephrine reuptake inhibitors (SNRIs) drugs that block the reuptake of serotonin and norepinephrine, 477, *477*
Serotonin synapses, and aggressive behaviors, 368–369
Set point a value that the body works to maintain, 295
activating effects of, 331–335
organizing effects of, 328–331
Sex diffferences, 343
in childhood behavior, 330–331
in the hypothalamus, 329–330
parental behavior, 336–337
activating effects of, 331–335
effects of on nonsexual characteristics, 334–335
organizing effects of, 328–331
Sex hormones
activating effects of, 331–335
effects of non-sexual characteristics, 334–335
organizing effects of, 328–331
parental behavior, 336–337
Sex-limited genes gene that exerts its effects primarily in one sex because of activation by androgens or estrogens, although members of both sexes may have the gene, 106–107
Sex-linked gene gene on either the X or the Y chromosome, 106–107, *106*
Sexsomnia, 281
Sexual activities, female-initiated, 333–334, *334*
Sexual appearance, intersexes and, 345–346
Sexual behavior, variations in
evolutionary interpretations of mating behavior, 341–342
gender identity and gender-differentiated behaviors, 343–346
sexual orientation, 346–350
Sexual development, disorders of, 343
Sexual differentiation, 328–331
Sexually dimorphic nucleus area in the anterior hypothalamus that is larger in males than in females and contributes to control of male sexual behavior, 329
Sexual orientation
behavioral and anatomical differences, 346
brain anatomy, 348–350
and genetics, 346–347
prenatal influences, 348
Sexual selection tendency for a gene to spread in the population if it makes individuals more appealing to the opposite sex, 341
SFO. *See* **Subfornical organ**
Sham-feeding procedure in which everything that an animal swallows leaks out a tube connected to the esophagus or stomach, 310
Shell shock. *See* **Post-traumatic stress disorder (PTSD)**
Shift work, 265
Short-term memory memory of events that have just occurred, 395–396
Short-term recovery from brain damage, 136–138
Sign language, 439, 440, 441, 442
Simple cell type of visual cortex cell that has a receptive held with fixed excitatory and inhibitory zones, 167, *168*
Simple receptive fields, 167–169
Single-cell mechanisms of invertebrate behavior change, 414–415
6-OHDA, 254
Skeletal muscles muscles that control movement of the body in relation to the environment, 228, *229*
Sleep. *See* Wakefulness and sleep
Sleep apnea impaired ability to breathe while sleeping, 279
Sleep disorders, 279–281
Sleep paralysis, 280
Sleep sex, 281
Sleep spindle 12 to 14 Hz brain waves in bursts that last at least half a second, 273
Sleep stages, *274*
brain function in REM sleep, 278–279
brain mechanisms of, 275–278
introduction to, 272–273
REM sleep, 273–274
sleep disorders, 279–281
Sleepwalking, 277, 281
Slow muscles, 230
Slow-twitch fibers muscle fibers that have less vigorous contractions and no fatigue, 230
Slow-wave sleep (SWS) stages 3 and 4 of sleep, which are occupied by slow, large-amplitude brain waves, 273
Smooth muscles those that control the digestive system and other organs, 228, *229*
SNRIs. *See* **Serotonin norepinephrine reuptake inhibitors (SNRIs)**
Socialization, 330
Social neuroscience the study of how genes, chemicals, and brain activity contribute to social behavior, 459–461
Society for Neuroscience Policies on the Use of Animals and Human Subjects in Research, 509–511
Sodium, crystal structure of, *505*
Sodium channels, 29–30, 32, 33–34, 90
Sodium gradients, 27–28, *28*
Sodium ions, 27–28, *30*
Sodium–potassium pump mechanism that actively transports sodium ions out of the cell while drawing in two potassium ions, 27, *28*
Sodium-specific hunger, 304
Solutes, 302
Soma (cell body) structure containing the nucleus, ribosomes, and mitochondria, 18
Somatic nervous system part of the PNS that consists of the axons conveying messages from the sense organs to the CNS and from the CNS to the muscles, 66, *67*
Somatosensory cortex, *140*, *204*, 358
Somatosensory receptors, 199–200, *200*
Somatosensory system sensory network that monitors the surface of the body and its movements, 198–202
Somnambulism, 277
Sound, 188–190
Sound localization, 194–195, *195*
Sound shadow, 194
Sound waves, *188*, *189*, *195*
Spatial memory, 402–403
Spatial neglect a tendency to ignore the left side of the body or the left side of objects, 454–456, *455*
Spatial rotation, *98*
Spatial summation combination of effects of activity from two or more synapses onto a single neuron, 41–43, *42*
Special experiences, effects of, 127–131
Specialization, fields of, *8*
Special training in adulthood, 128–129
Species differences in sleep, 285
Specificity property that highly active synapses become strengthened and less active synapses do not, 120, 415
Speech, brain activity during, *441*

Spinal cord part of the CNS; it communicates with all the sense organs and muscles except those of the head
connection to brain, 5, 239–241
disorders, *240*
formation of, 117, *117*
as part of the central nervous system, 66
in sagittal section of the brain, *73*
stimuli and spinal cord path, 202–203
in ventral surface, *74*
vertebrate nervous system structure, 68–69, *68*, *69*
Splanchnic nerves nerves that convey information about the nutrient contents of the stomach to the brain, 310
Split-brain operation
competition and cooperation, 428–429
hemispheric specializations in intact brains, 430–431
right hemisphere, 429–430
Split-brain people people who have undergone surgery to the corpus callosum, 426–429, *429*
Spontaneous firing rate a periodic production of action potentials even without synaptic input, 45
SRY the sex-determining region on the Y chromosome, 326
SSRIs. *See* **Selective serotonin reuptake inhibitors (SSRIs)**
Startle reflex response that one makes after a sudden, unexpected loud noise or similar sudden stimulus, 371, 372
Stem cells undifferentiated cells that divide and produce daughter cells that develop more specialized properties, 117–118, 254
Stereotaxic instrument a device for the precise placement of electrodes in the brain, 89, *89*
Steroid hormones hormones that contain four carbon rings, 327, *327*
Stimulant drugs, 468
Stimuli, and spinal cord paths, 202–203
Stimulus, consciousness of
binocular rivalry, 450–451
consciousness as a threshold phenomenon, 452
masking, 450
timing of consciousness, 452–453
unattended stimulus, 451–452
Stirrup, *189*, 190
St. John's wort, 478
Stomach, in regulation of feeding, 310
Strabismus (or strabismic amblyopia or lazy eye) a condition in which the eyes do not point in the same direction, 171–172
Stress the nonspecific response of the body to any demand made upon it; also defined as events that are interpreted as threatening
definition of, 383
and depression, *476*
general adaptation syndrome, 383
and the hypothalamus-pituitary-adrenal cortex axis, 383–386
immune system, 384–386
stress control, 386
Stretch reflex a reflexive contraction of a muscle in response to a stretch of that muscle, 231, *231*
Striate cortex, 82, 166
Striated muscles muscles that control movement of the body in relation to the environment, 228, *229*
Striatum forebrain structure composed of the caudate nucleus and putamen, which are important for certain aspects of movement, 243
String theory, 4
Stroke a temporary loss of normal blood flow to a brain area, 136–138, *137*, 142
Stroop effect the difficulty of saying the color of ink of a word instead of reading the word itself, 454
Subatomic particles, 505
Subfornical organ (SFO) brain structure adjoining the third ventricle of the brain, where its cells monitor blood volume and relay information to the preoptic area of the hypothalamus, 303
Substance abuse and addiction
cravings, 468
drug mechanisms, 466–469
predispositions, 469–471
and schizophrenia, 488
tolerance and withdrawal, 468–469
treatments, 471–472
Substance-induced psychotic disorder condition similar to schizophrenia, provoked by large, repeated doses of a drug, 494
Substantia nigra a midbrain structure that gives rise to a pathway releasing dopamine, 72, 252–253, *252*
Subthreshold stimulation, 29
Sulcus, *68*
Superior, *68*
Superior colliculus swelling on either side of the tectum; important to visual processing, 72, *73*
Supertasters, 215, *216*
Supplementary motor cortex area of the frontal cortex; active during preparation of a rapid sequence of movements, *236*, 237–238
Suprachiasmatic nucleus (SCN) part of the hypothalamus; provides the main control of the circadian rhythms for sleep and body temperature, 267–268, *267*
Supraoptic nucleus part of the hypothalamus that controls the release rate of vasopressin, 303
SWS. *See* **Slow-wave sleep**
Sylvian fissure, *440*
Sympathetic nervous system a network of nerves that prepare the organs for vigorous activity, 69–70, *70*, 122–123, 356–357, *356*
Synapse a specialized gap as a point of communication between two neurons
anatomy of, *51*
chemical events, 48–59
competition among axons, 121–122
definition of, 40
events in transmission at, *49*
formation of, 118
for pain and its inhibition, *205*
properties of, 40–44
relationship between EPSP, IPSP, and action potentials, 44–45
wiring diagram for, *45*
Synaptic activation, *42*
Synaptic cleft, 49, 52, *52*
Synaptic delay, *41*
Synaptogenesis formation of synapses, 118
Syndromal obesity, 318
Synesthesia the experience some people have in which stimulation of one sense evokes a perception of that sense and another one also, 221–222
Systematic desensitization, 378

Tabes dorsalis, *240*
Tangles, 405, *405*
Tardive dyskinesia a movement disorder characterized by tremors and other involuntary movements, 495, *496*
Taste, 212–216, *214*
Taste buds receptors on the tongue that detect certain chemicals, 212, *212*
Taste coding, 214–215
Taste receptors, 212–214
Taste sensitivity, 215
Tau protein part of the intracellular support structure of axons, 404–405
T cells, 384, *385*
Tectum roof of the midbrain, 72
Tegmentum intermediate level of the midbrain, 72
Temperature
and movement, *230*
and sleep, *263*
Temperature regulation
behavioral regulation, 296–297, *297*
body temperature control, 296–299
homeostasis and allostasis, 295
Temporal cortex, 124–125, *125*, 431
Temporal lobe the lateral portion of each hemisphere, near the temples, 5, *74*, *82*, 83–84
Temporal summation a cumulative effect of repeated stimuli within a brief time, 41, 42, *42*
Test Ban Treaty, 119
Testes sperm-producing organs, 326, *326*
Testicular feminization condition in which individuals with an XY chromosome pattern have the genital appearance of a female, 344
Testis, *58*
Testosterone an androgen chemical, 327, *327*, 328–332, 344, 368, *368*
Thalamus a pair of structures in the center of the forebrain
location of, *76*
overview of, 74–75, *74*, *75*
and pain, 203, *203*, *204*
in sagittal section of the brain, *73*
taste, *215*
in the visual system, *163*
Thiamine a B_1 vitamin necessary to use glucose, 23, 403–404
Thirst, 302–304
Threshold of excitation minimum amount of membrane depolarization necessary to trigger an action potential, 29
Thymine, 105
Thyroid hormones, *59*
Tickle, 201
TIM (timeless), 269, *269*
Timbre tone quality or complexity, dependent on the harmonics of the tone, 188
Timeless (TIM), 269, *269*
Time of arrival, 194, *194*
Tinnitus frequent or constant ringing in the ears, 193–194
Tissue plasminogen activator (tPA) drug that breaks up blood clots, 137
TMS. *See* **Transcranial magnetic stimulation**
Tone deafness, 191
Topoisomerases, 500
Touch, spinal pathways for, *203*
Touch path, *241*
Toxoplasma gondii, 372, 491
tPA. *See* **Tissue plasminogen activator**
Tract, *68*
Transcranial magnetic stimulation (TMS) the application of an intense magnetic field to a portion of the scalp, temporarily inactivating neurons below the magnet, 90, *96*
Transmitter-gated channels ion channel that opens temporarily when a neurotransmitter binds to it, 52
Transporters special membrane protein where reuptake occurs in the neurotransmitter, 55
Trichromatic theory (Young-Helmholtz theory) theory that color is perceived through the relative rates of response by three kinds of cones, each one maximally sensitive to a different set of wavelengths, 154–155

Tricyclic antidepressant drug that blocks the reuptake of catecholamines and serotonin by presynaptic terminals, 477, *477*
Tripartite synapse, 20
Trolley dilemma, 362, *363*
True hermaphrodites, 343
Tryptophan, 51, 105, 309
TSH-releasing hormone, 58, *58*
Turnover release and resynthesis of a neurotransmitter, 369
Twins, 108, 346–347, *347*, 490
2-AG (*sn*-2 arachidonylglycerol) chemical that binds to cannabinoid receptors, 56, *56*
Tympanic membrane the eardrum, 189–190, *189*
Type 1 diabetes, *312*
Type I (Type A) alcoholism alcohol abuse with gradual onset; only a weak genetic predisposition, 470
Type II (Type B) alcoholism alcohol abuse with rapid onset and a strong genetic basis, 470

Unattended stimulus, 451–452
Unconditioned response (UCR) response automatically evoked by an unconditioned stimulus, 392
Unconditioned stimulus (UCS) stimulus that automatically evokes an unconditioned response, 392, *393*, 394–395, *394*
Unconscious people, 453
Uncorrelated stimulation in the two eyes, 171–172
Units of movement, 232–233
Urbach-Wiethe disease, 374–375
U.S. Public Health Service Policy of Humane Care and Use of Laboratory Animals, 509
Utricle, 198

Vagus nerve tenth cranial nerve, which has branches to and from stomach and several other organs, 48, *48*, 310
Vallate papilla, *212*
Valproate, 483
Vas deferens, 326
Vasopressin (antidiuretic hormone) hormone released by posterior pituitary; raises blood pressure and enables kidneys to conserve water, 58, 59, 302, 336, *337*
Vegetative state condition in which someone has decreased brain activity and alternates between wakefulness and sleep but shows only limited responsiveness, such as increased heart rate in response to a painful stimulus, 272
Velocity, of an action potential, 31
Ventral toward the stomach, 5, *5*, 67, *68*
Ventral lateral nucleus, *75*
Ventral path, 177–178
Ventral posterior nucleus, *75*
Ventral stream visual paths in the temporal cortex that are specialized for identifying and recognizing objects; the "what" path, 177–178
Ventricles four fluid-filled cavities within the brain, 77, *77*
Ventromedial hypothalamic syndrome, 316
Ventromedial hypothalamus (VMH) region of the hypothalamus in which damage leads to faster stomach emptying and increased secretion of insulin, *315*, 316–317, *317*
Vertebrate nervous system structure
  autonomic nervous system, 69–71
  forebrain, 72–77
  hindbrain, 71
  midbrain, 71–72
  spinal cord, 68–69
  terminology, 66–68
  ventricles, 77
Vertebrate neurons, nourishment of, 23
Vertebrates, long-term potentiation in, 415–419
Vesicles tiny nearly spherical packets filled with neurotransmitter molecules, 51
Vestibular nucleus cluster of neurons in the brainstem, primarily responsible for motor responses to vestibular sensation, 241
Vestibular organ, 198
Vestibular sensation, 198, *199*
Vision
  brain processing of visual information, 162–173
  color vision, 153–158
  parallel processing in the visual cortex, 177–183
  visual coding, 148–158
Visual agnosia an inability to recognize objects despite otherwise satisfactory vision, 179
Visual coding
  eye and the connection to the brain, 149–152
  perceptions, general principles of, 148–149
  visual receptors, 152–153
Visual connections in the brain hemispheres, 425–426
Visual cortex, *163*
  analysis of shape, 178–181
  color perception, 181
  columnar organization of, 169–170
  columns in, *169*
  development of, 170–173
  motion perception, 181–183
  parallel processing in, 177–183
  ventral and dorsal paths, 177–178
Visual field area of the world that an individual can see at any time, 155, 424, *424*
Visual information, brain processing of
  further processing, 165–166
  primary visual cortex, 166–170
  in the retina, 162–165
Visual receptors, 152–153
Visual stimuli, 373
VMH. *See* **Ventromedial hypothalamus**
VNO. *See* **Vomeronasal organ**
Volley principle tenet that the auditory nerve as a whole produces volleys of impulses for a sound even though no individual axon approaches that frequency, 190
Voltage-gated channel membrane channel whose permeability to sodium (or some other ion) depends on the voltage difference across the membrane, 30
Voluntary movements, 232
Voluntary eye movements, 32–34
Vomeronasal organ (VNO) a set of receptors, located near, but separate from, the olfactory receptors, 220

Wakefulness and sleep
  altered sleep patterns and depression, 481–482
  and bipolar disorder, 483
  brain mechanisms, *276*
  functions of sleep, 284–288
  rhythms of waking and sleeping, 262–269
  and social time, *264*
  stages of sleep and brain mechanisms, 272–281
Waterfall illusion, 169
Water molecule, *505*
Water regulation, 302
Wavelenths, *153*, 154–155, *154*
Weight loss, and eating disorders, 318–319
Wernicke-Korsakoff syndrome. *See* **Korsakoff's syndrome**
Wernicke's aphasia condition characterized by poor language comprehension and impaired ability to remember the name of objects, *440*, 442–443, *443*
Wernicke's area portion of the brain located near the auditory cortex, associated with language comprehension, 442
White matter area of the nervous system consisting mostly of myelinated axons, 69, *69*, *169*
Williams syndrome condition in which the person has relatively good language abilities in spite of impairments in other regards, 438–439, *439*
Wisconsin Card Sorting Test, 492
Withdrawal, 468–469
Withdrawal effects of drug cessation, 468–469
Withdrawal response, 414, *414*, *415*
Wolffian ducts precursors to male internal structures, 326, *326*
Women
  activating effects, 332–334
  aggressive behaviors, 368
  brain size compared to men, 98
  brains of, *335*
  characteristcs sought in mates, 342
  and congenital adrenal hyperplasia (CAH), 344
  discrepancies of sexual appearance, 345–346
  effects of sex hormones on nonsexual characteristics, 334–335
  gender assignment and rearing, 344–345
  genitals, *326*, *328*
  interest in multiple mates, 341–342
  and jealousy, 342
  parental behavior, 336–337
  and pheromones, 220–221
  and schizophrenia, 489
  sex hormones, 328–331
  sexual activities, female-initiated, 333–334, *334*
  sexual orientation, 346–347
Working memory storage of memory while one is working with it, 397, 399, 488
X chromosome, 104, 106, 326, 327, 343, 344, 347
Y chromosome, 104, 106, 326, 327, 343, 344

Young-Helmholtz theory. *See* **Trichromatic theory**

Zeitgeber stimulus that resets the circadian rhythm, 264